MGMT¹²

PRINCIPLES OF MANAGEMENT

CHUCK WILLIAMS
Butler University

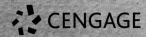
CENGAGE

Australia • Brazil • Canada • Mexico • Singapore • United Kingdom • United States

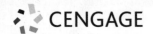

MGMT 12e
Chuck Williams

Senior Vice President, Higher Education & Skills Product: Erin Joyner

Product Director: Joe Sabatino

Product Manager: Heather Mooney

Content Manager: Amanda White

Product Assistant: Nick Perez

Marketing Manager: Audrey Wyrick

Marketing Coordinator: Alexis Cortez

Intellectual Property Analyst: Diane Garrity

Intellectual Property Project Manager: Carly Belcher

Production Service: MPS Limited

Senior Art Director: Bethany Bourgeois

Text Designer: Tippy McIntosh

Cover Designer: Lisa Kuhn, Curio Press, LLC/ Bethany Bourgeois

Cover Image: iStock.com/andresr

For product information and technology assistance, contact us at
Cengage Customer & Sales Support, 1-800-354-9706 or support.cengage.com.

For permission to use material from this text or product, submit all requests online at **www.cengage.com/permissions**.

Library of Congress Control Number: 2020914123

ISBN: 978-0-357-13772-7

Cengage
200 Pier 4 Boulevard
Boston, MA 02210
USA

Cengage is a leading provider of customized learning solutions with employees residing in nearly 40 different countries and sales in more than 125 countries around the world. Find your local representative at **www.cengage.com**.

To learn more about Cengage platforms and services, register or access your online learning solution, or purchase materials for your course, visit **www.cengage.com**.

Printed in the United States of America
Print Number: 01   Print Year: 2021

CHUCK WILLIAMS

MGMT¹² BRIEF CONTENTS

iStock.com/andresr

Contents

Part 3
Organizing

Wright Studio/Shutterstock.com

Part 4
Leading

Who is Danny/Shutterstock.com

Part 5
Controlling

Andrey_Popov/Shutterstock.com

1 | Management

LEARNING OUTCOMES

1-1 Describe what management is.

1-2 Explain the four functions of management.

1-3 Describe different kinds of managers.

1-4 Explain the major roles and subroles that managers perform in their jobs.

1-5 Assess managerial potential, based on what companies look for in managers.

1-6 Recognize the top mistakes that managers make in their jobs.

1-7 Describe the transition that employees go through when they are promoted to management.

1-8 Explain how and why companies can create competitive advantage through people.

1-1 MANAGEMENT IS …

Management issues are fundamental to any organization: How do we plan to get things done, organize the company to be efficient and effective, lead and motivate employees, and put controls in place to make sure plans are followed and goals are met? Good management is basic to starting a business, growing a business, and maintaining a business after it has achieved some measure of success.

To understand how important *good* management is, think about this. **Sears** dominated US retailing for a century.[1] Before Amazon, the Sears catalog sold everything from Christmas toys to 447 kinds of assemble-it-yourself houses![2] And, before Walmart Supercenters, there was a Sears store within 30 minutes of every American, where consumers picked up catalog orders and bought everything from clothes to furniture to Kenmore appliances.[3] But since 2010, despite raising $10.6 billion by selling its best brands (Lands End, Craftsman tools, and Diehard batteries) and

its 337 strongest stores, Sears has shrunk from 3,500 to 695 stores, laid off 250,000+ employees, lost $12 billion, and filed for bankruptcy in 2018.[4] With additional closings, just 182 Sears stores will remain in early 2020.[5]

Ah, bad managers and bad management. Is it any wonder that companies pay management consultants nearly $230 billion a year for advice on basic management issues such as how to outperform competitors to earn customers' business, lead people effectively, organize the company efficiently, and manage large-scale projects and

processes?[6] This textbook will help you understand some of the basic issues that management consultants help companies resolve. (And it won't cost you billions of dollars.)

Many of today's managers got their start welding on the factory floor, clearing dishes off tables, helping customers fit a suit, or wiping up a spill in aisle 3. Similarly, lots of you will start at the bottom and work your way up. There's no better way to get to know your competition, your customers, and your business. But whether you begin your career at the entry level or as a supervisor, your job as a manager is not to do the work but to help others do theirs. **Management** is getting work done through others.

Vineet Nayar, former CEO of IT services company HCL Technologies, doesn't see himself as the guy who has to do everything or have all the answers. Instead, he sees himself as "the guy who is obsessed with enabling employees to create value." Rather than coming up with solutions himself, Nayar creates opportunities for collaboration, for peer review, and for employees to give feedback on ideas and work processes. Says Nayar, "My job is to make sure everybody is enabled to do what they do well."[7]

Nayar's description of managerial responsibilities suggests that managers must also be concerned with efficiency and effectiveness in the work process. **Efficiency** is getting work done with a minimum of effort, expense, or waste. At **Maersk**, the world's largest container

Sears is so cash strapped that it has sold off its best brands, shut down hundreds of stores, and filed for bankruptcy.

Management getting work done through others

Efficiency getting work done with a minimum of effort, expense, or waste shipping company, Chief Operating Officer Soren Toft says, "Cutting idle time at ports is a big priority and challenge. It's like a Formula One pit stop. The faster we come in and out, the more time and money we save."[8] So Maersk digitally tracks each container (a 40-foot steel box loaded onto a railroad car or behind a semi-truck) and all the loading/unloading steps for its "Triple E" ships, which hold nearly 21,000 containers. Maersk's "Pit Stop" system ties into mobile phone apps so ships can easily share data with shore crews who position 2000-ton stacking cranes, shuttle carriers, and "truck-on" loaders to efficiently move the right container boxes on and off at each stop.[9] For example, the Madrid Maersk unloaded and reloaded 6,500 containers in just 59 hours in Antwerp, Belgium.[10]

Efficiency alone, however, is not enough to ensure success. Managers must also strive for **effectiveness**, which is accomplishing tasks that help fulfill organizational objectives, such as customer service and satisfaction. Hotel apps let customers pick rooms, ask for extra towels, and check in and out, but they don't help with hotel shuttles. Like most travelers, software executive Ken Montgomery says, "The last thing I want to do when getting off a flight is wait for a shuttle bus…."[11] Ray Bennett, Marriott's chief operations officer, says the shuttle "is probably the No. 1 or No. 2 pain point for customers."[12] After Marriott added GPS trackers to shuttles and tracking capabilities to its mobile app, phone calls to the front desk of the Dulles Airport Marriott dropped by 30 percent. Marriott general manager Keith McNeil says they're no longer apologizing "that the shuttle's not there. Just look at your phone and you see where it is."[13] The Marriott app also displays an accurate estimated time until pickup.

1-2 MANAGEMENT FUNCTIONS

Henri Fayol, who was a managing director (CEO) of a large steel company in the early 1900s, was one of the founders of the field of management. You'll learn more about Fayol and management's other key contributors when you read about the history of management in Chapter 2. Based on his 20 years of experience as a CEO, Fayol argued that "the success of an enterprise generally depends much more on the administrative ability of its leaders than on their technical ability."[14] A century later, Fayol's arguments still hold true. During a two-year study code-named Project Oxygen, Google analyzed performance reviews and feedback surveys to identify the traits of its best managers. According to Laszlo Bock, Google's former vice president for people operations, "We'd always believed that to be a manager, particularly on the engineering side, you need to be as deep or deeper a technical expert than the people who work for you. It turns out that that's absolutely the least important thing." What was most important? "Be a good coach." "Empower; Don't micromanage." "Be product and results-oriented." "Be a good communicator and listen to your team." "Be interested in [your] direct reports' success and well-being." In short, Google found what Fayol observed: administrative ability, or management, is key to an organization's success.[15]

According to Fayol, managers need to perform five managerial functions in order to be successful: planning, organizing, coordinating, commanding, and controlling.[16] Most management textbooks today have updated this list by dropping the coordinating function and referring to Fayol's commanding function as "leading." Fayol's management functions are thus known today in this updated form as planning, organizing, leading, and controlling. Studies indicate that managers who perform these management functions well are more successful, gaining promotions for themselves and profits for their companies. For example, the more time CEOs spend planning, the more profitable their companies are.[17] A 25-year study at AT&T found that employees with better planning and decision-making skills were more likely to be promoted into management jobs, to be successful as managers, and to be promoted into upper levels of management.[18]

The evidence is clear. Managers serve their companies well when they plan, organize, lead, and control. So we've organized this textbook based on these functions of management, as shown in Exhibit 1.1.

*Now let's take a closer look at each of the management functions: **1-2a planning, 1-2b organizing, 1-2c leading,** and **1-2d controlling.***

1-2a Planning

Planning involves determining organizational goals and a means for achieving them. As you'll learn in Chapter 5, planning is one of the best ways to improve performance. It encourages people to work harder, to work for extended periods, to engage in behaviors directly related to goal accomplishment, and to think of better ways to do their jobs. But most importantly, companies that plan

Effectiveness accomplishing tasks that help fulfill organizational objectives

Planning determining organizational goals and a means for achieving them

Exhibit 1.1
The Four Functions of Management

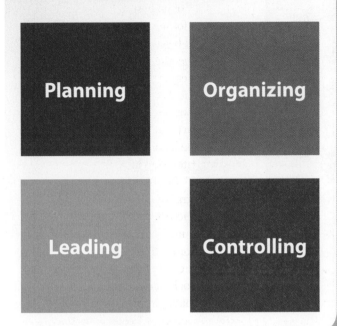

Planning	Organizing
Leading	**Controlling**

have larger profits and faster growth than companies that don't plan.

For example, the question "What business are we in?" is at the heart of strategic planning. You'll learn about this in Chapter 6. If you can answer the question "What business are you in?" in two sentences or less, chances are you have a very clear plan for your business. But getting a clear plan is not so easy. General Motors, Toyota, and Mercedes-Benz are in the business of making *combustion*-engine automobiles for individual consumers. But, for how much longer? The automotive industry is scrambling to catch up with Tesla, which sold 367,000 *electric* vehicles (EVs) in 2019, with new factories in China and Germany potentially raising production to a million *electric* cars a year.[19] Because of ride-hailing services like Uber and Lyft, just 80 percent of 20- to 24-year-olds had a driver's license in 2017 compared to 92 percent in 1983.[20] And for those who drive, car-sharing services are often less expensive, especially in major cities. Yandex Drive rents 7,000 cars in Moscow, Russia, for just 8 cents a minute. After calculating the cost of his car payment, insurance, fuel, repairs and parking, Muscovite Evgeny Barkov sold his car. He says, "Now, I'm just paying for usage."[21] Finally, with an estimated 23 million self-driving cars in the United States by 2035, even fewer people will need to own cars.[22] Toyota CEO Akio Toyoda says that adapting to these threats is "A matter of surviving or dying."[23]

You'll learn more about planning in Chapter 5 on planning and decision making, Chapter 6 on organizational strategy, Chapter 7 on innovation and change, and Chapter 8 on global management.

1-2b Organizing

Organizing is deciding where decisions will be made, who will do what jobs and tasks, and who will work for whom in the company. In other words, organizing is about determining how things get done. Online orders in which customers pick up their groceries in the store parking lot without setting foot in the store are just 3.5 percent of total grocery spending. But surging customer demand is forcing grocers to reorganize how things get done.[24] The first challenge, according to industry analyst Sucharita Kodali, is that unlike in warehouses, "Inventory is never where it's supposed to be (in the store). People (shoppers) move it around, and fast-moving items are never there."[25] The second is that store workers only collect 80 items an hour from grocery store aisles.[26] With online orders having doubled in the last year, **Walmart** couldn't keep up. So, it turned to **Alert Innovation**. Its Alphabot Automated Storage and Retrieval System (ASRS) reorganizes who does what. Installed in the 20,000-square-foot storerooms at the back of Walmart Supercenters, Alert Innovation's 24-foot-high system automatically moves items vertically and horizontally in automated carts from their stored locations to workstations where employees check and bag the items for pickup. According to Walmart senior manager Brian Roth, "Ultimately, this will lower dispense times, increase accuracy, and improve the entirety of online grocery (shopping)." Indeed, the Alphabot system allows Walmart associates to handle 800 items an hour, a 10-fold increase from aisle picking.[27] Roth concludes that the reorganization "will help free associates to focus on service and selling, while the technology handles the more mundane, repeatable tasks."[28]

You'll learn more about organizing in Chapter 9 on designing adaptive organizations, Chapter 10 on managing teams, Chapter 11 on managing human resources, and Chapter 12 on managing individuals and a diverse workforce.

> **Organizing** deciding where decisions will be made, who will do what jobs and tasks, and who will work for whom

alphaspirit/Shutterstock.com

What Happens When A Great Ceo Leaves?

Does good management matter? If so, how much? One way to answer this question (also see section 1-8 about creating competitive advantage through people) is to ask, "What happens when a great CEO leaves?" After the death of co-founder and CEO Steve Jobs in 2011, Apple continues to thrive under CEO Tim Cook, having become the most profitable and valuable private company in the world.[29] The opposite happened when Jeffrey Immelt succeeded legendary General Electric (GE) CEO Jack Welch in 2001, under whom GE had become the most profitable and admired companies of its time. After Immelt's 17 years as CEO, GE's stock was worth less than when he started and dropped another 40 percent after his departure as two subsequent CEOs downsized, froze pensions, and sold off roughly a third of GE's businesses to raise cash to stabilize the company.

So, what happens when CEOs leave? In a 15-year study across 284 firms, financial performance was on average 4 points lower. And that matters! Over

Bloomberg/Getty Images

Successor CEOs, who follow great CEOs, like GE's Jack Welch shown here, have much shorter tenure and are twice as likely to be fired.

10 years, a company starting with $100 million in annual revenues would grow to $179 million with 6 percent growth and just $122 million with 2 percent growth. Not surprisingly, successor CEOs have much shorter tenure and are twice as likely to be fired. So, yes, good management matters. And maintaining top company performance is just as difficult as achieving it in the first place.

Sources: P. Karlsson, M. Turner, and P. Gassmann, "Succeeding the Long-Serving Legend in the Corner Office," *Leadership*, May 15, 2019, accessed January 24, 2020, https://www.strategy-business.com/article/Succeeding-the-long-serving-legend-in-the-corner-office?gko=90171; M. Kolakowski, "The World's 10 Most Profitable Companies," *Investopedia*, July 25, 2019, accessed January 24, 2020, https://www.investopedia.com/the-world-s-10-most-profitable-companies-4694526; T. Gryta, J. Lublin and D. Beoit, "How Jeffrey Immelt's 'Success Theater' Masked the Rot at GE, *Wall Street Journal*, February 21, 2019, accessed January 24, 2020, https://www.wsj.com/articles/how-jeffrey-immelts-success-theater-masked-the-rot-at-ge-1519231067; T. Kilgore, "GE Freezing Pensions for 20,000 Employees," *MarketWatch*, October 8, 2019, accessed January 24, 2020, https://www.marketwatch.com/story/ge-freezing-pensions-for-20000-employees-2019-10-07; J. Snell, "Fun with Charts: Apple's Turnaround Decade," *Six Colors*, January 24, 2020, accessed January 25, 2020, https://sixcolors.com/post/2020/01/fun-with-charts-apples-turnaround-decade/.

1-2c Leading

Our third management function, **leading**, involves inspiring and motivating workers to work hard to achieve organizational goals. Inspiring people in large companies to take risks is a difficult leadership task. **Amazon**'s founder and CEO Jeff Bezos now faces this challenge. He says, "Amazon will be experimenting at the right scale for a company of our size if we occasionally have multibillion-dollar failures… We will work hard to make them good bets, but not all good bets will ultimately pay out. This kind of large-scale risk taking is part of the service we as a large company can provide to our customers and to society. The good news for shareowners is that a single big winning bet can more than cover the cost of many losers."[30]

You'll learn more about leading in Chapter 13 on motivation, Chapter 14 on leadership, and Chapter 15 on managing communication.

Leading inspiring and motivating workers to work hard to achieve organizational goals

Controlling monitoring progress toward goal achievement and taking corrective action when needed

1-2d Controlling

The last function of management, **controlling**, is monitoring progress toward goal achievement and taking corrective action when progress isn't being made. The basic control process involves setting standards to achieve goals, comparing actual performance to those standards, and then making changes to return performance to those standards. Inspecting, maintaining, and repairing equipment is a control process. For example, AT&T has 65,000 mobile phone towers that require regular inspections. However, even with advanced safety practices and equipment, workers who climb towers are twice as likely to die at work as most employees.[31] And with the tallest mobile phone towers nearly 1,000 feet high, climbing towers for regular inspections is dangerous. AT&T now uses a fleet of drones to inspect mobile phone towers. Using drones with powerful cameras that take high-resolution pictures with details fine enough to count bolt threads, it takes only a few minutes to inspect a cell tower. Pat Dempsey, who is in charge of maintenance at PSEG Power, says, "The fact you don't have to make a person climb that tower, from a safety standpoint, it's a game changer."[32] AT&T's Art Pregler, who runs the drone program, says the company has avoided 5,000 tower climbs in the last 18 months.[33]

You'll learn more about the control function in Chapter 16 on control, Chapter 17 on managing information, and Chapter 18 on managing service and manufacturing operations.

1-3 KINDS OF MANAGERS

Not all managerial jobs are the same. The demands and requirements placed on the CEO of Facebook are significantly different from those placed on the manager of your local Chipotle restaurant.

*As shown in Exhibit 1.2, there are four kinds of managers, each with different jobs and responsibilities: **1-3a top managers, 1-3b middle managers, 1-3c first-line managers,** and **1-3d team leaders.***

1-3a Top Managers

Top managers hold positions such as chief executive officer (CEO), chief operating officer (COO), chief financial officer (CFO), and chief information officer (CIO) and are responsible for the overall direction of the organization. Top managers have three major responsibilities.[34]

First, they are responsible for creating a context for change. **Kroger**, the Cincinnati-based grocery chain with 2,800 stores, was slow to embrace online ordering and parking-lot pickup for its customers. Kroger CEO Rodney McMullen said, "We've got to get our butts in gear. There was no doubt we were behind."[35] To catch up, Kroger is investing $4 billion for robot-based warehouses and digital shelves. Compared to paper price tags, which must be changed by hand, Wi-Fi- and Bluetooth-enabled digital shelves with high-definition screens (below each item) can instantly change prices and advertise sales specials storewide. They also generate revenue by displaying ads purchased by product manufacturers and make restocking easier by marking low-inventory items.[36] CEO McMullen said, "You have to start somewhere, and you have to learn."[37]

Indeed, in both Europe and the United States, 35 percent of all CEOs are eventually fired because of their inability to successfully change their companies.[38] Creating a context for change includes forming a long-range vision or mission for the company. When Satya Nadella became CEO of **Microsoft**, the company had blown opportunities in mobile phones, search engines and web advertising, and social media. It was entrenched, unable to move beyond its dominant product, Microsoft Windows.[39] Nadella's vision refocused Microsoft around cloud-based services. A former Microsoft executive said Satya "just started omitting 'Windows' from sentences… Suddenly, everything from Satya was 'cloud, cloud, cloud!'" Five years later, Azure, Microsoft's cloud platform, has grown from $3 billion to $34 billion in annual revenues. Microsoft Office, formerly a "buy once, upgrade often" software package, became a $99-a-year cloud-based service with 214 million subscribers.[40] Netflix CEO Reed Hastings commented, "I don't know of any other software company in the history of technology that fell onto hard times and has recovered so well."[41]

After that vision or mission is set, the second responsibility of top managers is to develop employees' commitment to and ownership of the company's performance. That is, top managers are responsible for creating employee buy-in. Amy Hood became Microsoft's CFO at a challenging time, just six months before Satya Nadella was appointed CEO. Goldman Sachs analyst Heather Bellini says, "Satya has done an excellent job, but people think of them as a package together."[42] One of Hood's regular responsibilities is speaking to new Microsoft employees. She tells them that while she's responsible for company finances, she sees her main responsibility as making them happy that they chose to work for Microsoft – in other words, employee buy-in. Says Hood, "My kids will tell you I practice counting, but my job is really a little different than that. I may have thought about it that way when I took the job almost five years ago. But now it's about creating an environment in which you all remember that you still want to pick us every day. That's my job as a CFO."[43]

Third, top managers must create a positive organizational culture through language and action, actively managing internal communication. Top managers impart company values, strategies, and lessons through what they do and say to others both inside and outside the company. Indeed, no matter what they communicate, it's critical for them to send and reinforce clear, consistent messages.[44]

Finally, top managers are responsible for monitoring their business environments. This means that top managers must closely monitor customer needs, competitors' moves, and long-term business, economic, and social trends. We'll review this in detail in section 1-4b, Informational Roles.

1-3b Middle Managers

Middle managers hold positions such as plant manager, regional manager, or divisional

Leszek Glasner/Shutterstock.com

> **Top managers** executives responsible for the overall direction of the organization
>
> **Middle managers** responsible for setting objectives consistent with top management's goals and for planning and implementing subunit strategies for achieving these objectives

Exhibit 1.2
What the Four Kinds of Managers Do

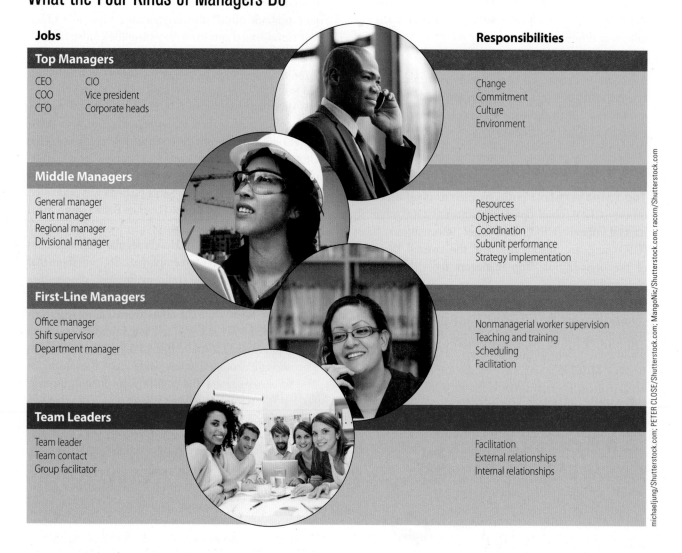

Jobs		Responsibilities
Top Managers		
CEO	CIO	Change
COO	Vice president	Commitment
CFO	Corporate heads	Culture
		Environment
Middle Managers		
General manager		Resources
Plant manager		Objectives
Regional manager		Coordination
Divisional manager		Subunit performance
		Strategy implementation
First-Line Managers		
Office manager		Nonmanagerial worker supervision
Shift supervisor		Teaching and training
Department manager		Scheduling
		Facilitation
Team Leaders		
Team leader		Facilitation
Team contact		External relationships
Group facilitator		Internal relationships

michaeljung/Shutterstock.com; PETER CLOSE/Shutterstock.com; MangoNic/Shutterstock.com; racorn/Shutterstock.com

manager. They are responsible for setting objectives consistent with top management's goals and for planning and implementing subunit strategies for achieving those objectives.[45] Or as one middle manager put it, a middle manager is "the implementer of the company's strategy" who figures out the "how" to do the "what."[46] Ryan Carson founded online learning company Treehouse Island without managers because he believed that his 100 employees could make decisions better and faster by themselves. However, that decision was severely tested when rapid growth resulted in 100,000 students enrolled in Treehouse Island's online courses. Employees, unsure of their responsibilities, became increasingly frustrated as endless meetings never seemed to result in meaningful action or decisions. Tasks and projects that were necessary to keep up with demand started to fall

behind schedule. Carson fixed the situation by creating roles for middle managers. "That [managerless] experiment broke," said Carson. "I just had to admit it."[47]

One specific middle management responsibility is to plan and allocate resources to meet objectives. A second major responsibility is to coordinate and link groups, departments, and divisions within a company. One middle manager described his job as "a man who can discuss strategy with [the] CXO at breakfast and [then] eat lunch with workers."[48]

A third responsibility of middle management is to monitor and manage the performance of the subunits and individual managers who report to them. Finally, middle managers are also responsible for implementing the changes or strategies generated by top managers. Why? Because they're closer to the managers and employees who work daily with suppliers to effectively and efficiently deliver the company's product or service. In short, they're closer to the people who can best solve problems and implement solutions.

How important are middle managers to company performance? A study of nearly 400 video-game companies conducted at the University of Pennsylvania's Wharton School of Business found that middle managers' effectiveness accounted for 22 percent of the differences in performance across companies. In fact, middle managers were three times as important as the video-game designers who develop game characters and storylines. Professor Ethan Mollick, who conducted the study, said that middle managers are the key to "making sure the people at the bottom and the top [of the organization] are getting what they need."[49] As for Treehouse Island, revenue is up, the number of instructional videos has increased, and response times to student questions have been cut in half. According to instructor Craig Dennis, things are "light years better" with middle managers in place.[50]

1-3c First-Line Managers

First-line managers hold positions such as office manager, shift supervisor, or department manager. The primary responsibility of first-line managers is to manage the performance of entry-level employees who are directly responsible for producing a company's goods and services. Thus, first-line managers are the only managers who don't supervise other managers. The responsibilities of first-line managers include monitoring, teaching, and short-term planning.

First-line managers encourage, monitor, and reward the performance of their workers. First-line managers are also responsible for teaching entry-level employees how to do their jobs. They also make detailed schedules and operating plans based on middle management's intermediate-range plans. In contrast to the long-term plans of top managers (three to five years out) and the intermediate plans of middle managers (6 to 18 months out), first-line managers engage in plans and actions that typically produce results within two weeks.[51] Consider the typical convenience store manager (e.g., 7-Eleven) who starts the day by driving past competitors' stores to inspect their gasoline prices and then checks the outside of his or her store for anything that might need maintenance, such as burned-out lights or signs, or restocking, such as windshield washer fluid and paper towels. Then comes an inside check, where the manager determines what needs to be done for that day. (Are there enough donuts and coffee for breakfast or enough sandwiches for lunch?) After the day is planned, the manager turns to weekend orders. After accounting for the weather (hot

wirojsid/123RF

or cold) and the sales trends at the same time last year, the manager makes sure the store will have enough beer, soft drinks, and snack foods on hand. Finally, the manager looks 7 to 10 days ahead for hiring needs. Because of strict hiring procedures (basic math tests, drug tests, and background checks), it can take that long to hire new employees. Said one convenience store manager, "I have to continually interview, even if I am fully staffed."[52]

1-3d Team Leaders

The fourth kind of manager is a team leader. This relatively new kind of management job developed as companies shifted to self-managing teams, which, by definition, have no formal supervisor. In traditional management hierarchies, first-line managers are responsible for the performance of nonmanagerial employees and have the authority to hire and fire workers, make job assignments, and control resources. In this new structure, the teams themselves perform nearly all the functions performed by first-line managers under traditional hierarchies.[53]

Team leaders are primarily responsible for facilitating team activities toward accomplishing a goal. This doesn't mean team leaders are responsible for team performance.

First-line managers responsible for training and supervising the performance of nonmanagerial employees who are directly responsible for producing the company's products or services

Team leaders managers responsible for facilitating team activities toward goal accomplishment

They aren't. The team is. Team leaders help their team members plan and schedule work, learn to solve problems, and work effectively with each other. A Walmart Supercenter has a store manager, assistant store managers, and department managers. Walmart, however, is changing that structure to focus on teams. Store managers will now manage six "business leads" responsible for store finances and hiring (who will be paid 10 percent more than assistant managers). Business leads will manage 8 to 10 "team leads" (starting pay, $18 an hour), who will manage sales associates.[54] The first reason behind the change is to improve associates' job satisfaction. Drew Holler, senior vice president of associate experience, says, "Associates like smaller teams, and they like having a connection with a leader. They want something they can own and to know if they are winning or losing every day. And today that does not always happen."[55] The second is to increase associate's decision-making authority. Holler says, "That is probably the game changer in this, we are pushing decisions down," including helping customers with returns, authorizing prices changes without management approval, and communicating with teams on other shifts.[56] CEO Doug McMillon says, "We will compete with technology but win with people."[57]

Relationships among team members and between different teams are crucial to good team performance and must be well managed by team leaders, who are responsible for fostering good relationships and addressing problematic ones within their teams. Getting along with others is much more important in team structures because team members can't get work done without the help of teammates. In other words, team leaders need to foster *civil behavior* based on politeness, respect, and positive regard. For two decades, Professor Christine Porath has studied the effects of workplace incivility. She stresses that leaders set the tone for their teams: "A study of cross-functional product teams revealed that when leaders treated members of their team well and fairly, the team members were more productive individually and as a team. They were also more likely to go above and beyond their job requirements. It all starts at the top. When leaders are civil, it increases performance and creativity, allows for early mistake detection and the initiative to take actions, and reduces emotional exhaustion."[58]

Team leaders are also responsible for managing external relationships. Team leaders act as the bridge or liaison between their teams and other teams, departments, and divisions in a company. For example, if a member of Team A complains about the quality of Team B's work, Team A's leader is responsible for solving the problem by initiating a meeting with Team B's leader. Together, these team leaders are responsible for getting members of both teams to work together to solve the problem. If it's done right, the problem is solved without involving company management or blaming members of the other team.[59]

In summary, because of these critical differences, team leaders who don't understand how their roles are different from those of traditional managers often struggle in their jobs.

You will learn more about teams in Chapter 10.

1-4 MANAGERIAL ROLES

Although all four types of managers engage in planning, organizing, leading, and controlling, if you were to follow them around during a typical day on the job, you would probably not use these terms to describe what they actually do. Rather, what you'd see are the various roles managers play. Professor Henry Mintzberg followed five American CEOs, shadowing each for a week and analyzing their mail, their conversations, and their actions. He concluded that managers fulfill three major roles while performing their jobs – interpersonal, informational, and decisional.[60]

In other words, managers talk to people, gather and give information, and make decisions. Furthermore, as shown in Exhibit 1.3, these three major roles can be subdivided into 10 subroles.

Let's examine each major role – 1-4a interpersonal roles, 1-4b informational roles, and 1-4c decisional roles – and their 10 subroles.

1-4a Interpersonal Roles

More than anything else, management jobs are people intensive. Estimates vary with the level of management, but most managers spend between two-thirds and four-fifths of their time in face-to-face communication with others.[61] Indeed, a 2018 *Harvard Business Review* study that tracked the time of 27 CEOs in 15-minute increments for three months (12 times longer than Mintzberg) concluded, "The top job in a company involves primarily face-to-face interactions, which took up 61 percent of the work time of the CEOs we studied."[62] If you're a loner, or if you consider dealing with people a pain, then you may not be cut out for management work. In fulfilling the interpersonal role of management, managers perform three subroles: figurehead, leader, and liaison.

Exhibit 1.3
Mintzberg's Managerial Roles

Interpersonal Roles
- Figurehead
- Leader
- Liaison

Informational Roles
- Monitor
- Disseminator
- Spokesperson

Decisional Roles
- Entrepreneur
- Disturbance Handler
- Resource Allocator
- Negotiator

Source: Adapted from "The Manager's Job: Folklore and Fact," by Mintzberg, H. *Harvard Business Review*, July–August 1975.

In the **figurehead role**, managers perform ceremonial duties such as greeting company visitors, speaking at the opening of a new facility, or representing the company at a community luncheon to support local charities. When Louis Vuitton Moët Hennessy (LVMH), the world's premiere maker of luxury goods, opened a new factory in Keene, Texas, CEO Bernard Arnault flew in from Paris to commemorate the event.[63]

In the **leader role**, managers spend 43 percent of their time motivating and encouraging workers to accomplish organizational objectives.[64] In competitive labor markets, motivating can mean eliminating what people dislike about their jobs. Each Dunkin' Donuts employee handwrites dozens of expiration labels every day, indicating the precise time, for instance, when coffee or pastries are no longer fresh. Workers hate this, so Dunkin' installed database-linked printers to automate the task. Morning shift leader Alexandra Guajardo said now, "I don't have to constantly be worried about other smaller tasks that were tedious. I can focus on other things that need my attention in the restaurant."[65]

In the **liaison role**, managers deal with people outside their units. Studies consistently indicate that managers spend as much time with outsiders as they do with their own subordinates and their own bosses. When Tom Watjen became CEO of **Unum**, a provider of benefits

insurance, his 30 top managers generally worked within their functions and regions, but not with others across the company. Watjen said, "You can't just send out a memo that says, 'Hey, you guys have to talk to one another,'" so he began promoting managers across units and functions.[66] And, he reminded them of the importance of their liaison roles, for instance, telling finance executives, "Your job is to help your business colleagues (in other areas) get the information to understand what's happening in their business."[67]

1-4b Informational Roles

Not only do managers spend most of their time in face-to-face contact with others, they spend much of it obtaining and sharing information. Mintzberg found that the managers in his study spent 40 percent of their time giving and getting information from others. In this regard, management can be viewed as gathering information by scanning the business environment and listening to others in face-to-face conversations, processing that information, and then sharing it with people both inside and outside the company. Mintzberg described three informational subroles: monitor, disseminator, and spokesperson.

In the **monitor role**, managers scan their environment for information, actively contact others for information, and, because of their personal contacts, receive a great deal of unsolicited information. Besides receiving firsthand information, managers monitor their environment by reading local newspapers and the *Wall Street Journal* to keep track of customers, competitors, and technological changes that may affect their businesses. Today's managers can subscribe to electronic monitoring and distribution services that track the news wires (Associated Press, Reuters, and so on) for stories and social media posts related to their businesses. These services deliver customized news that only includes topics the managers specify. Business Wire (www.businesswire.com) monitors and distributes daily news headlines from major industries (for example, automotive, banking and financial, health, high tech).[68] Glean (www.glean.info) does real-time monitoring of Twitter, Facebook, LinkedIn, and Instagram feeds, as well as 60,000 global news outlets in 250 languages in

Figurehead role the interpersonal role managers play when they perform ceremonial duties

Leader role the interpersonal role managers play when they motivate and encourage workers to accomplish organizational objectives

Liaison role the interpersonal role managers play when they deal with people outside their units

Monitor role the informational role managers play when they scan their environment for information

COMPANIES MUST IMPROVE AT SPOTTING MANAGEMENT TALENT

If you work in a large organization, getting anointed as a HIPO (high potential) is a mark of early success, as it indicates a strong belief in your management potential. Typically, HIPOs are thought to be in top 5 percent of those with management potential. However, follow-up research of 1,964 HIPOs from three organizations indicated that 12 percent were in the bottom quarter and that 42 percent overall were below average in management potential! Likewise, a study of 50,000 HIPO sales representatives found that stars who sold twice as much as their sales goals were more likely to be promoted to management. But, the total sales of sales teams they managed dropped by 7.5 percent! What went wrong?

While these non-HIPOs had technical and professional expertise, took initiative and produced results, honored their commitments, and fit their organizations' cultures, they weren't strategic and had difficulty motivating others. Were they bad employees? No, they were great individual contributors. But they weren't well suited for management. And putting them in managerial roles not only hurt them, but it also hurt employees and the company.

Illia Uriadnikov/123RF

Sources: J. Zenger & J. Folkman, "Companies Are Bad at Identifying High-Potential Employees," *Harvard Business Review*, February 20, 2017, accessed March 9, 2017, https://hbr.org/2017/02/companies-are-bad-at-identifying-high-potential-employees; S. Walker, "Why Superstars Make Lousy Bosses," *Wall Street Journal*, October 20, 2018, accessed January 24, 2020, https://www.wsj.com/articles/the-curse-of-the-superstar-boss-1540008001?mod=article_inline.

191 countries.[69] It also monitors posts to 190 million blogs, 64,000 message boards, 75,000 UseNet groups, and over 200 different video sharing sites.[70] Another site, Federal News Service (fednews.com), provides subscribers with precision alerts and monitoring of federal hearings (via complete transcripts), bills, and policy proposals that may affect their company or industry.[71]

Because of their numerous personal contacts and their access to subordinates, managers are often hubs for the distribution of critical information. In the **disseminator role**, managers share the information they have collected with their subordinates and others in the company. **Front** is a software company that facilitates effective teamwork by providing shared emails, inboxes and assignments, all within a powerful email/calendar platform. CEO and cofounder Mathilde Collin makes sure everyone is clear on Front's goals and plans. She says:

> At the beginning of every week, I also send an email to direct reports, I share what my goals of the week are. What I'm working on is also what they're working on. The way that our goal-setting works is that once the company OKRs (objectives and key results) are done, then every executive will work on their OKRs and those are shared [with their teams].[72]

Collin doesn't share goals that are personal or confidential (out of privacy concern for others) that "would raise more questions."[73] She says, "The way I think about transparency is: Good transparency will help solve problems, and bad transparency will create more questions and problems."[74]

In contrast to the disseminator role, in which managers distribute information to employees inside the company, managers in the **spokesperson role** share information with people outside their departments or companies. One of the most common ways that CEOs act as spokespeople for their companies is speaking at annual meetings and on conference calls with shareholders or boards of directors. CEOs also serve as spokespeople to the media when their companies are involved in major news stories. A **Southwest Airlines** passenger was killed when a jet engine exploded on route from

Disseminator role the informational role managers play when they share information with others in their departments or companies

Spokesperson role the informational role managers play when they share information with people outside their departments or companies

When a Southwest Airlines passenger was killed after a jet engine exploded, CEO Gary Kelly served as the company spokesperson and apologized to the deceased passenger's family.

In the **entrepreneur role**, managers adapt themselves, their subordinates, and their units to change. **General Motors** paid $1 billion in 2016 for Cruise Automation, a 40-person startup firm developing self-driving car technology.[76] GM has since raised $7 billion from outside investors and grown Cruise to 1,700 people.[77] GM says it will be cheaper to subscribe to Cruise's fleet of robot cars instead of purchasing cars or using ride hailing (like Lyft or Uber) or car sharing (like Zipcar).[78] CEO Dan Ammann said, "Our goal is to deliver something that can beat all of them."[79] Furthermore, he believes that, "The status quo of transportation is broken, and ... our need to find better solutions grows more urgent every day."[80] The Cruise Origin, an electric, self-driving car, without steering wheels or brake/acceleration pedals, was revealed in January 2020 in preparation for road testing and production.[81]

In the **disturbance handler role**, managers respond to pressures and problems so severe that they demand immediate attention and action. When hurricanes threaten Waffle House restaurants, the Waffle House Index indicates if a restaurant is open and serving a full menu (green), open, serving water and a reduced menu, but without power (yellow), or not open (red). Vice president Pat Warner says, "Our goal is always to be the last to close, first to open."[82] Jump teams from headquarters are sent ahead of the storms with emergency supplies and generators. Warner said, "A lot of times, especially after a big storm, we're the only ones still open because we've got generators. Right after storms, business is brisk. We have a lot of people come in and are only able to get their first hot meal at a Waffle House."[83]

In the **resource allocator role**, managers decide who will get what resources and how many resources they will get. After Apple, **Alphabet** (formerly Google) is the second most profitable company in the world. For years, it grew so fast, with revenues greatly exceeding costs, that budgets, much less budget discipline, didn't matter (if ever used at all). When founders Larry Page and Sergey Brin hired CFO Ruth Porat, they did so to get Alphabet's businesses to make and stick to their budgets. Former Alphabet Chairman Eric Schmidt admits, "Before

New York to Dallas. Minutes after the pilot reported problems, Southwest's senior leadership team began executing its emergency response plan. Within hours, a full plane containing accident response team members flew from Dallas, Southwest's headquarters, to Philadelphia where the plane made its emergency stop. While some assisted local workers or accident investigators, most cared for passengers, providing counseling, alternative travel arrangements and overnight hotel stays. CEO Gary Kelly, serving as company spokesperson, announced the incident and apologized to the deceased passenger's family. Said Kelly, "On behalf of the Southwest family, I want to extend my deepest sympathies for the family and the loved ones of our deceased customer. They are our immediate and primary concern, and we will do all that we can to support them during this difficult time."[75]

1-4c Decisional Roles

Mintzberg found that obtaining and sharing information is not an end in itself. Obtaining and sharing information with people inside and outside the company is useful to managers because it helps them make good decisions. According to Mintzberg, managers engage in four decisional subroles: entrepreneur, disturbance handler, resource allocator, and negotiator.

Entrepreneur role the decisional role managers play when they adapt themselves, their subordinates, and their units to change

Disturbance handler role the decisional role managers play when they respond to severe pressures and problems that demand immediate action

Resource allocator role the decisional role managers play when they decide who gets what resources and in what amounts

she was there, we had lost discipline."[84] Alphabet makes 95 percent of its revenue from online ads, meaning Google search, YouTube, and mobile ads (mostly on Android phones). But in the rest of Alphabet (Nest thermostats, Google Ventures, Google Fiber), expenses far exceed revenues. So Porat instilled discipline by cutting budgets, by approving video conferences rather than business travel, by charging the business units for using Alphabet's functions (legal, human resources, and public relations). Former Chairman Schmidt said, "The cost cutting is real, and it's the right thing to be done, and it's driven by [Porat]."[85]

In the **negotiator role**, managers negotiate schedules, projects, goals, outcomes, resources, and employee raises. Fifty of the largest US companies, including American Express, IBM, Marriott, Shell Oil, and Verizon Communications, have formed the **Health Transformation Alliance (HTA)** to negotiate lower drug and medical costs.[86] Kevin Cox, chief human resource office at American Express, says, "Even the most successful companies won't be able to afford the rising costs of health care in the not too distant future."[87] At a time when health care spending is increasing 6 to 8 percent per year, the HTA expects to lower drug costs by 15 percent for their 7 million employees. Kyu Rhee, IBM's chief health officer says, "This is the group that's paying the bill. We're not waiting for the public sector to come up with the solution – we have the skills and expertise to do this ourselves."[88]

1-5 WHAT COMPANIES LOOK FOR IN MANAGERS

I didn't have the slightest idea what my job was. I walked in giggling and laughing because I had been promoted and had no idea what principles or style to be guided by. After the first day, I felt like I had run into a brick wall. (Sales Representative #1)

Suddenly, I found myself saying, boy, I can't be responsible for getting all that revenue. I don't have the time. Suddenly you've got to go from [taking care of]

yourself and say now I'm the manager, and what does a manager do? It takes awhile thinking about it for it to really hit you . . . a manager gets things done through other people. That's a very, very hard transition to make. (Sales Representative #2)[89]

The preceding statements were made by two star sales representatives who, based on their superior performance, were promoted to the position of sales manager. At first, they lacked confidence in their ability to do their jobs as managers. Like most new managers, these sales managers suddenly realized that the knowledge, skills, and abilities that led to success early in their careers (and were probably responsible for their promotion into the ranks of management) would not necessarily help them succeed as managers. As sales representatives, they were responsible only for managing their own performance. But as sales managers, they were now directly responsible for supervising all the sales representatives in their sales territories. Furthermore, they were now directly accountable for whether those sales representatives achieved their sales goals. If performance in nonmanagerial jobs doesn't necessarily prepare you for a managerial job, then what does it take to be a manager?

When companies look for employees who could be good managers, they look for individuals who have technical skills, human skills, conceptual skills, and the motivation to manage.[90] Exhibit 1.4 shows the relative importance of these four skills to the jobs of team leaders, first-line managers, middle managers, and top managers.

Technical skills are the specialized procedures, techniques, and knowledge required to get the job done. For the sales managers described previously, technical skills involve the ability to find new sales prospects, develop accurate sales pitches based on customer needs, and close sales. For a nurse supervisor, technical skills include being able to insert an IV or operate a crash cart if a patient goes into cardiac arrest.

Technical skills are most important for team leaders and lower-level managers because they supervise the workers who produce products or serve customers. Team leaders and first-line managers need technical knowledge and skills to train new employees and help employees solve problems.

Negotiator role the decisional role managers play when they negotiate schedules, projects, goals, outcomes, resources, and employee raises

Technical skills the specialized procedures, techniques, and knowledge required to get the job done

Viorel Sima/Shutterstock.com

Love The Job? Your Boss Has Technical Skills

When companies look for employees who could be good managers, they look for technical, human and conceptual skills, and the motivation to manage. Technical skills are the specialized procedures, techniques, and knowledge required to get the job done. Technical skills are most important for team leaders and lower-level managers, and for training new employees and helping them solve problems. Generally, technical skills become less important as managers rise through the managerial ranks, but they are still important. The question is, why?

It turns out, employees are much happier if they work for a boss with technical skills. A study of 35,000 randomly selected employees in the United States and the United Kingdom found that, "having a highly competent boss is easily the largest positive influence on a typical worker's level of job satisfaction." Highly competent was defined as being able to do the employees job, working one's way up inside the company, and whether the employee felt the boss possessed technical competence.

So, yes, technical skills become less important the higher you go. But they always matter to those you manage.

Source: B. Artz, A. Goodall & A. Oswald, "If Your Boss Could Do Your Job, You're More Likely to Be Happy at Work," *Harvard Business Review*, December 29, 2016, accessed March 9, 2017, https://hbr.org/2016/12/if-your-boss-could-do-your-job-youre-more-likely-to-be-happy-at-work.

Technical knowledge and skills are also needed to troubleshoot problems that employees can't handle. Technical skills become less important as managers rise through the managerial ranks, but they are still important.

Human skills can be summarized as the ability to work well with others. Managers with human skills work effectively within groups, encourage others to express their thoughts and feelings, are sensitive to others' needs and viewpoints, and are good listeners and communicators. Human skills are equally important at all levels of management, from team leaders to CEOs.

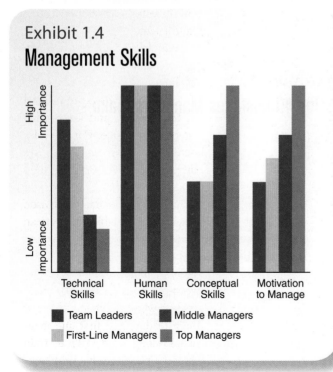

Exhibit 1.4
Management Skills

However, because lower-level managers spend much of their time solving technical problems, upper-level managers may actually spend more time dealing directly with people. On average, first-line managers spend 57 percent of their time with people, but that percentage increases to 63 percent for middle managers and 78 percent for top managers.[91]

Conceptual skills are the ability to see the organization as a whole, to understand how the different parts of the company affect each other, and to recognize how the company fits into or is affected by its external environment such as the local community, social and economic forces, customers, and the competition. Good managers have to be able to recognize, understand, and reconcile multiple complex problems and perspectives. In other words, managers have to be smart! In fact, intelligence makes so much difference for managerial performance that managers with above-average intelligence typically outperform managers of average intelligence by approximately 48 percent.[92] Clearly, companies need to be careful to promote smart workers into management. Conceptual skills increase in importance as managers rise through the management hierarchy.

Good management involves much more than intelligence, however. For example, making the department genius a manager can be disastrous if that genius lacks technical skills, human skills, or

Human skills the ability to work well with others

Conceptual skills the ability to see the organization as a whole, understand how the different parts affect each other, and recognize how the company fits into or is affected by its environment

one other factor known as the motivation to manage. **Motivation to manage** is an assessment of how motivated employees are to interact with superiors, participate in competitive situations, behave assertively toward others, tell others what to do, reward good behavior and punish poor behavior, perform actions that are highly visible to others, and handle and organize administrative tasks. Managers typically have a stronger motivation to manage than their subordinates, and managers at higher levels usually have a stronger motivation to manage than managers at lower levels. Furthermore, managers with a stronger motivation to manage are promoted faster, are rated as better managers by their employees, and earn more money than managers with a weak motivation to manage.[93]

1-6 MISTAKES MANAGERS MAKE

Another way to understand what it takes to be a manager is to look at the mistakes managers make. In other words, we can learn just as much from what managers shouldn't do as from what they should do. Exhibit 1.5 lists the top 10 mistakes managers make.

Several studies of US and British managers have compared *arrivers*, or managers who made it all the way to the top of their companies, with *derailers*, or managers who were successful early in their careers but were knocked off the fast track by the time they reached the middle to upper levels of management.[94] The researchers found that there were only a few differences between arrivers and derailers. For the most part, both groups were talented, and both groups had weaknesses. But what distinguished derailers from arrivers was that derailers possessed two or more fatal flaws with respect to the way they managed people. Although arrivers were by no means perfect, they usually had no more than one fatal flaw or had found ways to minimize the effects of their flaws on the people with whom they worked.

The top mistake made by derailers was that they were insensitive to others by virtue of their abrasive, intimidating, and bullying management style. The authors of one study described a manager who walked into his subordinate's office and interrupted a meeting by saying, "I need to see you." When the subordinate tried to explain that he was not available because he was in the middle of a

Chrisdorney/Shutterstock.com

Werner Heiber/Shutterstock.com

The top mistake made by derailers is having an abrasive, intimidating, and bullying management style.

Exhibit 1.5
Top 10 Mistakes Managers Make

1. Insensitive to others: abrasive, intimidating, bullying style
2. Cold, aloof, arrogant
3. Betrays trust
4. Overly ambitious: thinking of next job, playing politics
5. Specific performance problems with the business
6. Overmanaging: unable to delegate or build a team
7. Unable to staff effectively
8. Unable to think strategically
9. Unable to adapt to boss with different style
10. Overdependent on advocate or mentor

Source: M. W. McCall, Jr., and M. M. Lombardo, "What Makes a Top Executive?" *Psychology Today*, February 1983, 26–31.

Motivation to manage an assessment of how enthusiastic employees are about managing the work of others

meeting, the manager barked, "I don't give a damn. I said I wanted to see you now."[95] Not surprisingly, only 25 percent of derailers were rated by others as being good with people, compared to 75 percent of arrivers.

The second mistake was that derailers were often cold, aloof, or arrogant. Although this sounds like insensitivity to others, it has more to do with derailed managers being so smart, so expert in their areas of knowledge, that they treated others with contempt because they weren't experts, too.[96] For example, AT&T called in an industrial psychologist to counsel its vice president of human resources because she had been blamed for "ruffling too many feathers" at the company.[97] Interviews with the vice president's coworkers and subordinates revealed that they thought she was brilliant, was "smarter and faster than other people," "generates a lot of ideas," and "loves to deal with complex issues." Unfortunately, these smarts were accompanied by a cold, aloof, and arrogant management style. The people she worked with complained that she does "too much too fast," treats coworkers with "disdain," "impairs teamwork," "doesn't always show her warm side," and has "burned too many bridges."[98]

The third mistake made by derailers involved betraying a trust. Betraying a trust doesn't mean being dishonest. Instead, it means making others look bad by not doing what you said you would do when you said you would do it. That mistake, in itself, is not fatal because managers and their workers aren't machines. Tasks go undone in every company every day. There's always too much to do and not enough time, people, money, or resources to do it. The fatal betrayal of trust is failing to inform others when things will not be done right or on time. This failure to admit mistakes, failure to quickly inform others of the mistakes, failure to take responsibility for the mistakes, and failure to fix the mistakes without blaming others clearly distinguished the behavior of derailers from arrivers.

The fourth mistake was being overly political and ambitious. Managers who always have their eye on their next job rarely establish more than superficial relationships with peers and coworkers. In their haste to gain credit for successes that would be noticed by upper management, they make the fatal mistake of treating people as though they don't matter. An employee with an overly ambitious boss described him this way: "He treats employees coldly, even cruelly. He assigns blame without regard to responsibility and takes all the credit for himself. I once had such a boss, and he gave me a new definition of shared risk: If something I did was successful, he took the credit. If it wasn't, I got the blame."[99]

The fatal mistakes of being unable to delegate, build a team, and staff effectively indicate that many derailed managers were unable to make the most basic transition to managerial work: to quit being hands-on doers and get work done through others. In fact, according to an article in *Harvard Business Review*, up to 50 percent of new managers fail because they cannot make the transition from producing to managing.[100] Two things go wrong when managers make these mistakes. First, when managers meddle in decisions that their subordinates should be making – when they can't stop being doers – they alienate the people who work for them. Rich Dowd, founder of Dowd Associates, an executive search firm, admits to constantly monitoring and interrupting employees because they weren't doing the job "in the way I saw fit, even when their work was outstanding." According to Richard Kilburg of Johns Hopkins University, when managers interfere with workers' decisions, "You . . . have a tendency to lose your most creative people. They're able to say, 'Screw this. I'm not staying here.'"[101] Indeed, one employee told Dowd that if he was going to do her job for her, she would quit. Second, because they are trying to do their subordinates' jobs in addition to their own, managers who fail to delegate will not have enough time to do much of anything well. An office assistant to a Washington politician came in to work every day to find a long to-do list waiting on her desk, detailing everything she was expected to get done that day, along with how to do it, who to call, and when to give her boss updates on her progress. She said, "Sometimes, this list was three or four pages long. It must have taken him at least an hour to create."[102]

1-7 THE TRANSITION TO MANAGEMENT: THE FIRST YEAR

In her book *Becoming a Manager: Mastery of a New Identity*, Harvard Business School professor Linda Hill followed the development of 19 people in their first year as managers. Her study found that becoming a manager produced a profound psychological transition that changed the way these managers viewed themselves and others. As shown in Exhibit 1.6, the evolution of the managers' thoughts, expectations, and realities over the course of their first year in

Exhibit 1.6
Stages in the Transition to Management

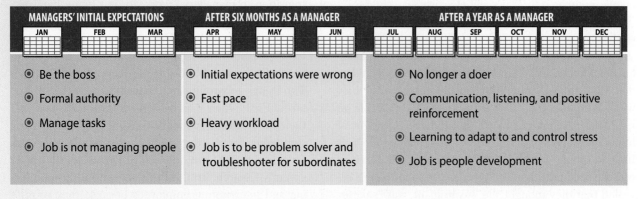

MANAGERS' INITIAL EXPECTATIONS			AFTER SIX MONTHS AS A MANAGER			AFTER A YEAR AS A MANAGER					
JAN	FEB	MAR	APR	MAY	JUN	JUL	AUG	SEP	OCT	NOV	DEC

MANAGERS' INITIAL EXPECTATIONS	AFTER SIX MONTHS AS A MANAGER	AFTER A YEAR AS A MANAGER
◉ Be the boss	◉ Initial expectations were wrong	◉ No longer a doer
◉ Formal authority	◉ Fast pace	◉ Communication, listening, and positive reinforcement
◉ Manage tasks	◉ Heavy workload	◉ Learning to adapt to and control stress
◉ Job is not managing people	◉ Job is to be problem solver and troubleshooter for subordinates	◉ Job is people development

Source: L.A. Hill, *Becoming a Manager: Mastery of a New Identity* (Boston: Harvard Business School Press, 1992).

management reveals the magnitude of the changes they experienced.

Initially, the managers in Hill's study believed that their job was to exercise formal authority and to manage tasks – basically being the boss, telling others what to do, making decisions, and getting things done. One of the managers Hill interviewed said, "Being the manager means running my own office, using my ideas and thoughts." Another said, "[The office is] my baby. It's my job to make sure it works."[103] In fact, most of the new managers were attracted to management positions because they wanted to be in charge. Surprisingly, the new managers did not believe that their job was to manage people. The only aspects of people management mentioned by the new managers were hiring and firing.

After six months, most of the new managers had concluded that their initial expectations about managerial work were wrong. Management wasn't just about being the boss, making decisions, and telling others what to do. The first surprise was the fast pace and heavy workload involved. Said one of Hill's managers, "This job is much harder than you think. It is 40 to 50 percent more work than being a producer!

Who would have ever guessed?" The pace of managerial work was startling, too. Another manager said, "You have eight or nine people looking for your time . . . coming into and out of your office all day long." A somewhat frustrated manager declared that management was "a job that never ended . . . a job you couldn't get your hands around."[104]

Informal descriptions like these are consistent with studies indicating that the average first-line manager spends no more than two minutes on a task before being interrupted by a request from a subordinate, a phone call, or an email. The pace is somewhat less hurried for top managers, who spend an average of approximately nine minutes on a task before having to switch to another. In practice, this means that supervisors may perform 30 tasks per hour, while top managers perform seven tasks per hour, with each task typically different from the one that preceded it. A manager described this frenetic level of activity by saying, "The only time you are in control is when you shut your door, and then I feel I am not doing the job I'm supposed to be doing, which is being with the people."[105]

The other major surprise after six months on the job was that the managers' expectations about what they should do as managers were very different from their subordinates' expectations. Initially, the managers defined their jobs as helping their subordinates perform their jobs well. For the managers, who still defined themselves as doers rather than managers, assisting their subordinates meant going out on sales calls or handling customer complaints. One manager said, "I like going out with the rep, who may need me to lend him my credibility as manager. I like the challenge, the joy in closing. I go out with the reps and we make the call and talk about the customer; it's fun."[106] But when new managers "assisted" in this way, their subordinates were resentful and viewed their help as interference. The subordinates wanted their managers to help them by solving problems that they couldn't solve themselves. After the managers realized this distinction, they embraced their role as problem solver and troubleshooter. Thus, they could help without interfering with their subordinates' jobs.

After a year on the job, most of the managers thought of themselves as managers and no longer as doers. In making the transition, they finally realized that people management was the most important part of their job. One of Hill's interviewees summarized the lesson that had taken him a year to learn by saying, "As many demands as managers have on their time, I think their primary responsibility is people development. Not production, but people development."[107] Another indication of how much their views had changed was that most of the managers now regretted the rather heavy-handed approach they had used in their early attempts to manage their subordinates. "I wasn't good at managing . . . , so I was bossy like a first-grade teacher." "Now I see that I started out as a drill sergeant. I was inflexible, just a lot of how-tos." By the end of the year, most of the managers had abandoned their authoritarian approach for one based on communication, listening, and positive reinforcement.

Finally, after beginning their year as managers in frustration, the managers came to feel comfortable with their subordinates, with the demands of their jobs, and with their emerging managerial styles. While being managers had made them acutely aware of their limitations and their need to develop as people, it also provided them with an unexpected reward of coaching and developing the people who worked for them. One manager said, "It gives me the best feeling to see somebody do something well after I have helped them. I get excited." Another stated, "I realize now that when I accepted the position of branch manager that it is truly an exciting vocation. It is truly awesome, even at this level; it can be terribly challenging and terribly exciting."[108]

1-8 COMPETITIVE ADVANTAGE THROUGH PEOPLE

If you look at the list of bestselling business books on Amazon, you'll find hundreds that explain precisely what companies need to do to be successful. Unfortunately, the best-selling business books tend to be faddish, changing dramatically every few years. One thing that hasn't changed, though, is the importance of good people and good management: companies can't succeed for long without them. Apple CEO Tim Cook agrees, saying, "I think about my day and weeks and months and years – I put them in three buckets: people, strategy, and execution. I sort of move between those on a daily basis as to where I put my time. I always think the most important one of those is people. If you don't get that one right, it doesn't matter what kind of energy you have in the other two – it's not enough."[109]

In his books *Competitive Advantage through People: Unleashing the Power of the Work Force* and *The Human Equation: Building Profits by Putting People First*, Stanford University business professor Jeffrey Pfeffer contends that what separates top-performing companies from their competitors is the way they treat their workforces – in other words, their management style.[110]

Pfeffer found that managers in top-performing companies used ideas such as employment security, selective hiring, self-managed teams and decentralization, high pay contingent on company performance, extensive training, reduced status distinctions (between managers and employees), and extensive sharing of financial information to achieve financial performance that, on average, was 40 percent higher than that of other companies. These ideas, which are explained in detail in Exhibit 1.7, help organizations develop workforces that are smarter, better trained, more motivated, and more committed than their competitors' workforces. And – as indicated by the phenomenal growth and return on investment earned by these companies – smarter, better trained, more motivated, and more committed workforces provide superior products and service to customers. Such customers keep buying and, by telling others about their positive experiences, bring in new customers.

According to Pfeffer, companies that invest in their people will create long-lasting competitive advantages that are difficult for other companies to duplicate. Other studies also clearly demonstrate that sound management practices can produce substantial advantages in

Exhibit 1.7
Competitive Advantage Through People: Management Practices

1. Employment Security – Employment security is the ultimate form of commitment companies can make to their workers. Employees can innovate and increase company productivity without fearing the loss of their jobs.

2. Selective Hiring – If employees are the basis for a company's competitive advantage, and those employees have employment security, then the company needs to aggressively recruit and selectively screen applicants in order to hire the most talented employees available.

3. Self-Managed Teams and Decentralization – Self-managed teams are responsible for their own hiring, purchasing, job assignments, and production. Self-managed teams can often produce enormous increases in productivity through increased employee commitment and creativity. Decentralization allows employees who are closest to (and most knowledgeable about) problems, production, and customers to make timely decisions. Decentralization increases employee satisfaction and commitment.

4. High Wages Contingent on Organizational Performance – High wages are needed to attract and retain talented workers and to indicate that the organization values its workers. Employees, like company founders, shareholders, and managers, need to share in the financial rewards when the company is successful. Why? Because employees who have a financial stake in their companies are more likely to take a long-run view of the business and think like business owners.

5. Training and Skill Development – Like a high-tech company that spends millions of dollars to upgrade computers or research and development labs, a company whose competitive advantage is based on its people must invest in the training and skill development of its people.

6. Reduction of Status Differences – A company should treat everyone, no matter what the job, as equal. There are no reserved parking spaces. Everyone eats in the same cafeteria and has similar benefits. The result is improved communication as employees focus on problems and solutions rather than on how they are less valued than managers.

7. Sharing Information – If employees are to make decisions that are good for the long-term health and success of the company, they need to be given information about costs, finances, productivity, development times, and strategies that was previously known only by company managers.

Source: J. Pfeffer, *The Human Equation: Building Profits by Putting People First* (Boston: Harvard Business School Press, 1996).

four critical areas of organizational performance: sales revenues, profits, stock market returns, and customer satisfaction.

In terms of sales revenues and profits, a study of nearly 1,000 US firms found that companies that use *just some* of the ideas shown in Exhibit 1.7 had $27,044 more sales per employee and $3,814 more profit per employee than companies that didn't. For a 100-person company, these differences amount to $2.7 million more in sales and nearly $400,000 more in annual profit! For a 1,000-person company, the difference grows to $27 million more in sales and $4 million more in annual profit![111]

Another study that considers the effect of investing in people on company sales found that poorly performing companies were able to improve their average return on investment from 5.1 to 19.7 percent and increase sales by $94,000 per employee. They did this by adopting management techniques as simple as setting performance expectations (establishing goals, results, and schedules), coaching (informal, ongoing discussions between managers and subordinates about what is being done well and what could be done better), reviewing employee performance (annual, formal discussion about results), and rewarding employee performance (adjusting salaries and bonuses based on employee performance and results).[112] Two decades of research across

92 companies indicates that the average increase in company performance from using these management practices is typically around 20 percent.[113] That fits with another study of 2,000 firms showing that an average improvement in management practices can produce a 10 to 20 percent increase in the total value of a company.[114] In addition to significantly improving the profitability of healthy companies, sound management practices can also turn around failing companies.

To determine how investing in people affects stock market performance, researchers matched companies on *Fortune* magazine's list of "100 Best Companies to Work for in America" with companies that were similar in industry, size, and – this is key – operating performance. Both sets of companies were equally good performers; the key difference was how well they treated their employees. For both sets of companies, the researchers found that employee attitudes such as job satisfaction changed little from year to year. The people who worked for the "100 Best" companies were consistently much more satisfied with their jobs and employers year after year than were employees in the matched companies. More importantly, those stable differences in employee attitudes were strongly related to differences in stock market performance. Over a three-year period, an investment in the "100 Best" would have resulted in an 82 percent

THE WORLD MANAGEMENT SURVEY: GOOD MANAGEMENT MATTERS EVERYWHERE

The World Management Survey (WMS) measures whether 12,000 companies in 34 countries "use (or don't use)" 18 specific management practices across four areas of management: operations management (creating maximum value for customers as efficiently as possible), performance monitoring (process documentation, key performance measures/reviews and consequences for missing targets), target setting (clear, appropriate goals connected to strategy at all levels), and talent management (stretch goals, coaching to improve poor performance, and investing to develop and keep talent).

donskarpo/Shutterstock.com

What can we learn from the WMS? First, while management seems simple, practicing good management is difficult. Just 6 percent of companies averaged a 4 or better on a 5-point scale. Second, companies that practiced good management performed better. Moving from the worst 10 percent to the top 10 percent results in "a $15 million increase in profits, 25 percent faster annual growth, and 75 percent higher productivity." Third, most managers were in denial, wildly overestimating how well managed their firms were. Fourth, the adoption of good management practices doesn't happen without top management's time and personal commitment. There are no shortcuts. Good management is hard. It happens only when leaders recognize, practice, and support the adoption of management ideas. But the great news is this: Good management produces results – everywhere.

Source: R. Sadun, N. Bloom & J. Van Reenen, "Why Do We Undervalue Competent Management?" *Harvard Business Review*," September–October 2017, accessed January 25, 2020, hbr.org/2017/09/why-do-we-undervalue-competent-management.

cumulative stock return compared with just 37 percent for the matched companies.[115] This difference is remarkable, given that both sets of companies were equally good performers at the beginning of the period.

Finally, research also indicates that managers have an important effect on customer satisfaction. Many people find this surprising. They don't understand how managers, who are largely responsible for what goes on inside the company, can affect what goes on outside the company. They wonder how managers, who often interact with customers under negative conditions (when customers are angry or dissatisfied), can actually improve customer satisfaction. It turns out that managers influence customer satisfaction through employee satisfaction. When employees are satisfied with their jobs, their bosses, and the companies they work for, they provide much better service to customers.[116] In turn, customers are more satisfied, too. In fact, customers of companies on *Fortune*'s list of "100 Best," where employees are much more satisfied with their jobs and their companies, have much higher customer satisfaction scores than do customers of comparable companies that are not on *Fortune*'s list. Over an eight-year period, that difference in customer satisfaction also resulted in a 14 percent annual stock market return for the "100 Best" companies compared to a 6 percent return for the overall stock market.[117]

You will learn more about the service-profit chain in Chapter 18 on managing service and manufacturing operations.

2 | The History of Management

LEARNING OUTCOMES

2-1 Explain the origins of management.

2-2 Explain the history of scientific management.

2-3 Discuss the history of bureaucratic and administrative management.

2-4 Explain the history of human relations management.

2-5 Discuss the history of operations, information, systems, and contingency management.

2-1 THE ORIGINS OF MANAGEMENT

Each day, managers are asked to solve challenging problems with limited time, people, and resources. Yet it's still their responsibility to get things done on schedule and within budget. Tell today's managers to "reward workers for improved production or performance," "set specific goals to increase motivation," or "innovate to create and sustain a competitive advantage," and they'll respond, "Duh! Who doesn't know that?" A mere 130 years ago, however, business ideas and practices were so different that today's widely accepted management ideas would have been as self-evident as space travel, smart phones, and flying drones. In fact, management jobs and careers didn't exist 130 years ago, so management was not yet a field of study. Now, of course, managers and management are such an important part of the business world that it's hard to imagine organizations without them.

So, if there were no managers 130 years ago, but you can't walk down the hall today without bumping into one, where did management come from?

Although we can find the seeds of many of today's management ideas throughout history, not until the past few centuries did systematic changes in the nature of work and organizations create a compelling need for managers.

2-1a Management Ideas and Practices throughout History

Examples of management thought and practice can be found throughout history.[1] For example, the earliest recorded instance of information management dates to ancient Sumer (modern Iraq), *circa* 8000–3000 BCE. Sumerian businesses used small clay tokens to calculate quantities of grain and livestock—and later, value-added goods such as perfume or pottery—that they owned and traded in temples and at city gates. Different shapes and sizes represented different types and quantities of goods. The tokens were also used to store data. They were kept in small clay envelopes, and the token shapes were impressed on the outside of the envelope to indicate what was inside. Eventually, someone figured out that it was easier to just write these symbols with a stylus on a tablet instead of using the tokens.

Here's what was written on one clay tablet from this era: "From Durhumit until Kaneš I incurred expenses of 5 minas of refined (copper), I spent 3 minas of copper until Wahšušana, I acquired and spent small wares for a value of 4 shekels of silver."[2] In the end, the new technology of *writing* led to more efficient management of the business of Sumerian temples.[3] Indeed, archaeologists have determined that most clay tablets of this time were "business letters, shipment documents, accounting records, seals and contracts."[4]

A task as enormous as building the great pyramids in Egypt was bound to present practical problems that would lead to the development of management ideas.

Egyptians recognized the need for planning, organizing, and controlling; for submitting written requests; and for consulting staff for advice before making decisions. The enormity of the task they faced is evident in the pyramid of King Khufu, which contains 2.3 million blocks of stone. Each block had to be quarried, cut to precise size and shape, cured (hardened in the sun), transported by boat for two to three days, moved to the construction site, numbered to identify where it would be placed, and then shaped and smoothed so that it would fit perfectly into place. It took 20,000 workers 23 years to complete this pyramid; more than 8,000 were needed just to quarry and transport the stones. A typical quarry expedition might include 100 army officers, 50 government and religious officials, and 200 members of the king's court to lead; 130 stonemasons to cut the stones; and 5,000 soldiers, 800 barbarians, and 2,000 bond servants to load and unload the stones from the ships.[5]

Exhibit 2.1 shows how other management ideas and practices throughout history relate to the management functions we discuss in this textbook.

2-1b Why We Need Managers Today

Working from 8:00 a.m. to 5:00 p.m., coffee breaks, lunch hours, crushing rush hour traffic, and endless emails and nonstop meetings are things we associate with today's working world. Work hasn't always been this way, however. In fact, the design of jobs and organizations has changed dramatically over the past 500 years. For most of humankind's history, for example, people didn't commute to work.[6] Work usually occurred in homes or on farms. In 1720, almost 80 percent of the 5.5 million people in England lived and worked in the country. And as recently as 1870, two-thirds of Americans earned their living from agriculture. Even most of those who didn't earn their living from agriculture didn't commute to work. Blacksmiths, furniture makers, leather goods makers, and other skilled tradespeople or craftspeople who formed trade guilds (the historical predecessors of labor unions) in England as early as 1093 typically worked out of shops in or next to their homes.[7] Likewise, cottage workers worked with each other out of small homes that were often built in a semicircle. A family in each cottage would complete a

Exhibit 2.1
Management Ideas and Practices throughout History

Time	Individual or Group	Planning	Organizing	Leading	Controlling	Contributions to Management Thought and Practice
5000 BCE	Sumerians				√	Written record keeping
4000 BCE to 2000 BCE	Egyptians	√	√		√	Planning, organizing, and controlling to build the pyramids; submitting requests in writing; making decisions after consulting staff for advice
1800 BCE	Hammurabi				√	Controls and using witnesses in legal cases
600 BCE	Nebuchadnezzar		√	√		Wage incentives and production control
500 BCE	Sun Tzu	√		√		Strategy and identifying and attacking opponents' weaknesses
400 BCE	Xenophon	√	√	√	√	Management as separate art
400 BCE	Cyrus		√	√	√	Human relations and motion study
175	Cato		√			Job descriptions
284	Diocletian		√			Delegation of authority
900	al-Farabi			√		Leadership traits
1100	Ghazali			√		Managerial traits
1418	Barbarigo		√			Different organizational forms/structures
1436	Venetians				√	Numbering, standardization, and interchangeability of parts
1500	Sir Thomas More			√		Critique of poor management and leadership
1525	Machiavelli		√	√		Cohesiveness, power, and leadership in organizations

Source: C. S. George Jr., *The History of Management Thought* (Englewood Cliffs, NJ: Prentice Hall, 1972).

different production step, and work passed from one cottage to the next until production was complete. With small, self-organized work groups, no commute, no bosses, and no common building, there wasn't a strong need for management.

During the Industrial Revolution (1750–1900), however, jobs and organizations changed dramatically.[8] First, unskilled laborers running machines began to replace high-paid, skilled artisans. This change was made possible by the availability of power (steam engines and, later, electricity) as well as numerous related inventions, including Darby's coke-smelting process and Cort's puddling and rolling process (both for making iron), as well as Hargreaves's spinning jenny and Arkwright's water frame (both for spinning cotton). Although artisans made entire goods by themselves by hand, this new production system was based on a division of labor: each worker, interacting with machines, performed separate, highly specialized tasks that were but a small part of all the steps required to make manufactured goods. Mass production was born as rope- and chain-driven assembly lines moved work to stationary workers who concentrated on performing one small task over and over again. While workers focused on their singular tasks, managers were needed to coordinate the different parts of the production system and optimize its overall performance. Productivity skyrocketed at companies that understood this. At **Ford Motor Company**, where the assembly line was developed, the time required to assemble a car dropped from 12.5 work hours to just 93 minutes after switching to mass production.[9]

Second, instead of being performed in fields, homes, or small shops, jobs occurred in large, formal organizations where hundreds, if not thousands, of people worked under one roof.[10] In 1849, for example, **Chicago Harvester** (the predecessor of International Harvester) ran the largest factory in the United States with just 123 workers. Yet by 1913, Henry Ford employed 12,000 employees in his Highland Park, Michigan, factory alone. Because the number of people working in manufacturing quintupled from 1860 to 1890, and individual factories employed so many workers under one roof, companies now had a strong need for disciplinary rules to impose order and structure. For the first time, they needed managers who knew how to organize large groups, work with employees, and make good decisions.

2-2 SCIENTIFIC MANAGEMENT

Before 1880, business educators taught only basic bookkeeping and secretarial skills, and no one published books or articles about management.[11] Today if you have a question about management, you can turn to dozens of academic journals (such as the Academy of Management's *Journal* or *Review*, *Administrative Science Quarterly*, the *Strategic Management Journal*, and the *Journal of Applied Psychology*), hundreds of business school and practitioner journals (such as *Harvard Business Review*, *MIT Sloan Management Review*, and the *Academy of Management Perspectives*), and thousands of other books and articles. In the next four sections, you will learn about some important contributors to the field of management and how their ideas shaped our current understanding of management theory and practice.

Bosses, who were hired by the company owner or founder, used to make decisions by the seat of their pants—haphazardly, without any systematic study, thought, or collection of information. If the bosses decided that workers should work twice as fast, little or no thought was given to worker motivation. If workers resisted, the bosses often resorted to physical beatings to get workers to work faster, harder, or longer. With no incentives for bosses and workers to cooperate with one another, both groups played the system by trying to take advantage of each other. Moreover, each worker did the same job in his or her own way with different methods and different tools. In short, there were no procedures to standardize operations, no standards by which to judge whether performance was good or bad, and no follow-up to determine whether productivity or quality actually improved when changes were made.[12]

This all changed, however, with the advent of **scientific management**, which involved thorough study and testing of different work methods to identify the best, most efficient ways to complete a job.

*Let's find out more about scientific management by learning about **2-2a Frederick W. Taylor, the father of scientific management; 2-2b Frank and Lillian Gilbreth and motion studies; and 2-2c Henry Gantt and his Gantt charts.***

2-2a Father of Scientific Management: Frederick W. Taylor

Frederick W. Taylor (1856–1915), the father of scientific management, began his career as a worker at **Midvale Steel Company**. He was promoted to patternmaker, supervisor, and then chief engineer. At Midvale, Taylor was deeply affected by his three-year struggle to get the men who worked for him to do, as he called it,

> **Scientific management**
> thoroughly studying and testing different work methods to identify the best, most efficient way to complete a job

Frederick W. Taylor was affected by his three-year struggle to get the men who worked for him to do, as he called it, "a fair day's work."

"a fair day's work." Taylor, who had worked alongside the men as a coworker before becoming their boss, said, "We who were the workmen of that shop had the quantity output carefully agreed upon for everything that was turned out in the shop. We limited the output to about, I should think, one third of what we could very well have done." Taylor explained that, as soon as he became the boss, "the men who were working under me . . . knew that I was onto the whole game of **soldiering**, or deliberately restricting output."[13] When Taylor told his workers, "I have accepted a job under the management of this company and I am on the other side of the fence . . . I am going to try to get a bigger output," the workers responded, "We warn you, Fred, if you try to bust any of these rates [a **rate buster** was someone who worked faster than the group] we will have you over the fence in six weeks."[14]

Soldiering when workers deliberately slow their pace or restrict their work output

Rate buster a group member whose work pace is significantly faster than the normal pace in his or her group

Over the next three years, Taylor tried everything he could think of to improve output. By doing the job himself, he showed workers that it was possible to produce more output. He hired new workers and trained them himself, hoping they would produce more. But "very heavy social pressure" from the other workers kept them from doing so. Pushed by Taylor, the workers began breaking their machines so that they couldn't produce. Taylor responded by fining them every time they broke a machine and for any violation of the rules, no matter how small, such as being late to work. Tensions became so severe that some of the workers threatened to shoot Taylor. Looking back at the situation, Taylor reflected, "It is a horrid life for any man to live, not to be able to look any workman in the face all day long without seeing hostility there and feeling that every man around one is his virtual enemy." He said, "I made up my mind either to get out of the business entirely and go into some other line of work or to find some remedy for this unbearable condition."[15]

The remedy that Taylor eventually developed was scientific management. Taylor, who once described scientific management as "seventy-five percent science and twenty-five percent common sense," emphasized that the goal of scientific management was to use systematic study to find the "one best way" of doing each task. To do that, managers had to follow the four principles shown in Exhibit 2.2. The first principle was to "develop a science" for each element of work. Study it. Analyze it. Determine the "one best way" to do the work. For example, one of Taylor's controversial proposals at the time was to give rest breaks to factory workers doing physical labor. We take morning, lunch, and afternoon breaks for granted, but in Taylor's day, factory workers were expected to work without stopping.[16] When Taylor said that breaks would increase worker productivity, no one believed him. Nonetheless, through systematic experiments, he showed that workers receiving frequent rest breaks were able to greatly increase their daily output.

Second, managers had to scientifically select, train, teach, and develop workers to help them reach their full potential. Before Taylor, supervisors often hired on the basis of favoritism and nepotism. Who you knew was often more important than what you could do. By contrast, Taylor instructed supervisors to hire "first-class" workers on the basis of their aptitude to do a job well. In one of the first applications of this principle, physical reaction times were used to select bicycle ball-bearing inspectors, who had to be able to examine ball bearings as fast as they were produced on a production line. For similar reasons, Taylor also recommended that companies train and develop their workers—a rare practice at the time.

Exhibit 2.2
Taylor's Four Principles of Scientific Management

First:	Develop a science for each element of a man's work, which replaces the old rule of thumb method.
Second:	Scientifically select and then train, teach, and develop the workman, whereas in the past, he chose his own work and trained himself as best he could.
Third:	Heartily cooperate with the men so as to ensure all of the work being done is in accordance with the principles of the science that has been developed.
Fourth:	There is an almost equal division of the work and the responsibility between the management and the workmen. The management take over all the work for which they are better fitted than the workmen, while in the past, almost all of the work and the greater part of the responsibility were thrown upon the men.

Source: F. W. Taylor, *The Principles of Scientific Management* (New York: Harper, 1911).

The third principle instructed managers to cooperate with employees to ensure that the scientific principles were actually implemented. Labor unrest was widespread at the time; the number of labor strikes against companies doubled between 1893 and 1904. As Taylor knew from personal experience, workers and management more often than not viewed each other as enemies. Taylor's advice ran contrary to the common wisdom of the day. He said, "The majority of these men believe that the fundamental interests of employees and employers are necessarily antagonistic. Scientific management, on the contrary, has for its very foundation the firm conviction that the true interests of the two are one and the same; that prosperity for the employer cannot exist through a long term of years unless it is accompanied by prosperity for the employee and vice versa; and that it is possible to give the workman what he most wants—high wages—and the employer what he wants—a low labor cost for his manufactures."[17]

Taylor's Rest Break Now Includes Napping and Sabbaticals

While rest breaks traditionally involve sitting or taking a brief walk, some employers now see a rest break as an opportunity for a quick snooze or a long sabbatical. Lampooned in movies and television, napping at work is nonetheless a proven way to increase focus, memory, and alertness on the job. A University of Michigan study found that a one-hour nap during the workday produced all those benefits—and more. But obtaining those benefits is not easy. Not only is it difficult to make time during hectic workdays, but finding a *place* to sleep can be challenging as well. Only 6 percent of companies have dedicated napping spaces, and many employees work in loud, crowded spaces with uncomfortable chairs.

But, if you can find a spot, when and how long should you nap? First, figure out the midpoint of your previous night's rest and add 12 hours. Second, sleep either for 20 or 90 minutes. Anything in between or longer will leave you groggy and ineffective, counteracting the point of the nap in the first place.

While naps are good for short-term focus and recharging, numerous studies show that taking extended sabbaticals, meaning three months or longer, produces lasting benefits of reduced stress and increased confidence, creativity, and psychological health. They're also an opportunity to develop the skills of interim managers who step in for those on extended leave. Human resource professor Maurice Mazerolle says, "The strategic use of sabbaticals can greatly enhance an organization's competitiveness." So, whether it's short naps or long sabbaticals, Frederick W. Taylor's observation that breaks are good for workers and managers is still relevant in the twenty-first century.

Sources: D. Burkus, "Research Shows That Organizations Benefit When Employees Take Sabbaticals," *Harvard Business Review*, August 10, 2017, accessed January 30, 2020, https://hbr.org/2017/08/research-shows-that-organizations-benefit-when-employees-take-sabbaticals; J. Dunne, "Need a Longer Holiday? In a Tight Labour Market Some Companies Offer Sabbaticals," *CBC News*, July 13, 2019, accessed January 30, 2020, https://www.cbc.ca/news/business/sabbaticals-human-resources-1.5208559; R. Greenfield, "Napping at Work Can Be So Exhausting," *Bloomberg Businessweek*, August 20, 2015, http://www.bloomberg.com/news/articles/2015-08-20/napping-at-work-can-be-so-exhausting, accessed March 26, 2016.

The fourth principle of scientific management was to divide the work and the responsibility equally between management and workers. Prior to Taylor, workers alone were held responsible for productivity and performance. But, said Taylor, "Almost every act of the workman should be preceded by one or more preparatory acts of the management, which enable him to do his work better and quicker than he otherwise could. And each man should daily be taught by and receive the most friendly help from those who are over him, instead of being, at the one extreme, driven or coerced by his bosses, and at the other left, to his own unaided devices."[18]

Above all, Taylor believed these principles could be used to determine a "fair day's work," that is, what an average worker could produce at a reasonable pace, day in and day out. After that was determined, it was management's responsibility to pay workers fairly for that fair day's work. In essence, Taylor was trying to align management and employees so that what was good for employees was also good for management. In this way, he believed, workers and managers could avoid the conflicts he had experienced at Midvale Steel.

Although Taylor remains a controversial figure among some academics who believe that his ideas were bad for workers, his key ideas have stood the test of time.[19] These include using systematic analysis to identify the best methods; scientifically selecting, training, and developing workers; promoting cooperation between management and labor; developing standardized approaches and tools; setting specific tasks or goals and then rewarding workers with financial incentives; and giving workers shorter work hours and frequent breaks. In fact, his ideas are so well accepted and widely used that we take most of them for granted. As eminent management scholar Edwin Locke said, "The point is not, as is often claimed, that he was 'right in the context of his time,' but is now outdated, but that *most of his insights are still valid today.*"[20]

2-2b Motion Studies: Frank and Lillian Gilbreth

The husband and wife team of Frank and Lillian Gilbreth are best known for their use of motion studies to simplify work, but they also made significant contributions to the employment of disabled workers and to the field of industrial psychology. Like Taylor, their early experiences significantly shaped their interests and contributions to management.

Though admitted to MIT, Frank Gilbreth (1868–1924) began his career as an

> **Motion study** breaking each task or job into its separate motions and then eliminating those that are unnecessary or repetitive

Frank and Lillian Gilbreth are best known for their use of motion studies to simplify work.

apprentice bricklayer. While learning the trade, he noticed the bricklayers using three different sets of motions—one to teach others how to lay bricks, a second to work at a slow pace, and a third to work at a fast pace.[21] Wondering which was best, he studied the various approaches and began eliminating unnecessary motions. For example, by designing a stand that could be raised to waist height, he eliminated the need to bend over to pick up each brick. Turning to grab a brick was faster and easier than bending down. By having lower-paid workers place all the bricks with their most attractive side up, bricklayers didn't waste time turning a brick over to find it. By mixing a more consistent mortar, bricklayers no longer had to tap each brick numerous times to put it in the right position. Together, Gilbreth's improvements raised productivity from 120 to 350 bricks per hour and from 1,000 bricks to 2,700 bricks per day.

As a result of his experience with bricklaying, Gilbreth and his wife, Lillian, developed a long-term interest in using motion study to simplify work, improve productivity, and reduce the level of effort required to safely perform a job. Indeed, Frank Gilbreth said, "The greatest waste in the world comes from needless, ill-directed, and ineffective motions."[22] **Motion study** broke each task or job into separate motions and then eliminated those that were unnecessary or repetitive. Because many motions were completed very quickly, the

Exhibit 2.3
Gantt Chart for Starting Construction on a New Headquarters

Tasks	Weeks	23 Sep to 29 Sep	30 Sep to 6 Oct	7 Oct to 13 Oct	14 Oct to 20 Oct	21 Oct to 27 Oct	28 Oct to 3 Nov	4 Nov to 10 Nov	11 Nov to 17 Nov	18 Nov to 25 Nov
Interview and select architectural firm		Architect by October 7								
Hold weekly planning meetings with architects				Planning with architects by November 4						
Obtain permits and approval from city							Permits and approval by November 11			
Begin preparing site for construction								Site preparation done by November 18		
Finalize loans and financing									Financing finalized by November 18	
Begin construction										Start building

Gilbreths used motion-picture films, then a relatively new technology, to analyze jobs. Most film cameras at that time were hand cranked and thus variable in their film speed, so Frank invented the microchrono-meter, a large clock that could record time to 1/2,000th of a second. By placing the microchonometer next to the worker in the camera's field of vision and attaching a flashing strobe light to the worker's hands to better identify the direction and sequence of key movements, the Gilbreths could use film to detect and precisely time even the slightest, fastest movements. Motion study typically yielded production increases from 25 to 300 percent.[23]

Taylor also strove to simplify work, but he did so by managing time rather than motion as the Gilbreths did.[24] Taylor developed time study to put an end to soldiering and to determine what could be considered a fair day's work. **Time study** worked by timing how long it took a "first-class man" to complete each part of his job. A standard time was established after allowing for rest periods, and a worker's pay would increase or decrease depending on whether the worker exceeded or fell below that standard.

Lillian Gilbreth (1878–1972) was an important contributor to management in her own right. She was the first woman to receive a PhD in industrial psychology, as well as the first woman to become a member of the Society of Industrial Engineers and the American Society of Mechanical Engineers. When Frank died in 1924, she continued the work of their management consulting company (which they had shared for over a dozen years). Lillian, who was concerned with the human side of work, was one of the first contributors to industrial psychology, originating ways to improve office communication, incentive programs, job satisfaction, and management training. Her work also convinced the government to enact laws regarding workplace safety, ergonomics, and child labor.

2-2c Charts: Henry Gantt

Henry Gantt (1861–1919) was first a protégé and then an associate of Frederick W. Taylor. Gantt is best known for the Gantt chart, but he also made significant contributions to management with respect to pay-for-performance plans and the training and development of workers. As shown in Exhibit 2.3, a **Gantt chart** visually indicates what tasks must be completed at which times in order to complete a project. It accomplishes this by showing time in various units on the x-axis and tasks on the y-axis. For example, Exhibit 2.3 shows that the following tasks must be completed by the following dates: in order to start construction on a new company

> **Time study** timing how long it takes good workers to complete each part of their jobs
>
> **Gantt chart** a graphical chart that shows which tasks must be completed at which times in order to complete a project or task

headquarters by the week of November 18, the architectural firm must be selected by October 7, architectural planning done by November 4, permits obtained from the city by November 11, site preparation finished by November 18, and loans and financing finalized by November 18.

Though simple and straightforward, Gantt charts were revolutionary in the era of seat-of-the-pants management because of the detailed planning information they provided. As Gantt wrote, "By using the graphical forms, [the Gantt chart's] value is very much increased, for the general appearance of the sheet is sufficient to tell how closely the schedule is being lived up to; in other words, whether the plant is being run efficiently or not."[25] Gantt said, "Such sheets show at a glance where the delays occur, and indicate what must have our attention in order to keep up the proper output." The use of Gantt charts is so widespread today that nearly all project management software and computer spreadsheets have the capability to create charts that track and visually display the progress being made on a project.

Finally, Gantt, along with Taylor, was one of the first to strongly recommend that companies train and develop their workers.[26] In his work with companies, he found that workers achieved their best performance levels if they were trained first. At the time, however, supervisors were reluctant to teach workers what they knew for fear that they could lose their jobs to more knowledgeable workers. Gantt overcame the supervisors' resistance by rewarding them with bonuses for properly training all of their workers. Said Gantt, "This is the first recorded attempt to make it in the financial interest of the foreman to teach the individual worker, and the importance of it cannot be overestimated, for it changes the foreman from a driver of men to their friend and helper."[27]

Gantt's approach to training was straightforward: "(1) A scientific investigation in detail of each piece of work, and the determination of the best method and the shortest time in which the work can be done. (2) A teacher capable of teaching the best method and the shortest time. (3) Reward for both teacher and pupil when the latter is successful."[28]

2-3 BUREAUCRATIC AND ADMINISTRATIVE MANAGEMENT

The field of scientific management developed quickly in the United States between 1895 and 1920 and focused on improving the efficiency of manufacturing facilities and their workers. At about the same time, equally important ideas about bureaucratic and administrative management were developing in Europe. German sociologist Max Weber (1864–1920)

Bureaucracy's "Iron Cage" Costs Companies Trillions

While Max Weber's ideas (fairness, efficiency, rules, and procedures) advanced business management, he correctly predicted bureaucracy's downside, saying, "Once fully established, bureaucracy is among those social structures which are the hardest to destroy."

So how much does bureaucracy's inefficiency, red tape, and incompetence cost companies? According to management professors Gary Hamel and Michele Zanini, in the United States alone its cost is $3 trillion a year, or 17 percent of GDP! A study of 7,000 *Harvard Business Review (HBR)* readers found that, on average, managers and employees wasted more than one day a week on "bureaucratic chores such as preparing reports, attending meetings, complying with internal requests, securing sign-offs and interacting with staff functions." Even worse, nearly two-thirds of those *HBR* readers said their companies had become *more* bureaucratic in the last few years.

If management ideas were supposed to improve business functioning and productivity, how is this so? Too many managers!

Twenty-four million US managers results in 1 manager for every 4.7 workers. Hamel and Zanini estimate that companies could easily double that to 1 manager for every 10 workers. With more people manufacturing products, providing services, or directly dealing with customers, and millions fewer managers pushing red tape rather than company goals, productivity could jump by 15 percent!

Christian Delbert/Shutterstock.com

Sources: G. Hamel & M. Zanini, "Excess Management Is Costing the US $3 Trillion Per Year," *Harvard Business Review Digital Articles,* September 5, 2016, accessed March 4, 2017, https://hbr.org/2016/09/excess-management-is-costing-the-us-3-trillion-per-year; G. Hamel & M. Zanini, "What We Learned about Bureaucracy from 7,000 HBR Readers," *Harvard Business Review,* August 10, 2017, accessed January 31, 2020, https://hbr.org/2017/08/what-we-learned-about-bureaucracy-from-7000 -hbr-readers; M. Weber, *The Protestant Ethic and the Spirit of Capitalism* (New York: Scribner's, 1958).

presented a new way to run entire organizations (bureaucratic management) in *The Theory of Social and Economic Organization*, published in 1922. Henri Fayol, an experienced French CEO, published his ideas about how and what managers should do in their jobs (administrative management) in *General and Industrial Management* in 1916.

*Let's find out more about the contributions Weber and Fayol made to management by learning about **2-3a bureaucratic management** and **2-3b administrative management**.*

2-3a Bureaucratic Management: Max Weber

Today, when we hear the term *bureaucracy*, we think of inefficiency and red tape, incompetence and ineffectiveness, and rigid administrators blindly enforcing nonsensical rules. When Weber first proposed the idea of bureaucratic organizations, however, these problems were associated with monarchies and patriarchies rather than bureaucracies. In monarchies, where kings, queens, sultans, and emperors ruled, and patriarchies, where a council of elders, wise men, or male heads of extended families ruled, the top leaders typically achieved their positions by virtue of birthright. For example, when the queen died, her oldest son became king, regardless of his intelligence, experience, education, or desire. Likewise, promotion to prominent positions of authority in monarchies and patriarchies was based on who you knew (politics), who you were (heredity), or ancient rules and traditions.

It was against this historical background of monarchical and patriarchal rule that Weber proposed the then-new idea of bureaucracy. *Bureaucracy* comes from the French word *bureaucratie*. Because *bureau* means desk or office and *cratie* or *cracy* means to rule, *bureaucracy* literally means to rule from a desk or office. According to Weber, **bureaucracy** is "the exercise of control on the basis of knowledge."[29] Rather than ruling by virtue of favoritism or personal or family connections, people in a bureaucracy would lead by virtue of their rational-legal authority—in other words, their knowledge, expertise, or experience. Furthermore, the aim of bureaucracy is not to protect authority but to achieve an organization's goals in the most efficient way possible.

Exhibit 2.4 shows the seven elements that, according to Weber, characterize bureaucracies. First, instead of hiring people because of their family or political connections or personal loyalty, they should be hired because their technical training or education qualifies them to do the job well. Second, along the same lines, promotion within the company should no longer be based on who

you know (politics) or who you are (heredity) but on your experience or achievements. And to further limit the influence of personal connections in the promotion process, *managers* rather than organizational owners should decide who gets promoted. Third, each position or job is part of a chain of command that clarifies who reports to whom throughout the organization. Those higher in the chain of command have the right, if they so choose, to give commands, act, and make decisions concerning activities occurring anywhere below them in the chain. Unlike in many monarchies or patriarchies, however, those lower in the chain of command are protected by a grievance procedure that gives them the right to appeal the decisions of those in higher positions. Fourth, to increase efficiency and effectiveness, tasks and responsibilities should be separated and assigned to those best qualified to complete them. Authority is vested in these task-defined positions rather than in people, and the authority of each position is clearly defined in order to reduce confusion and conflict. If you move to a different job in a bureaucracy, your authority increases or decreases commensurate with the responsibilities of that job. Fifth, because of his strong distaste for favoritism, Weber believed that an organization's rules and procedures should apply to all the members regardless of their position or status. Sixth, to ensure consistency and fairness over time and across different leaders and supervisors, all rules, procedures, and decisions should be recorded in writing. Finally, to reduce favoritism, "professional" managers rather than company owners should manage or supervise the organization.

When viewed in historical context, Weber's ideas about bureaucracy represent a tremendous improvement in how organizations should be run. Fairness supplanted favoritism, the goal of efficiency replaced the goal of personal gain, and logical rules and procedures took the place of traditions or arbitrary decision-making.

Today, however, after more than a century of experience, we recognize that bureaucracy has limitations as well. Weber called bureaucracy the "iron cage" and said, "Once fully established, bureaucracy is among those social structures which are the hardest to destroy."[30] In bureaucracies, managers are supposed to influence employee behavior by fairly rewarding or punishing employees for compliance or noncompliance with organizational policies, rules, and procedures. In reality, however, most employees would argue that bureaucratic managers emphasize punishment for noncompliance much more than rewards for compliance. Ironically, bureaucratic management was created to prevent just this type of managerial behavior.

Bureaucracy the exercise of control on the basis of knowledge, expertise, or experience

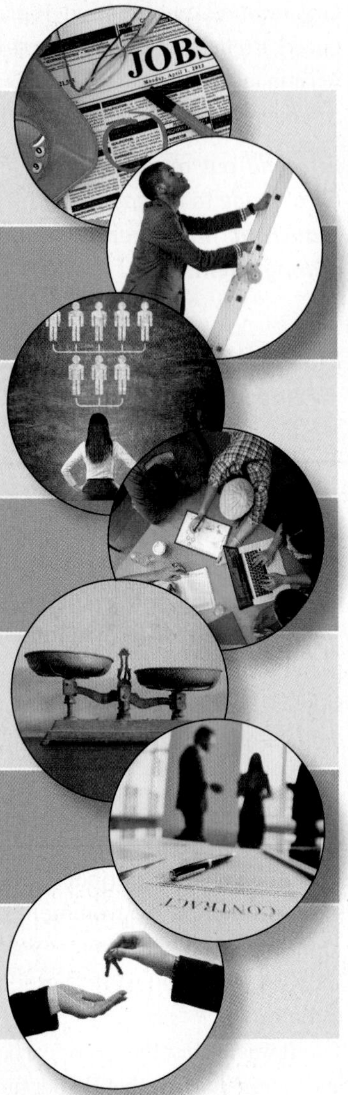

Maxx-Studio/Shutterstock.com; Wavebreakmedia/Shutterstock.com; ImageFlow/Shutterstock.com; Lucky Business/Shutterstock.com; XRoigs/Shutterstock.com; Pressmaster/Shutterstock.com; Andy Dean Photography/Shutterstock.com

Exhibit 2.4
Elements of Bureaucratic Organizations

Qualification-based hiring:	Employees are hired on the basis of their technical training or educational background.
Merit-based promotion:	Promotion is based on experience or achievement. Managers, not organizational owners, decide who is promoted..
Chain of command:	Each job occurs within a hierarchy, the chain of command, in which each position reports and is accountable to a higher position. A grievance procedure and a right to appeal protect people in lower positions.
Division of labor:	Tasks, responsibilities, and authority are clearly divided and defined.
Impartial application of rules and procedures:	Rules and procedures apply to all members of the organization and will be applied in an impartial manner, regardless of one's position or status.
Recorded in writing:	All administrative decisions, acts, rules, and procedures will be recorded in writing.
Managers separate from owners:	The owners of an organization should not manage or supervise the organization

Source: M. Weber, *The Theory of Social and Economic Organization*, trans. A. Henderson and T. Parsons (New York: The Free Press, 1947), 329–334.

2-3b Administrative Management: Henri Fayol

Though his work was not translated and widely recognized in the United States until 1949, Frenchman Henri Fayol (1841–1925) was as important a contributor to the field of management as Taylor. Like Taylor and the Gilbreths, Fayol's work experience significantly shaped his thoughts and ideas about management. But, whereas Taylor's ideas changed companies from the shop floor up, Fayol's ideas were shaped by his experience as a managing director (CEO) and generally changed companies from the board of directors down.[31] Fayol is best known for developing five functions of managers and 14 principles of management, as well as for his belief that management can and should be taught to others.

The most formative events in Fayol's business career came during his 20+ years as the managing director of Compagnie de Commentry-Fourchambault et Décazeville, commonly known as **Comambault**, a vertically integrated steel company that owned several coal and iron ore mines and employed 10,000 to 13,000 workers. Fayol was initially hired by the board of directors to shut down the "hopeless" steel company. The company was facing increased competition from English and German steel companies, which had lower costs, and from new steel mills in northern and eastern France, which were closer to major markets and thus could avoid the high shipping costs incurred by Fayol's company, located in central France.[32] In the five years before Fayol became CEO, production had dropped more than 60 percent, from 38,000 to 15,000 annual metric tons. Comambault had exhausted a key supply of coal needed for steel production, had already shut down one steel mill, and was losing money at another.[33] The company had quit paying dividends to shareholders and had no cash to invest in new technology, such as blast furnaces, that could lower its costs and increase productivity.

So the board hired Fayol as CEO to quickly dissolve and liquidate the business. But, after "four months of reflection and study," he presented the board with a plan, backed by detailed facts and figures, to save the company.[34] With little to lose, the board agreed. Fayol then began the process of turning the company around by obtaining supplies of key resources such as coal and iron ore; using research to develop new steel-alloy products; carefully selecting key subordinates in research, purchasing, manufacturing, and sales and then delegating responsibility to them; and cutting costs by moving the company to a better location closer to key markets.[35]

Looking back 10 years later, Fayol attributed his and the company's success to changes in management practices. He wrote, "When I assumed the responsibility for the restoration of Décazeville, I did not rely on my technical superiority. . . . I relied on my ability as an organizer [and my] skill in handling men."[36]

Based on his experience as a CEO, Fayol argued that "the success of an enterprise generally depends much more on the administrative ability of its leaders than on their technical ability."[37] And, as you learned in Chapter 1, Fayol argued that managers need to perform five managerial functions if they are to be successful: planning, organizing, coordinating, commanding, and controlling.[38] Because most management textbooks have dropped the coordinating function and now refer to Fayol's commanding function as "leading," these functions are widely known as planning (determining organizational goals and a means for achieving them), organizing (deciding where decisions will be made, who will do what jobs and tasks, and who will work for whom), leading (inspiring and motivating workers to work hard to achieve organizational goals), and controlling (monitoring progress toward goal achievement and taking corrective action when needed). In addition, according to Fayol, effective management is based on the 14 principles shown in Exhibit 2.5.

Exhibit 2.5
Fayol's 14 Principles of Management

1. **Division of work**
   Increase production by dividing work so that each worker completes smaller tasks or job elements.

2. **Authority and responsibility**
   A manager's authority, which is the "right to give orders," should be commensurate with the manager's responsibility. However, organizations should enact controls to prevent managers from abusing their authority.

3. **Discipline**
   Clearly defined rules and procedures are needed at all organizational levels to ensure order and proper behavior.

4. **Unity of command**
   To avoid confusion and conflict, each employee should report to and receive orders from just one boss.

5. **Unity of direction**
   One person and one plan should be used in deciding the activities to be carried out to accomplish each organizational objective.

6. **Subordination of individual interests to the general interests**
   Employees must put the organization's interests and goals before their own.

7. **Remuneration**
   Compensation should be fair and satisfactory to both the employees and the organization; that is, don't overpay or underpay employees.

8. **Centralization**
   Avoid too much centralization or decentralization. Strike a balance, depending on the circumstances and employees involved.

9. **Scalar chain**
   From the top to the bottom of an organization, each position is part of a vertical chain of authority in which each worker reports to just one boss. For the sake of simplicity, communication outside normal work groups or departments should follow the vertical chain of authority.

10. **Order**
    To avoid confusion and conflict, order can be obtained by having a place for everyone and having everyone in his or her place; in other words, there should be no overlapping responsibilities.

11. **Equity**
    Kind, fair, and just treatment for all will develop devotion and loyalty. This does not exclude discipline, if warranted, and consideration of the broader general interests of the organization.

12. **Stability of tenure of personnel**
    Low turnover, meaning a stable workforce with high tenure, benefits an organization by improving performance, lowering costs, and giving employees, especially managers, time to learn their jobs.

13. **Initiative**
    Because it is a "great source of strength for business," managers should encourage the development of initiative, or the ability to develop and implement a plan, in others.

14. *Esprit de corps*
    Develop a strong sense of morale and unity among workers that encourages coordination of efforts.

Sources: H. Fayol, *General and Industrial Management* (London: Pittman & Sons, 1949); M. Fells, "Fayol Stands the Test of Time," *Journal of Management History* 6 (2000): 345–360; C. Rodrigues, "Fayol's 14 Principles of Management Then and Now: A Framework for Managing Today's Organizations Effectively," *Management Decision* 39 (2001): 880–889.

DOING THE RIGHT THING

C.C. Spaulding: "Mr. Cooperation," African American CEO, and Early Contributor to Management

Thanks to new archival research by Professors Leon Prieto and Simone Phipps, Charles Clinton (C.C.) Spaulding is now recognized as a significant early contributor to the field of management. Spaulding, a successful African American business executive, was born 10 years (1874) after the end of the US Civil War and died 12 years (1952) before passage of the 1964 Civil Rights Act outlawing discrimination.

Like Henry Fayol and Chester Barnard, Spaulding's experience as president of the North Carolina Mutual Life Insurance Company—then the largest African American insurance company in the United States—shaped his views about management. However, Spaulding wrote his eight fundamental necessities of business administration in a 1927 article titled "The Administration of Big Business" before Barnard's (1938) and Fayol's (1949) ideas were first published in the United States. His ideas on conflict and cooperation are consistent with those of Mary Parker Follett, which were also published during the 1920s. Spaulding's eight fundamental necessities of management are, in the author's own words:

C.C. Spaulding is shown at left in this undated photo with Jessie Matthews Vann, editor and publisher of *The Pittsburgh Courier*.

» Necessity 1: Cooperation and Teamwork. "Not only should executives confer daily with each other, disclosing all the facts and circumstances attendant upon their operations, but they ought to keep constant check upon the activities and liabilities of their associates . . ."

» Necessity 2: Authority and Responsibility. "There must always be some responsible executive who must pass upon every issue that is fundamental; he must be the final authority from whom there is no appeal except to the entire group in conference."

» Necessity 3: Division of Labor. "Departmental divisions function separately under the direction of experts who may or may not be executive officers."

» Necessity 4: Adequate Manpower. "First and foremost success in business depends upon adequate manpower. Our schools are turning out only partially trained young people with no business experience whatsoever, and while many of them are good technicians they are for the most part helpless in their new jobs because there is little correlation between the classroom and the business office."

» Necessity 5: Adequate Capital. "Initial capital must not only be sufficient to commence operations, but must be sustaining over a given period . . . Even large scale corporations frequently dissipate their surplus earnings in hurried dividends instead of re-investing the surplus for the extension of the business."

» Necessity 6: Feasibility Analysis. "Frequently it happens that as soon as one person or group appears successful in a given line [of business] another person or group organizes a new enterprise in the same line without ascertaining the advisability of such a move, as reflected in the needs and resources of the community."

» Necessity 7: Advertising Budget. "[. . .] when it comes to advertising, a large number of our organizations are depriving themselves of the most effective means of propagation . . . Very few of these have an annual appropriation for advertisement."

» Necessity 8: Conflict Resolution. "Personal contact and business contact, if not properly directed and if not based on mutual goodwill and intelligence derived from a common sense education, will develop personal conflict and business conflict instead of personal cooperation and business cooperation."

Sources: L.C. Prieto & S.T.A. Phipps, "Re-discovering Charles Clinton Spaulding's 'The Administration of Big Business,' Insight Into Early 20th Century African-American Management Thought," *Journal of Management History* 22 (1) (2016): 73–90; A. Rutledge, "They call him 'Co-operation,'" *The Saturday Evening Post,* March 27, 1943, p. 15; C.C. Spaulding, "The Administration of Big Business," *The Pittsburgh Courier,* August, 13, 1927, 4; C.C. Spaulding, "The Administration of Big Business," *The Pittsburgh Courier,* August, 20, 1927, 8; H. Fayol, *General and Industrial Management* (London: Pittman & Sons, 1949); P. Graham, ed., *Mary Parker Follett—Prophet of Management: A Celebration of Writings from the 1920s* (Boston: Harvard Business School Press, 1995); C. I. Barnard, *The Functions of the Executive* (Cambridge, MA: Harvard University Press, 1938).

2-4 HUMAN RELATIONS MANAGEMENT

Iconic Bestiary/Shutterstock.com

As we have seen, scientific management focuses on improving efficiency; bureaucratic management focuses on using knowledge, fairness, and logical rules and procedures; and administrative management focuses on how and what managers should do in their jobs. The human relations approach to management focuses on *people*, particularly the psychological and social aspects of work. This approach to management sees people not as just extensions of machines but as valuable organizational resources in their own right. Human relations management holds that people's needs are important and that their efforts, motivation, and performance are affected by the work they do and their relationships with their bosses, coworkers, and work groups. In other words, efficiency alone is not enough. Organizational success also depends on treating workers well.

*Let's find out more about human relations management by learning about **2-4a Mary Parker Follett's theories of constructive conflict and coordination, 2-4b Elton Mayo's Hawthorne Studies,** and **2-4c Chester Barnard's theories of cooperation and acceptance of authority.***

2-4a Constructive Conflict and Coordination: Mary Parker Follett

Mary Parker Follett (1868–1933) was a social worker with a degree in political science who, in her 50s, after 25 years of working with schools and nonprofit organizations, began lecturing and writing about management and working extensively as a consultant for business and government leaders in the United States and Europe. Although her contributions were overlooked for decades, perhaps because she was a woman or perhaps because they were so different, many of today's "new" management ideas can clearly be traced to her work.

Follett believed that the best way to deal with conflict was not **domination**, where one side wins and the other loses, or **compromise**, where each side gives up some of what it wants, but integration. Said Follett, "There is a way beginning now to be recognized at least, and even occasionally followed: when two desires are *integrated*, that means that a solution has been found in which both desires have found a place that neither side has had to sacrifice anything."[39] So, rather than one side dominating the other or both sides compromising, the point of **integrative conflict resolution** is to have

both parties indicate their preferences and then work together to find an alternative that meets the needs of both. According to Follett, "Integration involves invention, and the clever thing is to recognize this, and not to let one's thinking stay within the boundaries of two alternatives which are mutually exclusive." Indeed, Follett's ideas about the positive use of conflict and an integrative approach to conflict resolution predate accepted thinking in the negotiation and conflict resolution literature by six decades (see the best-selling book *Getting to Yes: Negotiating Agreement without Giving In* by Roger Fisher, William Ury, and Bruce Patton).

Exhibit 2.6 summarizes Follett's contributions to management in her own words. She casts power as "with" rather than "over" others. Giving orders involves discussing instructions and dealing with resentment. Authority flows from job knowledge and experience rather than position. Leadership involves setting the tone for the team rather than being aggressive and dominating, which may be harmful. Coordination and control should be based on facts and information. In the end, Follett's contributions added significantly to our understanding of the human, social, and psychological sides of management. Peter Parker, the former chairman of the London School of Economics, said about Follett: "People often puzzle about who is the father of management. I don't know who the father was, but I have no doubt about who was the mother."[40]

2-4b Hawthorne Studies: Elton Mayo

Australian-born Elton Mayo (1880–1948) is best known for his role in the famous Hawthorne Studies at the **Western Electric Company**. The Hawthorne Studies were

Domination an approach to dealing with conflict in which one party satisfies its desires and objectives at the expense of the other party's desires and objectives

Compromise an approach to dealing with conflict in which both parties give up some of what they want in order to reach an agreement on a plan to reduce or settle the conflict

Integrative conflict resolution an approach to dealing with conflict in which both parties indicate their preferences and then work together to find an alternative that meets the needs of both

Exhibit 2.6

Mary Parker Follett says . . .

On constructive conflict . . .

"As conflict—difference—is here in this world, as we cannot avoid it, we should, I think, use it to work for us. Instead of condemning it, we should set it to work for us."

On power . . .

"It seems to me that whereas power usually means power-over, the power of some person or group over some other person or group, it is possible to develop the conception of power-with, a jointly developed power, a co-active, not a coercive power."

On the giving of orders . . .

"An advantage of not exacting blind obedience, of discussing your instructions with your subordinates, is that if there is any resentment, any come-back, you get it out into the open, and when it is in the open, you can deal with it."

On authority . . .

"Authority should go with knowledge and experience, that is where obedience is due, no matter whether it is up the line or down."

On leadership . . .

"Of the greatest importance is the ability to grasp a total situation. . . . Out of a welter of facts, experience, desires, aims, the leader must find the unifying thread. He must see a whole, not a mere kaleidoscope of pieces. . . . The higher up you go, the more ability you have to have of this kind."

On coordination . . .

"The most important thing to remember about unity is—that there is no such thing. There is only unifying. You cannot get unity and expect it to last a day—or five minutes. Every man in a business should be taking part in a certain process and that process is unifying."

On control . . .

"Central control is coming more and more to mean the co-relation of many controls rather than a superimposed control."

Source: M. Parker Follett, *Mary Parker Follett—Prophet of Management: A Celebration of Writings from the 1920s*, ed. P. Graham (Boston: Harvard Business School Press, 1995).

conducted in several stages between 1924 and 1932 at a Western Electric plant in Chicago. Although Mayo didn't join the studies until 1928, he played a significant role thereafter, writing about the results in his book *The Human Problems of an Industrial Civilization*.[41] The first stage of the Hawthorne Studies investigated the effects of lighting levels and incentives on employee productivity in the Relay Test Assembly Room, where workers took approximately a minute to put "together a coil, armature, contact springs, and insulators in a fixture and secure the parts by means of four machine screws."[42]

Two groups of six experienced female workers, five to do the work and one to supply needed parts, were separated from the main part of the factory by a 10-foot partition and placed at a standard work bench with the necessary parts and tools. Over the next five years, the experimenters introduced various levels and combinations of lighting, financial incentives, and rest pauses (work breaks) to study the effect on productivity. Curiously, however, production levels increased whether the experimenters increased or decreased the lighting, paid workers based on individual production or group production, or increased or decreased the number and length of rest pauses. In fact, Mayo and his fellow researchers were surprised that production steadily increased from 2,400 relays per day at the beginning of the study to 3,000 relays per day five years later. The question was: Why?

Mayo and his colleagues eventually concluded that two things accounted for the results. First, substantially more attention was paid to these workers than to workers in the rest of the plant. Mayo wrote, "Before every change of program [in the study], the group is consulted. Their comments are listened to and discussed; sometimes their objections are allowed to negate a suggestion. The group unquestionably develops a sense of participation in the critical determinations and becomes something of a social unit."[43]

For years, the "Hawthorne effect" has been *incorrectly* defined as increasing productivity by paying more attention to workers.[44] But it is not simply about attention from management. The Hawthorne effect cannot be understood without giving equal importance to the social units, which became intensely cohesive groups. Mayo said, "What actually happened was that six individuals became a team and the team gave itself wholeheartedly and spontaneously to cooperation in the experiment. The consequence was that they felt themselves to be participating freely and without afterthought, and they were happy in the knowledge that they were working without coercion from above or limits from below."[45]

For the first time, human factors related to work were found to be more important than the physical conditions or design of the work. Together, the increased attention from management and the development of a cohesive work group led to significantly higher levels of job satisfaction and productivity. In short, the Hawthorne Studies found that workers' feelings and attitudes affected their work.

The next stage of the Hawthorne Studies was conducted in the Bank Wiring Room, where "the group consisted of nine wiremen, three solderers, and two inspectors. Each of these groups performed a specific

iStock.com/PeopleImages

The Hawthorne effect showed that when management paid more attention to workers, productivity increased. But equal importance should be given to the social units, or teams, that were created, which demonstrated that human factors were more important than physical conditions or the work itself.

task and collaborated with the other two in completion of each unit of equipment. The task consisted of setting up the banks of terminals side-by-side on frames, wiring the corresponding terminals from bank to bank, soldering the connections, and inspecting with a test set for short circuits or breaks in the wire. One solderman serviced the work of the three wiremen."[46] While productivity increased in the Relay Test Assembly Room no matter what the researchers did, productivity dropped in the Bank Wiring Room. Again, the question was: Why?

Mayo and his colleagues found that the differences in performance were due to group dynamics. The workers in the Bank Wiring Room had been an existing work group for some time and had already developed strong negative norms that governed their behavior. For instance, despite a group financial incentive for production, the group members decided that they would wire only 6,000–6,600 connections a day (depending on the kind of equipment they were wiring), well below the production goal of 7,300 connections that management had set for them. Individual workers who worked at a faster pace were socially ostracized from the group or "binged" (hit on the arm) until they slowed their work pace. Thus, the group's behavior was reminiscent of the soldiering that Taylor had observed. Mayo concluded, "Work [was] done in accord with the group's conception of a day's work; this was exceeded by only one individual who was cordially disliked."[47]

In the end, the Hawthorne Studies demonstrated that the workplace was more complex than previously thought, that workers were not just extensions of machines, and that financial incentives weren't necessarily the most important motivator for workers. By highlighting the crucial role, positive or negative, that groups, group norms, and group behavior play at work, Mayo strengthened Follett's point about coordination—make just one change in an organization and others, some expected and some unexpected, will occur. Thanks to Mayo and his colleagues and their work on the Hawthorne Studies, managers better understood the effect that group social interactions, employee satisfaction, and attitudes had on individual and group performance.

2-4c Cooperation and Acceptance of Authority: Chester Barnard

Like Fayol, Chester Barnard (1886–1961) had experiences as a top executive that shaped his views of management. Barnard began his career in 1909 as an engineer and translator for **AT&T**, becoming a general manager at Pennsylvania Bell Telephone in 1922 and then president of New Jersey Bell Telephone in 1927.[48] Barnard's ideas, published in his classic book, *The Functions of the Executive*, influenced companies from the board of directors down. He is best known for his ideas about cooperation and the acceptance of authority.

Barnard proposed a comprehensive theory of cooperation in formal organizations. In fact, he defines an **organization** as a "system of consciously coordinated activities or forces of two or more persons."[49] In other words, organization occurs whenever two people work together for some purpose, whether it be classmates working together to complete a class project, Habitat for Humanity volunteers donating their time to build a house, or managers working with subordinates to reduce costs, improve quality, or increase sales. Barnard placed so much emphasis on cooperation because cooperation is *not* the normal state of affairs: "Failure to cooperate, failure of cooperation, failure of organization, disorganization, disintegration, destruction of organization—and reorganization—are characteristic facts of human history."[50]

According to Barnard, the extent to which people willingly cooperate in an organization depends on how workers perceive executive authority and whether they're willing to accept it. Many managerial requests or directives fall within a *zone of indifference* in which acceptance of managerial authority is automatic. For example, if your supervisor asks you for a copy of the monthly inventory report, and compiling and writing that report is part of your job, you think nothing of the request and automatically send it. In general, people will be indifferent to managerial directives or orders if they (1) are understood, (2) are consistent with the purpose of the organization, (3) are compatible with the people's personal interests, and (4) can actually be carried out by those people. Acceptance of managerial authority (i.e., cooperation) is not automatic, however. Ask people to do things contrary to the organization's purpose or to their own benefit and they'll put up a fight. While many people assume that managers have the authority to do whatever they want, Barnard, referring to the "fiction of superior authority," believed that workers ultimately grant managers their authority.

2-5 OPERATIONS, INFORMATION, SYSTEMS, AND CONTINGENCY MANAGEMENT

In this last section, we review four other significant historical approaches to management that have influenced how today's managers produce goods and services on a daily basis, gather and manage the information they need to understand their businesses and make good decisions, understand how the different parts of the company work together as a whole, and recognize when and where particular management practices are likely to work.

*To better understand these ideas, let's learn about **2-5a operations management, 2-5b information management, 2-5c systems management,** and **2-5d contingency management.***

2-5a Operations Management

In Chapter 18, you will learn about *operations management*, which involves managing the daily production of goods and services. In general, operations management uses a quantitative or mathematical approach to find ways to increase productivity, improve quality, and manage or reduce costly inventories. The most commonly used operations management tools and methods are quality control, forecasting techniques, capacity planning, productivity measurement and improvement, linear programming, scheduling systems, inventory systems, work measurement

Organization a system of consciously coordinated activities or forces created by two or more people

techniques (similar to the Gilbreths' motion studies), project management (similar to Gantt's charts), and cost-benefit analysis.[51]

Since the sixteenth century, skilled craftspeople made the lock, stock, and barrel of a gun by hand. After each part was made, a skilled gun finisher assembled the parts into a complete gun. But the gun finisher did not simply screw the different parts of a gun together, as is done today. Instead, each handmade part required extensive finishing and adjusting so that it would fit together with the other handmade gun parts. Hand-fitting was necessary because, even when made by the same skilled craftspeople, no two parts were alike. In fact, gun finishers played a role similar to that of fine watchmakers who meticulously assembled expensive watches—without them, the product simply wouldn't work. Today, we would say that these parts were low quality because they varied so much from one part to another.

All this changed in 1791 when the US government, worried about a possible war with France, ordered 40,000 muskets from private gun contractors. All but one contractor built handmade muskets assembled by skilled gun finishers who made sure that all the parts fit together. Thus, each musket was unique. If a part broke, a replacement part had to be handcrafted. But one contractor, Eli Whitney of New Haven, Connecticut (who is better known for his invention of the cotton gin), determined that if gun parts were made accurately enough, guns could be made with standardized, interchangeable parts. So he designed machine tools that allowed unskilled workers to make each gun part the same as the next. Said Whitney, "The tools which I contemplate to make are similar to an engraving on copper plate from which may be taken a great number of impressions perceptibly alike."[52] Years passed before Whitney delivered his 10,000 muskets to the US government. But he demonstrated the superiority of interchangeable parts to President-elect Thomas Jefferson in 1801 by quickly and easily assembling complete muskets from randomly picked piles of musket parts. Today, because of Whitney's ideas, most products, from cars to toasters to space shuttles, are manufactured using standardized, interchangeable parts.

But even with this advance, manufacturers still could not produce a part unless they had seen or examined it firsthand. Thanks to Gaspard Monge, a Frenchman of

modest beginnings, this soon changed. Monge's greatest achievement was his book *Descriptive Geometry*.[53] In it, he explained techniques for drawing three-dimensional objects on paper. For the first time, precise drawings permitted manufacturers to make standardized, interchangeable parts without first examining a prototype. Today, thanks to Monge, manufacturers rely on CAD (computer-aided design) and CAM (computer-aided manufacturing) to take three-dimensional designs straight from the computer to the factory floor.

Once standardized, interchangeable parts became the norm, and after parts could be made from design drawings alone, manufacturers ran into a costly problem that they had never faced before: too much inventory. *Inventory* is the amount and number of raw materials, parts, and finished products that a company has in its possession. In fact, large factories were accumulating parts inventories sufficient for two to three months, much more than they needed on a daily basis to run their manufacturing operations. A solution to this problem was found in 1905 when the Oldsmobile Motor Works in Detroit burned down.[54] Management rented a new production facility to get production up and running as quickly as possible after the fire. But because the new facility was much smaller, there was no room to store large stockpiles of inventory (which the company couldn't afford anyway as it was short on funds). Therefore, the company made do with what it called "hand-to-mouth inventories," in which each production station had only enough parts on hand to do a short production run. Because all of its parts suppliers were close by, Oldsmobile could place orders in the morning and receive them in the afternoon (even without telephones), just as with today's computerized just-in-time inventory systems. So, contrary to common belief, just-in-time inventory systems were not invented by Japanese manufacturers. Instead, they were invented out of necessity more than a century ago because of a fire.

2-5b Information Management

For most of recorded history, information has been costly, difficult to obtain, and slow to spread. Because of the immense labor and time it took to hand copy information, books, manuscripts, and written documents of any kind

FROM INDEX CARDS TO THE INTERNET AND GOOGLE

From 1735 to 1770, naturalist Carl Linnaeus, the founder of modern taxonomy, categorized 12,000 minerals, plants, and animals across 13 editions of his book, *Systema Naturae*. Rather than use notebooks to record his observations and data, he invented and used separate notecards. In a quickly changing field exploding with new information (sound familiar?), notecards provided flexibility to easily recategorize, add, or update information without having to change his other 12,000 observations.

The advantages of managing information by index cards were so great they gave birth in 1910 to Google's nondigital ancestor, Belgium's Mundaneum, which used 18 million index cards in 15,000 drawers for the purpose—like Google—of categorizing "all the information in the world."

In 1935, Paul Otlet, co-founder of the Mundaneum, clearly envisioned how notecards could lead to today's internet, writing, "From a distance, everyone will be able to read text, enlarged and limited to the desired subject, projected on an individual screen. In this way, everyone from his

andreykuzmin/123RF

armchair will be able to contemplate the whole of creation, in whole or in certain parts."

Sources: "History | Archives Centre," Mundaneum," accessed March 4, 2017, http://archives.mundaneum.org/en/history; "Google and Mundaneum Are Proud to Announce Their Collaboration," Mundaneum, accessed March 4, 2017, http://expositions.mundaneum.org/en/google-and-mundaneum-are-proud-announce-their-collaboration; British Society for the History of Science," Carl Linnaeus Invented The Index Card," *ScienceDaily*, June 16, 2009, accessed March 4, 2017, https://www.sciencedaily.com/releases/2009/06/090616080137.htm; J. Schifman, "How the Humble Index Card Foresaw the Internet," *Popular Mechanics*, February 11, 2016, accessed March 4, 2017, http://www.popularmechanics.com/culture/a19379/a-short-history-of-the-index-card/.

were rare and extremely expensive. Word of Joan of Arc's death in 1431 took 18 months to travel from France across Europe to Constantinople (now Istanbul, Turkey).

Consequently, throughout history, organizations have pushed for and quickly adopted new information technologies that reduce the cost or increase the speed with which they can acquire, store, retrieve, or communicate information. The first technologies to truly revolutionize the business use of information were paper and the printing press. In the fourteenth century, water-powered machines were created to pulverize rags into pulp to make paper. Paper prices, which were already lower than those of animal-skin parchments, dropped dramatically. Less than a half-century later, Johannes Gutenberg invented the printing press, which greatly reduced the cost and time needed to copy written information. In fifteenth-century Florence, Italy, a scribe would charge one florin (an Italian unit of money) to hand copy one document page. By contrast, a printer would set up and print 1,025 copies of the same document for just three florins. Within 50 years of its invention, Gutenberg's printing press cut the cost of information by 99.8 percent!

What Gutenberg's printing press did for publishing, the manual typewriter did for daily communication.

Before 1850, most business correspondence was written by hand and copied using the letterpress. With the ink still wet, the letter would be placed into a tissue-paper book. A hand press would then be used to squeeze the book and copy the still-wet ink onto the tissue paper. By the 1870s, manual typewriters made it cheaper, easier, and faster to produce and copy business correspondence. Of course, in the 1980s, slightly more than a century later, typewriters were replaced by personal computers and word processing software with the same results.

Finally, businesses have always looked for information technologies that would speed access to timely information. The Medici family, which opened banks throughout Europe in the early 1400s, used post messengers to keep in contact with their more than 40 branch managers. The post messengers, who predated the US Postal Service Pony Express by 400 years, could travel 90 miles per day, twice what average riders could cover, because the Medicis were willing to pay for the expense of providing them with fresh horses. This need for timely information also led companies to quickly adopt the telegraph in the 1860s, the telephone in the 1880s, and, of course, internet technologies in the past three decades.

THE HISTORY OF THE BAR CODE

In 1947, a Philadelphia grocery store owner was losing business due to slow checkout lines because prices were entered into cash registers one digit at a time. Inventor Joe Woodland heard about this problem from Bernard Silver (who had overheard the grocer's complaint). Inspired by Morse code, the idea for a bar code came to Woodland on a Florida beach: "I remember I was thinking about dots and dashes when I poked my four fingers into the sand and, for whatever reason—I didn't know—I pulled my hand toward me and I had four lines. I said 'Golly! Now I have four lines and they could be wide lines and narrow lines, instead of dots and dashes… Then, only seconds later, I took my four fingers—they were still in the sand and I swept them round into a circle." Woodland and Silver filed a patent in 1949 but stopped developing their circular bar code in 1952 due to unreliable technology.

In 1966, Kroger publicized a similar complaint, "Just dreaming a little… could an optical scanner read the price and total the sale… Faster service, more productive service is needed desperately. We solicit your help." In the early 1970s, seven companies formed the Ad Hoc Committee of the Universal Product Identification Code to encourage development. Building on Woodland and Silver's patent, RCA created a round bull's-eye bar code, but printers struggled with the circular design. At IBM, George Lauer simultaneously developed the rectangular bar code (which avoided those problems) that we use today. The first real-world use of Lauer's design, now called the Universal Product Code, or UPC symbol, was on a 10-pack of Wrigley's Juicy Fruit chewing gum at a Marsh's Supermarket in Troy, Ohio, in 1974. Within a decade, scanners and bar codes were widely used.

Sources: T. Harford, "How the Barcode Changed Retailing and Manufacturing," *BBC News*, January 23, 2017, accessed January 31, 2020, https://www.bbc.com/news/business-38498700; C. Stokel-Walker, "Beep Beep: The History of George Laurer and the Barcode," *OneZero*, December 10, 2019, accessed January 31, 2020, https://onezero.medium.com/beep-beep-the-history-of-george-laurer-and-the-barcode-3522a15405ea; G. Weightman, "The History of the Bar Code," *Smithsonian Magazine*, September 23, 2015, accessed January 31, 2020, https://www.smithsonianmag.com/innovation/history-bar-code-180956704/.

2-5c Systems Management

Today's companies are much more complex than they used to be. They are larger and employ more people. They most likely manufacture, service, *and* finance what they sell, not only in their home markets but in foreign markets throughout the world, too. They also operate in complex, fast-changing, competitive, global environments that can quickly turn competitive advantages into competitive disadvantages. How, then, can managers make sense of this complexity, both within and outside of their organizations?

One way to deal with organizational and environmental complexity is to take a systems view of organizations. The systems approach is derived from theoretical models in biology and social psychology developed in the 1950s and 1960s.[55] A **system** is a set of interrelated elements or parts that function as a whole. Rather than viewing one part of an organization as separate from the other parts, a systems approach encourages managers to complicate their thinking by looking for connections between the different parts of the organization. Indeed, one of the more important ideas in the systems approach to management is that organizational systems are composed of parts or **subsystems**, which are simply smaller systems within larger systems. Subsystems and their connections matter in systems theory because of the possibility for managers to create synergy. **Synergy** occurs when two or more subsystems working together can produce more than they can working apart. In other words, synergy occurs when $1 + 1 = 3$.

Systems can be open or closed. **Closed systems** can function without interacting with their environments. But nearly all organizations should be viewed as **open systems** that interact with their environments and depend on them for survival. Therefore, rather than viewing what goes on within the organization as separate from what goes on outside it, the systems approach encourages managers to look for connections between the different parts of the organization

System a set of interrelated elements or parts that function as a whole

Subsystems smaller systems that operate within the context of a larger system

Synergy when two or more subsystems working together can produce more than they can working apart

Closed systems systems that can sustain themselves without interacting with their environments

Open systems systems that can sustain themselves only by interacting with their environments, on which they depend for their survival

Exhibit 2.7
Systems View of Organizations

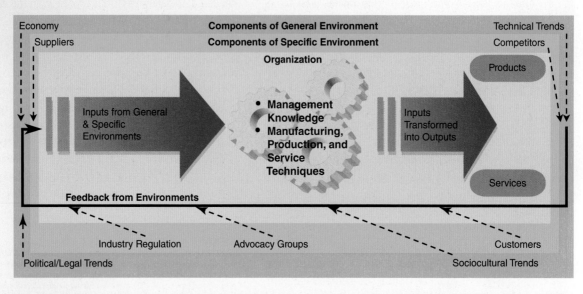

and the different parts of its environment. Exhibit 2.7 illustrates how the elements of systems management work together.

A systems view of organizations offers several advantages. First, it forces managers to view their organizations as part of and subject to the competitive, economic, social, technological, and legal/regulatory forces in their environments.[56] Second, it forces managers to be aware of how the environment affects specific parts of the organization. Third, because of the complexity and difficulty of trying to achieve synergies among different parts of the organization, the systems view encourages managers to focus on better communication and cooperation within the organization. Finally, it makes managers acutely aware that good internal management of the organization may not be enough to ensure survival. Survival also depends on making sure that the organization continues to satisfy critical environmental stakeholders such as shareholders, employees, customers, suppliers, governments, and local communities.

Contingency approach
holds that there are no universal management theories and that the most effective management theory or idea depends on the kinds of problems or situations that managers are facing at a particular time and place

2-5d Contingency Management

Earlier, you learned that the goal of scientific management was to use systematic study to find the one best way of doing each task and then use that one best way everywhere. The problem, as you may have gathered from reading about the various approaches to management, is that no one in management seems to agree on what that one best

way is. Furthermore, more than 130 years of management research has shown that there are clear boundaries or limitations to most management theories and practices. No management ideas or practices are universal. Although any theory or practice may work much of the time, none works all the time. How, then, is a manager to decide what theory to use? Well, it depends on the situation. The **contingency approach** to management clearly states that there are no universal management theories and that the most effective management theory or idea depends on the kinds of problems or situations that managers or organizations are facing at a particular time and place.[57] In short, the best way depends on the situation.

One of the practical implications of the contingency approach to management is that management is much harder than it looks. In fact, because of the clarity and obviousness of management theories (OK, most of them), students and workers often wrongly assume that a company's problems would be quickly and easily solved if management would take just a few simple steps. If this were true, few companies would have problems.

A second implication of the contingency approach is that managers need to look for key contingencies that differentiate today's situation or problems from yesterday's situation or problems. Moreover, it means that managers need to spend more time analyzing problems, situations, and employees before taking action to fix them. Finally, it means that as you read this text and learn about management ideas and practices, you need to pay particular attention to qualifying phrases such as "usually," "in these situations," "for this to work," and "under these circumstances." Doing so will help you identify the key contingencies that will help you become a better manager.

3 | Organizational Environments and Cultures

LEARNING OUTCOMES

3-1 Discuss how changing environments affect organizations.

3-2 Describe the four components of the general environment.

3-3 Explain the five components of the specific environment.

3-4 Apply the process that companies use to make sense of their changing environments.

3-5 Explain how organizational cultures are created and how they can help companies be successful.

3-1 CHANGING ENVIRONMENTS

This chapter examines the internal and external forces that affect business. We begin by explaining how the changes in external organizational environments affect the decisions and performance of a company. Next, we examine the two types of external organizational environments: the general environment that affects all organizations and the specific environment unique to each company. Then, we learn how managers make sense of their changing general and specific environments. The chapter finishes with a discussion of internal organizational environments by focusing on organizational culture. But first, let's see how the changes in external organizational environments can affect a company's decisions and performance.

External environments are the forces and events outside a company that have the potential to influence or affect it. Movie ticket sales have always fallen or risen with the quality of films in theaters. But sales maxed out at 1.6 billion tickets in 2002, falling steadily to 1.25 billion tickets in 2019.[1] With the popularity of streaming services like Netflix, Amazon Prime, and Hulu, along with a revamped HBO Max streaming app and new services like Disney+ and Apple TV+, many expect further declines. Movie theater chains, however, are trying two strategies to turn around sales. First, they are spending billions installing luxury seating in theaters. AMC, for example, committed $600 million to install wide, plush recliners into 1,800 theaters.[2] Rolando Rodriguez, CEO of Marcus Theatres (the fourth-largest US movie chain), which is doing the same, says, "If you're building a product for the next 20 years, you need to either renovate it or you build new."[3] Indeed, the Studio Movie Grill, with 30 theaters in 9 states, buys empty Sports Authority big-box stores, turning them into new theaters.[4] The second strategy is selling movie passes. For $20 a month, AMC's "Stub A-List" pass gives customers three movies a week, free online reservations with no processing fee and 10 percent off drinks and snacks. In just a year, AMC has signed up 750,000 subscribers who see more movies at a much lower cost.[5] However, AMC benefits as passholders buy more food and bring friends who buy full-price tickets.[6]

Let's examine the three basic characteristics of changing external environments: **3-1a environmental change; 3-1b environmental complexity; 3-1c resource scarcity;** *and* **3-1d the uncertainty that environmental change, complexity, and resource scarcity can create for organizational managers.**

> **External environments** all events outside a company that have the potential to influence or affect it

3-1a Environmental Change

Environmental change is the rate at which a company's general and specific environments change. In **stable environments**, the rate of environmental change is slow. The funeral business changes little from year to year. Families arrange for services for their loved ones with a funeral home, which then obtains a casket from one of three US manufacturers, cares for the remains, hosts a visitation or memorial service, and organizes the burial or cremation, by perhaps connecting the family with the cemetery or columbarium for purchase of a final resting place – all for an average price of $7,360 for viewing and burial and $6,260 for viewing and cremation. Although there have been some changes – such as cremation increasing from 4 percent in 1960 to 56 percent today, advances in embalming that are healthier (for the embalmer and the environment), and a small percentage of imported caskets (less than 10 percent) – the basic business of preparing bodies for burial, internment, or cremation hasn't changed significantly in over a century.[7]

Although the funeral industry has a stable environment, lumberyards compete in an surprisingly dynamic external environment. In **dynamic environments**, the rate of environmental change is fast. Tariffs on Canadian wood, widespread wildfires, wood-boring beetles and a chronic shortage of truck drivers all combined to drive lumber prices to an all-time high of $639 for 1,000 feet of wood. But, six months later, thanks to a slowdown in home construction arising from higher housing prices, rising interest rates, and widespread hurricanes, which prevented home construction throughout much of the southern United States, prices had dropped by nearly half to $329 per 1,000 feet. Stinson Dean, managing partner at Deacon Lumber Co., said, "We've got a lot of lumber we have to chew through

Tariffs on Canadian wood, widespread wildfires, wood-boring beetles and a shortage of truck drivers combined to drive lumber prices to an all-time high of $639 per 1,000 feet of wood. But six months later, thanks to rising interest rates and higher housing prices, lumber prices had fallen to $329 per 1,000 feet. Change is fast in this surprisingly dynamic environment.

laughingmango/iStock/Getty Images

before we can think about higher prices… Sawmills have to cut production."[8]

Although you might think that a company's external environment would be either stable or dynamic, research suggests that companies often experience both. According to **punctuated equilibrium theory**, companies go through long periods of stability (equilibrium) during which incremental changes occur; followed by short, complex periods of dynamic, fundamental change (revolutionary periods); and finishing with a return to stability (new equilibrium).[9]

The US airline industry is a classic example of punctuated equilibrium, as four times in the past 40 years it has experienced revolutionary periods followed by a temporary return to stability. The first, from mid-1979 to mid-1982, occurred immediately after airline deregulation in 1978. Prior to deregulation, the federal government controlled where airlines could fly, how much they could charge, when they could fly, and the number of flights they could have on a particular route. After deregulation, these choices were left to the airlines. The large financial losses during this period clearly indicate that the airlines had trouble adjusting to the intense competition from new airlines that occurred after deregulation. By mid-1982, however, profits returned to the industry and held steady until mid-1989.

Then, after experiencing record growth and profits, US airlines lost billions of dollars between 1989 and 1993 as the industry went through dramatic changes. Key expenses, including jet fuel and employee salaries, which

Environmental change the rate at which a company's general and specific environments change

Stable environment an environment in which the rate of change is slow

Dynamic environment an environment in which the rate of change is fast

Punctuated equilibrium theory the theory that companies go through long periods of stability (equilibrium), followed by short periods of dynamic, fundamental change (revolutionary periods), and then a new equilibrium

had held steady for years, suddenly increased. Furthermore, revenues, which had grown steadily year after year, suddenly dropped because of dramatic changes in the airlines' customer base. Business travelers, who had typically paid full-price fares, made up more than half of all passengers during the 1980s. However, by the late 1980s, the largest customer base had changed to leisure travelers, who wanted the cheapest flights they could get.[10] With expenses suddenly up, and revenues suddenly down, the airlines responded to these changes in their business environment by laying off 5 to 10 percent of their workers, canceling orders for new planes, and eliminating unprofitable routes. Starting in 1993 and lasting until 1998, these changes helped the airline industry achieve profits far in excess of their historical levels. The industry began to stabilize, if not flourish, just as punctuated equilibrium theory predicts.[11]

The third revolutionary period for the US airline industry began with the terrorist attacks of September 11, 2001, in which planes were used as missiles to bring down the World Trade Center towers and damage the Pentagon. The immediate effect was a 20 percent drop in scheduled flights, a 40 percent drop in passengers, and losses so large that the US government approved a $15 billion bailout to keep the airlines in business. Heightened airport security also affected airports, the airlines themselves, and airline customers. Five years after the 9/11 attacks, United Airlines, US Airways, Delta, and American Airlines had reduced staffing by 169,000 full-time jobs to cut costs after losing a combined $42 billion.[12] Due to their financially weaker position, the airlines restructured operations to take advantage of the combined effect of increased passenger travel, a sharply reduced cost structure, and a 23 percent reduction in the fleet to return their businesses to profitability.[13] But, just as the airlines were heading toward a more stable period of equilibrium in 2006 and 2007, the price of oil jumped dramatically, doubling, if not tripling, the price of jet fuel, which prompted the airlines to charge for luggage (to increase revenues and discourage heavy baggage) and cut flights using older, fuel-inefficient jets.

In 2013, however, stability largely returned. Compared to 2007, the airlines cut total seat capacity 14 percent; filled 83 percent of seats, up from

The US airline industry is a classic example of punctuated equilibrium, as four times in the past 40 years it has experienced revolutionary periods followed by a temporary return to stability.

ekapol/iStock/Getty Images

80 percent; and with stronger demand and fewer flights, saw round-trip fares rise by 4 percent, even after adjusting for inflation. In 2008 and 2009, US airlines collectively lost $26.3 billion, but by the beginning of 2020, they had logged their tenth consecutive year of profits.[14]

Multiple airline mergers – Delta and Northwest, United and Continental, Southwest and AirTran, and US Airways and American Airlines – reduced competition. As a result, the number of domestic flights dropped 6.8 percent from 2012 to 2015, while the number of available seats increased by 2.2 percent.[15]

The fourth and most severe revolutionary period began February 2020 as the coronavirus spread worldwide. Travel restrictions to and from specific countries quickly morphed into outright travel bans and strict shelter-in-place orders lasting two to three months. Global air traffic fell by 80 to 90 percent. Airlines grounded unused planes, retired older fuel inefficient jets, and pulled seats out of passenger jets to ship cargo instead. Without short-term government financial support, most airlines would have gone out of business with financial losses likely to exceed $84 billion in 2020 alone.[16] Will coronavirus vaccines under development arrive in time to safeguard travelers and restore demand for business and leisure travel, returning some semblance of industry stability? If not, the airline industry will likely shrink again to a much smaller footprint.

3-1b Environmental Complexity

Environmental complexity refers to the number and the intensity of external factors in the environment that affect organizations. **Simple environments** have few environmental factors, whereas **complex environments** have many environmental factors. The recreational boating industry is an excellent example of a relatively simple

Environmental complexity the number and the intensity of external factors in the environment that affect organizations

Simple environment an environment with few environmental factors

Complex environment an environment with many environmental factors

The boating industry is an excellent example of a simple external environment.

external environment. The number of boats in use has held steady between 12 million and 13 million vessels for two decades. Sales of fishing boats, jet skis, pontoon boats, and wake sport boats (for water skiing and wakeboarding) rise and fall with changes in the economy. Ninety-five percent of boats in use are less than 26 feet long. Likewise, international competition matters little, as 95 percent of recreational boats are made in the United States. While highly competitive (sales are split among 10 brands), the industry has few key environmental factors.[17]

At the other end of the spectrum, we find "less-than-truckload" (LTL) distribution companies with surprisingly complex environments. Order a sofa or other items too big or too heavy for United Parcel Service, FedEx, or the United States Postal Service (USPS), and they'll be delivered to your home by LTL trucking companies that traditionally deliver to businesses' loading docks. With LTL deliveries up 20 percent thanks to e-commerce and industry revenues now $9 billion a year, LTL firms are struggling with how to quickly and cheaply deliver heavy, bulky items via full-sized trucks that are too large for small neighborhood streets.[18] Paul Dugent, vice president of Estes Express Lines says, "Chances are, we're going to take out a mailbox."[19] Steven Gast, president of Wilson trucking says, "If you're the [online] seller, you're happy. If you're the guy delivering it, you're pulling your hair out." Wilson says, "Nobody's figured out the cost side. Everyone is scrambling."[20] Paul Thompson, chairman of Transportation Insight LLC, agrees, saying, "Home delivery is more finicky, more risky, and more costly."[21]

3-1c Resource Scarcity

The third characteristic of external environments is resource scarcity. **Resource scarcity** is the abundance or shortage of critical organizational resources in an organization's external environment. **Beyond Meat**'s vegetarian Impossible Burger gets rave reviews because many people think that it feels, looks, and tastes like real beef. Chelsea Donovan said, "Every single time I order it, I think they must have made a mistake and given me beef instead."[22] After customer visits increased by 17 percent when Burger King added Impossible Whoppers to its menu at 7,000 restaurants, Beyond Meat couldn't keep up.[23] Tim Sykes, group operations manager at Ruby's, said people left restaurants when told the Impossible Burger wasn't in stock. Said Sykes, "(It's) super frustrating. I've never had a product where I can't get it anywhere... We can normally source something creatively but it's (not available) nationwide."[24] Impossible Burger's CFO, David Lee, explained, "It will take us some time to get back into that synchronization of supply and demand."[25]

3-1d Uncertainty

As Exhibit 3.1 shows, environmental change, environmental complexity, and resource scarcity affect environmental **uncertainty**, which is how well managers can understand or predict the external changes and trends affecting their businesses. Starting at the left side of the exhibit, environmental uncertainty is lowest when environmental change and environmental complexity are at low levels, and resource scarcity is low (i.e., resources are plentiful). In these environments, managers feel confident that they can understand, predict, and react to the external forces that affect their businesses. By contrast, the right side of the exhibit shows that environmental uncertainty is highest when environmental change and complexity are extensive, and resource scarcity is a problem. In these environments, managers may not be confident that they can understand, predict, and handle the external forces affecting their businesses.

Resource scarcity the abundance or shortage of critical organizational resources in an organization's external environment

Uncertainty extent to which managers can understand or predict which environmental changes and trends will affect their businesses

Exhibit 3.1
Environmental Change, Environmental Complexity, and Resource Scarcity

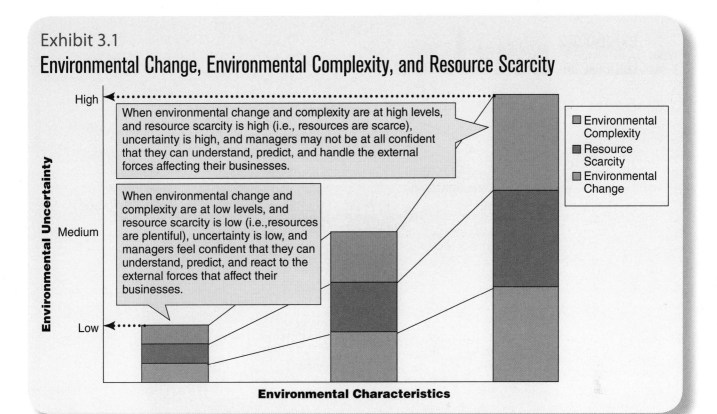

When environmental change and complexity are at high levels, and resource scarcity is high (i.e., resources are scarce), uncertainty is high, and managers may not be at all confident that they can understand, predict, and handle the external forces affecting their businesses.

When environmental change and complexity are at low levels, and resource scarcity is low (i.e.,resources are plentiful), uncertainty is low, and managers feel confident that they can understand, predict, and react to the external forces that affect their businesses.

Legend:
- Environmental Complexity
- Resource Scarcity
- Environmental Change

y-axis: Environmental Uncertainty (Low, Medium, High)
x-axis: Environmental Characteristics

3-2 GENERAL ENVIRONMENT

As Exhibit 3.2 shows, two kinds of external environments influence organizations: the general environment and the specific environment. The **general environment** consists of the economy and the technological, sociocultural, and political/legal trends that indirectly affect *all* organizations. Changes in any sector of the general environment eventually affect most organizations. For example, when the Federal Reserve lowers its prime lending rate, most businesses benefit because banks and credit card companies often lower the interest rates they charge for loans. Consumers, who can then borrow money more cheaply, might borrow more to buy homes, cars, refrigerators, and large-screen TVs.

Each organization also has a **specific environment** that is unique to that firm's industry and directly affects the way it conducts day-to-day business.

The specific environment, which will be discussed in detail in Section 3-3 of this chapter, includes customers, competitors, suppliers, industry regulation, and advocacy groups.

But first let's take a closer look at the four components of the general environment: 3-2a the economy and 3-2b the technological, 3-2c sociocultural, and 3-2d political/legal trends that indirectly affect all organizations.

3-2a Economy

The current state of a country's economy affects virtually every organization doing business there. In general, in a growing economy, more people are working, and wages are growing, and therefore consumers have relatively more money to spend. More products are bought and sold in a growing economy than in a static or shrinking economy. Although an individual firm's sales will not necessarily increase, a growing economy does provide an environment favorable to business growth. In contrast, in a shrinking economy, consumers have less money to spend, and relatively fewer products are bought and sold. Thus, a shrinking economy makes growth for individual businesses more difficult.

For three decades, the Chinese economy averaged 10 percent annual growth. This consistent growth spurred cargo companies to buy new ships to transport goods to and from China.[26] In 2008, however, China's growth rate began declining. China's growth slowed so much that by 2015, several global shipping companies started storing, selling, or scrapping much of their

General environment the economic, technological, sociocultural, and political/legal trends that indirectly affect all organizations

Specific environment the customers, competitors, suppliers, industry regulations, and advocacy groups that are unique to an industry and directly affect how a company does business

Exhibit 3.2
General and Specific Environments

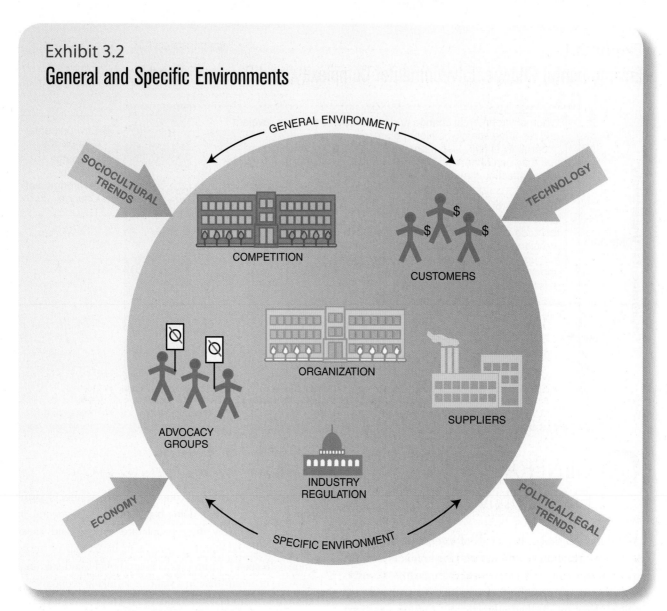

fleets.[27] In 2016, roughly 1,000 ships capable of transporting 52 million metric tons were dismantled and sold for scrap.[28] From 2015 to 2016, **International Shipcare** doubled its number of ships in dry dock from 51 to 102.[29] **Scorpio Bulkers**, which spent $1.5 billion in 2013 and 2014 to acquire new cargo ships, has had to sell them all at a loss of $400 million.[30] As China's economy maintained its slower growth, Shippers continued downsizing their fleets with 983 ships scrapped in 2017, 809 scrapped in 2018 and an estimated 684 scrapped in 2019.[31]

Because the economy influences basic business decisions, such as whether to hire more employees, expand production, or take out loans to purchase equipment, managers scan their economic environments for signs of significant change. Unfortunately, the economic statistics that managers

Business confidence indices indices that show managers' level of confidence about future business growth

rely on when making these decisions are notoriously poor predictors of *future* economic activity. Scott Wine, CEO of **Polaris Industries**, which makes motorcycles, snowmobiles, and off-road vehicles, says, "The so-called experts and global economists are proven as often to be wrong as right these days."[32] Steve Miller, CEO of **International Automotive Components Group**, agrees, saying, "You can't run your business with only one track in mind – which is the direction that forecasters and experts are telling you it will go."[33] So a manager who hired 10 more employees because forecasts suggested future growth, could very well have had to lay off those workers when the forecasted economic growth did not occur.

Because economic statistics can be poor predictors, some managers try to predict future economic activity by keeping track of business confidence. **Business confidence indices** show how confident actual managers are about future business growth. For example, the

"HAVE YOU HUGGED YOUR UNCERTAINTY MONSTER TODAY?"

Ninety-nine out of 100 managers will tell you they manage in conditions of high environmental uncertainty. Why? Because they're feeling the stress from competitors, from technological and regulatory changes in their industries, or from stretched supply chains that depend on suppliers halfway around the world. *Wall Street Journal* writer John Stoll writes, "Uncertainty is the monster that lives under the bed of every CEO. It waits until the door is shut and the lights are out, and even then, it bides its time. Pulses race, sweat beads, no move seems the right one." Environmental uncertainty is highest when environmental change and complexity are extensive, and resource scarcity is a problem. In these environments, as Stoll makes clear, managers often feel they cannot understand, predict, and handle the external forces affecting their businesses.

But he points out, should we always fear uncertainty? Is uncertainty always as bad as we make it out to be? Chet Pipkin, founder of Belkin International, says, "There is always unknown. [However, as] the unknown becomes known,

a choice is to expect it, welcome it, embrace it, and make choices that create a new competitive advantage." Carnival Cruise CEO Arnold Donald, whose company deals with hurricanes, tsunamis, extreme swings in exchange rates, geopolitical issues, and significant health risks (from noroviruses to the coronavirus), says that even if uncertainty is high, managers still need to deal with it. Donald says, "The problem is that shareholders don't care about the weather. We need to assume bad weather and make a plan to deal with that. We've got to ask ourselves, how are we going to organize so we can deliver?"

So, the next time you're feeling a bit overwhelmed with high environmental uncertainty, do as Stoll suggests, "Hug your uncertainty monster." It's probably not as scary as you think. And, there's no magic wand to wish it away. Give it a hug. Get busy figuring out how to solve your customers' problems.

Source: J. Stoll, "Hey CEOs, Have You Hugged the Uncertainty Monster Lately?" *Wall Street Journal*, September 14, 2019, accessed February 9, 2020, www.wsj.com/articles/hey-ceos-have-you-hugged-the-uncertainty-monster-lately-11568433606?mod=hp_lead_pos1.

Conference Board's CEO Confidence Index is a quarterly survey of 100 CEOs in large companies across a variety of different industries that examines attitudes regarding future growth in the economy or particular industries.[34] Another useful index is the *Wall Street Journal (WSJ)*/Vistage Small Business CEO Survey, which surveys small business CEOS about their sentiments regarding their general economy and how optimistic they are about future revenues, profitability, and business spending.[35] Managers often prefer business confidence indices to economic statistics because they know that other managers make business decisions that are in line with their expectations concerning the economy's future. So, if the Conference Board or *WSJ*/Vistage Small Business CEO Survey business confidence indices are dropping, a manager might decide against hiring new employees, increasing production, or taking out additional loans to expand the business.

3-2b Technological Component

Technology is the knowledge, tools, and techniques used to transform inputs (raw materials, information,

and so on) into outputs (products and services). For example, the inputs of optometrists, eyeglass designers, and optical engineers (knowledge) and the use of equipment such as lensometers and grinders for making prescription lenses (technology) transform metal, glass, and plastic (raw materials) into eyeglasses (the finished product). In the case of a service company such as an airline, the technology consists of equipment, including airplanes, repair tools, and computers, as well as the knowledge of mechanics, ticketers, and flight crews. The output is the service of transporting people from one place to another.

Changes in technology can help companies provide better products or produce their products more efficiently. Although technological changes can benefit a business, they can also threaten it. As discussed in Chapter 1, the expected shift from combustion- to electric-powered cars is a technological threat to automakers. Deloitte's Neal Ganguli says, "… companies and their

> **Technology** the knowledge, tools, and techniques used to transform inputs into outputs

Trust Experts, But Not about the Future

|| "If I were a gambler, I would take even money that England will not exist in the year 2000." After 20 years of testing 28,000 predictions made by experts, Professor Philip Tetlock clearly found that experts are not much better than chance when it comes to predicting the future. Why? Because they rely on assumptions that explain the past, but not the future. That 1971 prediction, by the way, was made by an expert, Stanford biologist Paul Erich, who, like the United Kingdom (i.e., England), is still around.

Source: M. Ridley, "Experts and the Future," Matt Ridley, July 31, 2016, accessed March 8, 2017, www.rationaloptimist.com/blog/experts-and-the-future/.

unions are going to have to figure out how to change themselves or risk becoming part of a shrinking bubble."[36] Even firms that change will have to downsize because it takes fewer parts and thus 40 percent fewer labor hours to assemble an electric car's engine and battery. AlixPartner's Mark Wakefield says, "You would fundamentally need less people."[37] Companies must embrace new technology and find effective ways to use it to improve their products and services or decrease costs. If they don't, they will lose out to companies that do.

3-2c Sociocultural Component

The sociocultural component of the general environment refers to the demographic characteristics, general behavior, attitudes, and beliefs of people in a particular society. Sociocultural changes and trends influence organizations in two important ways.

First, changes in demographic characteristics, such as the number of people with particular skills or the growth of or decline in the number of people with particular population characteristics (marital status, age, gender, ethnicity), affect how managers run their businesses. With the cruise industry growing just 3 to 4 percent per year, cruise lines are expanding to China where the market grew by 70 percent from 2013 to 2016. While 4.25 million Chinese took a cruise in 2018, that may rise to 10 million by 2030.[38] As a result, cruise lines are designing services specifically for Chinese consumers. Thatcher Brown, president of Dream Cruises, said, "We will have authentic Chinese food choices for our Chinese guests. And we have [a] Chinese dedicated spa, that's all about comfort and relaxation. There are things like mahjongg for grandma. Our whole environment caters to the Chinese preferences in many ways."[39]

Second, sociocultural changes in behavior, attitudes, and beliefs also affect the demand for a business's products and services. The aging of America may be responsible for changing attitudes that have led to a 30 percent drop in the sale of real Christmas trees. Today just 76 percent of households put up Christmas trees, compared to 90 percent in 1989. And, of those trees, just 21 percent are real compared to 47 percent in 1989.[40] Why? As families age and their children move out and have their own families, their parents, who are now grandparents, find it much easier and cheaper to put up the same artificial tree each year. Why spend $76 on average for a real tree every year when you can spend $150 to $250 once for a nice-looking artificial tree that lasts for decades?[41] The National Christmas Tree Association's Tim O'Connor said, "We did see significant market share loss to fake trees, particularly to baby boomers as their kids grew up and left home."[42] Consistent with these changes, Christmas tree farmers sold 30 million trees in 1997, 21 million in 2002, and just 15 million in 2018.[43] Hundreds of Christmas tree farms have gone out of business due to these sociocultural trends.

3-2d Political/Legal Component

The political/legal component of the general environment includes the legislation, regulations, and court decisions that govern and regulate business behavior. New laws and regulations continue to impose additional responsibilities on companies. Unfortunately, many managers are unaware of these new responsibilities. For example, under the 1991 Civil Rights Act (www.eeoc.gov/eeoc/history/35th/1990s/civilrights.html), if an employee is sexually harassed by anyone at work (a supervisor, a coworker, or even a customer), the company – not just the harasser – is potentially liable for damages, attorneys' fees, and back pay.[44] Under the

Family and Medical Leave Act (www.dol.gov/general/topic/benefits-leave/fmla), which applies to employers with 50 or more employees, employees who have been on the job one year are guaranteed 12 weeks of unpaid leave per year to tend to their own illnesses or to their elderly parents, a newborn baby, or a newly adopted child. Employees are guaranteed the same job, pay, and benefits when they return to work.[45] The most recent major regulation to affect US businesses is the Patient Protection and Affordable Care Act (www.hhs.gov/healthcare/about-the-law/index.html), which requires businesses with more than 100 full-time employees to offer affordable health-care insurance to full-time employees and their families. To demonstrate that they are complying, companies must file tax forms showing their individual employees' health-care costs on a monthly basis. Penalties for not filing proper tax forms can be up to $3,000 per employee.[46]

Many managers are also unaware of the potential legal risks associated with traditional managerial decisions about recruiting, hiring, and firing employees. Increasingly, businesses and managers are being sued for negligent hiring and supervision, defamation, invasion of privacy, emotional distress, fraud, and misrepresentation during employee recruitment.[47] More than 14,000 suits for wrongful termination (unfairly firing employees) are filed each year.[48] In fact, wrongful termination lawsuits increased by 77 percent during the 1990s.[49] Likewise, Equal Employment Opportunity Commission filings alleging wrongful discharge average around 22,750 cases per year.[50] One in four employers will at some point be sued for wrongful termination. It can cost $300,000 to settle such a case after it goes to court, but employers lose 50 to 70 percent of court cases,[51] and the former employee is awarded, on average, $1 million or more.[52] On the other hand, employers who settle before going to court typically pay just $10,000 to $100,000 per case.[53]

Not everyone agrees that companies' legal risks are too severe. Indeed, many believe that the government should do more to regulate and restrict business behavior and that it should be easier for average citizens to sue dishonest or negligent corporations. From a managerial perspective, the best medicine against legal risk is prevention. As a manager, it is your responsibility to educate yourself about the laws, regulations, and potential lawsuits that could affect your business. Failure to do so may put you and your company at risk of sizable penalties, fines, or legal charges.

3-3 SPECIFIC ENVIRONMENT

As you just learned, changes in any sector of the general environment (economic, technological, sociocultural, and political/legal) eventually affect most organizations. Each organization also has a specific environment that is unique to that firm's industry and directly affects the way it conducts day-to-day business. For instance, if your customers decide to use another product, your main competitor cuts prices 10 percent, your best supplier can't deliver raw materials, federal regulators mandate reductions in pollutants in your industry, or environmental groups accuse your company of selling unsafe products, the impact from the specific environment on your business is immediate.

*Let's examine how the **3-3a customer, 3-3b competitor, 3-3c supplier, 3-3d industry regulation,** and **3-3e advocacy group components of the specific environment affect businesses.***

3-3a Customer Component

Customers purchase products and services. Companies cannot exist without customer support. Monitoring customers' changing wants and needs is critical to business success. There are two basic strategies for monitoring customers: reactive and proactive.

Reactive customer monitoring involves identifying and addressing customer trends and problems after they occur. **IKEA** is known for its high value, inexpensive, need-to-be-assembled furniture in 300,000-square-foot stores located on the edge of major cities. However, it's difficult to shop at IKEA unless you have a car to transport your purchases and at least half a day's time to make your way through the massive stores. But after talking to customers at 50 different IKEA stores in 20 different markets, CEO Jesper Brodin said, "The story is the same. Very often they shop on their way to work in the subway, or after the kids have gone to bed.... We were still affordable and relevant, but the accessibility of IKEA was mainly through our flagship stores... [and because of that] we were seeing the risk of losing out on convenience shopping."[54] To make shopping easier, Ikea bought TaskRabbit (which assembles IKEA furniture for customers), put lockers outside existing stores for after-hours pickup, and located smaller stores in city centers that focus only on kitchens or living rooms.[55]

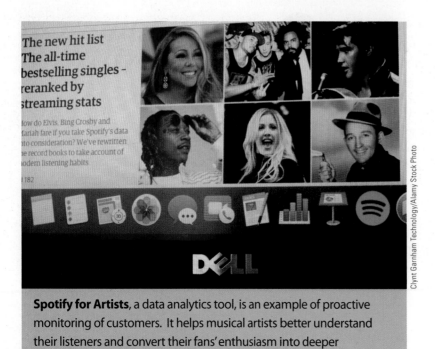

Clynt Garnham Technology/Alamy Stock Photo

Spotify for Artists, a data analytics tool, is an example of proactive monitoring of customers. It helps musical artists better understand their listeners and convert their fans' enthusiasm into deeper engagement.

One reactive strategy is to listen closely to customer complaints and respond to customer concerns. Companies that respond quickly to customer letters of complaint (i.e., reactive customer monitoring) are viewed much more favorably than companies that are slow to respond or never respond.[56] In particular, studies have shown that customers are much more likely to purchase products or services again from a company when that company sends a follow-up letter to thank the customer for writing; offers a sincere, specific response to the complaint (not a form letter, but an explanation of how the problem will be handled); and offers a small gift, coupons, or a refund to make up for the problem.[57]

Proactive monitoring of customers means identifying and addressing customer needs, trends, and issues *before* they occur. **Spotify** is the world's most popular subscription music service, with 124 million paying subscribers and 271 million ad-supported users.[58] Spotify for Artists, a data analytics tool, helps musical artists better understand their listeners and convert their fans' enthusiasm into deeper engagement. Spotify for Artists lists listeners' geographic locations, demographic information (such as gender and age), how they are listening (e.g. example, to a Spotify-curated playlist or to their own), when they are listening (down to the time of day), and even which playlists contain the artists' music. In addition, artists can now share music on Instagram and Snapchat with one click, and sell concert tickets and merchandise directly through Spotify.[59] For Spotify Chief Revenue Officer Jeff Levick, supporting artists with metrics and selling tools helps them understand their own audiences. "For artists, this can even give them the ability to better manage their tours. They can have the knowledge about where they should be playing certain songs, for example, rather than just doing the same set list everywhere."[60] This kind of information is particularly helpful for finding and catering to superfans. According to Spotify's vice president of product, Charlie Hellman, these fans "have a disproportionate impact on revenue: they're the people who'll buy tickets, VIP packages, merchandise, and will be the social evangelists for the band."[61]

3-3b Competitor Component

Competitors are companies in the same industry that sell similar products or services to customers. GM, Toyota, Honda, Volkswagen, Hyundai, and Ford all compete for automobile customers. Netflix, (Amazon) Prime Video, Disney+, HBO Max and Hulu (along with hundreds of cable channels) compete for TV viewers' attention. McDonald's, Burger King, Wendy's, Taco Bell, Chick-fil-A, and a host of others compete for fast-food customers' dollars. Often the difference between business success and failure comes down to whether your company is doing a better job of satisfying customer wants and needs than the competition. Consequently, companies need to keep close track of what their competitors are doing. To do this, managers perform a **competitive analysis**, which involves deciding who your competitors are, anticipating competitors' moves, and determining competitors' strengths and weaknesses.

Surprisingly, managers often do a poor job of identifying potential competitors because they tend to focus on only two or three well-known competitors with similar goals and resources.[62]

Another mistake managers may make when analyzing the competition is to underestimate potential

Competitors companies in the same industry that sell similar products or services to customers

Competitive analysis a process for monitoring the competition that involves identifying competitors, anticipating their moves, and determining their strengths and weaknesses

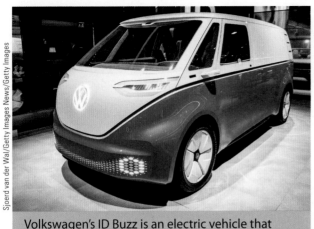
Volkswagen's ID Buzz is an electric vehicle that resembles their classic Microbus.

Staples is a prime example of a supplier.

competitors' capabilities. When this happens, managers don't take the steps they should to continue to improve their products or services. While GM, Toyota, and other global automakers are focused on catching Tesla in the electric vehicle market (EV), they should not underestimate Volkswagen's (VW's) potential. After producing 50,000 EVs in 2018 and 70,000 in 2019, VW plans to produce 1 million EVs a year by 2023 and 1.5 million by 2025, all under its newly named "ID" brand.[63] By contrast, Tesla produced 367,000 EVs in 2019 with plans to produce 1 million by 2025. VW has allocated $66 billion (about three times more than Tesla) toward the design, testing, and production of six ID models in 16 EV production facilities in the United States, Europe, and China. VW CEO Herbert Diess says, "We are quite optimistic that we still can keep the pace with Tesla and also at some stage probably overtake [it]."[64]

3-3c Supplier Component

Suppliers are companies that provide material, human, financial, and informational resources to other companies. US Steel buys iron ore from suppliers to make steel products. When IBM sells a mainframe computer, it also provides support staff, engineers, and other technical consultants to the company that bought the computer. If you're shopping for desks, chairs, and office supplies, chances are that Staples will be glad to help your business open a revolving charge account to pay for your purchases. When a clothing manufacturer has spent $100,000 to purchase new high-pressure water drills to cut shirt and pant patterns to precise sizes, the water drill manufacturer, as part of the purchase, will usually train the workers to use the machinery.

A key factor influencing the impact and quality of the relationship between companies and their suppliers is how dependent they are on each other.[65] **Supplier dependence** is the degree to which a company relies on that supplier because of the importance of the supplier's product to the company and the difficulty of finding other sources for that product. Over the last decade, China has produced 75 to 95 percent of all rare-earth metals.[66] That dominance made automotive companies almost exclusively dependent on Chinese suppliers for heavy rare-earth metals used to manufacture the magnets used in hybrid car engines.

Buyer dependence is the degree to which a supplier relies on a buyer because of the importance of that buyer to the supplier's sales and the difficulty of finding other buyers of its products. While South Korea-based Samsung dominates the OLED market for smartphone screens (that is, supplier dependence), it's also the case that Samsung's growing OLED business is highly dependent on its largest customer, Apple, which purchased an estimated 82 million OLED screens for iPhones in 2019.[67] Apple, however, has added two new OLED suppliers in the last 18 months, Korea's LG Display and China's BOE Technology Group, which could lead to fewer OLED orders for Samsung.[68]

Suppliers companies that provide material, human, financial, and informational resources to other companies

Supplier dependence the degree to which a company relies on a supplier because of the importance of the supplier's product to the company and the difficulty of finding other sources of that product

Buyer dependence the degree to which a supplier relies on a buyer because of the importance of that buyer to the supplier and the difficulty of finding other buyers for its products

Federal Regulatory Agencies and Commissions

Consumer Product Safety Commission

Reduces risk of injuries and deaths associated with consumer products, sets product safety standards, enforces product recalls, and provides consumer education **cpsc.gov**

Department of Labor

Collects employment statistics and administers labor laws concerning safe working conditions, minimum hourly wages and overtime pay, employment discrimination, and unemployment insurance **dol.gov**

Environmental Protection Agency

Reduces and controls pollution through research, monitoring, standard setting, and enforcement activities **epa.gov**

Equal Employment Opportunity Commission

Promotes fair hiring and promotion practices **eeoc.gov**

Federal Communications Commission

Regulates interstate and international communications by radio, television, wire, satellite, and cable **fcc.gov**

Federal Reserve System

As the nation's central bank, controls interest rates and money supply and monitors the US banking system to producea growing economy with able prices **federalreserve.gov**

Federal Trade Commission

Restricts unfair methods of business competition and misleading advertising and enforces consumer protection laws **ftc.gov**

Food and Drug Administration

Protects the nation's health by making sure food, drugs, and cosmetics are safe **fda.gov**

National Labor Relations Board

Monitors union elections and stops companies from engaging in unfair labor practices **nlrb.gov**

Occupational Safety and Health Administration

Saves lives, prevents injuries, and protects the health of workers **osha.gov**

Securities and Exchange Commission

Protects investors in the bond and stock markets, guarantees access to information on publicly traded securities, and regulates firms that sell securities or give investment advice **sec.gov**

A high degree of buyer or seller dependence can lead to **opportunistic behavior,** in which one party benefits at the expense of the other. Because of its online market dominance, Amazon pressures the suppliers (who sell products on Amazon.com) to cut prices. For example, if Amazon's search algorithms detect that an Amazon supplier is selling the same product for a penny less on another website, it removes the "Buy Now" and "Add to Cart" buttons for those products, often plunging sales by 75 percent.[69] Amazon chief executive of consumer sales, Jeff Wilke, responds, "If sellers weren't succeeding, they wouldn't be here."[70] Former Amazon Vice President David Glick says, "The secret of Amazon is we're happy to help you be very successful," but he admits, "You just have to kiss the ring." Bernie Thompson, founder of Plugables, a popular brand of computer accessories, says, "Every year it's been a ratchet tighter. We are dealing with a partner [Amazon] who can and will disrupt us for unpredictable reasons at any time."[71] And while we "built the company on Amazon... today our focus has to be getting diversification off Amazon."[72]

In contrast to opportunistic behavior, **relationship behavior** focuses on establishing a mutually beneficial, long-term relationship between buyers and suppliers.[73] General Motors has a well-earned reputation for opportunistic behavior toward its suppliers. Steve Kiefer, GM's purchasing chief, admits that GM's supplier relationships have been one sided in GM's favor. If material costs or currency exchange rates changed, significantly raising suppliers' costs, GM expected them to absorb the losses because they previously agreed to lower prices. But Kiefer, who used to work for Delphi Automotive PLC, one of GM's largest suppliers, is encouraging a mutually beneficial relationship by allowing suppliers to renegotiate their contracts when market conditions change significantly. Kiefer says that with GM's new relationship behavior is, " . . . adopting a simple formula that is more predictable and allows both sides to share in the ups and downs of those costs."[74] Scott Paradise, of Magna International, a GM supplier, welcomes the change, saying, "We now have a chance to recoup some of the costs you just weren't planning on hitting your business."[75]

Opportunistic behavior a transaction in which one party in the relationship benefits at the expense of the other

Relationship behavior the establishment of mutually beneficial, long-term exchanges between buyers and suppliers

3-3d Industry Regulation Component

While the political/legal component of the general environment affects all businesses, the **industry regulation** component consists of regulations and rules that govern the practices and procedures of specific industries, businesses, and professions. Airbnb, the home-sharing website, that helps homeowners earn extra money through short-term rentals of rooms, apartments, or homes, is facing regulatory push back from major cities. Regulators argue that Airbnb rentals reduce the supply of housing that could go to full-time renters or owners, thus driving expensive housing prices even higher. Accordingly, Paris makes **Airbnb** limit its hosts to 120 rental days a year. Airbnb's platform proactively helps hosts follow regulations by deactivating rental listings after that limit has been reached.[76] It also provides detailed information via its website with topics such as, "Night Limits in France: Frequently Asked Questions," and "Responsible Hosting in France," the latter of which covers topics like tourists taxes, regulations and permissions, the data Airbnb shares with local authorities, and the six steps required to register as an Airbnb host in Paris. Airbnb partner LegalPlace also provides hosts specialized legal assistance to maintain compliance with local regulations.[77]

The nearly 100 federal agencies and regulatory commissions can affect almost any kind of business. For example, according to the Consumer Products Safety Commission (CPSC), a child is injured every 24 minutes, or killed every two weeks, from furniture and TVs tipping over. The CPSC announced a recall of 29 million Ikea chests and dressers that were tip-over hazards. Accordingly, Ikea offered consumers a full refund or a free wall-anchoring kit.[78] IKEA reached a $50 million settlement with three families whose children were killed when its dressers tipped over.[79] IKEA subsequently developed a safety app and "Safer Homes" workshops to educate customers about the importance of using wall-anchoring kits to prevent tip-overs.[80]

3-3e Advocacy Groups

Advocacy groups are groups of concerned citizens who band together to try to influence the business practices of specific industries, businesses, and professions. The members of a group generally share the same point of view on a particular issue. For example, environmental advocacy groups might try to get manufacturers to reduce carbon emissions. Unlike the industry regulation component of the specific environment, advocacy groups cannot force organizations to change their practices. Nevertheless, they can use a number of techniques to try to influence companies, including public communications, media advocacy, web pages, blogs, and product boycotts.

The **public communications** approach relies on *voluntary* participation by the news media and the advertising industry to send out an advocacy group's message. Media advocacy is much more aggressive than the public communications approach. A **media advocacy** approach typically involves framing the group's concerns as public issues (affecting everyone); exposing questionable, exploitative, or unethical practices; and creating controversy that is likely to receive extensive news coverage.

A **product boycott** is a tactic in which an advocacy group actively tries to persuade consumers not to purchase a company's product or service. Often times, advocacy groups will combine media advocacy with boycotts. This not only draws attention to concerns a group has with a company's practices or products, but it also has the potential to reduce a company's revenues and profits.

Airbnb, which historically challenged local regulations in court, now works closely with local Airbnb hosts who rent rooms, apartments and homes, to follow local laws and regulations.

Industry regulation regulations and rules that govern the business practices and procedures of specific industries, businesses, and professions

Advocacy groups concerned citizens who band together to try to influence the business practices of specific industries, businesses, and professions

Public communications an advocacy group tactic that relies on voluntary participation by the news media and the advertising industry to get the advocacy group's message out

Media advocacy an advocacy group tactic that involves framing issues as public issues; exposing questionable, exploitative, or unethical practices; and forcing media coverage by buying media time or creating controversy that is likely to receive extensive news coverage

Product boycott an advocacy group tactic that involves protesting a company's actions by persuading consumers not to purchase its product or service

It's a Bird! It's a Plane! It's a Drone With Your Latte!

You have likely heard news stories about drones being used in both personal and commercial applications. But are drones a recreational hobby or mass-market commercial industry? According to the U.S. Federal Aviation Administration (FAA), the answer is both!

Drones for Personal Use.

After receiving nearly 250 reports of drones flying dangerously close to commercial air-crafts, the FCC moved swiftly to outline rules regarding personal use of the unmanned aircrafts. For example, the FCC now requires that all drones be registered with the organization.

Drone pilots who pay the $5 registration fee receive a unique identification number, which must appear on every drone that person owns. By classifying drones as aircrafts, regulators are sending the message that drones are more than toys. Indeed, the new regulations empower the FAA to penalize those who don't register their drones with fines of up to $250,000 and a three-year prison sentence.

Glenn Price/Shutterstock.com

Drones for Commercial Use.

As of January 2020, the FAA's new policy is that drones will be treated as a "special class" of aircraft, similar to passenger jets, cargo jet, helicopters and smaller private planes. As with those aircraft, the FAA will certify specific drone types and models for safety and specific commercial purposes. Eventually, the new Unmanned Aircraft Systems Traffic Management system will automatically track and manage drone traffic, keeping drones below 400 feet and well away from flight spaces for jets, planes and helicopters. So, one day, perhaps soon, you'll be able to order a Pumpkin Spice Latte from Starbucks and have a drone deliver it minutes later to your location.

Sources: C. Mims, "Your Drone-Delivered Coffee Is (Almost) Here," *Wall Street Journal,* March 30, 2019, accessed February 9, 2020, www.wsj.com/articles/your-drone-delivered-coffee-is-almost-here-11553918415?mod=djemCI; J. Nicas, "New Rules for Drone Owners," *Wall Street Journal,* December 15, 2015, B3; "The FAA Reminds You to Register Your Drone," Federal Aviation Administration, January 6, 2020, faa.gov; A. Pasztor, "FAA Moves Toward Certifying Specific Drones for Package Deliveries," *Wall Street Journal,* February 3, 2020, accessed February 9, 2020, www.wsj.com/articles/faa-moves-toward-certifying-specific-drones-for-package-deliveries-11580764882?mod=djemCIO.

Fifteen years ago, People for the Ethical Treatment of Animals (PETA), called for a boycott of Australia's multibillion-dollar wool industry with an ad campaign titled "Did your sweater cause a bloody butt?"[81] PETA wanted Australia's 55,000 sheep farmers to stop mulesing, which it considered cruel. Mulesing removes skin folds from a young sheep's rear end, usually without anesthesia, to prevent blowfly egg infestations (i.e., flystrike) that turn into flesh-eating maggots. Craig Johnston, an Australian farmer with 6,000 merino sheep, defended the practice, explaining "We don't mulesing to be cruel, we do it because it's the best husbandry practice available. Once a sheep suffers flystrike you are at a loss to do anything."[82] As a result of PETA's pressure, however, the Australian wool industry's trade group spent $30 million on research and programs to eliminate flystrike via selective breeding and chemicals.[83] The trade group also pushed for more humane treatment. Today, 85 percent of lambs that receive mulesing are treated for pain relief.[84]

PETA began another wool boycott a year ago. In the "Leave Wool Behind" campaign, actor Alicia Silverstone declared that shearing sheep to remove wool was cruel.[85] This time, the wool industry pushed back. On social media, Canadian farmer Quinton McEwan argued, "Farmers are responsible for shearing their sheep, because if

TENGKU BAHAR/AFP/Getty Images

Despite being harshly criticized and boycotted, the Australian wool industry maintains that shearing keeps sheep healthy by avoiding heat, stress, and maggot infestations.

the sheep's wool becomes over grown… their chance of becoming sick and immobile drastically increases. Shearing sheep is a huge part of keeping my sheep healthy."[86] And with merino sheep producing as much as 40 pounds of wool each year, Veterinarian Susana Meyers explained that unsheered sheep "can suffer heat stress, inability to feed babies, lack of vision, and maggot infestation."[87]

3-4 MAKING SENSE OF CHANGING ENVIRONMENTS

In Chapter 1, you learned that managers are responsible for making sense of their business environments. As our discussions of the general and specific environments have indicated, however, making sense of business environments is not an easy task.

Because external environments can be dynamic, confusing, and complex, managers use a three-step process to make sense of the changes in their external environments: **3-4a environmental scanning, 3-4b interpreting environmental factors,** *and* **3-4c acting on threats and opportunities.**

3-4a Environmental Scanning

Environmental scanning involves searching the environment for important events or issues that might affect an organization. Managers scan the environment to stay up-to-date on important factors in their industry and to reduce uncertainty. They want to know if demand will increase, or prices for key components will rise, and whether competitors sales are rising or falling. Amazon is scanning its environment to determine the key issues for becoming a major retailer of medical supplies. It brought hospital executives to headquarters to answer questions about adapting Amazon Business (where businesses sell to other businesses) for this purpose. The idea is to build a "marketplace" where, instead of contracting with one supplier, hospitals shopping on Amazon Business choose among multiple suppliers for each product. Chris Holt, who heads Amazon's global healthcare division, said, "We've been actively building out new capabilities and features."[88] Phyllis McCready, a hospital purchasing executive who spoke with Amazon, says product availability is key. She said, "It's a little different than being out of a size 6 dress. I can't be out of a six French catheter.

We can't be without supplies."[89] Amazon hopes to address that concern and gain significant industry experience via a pilot test with a large hospital system using Amazon Business to order medical supplies for its 150 outpatient facilities.[90]

Organizational strategies also affect environmental scanning. In other words, managers pay close attention to trends and events that are directly related to their company's ability to compete in the marketplace.[91] A key trend affecting many businesses is declining birthrates, down from 2.12 babies per woman before 2007, to 1.9 in 2007 to a 35-year low of 1.7 in 2018.[92] While seemingly small, in the United States alone that results in half a million fewer babies born each year. Jennifer Olson, vice president of strategy and business development at Children's Hospitals and Clinics of Minnesota, says, "We're just in a new era nationally and even globally where people are having fewer children."[93] Reg McLay, senior vice president of Babies "R" Us, says, "The assumption we'll make is that the market is not going to grow."[94] So Babies "R" Us will try to grow by taking market share from competitors. Hospitals are adapting, too, by slowly adding neonatal care units as career women delay childbirth into their late 30s.[95]

Finally, environmental scanning is important because it contributes to organizational performance. Environmental scanning helps managers detect environmental changes and problems before they become organizational crises.[96] Furthermore, companies whose CEOs do more environmental scanning have higher profits.[97] CEOs in better-performing firms scan their firms' environments more frequently and scan more key factors in their environments in more depth and detail than do CEOs in poorer-performing firms.[98]

3-4b Interpreting Environmental Factors

After scanning, managers determine what environmental events and issues mean to the organization. Typically, managers view environmental events and issues as either threats or opportunities. When managers interpret environmental events as threats, they take steps to protect the company from further harm. For over a century, dry cereal was found on nearly every breakfast table. At its peak, **Kellogg's** and its cast of cartoon cereal mascots held 45 percent of the market.[99] Today, Kellogg's cereal sales

> **Environmental scanning** searching the environment for important events or issues that might affect an organization

are dropping. Former Kroger grocery executive Tory Gundelach says, "It's not that people don't eat breakfast. It's more that they don't eat it the way they used to."[100] Instead of cereal, many consumers prefer a piece of fruit, a breakfast sandwich, a granola bar, or a protein shake, all of which can be eaten in their car or at their desk. Kellogg's CEO Steve Cahillane acknowledges the threat to the company, saying, "We've got big hurdles to overcome, but we're on it."[101] Kellogg's turnaround efforts are based on new flavors for old cereals, like Wild Berry Froot Loops and Strawberry Rice Krispies, and its first new cereal in decades, Happy Inside, which contains prebiotics and probiotics for health conscious consumers.[102] Kellogg's tried turning cereal into snacks at its Kellogg's NYC café, but closed the café after two years because consumers were not sufficiently interested in paying $1.50 for a dressed-up bowl of cereal topped with pistachios and lemon zest.[103]

By contrast, when managers interpret environmental threats as opportunities, they consider strategic alternatives for taking advantage of those events to improve company performance. With the world's population projected to grow from 7.3 billion in 2016 to 9.7 billion by 2050, farmers and food producers will need to produce an additional 455 million metric tons of meat to keep up with demand. Chicken is expected to account for the majority of that increase because of its mild taste, universal religious acceptance, and efficiency. Bringing a full-grown chicken to market requires just 30 percent of the water and feed needed to bring a cow to market.[104] Hoping to take advantage of the growing population and increased preference for chicken, Cargill has invested several billion dollars in new and expanded facilities. These high-tech operations feature automated, high-speed processing lines for breast deboning and production-line software that ensures that chicken portions are consistent in size and weight.[105] In Thailand, the company's network of more than 100 animal-friendly poultry farms has increased production 300 percent in just 10 years. Cargill is now able to ship 2.6 million birds from its Thailand operations to customers in Asia and Europe every week. This amounts to an additional 100 metric tons of chicken per year, or roughly 22 percent of the amount needed to feed an additional 2.4 billion people by 2050. Cargill expects to increase its capacity in Thailand another 30 percent in the near future, and also plans to develop a similarly sized network in sub-Saharan Africa to meet growing demand for meat across Africa's swelling urban centers.[106]

3-4c Acting on Threats and Opportunities

After scanning for information on environmental events and issues and interpreting them as threats or opportunities, managers have to decide how to respond to these environmental factors. Deciding what to do under conditions of uncertainty is always difficult. Managers can never be completely confident that they have all the information they need or that they correctly understand the information they have.

Because it is impossible to comprehend all the factors and changes, managers often rely on simplified models of external environments called cognitive maps. **Cognitive maps** summarize the perceived relationships between environmental factors and possible organizational actions. For example, the cognitive map shown in Exhibit 3.3 represents a small clothing-store owner's interpretation of her business environment. The map shows three kinds of variables. The first variables, shown as rectangles, are environmental factors, such as Amazon, Walmart, or Zara (the Spain-based retainer known for frequently refreshing the clothing designs it sells). The second variables, shown in ovals, are potential actions that the store owner might take, such as a low-cost strategy; a good-value, good-service strategy; or a "large selection of the latest fashions" strategy. The third variables, shown as trapezoids, are company strengths, such as low employee turnover, and weaknesses, such as small size.

The plus and minus signs on the map indicate whether the manager believes there is a positive or negative relationship between variables. For example, the manager believes that a low-cost strategy won't work because of Walmart and Amazon. Offering a large selection of the latest fashions would not work, either – not with the small size of the store and that nearby Zara. However, the manager believes that a good-value, good-service strategy would lead to success and profits due to

Vladislav Noseek/Shutterstock.com

Cognitive maps graphic depictions of how managers believe environmental factors relate to possible organizational actions

Exhibit 3.3
Cognitive Maps

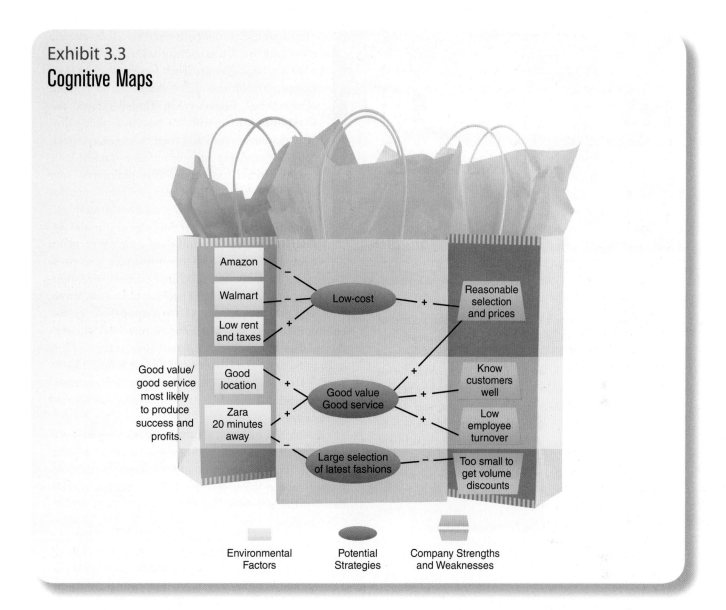

Environmental Factors   Potential Strategies   Company Strengths and Weaknesses

the store's low employee turnover, good knowledge of customers, reasonable selection of clothes at reasonable prices, and good location.

3-5 ORGANIZATIONAL CULTURES: CREATION, SUCCESS, AND CHANGE

We have been looking at trends and events outside of companies that have the potential to affect them. By contrast, the **internal environment** consists of the trends and events *within* an organization that affect the management, employees, and **organizational culture**. Internal environments are important because they affect what people think, feel, and do at work. The key component in internal environments is organizational culture, or the set of key values, beliefs, and attitudes shared by members of the organization.

Creating, maintaining, and changing organizational culture matters because research shows that positive, consistent culture improves company performance. In a six-year study of 95 automobile dealerships, Professor Michael Gillespie says, "We found that culture causes performance, not vice versa." Culture clearly comes first. Dealerships whose cultures

Internal environment the events and trends inside an organization that affect management, employees, and organizational culture

Organizational culture the values, beliefs, and attitudes shared by organizational members

Dealership culture can have an impact on auto sales.

did not improve were less profitable over the course of the study.[107] But dealerships, with positive cultures in the study's first few years usually had higher profits in the later years. It usually took, however, several years of change to an organizational culture to improve dealership performance as measured by customer satisfaction and dealer sales. "The culture of a sales department right now is to influence the customer satisfaction from that department two years from now, and that customer satisfaction is going to drive vehicle sales two years from that point," says Gillespie.[108] Gillespie and his co-authors concluded, " . . . that strong culture at the foundation can be a unique point of leverage for winning and retaining customers over time."[109] Leadership consultant David Grossman concludes, "Culture change today is at the heart of winning because it's so difficult for [other] employers to copy."[110]

*Let's take a closer look at **3-5a how organizational cultures are created and maintained, 3-5b the characteristics of successful organizational cultures,** and **3-5c how companies can accomplish the difficult task of changing organizational cultures.***

3-5a Creation and Maintenance of Organizational Cultures

A primary source of organizational culture is the company founder. Founders like Walt Disney (Disney) and Steve Jobs (Apple) created organizations in their own images and imprinted them with their beliefs, attitudes, and values. According to Professor Zeynep Ton,

Organizational stories stories told by organizational members to make sense of organizational events and changes and to emphasize culturally consistent assumptions, decisions, and actions

"The founder is in a better position than anyone else to say this is what our business is about, this is what we won't give up. They have to stick to their values 100 percent of the time, not 95 percent of the time." Founder Kip Tindell infused the **Container Store** with his personal philosophy, "Pay employees well and treat them with respect; consider suppliers and customers as family; have fun."[111] Tindell has turned that philosophy into seven Foundational Principles (see http://standfor.containerstore.com/our-foundation-principles/) that drive the Container Store's culture and actions. Not only are full-time employees given a week of training on the principles, the principles have also been printed on company shopping bags, T-shirts, and packing tape. One strong sign that the principles have shaped the company culture is the low rate of employee turnover. Whereas the median turnover rate for part-time retail workers is 75 percent, at the Container Store, it is only 10 percent.[112] How are values, attitudes, and beliefs sustained in organizational cultures? Answer: stories, heroes, and celebrations.

People tell **organizational stories** to make sense of organizational events and changes and to emphasize culturally consistent assumptions, decisions, and actions.[113] Silicon Valley entrepreneur, consultant, and author Steve Blank says:

It was in my third startup, Convergent Technologies, that I started to understand the power of a corporate culture. The values and basic beliefs of working in this crazy startup were embodied in the phrase that we were "The Marine Corps of Silicon Valley." If the notion of joining the Marine Corps of tech wasn't something that interested you, you didn't apply. If it was appealing…, you fought to get in. … [114] By the time I joined, the company already had a story of 'beating the impossible odds' and 'innovation on your feet' stories. It was already lore that the founders had pivoted from simply building an entire computer that fit on a single-circuit board with a newfangled Intel microprocessor to selling complete desktop workstations with an operating system and office applications (the precursor to the PC) to other computer companies. And

the CEO had done the pivot in front of a whiteboard of a customer who went from a "we're not interested" to a $45 million order in the same meeting.[115]

A second way in which organizational culture is sustained is by recognizing and celebrating heroes. By definition, **organizational heroes** are people admired for their qualities and achievements within the organization. Steve Blank again explains:

> For example, if a company values financial performance above all, its stories, myths, and rituals might include how a hero saved the company 5 percent from a supplier. Or if a company is focused on delivering breakthrough products, then the heroes, stories, and rituals will be about product innovation (e.g., the Apple legends of the Mac, iPod, and iPhone development).[116]

Finally, the last way of sustaining organizational culture is through ceremonies. **Organizational ceremonies** are gatherings in which symbolic acts commemorate or celebrate notable achievements or changes. Blank describes these cultural ceremonies at his third startup, Convergent Technologies:

> Finally, there were rituals and celebrations that accompanied each big order. Bells and gongs would ring. The CEO would hand out $100 bills and gave out a $25,000 on-the-spot bonus that was talked about for years. Once he even spray-painted an exhortation to ship a new product on time on our main hallway wall (so crude I can't even paraphrase it, but still remembered 30 years later). While my title, business card and job description described my job functions, these unwritten values, stories, heroes and rituals guided the behavior that was expected of me in my job.[117]

3-5b Successful Organizational Cultures

Research increasingly shows that organizational culture is related to organizational success. As shown in Exhibit 3.4, cultures based on adaptability, involvement, a clear mission, and consistency can help companies achieve higher sales growth, return on assets, profits, quality, and employee satisfaction.[118]

Adaptability is the ability to notice and respond to changes in the organization's environment. Cultures need to reinforce important values and behaviors, but a culture becomes dysfunctional if it prevents change. **Theranos** was paid nearly $1 billion by investors to produce a home

Exhibit 3.4
Keys to an Organizational Culture That Fosters Success

de2marco/Shutterstock.com

blood-testing device that would be fast, inexpensive, and capable of producing 240 kinds of test results, similar to commercial medical laboratories.[119] But after repeated failure to meet deadlines and burning through most of its startup funds, the company's assets were liquidated to pay creditors after federal prosecutors filed criminal fraud charges against founder Elizabeth Holmes and COO Sunny Balwani for exaggerating and making false statements about Theranos's technology and financial performance.[120] Security and Exchange Commission Co-Director Stephanie Avakian stated, "As a result of Holmes' alleged fraudulent conduct, she is being stripped of control of the company she founded, is returning millions of shares to Theranos, and is barred from serving as an officer or director of a public company for 10 years."[121] *Wall Street Journal* reporter John Carreyrou, who uncovered Theranos's problems, attributes its downfall to a dysfunctional culture that prevented change. Carreyrou wrote, "The biggest problem of all was the dysfunctional corporate culture in which it was being developed. Holmes and Balwani regarded anyone who raised a concern or an objection as a cynic and a nay-sayer. Employees who persisted in doing so were usually marginalized or fired, while sycophants were promoted."[122]

Organizational heroes people celebrated for their qualities and achievements within an organization

Organizational ceremonies gatherings in which symbolic acts commemorate or celebrate notable achievements or changes

ORGANIZATIONAL CULTURES: CULTS OR TATTOOS?

Organizational cultures are created by company founders, and perpetuated via organizational stories, heroes, and ceremonies. Successful organizational cultures can adapt to changes in organizational environments, involve employees through greater decision-making authority, are linked to the company's mission and purpose, and are consistent because the company actively defines and teaches organizational values, beliefs, and attitudes.

But at what point do successful organizational cultures cross the line into cultish cultures? Manfred Kets de Vries, a psychoanalyst and executive coach who has written about the psychopathologies of organizations for 40 years, says, "Healthy corporate cultures can easily turn into corporate cults, whether leaders intend for it to happen or not. Many of the companies we celebrate are treading that fine line; Apple, Tesla, Zappos, Southwest Airlines, Nordstrom, and Harley Davidson are a few examples. They have all built a cult-like following among their customers and, increasingly, are encouraging cultish behaviors in their workforces as well." According to Kets de Vries, what crosses the line is "the degree of control management exercises over employees' thinking and behavior." He warns, for example, about daily or weekly meetings where employees chant empty corporate slogans because it's required, not because they believe them. Or squashing individualism. Or working employees so hard they don't have meaningful personal lives.

What would Kets de Vries think about employees who tattooed themselves with company mottos or slogans? As

Olivier Le Moal/iStock/Getty Images

long it was voluntary, Kets de Vries wouldn't care. In fact, he might view them as a sign of a positive organizational culture. For example, Thomas Cameron so loves working at Red Hat, one of the world's largest software companies, that he had its insignia tattooed on his left forearm. After Red Hat announced that it was developing a new logo, he proclaimed, "I already have a place on my [other] arm picked out."

While choosing to get "tatted up" with the company logo can express commitment, considering family members' reactions might be wise. Anytime Fitness media director got a company tattoo like his co-workers but hid it from his wife for three days. He says she thought it was "sexy," but she says the tattoo proved he's a "knucklehead."

Sources: R. Feintzeig & K. Gee, "Nice Tattoo! I Didn't Know You Worked at Walmart," *Wall Street Journal*, March 2, 2018, accessed February 10, 2020, www.wsj.com/articles/nice-tattoo-i-didnt-know-you-worked-at-walmart-152000519; M. Kets de Vries, "Is Your Corporate Culture Cultish?" *Harvard Business Review*, May 10, 2019, accessed February 10, 2020, https://hbr.org/2019/05/is-your-corporate-culture-cultish.

In cultures that promote higher levels of *employee involvement* in decision-making, employees feel a greater sense of ownership and responsibility. We'll learn more about this in Chapter 9, in Section 9-2c about delegation of authority and 9-2d, degree of centralization. For now, it's enough to know that when employees are given more decision-making authority, they take greater ownership of their work and feel more positive responsibility about the results created by their work.

Company mission is the business's purpose or reason for existing. In organizational cultures with a clear company mission, the organization's strategic purpose and direction are apparent to everyone in the company. When managers are uncertain about their business environments, the mission helps guide the discussions, decisions, and behavior of the people in the company. BPV Capital Management is a Knoxville, Tennessee, mutual fund with 38 employees. Alluding to the common dream of owning a retirement home with wonderful weather and a great view, founder Mike West explains that "BPV" stands for "back porch vista"; BPV exists "to help American families retire well." More specifically, its mission is, "To ensure that investors who work hard and save have the opportunity to retire comfortably, regardless of net worth." Says West, "Our values and the promise that we make to every advisor and investor are driven by that core ideology."[123]

Finally, in **consistent organizational cultures**, the company actively defines and teaches organizational values, beliefs, and attitudes. Claudio Del Vecchio, who bought and turned around Brooks Brothers, a 200-year-old high-end clothing brand, agrees. As a CEO, he says, "I am here to reinforce a culture. I have to make sure that we are building a company that will last after me. I don't want to be here

Company mission a company's purpose or reason for existing

Consistent organizational culture a company culture in which the company actively defines and teaches organizational values, beliefs, and attitudes

Exhibit 3.5
Three Levels of Organizational Culture

SEEN
(Surface level)

- Symbolic artifacts such as dress codes
- Workers' and managers' behaviors
- What people say

HEARD
(Expressed values
and beliefs)

- How decisions are made and explained

BELIEVED
(Unconscious
assumptions and
beliefs)

- Widely shared assumptions and beliefs
- Buried deep below surface
- Rarely discussed or thought about

Anton Zabielskyi/Shutterstock.com

another 20 years. Forget about another 200 years. It's really about trying to build a culture that will last longer than the business. That will make it very hard for the next guy to screw it up."[124]

Having a consistent or strong organizational culture doesn't guarantee good company performance. When core beliefs are widely shared and strongly held, it is very difficult to bring about needed change. Consequently, companies with strong cultures tend to perform poorly when they need to adapt to dramatic changes in their external environments. Their consistency sometimes prevents them from adapting to those changes.[125]

3-5c Changing Organizational Cultures

As shown in Exhibit 3.5, organizational cultures exist on three levels.[126] On the first, or surface, level are the reflections of an organization's culture that can be seen and observed, such as symbolic artifacts (e.g., dress codes and office layouts) and workers' and managers' behaviors. Next, just below the surface, are the values and beliefs expressed by people in the company. You can't see these values and beliefs, but they become clear if you carefully listen to what people say and observe how decisions are made or explained. Finally, unconsciously held assumptions and beliefs about the company are buried deep below the surface. These are the unwritten views and rules that are so strongly held and so widely shared that they are rarely discussed or even thought about unless someone attempts to change them or unknowingly violates them. Changing such assumptions and beliefs can be very difficult. Instead, managers should focus on the parts of the organizational culture they can control. These include observable surface-level items, such as workers' behaviors, symbolic artifacts, and expressed values and beliefs, which can be influenced through employee selection. Let's see how these can be used to change organizational cultures.

One way of changing a corporate culture is to use behavioral addition or behavioral substitution to establish new patterns of behavior among managers and employees. **Behavioral addition** is the process of having

> **Behavioral addition** the process of having managers and employees perform new behaviors that are central to and symbolic of the new organizational culture that a company wants to create

Some 5,300 Wells Fargo bank employees and branch managers were fired after opening 2.1 million bank accounts and services that customers never approved.

managers and employees perform a new behavior, while **behavioral substitution** is having managers and employees perform a new behavior in place of another behavior. The key in both instances is to choose behaviors that are central to and symbolic of the old culture you're changing and the new culture that you want to create.[127] Unfortunately, reward systems sometimes encourage behaviors that run counter to desired cultural changes. When this happens, behavioral addition and substitution can produce the wrong behaviors. Professor Daniel Barron explains that, "When you're given a strong incentive, when a lot of money is on the line, you're going to move your behavior toward that."[128]

Because of aggressive sales goals, 5,300 Wells Fargo bank employees and branch managers were fired after opening 2.1 million bank accounts and services that customers never approved. Then CFO John Shrewsberry admitted the problems were caused by "people trying to meet minimum goals to hang onto their jobs."[129] Former CEO John Stumpf said incentives would no longer be linked to branch-level sales goals. "We think to the extent that some team members used a sales goal as a motivation to something that is inconsistent with our culture . . . [it's] just not worth it."[130] But three years later, after paying $1.5 billion in government penalties and $620 million in lawsuit settlements, Wells Fargo reportedly still linked rewards to aggressive sales goals. A *New York Times* report indicated that company debt collectors were expected to make 33 calls an hour and recoup $40,000 in unpaid consumer debt each month, up from 30 calls and $34,000.[131] Wells Fargo employee Mark Willie said, "For us front-line workers, there's an overwhelming sense of frustration. There is a general fear of retaliation for speaking out."[132] A former Wells Fargo salesperson, who exited the company to escape the pressure, said that managers would use "coded language" such as, "We're not helping enough customers."[133] Wells Fargo employee Alex Ross concluded, "There's a sense among the workers that most of the reforms the bank has made are very superficial and only being done for P.R. reasons."[134]

Another way in which managers can begin to change corporate culture is to change the **visible artifacts** of their old culture, such as the office design and layout, company dress code, and recipients (or nonrecipients) of company benefits and perks such as stock options, personal parking spaces, or the private company dining room. Ryanair is a Dublin-based airline that offers incredibly low rates. Ryanair led the way in charging passengers for every part of the flight experience, including $50 to print a boarding pass at the airport and a "no refunds" policy for canceled flights. Ryanair's brazen policies originate from its brash CEO, Michael O'Leary. Regarding passengers who forget to print boarding passes at home, O'Leary says, "We think they should pay 60 euros for being so stupid." Regarding canceled flights, he says, "You're not getting a refund, so **** off. We don't want to hear your sob stories. What part of 'no refund' don't you understand?"[135] Unfortunately, O'Leary's unabashed statements have rubbed off on the company's staffers, whose similarly negative attitudes discouraged customers from choosing the airline. To address the problem, Ryanair introduced the "Always Getting Better" campaign (also called the "Being Nicer" campaign) to change the company's focus from being cheap to providing a superior customer experience. The company reduced or eliminated some (but not all) of its fees; simplified online booking to require only 5 mouse clicks instead of 17; and introduced fully allocated seating to minimize congestion at the boarding gate. Previously, its "first-come, first-served" boarding strategy encouraged travelers to rush the gates to get better seats.[136] Crews were issued new, brightly colored uniforms, and the company moved its headquarters from a tired, dull facility to a cheerful building with colorful art on the walls. The changes dramatically improved company performance. In just one year, the number of Ryanair

Behavioral substitution the process of having managers and employees perform new behaviors central to the new organizational culture in place of behaviors that were central to the old organizational culture

Visible artifacts visible signs of an organization's culture, such as the office design and layout, company dress code, and company benefits and perks, such as stock options, personal parking spaces, or the private company dining room

Cultural Fit: Good Idea Or Legal Problem?

Zappos, the online shoe retailer, only hires people who fit its quirky culture. Zappos' Rick Jordan, head of talent acquisition, says, "People who are true fits to the culture and believe what we believe – they'll do anything for the business." While hiring for cultural fit makes sense, companies like Facebook see it as a "bias trap," and discourage managers from using it as a hiring criterion. Professor Lauren Rivera says, "In many organizations, it is this catchall for, 'I don't feel right about this person.'" If you use cultural fit, clearly define it and get approval from company attorneys so it helps make good, legal hiring decisions.

Source: R. Feintzeig, "'Culture Fit' May Be the Key to Your Next Job," *Wall Street Journal*, October 12, 2017, accessed March 8, 2017, www.wsj.com/articles/culture-fit-may-be-the-key-to-your-next-job-1476239784.

passengers increased 10 percent, and the load factor (the measurement of how full a jet is) reached 95 percent. O'Leary said, "If I'd known being nicer to customers was going to work so well, I'd have done it ages ago."[137]

Cultures can also be changed by hiring and selecting people with values and beliefs consistent with the company's desired culture. *Selection* is the process of gathering information about job applicants to decide who should be offered a job. As discussed in Chapter 11 on human resources, most selection instruments measure whether job applicants have the knowledge, skills, and abilities needed to succeed in their jobs. But companies are increasingly testing job applicants to determine how they fit with the company's desired culture by using selection tests, instruments, and exercises to measure these values and beliefs in job applicants. (See Chapter 11 for a complete review of

Changing corporate culture can go a long way in boosting employee morale.

applicant and managerial selection.) During the hiring process, Amazon uses a group of employees called *Bar Raisers*, who interview job candidates from other areas of the company, asking difficult and unexpected questions. Bar Raisers, who spend two to three hours on each job candidate, conducting phone and face-to-face interviews and participating in evaluation meetings, have the power to veto any applicant they've assessed. Founder Jeff Bezos started the Bar Raiser program to create a consistent corporate culture by "raising the bar" when it came to hiring talent. Rather than hiring people for particular jobs, Bezos asks Bar Raisers to focus on hiring people who can succeed in Amazon's culture. John Vlastelica, an HR consultant who worked at Amazon in its early days, says, "You want someone who can adapt to new roles in the company, not just someone who can fill the role that's vacant." Susan Harker, Amazon's vice president of global talent acquisition, says, "We want to be as objective and scientific in our hiring as possible. The point is to optimize our chances of having long-term employees." [138] And Bar Raisers do that "as an objective third party" in the hiring process whose primary responsibility is making sure that new hires fit Amazon's culture.[139]

Corporate cultures are very difficult to change. Consequently, there is no guarantee that any one approach – changing visible cultural artifacts, using behavioral substitution, or hiring people with values consistent with a company's desired culture – will change a company's organizational culture. The best results are obtained by combining these methods. Together, these are some of the best ways managers have for changing culture because they send the clear message to managers and employees that "the accepted way of doing things" has changed.

Finally, the lead authors in a special edition of the *Harvard Business Review* on organizational culture conclude, "Leading with culture may be among the few sources of sustainable competitive advantage left to companies today. Successful leaders will stop regarding culture with frustration and instead use it as a fundamental management tool."[140]

4 | Ethics and Social Responsibility

LEARNING OUTCOMES

4-1 Identify common kinds of workplace deviance.

4-2 Describe how the US Sentencing Commission Guidelines Manual for Organizations encourages ethical behavior, including how to calculate fines for unethical behavior.

4-3 Describe what influences ethical decision-making.

4-4 Apply the practical steps managers can take to improve ethical decision-making in real-world situations.

4-5 Explain to whom organizations are socially responsible.

4-6 Explain for what organizations are socially responsible.

4-7 Identify how organizations can respond to societal demands for social responsibility.

4-8 Explain whether social responsibility hurts or helps an organization's economic performance.

themacx/iStock/Getty Images

4-1 WORKPLACE DEVIANCE

Today, it's not enough for companies to make a profit. We also expect managers to make a profit by doing the right things. Unfortunately, no matter what managers decide to do, someone or some group will be unhappy with the outcome. Managers don't have the luxury of choosing theoretically optimal, win–win solutions that are obviously desirable to everyone involved. In practice, solutions to ethical and social responsibility problems aren't optimal. Often, managers must be satisfied with a solution that just makes do or does the least harm. Rights and wrongs are rarely crystal clear to managers charged with doing the right thing. The business world is much messier than that.[1]

Ethics is the set of moral principles or values that defines right and wrong for a person or group. Unfortunately, numerous studies have consistently produced distressing results about the state of ethics in today's business world. One global ethics study found that, even though business is substantially more trusted than government and that 75 percent of employees trust the company where they work (i.e., "my employer"), just 55 percent believe that management always tells the truth, and only 47 percent believe that CEOs can be believed.[2] Another study found that just 25 percent trust business leaders to honestly correct mistakes and that less than 20 percent believed that business leaders would be truthful and make ethical decisions.[3] The Ethics & Compliance Initiative's *Global* Business Ethics Survey across 18 countries found that:

» 22 percent of employees were pressured to commit unethical acts.

» 33 percent of employees observed unethical behavior.

» 62 percent of employees observing unethical behavior reported it to company officials.

» 36 percent of those reporting unethical behavior experienced retaliation for doing so (see the discussion of whistle-blowing in Section 4-4d).[4]

The Ethics & Compliance Initiative's *National* Business Ethics Survey (for US companies) also found that 24 percent of unethical behavior was committed by senior managers, while 60 percent was committed by managers (of all kinds).[5]

Fortunately, some studies contain good news about workplace ethics. When people believe their work environment is ethical, they are six times more likely to stay with that company than if they believe they work in an unethical environment.[6] In fact, a survey by Deloitte reported that employees who were considering leaving their jobs cited "loss of trust" as the

Ethics the set of moral principles or values that defines right and wrong for a person or group

FABRICE COFFRINI/Getty Images

Matthias Mueller, CEO of the Volkswagen group, has called for the company to learn from its mistakes following the devastating financial impact of an emission test cheating scandal.

behaviors like these, which researchers call *workplace deviance*, may cost companies as much as $4 trillion a year, or roughly 5 percent of their revenues.[10]

Workplace deviance is unethical behavior that violates organizational norms about right and wrong. As Exhibit 4.1 shows, workplace deviance can be categorized by how deviant the behavior is, from minor to serious, and by the target of the deviant behavior, either the organization or particular people in the workplace.[11]

Company-related deviance can affect both tangible and intangible assets. One kind of workplace deviance,

greatest factor.[7] One study asked 444 white-collar workers which qualities they considered to be important in company leaders. The results? Honesty (30 percent) and communication (22 percent) ranked by far the highest. Interestingly, these two qualities also ranked highest as areas in which business leaders needed to improve—16 percent of respondents said that leaders need to improve their honesty, and 11 percent cited communication.[8] Michael Gould, Bloomingdale's CEO of 22 years, agreed, saying, "To me, the fundamental basis of leadership is trust. If you don't have trust, you have no leadership."[9] In short, much needs to be done to make workplaces more ethical, but – and this is very important – most managers and employees want this to happen.

Ethical behavior follows accepted principles of right and wrong. Depending on the study, one-third to three-quarters of all employees admit that they have stolen from their employers, committed computer fraud, embezzled funds, vandalized company property, sabotaged company projects, faked injuries to receive workers' compensation benefits or insurance, or been "sick" from work when they weren't really sick. Experts estimate that unethical

Ethical behavior behavior that conforms to a society's accepted principles of right and wrong

Workplace deviance unethical behavior that violates organizational norms about right and wrong

Exhibit 4.1
Types of Workplace Deviance

Organizational

Production Deviance
- Leaving early
- Taking excessive breaks
- Intentionally working slowly
- Wasting resources

Property Deviance
- Sabotaging equipment
- Accepting kickbacks
- Lying about hours worked
- Stealing from company

Minor ← → Serious

Political Deviance
- Showing favoritism
- Gossiping about coworkers
- Blaming coworkers
- Competing nonbeneficially

Personal Aggression
- Sexual harassment
- Verbal abuse
- Stealing from coworkers
- Endangering coworkers

Interpersonal

Source: Adapted from "A Typology of Deviant Workplace Behaviors" (Figure), S. L. Robinson and R. J. Bennett. *Academy of Management Journal* 38 (1995).

called **production deviance**, hurts the quality and quantity of work produced. Examples include leaving early, taking excessively long work breaks, intentionally working slower, or wasting resources. A Salary.com study found that 89 percent of employees admit to wasting time at work, with 62 percent wasting 30 minutes to an hour, 22 percent wasting two to three hours, and 4 percent wasting four to five hours per day.[12] The most accomplished time wasters secretly brought their pet birds to the office, hid under boxes to scare coworkers, and held wrestling matches with other employees. A female employee wasted time by shaving her legs in the women's restroom.[13] The biggest source of workplace deviance, however, is probably *cyberloafing*, wasting time on the job with nonwork-related social-media sites and apps like Facebook, Twitter, Instagram, or SnapChat, as well as surfing nonwork-related retail sites like Amazon.com. Amazingly, participants in a Kansas State University study admitted to wasting 60 to 80 percent of their work time online! Cyberloafing is estimated to cost US businesses $85 billion a year in lost productivity.[14]

Property deviance is unethical behavior aimed at company property or products. Examples include sabotaging, stealing, or damaging equipment or products, and overcharging for services and then pocketing the difference. A study of 1 million visits to self-service checkout lanes, in which customers and not store employees scanned products at store registers, found that only 86 percent of items were scanned. Consumers did not scan 850,000 items out of the 6 million items brought to the self-service checkout lanes, leaving retailers 4 percent short of what they should have been paid. Study researchers concluded, "Retailers could find themselves accused of making theft so easy that

The biggest type of workplace deviance is spending time on personal social media sites and surfing nonwork-related retail sites.

some customers who would normally – and happily – pay are tempted to commit crime, especially when they feel 'justified' in doing it."[15]

Organizational employees, however, do a significant amount of property deviance themselves. **Employee shrinkage**, when employees steal company merchandise, accounts for 23 percent of theft from US retailers and costs $9.76 billion a year.[16] Examples include an employee who stole $240,000 of printer ink, which he tried to resell on eBay, and a delivery driver who stole $90,000 of designer cakes from a New York City bakery.[17] The good news is that employee shrinkage is down by nearly half in the last 5 years. The bad news is that employee theft still costs US retailers more than shoplifters do![18] A survey of 20 large retailers across 13,674 stores found that 1 out of 40 employees is caught stealing each year and that a dishonest employee steals 4.5 times as much as the typical shoplifter.[19] Likewise, 58 percent of office workers acknowledge taking company property for personal use, according to a survey conducted for lawyers.com. "Sweethearting" occurs when employees discount or don't ring up merchandise their family or friends bring to the cash register. Sweethearting costs the retail service industry (i.e., restaurants, hotels, hair salons, car washes, and so on) $60 billion annually.[20] Sixty-seven percent of employees admit to sweethearting, primarily in hopes of receiving similar deals and discounts from the customers to whom they had extended a sweetheart deal.[21] In "dumpster diving," employees unload trucks, stash merchandise in a dumpster, and then retrieve it after work.[22]

Although production and property deviance harm companies, political deviance and personal aggression are unethical behaviors that hurt particular people within companies. **Political deviance** is using one's influence to harm others in the company. Examples include making decisions based on favoritism rather than performance, spreading rumors about coworkers, or blaming others for mistakes they didn't make. **Personal aggression** is hostile or aggressive behavior toward others. Examples include sexual harassment, verbal abuse, stealing from coworkers, or personally threatening coworkers. Another kind of personal aggression is workplace violence.

Production deviance unethical behavior that hurts the quality and quantity of work produced

Property deviance unethical behavior aimed at the organization's property or products

Employee shrinkage employee theft of company merchandise

Political deviance using one's influence to harm others in the company

Personal aggression hostile or aggressive behavior toward others

Fortunately, like nearly all kinds of crime, workplace violence has dropped significantly since 1993, when 16 of every 1,000 employees experienced nonfatal workplace violence. Today, the rate has dropped to just 2.1 incidents per 10,000 full-time retail workers and 4.4 incidents per 10,000 full-time workers in nonretail jobs.[23] Furthermore, the rate of workplace violence is one-third the level of nonworkplace violence. So, overall, you are less likely to encounter violence at work. Still, 453 people were killed at work as a result of workplace violence in 2018, the most recent year for which data are available. That means 8.6 percent of workplace deaths are homicides.[24] For more information on workplace violence, see the Bureau of Labor Statistics website, www.bls.gov/iif/osh_wpvs.htm.

4-2 US SENTENCING COMMISSION *GUIDELINES MANUAL* FOR ORGANIZATIONS

A male supervisor is sexually harassing female coworkers. A sales representative offers a $25,000 kickback to persuade an indecisive customer to do business with his company. A company president secretly meets with the CEO of her biggest competitor, and they agree not to compete in markets where the other has already established customers. Each of these behaviors is clearly unethical (and, in these cases, also illegal). Historically, if management was unaware of such activities, the company could not be held responsible for them. Since 1984, however, when the US Sentencing Commission was created, the *Guidelines Manual* established that companies can be prosecuted and punished *even if management didn't know about the unethical behavior*. Penalties can be substantial, with maximum fines approaching a whopping $600 million.[25] Later changes to the Sentencing Commission *Guidelines Manual* resulted in much stricter ethics training requirements and emphasized the importance of creating a legal and ethical company culture.[26]

*Let's examine **4-2a to whom the guidelines apply and what they cover** and **4-2b how, according to the guidelines, an organization can be punished for the unethical behavior of its managers and employees.***

4-2a Who, What, and Why?

Nearly all businesses are covered by the US Sentencing Commission's Guidelines Manual. This includes nonprofits, partnerships, labor unions, unincorporated organizations and associations, incorporated organizations, and even pension funds, trusts, and joint stock companies. If your organization can be characterized as a business (remember, nonprofits count, too), then it is subject to these guidelines.[27] For example, World Vision, a nonprofit Christian humanitarian aid organization, has a compliance program based on the US Sentencing Commission's *Guidelines Manual*. The program includes regular audits, a code of conduct, ethics standards, and anti-bribery and corruption policies (because much of its humanitarian work is carried out in third-world countries).[28]

The guidelines cover offenses defined by federal laws such as invasion of privacy, price fixing, fraud, customs violations, antitrust violations, civil rights violations, theft, money laundering, conflicts of interest, embezzlement, dealing in stolen goods, copyright infringements, extortion, and more. But it's not enough merely to stay within the law. The purpose of the guidelines is not just to punish companies *after* they or their employees break the law but also to encourage companies to take proactive steps that will discourage or prevent white-collar crime *before* it happens. The guidelines also give companies an incentive to cooperate with and disclose illegal activities to federal authorities.[29]

4-2b Determining the Punishment

The Sentencing Commission Guidelines impose smaller fines on companies that take proactive steps to encourage ethical behavior or voluntarily disclose illegal activities to federal authorities. Essentially, the law uses a carrot-and-stick approach. The stick is the threat of heavy fines that can total millions of dollars. The carrot is a greatly reduced fine, but only if the company has started an effective compliance program (discussed next) to encourage ethical behavior *before* the illegal activity occurs and then cooperates with the investigation.[30] The method used to determine a company's punishment illustrates how this works.

As shown in Exhibit 4.2, the first step is to compute the *base fine* by determining what *level of offense* (that is, its seriousness) has occurred. The level of the offense varies depending on the kind of crime, the loss incurred by the victims, and how much planning went into the crime. For example, simple fraud is a level 6 offense (there are 38 levels in all). But if the victims of that fraud lost more than $5 million, that level 6 offense becomes a level 22 offense. Moreover, anything beyond minimal planning to commit the fraud results in an increase of two levels to a level 24 offense. How much difference would this make to a company? As Exhibit 4.2 shows, crimes at or below level 6 incur a base fine of $8,500, whereas the base fine for level 24 is $3.5 million, a difference of $3,491,500! The base fine for level 38, the top-level offense, is a hefty $150 million.

After assessing a *base fine*, a judge computes a culpability score, which is a way of assigning blame to the company. Culpability scores generally range from 0 to 10. The judge starts with a culpability score of 5 and then adjusts up or down based on several factors.[31]

Factors that increase the culpability score:

» *The number of employees and high-level managers involved in misconduct* – add 1 to 5 points.
» *The organization's prior history of misconduct* – add 1 to 2 points.
» *Whether the unethical behavior violated a previous judicial order or condition of probation* – add 1 to 2 points.
» *Whether the organization willfully obstructed or attempted to obstruct the investigation into its unethical behavior* – add 3 points.

Factors that reduce the culpability score:

» *The organization had an effective compliance and ethics program in place* – subtract 3 points.
» *The organization (a) self-reported its offense, (b) fully cooperated with the investigation, and (c) took full responsibility for its misconduct*:

    – If all (a, b, and c), subtract 5 points.
    – If (b) fully cooperated and (c) took full responsibility, subtract 2 points.
    – If (c) took full responsibility, subtract 1 point.

The culpability score then determines the minimum or maximum multiplier applied to the base fine.[32] As shown above, the multiplier rises directly with increases in culpability. The more blame a company deserves for unethical misconduct, the higher the multiplier and therefore the higher the fine.

Culpability Score	Minimum Multiplier	Maximum Multiplier
10 or more	2.00	4.00
9	1.80	3.60
8	1.60	3.20
7	1.40	2.80
6	1.20	2.40
5	1.00	2.00
4	0.80	1.60
3	0.60	1.20
2	0.40	0.80
1	0.20	0.40
0 or less	0.05	0.20

Let's return to our level 24 fraud offense where the base fine is $3,500,000 and compare how this would work for two companies. Remember, with all companies, a judge starts with a culpability score of 5 and adjusts up or down, depending on the circumstances. In this example, shown in Exhibit 4.2, Company 1 has no compliance and ethics program in place, but end ups with a culpability score of 0 after 5 points are subtracted because it self-reported its offense, fully cooperated with the investigation, and took full responsibility for its misconduct. With a "0 or less" culpability score, the multiplier is a minimum of 0.05 and a maximum of 0.20. So, for a level 24 offense with a base fine of $3.5 million, Company 1 will be fined at least $175,000 ($3,500,000 × 0.05) and no more than $700,000 ($3,500,000 × 0.02).

On the other hand, Company 2 in our example, ends up with a culpability score of 10. The judge started with a culpability score of five, but added 2 points for top management involvement in the misconduct and 3 additional points for obstructing the investigation into the company's behavior. With a "10 or more" culpability score, the multipliers are much larger with a minimum of 2.00 and a maximum of 4.00. So for a level 24 offense with a base fine of $3.5 million, Company 2 will be fined at least 7 million ($3,500,000 × 2.0), and a maximum of $14 million ($3,500,000 × 4.0).

The difference is even greater for level 38 offenses where the base fine is $150,000,000. As

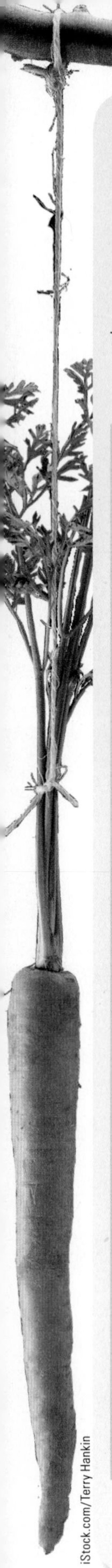

Exhibit 4.2

Offense Levels, Base Fines, Culpability Scores, and Multipliers: An Example of Possible Total Fines under the US Sentencing Commission Guidelines for Organizations

Offense Level	Base Fine	Company 1 Culpability Score of 0 or Less		Company 2 Culpability Score of 10 or More	
		Minimum Multiplier 0.05	Maximum Multiplier 0.20	Minimum Multiplier 2.00	Maximum Multiplier 4.00
6 or less	$8,500	$425	$1,700	$17,000	$34,000
7	$15,000	$750	$3,000	$30,000	$60,000
8	$15,000	$750	$3,000	$30,000	$60,000
9	$25,000	$1,250	$5,000	$50,000	$100,000
10	$35,000	$1,750	$7,000	$70,000	$140,000
11	$50,000	$2,500	$10,000	$100,000	$200,000
12	$70,000	$3,500	$14,000	$140,000	$280,000
13	$100,000	$5,000	$20,000	$200,000	$400,000
14	$150,000	$7,500	$30,000	$300,000	$600,000
15	$200,000	$10,000	$40,000	$400,000	$800,000
16	$300,000	$15,000	$60,000	$600,000	$1,200,000
17	$450,000	$22,500	$90,000	$900,000	$1,800,000
18	$600,000	$30,000	$120,000	$1,200,000	$2,400,000
19	$850,000	$42,500	$170,000	$1,700,000	$3,400,000
20	$1,000,000	$50,000	$200,000	$2,000,000	$4,000,000
21	$1,500,000	$75,000	$300,000	$3,000,000	$6,000,000
22	$2,000,000	$100,000	$400,000	$4,000,000	$8,000,000
23	$3,000,000	$150,000	$600,000	$6,000,000	$12,000,000
24	$3,500,000	$175,000	$700,000	$7,000,000	$14,000,000
25	$5,000,000	$250,000	$1,000,000	$10,000,000	$20,000,000
26	$6,500,000	$325,000	$1,300,000	$13,000,000	$26,000,000
27	$8,500,000	$425,000	$1,700,000	$17,000,000	$34,000,000
28	$10,000,000	$500,000	$2,000,000	$20,000,000	$40,000,000
29	$15,000,000	$750,000	$3,000,000	$30,000,000	$60,000,000
30	$20,000,000	$1,000,000	$4,000,000	$40,000,000	$80,000,000
31	$25,000,000	$1,250,000	$5,000,000	$50,000,000	$100,000,000
32	$30,000,000	$1,500,000	$6,000,000	$60,000,000	$120,000,000
33	$40,000,000	$2,000,000	$8,000,000	$80,000,000	$160,000,000
34	$50,000,000	$2,500,000	$10,000,000	$100,000,000	$200,000,000
35	$65,000,000	$3,250,000	$13,000,000	$130,000,000	$260,000,000
36	$80,000,000	$4,000,000	$16,000,000	$160,000,000	$320,000,000
37	$100,000,000	$5,000,000	$20,000,000	$200,000,000	$400,000,000
38 or more	$150,000,000	$7,500,000	$30,000,000	$300,000,000	$600,000,000

Source: US Sentencing Commission, *Guidelines Manual*, §3E1.1 (November 2015), accessed February 18, 2020, www.ussc.gov/sites/default/files/pdf/guidelines-manual /2015/GLMFull.pdf; "Primer: Fines Under the Organizational Guidelines," US Sentencing Commission, February 2019, accessed February 18, 2020, www.ussc.gov/sites /default/files/pdf/training/primers/2019_Primer_Organizational_Fines.pdf;

iStock.com/Terry Hankin

shown at the bottom of Exhibit 4.2, Company 1 with a "0 or less" culpability score is fined no less than $7.5 million ($150,000,000 × 0.05) and no more than $30,000,000 ($150,000,000 × 0.20). In contrast, Company 2 with the maximum "10 or more" culpability score is fined a minimum of $300 million ($150,000,000 × 2.00) and a maximum of $600 million ($150,000,000 × 4.00). These differences clearly show the importance of having a compliance program in place, self-reporting the offense, fully cooperating with the investigation, and taking full responsibility for misconduct, all of which greatly reduce the multiplier applied to the base fine.

In 2018, the last year for which data are available, 99 companies, down significantly from 181 in 2015, 132 in 2016, and 131 in 2017, were charged under the US Sentencing Commission Guidelines. Ninety-five percent pleaded guilty. Twenty-five percent were ordered to develop a compliance program (see next paragraph). Ninety percent were ordered to pay fines, with an average fine of nearly $2.4 million. Thirty-six percent were ordered to pay restitution, with an average payment of $4.7 million to those harmed by the company's misconduct.[33]

Fortunately for companies that want to avoid paying these stiff fines, the US Sentencing Guidelines clearly spell out the seven necessary components of an effective compliance program.[34] Exhibit 4.3 lists those components. Caremark International, a managed-care service provider in Delaware, pleaded guilty to criminal charges related to its physician contracts and improper patient referrals. When shareholders sued the company for negligence and poor management, the Delaware court dismissed the case, ruling that the company's ethics compliance program, built on the components described in Exhibit 4.3, was a good-faith attempt to monitor employees and that the company did not knowingly allow illegal and unethical behavior to occur. The court went on to rule that a compliance program based on the US Sentencing *Guidelines Manual* was enough to shield the company from liability.[35]

4-3 INFLUENCES ON ETHICAL DECISION-MAKING

Consider this case study, based on a real-life dilemma regarding an experimental antiviral drug called brincidofovir, made by Chimerix. This drug could be an effective treatment for a range of virulent viruses, including Ebola, smallpox, and the adenovirus, which is thought to cause the common cold. The CEO of Chimerix was contacted by the family of Josh Hardy, a seven-year-old boy who underwent a marrow stem cell transplant to treat kidney cancer. While being treated for cancer, Josh contracted a life-threatening respiratory virus that the family hoped could be treated with brincidofovir. Unfortunately, drug companies must often reserve their limited drug supply for clinical trials needed to secure Food and Drug Administration (FDA) approval and bring drugs to market. After being declined three times for the drug, the family decided to conduct a social media campaign. More than 32,000 tweets using the hashtag #savejosh were posted worldwide. Nonprofit group Kids v Cancer publicized the campaign, and its director made a public statement that it is "profoundly unethical" for Chimerix to not give Josh the drug. The company was condemned on social

Exhibit 4.3

Compliance Program Steps from the US Sentencing Commission *Guidelines Manual*

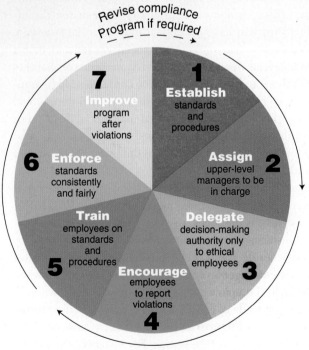

Sources: D. R. Dalton, M. B. Metzger, and J. W. Hill, "The 'New' US Sentencing Commission Guidelines: A Wake-up Call for Corporate America," *Academy of Management Executive* 8 (1994): 7–16; "US Sentencing Commission, *Guidelines Manual*, Chapter Eight – Sentencing of Organizations," US Sentencing Commission, November 1, 2014, accessed February 18, 2020, www.ussc.gov/sites/default/files/pdf/guidelines-manual/2014/CHAPTER_8.pdf.

media, and according to the Federal Bureau of Investigation (FBI), the CEO Kenneth Moch received several credible death threats.[36] As Chimerix's CEO, what would be the ethical thing to do?

Although some ethical issues are easily solved, many do not have clearly right or wrong answers. But even though the answers are rarely clear, managers do need to have a clear sense of *how* to arrive at an answer in order to manage this ethical ambiguity well. The following sections will examine this case study from several perspectives to consider how a situation like this might be resolved.

*The ethical answers that managers choose depend on **4-3a the ethical intensity of the decision, 4-3b the moral development of the manager,** and **4-3c the ethical principles used to solve the problem.***

4-3a Ethical Intensity of the Decision

Managers don't treat all ethical decisions the same. Chimerix's CEO, who has to decide if the company's drug treatment will go to Josh or to another ill (perhaps dying) person who has been waiting for the company's clinical trial to begin, is going to treat that decision much more seriously than the decision of how to deal with an assistant who has been taking paper home for use in a personal printer. These decisions differ in their **ethical intensity**, or the degree of concern people have about an ethical issue. When addressing an issue of high ethical intensity, managers are more aware of the impact their decision will have on others. They are more likely to view the decision as an ethical or moral decision than as an economic decision. They are also more likely to worry about doing the right thing.

Six factors must be considered when determining the ethical intensity of an action, as shown in Exhibit 4.4. **Magnitude of consequences** is the total harm or benefit derived from an ethical decision. The more people who are harmed or the greater the harm to those people, the larger the consequences. **Social consensus** is agreement on whether behavior is bad or good. **Probability of effect** is the chance that something will happen that results in harm to others. If we combine these factors, we can see the effect they can have on ethical intensity. For example, if there is *clear agreement* (social consensus) that a managerial decision or action is *certain* (probability of effect) to have *large negative consequences* (magnitude of consequences) in some way, then people will be highly concerned about that managerial decision or action, and ethical intensity will be high.

Temporal immediacy is the time between an act and the consequences the act produces. Temporal immediacy is stronger if a manager has to lay off workers next week as opposed to three months from now. **Proximity of effect** is the social, psychological, cultural, or physical distance of a decision maker from those affected by his or her decisions. Thus, proximity of effect is greater when a manager lays off employees he knows than when he lays off employees he doesn't know. Finally, whereas the magnitude of consequences is the total effect across all people, **concentration of effect** is how much an act affects the average person. For instance, eliminating health care coverage for 100 employees has a greater concentration of effect than reducing the health care benefits for 1,000 employees by 10 percent.

Ethical intensity the degree of concern people have about an ethical issue

Magnitude of consequences the total harm or benefit derived from an ethical decision

Social consensus agreement on whether behavior is bad or good

Probability of effect the chance that something will happen that results in harm to others

Temporal immediacy the time between an act and the consequences the act produces

Proximity of effect the social, psychological, cultural, or physical distance between a decision maker and those affected by his or her decisions

Concentration of effect the total harm or benefit that an act produces on the average person

Exhibit 4.4
Six Factors that Contribute to Ethical Intensity

Magnitude of consequences
Social consensus
Probability of effect
Temporal immediacy
Proximity of effect
Concentration of effect

Source: Academy of Management; P.O. Box 3020, Briar Cliff Manor, NY, 10510-8020. T.M. Jones, "Ethical Decision Making by Individuals in Organizations: An Issue Contingent Model," *Academy of Management Review* 16 (1991) 366–395;

Ethical Dilemmas? Could vs. Should

*R*ight vs. right ethical dilemmas between two ethical principles or two important goals are the most common and difficult to solve. Your frequently late best friend asks you to not tell the boss they were late. Do you lie to protect your best friend or tell the truth knowing they might be fired? Usually, we think about what we *should do. Should* focuses decision makers on the costs and benefits of each alternative. But when you're stuck between two important goals or principles, ask, "What *could* I do?" instead.

Could helps you expand the number of ethical solutions, greatly increasing the chance of not sacrificing one ethical alternative for another. So, the next time you find yourself in an ethical dilemma, try asking, "What *could* I do?"

Sources: "Facing an Ethical Dilemma? Try This Approach," *Academy of Management Insights*, accessed February 22, 2020, https://journals.aom.org/doi/10.5465/amj.2014.0839.summary; T. Zhang, F. Gino & J. Margolis, "Does 'Could' Lead to Good? On the Road to Moral Insight," *Academy of Management Journal* 61 (2018): 857–895.

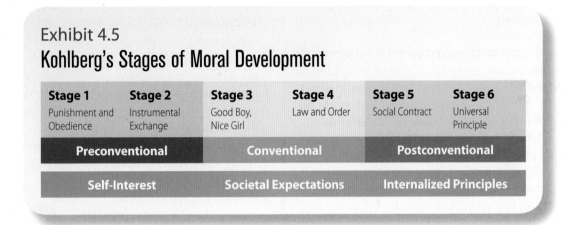

Exhibit 4.5
Kohlberg's Stages of Moral Development

Stage 1 Punishment and Obedience	Stage 2 Instrumental Exchange	Stage 3 Good Boy, Nice Girl	Stage 4 Law and Order	Stage 5 Social Contract	Stage 6 Universal Principle
Preconventional		Conventional		Postconventional	
Self-Interest		Societal Expectations		Internalized Principles	

Which of these six factors has the most impact on ethical intensity? Studies indicate that managers are much more likely to view decisions as ethical issues when the magnitude of consequences (total harm) is high and there is a social consensus (agreement) that a behavior or action is bad.[37]

4-3b Moral Development

It's Friday. Another long week of classes and studying is over, and all you want to do is sit down and relax. "A movie sounds good," you think to yourself, but you don't want to spend $12 to trek down to the megaplex, plus another $25 on popcorn, snacks, and drinks. And, while it would cost less than a $2 to rent a DVD, you're too tired to make the short trip down to the corner drug-store's Redbox machine. Your best friend says he's got the perfect solution and gives you the URL of a piracy website that streams all the latest blockbuster movies and TV shows for free.[38] Or, you could just use your old roommate's "pirated" Disney+ streaming password.[39] Disney+ and

the writers, actors, and producers who made the movie won't earn a dime either way. Furthermore, it's illegal to download or watch streamed copies of pirated shows via piracy websites or a streaming service you didn't pay for. But how will the movie studios or Disney+ ever find out? Are the cops going to come through your door because you watched a pirated copy of *Avengers: Endgame?* Will you watch the movie? What are you going to do?

In part, according to psychologist Lawrence Kohlberg, your decision will be based on your level of moral development. Kohlberg identified three phases of moral development, with two stages in each phase (see Exhibit 4.5).[40] At the **preconventional level of moral development**, people decide based on selfish reasons. For example, if you are in Stage 1, the punishment and obedience stage, your primary concern will be to avoid trouble for yourself. So, you won't watch the pirated movie

Preconventional level of moral development the first level of moral development, in which people make decisions based on selfish reasons

on the piracy website or Disney+ because you are afraid of being caught and punished. Yet, in Stage 2, the instrumental exchange stage, you worry less about punishment and more about doing things that directly advance your wants and needs. So, you will watch the pirated movie.

People at the **conventional level of moral development** make decisions that conform to societal expectations. In other words, they look outside themselves to others for guidance on ethical issues. In Stage 3, the "good boy, nice girl" stage, you normally do what the other "good boys" and "nice girls" are doing. If everyone else is watching the pirated movie on that piracy website or Disney+, you will, too. But if they aren't, you won't either. In the law and order stage, Stage 4, you again look for external guidance and do whatever the law permits, so you won't watch a pirated version of the movie.

People at the **postconventional level of moral development** use internalized ethical principles to solve ethical dilemmas. In Stage 5, the social contract stage, you will refuse to watch the pirated movie on that website or Disney+ because, as a whole, society is better off when the rights of others – in this case, the rights of actors, producers, directors, writers and Disney+ – are not violated. In fact, streaming services and Hollywood studios lose an estimated $29 billion a year to piracy.[41] In Stage 6, the universal principle stage, you might or might not watch the pirated movie, depending on your principles of right and wrong. Moreover, you will stick to your principles even if your decision conflicts with the law (Stage 4) or what others believe is best for society (Stage 5). For example, those with socialist or communist beliefs would probably choose to watch the pirated movie on the piracy website or Disney+ because they believe goods and services should be owned by society rather than by individuals and corporations.

Kohlberg believed that people would progress sequentially from earlier stages to later stages as they became more educated

and mature. But only 20 percent of adults ever reach the postconventional stage of moral development, where internal principles guide their decisions. Most adults are in the conventional stage of moral development, in which they look outside themselves to others for guidance on ethical issues. This means that most people in the workplace look to and need leadership when it comes to ethical decision-making.[42]

4-3c Principles of Ethical Decision-Making

Beyond an issue's ethical intensity and a manager's level of moral maturity, the particular ethical principles that managers use will also affect how they solve ethical dilemmas. Unfortunately, there is no one ideal principle to use in making ethical business decisions.

According to professor LaRue Hosmer, a number of different ethical principles can be used to make business decisions: long-term self-interest, religious injunctions, government requirements, individual rights, personal virtue, distributive justice, and utilitarian benefits.[43] All of these ethical principles encourage managers and employees to take others' interests into account when making ethical decisions. At the same time, however, these principles can lead to very different ethical actions, as we can see by using these principles to decide what Chimerix might do regarding its decision to give brincidofovir to Josh Hardy.

POSTCONVENTIONAL LEVEL OF MORAL DEVELOPMENT

CONVENTIONAL LEVEL OF MORAL DEVELOPMENT

PRECONVENTIONAL LEVEL OF MORAL DEVELOPMENT

iStock.com/Mikhail Tolstoy

According to the **principle of long-term self-interest**, you should never take any action that is not in your or your organization's long-term self-interest. Although this sounds as if the principle promotes selfishness, it doesn't. What we do to maximize our long-term interests (save more, spend less, exercise every day, watch what we eat) is often very different from what we do to maximize short-term interests (max out our credit cards, be couch potatoes, eat whatever we want). The cost to bring a drug to market has more than doubled in the last decade. According to research conducted by the Tufts Center for the Study of Drug Development, the average cost of launching a new drug is $2.9 billion.[44] For a small, 55-employee company like **Chimerix**, every development dollar counts. At the time of Hardy's request, Chimerix had no FDA-approved drugs, no source of revenue beyond investor funding, and a $173 million deficit. For any pharmaceutical company, distributing experimental drugs for free represents a significant donation. For Chimerix, it would be especially costly because the company's survival depends on its ability to bring effective drug therapies to market.[45] So, based on long-term self-interest, Chimerix should refuse individual requests for its experimental drugs.

According to the **principle of religious injunctions**, you should never take an action that is unkind or that harms a sense of community, such as the positive feelings that come from working together to accomplish a commonly accepted goal. Using this principle, Chimerix would have given Josh the treatment – even if it would have damaged the company financially.

According to the **principle of government requirements**, the law represents the minimal moral standards of society, so you should never take any action that violates the law. To obtain approval for an experimental drug from the FDA, companies must follow strict protocols and must meet specific regulatory requirements. When the Hardy family first approached Chimerix, the drug was already in its last stages of clinical trials and had not yet been approved for use. Based on the principle of government requirements, Chimerix should have denied the Hardys' request because Josh was not enrolled in the trials and could not legally receive the drug.

The **principle of individual rights** holds that you should never take an action that infringes on others' agreed-upon rights. At the time the brincidofovir request was made for Hardy, Chimerix was preparing to begin its Phase III trials in hopes of receiving final FDA approval in 2017.[46] While many on social media argued it was wrong for Chimerix not to give Josh the drug, the significant cost of doing so would infringe on the individual rights of investors (who expect

their funds to be used prudently to produce a reasonable financial return), and patients who were already enrolled in Phase III trials (who might not receive treatment because of limited supply). Because of these violations, Chimerix should not give Josh Hardy the treatment.

The **principle of personal virtue** holds that you should never do anything that is not honest, open, and truthful and that you would not be glad to see reported in the newspapers or on TV. Using the principle of personal virtue, Chimerix would have quietly allocated treatment doses of brincidofovir for Josh Hardy. Had it done so, it might have avoided the

UNETHICAL AMNESIA: WHY UNETHICAL WORKERS CAN LIVE WITH THEMSELVES

*//*I hope you can sleep at night!" is what we might (or would like) to say to someone acting unethically or making unethical decisions. But, thanks to *unethical amnesia*, people who are repeatedly unethical generally forget that they were,

which makes it easier to continue being unethical. When recalled, memories of unethical behavior are remembered less clearly than ethical behavior, which is easily and accurately remembered. So why do unethical workers have a "clear conscious?" Because they can't remember.

Source: F. Gina & M. Kouchaki, "We're Unethical at Work Because We Forget Our Misdeeds," *Harvard Business Review*, May 18, 2016, accessed March 21, 2017, https:// hbr.org/2016/05/were-unethical-at-work-because-we-forget-our-misdeeds.

Principle of long-term self-interest an ethical principle that holds that you should never take any action that is not in your or your organization's long-term self-interest

Principle of religious injunctions an ethical principle that holds that you should never take any action that is not kind and that does not build a sense of community

Principle of government requirements an ethical principle that holds that you should never take any action that violates the law, for the law represents the minimal moral standard

Principle of individual rights an ethical principle that holds that you should never take any action that infringes on others' agreed-upon rights

Principle of personal virtue an ethical principle that holds that you should never do anything that is not honest, open, and truthful and that you would not be glad to see reported in the newspapers or on TV

social media firestorm and the subsequent publication of an article in *Bloomberg Business Week,* which brought the story to even more people.

Under the **principle of distributive justice**, you should never take any action that harms the least fortunate among us in some way. This principle is designed to protect the poor, the uneducated, and the unemployed. Josh Hardy could certainly be considered vulnerable. Having fought kidney cancer since he was a baby, he contracted a life-threatening virus after receiving a marrow stem cell transplant targeting the cancer. Chimerix had a drug on hand that had been shown effective in the treatment of such viruses. Would the company want to be seen as having a cure and intentionally withholding it? The principle of distributive justice says it would not.

Finally, the **principle of utilitarian benefits** states that you should never take an action that does not result in greater good for society. In short, you should do whatever creates the greatest good for the greatest number. Chimerix had previously given 430 patients brincidofovir for compassionate use. That program, however, was funded by the government. When funding ended, Chimerix reallocated all of its remaining doses of the drug to the formal trials required for FDA approval. Allocating any doses to Josh might have jeopardized the FDA approval process by reducing the number of doses available for use in the formal trials. Fewer individuals would be able to participate in the trials, potentially requiring additional trial rounds, delaying approval, and preventing distribution of the life-saving drug to even more people suffering from life-threatening viral infections. Thus, according to the principle of utilitarian benefit, Chimerix would be obligated to put the larger group's interests first and deny the Hardy family's request. Chimerix CEO Kenneth Moch echoed this principle, saying, "If it were my child, would I do what the Hardys did? Absolutely, yes. As the CEO, I have to think about not just the individual but the many."[47]

So, what did Moch decide to do? He factored in many of the concerns raised by these ethical principles and worked with the FDA to create a separate clinical trial for brincidofovir with Josh Hardy as its first patient. Within a week of receiving the drug, Josh's condition improved and he was discharged from the hospital. Three weeks into the trial, however, Moch was replaced as CEO of Chimerix. He said he would have "loved to continue to be the CEO, but the board thought otherwise."[48] Josh Hardy died two years later, at the age of 10, from complications related to his cancer.[49]

 # 4-4 PRACTICAL STEPS TO ETHICAL DECISION-MAKING

Companies are putting more emphasis on ethical decision-making. For example, 89 percent now provide ethics training; 67 percent include ethical conduct as a standard part of performance evaluations; and 88 percent communicate internally about disciplinary actions that are taken when unethical behavior occurs.[50]

*Managers can encourage more ethical decision-making in their organizations by **4-4a carefully selecting and hiring ethical employees, 4-4b establishing a specific code of ethics, 4-4c training employees to make ethical decisions, and 4-4d creating an ethical climate.***

4-4a Selecting and Hiring Ethical Employees

As an employer, how can you increase your chances of hiring honest employees, the kind who would return a wallet filled with money to its rightful owner? **Overt integrity tests** estimate job applicants' honesty by asking them directly what they think or feel about theft or about punishment of unethical behaviors.[51] For example, an employer might ask an applicant, "Would you ever consider buying something from somebody if you knew the person had stolen the item?" or "Don't most people steal from their companies?" Surprisingly, unethical people will usually answer "yes" to such questions because they believe that the world is basically dishonest and that dishonest behavior is normal.[52]

Personality-based integrity tests indirectly estimate job applicants' honesty by measuring psychological traits such as dependability and conscientiousness. For example, prison inmates serving time for

Principle of distributive justice an ethical principle that holds that you should never take any action that harms the least fortunate among us: the poor, the uneducated, the unemployed

Principle of utilitarian benefits an ethical principle that holds that you should never take any action that does not result in greater good for society

Overt integrity test a written test that estimates job applicants' honesty by directly asking them what they think or feel about theft or about punishment of unethical behaviors

Personality-based integrity test a written test that indirectly estimates job applicants' honesty by measuring psychological traits, such as dependability and conscientiousness

white-collar crimes (counterfeiting, embezzlement, and fraud) scored much lower than a comparison group of middle-level managers on scales measuring reliability, dependability, honesty, conscientiousness, and abiding by rules.[53] These results show that companies can selectively hire and promote people who will be more ethical.

4-4b Codes of Ethics

Today, almost all large corporations have an ethics code in place. In fact, to be listed on the New York Stock Exchange, a company must "adopt and disclose a code of business conduct and ethics for directors, officers, and employees."[54] Even if a company has a code of ethics, two things must still happen if those codes are to encourage ethical decision-making and behavior.[55] First, a company must communicate its code to others both inside and outside the company.

Second, in addition to having an ethics code with general guidelines such as "do unto others as you would have others do unto you," management must also develop practical ethical standards and procedures specific to the company's line of business. ADP (Automatic Data Processing), a global provider of HR, payroll, time tracking, tax and benefits solutions, does business in 140 countries. Visitors to ADP's website can download its "Code of Business Conduct & Ethics" or its "Anti-Bribery Policy."[56] The code and other extensive policies set specific ethical standards on topics ranging from conflicts of interest to gifts, bribes, and kickbacks to covering up mistakes and falsifying records. For example, the code specifically states, "Mistakes should never be covered up, but should be immediately fully disclosed and corrected. Falsification of any ADP, client or third-party record is prohibited. If you are uncertain about whether a mistake has been made, you should seek guidance from your immediate supervisor or manager." ADP has a strict anti-bribery policy against "improper or unethical payments" to influence business decisions. However, items not exceeding $25 in value, "such as ADP logo pen and pencil sets, shirts, hats, and other similar items" may be given to government officials, but not more than once per year.[57] Specific codes of ethics such as this make it much easier for employees to decide what to do when they want to do the right thing. And when employees make decisions based on organizational values and standards, such as those found in codes of conduct, they are 11 times more likely to produce ethical outcomes for their companies.[58]

iStock.com/Nuzhdin

4-4c Ethics Training

In addition to establishing ethical standards for the company, managers must sponsor and be involved in ethics and compliance training in order to create an ethical company culture.[59] The first objective of ethics training is to develop employees' awareness of ethics.[60] The problem, according to Professor Yuval Feldman, is "that employees have a 'blind spot' that prevents them from seeing the ethical and legal meaning of their own behavior."[61] This means helping employees recognize which issues are ethical issues and then avoiding rationalizing unethical behavior by thinking, "This isn't really illegal or immoral" or "No one will ever find out."

Several companies have created board games, produced videos, or invited special speakers to improve awareness of ethical issues.[62] Howard Winkler, project manager for ethics and compliance at Southern Co., an Atlanta-based energy provider, even had a convicted felon come in to talk about how small ethical compromises eventually lead to bigger unethical behavior, such as fraud, the charges that sent him to jail for five years. "It created an enormous impression," Winkler says, because, "This person didn't start out his career looking to commit fraud. The main message was that once you make the first ethical compromise, you are embarking on a path that can lead all the way to a prison cell."[63] Winkler also regularly creates opportunities for senior executives to speak with employees about ethics issues. This multifaceted approach appears to be working, as internal surveys indicate that 93 percent of employees recognize that their continued career at Southern "depends on my ethical behavior."

"When I first began prosecuting corruption, I expected to walk into rooms and find the vilest people. I was shocked to find ordinarily good people I could well have had coffee with that morning." Why Ethical People Make Unethical Choices

The second objective for ethics training programs is to achieve credibility with employees. Not surprisingly, employees can be highly suspicious of management's reasons for offering ethics training. Some companies have hurt the credibility of their ethics programs by having outside instructors and consultants conduct the classes.[64] Employees often complain that outside instructors and consultants are teaching theory that has nothing to do with their jobs and the practical dilemmas they actually face on a daily basis. CA Technologies made its ethics training practical and relevant by creating a series of comical training videos with a fictional manager, Griffin Peabody, who was shown interacting with CA Technologies employees and managers in real business situations. Chief ethics officer Joel Katz says, "Over the years, we have created a library of funny videos involving Griffin that cover topics ranging from appropriate workplace conduct to anti-corruption to insider trading. While some of the videos are admittedly silly and a bit over the top, we have received overwhelmingly positive feedback from our employees about the Griffin character. Employees also reported that they had retained more from the Griffin videos because they were fully engaged in the course content due to the use of humor. We have also gotten many YouTube hits on these videos along with requests from other companies to use them in their own compliance training offerings."[65]

Ethics training becomes even more credible when top managers teach the initial ethics classes to their subordinates who in turn teach their subordinates.[66] At **Intuitive Research and Technology Corp.**, an engineering services company in Huntsville, Alabama, Harold "Hal" Brewer, the company's co-founder and president, is the company's ethics champion. Every new employee attends a session called "Let's Talk Ethics with Hal," led by Brewer and the director of human resources, Juanita Phillips. Brewer explains how employees' decisions impact the company, situations they will likely encounter with outside organizations they do business with, and then how to respond. What effect does having the co-founder and president talk

to every employee about ethics? Philips says about Hal, "He makes it clear that he is the ethics officer. His strength is that he means every word of it, and he shows it in how he lives every day in terms of running the company.[67] Michael Hoffman, executive director for the Center for Business Ethics at Bentley University, says that having managers teach ethics courses greatly reinforces the seriousness with which employees treat ethics in the workplace.[68]

The third objective of ethics training is to teach employees a practical model of ethical decision-making. A basic model should help them think about the consequences their choices will have on others and consider how they will choose between different solutions. Exhibit 4.6 presents a basic model of ethical decision-making.

The overarching goals of ethics training are to develop employees' awareness of ethics, achieve credibility with employees, and teach employees a practical model of ethical decision-making.

Mangostar/Shutterstock.com

4-4d Ethical Climate

Organizational culture is key to fostering ethical decision-making. The 2018 National Business Ethics Survey found striking differences between companies with strong ethical cultures (where core beliefs are widely shared and strongly held) and companies with weak ethical cultures (where core beliefs are not widely shared or strongly held). Employees in strong ethical cultures are *much less likely* to observe abusive behavior (15 percent vs. 60 percent in weak ethical cultures), workplace discrimination (9 percent vs. 41 percent in weak ethical cultures), and sexual harassment (10 percent vs. 31 percent in weak ethical cultures) and be pressured to compromise standards (19 percent vs. 50 percent in weak ethical cultures).[69] Employees of companies with strong ethical cultures are also much *more likely* to report misconduct that they observe (87 percent vs. 32 percent in weak ethical cultures).[70]

The first step in establishing an ethical climate is for managers, especially top managers, to act ethically themselves. It's no surprise that in study after study, when researchers ask, "What is the most important influence on your ethical behavior at work?" the answer comes back, "My manager."

Chatbots Could Be a Better Way to Apply Ethical Codes of Conduct

Effective codes of ethics are communicated inside and outside the company and provide practical standards and procedures specific to your business. Accenture, a global consulting firm, developed a chatbot named COBE to meet the challenge of getting 460,000 employees in 120 countries to follow its ethics code. Short for Code of Business Ethics, COBE simplifies Accenture's ethics code by focusing on desired behaviors, quickly guiding employees to relevant information, and making ethics more engaging and personalized. COBE acts like the messaging app on your smartphone and responds in natural language. Type "A competitor wants to meet me for coffee to talk about an opportunity I'm working on," and COBE responds, "Make sure you never collaborate with competitors on how to price services or whether to pursue opportunities in a particular market." COBE, which is completely confidential, has chatted with employees 61,000 times, increased visits to Accenture's ethics website by twenty-fold, and helped employees finish ethics training twice as fast.

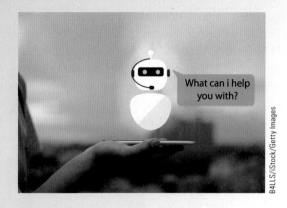

What can i help you with?

B4LLS/iStock/Getty Images

Sources: "Meet the Chatbot That Makes Ethics People-Friendly," Accenture Code of Business Ethics, accessed February 22, 2020, www.accenture.com/us-en/success -code-business-ethics; L. Muszynski, "Revolutionizing HR with Automated Digital Assistants," *HR.com*, February 6, 2019, accessed February 22, 2020, www .hr.com/en/magazines/all_articles/revolutionizing-hr-with-automated-digital -assistan_jru0m3xq.html; E. Olson, "Accenture GC: Anti-Corruption Goes Companywide with Tech Platform," *Bloomberg Law: Big Law Business*, May 25, 2018, accessed February 22, 2020, https://biglawbusiness.com/accenture-gc-anti- corruption-goes-companywide-with-tech-platform; S. Rubenfield, "Accenture Tries Chatbot for Code of Conduct," *Wall Street Journal*, January 24, 2018, accessed February 22, 2020, https://blogs.wsj.com/riskandcompliance/2018/01/24/ accenture-tries-chatbot-for-code-of-conduct/.

Exhibit 4.6
A Basic Model of Ethical Decision-Making

1. **Identify the problem.** What makes it an ethical problem? Think in terms of rights, obligations, fairness, relationships, and integrity. How would you define the problem if you stood on the other side of the fence?

2. **Identify the constituents.** Who has been hurt? Who could be hurt? Who could be helped? Are they willing players, or are they victims? Can you negotiate with them?

3. **Diagnose the situation.** How did it happen in the first place? What could have prevented it? Is it going to get worse or better? Can the damage now be undone?

4. **Analyze your options.** Imagine the range of possibilities. Limit yourself to the two or three most manageable. What are the likely outcomes of each? What are the likely costs? Look to the company mission statement or code of ethics for guidance.

5. **Make your choice.** What is your intention in making this decision? How does it compare with the probable results? Can you discuss the problem with the affected parties before you act? Could you disclose without qualm your decision to your boss, the CEO, the board of directors, your family, or society as a whole?

6. **Act.** Do what you have to do. Don't be afraid to admit errors. Be as bold in confronting a problem as you were in causing it.

Source: L. A. Berger, "Train All Employees to Solve Ethical Dilemmas," *Best's Review – Life-Health Insurance Edition* 95 (1995): 70–80

A second step in establishing an ethical climate is for top management to be active in and committed to the company ethics program.[71] Top managers who consistently talk about the importance of ethics and back up that talk by participating in their companies' ethics programs send the clear message that ethics matter. When management engages and communicates about ethical issues, employees are less likely to break rules and more likely to report ethical violations.[72] Business writer Dayton Fandray says, "You can have ethics offices and officers and training programs and reporting systems, but if the CEO doesn't seem to care, it's all just a sham. It's not surprising to find that the companies that really do care about ethics make a point of including senior management in all of their ethics and compliance programs."[73] Alphabet CEO Sundar Pichai agrees, saying, "It's the job of the CEO to be chief ethics officer."[74]

A third step is to put in place a reporting system that encourages managers and employees to report potential ethics violations. **Whistleblowing**, that is, reporting others' ethics violations, is a difficult step for most people to take.[75] Professor Elizabeth Morrison says, "You have to confront the two fundamental challenges preventing employees from speaking up. The first is the natural feeling of futility – feeling like speaking up isn't worth the effort or that anyone wants to hear it. The second is the natural fear that speaking up will lead to retribution or harsh reactions."[76] Indeed, in large companies without an effective compliance program, 62 percent of workers have observed unethical behavior, 32 percent of those have reported the misconduct, and 59 percent of those who reported the unethical behavior experienced some kind of retaliation.[77]

Reid Bigland, former head of US sales for Fiat Chrysler, filed a whistleblower lawsuit against the company, claiming his pay was cut 90 percent because he cooperated with a Securities and Exchange Commission (SEC) investigation into the company.[78] The SEC found the following:

> *FCA US inflated new vehicle sales results by paying dealers to report fake vehicle sales and maintaining a database of actual but unreported sales, which employees often referred to as a "cookie jar." In months when the growth streak would have ended or when FCA US fell short of other targets, FCA US dipped into the "cookie jar" and reported old sales as if they had just occurred."[79]*

Fiat Chrysler paid the SEC $40 million to settle these charges. Bigland alleged that Fiat Chrysler withheld more than $2 million in performance bonuses in retaliation for his whistleblower lawsuit. Chrysler initially disputed the whistleblower lawsuit, but then settled the case out of court.[80]

A 2014 ruling by the US Supreme Court greatly expands protections for whistleblowers. The Court declared

thodonal88/Shutterstock.com

that the strong whistleblower protections built into the 2002 Sarbanes-Oxley Act, which apply to employees of publicly traded companies, should also apply to the employees of contractors and subcontractors that work with those public companies. This ruling extends whistleblower protection laws beyond the 5,000 publicly traded companies covered by Sarbanes-Oxley to an additional 6 million private companies.[81] A 2018 US Supreme Court ruling clarified that in public companies, which the SEC requires to make accurate, detailed reports of financial performance, whistleblowers are protected by law only if they also report ethics violations to the Office of the Whistleblower at the SEC (www.sec.gov/whistleblower).[82]

To encourage employees to report ethics violations, that is, to act as whistleblowers, many companies have installed confidential ethics hotlines. Employees at ADP, which has the extensive code of ethics discussed earlier, can anonymously report ethics violations via phone or website, both of which are staffed by EthicsPoint, an independent, third-party provider.[83] Anonymous reporting is critical as it helps whistleblowers avoid retaliation by their companies or managers. Retaliation typically occurs within three weeks of reporting an ethical violation.[84]

The factor that does the most to discourage whistleblowers from reporting problems is lack of company action on their complaints.[85] Thus, the final step in developing an ethical climate is for management to fairly and consistently punish those who violate the company's code of ethics. The key, says Paychex CEO Martin Mucci, is "to deal with it quickly, severely, and publicize it."[86] Says Mucci, "Our employees know that if they are caught cheating in any way, even if only to make a few dollars or improve their scores, they will most likely be terminated. Then we review that with the entire management team. We have done that with managers of locations, top sales representatives – we don't treat anyone differently."[87] And when employees believe they will be held accountable for wrongdoing, they are 12 times more likely to act ethically.[88] Amazingly, though, not all companies fire ethics violators. In fact, 8 percent of surveyed companies admit that they would promote top performers even if they violated ethical standards.[89]

Whistleblowing reporting others' ethics violations to management or legal authorities

4-5 TO WHOM ARE ORGANIZATIONS SOCIALLY RESPONSIBLE?

Social responsibility is a business's obligation to pursue policies, make decisions, and take actions that benefit society.[90] Unfortunately, because there are strong disagreements over to whom and for what in society organizations are responsible, it can be difficult for managers to know what is or will be perceived as socially responsible corporate behavior. After a terrorist attack killed 14 people, the US government asked Apple to break into the attacker's encrypted iPhone. In a public letter to its customers (see www.apple.com/customer-letter/), CEO Tim Cook stated, "While we believe the FBI's intentions are good, it would be wrong for the government to force us to build a backdoor into our products. And ultimately, we fear that this demand would undermine the very freedoms and liberty our government is meant to protect." District Attorney Cyrus Vance Jr. criticized Apple, saying, "Apple and Google are their own sheriffs. There are no rules." In a similar 2020 case, Apple again refused the FBI request to decrypt another attacker's phone.[91] Are Apple's refusals principled and to society's benefit, or will its lack of cooperation harm, if not eventually endanger, others?[92]

There are two perspectives regarding to whom organizations are socially responsible: the shareholder model and the stakeholder model. According to the late Nobel Prize-winning economist Milton Friedman, the only social responsibility that organizations have is to satisfy their owners, that is, company shareholders. This view – called the **shareholder model** – holds that the only social responsibility that businesses have is to maximize profits. By maximizing profit, the firm maximizes shareholder wealth and satisfaction. More specifically, as profits rise, the company stock owned by shareholders generally increases in value.

Friedman argued that it is socially irresponsible for companies to divert time, money, and attention from maximizing profits to social causes and charitable organizations. The first problem, he believed, is that organizations cannot act effectively as moral agents for all company shareholders. Although shareholders are likely to agree on investment issues concerning a company, it's highly unlikely that they have common views on what social causes a company should or should not support.

The second major problem, Friedman said, is that the time, money, and attention diverted to social causes undermine market efficiency.[93] In competitive markets, companies compete for raw materials, talented workers, customers, and investment funds. A company that spends money on social causes will have less money to purchase quality materials or to hire talented workers who can produce a valuable product at a good price. If customers find the company's product less desirable, its sales and profits will fall. If profits fall, the company's stock price will decline, and the company will have difficulty attracting investment funds that could be used to fund long-term growth. In the end, Friedman argues, diverting the firm's money, time, and resources to social causes hurts customers, suppliers, employees, and shareholders. Russell Roberts, an economist and research fellow at Stanford University's Hoover Institution, agrees, saying, "Doesn't it make more sense to have companies do what they do best, make good products at fair prices, and then let consumers use the savings for the charity of their choice?"[94]

By contrast, under the **stakeholder model**, management's most important responsibility is the firm's long-term survival (not just maximizing profits), which is achieved by satisfying the interests of multiple corporate stakeholders (not just shareholders).[95] **Stakeholders** are persons or groups with a legitimate interest in a company.[96] Because stakeholders are interested in and affected by the organization's actions, they have a stake in what those actions are. Marc Benioff, founder and CEO of SalesForce.com, says, "The next generation of CEOs must advocate for all stakeholders – employees, customers, community, the environment, everybody… not just shareholders."[97] "I even consider the communities that we live in are stakeholders. The environment is a stakeholder."[98] Because of the importance that Benioff places on stakeholders, Salesforce has a "1-1-1" philosophy in which it donates 1 percent of its founding stock (for grants supporting technology innovation in nonprofit and youth programs), 1 percent of employees' time (giving each employee 6 paid days of volunteer time each year), and 1 percent of its product (donation or discounting of SalesForce's customer relationship management services) each year.[99] So far, says Benioff, "…we have given more than $240 million in grants, 3.5 million hours of community service, and provided product donations for more than 39,000 nonprofits and

---

Social responsibility a business's obligation to pursue policies, make decisions, and take actions that benefit society

Shareholder model a view of social responsibility that holds that an organization's overriding goal should be profit maximization for the benefit of shareholders

Stakeholder model a theory of corporate responsibility that holds that management's most important responsibility, long-term survival, is achieved by satisfying the interests of multiple corporate stakeholders

Stakeholders persons or groups with a stake, or legitimate interest, in a company's actions

education institutions.."[100] In the end, he says, "The business of business is improving the state of the world.[101]

Stakeholder groups may try to influence the firm to advance their interests. Exhibit 4.7 shows the various stakeholder groups that the organization must satisfy to assure its long-term survival. Being responsible to multiple stakeholders raises two basic questions. First, how does a company identify organizational stakeholders? Second, how does a company balance the needs of different stakeholders? Distinguishing between primary and secondary stakeholders can help to answer these questions.[102]

Some stakeholders are more important to the firm's survival than others. **Primary stakeholders** are groups on which the organization depends for its long-term survival; they include shareholders, employees, customers, suppliers, governments, and local communities. When managers are struggling to balance the needs of different stakeholders, the stakeholder model suggests that the needs of primary stakeholders take precedence over the needs of secondary stakeholders. But among primary stakeholders, are some more important than others? According to the life cycle theory of organizations, the answer is yes. In practice, the answer is also yes, as CEOs typically give somewhat higher priority to shareholders, employees, and customers than to suppliers, governments, and local communities, no matter what stage of the life cycle a company is in.[103] Addressing the concerns of primary stakeholders is important because if a stakeholder group becomes dissatisfied and terminates its relationship with the company, the company could be seriously harmed or go out of business.

Secondary stakeholders, such as the media and special interest groups, can influence or be influenced by the company. Unlike the primary stakeholders, however, they do not engage in regular transactions with the company and are not critical to its long-term survival. Meeting the needs of primary stakeholders is therefore usually more important than meeting the needs of secondary stakeholders. Nevertheless, secondary stakeholders are still important because they can affect public perceptions and opinions about socially responsible behavior.

So, to whom are organizations socially responsible? Many commentators, especially economists and financial analysts, continue to argue that organizations are responsible only to shareholders. For example, the Council of Institutional Investors (CII) says, "To achieve long-term shareholder value, it is critical to respect stakeholders, but also to have clear accountability to company owners. Accountability to everyone means accountability to no one."[104] Likewise, Professors Michael Mauboussin and Alfred Rappaport argue that "balancing stakeholder interests sounds like an entirely reasonable idea. But it cannot serve as a company's singular governing objective because it is impossible to simultaneously satisfy the interests of all stakeholders."[105] CII's executive director Ken Bertsch says, "There has to be a north star, and it's long-term shareholder value,"[106]

Primary stakeholder any group on which an organization relies for its long-term survival

Secondary stakeholder any group that can influence or be influenced by a company and can affect public perceptions about the company's socially responsible behavior

Exhibit 4.7
Stakeholder Model of Corporate Social Responsibility

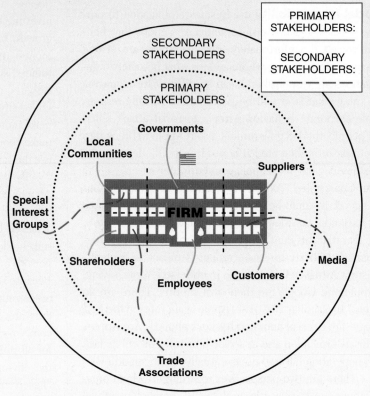

Source: Academy of Management, P.O. Box 3020, Briar Cliff Manor, NY, 10510-8020. "The Stakeholder Theory of the Corporation: Concepts, Evidence and Implications" (Figure), T. Donaldson and L. E. Preston, *Academy of Management Review* 20 (1995).

Increasingly, however, top managers have come to believe that they and their companies must be socially responsible to their stakeholders. The Business Roundtable represents the CEOs of "America's leading companies," which employ 15 million people. In August 2019, it changed its support from the shareholder model to the stakeholder model. Its revised "Statement on the Purpose of a Corporation"

Minerva Studio/Shutterstock.com

declared that "we share a fundamental commitment to all of our stakeholders."[107] Signed by 181 CEOs, the statement made clear commitments to delivering value to customers, investing in employees, dealing fairly and ethically with suppliers, supporting the communities in which they work, and generating long-term value for shareholders.[108] Mastercard's Ajay Banga, one of the 181 CEOs who signed the Conference Board's "Purpose of a Corporation" says, "Yes, we have to make our margins, be competitive on price, drive profit, grow. That's the textbook definition of capitalism, and that's what you'll see if you're only looking a few feet ahead of you. But when you raise your eyes a little and recognize that most companies and nations survive on people making and spending money, you realize that you're part of an interconnected system. Giving people a lift, expanding the middle class, helping them thrive and grow will also do the same for you."[109]

Today, surveys show that as many as 80 percent of top-level managers believe that it is unethical to focus just on shareholders. Thirty-five states have changed their laws to allow company boards of directors to consider the needs of employees, creditors, suppliers, customers, and local communities, as well as those of shareholders.[110]

Although there is not complete agreement, a majority of opinion makers would argue that companies must be socially responsible to their stakeholders.

4-6 FOR WHAT ARE ORGANIZATIONS SOCIALLY RESPONSIBLE?

If organizations are to be socially responsible to stakeholders, what are they to be socially responsible *for*? Companies can best benefit their stakeholders by fulfilling their economic, legal, ethical, and discretionary responsibilities. Economic and legal responsibilities are at the bottom of the pyramid because

they play a larger part in a company's social responsibility than do ethical and discretionary responsibilities. However, the relative importance of these various responsibilities depends on society's expectations of corporate social responsibility at a particular point in time.[111] A century ago, society expected businesses to meet their economic and legal responsibilities and little else. Today, when society judges whether businesses are socially responsible, ethical and discretionary responsibilities are considerably more important than they used to be.

Historically, **economic responsibility**, or making a profit by producing a product or service valued by society, has been a business's most basic social responsibility. Organizations that don't meet their financial and economic expectations come under tremendous pressure. For example, company boards are quick these days to fire CEOs. Typically, all it takes is two or three bad quarters in a row. William Rollnick, who became acting chairman of Mattel after the company fired its previous CEO, says, "There's zero forgiveness. You screw up and you're dead."[112] According to the Conference Board, 16 to 29 percent of CEOs of large companies are fired each year.[113] However, CEO firings reached an all-time high of 30.5 percent in 2018 among large Standard and Poor 500 companies (as measured by stock market value).[114]

Legal responsibility is a company's social responsibility to obey society's laws and regulations as it tries to meet its economic responsibilities. Volkswagen clearly violated its legal responsibilities after admitting to using software to falsify emissions tests for vehicles with diesel engines. It agreed to pay $22 billion in settlements and fines in the United States, including payments of $5,000 to $10,000 to each owner of a VW diesel car and $4.3 billion in civil and criminal penalties. "Volkswagen deeply regrets the behavior that gave rise to the diesel crisis," the company said in a statement. "The agreements that we have reached with the US government reflect our determination to address misconduct that went against all of the values Volkswagen holds so dear."[115] So far Volkswagen's total global payments for fines, penalties and settlements to owners of its diesel cars come to $33.6 billion. However, it has also set aside an additional $10 billion for possible future claims.[116]

> **Economic responsibility** a company's social responsibility to make a profit by producing a valued product or service
>
> **Legal responsibility** a company's social responsibility to obey society's laws and regulations

IF YOU HAVE ANY ALLERGIES, PLEASE ASK THE MANAGER…"

After buying a sandwich at Pret a Manger, a popular UK restaurant chain known for selling fresh, organic food, 15-year-old Natasha Edan-Laperouse died from an allergic reaction to the sesame seeds that she did not know were mixed into the bread dough. Multiple EpiPen injections and emergency care were not enough to save her life. Her father said, "Natasha and I relied on food information [on the label] and saw no need to ask Pret counter staff if any other information was needed." Pret's practice of posting signs encouraging customers with allergies to "Ask the Manager…" was consistent with existing regulations. However, in the year prior to Natasha's death, six other people suffered severe allergic reactions from the same sandwich, four of which required hospital care. Still, Pret continued to rely on "Ask the Manager…" signs to warn at risk customers. After cooperating with the investigation into her death, Pret CEO Clive Schlee said, "I want to say again how deeply sorry we are for the loss of Natasha." Pret now requires full ingredient labeling, including allergens, on all products.

Did Pret a Manger handle the crisis responsibly? Did it do right by customers and fix the problem for the long term? Would you be concerned about eating at Pret a Manger today if you had serious food allergies?

Sources: Telegraph Reporters, "Pret a Manger Was Warned about Six Baguette Allergy Cases a Year Before Girl's Death, Inquest Told," *The Telegraph*, September 25, 2018, accessed February 22, 2020, www.telegraph.co.uk

After six people suffered severe allergic reactions from the same sandwich, with four needing hospital care, Pret a Manger continued using this "Allergies?... Please ask the Manager…" warning sign.

/news/2018/09/25/pret-manger-warned-six-baguette-allergy-cases-year-girls-death/; Telegraph Reporters, "Pret a Manger to Introduce Full Ingredient Labelling After Teenager's Allergy Death," *The Telegraph*, October 3, 2018, accessed February 22, 2020, www.telegraph.co.uk/news/2018/10/03/pret-manger-introduce-full-ingredient-labelling-teenagers-allergy/; V. Ward, "Phone Held to the Ear of Girl Who Died After Eating a Pret a Manger Baguette So Her Mother Could Say Goodbye, Inquest Hears," The Telegraph, September 24, 2018, accessed February 22, 2020, www.telegraph.co.uk/news/2018/09/24/girl-died-eating-pret-manger-baguette-begged-daddy-help-inquest/.

Ethical responsibility is a company's social responsibility to not violate accepted principles of right and wrong when conducting its business. Two years ago, Apple admitted to slowing down processors in older iPhones to extend battery life. It responded with a public apology, explained that slowing down processors on older phones was done to prevent unexpected shutdowns, and that it would take care of customers with older phones by cutting the cost of a replacement battery from $79 to $29.[117] While correcting a mistake at company expense was the right thing to do, financial analysts estimated that 16 million customers would buy battery replacements instead of buying new iPhones.[118] With the average iPhone costing $700 at the time, Apple gave up approximately $11.2 billion in new iPhone sales for $464 million in fees for battery replacements. In other words, Apple did the right thing at a cost of $10.7 billion in lost revenue. Bloomberg reporter Shira Ovide wrote Apple's "decision to do the right thing for customers will be bad for business."[119] And then she bought a replacement battery, explaining, "I probably wouldn't have replaced the 6s model I bought more than two years ago any time soon. But I'm definitely not going to buy a new one now that I can just freshen it with a low-cost new power pack."[120]

Discretionary responsibilities pertain to the social roles that businesses play in society beyond their economic, legal, and ethical responsibilities. When a million-acre wildfire destroyed the town of Fort McMurray in Alberta, Canada, 88,000 citizens were ordered to evacuate from their homes; 2,400 buildings, including 1,800 homes, were destroyed.[121] Thankfully, no one died. As recovery efforts began, local companies stepped in with donations, contributions, and other forms of valuable assistance. According to Professor Steven Horowitz, "The oil companies provided free food and shelter to over 25,000 people. When the fires cut off easy road access to the small community of Fort McKay First Nation, Brion Energy began trucking in perishable foods daily. Imperial Oil donated 20,000 liters of gasoline to the relief efforts and Shell Albian Aerodrome rounded up evacuees on buses and, along with Suncor's Firebag Aerodrome, evacuated over 7,000 people on company-chartered commercial jets using their private airstrips."[122] Reporter Tristin Hopper says that, "Alberta's oil producers effectively turned themselves into multimillion-dollar humanitarian organizations at the drop of a hat."[123]

Carrying out discretionary responsibilities such as these is voluntary. Companies are not considered unethical if they don't perform them. Today, however, corporate stakeholders expect companies to do much more than in the past to meet their discretionary responsibilities.

 # 4-7 RESPONSES TO DEMANDS FOR SOCIAL RESPONSIBILITY

Social responsiveness refers to a company's strategy to respond to stakeholders' economic, legal, ethical, or discretionary expectations concerning social responsibility. A social responsibility problem exists whenever company actions do not meet stakeholder expectations. One model of social responsiveness identifies four strategies for responding to social responsibility problems: reactive, defensive, accommodative, and proactive. These strategies differ in the extent to which the company is willing to act to meet or exceed society's expectations.

A company using a **reactive strategy** will do less than society expects. When Google discovered that the private data of 500,000 Google+ users had been wrongly shared with outside developers for three years, the issue was fixed and then referred to Google's Privacy and Data Protection office for review. According to a *Wall Street Journal* investigation, "Internal lawyers advised that Google wasn't legally required to disclose the incident to the public… [and that the lawyers] …didn't believe notifying users would give any actionable benefit…"[124] Furthermore, letting the public know about the issue "almost guarantees [CEO] Sundar [Pichai] will testify before Congress" and would lead to "immediate regulatory interest."[125] CEO Pichai approved the recommendation to not reveal the improper data access to the public. Google shut down Google+ after the *Wall Street Journal* report, but appeared more interested in protecting its reputation than letting customers know about the mistake.

By contrast, a company using a **defensive strategy** would admit responsibility for a problem but would do the least required to meet societal expectations. For example, customers expect at the very least that retailers will sell safe products. **Walmart** has long required suppliers to test products for safety at Walmart-approved labs. Target makes suppliers prove their products exceed government standards. But Amazon hasn't required new third-party sellers on its website to prove the safety of their products until recently.[126] For example, the US Environmental Protection Agency (EPA) penalized **Amazon** for nearly 4,000 violations dating back to 2013 "for selling and distributing imported pesticide products that were not licensed for sale in the United States."[127] Furthermore, the *Wall Street Journal* found over 4,000 other products declared unsafe by various federal agencies for sale on Amazon, including safety helmets, fraudulently listed as meeting Department of Transportation safety requirements.[128] An Amazon spokesperson stated, "Safety is a top priority at Amazon. When a concern arises, we move quickly to protect customers and work directly with sellers, brands, and government agencies."[129] When notified, Amazon promptly removes such products from its website. But hundreds of them returned weeks later with different sellers, different product names, and different packaging. Mike Schade, of the nonprofit Safer Chemicals Healthy Families, says, "They clearly need to do a better job of setting up a system to police their supply chain."[130]

A company using an **accommodative strategy** will accept responsibility for a problem and take a progressive approach by doing all that could be expected to solve the problem. Amazon is now using an accommodative strategy for dealing with counterfeit products sold by third-party sellers on its website. (Similar new programs will also help it significantly reduce the sale of unsafe products discussed above.) For example, rather than waiting to accumulate data, it now contacts US and European authorities each time it confirms the sale of a counterfeit product.[131] Amazon has

Social responsiveness a company's strategy to respond to stakeholders' economic, legal, ethical, or discretionary expectations concerning social responsibility

Reactive strategy a social responsiveness strategy in which a company does less than society expects

Defensive strategy a social responsiveness strategy in which a company admits responsibility for a problem but does the least required to meet societal expectations

Accommodative strategy a social responsiveness strategy in which a company accepts responsibility for a problem and does all that society expects to solve that problem

WHAT PRICE DO CUSTOMERS PUT ON SOCIAL RESPONSIBILITY?

When the Boston Tea Party coffee chain banned single-use paper cups, it required customers to bring reusable cups (for which they get a 25 cent discount), drink coffee in the store using a porcelain mug, or pay a deposit on a portable coffee mug that could be returned to any of their 21 stores. This prevented 125,000 paper cups from being thrown away, but sales of takeaway coffee fell by 25 percent. Owner Sam Roberts said that despite the costs to the company, "…we want this to be a call to action to other companies." The most damaging way to put a price on social responsibility, however, is by losing public trust. After studying 7,000 companies in 20 industries, Global consulting firm Accenture found that "reputational damage" from unethical or socially irresponsible corporate behavior costs companies $180 billion a year in lost revenue. Do "something wrong" and your customers will look elsewhere. Revenues and profits will decline. Today, ethical and socially responsible behaviors are not only better ways to do business, they are also clearly "better for business."

Rosie Parsons/Alamy Stock Photo

Sources: Accenture Strategy, "The Bottom Line on Trust: Achieve Competitive Agility," Accenture, 2018, accessed February 23, 2020, www.accenture. com/_acnmedia/thought-leadership-assets/pdf/accenture-competitive-agility-index.pdf; A. Ellison, "Boston Tea Party's Coffee Sales Drain Away After It Bans Single-Use Cups," The Times, April 3, 2019, accessed February 23, 2020, www.thetimes.co.uk/article/boston-tea-party-s-coffee-sales-drain-away-after-it-bans-single-use-cups-gdcsfw0dl; M. Sun, "What Loss of Trust Costs Companies in Dollars and Cents," Wall Street Journal, October 31, 2018, accessed February 23, 2020, https://blogs.wsj.com/riskandcompliance/2018/10/31/what-loss-of-trust-costs-companies-in-dollars-and-cents/.

also introduced the following new programs to aggressively battle counterfeiting:[132]

» Brand Registry (https://brandservices.amazon.com/). A trademark and copyright protection system that makes it easy to find counterfeit products.

» Project Zero (https://brandservices.amazon.com/projectzero). This gives brands in the Brand Registry the ability to remove counterfeit listings from Amazon.

» Transparency (https://brandservices.amazon.com/transparency). QR-like codes are used to "ensure only authentic units are shipped to customers."

» Intellectual Property Accelerator (https://blog.aboutamazon.com/policy/amazon-intellectual-property-accelerator). This helps smaller brands obtain intellectual property and brand protection.

Proactive strategy a social responsiveness strategy in which a company anticipates a problem before it occurs and does more than society expects to take responsibility for and address the problem

» Utility Patent Neutral Evaluation Program. Patent owners pay a $4,000 fee and Amazon chooses a neutral patent lawyer to settle the dispute. If the patent holder wins, they get their fee back and the knockoff produce is removed from Amazon. The entire process takes no more than two months.[133]

Finally, a company using a **proactive strategy** will anticipate responsibility for a problem before it occurs, do more than expected to address the problem, and lead the industry in its approach. McDonald's has stopped selling menu items made from chickens treated with antibiotics. Scientists and doctors have long warned that treating livestock with antibiotics to prevent infections before they occur is accelerating the development of antibiotic-resistant bacteria. Indeed, 2 million Americans a year develop bacterial infections resistant to antibiotics, and, according to the Centers for Disease Control and Prevention (CDC), 23,000 of them will die. McDonald's made these changes even though it significantly increased its costs (antibiotic-free chickens are two to three times more expensive to raise).[134] Now it has begun working with its largest beef suppliers to do the same thing.[135] Because cattle live about 18 months before processing, compared to five to seven weeks for chickens, there's a much greater risk of infection.[136] Sourcing beef not treated with antibiotics is therefore much more difficult.[137] Similar to the poultry industry, McDonald's size is expected to broadly influence the beef industry to change the practice of raising cattle with antibiotics.

4-8 SOCIAL RESPONSIBILITY AND ECONOMIC PERFORMANCE

One question that managers often ask is, "Does it pay to be socially responsible?" In previous editions of this textbook, the answer was no, as early research indicated that there was not an inherent relationship between social responsibility and economic performance.[138] Recent research, however, leads to different conclusions. There is no trade-off between being socially responsible and economic performance.[139] And there is a small, positive relationship between being socially responsible and economic performance that strengthens with corporate reputation.[140] Let's explore what each of these results means.

First, there is no trade-off between being socially responsible and economic performance.[141] Being socially responsible usually won't make a business less profitable. What this suggests is that the costs of being socially responsible – and those costs can be high, especially early on – can be offset by a better product or corporate reputation, which results in stronger sales or higher profit margins. When businesses enhance their reputations by being socially responsible, they hope to maximize *willingness to pay,* that is, customers paying more for products and services that are socially responsible. Much more expensive organic, grass-fed, antibiotic-free beef that takes longer to make weight (20 to 24

Ahturner/Shutterstock.com

months versus 16 to 18 months) is an example of maximizing willingness to pay. But, according to Pat Brown, CEO of Impossible Foods, maker of the Incredible Burger, a plant-based product that feels, looks, and tastes like real beef, broad consumer acceptance will only happen when socially responsible products are similar, if not lower, in price. Says Brown, "What we need to do [at Impossible Foods] is get to the point where animal food as a technology no longer works because the economic model is no longer viable [compared to our products.]"[142]

Second, it usually *does* pay to be socially responsible, and that relationship becomes stronger, particularly when a company or its products have a strong reputation for social responsibility.[143] Finally, even if there is generally a small positive relationship between social responsibility and economic performance that becomes stronger when a company or its products have a positive reputation for social responsibility, and even if there is no trade-off between being socially responsible and economic performance, there is no guarantee that socially responsible companies will be profitable. Simply put, socially responsible companies experience the same ups and downs in economic performance that traditional businesses do. Panera Bread, which has over 2,000 popular bakery-cafes in the United States, has closed the fifth and last Panera Cares restaurant. Panera Cares restaurants were identical to Panera Bread restaurants, except that Panera Cares customers could pay what they wanted for their food. For a Panera Cares restaurant to cover its costs, 20 percent of customers would need to pay more, 60 percent would need to pay regular prices, and then 20 percent would be able to pay less.[144] The five now closed Panera Cares restaurants were part of Panera's nonprofit organization and were established as a gift to five different communities, according to former CEO Ron Shaich. But, in the end, Panera Cares restaurants lost too much money because customers paid only 85 percent of suggested menu prices.[145] Shaich explained, "The nature of the economics did not make sense."[146] Being socially responsible might be the right thing to do, and it is usually associated with increased profits, but it doesn't guarantee business success.

PART 2

5 | Planning and Decision-Making

PeopleImages/E+/Getty Images

LEARNING OUTCOMES

5-1 Discuss the benefits and pitfalls of planning.

5-2 Outline the steps for creating an effective plan.

5-3 Discuss how companies can use plans at all management levels, from top to bottom.

5-4 Use the steps and avoid the limits to rational decision-making.

5-5 Explain how group decisions and group decision-making techniques can improve decision-making.

5-1 BENEFITS AND PITFALLS OF PLANNING

Even inexperienced managers know that planning and decision-making are central parts of their jobs. Figure out what the problem is. Generate potential solutions or plans. Pick the best one. Make it work. Experienced managers, however, know how hard it really is to make good plans and decisions. One seasoned manager says, "I think the biggest surprises are the problems. Maybe I had never seen it before. Maybe I was protected by my management when I was in sales. Maybe I had delusions of grandeur, I don't know. I just know how disillusioning and frustrating it is to be hit with problems and conflicts all day and not be able to solve them very cleanly."[1]

> **Planning** choosing a goal and developing a strategy to achieve that goal

Planning is choosing a goal and developing a method or strategy to achieve that goal. With 785 warehouse stores, 100 million fee-paying members, $149 billion in annual revenue, and 243,000 employees, **Costco** is the second largest retailer in the world.[2] Since its founding, Costco's plan has been to

sell branded products for no more than 14 percent over cost and its Kirkland Signature house brands for no more than 15 percent over cost. Its carefully selected, high-quality goods are marked up an average of 11 percent, compared to 35 percent at The Home Depot and Lowes, 30 percent at grocery stores, and 24 percent at Walmart.[3] So, how does Costco exceed its aggressive price goals? By generally selling one high-quality item in each product category, which it buys at higher volumes, and thus lower costs, and sells straight off shipping pallets.[4] A Costco warehouse has roughly 4,000 items compared to 30,000 at a supermarket. CEO Craig Jelinek says, "We run a tight operation with extremely low overhead, which enables us to pass dramatic savings to our members."[5]

Costco has a clear, successful plan. What about you? Are you one of those naturally organized people who always makes a daily to-do list and never misses a deadline because you keep track of everything with written lists, a spreadsheet, or task management apps like Todoist, Trello, or Microsoft To Do? Or are you one of those flexible, creative, go-with-the-flow people who dislikes planning and organizing because it restricts your freedom, energy, and performance? Some people are natural planners. They love it and only see its benefits. Others dislike planning and only see its disadvantages. It turns out that *both* views have real value.

*Planning has advantages and disadvantages. Let's learn about **5-1a the benefits** and **5-1b the pitfalls of planning**.*

5-1a Benefits of Planning

Planning offers several important benefits: intensified effort, persistence, direction, and creation of task strategies.[6] First, managers and employees put forth greater effort when following a plan. Take two workers. Instruct one to "do your best" to increase production, and instruct the other to achieve a 2 percent increase in production each month. Research shows that the one with the specific plan will work harder.[7]

Second, planning leads to persistence, that is, working hard for long periods. In fact, planning encourages persistence even when there may be little chance of short-term success.[8] McDonald's founder Ray Kroc, a keen believer in the power of persistence, had this quotation from President Calvin Coolidge hung in all of his executives' offices: "Nothing in the world can take the place of persistence. Talent will not; nothing is more

As American President Calvin Coolidge said, "Nothing in the world can take the place of persistence."

common than unsuccessful men with talent. Genius will not; unrewarded genius is almost a proverb. Education will not; the world is full of educated derelicts. Persistence and determination alone are omnipotent."[9]

The third benefit of planning is direction. Ken Allen, former CEO of **DHL Express** says, "For executives, the question of 'what to do' is often better thought of as 'what not to do.' Every day half a dozen opportunities land on my desk that promise to be the next big thing, but successful managers know how to turn down opportunities that could distract from the sector where they can deliver the most value."[10] Allen says when DHL was losing $110 million a month, "Our turnaround strategy was based on one central tenet: focus. DHL Express would have the single focus of being the world's premier international express shipping company," shipping packages to and from 220 countries.[11]

The fourth benefit of planning is that it encourages the development of task strategies. In other words, planning not only encourages people to work hard for extended periods and to engage in behaviors directly related to goal accomplishment, it also encourages them to think of better ways to do their jobs. Finally, perhaps the most compelling benefit of planning is that it has been proven to work for both companies and individuals. On average, companies with plans have larger profits and grow much faster than companies without plans.[12] The same holds true for individual managers and employees: There is no better way to improve the performance of the people who work in a company than to have them set goals and develop strategies for achieving those goals.

5-1b Pitfalls of Planning

Despite the significant benefits associated with planning, it is not a cure-all. Plans won't fix all organizational problems. In fact, many management authors and consultants believe that planning can harm companies in several ways.[13]

The first pitfall of planning is that it can impede change and prevent or slow needed adaptation. Sometimes companies become so committed to achieving the goals set forth in their plans or on following the strategies and tactics spelled out in them that they fail to see that their plans aren't working or that their goals need to change. In 2015, only 25 percent of the makers of luxury Swiss mechanical watches thought Apple's new smart watch would have a "meaningful impact" on sales.[14] But by the end of 2015, sales had dropped by

Apple watch sales grew from 12 million watches in 2016 to 31 million in 2019.

$2 billion, or 1.6 percent. By the end of 2016, sales had fallen again, by 9.9 percent, or nearly $19 billion.[15] To avoid price discounts, Swiss watch makers bought back nearly 10 percent of unsold watch inventory from retailers and dismantled those watches for parts.[16] Analysts estimate that Apple sold nearly 12 million Apple Watches in 2016, accounting for half the market share and 80 percent of the profits in global smart watches.[17] Will luxury buyers come back to mechanical watches? In 2019, 20.6 million Swiss mechanical watches were sold, down from 28.1 million in 2015.[18] Apple Watch sales, however, grew from 12 million watches in 2016 to 22.5 million in 2018 and then 31 million in 2019.[19] Strategy Analytics Neil Mawson says, the Swiss mechanical watch industry is "in a bit of a mess at the moment – it's recording its lowest level of output since the 1980s."[20]

The second pitfall is that planning can create a false sense of certainty. Planners sometimes feel that they know exactly what the future holds for their competitors, their suppliers, and their companies. However, all plans are based on assumptions: National home prices never go down. Eurozone countries don't default. Saudi Arabia won't let the price of oil crash. China's demand for raw materials is infinite. Unemployment rates, peaking at 10 percent, will bottom out at 5 percent. The Federal bank interest rate, which fell to 0.25 percent in the Great Recession, will bounce back to 4.2 percent.

For plans to work, the assumptions on which they are based must hold true. If the assumptions turn out to be false, then the plans based on them are likely to fail. Indeed, according to the *Wall Street Journal's* Greg Ip, the assumptions just listed were "some of the most cherished assumptions of investors and policy makers in the past decade, assumptions that have underpinned trillions of dollars of investment and debt."[21] And they were all completely wrong:[22] Home prices crashed. Greece defaulted on loans. Oil prices dropped to near historic lows. China's economy slowed. Unemployment dropped to 3.5 percent and the Fed hasn't raised interest rates above 2.44 percent in the last 10 years. Of course, none of those investors and policy makers anticipated the coronavirus and its effects on businesses and financial markets.

The third potential pitfall of planning is the detachment of planners. In theory, strategic planners and top-level managers are supposed to focus on the big picture and not concern themselves with the details of implementation (that is, carrying out the plan). According to management professor Henry Mintzberg, detachment leads planners to plan for things they don't understand.[23] Plans are meant to be guidelines for action, not abstract theories. Consequently, planners need to be familiar with the daily details of their businesses if they are to produce plans that can work. A study of 3,620 strategic decisions based on clear strategic plans and rules found that it took managers roughly 19 attempts (i.e., the same kind of decision made 19 times over a number of years) to reliably make good decisions where performance stabilized at a high level![24] The lesson is clear: It takes a long time to get good at making complex decisions based on plans. It would likely, however, take much longer for detached planners who do not have the same opportunity to learn from the repeated decisions made by company managers in this study.

5-2 HOW TO MAKE A PLAN THAT WORKS

Planning is a double-edged sword. If done right, planning brings about tremendous increases in individual and organizational performance. If planning is done wrong, however, it can have just the opposite effect and harm individual and organizational performance.

*In this section, you will learn how to make a plan that works. As depicted in Exhibit 5.1, planning consists of **5-2a setting goals, 5-2b developing commitment to the goals, 5-2c developing effective action plans, 5-2d tracking progress toward goal achievement,** and **5-2e maintaining flexibility in planning.***

5-2a Setting Goals

The first step in planning is to set goals. To direct behavior and increase effort, goals need to be specific and challenging.[25] For example, deciding to "increase sales this year" won't direct and energize workers as much as deciding to "increase North American sales by 4 percent in the next six months." Specific, challenging goals provide a target for which to aim and a standard against which to measure success.

One way of writing effective goals for yourself, your job, or your company is to use the S.M.A.R.T. guidelines. **S.M.A.R.T. goals** are **S**pecific, **M**easurable, **A**ttainable, **R**ealistic, and **T**imely.[26] With annual sales of $68 billion, Cincinnati-based **Procter & Gamble** (P&G) is a global leader in consumer products in 180 countries. Its size, however, made managing growth difficult. To combat this difficulty, in 2013, CEO A.G. Lafley established a goal of cutting P&G's massive brand portfolio of roughly 165 brands

> **S.M.A.R.T. goals** goals that are specific, measurable, attainable, realistic, and timely

Exhibit 5.1
How to Make a Plan That Works

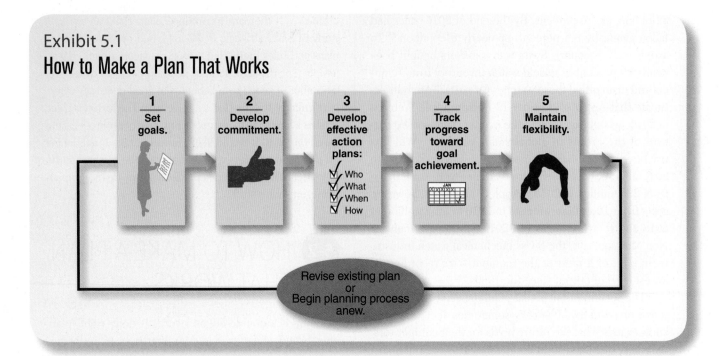

| 1 Set goals. | 2 Develop commitment. | 3 Develop effective action plans: ✓ Who ✓ What ✓ When ✓ How | 4 Track progress toward goal achievement. | 5 Maintain flexibility. |

Revise existing plan or Begin planning process anew.

to 65 core brands, organized into 10 key categories, by 2016.[27] Let's see how P&G's objectives measure up to the S.M.A.R.T. guidelines for goals.

First, is the goal *Specific*? Yes, as opposed to saying that it wants to be smaller, P&G identified exactly how many brands it wanted in its portfolio by 2016—its 65 best-selling brands. Is the goal *Measurable*? Yes, P&G's best-performing brands generated 95 percent of its profits, which were growing faster than the rest of P&G, while its poorer performing brands had sales and profits that were shrinking 3 percent and 16 percent per year, respectively.[28] Whether the goal is *Attainable* depends on many factors. First, P&G needed to find potential buyers for the 100 brands it was selling. After it identified potential buyers, they had to agree on a purchase price (a complex task with billion-dollar businesses). Then, it had to clear the financial and legal hurdles involved in transferring ownership of each brand. But major merger and acquisitions transactions aren't new, certainly for P&G, and those issues were not problematic. Finally, while the goals were ambitious, they are *Timely*. When P&G announced the goal in 2013, it gave itself three years to divest 50 of the 100 brands it has identified for sale. In 2016, it had successfully sold 43 beauty brands, including Clairol and Cover Girl, to Coty for $12.5 billion.[29] By 2018, P&G had achieved the goal of downsizing to 65 brands.[30] While it took three years longer than planned, the result was a slimmed down, more focused company with 60 percent fewer product categories,

Goal commitment the determination to achieve a goal

70 percent fewer brands, and 50 percent fewer kinds of manufacturing facilities.[31]

5-2b Developing Commitment to Goals

Just because a company sets a goal doesn't mean that people will try to accomplish it. If workers don't care about a goal, that goal won't encourage them to work harder or smarter. Thus, the second step in planning is to develop commitment to goals.[32]

Goal commitment is the determination to achieve a goal. Commitment to achieve a goal is not automatic. Managers and workers must choose to commit themselves to a goal. Edwin Locke, professor emeritus of management at the University of Maryland and the foremost expert on how, why, and when goals work, tells a story about an overweight friend who lost 75 pounds. Locke says, "I asked him how he did it, knowing how hard it was for most people to lose so much weight." His friend responded, "Actually, it was quite simple. I simply decided that I *really wanted* to do it."[33] Put another way, goal commitment is really wanting to achieve a goal.

So how can managers bring about goal commitment? The most popular approach is to set goals participatively. Rather than assigning goals to workers ("Johnson, you've got till Tuesday of next week to redesign the flux capacitor so it gives us 10 percent more output"), managers and employees choose goals together. The goals are more likely to be realistic and attainable if employees participate in setting them. Another technique for gaining

Does "Plan B" Kill Goal Commitment?

Standard advice is to have a "Plan B" in in case "Plan A" doesn't work. However, developing "Plan B" might reduce your commitment—and chance of success—with Plan A.

In three studies, Professors Jihae Shin and Katherine Milkman had college students do a series of tasks for which they could be rewarded with a snack. But some of the students were told to think about other places on campuses where they might get free food if they weren't successful at their tasks, that is, Plan B. Milkman said, "When people were prompted to think about another way to achieve the same high-level outcome in case they failed in their primary goal, they worked less hard and did less well."

So, if you really want to succeed with Plan A, be cautious when asked, "What's Plan B?" At the very least, says Shin, "You might want to delay making a backup plan until after you have done everything you can to achieve your primary goal."

Source: Knowledge@ Wharton, "The Downside of a Backup Plan – and What to Do About It," University of Pennsylvania, The Wharton School of Business, June 2, 2016, accessed March 25, 2017, http://knowledge.wharton.upenn.edu/article/the-downsideof-making-a-backup-plan/; R. Silverman, "Plan A' Works Better When There's No 'Plan B,'" *Wall Street Journal*, August 16, 2016, accessed March 25, 2017, https://www.wsj.com/articles/plan-a-works-better-when-theres-no-plan-b-1471356000.

commitment to a goal is to make the goal public. For example, college students who publicly communicated their semester grade goals ("This semester, I'm shooting for a 3.5") to important people in their lives (usually a parent or sibling) were much more committed to achieving their grades than those who did not. Still another way to increase goal commitment is to obtain top management's support. Top management can show support for a plan or program by providing funds, speaking publicly about the plan, or participating in the plan itself.

5-2c Developing Effective Action Plans

The third step in planning is to develop effective action plans. An **action plan** lists the specific steps (how), people (who), resources (what), and time period (when) for accomplishing a goal. The top goal for Mark Tritton, the new CEO at **Bed Bath & Beyond** (BB&B), is to declutter stores by reducing the number of items it sells. The problem is overwhelmed customers who, he says, suffer from "purchase paralysis." The steps (how) are straightforward—reduce the number of products in each product category. For example, sales jumped after reducing the number of can openers it sells from 12 to 3. The people (who) are responsible for deciding which products to keep will be corporate product managers and store managers. In terms of resources (what), BB&B has $900 million in cash but hopes to raise an additional $252 million by selling 1-800Flowers.com. Those funds will easily pay for needed investments in purchasing and supply chain management. The time period (when) is one year. But there is more to do. Tritton says, "We are making substantial moves. But we are early in our turnaround. This is phase one."[34]

5-2d Tracking Progress

The fourth step in planning is to track progress toward goal achievement. There are two accepted methods of tracking progress. The first is to set proximal goals and distal goals. **Proximal goals** are short-term goals or subgoals, whereas **distal goals** are long-term or primary goals.[35]

When Tesla launched a plan to produce 1 million electric vehicles (EVs) by 2025 (the distal goal), doubling its 2020 production of 500,000 cars, managers identified the following three proximal goals to get there:

1. In 2021, complete Berlin, Germany, factory; start production of batteries, power trains, and seats. Add capability to assemble cars later.

2. In 2023, manufacture 250,000 EVs per year at Shanghai, China, factory, which started production in 2019.

3. In 2025, manufacture 250,000 EVs in Berlin, Germany.[36]

The second method of tracking progress is to gather and provide performance feedback. Regular, frequent performance feedback allows workers and managers to track their progress toward goal achievement and make adjustments in effort, direction, and strategies.[37] Exhibit 5.2 shows the impact of feedback on safety behavior at a large bakery company with a worker safety record that was two-and-a-half times worse than the industry average. During the baseline period, workers in the wrapping department,

> **Action plan** a plan that lists the specific steps, people, resources, and time period needed to attain a goal
>
> **Proximal goals** short-term goals or subgoals
>
> **Distal goals** long-term or primary goals

Exhibit 5.2
Effects of Goal Setting, Training, and Feedback on Safe Behavior in a Bread Factory

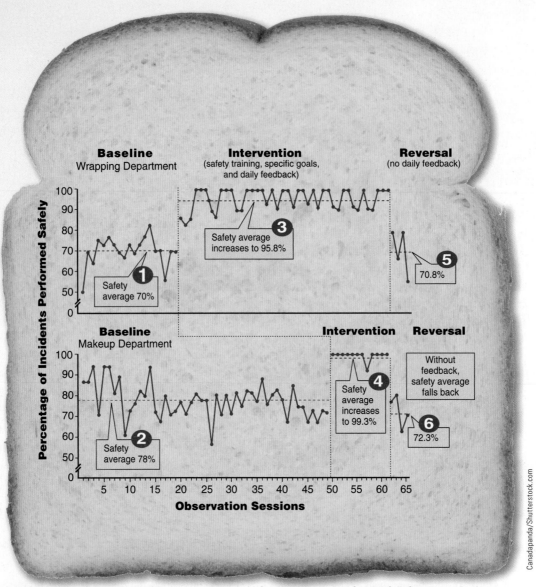

Source: J. Komaki, K. D. Barwick, and L. R. Scott. "A Behavioral Approach to Occupational Safety: Pinpointing and Reinforcing Safe Performance in a Food Manufacturing Plant," *Journal of Applied Psychology* 63 (1978).

who measure and mix ingredients, roll the bread dough, and put it into baking pans, performed their jobs safely about 70 percent of the time (see 1 in Exhibit 5.2). The baseline safety record for workers in the makeup department, who bag and seal baked bread and assemble, pack, and tape cardboard cartons for shipping, was somewhat better at 78 percent (see 2 in Exhibit 5.2). The company then gave workers 30 minutes of safety training, set a goal of 90 percent safe behavior, and then provided daily feedback (such as a chart similar to Exhibit 5.2). Performance improved

dramatically. During the intervention period, safely performed behaviors rose to an average of 95.8 percent for wrapping workers (see 3 in Exhibit 5.2) and 99.3 percent for workers in the makeup department (see 4 in Exhibit 5.2), and never fell below 83 percent. Thus, the combination of training, a challenging goal, and feedback led to a dramatic increase in performance. The importance of feedback alone can be seen in the reversal stage, when the company quit posting daily feedback on safe behavior. Without daily feedback, the percentage of safely performed behaviors

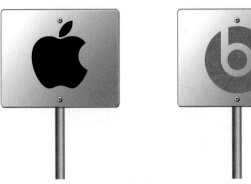

grzegorz knec/Alamy Stock Photo

returned to baseline levels –70.8 percent for the wrapping department (see 5 in Exhibit 5.2) and 72.3 percent for the makeup department (see 6 in Exhibit 5.2). For planning to be effective, workers need both a specific, challenging goal and regular feedback to track their progress. In fact, additional research indicates that the effectiveness of goal setting can be doubled by the addition of feedback.[38]

5-2e Maintaining Flexibility

Because action plans are sometimes poorly conceived and goals sometimes turn out not to be achievable, the last step in developing an effective plan is to maintain flexibility. One method of maintaining flexibility while planning is to adopt an options-based approach.[39] The goal of **options-based planning** is to keep options open by making small, simultaneous investments in many alternative plans. Then, when one or a few of these plans emerge as likely winners, you invest even more in these plans while discontinuing or reducing investment in the others. Apple has followed an options-based plan for acquisitions for over a decade. CEO Tim Cook said, "We acquire everything that we need that can fit and has a strategic purpose to it. And so we acquire a company, on average, every two to three weeks."[40] Consistent with options-based planning, 75 percent of Apple's acquisitions are small startup companies purchased with the hope of adding specific technological capabilities to Apple products.[41] Examples include Apple's acquisition of Stamplay, an API integration developer that Apple might use to spread the use of Apple Pay, or Silk Labs, which develops artificial intelligence software that works on small computerized devices.[42] Apple does make a small number of larger acquisitions to directly create or improve Apple services or products. For example, Apple's purchase of Beats music was the foundation for creating Apple Music. Likewise, Apple's purchase of Intel's smartphone modem business was used to bring the development and manufacture of 5G modems in house.[43]

In part, options-based planning is the opposite of traditional planning. Whereas the purpose of an action plan is to commit people and resources to a particular course of action, the purpose of options-based planning is to leave those commitments open by maintaining **slack resources**—that is, a cushion of resources, such as extra time, people, money, or production capacity, that can be used to address and adapt to unanticipated changes, problems, or opportunities.[44] Holding options open gives you choices. And choices, combined with slack resources, give you flexibility. Because it can take a year and a half to receive new equipment, US power companies are funding **Grid Assurance, LLC**, which buys and holds extra electrical transformers and circuit breakers to be used for emergencies when damaged power generating and transmission equipment needs replacing. Grid Assurance will also locate key equipment in secure, undisclosed locations. In case of a terrorist attack, "The last thing we want is for someone to do a physical attack and wipe out our spares," says Scott Moore, vice president of transmission engineering for American Electric Power.[45] Grid Assurance provides the equivalent of catastrophic insurance, giving power companies the extra resources needed to survive unanticipated disruptions and breakdowns. So far, 31 companies providing power in 23 states now subscribe and support Grid Assurance.[46]

5-3 PLANNING FROM TOP TO BOTTOM

Planning works best when the goals and action plans at the bottom and middle of the organization support the goals and action plans at the top of the organization. In other words, planning works best when everybody pulls in the same direction. Exhibit 5.3 illustrates this planning continuity, beginning at the top with a clear definition of the company purpose and ending at the bottom with the execution of operational plans.

*Let's see how **5-3a top managers create the organization's purpose statement and strategic objective, 5-3b middle managers develop tactical plans and use management by objectives to motivate employee efforts toward the overall purpose and strategic objective,** and **5-3c first-level managers use operational, single-use, and standing plans to implement the tactical plans.***

Options-based planning maintaining planning flexibility by making small, simultaneous investments in many alternative plans

Slack resources a cushion of extra resources that can be used with options-based planning to adapt to unanticipated changes, problems, or opportunities

Exhibit 5.3
Planning from Top to Bottom

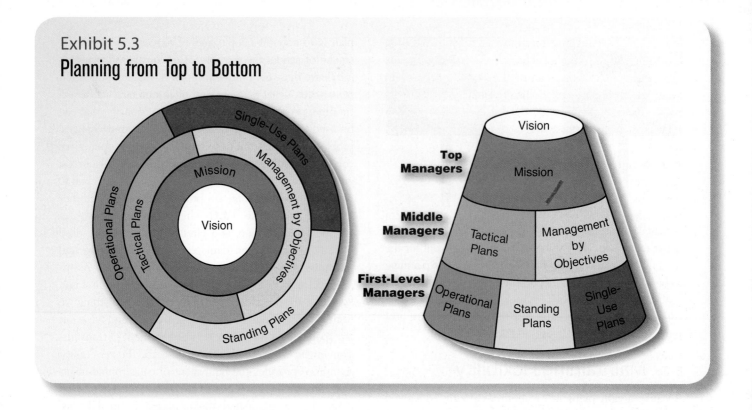

5-3a Starting at the Top

Top management is responsible for developing long-term **strategic plans** that make clear how the company will serve customers and position itself against competitors in the next two to five years. The average cost for eyeglass frames is $127.[47] Add prescription lenses and the average cost rises to $238.[48] Add thinner lenses (for strong prescriptions), transitions coating (to make clear lenses darken in the sun), progressive lenses (for reading, computer use, and distance), and the cost easily rises to $400+. The strategic plan of **EyeBuyDirect. com** (owned by Essilor Luxottica, the world's largest maker of frames and lenses) is to offer the widest variety of frames for half the cost of brick-and-mortar optical stores.[49] Its virtual "TRY ON" tool uses selfies to show how you'll look in various frames. At EyeBuyDirect, a standard pair of glasses runs $50 for weak prescriptions and $100 for strong prescriptions. Bifocals are just $29 for bifocals, and progressives run $49 to $69. Shipping is free for orders over $99. Returns are free for 14 days. *The Wirecutter*, a product review website, says EyeBuyDirect is the best place to buy glasses online "when compared with the prominent competition."[50]

Strategic plans overall company plans that clarify how the company will serve customers and position itself against competitors over the next two to five years

Purpose statement a statement of a company's purpose or reason for existing

Strategic planning begins with the creation of an organizational purpose. A **purpose statement**, which is often referred to as an organizational mission or vision, is a statement of a company's purpose or reason for existing.[51] Purpose statements should be brief—no more than two sentences. They should also be enduring, inspirational, clear, and consistent with widely shared company beliefs and values. An excellent example of a well-crafted purpose statement is that of cosmetics company **Avon**: "To be the company that best understands and satisfies the product, service and self-fulfillment needs of women—globally."[52] It guides everyone in the organization and provides a focal point for the delivery of beauty products and services to its customers, women around the world. The purpose is the same whether Avon is selling lipstick to women in India, shampoo packets to women in the Amazon, or jewelry to women in the United States. Despite these regional differences in specific strategy, the overall goal—understanding the needs of women globally—does not change. Other examples of organizational purpose statements that have been particularly effective include Walt Disney Company's "to make people happy," Schlage Lock Company's "to make the world more secure," and *Highlights*, the long-running magazine for children, "fun with a purpose."[53]

Collins and Porras explain that: "A mission is a clear and compelling goal that serves to unify an organization's efforts. An effective mission must stretch and challenge the organization, yet be achievable." However, many others define *mission* as an organization's purpose. To avoid confusion, we use Collins and Porras's term *purpose statement*, meaning a clear statement of an organization's purpose or reason for existence. Furthermore, we will continue to use their definition of a mission (that is "a clear and compelling goal . . .") but instead call it "the strategic objective." The **strategic objective**, which flows from the purpose, is a more specific goal that unifies company-wide efforts, stretches and challenges the organization, and possesses a finish line and a time frame.[54]

For example, at **Edwards Lifesciences**, the purpose or reason for existence is "Providing innovative solutions for people fighting cardiovascular disease." The strategic objective, which flows from that purpose, is to be "the global leader in patient-focused medical innovations for structural heart disease, as well as critical care and surgical monitoring."[55] Consistent with that strategic objective, Edwards Lifesciences leads the market in surgical heart valves for structural heart disease, and hemodynamic monitoring (measuring blood pressure inside the heart, arteries and veins) for critically ill and high-risk surgical patients.[56]

Once the strategic objective has been accomplished, a new one should be chosen, However, the new strategic objective must grow out of the organization's purpose, which does not change significantly over time. There are two ways to choose the new strategic objective, retrospectively and prospectively.[57] A *retrospective strategic objective* looks to the company's past for guidance on what to do or not do in the future. Sixty-year-old Miles Edwards founded Edwards Lifesciences in 1958 after retiring from a career in engineering. Twice during his teenage years, Edwards suffered from rheumatic fever, which can scar heart valves and lead to heart failure. That personal experience, combined with his expertise in hydraulics and fuel pumps in which he earned 63 patents, led to him developing the first artificial heart valve.[58] Edwards Lifesciences' current strategic objective is retrospective and clearly linked to its founder and why he started the company.

A *prospective strategic objective* looks to the future, asks "Where can we go?" not "Where have we been?" and is often used when there are strong reasons for strategic change, such as shrinking market share or sustained financial losses. The challenge with prospective strategic objectives is to choose a new path, but one not completely divorced from the organization's purpose. Instead, the company finds a new way to fulfill that purpose. From

With sales plummeting over a four-year period, Arby's added more sandwiches to their menu to appease younger consumers.

its start in 1964, **Arby's**, the fast-food chain, was simply known as "Arby's Roast Beef Sandwich (is Delicious)." And that served Arby's well for nearly 30 years, after which salads, chicken, and corned beef were added to its menu.[59] New Arby's President Rob Lynch said, "Our customers were not loving Arby's for a very long time. We had lost about $150,000 per restaurant in sales over a four-year period, which, for a brand of our size, is essentially catastrophic."[60] Lynch searched Arby's history, finding a clear purpose of serving high-quality meat sandwiches ("Arby's. We Have The Meats.") and a track record of innovation (first to offer free refills and "lite," lower-calorie menu items). Putting those together, Arby's adopted a new prospective strategic objective made clear in its new tagline, "Arby's. We Have The Meats…for Sandwiches."[61] Arby's marketing chief Jim Taylor said,

Strategic objective a more specific goal that unifies company-wide efforts, stretches and challenges the organization, and possesses a finish line and a time frame

"Younger people don't eat roast beef as much. We want to bring in some younger consumers who love sandwiches."[62] Now, with 17 different sandwiches on its menu, using various kinds of beef, pork, chicken, and turkey, Arby's new strategic objective has given it a different way to fulfill its purpose.

5-3b Bending in the Middle

Middle management is responsible for developing and carrying out tactical plans to accomplish the organization's strategic objective. **Tactical plans** specify how a company will use resources, budgets, and people to accomplish specific goals related to its strategic objective for the next five years. Whereas strategic plans and objectives are used to focus company efforts over the next two to five years, tactical plans and objectives are used to direct behavior, efforts, and attention over the next six months to two years. **Hostess** sells nearly $1.3 billion a year in Twinkies, Cupcakes, HoHos, Ding Dongs, and other snack cakes in more than 100,000 convenience stores across the United States. But according to former CEO Bill Toler, Hostess was 20,000 stores shy of reaching its strategic objective: "To be sold everywhere a candy bar is sold, whether it's an airport kiosk, or a vending machine."[63] To achieve that objective, Hostess's tactical plans included expanding in the United States, broadening distribution in Europe and the Caribbean, and launching new distribution in Mexico and Canada. Hostess also extended its brand name into ice cream with products like the Twinkies Cone, Twinkies Ice Cream, the Ding Dongs [ice cream] Sandwich, and the Sno Balls Bar (on a stick).[64] New CEO Andrew Callahan says, "When we come out with products that are convenient, that consumers love and that satisfy consumer needs, we're successful."[65]

iStock.com/LynnSeeden

Management by objectives is a management technique often used to develop and carry out tactical plans. **Management by objectives** is a four-step process in which managers and their employees (1) discuss possible goals; (2) collectively select goals that are challenging, attainable, and consistent with the company's overall goals; (3) jointly develop tactical plans that lead to the accomplishment of tactical goals and objectives; and (4) meet regularly to review progress toward accomplishment of those goals. **Kimberly-Clark**, the maker of diapers, tissues, and other consumer products, was a low-pressure workplace in which, according to retired sales director Rick Herbert, "A lot of people [meaning poor performers] could and would hide in the weeds."[66] But the company has now switched to a performance management system, a variant of MBO, in which personalized goals and tracking data are used to closely monitor performance. Says Herbert, "People can't duck and hide in the same way they could in the past." Instead of once-a-year reviews, feedback regarding goal progress and personal improvement is real-time and continuous. Engineer Stephanie Martin says, "We have to routinely shuffle the resources and say, what's the most important thing we need to do today, this week, this month, to drive this objective?"[67]

5-3c Finishing at the Bottom

Lower-level managers are responsible for developing and carrying out **operational plans**, which are the day-to-day plans for producing or delivering the organization's products and services. Operational plans direct the behavior, efforts, and priorities of operative employees for periods ranging from 30 days to six months. There are three kinds of operational plans: single-use plans, standing plans, and budgets.

Single-use plans deal with unique, one-time-only events. Since 1935, Tokyo's Tsukiji fish market has been located in Ginza, Tokyo's high-end shopping, restaurant and entertainment district. On a typical day, 42,000 tourists and 3.6 million pounds of fish pass through the market. Under a single-use plan that was 20 years in development, the Tsukiji fish market moved to a new location much closer to Tokyo Bay.[68] Unlike the old market, the new one has full temperature controls throughout, as well as closed buildings to prevent

Tactical plans plans created and implemented by middle managers that direct behavior, efforts, and attention over the next six months to two years

Management by objectives a four-step process in which managers and employees discuss and select goals, develop tactical plans, and meet regularly to review progress toward goal accomplishment

Operational plans day-to-day plans, developed and implemented by lower-level managers, for producing or delivering the organization's products and services over a 30-day to six-month period

Single-use plans plans that cover unique, one-time-only events

possible contamination from birds, insects, and rodents. It meets global food safety standards set by the International HACCP (Hazard Analysis Critical Control Points) Alliance.[69] The total cost of moving to the new fish market, which is 1.7 times larger, came to $5.1 billion.[70]

Unlike single-use plans that are created, carried out once, and then never used again, **standing plans** save managers time because after the plans are created, they can be used repeatedly to handle frequently recurring events. If you encounter a problem that you've seen before, someone in your company has probably written a standing plan that explains how to address it. When a snowstorm hit Atlanta in 2014, **Delta Airlines** transformed a Boeing 767 into sleeping quarters for stranded employees. Instead of going to the airport hotel—or to uncomfortable cots in the terminal—employees slept on the plane's business class lie-flat seats and were rested and ready when the runways were clear in the morning. The contingency plan was so successful that Delta added it to its standard storm-response planning in 2015. Using a standing plan rather than reinventing the wheel allows Delta to save time. Delta's senior vice president of operations, Dave Holtz, says, "We don't want to limit our ability to get customers going because employees can't get there."[71] There are three kinds of standing plans: policies, procedures, and rules and regulations.

Policies indicate the general course of action that company managers should take in response to a particular event or situation. A well-written policy will also specify why the policy exists and what outcome the policy is intended to produce.[72] When bad weather threatened flights, the old policy followed by the airlines was to take care of frequent fliers first, finding them alternative routes to their destinations. As for everyone else, well, with limited seats available on any particular travel day, large numbers of travelers were guaranteed to be stuck at the airport. Now, however, the policy is to electronically issue passengers flexible weather waivers several days in advance of disruptive weather. The waivers allow passengers to cancel their flights (with a full refund), fly several days before or after their ticketed travel date, or, even fly out of or to nearby airports where flights are still operating, all without typical changes fees of $200 or more per ticket. Delta spokesperson Michael Thomas explained, "We used to just rebook passengers on the next available flight. Now we let them choose."[73]

Procedures are more specific than policies because they indicate the series of steps that should be taken in response to a particular event. All commercial airplanes require regular cleaning. With no regulatory standards, airlines set their own procedures.

Money sends a clear message about your priorities. Budgets act as a language for communicating your goals to others.

iStock.com/FredFroese

At **Singapore Airlines**, which flies longer international flights, a 12-person team takes roughly 40 minutes to clean a Boeing 777-300 jet during a normal stopover. At **United Airlines**, most domestic flights require a quick turn (30 minutes or less), so the cleaning procedures focus on the following tasks:

» Removing visible trash and cleaning out the seat-back pockets

» Cleaning and restocking the bathrooms and galleys

» Pulling up the armrests

» Wiping crumbs off seats

» Cleaning large spills

In addition to between flights, United conducts more thorough overnight cleanings (vacuuming and cleaning restrooms and galleys) and "deep cleanings," in which the plane is "scrubbed from nose to tail," every 35 to 55 days.[74]

Standing plans plans used repeatedly to handle frequently recurring events

Policies standing plans that indicate the general course of action that should be taken in response to a particular event or situation

Procedures standing plans that indicate the specific steps that should be taken in response to a particular event

Rules and regulations are even more specific than procedures because they specify what must happen or not happen. They describe precisely how a particular action should be performed. For example, for security issues and worries about drug interactions, most hospitals prohibit patients from bringing medications from home. At the MD Anderson Cancer Center in Houston, admitting nurses must follow this regulation: "All medications brought into the hospital upon admission should be returned home whenever possible. Nursing personnel carrying out the admission procedure should determine whether the patient has brought any medication with him/her from home. Such medications should be placed in tamper-proof bags and placed in a secured area in the nursing unit."[75]

After single-use plans and standing plans, budgets are the third kind of operational plan. **Budgeting** is quantitative planning because it forces managers to decide how to allocate available money to best accomplish company goals. According to Jan King, author of *Business Plans to Game Plans*, "Money sends a clear message about your priorities. Budgets act as a language for communicating your goals to others." A more detailed discussion of budgets can be found in Chapter 16, Section 16-3b, "The Financial Perspective: Controlling Budgets, Cash Flows, and Economic Value Added."

5-4 STEPS AND LIMITS TO RATIONAL DECISION-MAKING

Decision-making is the process of choosing a solution from available alternatives.[76] **Rational decision-making** is a systematic process in which managers define problems, evaluate alternatives, and choose optimal solutions that provide maximum benefits to their organizations. Thus, for example, your boss comes to you requesting that you define and evaluate the various options for the company's social media strategy; after all, you tweet and use Facebook, Instagram, SnapChat, Reddit, and so on and he doesn't even know how to reboot his computer. Furthermore, your solution has to be optimal. Because budgets and expertise are limited, the company gets one, maybe two, tries to make its social media strategy work. If you choose incorrectly, the company's investment will just go to waste, without increasing sales and market share. What would you recommend?

Let's learn more about each of these: **5-4a define the problem, 5-4b identify decision criteria, 5-4c weigh the criteria, 5-4d generate alternative courses of action, 5-4e evaluate each alternative, and 5-4f compute the optimal decision.** *Then we'll consider* **5-4g limits to rational decision-making.**

5-4a Define the Problem

The first step in decision-making is identifying and defining the problem. A **problem** exists when there is a gap between a desired state (what is wanted) and an existing state (the situation you are actually facing). You're in charge of ordering the pharmaceutical drugs used in your hospital system. You buy the drugs that doctors and nurses need for treating patients from wholesalers and are paid by insurers who negotiate a fixed reimbursement rate for those patients. When drug prices jump unexpectedly, such as when Valeant Pharmaceuticals increased the price of Nitropress and Isuprel (both used for treating heart-related health issues) by 200 to 500 percent, the hospital end ups absorbing the entire cost increase. In other words, there's a huge gap between what you budgeted to pay for particular drugs like Nitropress and Isuprel, and the much-higher price that you're actually paying when pharmaceutical firms suddenly raise prices.[77]

The presence of a gap between an existing state and a desired state is no guarantee that managers will make decisions to solve problems. Three things must occur for this to happen.[78] First, managers have to be aware of the gap. They have to know there is a problem before they can begin solving it. For example, after noticing that people were spending more money on their pets, a new dog food company created an expensive, high-quality dog food. To emphasize its quality, the dog food was sold in cans and bags with gold labels, red letters, and detailed information about its benefits and nutrients. Yet the product did not sell very well, and the company went out of business in less than a year. Its founders didn't understand why. When they asked a manager at a competing dog food company what their biggest mistake had been, the

Rules and regulations standing plans that describe how a particular action should be performed or what must happen or not happen in response to a particular event

Budgeting quantitative planning through which managers decide how to allocate available money to best accomplish company goals

Decision-making the process of choosing a solution from available alternatives

Rational decision-making a systematic process of defining problems, evaluating alternatives, and choosing optimal solutions

Problem a gap between a desired state and an existing state

answer was, "Simple. You didn't have a picture of a dog on the package."[79] This problem would have been easy to solve if management had only been aware of it.

Being aware of a problem isn't enough to begin the decision-making process. Managers have to be motivated to reduce the gap between a desired and an existing state. Whether the cause is conflict avoidance, lack of confidence, or disorganization, some managers lack the motivation to solve difficult problems. Economists would say that these managers enjoy the "quiet life instead of making hard decisions or taking on difficult tasks.[80] Others call the unwillingness to face up to difficult problems "under management."[81] Management consultant and author Ron Carucci says, "Too many leaders avoid making tough calls. In an effort not to upset others or lose status in the eyes of their followers, they concoct sophisticated justifications for putting off difficult decisions, and the delay often does far more damage than whatever fallout they were trying to avoid. In fact, hard decisions often get more complicated when they're deferred. And as a leader gets more senior, the need to make hard calls only intensifies. In our 10-year longitudinal study of more than 2,700 leaders, 57 percent of newly appointed executives said that decisions were more complicated and difficult than they expected."[82]

Finally, it's not enough to be aware of a problem and be motivated to solve it. Managers must also have the knowledge, skills, abilities, and resources to fix the problem. So how do hospitals solve the problem of sudden price increases for pharmaceuticals (that is, closing the gap between what they budgeted to pay for drugs and the higher prices they actually pay when pharmaceutical companies unexpectedly raise prices). When Nitropress and Isuprel prices jumped by 200 to 500 percent, MedStar Washington Hospital Center in Washington, DC, switched from Nitropress to a cheaper, but identical generic drug and repackaged Isuprel from a onetime use ampule (used for injections), much of which was wasted, into five dosages. Savings amounted to $1.7 million a year.[83]

5-4b Identify Decision Criteria

Decision criteria are the standards used to guide judgments and decisions. Typically, the more criteria a potential solution meets, the better that solution will be. Again, imagine your boss asks you to determine the best options for the company's social media strategy. What general factors would be important when selecting one social media tool over another? Are you trying to increase your search rankings? Provide customer support? Are you trying to reach a particular target market? Is it young single women ages 18–25 or, perhaps, married women ages 25–35? Are you reaching out directly to consumers or to businesses (i.e., business-to-business)? Will your strategy focus on visual content, demonstrations, or detailed, complex knowledge? Answering questions like these will help you identify the criteria that will guide the social media strategy you recommend.

5-4c Weigh the Criteria

After identifying decision criteria, the next step is deciding which criteria are more or less important. Although there are numerous mathematical models for weighing decision criteria, all require the decision maker to provide an initial ranking of the criteria. Some use **absolute comparisons**, in which each criterion is compared with a standard or is ranked on its own merits. For example, *Consumer Reports* uses these criteria when it rates and recommends new cars: predicted reliability, current owners' satisfaction, predicted depreciation (the price you could expect if you sold the car), ability to avoid an accident, fuel economy, crash protection, acceleration, ride, and front seat comfort.[84]

Different individuals will rank these criteria differently, depending on what they value or require in a car. Exhibit 5.4 shows the absolute weights that someone buying a car might use. Because these weights are absolute, each criterion is judged on its own importance using a five-point scale, with five representing "critically important" and one representing "completely unimportant." In this instance, predicted reliability, fuel economy, and front seat comfort were rated most important, and acceleration and predicted depreciation were rated least important.

> **Decision criteria** the standards used to guide judgments and decisions
>
> **Absolute comparisons** a process in which each decision criterion is compared to a standard or ranked on its own merits

Exhibit 5.4
Absolute Weighting of Decision Criteria for a Car Purchase

5 critically important
4 important
3 somewhat important
2 not very important
1 completely unimportant

1. Predicted reliability	1	2	3	4	(5)
2. Owner satisfaction	1	(2)	3	4	5
3. Predicted depreciation	(1)	2	3	4	5
4. Avoiding accidents	1	2	3	(4)	5
5. Fuel economy	1	2	3	4	(5)
6. Crash protection	1	2	3	(4)	5
7. Acceleration	(1)	2	3	4	5
8. Ride	1	2	(3)	4	5
9. Front seat comfort	1	2	3	4	(5)

Another method uses **relative comparisons**, in which each criterion is compared directly with every other criterion.[85] Professor Jordan Ellenberg emphasizes that not *comparing* the data associated with each option is a fundamental mistake. He says, "A number by itself is often meaningless; it is the comparison between numbers that carries the force."[86] Exhibit 5.5 shows six criteria that someone might use when buying a house. Moving down the first column of Exhibit 5.5, we see that the length of time of the daily commute has been rated less important (−1) than school system quality; more important (+1) than having an in-ground pool, a sun room, or a quiet street; and just as important as the house being brand new (0). Total weights, which are obtained by summing the scores in each column, indicate that the school system quality and daily

Relative comparisons a process in which each decision criterion is compared directly with every other criterion

commute are the most important factors to this home buyer, while an in-ground pool, sun room, and a quiet street are the least important. So, with relative comparisons, criteria are directly compared with each other.

5-4d Generate Alternative Courses of Action

After identifying and weighting the criteria that will guide the decision-making process, the next step is to identify possible courses of action that could solve the problem. In general, at this step, the idea is to generate as many alternatives as possible. Let's assume that you're trying to select a city in Europe to be the location of a major office. After meeting with your staff, you generate a list of possible alternatives: Amsterdam, the Netherlands; Barcelona or Madrid, Spain; Berlin, Dusseldorf, Frankfurt, or Munich, Germany; Brussels, Belgium; London, England; and Paris, France.

5-4e Evaluate Each Alternative

The next step is to systematically evaluate each alternative against each criterion. Because of the amount of information that must be collected, this step can take much longer and be much more expensive than other steps in the decision-making process. When selecting a European city for your office, you could contact economic development offices in each city, systematically interview businesspeople or executives who operate there, retrieve and use published government data on each location, or rely on published studies such as Cushman & Wakefield's *European Cities Monitor*, which conducted a survey of more than 500 senior European

Exhibit 5.5
Relative Comparison of Home Characteristics

Home Characteristics	L	SSQ	IP	SR	QS	NBH
Daily commute (L)		+1	−1	−1	−1	0
School system quality (SSQ)	−1		−1	−1	−1	−1
In-ground pool (IP)	+1	+1		0	0	+1
Sun room (SR)	+1	+1	0		0	0
Quiet street (QS)	+1	+1	0	0		0
Newly built house (NBH)	0	+1	−1	0	0	
Total weight	(+2)	(+5)	(−3)	(−2)	(−2)	(0)

executive who rated 34 European cities on 12 business-related criteria.[87]

No matter how you gather the information, once you have it, the key is to use that information systematically to evaluate each alternative against each criterion. Exhibit 5.6 shows how each of the 10 cities on your staff's list fared with respect to each of the 12 criteria (higher scores are better), from qualified staff to freedom from pollution. Although London has the most qualified staff, the best access to markets and telecommunications, and is the easiest city to travel to and from, it is also one of the most polluted and expensive cities on the list. Paris offers excellent access to markets and clients, but if your staff is multi-lingual, Brussels might be a better choice.

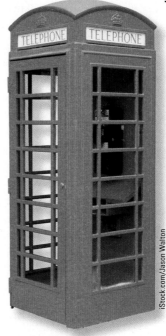

iStock.com/Jason Walton

5-4f Compute the Optimal Decision

The final step in the decision-making process is to compute the optimal decision by determining the optimal value of each alternative. This is done by multiplying the rating for each criterion (Step 5-4e) by the weight for that criterion (Step 5-4c), and then summing those scores for each alternative course of action that you generated (Step 5-4d). For example, the 500 executives participating in Cushman & Wakefield's survey of the best European cities for business rated the 12 decision criteria in terms of importance, as shown in the first row of Exhibit 5.6. Access to markets, qualified staff, telecommunications, and easy travel to and from the city

Exhibit 5.6
Criteria Ratings Used to Determine the Best Location for a New Office

Criteria Weights:	Access to Markets 0.60	Qualified Staff 0.53	Telecom- munications 0.52	Easy to Travel to/from City 0.42	Cost & Value of Office Space 0.33	Cost of Staff 0.32	Available Office Space 0.25	Languages Spoken 0.21	Business Climate 0.20	Travel within City 0.20	Quality of Life 0.16	Freedom from Pollution 0.16	Weighted Average	Ranking
Amsterdam	0.42	0.40	0.39	0.68	0.30	0.19	0.30	0.96	0.47	0.34	0.44	0.63	1.72	5
Barcelona	0.23	0.32	0.16	0.29	0.52	0.59	0.52	0.23	0.31	0.47	1.08	0.42	1.45	8
Berlin	0.44	0.39	0.41	0.35	0.78	0.40	0.79	0.50	0.34	0.78	0.38	0.29	1.85	4
Brussels	0.46	0.43	0.37	0.48	0.44	0.17	0.42	0.98	0.37	0.29	0.41	0.27	1.65	7
Dusseldorf	0.30	0.30	0.23	0.21	0.37	0.14	0.28	0.18	0.17	0.22	0.20	0.26	0.97	10
Frankfurt	0.68	0.57	0.70	1.17	0.38	0.11	0.44	0.57	0.38	0.35	0.17	0.18	2.16	3
London	1.50	1.36	1.27	1.79	0.27	0.10	0.42	1.48	0.55	1.26	0.46	0.15	4.03	1
Madrid	0.45	0.46	0.27	0.41	0.52	0.61	0.67	0.22	0.29	0.53	0.67	0.13	1.70	6
Munich	0.34	0.47	0.48	0.37	0.18	0.03	0.18	0.30	0.22	0.47	0.62	0.57	1.36	9
Paris	1.09	0.84	0.89	1.36	0.22	0.10	0.37	0.58	0.30	1.07	0.52	0.12	2.83	2

Source: "European Cities Monitor 2011," *Cushman & Wakefield*, 2011, accessed 27 May 2013. http://www.berlin-partner.de/fileadmin/user_upload/01_chefredaktion/02 _pdf/studien-rankings/2011/Cushman%20&%20Wakefield%20-%20European%20Cities%20Monitor%20%282011%20english%29.pdf

were the four most important factors, while quality of life and freedom from pollution were the least important factors. To calculate the optimal value for Paris, the weight for each category is multiplied by its score in each category (.53 × .84 in the qualified staff category, for example). Then all of these scores are added together to produce the optimal value, as follows:

$$(.60 \times 1.09) + (.53 \times .84) + (.52 \times .89) +$$
$$(.42 \times 1.36) + (.33 \times .22) + (.32 \times .10) +$$
$$(.25 \times .37) + (.21 \times .58) + (.20 \times .30) +$$
$$(.20 \times 1.07) + (.16 \times .52) + (.16 \times .12) = 2.83$$

Because London has a weighted average of 4.03 compared to 2.83 for Paris and 2.16 for Frankfurt (the cities with the next-best ratings), London clearly ranks as the best location for your company's new European office because of its large number of qualified staff; easy access to markets; outstanding ease of travel to, from, and within the city; excellent telecommunications; and top-notch business climate.

5-4g Limits to Rational Decision-Making

In general, managers who diligently complete all six steps of the rational decision-making model will make better decisions than those who don't. So, when they can, managers should try to follow the steps in the rational decision-making model, especially for big decisions with long-range consequences. Chapter 17, "Managing Information," also addresses the limits of rational decisions, but does so by examining how models and algorithms can help managers make better, faster decisions (see Section 17-4c on sharing knowledge and expertise).

To make completely rational decisions, managers would have to operate in a perfect world with no real-world constraints. Of course, it never actually works like that in the real world. Managers face time and money constraints. They often don't have time to make extensive lists of decision criteria. And they often don't have the resources to test all possible solutions against all possible criteria.

In theory, fully rational decision makers **maximize** decisions by choosing the optimal solution. In practice, however, limited resources along with attention, memory, and expertise problems make it nearly impossible for managers to maximize decisions. Consequently, most managers don't maximize—they satisfice. Whereas maximizing is choosing the

Maximize choosing the best alternative

Satisficing choosing a "good-enough" alternative

best alternative, **satisficing** is choosing a "good-enough" alternative.

In the opening to this section, your boss comes to you asking for a recommendation on the best options for the company's social media strategy. With so many options and the fast pace of change, deciding isn't easy. In other words, there's no optimal solution that will satisfy all criteria. For instance, if you're trying to increase your search rankings, you should use Facebook and YouTube, both of which are directly linked to Facebook and Google search algorithms. If you're interested in providing customer support, then pay close attention to what your customers are saying on Facebook and Twitter, and reach out to them when they're having problems or are dissatisfied. If your target market is teenagers, use Instagram and SnapChat. If it is young single women ages 18–25, use Facebook, SnapChat, or Instagram. If it's married women ages 25–35, use Pinterest and Instagram. If reaching out directly to consumers, use Pinterest and Facebook, but if reaching out to businesses, use LinkedIn and Twitter. Finally, if your strategy focuses on visual content, use Pinterest and Instagram; if your intent is to demonstrate what your product or service does, use YouTube; and if you've got detailed, complex knowledge, use Twitter and blogs.[88] Your decision will be complete when you find a "good-enough alternative" that does the best job of meeting your decision criteria.

5-5 USING GROUPS TO IMPROVE DECISION-MAKING

A survey of 2,044 human resources and organizational leaders found that 84 percent of companies used teams for special projects, while 74 percent used teams to address departmental issues and innovation.[89] In other words, groups were used to solve problems and make decisions. Companies rely so heavily on groups to make decisions because when done properly, group decision-making can lead to much better decisions than those typically made by individuals. In fact, numerous studies show that groups consistently outperform individuals on complex tasks.

*Let's explore the **5-5a advantages and pitfalls of group decision-making** and see how the following group decision-making methods—**5-5b structured conflict, 5-5c the nominal group technique, 5-5d the Delphi technique,** and **5-5e electronic brainstorming**—can be used to improve decision-making.*

5-5a Advantages and Pitfalls of Group Decision-Making

Groups can do a much better job than individuals in two important steps of the decision-making process: defining the problem and generating alternative solutions. Still, group decision-making is subject to some pitfalls that can quickly erase these gains. One possible pitfall is groupthink. **Groupthink** occurs in highly cohesive groups when group members feel intense pressure to agree with each other so that the group can approve a proposed solution.[90] Because groupthink leads to consideration of a limited number of solutions and restricts discussion of any considered solutions, it usually results in poor decisions. Groupthink is most likely to occur under the following conditions:

» The group is insulated from others with different perspectives.

» The group leader begins by expressing a strong preference for a particular decision.

» The group has no established procedure for systematically defining problems and exploring alternatives.

» Group members have similar backgrounds and experiences.[91]

A second potential problem with group decision-making is that it takes considerable time. Reconciling schedules so that group members can meet takes time. Furthermore, it's a rare group that consistently holds productive, task-oriented meetings to effectively work through the decision-making process. Some of the most common complaints about meetings (and thus group decision-making) are that the meeting's purpose is unclear, participants are unprepared, critical people are absent or late, conversation doesn't stay focused on the problem, and no one follows up on the decisions that were made.

A third possible pitfall to group decision-making is that sometimes one or two people, perhaps the boss or a strong-willed, vocal group member, can dominate group discussions and limit the group's consideration of different problem definitions and alternative solutions. This may be more likely to happen when subject matter experts are part of groups. The pitfall is that subject matter experts dominate and limit group discussion as non-experts in the group defer to "expert" judgment. Doing so often results in much poorer quality decisions.[92] And, unlike individual decisions where people feel personally responsible for making a good choice, another potential problem is that group members may not feel accountable for the decisions made and actions taken by the group.

"Today's theme is 'Getting Beyond Group Think.'"

Ironically, a fourth pitfall to group decision-making is equality bias, which causes individuals to treat all group members as equally competent. More highly competent people tend to underestimate their abilities, while less competent people overestimate theirs. A recent study showed that even though the more competent person in a pair of study participants was correct over 70 percent of the time, the more competent person would agree to the less competent partner's decision roughly 40 percent of the time. Likewise, the less competent person in the pair would agree with the more competent partner's choice only 50 percent of the time, even though the other person was correct over 70 percent of the time. Study author Professor Bahudar Bahrami noted, "Even when we showed them exactly how competent they each were, they still gave each other more or less equal say. Incredibly, this still continued when people were rewarded with real money for making correct decisions." Bahrami suggests two key reasons for equality bias. First, individuals do not want to exclude the other group members by asserting their competence. Second, individuals may be reluctant to take responsibility for group decisions.[93]

Although these pitfalls can lead to poor decision-making, this doesn't mean that managers should avoid using groups to make decisions. When done properly, group decision-making can lead to much better decisions. The pitfalls of group decision-making are not inevitable. Managers can overcome most of them by using the various techniques described next.

5-5b Structured Conflict

Most people view conflict negatively. Professor Charlan Nemeth, author of *In Defense of Trouble-makers: The Power of*

> **Groupthink** a barrier to good decision-making caused by pressure within the group for members to agree with each other

Dissent in Life and Business, explains, "Most people are afraid and they don't speak up. Companies have that problem all the time. And the research really shows us that that even if it's wrong, the fact that the majority or the consensus is challenged actually stimulates thinking."[94] Yet the right kind of conflict can lead to much better group decision-making. There are two basic kinds of conflict.

C-type conflict, or "cognitive conflict," focuses on problem- and issue-related differences of opinion.[95] In c-type conflict, group members disagree because their different experiences and expertise lead them to view the problem and its potential solutions differently. C-type conflict is also characterized by a willingness to examine, compare, and reconcile those differences to produce the best possible solution. Victor Ho, the CEO and co-founder of **Five Stars**, a customer loyalty network for small and medium businesses, who worked for **McKinsey & Company**, a global consulting firm, said, "The strongest lesson I learned at McKinsey that I now share with every new hire is what they call the 'obligation to dissent.' It means that the youngest, most junior person in any given meeting is the most capable to disagree with the most senior person in the room."[96] **Netflix** CEO Reed Hastings says, "We want people to speak the truth and we say, 'To disagree silently is disloyal. It's not OK to let a decision go through without saying your piece. We're very focused on trying to get good decisions with a good debate."[97]

By contrast, **a-type conflict**, meaning "affective conflict," refers to the emotional reactions that can occur when disagreements become personal rather than professional. A-type conflict often results in hostility, anger, resentment, distrust, cynicism, and apathy. Unlike c-type conflict, a-type conflict undermines team effectiveness by preventing teams from engaging in the activities characteristic of c-type conflict that are critical to team effectiveness. Examples of a-type conflict statements are "your idea," "our idea," "my department," "you don't know what you are talking about," or "you don't understand our situation."

Rather than focusing on issues and ideas, these statements focus on individuals.[98]

The **devil's advocacy** approach can be used to create c-type conflict by assigning an individual or a subgroup the role of critic. The following five steps establish a devil's advocacy program:

1. Generate a potential solution.

2. Assign a devil's advocate to criticize and question the solution.

3. Present the critique of the potential solution to key decision makers.

4. Gather additional relevant information.

5. Decide whether to use, change, or not use the originally proposed solution.[99]

When properly used, the devil's advocacy approach introduces c-type conflict into the decision-making process. Contrary to the common belief that conflict is bad, studies show that these methods lead not only to less a-type conflict but also to improved decision quality and greater acceptance of decisions after they have been made.[100] **Ariel Investments**, which was recently ranked the best investment fund for mid-cap stocks, assigns a devil's advocate for each investing decision. Timothy Fidler, Ariel's director of research and co-manager of the Ariel Appreciation Fund, says, "The devil's advocate role ensures that arguments [about investing decisions] are fresh."[101] Each member of Ariel's investment teams takes turns as the devil's advocate. Says Fidler, "We get along well as a team, so we assign the devil's advocate's job because it enables that person to yell and argue."[102]

Another method of creating c-type conflict is **dialectical inquiry**, which creates c-type conflict by forcing decision makers to state the assumptions of a proposed solution (a thesis) and then generate a solution that is the opposite (antithesis) of the proposed solution. The five steps of the dialectical inquiry process are:

1. Generate a potential solution.

2. Identify the assumptions underlying the potential solution.

3. Generate a conflicting counterproposal based on the opposite assumptions.

4. Have advocates of each position present their arguments and engage in a debate in front of key decision makers.

5. Decide whether to use, change, or not use the originally proposed solution.[103]

C-type conflict (cognitive conflict) disagreement that focuses on problem- and issue-related differences of opinion

A-type conflict (affective conflict) disagreement that focuses on individuals or personal issues

Devil's advocacy a decision-making method in which an individual or a subgroup is assigned the role of critic

Dialectical inquiry a decision-making method in which decision makers state the assumptions of a proposed solution (a thesis) and generate a solution that is the opposite (antithesis) of that solution

5-5c Nominal Group Technique

Nominal means "in name only." Accordingly, the **nominal group technique** (NGT) received its name because it begins with a quiet time in which group members independently write down as many problem definitions and alternative solutions as possible. In other words, the NGT begins by having group members act as individuals. After the quiet time, the group leader asks each member to share one idea at a time with the group. As they are read aloud, ideas are posted on flip charts or wallboards for all to see. This step continues until all ideas have been shared. In the next step, the group discusses the advantages and disadvantages of the ideas. The NGT closes with a second quiet time in which group members independently rank the ideas presented. Group members then read their rankings aloud, and the idea with the highest average rank is selected.[104]

IBM manager Phil Gilbert used the NGT when his team developed a new email tool called IBM Verse. Instead of instructing them to come up with the next big thing in email, Gilbert had them spend 10 minutes quietly writing down what they disliked about email on sticky notes—one idea per note, and no talking. As people finished writing, they stuck their notes on a big whiteboard until there weren't any more to post. The team leader then organized the sticky notes into logical groupings for review. Then the team left (Gilbert says sometimes briefly or for days). When they returned to the whiteboard, they brought additional ideas. Regarding the NGT process, Gilbert says, "It makes for better teams, and it leads to better outcomes. When you give voice to more people, the best ideas win, not the loudest ones."[105]

The nominal group technique improves group decision-making by decreasing a-type conflict. But it also restricts c-type conflict. Consequently, the nominal group technique typically produces poorer decisions than the devil's advocacy and dialectical inquiry approaches. Nonetheless, more than 80 studies have found that nominal groups produce better ideas than those produced by traditional groups.[106]

5-5d Delphi Technique

In the **Delphi technique**, the members of a panel of experts respond to questions and to each other until reaching agreement on an issue. The first step is to assemble a panel of experts. Unlike other approaches to group decision-making, however, it isn't necessary to bring the panel members together in one place. Because the Delphi technique does not require the experts to leave their offices or disrupt their schedules, they are more likely to participate.

The second step is to create a questionnaire consisting of a series of open-ended questions for the group. In the third step, the group members' written responses are analyzed, summarized, and fed back to the group for reactions until the members reach agreement. Asking group members why they agree or disagree is important because it helps uncover their unstated assumptions and beliefs. Again, this process of summarizing panel feedback and obtaining reactions to that feedback continues until the panel members reach agreement.

5-5e Electronic Brainstorming

Brainstorming, in which group members build on others' ideas, is a technique for generating a large number of alternative solutions. Brainstorming has four rules:

1. The more ideas, the better.

2. All ideas are acceptable, no matter how wild or crazy they might seem.

3. Other group members' ideas should be used to come up with even more ideas.

4. Criticism or evaluation of ideas is not allowed.

Although brainstorming is great fun and can help managers generate a large number of alternative solutions, it does have a number of disadvantages. Fortunately, **electronic brainstorming**, in which group members use computers to communicate and generate alternative solutions,

Nominal group technique a decision-making method that begins and ends by having group members quietly write down and evaluate ideas to be shared with the group

Delphi technique a decision-making method in which members of a panel of experts respond to questions and to each other until reaching agreement on an issue

Brainstorming a decision-making method in which group members build on each others' ideas to generate as many alternative solutions as possible

Electronic brainstorming a decision-making method in which group members use computers to build on each others' ideas and generate as many alternative solutions as possible

Maximize Your Life Decisions Using a Spreadsheet

Maximizers, according to the *Wall Street Journal's* Elizabeth Bernstein, "like to take their time and weigh a wide range of options—sometimes every possible one—before choosing." Satisficers, on the other hand, "would rather be fast than thorough; they prefer to quickly choose the option that fills the minimum criteria."

Most of us are satisficers. But should we really make major life decisions based on what meets "minimum criteria?" Probably not. When it comes to the decisions that matter, it is in your best interest to weigh the costs and benefits of all available choices. This may sound like a daunting task, but a simple spreadsheet can help you evaluate your alternatives quickly and easily.

Suppose you're looking for a new apartment. First, list the criteria you're looking for (location, cost, spaciousness) in the left-hand column and list your various alternatives at the top. As you gather information, rate each alternative against the criteria on a scale of 1–5

(1 being worst and 5 being best). Psychologist Fjola Helgadottir has used this spreadsheet method to "run 4 marathons, climb Mt Kilimanjaro, travel the world, and complete 4 university degrees." Likewise, Terese Lawry and Jacob Falkovich used a spreadsheet with 22 weighted criteria for deciding which apartment to rent in New York City. Falkovich said, "Without weighting criteria, people just start being like, 'I refuse to live without a dishwasher.' How much is it worth for you —– $100 a month, $200 a month?" For example, Falkovich was willing to walk up three flights of stairs, byut Lawry countered by asking whether that would work when they had children. The compromise? An elevator was weighted 4 of 10, compared to 10 for apartment size and 1 for in-house laundry. The two-bedroom, two-bathroom apartment they rented scored 238 in their spreadsheet, compared to 180 to 215 for other apartments. Falkovich concluded, "When I tell people about the [decision] matrix, their intuition is that I'm outsourcing my heart. But my heart is confused. I need to put my desires in a more organized structure. Goal factoring and decision matrices help you realize what's missing and what you care about." What could a spreadsheet help you decide to do with your life?

Sources: K. Velsey, "The Best Way to Pick an Apartment? Try a Decision Matrix," *New York Times*, accessed March 1, 2020, https://www.nytimes.com/2020/01/06/realestate /the-best-way-to-pick-an-apartment-try-a-decision-matrix.html; F. Helgadottir, "How Excel Can Help You Achieve Goals," The *AI-Therapy Blog*, August 27, 2012, accessed May 7, 2016, https://www.ai-therapy.com/blog/how-excel-can-help-you-achieve-goals/; R. Sanghani, "How Excel Spreadsheets Can Help You Make Major Life Decisions," *The Telegraph*, January 4, 2016, accessed May 7, 2016, http://www.telegraph.co.uk /women/life/how-excel-spreadsheets-can-help-you-make-major-life-decisions/; E. Bernstein, "How You Make Decisions Says a Lot About How Happy You Are," *Wall Street Journal*, October 6, 2014, accessed May 7, 2016, http://www.wsj.com/articles /how-you-make-decisions-says-a-lot-about-how-happy-you-are-1412614997.

overcomes the disadvantages associated with face-to-face brainstorming.[107]

The first disadvantage that electronic brainstorming overcomes is **production blocking**, which occurs when you have an idea but have to wait to share it because someone else is already presenting an idea to the group. During this short delay, you may forget your idea or decide that it really wasn't worth sharing. Production blocking doesn't happen with electronic brainstorming. All group members are seated at computers, so everyone can type in ideas whenever they occur. There's no waiting for your turn to be heard by the group.

The second disadvantage that electronic brainstorming overcomes is **evaluation apprehension**, that is, being afraid of what others will think of your ideas. An employee suffering from evaluation apprehension described this incident: "...for the thousandth time, I was in a meeting where I thought I had a great solution to a complicated problem my team is facing, and I was right. How do I know? Because I didn't say a word, but the guy sitting next to me suggested the same thing I was thinking – and, as a result, got put in charge of a project I'd love to have been assigned."[108]

Production blocking a disadvantage of face-to-face brainstorming in which a group member must wait to share an idea because another member is presenting an idea

Evaluation apprehension fear of what others will think of your ideas

With electronic brainstorming, all ideas are anonymous. When you type in an idea and press the Enter key to share it with the group, group members see only the idea. Furthermore, many brainstorming software programs also protect anonymity by displaying ideas in random order. So, if you laugh maniacally while you type "Cut top management's pay by 50 percent!" and then press the Enter key, it won't show up immediately on everyone's screen. This makes it doubly difficult to determine who is responsible for which comments.

In the typical layout for electronic brainstorming, all participants sit in front of computers around a U-shaped table. This configuration allows them to see their computer screens, the other participants, a large main screen, and a meeting leader or facilitator. Step 1 in electronic brainstorming is to anonymously generate as many ideas as possible. Groups commonly generate 100 ideas in a half-hour period. Step 2 is to edit the generated ideas, categorize them, and eliminate redundancies. Step 3 is to rank the categorized ideas in terms of quality. Step 4, the last step, has three parts: generate a series of action steps, decide the best order for accomplishing these steps, and identify who is responsible for each step. All four steps are accomplished with computers and electronic brainstorming software.[109]

Studies show that electronic brainstorming is much more productive than face-to-face brainstorming. Four-person electronic brainstorming groups produce 25 to 50 percent more ideas than four-person regular brainstorming groups, and 12-person electronic brainstorming groups produce 200 percent more ideas than regular groups of the same size! In fact, because production blocking (having to wait your turn) is not a problem in electronic brainstorming, the number and quality of ideas generally increase with group size.[110]

Even though it works much better than traditional brainstorming, electronic brainstorming has disadvantages, too. An obvious problem is the expense of computers, networks, software, and other equipment. As these costs have dropped, however, electronic brainstorming has become cheaper.

Another problem is that the anonymity of ideas may bother people who are used to having their ideas accepted by virtue of their position (that is the boss). On the other hand, one CEO said, "Because the process is anonymous, the sky's the limit in terms of what you can say, and, as a result, it is more thought-provoking. As a CEO, you'll probably discover things you might not want to hear but need to be aware of."[111]

A third disadvantage is that outgoing individuals who are more comfortable expressing themselves verbally may find it difficult to express themselves in writing. Finally, the most obvious problem is that participants have to be able to type. Those who can't type, or who type slowly, may be easily frustrated and find themselves at a disadvantage compared to experienced typists.

6 | Organizational Strategy

LEARNING OUTCOMES

6-1 Explain the steps for creating a sustainable competitive advantage and why having such an advantage is so important.

6-2 Describe the steps involved in the strategy-making process.

6-3 Explain the different kinds of corporate-level strategies and when each should be used.

6-4 Describe the different kinds of industry-level strategies and how they affect competition.

6-5 Explain the components and kinds of firm-level strategies and the ways in which firms attack competitors or respond to competitive attacks.

courtneyk/E+/Getty Images

6-1 SUSTAINABLE COMPETITIVE ADVANTAGE

If you wake up each morning by turning off the morning alarm on your smartphone/tablet and then—device in hand—immediately check your email, news, sports scores or social media, well, you're just like billions of people around the world. And if the smartphone or tablet you're using is an Apple iPhone or iPad, know that there are 1.5 billion other iPhones and iPads used every day.[1] It is not an understatement to argue that Apple's introductions of the iPhone in 2007 and the iPad in 2010 transformed the tech industry, if not the world. The iPhone alone devastated Blackberry, Nokia, and Motorola, which once dominated cell phones sales, as well as digital camera makers, whose sales fell from 121 million in 2010 to 15.2 million in 2019.[2] Apple's success, however, brought new competitors as Samsung, Oppo, and Google sold smartphones and tablets using Google's Android operating system. While the iPhone holds just 20 percent

of the global smartphone market and the iPad has 37 percent of the global tablet market, Apple earns 70 to 90 percent of industry profits.[3] Because of that dominance, Apple's annual profit surged from $2 billion in 2006 to $53.5 billion in 2015.[4] But, on average, Apple's enormous profits have not risen since 2015.[5] Apple's days of double digit growth may be over now that half the people on Earth wake up with smartphones.[6]

While still one of the most profitable businesses in the world, how can a company like Apple, which dominates a particular industry, maintain its competitive advantage against strong, well-financed competitors? What steps can Apple and other companies take to better manage their strategy-making process?

Resources are the assets, capabilities, processes, employee time, information, and knowledge that an organization controls. Firms use their resources to improve organizational effectiveness and efficiency. Resources are critical to organizational strategy because they can help companies create and sustain an advantage over competitors.[7]

> **Resources** the assets, capabilities, processes, employee time, information, and knowledge that an organization uses to improve its effectiveness and efficiency and create and sustain competitive advantage

Organizations can achieve a **competitive advantage** by using their resources to provide greater value for customers than competitors can. The goal of most organizational strategies is to create and then sustain a competitive advantage. A competitive advantage becomes a **sustainable competitive advantage** when other companies cannot duplicate the value a firm is providing to customers. Sustainable competitive advantage is *not* the same as a long-lasting competitive advantage, though companies obviously want a competitive advantage to last a long time. Instead, a competitive advantage is *sustained* if competitors have tried unsuccessfully to duplicate the advantage and have, for the moment, stopped trying to duplicate it. It's the corporate equivalent of your competitors saying, "We give up. You win. We can't do what you do, and we're not even going to try to do it anymore." Four conditions must be met if a firm's resources are to be used to achieve a sustainable competitive advantage. The resources must be valuable, rare, imperfectly imitable, *and* nonsubstitutable.

Valuable resources allow companies to improve their efficiency and effectiveness. Unfortunately, changes in customer demand and preferences, competitors' actions, and technology can make once-valuable resources much less valuable. For example, the iPhone and iPad's initial competitive advantage came largely from their sleek, attractive designs, then-unique touchscreens, the intuitive easy-to-use iOS operating system, and a large selection of apps via the centralized and secure App Store in which independent **Apple** software developers have sold $155 billion worth of apps since 2008.[8] But, today, all of these features are available from Apple's competitors in similar products for much less than what Apple charges. In other words, unlike in 2007 and 2010 when the iPhone and iPad were introduced, these features by themselves are now commonplace and no longer provide Apple a competitive advantage.[9]

For sustained competitive advantage, valuable resources must also be rare resources. Think about it: How can a company sustain a competitive advantage if all of its competitors have similar resources and capabilities? Consequently, **rare resources**, resources that are not controlled or possessed by many competing firms, are necessary to sustain a competitive advantage. Today, Apple's most valuable resources are not found in its product designs or features (touchscreen, intuitive, and easy-to-use, etc.), but in the seamless way in which Apple's products and services work together. Apple is the only tech company that designs and controls its own hardware *and* software, thus ensuring that they are not only custom built for each other but that all of its hardware and software products work seamlessly together. This integration strategy rests on Apple's ability to use its core capabilities in hardware *and* software design to create more value for the customer who owns nothing but Apple gear.[10]

For example, consider the iPhone user who buys an Apple Watch because it shares and syncs health data, reminders, messages, podcasts, music and apps with the iPhone. Or the Apple customer who buys Apple's wireless AirPods, which seamlessly pair with the iPad, iPhone, Mac computers, Apple TV, and Apple Watch. Contrast that with someone in the Android/Windows world who buys an Android phone from Google, an Android watch from Oppo, a Dell PC running Windows 10, a Windows tablet, an Amazon TV device, and Samsung Galaxy Buds (wireless earbuds).[11] Which consumer will have an easier time getting their technology to work together?[12] A clear sign of the success of Apple's integration strategy and the value it holds for Apple customers is that in just five years its "wearables" business, meaning the Apple Watch and AirPods, has grown to "the size of a Fortune 150 company" worth roughly $21 billion a year in annual revenue and 10 percent of Apple's profits.[13] Likewise, the services side of Apple's integration strategy produces $46 billion a year in annual revenue and 20+ percent of Apple's profits. Services revenue comes from Apple customers who pay monthly or yearly subscriptions for Apple Music, Apple Arcade, Apple News Plus, and iCloud storage, or who purchase apps from the App Store or use Apple Pay to make secure purchases.[14]

Valuable and rare resources can create temporary competitive advantage. For sustained competitive advantage, however, other firms must be unable to imitate or find substitutes for those valuable, rare resources. **Imperfectly imitable resources** are those resources that are impossible or extremely costly or difficult to duplicate. Microsoft, Google, Amazon, and other Apple competitors buy standard "off the shelf" computer chips from Intel and other chipmakers. Because they all use the same chip architectures, none has an advantage with the "digital engines" that power their devices. By contrast, for over a decade, Apple's semiconductor team has designed the unique chips used in Apple iPhones, the latest being the A13 Bionic chip used in iPhone 11s. Why does this matter in terms of strategy? Because it would take billions in investment and 5 to 10 years for competitors to catch up. Because the A13 chips are faster than the off-the-shelf chips from traditional semiconductor companies and provide an extra five hours of battery life per day.[15] Because Apple takes the chips first designed for iPhones and then reuses them in other devices, such as iPads, Apple TVs, and Apple Watches.

Furthermore, Apple paid $1 billion to acquire Intel's smartphone modem-chip business. Instead of continuing to buy smartphone modems from Qualcomm and Intel (prior to the acquisition), this gives Apple in-house control to design and manufacture custom 4G and 5G modems just for iPhones and iPads.[16] As with its A13 chips, the goal is to develop smaller, more powerful, and more efficient smartphone modems that extend battery life, which is another imperfectly imitable resource that would be extremely costly and difficult for Apple's competitors to match.

Valuable, rare, imperfectly imitable resources can produce sustainable competitive advantage only if they are also **nonsubstitutable resources**, meaning that no other resources can replace them and produce similar value or competitive advantage. From 2007 to 2012, Google Maps was the iPhone's dominant navigation app. Nothing else on the iPhone provided the simple, accurate, easy-to-use navigation found in Google Maps.[17] With 7,000 people working on Google Maps as "street view drivers, people flying planes, people drawing maps, people correcting listings, and people building new products," Google Maps was a nonsubstitutable navigation resource on the iPhone.[18] Apple set out to change that in 2012 when it released Apple Maps for iOS. However, it was so bad and inaccurate that CEO Tim Cook apologized, telling iPhone owners to use other maps while Apple Maps was being fixed.[19] By June 2015, after acquiring a number of mapping software companies, fixing incorrect map data, and better matching the functionality found in Google Maps, Apple reported that iPhone owners used the Apple Maps app 5 billion times per week, 3.5 times more than Google Maps.[20] In 2018, Apple sent thousands of vans with ground-level lidar scanners onto roads all over the world to create new, highly detailed maps that were in some ways better than Google's.[21] The "new" Apple Maps, rolled out in 2019 and 2020, has new features like Look Around (similar to Google Street View), Share ETA, which automatically shares your arrival time with whomever you designate, real-time transit data, and directions for subways and buses, flight status information automatically detected in Apple Mail, Wallet, and Calendar that displays departure time, and terminal and gate locations.[22] Does this mean that Apple Maps has a sustainable competitive advantage over Google Maps? No. But it does mean that Apple Maps is an increasingly good substitute for Google Maps, and that Google Maps may be losing its sustainable competitive advantage among iPhone users.[23]

In summary, Apple reaped the early rewards of a first-mover advantage when it introduced the iPhone and iPad. However, if you want a tablet or smartphone with a touchscreen, easy-to-use operating system, and a large selection of apps, Apple's competitors now sell them for much less. Today, Apple's competitive advantage is based on an integration strategy in which all of Apple's products work better together (i.e., fast-growing services and "wearables"), as well as the in-house design and manufacture of imperfectly imitable computer chips and modems that maximize the speed, battery life, and functions of Apple products. These strategic moves are incredibly difficult and expensive for competitors to duplicate. However, as demonstrated by the stumble of Apple Maps; its weakness in China, where it has just 12 percent of the market; its cost-prohibitive prices in fast-growing markets like India; and its overreliance on stagnant iPhone sales, which make up two-thirds of its profits, Apple faces significant challenges.[24] Apple needs to continue developing and improving its products and services or risk losing its sustainable competitive advantage to global competitors intent on unseating its market leadership.

 # STRATEGY-MAKING PROCESS

To create a sustainable competitive advantage, a company must have a strategy.[25] Exhibit 6.1 displays the three steps of the strategy-making process:

6-2a assess the need for strategic change, 6-2b conduct a situational analysis, and then **6-2c choose strategic alternatives.** Let's examine each of these steps in more detail.

Nonsubstitutable resource a resource that produces value or competitive advantage and has no equivalent substitutes or replacements

6-2a Assessing the Need for Strategic Change

The external business environment is much more turbulent than it used to be. With customers' needs constantly growing and changing, and with competitors working harder, faster, and smarter to meet those needs, the first step in creating a strategy is determining the need for strategic change. In other words, the company should determine whether it needs to change its strategy to sustain a competitive advantage.[26]

Determining the need for strategic change might seem easy to do, but it's really not. There's a great deal of uncertainty in strategic business environments. Furthermore, top-level managers are often slow to recognize the need for strategic change, especially at successful companies that have created and sustained competitive advantages. Because they are acutely aware of the strategies that made their companies successful, they continue to rely on those strategies, even as the competition changes. In other words, success often leads to **competitive inertia**—a reluctance to change strategies or competitive practices that have been successful in the past.

HBO has produced some of the best and edgiest multiyear TV series, such as *The Sopranos*, *Sex and the City*, *The Wire*, and *Game of Thrones*. For four decades HBO dominated cable/satellite TV in terms of viewers, revenue, and Emmy awards. That long-term success, however, led to competitive inertia that resulted in HBO largely missing the dramatic shift to TV streaming services. Jamyn Edis, former vice president of HBO, said that "long-term contracts written before the dawn of digital," "30-year career executives with no incentive" to change, and an attitude characterized as "an institutional distaste for technology – [because] 'we're in the content business,'" all prevented HBO from recognizing the need for strategic change.[27] Early on, HBO broadly considered asking its corporate owner Time Warner, now **Warner Media, LLC**, to buy Netflix for $1 billion. Then Chief Information Officer Michael Gabriel said the idea was shot down: "There was a belief that Netflix was going to implode either due to the escalating costs with the [business] model or due to content no longer being licensed to them."[28] HBO made two attempts, neither with much financial support or top management commitment, to develop streaming services. HBO Go, for existing cable TV subscribers, famously crashed during a *Game of Thrones* season premiere. HBO Now, for new customers who wanted access via streaming, eventually earned 8 million subscribers in 2019 – compared to 167 million for Netflix.[29] HBO Max, HBO's third attempt at a streaming service, launched in May 2020, but only after a significant corporate shakeup which saw its longtime CEO leave.[30]

Besides being aware of the dangers of competitive inertia, what can managers do to improve the speed and accuracy with which they determine the need for strategic change? One method is to actively look for signs of strategic dissonance. **Strategic dissonance** is a discrepancy between a company's intended strategy and the strategic actions managers take when actually implementing that strategy.[31]

Brian Halligan, founder of **HubSpot**, a software services company that provides marketing, sales, and

Competitive inertia a reluctance to change strategies or competitive practices that have been successful in the past

Strategic dissonance a discrepancy between a company's intended strategy and the strategic actions managers take when implementing that strategy.

Exhibit 6.1
Three Steps of the Strategy-Making Process

Step 1	Step 2	Step 3
Assess Need for Strategic Change.	Conduct Situational Analysis.	Choose Strategic Alternatives.

Step 1:
- Avoid Competitive Inertia.
- Look for Strategic Dissonance (Are strategic actions consistent with the company's strategic intent?).

Step 2:
INTERNAL ENVIRONMENT
- Strengths
  - Distinctive Competence
  - Core Capability
- Weaknesses

EXTERNAL ENVIRONMENT
- Opportunities
  - Environmental Scanning
  - Strategic Groups
  - Shadow-Strategy Task Force
- Threats

Step 3:
- Risk-Avoiding Strategies
- Strategic Reference Points
- Risk-Seeking Strategies

HBO NOW, a stand-alone streaming service, was introduced for customers who want access to HBO movies and shows, but do not have a cable TV package.

service "hubs" for companies, says "When HubSpot was in its earliest stages, I used to say yes to almost anything: new features, new initiatives, new ideas. It empowered my team to move fast and get things done."[32] But as the company grew, saying yes to everything often scattered peoples' time and efforts on nonstrategic actions. Lorrie Norrington, a HubSpot board member, told him, "You have half-baked projects all over the place. You need to add the word no to your management vocabulary."[33] To make sure that new ideas line up with HubSpot's intended strategy, they must include a project proposal that follows a one-page "MSPOT" format. Halligan says with MSPOT, "We articulate our **M**ission, the constituencies we **S**erve, the **P**lays we're going to run this year, the plays we are going to **O**mit, and how we will **T**rack our progress."[34] The most painful

HubSpot's employees must follow the MSPOT format when submitting ideas, to ensure projects align with the company's strategy.

and important are omissions, which Halligan says "are usually excellent ideas with high potential" that we should *not* do "because we are better off doing [just] a few [strategic] things well."[35]

Note, however, that strategic dissonance is not the same thing as when a strategy does not produce the results that it's supposed to. **Airbus** created the wide-body, double-decker A380, the largest passenger jet in the world capable of flying 853 passengers. The idea was that airlines would use the A380 for their most profitable, heavily traveled, long-haul international flights. But even with low jet fuel prices, the A380 is expensive to operate, which means it has to fly as full as possible to cover costs. So, airlines canceled orders and leases for the A380. Airbus delivered 27 planes in 2016, 14 in 2017, 12 in 2018 and just 8 in 2019.[36] Production of the A380 will stop in 2021. Airbus CEO Tom Enders said, "If you have a product that nobody wants anymore or you can only sell below production costs, you have to stop it, as painful as it is."[37]

6-2b Situational Analysis

A situational analysis can also help managers determine the need for strategic change. A **situational analysis**, also called a **SWOT analysis**, for *strengths, weaknesses, opportunities*, and *threats*, is an assessment of the strengths and weaknesses in an organization's internal environment and the opportunities and threats in its external environment.[38] Ideally, as shown in Step 2 of Exhibit 6.1, a SWOT analysis helps a company determine how to increase internal strengths and minimize internal weaknesses while maximizing external opportunities and minimizing external threats.

An analysis of an organization's internal environment, that is, a company's strengths and weaknesses, often begins with an assessment of its distinctive competencies and core capabilities. A **distinctive competence** is something that a company can make, do, or perform better than its competitors. For example, *Consumer Reports* magazine consistently ranks Porsche, Subaru, and Mazda cars as tops in quality, reliability, and owner satisfaction.[39] Similarly, *PC Magazine* ranked Intuit's TurboTax the best tax-preparation software for its user experience, thorough coverage of tax topics, and robust help resources.[40]

Situational (SWOT) analysis an assessment of the strengths and weaknesses in an organization's internal environment and the opportunities and threats in its external environment

Distinctive competence what a company can make, do, or perform better than its competitors

Shadow-Strategy Task Force

When looking for threats and opportunities, many managers focus on competitors in the external environment. Others, however, prefer to examine the internal environment through a **shadow-strategy task force**. This strategy involves a company actively seeking out its own weaknesses and then thinking like its competitors, trying to determine how they can be exploited for competitive advantage. To make sure that the task force challenges conventional thinking, its members should be independent-minded, come from a variety of company functions and levels, and have the access and authority to question the company's current strategic actions and intent.

Source: W. B. Werther, Jr., and J. L. Kerr, "The Shifting Sands of Competitive Advantage," *Business Horizons* (May–June 1995): 11–17.

Whereas distinctive competencies are tangible—for example, a product or service is faster, cheaper, or better—the core capabilities that produce distinctive competencies are not. **Core capabilities** are the less visible, internal decision-making routines, problem-solving processes, and organizational cultures that determine how efficiently inputs can be turned into outputs. Distinctive competencies cannot be sustained for long without superior core capabilities.

The distinctive competence of gourmet grocers like Earth Fare, Lucky's Market, and Fairway Market, or what they did better than competitors, was sell organic, imported, and unique foods not available at most grocery stores. Fairway Market says, "We were always first to offer unique, different, imported, things-you-didn't-know-existed foodstuffs."[41] Because larger grocery chains like Kroger and Whole Foods now sell the same foods for much less, Earth Fare, Lucky's, and Fairway have all filed for bankruptcy. Don Fitzgerald, a former merchandise manager at Kroger's Mariano's stores, says, "What was special 10 years ago isn't special anymore."[42] The core capability that Kroger, Aldi, and Whole Foods (owned by Amazon) have that the gourmet grocers do not is their sophisticated ordering and logistics systems to inexpensively source organic, imported, and unique foods. Andrew Erace, who closed his Green Aisle Grocery stores after Amazon bought Whole Foods, said, "I can't compete with that. I don't have the technology to implement for our small shops."

After examining internal strengths and weaknesses, the second part of a situational analysis is to look outside the company and assess the opportunities and threats in the external environment. In Chapter 3, you learned that *environmental scanning* involves searching the environment for important events or issues that might affect the organization, such as pricing trends or new products and technology. In situational analysis, however, managers use environmental scanning to identify specific opportunities and threats that can either improve or harm the company's ability to sustain its competitive advantage. Identification of strategic groups and formation of shadow-strategy task forces are two ways to do this (see box "Shadow-Strategy Task Force").

Strategic groups are not groups that actually work together. They are companies—usually competitors—that managers closely follow. More specifically, a **strategic group** is a group of other companies within an industry against which top managers compare, evaluate, and benchmark their company's strategic threats and opportunities.[43] (*Benchmarking* involves identifying outstanding practices, processes, and standards at other companies and adapting them to your own company.) Typically, managers include companies as part of their strategic group if they compete directly with those companies for customers or if those companies use strategies similar to theirs. The US home improvement industry has annual sales in excess of $405 billion. This market is divided into professional and consumer markets, both of which were forecast to grow roughly 4.1 percent in 2019.[44] It's likely that the managers at **The Home Depot**, the largest US home improvement and hardware retailer, assess strategic threats and opportunities by comparing their company to a strategic group consisting of the other major home improvement supply companies.

Shadow-strategy task force a committee within a company that analyzes the company's own weaknesses to determine how competitors could exploit them for competitive advantage

Core capabilities the internal decision-making routines, problem-solving processes, and organizational cultures that determine how efficiently inputs can be turned into outputs

Strategic group a group of companies within an industry against which top managers compare, evaluate, and benchmark strategic threats and opportunities

Exhibit 6.2

Core and Secondary Firms in the Home Improvement Industry

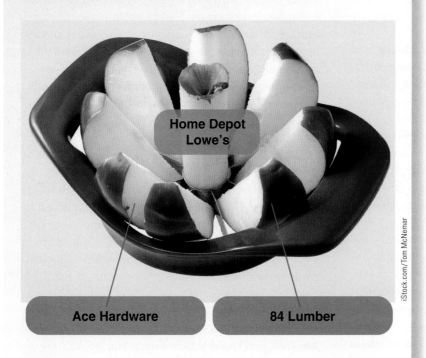

iStock.com/Tom McNemar

	# of Stores	# of States	Countries	Size of Typical Store (sq. feet)
Home Depot	2,291	50	3	104,000
Lowe's	1,977	50	2	112,000
Ace Hardware	5,366	50	65	10,000–14,000
84 Lumber	250	30	1	33,000

Exhibit 6.2 shows the number of stores, the size of the typical new store, and the overall geographic distribution (states, countries) of Home Depot stores compared with Lowe's, Ace Hardware, and 84 Lumber.

In fact, when scanning the environment for strategic threats and opportunities, managers tend to categorize the different companies in their industries as core, secondary, and transient firms.[45] **Core firms** are the central companies in a strategic group. The Home Depot operates 2,291 stores covering all 50 states, Puerto Rico, the US Virgin Islands, Guam, Mexico, and Canada. The company has more than 400,000 employees and annual revenues of $110 billion. By comparison, **Lowe's** has more than 1,977 stores and 300,000 employees in the United States and Canada; stocks about 36,000 products in

each store; and has annual revenues of $72 billion.[46] Clearly, Lowe's is the closest competitor to The Home Depot and is the core firm in Home Depot's strategic group. Even though **Ace Hardware** has more stores (5,366) than Home Depot and appears to be a bigger multinational player (65 different countries), Ace's different franchise structure and small, individualized stores (10,000–14,000 square feet, with each store laid out differently with a different mix of products) with 76,000 employees keep it from being a core firm in Home Depot's strategic group.[47] Likewise, Home Depot's management probably doesn't include Aubuchon Hardware in its core strategic group, because Aubuchon has only 100+ stores in New England and upstate New York.[48]

When most managers scan their environments for strategic threats and opportunities, they concentrate on the strategic actions of core firms, not unrelated firms such as Aubuchon. Where does a firm like Ace Hardware fit in? As a retailer-owned cooperative, Ace Hardware is a network of independently owned stores. Ace describes its strategy this way: "While other stores have become large and impersonal, at Ace, we've remained small and very personal."[49]

Secondary firms are firms that use strategies related to but somewhat different from those of core firms. **84 Lumber** has nearly 250 stores in 30+ states, but even though its stores are open to the public, the company focuses on supplying professional contractors, to whom it sells 85 percent of its products. Without the wide variety of products on the shelves or assistance available to the average consumer, people without expertise in building or remodeling probably don't find 84 Lumber stores very accessible. The Home Depot would most likely classify 84 Lumber as a secondary firm in its strategic group analysis.[50] Managers need to be aware of the potential

Core firms the central companies in a strategic group

Secondary firms the firms in a strategic group that follow strategies related to but somewhat different from those of the core firms

threats and opportunities posed by secondary firms, but they usually spend more time assessing the threats and opportunities associated with core firms.

6-2c Choosing Strategic Alternatives

After determining the need for strategic change and conducting a situational analysis, the last step in the strategy-making process is to choose strategic alternatives that will help the company create or maintain a sustainable competitive advantage. According to *strategic reference point theory*, managers choose between two basic alternative strategies. They can choose a conservative, *risk-avoiding strategy* that aims to protect an existing competitive advantage. Or they can choose an aggressive, *risk-seeking strategy* that aims to extend or create a sustainable competitive advantage.

The choice to seek risk or avoid risk typically depends on whether top management views the company as falling above or below strategic reference points. **Strategic reference points** are the targets that managers use to measure whether their firm has developed the core competencies that it needs to achieve a sustainable competitive advantage. If a hotel chain decides to compete by providing superior quality and service, then top management will track the success of this strategy through customer surveys or ratings on influential websites like TripAdvisor. If a hotel chain decides to compete on price, it will use services like MonitorHotels.com to check the prices of other hotels. The competitors' prices are the hotel managers' strategic reference points against which to compare their own pricing strategy. If competitors can consistently underprice them, then the managers need to determine whether their staff and resources have the core competencies to compete on price.

As shown in Exhibit 6.3, when a company is performing above or better than its strategic reference points, top management will typically be satisfied with the company's strategy. Ironically, this satisfaction tends to make top management conservative and risk-averse. Because the company already has a sustainable competitive advantage, the worst thing that could happen would be to lose it, so new issues or changes in the company's external environment are viewed as threats. By contrast, when a company is performing below or worse than its strategic reference points, top management will typically be dissatisfied with the company's strategy. In this instance, managers are much more likely to choose a daring, risk-taking strategy. If the current strategy is producing substandard results, the company has nothing to lose by switching to risky new strategies in the hope that it can create a sustainable competitive advantage. Managers of companies in this situation view new issues or changes in the external environment as opportunities for potential gain.

Strategic reference point theory is not deterministic, however. Managers are not predestined to choose risk-averse or risk-seeking strategies for their companies. In fact, one of the most important elements of the theory is that managers *can* influence the strategies chosen by their company by *actively changing and adjusting* the strategic reference points they use to judge strategic performance. If a company has become complacent after consistently surpassing its strategic reference points, then top management can change from a risk-averse to a risk-taking orientation by raising or changing the standards of performance (that is, the strategic reference points).

Walmart is the largest grocer in the United States. If it had become complacent, that all changed when **Amazon** purchased Whole Foods Market with the intention of entering and dominating the grocery business.[51] In response, it began changing its strategic references points with a "Produce 2.0" strategy to revamp its produce departments. Walmart's executive vice president Charles Redfield admitted, "We knew we were not meeting customers' expectations for quality..."[52] Groceries account for 56 percent of Walmart's sales, and the produce section is the second most profitable department besides meat. Furthermore, Walmart customers who buy fruits and vegetables spend 55 percent more when shopping.[53] So it's critical that Walmart get Produce 2.0 right. To do so, it is improving the quality and assortment of its produce, putting a wider selection of organics in one easy-to-find location, and widening produce aisles. Redfield said, "We're [also] using colorful, abundantly filled displays to highlight freshness and the quality of our items – for example, large bins of ripe, red tomatoes and sizable displays of seasonal items like squash and pumpkins."[54]

So even when (perhaps *especially* when) companies have achieved a sustainable competitive advantage, top managers must adjust or change strategic reference points to challenge themselves and their employees to develop new core competencies for the future. In the long run, effective organizations will frequently revise their strategic reference points to better

Strategic reference points the strategic targets managers use to measure whether a firm has developed the core competencies it needs to achieve a sustainable competitive advantage

Exhibit 6.3
Strategic Reference Points

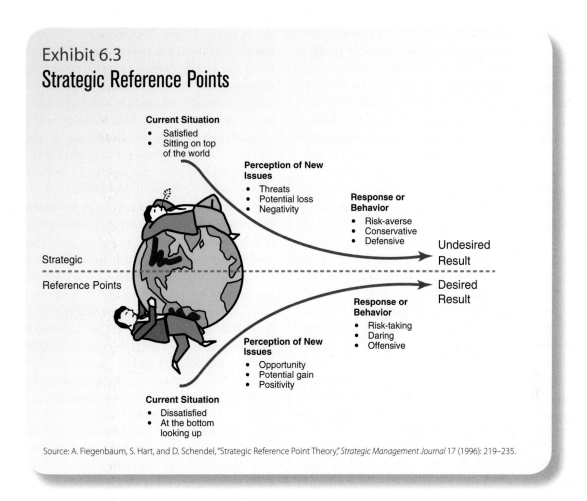

Source: A. Fiegenbaum, S. Hart, and D. Schendel, "Strategic Reference Point Theory," *Strategic Management Journal* 17 (1996): 219–235.

focus managers' attention on the new challenges and opportunities that occur in their ever-changing business environments.

6-3 CORPORATE-LEVEL STRATEGIES

To formulate effective strategies, companies must be able to answer these basic questions:

» What business are we in?

» How should we compete in this industry?

» Who are our competitors, and how should we respond to them?

These simple but powerful questions are at the heart of corporate-, industry-, and firm-level strategies.

Corporate-level strategy is the overall organizational strategy that addresses the question, "What business or businesses are we in or should we be in?" Southwest Airlines wants to be "the world's most loved, most efficient, and most profitable airline."[55] Ted.com,

famous for its TED Talks, is in business to "spread information."[56] Dr. Pepper is in the "refreshment beverage business."[57]

There are two major approaches to corporate-level strategy that companies use to decide which businesses they should be in: **6-3a portfolio strategy** *and* **6-3b grand strategies.**

6-3a Portfolio Strategy

One of the standard strategies for stock market investors is **diversification**, or owning stocks in a variety of companies in different industries. The purpose of this strategy is to reduce risk in the overall stock portfolio (the entire collection of stocks). The basic idea is simple: If you invest in

Corporate-level strategy the overall organizational strategy that addresses the question "What business or businesses are we in or should we be in?"

Diversification a strategy for reducing risk by buying a variety of items (stocks or, in the case of a corporation, types of businesses) so that the failure of one stock or one business does not doom the entire portfolio

10 companies in 10 different industries, you won't lose your entire investment if one company performs poorly. Furthermore, because they're in different industries, one company's losses are likely to be offset by another company's gains. Portfolio strategy is based on these same ideas. We'll start by taking a look at the theory and ideas behind portfolio strategy and then proceed with a critical review, which suggests that some of the key ideas behind portfolio strategy are *not* supported.

Portfolio strategy is a corporate-level strategy that minimizes risk by diversifying investment among various businesses or lines.[58] Just as a diversification strategy guides an investor who invests in a variety of stocks, portfolio strategy guides the strategic decisions of corporations that compete in a variety of businesses. For example, portfolio strategy could be used to guide the strategy of a company such as 3M, which makes 60,000 products for four different business groups: Consumer (Post-Its, Scotch tape, cleaning products, retail abrasives, and paints); Health Care (medical, surgical, and dental products, skin and wound care, and food safety); Safety & Industrial (safety and security products, tapes, abrasives, adhesives, specialty materials, filtration systems); and Transportation & Electronics (reflective signage, auto electrification solutions).[59]

Just as investors consider the mix of stocks in their stock portfolio when deciding which stocks to buy or sell, managers following portfolio strategy try to acquire companies that fit well with the rest of their corporate portfolio and to sell those that don't. **Bombardier**, which invented the first ski-steered snowmobile in 1937, acquired train manufacturers in the 1970s and jet plane manufacturers in the 1980s. It then sold the recreational division containing its original snowmobile business in 2003. Two years ago, it sold its train division, which made subway cars and high-speed trains, to Alstom SA, a French train and tram manufacturer, for $6.6 billion. Bombardier CEO Alain Bellemare said, "We had two great businesses, and one had to go."[60]

First, according to portfolio strategy, the more businesses in which a corporation competes, the smaller its overall chances of failing. Think of a corporation as a stool and its businesses as the legs of the stool. The more legs or businesses added to the stool, the less likely it is to tip over. Using this analogy, portfolio strategy reduces 3M's risk of failing because the corporation's survival depends on essentially four different business sectors. Managers employing portfolio strategy can either develop new businesses internally or look for **acquisitions**, that is, other companies to buy. Either way, the goal is to add legs to the stool.

Second, beyond adding new businesses to the corporate portfolio, portfolio strategy predicts that companies can reduce risk even more through **unrelated diversification**—creating or acquiring companies in completely unrelated businesses (more on the accuracy of this prediction later). According to portfolio strategy, when businesses are unrelated, losses in one business or industry should have minimal effect on the performance of other companies in the corporate portfolio. For example, **Newell Brands**, founded in 1903 as a curtain rod manufacturer, acquired dozens of companies, including Sharpie markers, Rubbermaid Brands (famous for rubber/plastic kitchen storage containers), Baby Jogger (which makes strollers for active parents), and Elmer's Glue. It took its strategy of buying unrelated business even further two years ago, paying $15 billion to acquire Jarden, which owned a canning company, Coleman outdoors products, Sunbeam appliances, First Alert safety products, Mr. Coffee, K2 winter sports, Marker winter sports, Marmot outdoor clothing, and sporting goods companies Rawlings and Volkl, as well as Crock-Pot, Yankee Candles, and Bicycle Playing Cards.[61] That combination of businesses is clearly unrelated diversification.

Because most internally grown businesses tend to be related to existing products or services, portfolio strategy suggests that acquiring new businesses is the preferred method of unrelated diversification.

Third, investing the profits and cash flows from mature, slow-growth businesses into newer, faster-growing businesses can reduce long-term risk. The best-known portfolio strategy for guiding investment in a corporation's businesses is the Boston Consulting Group (BCG) matrix.[62] The **BCG matrix** is a portfolio strategy that managers use to categorize their corporation's businesses by growth rate and relative market share, which helps them decide how to invest corporate funds. The matrix, shown in Exhibit 6.4, separates businesses into four categories based on how fast the market is growing (high growth or low growth) and the size of the business's share of that market (small or large). **Stars** are companies that have a large share of a fast-growing market. To take advantage of a star's fast-growing market and its strength in that market (large share), the corporation must invest substantially in it. The investment is usually worthwhile, however, because many

---

Portfolio strategy a corporate-level strategy that minimizes risk by diversifying investment among various businesses or product lines

Acquisition the purchase of a company by another company

Unrelated diversification creating or acquiring companies in completely unrelated businesses

BCG matrix a portfolio strategy developed by the Boston Consulting Group that categorizes a corporation's businesses by growth rate and relative market share and helps managers decide how to invest corporate funds

Star a company with a large share of a fast-growing market

stars produce sizable future profits. **Question marks** are companies that have a small share of a fast-growing market. If the corporation invests in these companies, they may eventually become stars, but their relative weakness in the market (small share) makes investing in question marks riskier than investing in stars. **Cash cows** are companies that have a large share of a slow-growing market. Companies in this situation are often highly profitable, hence the name *cash cow*. Finally, **dogs** are companies that have a small share of a slow-growing market. As the name suggests, having a small share of a slow-growth market is often not profitable.

Because the idea is to redirect investment from slow-growing to fast-growing companies, the BCG matrix starts by recommending that while the substantial cash flows from cash cows last, they should be reinvested in stars (see 1 in Exhibit 6.4) to

Exhibit 6.4
Boston Consulting Group Matrix

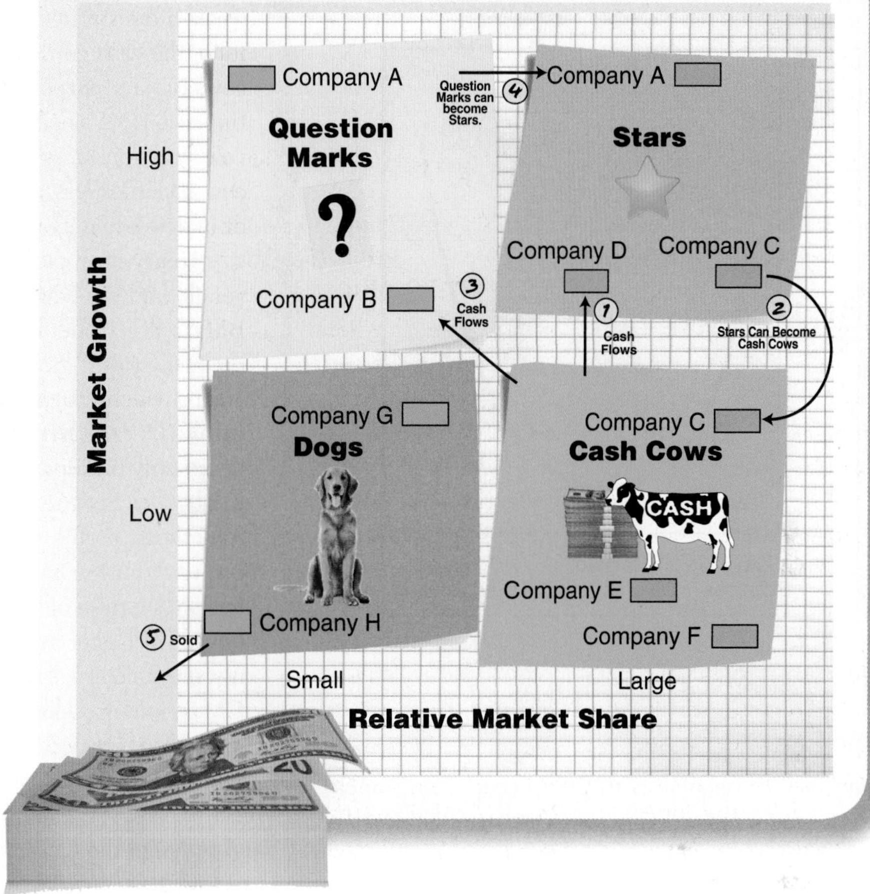

Question mark-Flat Design/Shutterstock.com/Star-Olga Knutova/Shutterstock.com/Dog-Andresr/Shutterstock.com/Cow-SoRad/Shutterstock.com/Money next to cow-iStock.com/Mosichev/Money in lower left corner-iStock.com/Claudio Baldin/Graph paper background-iStock.com/Post-it notes-iStock.com/subjug

help them grow even faster and obtain even more market share. Using this strategy, current profits help produce future profits. Over time, as their market growth slows, some stars may turn into cash cows (see 2). Cash flows should also be directed to some question marks (see 3). Though riskier than stars, question marks have great potential because of their fast-growing market. Managers must decide which question marks are most likely to turn into stars and therefore warrant further investment and which ones are too risky and should be sold. Over time, managers hope some question marks will become stars as their small markets become large ones (see 4). Finally, because dogs lose money, the corporation should "find them new owners" or "take them to the pound." In other words, dogs should either be sold to other companies or closed down and liquidated for their assets (see 5).

Although the BCG matrix and other forms of portfolio strategy are relatively popular among managers, portfolio strategy has some drawbacks. The most significant drawback is that contrary to the predictions of portfolio

strategy, the evidence suggests that acquiring unrelated businesses is *not* useful. As shown in Exhibit 6.5, there is a U-shaped relationship between diversification and risk.[63] The left side of the curve shows that single businesses with no diversification are extremely risky (if the single business fails, the entire business fails). So, in part, the portfolio strategy of diversifying is correct—competing in a variety of different businesses can lower risk. However, portfolio strategy is partly wrong, too—the right side of the curve shows that conglomerates composed of completely unrelated businesses are even riskier than single, undiversified businesses. Indeed, Newell Brands has struggled to make its very different businesses work well together.[64]

A second set of problems with portfolio strategy has to do with the

Question mark a company with a small share of a fast-growing market

Cash cow a company with a large share of a slow-growing market

Dog a company with a small share of a slow-growing market

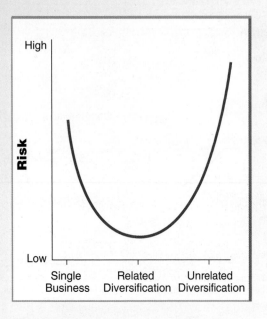

Exhibit 6.5
U-Shaped Relationship between Diversification and Risk

Source: M. Lubatkin & P.J. Lane, "Psst! . . . The Merger Mavens Still Have It Wrong," *Academy of Management* Executive 10 (1996) 21–39.

dysfunctional consequences that can occur when companies are categorized as stars, cash cows, question marks, or dogs. Contrary to expectations, the BCG matrix often yields incorrect judgments about a company's potential. In other words, managers using the BCG matrix aren't very good at accurately determining which companies should be categorized as stars, cash cows, questions marks, or dogs. The most common mistake is simply miscategorizing highly profitable companies as dogs.[65] In part, this is because the BCG matrix relies on past performance (previous market share and previous market growth), which is a notoriously poor predictor of future company performance. More worrisome, however, is research that indicates the BCG matrix actually makes managers worse at judging the future profitability of a business. A study conducted in six countries over five years gave managers and business students clear information about the current and future profits (that is, slow or fast growth) of three companies and asked them to select the one that would be most successful in the future. Although not labeled this way, one company was clearly a star, another was a dog, and the last was a cash cow. Just exposing people to the ideas in the BCG

Related diversification
creating or acquiring companies that share similar products, manufacturing, marketing, technology, or cultures

matrix led them to incorrectly categorize less-profitable businesses as the most successful businesses 64 percent of the time, while actually *using* the BCG matrix led to making the same mistake 87 percent of the time.[66]

Furthermore, using the BCG matrix can also weaken the strongest performer in the corporate portfolio: the cash cow. As funds are redirected from cash cows to stars, corporate managers essentially take away the resources needed to take advantage of the cash cow's new business opportunities. As a result, the cash cow becomes less aggressive in seeking new business or in defending its present business.

Heavy-duty pickup trucks like the Chevrolet Silverado and the GMC Sierra that cost more than many BMWs are General Motors (GM) cash cows. Industry analyst Jeff Schuster said, "These vehicles have among the highest margins in the business."[67] GM earns $65 billion each year from pickup trucks, but heavy-duty pickups, which produce an average profit of $12,000 each, generate $2 billion in profits each year.[68] And those profits from heavy-duty pickup trucks, in turn, pay for the $1 billion a year in development costs for GM's Cruise electric self-driving cars. Industry analyst Jeff Schuster says that at GM, "You have no tomorrow if you don't sell these trucks today."[69] In other words, GM is running a classic BCG matrix strategy, redirecting profits from cash cows to a future star, the GM Cruise. Has GM stopped investing in its cash cow heavy-duty pickups? Not yet, as it invested nearly $2 billion to update and redesign the Chevy Silverado and GMC Sierra pickups in 2019.[70]

Finally, labeling a top performer as a cash cow can harm employee morale. Cash cow employees realize that they have inferior status and that instead of working for themselves, they are now working to fund the growth of stars and question marks.

So, what kind of portfolio strategy does the best job of helping managers decide which companies to buy or sell? The U-shaped curve in Exhibit 6.5 indicates that, contrary to the predictions of portfolio strategy, the best approach is probably **related diversification**, in which the different business units share similar products, manufacturing, marketing, technology, or cultures. The key to related diversification is to acquire or create new companies with core capabilities that complement the core capabilities of businesses already in the corporate portfolio. For example, **Inspire Brands**, parent of Arby's Restaurant Group, merged with casual dining chain Buffalo Wild Wings in a $2.9 billion deal.[71] Inspire Brands then paid $2.3 billion to buy Sonic Corp, which runs Sonic drive-in restaurants.[72] Both deals are examples of related diversification.

HOTELS RESPOND: FIGHTING BACK AGAINST EXPEDIA AND AIRBNB

Travelers use Airbnb.com to rent private rooms, flats, or houses directly from homeowners. Roughly a third of leisure travelers choose private accommodations, like those through Airbnb, over hotels. Thirty-one percent of business travelers have done the same in the last two years. Likewise, 81 percent of hotel rooms are booked through online travel sites like Expedia.com. When that happens, hotel chains pay travel sites a 15 to 25 percent commission, which means they make make less money per room. Hotels are fighting back by offering discounts and benefits to customers enrolled in hotel member rewards accounts who make direct room reservations using the hotel's website. Hilton's "Stop Clicking Around" plan offered 10 percent member discounts, whereas Marriott's "It Pays to Be Direct" plan offered 2 to 5 percent discounts. Members benefit from "best price guarantees" on hotel websites. Hotels benefit because member discounts are smaller than commissions paid to travel sites. Hotels also offer members additional benefits that are only available through direct reservations on hotel websites, such as free Wi-Fi, digital check-in, and rewards points than can be used to pay for future reservations.

Source: R. Chhatwal, "Marriott And Hilton Fight Back Against Priceline And Expedia," Seeking Alpha, March 21, 2016, accessed April 1, 2017, https://seekingalpha.com/article/3959946-marriott-hilton-fight-back-priceline-expedia; D. Fitzgerald, "Hotels Turn to 'Member' Discounts to Battle Travel Websites," Wall Street Journal, July 7, 2016, accessed April 1, 2017, https://www.wsj.com/articles/hotels-turn-to-member-discounts-to-battle-travel-websites-1467907475; E. Glusac, "Hotels vs.

Airbnb: Let the Battle Begin," New York Times, July 20, 2016, accessed April 1, 2017, https://www.nytimes.com/2016/07/24/travel/airbnb-hotels.html.

We began this section with the example of 3M and its 60,000 products sold in four different business groups. While seemingly different, most of 3M's product divisions are based in some fashion on its distinctive competencies in adhesives and tape (for example, wet or dry sandpaper, Post-It notes, Scotchgard fabric protector, transdermal skin patches, and reflective material used in traffic signs). Furthermore, all of 3M's divisions share its strong corporate culture that promotes and encourages risk taking and innovation. In sum, in contrast to a single, undiversified business or unrelated diversification, related diversification reduces risk because the different businesses can work as a team, relying on each other for needed experience, expertise, and support.

6-3b Grand Strategies

A **grand strategy** is a broad strategic plan used to help an organization achieve its strategic goals.[73] Grand strategies guide the strategic alternatives that managers of individual businesses or subunits may use in deciding what businesses they should be in. There are three kinds of grand strategies: growth, stability, and retrenchment/recovery.

The purpose of a **growth strategy** is to increase profits, revenues, market share, or the number of places (stores, offices, locations) in which the company does business. Companies can grow in several ways. They can grow externally by merging with or acquiring other companies in the same or different businesses. **Marriott International**, with hotel brands such as Marriott, JW Marriott, Courtyard, and Renaissance, paid

> **Grand strategy** a broad corporate-level strategic plan used to achieve strategic goals and guide the strategic alternatives that managers of individual businesses or subunits may use
>
> **Growth strategy** a strategy that focuses on increasing profits, revenues, market share, or the number of places in which the company does business

$12.2 billion to acquire Starwood Hotels & Resorts, which is known for its Westin, St. Regis, Sheraton, and Meridien hotels, among others. Marriott's CEO Arne M. Sorenson said, "We've got an ability to offer just that much more choice. A choice in locations, a choice in the kind of hotel, a choice in the amount a customer needs to spend."[74] Starwood's CEO Adam Aron agreed, noting that, "To be successful in today's lodging space, a wide distribution of brands and hotels across price points is critical. Today, size matters."[75] With the acquisition completed, Marriott International has become the largest hotel business in the world, with $4 billion in revenue, 1.4 million rooms, and 30 well-regarded hotel brands with 7,300 properties in 131 countries.[76]

Another way to grow is internally, directly expanding the company's existing business or creating and growing new businesses. Go to Amazon.com. Type "batteries" into the search box. Go ahead. Your smartphone is right there. I'll wait. OK, what did you find? If your search results were like mine and *New York Times* reporter Julie Creswell, 10 of the first 20 battery brands in the search results were Amazon's private-label AmazonBasics batteries, all as highly rated as Energizer and Duracell batteries, but much cheaper.[77] Can you guess which battery more people are likely to buy? Amazon pays a supplier to make the batteries and then puts the AmazonBasics label on them. It does that with 2,800 other AmazonBasics products, 88 percent of which cost less than $50.[78] Sales of AmazonBasics products, which represent internal growth, are expected to grow from $7.5 billion in 2018 to more than $25 billion in 2022.[79]

The purpose of a **stability strategy** is to continue doing what the company has been doing, just doing it better. Companies following a stability strategy try to improve the way in which they sell the same products or services to the same customers. Vanguard Group, one of the world's largest investment firms was designed at its founding in 1975 to offer low-cost investing options. Because it is client-owned, it returns profits to customers by lowering costs. Vanguard's stability strategy to reduce costs means that Vanguard's investment fees have dropped from $0.89 per $100 in 1975 to $0.10 today. Since the typical investment fund charges $0.58 per $100 invested in 2020, an investor with $100,000 invested would save $480 in fees per year with Vanguard.[80]

The purpose of a **retrenchment strategy** is to turn around very poor company performance by shrinking the size or scope of the business or, if a company is in multiple businesses, by closing or shutting down different lines of the business. The first step of a typical retrenchment strategy might include making significant cost reductions: laying off employees; closing poorly performing stores, offices, or manufacturing plants; or closing or selling entire lines of products or services.[81] A decade ago, GameStop sold video-game discs for personal computers (PC) and game consoles, such as the PlayStation (PS) or Xbox, that could only be purchased and picked up at its 6,000 stores. GameStop sold each game twice, first as a new game and again as a used game (after the original buyer traded the game in for store credit). Today, most video games are played online, on smartphones, on tablets, and, of course, on PCs and game consoles. *Business Insider's* Clancy Morgan says, "Sony, Microsoft, and Nintendo all sell their games digitally. You can buy them right from the console without even having to get off the couch and if you want a physical copy of a game, you can order it off of Amazon. Got Prime? It'll be there in two days."[82] GameStop shifted to selling digital PS and Xbox games online, but PS digital download codes are now only available through Sony.[83] After losing $673 million in 2018 and $471 million in 2019, GameStop is closing 200 of its 5,700 stores. This follows the closing of 150 stores three years ago.[84]

After cutting costs and reducing a business's size or scope, the second step in a retrenchment strategy is recovery. **Recovery** consists of the strategic actions that a company takes to return to a growth strategy. This two-step process of cutting and recovery is analogous to pruning roses. Prior to each growing season, roses should be cut back to two-thirds their normal size. Pruning doesn't damage the roses; it makes them stronger and more likely to produce beautiful, fragrant flowers. The retrenchment-and-recovery process is similar.

Like pruning, the cuts are made as part of a recovery strategy intended to allow companies to eventually return to a successful growth strategy. When company performance drops significantly, a strategy of retrenchment and recovery may help the company return to a successful growth strategy.

Stability strategy a strategy that focuses on improving the way in which the company sells the same products or services to the same customers

Retrenchment strategy a strategy that focuses on turning around very poor company performance by shrinking the size or scope of the business

Recovery the strategic actions taken after retrenchment to return to a growth strategy

Exhibit 6.6
Porter's Five Industry Forces

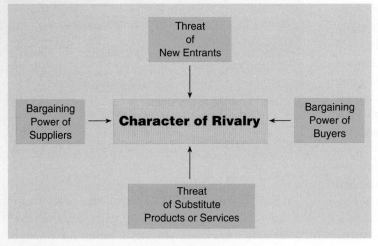

Source: Based on the Simon & Schuster, Inc. Porter, M. E. *Competitive Strategy: Techniques for Analyzing Industries and Competitors.* New York: Free Press, 1980.

6-4 INDUSTRY-LEVEL STRATEGIES

Industry-level strategy addresses the question, "How should we compete in this industry?"

Let's find out more about industry-level strategies by discussing **6-4a the five industry forces that determine overall levels of competition in an industry** *as well as* **6-4b the positioning strategies** *and* **6-4c adaptive strategies that companies can use to achieve sustained competitive advantage** *and* **above-average profits.**

6-4a Five Industry Forces

According to Harvard professor Michael Porter, five industry forces determine an industry's overall attractiveness and potential for long-term profitability: the character of the rivalry, the threat of new entrants, the threat of substitute products or services, the bargaining power of suppliers, and the bargaining power of buyers. The stronger these forces, the less attractive the industry becomes to corporate investors because it is more difficult for companies to be profitable. Porter's industry forces are illustrated in Exhibit 6.6. Let's examine how these forces are bringing changes to several kinds of industries.

Character of the rivalry is a measure of the intensity of competitive behavior among companies in an industry. Is the competition among firms aggressive and cutthroat, or do competitors focus more on serving customers than on attacking each other? Both industry attractiveness and profitability decrease when rivalry is cutthroat. Marriott International has 410 luxury hotels in operation, such as JW Marriott and Ritz-Carlton, with another 190 soon to open. **InterContinental Hotel Group, IHG**, has 296 luxury hotels with 109 in development. **Hyatt** has 130 luxury hotels, with 80 in development. This intense level of competition has **Hilton Hotels and Resorts**, with just 65 luxury hotels and 30 soon to open, scrambling to catch up. Hilton Executive Vice President Martin Rinck admits, "We were a little bit later to the game."[85]

The **threat of new entrants** is a measure of the degree to which barriers to entry make it easy or difficult for new companies to get started in an industry. If new companies can enter the industry easily, then competition will increase, and prices and profits will fall. Quip electric toothbrushes, Allbirds sneakers, ThirdLove bras, Ritual vitamins, Glossier makeup, Farmer's Dog pet food, and Warby Parker glasses are all examples of direct-to-consumer companies that took $17 billion in sales away from big consumer brands like Gillette and Unilever by significantly cutting product prices. All are in industries with low barriers to entry. Neil Blumenthal, Warby Parker co-founder, said, "It's never been cheaper to start a business…"[86]

On the other hand, if there are sufficient barriers to entry, such as large capital requirements to buy expensive equipment or plant facilities or the need for specialized knowledge, then competition will be weaker, and prices and profits will generally be higher. The automobile industry has traditionally had a high barrier to entry. So, when Tesla entered the market in 2003 to manufacture a completely electric sports car, it was

Industry-level strategy a corporate strategy that addresses the question, "How should we compete in this industry?"

Character of the rivalry a measure of the intensity of competitive behavior between companies in an industry

Threat of new entrants a measure of the degree to which barriers to entry make it easy or difficult for new companies to get started in an industry

the first new car company in a generation. With billions of dollars in startup funding, the company hired thousands of engineers, built new manufacturing facilities, and created a complex supply chain to source, manufacture, and assemble 10,000 component parts. Seventeen years later, at the beginning of 2020, Tesla is growing faster than any other auto manufacturer, and has finally earned its first annual profit. To build new factories and achieve that growth, it has burned through $100 million a month in expenses since going public in 2010.[87] But, other than the GM Cruise, a startup that GM purchased, there have been no other new entrants in the automobile industry because the barriers to entry are just too high.[88]

The **threat of substitute products or services** is a measure of the ease with which customers can find substitutes for an industry's products or services. If customers can easily find substitute products or services, the competition will be greater, and profits will be lower. If there are few or no substitutes, competition will be weaker, and profits will be higher. Overnight delivery companies like UPS and DHL deliver millions of items every day. What would happen to these businesses if, instead of buying products and having them delivered, people could use 3-D printers to manufacture what they needed right at work or home? This new technology led **UPS** Chief Information Officer Dave Barnes to wonder, "Should we be threatened by it or should we endorse it?[89] To answer that question, UPS created a 3-D printing test center at its Louisville, Kentucky hub. There, UPS tested the feasibility of local production and delivery of 3-D printed items. The center's 100 industrial 3-D printers create everything from iPhone cases to replacement parts for UPS's fleet of Airbus A300 jets. DHL's initial studies show that 2 to 4 percent of shipped products can reliably be 3D printed.[90] Because initial testing was so successful, UPS now offers 3D printing in 100 stores, printing items such as, "engineering parts, functional prototypes, acting props, architectural models, fixtures for cameras, lights and cables…Most items that are smaller than a breadbox and can be made out of single color of plastic are perfect for 3D printing"[91]

By leasing its own fleet of trucks, Amazon saves as much as 40 percent on shipping costs.

Jarek Kilian/Shutterstock.com

Bargaining power of suppliers is a measure of the influence that suppliers of parts, materials, and services to firms in an industry have on the prices of these inputs. When companies can buy parts, materials, and services from numerous suppliers, the companies will be able to bargain with the suppliers to keep prices low. On the other hand, if there are few suppliers, or if a company is dependent on a supplier with specialized skills and knowledge, then the suppliers will have the bargaining power to dictate price levels. On the flip side, the **bargaining power of buyers** is a measure of the influence that customers have on the firm's prices. If a company sells a popular product or service to multiple buyers, then the company has more power to set prices. By contrast, if a company is dependent on just a few high-volume buyers, those buyers will typically have enough bargaining power to dictate prices.

We can see how the bargaining power of suppliers and buyers changes by examining the relationship between Amazon and its key delivery suppliers, UPS and FedEx. Since 2009, Amazon's shipping costs have risen each year, from 7.5 percent of sales to 10.8 percent of sales, indicating UPS and FedEx's growing supplier bargaining power. Amazon relies on them for package delivery, especially to Amazon Prime customers, who pay $119 a year for two-day, no charge deliveries.[92] Prime members, who buy three times as much from Amazon as non-Prime customers, drove Amazon's revenue growth from $89 billion in 2014 to $280.5 billion in 2019.[93] As Amazon has grown, it has reinvested profits into establishing 175 warehouses, and leasing 70 Boeing 767s for "Prime Air" logistics and thousands of "Prime Now" trucks, the latter of which promise free two-hour delivery.[94] Why does

Threat of substitute products or services a measure of the ease with which customers can find substitutes for an industry's products or services

Bargaining power of suppliers a measure of the influence that suppliers of parts, materials, and services to firms in an industry have on the prices of these inputs

Bargaining power of buyers a measure of the influence that customers have on a firm's prices

Amazon appear to be establishing its own delivery service capabilities? It has reduced the average shipping cost by 40 percent. With these moves, Amazon's bargaining power as a buyer is clearly getting stronger. Amazon's demand for greater shipping volumes at much lower prices led FedEx to not renew its Amazon contract, which was worth $900 million a year. Instead, FedEx will deliver packages for Amazon's competitors, like Walmart and Target.[95]

6-4b Positioning Strategies

After analyzing industry forces, the next step in industry-level strategy is to protect your company from the negative effects of industry-wide competition and to create a sustainable competitive advantage. According to Michael Porter, there are three positioning strategies: cost leadership, differentiation, and focus.

Cost leadership means producing a product or service of acceptable quality at consistently lower production costs than competitors so that the firm can offer the product or service at the lowest price in the industry. Cost leadership protects companies from industry forces by deterring new entrants, who will have to match low costs and prices. Cost leadership also forces down the prices of substitute products and services, attracts bargain-seeking buyers, and increases bargaining power with suppliers, who have to keep their prices low if they want to do business with the cost leader. With entry-level surfboards costing $300 and top-of-the-line, handmade longboards going for $1,000 or more, surfing is expensive. Those high prices inspired Matt Zilinskas to create Wavestorm, an 8-foot, mass-produced soft-foam surfboard that sells for $99 at Costco. Now the industry's best-selling surfboard, Wavestorm's sales are so strong that other retailers have stopped selling more expensive soft-foam boards altogether. "Why even bother when you can go to Costco [and get one for] $100?" said Cody Quarress, manager at the Huntington Surf & Sport.[96] Zilinkas has received complaints from competitors, but he sees his product as beneficial to the industry: "How many of the hundreds of thousands of people who bought our board have moved on to higher-end product? Ask any surfer in the water about Wavestorm. They probably own one."[97]

Differentiation means making your product or service sufficiently different from competitors' offerings that customers are willing to pay a premium price for the extra value or performance that it provides. Differentiation protects companies from industry forces by reducing the threat of substitute products.

It also protects companies by making it easier to retain customers and more difficult for new entrants trying to attract new customers. At **Boyds**, a family-owned, four-story high-end clothing store in Philadelphia, manager Chris Phillips greets customers at the elevator, directing them to the salesperson who can help them with dress shirts, shoes, blazers, suits, or casual clothes.[98] Customer Philip Scotti says, "It's how it should be. They actually wait on you."[99] Thirty-nine full-time tailors working on the fifth floor do free alterations. Customers often work with the same salesperson, who keeps a complete historical record of preferences and purchases. Hall of Fame basketball player Julius Erving says, "They always had somebody who would make sure everything was just so: sleeve length, cuff length. They know what you like."[100] Marc Brownstein, who has been shopping at Boyds for four decades, says, "They'll deliver to your house, to your office. You park for free. You know what parking costs in the center of Philadelphia? They're going to out-work and out-service everyone else."[101] Philip Scotti said, "I wish all stores were like this. There's not many left."[102]

With a **focus strategy**, a company uses either cost leadership or differentiation to produce a specialized product or service for a limited, specially targeted group of customers in a particular geographic region or market segment. Focus strategies typically work in market niches that competitors have overlooked or have difficulty serving. Cable channel HGTV shows *House Hunters Renovation, Property Brothers, and Love It or List It?* have a common theme: A couple shops for an outdated house, buying one of the several homes shown to viewers. The contractor takes out a wall, creating an open floor plan, and has an overbudget surprise. The couple moves in, crying with joy at the redesign of their beautiful home. HGTV's target customer is very specific. She's a college-educated suburbanite with an $84,000 household income and an insatiable interest in home improvement. Chief Programming Officer Kathleen Finch

Cost leadership the positioning strategy of producing a product or service of acceptable quality at consistently lower production costs than competitors can, so that the firm can offer the product or service at the lowest price in the industry

Differentiation the positioning strategy of providing a product or service that is sufficiently different from competitors' offerings that customers are willing to pay a premium price for it

Focus strategy the positioning strategy of using cost leadership or differentiation to produce a specialized product or service for a limited, specially targeted group of customers in a particular geographic region or market segment

Can Disney And Netflix Be Frenemies?

The Walt Disney Company owns these major TV networks: ESPN (20+), ABC (4), FX (4), Disney Channels (4), National Geographic (4), A&E (3), Lifetime Entertainment (3), and the History Network (4). But now that it has started the Disney+ streaming service, signing 29 million subscribers in its first month, Disney finds itself competing with the streaming services to which it used to license TV shows and movies. At first, Disney decided to no longer accept TV ads from its new streaming rivals. After all, why promote the competition? But it reversed that policy after striking "frenemy" compromises with all but one streaming service, Netflix, the dominant industry player with 167 million subscribers. With the exception of ESPN, no Disney TV networks will accept Netflix advertising. Netflix admits this could hurt its business, saying, "If the available marketing channels are curtailed, our ability to attract new members may be adversely affected." So, Disney and Netflix can't even be frenemies – especially since Disney "ghosted" Netflix.

Source: A. Bruell & S. Vranica, "Disney Bans Netflix Ads as Streaming's Marketing Wars Intensify," *Wall Street Journal*, October 4, 2019, accessed March 19, 2020, https://www.wsj.com/articles/disney-bans-netflix-ads-as-streamings-marketing-wars-intensify-11570199291.

says, "We super-serve our viewer what she likes, and we give her more and more of it." HGTV's focus strategy works. As the third-most popular cable network, it delivers twice as much web traffic for advertisers like Wayfair, an online retailer of furniture, home furnishings, and decor.[103]

26-4c Adaptive Strategies

Adaptive strategies are another set of industry-level strategies. Although the aim of positioning strategies is to minimize the effects of industry competition and build a sustainable competitive advantage, the purpose of adaptive strategies is to choose an industry-level strategy that is best suited to changes in the organization's external environment. There are four kinds of adaptive strategies: defenders, prospectors, analyzers, and reactors.[104]

Defenders seek moderate, steady growth by offering a limited range of products and services to a well-defined set of customers. In other words, defenders aggressively "defend" their current strategic position by doing the best job they can to hold on to customers in a particular market segment. Chances are, the printer next to your computer is made by **Hewlett-Packard (HP)**. HP doesn't make money when you buy that printer; it makes money when you buy printer cartridges, such as the $45 HP 950XL black cartridge and the $70 HP 951 cyan/magenta/yellow cartridge (my HP printer requires both). While slowing shrinking, the printer supply business is still worth $35 billion annually because we're still printing 3.2 trillion pages a year. HP's printer supply business sells $12.9 billion of ink cartridges annually, accounting for nearly two-thirds of HP's profits.[105] HP defends this business with a subscription cartridge replacement program with 6 million members, and by aggressively using HP technology to make competitors' ink cartridges without "genuine HP chips" incompatible with HP printers.

Prospectors seek fast growth by searching for new market opportunities, encouraging risk taking, and being the first to bring innovative new products to market. Prospectors are analogous to gold miners who "prospect" for gold nuggets (that is, new products) in hope that the nuggets will lead them to a rich deposit of gold (i.e., fast growth). Toyota, a global auto manufacturer, invested $394 million in Joby Aviation, a startup company that is developing an electric vertical takeoff and landing (eVTOL) air taxi that will lift off and land like a helicopter but fly like an airplane. Toyota CEO Akio Toyoda said, "Air transportation has been a long-term goal for Toyota, and while we continue our work in the automobile business, this agreement sets our sights to the sky. As we take up the challenge of air transportation together with Joby, an innovator in the emerging eVTOL space, we tap the potential to revolutionize future transportation and life."[106]

Defenders companies using an adaptive strategy aimed at defending strategic positions by seeking moderate, steady growth and by offering a limited range of high-quality products and services to a well-defined set of customers

Prospectors companies using an adaptive strategy that seeks fast growth by searching for new market opportunities, encouraging risk taking, and being the first to bring innovative new products to market

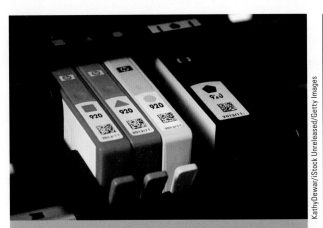

HP makes money off of ink cartridge sales. These can be purchased in stores, online, or through a subscription replacement program.

Analyzers are the blend of the defender and prospector strategies. They seek moderate, steady growth and limited opportunities for fast growth. Analyzers are rarely first to market with new products or services. Instead, they try to simultaneously minimize risk and maximize profits by following or imitating the proven successes of prospectors. Encouraged by founder and CEO Mark Zuckerberg to not be "too proud to copy," Facebook admits to using an analyzer strategy in copying the key features of Snapchat, the popular social media app in which users share pictures and videos.[107] Facebook has copied Snapchat's features multiple times:

» Snapchat opens in camera view. Facebook made the camera available with one swipe.

» Facebook added the one-swipe capability to take and post picture and videos to its Instagram, WhatsApp, and Messenger apps.

» Similar to Snapchat stories, it named these features Facebook Stories.

» Just like in Snapchat, users can choose to create photos and stories that only exist for 24 hours.[108]

» Facebook created Threads that lets Instagram users share photos and videos privately with friends, copying Snapchat's private stories.[109]

Facebook's adoption of Snapchat features has significantly slowed Snapchat's user growth. Instagram has 500 million daily users, while Snapchat's daily user base is 218 million.[110]

Finally, unlike defenders, prospectors, or analyzers, **reactors** do not follow a consistent strategy. Rather than anticipating and preparing for external opportunities and threats, reactors tend to react to changes in their external environment after they occur. Not surprisingly, reactors tend to be poorer performers than defenders, prospectors, or analyzers. A reactor approach is inherently unstable, and firms that fall into this mode of operation must change their approach or face almost certain failure.

6-5 FIRM-LEVEL STRATEGIES

Apple unveils its Apple Watch with advanced fitness tracking and FitBit counters with the Versa 2, which has a color touchscreen and syncs automatically with your phone (and looks like an Apple Watch). Starbucks Coffee opens a store, and nearby locally run coffeehouses respond by improving service, increasing portions, and holding the line on prices. In the German luxury car industry, **BMW**, **Audi**, and **Mercedes** have an intense three-way rivalry that goes well beyond sales volume to include investments in technology, quality rankings, and profitability. According to one Audi executive, to get approval for a new project, "I just have to say BMW is already doing it, and it goes through." The rivalry is just as heated over at BMW. When it comes to Audi, one BMW executive said, "We like to stick it to them."[111] Attack and respond, respond and attack. **Firm-level strategy** addresses the question, "How should we compete against a particular firm?"

Let's find out more about the firm-level strategies (direct competition between companies) by reading about 6-5a the basics of direct competition and 6-5b the strategic moves involved in direct competition between companies.

6-5a Direct Competition

Although Porter's five industry forces indicate the overall level of competition in an industry, most companies do not compete directly with all the firms in their industry. For example, McDonald's and Red Lobster are both in the restaurant business, but no one would characterize them as competitors. McDonald's offers low-cost, convenient fast

Analyzers companies using an adaptive strategy that seeks to minimize risk and maximize profits by following or imitating the proven successes of prospectors

Reactors companies that do not follow a consistent adaptive strategy but instead react to changes in the external environment after they occur

Firm-level strategy a corporate strategy that addresses the question, "How should we compete against a particular firm?"

food in a seat-yourself restaurant, while Red Lobster offers mid-priced seafood dinners complete with servers and a bar.

Instead of competing with an entire industry, most firms compete directly with just a few companies within it. **Direct competition** is the rivalry between two companies offering similar products and services that acknowledge each other as rivals and take offensive and defensive positions as they act and react to each other's strategic actions.[112] Two factors determine the extent to which firms will be in direct competition with each other: market commonality and resource similarity. **Market commonality** is the degree to which two companies have overlapping products, services, or customers in multiple markets. The more markets in which there is product, service, or customer overlap, the more intense the direct competition between the two companies. **Resource similarity** is the extent to which a competitor has similar amounts and kinds of resources, that is, similar assets, capabilities, processes, information, and knowledge used to create and sustain an advantage over competitors. From a competitive standpoint, resource similarity means that your direct competitors can probably match the strategic actions that your company takes.

Exhibit 6.7 shows how market commonality and resource similarity interact to determine when and where companies are in direct competition.[113] The overlapping area in each quadrant (between the triangle and the rectangle, or between the differently colored rectangles) depicts market commonality. The larger the overlap, the greater the market commonality. Shapes depict resource similarity, with rectangles representing one set of competitive resources and triangles representing another. Quadrant I shows two companies in direct competition because they have similar resources at their disposal and a high degree of market commonality.

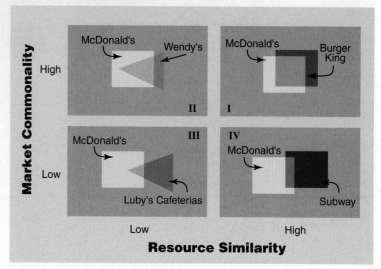

Exhibit 6.7
A Framework of Direct Competition

Source: M. Chen, "Competitor Analysis and InterFirm Rivalry: Toward a Theoretical Integration," *Academy of Management Review* 21 (1996): 100–134.

These companies try to sell similar products and services to similar customers. **McDonald's** intends to intensify its direct competition with **Burger King (BK)** by partnering with DoorDash, GrubHub, and Uber Eats.[114] In its top five markets, 75 percent of the population lives within three miles of a McDonald's. Globally, one billion people live within 10 minutes of a McDonald's. Senior Vice President Lucy Brady said, "Delivery is the most significant disruption in the restaurant industry in our lifetime."[115]

In Quadrant II, the overlapping parts of the triangle and rectangle show two companies going after similar customers with some similar products or services but doing so with different competitive resources. McDonald's and **Wendy's** restaurants would fit here. Wendy's is after the same lunchtime and dinner crowds that McDonald's is. Nevertheless, with its more expensive hamburgers, fries, shakes, and salads, Wendy's is less of a direct competitor to McDonald's than Burger King is. For example, Wendy's has recently rebranded itself more like a casual dining restaurant, redesigning its locations with lounge seating, fireplaces, Wi-Fi, and digital menu boards.[116] However, after failing in an attempt to compete against McDonald's with breakfast food in 2012, Wendy's will again take on McDonald's by expanding its breakfast menu, adding a Breakfast Baconator sandwich, a chicken biscuit sandwich, and

Direct competition the rivalry between two companies that offer similar products and services, acknowledge each other as rivals, and act and react to each other's strategic actions

Market commonality the degree to which two companies have overlapping products, services, or customers in multiple markets

Resource similarity the extent to which a competitor has similar amounts and kinds of resources

McDonald's has partnered with UberEats to beef up its competitive edge.

a Frosty-ccino flavored iced coffee, made with creamer from Wendy's Frosty shakes.[117]

Even though it competes less directly with Wendy's, McDonald's took aim at Wendy's by switching from frozen to fresh beef in its Quarter Pounder hamburgers.[118] Wendy's has long touted its fresh beef as a key difference. Indeed, when McDonald's announced the change to fresh beef, Wendy's tweeted, "So you'll still use frozen beef in MOST of your burgers in ALL of your restaurants? Asking for a friend."[119]

In Quadrant III, the very small overlap shows two companies with different competitive resources and little market commonality. McDonald's and **Luby's** cafeterias fit here. Although both are in the fast-food business, there's almost no overlap in terms of products and customers. Luby's sells baked chicken, turkey, roasts, meat loaf, and vegetables, none of which are available at McDonald's. Furthermore, Luby's customers aren't likely to eat at McDonald's. In fact, Luby's is not really competing with other fast-food restaurants, but with eating at home. Company surveys show that close to half of its customers would have eaten at home, not at another restaurant, if they hadn't come to Luby's.[120]

Finally, in Quadrant IV, the small overlap between the two rectangles shows that McDonald's and **Subway** compete with similar resources but with little market commonality. In terms of resources, sales at McDonald's are much larger, but Subway has grown substantially in the past decade and now has 41,600 stores in 103 countries, compared to McDonald's with 35,461 stores in more than 118 countries.[121]

Though Subway and McDonald's compete, they aren't direct competitors in terms of market commonality in the way that McDonald's and Burger King are because Subway, unlike McDonald's, sells itself as a provider of healthy fast food. Thus, the overlap is much smaller in Quadrant IV than in Quadrant I. With detailed nutritional information available in its stores, and its close relationships with the American Heart Association, the American College of Cardiologists, and Heart Research UK, Subway has long focused on healthy eating and well being.[122]

6-5b Strategic Moves of Direct Competition

While corporate-level strategies help managers decide what business to be in, and industry-level strategies help them determine how to compete within an industry, firm-level strategies help managers determine when, where, and what strategic actions should be taken against a direct competitor. Firms in direct competition can make two basic strategic moves: attack and response. These moves occur all the time in virtually every industry, but they are most noticeable in industries where multiple large competitors are pursuing customers in the same market space.

An **attack** is a competitive move designed to reduce a rival's market share or profits. Burger King attacked McDonald's with a unique price-cutting promotion in which it sold its bestselling sandwich, the Whopper, for one cent. But to get that low price via the "Whopper Detour" promotion, customers had to use the BK app at a McDonald's, or more specifically, within 600 feet of a McDonald's. *The Motley Fool's* Nicholas Rossolillo did just that:

> *I went to McDonald's first, location-services equipped so my phone knew I was in range, and ordered my penny Whopper. The coupon applied itself, prompted me to set up an account, asked if I wanted emailed news and deals (nope), and asked for payment information. Next stop, Burger King, where dine-in, pickup, or drive-through could be selected. Not bad for an almost-free lunch.*[123]

Within days, 50,000 people downloaded the BK app to buy their penny Whopper.[124]

Attack a competitive move designed to reduce a rival's market share or profits

T-Mobile has launched a strategic initiative aimed at removing key restrictions found in its competitors' wireless services.

A **response** is a countermove, prompted by a rival's attack, that is designed to defend or improve a company's market share or profit. There are two kinds of responses.[125] The first is to match or mirror your competitor's move. This is what McDonald's did when it responded to BK with a one-cent Big Mac. But that was only for delivery via DoorDash, which costs $6 ($4 for the DoorDash delivery and $2 for a suggested tip for the DoorDash driver).[126] Yes, McDonald's responded, but BK customers got the better deal with a true penny Whopper.

The second kind of response, however, is to respond along a different dimension from your competitor's move or attack. Wireless carriers, such as AT&T and Verizon, have typically responded to competitors' attacks by cutting prices, expanding coverage, or speeding up their networks. T-Mobile, once the smallest of the major wireless carriers, faired poorly on those dimensions, losing 2 million customers.[127] In the past six years, however, T-Mobile has grown from 33 million to 86 million customers, increasing its share of the US wireless market from 10 to 16.4 percent.[128] The company achieved this remarkable growth by

Response a competitive countermove, prompted by a rival's attack, to defend or improve a company's market share or profit

responding with an "uncarrier" strategy that removes key restrictions found in its competitors' wireless services.[129] Overage charges? Not at T-Mobile, which offers unlimited minutes and texts. Exorbitant roaming charges for international plans? T-Mobile charges a meager 20 cents per minute for international calls, while providing unlimited international data and texts at no extra charge in 140 countries. Moreover, with 35 percent of US international calls and 55 percent of US international travel to Mexico and Canada, T-Mobile has consolidated all three countries into one North American market in which access to data plans, 4G LTE fast connections, and calling are included—at no extra cost—for T-Mobile customers. Finally, are low data caps preventing music and streaming video on your phone? T-Mobile One introduced unlimited data, with music and HD streaming. T-Mobile then cut the price of its unlimited plans by including sales taxes and regulator fees in the advertised prices (not in addition to), and by reducing plans $5 a month if customers used autopay and by $10 a month when a phone uses less than 2GB a month (T-Mobile Kickback.)[130]

Market commonality and resource similarity determine the likelihood of an attack or response, that is, whether a company is likely to attack a direct competitor or to strike back with a strong response when attacked. When market commonality is large, and companies have overlapping products, services, or customers in multiple markets, there is less motivation to attack and more motivation to respond to an attack. The reason for this is straightforward: When firms are direct competitors in a large number of markets, they have a great deal at stake.

Airlines Air France-KLM and Lufthansa once dominated highly lucrative routes between Europe's and Asia's largest cities. That is, until Middle Eastern carriers such as Emirates Airlines and Etihad Airways attacked their market shares and profits by offering high-end amenities such as private suites, onboard showers, and a bar in first class. The European carriers quickly took note, with Air France-KLM CEO Alexandre de Juniac saying, "The Gulf carriers have significantly captured market share."[131] Market commonality is extensive in the airline industry. With so much at stake, Germany-based Lufthansa responded by spending $3.4 billion for 650 new first-class seats, 7,000 business-class seats that lie flat (for sleeping), and upgrades to premium economy seating and in-flight entertainment. Air France-KLM responded similarly, spending $1.1 billion to install private, first-class suites on 44 planes and replace economy-class seating.[132]

Whereas market commonality affects the likelihood of an attack or a response to an attack, resource similarity largely affects response capability, that is, how quickly and forcefully a company can respond to an attack. When resource similarity is strong, the responding firm will generally be able to match the strategic moves of the attacking firm. Consequently, a firm is less likely to attack firms with similar levels of resources because it is unlikely to gain any sustained advantage when the responding firms strike back. On the other hand, if one firm is substantially stronger than another (i.e., there is low resource similarity), then a competitive attack is more likely to produce sustained competitive advantage.

In general, the more moves (i.e., attacks) a company initiates against direct competitors, and the greater a company's tendency to respond when attacked, the better its performance. More specifically, attackers and early responders (companies that are quick to launch a retaliatory attack) tend to gain market share and profits at the expense of late responders. This is not to suggest that a full-attack strategy always works best. In fact, attacks can provoke harsh retaliatory responses.

Amazon uses automated pricing algorithms to search competitors' retail websites for prices. When competitors lower prices, Amazon retaliates by aggressively lowering its prices to match or beat competitors' prices. For example, the Star Shower Motion is a light projector sold during holiday season, which projects decorative light patterns on the outside of homes. It sells to retailers for a wholesale price of $30, retails for a suggested price of $49.99, and thus offers the possibility of a $19.99 profit. But once Amazon's algorithm found lower prices on competitors' websites, it began cutting Amazon's price. When competitors repeated lowered prices in response, the algorithm eventually cut Amazon's price to just below $31, or less than a dollar above cost. A. J. Khubani, CEO of Telebrands, which sells the Star Shower Motion, said that traditional brick-and-mortar retailers were angry that Amazon retaliated by cutting the price to $31. He said, "Keeping everybody happy while we are selling on Amazon has become a challenge."[133]

Amazon's aggressive retaliatory responses, driven by its web search algorithm, followed by competitors' retaliatory price cuts, followed by more retaliatory price cutting from Amazon, eliminated all of the profit [after shipping costs] on the hot-selling Star Shower Motion projector. Because the pricing algorithm does this so often, Amazon calls these CRaP products, meaning "Can't Realize a Profit."[134] Despite the hit to its bottom line, Amazon has no plans to stop selling CRaP products. Amazon spokesperson Julie Law said, "We find the lowest prices and meet or beat them every day."[135] Consequently, when deciding when, where, and what strategic actions to take against a direct competitor, managers should always consider the possibility of retaliation.

7 | Innovation and Change

Photobank gallery/Shutterstock.com

LEARNING OUTCOMES

7-1 Explain why innovation matters to companies.

7-2 Outline the steps for the different methods that managers can use to effectively manage innovation in their organizations.

7-3 Discuss why not changing can lead to organizational decline.

7-4 Discuss the different methods that managers can use to better manage change as it occurs.

7-1 WHY INNOVATION MATTERS

As you approach your office parking garage, the LED lights inside brighten. Prompted by an app on your smartphone, the garage camera matches your license plate to your personnel record, raises the gate, and locates a parking space. Inside the office, the same app finds a desk based on your schedule and preferences (standing desk, sitting desk, work booth, concentration room, meeting room, or who you're working with that day). Before setting off to your desk, you drop your coat and personal belongings in an empty locker (indicated by a green light), using your ID badge to unlock it. As you arrive at your desk, the temperature and lighting automatically adjust to the personal preferences you set in the app. A central dashboard collects data on everything from energy usage to when the espresso machines—which, naturally, remember how you like your coffee— need to be refilled. The north-facing exterior wall is glass, while the

south-facing exterior wall is composed of an alternating pattern of windows and solar panels that generate more electricity than the building uses. And when everyone leaves for the day (with pre-ordered evening meals delivered to their desks so they don't have to grocery shop on the way home), small security robots begin their patrol while other robots clean the rooms that were most heavily used that day.[1] Sound futuristic? It's not. This is routine at **the Edge,** a smart building in Amsterdam where a complex network of cables and 28,000 sensors connects the building, its mechanical structures (heating, ventilation, plumbing, and electricity), technological systems, and occupants via a smartphone app.[2] **Organizational innovation** is the successful implementation of creative ideas, like the construction of the Edge office building in Amsterdam (http://ovgrealestate. com/project-development/the-edge).

Organizational innovation the successful implementation of creative ideas in organizations

In an article reviewing the advance of technology from 2009 to 2019, *Wall Street Journal* columnist Andy Kessler wrote, "In 2009 we wore analog watches, had landline phones, hung out in bookstores, and even hailed taxis. Ah, the good old days. Please don't make us go back."[3] Similarly, today, we can only guess what changes technological innovations will bring in the next 10 years. Will the smartphones in our pockets be replaced with smart glasses or smart contact lenses that operate by voice and where your eyes look on a screen that only you can see? Will solar power and wind power get cheap and efficient enough so that your home can have a standalone power source off the main electrical grid? Will fully automated, self-driving cars chauffeur you to the office (as you work in the back seat on a computing tablet via a 5G or 6G wireless connection that is a hundred to thousands of times faster than 4G)? Or will you fly to work via air taxis above previously congested roads and freeways?[4] Will you commute from your apartment in New York City to your job in Washington D.C. in just 29 minutes via one of Elon Musk's hyperloops at 700+ miles per hour?[5] Or will you work virtually from home with a 3D holographic version of Zoom so it seems as if the people you're videoconferencing with are sitting next to you? Who knows? The only thing we do know about the next 10 years is that innovation will continue to change our lives.

Let's begin our discussion of innovation by learning about 7-1a technology cycles and 7-2b innovation streams.

7-1a Technology Cycles

In Chapter 3, you learned that technology consists of the knowledge, tools, and techniques used to transform inputs (raw materials and information) into outputs (products and services). A **technology cycle** begins with the birth of a new technology and ends when that technology reaches its limits and dies as it is replaced by a newer, substantially better technology.[6] For example, technology cycles occurred when air conditioners supplanted fans, when Henry Ford's Model T replaced horse-drawn carriages, when planes replaced trains as a means of cross-country travel, when vaccines that prevented diseases replaced medicines designed to treat them, and when battery-powered wristwatches replaced mechanically powered, stem-wound wristwatches.

From Gutenberg's invention of the printing press in 1448 to the rapid advance of the Internet, studies of hundreds of technological innovations have shown that nearly all technology cycles follow the typical **S-curve pattern of innovation** shown in Exhibit 7.1.[7] Early in a technology cycle, there is still much to learn so progress is slow, as depicted by point A on the S-curve. The flat slope indicates that increased effort (in terms of money or research and development) brings only small improvements in technological performance.

Fortunately, as the new technology matures, researchers figure out how to get better performance from it. This is represented by point B of the S-curve in Exhibit 7.1. The steeper slope indicates that small amounts of effort will result in significant increases in performance. At point C, the flat slope again indicates that further efforts to develop this particular technology will result in only small increases in performance. More importantly, however, point C indicates that the performance limits of that particular technology are being reached. In other words, additional significant improvements in performance are highly unlikely.

Intel's technology cycles have followed this pattern. **Intel** spends billions to develop new computer chips and to build new facilities to produce them. Intel has found that the technology cycle for its integrated circuits is about three years. In each three-year cycle, Intel spends billions to introduce a new chip, improves the chip by making it a little bit faster each year, and then replaces that chip at the end of the cycle with a brand-new, different chip that is substantially faster than the old chip. At first, though (point A), the billions Intel spends typically produce only small improvements in performance. But after six months to a year with a new chip design, Intel's engineering and

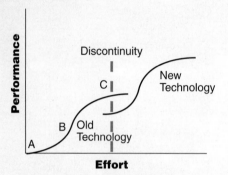

Exhibit 7.1
S-Curves and Technological Innovation

Source: R. N. Foster, Innovation: *The Attacker's Advantage* (New York: Summitt, 1986).

Technology cycle a cycle that begins with the birth of a new technology and ends when that technology reaches its limits and is replaced by a newer, substantially better technolog

S-curve pattern of innovation a pattern of technological innovation characterized by slow initial progress, then rapid progress, and then slow progress again as a technology matures and reaches its limits

production people typically figure out how to make the new chips much faster than they were initially (point B). Yet, despite impressive gains in performance, Intel is unable to make a particular computer chip run any faster because the chip reaches its design limits.

After a technology has reached its limits at the top of the S-curve, significant improvements in performance usually come from radical new designs or new performance-enhancing materials. In Exhibit 7.1, that new technology is represented by the second S-curve. The changeover or discontinuity between the old and new technologies is represented by the dotted line. At first, the old and new technologies will likely coexist. Eventually, however, the new technology will replace the old technology. When that happens, the old technology cycle will be complete and a new one will have started. The changeover between newer and older computer chip designs typically takes about one year. Over time, improving existing technology (tweaking the performance of the current technology cycle), combined with replacing old technology with new technology cycles (that is, new, faster computer chip designs replacing older ones), has increased the speed of computer processors by a factor of 2.2 million! Today's superpowerful 64-bit processors, which provide instantaneous processing and results, have 10 billion transistors compared to 3.1 million transistors for 1990s 32-bit processors, 275,000 transistors for the earliest 1980s 32-bit processors, or just 4,500 transistors for the 8-bit processors, which began personal computing in the 1970s.[8]

Though the evolution of Intel's chips has been used to illustrate S-curves and technology cycles, it's important to note that technology cycles and technological innovation don't necessarily involve faster computer chips or electric automobiles. Remember, *technology* is simply the knowledge, tools, and techniques used to transform inputs into outputs. So, a technology cycle occurs whenever there are major advances or changes in the *knowledge*, *tools*, and *techniques* of a field or discipline, whatever it may be.

For example, one of the most important technology cycles in the history of civilization occurred in 1859, when 1,300 miles of central sewer line were constructed throughout London to carry human waste to the sea more than 11 miles away. This extensive sewer system replaced the widespread practice of dumping raw sewage directly into streets, where people walked through it and where it drained into public wells that supplied drinking water. Though the relationship between raw sewage and cholera wasn't known at the time, preventing waste runoff from contaminating water supplies stopped the spread of that disease, which had killed millions of people for centuries in cities throughout the world.[9] Safe water supplies immediately translated into better health and longer life expectancies. Indeed, readers of the *British Medical* Journal "chose the introduction of clean water and sewage disposal" as the most important medical advancement since 1840.[10] The water you drink today is safe thanks to this technological breakthrough. So, when you think about technology cycles, don't automatically think "high tech." Instead, broaden your perspective by considering advances or changes in *any* kind of knowledge, tools, and techniques.

7-1b Innovation Streams

In Chapter 6, you learned that organizations can create *competitive advantage* for themselves if they have a *distinctive competence* that allows them to make, do, or perform something better than their competitors. A competitive advantage becomes sustainable if other companies cannot duplicate the benefits obtained from that distinctive competence. Technological innovation, however, can enable competitors to duplicate the benefits obtained from a company's distinctive advantage. It can also quickly turn a company's competitive advantage into a competitive disadvantage.

Thirty years ago, digital cameras began replacing film-based technology. But with digital camera sales having peaked at 120 million cameras in 2008 and crashed to 15.2 million cameras in 2019, digital camera makers are losing their competitive advantage to smartphones with HD photo and video capabilities far better than basic digital cameras.[11] Shigenobu Nagamori, CEO of Nidec, which makes electric motors used in consumer electronics, says that thanks to smartphones, we should, "assume that the inexpensive cameras are dead, just like PCs."[12] Tsugio Tsuchiya, a general manager at Tamron that makes lenses for more advanced digital single-lens reflex cameras (DSLRs), worries that, "Smartphones pose a threat not just to compact cameras but entry-level DSLRs," which start at $400 and use interchangeable lenses, such as telescoping zooms.[13] Indeed, in fall of 2019 Apple's iPhone 11 pro incorporated three 12-megapixel sensors to work with three lenses, a 13mm ultra-wide, a 26mm for "normal" pictures and a 56mm 2x optical zoom, which makes objects look twice as big. All three of those lenses can also be zoomed further with a 10x software zoom function.[14]

Peter Gudella/Shutterstock.com

Exhibit 7.2
Innovation Streams: Technology Cycles over Time

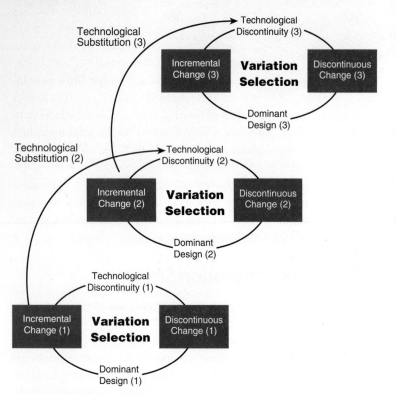

Source: Adapted from M. L. Tushman, P. C. Anderson, and C. O'Reilly, "Technology Cycles, Innovation Streams and Ambidextrous Organizations: Organization Renewal Through Innovation Streams and Strategic Change," *On Managing Strategic Innovation and Change*, eds. M. L. Tushman and P. C. Anderson (New Oxford Press, 1997) 3–23.

Innovation streams patterns of innovation over time that can create sustainable competitive advantage

Technological discontinuity the phase of an innovation stream in which a scientific advance or unique combination of existing technologies creates a significant breakthrough in performance or function

Discontinuous change the phase of a technology cycle characterized by technological substitution and design competition

Technological substitution the purchase of new technologies to replace older ones

Design competition competition between old and new technologies to establish a new technological standard or dominant design

Companies that want to sustain a competitive advantage must understand and protect themselves from the strategic threats of innovation. Over the long run, the best way for a company to do that is to create a stream of its own innovative ideas and products year after year. Consequently, we define **innovation streams** as patterns of innovation over time that can create sustainable competitive advantage.[15] Exhibit 7.2 shows a typical innovation consisting of a series of technology cycles.

Recall that a technology cycle begins with a new technology and ends when that technology is replaced by a newer, substantially better technology. The innovation stream in Exhibit 7.2 shows three such technology cycles.

An innovation stream begins with a **technological discontinuity**, in which a scientific advance or a unique combination of existing technologies creates a significant breakthrough in performance or function. Imagine the inefficiency of just one train running on the train track between two cities. It goes to the first, returns to the second, and so on. That, however, is exactly how elevators work, up to the top, down to the bottom, just one car per elevator shaft. **ThyssenKrupp**, maker of the Multi elevator, solved that problem by replacing the steel safety cable and pulleys used to move elevators with magnetic levitation (similar to that used on high-speed trains) that allows elevators cars to "float" to their destinations. This not only reduces the space needed for elevators by 25 percent but, without cables, multiple cars can use the same shaft, just like a subway line, and they can even move horizontally, from one side of a building to another, all of which will allow the design of wider, uniquely shaped buildings.[16] Thyssenkrupp vice president Brad Nemeth said, "The sideways capability will allow passengers to now move to all parts of a building, significantly increasing efficiency."[17]

Technological discontinuities are followed by a **discontinuous change**, which is characterized by technological substitution and design competition. **Technological substitution** occurs when customers purchase new technologies to replace older technologies. Besides digital cameras, smartphones have replaced these older technologies in the last decade: landlines, pay phones, and walkie-talkies; timers and alarm clocks; photo albums, maps and GPS devices; address books, calendars, and business cards; radios, CDs, and portable MP3 players; voice recorders and notepads; printed books, newspapers and magazines; and finally, emergency flashlights, calculators, and barcode scanners.[18]

Discontinuous change is also characterized by **design competition,** in which the old technology and several different new technologies compete to establish a new technological standard or dominant design. Because of large investments in old technology and because the new and old technologies are often incompatible with each other, companies and consumers are reluctant to switch to a different technology during a design competition. For example, the telegraph was so widely used as a means of communication in the late 1800s that at first almost no one understood why telephones would be a better way to communicate. It's hard to envision today, with everyone constantly checking cell phones for email, texts, voice mails, and social media, but as Edwin Schlossberg explains in his book *Interactive Excellence*, "People could not imagine why they would want or need to talk immediately to someone who was across town or, even more absurdly, in another town. Although people could write letters to one another, and some could send telegraph messages, the idea of sending one's voice to another place and then instantly hearing another voice in return was simply not a model that existed in people's experience. They also did not think it was worth the money to accelerate sending or hearing a message."[19] In addition, during design competition, the older technology usually improves significantly in response to the competitive threat from the new technologies; this response also slows the changeover from older to newer technologies.

Discontinuous change is followed by the emergence of a **dominant design**, which becomes the new accepted market standard for technology.[20] Dominant designs emerge in several ways. One is critical mass, meaning that a particular technology can become the dominant design simply because most people use it – for example, Blu-ray beating out HD-DVD to become the dominant design for high definition video.[21] Critical mass determined the dominant design for wireless device charging, where instead of plugging in your device to recharge, you simply place it on top of a recharging station containing magnetic charging coils. Over the last decade, the following three different wireless charging technologies were trying to become the dominant standard:

» the Power Matters Alliance (PMA) backing Duracell's Powermat;

» the Alliance for Wireless Power (A4WP) and its Rezence charging mats;

» and the Wireless Power Consortium (WPC) and its Qi charging mats.

However, PMA and A4WP joined forces in 2015 under the Powermat name to create a combined standard for wireless charging devices.[22] Then in 2018, Powermat joined the WPC and its Qi standard. Powermat CEO Elad Dubzinski said, "Qi has become the dominant wireless charging standard on the market."[23] Today, 90 percent of wireless charging products are based on

Qi technology. Again, why does this matter? It matters because the market for wireless charging, estimated at $2.6 billion, is projected to increase to $21 billion by 2023.[24] In other words, becoming the dominant standard is worth billions to the winner.

The best technology doesn't always become the dominant design because a number of other factors come into play. For instance, a design can become dominant if it solves a practical problem. The QWERTY keyboard (named for the top left line of letters) became the dominant design for typewriters because it slowed typists who, by typing too fast, caused mechanical typewriter keys to jam. Though computers can easily be switched to the Dvorak keyboard layout, which doubles typing speed and cuts typing errors in half, QWERTY lives on as the standard keyboard. In this instance, the QWERTY keyboard solved a problem that, with computers, is no longer relevant. Yet it remains the dominant design not because it is the best technology but because most people learned to type that way and continue to use it.

Dominant designs can also emerge through independent standards bodies. The International Telecommunication Union (ITU) (www.itu.ch) is an independent organization that establishes standards for the communications industry. The ITU was founded in Paris in 1865 because European countries all had different telegraph systems that could not communicate with each other. Messages crossing borders had to be transcribed from one country's system before they could be coded and delivered on another. After three months of negotiations, 20 countries signed the International Telegraph Convention, which standardized equipment and instructions, enabling telegraph messages to flow seamlessly from country to country. Today, as in 1865, various standards

> **Dominant design** a new technological design or process that becomes the accepted market standard

Luna Display: When Apple "Sherlocks" Your Product

Luna Display uses apps and a $50 hardware dongle to turn iPads into second screens for Mac computers. Whether you're at the office or on the road, if you have an iPad you've got a second screen. However, Apple recently copied or *sherlocked* Luna Display with Sidecar, which allows Mac users to "use your iPad as a second display." Luna Display's marketing director Savannah Reising wrote, "For our team of just 13 people, it was devastating news. Watching Apple present Sidecar to the world was like seeing years of hard work flash before your eyes while someone else takes credit for it." So, what did Luna Display do?

First, it recognized that instead of worrying about competitors, it should have been worrying about Apple. Reising said, Apple "...ordered thousands of dollars' worth of our hardware, and we naively thought it was because they were interested in our product. It turns out that they were... just not in the way we were thinking." Second, it added functions to Luna Display that are not in Sidecar. Third, it focused on their AstroPad Studio app, which allows artists to draw with precision in Mac apps using the Apple Pencil on their iPads. Finally, it reengineered using a cross-platform programming language that works on Macs *and* Windows and Linux computers, as well as Android tablets.

AVN Photo Lab/Shutterstock.com

When your product gets sherlocked, Reising advises, "Refocus your energy on your users by stopping to listen to what they're asking for; harness your team's agile spirit; lean in to your vulnerabilities; and double-down on what you do best."

Sources: Apple Support, "Use your iPad as a second display for your Mac with Sidecar," Apple, January 28, 2020, accessed March 29, 2020, https://support.apple.com/en-us/HT210380; M. Ronge, "Why We're Bringing Astropad Cross-Platform with Rust," Astropad, October 7, 2019, accessed March 29, 2020, https://astropad.com/why-rust/; S. Reising, "What To Do When You Get Sherlocked by Apple," Astropad, October 7, 2019, accessed March 29, 2020, https://astropad.com/sherlocked-by-apple/.

---

are proposed, discussed, negotiated, and changed until agreement is reached on a final set of standards that communication industries (internet, telephony, satellites, radio) will follow worldwide.

For example, the telecommunications industry is close to agreeing on standards for 5G, or fifth-generation, service on mobile devices, but the ITU is scheduled to finalize its IMT-2020 global standards in 2020.[25] Telecom operators are hoping for a 5G standard data-transmission speed of 1–10 gigabits per second, fast enough to download high-def movies within seconds. Another desired 5G standard is for two 5G devices to communicate with each other with a latency (or wait time) of just 1 millisecond, down from 50 milliseconds with 4G.[26] Shorter 5G latencies would allow doctors in remote hospitals to conduct life-saving robotics-based surgeries on patients in other locations and the operation of driverless cars. It's estimated that it will take seven years and $275 billion for US wireless providers to make the change from 4G to 5G.[27]

Technological lockout
the inability of a company to competitively sell its products because it relies on old technology or a nondominant design

No matter how it happens, the emergence of a dominant design is a key event in an innovation stream. First, the emergence of a dominant design indicates that there are winners and losers. Technological innovation is both competence enhancing and competence destroying. Companies that bet on the now-dominant design usually prosper. By contrast, when companies bet on the wrong design or the old technology, they may experience **technological lockout**, which occurs when a new dominant design (that is, a significantly better technology) prevents a company from competitively selling its products or makes it difficult to do so.[28] Adobe's Flash software, which supports animation and video on web pages and ads, was once ubiquitous in website design, including video streaming platforms YouTube and Netflix. In 2010, due to resource intensity and security issues, Apple stopped supporting Flash on iPhones and iPads. By 2015, YouTube, Facebook, and Netflix had removed Flash, opting for the new HTML5 video standard.[29] In 2017, Google's Chrome Browser stopped automatically running Flash (unless users configured it).[30] Then when Google, Microsoft and Apple indicated they would completely stop Flash from working

NEED INNOVATION? OFFER A PRIZE

Frustrated with the slow pace of innovation, companies and governments are awarding $2 billion a year in 30,000 innovation competitions. Zeniz Tata of XPrize, which runs innovation competitions on behalf of major corporations and foundations, says, "A prize allows for crazy open innovation to test a new idea, to take a gamble, to take a risk which you cannot do with grant money." XPrize is currently offering a $20 million prize for turning CO_2 emissions into a valuable product and $7 million to create a handheld "tricorder" that scans peoples' health for 13 conditions. Other competitions offer prizes for creating a delivery drone ($50,000) or a new use for canned tuna fish ($5,000 from a French food supplier). So, do you need innovation fast? Hold a competition and offer prize money!

Source: L. Chapman, "These Hackathon Hustlers Make Their Living from Corporate Coding Contests," *Bloomberg*, April 4, 2017, accessed April 5, 2017, https://www.bloomberg.com/news/features/2017-04-04/these-hackathon-hustlers-make-their-living-from-corporate-coding-contests; "What Is an XPrize?" XPrize, accessed April 5, 2017, http://www.xprize.org/about.

W. Scott McGill/123RF

with future versions of their web browsers, Adobe announced it would stop supporting Flash as a product. "We will stop updating and distributing the Flash Player at the end of 2020 and encourage content creators to migrate any existing Flash content to these new open formats."[31] Technological lockout is a serious threat, as more companies are likely to go out of business in a time of discontinuous change and changing standards than in an economic recession or slowdown.

Second, the emergence of a dominant design signals a shift from design experimentation and competition to **incremental change,** a phase in which companies innovate by lowering the cost and improving the functioning and performance of the dominant design. For example, manufacturing efficiencies enable Intel to cut the cost of its chips by one-half to two-thirds during a technology cycle, while doubling or tripling their speed. This focus on improving the dominant design continues until the next technological discontinuity occurs.

7-2 MANAGING INNOVATION

One consequence of technology cycles and innovation streams is that managers must be equally good at managing innovation in two very different circumstances. First, during discontinuous change, companies must find a way to anticipate and survive the technological changes that can suddenly transform industry leaders into losers and industry unknowns into powerhouses. Companies that can't manage innovation following technological discontinuities risk quick organizational decline and dissolution. Second, after a new dominant design emerges following discontinuous change, companies must manage the very different process of incremental improvement and innovation. Companies that can't manage incremental innovation slowly deteriorate as they fall further behind industry leaders.

Unfortunately, what works well when managing innovation during discontinuous change doesn't work well when managing innovation during periods of incremental change (and vice versa).

Consequently, to successfully manage innovation streams, companies need to be good at three things: 7-2a managing sources of innovation, 7-2b managing innovation during discontinuous change, and 7-2c managing innovation during incremental change.

> **Incremental change** the phase of a technology cycle in which companies innovate by lowering costs and improving the functioning and performance of the dominant technological design

7-2a Managing Sources of Innovation

Innovation comes from great ideas. So, a starting point for managing innovation is to manage the sources of innovation, that is, where new ideas come from. One place where new ideas originate is with brilliant inventors. But only a few companies have the likes of a Thomas Edison, Alexander Graham Bell, or Nikola Tesla. Given that great thinkers and inventors are in short supply, what might companies do to ensure a steady flow of good ideas?

Well, when we say that innovation begins with great ideas, we're really saying that innovation begins with creativity. As we defined it at the beginning of this chapter, creativity is the production of novel and useful ideas.[32] Although companies can't command employees to be creative ("You *will* be more creative!"), they can jump-start innovation by building **creative work environments** in which workers perceive that creative thoughts and ideas are welcomed and valued. As Exhibit 7.3 shows, creative work environments have six components that encourage creativity: challenging work, organizational encouragement, supervisory encouragement, work group encouragement, freedom, and a lack of organizational impediments.[33]

Work is *challenging* when it requires effort, demands attention and focus, and is perceived as important to others in the organization. According to researcher Mihaly Csikszentmihalyi (pronounced ME-high-ee CHICK-sent-me-high-ee), challenging work promotes creativity because it creates a rewarding psychological experience known as "flow." **Flow** is a psychological state of effortlessness, in which you become completely absorbed in what you're doing and time seems to fly. When flow occurs, who you are and what you're doing become one. Csikszentmihalyi first encountered flow when studying artists: "What struck me by looking at artists at work was their tremendous focus on the work, this enormous involvement, this forgetting of time and body. It wasn't justified by expectation of rewards, like, 'Aha, I'm going to sell this painting.'"[34] Csikszentmihalyi has found that chess players, rock climbers, dancers, surgeons, and athletes regularly experience flow, too. Today, achieving flow is increasingly challenging. For example, employees say that their biggest distractions are coworkers talking loudly on the phone or to others nearby.[35] Likewise, a study by Professor Gloria Mark at the University of California, Irvine, found that workers focus on their computer screen an average of 1 minute 15 seconds before shifting their attention, down from 2 minutes 18 seconds in 2008. Professor Mark's research also shows that workers suffer from self-inflicted digital distractions such as visiting Facebook an average of 21 times per day and checking email 74 times per day.[36] Flow can't be achieved when employees constantly interrupt their work or are frequently distracted by others.

Removing distractions assists in creating an environment conducive to flow. Another key part of creating flow experiences, and thus creative work environments, is to achieve a balance between skills and task challenge. Workers become bored when they can do more than is required of them. Or, they become anxious when their skills aren't sufficient to accomplish a task. When skills and task challenges are balanced, however, flow and creativity can occur.

A creative work environment requires three kinds of encouragement: organizational, supervisory, and work group. *Organizational encouragement* of creativity occurs when management encourages risk taking and new ideas, supports and fairly evaluates new ideas, rewards and recognizes creativity, and encourages the sharing of new ideas throughout different parts of the company. **GE Healthcare** honors teams who have "dared to try new things and learned from failure." The idea is not to reward failure but to encourage risk taking and the sharing of new ideas. GE spokesperson Laura Paredes

Exhibit 7.3
Components of Creative Work Environments

Source: T. M. Amabile, R. Conti, H. Coon, J. Lazenby, and M. Herron, "Assessing the Work Environment for Creativity," *Academy of Management Journal* 39 (1996): 1154–1184.

Creative work environments workplace cultures in which workers perceive that new ideas are welcomed, valued, and encouraged

Flow a psychological state of effortlessness, in which you become completely absorbed in what you're doing, and time seems to pass quickly

says that GE Healthcare employees formalized the sharing process through a short event it called "Failcon," at which people shared the lessons they learned from failed ideas and efforts.[37] Likewise, failure is also celebrated at X, Alphabet's (**Alphabet** is Google's corporate name) research and development lab, which is also called the *moonshot factory*. Because of the extreme difficulty of X's projects, from self-driving cars to trying to get fuel from seawater, there is a strong expectation that success will be preceded by multiple failures. So, like at GE Healthcare, X encourages risk taking by celebrating failure. One way that's done is by letting employees put stickers of crumpled paper (signifying that it's time to go back to the proverbial drawing board) on their laptops whenever they abandon ideas or methods that weren't working.[38] Astro Teller, X's Captain of Moonshots, says, "We keep people brave by rewarding teams that kill their projects. We see killing projects as a normal part of doing business because it means we can go faster and take on ideas that are more promising."[39]

Supervisory encouragement of creativity occurs when supervisors provide clear goals, encourage open interaction with subordinates, and actively support development teams' work and ideas. When it comes to clear goals, MIT's Andrew McAfee says *be specific*. He says goals such as, "We need to figure out why so many people are leaving our site before completing a transaction," or, "How can we increase sales to women in their 30s?" are much better at generating innovations than broad goals such as, "What should our next great idea be?"[40] **Malta**, an Alphabet X lab spinoff, began with the goal of creating "low-cost, long-duration energy storage" for solar and wind energy.[41] Because it's not always windy or sunny, solar and wind energy must be used when generated, stored for later use, or lost. Because of inefficient power storage technology, 30 percent or more of stored solar and wind energy is lost every day.[42] Malta takes solar- and wind-generated electricity, converts and stores it as heat in large steel tanks of molten salt, and then reverses the process when needed to produce electricity. Unlike lithium batteries, Malta's molten salt tanks can store energy for weeks with much less energy loss. Furthermore, Malta's storage tank technology will last up to 20 years, or twice as long as lithium batteries.[43]

Work group encouragement occurs when group members have diverse experience, education, and backgrounds, and the group fosters mutual openness to ideas; positive, constructive challenge to ideas; and shared commitment to ideas. *Freedom* means having autonomy over one's day-to-day work and a sense of ownership and control over one's ideas. Numerous studies have indicated that creative ideas thrive under conditions of freedom.

To foster creativity, companies may also have to *remove impediments* to creativity from their work environments. Internal conflict and power struggles, rigid management structures, and a conservative bias toward the status quo can all discourage creativity. They create the perception that others in the organization will decide which ideas are acceptable and deserve support. One of the biggest impediments to creativity is a lack of time to be curious, to read broadly, to think, and to actually work on creative tasks and projects. Regular job requirements always push creativity to the bottom of the to-do list. Why? Because according to one executive, companies are "organized to deliver predictable, reliable results – and that's exactly the problem."[44] Perhaps the best way to remove time as an impediment to creativity is to give employees time to *not* do their jobs. At Singapore-based DBS Bank, technology employees follow the 70:20:10 rule. Software developers spend 70 percent of their time on their normal job responsibilities, 20 percent

DBS Bank software developers follow the 70:20:10 rule when it comes to time on task. The majority of their time is spent on normal job responsibilities. The remaining time is spent on improvements and exploration of their their own ideas.

of their time on ways to improve the work done in their teams and departments, and 10 percent of their time on whatever experiments and ideas they want to explore. DBS reinforces the importance of the 70:20:10 rule by having software developers share their projects and experiments with others.[45]

7-2b Experiential Approach: Managing Innovation during Discontinuous Change

A study of 72 product development projects (that is, innovation) in 36 computer companies across the United States, Europe, and Asia sheds light on how to manage innovation. Companies that succeeded in periods of discontinuous change (characterized by technological substitution and design competition, as described earlier) typically followed an experiential approach to innovation.[46] The **experiential approach to innovation** assumes that innovation is occurring within a highly uncertain environment and that the key to fast product innovation is to use intuition, flexible options, and hands-on experience to reduce uncertainty and accelerate learning and understanding. The experiential approach to innovation has five aspects: design iterations, testing, milestones, multifunctional teams, and powerful leaders.[47]

An *iteration* is a repetition. So, a **design iteration** is a cycle of repetition in which a company tests a prototype of a new product or service, improves on the design, and then builds and tests the improved product or service prototype. A **product prototype** is a full-scale working model that is being tested for design, function, and reliability. **Testing** is a systematic comparison of different product designs or design iterations. Companies that want to create a new dominant design following a technological discontinuity quickly build, test, improve, and retest a series of different product prototypes. Procter & Gamble (P&G) went through hundreds of design iterations to test prototypes for its nontoxic Zevo bug traps, which use "multi-spectrum light technology and a body heat attractant" to lure and trap bugs.[48] P&G tested different light wavelengths, releasing flies and other insects in a tiny tent to see which of two wavelengths attracted more bugs.[49] "Winning" prototypes were tested against other light wavelengths until the most effective one was found. Likewise, it tested 50 different iterations of the cover for its sticky replaceable cartridge, looking for a design with big enough openings for bugs to pass through, and, a plastic color that balanced showing enough light to attract bugs with enough opacity to prevent consumers from seeing the gross collection of accumulated dead bugs.[50]

By trying a number of very different designs or making successive improvements and changes in the same design, frequent design iterations reduce uncertainty and improve understanding. Simply put, the more prototypes you build, the more likely you are to learn what works and what doesn't. Also, when designers and engineers build a number of prototypes, they are less likely to fall in love with a particular prototype. Instead, they'll be more concerned with improving the product or technology as much as they can. Testing speeds up and improves the innovation process, too. When two very different design prototypes are tested against each other, or the new design iteration is tested against the previous iteration, product design strengths and weaknesses quickly become apparent. Likewise, testing uncovers errors early in the design process when they are easiest to correct. Finally, testing accelerates learning and understanding by forcing engineers and product designers to examine hard data about product performance. When there's hard evidence that prototypes are testing well, the confidence of the design team grows. Also, personal conflict between design team members is less likely when testing focuses on hard measurements and facts rather than on personal hunches and preferences.

Milestones are formal project review points used to assess progress and performance. For example, a company that has put itself on a 12-month schedule to complete a project might schedule milestones at the three-month, six-month, and nine-month points on the schedule. By making people regularly assess what they're doing, how well they're performing, and whether they need to take corrective action, milestones provide structure to the general chaos that follows technological discontinuities. Regularly meeting milestones gives people a sense of accomplishment and can shorten the innovation process by creating a sense of urgency that keeps people on task.

Experiential approach to innovation an approach to innovation that assumes a highly uncertain environment and uses intuition, flexible options, and hands-on experience to reduce uncertainty and accelerate learning and understanding

Design iteration a cycle of repetition in which a company tests a prototype of a new product or service, improves on that design, and then builds and tests the improved prototype

Product prototype a full-scale, working model that is being tested for design, function, and reliability

Testing the systematic comparison of different product designs or design iterations

Milestones formal project review points used to assess progress and performance

At X, Alphabet's research and development lab known as the "moonshot factory," project milestones must be achieved before receiving additional funding or staff. One of the key milestones is called Foundry because it requires project engineers to develop business plans for their technologies. For example, X's Foghorn project was created to develop carbon-neutral fuel from seawater. With the world's unlimited supply of seawater, the potential was huge. However, after two years, X killed the project at the Foundry milestone because it wasn't viable as a business. Costs were substantially higher than gasoline and the technology, in early research stages, was moving too slowly.[51] X pays team members "failure bonuses" for shutting down projects that won't make it to the Foundry milestone. When a team of 30 engineers shut down a two-year-old project, Astro Teller, X's Captain of Moonshots praised them publicly, saying, "Thank you! By ending their project, this team has done more to speed up innovation at X this month than any other team in this room."[52]

Multifunctional teams are work teams composed of people from different departments. Multifunctional teams accelerate learning and understanding by mixing and integrating technical, marketing, and manufacturing activities. By involving all key departments in development from the start, multifunctional teams speed innovation through early identification of new ideas or problems that would typically not have been generated or addressed until much later. Under the code name "Titan," Apple has a multifunctional project team of 500+ people working to develop the code to control the steering, breaking, safety, and navigation system for self-driving cars. The large project team is composed of software engineers developing apps to link vision sensors to driving systems, regulatory specialists with experience in auto industry rules, and coding specialists hired away from QNX, which develops automotive "infotainment system" software.[53] Apple has also hired engineers and programmers and operations managers from Tesla, employees from A123 Systems with expertise in batteries for electric vehicles, and engineers who worked on autonomous vehicles at NVIDIA and Waymo.[54]

Powerful leaders provide the vision, discipline, and motivation to keep the innovation process focused, on time, and on target. Powerful leaders are able to get resources when they are needed, are typically more experienced, have high status in the company, and are held directly responsible for the products' success or failure. On average, powerful leaders can get innovation-related projects done nine months faster than leaders with little power or influence.

Astro Teller, "Captain of Moonshots" at X, rewards employees for quick failures, which speed up overall innovation.

7-2c Compression Approach: Managing Innovation during Incremental Change

Although the experiential approach is used to manage innovation in highly uncertain environments during periods of discontinuous change, the compression approach is used to manage innovation in more certain environments during periods of incremental change. While the goals of the experiential approach are significant improvements in performance and the establishment of a *new* dominant design, the goals of the compression approach are lower costs and incremental improvements in the performance and function of the *existing* dominant design.

The general strategies in each approach are different, too. With the experiential approach, the general strategy is to build something new, different, and substantially better. Because there's so much uncertainty—no one knows which technology will become the market leader—companies adopt a winner-take-all approach by trying to create the market-leading, dominant design. With the compression approach, the general strategy is to compress the time and steps needed to bring about small, consistent improvements in performance and functionality. Because a dominant technology design already exists, the general strategy is to continue improving the existing technology as rapidly as possible. For example, **Mazda's** Skyactiv-X gas-powered engine gets 50 to 60 MPG

Multifunctional teams work teams composed of people from different departments

in a Mazda 3, compared to 30 to 36 MPG in a Mazda 3 equipped with a standard Mazda gas engine. The Skyactiv-X engine uses spark-controlled compression ignition with an extremely lean air/fuel mix, similar to diesel engines. It runs like a normal gas engine when starting, accelerating and at high speeds, but spark-controlled compression kicks in for steady speeds, slow acceleration, and moderate speeds.[55] AutoPacific's Ed Kim, an industry analyst, says, "Gasoline engines are going to remain very, very relevant for a long time," especially with significant performance improvements like these.[56]

In short, a **compression approach to innovation** assumes that innovation is a predictable process, that incremental innovation can be planned using a series of steps, and that compressing the time it takes to complete those steps can speed up innovation. The compression approach to innovation has five aspects: planning, supplier involvement, shortening the time of individual steps, overlapping steps, and multifunctional teams.[57]

In Chapter 5, *planning* was defined as choosing a goal and a method or strategy to achieve that goal. When *planning for incremental innovation*, the goal is to squeeze or compress development time as much as possible, and the general strategy is to create a series of planned steps to accomplish that goal. Planning for incremental innovation helps avoid unnecessary steps and enables developers to sequence steps in the right order to avoid wasted time and delays between steps. Planning also reduces misunderstandings and improves coordination.

Most planning for incremental innovation is based on the idea of generational change. **Generational change** occurs when incremental improvements are made to a dominant technological design such that the improved version of the technology is fully backward compatible with the older version.[58] All Wi-Fi routers and devices are based on the 802.11 standard established by the Wi-Fi Alliance. First there was the 802.11b (1999), followed by 802.11a (1999), 802.11g (2003), 802.11n (2009), and 802.11ac (2014). Each was faster and more reliable than its predecessor. To avoid confusion (Is ac faster than g?), the Wi-Fi Alliance renamed those standards Wi-Fi 1 to Wi-Fi 5.[59] The Wi-Fi router you have is probably Wi-Fi 5. But Wi-Fi 6, which is at least 30 percent faster, is now available, and is backward compatible with all Wi-Fi devices. Older smartphones using Wi-Fi 4 or 5 will work with Wi-Fi 6, but not as fast as Wi-Fi 6 smartphones like Apple's iPhone 11.[60]

farakos/iStock/Getty Images

Because the compression approach assumes that innovation can follow a series of preplanned steps, one of the ways to shorten development time is *supplier involvement*. Delegating some of the preplanned steps in the innovation process to outside suppliers reduces the amount of work that internal development teams must do. Plus, suppliers provide an alternative source of ideas and expertise that can lead to better designs. Even though **Apple** develops most of its innovations in house, it does rely on suppliers for innovation as well. The prospect of landing a large contract and supplying a crucial component to a company like Apple drives suppliers to build out their own research and development capabilities. Professor Ram Mudambi believes that Apple's size and component budget ($40.1 billion in 2019) motivate suppliers to pitch their biggest breakthroughs to the company: "Suppliers are racing with each other to get Apple's business, and part of the racing they are doing is spending more on R&D."[61]

Another way to shorten development time is simply to *shorten the time of individual steps* in the innovation process. It normally takes **McCormick**, the spice and seasoning company, about a year to develop and test new spice and seasoning flavors. McCormick's scientists start with the 10,000 ingredients already used in its product lines and then systematically test combinations of 500 ingredients before completing a new recipe, which might contain two dozen ingredients.[62] However, McCormick is shortening this step by as much as 70 percent by partnering with IBM to use artificial intelligence. Instead of testing 150 new recipes to arrive at the final product, artificial intelligence processes data from tens of thousands of previous tests, standard ingredient combinations found in products sold all around the world, and recipe characteristics (price, natural ingredients, used for cooking or after cooking seasoning) to give McCormick's scientists a much smaller number of promising ingredient combinations to consider. IBM's Robin Lougee, who is working with McCormick, said, "We're able to explore the flavors in a way that is perhaps a little bit more broad than they would have because it's impossible for them to know the thousands of ingredients that McCormick has available and be familiar with them. There is so much data that a human can't read all of it."[63]

James F. Qunn Krt/Newscom

In a sequential design process, each step must be completed before the next step begins. But sometimes multiple development steps can be performed at the same time. *Overlapping steps* shorten the development process by reducing delays or waiting time between steps.

7-3 ORGANIZATIONAL DECLINE: THE RISK OF NOT CHANGING

Founded in 1921 in Boston as a store for ham radio enthusiasts, **RadioShack** grew to more than 7,000 stores by stocking a wide range of components used to build or repair various electronic devices. In fact, before starting Apple, co-founders Steve Jobs and Steve Wozniak bought parts at RadioShack to make a "blue-box" device that illegally switched on free long-distance calling (which mattered when long-distance calls were 40 cents a minute).[64] RadioShack's growth was first propelled by hobbyists (nerds like Jobs and Wozniak), then by battery sales, computers, and cell phones. The TRS-80, introduced in 1977, was one of the first broadly popular PCs. Following computers, which it stopped making in 1993, its next growth cycle came from cell phones. The phone companies at first relied on RadioShack to sign up and service customers, but this changed as they eventually established their own retail stores. RadioShack moved away from its focus on serving technology power users and hobbyists by opening unsuccessful big-box electronics and appliance stores, such as Computer City

and Incredible Universe, on which it lost hundreds of millions of dollars in the 1990s. Outmaneuvered by BestBuy in brick-and-mortar retailing, and never really competitive on the Web, RadioShack filed for bankruptcy in spring 2015 after losing $936 million since 2011, the last year it was profitable.[65]

Businesses operate in a constantly changing environment. Recognizing and adapting to internal and external changes can mean the difference between continued success and going out of business. Companies that fail to change run the risk of organizational decline.[66] **Organizational decline** occurs when companies don't anticipate, recognize, neutralize, or adapt to the internal or external pressures that threaten their survival. CEO of **Netflix** Reed Hastings, whose company successfully bridged from its DVD-by-mail business to Internet streaming, said, "Most companies that are great at something—AOL dial-up or Borders bookstores—do not become great at new things people want (streaming for us) because they are afraid to hurt their initial business. Eventually, these companies realize their error of not focusing enough on the new thing, and then the company fights desperately and hopelessly to recover. Companies rarely die from moving too fast, and they frequently die from moving too slowly."[67] In other words, decline occurs when organizations don't recognize the need for change. There are five stages of organizational decline: blinded, inaction, faulty action, crisis, and dissolution.

In the *blinded stage*, decline begins because key managers fail to recognize the internal or external changes that will harm their organizations. This blindness may be due to a simple lack of awareness about changes or an inability to understand their significance. It may also come from the overconfidence that can develop when a company has been successful.

In the *inaction stage*, as organizational performance problems become more visible, management may recognize the need to change but still take no action. The managers may be waiting to see if the problems will correct themselves. Or, they may find it difficult to change the practices and policies that previously led to success. Possibly, too, they wrongly assume that they can easily correct the problems, so they don't feel the situation is urgent.

> **Organizational decline**
> a large decrease in organizational performance that occurs when companies don't anticipate, recognize, neutralize, or adapt to the internal or external pressures that threaten their survival

"RadioShacks filed for bankruptcy in 2015 and was acquired by its largest lender, hedge fund, Standard General." And then filed for bankruptcy again in 2017!

In the *faulty action stage*, faced with rising costs and decreasing profits and market share, management will announce belt-tightening plans designed to cut costs, increase efficiency, and restore profits. In other words, rather than recognizing the need for fundamental changes, managers assume that if they just run a tighter ship, company performance will return to previous levels.

In the *crisis stage*, bankruptcy or dissolution (breaking up the company and selling its parts) is likely to occur unless the company completely reorganizes the way it does business. At this point, however, companies typically lack the resources to fully change how they run their businesses. Cutbacks and layoffs will have reduced the level of talent among employees. Furthermore, talented managers who were savvy enough to see the crisis coming will have found jobs with other companies, often with competitors. At this stage, hoping to generate enough cash to fund a much-needed redesign of its remaining stores, RadioShack took out $835 million in loans and closed 1,100 stores, However, during the 2014 holiday season, its corporate finances amounted to the equivalent of just $15,000 of cash per store.[68]

In the *dissolution stage*, after failing to make the changes needed to sustain the organization, the company is dissolved through bankruptcy proceedings or by selling assets to pay suppliers, banks, and creditors. At this point, a new CEO may be brought in to oversee the closing of stores, offices, and manufacturing facilities; the final layoff of managers and employees; and the sale of assets. It is important to note that decline is reversible at each of the first four stages and that not all companies in decline reach final dissolution. RadioShack declared bankruptcy in February 2015, and was acquired by its largest lender, hedge fund Standard General. Initially, 1,700 stores remained open, with 1,400 featuring Sprint/RadioShack signage and branding. Sprint used one-third of each store to sell and display Sprint mobile phones and related products.[69] By 2017, Radio Shack filed for bankruptcy again, laying off headquarters staff, closing 200 stores, and "evaluating options" on the remaining stores.[70] In 2018, RadioShack emerged from bankruptcy with just 400 stores, but struck an agreement with HobbyTown USA to open "RadioShack Express" stores-within-a-store in 100 of HobbyTown's 140 locations.[71]

When Everything Must Go: The Last Stop in Organizational Decline

Jerry Robertson is the business specialist you bring in when your retail store hits the last stop in organizational decline, the dissolution stage when assets are sold to pay suppliers, banks, and creditors. When Robertson closes a store – and he's closed 90 – he works alone, six days a week for typically seven weeks. Since he is paid a fee plus a percentage of sales, his job is to find that middle ground between selling everything too cheaply and getting stuck with unsold inventory because prices weren't slashed low enough to draw in shoppers. He typically starts with a 13 percent discount to bring in the early bargain hunters, and then slashes prices more aggressively as the closing date nears. When store managers resist, he tells them either sell it now for $10 or toss it in the trash for nothing when we close. If Robertson's job bothers you, it shouldn't. Dissolution is the ultimate business garage sale, the epitome of asset recycling. Nothing goes to waste, but everything must go.

Source: C. Cutter, "Everything Must Go: Record Pace of Shut Stores Fuels Business for 'the Closers," *Wall Street Journal*, January 2, 2020, accessed March 29, 2020, https://www.wsj.com/articles/everything-must-go-record-pace-of-shut-stores-fuels-business-for-the-closers-11578001910.

7-4 MANAGING CHANGE

According to social psychologist Kurt Lewin, change is a function of the forces that promote change and the opposing forces that slow or resist change.[72] **Change forces** lead to differences in the form, quality, or condition of an organization over time. In contrast to change forces, **resistance forces** support the status quo, that is, the existing conditions in an organization. Change is difficult under any circumstances. When Paul Cannon's law firm replaced the out-of-date software it used for managing calendars, documents, time tracking, and client portals and billing, he was surprised how strongly the change was resisted. Some attorneys and employees refused to watch the new systems training videos. Others continued using the old software. And others produced costly mistakes by applying the steps in the old system to the new one. Cannon said, "One thing I learned from all this is that a lot of people are afraid of change, because they're afraid of making a mistake. They know how to do their jobs under the old system. Even if it's cumbersome and inefficient, it's comfortable. And comfort equals security."[73]

Resistance to change is caused by self-interest, misunderstanding and distrust, and a general intolerance for change.[74] People resist change out of *self-interest* because they fear that change will cost or deprive them of something they value. Resistance might stem from a fear that the changes will result in a loss of pay, power, responsibility, or even perhaps one's job.

People also resist change because of *misunderstanding and distrust*; they don't understand the change or the reasons for it, or they distrust the people—typically management—behind the change. Resistance isn't always visible at first. In fact, some of the strongest resisters may initially support the changes in public, nodding and smiling their agreement, but then ignoring the changes in private and doing their jobs as they always have. Management consultant Michael Hammer calls this deadly form of resistance the "Kiss of Yes."[75]

Resistance may also come from a generally low tolerance for change. Some people are simply less capable of handling change than others. People with a *low tolerance for change* feel threatened by the uncertainty associated with change and worry that they won't be able to learn the new skills and behaviors needed to successfully negotiate change in their companies.

Because resistance to change is inevitable, successful change efforts require careful management.

*In this section, you will learn about **7-4a managing resistance to change, 7-4b what not to do when leading organizational change,** and **7-4c different change tools and techniques.***

Roman Märzinger/AGE Fotostock

The Kiss of Yes occurs when some of the strongest resisters support changes in public, but then ignore them in private.

7-4a Managing Resistance to Change

According to psychologist Kurt Lewin, managing organizational change is a basic process of unfreezing, change intervention, and refreezing. **Unfreezing** is getting the people affected by change to believe that change is needed. During the **change intervention** itself, workers and managers change their behavior and work practices. **Refreezing** is supporting and reinforcing the new changes so that they stick.

Resistance to change is an example of frozen behavior. Given the choice

Change forces forces that produce differences in the form, quality, or condition of an organization over time

Resistance forces forces that support the existing conditions in organizations

Resistance to change opposition to change resulting from self-interest, misunderstanding and distrust, and a general intolerance for change

Unfreezing getting the people affected by change to believe that change is needed

Change intervention the process used to get workers and managers to change their behaviors and work practices

Refreezing supporting and reinforcing new changes so that they stick

between changing and not changing, most people would rather not change. Because resistance to change is natural and inevitable, managers need to unfreeze resistance to change to create successful change programs. The following methods can be used to manage resistance to change: education and communication, participation, negotiation, top management support, and coercion.[76]

When resistance to change is based on insufficient, incorrect, or misleading information, managers should *educate* employees about the need for change and *communicate* change-related information to them. Managers must also supply the information, funding, or other support employees need to make changes. For example, resistance to change can be particularly strong when one company buys another company. This is because one company in the merger usually has a higher status due to its size or its higher profitability or the fact that it is the acquiring company. These status differences are important to managers and employees, particularly if they're in the lower status company, who worry about retaining their jobs or influence after the merger. That fear or concern can greatly increase resistance to change.[77] When PMA Companies, an insurance risk management firm, was acquired by Old Republic International, an insurance company, PMA's CEO Vince Donnelly communicated frequently with PMA's employees about the merger. Four months before the acquisition became official, he traveled to each of the company's 20 offices and gave employees a detailed description of how their day-to-day operations would change and why the acquisition was good for everyone involved. He also held quarterly updates with employees via videoconference. Said Donnelly, "It's not just one and done. Communication needs to be continual. You need to continue to reinforce the messages that you want people to internalize. So, you need to understand that communication is a continuous process and not something that you do just once." He went on to say, "What you are asking people to do is trust you, [trust] that you have the best interest of everybody in mind, and [trust that] when there is news to tell, you're going to hear it directly from the CEO—good, bad, or indifferent."[78]

Another way to reduce resistance to change is to have those affected by the change *participate in planning and implementing the change process.* Employees who participate have a better understanding of the

Coercion the use of formal power and authority to force others to change

change and the need for it. Furthermore, employee concerns about change can be addressed as they occur if employees participate in the planning and implementation process. It took Kaiser Permanente, a large healthcare provider, five years to transition from paper records to digital medical records and telemedicine services (for patients in remote locations). CEO Bernard Tyson said:

The biggest problem was our physicians had a bond with the patient. It was the personal touch, the personal voice, the personal phone call. The physician is the advocate of the patient. Then you have the nurses and others. And they had a way of working. There was a lot of concern about breaking that trusted relationship, a lot of questions as to whether it would really work in the health-care industry. It took a lot of buy-in, and conversations and engaging the physicians in particular but the other health-care workers, too. So, ultimately, it wasn't done to them. They were a part of it. But I would not kid you. It was extremely difficult.[79]

Employees are also less likely to resist change if they are allowed *to discuss and agree on who will do what* after change occurs. Craig Durosko, founder of **Sun Design Home Remodeling Specialists** in Burke, Virginia, says, "Unfortunately, the way most employees find out when a company isn't doing well is when their paychecks bounce or when they show up and the front doors are locked. When changes go down and they don't know about it, they can't do anything about it." So, when Sun Design's business shrank dramatically during the Great Recession, Durosko explained the problem, shared detailed financial information, and then asked his employees what could be done to minimize losses. He says, "No less than 20 employees gave line-by-line specific *things they could do* to make a difference.[80]

Resistance to change also decreases when change efforts receive *significant managerial support.* Managers must do more than talk about the importance of change, though. They must provide the training, resources, and autonomy needed to make change happen. Finally, resistance to change can be managed through **coercion**, or the use of formal power and authority to force others to change. Because of the intense negative reactions it can create (for example, fear, stress, resentment, sabotage of company products), coercion should be used only when a crisis exists or when all other attempts to reduce resistance to change have failed.

7-4b What Not to Do When Leading Change

So far, you've learned about the basic change process (unfreezing, change intervention, refreezing) and managing resistance to change. Harvard Business School professor John Kotter argues that knowing what *not* to do is just as important as knowing what to do when it comes to achieving successful organizational change.[81]

Managers commonly make predictable errors when they lead change. The first two errors occur during the unfreezing phase, when managers try to get the people affected by change to believe that change is really needed. The first and potentially most serious error is *not establishing a great enough sense of urgency*. In fact, Kotter estimates that more than half of all change efforts fail because the people affected are not convinced that change is necessary. People will feel a greater sense of urgency if a leader in the company makes a public, candid assessment of the company's problems and weaknesses.

In Chapter 5 you learned that DHL Express, a global shipping and delivery company, was losing $110 million a month. Here's how Ken Allen, former CEO, first communicated the urgency of the situation to DHL's upper managers:

> Our performance across all major markets was deteriorating, and without a fundamental overhaul, our losses were posed to threaten the profitability of the entire **Deutsche Post DHL Group**. Three hundred and fifty company leaders had gathered in Cincinnati to confront this challenge head-on. *As the meeting began, a beating heart appeared on an immense screen at the back of the stage. Strong and steady at first, the pounding heartbeats grew further apart, faltered, and then ceased altogether. You could have heard a pin drop. I knew I had the crowd's attention. Now I needed to convey that we had only two choices: act or face extinction.*[82]

The second mistake that occurs in the unfreezing process is *not creating a powerful enough coalition*. Change often starts with one or two people. But change has to be supported by a critical and growing group of people to build enough momentum to change an entire department, division, or company. Besides top management, Kotter recommends that key employees, managers, board members, customers, and even union leaders be members of a *core change coalition* that guides and supports organizational change. Italy-based **Stora Enso** was the world's leading forestry, pulp and paper company.[83] But when digitalization drove down demand for paper, then CEO Jouko Karvinen created a powerful coalition to turn Stora Enso into a global renewable materials company. Instead of turning to senior managers, he created a Pathbuilder team, which he called a "shadow cabinet," to rewrite the firm's purpose and value statements, recommend strategic ideas to upper management, and to disrupt and digitalize Stora Enso's old ways of getting things done. Out of 250 applicants, 16 people from different levels and areas of the company were selected to be Pathbuilders. Karvinen said, "It was this mix of perspectives that allowed us to come up with unconventional yet implementable ideas and recommendations."[84] Working with senior management, Pathbuilders were then charged to find solutions to "mission-critical" problems.

The next four errors that managers make occur during the change phase, when a change intervention is used to try to get workers and managers to change their behavior and work practices. *Lacking a vision* for change is a significant error at this point. As you learned in Chapter 5, a *vision* (defined as a *purpose statement* in Chapter 5) is a statement of a company's purpose or reason for existing. A vision for change makes clear where a company or department is headed and why the change is occurring. Change efforts that lack vision tend to be confused, chaotic, and contradictory. By contrast, change efforts guided by visions are clear, easy to understand, and can be effectively explained in five minutes or less.

Undercommunicating the vision by a factor of 10 is another mistake in the change phase. According to Kotter, companies mistakenly hold just one meeting to announce the vision. Or, if the new vision receives heavy emphasis in executive speeches or company newsletters, senior management then undercuts the vision by behaving in ways contrary to it. Successful communication of the vision requires that top managers link everything the company does to the new vision and that they "walk the talk" by behaving in ways consistent with the vision. Furthermore, even companies that begin change with a clear vision sometimes make the mistake of *not removing obstacles to the new vision*. They leave formidable barriers to change in place by failing to redesign jobs, pay plans, and technology to support the new way of doing things. When **FMC**, an agricultural sciences company, acquired DuPont's crop protection business, it developed a "Nature of Next" plan to communicate the reason and the vision for the acquisition to its 5000+ employees. Employees learned the acquisition would make FMC the fifth-largest global crop protection company, that it would expand the number of countries in which FMC did business, that cross-selling opportunities were huge since 80 percent of customers had relationships

When FMC acquired DuPont's crop protection business in 2017, it made them the 5th largest crop protection company globally.

Randy Duchaine/Alamy Stock Photo

phase. Managers typically declare victory right after the first large-scale success in the change process. Declaring success too early has the same effect as draining the gasoline out of a car: It stops change efforts dead in their tracks. With success declared, supporters of the change process stop pushing to make change happen. After all, why push when success has been achieved? Rather than declaring victory, managers should use the momentum from short-term wins to push for even bigger or faster changes. This maintains urgency and prevents change supporters from slacking off before the changes are frozen into the company's culture.

The last mistake that managers make is *not anchoring changes in the corporation's culture*. An *organization's culture* is the set of key values, beliefs, and attitudes shared by organizational members that determines the accepted way of doing things in a company. As you learned in Chapter 3, changing cultures is extremely difficult and slow. According to Kotter, two things help anchor changes in a corporation's culture. The first is directly showing people that the changes have actually improved performance. The second is to make sure that the people who get promoted fit the new culture. If they don't, it's a clear sign that the changes were only temporary.

7-4c Change Tools and Techniques

Imagine that your boss came to you and said, "All right, genius, you wanted it. You're in charge of turning around the division." Where would you begin? How would you encourage change-resistant managers to change? What would you do to include others in the change process? How would you get the change process off to a quick start? Finally, what approach would you use to promote long-term effectiveness and performance? Results-driven change, Agile change methods, the General Electric fastworks approach, and organizational development are different change tools and techniques that can be used to address these issues.

One of the reasons that organizational change efforts fail is that they are activity oriented rather than results oriented. In other words, they focus primarily on changing company procedures, management philosophy, or employee behavior. Typically, there is much buildup and preparation as consultants are brought in, presentations are made, books are read, and employees and managers are trained. There's a tremendous emphasis on doing things the new way. But, with all the focus on "doing," almost no attention is paid to *results*, to seeing if all this activity has actually made a difference.

with FMC or DuPont (but not both), that it would raise FMC's manufacturing capability from 12 to 26 manufacturing facilities, and that it would significantly strengthen FMC's research and development efforts, adding 21 new insecticides, herbicides, and fungicides.[85] Furthermore, 150 FMC employees were nominated by their bosses to be members of the Change Champion Network that amplified top management's communication by actively discussing the merger with their colleagues, answering questions, and elevating important issues and concerns to FMC's leaders.[86]

Another error in the change phase is *not systematically planning for and creating short-term wins*. Most people don't have the discipline and patience to wait two years to see if the new change effort works. Change is threatening and uncomfortable, so people need to see an immediate payoff if they are to continue to support it. Kotter recommends that managers create short-term wins by actively picking people and projects that are likely to work extremely well early in the change process.

The last two errors that managers make occur during the refreezing phase, when attempts are made to support and reinforce changes so that they stick. *Declaring victory too soon* is a tempting mistake in the refreezing

Sara De Marco/Shutterstock.com

Another advantage of results-driven change is that managers introduce changes in procedures, philosophy, or behavior only if they are likely to improve measured performance. In other words, managers and workers actually test to see if changes make a difference. A third advantage of results-driven change is that quick, visible improvements motivate employees to continue to make additional changes to improve measured performance. Exhibit 7.4 describes the basic steps of results-driven change.

Agile change is a results-driven change method that uses daily standup meetings or "huddles" to review the progress of fast-moving multidisciplinary teams or "Scrums" who break problems into small, clearly defined parts that team members work on in sprints.[90] It is similar to the design iteration and prototype testing found in the compression approach to innovation discussed in Section 7-2c of this chapter. At its core, Agile change is iterative and focuses on speed and daily accountability for results. This means that quickly-made changes (i.e., sprints) are tested and reviewed on a daily basis (daily standups are 15- to 20-minutes long), adjusted based on what's learned, and then tested and reviewed again and again until a product design is finished or a customer problem is solved. **Campbell**, best known for Campbell's Soups, used agile change to reduce the time it takes to develop new food products from two years to nine months. Craig Slavtcheff, vice president and head of research and development at Campbell, said, "We searched outside the [consumer-packaged goods] world and looked at companies where innovation speed was a critical factor for success, and that's how we arrived on agile methodology as a tool."[91] Agile change methods are frequently used in product development or to solve customer problems.

General Electric fastworks approach is another kind of results-driven change. With fastworks, companies improve results in an uncertain business environment by quickly experimenting with new ideas to

By contrast, **results-driven change** supplants the emphasis on activity with a laser-like focus on quickly measuring and improving results.[87] At Zara, the Spain-based retailer known for "fast fashion," 350 designers send brand-new styles to stores and Zara.com twice a week. Because designers get daily data on what's selling, they can react to fashion trends by going from concept to ready-for-sale clothing in just three weeks. If daily reports show surging demand for particular products, Zara airlifts them (the most expensive way to ship) to get them in stores as fast as possible.[88] Furthermore, retailers don't need anyone's approval to make changes. They decide on the spot. Ann Critchlow, an analyst at Société Générale, says, "The root of Inditex's success [Inditex own's Zara] is its predominantly short lead time, which gives a greater level of newness to its collections."[89]

Exhibit 7.4
How to Create a Results-Driven Change Program

1. Set measurable, short-term goals to improve performance.
2. Make sure your action steps are likely to improve measured performance.
3. Stress the importance of immediate improvements.
4. Solicit help from consultants and staffers to achieve quick improvements in performance.
5. Test action steps to see if they actually yield improvements. If they don't, discard them and establish new ones.
6. Use resources you have or that can be easily acquired. It doesn't take much.

Source: R. H. Schaffer and H. A. Thomson, "Successful Change Programs Begin with Results," *Harvard Business Review on Change* (Boston: Harvard Business School Press, 1998), 189–213.

Results-driven change change created quickly by focusing on the measurement and improvement of results

Agile change using daily standups, or "huddles," to review the progress of multidisciplinary teams or "Scrums," who break problems into small, clearly defined parts that team members work on in sprints

General Electric fastworks quickly experimenting with new ideas to solve customer problems and learn from repeated tests and improvements

solve customer problems and learn from repeated tests and improvements. Because things change quickly in uncertain business environments, the idea is to move as fast, if not faster than competitors. For example, it normally takes GE Healthcare two to four years to bring a new PET/CT scanner to market. But because of customer feedback under fastworks, it cut development time in half.[92] GE fastworks is similar to Agile change. If there's a meaningful difference in practice, it might be that GE fastworks gives top management more say in deciding where to focus change efforts, whereas Agile change methods typically require top managers to give that authority to Agile teams or Scrums.[93]

Fastworks also focuses on solving customer problems. Viv Goldstein, director of innovation acceleration at GE Corporate, says, "We don't assume that we know what features create the best solution. We start speaking to customers much earlier in the cycle so we can test solutions quickly and inexpensively . . . It's about achieving customer outcomes, as opposed to selling products."[94]

Finally, repeated testing and improvements depend on putting a minimum viable product in front of customers. When GE Appliances was redesigning its high-end Monogram refrigerators, it listened to feedback from home designers and then built a new refrigerator (that is, a minimum viable product). Customers disliked it because the stainless steel was too dark. They fixed that. Next, customers disliked the lighting. GE fixed that. After six prototypes, GE built 75 versions for broader testing and feedback. Five versions later, it was ready to begin manufacturing. Fastworks resulted in a refrigerator developed in half the time, for half the cost, and which is selling twice as fast as the typical new model.[95]

Organizational development is a philosophy and collection of planned change interventions designed to improve an organization's long-term health and performance. Organizational development takes a long-range approach to change; assumes that top management support is necessary for change to succeed; creates change by educating workers and managers to change ideas, beliefs, and behaviors so that problems can be solved

Organizational development a philosophy and collection of planned change interventions designed to improve an organization's long-term health and performance

Change agent the person formally in charge of guiding a change effort

Exhibit 7.5
General Steps for Organizational Development Interventions

1. Entry	A problem is discovered, and the need for change becomes apparent. A search begins for someone to deal with the problem and facilitate change.
2. Startup	A change agent enters the picture and works to clarify the problem and gain commitment to a change effort.
3. Assessment & feedback	The change agent gathers information about the problem and provides feedback about it to decision makers and those affected by it.
4. Action planning	The change agent works with decision makers to develop an action plan.
5. Intervention	The action plan, or organizational development intervention, is carried out.
6. Evaluation	The change agent helps decision makers assess the effectiveness of the intervention.
7. Adoption	Organizational members accept ownership and responsibility for the change, which is then carried out through the entire organization.
8. Separation	The change agent leaves the organization after first ensuring that the change intervention will continue to work.

Source: W. J. Rothwell, R. Sullivan, and G. M. McLean, *Practicing Organizational Development: A Guide for Consultants* (San Diego: Pfeiffer & Co., 1995)

in new ways; and emphasizes employee participation in diagnosing, solving, and evaluating problems.[96] As shown in Exhibit 7.5, organizational development interventions begin with the recognition of a problem. Then, the company designates a **change agent** to be formally in charge of guiding the change effort. This person can be someone from within the company or a professional consultant. The change agent clarifies the problem, gathers information, works with decision makers to create and implement an action plan, helps to evaluate the plan's effectiveness, implements the plan throughout the company, and then leaves (if from outside the company) after making sure the change intervention will continue to work.

Organizational development interventions are aimed at changing large systems, small groups, or

Exhibit 7.6
Types of Organizational Development Interventions

Large-System Interventions

Sociotechnical systems	An intervention designed to improve how well employees use and adjust to the work technology used in an organization.
Survey feedback	An intervention that uses surveys to collect information from the members of the system, reports the results of that survey to the members, and then uses those results to develop action plans for improvement.

Small-Group Interventions

Team building	An intervention designed to increase the cohesion and cooperation of work group members.
Unit goal setting	An intervention designed to help a work group establish short- and long-term goals.

Person-Focused Interventions

Counseling/coaching	An intervention designed so that a formal helper or coach listens to managers or employees and advises them on how to deal with work or interpersonal problems.
Training	An intervention designed to provide individuals with the knowledge, skills, or attitudes they need to become more effective at their jobs.

Source: W. J. Rothwell, R. Sullivan, and G. M. McLean, *Practicing Organizational Development: A Guide for Consultants* (San Diego: Pfeiffer & Co., 1995).

people.[97] More specifically, the purpose of *large-system interventions* is to change the character and performance of an organization, business unit, or department. *Small-group intervention* focuses on assessing how a group functions and helping it work more effectively to accomplish its goals. *Person-focused intervention* is intended to increase interpersonal effectiveness by helping people to become aware of their attitudes and behaviors and to acquire new skills and knowledge. Exhibit 7.6 describes the most frequently used organizational development interventions for large systems, small groups, and people.

8 | Global Management

8-1 GLOBAL BUSINESS, TRADE RULES, AND TRADE AGREEMENTS

Business is the buying and selling of goods or services. Buying this textbook was a business transaction. So was buying your first car and getting paid for babysitting or for mowing lawns. **Global business** is the buying and selling of goods and services by people from different countries. The Apple iPhone sitting on my desk while writing this chapter was purchased from an Apple Store in Indiana. The components of that iPhone, the touch screen, camera lenses, microphone, and the hard drive for storage, were made by 200 suppliers around the world. Once assembled in China, my iPhone was flown by United Parcel Service (UPS) or FedEx to Anchorage, Alaska (for refueling), before arriving in Louisville, Kentucky, where it was sorted for truck delivery to the Apple Store.[1]

Global business the buying and selling of goods and services by people from different countries

Global business presents its own set of challenges for managers. How can you be sure that the way you run your business in one country is the right way to run that business in another? This chapter discusses how organizations answer that question. We will start by examining global business in two ways: first exploring its impact on US businesses and then reviewing the basic rules and agreements that govern global trade. Next, we will examine how and when companies go global by examining the trade-off between consistency and adaptation and discussing how to organize a global company. Finally, we will look at how companies decide where to expand globally, including finding the best business climate, adapting to cultural differences, and better preparing employees for international assignments.

In addition to the previous iPhone example, if you want other demonstrations of the impact of global business, look at the tag on your shirt, the inside of your shoes, and the inside of your digital camera (take out your battery). Chances are, all of these items were made in different places around the world. As I write this, my shirt, shoes, and digital camera were made in Thailand, China, and Korea. Where were yours made?

Let's learn more about **8-1a the impact of global business, 8-1b how tariff and nontariff trade barriers have historically restricted global business, 8-1c how today global and regional trade agreements are reducing those trade barriers worldwide**, *and* **8-1d how consumers are responding to those changes in trade rules and agreements.**

8-1a The Impact of Global Business

Multinational corporations (MNCs) are corporations that own businesses in two or more countries. Motorcycle maker **Harley-Davidson** is headquartered in Milwaukee, Wisconsin, and has US assembly plants in Pennsylvania, Missouri, and Wisconsin. But with manufacturing plants in Australia, Brazil, India and Thailand, and regional offices in 21 countries, Harley-Davidson, a brand considered to be quintessentially American, is a multinational corporation.[2]
Harley-Davidson's goal is to have international sales account for half of revenues by 2027.[3] Consistent

> **Multinational corporation**
> a corporation that owns businesses in two or more countries

with that goal, Harley's international sales have risen from 22 percent in 2007 to 38 percent in 2017 to 48 percent in 2019.[4] Harley-Davidson isn't unique. There are 30,000-plus MNCs around the world. The 100 largest MNCs, on average, have 500 foreign facilities/offices located in 50 different countries![5] The Organisation for Economic Co-operation and Development (OECD), representing 34 countries that discuss and develop economic and social policy, estimates that MNCs produce half of global exports, employ 25 percent of the world's workers, and generate a third of the world's gross domestic product.[6]

Another way to appreciate the impact of global business is by considering direct foreign investment. **Direct foreign investment** occurs when a company builds a new business or buys an existing business in a foreign country. Italian candy maker Ferraro International SA made a direct foreign investment in the United States when it paid $2.8 billion for Nestle's US chocolate business.[7]

Of course, companies from many other countries also own businesses in the United States. As Exhibit 8.1 shows, companies from the United Kingdom, Canada, Japan, the Netherlands, Luxembourg, Germany, Switzerland, and France have the largest direct foreign investment in the United States. Overall, foreign companies invest more than $4.3 trillion a year to do business in the United States.

But direct foreign investment in the United States is only half the picture. US companies have also made large direct foreign investments in countries throughout the world. Atlanta-based **Coca-Cola**, which makes and distributes sparkling soft drinks, bottled water, and juice, dairy and plant-based drinks, paid $5.1 billion to buy Costa Limited from UK-based Whitbread PLC. Costa Limited, which is better known as Costa Coffee, has 3,800 retail coffee shops in 32 countries, including China.[8] Industry analyst Jonathan Davison of Global Data said, "The (Costa Coffee) chain might be the biggest in the United Kingdom, but it lags well behind **Starbucks** globally. Coca-Cola's distribution muscle will no doubt help close the gap and boost sales significantly in the long run."[9]

As Exhibit 8.2 shows, US companies have made their largest direct foreign investments in the Netherlands, the United Kingdom (UK), Luxembourg, France, Ireland, Canada, UK Caribbean Islands and Switzerland. Overall, US companies invest more than $5.95 trillion a year to do business in other countries.

So, whether foreign companies invest in the United States or US companies invest abroad, direct foreign investment is an increasingly important and common method of conducting global business.

Direct foreign investment a method of investment in which a company builds a new business or buys an existing business in a foreign country

Exhibit 8.1
Direct Foreign Investment in the United States

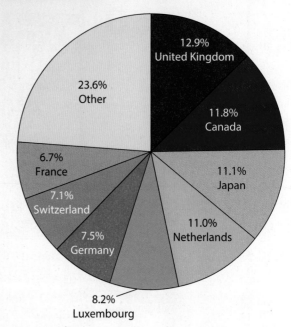

Source: "Foreign Direct Investment Position in the United States on a Historical-Cost Basis, 2018," Bureau of Economic Analysis: US Department of Commerce, March 19, 2020, apps.bea.gov/international/xls/fdius-current/fdius-detailed-industry-2008-2018.xlsx.

Exhibit 8.2
US Direct Foreign Investment Abroad

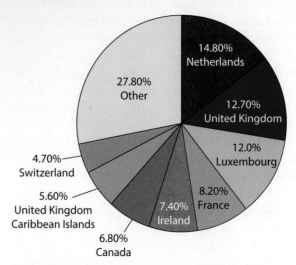

Source: "US Direct Investment Abroad: Direct Investment Position on a Historical-Cost Basis by Detailed Country, 2009–2018," Bureau of Economic Analysis: US Department of Commerce, March 19, 2020, apps.bea.gov/international/xls/usdia-current/usdia-detailedcountry-2009-2018.xlsx.

8-1b Trade Barriers

Although today's consumers usually don't care where the products they buy come from (more on this in Section 8-1d), national governments have traditionally preferred that consumers buy domestically made products in hopes that such purchases would increase the number of domestic businesses and workers. In fact, governments have done much more than hope that you will buy from domestic companies. Historically, governments have actively used **trade barriers** to make it much more expensive or difficult (or sometimes impossible) for consumers to buy or consume imported goods. The percentage has recently varied because of tariff threats between China and the United States, but the Chinese government has added a 15 to 40 percent tariff to automobiles imported to China over the last few years. Imports make up just 4.1 percent of the 27.8 million cars sold annually in China, a percentage that has changed little in 20 years.[10] Consultant Michael Dunne says, "There might as well be a sign saying: Imports not welcome."[11] By establishing these restrictions and taxes, the Chinese government is engaging in **protectionism**, which is the use of trade barriers to protect local companies and their workers from foreign competition. According to trade monitoring group Global Trade Alert, 1900 protectionist measures have been put in place by governments around the world since 2008.[12]

Governments have used two general kinds of trade barriers: tariff and nontariff barriers. A **tariff** is a direct tax on imported goods. Tariffs increase the cost of imported goods relative to that of domestic goods. Because of retaliatory tariffs on Chinese goods, US consumers paid an estimated $70 billion in tariffs on $250 billion of products imported from China.[13] For example, the US tariffs on imported Chinese washing machines alone cost US consumers an extra $1.5 billion.[14]

Nontariff barriers are nontax methods of increasing the cost or reducing the volume of imported goods. There are five types of nontariff barriers: quotas, voluntary export restraints, government import standards, government subsidies, and customs valuation/classification. Because there are so many different kinds of nontariff barriers, they can be an even more potent method of shielding domestic industries from foreign competition.

Quotas are specific limits on the number or volume of imported products. For example, to avoid US tariffs on imported steel, South Korea amended its US trade agreement to limit its exports to 70 percent of the average amount of steel imported to the United States, or 2.63 million tons per year.[15] Likewise, the Chinese government only allows 34 imported movies each year. China also limits the amount of foreign content available on video-streaming websites to no more than 30 percent. To get around the quota, films must be at least partially shot in China, cofinanced by a Chinese firm, and have some Chinese cultural elements.[16]

Like quotas, **voluntary export restraints** limit the amount of a product that can be imported annually. The difference is that the exporting country rather than the importing country imposes restraints. Usually, however, the "voluntary" offer to limit exports occurs because the importing country has implicitly threatened to impose quotas. For example, to protect Brazilian auto manufacturers from less expensive Mexican-made cars, the Brazilian government convinced Mexico to "voluntarily" restrict auto exports to Brazil to no more than $1.55 billion a year for three years.[17] According to the World Trade Organization ([WTO] see the discussion in Section 8-1c), however, voluntary export restraints are illegal and should not be used to restrict imports.[18]

In theory, **government import standards** are established to protect the health and safety of citizens. In reality, such standards are often used to restrict or ban imported goods. Europe bans imports of hormone-treated US-raised beef due to alleged health risks to European Union (EU) citizens. However, the WTO ruled that the EU's ban is not based on scientific evidence, and that the EU should

> Countries place tariffs on exports to discourage manufacturers from sending domestically produced goods overseas.

Trade barriers government-imposed regulations that increase the cost and restrict the number of imported goods

Protectionism a government's use of trade barriers to shield domestic companies and their workers from foreign competition

Tariff a direct tax on imported goods

Nontariff barriers nontax methods of increasing the cost or reducing the volume of imported goods

Quota a limit on the number or volume of imported products

Voluntary export restraints voluntarily imposed limits on the number or volume of products exported to a particular country

Government import standard a standard ostensibly established to protect the health and safety of citizens but, in reality, is often used to restrict imports

open its markets to American beef imports.[19] After the United States threatened retaliation with 100 percent tariffs on select EU imports, the EU signed an agreement with the United States that would increase the amount of imported US beef by 46 percent the first year, rising to 90 percent more after seven years. However, that beef will be processed by 17 US slaughterhouses preapproved by the EU to export hormone-free beef to Europe.[20]

Many nations also use **subsidies**, such as long-term, low-interest loans, cash grants, and tax deferments, to develop and protect companies in special industries. In 2016, the WTO ruled that the EU illegally provided billions in subsidies to Airbus Group SE, a European conglomerate that designs and manufactures passenger jets. The office of the US Trade Representative said, "The EU did not come into compliance with respect to the subsidies previously found, and it further breached WTO rules by granting more than $4 billion in new subsidized financing for the A350XWB (Airbus's long-haul plane)."[21] US Trade Representative Michael Froman said, "EU aircraft subsidies have cost American companies tens of billions of dollars in lost revenue."[22] The United States indicated that Airbus received EU subsidies totaling $22 billion and that it would seek $10 billion a year in retaliatory tariffs.[23] In 2019, the WTO ruled that the US could recoup $7.5 billion a year in damages through tariffs on EU products imported to the United States.[24]

The last type of nontariff barrier is **customs classification**. As products are imported into a country, they are examined by customs agents, who must decide which of nearly 9,000 categories

Festive Articles

Apparel

kurhan/Shutterstock.com

they should be classified into (see the Official Harmonized Tariff Schedule of the United States at www.usitc.gov for more information). The category assigned by customs agents can greatly affect the size of the tariff and whether the item is subject to import quotas. For example, the US Customs Service classifies the various parts of a Santa Claus costume differently. The beard, wig, and hat are classified as "festive articles," which are defined as "flimsy, nondurable, and not normal articles of wearing apparel." Festive articles are exempt from import duties. The jacket, pants, gloves, and toy sacks, however, are considered apparel. They carry tariffs from 10 to 32 percent.[25]

8-1c Trade Agreements

Thanks to the trade barriers described previously, buying imported goods has often been much more expensive and difficult than buying domestic goods. During the 1990s, however, the regulations governing global trade were transformed. The most significant change was that 124 countries agreed to adopt the **General Agreement on Tariffs and Trade (GATT)**. GATT, which existed from 1947 to 1995, was an agreement to regulate trade among (eventually) more than 120 countries, the purpose of which was "substantial reduction of tariffs and other trade barriers and the elimination of preferences."[26] GATT members engaged in eight rounds of trade negotiations, with the Uruguay Round signed in 1994 and going into effect in 1995. Although GATT itself was replaced by the **World Trade Organization (WTO)** in 1995, the changes that it made continue to encourage international trade. Today, the WTO and its member countries are negotiating what's known as the Doha Round, which seeks to advance trade opportunities for developing countries in areas ranging from agriculture to services to intellectual property rights. The WTO, headquartered in Geneva, Switzerland, administers trade agreements, provides a forum for trade negotiations, handles trade disputes, monitors national trade policies, and offers technical assistance and training for developing countries for its 164 member countries.

Through tremendous decreases in tariff and nontariff barriers, the Uruguay round of GATT made it

Subsidies government loans, grants, and tax deferments given to domestic companies to protect them from foreign competition

Customs classification a classification assigned to imported products by government officials that affects the size of the tariff and the imposition of import quotas

General Agreement on Tariffs and Trade (GATT) a worldwide trade agreement that reduced and eliminated tariffs, limited government subsidies, and established protections for intellectual property

World Trade Organization (WTO) the successor to GATT; the only international organization dealing with the global rules of trade between nations; its main function is to ensure that trade flows as smoothly, predictably, and freely as possible

Exhibit 8.3
World Trade Organization

WORLD TRADE
ORGANIZATION

Location: Geneva, Switzerland
Established: January 1, 1995
Created by: Uruguay Round
negotiations (1986–1994)
Membership: 164 members
representing 98 percent of world trade
Budget: 197 million Swiss
francs for 2019
Secretariat staff: 625
Head: Roberto Azevêdo
(Director-General)

Functions:
- Administering WTO trade agreements
- Forum for trade negotiations
- Handling trade disputes
- Monitoring national trade policies
- Technical assistance and training for developing countries
- Cooperation with other international organizations

Source: "Fact File: What Is the WTO?" *World Trade Organization*, accessed April 4, 2020, www.wto.org/english/thewto_e/whatis_e/whatis_e.htm.

much easier and cheaper for consumers in all countries to buy foreign products. First, tariffs were cut 40 percent on average worldwide by 2005. Second, tariffs were eliminated in 10 specific industries: beer, alcohol, construction equipment, farm machinery, furniture, medical equipment, paper, pharmaceuticals, steel, and toys. Third, stricter limits were put on government subsidies (see the discussion of subsidies in Section 8-1b). Fourth, the Uruguay round of GATT established protections for intellectual property, such as trademarks, patents, and copyrights. In 2017, the WTO's Trade Facilitation Agreement (TFA), which simplifies and standardizes customs procedures around the world, went into effect. The WTO estimates that countries that implement the TFA may cut their trade costs by 14 percent and reduce how long it takes to import and export goods by 47 percent and 91 percent, respectively.[27]

Protection of intellectual property has become an increasingly important issue in global trade because of widespread product piracy. For example, the International Federation of the Phonographic Industry estimates that 23 percent of internet users access "illegal stream ripping services – the leading form of music piracy."[28] Likewise, according to BSA The Software Alliance, 37 percent of all software used in the world is pirated, and malware embedded in unlicensed software costs companies $359 billion a year.[29] Product piracy is also costly to the movie industry,

as movie studios and theaters, as well as video/DVD distributors, lose $29 billion each year to pirates.[30] For example, the piracy site iStreamItAll charged "subscribers" $19.99 a month for access to 11,000 films and 118,000 TV episodes, "dwarfing the amount of content available on … Netflix, Hulu and Amazon Prime Video."[31]

Finally, trade disputes between countries now are fully settled by the WTO's Appellate Body.[32] In the past, countries could use their veto power to cancel a panel's decision. For instance, the French government routinely vetoed rulings that its large cash grants to French farmers constituted unfair subsidies. Now, however, countries that are members of the WTO no longer have veto power. Thus, WTO rulings are complete and final. Exhibit 8.3 provides a brief overview of the WTO and its functions.

The second major development that has reduced trade barriers has been the creation of **regional trading zones**, or zones in which tariff and nontariff barriers are reduced or eliminated for countries within the trading zone. The largest and most important trading zones are:

» Africa: African Free Trade Zone Agreement (AFTZ) and Tripartite Free Trade Area (TFTA)

» Asia: Association of Southeast Asian Nations (ASEAN), Asia-Pacific Economic Cooperation (APEC)

» Central America: Dominican Republic-Central America Free Trade Agreement (CAFTA-DR)

» Europe: The Maastricht Treaty (EU, European Union)

» North America: United States–Mexico–Canada Agreement (USMCA)

» South America: Southern Common Market Free Trade Agreement (MERCOSUR)

The map in Exhibit 8.4 shows the extent to which free-trade agreements govern global trade. It does not include agreements between individual countries, such as between the United States and Japan, nor side agreements that regional trade zones strike with individual countries, such as between the EU and Japan.[33]

Regional trading zones
areas in which tariff and nontariff barriers on trade between countries are reduced or eliminated

Exhibit 8.4
Global Map of Regional Trade Agreements

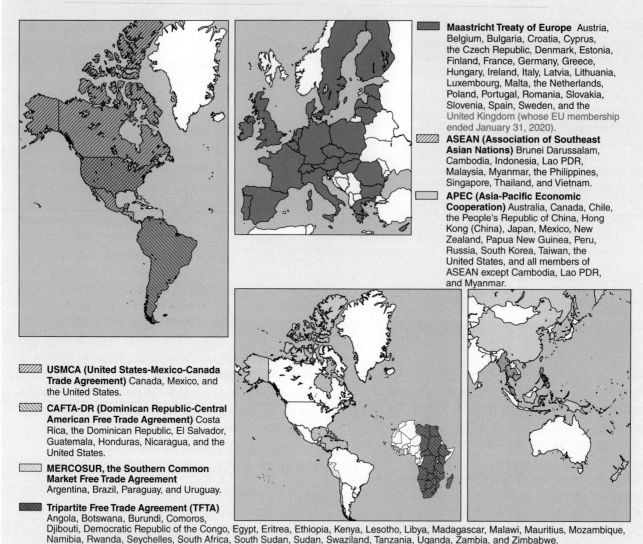

Maastricht Treaty of Europe Austria, Belgium, Bulgaria, Croatia, Cyprus, the Czech Republic, Denmark, Estonia, Finland, France, Germany, Greece, Hungary, Ireland, Italy, Latvia, Lithuania, Luxembourg, Malta, the Netherlands, Poland, Portugal, Romania, Slovakia, Slovenia, Spain, Sweden, and the United Kingdom (whose EU membership ended January 31, 2020).

ASEAN (Association of Southeast Asian Nations) Brunei Darussalam, Cambodia, Indonesia, Lao PDR, Malaysia, Myanmar, the Philippines, Singapore, Thailand, and Vietnam.

APEC (Asia-Pacific Economic Cooperation) Australia, Canada, Chile, the People's Republic of China, Hong Kong (China), Japan, Mexico, New Zealand, Papua New Guinea, Peru, Russia, South Korea, Taiwan, the United States, and all members of ASEAN except Cambodia, Lao PDR, and Myanmar.

USMCA (United States-Mexico-Canada Trade Agreement) Canada, Mexico, and the United States.

CAFTA-DR (Dominican Republic-Central American Free Trade Agreement) Costa Rica, the Dominican Republic, El Salvador, Guatemala, Honduras, Nicaragua, and the United States.

MERCOSUR, the Southern Common Market Free Trade Agreement Argentina, Brazil, Paraguay, and Uruguay.

Tripartite Free Trade Agreement (TFTA) Angola, Botswana, Burundi, Comoros, Djibouti, Democratic Republic of the Congo, Egypt, Eritrea, Ethiopia, Kenya, Lesotho, Libya, Madagascar, Malawi, Mauritius, Mozambique, Namibia, Rwanda, Seychelles, South Africa, South Sudan, Sudan, Swaziland, Tanzania, Uganda, Zambia, and Zimbabwe.

In 1992, Belgium, Denmark, France, Germany, Greece, Ireland, Italy, Luxembourg, the Netherlands, Portugal, Spain, and the United Kingdom adopted the **Maastricht Treaty of Europe**. The purpose of this treaty was to transform their 12 different economies and 12 currencies into one common economic market, called the EU, with one common currency. On January 1, 2002, a single common currency, the euro, went into circulation in 12 of the EU's members (Austria, Belgium, Finland, France, Germany, Greece, Ireland, Italy, Luxembourg, the Netherlands, Portugal, and Spain). Austria, Finland, and Sweden joined the EU in 1995, followed by Cyprus, the Czech Republic, Estonia, Hungary, Latvia, Lithuania, Malta, Poland, Slovakia, and Slovenia in 2004; Bulgaria and Romania in 2007; and Croatia in 2013, bringing the total membership to 28 countries.[34] Albania, Macedonia, Montenegro, Serbia, and Turkey have applied and are being considered for membership. In what became known as Brexit (i.e., Great Britain exiting the EU), the United Kingdom voted in June 2016 to leave the EU.[35] Brexit became official January 31, 2020, but the United Kingdom will continue to follow all EU laws, rules, and regulations during a transition period ending December 31, 2020. The United Kingdom and the EU are negotiating a trade agreement to govern trade after this transition.[36]

Maastricht Treaty of Europe a regional trade agreement among most European countries

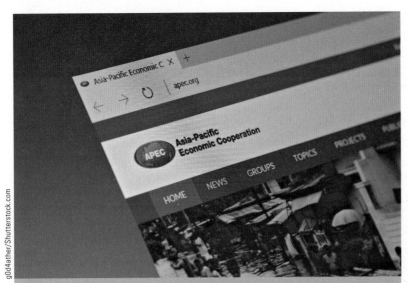

APEC, the Asian-Pacific Economic Cooperation, is one of the two largest regional trading groups in Asia.

the three countries from increasing existing tariffs or introducing new ones. Overall, combined Mexican and Canadian exports to the United States increased 349 percent since NAFTA went into effect. US combined exports to Mexico and Canada rose 287 percent, growing twice as fast as US exports to any other part of the world.[37] In fact, Mexico and Canada now account for 34 percent of all US exports.[38]

A few of the significant changes from NAFTA to the USMCA include fewer restrictions on agricultural imports, such as dairy, chicken, and eggs; 62.5 percent of automotive vehicles, rising to 75 percent over a number of years, must be made in North America to qualify for zero tariffs; increased copyright protections from 50 years to 75 years; and reduced protections on drugs and other pharmaceutical products.[39]

CAFTA-DR, the **Dominican Republic–Central America Free Trade Agreement** among the United States, the Dominican Republic, and the Central American countries of Costa Rica, El Salvador, Guatemala, Honduras, and Nicaragua, went into effect in August 2005. With a combined population of 57 million, the CAFTA-DR countries together are the eighteenth-largest US export market in the world. US companies export nearly $32 billion in goods each year to the CAFTA-DR countries.[40]

Free trade agreements in South America are in transition. The *Union of South American Nations (UNASUR)* Constitutive Treaty, which united all the countries in South America, ceased functioning in 2019 as all but three countries suspended their membership.[41] **MERCOSUR**, the Southern Common Market free trade agreement among the primary countries of Argentina, Brazil, Paraguay, and Uruguay, went into effect in 1991. MERCOSUR's associated countries, Bolivia (in the process of becoming a primary country), Chile, Colombia, Ecuador, Guyana, Peru, and Surinam receive reduced tariffs, but not the free trade or access accorded

Prior to the treaty, trucks carrying products were stopped and inspected by customs agents at each border. Furthermore, because the required paperwork, tariffs, and government product specifications could be radically different in each country, companies often had to file 12 different sets of paperwork, pay 12 different tariffs, produce 12 different versions of their basic product to meet various government specifications, and exchange money in 12 different currencies. Likewise, open business travel, which we take for granted in the United States, was complicated by inspections at each border crossing. If you lived in Germany but worked in Luxembourg, your car was stopped and your passport was inspected twice every day as you traveled to and from work. Also, every business transaction required a currency exchange – for example, from German deutschemarks to Italian lira, or from French francs to Dutch guilders. Imagine all of this happening to millions of trucks, cars, and workers each day, and you can begin to appreciate the difficulty and cost of conducting business across Europe before the Maastricht Treaty. For more information about the Maastricht Treaty, the EU, and the euro, see http://europa.eu.

USMCA, the **United States–Mexico–Canada Agreement** went into effect on June 1, 2020. The USMCA updates and replaces NAFTA, the North American Free Trade Agreement among the United States, Canada, and Mexico, which went into effect on January 1, 1994. More than any other regional trade agreement, NAFTA liberalized trade between countries so that businesses can plan for one market (North America) rather than for three separate markets. One of NAFTA's most important achievements was to eliminate most product tariffs *and* prevent

United States–Mexico–Canada Agreement (USMCA) a regional trade agreement among the United States, Canada, and Mexico

Dominican Republic–Central America Free Trade Agreement (CAFTA-DR) a regional trade agreement among Costa Rica, the Dominican Republic, El Salvador, Guatemala, Honduras, Nicaragua, and the United States

Southern Common Market (MERCOSUR) a regional trade agreement among the primary countries of Argentina, Brazil, Paraguay, and Uruguay, with associated countries, Bolivia, Chile, Colombia, Ecuador, Guyana, Peru, and Surinam

g0d4ather/Shutterstock.com

primary members.[42] With a combined population of 268 million, the four primary members of MERCOSUR are together the fifth largest trading market in the world with a combined gross domestic product (GDP) of $3.4 trillion.[43]

ASEAN, the **Association of Southeast Asian Nations**, and **APEC**, the **Asia-Pacific Economic Cooperation**, are the two largest and most important regional trading groups in Asia. ASEAN is a trade agreement among Brunei Darussalam, Cambodia, Indonesia, Lao PDR, Malaysia, Myanmar, the Philippines, Singapore, Thailand, and Vietnam, which form a market of more than 649 million people with a combined GDP of $2.98 trillion. US trade with ASEAN countries exceeds $234 billion a year.[44]

In fact, the United States is ASEAN's third-largest trading partner (China is its largest), and ASEAN's member nations constitute the fourth-largest trading partner of the United States. An ASEAN free-trade area was established in 2015 for the six original countries (Brunei Darussalam, Indonesia, Malaysia, the Philippines, Singapore, and Thailand), and in 2018 for the newer member countries (Cambodia, Lao PDR, Myanmar, and Vietnam). All 10 nations have committed to develop a "deeply integrated and highly cohesive ASEAN economy" by 2025.[45]

APEC is a broad agreement that includes Australia, Canada, Chile, the People's Republic of China, Hong Kong, Japan, Mexico, New Zealand, Papua New Guinea, Peru, Russia, South Korea, Taiwan, the United States, and all the members of ASEAN except Cambodia, Lao PDR, and Myanmar. APEC's 21 member countries have a total population of 2.9 billion people and combined GDP of more than $51.3 trillion.[46]

APEC countries began reducing trade barriers in 2000, though all the reductions will not be completely phased in until 2020.[47]

The **Tripartite Free Trade Agreement (TFTA)** is an African trade agreement proposed in 2015. Currently signed by 22 of its 27 member states and awaiting ratification, the TFTA's ultimate goal is to create a free trade area across all 54 African Union states.[48] As of February 2020, only eight countries – Burundi, Kenya, Egypt, Rwanda, Uganda, South Africa, Namibia, and Botswana – have ratified the TFTA. Six more countries must ratify the agreement before trade provisions go into effect.[49]

8-1d Consumers, Trade Barriers, and Trade Agreements

The average worker earns nearly $48,280 in Finland, $55,490 in Sweden, $80,610 in Norway, and $63,080 in the United States.[50] However, in order to get a more meaningful comparison, we need to adjust these incomes for purchasing power – that is, how much workers can buy in those countries based on what they earn. When we do, the Finnish income is worth $48,580, the Swedish $54,030, the Norwegian $68,310 (a huge drop!), and the American $63,690.[51] In other words, Americans, who are ranked eleventh in the world on this dimension can buy much more with their incomes than those in many other countries.[52]

One reason that Americans get more for their money is that the US marketplace is the second-most competitive in the world (behind Singapore). The US economy has historically been one of the easiest for foreign countries to enter.[53] Although some US industries, such as textiles, have been heavily protected from foreign competition by trade barriers, for the most part, American consumers (and businesses) have had plentiful choices among American-made and foreign-made products. More important, the high level of competition between foreign and domestic companies that creates these choices helps keep prices low in the United States. Furthermore, it is precisely the lack of choice and the low level of competition that keep prices higher in countries that have not been as open to foreign companies and products. But even though the US economy is one

iStock.com/kevinjeon00

Protectionism or Accuracy in Advertising? "It's The F-Word We Can't Say"

Sartori Cheese is a fourth-generation family-owned business in Plymouth, Wisconsin. *Businessweek* magazine featured its Parmesan cheese among "Products that Rival Europe's Best." But when Sartori began exporting *to* Europe, it changed the name from Parmesan to "Sarmesan" cheese. Why? Because European Union regulations permit local names to be used for products made only in those areas – in this case, the Parma, Reggio Emilia, Modena, Mantua, and Bologna regions of Italy. Likewise, because only Greek feta cheese can be called "feta," Arla Foods, one of the world's largest dairy companies, has to call its feta cheese "white cheese" or "salad cheese." Arla's communication director Theis Brogger says, "It's the F-word we can't say." To avoid confusion, he says, "We make sure there is a large photo of the cheese on the outside."

Prostock-Studio/iStock/Getty Images

Sources: "Quality Schemes Explained," European Commission, accessed April 9, 2020, ec.europa.eu/info/food-farming-fisheries/food-safety-and-quality/certification/quality-labels/quality-schemes-explained_en#geographicalindications; "About Us – SartoriCheese.com," Sartori Cheese, accessed April 9, 2020, www.sartoricheese.com/about-us.html; L. Craymer, "When U.S. Cheese Goes Overseas, It Needs a Fake ID," *Wall Street Journal*, May 3, 2018, accessed April 9, 2020, www.wsj.com/articles/u-s-cheese-makers-are-having-a-cow-about-naming-rights-1525358957?mod=djemRiskCompliance.

of the most competitive in the world, new tariffs instituted over the last few years now cost American consumers an additional $70 billion a year.[54] Why? Because businesses raise prices to pass the cost of tariffs directly to consumers.

So why do trade barriers and free-trade agreements matter to consumers? They're important because free-trade agreements increase choices, competition and purchasing power, what people pay for food, clothing, necessities, and luxuries. Indeed, in the United States, free trade lowers prices 29 percent for middle-income consumers, 62 percent for the poorest consumers, and $18,000 a year on average for American households.[55] Accordingly, today's consumers rarely care where their products and services come from. From seafood to diamonds, people don't care where products are from – they just want to know which brand or kind is a better value.[56] And, while the coronavirus pandemic may change attitudes toward global trade, a Gallup poll in February 2020 found that 79 percent of Americans also see global trade as "an opportunity for economic growth through increased US exports."[57]

Finally, why do trade barriers and free-trade agreements matter to managers? The reason, as you're about to read, is that while free-trade agreements create new business opportunities, they also intensify competition, and addressing that competition is a manager's job.

8-2 CONSISTENCY OR ADAPTATION?

After a company has decided that it *will* go global, it must decide *how* to go global. For example, if you decide to sell in Singapore, should you try to find a local business partner who speaks the language, knows the laws, and understands the customs and norms of Singapore's culture? Or should you simply export your products from your home country? What do you do if you are also entering Eastern Europe, perhaps starting in Hungary? Should you use the same approach in Hungary that you use in Singapore?

In this section, we return to a key issue: How can you be sure that the way you run your business in one country is the right way to run that business in another? In other words, how can you strike the right balance between global consistency and local adaptation?

Global consistency means that a multinational company with offices, manufacturing plants, and distribution facilities in different countries uses the same rules, guidelines, policies, and procedures to run all of those offices, plants, and facilities. Managers at

> **Global consistency** when a multinational company has offices, manufacturing plants, and distribution facilities in different countries and runs them all using the same rules, guidelines, policies, and procedures

company headquarters value global consistency because it simplifies decisions. For example, the *Love Island* TV show, which originated in the United Kingdom, also produces nearly identical versions of the show for Australia, Belgium/ the Netherlands, Denmark, Finland, Germany, Hungary, New Zealand, Poland, Sweden, Norway, and the United States.[58] If you turn the volume down so you can't hear the different languages spoken by the contestants from each country, the only noticeable difference would be that each show uses a unique luxury home for taping the reality show. However, half of those are located in Spain. Otherwise, each show consists of various games, interviews, and made-for-TV "dramatic" moments to find "real" romance among the participants.[59]

By contrast, a company following a policy of **local adaptation** modifies its standard operating procedures to adapt to differences in foreign customers, governments, and regulatory agencies. **Amazon** chose local adaptation to grow its video services in India by developing new shows specifically for Indian viewers. Roy Price, chief of Amazon Studios, said, "You can have a global service, but there are no global customers. There are only local customers."[60] Amazon released 10 original shows in 2019, made just for Indian viewers. For example, *The Family Man* is about a middle-class father who ostensibly balances his family responsibilities with his government desk job. But, unbeknownst to his family, he's really a spy trying to protect India.[61] Local adaptation is typically preferred by local managers who are charged with making the international business successful in their countries.

If companies lean too much toward global consistency, they run the risk of using management procedures poorly suited to particular countries' markets, cultures, and employees (i.e., a lack of local adaptation). Walmart became the world's largest retailer by building hypermarkets with a full-sized grocery and a full-sized discount department store. But that strategy has struggled overseas. Professor Flavio Tayra said, "Ever since it entered Brazil, Walmart has found it difficult to integrate itself into the market. It occupies a modest space here given all the potential

it has."[62] Traffic is notoriously bad in Brazil's large cities, so getting to Walmart stores located in city outskirts (because of their large size) is frustrating. Also, bargain-hunting Brazilians prefer "cash and carries" retailers selling heavily discounted goods in bulk. While they might visit cash and carries once a month, Brazilians shop for groceries several times a week at smaller, neighborhood grocers. Despite spending $320 million to upgrade its hypermarkets, Walmart ended up selling an 80 percent ownership share of its Brazilian operations to Advent International, which renamed the stores "Grupo Big."[63] Walmart reported a $4.5 billion loss for on the sale.[64]

If, however, companies focus too much on local adaptation, they run the risk of losing the cost effectiveness and productivity that result from using standardized rules and procedures throughout the world.[65] While **McDonald's** offers burgers and fries around the world, it relies on local adaptation to adjust its menu to global consumers' tastes. For example, it serves waffle fries in Austria, cheesy bacon fries in Belgium, and potato wedges in Indonesia.[66] To best serve global palates, it tries to source most ingredients locally. But, in many countries, it can take years to find reliable suppliers, leaving McDonald's with the more expensive option of importing food ingredients from dependable overseas suppliers. After 30 years of doing this in Russia, McDonald's brought in a Dutch firm, Lamb Weston/ Meijer, a global supplier of high-quality potatoes, to teach Russian farmers how to grow potatoes to McDonald's standards and high volumes. Roman Bezdudny, who worked for McDonald's in Russia as a regional marketing manager, said, "No one could get the french fries right, to get that golden crisp that it took years to perfect."[67]

> Walmart became the world's largest retailer by building hypermarkets with a full-sized grocery and a full-sized discount department store, but it sold an 80 percent share of its Brazilian operations to Advent International, losing $4.5 billion on the sale.

8-3 FORMS FOR GLOBAL BUSINESS

Besides determining whether to adapt organizational policies and procedures, a company must also determine how to organize itself for successful entry into foreign markets.

BMW's plant in Spartanburg, SC, is the largest auto manufacturing plant in the world.

*Historically, companies have generally followed the phase model of globalization, in which a company makes the transition from a domestic company to a global company in the following sequential phases: **8-3a exporting, 8-3b cooperative contracts, 8-3c strategic alliances,** and **8-3d wholly owned affiliates.** At each step, the company grows much larger, uses those resources to enter more global markets, is less dependent on home-country sales, and is more committed in its orientation to global business. Some companies, however, do not follow the phase model of globalization. Some skip phases on their way to becoming more global and less domestic. Others don't follow the phase model at all. These are known as **8-3e global new ventures.** This section reviews these forms of global business.[68]*

8-3a Exporting

When companies produce products in their home countries and sell those products to customers in foreign countries, they are **exporting**. Exporting as a form of global business offers many advantages. It makes the company less dependent on sales in its home market and provides a greater degree of control over research, design, and production decisions. The largest auto manufacturing plant in the world in Spartanburg, South Carolina, is owned by German-based BMW. Opened in 1994, BMW's Spartanburg plant, which employs 11,000 people produced 411,620 cars in 2019.[69] Seventy percent of the X3, X4, X5, and X6 BMWs produced there are exported outside the United States to 125 different countries. BMW's

cumulative investment in Spartanburg is $10.6 billion. In 25 years of production, the plant has produced 4.9 million cars.[70]

Though advantageous in a number of ways, exporting also has its disadvantages. The primary disadvantage is that many exported goods are subject to tariff and nontariff barriers that can substantially increase their final cost to consumers. The second disadvantage is that transportation costs can significantly increase the price of an exported product. Chinese regulations require live imported animals to be slaughtered within 55 miles of their point of entry. To meet China's growing demand for fresh beef, Australian ranchers have begun flying cattle on 747 jumbo jets to ports of entry thousands of miles inland. By switching from ships to jets, exporters have been able to expand the market for fresh beef in inland China.[71] The final disadvantage of exporting is that exporters depend on foreign importers for product distribution. If, for example, the foreign importer makes a mistake on the paperwork that accompanies a shipment of imported goods, those goods can be returned to the foreign manufacturer at the manufacturer's expense.

8-3b Cooperative Contracts

When an organization wants to expand its business globally without making a large financial commitment to do so, it may sign a **cooperative contract** with a foreign business owner who pays the company a fee for the right to conduct that business in his or her country. There are two kinds of cooperative contracts: licensing and franchising.

Under a **licensing** agreement, a domestic company, the *licensor*, receives royalty payments for allowing another company, the *licensee*, to produce its product, sell its service, or use its brand name in a particular foreign market. For example, *Peppa Pig*, an animated TV show for preschoolers that originated in the United Kingdom (but is now owned by US-based Hasbro), licenses

Exporting selling domestically produced products to customers in foreign countries

Cooperative contract an agreement in which a foreign business owner pays a company a fee for the right to conduct that business in his or her country

Licensing an agreement in which a domestic company, the licensor, receives royalty payments for allowing another company, the licensee, to produce the licensor's product, sell its service, or use its brand name in a specified foreign market

Franchisees pay McDonald's an initial franchise fee of $45,000 to get the rights to operate a restaurant.

overexposure. Luxury fashion brands like Louis Vuitton, Celine, Gucci, Yves Saint Laurent, and Burberry recently ended long-term licensing agreements, citing a lack of control over the products sold under their brand names. **Burberry** ended a 45-year agreement with its Japanese licensee, Sanyo Shokai, because the company opened hundreds of stores and flooded Japan with too many moderately-priced items. After canceling the contract, Burberry reduced the number of Japanese stores from more than 400 to two dozen and replaced Sanyo Shokai's mid-tier products with ones costing up to 10 times more. According to CEO for Burberry in Asia, Pascal Perrier, "The license has been suffering from overexposure. We will never do that again."[74] An additional disadvantage is that licensees can eventually become competitors, especially when a licensing agreement includes access to important technology or proprietary business knowledge.

A **franchise** is a collection of networked firms in which the manufacturer or marketer of a product or service, the *franchisor*, licenses the entire business to another person or organization, the *franchisee*. For the price of an initial franchise fee plus royalties, franchisors provide franchisees with training, assistance with marketing and advertising, and an exclusive right to conduct business in a particular location. Most franchise fees run between $5,000 and $45,000. Franchisees pay McDonald's, one of the largest franchisors in the world, an initial franchise fee of $45,000. Another $1,263,000 to $2,235,000 is needed beyond that to pay for food inventory, kitchen equipment, construction, landscaping, and other expenses (the cost varies by location). While franchisees typically borrow part of this cost from a bank, McDonald's requires applicants to have over $500,000 in nonborrowed assets and requires a 25 to 40 percent cash down payment for the initial investment.[75] Typical royalties run from 4 percent of gross sales (plus rent at 8.5 percent) to 15 percent based on location and revenue.[76] So franchisors are well rewarded for the help they provide to franchisees. More than 400 US companies franchise their businesses to foreign franchise partners.

merchandise rights around the world.[72] In the United States, CSS Industries is licensed to make Peppa Pig "exchange products and accessories" for Valentine's Day and Easter, while PTI group is licensed to make Peppa Pig "character treat buckets" for Halloween. Likewise, Amscan makes Peppa Pig "tableware, decorations, favors and invitations" for parties, while Kurt S. Adler makes Peppa Pig Christmas decorations and ornaments.[73]

One of the most important advantages of licensing is that it allows companies to earn additional profits without investing more money. As foreign sales increase, the royalties paid to the licensor by the foreign licensee increase. Moreover, the licensee, not the licensor, invests in production equipment and facilities to produce the product. Licensing also helps companies avoid tariff and nontariff barriers. Because the licensee manufactures the product within the foreign country, tariff and nontariff barriers don't apply.

The biggest disadvantage associated with licensing is that the licensor gives up control over the quality of the product or service sold by the foreign licensee. Unless the licensing agreement contains specific restrictions, the licensee controls the entire business from production to marketing to final sales. Many licensors include inspection clauses in their license contracts, but closely monitoring product or service quality from thousands of miles away can be difficult.

An overeager licensor can dilute the value of a brand or damage the brand's reputation through

> **Franchise** a collection of networked firms in which the manufacturer or marketer of a product or service, the franchisor, licenses the entire business to another person or organization, the franchisee

Despite franchising's many advantages, franchisors face a loss of control when they sell businesses to franchisees who are thousands of miles away. Connaught Partners opened the first McDonald's in India in 1996 and eventually grew to 169 restaurants. McDonald's said that franchise agreement violations prompted it to terminate Connaught's franchises and stop suppliers from sourcing burgers, fries, and other key ingredients. While the case was in court, Connaught found new suppliers and kept the restaurants running without McDonald's support. After five years, McDonald's bought out Connaught in an out-of-court settlement.[77]

Although there are exceptions, franchising success may be somewhat culture-bound. Because most global franchisors begin by franchising their businesses in similar countries or regions (Canada is by far the first choice for US companies taking their first step into global franchising), and because 65 percent of franchisors make absolutely no change in their business for overseas franchisees, that success may not generalize to cultures with different lifestyles, values, preferences, and technological infrastructures.

Here are some examples, though, of companies that have adapted to different cultures. In Hong Kong, Pizza Hut's "flying fish roe salmon cream cheese pizza" is topped with shrimp, crayfish, clams, and scallops. In Australia it serves a hot-dog stuffed crust pizza. And in South Korea it serves a dessert stuffed crust (cream cheese, cranberry or cinnamon apple nut) pizza with sausage, steak, bacon, and calamari toppings. Burger King offers the "SufganiKing" whopper with two fried donut halves for the bun in Israel, the "Meatatarian" burger with bacon, chicken, beef, cheese, and barbecue sauce in New Zealand, and the "Kuro" (black) burger with a black charred bun, black cheese made from charcoaled bamboo, and black sauce from black squid ink in Japan.[78]

8-3c Strategic Alliances

Companies forming **strategic alliances** combine key resources, costs, risks, technology, and people. Airbnb, the reservation site for people renting rooms, apartments and

In Japan, Burger King offers the "Kuro" (black) burger with a black charred bun, black cheese made from charcoaled bamboo, and black sauce from black squid ink.

homes to travelers, makes it easy for Chinese customers to pay for reservations by partnering with Alipay, the Chinese version of PayPal, and with Tencent, the owner of WeChat, the dominant messaging and social group app in China that can also be used to pay bills and make online purchases via TenPay (Tencent's version of PayPal).[79] The most common strategic alliance is a **joint venture**, which occurs when two existing companies collaborate to form a third company or engage in a clearly defined business activity. US-based Walmart and Rakuten, Japan's largest online retailer, formed a joint venture to sell groceries online in Japan, and ebooks and audiobooks in the United States.[80]

One of the advantages of global joint ventures is that, like licensing and franchising, they help companies avoid tariff and nontariff barriers to entry. Another advantage is that companies participating in a joint venture bear only part of the costs and the risks of that business. Many companies find this attractive because of the expense of entering foreign markets or developing new products. Global joint ventures can be especially advantageous to smaller local partners who link up with larger, more experienced foreign firms that can bring advanced management, resources, and business skills to the joint venture.

Global joint ventures are not without problems, though. Because companies share costs and risks with their joint venture partners, they must also share profits. Managing global joint ventures can also be difficult because they represent a merging of four cultures: the country and the organizational culture of the first partner, and the country and the organizational culture of the second partner. Often, to be fair to all involved, each partner in the global joint venture will have equal ownership and power. But this can result in power struggles and a lack of leadership. Because of these problems, companies forming global joint ventures should carefully develop detailed contracts that specify the obligations of each party. US-based Simon Property, the world's largest shopping mall developer, has had two unsuccessful joint ventures in China. Its first joint venture with US-based investment firm Morgan Stanley and a state-owned Chinese company to build shopping malls in China ended with Simon selling its shares in the business back to its partners. Two years later Simon agreed to form a joint venture with a China-based developer, Bailian Group, to build high-end outlet centers in China. But nothing resulted from that agreement, either.[81]

Strategic alliance an agreement in which companies combine key resources, costs, risks, technology, and people

Joint venture a strategic alliance in which two existing companies collaborate to form a third, independent company or engage in a clearly defined business activity

8-3d Wholly Owned Affiliates (Build or Buy)

Approximately one-third of multinational companies enter foreign markets through wholly owned affiliates. China-based Golden Dragon Precise Copper Tube Group entered the US market by building a $120 million pipe factory in Wilcox, Alabama. The company's US subsidiary, GD Copper, is completely owned by the Chinese parent company.[82] Unlike licensing arrangements, franchises, or joint ventures, **wholly owned affiliates**, such as American Standard Brands and GROHE, are 100 percent owned by their parent company, in this case, Lixil.

The primary advantage of wholly owned businesses is that the parent company receives all of the profits and has complete control over the foreign facilities. The biggest disadvantage is the expense of building new operations or buying existing businesses. Although the payoff can be enormous if wholly owned affiliates succeed, the losses can be immense if they fail because the parent company assumes all of the risk. As part of an $11 billion restructuring, US-based **Ford Motor Company** closed six European manufacturing facilities, putting 12,000 employees out of work. Ford's European president Stuart Rowley said, "Separating employees and closing plants are the hardest decisions we make. We are moving forward and focused on building a long-term sustainable future."[83] Rowley suggested that more cuts could be made, saying, "Where a product line either does not contribute to our cash flow or is adverse to our CO_2 (environmental regulation) compliance, we will consider actions."[84]

8-3e Global New Ventures

Companies used to evolve slowly from small operations selling in their home markets to large businesses selling to foreign markets. Furthermore, as companies went global, they usually followed the phase model of globalization. The following three trends have combined to allow companies to skip the phase model when going global:

1. Quick, reliable air travel can transport people to nearly any point in the world within one day.

2. Low-cost communication technologies such as email, teleconferencing via Zoom or Skype, and cloud computing make it easier to communicate with global customers, suppliers, managers, and employees.

3. There is now a critical mass of businesspeople with extensive personal experience in all aspects of global business.[85]

This combination of developments has made it possible to start companies that are global from inception. With sales, employees, and financing in different countries, **global new ventures** are companies that are founded with an active global strategy.[86]

Although there are several different kinds of global new ventures, all share two common factors. First, the company founders successfully develop and communicate the company's global vision from inception. Second, rather than going global one country at a time, new global ventures bring a product or service to market in several foreign markets at the same time. **Stripe**, a digital platform that helps companies process payments from anywhere in the world, was founded as a global new venture. While headquartered in San Francisco, it has 14 global offices, including Dublin, London, Paris, Singapore, and Tokyo. Stripe's customers include some of the biggest companies in the world – Amazon, Google, and Microsoft – but millions of smaller companies in 36 countries also use Stripe.[87] As it grows, Stripe will do most of its hiring outside the United States. CEO Patrick Collison said, "There's so much that's market- and country-specific about money. We don't want to be this San Francisco company that swaggers in, thinks it knows everything, and has all the answers."[88]

> Purchasing power is growing in countries such as India and China, which have low average levels of income.

8-4 FINDING THE BEST BUSINESS CLIMATE

When deciding where to go global, companies try to find countries or regions with promising business climates.

*An attractive global business climate **8-4a positions the company for easy access to growing markets, 8-4b is an effective but cost-efficient place to build an office or manufacturing facility,** and **8-4c minimizes the political risk to the company.***

Wholly owned affiliates foreign offices, facilities, and manufacturing plants that are 100 percent owned by the parent company

Global new ventures new companies that are founded with an active global strategy and have sales, employees, and financing in different countries

8-4a Growing Markets

The most important factor in an attractive business climate is access to a growing market. Two factors help companies determine the growth potential of foreign markets: purchasing power and foreign competitors.

Purchasing power is measured by comparing the relative cost of a standard set of goods and services in different countries. For example, a Starbucks' tall latte costs $6.05 in Copenhagen, Denmark. Because that same tall latte costs $4.30 in New York City (and less in most other places in the United States), the average American has more purchasing power than the average Dane.[89] Purchasing power is growing in countries such as India and China, which have low average levels of income. This is because basic living expenses such as food and shelter are very inexpensive in those countries, so consumers still have money to spend after paying for necessities, especially as salaries increase thanks to demand from international trade (see box "Paying for a 'Mac Attack'").

Consequently, countries with high and growing levels of purchasing power are good choices for companies looking for attractive global markets. As Exhibit 8.5 shows, the number of cars per 1,000 people in a country rises directly with purchasing power. For example, in India, China, Israel, and Germany, where the respective average annual purchasing power is $7,680, $18,170, $39,940, and $54,560 per year, the number of cars per 1,000 people increases, respectively, from 22 to 181 to 384 to 589. The more purchasing power people have, the more likely they are to buy cars for themselves and family members. Is purchasing power a perfect predictor of an attractive global market? No. Other factors, such as government regulations, or the cost and convenience of public transportation, also influence car sales. For instance, while China's car sales have grown from 4 million cars a year in 2005 to 25.8 million cars in 2019 as purchasing power more than doubled, it's unlikely

> **Purchasing power** the relative cost of a standard set of goods and services in different countries

Exhibit 8.5
How Car Purchases Vary with Purchasing Power Around the World

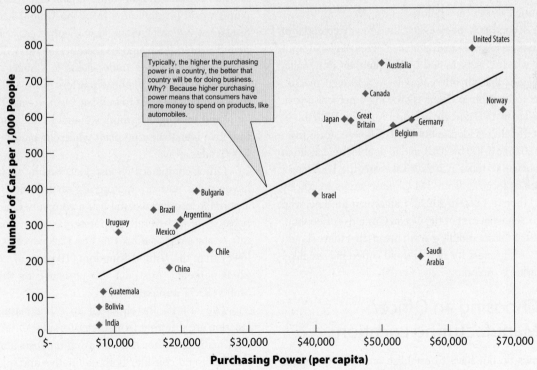

Typically, the higher the purchasing power in a country, the better that country will be for doing business. Why? Because higher purchasing power means that consumers have more money to spend on products, like automobiles.

Sources: "GNI Per Capita Ranking, Atlas Method and PPP Based," *The World Bank*, December 23, 2019, accessed April 7, 2020, databank.worldbank.org/data/download/GNIPC.pdf; "List of Countries by Vehicles Per Capita," *Wikipedia*, March 8, 2020, accessed April 7, 2020, en.wikipedia.org/wiki/List_of_countries_by_vehicles_per_capita.

PAYING FOR A "MAC ATTACK"

Every year, *The Economist* magazine produces the Big Mac Index to illustrate differences in purchasing power across countries. By comparing the price of a single item, in this case, a Big Mac from McDonald's which should cost roughly the same amount anywhere it's sold, the index shows how much (or how little) consumers in each country get for their money. According to the latest index, a Big Mac costs an average of $5.67 in the United States. The average cost jumps to $6.71 in Switzerland and $5.97 in Norway, meaning that residents of these countries get less for their money than US residents do. Conversely, the average cost of a Big Mac is $5.44 in Sweden, $3.47 in Saudi Arabia, $2.90 in Poland, $2.65 in India, and just $2.20 in Russia, where, as measured by the Big Mac Index, consumers should have more purchasing power.

Tooykrub/Shutterstock.com

Source: "The Big Mac Index," *Economist*, January 15, 2020, accessed April 10, 2020, http://www.economist.com/content/big-mac-index/.

that additional increases in Chinese purchasing power will lead to similar growth in car sales. Terrible pollution and traffic have prompted city governments in locations like Beijing and Shanghai to strongly limit the number of cars on their roads.[90] So, while car sales will likely continue to grow in China along with purchasing power, the increase will be much slower than before.[91]

The second part of assessing the growth potential of global markets involves analyzing the degree of global competition, which is determined by the number and quality of companies that already compete in a foreign market. Coffee consumption in China is growing 7 percent a year, compared to just 0.9 percent in North America. With this in mind, Starbucks decided to double its Chinese stores from 1,700 in 2015 to 3,400 by 2019, and to double them again to more than 6,000 stores in 2022.[92] Likewise, the UK's Costa Coffee plans to grow from 344 Chinese stores to 900 by 2020 and then to 1,200 in 2022.[93] Californian Jim Lee, who moved to Shanghai to start the Ocean Grounds coffee shop, believes that this incredible growth means that there should be plenty of business for new and old coffee houses alike. "This market is exploding," says Lee.[94]

8-4b Choosing an Office/ Manufacturing Location

Companies do not have to establish an office or manufacturing location in each country they enter. They can license, franchise, or export to foreign markets, or they can serve a larger region from one country. But there are many reasons why a company might choose to establish a location in a foreign country. Some foreign offices are established through global mergers and acquisitions, and some are established because of a commitment to grow in a new market. After establishing two manufacturing and research facilities in Singapore over the last decade, British inventor James Dyson is moving his company's world headquarters from the United Kingdom to Singapore, where Dyson's new electric car will also be manufactured.[95] Singapore's membership in ASEAN gives Dyson's products free trade access to China's enormous markets. Regarding the headquarters move and the company's ambitious plans to build an electric car, Dyson said, "it would be stupid to think we could build our own automotive manufacturing plant while our management sat 7,000 miles away."[96]

Other companies choose locations by seeking a tax haven or as part of creating a global brand. Ireland is a popular location to establish a company headquarters because of its overall corporate tax rate (country tax rate + state/regional tax rate) of 12.5 percent, which is lower than the United Kingdom (19 percent), Germany (29.9 percent), Australia (30 percent), or the United States (25.77 percent).[97]

The criteria for choosing an office/manufacturing location are different from the criteria for entering a foreign market. Rather than focusing on costs alone, companies should consider both qualitative and quantitative factors. Two key qualitative factors are workforce quality and company strategy. Workforce quality is important because it is often difficult to find workers with the specific skills, abilities, and experience that a company needs

American manufacturer Wrangler is headquartered in Greensboro, NC, but sources products from Ethiopia.

exclusively for foreign investors in the apparel industry and is building a railroad through neighboring Djibouti to give its landlocked country access to a seaport. M. Raghuraman, CEO of Brandix, Sri Lanka's largest clothing exporter, is interested in Ethiopia as a manufacturing location because "Ethiopia seems to be the best location from a government, labor, and (electrical) power point of view.[100]

Companies rely on studies such as FM Global's annually published "Resilience Index" to compare business climates throughout the world.[101] Exhibit 8.6 offers a quick overview of the best cities for business based on a variety of criteria. This information is a good starting point if your company is trying to decide where to put an international office or manufacturing plant.

to run its business. Workforce quality is one reason that many companies doing business in Europe locate in the Netherlands. Workers in the Netherlands are the most linguistically gifted in Europe, with 77 percent trilingual (speaking Dutch, English, and a third language) and 90 percent bilingual (Dutch and English). Comparable numbers across Europe are 25 percent and 54 percent.[98] Furthermore, compared to 63 countries worldwide, the Netherlands ranks ninth in terms of the supply of skilled labor, third for workers with financial skills, and second for competent senior managers (the United States ranks twenty-fifth, tenth, and tenth, respectively).[99]

A company's strategy is also important when choosing a location. For example, a company pursuing a low-cost strategy may need plentiful raw materials, low-cost transportation, and low-cost labor. A company pursuing a differentiation strategy (typically a higher-priced, better product or service) may need access to high-quality materials and a highly skilled and educated workforce.

Quantitative factors such as the kind of facility being built, tariff and nontariff barriers, exchange rates, and transportation and labor costs should also be considered when choosing an office/manufacturing location. Low costs and short distances from field to factory are critical success factors for every manufacturer. That's why VF Corporation, owner of brands such as Wrangler, North Face, and Timberland, is sourcing products from Ethiopia. In addition to having the ability to go from fiber to factory in one country, Ethiopia also boasts a low average salary for garment workers ($21 per month versus up to $297 per month in China), low energy costs, and a free-trade agreement with the United States. The Ethiopian government built a $250 million industrial park

8-4c Minimizing Political Risk

When managers think about political risk in global business, they envision burning factories and riots in the streets. Although political events such as these receive dramatic and extended coverage in the media, the political risks that most companies face usually are not covered as breaking stories on Fox News or CNN. Nonetheless, the negative consequences of ordinary political risk can be just as devastating to companies that fail to identify and minimize that risk.[102]

When conducting global business, companies should attempt to identify two types of political risk: political uncertainty and policy uncertainty.[103] **Political uncertainty** is associated with the risk of major changes in political regimes that can result from war, revolution, death of political leaders, social unrest, or other influential events. **Policy uncertainty** refers to the risk associated with changes in laws and government policies that directly affect the way foreign companies conduct business.

Policy uncertainty is the most common—and perhaps most frustrating—form of political risk in global business, especially when changes in laws and government policies directly undercut sizable investments made by foreign companies. Shortly after Walmart paid $16 billion to buy a 77% stake in Flipkart,

Political uncertainty the risk of major changes in political regimes that can result from war, revolution, death of political leaders, social unrest, or other influential events

Policy uncertainty the risk associated with changes in laws and government policies that directly affect the way foreign companies conduct business

Exhibit 8.6
World's Best Countries for Business

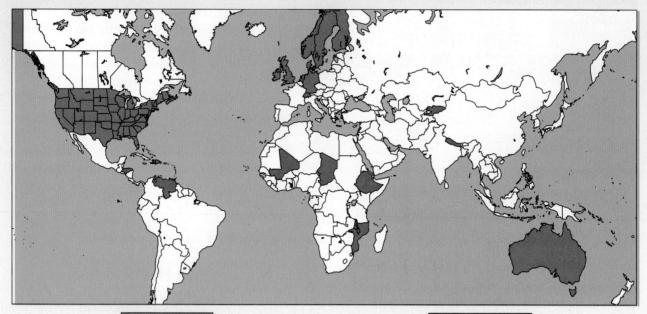

Best 10 Countries		Worst 10 Countries	
1. Norway	6. Sweden	1. Haiti	6. Kyrgyzstan
2. Denmark	7. Luxembourg	2. Venezuela	7. Lebanon
3. Switzerland	8. Australia	3. Ethiopia	8. Mali
4. Germany	9. United States	4. Chad	9. Nepal
5. Finland	10. United Kingdom	5. Mozambique	10. Honduras

Source: "2019 FM Global Resilience Index," *FM Global*, accessed April 8, 2020, www.fmglobal.com/research-and-resources/tools-and-resources/resilienceindex.

India's biggest online retailer, the Indian government substantially changed the regulations for foreign-owned online stores:[104]

» To protect Indian "mom and pop" stores from competition, foreign-owned online stores were told to stop discounting prices.

» To generate sales for Indian firms, foreign-owned online stores were prevented from selling their own online inventory to Indian consumers.

» To create demand for Indian data storage companies, foreign-owned online stores are required to locally store the huge amounts of data generated from sales to Indian consumers.[105]

A spokesperson for India's prime minister denied that the changes were protectionist and that India welcomed direct foreign investment from firms like Walmart and Amazon. Six months later, Walmart sold its 28 Indian stores to Indian-based Flipkart to avoid these restrictive regulations.[106]

Several strategies can be used to minimize or adapt to the political risk inherent in global business. An *avoidance strategy* is used when the political risks associated with a foreign country or region are viewed as too great. If firms are already invested in high-risk areas, they may divest or sell their businesses. If they have not yet invested, they will likely postpone their investment until the risk shrinks.

Exhibit 8.7 shows the long-term political stability of various countries in the Middle East (higher scores indicate less political risk). The following factors, which were used to compile these ratings, indicate greater political risk: government instability, poor socioeconomic conditions, internal or external conflict, military involvement in politics, religious and ethnic tensions, high foreign debt as a percentage of GDP, exchange rate instability, and high inflation.[107] An avoidance strategy would likely be used for the riskiest countries shown in Exhibit 8.7, such as Lebanon, Iran, Egypt, Bahrain and Saudi Arabia but might not be needed for the less risky countries, such as Oman or the United Arab Emirates. Risk conditions

Exhibit 8.7
Overview of Political Risk in the Middle East

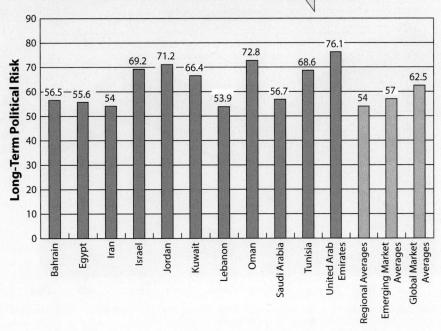

Higher scores indicate less long-term political risk, which is calculated by estimating government instability, socioeconomic conditions, internal or external conflict, military involvement in politics, religious and ethnic tensions, foreign debt as a percent of GDP, exchange rate instability, and whether there is high inflation.

Country	Long-Term Political Risk
Bahrain	56.5
Egypt	55.6
Iran	54
Israel	69.2
Jordan	71.2
Kuwait	66.4
Lebanon	53.9
Oman	72.8
Saudi Arabia	56.7
Tunisia	68.6
United Arab Emirates	76.1
Regional Averages	54
Emerging Market Averages	57
Global Market Averages	62.5

Source: "BMI Research: United Arab Emirates Country Risk Report, 2020 Q1, Issue 1," *Fitch Solutions*, accessed April 9, 2020; "BMI Research: Israel Country Risk Report, 2020 Q1, Issue 1," *Fitch Solutions*, accessed April 9, 2020.

and factors change, so be sure to make risk decisions with the latest available information from resources such as the PRS Group (www.prsgroup.com), which supplies information about political risk to 80 percent of *Fortune* 500 companies.

Control is an active strategy to prevent or reduce political risks. Firms using a control strategy lobby foreign governments or international trade agencies to change laws, regulations, or trade barriers that hurt their business in that country. Ten thousand of the 16,000 requests made in 2019 by US companies seeking exemptions from $200 billion worth of new 30 percent tariffs imposed on Chinese goods came from Arrowhead Engineered Products in Blaine, Minnesota.[108] Arrowhead imports aftermarket replacement parts for cars, trucks, lawn mowers, motorcycles and other engines, all of which are made in China. Because similar parts are no longer made in the United States, Arrowhead contacted its local congressional representative for help. When told to be as specific as possible, the company ended up filing exemption appeals

for every starter, solenoid, spark plug, etc., it imports from China. Because of the direct risk to Arrowhead's low cost business model, CEO John Mosunic said, "We basically put everything else on the back burner" to file these appeals.[109]

Another method for dealing with political risk is *cooperation*, which involves using joint ventures and collaborative contracts, such as franchising and licensing. Although cooperation does not eliminate the political risk of doing business in a country, it can limit the risk associated with foreign ownership of a business. For example, a German company forming a joint venture with a Chinese company to do business in China may structure the joint venture contract so that the Chinese company owns 51 percent or more of the joint venture. Doing so qualifies the joint venture as a Chinese company and exempts it from Chinese laws that apply to foreign-owned businesses. However, cooperation cannot always protect against *policy risk* if a foreign government changes its laws and policies to directly affect the way foreign companies conduct business.

Exhibit 8.8
Hofstede's Six Cultural Dimensions

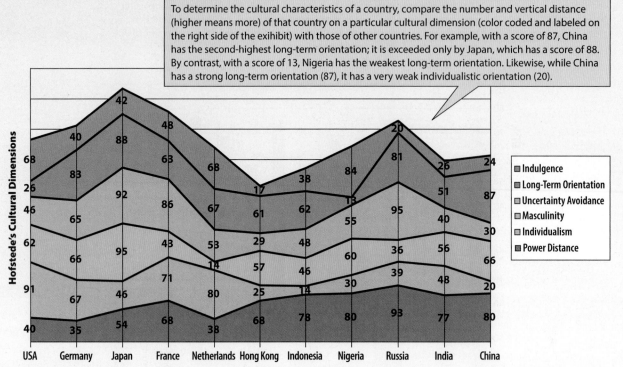

To determine the cultural characteristics of a country, compare the number and vertical distance (higher means more) of that country on a particular cultural dimension (color coded and labeled on the right side of the exihibit) with those of other countries. For example, with a score of 87, China has the second-highest long-term orientation; it is exceeded only by Japan, which has a score of 88. By contrast, with a score of 13, Nigeria has the weakest long-term orientation. Likewise, while China has a strong long-term orientation (87), it has a very weak individualistic orientation (20).

Source: G. H. Hofstede, "Cultural Constraints in Management Theories," *Academy of Management Executive* 7, no. 1 (1993): 81–94; G. Hofstede and G. J. Hofstede, "Dimension Data Matrix," accessed April 9, 2020,, http://www.geerthofstede.eu/dimension-data-matrix.

8-5 BECOMING AWARE OF CULTURAL DIFFERENCES

National culture is the set of shared values and beliefs that affects the perceptions, decisions, and behavior of the people from a particular country. The first step in dealing with culture is to recognize that there are meaningful differences. In recent years, Indian companies have targeted a group of mid-sized, independent, often family-owned, German companies (called Mittlestand) for acquisition. When Rail.One GmbH was acquired by PCM Group, an Indian conglomerate, the new owners didn't change the Bavarian management because, says PCM Chairman Kamal Mittal, "We didn't want to disturb the

National culture the set of shared values and beliefs that affects the perceptions, decisions, and behavior of the people from a particular country

business."[110] Professor Geert Hofstede spent 20 years studying cultural differences in 53 different countries. His research shows that there are six consistent cultural dimensions across countries: power distance, individualism, masculinity, uncertainty avoidance, short-term versus long-term orientation, and indulgence versus restraint.[111]

Power distance is the extent to which people in a country accept that power is distributed unequally in society and organizations. In countries where power distance is weak, such as Denmark and Sweden, employees don't like their organization or their boss to have power over them or tell them what to do. They want to have a say in decisions that affect them. As Exhibit 8.8 shows, Russia, China, and Nigeria, with scores of 93, 80, and 80, respectively, are much stronger in power distance than Germany (35), the Netherlands (38), and the United States (40).

Individualism is the degree to which societies believe that individuals should be self-sufficient. In individualistic societies, employees put loyalty to themselves first and loyalty to their company and work group second. In Exhibit 8.8, the United States (91), the Netherlands (80), France (71), and Germany (67) are the strongest in individualism, while Indonesia (14), China (20), and Hong Kong (25) are the weakest.

Masculinity and *femininity* capture the difference between highly assertive and highly nurturing cultures. Masculine cultures emphasize assertiveness, competition, material success, and achievement, whereas feminine cultures emphasize the importance of relationships, modesty, caring for the weak, and quality of life. In Exhibit 8.8, Japan (95), Germany (66), and China (66) have the most masculine orientations, while the Netherlands (14) has the most feminine orientation. Manu Parpia, the CEO of Geometric, Ltd., the Indian company that acquired German engineering company 3Cap, noted that, compared to India, "German culture is more precise, very process oriented (and) quite blunt. The emphasis on process in India is much lower because if you focused on process, nothing would get done."[112]

The cultural difference of *uncertainty avoidance* is the degree to which people in a country are uncomfortable with unstructured, ambiguous, unpredictable situations. In countries with strong uncertainty avoidance, such as Greece and Portugal, people tend to be aggressive and emotional and seek security rather than uncertainty. In Exhibit 8.8, Russia (95), Japan (92), and France (86) are strongest in uncertainty avoidance, while Hong Kong (29) and China (30) are the weakest. Rail. One CEO Jochen Riepl has noticed this dimension playing itself out during meetings with PCM officials. "In India, a 'no' is a kind of invitation to start a discussion. In Germany, a 'no' is a 'no,'" he says.[113]

The cultural dimension of *short-term/long-term orientation* addresses whether cultures are oriented to the present and seek immediate gratification or to the future and defer gratification. Not surprisingly, countries with short-term orientations are consumer-driven, whereas countries with long-term orientations are savings-driven. In Exhibit 8.8, Japan (88) and China (87) have very strong long-term orientations, while Nigeria (13) and the United States (26), have very strong short-term orientations.

The cultural dimension of *indulgence versus restraint* addresses the degree to which a society allows relatively free gratification of basic drives related to

sh_lisong/123RF

While the magical experience of Disney translated easily for visitors, some words and phrases did not as easily bridge the cultural divide at Disneyland Shanghai.

enjoying life and having fun versus strict social norms that regulate and suppress gratification of needs and wants. Nigeria (81), the United States (68), and the Netherlands (68) are strongest in indulgence, while Hong Kong (17), Russia (20), and China (24) practice the most restraint. Part of what makes Mittelstand companies comfortable with new Indian owners is that Indian bidders usually offer long-term commitments. Attorney Christopher Wright says of Indian investors, "They tend to have a long-term vision and (that) gives German companies some assurance.[114]

To generate a graphical comparison of two different countries' cultures, go to www.hofstede-insights.com/country-comparison/. Select a "Country" from the dropdown list, and then select a "Comparison Country." A graph comparing the countries on each of Hofstede's six cultural differences will be generated automatically.

Cultural differences affect perceptions, understanding, and behavior. Recognizing cultural differences is critical to succeeding in global business. Nevertheless, as Hofstede pointed out, descriptions of cultural differences are based on averages—the average level of uncertainty avoidance in Portugal, the average level of power distance in Argentina, and so forth. Accordingly, says Hofstede, "If you are going to spend time with a Japanese colleague, you shouldn't assume that overall cultural statements about Japanese society automatically apply to this person."[115] Similarly, cultural beliefs may differ significantly from one part of a country to another.[116]

After becoming aware of cultural differences, the second step is deciding how to adapt your company to those differences. Unfortunately, studies investigating the effects of cultural differences on management practices point more to difficulties than to easy solutions.

Another difficulty is that cultural values are changing, albeit slowly, in many parts of the world. The fall of communism in Eastern Europe and the former Soviet Union, and broad economic reforms in China, produced sweeping changes on two continents in the past four decades. Thanks to increased global trade resulting from free-trade agreements and trillions of dollars of direct foreign investment, major economic transformations are well under way in India, Southeast Asia, Central and South America, and are beginning to take shape in Africa. Consequently, when trying to adapt management practices to cultural differences, companies must ensure that they are not basing their adaptations on outdated and incorrect assumptions about a country's culture.

8-6 PREPARING FOR AN INTERNATIONAL ASSIGNMENT

When Atlanta native Joanna Maddox was first in Argentina, she was invited to an asado, or Argentinian barbecue, scheduled for 8 p.m. Not wanting to be late, she arrived at 7:30 p.m. The catering chef explained that in Argentina, "you *never* arrive *early* to an asado."[117] When Argentinian guests arrived after 9 p.m., Maddox said, "Not a single apology was given for arriving late."[118] And because drinks and appetizers weren't served until 9:30 p.m., Maddox, who usually ate much earlier, said she was so hungry she could "eat the tablecloth." Dinner was eventually served at 10:30 p.m. Now, however, Maddox has adjusted to Argentina's cultural expectations regarding time. Today, she says, "when I make plans to meet my Argentine friends for coffee or lunch, all I have to do is add an hour to our meeting time and voila, I will be on time."[119]

If you become an **expatriate**, someone who lives and works outside his or her native country, chances are you'll run into cultural surprises just like Joanna Maddox did in Argentina. The difficulty of adjusting to language, cultural, and social differences is the primary reason for expatriate failure in overseas assignments. For example, although there

Expatriate someone who lives and works outside his or her native country

have recently been disagreements among researchers about these numbers, it is probably safe to say that 5 to 20 percent percent of American expatriates sent abroad by their companies will return to the United States before they have successfully completed their assignments.[120] Of those who do complete their international assignments, about one-third are judged by their companies to be no better than marginally effective.[121] Because even well-planned international assignments can cost as much as three to five times an employee's annual salary, failure in those assignments can be extraordinarily expensive.[122] Furthermore, while it is difficult to find reliable indicators, studies typically show that 8 to 25 percent of expatriate managers leave their companies following an international assignment.[123]

*The chances for a successful international assignment can be increased through **8-6a language and cross-cultural training** and **8-6b consideration of spouse, family, and dual-career issues.***

8-6a Language and Cross-Cultural Training

Predeparture language and cross-cultural training can reduce the uncertainty that expatriates feel, the misunderstandings that take place between expatriates and natives, and the inappropriate behaviors that expatriates unknowingly commit when they travel to a foreign country. In fact, simple things such as using a phone, locating a public toilet, asking for directions, finding out how much things cost, paying for things, exchanging greetings, or understanding what people want can become tremendously complex when expatriates don't know a foreign language or a country's customs and cultures. Hong Kong-based *Bloomberg* reporter Shelly Banjo ran into an issue on temporary assignment in Beijing, China. She said, "As a foreigner without a bank account or phone number from mainland China, once I landed in Beijing I was locked out of WeChat's pay function. Ditto for Alibaba's Alipay, the other big pay app with about 520 million users. I could use both services in Hong Kong, but not in Beijing. In order to do so, I would need a Chinese bank account… Still, I completely underestimated how difficult this would make daily life."[124] Without WeChat or Alipay, she found it nearly impossible to hail a taxi or Didi Chuxiing (China's Uber). Cash and foreign credit cards were rarely accepted at restaurants or convenience stores. WeChat Pay and Alipay were so pervasive in China's nearly cashless economy that beggars use them to accept street donations.[125]

Expatriates who receive predeparture language and cross-cultural training make faster adjustments to foreign

Expats Leave As Squares, Try to Fit in as Circles, and Come Back as Triangles

Working and living abroad changes expatriates. First is the challenge of leaving home, family, and friends, moving from one culture (squares) to fit into a new culture (circles). And that challenge can be harder for the so-called "trailing spouse." Petra Trudell, who gave up her job as a reporter to move with her husband to Japan says, "My own turning point came when I first met the wife of my husband's boss. They are fellow Americans who hadn't been in Japan much longer than us, and we met for dinner while my husband and I were still in temporary housing. She looked at me and asked how I was doing. When I gave the polite answer, dancing around my own insecurities, she did something I didn't expect: She congratulated me. She told me not to feel badly about wanting to stay inside and feeling overwhelmed."

Most expats and their families do adjust to their new cultures. Many thrive and learn to love their new homes and neighbors, eventually taking as their own some of the customs and norms of those new cultures. In that process, they become triangles, a hybrid between their original culture (squares) and their new culture (circles). And that becomes most apparent to them when they return home. Relocation specialist Naomi Hattaway, who moved with her family to India and then Singapore and back to the United States, says, "During my time abroad, my horizons were expanded, but when we returned home to the US, I found myself struggling with fitting in. I felt like a misfit." So, she took to blogging to share her thoughts and feelings, forming the "I am a Triangle" group on Facebook, which grew from 30 to 6,300 members. One Facebook participant wrote, "Being home and near family has been great, but outside of that, everything is a challenge. I feel completely foreign to the local culture, and have a hard time connecting with people . . . [But] I have been reading posts and comments and I already feel better, seeing the community and support here in this group."

Becoming an expat changes you. As Petra Trudell eventually learned in Japan, "it's not always an easy life, but there's no disputing it's a good life." Even when you're a triangle returning home to squares.

Sources: N. Hattaway, "Shaping Up in an Expat World: We're All 'Triangles' Now," *Wall Street Journal*, September 13, 2016, accessed April 10, 2017, blogs.wsj.com/expat/2016/09/13/shaping-up-in-an-expat-world-were-all-triangles-now/; P. Trudell, "Portrait of a Trailing Spouse: Dependent, Dejected and Learning to Give Herself Some Slack," *Wall Street Journal*, July 6, 2015, accessed April 10, 2017, WSJ, blogs.wsj.com/expat/2015/07/06/portrait-of-a-trailing-spouse-dependent-dejected-and-learning-to-give-herself-some-slack/.

cultures and perform better on their international assignments.[126] Unfortunately, only a third of the managers who go on international assignments are offered any kind of predeparture training, and only half of those actually participate in the training![127] Suzanne Bernard, director of international mobility at Bombardier Aerospace in Canada, says, "We always offer cross-cultural training, but it's very seldom used by executives leaving in a rush at the last minute."[128] This is somewhat surprising given the failure rates for expatriates and the high cost of those failures. Furthermore, with the exception of some language courses, predeparture training is not particularly expensive or difficult to provide. Three methods can be used to prepare workers for international assignments: documentary training, cultural simulations, and field experiences.

Documentary training focuses on identifying specific critical differences between cultures. France-based fashion company L'Oreal values direct communication so much that it offers a "Managing Confrontation" course for global employees who come from cultures with different communication norms. One Chinese employee said, "We don't do this type of debate traditionally in China, but these trainings have taught us a method of expressing diverging opinions, which we have all come to practice and appreciate, even in meetings made up of only Chinese."[129]

After learning specific critical differences through documentary training, trainees can participate in *cultural simulations*, in which they practice adapting to cultural differences. EMC, a global provider of information storage solutions, uses cultural simulations to train its people. In its early days before it was acquired by Dell computer, EMC was largely based in the United States, but with research labs, offices, and customers on every continent, cross-cultural interactions are a daily part of business. EMC's cultural simulations use photos and audio and video clips to present real-world situations. EMC employees must decide what to do and then learn what happened as a result of their choices. Whether it's interacting with customers or dealing with EMC employees from other countries, at every step they have the opportunity to learn good and bad methods of responding to cultural differences. EMC requires its worldwide workforce of 40,500 people to regularly use the cultural simulations. Louise Korver-Swanson, EMC's global head

After learning specific critical differences through documentary training, trainees can participate in cultural simulations, in which they practice adapting to cultural differences.

Photographee.eu/Shutterstock.com

of executive development, said, "This is about ensuring that we're truly a global company. We need everyone in the organization to be tuned in."[130]

Finally, *field simulation* training, a technique made popular by the US Peace Corps, places trainees in an ethnic neighborhood for three to four hours to talk to residents about cultural differences. For example, a US electronics manufacturer prepared workers for assignments in South Korea by having trainees explore a nearby South Korean neighborhood and talk to shopkeepers and people on the street about South Korean politics, family orientation, and day-to-day living.

8-6b Spouse, Family, and Dual-Career Issues

Not all international assignments are difficult for expatriates and their families, but the evidence clearly shows that how well an expatriate's spouse and family adjust to the foreign culture is the most important factor in determining the success or failure of an international assignment.[131] In fact, a *Harvard Business Review* study found

{ Evidence shows that how well an expatriate's family adjusts to a foreign culture is the most important factor in determining the success of an international assignment. }

that 32 percent of those offered international assignments turned them down because they did not want their families to have to relocate, while 28 percent turned them down "to protect their marriages."[132] Unfortunately, despite its importance, there has been little systematic research on what does and does not help expatriates' families successfully adapt. A number of companies, however, have found that adaptability screening and intercultural training for families can lead to more successful overseas adjustment.

Adaptability screening is used to assess how well managers and their families are likely to adjust to foreign cultures. For example, Prudential Relocation Management's international division has developed an "Overseas Assignment Inventory" (OAI) to assess a spouse and family's open-mindedness, respect for others' beliefs, sense of humor, and marital communication. The OAI was initially used to help the US Peace Corps, the US Navy, and the Canadian International Development Agency select people who could adapt well in foreign cultures. Success there led to its use in helping companies assess whether managers and their spouses were good candidates for international assignments.[133] Likewise, Pennsylvania-based AMP, a worldwide producer of electrical connectors, conducts extensive psychological screening of expatriates and their spouses when making international assignments. But adaptability screening does not just involve a company assessing an employee; it can also involve an employee screening international assignments for desirability. Because more employees are becoming aware of the costs of international assignments (spouses having to give up or change jobs, children having to change schools, everyone having to learn a new language), some companies are willing to pay for a preassignment trip so the employee and his or her spouse can investigate the country *before* accepting the international assignment.[134]

Only 40 percent of expatriates' families receive language and cross-cultural training, yet such training is just as important for the families of expatriates as for the expatriates themselves.[135] In fact, it may be more important because, unlike expatriates, whose professional jobs often shield them from the full force of a country's culture, spouses and children are fully immersed in foreign neighborhoods and schools. Households must be run, shopping must be done, and bills must be paid.

When Judy Holland's husband was transferred to Shanghai, his company sent the family to a two-day cultural immersion class in the United Kingdom, where the family learned about business etiquette, the cultural importance of the number 8, the Chinese zodiac, and how to eat with chopsticks. The class even prepared the Hollands for differences they might not have anticipated, such as, in China, it's uncommon to find men's shoes in sizes larger than a US 9.5 (Holland's husband wore a US 11.5). Holland was grateful for the instruction, saying, "Nothing can fully prepare you for China, but it certainly took the shock out of arriving." Soon after arriving, however, her sense of confidence eroded. "I remember standing in a house with no furniture, not knowing anyone, and wishing they had buddied me up with someone from my husband's company."[136]

In addition to helping families prepare for the cultural differences they will encounter, language and cross-cultural training can help reduce uncertainty about how to act and decrease misunderstandings between expatriates and their families and locals. For example, in the West, people enjoy a fairly large circle of personal space and are only comfortable with family and intimate friends being within inches of their bodies. But in China, where personal space is measured in inches and not feet, the constant jostling by strangers can be perceived as an encroachment and unhinge many Westerners. New Zealander Marita Light, who spent five years in China, found that recalibrating her expectations and being intentionally open helped. "Letting go of my judgments and consciously being more open enabled more creativity in how I dealt with awkward situations. It was a much more rewarding way to live in China."[137]

PART 3

9 | Designing Adaptive Organizations

LEARNING OUTCOMES

9-1 Describe the departmentalization approaches to organizational structure.

9-2 Explain organizational authority.

9-3 Outline the steps for using the different methods for job design.

9-4 Explain the methods that companies are using to redesign internal organizational processes (i.e., intraorganizational processes).

9-5 Describe the methods that companies are using to redesign external organizational processes (i.e., interorganizational processes).

9-1 DEPARTMENTALIZATION

Organizational structure is the vertical and horizontal configuration of departments, authority, and jobs within a company. Organizational structure is concerned with questions such as "Who reports to whom?" and "Who does what?" and "Where is the work done?" When Swiss-based **ABB Ltd.** sold its power-grid unit for $11 billion, it rearranged the organizational structure to increase accountability. CEO Ulrich Spiesshofer said, "We want to have absolutely clear responsibilities. People need to own a business and they need to have global, undiluted responsibility to run their businesses, set priorities and really make sure you're lined up against competition."[1] To do that, it replaced the previous structure, organized by country and region, with four divisions organized by business:[2]

> **Organizational structure** the vertical and horizontal configuration of departments, authority, and jobs within a company

» Electrification – supporting the power industry, with 53,000 employees and $12.7 billion in revenue;

» Industrial automation – supporting manufacturers, with 22,000 employees and $6.3 billion in revenue;

» Motion – producing drives motors, generators, and mechanical power transmissions, with 20,000 employees and $6.5 billion in revenue;

» Robotics and discrete automation – supporting machine and factory automation, with 10,000 employees and $3.3 billion in revenue.

The goal is to make ABB Ltd. more innovative and responsive to customers and competitors. Said CEO Spiesshofer, "We're going towards a fully global entrepreneur model. That's really a massive, massive change to the operational DNA of ABB."[3]

You can see ABB Ltd.'s new organizational structure in Exhibit 9.1. In the first half of the chapter, you will learn about the traditional vertical and horizontal approaches to organizational structure, including departmentalization, organizational authority, and job design.

An **organizational process** is the collection of activities that transform inputs into outputs that customers value.[4] Organizational process asks, "How do things get done?" For example, **Microsoft** uses basic internal and external processes, shown in Exhibit 9.2, to write computer software. The process starts when Microsoft gets feedback from customers through the Windows Insider Program and the Windows Insider Program for Business.[5] This information helps Microsoft understand customers' needs and problems and identify important software issues and needed changes. Microsoft then rewrites the software, testing it internally at the company and then externally through its beta testing process in which customers in its Windows Insider programs provide extensive feedback used to improve the software. Millions of people around the world participate as Microsoft Insiders. Using the Feedback Hub App they report bugs that crash programs and indicate what changes and functionality they want.[6] After final corrections are made, Microsoft distributes the officially updated version

> **Organizational process** the collection of activities that transforms inputs into outputs that customers value

Exhibit 9.1
Organizational Chart at ABB Ltd.

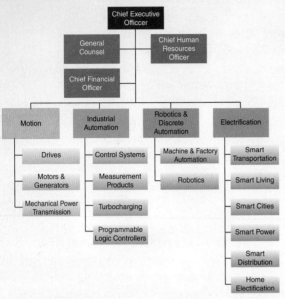

Source: "ABB Fact Sheets," ABB Group, February 2020 update, accessed April 12, 2020, new.abb.com/docs/default-source/investor-center-docs/abb-fact-sheets. pdf. "Industrial Automation business," ABB Group, accessed April 12, 2020, new.abb. com/about/our-businesses/industrial-automation; "Motion Business," ABB Group, accessed April 12, 2020, new.abb.com/about/our-businesses/motion; "Robotics & Discrete Automation Business," ABB Group, accessed April 12, 2020, new.abb. com/about/our-businesses/robotics-and-discrete-automation; "Smart Industry | ABB," ABB Group, accessed April 12, 2020, new.abb.com/about/our-businesses/ electrification/smart-industry/.

to its broader base of customers using Windows 10 on a billion devices.[7] The feedback process never ends, however, because as soon as Microsoft releases a new version of Windows, that release is followed by a beta version for testing and feedback from Microsoft's Windows Insiders.[8]

This process view of Microsoft, which focuses on how things get done, is very different from the hierarchical view of ABB Ltd, which focuses on accountability, responsibility, and positions within the chain of command. In the second half of the chapter, you will learn how companies use reengineering and empowerment to redesign their internal organizational processes. The chapter ends with a discussion about the ways in which companies are redesigning their external processes, that is, how they are changing to improve their interactions with those outside the company. In that discussion, you will explore the basics of modular and virtual organizations.

Traditionally, organizational structures

Departmentalization
subdividing work and workers into separate organizational units responsible for completing particular tasks

have been based on some form of departmentalization. **Departmentalization** is a method of subdividing work and workers into separate organizational units that take responsibility for completing particular tasks.[9] **Pfizer**, a global pharmaceutical company, has separate divisions for creating new drugs, for consumer health care, including over-the-counter (OTC) drugs, and an established medicines division for already developed drugs like Viagra and Lipitor.[10]

Traditionally, organizational structures have been created by departmentalizing work according to five methods: 9-1a functional, 9-1b product, 9-1c customer, 9-1d geographic, and 9-1e matrix.

9-1a Functional Departmentalization

One of the most common organizational structures is functional departmentalization. Companies tend to use this structure when they are small or just starting out, but nearly a quarter of large companies (50,000 or more employees) also use functional

Exhibit 9.2
Process View of Microsoft's Organization

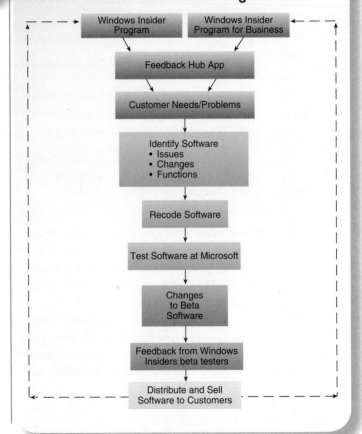

Exhibit 9.3
Functional Departmentalization

Insurance Company

Sales	Information Systems
Accounting	Human Resources
Life Insurance	Auto Insurance
Home Insurance	Health Insurance

Advertising Agency

Sales	Information Systems
Accounting	Human Resources
Art Department	Print Advertising
Creative Department	Internet Advertising

department take responsibility for producing accurate revenue and expense figures, the engineers in research and development can focus their efforts on designing a product that is reliable and simple to manufacture. Second, it lowers costs by reducing duplication. When the engineers in research and development come up with a fantastic new product, they don't have to worry about creating an aggressive advertising campaign to sell it. That task belongs to the advertising experts and sales representatives in marketing. Third, with everyone in the same department having similar work experience or training, communication and coordination are less problematic for departmental managers.

At the same time, functional departmentalization has a number of disadvantages. To start, cross-department coordination can be difficult. Managers and employees are often more interested in doing what's right for their function than in doing what's right for the entire organization. A good example is the traditional conflict between marketing and manufacturing. Marketing typically pushes for spending more money to make more products with more capabilities to meet customer needs. By contrast, manufacturing pushes for fewer products with simpler designs so that manufacturing facilities can ship finished products on time and keep costs within expense budgets. As companies grow, functional departmentalization may also lead to slower decision making and produce managers and workers with narrow experience and expertise.

departmentalization.[11] **Functional departmentalization** organizes work and workers into separate units responsible for particular business functions or areas of expertise. A common functional structure might have individuals organized into accounting, sales, marketing, production, and human resource departments.

Not all functionally departmentalized companies have the same functions. The insurance company and the advertising agency, shown in Exhibit 9.3, both have sales, accounting, human resources, and information systems departments, as indicated by the pale orange boxes. The purple and green boxes indicate the functions that are different. As would be expected, the insurance company has separate departments for life, auto, home, and health insurance. The advertising agency has departments for artwork, creative work, print advertising, and internet advertising. So, the functional departments in a company that uses functional structure depend, in part, on the business or industry a company is in.

Functional departmentalization has some advantages. First, it allows work to be done by highly qualified specialists. While the accountants in the accounting

9-1b Product Departmentalization

Product departmentalization organizes work and workers into separate units responsible for producing particular products or services. Exhibit 9.4 shows the product departmentalization structure used by **Raytheon Technologies**, which is organized along four different areas, each with its own product line:

» Collins Aerospace (aerostructures, avionics, interiors, mechanical systems, mission systems, and power & controls)

» Pratt & Whitney jet engines (Pratt & Whitney commercial engines, Pratt & Whitney military engines, Pratt & Whitney helicopter engines, and Pratt & Whitney auxiliary power units)

Functional departmentalization organizing work and workers into separate units responsible for particular business functions or areas of expertise

Product departmentalization organizing work and workers into separate units responsible for producing particular products or services

Exhibit 9.4
Product Departmentalization: Raytheon Technologies

Collins Aerospace				Pratt & Whitney				Raytheon Intelligence & Space	Raytheon Missiles & Defense
Aerostructures Mechanical Systems	Avionics Mission Systems	Interiors Power & Controls		Pratt & Whitney Commercial Engines	Pratt & Whitney Military Engines	Pratt & Whitney Helicopter Engines	Pratt & Whitney Auxillary Power Units	Air dominance, space solutions, cybersecurity, communications and navigation, air traffic management and weather planning, modernization/ training/mission support, and advanced technology.	Air warfare, defending against unmanned aircraft (drones), missile defense, land and naval warfare, hypersonic.
— Communications — Customer & Account Management — Digital Technology — Engineering & Technology — Finance — Human Resources — General Counsel — Operations & Quality — Strategic Development				— Communications — Environment, Health & Safety — Engineering — Finance — General Counsel — Human Resources — Information Technology — Supply Chain, and Manufacturing — Sales, Marketing and Customer Support — Transformation & Strategy — Quality					

Sources: "Key Facts: Explore our Businesses," Raytheon Technologies, accessed April 13, 2020, www.rtx.com/Our-Company/key-facts; "Collins Aerospace Fact Sheet," Collins Aerospace, April 2020, accessed April 13, 2020, www.collinsaerospace.com/-/media/project/collinsaerospace/collinsaerospace-website/newsroom/files /collins_aerospace_fact-sheet.pdf?; "Leadership," Collins Aerospace, accessed April 13, 2020, www.collinsaerospace.com/who-we-are/leadership; "Products & Services - Pratt & Whitney," Pratt & Whitney, accessed April 13, 2020, prattwhitney.com/products-and-services; "MediaRoom - Leadership Bios," Pratt & Whitney," accessed April 13, 2020, newsroom.prattwhitney.com/leadership-bios; "What We Do," Raytheon Intelligence & Space, accessed April 13, 2020, www.raytheonintelligenceandspace.com/capabilities; "What We Do," Raytheon Missiles & Defense, accessed April 13, 2020, www.raytheonmissilesanddefense.com/capabilities.

» Raytheon Intelligence & Space (air dominance, space solutions, cybersecurity, communications and navigation, air traffic management and weather planning, modernization/training/mission support, and advanced technology)

» Raytheon Missiles & Defense (air warfare, defending against unmanned aircraft (drones), missile defense, land and naval warfare, hypersonic)

One of the advantages of product departmentalization is that, like functional departmentalization, it allows managers and workers to specialize in one area of expertise. Unlike the narrow expertise and experiences in functional departmentalization, however, managers and workers develop a broader set of experiences and expertise related to an entire product line. Likewise, product departmentalization makes it easier for top managers to assess work-unit performance. Because of the clear separation of their four different product divisions, Raytheon Technologies' top managers can easily compare the performance of Collins Aerospace division and the Pratt & Whitney aircraft engines division. In 2019, Collins Aerospace sales and profits ($26 billion and $4.4 billion) were slightly larger than Pratt & Whitney's ($20.9 billion and $1.8 billion).[12]

Finally, decision making should be faster because managers and workers are responsible for the entire product line rather than for separate functional departments; in other words, there are fewer conflicts compared to functional departmentalization.

The primary disadvantage of product departmentalization is duplication. You can see in Exhibit 9.4 that both Collins Aerospace and the Pratt & Whitney division have communications, engineering, finance, human resources, legal (general counsel), quality and strategy departments. Duplication like this often results in higher costs. If Raytheon Technologies was organized by function, one legal department would handle matters for four product divisions.

A second disadvantage is the challenge of coordinating across the different product departments. Raytheon Technologies might have difficulty standardizing its policies and procedures in product departments as different as, for example, Pratt & Whitney helicopter engines and Raytheon Intelligence & Spaces cybersecurity and space solutions divisions.

9-1c Customer Departmentalization

Customer departmentalization organizes work and workers into separate units responsible for particular kinds of customers. For example, as Exhibit 9.5 shows, **Verizon**, the largest American telecommunications provider, is organized into departments by type of customer:

» Verizon Consumer (wired data and voice, wireless data and voice, and wireless wholesale)

» Verizon Business (wired and wireless enterprise, small and medium business wired wholesale and Verizon Connect)

» Verizon Media (content, advertising and technology)[13]

Customer departmentalization organizing work and workers into separate units responsible for particular kinds of customers

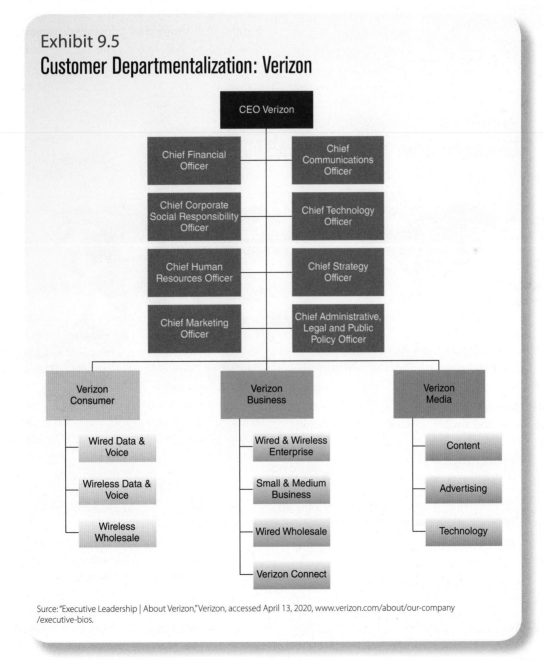

Exhibit 9.5
Customer Departmentalization: Verizon

Surce: "Executive Leadership | About Verizon," Verizon, accessed April 13, 2020, www.verizon.com/about/our-company/executive-bios.

The primary advantage of customer departmentalization is that it focuses the organization on customer needs rather than on products or business functions. Furthermore, creating separate departments to serve specific kinds of customers allows companies to specialize and adapt their products and services to customer needs and problems. The primary disadvantage of customer departmentalization is that, like product departmentalization, it leads to duplication of resources. This is why Verizon also has eight "corporate" functions – finance, communication, social responsibility, technology, human resources, strategy, marketing, and administrative/legal/public policy – that support each of its

three customer departments, and avoids the disadvantage of duplication common to customer departmentalization structures. It can be difficult to achieve coordination across different customer departments, as is also the case with product departmentalization. Finally, the emphasis on meeting customers' needs may lead workers to make decisions that please customers but hurt the business.

9-1d Geographic Departmentalization

Geographic departmentalization organizes work and workers into separate units responsible for doing business in particular geographic areas. Exhibit 9.6 shows the geographic departmentalization used by **AB InBev**, the largest beer brewer in

> **Geographic departmentalization**
> organizing work and workers into separate units responsible for doing business in particular geographic areas

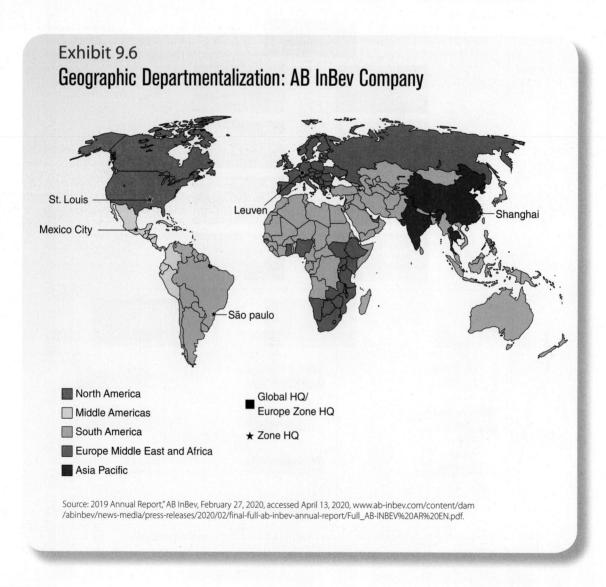

Exhibit 9.6
Geographic Departmentalization: AB InBev Company

St. Louis
Mexico City
Leuven
Shanghai
São paulo

■ North America
□ Middle Americas
□ South America
■ Europe Middle East and Africa
■ Asia Pacific

■ Global HQ/ Europe Zone HQ
★ Zone HQ

Source: 2019 Annual Report," AB InBev, February 27, 2020, accessed April 13, 2020, www.ab-inbev.com/content/dam /abinbev/news-media/press-releases/2020/02/final-full-ab-inbev-annual-report/Full_AB-INBEV%20AR%20EN.pdf.

the world. AB InBev has operations in 50 countries, 170,000 employees, and annual revenue of $52.3 billion.[14] As shown in Exhibit 9.6, AB InBev has five regional groups: North America, Middle Americas, South America, Europe/Middle East/Africa, and Asia Pacific. Each of these regions would be a sizable company by itself. The smallest region, Europe/Middle East/Africa, for instance, sold 87 million hectoliters of beverages for an estimate annual revenue of $8.36 billion.[15]

The primary advantage of geographic departmentalization is that it helps companies respond to the demands of different markets. This can be especially important when the company sells in different countries. For example, while AB InBev has three brands sold worldwide (Budweiser, Stella Artois, and Corona), and five sold in multiple countries (Beck's, Castle, Hoegaarden, Leffe, and Michelob Ultra), most of its brands are local. You'll find the Antarctica and Brahma brands in Brazil, the Belle-Vue and Jupiler brands in Belgium, and the Sibirskaya Korona and Klinskoye brands in Russia.[16]

Another advantage is that geographic departmentalization can reduce costs by locating unique organizational resources closer to customers. For instance, it is cheaper in the long run for AB InBev to build bottling plants in each region than to, for example, transport beer to Mexico, where it has 10 beverage plants, after it has been brewed and bottled in Brazil, where it has 34 beverage plants.[17]

The primary disadvantage of geographic departmentalization is that it can lead to duplication of resources. For example, while it may be necessary to adapt products and marketing to different geographic locations, it's doubtful that AB InBev needs significantly different inventory tracking systems from location to location. Also, even more than with the other forms of departmentalization, it can be difficult to coordinate departments that are literally thousands of miles from each other and whose managers have very limited contact with each other.

9-1e Matrix Departmentalization

Matrix departmentalization is a hybrid structure in which two or more forms of departmentalization are used together. The most common matrix combines the product and functional forms of departmentalization, but other forms may also be used. Exhibit 9.7 shows the matrix structure used by Procter & Gamble, which has 97,000 employees working in 80 different countries. Across the top of Exhibit 9.7, you can see that the company uses a product sector structure where it groups its 22 billion-dollar and 20 half-billion-dollar brands (Pampers, Tampax, Pantene, Olay, Charmin, Crest, Metamucil, Venus, Gillette, Tide, and Swiffer are shown for illustration) into six units:

» Baby and Feminine Care

» Beauty

» Family Care and Procter & Gamble (P&G) Ventures

» Health Care

» Grooming

» Fabric & Home Care.[18]

> **Matrix departmentalization** a hybrid organizational structure in which two or more forms of departmentalization, most often product and functional, are used together

Exhibit 9.7
Matrix Departmentalization: Procter & Gamble

		Product Sector Units												
		Baby and Feminine Care		Beauty		Family Care & P&G Ventures		Health Care		Grooming		Fabric & Home Care		
		Baby Care	Feminine Care	Hair Care	Skin & Personal Care	Family Care	P&G Ventures	Oral Care	Personal Health Care	Female	Male	Fabric Care	Home Care	
Market Operations	Customer Teams	Pampers	Tampax	Pantene	Olay	Charmin	Chronic Skin Conditions	Crest	Metamucil	Venus	Gillette	Tide	Swiffer	(1) Focus Markets
	Transportation	Pampers	Tampax	Pantene	Olay	Charmin	Non-Toxic Home & Garden	Crest	Metamucil	Venus	Gillette	Tide	Swiffer	or
	Warehousings	Pampers	Tampax	Pantene	Olay	Charmin	Women's Wellness	Crest	Metamucil	Venus	Gillette	Tide	Swiffer	(2) Enterprise Markets
	Logistics	Pampers	Tampax	Pantene	Olay	Charmin	Menopause	Crest	Metamucil	Venus	Gillette	Tide	Swiffer	
	Marketing	Pampers	Tampax	Pantene	Olay	Charmin	Male Wellness	Crest	Metamucil	Venus	Gillette	Tide	Swiffer	
	Corporate Services	Pampers	Tampax	Pantene	Olay	Charmin	Active Aging	Crest	Metamucil	Venus	Gillette	Tide	Swiffer	

Source: "P&G Corporate Structure," Procter & Gamble, accessed April 13, 2020, https://us.pg.com/structure-and-governance/corporate-structure/; "P&G Brands and Products," Procter & Gamble," accessed April 13, 2020, https://us.pg.com/brands/#Home-Care; "P&G at a Glance," Procter & Gamble, accessed April 13, 2020, www.pginvestor.com/PG-at-a-Glance/Index?KeyGenPage=1073748355.

Each of these six product sector units, such as Baby and Feminine Care, is judged as a standalone business with sales, cash flow, and profit expectations. The left side of the figure shows that the company also uses a functional structure – customer teams, transportation, warehousing, logistics, marketing, and corporate services (i.e., human resources, legal, accounting, etc.) – which support the "Market Operations" in each of the six product sector units. The right side of the figure shows the two global regions in which P&G sells its products, Focus Markets, such as the United States, Canada, Western Europe, and Asia, that account for 80 percent of sales, and Enterprise Markets, such as Mexico, Central and South America, Eastern Europe, Africa, the Middle East and Australia, which are "important to the future of P&G because of their attractive market growth rates."[19]

The white boxes in Exhibit 9.7 represent the matrix structure created by the combination of the product and functional structures. For example, P&G's Fabric & Home Care product sector unit (on the far right) would work with Market Operations customer teams to sell, market, and distribute Tide detergent and Swiffer floor cleaning products in Focus Markets and Enterprise Markets across the world. Market Operations functions helps each of the six product sector units work with suppliers, keep transportation, warehouse, and logistics costs down, effectively market products, and, through corporate services, hire employees, bill customers, and pay suppliers. Matrix combinations are shown for Pampers, Tampax, Pantene, Olay, Charmin, various P&G Ventures (to create new products), Crest, Metamucil, Venus, Gillette, Tide and Swiffer within each of P&G's six product sector units.

Several things distinguish matrix departmentalization from the other traditional forms of departmentalization.[20] First, most employees report to two bosses, one from each core part of the matrix. For example, in Exhibit 9.7 a manager on the Pampers team (far left) responsible for marketing would report to a boss in the

Baby Care segment of the Baby and Feminine Care product unit as well as to a manager in Market Operations. Second, by virtue of their hybrid design, matrix structures lead to much more cross-functional interaction than other forms of departmentalization. In fact, while matrix workers are typically members of only one functional department (based on their work experience and expertise), they are also commonly members of several ongoing project, product, or customer groups. Third, because of the high level of cross-functional interaction, matrix departmentalization requires significant coordination between managers in the different parts of the matrix. In particular, managers have the complex job of tracking and managing the multiple demands (project, product, customer, or functional) on employees' time.

All Tide products are part of the Fabric & Home Care business unit at P&G.

Rmnoa357/Shutterstock.com

The primary advantage of matrix departmentalization is that it allows companies to efficiently manage large, complex tasks such as researching, developing, and marketing pharmaceuticals or carrying out complex global businesses. Efficiency comes from avoiding duplication. For example, rather than having an entire transportation function for each product, the company simply assigns and reassigns workers from the transportation department in Market Operations at P&G when and where they are needed to distribute products. More specifically, an employee may simultaneously be part of five different ongoing projects but may be actively completing work on only a few projects at a time. Another advantage is the pool of resources available to carry out large, complex tasks. Because of the ability to quickly pull in expert help from all the functional areas of the company, matrix project managers have a much more diverse set of expertise and experience at their disposal than managers in the other forms of departmentalization.

The primary disadvantage of matrix departmentalization is the high level of coordination required to manage the complexity involved in running large, ongoing projects at various levels of completion. Matrix structures are notorious for confusion and conflict between project bosses in different parts of the matrix. Disagreements or misunderstandings about schedules, budgets, available resources, and the availability of employees with particular functional expertise are common in matrix structures. Because of

these problems, many matrix structures evolve from a **simple matrix**, in which managers in different parts of the matrix negotiate conflicts and resources directly, to a **complex matrix**, in which specialized matrix managers and departments are added to the organizational structure. In a complex matrix, managers from different parts of the matrix might report to the same matrix manager, who helps them sort out conflicts and problems.

9-2 ORGANIZATIONAL AUTHORITY

The second part of traditional organizational structures is authority. **Authority** is the right to give commands, take action, and make decisions to achieve organizational objectives.[21]

Traditionally, organizational authority has been characterized by the following dimensions: 9-2a chain of command, 9-2b line versus staff authority, 9-2c delegation of authority, and 9-2d degree of centralization.

Simple matrix a form of matrix departmentalization in which managers in different parts of the matrix negotiate conflicts and resources

Complex matrix a form of matrix departmentalization in which managers in different parts of the matrix report to matrix managers, who help them sort out conflicts and problems

Authority the right to give commands, take action, and make decisions to achieve organizational objectives

9-2a Chain of Command

Consider again the AB InBev organizational structure. A manager in any of the corporation's geographical divisions ultimately reports to the head of that division. That division head, in turn, reports to the AB InBev's CEO Carlos Brito. This line, which vertically connects every job in the company to higher levels of management, represents the chain of command. The **chain of command** is the vertical line of authority that clarifies who reports to whom throughout the organization. People higher in the chain of command have the right, *if they so choose*, to give commands, take action, and make decisions concerning activities occurring anywhere below them in the chain. In the following discussion about delegation and decentralization, you will learn that managers don't always choose to exercise their authority directly.[22]

One of the key assumptions underlying the chain of command is **unity of command**, which means that workers should report to just one boss.[23] In practical terms, this means that only one person can be in charge at a time. Matrix organizations, in which employees have two bosses, automatically violate this principle. This is one of the primary reasons that matrix organizations are difficult to manage. Unity of command serves an important purpose: to prevent the confusion that might arise when an employee receives conflicting commands from two different bosses.

Companies don't necessarily have to have a matrix organization to violate unity of command – they can do so by appointing two CEOs. While co-CEO arrangements sometimes work well, they are rare and often short-lived because, according to research from Professor Lindred Greer, having co-CEOs "causes conflict," leads to "negative performance by (executive) teams," and may likely result in the development of "hostile mindsets" as the co-CEOs struggle to work together.[24] With market share and profits declining, Whole Foods abandoned its co-CEO arrangement. Analyst Brian Yarbrough commented, "When business is going great, there aren't a lot of disagreements, and it can work. But when times get tough, that's when you start to bump heads."[25] Deutsche Bank's co-CEOs resigned abruptly after a series of financial mistakes and regulatory penalties.[26] Nordstrom, Oracle, and Salesforce also abandoned their co-CEO arrangements within the last year, returning to the more traditional – and workable – single CEO model.[27]

Gajus/Shutterstock.com

9-2b Line versus Staff Authority

A second dimension of authority is the distinction between line and staff authority. **Line authority** is the right to command immediate subordinates in the chain of command. For example, ABB Ltd. CEO Peter Voser has line authority over the president of the company's Industrial Automation division. Voser can issue orders to that division president and expect them to be carried out. In turn, the president of the Industrial Automation division can issue orders to his subordinates, who run the control systems, turbocharging, and logic controllers businesses, and expect them to be carried out. By contrast, **staff authority** is the right to advise but not command others who are not subordinates in the chain of command. For example, a manager in human resources at ABB Ltd. might advise the manager in charge of the Robotics & Discrete Automation group on a hiring decision but cannot order him or her to hire a certain applicant.

The terms *line* and *staff* are also used to describe different functions within the organization. A **line function** is an activity that contributes directly to creating or selling the company's products. So, for example, activities that take place within the manufacturing and marketing departments would be considered line functions. A **staff function**, such as accounting, human resources, or legal services, does not contribute directly to creating or selling the company's products but instead supports line activities. For example, marketing managers might consult with the legal staff to ensure the wording of an advertisement is within the law.

Chain of command the vertical line of authority that clarifies who reports to whom throughout the organization

Unity of command a management principle that workers should report to just one boss

Line authority the right to command immediate subordinates in the chain of command

Staff authority the right to advise, but not command, others who are not subordinates in the chain of command

Line function an activity that contributes directly to creating or selling the company's products

Staff function an activity that does not contribute directly to creating or selling the company's products but instead supports line activities

9-2c Delegation of Authority

Managers can exercise their authority directly by completing tasks themselves, or they can choose to pass on some of their authority to subordinates. **Delegation of authority** is the assignment of direct authority and responsibility to a subordinate to complete tasks for which the manager is normally responsible.

When a manager delegates work, three transfers occur, as illustrated in Exhibit 9.8. First, the manager transfers full responsibility for the assignment to the subordinate. At Apple, when you've been delegated to a certain task, you become the DRI, or the "directly responsible individual." As a former Apple employee explains, "Any effective meeting at Apple will have an action list. Next to each action item will be the DRI," who of course, is responsible for completing that delegated responsibility. Furthermore, when you're trying to figure out who to contact to get something done in Apple's corporate structure, people simply ask, "Who's the DRI on that?"[28] TripAdvisor's Matthew Mamet says, "When I'm the DRI on a task, it can sometimes come with a bit of apprehension (*Gulp*, not 100% sure how I'm going to do that . . .but ok I'll figure it out), or maybe with a bit of grumbling (oh man, I guess I gotta do that, too), but being the DRI always comes with a sense of responsibility to the team."[29]

Many managers, however, find giving up full responsibility somewhat difficult. When Lori Lord was COO of **Spectrum Health Care**, she stayed up all night writing and reviewing 400-page requests for proposals (RFPs), upon which the company's sales and growth depended. Lord maintained tight control over the RFPs because she considered them critical to the company's success and believed that she was the only person who could do it right. "These were so important for our organization and I wouldn't let anyone else put the document(s) together."[30]

One reason it is difficult for some managers to delegate is that they often fear that the task won't be done as well as if they did it themselves. However, one CEO says, "If you can delegate a task to somebody who can do it 75 percent to 80 percent as well as you can today, you delegate it immediately." Why? Many tasks don't need to be done perfectly; they just need to be *done*. And delegating tasks that someone else can do frees managers to assume other important responsibilities. Indeed, *Leadership* author John C. Maxwell says, "If you want to do a few small things right, do them yourself. If you want to do great things and make a big impact, learn to delegate."[31] After Lori Lord learned to delegate the RFP review along with other day-to-day

Exhibit 9.8
Delegation: Responsibility, Authority, and Accountability

Source: C. D. Pringle, D. F. Jennings, and J. G. Longenecker, *Managing Organizations: Functions and Behaviors* (Columbus, Ohio: Merrill Publishing, 1984).

activities, she could attend key meetings, focus on the future of the organization, and concentrate on growth, all activities critical to her new role as the company's CEO. She says that she lost five years of her life from not delegating and that now, "I'm glad I don't have to be here at 3 a.m. anymore."[32]

Delegating authority can generate a related problem: micromanaging. Sometimes managers delegate only to interfere later with how the employee is performing the task. But delegating full responsibility means that the employee – not the manager – is now completely responsible for task completion. Good managers need to trust their subordinates to do the jobs and tasks they delegate.

The second transfer that occurs with delegation is that the manager gives the subordinate full authority over the budget, resources, and personnel needed to do the job. To do the job effectively, subordinates must have the same tools and information at their disposal that managers had when they were responsible for the same task. In other words, for delegation to work, delegated authority must be commensurate with delegated responsibility.

The third transfer that occurs with delegation is the transfer of accountability. The subordinate now has the authority and responsibility to do the job and, in return, is accountable for getting the job done. In other words, managers delegate their managerial authority and responsibility to subordinates in exchange for results.

Delegation of authority the assignment of direct authority and responsibility to a subordinate to complete tasks for which the manager is normally responsible

9-2d Degree of Centralization

Centralization of authority is the location of most authority at the upper levels of the organization. In a centralized organization, managers make most decisions, even the relatively small ones. Store managers at Whole Foods' 500+ locations were long responsible for deciding what to sell in their own stores. To compete more efficiently against Walmart, Kroger, and Costco, however, **Whole Foods** centralized purchasing responsibilities for meat, produce, and many nonperishable items at the company's Austin, Texas, headquarters. Co-CEO John Mackey says of the change, "We want to evolve the structure in such a way that we take out redundancy and waste."[33] Likewise, after Amazon purchased Whole Foods, hundreds of in-store marketing staff were laid off as Amazon took centralized control of marketing.[34] Not surprisingly, Amazon heavily markets Whole Foods to the 150 million Amazon Prime members who pay $119 a year for free two-day shipping, Prime Video and Prime Music, etc.[35] Amazon Prime members get an extra 10 percent off of Whole Foods sales items and up to 50 percent off on 30+ weekly "Prime member deals," both via the Whole Foods Market app at checkout.[36]

Decentralization is the location of a significant amount of authority in the lower levels of the organization. An organization is decentralized if it has a high degree of delegation at all levels. In a decentralized organization, workers closest to problems are authorized to make the decisions necessary to solve the problems on their own.

At Gap, a struggling clothes retailer, former CEO Art Peck instituted decentralization to produce faster, more effective decisions. Peck first eliminated signoffs that slowed decisions. Brand merchants acting as fashion collection editors no longer approved every product category. Step two was pushing decision-making authority out to those closest to problems. For example, Gap's foreign suppliers, who make most of the clothes sold in Gap stores, were authorized to make decisions on items like men's dress shirts.[37]

Decentralization has a number of advantages. It develops employee capabilities throughout the company and leads to faster decision making and more satisfied customers and employees. Furthermore, a study of 1,000 large companies found that companies with a high degree of

Volkswagen will apply standardization to decrease costs on production of its popular Golf model.

decentralization outperformed those with a low degree of decentralization in terms of return on assets (6.9 versus 4.7 percent), return on investment (14.6 versus 9.0 percent), return on equity (22.8 versus 16.6 percent), and return on sales (10.3 versus 6.3 percent). Surprisingly, the same study found that few large companies actually are decentralized. Specifically, only 31 percent of employees in these 1,000 companies were responsible for recommending improvements to management. Overall, just 10 percent of employees received the training and information needed to support a truly decentralized approach to management.[38]

With results like these, the key question is no longer *whether* companies should decentralize, but *where* they should decentralize. One rule of thumb is to stay centralized where standardization is important and to decentralize where standardization is unimportant. **Standardization** is solving problems by consistently applying the same rules, procedures, and processes. Volkswagen (VW) is one of the largest automakers in the world with a dozen brands (Volkswagen Passenger Cars, Audi, SEAT, ŠKODA, Bentley, Bugatti, Lamborghini, Porsche, Ducati, Volkswagen Commercial Vehicles, Scania trucks and buses, and MAN trucks and buses), 671,000 employees, 124 factories, and 365 different vehicles![39] Running a company this size is enormously complex. For example, the VW Golf, long one of the company's best-selling models, was made with 89 different steering wheels and 24 different radiator grilles. Using that many varieties for the same part not only increases costs it decreases quality and reliability. So, VW turned to standardization to use a small number of standard parts across different car platforms, eliminating 15,000 different parts in the process. That, combined with job cuts, will reduce costs by $4 billion a year.[40]

Centralization of authority the location of most authority at the upper levels of the organization

Decentralization the location of a significant amount of authority in the lower levels of the organization

Standardization solving problems by consistently applying the same rules, procedures, and processes

9-3 JOB DESIGN

Could you stand to do the same simple tasks an average of 50 times per hour, 400 times per day, 2,000 times per week, 8,000 times per month? Few can. Fast-food workers rarely stay on the job more than six months. In fact, McDonald's and other fast-food restaurants have well over 70 percent employee turnover each year.[41] As a drive-through employee at McDonald's, you would repeatedly perform the following steps:

1. Say, "Welcome to McDonald's. May I have your order please?"

2. Listen to the order. Repeat it for accuracy. State the total cost. "Please drive to the second window."

3. Take the money or credit card. Make change or swipe the card.

4. Give customers cups, straws, napkins, and condiments.

5. Give customers food.

6. Say, "Thank you for coming to McDonald's."

In this section, you will learn about **job design**– the number, kind, and variety of tasks that individual workers perform in doing their jobs.

*You will learn **9-3a why companies continue to use specialized jobs such as the McDonald's drive-through job** and **9-3b how job rotation, job enlargement, job enrichment**, and **9-3c the job characteristics model are being used to overcome the problems associated with job specialization.***

9-3a Job Specialization

Job specialization occurs when a job is composed of a small part of a larger task or process. Specialized jobs are characterized by simple, easy-to-learn steps; low variety; and high repetition, such as the McDonald's drive-through window job just described. One of the clear disadvantages of specialized jobs is that, being so easy to learn, they quickly become boring. This, in turn, can lead to low job satisfaction and high absenteeism and employee turnover, all of which are very costly to organizations.

Why, then, do companies continue to create and use specialized jobs? The primary reason is that specialized jobs are very economical. As we learned from Frederick W. Taylor and Frank and Lillian Gilbreth in Chapter 2, after a job has been specialized, it takes little time to learn and master. Consequently, when experienced workers quit or are absent, the company can replace them with new employees and lose little productivity. For example, next time you're at McDonald's, notice the labeled pictures of the food on the touchscreen cash registers. These labeled pictures make it easy for McDonald's trainees to quickly learn to take orders. Likewise, to simplify and speed operations at the drive-through, the drink dispensers are set to automatically fill drink cups. Put a medium cup below the dispenser. Punch the medium drink button. The soft-drink machine then fills the cup to within a half-inch of the top, while the worker goes to get your fries. At McDonald's, every task has been simplified in this way. Because the work is designed to be simple, wages can remain low because it isn't necessary to pay high salaries to attract highly experienced, educated, or trained workers.

9-3b Job Rotation, Enlargement, and Enrichment

Because of the efficiency of specialized jobs, companies are often reluctant to eliminate them. Consequently, job redesign efforts have focused on modifying jobs to keep the benefits of specialized jobs while reducing their obvious costs and disadvantages. Three methods – job rotation, job enlargement, and job enrichment – have been used to try to improve specialized jobs.[42]

Job rotation attempts to overcome the disadvantages of job specialization by periodically moving workers from one specialized job to another to give them more variety and the opportunity to use different skills. For example, an office receptionist who does nothing but answer phones could be systematically rotated to a different job, such as typing, filing, or data entry, every day or two. Likewise, the "mirror attacher" in an automobile plant might attach mirrors in the first half of the work shift and then install bumpers during the second half. Because employees simply switch from one specialized job to another, job rotation allows companies to retain the economic benefits of specialized work. At the same time, the greater variety of tasks makes the work less boring and more satisfying for workers.

Another way to counter the disadvantages of specialization is to enlarge the job. **Job enlargement** increases the number of different tasks that

> **Job design** the number, kind, and variety of tasks that individual workers perform in doing their jobs
>
> **Job specialization** job composed of a small part of a larger task or process
>
> **Job rotation** periodically moving workers from one specialized job to another to give them more variety and the opportunity to use different skills
>
> **Job enlargement** increasing the number of different tasks that a worker performs within one particular job

Exhibit 9.9
Job Characteristics Model

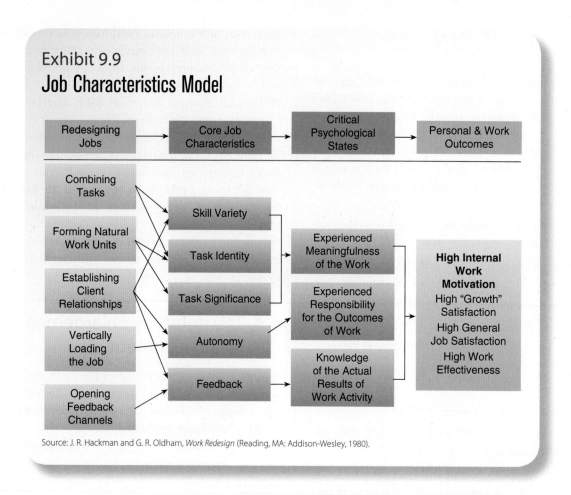

Source: J. R. Hackman and G. R. Oldham, *Work Redesign* (Reading, MA: Addison-Wesley, 1980).

a worker performs within one particular job. Instead of being assigned just one task, workers with enlarged jobs are given several tasks to perform. For example, an enlarged "mirror attacher" job might include attaching the mirror, checking to see that the mirror's power adjustment controls work, and then cleaning the mirror's surface. Though job enlargement increases variety, many workers report feeling more stress when their jobs are enlarged. Consequently, many workers view enlarged jobs as simply more work, especially if they are not given additional time to complete the added tasks.

Job enrichment attempts to overcome the deficiencies in specialized work by increasing the number of tasks *and* by giving workers the authority and control to make meaningful decisions about their work.[43]

Job enrichment increasing the number of tasks in a particular job and giving workers the authority and control to make meaningful decisions about their work

Job characteristics model (JCM) an approach to job redesign that seeks to formulate jobs in ways that motivate workers and create positive work outcomes

Internal motivation motivation that comes from the job itself rather than from outside rewards

9-3c Job Characteristics Model

In contrast to job rotation, job enlargement, and job enrichment, which focus on providing variety in job tasks, the **job characteristics model (JCM)** is an approach to job redesign that seeks to formulate jobs in ways that motivate workers and create positive work outcomes.[44]

As shown in Exhibit 9.9, the primary goal of the model is to create jobs that result in positive personal and work outcomes, such as internal work motivation, satisfaction with one's job, and work effectiveness. Of these, the central concern of the JCM is internal motivation. **Internal motivation** is motivation that comes from the job itself rather than from outside rewards such as a raise or praise from the boss. If workers feel that performing the job well is itself rewarding, then the job has internal motivation. Statements such as "I get a nice sense of accomplishment" or "I feel good about myself and what I'm producing" are examples of internal motivation.

In Exhibit 9.9, you can see that the JCM specifies three critical psychological states that must occur for work to be internally motivating. First, workers must *experience the work as meaningful*; that is, they must view their job as being important. Second, they must *experience responsibility for work outcomes* – they must feel personally responsible for the work being done well. Third, workers must have *knowledge of results*; that is, they must know how well they are performing their jobs. All three critical psychological states must occur for work to be internally motivating.

For example, grocery store cashiers usually have knowledge of results. When you're slow, your checkout line grows long. If you make a mistake, customers point it out: "No, I think got scanned three times. I only bought two." Likewise, cashiers experience responsibility for work outcomes. At the end of the day, the register is totaled, and the money is counted. Ideally, the money matches the total sales in the register. If the money in the till is less than what's recorded in the register, most stores make the cashier pay the difference. Consequently, most cashiers are very careful to avoid being caught short at the end of the day. Nonetheless, despite knowing the results and experiencing responsibility for work outcomes, most grocery store cashiers (at least where I shop) aren't internally motivated because they don't experience the work as meaningful. With scanners, it takes little skill to learn or do the job. Anyone can do it. In addition, cashiers have few decisions to make, and the job is highly repetitive.

What kinds of jobs produce the three critical psychological states? Moving another step to the left in Exhibit 9.9, you can see that these psychological states arise from jobs that are strong on five core job characteristics: skill variety, task identity, task significance, autonomy, and feedback. **Skill variety** is the number of different activities performed in a job. **Task identity** is the degree to which a job, from beginning to end, requires completion of a whole and identifiable piece of work. **Task significance** is the degree to which a job is perceived to have a substantial impact on others inside or outside the organization. **Autonomy** is the degree to which a job gives workers the discretion, freedom, and independence to decide how and when to accomplish the work. Finally, **feedback** is the amount of information the job provides to workers about their work performance.

To illustrate how the core job characteristics work together, let's use them to more thoroughly assess why the McDonald's drive-through window job is not particularly satisfying or motivating. To start, skill variety is low. Except for the size of an order or special requests ("no onions"), the process is the same for each customer. At best, task identity is

moderate. Although you take the order, handle the money or credit card, and deliver the food, others are responsible for a larger part of the process – preparing the food. Task identity will be even lower if the McDonald's has two drive-through windows because each drive-through window worker will have an even more specialized task. The first is limited to taking the order and making change, while the second just delivers the food.

Task significance, the impact you have on others, is probably low. Autonomy is also very low: McDonald's has strict rules about dress, cleanliness, and procedures. But the job does provide immediate feedback such as positive and negative customer comments, car horns honking, the amount of time it takes to process orders, and the number of cars in the drive-through. With the exception of feedback, the low levels of the core job characteristics show why the drive-through window job is not internally motivating for many workers.

What can managers do when jobs aren't internally motivating? The far left column of Exhibit 9.9 lists five job redesign techniques that managers can use to strengthen a job's core characteristics. *Combining tasks* increases skill variety and task identity by joining separate, specialized tasks into larger work modules. For example, some trucking firms are now requiring truck drivers to load their rigs as well as drive them. The hope is that involving drivers in loading will ensure that trucks are properly loaded, thus reducing damage claims.

Work can be formed into *natural work units* by arranging tasks according to logical or meaningful groups. Although many trucking companies randomly assign drivers to trucks, some have begun assigning drivers to particular geographic locations (e.g., the Northeast or Southwest) or to truckloads that require special driving skill (e.g., oversized loads or hazardous chemicals). Forming natural work units increases task identity and task significance.

Skill variety the number of different activities performed in a job

Task identity the degree to which a job, from beginning to end, requires the completion of a whole and identifiable piece of work

Task significance the degree to which a job is perceived to have a substantial impact on others inside or outside the organization

Autonomy the degree to which a job gives workers the discretion, freedom, and independence to decide how and when to accomplish the job

Feedback the amount of information the job provides to workers about their work performance

Establishing client relationships increases skill variety, autonomy, and feedback by giving employees direct contact with clients and customers. In some companies, truck drivers are expected to establish business relationships with their regular customers. When something goes wrong with a shipment, customers are told to call drivers directly.

Vertical loading means pushing some managerial authority down to workers. For truck drivers, this means that they have the same authority as managers to resolve customer problems. In some companies, if a late shipment causes problems for a customer, the driver has the authority to fully refund the cost of that shipment without first obtaining management's approval.

The last job redesign technique offered by the model, *opening feedback channels*, means finding additional ways to give employees direct, frequent feedback about their job performance. For example, with advances in electronics, many truck drivers get instantaneous data as to whether they're on schedule and driving their rigs in a fuel-efficient manner. Likewise, the increased contact with customers also means that many drivers now receive monthly data on customer satisfaction.

 ## 9-4 INTRAORGANIZATIONAL PROCESSES

defined jobs and responsibilities; loosely defined, frequently changing roles; and decentralized authority and horizontal communication based on task knowledge. This type of organization works best in dynamic, changing business environments.

The organizational design techniques described in the first half of this chapter – departmentalization, authority, and job design – are better suited for mechanistic organizations and the stable business environments that were more prevalent before 1980. By contrast, the organizational design techniques discussed in the second part of the chapter, are more appropriate for organic organizations and the increasingly dynamic environments in which today's businesses compete. The key difference between these approaches is that mechanistic organizational designs focus on organizational structure, whereas organic organizational designs are concerned with **intraorganizational process**, which is the collection of activities that take place within an organization to transform inputs into outputs that customers value.

*Let's take a look at how companies are **using 9-4a reengineering** and **9-4b empowerment to redesign intraorganizational processes like these.***

9-4a Reengineering

In their best-selling book *Reengineering the Corporation*, Michael Hammer and James Champy define **reengineering** as "the *fundamental* rethinking and *radical* redesign of business *processes* to achieve *dramatic* improvements in critical, contemporary measures of performance, such as cost, quality, service and speed."[46] Hammer and Champy further explained the four key words shown in italics in this definition. The first key word is *fundamental*. When reengineering organizational designs, managers must ask themselves, "Why do we do what we do?" and "Why do we do it the way we do?" The usual answer is "Because that's the way we've always done it." The second key word is *radical*. Reengineering is about significant change, about starting over by throwing out the old ways of getting work done. The third key word is *processes*. Hammer and Champy noted that "most business people are not process oriented; they are focused on tasks, on jobs, on people, on structures, but not on processes." The fourth key word is *dramatic*. Reengineering is about achieving quantum improvements in company performance.

An example from IBM Credit's operation illustrates how work can be reengineered.[47] **IBM Credit** lends businesses money to buy IBM computers. Previously, the loan

Mechanistic organization an organization characterized by specialized jobs and responsibilities; precisely defined, unchanging roles; and a rigid chain of command based on centralized authority and vertical communication

Organic organization an organization characterized by broadly defined jobs and responsibilities; loosely defined, frequently changing roles; and decentralized authority and horizontal communication based on task knowledge

Intraorganizational process the collection of activities that take place within an organization to transform inputs into outputs that customers value

Reengineering fundamental rethinking and radical redesign of business processes to achieve dramatic improvements in critical measures of performance, such as cost, quality, service, and speed

More than 40 years ago, Tom Burns and G. M. Stalker described how two kinds of organizational designs, mechanistic and organic, are appropriate for different kinds of organizational environments.[45] **Mechanistic organizations** are characterized by specialized jobs and responsibilities; precisely defined, unchanging roles; and a rigid chain of command based on centralized authority and vertical communication. This type of organization works best in stable, unchanging business environments. By contrast, **organic organizations** are characterized by broadly

Mechanistic or Organic Organizations: Which did Better During the Coronavirus Pandemic?

Before the global coronavirus lockdown, Nitin Nohria, Dean of the Harvard Business School, asked which organization would do better "in a sustained crisis such as a pandemic."

▶ Organization 1: Hierarchical, centralized leadership, tightly coupled (greater interdependence among parts), concentrated workforce, specialists, policy and procedure driven, or

▶ Organization 2: Networked, distributed leadership, loosely coupled (less interdependence), dispersed workforce, cross-trained generalists, guided by simple yet flexible rules.

Organization 1 is clearly mechanistic, while organization 2 is obviously organic. You know the answer, don't you? Nohria did, too, "Organization 2 is clearly better positioned to respond to evolving, unpredictable threats." Why? The ability to shift work from one location to another, to repurpose manufacturing or services to new uses (i.e., from autos to ventilators, from Google searches to apps that do network tracing and virus exposure tracking), from reliance on one leadership team to multiple leadership teams focusing on different tasks and processes, to the abandonment of strict rules and procedures to the adoption of general guidelines and principles, all to figure out new solutions in days, not months or years, clearly make organic organizational structures superior in pandemics.

Students often find organizational structures and processes to be a dry topic. But now that the world has been through the

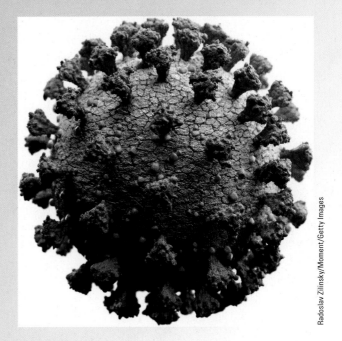

Radoslav Zilinsky/Moment/Getty Images

coronavirus pandemic, it should be obvious that organizational structures and processes *really* matter.

Source: N. Nohria, "What Organizations Need to Survive a Pandemic," *Harvard Business Review*, January 30, 2020, accessed April 15, 2020, https://hbr.org/2020/01/what-organizations-need-to-survive-a-pandemic.

---

process began when an IBM salesperson called the home office to obtain credit approval for a customer's purchase. The first department involved in the process took the credit information over the phone from the salesperson and recorded it on the credit form. The credit form was sent to the credit checking department, then to the pricing department (where the interest rate was determined), and on through a total of five departments. In all, it took the five departments six days to approve or deny the customer's loan. Of course, this delay cost IBM business. Some customers got their loans elsewhere. Others, frustrated by the wait, simply canceled their orders.

Finally, two IBM managers decided to walk a loan straight through each of the departments involved in the process. At each step, they asked the workers to stop what they were doing and immediately process their loan application. They were shocked by what they found. From start to finish, the entire process took just 90 minutes! The six-day turnaround time was almost entirely due to delays in handing off the work from one department to another. The solution: IBM redesigned the process so that one person, not five people in five separate departments, handles the entire loan approval process without any handoffs. The results were indeed dramatic. Reengineering the credit process reduced approval time from six days to four hours and allowed IBM Credit to increase the number of loans it handled by a factor of 100!

With everything digitalized, can reengineering produce the same kinds of gains today? In an identical situation, the

WHY?

Marta Design/Shutterstock.com

Democratize the Workplace to Empower Workers?

At some companies, small and large decisions are made not by managers, but by a worker vote. At software company **InContext**, for example, workers recently voted on whether to have standing desks, cubicles, or open tables. After organizing visits to two locations, marketing technology firm **MediaMath** let workers decide the location of its new headquarters. Employees at 1Sale.com voted on whether the company should continue to pay for employee lunches, or whether it should use that money to lower the cost of health insurance. According to 1Sale's Shmuli Bortunk, "They asked us, do you prefer to have your belly full or your wallet full?" While voting can take more time, it can also empower employees and improve morale. With democratized decisions, says InContext Product manager Mackenzie Siren, "People feel like they have a real voice."

Source: R. Silverman, "Workplace Democracy Catches On," *Wall Street Journal*, March 27, 2016, accessed April 29, 2016, www.wsj.com/articles/workplace-democracy-catches-on-1459117910.

Business Development Bank of Canada (BDC) developed seven iPad apps to increase the efficiency of its credit loan process as it collected business information for making loan decisions. The most used app, PDC Express Loan, saved the bank 8 hours on each loan! And, just like IBM, the BDC reduced the length of the loan process from 10 days to 30 minutes by using apps to reengineer its loan processes and steps![48]

Why does reengineering yields such big gains? First, because most things in organizations are done because of momentum – they've always been done a particular way, or because they solved an old problem. Legacy computer systems frequently dictate or restrict the steps in any process. A manager involved in process reengineering said, "Everything I see around here was developed because of specific issues that popped up, and it was all done ad hoc and added onto each other. It certainly wasn't engineered."[49] Second,

reengineering helps managers see how everything *across* the organization fits together. Another manager with reengineering experience explained, "It was like the sun rose for the first time. … I saw the bigger picture. [Before] I only thought of things in the context of my span of control."[50]

In other words, reengineering changes an organization's orientation from vertical to horizontal. Instead of taking orders from upper management, lower- and middle-level managers and workers take orders from a customer who is at the beginning and end of each process. Instead of running independent functional departments, managers and workers in different departments take ownership of cross-functional processes. Instead of simplifying work so that it becomes increasingly specialized, reengineering complicates work by giving workers increased autonomy and responsibility for complete processes.

In essence, reengineering changes work by changing **task interdependence**, the extent to which collective action is required to complete an entire piece of work. As shown in Exhibit 9.10, there are three kinds of task interdependence.[51] In **pooled interdependence**, each job or department contributes to the whole independently. In **sequential interdependence**, work must be performed in succession because one group's or job's outputs become the inputs for the next group or job. Finally, in **reciprocal interdependence**, different

Task interdependence the extent to which collective action is required to complete an entire piece of work

Pooled interdependence work completed by having each job or department independently contribute to the whole

Sequential interdependence work completed in succession, with one group's or job's outputs becoming the inputs for the next group or job

Reciprocal interdependence work completed by different jobs or groups working together in a back-and-forth manner

Exhibit 9.10
Reengineering and Task Interdependence

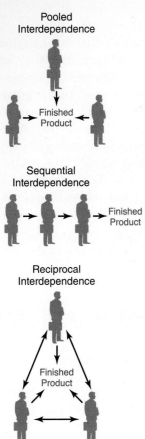

Pooled Interdependence

Sequential Interdependence

Reciprocal Interdependence

from three weeks to three days, Levi Strauss ended an $850 million reengineering project because of the fear and turmoil it created in the company's workforce. One low point occurred when Levi management, encouraged by its reengineering consultants, told 4,000 workers that they would have to "reapply for their jobs" as the company shifted from its traditional vertical structure to a process-based form of organizing. Thomas Kasten, Levi Strauss's vice president for reengineering and customer service at that time, says, "We felt the pressure building up [over reengineering efforts], and we were worried about the business."[53] Today, even reengineering gurus Hammer and Champy admit that roughly 70 percent of all reengineering projects fail because of the effects on people in the workplace. Says Hammer, "I wasn't smart enough about that [the people issues]. I was reflecting my engineering background and was insufficiently appreciative of the human dimension. I've [now] learned that's critical."[54]

9-4b Empowerment

Another way of redesigning intraorganizational processes is through empowerment. **Empowering workers** means permanently passing decision-making authority and responsibility from managers to workers. For workers to be fully empowered, companies must give them the information and resources they need to make and carry out good decisions and then reward them for taking individual initiative.[55] In other words, employees won't feel very empowered if they constantly have someone looking over their shoulders. Warby Parker, the online eyeglasses company, wanted to use computer programmers more effectively. So, it empowered employees through its new three-step Warbles system, which was designed by two programming teams. First, anyone can nominate projects that they feel deserve programmers' time and attention. Second, company managers assign points to projects based on perceived value. It's thought that managers' responsibilities make them more likely to identify projects with the broadest impact. Third, programmers decide which projects to work on and are rewarded for choosing higher value projects (with more points). CEO Dave Gilboa says that Warbles, "ensures we're getting a lot of value out of the tech team." Best of all, "Our engineers are much happier; they love

Empowering workers
permanently passing decision-making authority and responsibility from managers to workers by giving them the information and resources they need to make and carry out good decisions

jobs or groups work together in a back-and-forth manner to complete the process. By reducing the handoffs between different jobs or groups, reengineering decreases sequential interdependence. Likewise, reengineering decreases pooled interdependence by redesigning work so that formerly independent jobs or departments now work together to complete processes. Finally, reengineering increases reciprocal interdependence by making groups or individuals responsible for larger, more complete processes in which several steps may be accomplished at the same time.

As an organizational design tool, reengineering promises big rewards, but it has also come under severe criticism. The most serious complaint is that because it allows a few workers to do the work formerly done by many, reengineering is simply a corporate code word for cost cutting and worker layoffs.[52] For this reason, detractors claim that reengineering hurts morale and performance. Even though ordering times were reduced

Warby Parker CEO Dave Gilboa says that allowing the company's tech team to choose which programs it will work on maximizes their happiness and productivity.

the idea that they have autonomy and they can select ideas that they find most interesting."[56]

When workers are given the proper information and resources and are allowed to make good decisions, they experience strong feelings of empowerment. **Empowerment** is a feeling of intrinsic motivation in which workers perceive their work to have meaning and perceive themselves to be competent, having an impact, and capable of self-determination.[57] Work has meaning when it is consistent with personal standards and beliefs. Workers feel competent when they believe they can perform an activity with skill. The belief that they are having an impact comes from a feeling that they can affect work outcomes. A feeling of self-determination arises from workers' belief that they have the autonomy to choose how best to do their work.

Empowerment can lead to changes in organizational processes because meaning, competence, impact, and self-determination produce empowered employees who take active rather than passive roles in their work. At Ritz-Carlton hotels, all employees are empowered to spend up to $2,000 to solve customer service issues.[58] That's not $2,000 per year or $2,000 per day, it's $2,000 per incident. And, employees can spend that $2,000 without asking for managerial approval.[59] Bob Kharazmi, Ritz-Carlton's CEO, shares the powerful story of a wheelchair-bound guest who, overheard by a pool attendant, told her husband she wished they could have dinner on the beach. On his own, without management approval, the pool attendant worked with hotel engineering to build a wooden walkway over the sand and the kitchen to set up a table to serve the delighted couple dinner.[60]

9-5 INTERORGANIZATIONAL PROCESSES

An **interorganizational process** is a collection of activities that occur *among companies* to transform inputs into outputs that customers value. In other words, many companies work together to create a product or service that keeps customers happy. Nutella, the chocolate and hazelnut spread, is headquartered in Italy, has five factories in Europe, two in South America, and one each in Russia, North America, and Australia. Those factories work with suppliers in Turkey (hazelnuts), Malaysia (palm oil), Nigeria (cocoa), Brazil (sugar), and France (vanillin). The 401,500 tons of Nutella produced each year are then sold to grocers by sales offices and sales brokers in 160 different countries.[61]

In this section, you'll explore interorganizational processes by learning about 9-5a modular organizations and 9-5b virtual organizations.

9-5a Modular Organizations

Virgin America airline's CEO David Cush says, "We will outsource every job that we can that is not customer-facing."[62] Except for the core business activities that they can perform better, faster, and cheaper than others, **modular organizations** outsource all remaining business activities to outside companies,

Empowerment feeling of intrinsic motivation in which workers perceive their work to have impact and meaning and perceive themselves to be competent and capable of self-determination

Interorganizational process a collection of activities that take place among companies to transform inputs into outputs that customers value

Modular organization an organization that outsources noncore business activities to outside companies, suppliers, specialists, or consultants

Jim Spellman/WireImage/Getty Images

Exhibit 9.11
Modular Organization

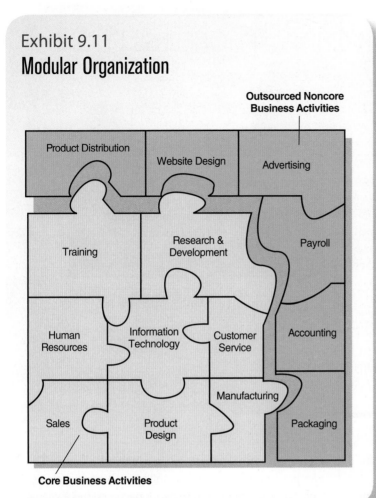

Outsourced Noncore Business Activities

Product Distribution · Website Design · Advertising · Training · Research & Development · Payroll · Human Resources · Information Technology · Customer Service · Accounting · Sales · Product Design · Manufacturing · Packaging

Core Business Activities

employees to the 125,000 employees already working at its 125 US warehouses and shipping hubs.[63] Amazon does not hire these seasonal workers itself, however. Instead, it contracts with Integrity Staffing Solutions to provide short-term labor. Integrity handles background checks, tax filings, payroll, unemployment, and other legal issues, saving Amazon roughly $200 million a year on payroll taxes alone. According to former Integrity manager Robert Capo Jr., "If Amazon [was] going to do this themselves, they would have to build an entire different infrastructure."[64] To obtain cost advantages, however, modular organizations need reliable partners – vendors and suppliers with whom they can work closely and can trust.

Modular organizations have disadvantages, too. The primary disadvantage is the loss of control that occurs when key business activities are outsourced to other companies. Also, companies may reduce their competitive advantage in two ways if they mistakenly outsource a core business activity. First, as a result of competitive and technological change, the noncore business activities a company has outsourced may suddenly become the basis for competitive advantage. Second, related to that point, suppliers to whom work is outsourced can sometimes become competitors.

suppliers, specialists, or consultants. The term *modular* is used because the business activities purchased from outside companies can be added and dropped as needed, much like adding pieces to a three-dimensional puzzle. Exhibit 9.11 depicts a modular organization in which the company has chosen to keep training, human resources, sales, product design, manufacturing, customer service, research and development, and information technology as core business activities but has outsourced the noncore activities of product distribution, web page design, advertising, payroll, accounting, and packaging.

The primary advantage of modular organizations is that they can cost significantly less to run than traditional organizations because they pay for outsourced labor, expertise, or manufacturing capabilities only when needed. Due to a surge in online holiday shopping, **Amazon's** fourth quarter revenue is consistently 50 percent higher than that of any other quarter throughout the year. To handle the increase in shipping this creates, Amazon adds 200,000 temporary

9-5b Virtual Organizations

In contrast to modular organizations, in which the interorganizational process revolves around a central company, a **virtual organization** is part of a network in which *many* companies share skills, costs, capabilities, markets, and customers with each other. Exhibit 9.12 shows a virtual organization in which, for today, the parts of a virtual company consist of product design, purchasing, manufacturing, advertising, and information technology. Unlike modular organizations, in which the outside organizations are tightly linked to one central company, virtual organizations work with some companies in the network alliance, but not with all. So, whereas a puzzle with various pieces is a fitting metaphor for a modular organization, a potluck dinner is an appropriate metaphor for

> **Virtual organization** an organization that is part of a network in which many companies share skills, costs, capabilities, markets, and customers to collectively solve customer problems or provide specific products or services

EMPTY DESKS BUT NEVER EMPTY "PHONELESS PHONE BOOTHS"

In a study of 10,000 global workers, 95 percent wanted more privacy at work, 85 percent loathed their open office plans, and 31 percent had to leave the office to get work done. This is why the phoneless phone booths (PPB) in open office spaces are never empty. A PPB is a small, private, quiet room with glass doors and a booth or table and chairs. They're supposed to be used for mobile phone conversations that would disrupt coworkers. Indeed, one of the most disruptive aspects of open offices is the *halfversation,* in which coworkers hear one side of a phone conversation, only to be distracted as their brains work to fill in the other half. The only problem with PPBs is they're always full. Elizabeth Tobey, marketing director for Code Ocean, a research collaboration platform, says, "People are always camped out in them." Kyle DeMilo says that's the point, "You move in with your laptop, cellphone, and maybe a snack. You can't crank out something with good grammar when the person behind you is slurping their soup."

Sources: J. Gross, "Can 'phone booths' solve the problem of open-plan offices?" *BBC Worklife*, August 9, 2019, accessed April 15, 2020, www.bbc.com/worklife/article/20190802-can-phone-booths-solve-privacy-issues-in-open-plan-offices; J. Medina & R. Mullenix, "How Neuroscience Is Optimizing the Office," *Wall Street Journal*, May 1, 2018, accessed April 15, 2020, www.wsj.com/articles/how-neuroscience-is-optimizing-the-office-1525185527; S. Needleman, "The Best Spot in the Office Is a Phone Booth – If You Can Get Into One," *Wall Street Journal*, November 27, 2018, accessed April 15, 2020, www.wsj.com/articles/the-best-spot-in-the-office-is-a-phone-boothif-you-can-get-into-one-1543333379.

a virtual organization. All participants bring their finest food dish but eat only what they want.

Another difference is that the working relationships between modular organizations and outside companies tend to be more stable and longer lasting than the shorter, often temporary, relationships found

Exhibit 9.12
Virtual Organizations

among the virtual companies in a network alliance. The composition of a virtual organization is always changing. The combination of network partners that a virtual corporation has at any one time depends on the expertise needed to solve a particular problem or provide a specific product or service. For instance, today the business might need to focus on advertising and product design, as shown in Exhibit 9.12, but tomorrow, the business could want something completely different. In this sense, the term "virtual organization" means the organization that exists "at the moment."

Virtual organizations have a number of advantages. They let companies share costs, and because members can quickly combine their efforts to meet customers' needs, they are fast and flexible. Finally, because each member of the network alliance is the best at what it does, virtual organizations should in theory provide better products and services in all respects.

As with modular organizations, a disadvantage of virtual organizations is that after work has been outsourced, it can be difficult to control the quality of work done by network partners. The greatest disadvantage, however, is that tremendous managerial skills are required to make a network of independent organizations work well together, especially because their relationships tend to be short and based on a single task or project. Virtual organizations are using two methods to solve this problem. The first is to use a *broker*. In traditional, hierarchical organizations, managers plan, organize, and control. But with the horizontal, interorganizational processes that characterize virtual organizations, the job of a broker is to create and assemble the knowledge, skills, and resources from different companies for outside parties, such as customers.[65] The second way to make networks of virtual organizations more manageable is to use a *virtual organization agreement* that, somewhat like a contract, specifies the schedules, responsibilities, costs, payouts, and liabilities for participating organizations.[66]

10 | Managing Teams

LEARNING OUTCOMES

10-1 Explain the good and bad of using teams.

10-2 Summarize the different kinds of teams.

10-3 Identify the general characteristics of work teams.

10-4 Outline the steps for enhancing work team effectiveness.

REDPIXEL.PL/Shutterstock.com

10-1 THE GOOD AND BAD OF USING TEAMS

Ninety-one percent of organizations are significantly improving their effectiveness by using work teams.[1] Procter & Gamble and Cummins Engine began using teams in 1962 and 1973, respectively. Boeing, Caterpillar, Champion International, Ford Motor Company, 3M, and General Electric established work teams in the mid- to late-1980s. Today, most companies use teams to tackle a variety of issues.[2] "Teams are ubiquitous. Whether we are talking about software development, Olympic hockey, disease outbreak response, or urban warfare, teams represent the critical unit that 'gets things done' in today's world."[3]

Work team a small number of people with complementary skills who hold themselves mutually accountable for pursuing a common purpose, achieving performance goals, and improving interdependent work processes

Work teams consist of a small number of people with complementary skills who hold themselves mutually accountable for pursuing a common purpose, achieving performance goals, and improving interdependent work processes.[4] By this definition, computer programmers working on separate projects in the same department of a company would not be considered a team. To be a team, the programmers would have to be interdependent and share responsibility and accountability for the quality and amount of computer code they produced.[5] Teams are becoming more important in many industries because they help organizations respond to specific problems and

challenges.[6] Though work teams are not the answer for every situation or organization, if the right teams are used properly and in the right settings, teams can dramatically improve company performance over more traditional management approaches while also instilling a sense of vitality in the workplace that is otherwise difficult to achieve.

Let's begin our discussion of teams by learning about **10-1a the advantages of teams, 10-1b the disadvantages of teams,** *and* **10-1c when to use and not use teams.**

10-1a The Advantages of Teams

Companies are making greater use of teams because teams have been shown to improve customer satisfaction, product and service quality, speed and efficiency in product development, employee job satisfaction, and decision-making.[7] For example, one survey indicated that 80 percent of companies with more than 100 employees use teams, and 90 percent of all US employees work part of their day in a team.[8] In fact, according to recent research, workers spend 50 percent more time in collaborative activities compared to just 20 years ago![9]

Teams help businesses increase *customer satisfaction* in several ways. One way is to create work teams that are trained to meet the needs of specific customers. 3D printing, also called additive manufacturing because one thin layer is added at a time, is now part of the production process in aviation, energy, pharmaceuticals, cars, and more. A survey of 900 manufacturers found that 14 percent use 3D printing today, and 48 percent plan to use it within a decade. Because legal issues related to additive manufacturing are different from those related to traditional manufacturing, the law practice of **Hunton & Williams** developed a cross-functional team of attorneys to assist clients adopting this new technology. Rather than seek out legal advice from several independent lawyers and then try to piece all the information together themselves, clients with significant investments in 3D printing can access a range of experts on product liability, taxes, intellectual property, insurance, litigation – and more – with just one phone call.[10]

Teams also help firms improve *product and service quality* in several ways.[11] In contrast to traditional organizational structures, in which management is responsible for organizational outcomes and performance, teams take direct responsibility for the quality of the products and service they produce and sell. Once considered a

COLLABORATION TOOL OVERLOAD IS KILLING TEAMS

A multitude of ways to communicate, from intranet discussion platforms to company chat programs like Slack and Google Chat, video meeting apps like Zoom, and Google Meet, and file-sharing apps like Google Drive and Dropbox overwhelm today's work teams. Forrester Research's Craig Le Clair says, "Workers don't want nine collaboration platforms." Add email to the list and it's the equivalent of having 10 different inboxes!

Seeking a simpler approach, J. Walter Thompson adopted Microsoft Teams, a threaded chat-based tool with video meeting capabilities integrated into Office365, which means that Office Apps like Excel, Word, and PowerPoint, and file storage and sharing like Microsoft's OneDrive, are available without leaving Teams.

Slack, which originated this way of communicating, has even greater functionality. Users can access file storage, task managers, phone and video calls, calendars and meeting scheduling, sales and accounting – 1,000 apps in all – without leaving Slack. Slack users report a one-third increase in productivity, a 49-percent drop in email, and 25 percent fewer meetings.

Kill collaboration tool overload. Make your teams more effective.

Zull Must/Shutterstock.com

Sources: J. Greene, "Beware Collaboration-Tool Overload," *Wall Street Journal*, March 12, 2017, accessed April 15, 2017, www.wsj.com/articles/beware-collaboration-tool-overload-1489370400; J. Nadler, "How to Survive Team Collaboration Tool Overload," Mitel, September 22, 2016, accessed April 15, 2017, www.mitel.com/blog/smb/2016/09/how-survive-team-collaboration-tool-overload.

---

solo career, over-the-road (OTR) truck drivers are increasingly pairing up to keep trucks moving more than 20 hours a day. Team driver Gary Helms says that he and his partner only stop for fuel, food, and a shower – otherwise, "We want the truck to move."[12] With state regulations limiting truck drivers to no more than 11 hours a day of driving, a single driver can cover roughly 500 miles per day. Driver teams, however, can cover 1,000 miles a day, which makes them incredibly valuable to online retailers and the organic-grocery industry, both of which promise customers fast delivery and fresh products. Driver teams are so valuable, in fact, that companies are willing to pay them $6 per mile – three times the normal price. According to transportation analyst Donald Broughton, driver teams provide freight speeds at a fraction of the price of alternative delivery methods.[13]

Another reason for using teams is that teamwork often leads to increased *job satisfaction*.[14] Teamwork can be more satisfying than traditional work because it gives workers a chance to improve their skills. This is often accomplished through **cross-training**, in which team members are taught how to do all or most of the jobs performed by the other team members. The advantage for the organization is that cross-training allows a team to function normally when one member is absent, quits, or is transferred. The advantage for workers is that cross-training broadens their skills and increases their capabilities while also making their work more varied and interesting.

Teamwork is also satisfying because work teams often receive proprietary business information that typically is available only to managers. **Atomic Object** is an employee-owned software company with an "open books" philosophy, which gives team members full access to financial information. Each quarter, founder Carl Erickson shares incomes statements and financial projections and explains how employee bonuses are determined. Financial data are accessible to all via spreadsheets and financial modeling tools to create better understanding about what makes Atomic profitable. Vice president and managing partner Shawn Crowley says each team "has a large key performance indicator (KPI)

Cross-training training team members to do all or most of the jobs performed by the other team members

monitor that displays . . . marketing and financial metrics. Openly showing our individual contributions allows us to see how we are performing against expectations and keeps us accountable to each other."[15] This means that Atomic's team members act like business owners. Said team member Brittany Hunter, "I don't mentally check out at 5 p.m. My mind is often going late into the night about things I can do to improve Atomic or promote it to outsiders, ways I can serve my clients better, how to solve hard problems on my projects."[16]

Team members also gain job satisfaction from unique leadership responsibilities that are not typically available in traditional organizations. Finally, teams share many of the advantages of group decision making discussed in Chapter 5. For instance, because team members possess different knowledge, skills, abilities, and experiences, a team is able to view problems from multiple perspectives. This diversity of viewpoints increases the odds that team decisions will solve the underlying causes of problems and not just address the symptoms. The increased knowledge and information available to teams also make it easier for them to generate more alternative solutions, a critical part of improving the quality of decisions. Because team members are involved in decision-making processes, they are also likely to be more committed to making those decisions work. In short, teams can do a much better job than individuals in two important steps of the decision-making process: defining the problem and generating alternative solutions.

10-1b The Disadvantages of Teams

Although teams can significantly improve customer satisfaction, product and service quality, speed and efficiency in product development, employee job satisfaction, and decision-making, using teams does not guarantee these positive outcomes. In fact, if you've ever participated in team projects in your classes, you're probably already aware of some of the problems inherent in work teams. Despite all of their promise, teams and teamwork are also prone to these significant disadvantages: initially high turnover, social loafing, and the problems associated with group decision-making.

The first disadvantage of work teams is *initially high turnover*. Teams aren't for everyone, and some workers balk at the responsibility, effort, and learning required in team settings. When **Zappos**, the online shoe company changed from a traditional to a team-based structure where there are no bosses and no titles and employees manage themselves, it offered everyone in the company three months of severance pay to leave if they decided that it wasn't right for them. Turns out that of its 1,500 employees, 14 percent decided to leave. After 10 months, that figure had risen to 18 percent overall and 38 percent among members of a special technology team charged with migrating Zappos's website to Amazon servers. Zappos's John Bunch, who is managing the transition, said, "Whatever the number of people who took the offer was the right number as they made the decision that was right for them and right for Zappos."[17]

Social loafing is another disadvantage of work teams. **Social loafing** occurs when workers withhold their efforts and fail to perform their share of the work.[18] A nineteenth-century French engineer named Maximilian Ringlemann first documented social loafing when he found that one person pulling on a rope alone exerted an average of 139 pounds of force on the rope. In groups of three, the average force dropped to 117 pounds per person. In groups of eight, the average dropped to just 68 pounds per person. Ringlemann concluded that the larger the team, the smaller the individual effort. In fact, social loafing is more likely to occur in larger groups where identifying and monitoring the efforts of individual team members can be difficult.[19] In other words, social loafers count on being able to blend into the background, where their lack of effort isn't easily spotted.

lenetstan/Shutterstock.com

> **Social loafing** behavior in which team members withhold their efforts and fail to perform their share of the work

Exhibit 10.1
When to Use and When Not to Use Teams

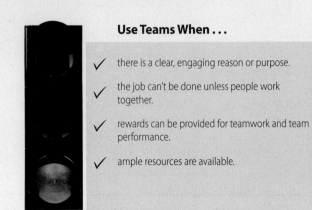

Use Teams When . . .

✓ there is a clear, engaging reason or purpose.

✓ the job can't be done unless people work together.

✓ rewards can be provided for teamwork and team performance.

✓ ample resources are available.

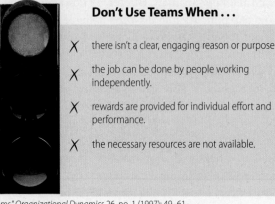

Don't Use Teams When . . .

✗ there isn't a clear, engaging reason or purpose.

✗ the job can be done by people working independently.

✗ rewards are provided for individual effort and performance.

✗ the necessary resources are not available.

iStock.com/Tunart

Source: R. Wageman, "Critical Success Factors for Creating Superb Self-Managing Teams," *Organizational Dynamics* 26, no. 1 (1997): 49–61.

From team-based class projects, most students already know about social loafers or "slackers," who contribute poor, little, or no work whatsoever. Not surprisingly, a study of 250 student teams found that the most talented students are typically the least satisfied with teamwork because of having to carry slackers and do a disproportionate share of their team's work.[20] A similar study of virtual teams (where team members work remotely) found that social loafing is higher among team members who are stretched by high levels of nonwork obligations (such as family, volunteering, and community work).[21] Perceptions of fairness are negatively related to the extent of social loafing within teams.[22]

Finally, teams share many of the *disadvantages of group decision making* discussed in Chapter 5, such as groupthink. In *groupthink*, members of highly cohesive groups feel intense pressure not to disagree with each other so that the group can approve a proposed solution. Because groupthink restricts discussion and leads to consideration of a limited number of alternative solutions, it usually results in poor decisions. Also, team decision-making takes considerable time, and team meetings can often be unproductive and inefficient. Another possible pitfall is *minority domination*, where just one or two people dominate team discussions, restricting consideration of different problem definitions and alternative solutions. Minority domination is especially likely to occur when the team leader talks so much during team discussions, effectively discouraging other team members from speaking up. When that happens, team performance drops significantly.[23] Finally, team members may not feel accountable for the decisions and actions taken by the team.

10-1c When to Use Teams

As the two previous subsections made clear, teams have significant advantages *and* disadvantages. Therefore, the question is not whether to use teams, but *when* and *where* to use teams for maximum benefit and minimum cost. As Doug Johnson, associate director at the Center for Collaborative Organizations at the University of North Texas, puts it, "Teams are a means to an end, not an end in themselves. You have to ask yourself questions first. Does the work require interdependence? Will the team philosophy fit company strategy? Will management make a long-term commitment to this process?"[24] Exhibit 10.1 provides some additional guidelines on when to use or not use teams.[25]

First, teams should be used when there is a clear, engaging reason or purpose for using them. Too many companies use teams because they're popular or because the companies assume that teams can fix all problems. Teams are much more likely to succeed if they know why they exist and what they are supposed to accomplish, and they are more likely to fail if they don't.

Second, teams should be used when the job can't be done unless people work together. This typically means that teams are needed when tasks are complex, require multiple perspectives, or require repeated interaction with others to complete. Because of the enormous complexity of today's cars, you would think that auto companies routinely use interconnected design teams. After all, the typical car has 30,000 parts, 80 different computer modules, indicators sensing how close other cars are when parking or going 70 mph, and the ability to automatically adjust braking, cornering, gas mileage, and acceleration. But auto companies don't routinely use interconnected design teams, as most designers are responsible for separate sections or parts of the car. Achim Badstübner, head of **Audi Group** exterior design, says, "We tend to make the mistake that we have an exterior department, an interior department and a technology department, and they all know what they're doing but the connection is not so good." Audi, however, takes a team approach. Badstübner says, "I think it's very important to basically lock them in one room, literally speaking. Then there is an interaction: you talk to the guy who does seats and he tells you something about his expertise and you might take something from him that helps you to develop a new wheel, for example." Badstübner says by connecting the teams, "you get a different result because through this method you get the best of every brain. I think you can't survive if you just depend on one brain to do a complex thing like (design) a car."[26]

Third, teams should be used when rewards can be provided for teamwork and team performance. Rewards that depend on team performance rather than individual performance are the key to rewarding team behaviors and efforts. You'll read more about team rewards later in the chapter, but for now it's enough to know that if the type of reward (individual versus team) is not matched to the type of performance (individual versus team), teams won't work.

10-2 KINDS OF TEAMS

*Let's continue our discussion of teams by learning about the different kinds of teams that companies such as Google and Maytag use to make themselves more competitive. We look first at **10-2a** how teams differ in terms of autonomy, which is the key dimension that makes one team different from another, and then at **10-2b** some special kinds of teams.*

10-2a Autonomy, the Key Dimension

Teams can be classified in a number of ways, such as permanent or temporary, or functional or cross-functional. However, studies indicate that the amount of autonomy possessed by a team is the key difference among teams.[27] *Autonomy* is the degree to which workers have the discretion, freedom, and independence to decide how and when to accomplish their jobs. Exhibit 10.2 shows how five kinds of teams differ in terms of autonomy. Moving left to right across the autonomy continuum at the top of the exhibit, traditional work groups and employee involvement groups have the least autonomy, semi-autonomous work groups have more autonomy, and, finally, self-managing teams and self-designing teams have the most autonomy. Moving from bottom to top along the left side of the exhibit, note that the number of responsibilities given to each kind of team increases directly with its autonomy. Let's review each of these kinds of teams and their autonomy and responsibilities in more detail.

The smallest amount of autonomy is found in **traditional work groups**, where two or more people work together to achieve a shared goal. In these groups, workers are responsible for doing the work or executing the task, but they do not have direct responsibility or control over their work. Workers report to managers, who are responsible for their performance and have the authority to hire and fire them, make job assignments, and control resources. For instance, suppose that an experienced worker blatantly refuses to do his share of the work, saying, "I've done my time. Let the younger employees do the work." In a team with high autonomy, the responsibility of getting this employee to put forth his fair share of effort would belong to his teammates. But, in a traditional work group, that responsibility belongs to the boss or supervisor. The supervisor in this situation calmly confronted the employee and told him, "We need your talent, [and] your knowledge of these machines. But if you won't work, you'll have to go elsewhere." Within days, the employee's behavior improved.[28]

Employee involvement teams, which have somewhat more autonomy, meet on company time on a weekly or monthly basis to provide advice or make suggestions to management concerning specific issues such as plant safety, customer relations, or product quality.[29] Though they offer advice and suggestions, they do not have the authority to make decisions. Membership on these teams is often voluntary, but members may be selected because of their expertise. The idea behind employee involvement teams is that the

Traditional work group a group composed of two or more people who work together to achieve a shared goal

Employee involvement team team that provides advice or makes suggestions to management concerning specific issues

Exhibit 10.2
Team Autonomy Continuum

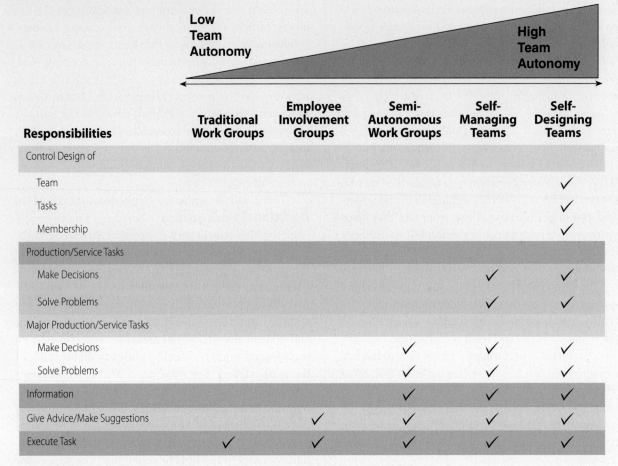

		High Team Autonomy			
Responsibilities	**Traditional Work Groups**	**Employee Involvement Groups**	**Semi-Autonomous Work Groups**	**Self-Managing Teams**	**Self-Designing Teams**
Control Design of					
Team					✓
Tasks					✓
Membership					✓
Production/Service Tasks					
Make Decisions				✓	✓
Solve Problems				✓	✓
Major Production/Service Tasks					
Make Decisions			✓	✓	✓
Solve Problems			✓	✓	✓
Information			✓	✓	✓
Give Advice/Make Suggestions		✓	✓	✓	✓
Execute Task	✓	✓	✓	✓	✓

The top-left of the continuum is labeled "Low Team Autonomy."

Sources: R. D. Banker, J. M. Field, R. G. Schroeder, and K. K. Sinha, "Impact of Work Teams on Manufacturing Performance: A Longitudinal Field Study," *Academy of Management Journal* 39 (1996): 867–890; J. R. Hackman, "The Psychology of Self-Management in Organizations," in *Psychology and Work: Productivity, Change, and Employment*, ed. M. S. Pallak and R. Perlof (Washington, D.C.: American Psychological Association), 85–136.

people closest to the problem or situation are best able to recommend solutions. For more than three years, production of Boeing's 787 Dreamliner (not the Boeing 737 Max, which was grounded for safety reasons) was delayed by multiple problems – parts shortages, improper installation, failed test flights, and more. Because of production delays, Boeing must build 10 planes per month, up from the typical two and a half planes. To meet this aggressive goal, it established nearly 200 employee involvement teams to analyze the way 787s are assembled and make changes to maximize efficiency. For example, one employee involvement team found that ducts already installed in the plane were being damaged because workers were kicking and stepping on them while doing other work. The damaged ducts then had to be removed and replaced. The team recommended that temporary covers be placed over the ducts, thus eliminating delays and reducing costs.[30]

Rawpixel.com/Shutterstock.com

Working from Home? Practical Tips for Zoom Virtual Meetings

» Test your setup by previewing your webcam and checking your audio and microphone recording levels (your cheapy plug-in ear buds/microphone should work fine). If your internet speed is slow, back down to audio only. Check the camera angle, remove what's in the background that shouldn't be. Make sure your lighting is in front of you and not behind you, which will shadow your face.

» Remember to look at the camera, not the person on the screen. If needed, elevate your laptop on a box or stack of books to center your face on the screen at a normal viewing angle.

» Mute your microphone when joining a meeting. Unmute the mic when you talk. This helps avoid noises from barking dogs or loud family members. Also, put your phone in vibration mode.

» Don't app switch out of Zoom. After 30 seconds, Zoom lets the virtual meeting host know that you're no longer active. It's like getting caught playing solitaire on your phone in a real meeting. So, don't do it. Maintain your attention.

» Turn on the security settings to avoid getting "zoom bombed" by outsiders (sometimes with pornography!). Look for the security padlock icon, where you can "lock the room" after starting, remove unwanted participants, and limit screen sharing. Passwords are on by default, as is "Waiting Room," which means only the host can admit people to the meeting.

» Finally, for fun, choose a photo for a virtual background, such as a photo of your real office or a place you've traveled. Or, invite a llama or a goat to your next Zoom meeting for less than $100. See www.sweetfarm.org/goat-2-meeting.

Sources: "Goat 2 Meeting," SweetFarm, accessed April 22, 2020, www.sweet-farm.org/goat-2-meeting; B. Chen, "The Dos and Don'ts of Online Video Meetings," *New York Times*, accessed April 22, 2020, www.nytimes.com/2020/03/25/technology/personaltech/online-video-meetings-etiquette-virus.html; T-P Chen, "A Bed. A Kiss. A Potato. Video Calls Reveal So Much About Your Colleagues," *Wall Street Journal*, April 8, 2020, accessed April 22, 2020, www.wsj.com/articles/a-bed-a-kiss-a-potato-video-calls-reveal-so-much-about-your-colleagues-11586361133; J. Lasky, "How to Look Your Best on a Webcam," *New York Times*, March 25, 2020, accessed April 22, 2020, www.nytimes.com/2020/03/25/realestate/coronavirus-webcam-appearance.html; T. Lorenz, "'Zoombombing': When Video Conferences Go Wrong," *New York Times*, April 7, 2020, accessed April 22, 2020, www.nytimes.com/2020/03/20/style/zoombombing-zoom-trolling.html; N. Nguyen, "Don't Get Bombed: How to Host Zoom Meetings, Hangouts, Houseparty and More," *Wall Street Journal*, April 2, 2020, accessed April 22, 2020, www.wsj.com/articles/dont-get-bombed-how-to-host-zoom-meetings-hangouts-houseparty-and-more-11585819821?mod=searchresults&page=1&pos=7; T. Warren, "Zoom Releases 5.0 Update With Security and Privacy Improvements," *The Verge*, April 22, 2020, accessed April 23, 2020, www.theverge.com/2020/4/22/21230962/zoom-update-security-privacy-features-improvements-download.

Semiautonomous work groups not only provide advice and suggestions to management but also have the authority to make decisions and solve problems related to the major tasks required to produce a product or service. Semiautonomous groups regularly receive information about budgets, work quality and performance, and competitors' products. Furthermore, members of semiautonomous work groups are typically cross-trained in a number of different skills and tasks. In short, semiautonomous work groups give employees the authority to make decisions that are typically made by supervisors and managers.

That authority is not complete, however. Managers still play a role, though one that is much reduced compared with traditional work groups, in supporting the work of semiautonomous work groups. The role a manager plays on a team usually evolves over time. "It may start with helping to transition problem-solving responsibilities to the team, filling miscellaneous requests for the team, and doing ad hoc tasks," says Steven Hitchcock, president of Axis Performance Advisors in Portland, Oregon. Later, the team may develop into a mini-enterprise, and the former manager becomes externally focused – sort of an account manager for the customer. Managers have to adjust what they do based on the sophistication of the team.[31] A lot of what managers of semiautonomous work groups do is ask good questions, provide resources, and facilitate performance of group goals.

Self-managing teams are different from semi-autonomous work groups in that team members manage and control *all* of the major tasks *directly related* to production of a product or service without first getting approval from management. This includes managing and controlling the acquisition of materials, making a product or providing a service, and ensuring timely delivery. Spotify, the streaming music company, organizes its 2,000 employees into self-organizing teams called squads. No larger than eight people, squads are completely responsible for a particular product function, like search algorithms, and decide what to do, how to do it, who to work with (other squads), and select their leaders.

> **Semiautonomous work group** a group that has the authority to make decisions and solve problems related to the major tasks of producing a product or service

> **Self-managing team** a team that manages and controls all of the major tasks of producing a product or service

Squads receive feedback from other squads and customers, and conduct postmortems every few weeks to analyze what is or is not working. All of these decisions are made without management's input or approval.[32]

The use of self-managing teams has significantly increased productivity at a number of other companies, increasing quality by 12 percent at AT&T, reducing errors by 13 percent at FedEx, and helping 3M increase production by 300 percent at one of its manufacturing plants.[33] Seventy-two percent of *Fortune* 1,000 companies have at least one self-managing team, up from 28 percent in 1987.[34]

Self-designing teams have all the characteristics of self-managing teams, but they can also control and change the design of the teams themselves, the tasks they do and how and when they do them, and the membership of the teams. **Valve**, a Bellevue, Washington, maker of video games, which describes itself as "Boss-free since 1996," has no managers.[35] In fact, the company defines "manager" in its employee handbook as, "The kind of people we don't have any of. So, if you see one, tell somebody, because it's probably the ghost of whoever was in this building before us."[36] "We do have a founder/president, but even he isn't your manager. This company is yours to steer – toward opportunities and away from risks. You have the power to green-light projects. You have the power to ship projects."[37] But what makes Valve's team self-designing (and not just self-managing), is that they control and change the teams themselves by deciding who gets hired, fired, promoted, and what they get paid (which is determined by peer rankings regarding contributions to team projects).[38]

While virtual teams have been common for years, many more employees found themselves relying heavily on group communication software to conduct business during the coronavirus pandemic.

Cabeca de Marmore/Shutterstock.com

10-2b Special Kinds of Teams

Companies are also increasingly using several other kinds of teams that can't easily be categorized in terms of autonomy: cross-functional teams, virtual teams, and project teams. Depending on how these teams are designed, they can be either low- or high-autonomy teams.

Cross-functional teams are intentionally composed of employees from different functional areas of the organization.[39] Because their members have different functional backgrounds, education, and experience, cross-functional teams usually attack problems from multiple perspectives and generate more ideas and alternative solutions, all of which are especially important when trying to innovate or solve problems creatively.[40] Cross-functional teams can be used almost anywhere in an organization and are often used in conjunction with matrix and product organizational structures (see Chapter 9). They can also be used either with part-time or temporary team assignments or with full-time, long-term teams. Starmark, a Fort Lauderdale, Florida, advertising agency, replaced its traditional department structure where, for example, ad copy was written and then handed over to the graphics department, with cross-functional teams consisting of a creative director, a copy writer, a data analyst for digital media metrics, a media and digital specialist, and an artist who guides or does the graphics work.[41]

Virtual teams are groups of geographically and/or organizationally dispersed coworkers who use a combination of telecommunications and information technologies to accomplish an organizational task.[42] Virtual teams were increasingly common, used by 28 percent of US-based corporations and 66 percent of multinational firms.[43] But with the coronavirus pandemic, virtual teams connecting via Zoom, Google Meet, or Microsoft Teams were suddenly used by most companies around the world. For example, because of "shelter in place" work restrictions, Pat Brown, CEO

Exhibit 10.3
Tips for Managing Virtual Teams

1. Establish clear expectations for communication, availability during offices hours, and frequency of check-ins.

2. Establish clear goals and milestones to help remote workers stay on track and accountable to the team.

3. Help team members set clear boundaries between work and family spaces.

4. Assign employees who have many outside obligations to teams whose members mostly have few nonwork obligations.

5. Ensure that team members have access to technology tools such as teleconferencing, file-sharing services, online meeting services, and collaboration portals.

6. Facilitate face-to-face communication with video conferencing or by requiring members of remote teams to work on-site several days each month.

7. Ensure the task is meaningful to the team and the company.

8. When building a virtual team, solicit volunteers as much as possible.

Sources: S. J. Perry, et al., "When Does Virtuality Really Work? Examining the Role of Work-Family and Virtuality in Social Loafing," *Journal of Management* 42 (2016), 449–479; C. Brooks, "4 Ways to Manage Remote Employees," *Business News Daily*, April 23, 2014, accessed April 30, 2016, http://www.businessnewsdaily.com/8895-remote-team-work.html.

of Impossible Foods, which makes plant-based meat, worked virtually with his executive team for nearly three months out of a spare room once used by his now-grown son. He said, "I do most of my business through this tiny portal in Isaac's room."[44] Members of virtual teams rarely meet face-to-face; instead, they use email, videoconferencing, and group communication software like Zoom. Virtual teams can be employee involvement teams, self-managing teams, or nearly any kind of team discussed in this chapter. Virtual teams are often (but not necessarily) temporary teams that are set up to accomplish a specific task.

Virtual teams are highly flexible because employees can work with each other regardless of physical location or time zones, but they're also much more complex than face-to-face teams when it comes to purpose, communication, and trust. Virtual teams often suffer from a lack of understanding regarding the team's purpose and team member roles. Dave Davis of RedFly Marketing has managed virtual teams for more than a decade and says, "You'd be surprised how many people will wait until halfway through a project to admit they don't understand something."[45] Because of distance and different time zones, 38 percent of virtual team members cite communication as their biggest challenge. Joe McCann says, CEO of NodeSource,

a JavaScript software company, says "It's a pain..., I'm gonna be honest. If everybody was in North America, it would be easier. We have an influential gentleman employee in Australia, so every Monday at 6 p.m. when I'd like to be winding down my day I have to have a very focused call."[46] Digital communication (email, IM, virtual conferencing) accounts for 63 percent of communication on virtual teams, yet 23 percent of team members find that long email discussion threads threaten (rather than help) effective project communication.[47] So, it's important for members to know when to use different communication media. Mary Ellen Slater, a manager at **Reputation Capital**, says, "At Rep Cap, we IM each other throughout the day, but there are times when a phone call or face-to-face meeting is better. A new project or something that deviates from our usual process may merit a phone call."[48] Finally, trust is critical for virtual teams to be successful. Andrea Rozman, owner of Your Gal Friday, a company that provides virtual personal assistants, says, "You have to take that leap of faith. You have to believe that once you hand them the work, they will do it, and get it done on time."[49] See Exhibit 10.3 for more information on managing virtual teams.

Project teams are created to complete specific, onetime projects or tasks within a limited time.[50] Project teams are often used to develop new products, significantly improve existing products, roll out new information systems, or build new factories or offices. The project team is typically led by a project manager who has the overall responsibility for planning, staffing, and managing the team, which usually includes employees from different functional areas. Effective project teams demand both individual and collective responsibility.[51] One advantage of project teams is that drawing employees from different functional areas can reduce or eliminate communication barriers. In turn, as long as team members feel free to express their ideas, thoughts, and concerns, free-flowing communication encourages cooperation among separate departments and typically speeds up the design process.[52] Another advantage of project teams is their flexibility. When projects are finished, project team members either move on to the next project or return to their functional units. For example, publication of this book required designers, editors, page compositors, and web designers, among others. When the task was finished, these people applied their skills to other textbook projects. Because of this flexibility, project teams are often used with the matrix organizational designs discussed in Chapter 9.

Project team a team created to complete specific, onetime projects or tasks within a limited time

WORK TEAM CHARACTERISTICS

"Why did I ever let you talk me into teams? They're nothing but trouble."[53] Lots of managers have this reaction after making the move to teams. Many don't realize that this reaction is normal, both for them and for workers. In fact, such a reaction is characteristic of the *storming* stage of team development (discussed in Section 10-3e). Managers who are familiar with these stages and with the other important characteristics of teams will be better prepared to manage the predictable changes that occur when companies make the switch to team-based structures.

*Understanding the characteristics of work teams is essential for making teams an effective part of an organization. Therefore, in this section you'll learn about **10-3a team norms, 10-3b team cohesiveness, 10-3c team size, 10-3d team conflict,** and **10-3e the stages of team development**.*

10-3a Team Norms

Over time, teams develop **norms**, which are informally agreed-on standards that regulate team behavior.[54] Norms are valuable because they let team members know what is expected. One of the key ways in which norms develop is by observing nearby team members. A two-year study in which 2,000 workers were randomly assigned to locations within offices found that ten percent of an employee's productivity, effectiveness, and work quality was determined by who they sat next to. When an average performer was replaced by a top performer, the workers seated nearby increased their performance by ten percent. Likewise, when productive workers (fast, but lacking quality) sat next to quality workers (superior work done slowly), quality workers became 13 percent more productive (faster) and productive workers were 17 percent more effective (higher quality).[55] In other words, one of the ways in which team members know what is expected of them (i.e., norms) is by taking immediate cues from those around them.

Studies indicate that norms are one of the most powerful influences on work behavior because they regulate the everyday actions that allow teams to function effectively. Team norms are often associated with positive

Norms informally agreed-on standards that regulate team behavior

TEN MINUTES, TEAM HUDDLES AND POSITIVE NORMS

It is critical for teams to establish positive norms early and reinforce them. At the Rotterdam Eye Hospital in The Netherlands, each shift begins with busy medical providers using a "team-start" huddle to share names and responsibilities, rate their moods (good, OK, or stressed), and discuss shift issues (particular patients in need of special care). The huddle ends with two team members drawing a card to test their knowledge, such as "What are the five steps in hand hygiene?" or to ask them to report back at the end of a shift, "Are we avoiding the common mistakes often made when preparing medications?" Reinforcing team care norms has improved patient safety, caregiver job satisfaction, and team commitment ("I now feel part of the caregiver team").

Source: R. van der Heijde & D. Deichmann, "How One Hospital Improved Patient Safety in 10 Minutes a Day," *Harvard Business Review*, October 30, 2018, accessed April 22, 2020, https://hbr.org/2018/10/how-one-hospital-improved-patient-safety-in-10-minutes-a-day.

outcomes such as stronger organizational commitment, more trust in management, and stronger job and organizational satisfaction.[56] Effective work teams develop norms about the quality and timeliness of job performance, absenteeism, safety, and honest expression of ideas and opinions.

At **Alphabet**, a special task force called Project Aristotle spent four years reviewing published research on teams, as well as analyzing internal data on 180 Google work teams.[57] Unable to find identifiable patterns related to the sizes, skills, or tenures of teams or their team members, Project Aristotle eventually found that Google's most successful teams had positive norms with high levels of psychological safety, a concept that Harvard Business School professor Amy Edmondson defines as "a sense of confidence that the team will not embarrass, reject or punish someone for speaking up . . . the team is safe for interpersonal risk-taking."[58] Building on that study, a team of researchers led by Carnegie Mellon professor Anita Woolley found that the best-performing teams engaged in conversational turn-taking. Woolley explained, "As long as everyone got a chance to talk, the team did well. But if only one person or a small group spoke all the time, the collective intelligence (of the team)

MINNESOTA VIKINGS' DONUT CLUB RULES

1. Players always buy. The players rotate during the regular season, but the trainers and staff never buy, since the donuts are a nod of appreciation to them.
2. Lateness will not be tolerated.
3. Do not touch the donuts before the designated time. Do not eat the donuts before the designated time. (The boxes open at 7:50 a.m., but no one can touch until 8 a.m. There are penalties.)
4. Finish the donut.
5. Attendance counts.
6. Wear your colors with pride. (There's a club T-shirt.)
7. Once a member of Donut Club, always a member of Donut Club.

iStock.com/pjohnson1

declined.[59] Woolley's findings are consistent with the previously discussed research showing that overly dominant team leaders minimized discussion and hurt team performance.

Norms can also influence team behavior in negative ways. For example, most people would agree that damaging organizational property; saying or doing something to hurt someone at work; intentionally doing one's work badly, incorrectly, or slowly; griping about coworkers; deliberately bending or breaking rules; and doing something to harm the company or boss are negative behaviors. A study of workers from 34 teams in 20 different organizations found that teams with negative norms strongly influenced their team members to engage in these negative behaviors. In fact, the longer individuals were members of a team with negative norms and the more frequently they interacted with their teammates, the more likely they were to perform negative behaviors. Because team norms typically develop early in the life of a team, these results indicate how important it is for teams to establish positive norms from the outset.[60]

10-3b Team Cohesiveness

Cohesiveness is another important characteristic of work teams. **Cohesiveness** is the extent to which team members are attracted to a team and motivated to remain in it.[61] What can be done to promote team cohesiveness? First, make sure that all team members are present at team meetings and activities. Team cohesiveness suffers when members are allowed to withdraw from the team and miss team meetings and events.[62] Second, create additional opportunities for teammates to work together by rearranging work schedules and creating common workspaces. Bank of America discovered the value of cohesive teams when it did a study tracking employee behavior. When Bank of America experimented by having call center employees wear sensors monitoring their movements throughout the office, it found that the most productive employees were in cohesive teams that communicated frequently. So, to encourage more interaction, it scheduled team members to all have breaks at the same time, rather than solo breaks. As a result, worker productivity rose 10 percent.[63] When task interdependence is high, and team members have lots of chances to work together, team cohesiveness tends to increase.[64] Third, engaging in nonwork activities as a team can help build cohesion. The NFL's Minnesota Vikings "Donut Club" is a key way in which the team builds cohesiveness among players. Head trainer Eric Sugarman says, "It's for the guys who aren't injured (who pay for the donuts) to be able to support the guys who get mandatory treatment all week (who eat the donuts)." The Donut Club, which meets every Saturday at 7:50 a.m., has a few key rules. Don't be late. Sugarman says, "The Donut Club waits for nobody." Do not touch or eat the donuts

Cohesiveness the extent to which team members are attracted to a team and motivated to remain in it

SHOOTING THE BOSS: WHEN PAINTBALL WRECKED TEAM BUILDING

"At a previous job, our boss would sometimes take us bowling. This time, though, he wanted to go paint-balling. I'm not a good shot, and I wasn't aiming for him, but my paintball went awry. The next thing I knew, he was on the floor. The game was stopped, the ambulance came, and people started talking about potential liver rupture and damage to his kidneys. He was OK. A preexisting condition had flared up. After the event, he told me it wasn't my fault, but I felt horrible and left the company six weeks later."

Source: K. Morrell, "What's Your Most Awkward-Team-Building Experience?" *Bloomberg*, April 5, 2017, accessed April 15, 2017, www.bloomberg.com/news/articles/2017-04-05/what-s-your -most-awkward-team-building-experience.

before 8:00 a.m. Sugarman calls this 10 minutes "basically, a donut viewing." Retired quarterback Gus Frerrote, who started buying the donuts, said, "I love that there are rules. That's what makes the game fun. It's really nice to have a common bond about something stupid like that."[65] Finally, companies build team cohesiveness by making employees feel that they are part of an organization.

10-3c Team Size

The relationship between team size and performance appears to be curvilinear. Very small or very large teams may not perform as well as moderately sized teams. Amazon CEO Jeff Bezos tends to prefer small teams, saying, "If I see more than two pizzas for lunch, the team is too big."[66] For most teams, the right size is somewhere between six and nine members.[67] A team of this size is small enough for the team members to get to know each other and for each member to have an opportunity to contribute in a meaningful way to the success of the team. At the same time, the team is large enough to take advantage of team members' diverse skills, knowledge, and perspectives. It is also easier to instill a sense of responsibility and mutual accountability in teams of this size.[68] The *Wall Street Journal*'s Sue Shellenbarger says managers invite too many people to meetings. For analyzing possible causes of problems, invite four to six people.[69] Bain & Company's Michael Mankins follows the "rule of seven," which says the chances of making good decisions drop 10 percent for every person beyond seven. Says Mankins, "By the time you get 17 people, the chances of your actually making a decision are zero."[70] So, for making decisions, invite 4 to 7.

Team size has a significant impact on the value of a company as well. Among companies with a market capitalization of $10 billion or more, those with smaller boards of directors outperform their peers by 8.5 percent, and those with larger boards underperform their peers by nearly 11 percent. With only seven directors, Netflix's board was able to spend nine months discussing a potential price increase. Director Jay Hoag says, "We get in-depth. That's easier with a small group." Netflix outperforms its sector peers by 32 percent.[71]

When teams get too large, team members find it difficult to get to know one another, and the team may splinter into smaller subgroups. When this occurs, subgroups sometimes argue and disagree, weakening overall team cohesion. As teams grow, there is also a greater chance of *minority domination*, where just a few team members dominate team discussions. Even if minority domination doesn't occur, larger groups may not have time for all team members to share their input. And when team members feel that their contributions are unimportant or not needed, the result is less involvement, effort, and accountability to the team.[72] Large teams also face logistical problems such as finding an appropriate time or place to meet. Finally, the incidence of social loafing, discussed earlier in the chapter, is much higher in large teams.

Just as team performance can suffer when a team is too large, it can also be negatively affected when a team is too small. Teams with just a few people may lack the diversity of skills and knowledge found in larger teams. Also, teams that are too small are unlikely to gain the advantages of team decision-making (multiple perspectives, generating more ideas and alternative solutions, and stronger commitment) found in larger teams.

What signs indicate that a team's size needs to be changed? If decisions are taking too long, if the team has difficulty making decisions or taking action, if a few members dominate the team, or if the commitment or efforts of team members are weak, chances are the team is too big. In contrast, if a team is having difficulty coming up with ideas or generating solutions, or if the team does not have the expertise to address a specific problem, chances are the team is too small.

10-3d Team Conflict

Conflict and disagreement are inevitable in most teams. But this shouldn't surprise anyone. From time to time, people who work together are going to disagree about what and how things get done. What causes conflict in teams? Although almost anything can lead to conflict – casual remarks that unintentionally offend a team member or fighting over scarce resources – the primary cause of team conflict is disagreement over team goals and priorities.[73] Other common causes of team conflict include disagreements over task-related issues, interpersonal incompatibilities, and simple fatigue.

Though most people view conflict negatively, the key to dealing with team conflict is not avoiding it, but rather making sure that the team experiences the right kind of conflict. In Chapter 5, you learned about *c-type conflict*, or *cognitive conflict*, which focuses on problem-related differences of opinion, and *a-type conflict*, or *affective conflict*, which refers to the emotional reactions that can occur when disagreements become personal rather than professional.[74] Cognitive conflict is strongly associated with improvements in team performance, whereas affective conflict is strongly associated with decreases in team performance.[75] Why does this happen? With cognitive conflict, team members disagree because their different experiences and expertise lead them to different views of the problem and solutions. Indeed, managers who participated on teams that emphasized cognitive conflict described their teammates as "smart," "team players," and "best in the business." They described their teams as "open," "fun," and "productive." One manager summed up the positive attitude that team members had about cognitive conflict by saying, "We scream a lot, then laugh, and then resolve the issue."[76] Thus, cognitive conflict is also characterized by a willingness to examine, compare, and reconcile differences to produce the best possible solution.

By contrast, affective conflict often results in hostility, anger, resentment, distrust, cynicism, and apathy. Managers who participated on teams that experienced affective conflict described their teammates as "manipulative," "secretive," "burned out," and "political."[77] Dana Browlee, who runs a corporate training company in Atlanta, gives the example of the naysayer, who, "whatever you bring up, it will never work," and the silent plotter, who she says, "may be the quiet person sitting in the back, but as soon as the (team) meeting is over, they're over by the Coke machine, planning your demise."[78] Not surprisingly, affective conflict can make people uncomfortable and cause them to withdraw and decrease their commitment to a team.[79] Affective conflict also lowers the satisfaction of team members, may lead to personal hostility between coworkers, and can decrease team cohesiveness.[80] So, unlike cognitive conflict, affective conflict undermines team performance by preventing teams from engaging in the kinds of activities that are critical to team effectiveness.

So, what can managers do to manage team conflict? First, they need to realize that emphasizing cognitive conflict alone won't be enough. Studies show that cognitive and affective conflicts often occur together in a given team activity! Sincere attempts to reach agreement on a difficult issue can quickly deteriorate from cognitive to affective conflict if the discussion turns personal, and tempers and emotions flare. While cognitive conflict is clearly the better approach to take, efforts to engage in cognitive conflict should be managed well and checked before they deteriorate, causing the team to become unproductive.

Can teams disagree and still get along? Fortunately, they can. In an attempt to study this issue, researchers examined team conflict in 12 high-tech companies. In four of the companies, work teams used cognitive conflict to address work problems but did so in a way that minimized the occurrence of affective conflict.[81]

There are several ways teams can have a "good fight."[82] First, work with more, rather than less, information. A senior retail executive said, "Disagreement is great as long as it's fact-based."[83] If data are plentiful, objective, and up-to-date, teams will focus on issues,

Exhibit 10.4
Stages of Team Development

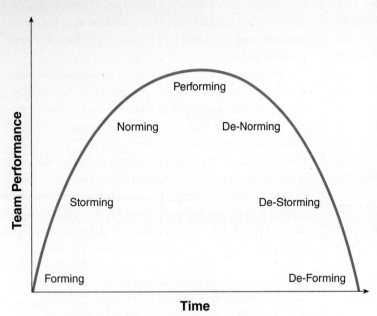

Sources: J. F. McGrew, J. G. Bilotta, and J. M. Deeney, "Software Team Formation and Decay: Extending the Standard Model for Small Groups," *Small Group Research* 30, no. 2 (1999): 209–234; B. W. Tuckman, "Development Sequence in Small Groups," *Psychological Bulletin* 63, no. 6 (1965): 384–399.

cohesion, and just makes being in teams fun. Fifth, maintain a balance of power by involving as many people as possible in the decision process. And, sixth, resolve issues without forcing a consensus. Consensus means that everyone must agree before decisions are finalized. Effectively, requiring consensus gives everyone on the team veto power. Nothing gets done until everyone agrees, which, of course, is nearly impossible. As a result, insisting on consensus usually promotes affective rather than cognitive conflict. If team members can't agree after constructively discussing their options, it's better to have the team leader make the final choice. Most team members can accept the team leader's choice if they've been thoroughly involved in the decision process.

10-3e Stages of Team Development

As teams develop and grow, they pass through four stages of development. As shown in Exhibit 10.4, those stages are forming, storming, norming, and performing.[85]

Although not every team passes through each of these stages, teams that do tend to be better performers.[86] This holds true even for teams composed of seasoned executives. After a period of time, however, if a team is not managed well, its performance may start to deteriorate as the team begins a process of decline and progresses through the stages of de-norming, de-storming, and de-forming.[87]

Forming is the initial stage of team development. This is the getting-acquainted stage in which team members first meet each other, form initial impressions, and try to get a sense of what it will be like to be part of the team. Some of the first team norms will be established during this stage as team members begin to find out what behaviors will and won't be accepted by the team. During this stage, team leaders should allow time for team members to get to know each other, set early ground rules, and begin to set up a preliminary team structure.

Conflicts and disagreements often characterize the second stage of team development, **storming**. As team members begin working together, different personalities and work styles may clash. Team members become more assertive at this stage and more willing to state opinions. This is also the stage when team members jockey for

not personalities. Second, develop multiple alternatives to enrich debate. Focusing on multiple solutions diffuses conflict by getting the team to keep searching for a better solution. Positions and opinions are naturally more flexible with five alternatives than with just two.

Third, establish common goals. Remember, most team conflict arises from disagreements over team goals and priorities. For example, says consultant and author Al Pittampalli, "Imagine a software team who gathers to discuss a disgruntled VIP customer, threatening, quite publicly, to jump ship to a competitor. While one attendee thinks the path forward is obvious and focuses on crafting an implementation plan..., another is intent on generating alternative solutions..., while yet another attendee is still trying to figure out whether the exit of this pompous hellion is, in fact, even a problem..."[84] Therefore, common goals encourage collaboration and minimize conflict over a team's purpose.

Fourth, inject humor into the workplace. Humor relieves tension, builds

Forming the first stage of team development, in which team members meet each other, form initial impressions, and begin to establish team norms

Storming the second stage of development, characterized by conflict and disagreement, in which team members disagree over what the team should do and how it should do it

To effectively motivate teams:

1. Teams must have a high degree of autonomy.

2. Teams must be empowered with control of resources.

3. Teams need structural accommodation.

4. Teams need bureaucratic immunity.

iStock.com/RoscoPhoto

At this point, members should be fully committed to the team and think of themselves as members of a team and not just employees. Team members often become intensely loyal to one another at this stage and feel mutual accountability for team successes and failures. Trivial disagreements, which can take time and energy away from the work of the team, should be rare. At this stage, teams get a lot of work done, and it is fun to be a team member.

The team should not become complacent, however. Without effective management, its performance may begin to decline as the team passes through the stages of **de-norming**, **de-storming**, and **de-forming**.[88] John Puckett, manufacturing vice president for circuit-board manufacturer XEL Communications, says, "The books all say you start in this state of chaos and march through these various stages, and you end up in this state of ultimate self-direction, where everything is going just great. They never tell you it can go back in the other direction, sometimes just as quickly."[89]

10-4 ENHANCING WORK TEAM EFFECTIVENESS

*Making teams work is a challenging and difficult process. Nonetheless, companies can increase the likelihood that teams will succeed by carefully managing **10-4a the setting of team goals and priorities** and **10-4b how work team members are selected, 10-4c trained,** and **10-4d compensated.**[90]*

position and try to establish a favorable role for themselves on the team. In addition, team members are likely to disagree about what the group should do and how it should do it. Team performance is still relatively low, given that team cohesion is weak and team members are still reluctant to support each other. Because teams that get stuck in the storming stage are almost always ineffective, it is important for team leaders to focus the team on team goals and on improving team performance. Team members need to be particularly patient and tolerant with each other in this stage.

During **norming**, the third stage of team development, team members begin to settle into their roles as team members. Positive team norms will have developed by this stage, and teammates should know what to expect from each other. Petty differences should have been resolved, friendships will have developed, and group cohesion will be relatively strong. At this point, team members will have accepted team goals, be operating as a unit, and, as indicated by the increase in performance, be working together effectively. This stage can be very short and is often characterized by someone on the team saying, "I think things are finally coming together." Note, however, that teams may also cycle back and forth between storming and norming several times before finally settling into norming.

In the last stage of team development, **performing**, performance improves because the team has finally matured into an effective, fully functioning team.

10-4a Setting Team Goals and Priorities

In Chapter 5, you learned that having specific, measurable, attainable, realistic, and timely (S.M.A.R.T.) goals is one of the most effective means for improving

Norming the third stage of team development, in which team members begin to settle into their roles, group cohesion grows, and positive team norms develop

Performing the fourth and final stage of team development, in which performance improves because the team has matured into an effective, fully functioning team

De-norming a reversal of the norming stage, in which team performance begins to decline as the size, scope, goal, or members of the team change

De-storming a reversal of the storming phase, in which the team's comfort level decreases, team cohesion weakens, and angry emotions and conflict may flare

De-forming a reversal of the forming stage, in which team members position themselves to control pieces of the team, avoid each other, and isolate themselves from team leaders

individual job performance. Fortunately, team goals also improve team performance. In fact, team goals lead to much higher team performance 93 percent of the time.[91]

Why is setting *specific* team goals so critical to team success? One reason is that increasing a team's performance is inherently more complex than just increasing one individual's job performance. For instance, consider that any team is likely to involve at least four different kinds of goals: each member's goal for the team, each member's goal for himself or herself on the team, the team's goal for each member, and the team's goal for itself.[92] In other words, without a specific goal for the team itself (the last of the four goals listed), team members may head off in all directions at once pursuing these other goals. Consequently, setting a specific goal *for the team* clarifies team priorities by providing a clear focus and purpose.

Challenging team goals affect how hard team members work. In particular, they greatly reduce the incidence of social loafing. When faced with difficult goals, team members necessarily expect everyone to contribute. Consequently, they are much more likely to notice and complain if a teammate isn't doing his or her share. In fact, when teammates know each other well, when team goals are specific, when team communication is good, and when teams are rewarded for team performance (discussed later in this section), there is only a 1 in 16 chance that teammates will be social loafers.[93]

What can companies and teams do to ensure that team goals lead to superior team performance? One increasingly popular approach is to give teams stretch goals. *Stretch goals* are extremely ambitious goals that workers don't know how to reach.[94] Indian-based Tata Steel's stretch goal is a 25 percent profit margin. Managing Director TV Narendran said, "Tata Steel has always had a rich history of setting steep targets which we may not know how to achieve. But that is how innovation comes about. Because if we know how to achieve the target, then it is only about execution. If you want to get people to think out of the box, then you have to have those stretch targets."[95] Likewise, CEO Jim Snee says Hormel Foods' goal is to make 15 percent of revenues from products no more than five years old. Says Snee, "The 15 percent is a very aggressive number. It's a stretch goal for our organization."[96] Hormel also aims to increase sales

and profits by 5 percent and 10 percent, respectively, each year.

Four things must occur for stretch goals to effectively motivate teams.[97] First, teams must have a high degree of autonomy or control over how they achieve their goals. Second, teams must be empowered with control of resources, such as budgets, workspaces, computers, or whatever else they need to do their jobs. Third, teams need structural accommodation. **Structural accommodation** means giving teams the ability to change organizational structures, policies, and practices if doing so helps them meet their stretch goals. Finally, teams need bureaucratic immunity. **Bureaucratic immunity** means that teams no longer have to go through the frustratingly slow process of multilevel reviews and sign-offs to get management approval before making changes. Once granted bureaucratic immunity, teams are immune from the influence of various organizational groups and are accountable only to top management. **Experian**, a credit reporting company, helps organizations and banks make lending decisions and individuals manage credit scores. Experian's Eric Haller went to his boss with a unique proposal to find out customers' unsolved problems (such as how to lend to people with no credit history), fix them, and turn those solutions into new product lines. His boss replied, "I've wanted to do this for years, so I'll give you the money if you can find the people."[98] With three years of guaranteed funding and just one requirement, a biannual performance report, Haller formed Experian DataLabs and hired his "navy seals of data science."[99] With freedom thanks to bureaucratic immunity, Experian DataLabs has grown in six years from 8 to 40 data scientists and now earns eight-figure revenues.[100]

10-4b Selecting People for Teamwork

University of Southern California management professor Edward Lawler says, "People are very naive about how easy it is to create a team. Teams are the Ferraris of work design. They're high performance but high maintenance and expensive."[101] It's almost impossible to have an effective work team without carefully selecting people who are suited for teamwork or for working on a particular team. A focus on teamwork (individualism-collectivism), team level, and team diversity can help companies choose the right team members.[102]

Structural accommodation the ability to change organizational structures, policies, and practices in order to meet stretch goals

Bureaucratic immunity the ability to make changes without first getting approval from managers or other parts of an organization

Exhibit 10.5
The Team Player Inventory

		Strongly Disagree				Strongly Agree
1.	I enjoy working on team/group projects.	1	2	3	4	5
2.	Team/group project work easily allows others to not pull their weight.	1	2	3	4	5
3.	Work that is done as a team/group is better than work done individually.	1	2	3	4	5
4.	I do my best work alone rather than in a team/group.	1	2	3	4	5
5.	Team/group work is overrated in terms of the actual results produced.	1	2	3	4	5
6.	Working in a team/group gets me to think more creatively.	1	2	3	4	5
7.	Teams/groups are used too often when individual work would be more effective.	1	2	3	4	5
8.	My own work is enhanced when I am in a team/group situation.	1	2	3	4	5
9.	My experiences working in team/group situations have been primarily negative.	1	2	3	4	5
10.	More solutions/ideas are generated when working in a team/group situation than when working alone.	1	2	3	4	5

Reverse score items 2, 4, 5, 7, and 9. Then add the scores for items 1 to 10. Higher scores indicate a preference for teamwork, whereas lower total scores indicate a preference for individual work.

Source: T. J. B. Kline, "The Team Player Inventory: Reliability and Validity of a Measure of Predisposition Toward Organizational Team-Working Environments," *Journal for Specialists in Group Work* 24, no. 1 (1999): 102–112.

Are you more comfortable working alone or with others? If you strongly prefer to work alone, you may not be well suited for teamwork. Studies show that job satisfaction is higher in teams when team members prefer working with others.[103] An indirect way to measure someone's *preference for teamwork* is to assess the person's degree of individualism or collectivism. **Individualism-collectivism** is the degree to which a person believes that people should be self-sufficient and that loyalty to one's self is more important than loyalty to one's team or company.[104] *Individualists*, who put their own welfare and interests first, generally prefer independent tasks in which they work alone. In contrast, *collectivists*, who put group or team interests ahead of self-interests, generally prefer interdependent tasks in which they work with others. Collectivists would also rather cooperate than compete and are fearful of disappointing team members or of being ostracized from teams. Given these differences, it makes sense to select team members who are collectivists rather than individualists. In fact, many companies use individualism-collectivism as an initial screening device for team members. If team diversity is desired, however, individualists may also be appropriate, as discussed next. To determine your preference for teamwork, take the Team Player Inventory shown in Exhibit 10.5.

Team level is the average level of ability, experience, personality,

Building an effective team means selecting people who are suited for teamwork.

Individualism-collectivism the degree to which a person believes that people should be self-sufficient and that loyalty to one's self is more important than loyalty to team or company

Team level the average level of ability, experience, personality, or any other factor on a team

Narcissism: There's No "N" in Team Chemistry

There's no "I" in team. There's no "N," either. "N" stands for narcissist, a person with "an excessive interest in or admiration of themselves." Narcissists are often arrogant, lack empathy for others, and think of themselves first – and always. Narcissists may be talented, but they aren't exactly great teammates. An innovative study of the National Basketball Association (NBA) found that teams with more narcissistic players didn't play as well together and had worse records than NBA teams with less talented, but more team-oriented players. Championship teams often have a special "team chemistry," where players sacrifice personal statistics for team success, or take reduced roles so the team can gain better offensive or defensive matchups. What if, in reality, team chemistry is simply a lack of narcissism and an abundance of team orientation and self-sacrifice? It's almost impossible to have an effective work team without carefully selecting people suited for teamwork. So, when picking team members, say no to narcissists.

Source: E. Grijalva, T. Maynes, K. Badura and S. Whiting, "Examining the "I" in Team: A Longitudinal Investigation of the Influence of Team Narcissism Composition on Team Outcomes in the NBA," *Academy of Management Journal* 63, no. 1 (2020): 7–33.

or any other factor on a team. For example, a high level of team experience means that a team has particularly experienced team members. This does not mean that every member of the team has considerable experience, but that enough team members do to significantly raise the average level of experience on the team. Team level is used to guide selection of teammates when teams need a particular set of skills or capabilities to do their jobs well. For example, **SAP**, a German software company, has struggled to deliver cloud-based solutions and hopes to replicate a team approach to innovation pioneered by Xerox Parc in the 1970s. So, it hired Alan Kay, a renowned technologist who was a computer scientist at Xerox Parc, to build a similar high-level team. So far, Kay recruited 20 polymathic technologists, funded their research projects, and gave them the independence to work alone to pursue their research interests.[105] (A polymath is someone who is a genius in more than one field.) Kay understood the risks of having too many "stars." Based on his research on NBA teams, management professor Adam Galinsky says, "If you have too many people (on teams), and they all want to be stars, coordination (on the team) goes down. But if you have a bunch of star programmers all working on their own projects, and they don't need to integrate their programs with each other, then more stars is probably better."[106]

Whereas team level represents the average level or capability on a team, **team diversity** represents the variances or differences in ability, experience, personality, or any other factor on a team.[107] From a practical perspective, why is team diversity important? Professor Alex Pentland's research at MIT's Human Dynamics lab shows that the most successful teams, (1) talk with everyone on the team, balancing talking with listening, (2) have a diversity of ideas and team members who are open to new ideas, and (3) are goal oriented. Pentland says, "You need everyone exploring slightly different things, but doing in the same direction."[108] Team diversity ensures that strong teams not only have talented members (that is, a high team level), but those talented members also have different abilities, experiences, and personalities from which to view and solve problems.

It typically takes 18 to 36 months and billions of dollars to develop new car models. So, auto manufacturers take the product development process seriously, making sure there is team diversity among those selected for product development teams. The head of product development at one auto manufacturer said, "We are very careful about who we select. We get the people with the right functional backgrounds, who have consistently done innovative work, and we make sure there is a mix of them from different backgrounds and that they are different ages."[109]

After the right team has been put together in terms of individualism-collectivism, team level, and team diversity, it's important to keep the team together as long as practically possible. Interesting research by the National Transportation Safety Board (NTSB) shows that 73 percent of serious mistakes made by jet cockpit crews are made the very first day that a crew flies together as a team and that 44 percent of serious mistakes occur on their very first flight together that day (pilot teams fly two to three flights per day). Moreover, research has shown that fatigued pilot crews who have worked together before make significantly fewer errors than rested crews who have never worked together.[110] Their experience working

> **Team diversity** the variances or differences in ability, experience, personality, or any other factor on a team

together helps them overcome their fatigue and outperform new teams that have not worked together before. So, after you've created effective teams, keep them together as long as possible.

10-4c Team Training

After selecting the right people for teamwork, you need to train them. To be successful, teams need significant training, particularly in interpersonal skills, decision-making and problem-solving skills, conflict resolution skills, and technical training. Organizations that create work teams *often underestimate the amount of training* required to make teams effective. This mistake occurs frequently in successful organizations where managers assume that if employees can work effectively on their own, they can work effectively in teams. In reality, companies that successfully use teams provide thousands of hours of training to make sure that teams work. Stacy Myers, a consultant who helps companies implement teams, says, "When we help companies move to teams, we also require that employees take basic quality and business knowledge classes as well. Teams must know how their work affects the company, and how their success will be measured."[111]

Most commonly, members of work teams receive training in interpersonal skills. **Interpersonal skills** such as listening, communicating, questioning, and providing feedback enable people to have effective working relationships with others. Consultant Peter Grazier, founder of **Teambuilding Inc.**, says, "Teams have told us that if they had to do it over again, they would have more of the people skills up front. They don't struggle with the technical stuff. They tend to struggle with the people skills."[112] Because of teams' autonomy and responsibility, many companies also give team members training in *decision-making and problem-solving skills* to help them do a better job of cutting costs and improving quality and customer service. Many organizations also teach teams *conflict resolution skills*. Teambuilding Inc.'s Grazier explains that "the diversity of values and personalities makes a team powerful, but it can be the greatest source of conflict. If you're a detail person, and I'm not, and we get on a team, you might say that we need more analysis on a problem before making a decision, (while I) may want to make a decision (right away). But, if I've been trained in problem-solving and conflict resolution, then I look at your detail (focus) as something that is needed in a team because it's a shortcoming of mine."[113] Liane Davey, co-founder of 3COze, a team communication consulting firm, says you see, ". . . the light bulbs going on as people realize, 'You mean, I'm supposed to fight with that person?' Yes! 'And when he's disagreeing with me, it's not because he's a jerk or trying to annoy me?' Right!"[114]

Firms must also provide team members with the *technical training* they need to do their jobs, particularly if they are being cross-trained to perform all of the different jobs on the team. Before teams were created at Milwaukee Mutual Insurance, separate employees performed the tasks of rating, underwriting, and processing insurance policies. After extensive cross-training, however, each team member can now do all three jobs.[115] Cross-training is less appropriate for teams of highly skilled workers. For instance, it is unlikely that a group of engineers, computer programmers, and systems analysts would be cross-trained for each other's jobs.

Team leaders need training, too, as they often feel unprepared for their new duties. New team leaders face myriad problems ranging from confusion about their new roles as team leaders (compared with their old jobs as managers or employees) to not knowing where to go for help when their teams have problems. The solution is extensive training. Overall, does team training work? One study found that across a wide variety of settings, tasks, team types, and 2,650 teams in different organizations, team training was positively related to team performance outcomes.[116] A similar analysis of healthcare team training based on nearly 44,000 people across 47 organizations found even stronger results.[117] Training teams makes them much more effective. And with healthcare teams, training saves lives!

10-4d Team Compensation and Recognition

Compensating teams correctly is very difficult. For instance, one survey found that only 37 percent of companies were satisfied with their team compensation plans and even fewer, just 10 percent, reported being "very positive."[118] One of the problems, according to Susan Mohrman of the Center for Effective Organizations at the University of Southern California, is that "there is a very strong set of beliefs in most organizations that people should be paid for how well they do. So, when people first get put into team-based organizations, they really balk at being paid for how well the team does. It sounds illogical to them. It sounds like their individuality and their sense of self-worth are being threatened."[119] Consequently, companies need to carefully choose

> **Interpersonal skills** skills, such as listening, communicating, questioning, and providing feedback, that enable people to have effective working relationships with others

a team compensation plan and then fully explain how teams will be rewarded. One basic requirement for team compensation to work is that the level of rewards (individual versus team) must match the level of performance (individual versus team).

Employees can be compensated for team participation and accomplishments in three ways: skill-based pay, gainsharing, and nonfinancial rewards. **Skill-based pay** programs pay employees for learning additional skills or knowledge.[120] These programs encourage employees to acquire the additional skills they will need to perform multiple jobs within a team and to share knowledge with others within their work groups.[121] For example, at the Patience & Nicholson (P&N) drill bit factory in Kaiapoi, New Zealand, workers produce 50,000 drill bits a day for export to Australia, Taiwan, Thailand, and other locations primarily in Asia. P&N uses a skill-based pay system. As employees learn how to run the various machines required to produce drill bits, their pay increases. According to operations manager Rick Smith, workers who are dedicated to learning can increase their pay by $6 an hour over the course of three or four years.[122]

In **gainsharing** programs, companies share the financial value of performance gains, such as productivity increases, cost savings, or quality improvements, with their workers.[123] *Nonfinancial rewards* are another way to reward teams for their performance. These rewards, which can range from vacations to T-shirts, plaques, and coffee mugs, are especially effective when coupled with management recognition, such as awards, certificates, and praise.[124] Nonfinancial awards tend to be most effective when teams or team-based interventions, such as total quality management (see Chapter 18), are first introduced.[125]

Which team compensation plan should your company use? In general, skill-based pay is most effective for self-managing and self-directing teams performing complex tasks. In these situations, the more each team member knows and can do, the better the whole team performs. By contrast, gainsharing works best in relatively stable environments where employees can focus on improving productivity, cost savings, or quality.

A final word on enhancing work team effectiveness: It takes time. A four-year study of semi-autonomous teams, which have the authority to make decisions and solve problems (see Section 10-2a), found that labor productivity in 20 manufacturing plants of a Fortune 500 company rose for the first two years compared to control groups that had not yet switched to teams, dropped in year three, and then rose even higher in year four. Likewise, the rate of inventory turnover (higher turnover indicates less inventory, which is better – See Chapter 18) dropped steadily for three years compared to control groups before rising quickly in year four to substantially better performance. The authors concluded that adapting to teams is "a long process and may not be completed in a short time period."[126] Teams are not a quick payoff. They are a long-term investment with high potential returns when used in the right place and backed by substantial management support and financial investment.

Skill-based pay compensation system that pays employees for learning additional skills or knowledge

Gainsharing a compensation system in which companies share the financial value of performance gains, such as increased productivity, cost savings, or quality, with their workers

11 | Managing Human Resource Systems

LEARNING OUTCOMES

11-1 Explain how different employment laws affect human resource practice.

11-2 Outline how companies should use recruiting to find qualified job applicants.

11-3 Describe the selection techniques and procedures that companies use when deciding which applicants should receive job offers.

11-4 Explain how to align various training needs with the appropriate training methods.

11-5 Outline the steps for using performance appraisals to give meaningful performance feedback.

11-6 Describe basic compensation strategies, and discuss the four kinds of employee separations.

Andrey_Popov/Shutterstock.com

11-1 EMPLOYMENT LEGISLATION

Human resource management (HRM), or the process of finding, developing, and keeping the right people to form a qualified workforce, is one of the most difficult and important of all management tasks. This chapter is organized around the three parts of the human resource management process shown in Exhibit 11.1: attracting, developing, and keeping a qualified workforce.

This chapter will walk you through the steps of the HRM process. We explore how companies use recruiting and selection techniques to attract and hire qualified employees to fulfill human resource needs. The next part of the chapter discusses how training and performance appraisal can develop the knowledge, skills, and abilities (KSAs) of the workforce. The chapter concludes with a review of compensation and employee separation, that is, how companies can keep their best workers through effective compensation practices and how they can manage the separation process when employees leave the organization.

Before we explore how human resource systems work, you need to understand the complex legal environment in which they exist. So, we'll begin the chapter by reviewing the federal laws that govern human resource management decisions.

"What was your last salary?" used to be the final question in the hiring process right before a job offer. Out of concern that asking about salary perpetuates

Human resource management (HRM) the process of finding, developing, and keeping the right people to form a qualified workforce

smaller salaries for women (who have lower salaries on average) and age discrimination (as older workers with higher salaries are screened out of the hiring process), 18 states and 21 cities have passed laws preventing employers from asking job applicants about salary histories.[1] Vice president Christina Wong of Philadelphia-based ESM Productions says not asking about prior salaries makes it difficult for ESM, which hires crews and designers who run conferences and concerts worldwide, to determine appropriate market rates.[2] So, what are employers to do? They don't want to overpay employees, exceeding budgets and creating internal equity issues. But they also don't want to violate the law or discriminate when setting wages. Carolyn Cowper, vice president at The Segal Group consultants in New York City, says, "Shift the conversation to the candidate's salary expectations rather than salary history..."[3] Other companies now communicate specific salary ranges (such as "$65,000 to $75,000") in job recruiting ads. Caroline King, chief people officer at the Atlanta-based Lucas Group, says, "It can be better to be forthcoming with salary ranges and what the company feels is the market value of the job."[4]

As the "last salary" example illustrates, the human resource planning process occurs in a complicated and changing legal environment.

*Let's explore employment legislation by reviewing **11-1a the major federal employment laws that affect human resource practice, 11-1b how the concept of adverse impact is related to employment discrimination**, and **11-1c the laws regarding sexual harassment in the workplace.***

11-1a Federal Employment Laws

Exhibit 11.2 lists the major federal employment laws and their websites, where you can find more detailed information. The Fair Labor Standards Act (FLSA), administered by the Department of Labor (DOL), establishes minimum wage, overtime pay, record keeping, and youth employment standards for the private sector, as well as for federal, state, and local governments. (As such, the FLSA pertains to compensation issues discussed in Section 11-6a.) Except for the Family and Medical Leave Act and the Uniformed Services Employment and Reemployment Rights Act, which are both administered

Exhibit 11.1
The Human Resource Management Process

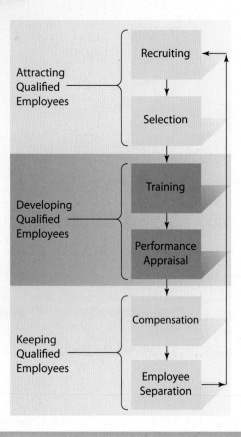

Attracting Qualified Employees

Recruiting

Selection

Developing Qualified Employees

Training

Performance Appraisal

Keeping Qualified Employees

Compensation

Employee Separation

Bona fide occupational qualification (BFOQ) an exception in employment law that permits sex, age, religion, and the like to be used when making employment decisions, but only if they are "reasonably necessary to the normal operation of that particular business." BFOQs are strictly monitored by the Equal Employment Opportunity Commission

by the DOL, all of these laws are administered by the Equal Employment Opportunity Commission (EEOC, www.eeoc.gov). The general effect of this body of law, which is still evolving through court decisions, is that employers may not discriminate in employment decisions on the basis of sex, sexual orientation, gender identity, age, religion, color, national origin, race, disability, or genetic history.[5] The intent is to make these factors irrelevant in employment decisions. Stated another way, employment decisions should be based on factors that are "job related," "reasonably necessary," or a "business necessity" for successful job performance.

The only time that sex, age, religion, and the like can be used to make employment decisions is when they are considered a bona fide occupational qualification. Title VII of the 1964 Civil Rights Act says that it is legal to hire and employ someone on the basis of sex, religion, or national origin when there is a **bona fide occupational qualification (BFOQ)** that is "reasonably necessary to the normal operation of that particular business." A Baptist church hiring a new minister can reasonably specify that being a Baptist rather than a Catholic or Presbyterian is a BFOQ for the position. However, it's unlikely that the church could specify race or national origin as a BFOQ. In general, the courts and the EEOC take a hard look when a business claims that sex, sexual orientation, gender identity, age, religion, color, national origin, race, or disability is a BFOQ. For example, citing BFOQs, the producers of the Broadway musical *Hamilton*, advertised auditions for "nonwhite performers," claiming, "It is essential to the storytelling. . . that the principal roles, which were written for nonwhite characters (excepting King George), be performed by nonwhite actors." The EEOC's Compliance Manual clearly states, however, that, "race and color can never be BFOQs."[6] At the urging of the Actor's Equity Association, auditions were opened to actors of all races and colors.[7]

It is important to understand, however, that these laws apply to the entire HRM process and not just to selection decisions (for example, hiring or promotion). These laws also cover all training and development activities, performance appraisals, terminations, and compensation decisions. Employers who use sex, sexual orientation, gender identity, age, race/ethnicity, or religion to make employment-related decisions when those factors are unrelated to an applicant's or employee's ability to perform a job may face charges of discrimination from employee lawsuits or the EEOC.

In addition to the laws presented in Exhibit 11.2, there are two other important sets of federal laws: labor laws and the laws and regulations governing safety standards. Labor laws regulate the interaction between management and labor unions that represent groups of employees. These laws guarantee employees the right to form and join unions of their own choosing. For more information about labor laws, see the National Labor Relations Board (NLRB) at www.nlrb.gov.

The Occupational Safety and Health Act (OSHA) requires that employers provide employees with a workplace that is "free from recognized hazards that are causing or are likely to cause death or serious physical harm." This law is administered by the Occupational Safety and Health Administration (which, like the act, is referred to as OSHA). OSHA sets safety and health standards for employers and conducts inspections to determine whether those standards are being met. Employers who do not meet OSHA standards may be

Exhibit 11.2
Summary of Major Federal Employment Laws

Fair Labor Standards Act (FLSA) of 1938	www.dol.gov/whd/flsa/index.htm	Establishes the federal minimum wage and rules related to overtime pay (eligibility and rates), recordkeeping, and child labor.
Equal Pay Act of 1963	www.eeoc.gov/laws/statutes/epa.cfm	Prohibits unequal pay for males and females doing substantially similar work.
Title VII of the Civil Rights Act of 1964	www.eeoc.gov/laws/statutes/titlevii.cfm	Prohibits employment discrimination on the basis of race, color, religion, sex, sexual orientation, gender identity, or national origin.
Age Discrimination in Employment Act of 1967	www.eeoc.gov/laws/statutes/adea.cfm	Prohibits discrimination in employment decisions against persons age 40 and older.
Pregnancy Discrimination Act of 1978	www.eeoc.gov/laws/statutes/pregnancy.cfm	Prohibits discrimination in employment against pregnant women.
Americans with Disabilities Act of 1990	www.eeoc.gov/laws/statutes/ada.cfm	Prohibits discrimination on the basis of physical or mental disabilities.
Civil Rights Act of 1991	www.eeoc.gov/laws/statutes/cra-1991.cfm	Strengthened the provisions of the Civil Rights Act of 1964 by providing for jury trials and punitive damages.
Family and Medical Leave Act of 1993	www.dol.gov/whd/fmla/index.htm	Permits workers to take up to 12 weeks of unpaid leave for pregnancy and/or birth of a new child, adoption, or foster care of a new child; illness of an immediate family member; or personal medical leave.
Uniformed Services Employment and Reemployment Rights Act of 1994	https://www.dol.gov/agencies/vets/programs/userra	Prohibits discrimination against those serving in the armed forces reserve, the National Guard, and other uniformed services; guarantees that civilian employers will hold and then restore civilian jobs.
Genetic Information Nondiscrimination Act of 2008	www.eeoc.gov/laws/types/genetic.cfm	Prohibits discrimination on the basis of genetic information.

fined.[8] OSHA has repeatedly fined The Dollar Tree retail chain for stacking boxes in "unstable piles that block aisles, reach precarious heights and, most seriously, block emergency exits."[9] Dollar Tree paid an $825,000 fine in 2015, but has been cited 150 more times for $898,000 in fines, which it is contesting.[10] Former OSHA head David Michael explains, "Management would send in large quantities of goods to be sold, but the stores didn't have enough storage space."[11]

For more information about OSHA, see www.osha.gov.

11-1b Adverse Impact and Employment Discrimination

The EEOC has investigatory, enforcement, and informational responsibilities. Therefore, it investigates charges of discrimination, enforces the employment discrimination laws in federal court, and publishes guidelines that organizations can use to ensure they are in compliance with the law. One of the most important guidelines, jointly issued by the EEOC, the US Department of Labor, the US Department of Justice, and the federal Office of Personnel Management, is the *Uniform Guidelines on Employee Selection Procedures*, which can be read in their entirety at www.uniformguidelines.com/uniform-guidelines.html. These guidelines define two important criteria, disparate treatment and adverse impact, which are used in determining whether companies have engaged in discriminatory hiring and promotion practices.

Disparate treatment, which is *intentional* discrimination, occurs when people,

Disparate treatment intentional discrimination that occurs when people are purposely not given the same hiring, promotion, or membership opportunities because of their race, color, sex, sexual orientation, gender identity, age, ethnic group, national origin, or religious beliefs despite being qualified, are *intentionally* not given the same hiring, promotion, or membership opportunities as other employees because of their race, color, age, sex, sexual orientation, gender identity, ethnic group, national origin, or religious beliefs.[12] Bobby Nickel, a former facilities manager at Staples, the office supply retailer, was awarded $26 million by a jury that found Staples guilty of harassing him by calling him an "old coot" and an "old goat" and firing him because he was an older employee with a higher salary.[13]

Legally, a key element of discrimination lawsuits is establishing motive, meaning that the employer intended to discriminate. If no motive can be established, then a claim of disparate treatment may actually be a case of adverse impact. **Adverse impact**, which is *unintentional* discrimination, occurs when members of a particular race, sex, sexual orientation, gender identity, age, or ethnic group are *unintentionally* harmed or disadvantaged because they are hired, promoted, or trained (or any other employment decision) at substantially lower rates than others.

At **Texas Roadhouse** restaurants, front-of-house employees (servers, bartenders, and hosts) are required to line dance during shifts, wear jeans, and work nights and weekends. The company hires younger workers for these positions – even though it produces a statistically adverse impact on older workers – because it considers such activities to be BFOQs.[14] The EEOC filed a class action lawsuit against the restaurant chain for discrimination, which Texas Roadhouse settled by paying the EEOC $12 million

Citing BFOQs, the producers of the Broadway musical *Hamilton* originally advertised auditions for "nonwhite performers," but at the urging of the Actor's Equity Association, auditions were opened to actors of all races and colors.

that went to workers ages 40 and over who applied but did not get those positions.[15] The EEOC noted that only 1.9 percent of Texas Roadhouse's front-of-house employees were over the age of 40, a figure "well below the protected age group's representation in the general population of defendants' locations, well below the protected age group's representation in Bureau of Labor statistics data for such positions within the industry, and well below the protected age group's representation in the pool of applicants for positions with defendants."[16] How do courts determine what constitutes "well below?"

The courts and federal agencies use the **four-fifths (or 80 percent) rule** to determine if adverse impact has occurred. Adverse impact is determined by calculating the impact ratio, which divides the decision rate for a protected group of people by the decision rate for a nonprotected group (usually white males). If the impact ratio is less than 80 percent, then adverse impact may have occurred. For example, if 20 out of 100 black applicants are hired (20/100 = 20%), but 60 white applicants are hired (60/100 = 60%), then adverse impact has occurred because the impact ratio is less than 80 percent (.20/.60 = 33%).

Violation of the four-fifths rule is not an automatic indication of discrimination, however. If an employer can demonstrate that a selection procedure or test is valid, meaning that the test accurately predicts job performance or that the test is job related because it assesses applicants on specific tasks actually used in the job, then the organization may continue to use the test. If validity cannot be established, however, then a violation of the four-fifths rule may likely result in a lawsuit brought by employees, job applicants, or the EEOC itself.

11-1c Sexual Harassment

According to the EEOC, **sexual harassment** is a form of discrimination in which unwelcome sexual advances, requests for sexual favors, or other verbal or physical conduct of a sexual nature occurs. Awareness regarding

Adverse impact unintentional discrimination that occurs when members of a particular race, sex, sexual orientation, gender identity, or ethnic group are unintentionally harmed or disadvantaged because they are hired, promoted, or trained (or any other employment decision) at substantially lower rates than others

Four-fifths (or 80 percent) rule a rule of thumb used by the courts and the EEOC to determine whether there is evidence of adverse impact; a violation of this rule occurs when the impact ratio (calculated by dividing the decision ratio for a protected group by the decision ratio for a nonprotected group) is less than 80 percent, or four-fifths

Sexual harassment a form of discrimination in which unwelcome sexual advances, requests for sexual favors, or other verbal or physical conduct of a sexual nature occurs while performing one's job

sexual harassment increased substantially because of the #MeToo movement in which public accusations of harassment have resulted in hundreds of powerful men losing their jobs since 2018.[17] From a legal perspective, there are two kinds of sexual harassment, quid pro quo and hostile work environment.[18]

Quid pro quo sexual harassment occurs when employment outcomes, such as hiring, promotion, or simply keeping one's job, depend on whether an individual submits to being sexually harassed. For example, in a quid pro quo sexual harassment lawsuit against Stones River Medical Group, a woman hired as the assistant office manager was pressured for sex by a doctor beginning her first month on the job. The doctor provided her medications, threatened her with violence if she ended the sexual relationship, placing her on leave when she did so, and only hired her back after she resumed their sexual relationship. This made it a quid pro quo case by linking sexual acts to economic outcomes. She again ended their sexual relationship and was fired five days later. A jury awarded her a $2.3 million settlement.[19]

A **hostile work environment** occurs when unwelcome and demeaning sexually related behavior creates an intimidating, hostile, and offensive work environment. In contrast to quid pro quo cases, a hostile work environment may not result in economic injury. However, it can lead to psychological injury when the work environment becomes stressful. Zillow, a real estate website that estimates the value or sales prices of for-sale homes, settled a federal lawsuit alleging a hostile work environment and a "frat house" culture. A sales manager referred to a female worker as "Rachel 2.0," because she was like, "Rachel but with bigger breasts and less miles on her."[20] This sales manager, who was fired by Zillow one day after a hostile work environment lawsuit was filed in federal court, allegedly sent the female worker sexually explicit messages, with one including a picture of a penis. An IT technician, asked to help a female employee reset a password, responded, "Only trade password for boob pix. Haha."[21]

Finally, what should companies do to make sure that sexual harassment laws are followed and not violated?[22] First, respond immediately when sexual harassment is reported. A quick response encourages victims of sexual harassment to report problems to management rather than to lawyers or the EEOC. Moreover, a quick and fair investigation may serve as a deterrent to future harassment. A lawyer for the EEOC says, "Worse than having no sexual harassment policy is a policy that is not followed. It's merely window dressing. You wind up with destroyed morale when people who come forward are ignored, ridiculed, retaliated against, or nothing happens to the harasser."[23] Indeed, two-thirds of those filing sexual harassment claims with the EEOC report company retaliation, such as shift changes, job transfers or firings.[24]

Then take the time to write a clear, understandable sexual harassment policy that is strongly worded, gives specific examples of what constitutes sexual harassment, spells outs sanctions and punishments, and is widely publicized within the company. This lets potential harassers and victims know what will not be tolerated and how the firm will deal with harassment should it occur.

Next, establish clear reporting procedures that indicate how, where, and to whom incidents of sexual harassment can be reported. The best procedures ensure that a complaint will receive a quick response, that impartial parties will handle the complaint, and that the privacy of the accused and accuser will be protected. At DuPont, Avon, and Texas Industries, employees can call a confidential hotline 24 hours a day, 365 days a year.[25]

Finally, managers should also be aware that most states and many cities or local governments have their own employment-related laws and enforcement agencies. So, compliance with federal law is often not enough. In fact, organizations can be in full compliance with federal law and at the same time be in violation of state or local sexual harassment laws. In particular, today's companies are challenged to comply with changing city and state laws regarding paid sick leave (69 percent), marijuana legalization (54 percent) and background checks (52 percent).[26]

Rommel Canlas/Shutterstock.com

Quid pro quo sexual harassment a form of sexual harassment in which employment outcomes, such as hiring, promotion, or simply keeping one's job, depend on whether an individual submits to sexual harassment

Hostile work environment a form of sexual harassment in which unwelcome and demeaning sexually related behavior creates an intimidating and offensive work environment

RECRUITING

Patty McCord, Netflix's chief talent officer for 14 years, said:

> ...we had a saying: "Always be recruiting!" ... The interview and hiring process gives a powerful first impression about how your company operates, for good or bad. So I had an ironclad rule that if people saw a stranger sitting alone at headquarters waiting for an interview, they should stop and say, "Hi, I'm ____. Are you here for an interview? Let's look at your schedule, and I'll help you find the next person." If I was late coming to meet with a candidate and said, "Sorry – I hope someone talked to you," he or she would say, "Six people talked to me."[27]

McCord explains, "Candidates are evaluating you, just as you're evaluating them. People forget that. Our goal was to have every person who came for an interview walk away wanting the job. Even if we hated candidates, we wanted them to think, 'Wow, that was an incredible experience.' It was efficient, it was effective, it was on time, the questions were relevant, everyone was smart, and I was treated with dignity."[28]

Recruiting is the process of developing a pool of qualified job applicants.

Let's examine 11-2a what job analysis is and how it is used in recruiting, 11-2b how companies use internal recruiting, and 11-2c external recruiting to find qualified job applicants.

11-2a Defining the Job

Job analysis is a "purposeful, systematic process for collecting information on the important work-related aspects of a job."[29] A job analysis typically collects four kinds of information:

» Work activities, such as what workers do and how, when, and why they do it

» The tools and equipment used to do the job

» The context in which the job is performed, such as the actual working conditions or schedule

» The personnel requirements for performing the job, meaning the knowledge, skills, and abilities needed to do a job well[30]

Job analysis information can be collected by having job incumbents and/or supervisors complete questionnaires about their jobs, by direct observation, by interviews, or by videoing employees as they perform their jobs.

Job descriptions and job specifications are two of the most important results of a job analysis. A **job description** is a written description of the basic tasks, duties, and responsibilities required of an employee holding a particular job. **Job specifications**, which are often included as a separate section of a job description, are a summary of the qualifications needed to successfully perform the job. Exhibit 11.3 shows a job description for a second-shift warehouse manager at AmerisourceBergen, a medication delivery and logistics company.

Because a job analysis specifies what a job entails as well as the knowledge, skills, and abilities that are needed to do the job well, companies must complete a job analysis *before* beginning to recruit job applicants. According to Netflix's Patty McCord, the worst mistake with written job descriptions is "the hiring manager, not thinking very hard about what problem they need this person to solve, comes up with a [quick] job description" *without* conducting a job analysis.[31] Author and consultant Whitney Johnson says managers make the mistake of, "copy-paste recruitment" in which they simply copy and paste the old job description into the recruiting advertisement rather than first conducting a new job analysis and then rewriting the job description.[32]

Job analyses, job descriptions, and job specifications are the foundation on which all critical human resource activities are built. They are used during recruiting and selection to match applicant qualifications with the requirements of the job. Software company **SAP** uses artificial intelligence to teach "a computer how to spot patterns and make connections by showing it a massive volume of data."[33] SAP Resume Matching reads thousands of job descriptions and specifications on the internet to identify the KSAs for a variety of jobs. SAP's chief innovation officer said, "Recruiters spend 60 percent of their time reading CVs. Why should a person read 300 resumes if a machine can propose the top 10?"[34]

Job analyses, job descriptions, and job specifications also help companies meet the legal requirement that their human resource decisions be job related. To be judged *job related*, recruitment, selection, training, performance appraisals, and employee separations must be

---

Recruiting the process of developing a pool of qualified job applicants

Job analysis a purposeful, systematic process for collecting information on the important work-related aspects of a job

Job description a written description of the basic tasks, duties, and responsibilities required of an employee holding a particular job

Job specifications a written summary of the qualifications needed to successfully perform a particular job

Exhibit 11.3

Job Description for a Second-Shift Warehouse Supervisor at AmerisourceBergen

The primary role is hiring, termination, direction, and performance of associates. Also responsible for warehouse functional areas, such as receiving, shipping, returns, picking, packing, checking, stocking, order filling, and verification and record keeping of shipments of controlled healthcare substances. The warehouse uses radio-frequency (RF) devices for many of these tasks. Also responsible for ensuring that all safety guidelines are followed.

Primary Duties and Responsibilities:

» Direct workflow, motivate, train, and monitor the performance of warehouse associates.

» Monitor work processes and suggest modifications to improve productivity and efficiency and reduce costs; implement changes as directed or needed.

» Support compliance with all appropriate policies, procedures, safety rules, and DEA regulations.

» Coach employees to support their personal and professional development.

» Supervise the receipt of merchandise, ensuring that only products intended for the Distribution Center are accepted by the receiving clerks; ensure that daily logs are accurately maintained.

» Oversee department staff in counting, weighing and identifying items being shipped; check materials against invoices, bills of lading, customer orders, and similar documents.

» Oversee the department staff in filling orders, double-checking, and shipping controlled substances with the assistance of cage/vault clerks or order fillers.

» Maintain all records of the delivery process such as time, date, quantity, source, and destination of materials shipped.

» Oversee the manifests of routes and departures to ensure customers receive their merchandise in a timely manner.

» Interact with customers in resolving delivery or order-filling issues.

Source: "Job Description – Warehouse Manager, 2nd Shift," AmerisourceBergen, accessed May 3, 2020, https://abccareers.taleo.net/careersection/2/jobdetail.ftl?job=000020XI&tz=GMT-04%3A00&tzname=America%2FIndianapolis.

iStockphoto.com/Kendall Griffin

valid and be directly related to the important aspects of the job, as identified by a careful job analysis. For example, SAP's Resume Matching validated what it learned by using the KSAs it identified to evaluate anonymous resumes (with no names or identifying demographics) of actual job applicants who were rejected, made the first cut of promising candidates, interviewed, or were eventually hired by managers in a variety of companies.[35] The questions asked in an interview should also be based on the most important work activities identified by a job analysis. Likewise, during performance appraisals, employees should be evaluated in areas that a job analysis has identified as the most important in a job.

In fact, in *Griggs v. Duke Power Co.* and *Albemarle Paper Co. v. Moody*, the US Supreme Court stated that companies should use job analyses to help establish the job relatedness of their human resource procedures.[36] The EEOC's *Uniform Guidelines on Employee Selection Procedures* also recommend that companies base their human resource procedures on job analysis.

11-2b Internal Recruiting

Internal recruiting is the process of developing a pool of qualified job applicants from people who already work in the company. Internal recruiting, sometimes called "promotion from within," improves employee commitment, morale, and motivation. Recruiting current employees also reduces recruitment start-up time and costs, and because employees are already familiar with the company's culture and procedures, they are more likely to succeed in new jobs. Crédit Suisse was posting less than half of its open jobs internally until it discovered that

> **Internal recruiting** the process of developing a pool of qualified job applicants from people who already work in the company

Artificial Intelligence Transforming Human Resource Management

As you'll learn in Chapter 17, artificial intelligence, or AI, is the capability of computerized systems to use feedback to learn and adapt through experience. Here's how AI is transforming all parts of human resource management:

» *Chatbot/text message recruiting.* AI chatbots answer applicant questions via text messaging in 100+ languages, do basic screening such as asking how much experience a candidate has, and automate interview schedules.

» *Resume screening.* The most common use of AI in HR is screening resumes, by scanning resumes for key words indicating job-related KSAs. AI systems rank applicants in terms of potential, recommending who should be interviewed.

» *Phone/video screening interviews.* AI grades phone or video responses to early screening questions, leading to better hiring decisions by ensuring that candidates are asked the same structured interview questions. Audio and video responses are easily reviewed by decision makers. The challenge for candidates is that there isn't a human being on the other end of the interview.

» *Deep background checks.* AI checks social media histories for potentially toxic behavior, like racism, criminal behavior or violence. There are legal risks if nonjob-related information is used. See Section 11-3b.

» *Training needs assessment.* AI recommends training programs after administering and scoring needs assessment tests, or comparing work histories to the KSAs needed in various career paths.

» *Performance appraisals.* AI compares results to goals, providing developmental feedback for improvement or more formal evaluations of performance.

» *Termination.* Amazon has used AI to automatically track and then fire employees in order fulfillment warehouses for not meeting productivity goals. While managers can override the program, the AI system generates performance warnings and terminations.

graphicwithart/Shutterstock.com

» *Turnover.* AI uses changes in survey responses and performance, increases in absenteeism, work histories, and promotion rates to let managers know who is likely to quit, giving them the opportunity to keep the employee or plan for their replacement.

How well do AI systems work? Frida Polli, cofounder of Pymetrics, an AI HR service provider, says, "AI Is like teenage sex. Everyone says they're doing it, and nobody really knows what it is." Professor Ifeoma Ajunwa says AI "is here to stay," but is "still a blunt tool." Accordingly, says John Jersin, vice president of product management at LinkedIn Talent Solutions, "There should always be a human in the loop when there are important decisions about hiring being made."

Sources: M. Aspan, "How A.I. Is Changing Hiring and Transforming HR," *Fortune*, January 20, 2020, accessed May 2, 2020, fortune.com/longform/hr-technology-ai-hiring-recruitment/; S. Castellanos, "HR Departments Turn to AI-Enabled Recruiting in Race for Talent," *Wall Street Journal*, March 14, 2019, accessed May 2, 2020, www.wsj.com/articles/hr-departments-turn-to-ai-enabled-recruiting-in-race-for-talent-11552600459; C. Cutter, "Your Next Job Interview May Be With a Robot," *Wall Street Journal*, November 28, 2018, accessed May 2, 2020, www.wsj.com/articles/its-time-for-your-job-interview-youll-be-talking-to-yourself-1543418495; R. Heilweil, "Job Recruiters Are Using AI in Hiring," *Vox – Recode*, December 12, 2019, accessed May 2, 2020, www.vox.com/recode/2019/12/12/20993665/artificial-intelligence-ai-job-screen; C. Lecher, "How Amazon Automatically Tracks and Fires Warehouse Workers for 'Productivity,'" *The Verge*, April 25, 2019, accessed May 2, 2020, www.theverge.com/2019/4/25/18516004/amazon-warehouse-fulfillment-centers-productivity-firing-terminations; S. Shellenbarger, "Make Your Job Application Robot-Proof," *Wall Street Journal*, December 16, 2019, accessed May 2, 2020, www.wsj.com/articles/make-your-job-application-robot-proof-11576492201.

those taking a new job within the company were more likely to stay long term. So, it now posts 80 percent of its openings internally – even cold-calling employees to let them know when jobs have opened. Doing so has resulted in promotions for 300 of its people. William Wolf, the bank's global head of talent acquisition and development, says, "We believe we've saved a number of them from taking jobs at other banks."[37] Because of strong results like these, Wharton professor Peter Cappelli recommends that *all* job openings be posted internally.[38]

Job posting and career paths are two methods of internal recruiting. *Job posting* is a procedure for advertising job openings within the company to existing employees. A job description and requirements are typically posted on a bulletin board, in a company newsletter, or in an internal computerized job bank that is accessible only to employees. Job posting helps organizations discover hidden talent, allows employees to take responsibility for career planning, and makes it easier for companies to retain talented workers who are dissatisfied in their current jobs and would otherwise leave the company.[39] In fact, a LinkedIn survey of workers who changed jobs found that 42 percent would have stayed with their former employers if a relevant position had been available.[40] LinkedIn vice president Parker Barrile says it's often the case that, "People quit their job, not the company."[41]

A study of 70 large global companies found that organizations that formalize internal recruiting and job posting have a lower average rate of turnover (11 percent) compared to companies that don't (15 percent).[42] Likewise, a University of Pennsylvania study found external hires generally are more costly, less reliable hires. Specifically, external hires get paid 18 to 20 percent more than internal hires, are 61 percent more likely to be fired, and are 21 percent more likely to quit their jobs.[43] Furthermore, in a large US investment bank, it took external hires three years to achieve the same performance as internal hires, who were already familiar with the organization's culture and procedures.[44]

A *career path* is a planned sequence of jobs through which employees may advance within an organization. According to Brian Hoyt of RetailMeNot, an online coupon company in Austin, Texas, "Workers were saying, 'It isn't enough for me to work at a fun internet company,' . . . they wanted to know where their career was going."[45] So the company revamped its internal recruiting system, adding to each job posting a detailed list of responsibilities, required competencies, and skills needed to get each job. Garrett Bircher, an associate product manager, said that when he when was hired, the company lacked a coherent approach. "Now, I feel more secure," he says. "I know four jobs ahead of me now where I want to go and what it takes to get there."[46]

Career paths help employees focus on long-term goals and development while also helping companies increase employee retention. Jennifer Hanna started at Whirlpool, an appliance manufacturer, after graduating high school 20 years ago. She said, "I wanted to find a company that would invest in me at the age of 18."[47] Whirlpool paid for her community college, promoted her, and, recognizing her managerial potential, encouraged her to get an MBA. After working in a number of Whirlpool factories, today she manages the 1,000-person factory that makes Whirlpool's bestselling KitchenAid mixers. Maggie Hammaker, who works for Hanna, supervises 100 people. When she joined Whirlpool after high school, she said, "It was just a job." But, with training and guidance and a clear career path, Hammaker says, "It's not a dead-end job anymore."[48] Career paths can help employees gain a broad range of experience, which is especially useful at higher levels of management.

11-2c External Recruiting

External recruiting is the process of developing a pool of qualified job applicants from outside the company. As the world literally came to a standstill, the coronavirus put 26 million Americans out of work in one month.[49] But, hundreds of thousands of jobs opened up within days as Amazon, Walmart, Kroger, and CVS pharmacies saw their still-open, "essential" businesses surge. Jeff Lackey, CVS's chief recruiter partnered with Gap, Hilton hotels, and Delta Airlines, who had furloughed many of their workers, telling them: "I want your people."[50] Lackey said, "I'm grateful for the spirit of the partnerships. I tell people, we have only one enemy right now, and it's the virus."[51] CVS created dedicated hiring websites for furloughed employees at those companies, shortening the hiring process to just a day or two for each of the 50,000 new hires.

External recruitment methods include advertising (newspapers, magazines, direct mail, radio, podcasting, or television), employee referrals (asking current employees to recommend possible job applicants), walk-ins (people who apply on their own), outside organizations (universities, technical/trade schools, professional societies), employment services (state or private employment agencies, temporary help agencies, and professional search firms), special events (career conferences or job fairs), internet job sites (CareerBuilder.com, Glassdoor.com, Indeed.com, and Monster.com), industry recruiting apps and social media recruiting sites (LinkedIn and Facebook), as well as career portals on company websites.

Which external recruiting method should you use? Historically, studies show that employee referrals, walk-ins, advertisements, and state employment agencies tend to be used most frequently for office/clerical and production/service employees. By contrast, advertisements and college/university recruiting are used most frequently for professional/technical employees. When recruiting managers, organizations tend to rely most heavily on advertisements, employee referrals, and search firms.[52]

External recruiting the process of developing a pool of qualified job applicants from outside the company

Recently, social media recruiting sites, industry-specific job boards and recruiting apps have displaced generalist job boards and newspapers as the most popular external recruiting methods. **Facebook**'s job search platform is used effectively to recruit lower-skilled workers, and sites such as **LinkedIn** and **theLadders .com** tend to attract more highly skilled or senior-level job seekers.[53] Even though 67 percent of people seeking jobs through social media use Facebook, LinkedIn continues to be where recruiters look for promising candidates. A recent survey found that a whopping 92 percent of recruiters use social media recruiting sites for outreach – 87 percent of whom use LinkedIn.[54] The industry-specific Pared app is used in the food industry to hire dishwashers, prep cooks, servers, baristas, etc., often for short-term employment needs. Workers use the app to submit two references and their work history. Pared's algorithms prescreens and matches experienced applicants to openings at over 10,000 restaurants.[55]

One of the biggest trends in recruiting is identifying passive candidates, people who are not actively seeking a job but who might be receptive to a change. Why pursue passive candidates? About half of all workers would be willing to change jobs if recruited by another company.[56] Apps such as Entelo search 50 sources across the web for information about passive candidates, such as job title, experience, or professional achievements. Recruiters then improve search accuracy after each wave of data matching by indicating whether the identified candidates fit. Becky McCullough, who runs recruiting at digital marketer HubSpot, says, "It has set new benchmarks for response rate," meaning the percentage of passive candidates who respond with interest when contacted by HubSpot, "and we can a/b test various outreach tactics" to see what recruiting methods work best.[57]

Some companies are even hosting virtual job fairs, where job applicants click on recruiting booths to learn about the company, see the kinds of available jobs, and speak with company representatives via video chat or instant message. Because they don't need to send HR representatives on long trips and can interact with potential hires from all over the world, Boeing, Progressive, Citibank, and Amazon have found virtual job fairs to be an efficient, cost-effective way to find qualified candidates. Still an important part of external recruiting, job fairs are being repositioned as

branding events. With nearly half of its US workforce expected to retire by 2025, the insurance and risk management industry is aggressively recruiting younger workers. **Allstate** bolsters its campus recruiting and job fairs with trivia nights, free food, and hackathons to attract computer science majors. And instead of wearing business suits, its campus recruiters wear T-shirts emblazoned with "Jobhunting is Mayhem," a reference to the star character in its popular ad campaign.[58]

11-3 SELECTION

After the recruitment process has produced a pool of qualified applicants, the selection process is used to determine which applicants have the best chance of performing well on the job. From the initial review of applicants to phone screening (seven days) to group interviews (six days) to personality and skills testing, it takes an average of 23 to 29 days to screen potential applicants and hire a new employee.[59] But in one of the strongest job markets in decades (before the coronavirus), companies began shrinking the screening process to days, if not hours, fearful of losing good applicants to other employers. When Jamari Powell applied for a job at Macy's in Portland, Oregon, he received an email the next day saying, "We're calling soon, so answer the phone."[60] After a 25-minute phone interview, he was offered the job – without an onsite interview. Powell said, "It was a little weird…It kind of feels like a scam almost." But with 1 million more job openings than applicants, speed pushed aside the many of the typical steps that companies take when assessing job applicants.

Selection is the process of gathering information about job applicants to decide who should be offered a job. To make sure that selection decisions are accurate and legally defensible, the EEOC's *Uniform Guidelines on Employee Selection Procedures* recommend that all selection procedures be validated. **Validation** is the process of determining how well a selection test or procedure predicts future job performance. The better or more accurate the prediction of future job performance, the more valid a test is said to be. Unfortunately, only about one-third of companies know the validity of their selection tests, which effectively means they're just hoping or guessing that their selection procedures help them hire better employees.[61]

*Let's examine common selection procedures such as **11-3a application forms and résumés, 11-3b references and background checks, 11-3c selection tests**, and **11-3d interviews**.*

Selection the process of gathering information about job applicants to decide who should be offered a job

Validation the process of determining how well a selection test or procedure predicts future job performance; the better or more accurate the prediction of future job performance, the more valid a test is said to be

11-3a Application Forms and Résumés

The first selection devices that most job applicants encounter when they seek a job are application forms and résumés. Both contain similar information about an applicant, such as name, address, job and educational history, and so forth. Though an organization's application form often asks for information already provided by the applicant's résumé, most organizations prefer to collect this information in their own format for entry into a **human resource information system (HRIS)**.

Employment laws apply to application forms just as they do to all selection devices. Application forms may ask applicants only for valid, job-related information. Nonetheless, application forms commonly ask applicants for non-job-related information such as marital status, maiden name, age, or date of high school graduation. One study found that 73 percent of organizations had application forms that violated at least one federal or state law.[62] Likewise, interviewers may not ask about medical histories or genetics, religious beliefs, or citizenship. Exhibit 11.4 provides a more detailed explanation and list of the kinds of information that companies may *not* request in application forms, during job interviews, or in any other part of the selection process.

Courts will assume that you use all of the information you request of applicants even if you actually don't. Be sure to ask only those questions that relate directly to the candidate's ability and motivation to perform the job. Furthermore, using social media such as Facebook and LinkedIn at the initial stage of the hiring process can give employers access to information they're not allowed to obtain directly from applicants. Attorney James McDonald says, "I advise employers that it's not a good idea to use social media as a screening tool. You need to control the information you receive so you're only getting information that is legal for you to take into accounting."[63]

Résumés also pose problems for companies, but in a different way. A CareerBuilder survey of hiring managers found that 58 percent had found a lie on a résumé, with the most common being embellished skills, employment dates, job titles, academic degrees, and the companies for which one has supposedly worked. Applicants in financial services (73 percent), leisure and hospitality (71 percent), and IT and health care (both 63 percent) were the most likely to have lies caught on resumes.[64] Scott Samuels, CEO of Horizon Hospitality, says, "It's an epidemic. More and more people feel like they can get away with lying because they think no one is going to check and verify. It's rampant."[65] Therefore, managers should verify the information collected via résumés and application forms by comparing it with additional information collected during interviews

Exhibit 11.4
Don't Ask! Topics to Avoid in an Interview

1. **Children.** Don't ask applicants if they have children, plan to have them, or have or need child care. Questions about children can unintentionally single out women.

2. **Age.** Because of the Age Discrimination in Employment Act, employers cannot ask job applicants their age during the hiring process. Because most people graduate high school at the age of 18, even asking for high school graduation dates could violate the law.

3. **Disabilities.** Don't ask if applicants have physical or mental disabilities. According to the Americans with Disabilities Act, disabilities (and reasonable accommodations for them) cannot be discussed until a job offer has been made.

4. **Physical characteristics.** Don't ask for information about height, weight, or other physical characteristics. Questions about weight could be construed as leading to discrimination toward overweight people, and studies show that they are less likely to be hired in general.

5. **Name.** Yes, you can ask an applicant's name, but you cannot ask a female applicant for her maiden name because it indicates marital status. Asking for a maiden name could also lead to charges that the organization was trying to establish a candidate's ethnic background.

6. **Citizenship.** Asking applicants about citizenship could lead to claims of discrimination on the basis of national origin. However, according to the Immigration Reform and Control Act, companies may ask applicants if they have a legal right to work in the United States.

7. **Lawsuits.** Applicants may not be asked if they have ever filed a lawsuit against an employer. Federal and state laws prevent this to protect whistle-blowers from retaliation by future employers.

8. **Arrest records.** Applicants cannot be asked about their arrest records. Arrests don't have legal standing. However, if laws allow, applicants can be asked whether they have been convicted of a crime.

9. **Smoking.** Applicants cannot be asked if they smoke. Smokers might be able to claim that they weren't hired because of fears of higher absenteeism and medical costs. However, they can be asked if they are aware of company policies that restrict smoking at work.

10. **AIDS/HIV.** Applicants can't be asked about AIDS, HIV, or any other medical condition, including genetics. Questions of this nature would violate the Americans with Disabilities Act, as well as federal and state civil rights laws.

11. **Religion.** Applicants can't be asked about religious beliefs. Questions of this nature would violate federal and state civil rights laws.

12. **Genetic information.** Employers should avoid asking about genetic test results or family medical history. This would violate the Genetic Information Nondiscrimination Act, or GINA, which was designed to help encourage people to get more genetic screening done without the fear of employers or insurers using that information to deny employment or coverage.

Sources: J. S. Pouliot, "Topics to Avoid with Applicants," *Nation's Business* 80, no. 7 (1992): 57; M. Trottman, "Employers Beware When Asking about Workers' Health," *Wall Street Journal*, July 22, 2013, accessed July 9, 2014, blogs.wsj.com/atwork/2013/07/22/employers-beware-when-asking-about-workers-health/; L. Weber, "Hiring Process Just Got Dicier," *Wall Street Journal*, July 3, 2014, accessed July 9, 2014, www.wsj.com/articles/hiring-process-just-got-dicier-1404255998.

> **Human resource information system (HRIS)** a computerized system for gathering, analyzing, storing, and disseminating information related to the HRM process

and other stages of the selection process, such as references and background checks, which are discussed next.

11-3b References and Background Checks

Nearly all companies ask an applicant to provide **employment references**, such as the names of previous employers or coworkers, whom they can contact to learn more about the candidate. **Background checks** are used to verify the truthfulness and accuracy of information that applicants provide about themselves and to uncover negative, job-related background information not provided by applicants. Background checks are conducted by contacting "educational institutions, prior employers, court records, police and governmental agencies, and other informational sources, either by telephone, mail, remote computer access, or through in-person investigations."[66] For example, in the United States, drivers for the Uber and Lyft ride-sharing services undergo background screening by Checkr, a company that runs each applicant's name through seven years of federal and county background checks, sex offender registries, and motor vehicle records. Checkr, which runs 800,000 checks a month, completes background checks in less than one day.[67] Commercial truck drivers get an even more thorough background check called "Drive-a-Check," or "DAC." DAC reports, which are completed by HireRight, examine work histories, driving accidents, and reliability in terms of completing scheduled deliveries. One negative incident is usually enough to prevent a hire. Independent trucker Jeff Bailey said, "If a company uses DAC and you have a bad DAC, you're not hired."[68]

Unfortunately, previous employers are increasingly reluctant to provide references or background check information for fear of being sued by previous employees for defamation.[69] If former employers provide potential employers with unsubstantiated information that damages applicants' chances of being hired, applicants can (and do) sue for defamation. As a result, 54 percent of employers will not provide information about previous employees.[70] Many provide only dates of employment, positions held, and date of separation.

When previous employers decline to provide meaningful references or background information,

they put other employers at risk of *negligent hiring* lawsuits, in which an employer is held liable for the actions of an employee who would not have been hired if the employer had conducted a thorough reference search and background check.[71] Heyl Logistics hired Washington Transportation, a trucking firm, to deliver bottled water, but its driver took drugs, fell asleep, hit a truck, and killed another driver. The killed driver's family sued Heyl Logistics for negligent hiring, alleging it should have known that Washington Transportation operated without a license, did not test its drivers for drug use, and carried no insurance. Heyl was found guilty, Washington Transportation's driver was sent to prison for negligent homicide and driving under the influence, and the family was awarded $5.2 million in punitive damages.[72]

With previous employers generally unwilling to give full, candid references and with negligent hiring lawsuits awaiting companies that don't get such references and background information, what can companies do? They can conduct online criminal record checks, especially if the job for which the person is applying involves money, drugs, safety, control over valuable goods, or access to the elderly, people with disabilities, or people's homes.[73] Requiring criminal record checks may prompt some applicants to withdraw from the hiring process. Jeff Russow owns Avalanche Roofing & Exteriors in Colorado Springs. He says that for many of the people he recruits to apply for jobs with his company, "As soon as I say 'criminal background check,' 'drug test,' they're out the door."[74]

While companies are legally entitled to use criminal background checks at some point in the hiring process, they should follow "ban-the-box" (such as "check here if you have a criminal record") laws, which typically restrict employers from asking applicants about criminal records on *initial* application forms.[75] Many ban-the-box laws, however, such as the Fair Chance to Compete for Jobs Act of 2019, which applies to the US federal government and its contractors, prevent employers from asking about criminal background histories until *after* conditional job offers have been made.[76] At this point, applicants must still pass background and criminal record checks, additional reference checks, and a medical exam. Thirty-five states and 150 cities and counties also have "ban the box" laws.[77]

As suggested above, after a conditional job offer has been made, keep digging for additional information to verify applicant qualifications and truthfulness. Ask applicants to provide additional references and to sign a waiver that permits you to check those references, run

---

Employment references sources such as previous employers or coworkers who can provide job-related information about job candidates

Background checks procedures used to verify the truthfulness and accuracy of information that applicants provide about themselves and to uncover negative, job-related background information not provided by applicants

a more complete background check, or contact anyone else with knowledge of their work performance or history. Likewise, ask applicants if there is anything they would like the company to know or if they expect you to hear anything unusual when contacting references.[78] This in itself is often enough to get applicants to share information they typically withhold. When you've finished checking, keep the findings confidential to minimize the chances of a defamation charge. Always document all reference and background checks, noting who was called and what information was obtained. Document everything, not just information you received. To reduce the likelihood that negligent hiring lawsuits will succeed, it's particularly important to document even which companies and people refused to share reference checks and background information.

Finally, consider hiring private investigators to conduct background checks, which can often uncover information missed by traditional background checks. For example, while traditional background checks should be able to verify applicants' academic credentials, a private investigator hired by the *Wall Street Journal* found that 7 out of 358 senior executives at publicly traded firms had falsified claims regarding the college degrees they had earned."[79] Likewise, private investigators can potentially identify when applicants hire companies that provide fake references from fake bosses (to avoid negative references from previous employers). Indeed, one such business claims, "We can replace a supervisor with a fictitious one, alter your work history, provide you with a positive employment reputation, and give you the glowing reference you need."[80]

11-3c Selection Tests

Selection tests give organizational decision makers a chance to know who will likely do well in a job and who won't. Prehiring assessments are growing in popularity, with 57 percent of large US employers using some sort of prehiring test to ensure a better fit. "The incentives to screen before hiring have increased over time, while costs have declined," says economist Steve Davis. "Both those things are encouraging employers to move away [from] what was essentially a trial employment situation to just screening out people in advance.[81] The basic idea behind selection testing is to have applicants take a test that measures something directly or indirectly related to doing well on the job. The selection tests discussed here are specific ability tests, cognitive ability tests, biographical data, personality tests, work sample tests, and assessment centers.

Specific ability tests measure the extent to which an applicant possesses the particular kind of ability

Exhibit 11.5
Clerical Test Items Similar to Those Found on the Minnesota Clerical Test

	Numbers/Letters		Same	
1	3468251	3467251	Yes	No
			O	O
2	4681371	4681371	Yes	No
			O	O
3	7218510	7218520	Yes	No
			O	O
4	ZXYAZAB	ZXYAZAB	Yes	No
			O	O
	ALZYXMN	ALZYXNM	Yes	No
5			O	O
	PRQZYMN	PRQZYMN	Yes	No
6			O	O

Source: N. W. Schmitt and R. J. Klimoski, *Research Methods in Human Resource Management* (Mason, OH: South-Western, 1991).

needed to do a job well. Specific ability tests are also called **aptitude tests** because they measure aptitude for doing a particular task well. For example, if you took the SAT to get into college, then you've taken the aptly named Scholastic Aptitude Test, which is one of the best predictors of how well students will do in college (that is, scholastic performance).[82] Specific ability tests also exist for mechanical, clerical, sales, and physical work. For example, clerical workers have to be good at accurately reading and scanning numbers as they type or enter data. Exhibit 11.5 shows items similar to the Minnesota Clerical Test, in which applicants have only a short time to determine if the two columns of numbers and letters are identical. Applicants who are good at this are likely to do well as clerical or data entry workers.

Cognitive ability tests measure the extent to which applicants have abilities in perceptual speed, verbal comprehension, numerical aptitude, general

Specific ability tests (aptitude tests) tests that measure the extent to which an applicant possesses the particular kind of ability needed to do a job well

Cognitive ability tests tests that measure the extent to which applicants have abilities in perceptual speed, verbal comprehension, numerical aptitude, general reasoning, and spatial aptitude

reasoning, and spatial aptitude. In other words, these tests indicate how quickly and how well people understand words, numbers, logic, and spatial dimensions. Although specific ability tests predict job performance in only particular types of jobs, cognitive ability tests accurately predict job performance in almost all kinds of jobs.[83] Why is this so? The reason is that people with strong cognitive or mental abilities are usually good at learning new things, processing complex information, solving problems, and making decisions, and these abilities are important in almost all jobs.[84] In fact, cognitive ability tests are almost always the best predictors of job performance. Consequently, if you were allowed to use just one selection test, a cognitive ability test would be the one to use.[85] (In practice, though, companies use a battery of different tests because doing so leads to much more accurate selection decisions.)

Biographical data, or **biodata**, are extensive surveys that ask applicants questions about their personal backgrounds and life experiences. The basic idea behind biodata is that past behavior (personal background and life experience) is the best predictor of future behavior. For example, during World War II, the US Air Force had to test tens of thousands of men without flying experience to determine who was likely to be a good pilot. Because flight training took several months and was very expensive, quickly selecting the right people for training was important. After examining extensive biodata, the Air Force found that one of the best predictors of success in flight school was whether students had ever built model airplanes that actually flew. This one biodata item was almost as good a predictor as the entire set of selection tests that the air force was using at the time.[86]

Most biodata questionnaires have more than 100 items that gather information about habits and attitudes, health, interpersonal relations, money, what it was like growing up in your family (parents, siblings, childhood years, teen years), personal habits, current home (spouse, children), hobbies, education and training, values, preferences, and work.[87] In general, biodata are very good predictors of future job performance, especially in entry-level jobs.

You may have noticed that some of the information requested in biodata surveys is related to those topics employers should avoid in applications, interviews, or other parts of the selection process. This information can be requested in biodata questionnaires provided that the company can demonstrate that the information is job related (i.e., valid) and does not result in adverse impact against protected groups of job applicants. Biodata surveys should be validated and tested for adverse impact before they are used to make selection decisions.[88]

An individual's *personality* is made up of a relatively stable set of behaviors, attitudes, and emotions displayed over time. In short, it is personality that makes people different from each other. A **personality test** measures the extent to which an applicant possesses different kinds of job-related personality dimensions. Personality tests allow employers to gauge a candidate's personality traits, cultural fit, and even compatibility with a team. In Chapter 12, you will learn that there are five major personality dimensions related to work behavior: extraversion, emotional stability, agreeableness, conscientiousness, and openness to experience.[89] Of these, only conscientiousness – the degree to which someone is organized, hardworking, responsible, persevering, thorough, and achievement oriented – predicts job performance across a wide variety of jobs.[90] A lifetime study measured the personality traits of high IQ (top 0.5 percent) students in grades 1 through 8 in 1921 and 1922, tracking them until 1991. Over those 70 years, it found that men who were above average in conscientiousness earned $16.7 percent more ($567,000) over their working lives.[91] Conscientiousness tests work especially well in combination with cognitive

Biographical data (biodata)
extensive surveys that ask applicants questions about their personal backgrounds and life experiences

Personality test an assessment that measures the extent to which an applicant possesses different kinds of job-related personality dimensions

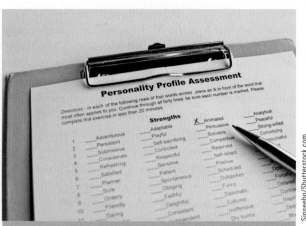

Personality tests measure the extent to which applicants possess different kinds of job-related personality dimensions.

ability tests, allowing companies to select applicants who are hardworking, organized, responsible, and smart!

Although increasingly prevalent, personality tests are not infallible. Charles Handler, a hiring consultant, admits assessments can't catch everything, saying, "There will be false positives, people who get through who shouldn't, and false negatives, someone who should've got through that didn't."[92]

Work sample tests, also called *performance tests*, require applicants to perform tasks that are actually done on the job. So, unlike specific ability tests, cognitive ability tests, biographical data surveys, and personality tests, which are indirect predictors of job performance, work sample tests directly measure job applicants' capability to do the job. For example, a candidate applying to be a pharmacist might be asked to consult medical databases and accurately fill prescriptions. An applicant for a sales position might have to role-play a sales pitch.

The Citadel financial firm hosts "'datathons' – contests in which undergraduate and graduate students who we would consider for artificial intelligence, technology, and data science roles at our firm have the chance to compete for a cash prize, while we use observable and measurable criteria to evaluate their performance."[93] Citadel's chief people and talent officers said, "Think about it: If you were an NFL scout, would you ask a prospective wide receiver to describe how he made catches in college? Or would you ask him to run a few routes with your QB and watch how he handles those tosses?"[94] Work sample tests are generally very good at predicting future job performance; however, they can be expensive to administer and can be used for only one kind of job. For example, an auto dealership could not use a work sample test for mechanics as a selection test for sales representatives.

Assessment centers use a series of job-specific simulations that are graded by multiple trained observers to determine applicants' ability to perform managerial work. Unlike the previously described selection tests that are commonly used for specific jobs or entry-level jobs, assessment centers are most often used to select applicants who have high potential to be good managers. For example, Walmart is using a visual reality (VR) skills assessment as one part of deciding who to promote into middle management. Via VR headsets, applicants respond to common managerial situations, such as handling conflict with employees or deciding which work takes priority when under deadlines and shorthanded. Drew Holler, Walmart's senior vice president of associate experience, said, "What we're trying to do is understand the capacity of the individual from a leadership perspective and how they view situations."[95]

Exhibit 11.6
In-Basket Item for an Assessment Center for Store Managers

```
February 28
Sam & Dave's Discount Warehouse
Orange, California

Dear Store Manager,

Last week, my children and I were shopping in your store.
After doing our grocery shopping, we stopped in the
electronics department and asked the clerk, whose name
is Donald Block, to help us find a copy of the latest
version of the Madden NFL video game. Mr. Block was rude,
unhelpful, and told us to find it for ourselves as he
was busy.

I've been a loyal customer for over six years and expect
you to immediately do something about Mr. Block's
behavior. If you don't, I'll start doing my shopping
somewhere else.

Sincerely,
Margaret Quinlan
```

Source: Adapted from N. W. Schmitt and R. J. Klimoski, *Research Methods in Human Resource Management* (Mason, OH: South-Western 1991).

Assessment centers often last two to five days and require participants to complete a number of tests and exercises that simulate managerial work.

Some of the more common assessment center exercises are in-basket exercises, role-plays, small-group presentations, and leaderless group discussions. An *in-basket exercise* is a test in which an applicant is given a manager's in-basket containing emails, voice messages, organizational policies, and other communications normally received by and available to managers. Applicants have a limited time to read through the in-basket, prioritize the items, and decide how to deal with each item. Experienced managers then score the applicants' decisions and recommendations. Exhibit 11.6 shows an item that could be used in an assessment center for evaluating applicants for a job as a store manager.

In a *leaderless group discussion*, another common assessment center exercise, a group of six applicants is given approximately two hours to solve a problem, but no one is put in charge (hence the name *leaderless* group discussion). Trained observers watch and score each participant on the extent to

Work sample tests tests that require applicants to perform tasks that are actually done on the job

Assessment centers a series of managerial simulations, graded by trained observers, that are used to determine applicants' capability for managerial work

which he or she facilitates discussion, listens, leads, persuades, and works well with others.

Are tests perfect predictors of job performance? No, they aren't. Some people who do well on selection tests will do poorly in their jobs. Likewise, some people who do poorly on selection tests (and therefore weren't hired) would have been very good performers. Nonetheless, valid tests will minimize selection errors (hiring people who should not have been hired and not hiring people who should have been hired) while maximizing correct selection decisions (hiring people who should have been hired and not hiring people who should not have been hired). Charles Handler, president of Rocket-Hire, a consulting firm on selection tests, says, "Predicting what humans will do is really . . . hard. Tests are a predictor and better than a coin toss, but you have to be realistic about them."[96] In short, tests substantially increase the chances that you'll hire the right person for the job, that is, someone who turns out to be a good performer. So, although tests aren't perfect, almost nothing predicts future job performance as well as the selection tests discussed here.

11-3d Interviews

In **interviews**, company representatives ask job applicants job-related questions to determine whether they are qualified for the job. Interviews are probably the most frequently used and relied on selection device. There are several basic kinds of interviews: unstructured, structured, and semistructured.

In **unstructured interviews**, interviewers are free to ask applicants anything they want, and studies show that they do. Because interviewers often disagree about which questions should be asked during interviews, different interviewers tend to ask applicants very different questions.[97] Furthermore, individual interviewers even seem to have a tough time asking the same questions from one interview to the next. This high level of variety can make things difficult. As a result, while unstructured interviews do predict job performance with some success, they are about half as accurate as structured interviews at predicting which job applicants should be hired.[98]

tsyhun/Shutterstock.com

By contrast, with **structured interviews**, standardized interview questions are prepared ahead of time so that all applicants are asked the same job-related questions.[99] Structuring interviews also ensures that interviewers ask only for important, job-related information. Not only are the accuracy, usefulness, and validity of the interview improved, but the chances that interviewers will ask questions about topics that violate employment laws (see Exhibit 11.4) are reduced.

Laszlo Bock, Google's former head of human resources, explains why structured interviews are so effective: ". . . think about the last five people you interviewed for a similar job. Did you give them similar questions or did each person get different questions? Did you cover everything you needed to with each of them, or did you run out of time? Did you hold them to exactly the same standard, or were you tougher on one because you were tired, cranky, and having a bad day? Did you write up detailed notes so that other interviewers could benefit from your insights? A concise hiring rubric [via structured interviews containing the same questions] addresses all these issues because it distills messy, vague, and complicated work situations down to measurable, comparable results."[100]

Four kinds of questions are typically asked in structured interviews. Situational questions ask applicants how they would respond in a hypothetical situation ("What would you do if . . .?"). These questions are more appropriate for hiring new graduates, who are unlikely to have encountered real-work situations because of their limited work experience. Behavioral questions ask applicants what they did in previous jobs that were similar to the job for which they are applying ("In your previous jobs, tell me about . . ."). These questions are more appropriate for hiring experienced individuals. Background questions ask applicants about their work experience, education, and

Interview a selection tool in which company representatives ask job applicants job-related questions to determine whether they are qualified for the job

Unstructured interviews interviews in which interviewers are free to ask the applicants anything they want

Structured interviews interviews in which all applicants are asked the same set of standardized questions, usually including situational, behavioral, background, and job-knowledge questions

Exhibit 11.7
Guidelines for Conducting Effective Structured Interviews

Interview Stage	What to Do

Planning the Interview

- Identify and define the knowledge, skills, abilities, and other (KSAO) characteristics needed for successful job performance.
- For each essential KSAO, develop key behavioral questions that will elicit examples of past accomplishments, activities, and performance.
- For each KSAO, develop a list of things to look for in the applicant's responses to key questions.

Conducting the Interview

- Create a relaxed, nonstressful interview atmosphere.
- Review the applicant's application form, résumé, and other information.
- Allocate enough time to complete the interview without interruption.
- Put the applicant at ease; don't jump right into heavy questioning.
- Tell the applicant what to expect. Explain the interview process.
- Obtain job-related information from the applicant by asking those questions prepared for each KSAO.
- Describe the job and the organization to the applicant. Applicants need adequate information to make a selection decision about the organization.

After the Interview

- Immediately after the interview, review your notes and make sure they are complete.
- Evaluate the applicant on each essential KSAO.
- Determine each applicant's probability of success, and make a hiring decision.

Source: B. M. Farrell, "The Art and Science of Employment Interviews," *Personnel Journal* 65 (1986): 91–94.

other qualifications ("Tell me about the training you received at . . ."). Job-knowledge questions ask applicants to demonstrate their job knowledge (for example, nurses might be asked, "Give me an example of a time when one of your patients had a severe reaction to a medication. How did you handle it?").[101]

Semistructured interviews lie between structured and unstructured interviews. A major part of the semistructured interview (perhaps as much as 80 percent) is based on structured questions, but some time is set aside for unstructured interviewing to allow the interviewer to probe into ambiguous or missing information uncovered during the structured portion of the interview.

How well do interviews predict future job performance? Contrary to what you've probably heard, recent evidence indicates that even unstructured

interviews do a fairly good job.[102] When conducted properly, however, structured interviews can lead to much more accurate hiring decisions than unstructured interviews. In some cases, the validity of structured interviews can rival that of cognitive ability tests.

But even more important because interviews are especially good at assessing applicants' interpersonal skills, they work particularly well with cognitive ability tests. Combining the two – using structured interviews together with cognitive ability tests to identify smart people who work well with others – leads to even better selection decisions than using either alone.[103] Exhibit 11.7 provides a set of guidelines for conducting effective structured employment interviews.

Virtual Realty Training Is Here

Talespin, a provider of virtual reality (VR) training, created Barry, an employee with substandard performance. Your task: Fire Barry. CEO Kyle Jackson says, "Almost every single person we put through that experience [of firing Barry] had an emotional reaction. We've had people take the headset off saying, 'I just can't do this. I'm just too uncomfortable.'"

Jeremey Bailenson, head of Stanford's Virtual Human Interactive Lab, says, "When you go into VR you forget the physical world. I've had CEOs of Fortune 100 companies be in front of their entire C-suite in the room – and when they get into a VR conversation with an employee, it's as though no one else is there. One CEO, a tear ran down his face and out of the headset because he had to fire someone."

Walmart purchased 17,000 VR headsets for 45 training modules, such as leadership training, dealing with difficult customers, or handling the crowds that storm Black Friday sales.

VR isn't just for gaming. VR will be part of your professional training.

Wavebreakmedia Ltd FUS1607/Alamy Stock Photo

Sources: N. Gagliordi, "Walmart deploys 17,000 Oculus Go Headsets to Train Its Employees," *ZDNet*, September 20, 2018, accessed May 3, 2020, www.zdnet .com/article/walmart-deploys-17000-oculus-go-headsets-to-train-its -employees/; J. Incao, "How VR Is Transforming the Way We Train Associates," Walmart, September 20, 2018, accessed May 3, 2020, corporate.walmart .com/newsroom/innovation/20180920/how-vr-is-transforming-the-way-we -train-associates; S. Melendez, "Want to Protect Your Job? VR Training Can Help," *Wall Street Journal*, August 29, 2019, accessed May 3, 2020, www.wsj .com/articles/want-to-protect-your-job-vr-training-can-help-11567094850; P . Rubin, "Boss Acting Nicer Recently? You May Have VR to Thank," *Wired*, February 28, 2019, accessed May 3, 2020, www.wired.com/story/vr-soft-skills/?CNDID =49330717&CNDI%E2%80%A6ailing=WIRED%20NL%20030319%20(1)&utm _medium=email&utm_source=nl.

11-4 TRAINING

According to the American Society for Training and Development, a typical investment in training increases productivity by an average of 17 percent, reduces employee turnover, and makes companies more profitable.[104] This is why communication giant AT&T is spending $1 billion to retrain 100,000 of its workers.[105] Giving employees the knowledge and skills they need to improve their performance is just the first step in developing employees, however. The second step – and not enough companies do this – is giving employees formal feedback about job performance (which we will discuss in Section 11-5).

Training means providing opportunities for employees to develop the job-specific skills, experience, and knowledge they need to do their jobs or improve their performance. Globally, companies spend an estimated $366 billion a year on training.[106]

Training developing the skills, experience, and knowledge employees need to perform their jobs or improve their performance

Needs assessment the process of identifying and prioritizing the learning needs of employees

*To make sure those training dollars are well spent, companies need to **11-4a determine specific training needs**, **11-4b select appropriate training methods**, and **11-4c evaluate training**.*

11-4a Determining Training Needs

Needs assessment is the process of identifying and prioritizing the learning needs of employees. Needs assessments can be conducted by identifying performance deficiencies, listening to customer complaints, surveying employees and managers, or formally testing employees' skills and knowledge. For example, JPMorgan Chase bank assesses IT employees' skills via its "skills passport" program, generating a customized list of training courses and job activities to strengthen and broaden each employee's technical capabilities.[107]

Note that training should never be conducted without first performing a needs assessment. Sometimes, training isn't needed at all or isn't needed for all employees. Unfortunately, however, many organizations simply require all employees to attend training whether they need to or not. As a result, employees who are not interested or don't need the training may react negatively during or after training. Likewise, employees who should be sent for training but aren't may also react negatively. Consequently, a needs assessment is an important tool for deciding who should or should not attend training. In fact, employment law restricts employers from discriminating on the basis of age, sex, sexual orientation, gender identity, race, color, religion, national origin, or disability when selecting training participants. Just like hiring

Exhibit 11.8
Training Objectives and Methods

Training Objective	Training Methods
Impart Information and Knowledge	▶ *Films and videos.* Films and videos present information, illustrate problems and solutions, and effectively hold trainees' attention.
	▶ *Lectures.* Trainees listen to instructors' oral presentations.
	▶ *Planned readings.* Trainees read about concepts or ideas before attending training.
Develop Analytical and Problem-Solving Skills	▶ *Case studies.* Cases are analyzed and discussed in small groups. The cases present a specific problem or decision, and trainees develop methods for solving the problem or making the decision.
	▶ *Coaching and mentoring.* Coaching and mentoring of trainees by managers involves informal advice, suggestions, and guidance. This method is helpful for reinforcing other kinds of training and for trainees who benefit from support and personal encouragement.
	▶ *Group discussions.* Small groups of trainees actively discuss specific topics. The instructor may perform the role of discussion leader.
Practice, Learn, or Change Job Behaviors	▶ *On-the-job training.* New employees are assigned to experienced employees. The trainee learns by watching the experienced employee perform the job and eventually by working alongside the experienced employee. Gradually, the trainee is left on his or her own to perform the job.
	▶ *Role-playing.* Trainees assume job-related roles and practice new behaviors by acting out what they would do in job-related situations.
	▶ *Simulations, virtual reality, and games.* Experiential exercises place trainees in realistic job-related situations and give them the opportunity to experience a job-related condition in a relatively low-cost setting. The trainee benefits from simulated or actual hands-on experience before actually performing the job, where mistakes may be more costly.
	▶ *Vestibule training.* Procedures and equipment similar to those used in the actual job are set up in a special area called a ***vestibule.*** The trainee is then taught how to perform the job at his or her own pace without disrupting the actual flow of work, making costly mistakes, or exposing the trainee and others to dangerous conditions.
Impart Information and Knowledge; Develop Analytical and Problem-Solving Skills; and Practice, Learn, or Change Job Behaviors	▶ *Computer-based learning.* Interactive videos, teleconferencing, apps, and web-based learning may be combined to present multimedia-based training.

Source: A. Fowler, "How to Decide on Training Methods," *People Management* 25, no. 1 (1995): 36.

decisions, the selection of training participants should be based on job-related information.

11-4b Training Methods

Assume that you're a training director for a hospital system and that you're in charge of making sure all employees in the biocontaminant unit can safely treat patients with Ebola.[108] Exhibit 11.8 lists a number of training methods you could use: films and videos, lectures, planned readings, case studies, coaching and mentoring, group discussions, on-the-job training, role-playing, simulations, virtual reality, and games, vestibule training, and computer-based learning. Which method would be best?

To choose the best method, you should consider a number of factors, such as the number of people to be trained, the cost of training, and the objectives of the training. For instance, if the training objective is to impart information or knowledge to trainees, then you should use films and videos, lectures, and planned readings. In our example, trainees might read a manual or attend/view a lecture about how to put on and remove personal protective gear.

If developing analytical and problem-solving skills is the objective, then use case studies, coaching and mentoring, and group discussions. In our example, trainees might view a video documenting how a team handled

More and more companies are turning towards e-learning to save costs and time typically associated with training. Employees no longer have to travel to receive their training, and can take advantage of online training modules when it is convenient to them.

exposure to the disease, talk with first responders who have worked in West Africa, and discuss what they would do in a similar situation.

If practicing, learning, or changing job behaviors is the objective, then use on-the-job training, role-playing, simulations, virtual reality and games, and vestibule training. Employees at the biocontainment unit of the University of Texas Southwestern Medical Center (UTSMC) role-play putting on and taking off their protective gear. Because of the number of steps involved, this is done in teams to ensure compliance so as to prevent the spread of the deadly disease. UTSMC sprays fake patients used during the training with spicy, peppery Tabasco sauce. Dr. Bruce Myer says that if doctors and nurses get Tabasco on their skin, "it gives immediate feedback," to let them know a potentially deadly mistake has just been made.[109]

If training is supposed to meet more than one of these objectives, then your best choice may be to combine one of the previous methods with computer-based training. According to chief people officer Mike Fenlon and digital talent leader Sara McEneaney, global accounting firm PwC combines training methods when developing digital skills: "We develop digital fitness through tech-enabled learning–including podcasts, gamification, immersive skill building, multimedia content, and quizzes pushed through mobile platforms."[110]

These days, most companies have adopted computer-based e-learning." E-learning offers several advantages. Because employees don't need to leave their jobs, travel costs are greatly reduced. Also, because employees can take training modules when it is convenient (i.e., they don't have to fall behind at their jobs to attend week-long training courses), workplace productivity should increase, and employee stress should decrease. And, if a company's technology infrastructure can support it, e-learning can be much faster than traditional training methods.

There are, however, several disadvantages to e-learning. First, despite its increasing popularity, it's not always the appropriate training method. E-learning can be a good way to impart information, but it isn't always as effective for changing job behaviors or developing problem-solving and analytical skills. Second, e-learning requires a significant investment in computers and high-speed internet and network connections for all employees. Finally, though e-learning can be faster, many employees find it so boring and unengaging that they may choose to do their jobs rather than complete e-learning courses when sitting alone at their desks. E-learning may become more interesting, however, as more companies incorporate interactivity, gamification, or virtual reality into e-learning courses.

Adobe, which makes digital creativity, photo/video, publishing and document apps, follows three rules when creating e-learning for its 22,000 employees:[111]

1. *Less is more.* Limit each e-learning session to three points. Daniele Clark, senior director of global talent development, says, "What do you most want employees to know about a given topic and use in their jobs? What are the three essential takeaways?"[112]

2. *Avoid one-way communication.* Says Clark, "People won't be engaged. They'll spend half the session checking their phones."[113] So, make half of each session interactive with polls, audience comments, and questions that invite audience participation.

3. *After e-learning, use an online coaching platform with messaging and video chats to show people how to use what they've learned.* Says Clark, Adobe's

Rawpixel.com/Shutterstock.com

platform, Pluma, "has been great for helping people see how to apply the training they're getting online to specific situations, and to their own careers."[114]

11-4c Evaluating Training

After selecting a training method and conducting the training, the last step is to evaluate the training. Training can be evaluated in four ways: on *reactions* (how satisfied trainees were with the program), on *learning* (how much employees improved their knowledge or skills), on *behavior* (how much employees actually changed their on-the-job behavior because of training), or on *results* (how much training improved job performance, such as increased sales or quality, or decreased costs).[115] In general, training provides meaningful benefits for most companies if it is done well. For example, a study by the American Society for Training and Development shows that a training budget as small as $680 per employee can increase a company's total return on investment by 6 percent.[116] Chuck Runyon, CEO of Anytime Fitness, which has 4,500 locations, says, "The only thing worse than training people and having them leave is not training people and having them stay."[117]

11-5 PERFORMANCE APPRAISAL

Performance appraisal is the process of assessing how well employees are doing their jobs. Most employees and managers intensely dislike the performance appraisal process. In fact, 65 percent of employees are dissatisfied with their performance appraisal process. Likewise, according to the Society for Human Resource Management, 95 percent of human resource managers are dissatisfied with their companies' performance appraisal systems. Sixteen percent of companies, including Accenture, Microsoft Adobe, and General Electric (GE), have abolished their performance appraisal systems altogether.[118] GE head of human resources Susan Peters explains the reason for the change this way: "It existed in more or less the same form since I started at the company in 1979, but we think over many years it had become more a ritual than moving the company upwards and forwards."[119]

On the other hand, Paul Rubenstein, a partner at global human resources consulting firm Aon Hewitt, says, "If you get rid of the performance ratings, how are you going to get rid of a fair and equitable and measurable system to blame the distribution of pay on? Because why

did performance ratings come into existence? So, there's some mechanism to force pay decisions. People wonder, which came first, the rating or the pay decision?"[120] Consulting firm CEB surveyed 9,000 managers and employees in 18 countries and found that employees were 14 percent less satisfied when companies dropped performance appraisals. The experience, according to CEB's Brian Kropp, "is pretty negative." Managers devote less time to performance issues and, without clarity regarding performance levels, employees often said, "my manager's just going to give more money to the person he likes."[121]

Indeed, performance appraisals are used for four broad purposes: making administrative decisions (for example, pay increase, promotion, retention), providing feedback for employee development (e.g., performance, developing career plans), evaluating human resource programs (e.g., validating selection systems), and for documentation purposes (e.g., documenting performance ratings and decisions based on those ratings).[122]

*Let's explore how companies can avoid some of these problems with performance appraisals by **11-5a accurately measuring job performance** and **11-5b effectively sharing performance feedback with employees**.*

11-5a Accurately Measuring Job Performance

Workers often have strong doubts about the accuracy of their performance appraisals – and they may be right. For example, it's widely known that assessors are prone to errors when rating worker performance. Three of the most common rating errors are central tendency, halo, and leniency. *Central tendency error* occurs when assessors rate all workers as average or in the middle of the scale. *Halo error* occurs when assessors rate all workers as performing at the same level (good, bad, or average) in all parts of their jobs. *Leniency error* occurs when assessors rate all workers as performing particularly well. One of the reasons managers make these errors is that they often don't spend enough time gathering or reviewing performance data. Facebook reduces appraisal errors by having managers work together to finalize appraisal ratings. "Managers sit together and discuss their reports face-to-face, defending and championing, debating and deliberating, and incorporating peer feedback. Here, the goal is to minimize the 'idiosyncratic rater effect' – also

> **Performance appraisal** the process of assessing how well employees are doing their jobs

known as personal opinion. (This way) people aren't unduly punished when individual managers are hard graders or unfairly rewarded when they're easy graders."[123] A slightly different approach is the use of *calibration committees* in which higher-level managers review and adjust ratings made by lower level managers for consistency. One study found that 25 percent of ratings were adjusted, with 80 percent of adjusted ratings lowered because of leniency error.[124]

What can be done to minimize rating errors and improve the accuracy with which job performance is measured? In general, two approaches have been used: improving performance appraisal measures themselves and training performance raters to be more accurate.

One of the ways companies try to improve performance appraisal measures is to use as many objective performance measures as possible. **Objective performance measures** are measures of performance that are easily and directly counted or quantified. Common objective performance measures include output, scrap, waste, sales, customer complaints, and rejection rates.

But when objective performance measures aren't available (and frequently they aren't), subjective performance measures have to be used instead. **Subjective performance measures** require that someone judge or assess a worker's performance. The most common kind of subjective performance measure is the graphic rating scale (GRS), as shown in Exhibit 11.9. Graphic rating scales are most widely used because they are easy to construct, but they are very susceptible to rating errors.

A popular alternative to graphic rating scales is

PlusONE/Shutterstock.com

the **behavior observation scale (BOS)**. BOSs requires raters to rate the frequency with which workers perform specific behaviors representative of the job dimensions that are critical to successful job performance. Exhibit 11.9 shows a BOS for two important job dimensions for a retail salesperson: customer service and money handling. Notice that each dimension lists several specific behaviors characteristic of a worker who excels in that dimension of job performance. (Normally, the scale would list 7 to 12 items per dimension, not 3, as in the exhibit.) Notice also that the behaviors are good behaviors, meaning they indicate good performance, and the rater is asked to judge how frequently an employee engaged in those good behaviors. The logic behind the BOS is that better performers engage in good behaviors more often.

Not only do BOSs work well for rating critical dimensions of performance, but studies also show that managers strongly prefer BOSs for giving performance feedback; accurately differentiating between poor, average, and good workers; identifying training needs; and accurately measuring performance. And in response to the statement, "If I were defending a company, this rating format would be an asset to my case," attorneys strongly preferred BOSs over other kinds of subjective performance appraisal scales.[125]

The second approach to improving the measurement of workers' job performance is **rater training**. The most effective is frame-of-reference training, in which a group of trainees learn how to do performance appraisals by watching a video of an employee at work. Next, they evaluate the performance of the person in the video. A trainer (an expert in the subject matter) then shares his or her evaluations, and trainees' evaluations are compared with the expert's. The expert then explains the rationales behind his or her evaluations. This process is repeated until the differences in evaluations given by trainees and evaluations by the expert are minimized. The underlying logic behind the frame-of-reference training is that by adopting the frame of reference used by an expert, trainees will be able to accurately observe, judge, and use relevant appraisal scales to evaluate the performance of others.[126]

Objective performance measures measures of job performance that are easily and directly counted or quantified

Subjective performance measures measures of job performance that require someone to judge or assess a worker's performance

Behavior observation scales (BOSs) rating scales that indicate the frequency with which workers perform specific behaviors that are representative of the job dimensions critical to successful job performance

Rater training training performance appraisal raters in how to avoid rating errors and increase rating accuracy

Exhibit 11.9
Subjective Performance Appraisal Scales

Graphic Rating Scale

	Very poor	Poor	Average	Good	Very good
Example 1: Quality of work performed is	1	2	3	4	5

	Very poor (20% errors)	Poor (15% errors)	Average (10% errors)	Good (5% errors)	Very good (less than 5% errors)
Example 2: Quality of work performed is	1	2	3	4	5

Behavioral Observation Scale

Dimension: Customer Service

	Almost Never				Almost Always
1. Greets customers with a smile and a "hello."	1	2	3	4	5
2. Calls other stores to help customers find merchandise that is not in stock.	1	2	3	4	5
3. Promptly handles customer concerns and complaints.	1	2	3	4	5

Dimension: Money Handling

	Almost Never				Almost Always
1. Accurately makes change from customer transactions..	1	2	3	4	5
2. Accounts balance at the end of the day, no shortages or surpluses.	1	2	3	4	5
3. Accurately records transactions in computer system.	1	2	3	4	5

11-5b Sharing Performance Feedback

After gathering accurate performance data, the next step is to share performance feedback with employees. Unfortunately, even when performance appraisal ratings are accurate, the appraisal process often breaks down at the feedback stage. Employees become defensive and dislike hearing any negative assessments of their work, no matter how small. Managers become defensive, too, and dislike giving appraisal feedback as much as employees dislike receiving it. In response, many companies are asking managers to ease up on harsh feedback and instead accentuate the positive by focusing on employee strengths. In the past, Michelle Russell of **Boston Consulting Group** says, "We would bring them in and beat them down a bit."[127] Some employees would suffer a crisis of confidence and performance and then quit. At **Intel**, telling employees they "need improvement"

deflates morale, says HR manager Devra Johnson, "We call them the walking wounded."[128]

What can be done to overcome the inherent difficulties in performance appraisal feedback? To start, be mindful of being overly critical and making employees so defensive that they quit listening. Professor Samuel Culbert, author of *Get Rid of the Performance Review!* explains, "When it comes time for an annual performance review, the employee walks in the room and wants to hear the good things they've done, the contributions and sacrifices they've made, have been seen, valued, and they're going to be rewarded. And the boss walks in the room to tell the individual their faults."[129]

The top half of Exhibit 11.10 offers some suggestion for being less negative and more positive in feedback sessions. Also, because performance appraisal ratings have traditionally been the judgments of just one person,

Exhibit 11.10
How and What to Discuss in a Performance Appraisal Feedback Session

How to Discuss Performance Feedback

	A	B
1	Don't say...	Instead say...
2	"What are we stuck on?"	"What are we doing really well?"
3	"Nice work."	"You show great promise with...."
4	"You need to get better at...."	"This is another way that's been successful."
5	"We can't do this."	"We haven't done this yet."

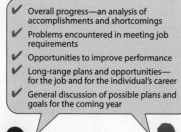

- ✓ Overall progress—an analysis of accomplishments and shortcomings
- ✓ Problems encountered in meeting job requirements
- ✓ Opportunities to improve performance
- ✓ Long-range plans and opportunities—for the job and for the individual's career
- ✓ General discussion of possible plans and goals for the coming year

Source: H. H. Meyer, "A Solution to the Performance Appraisal Feedback Enigma," *Academy of Management Executive* 5, no. 1 (1991): 68–76; R. Feintzeig, "Everything Is Awesome! Why You Can't Tell Employees They're Doing a Bad Job." *Wall Street Journal*, February 10, 2015, accessed May 7, 2015, www.wsj.com/articles/everything-is-awesome-why-you-cant-tell-employees-theyre-doing-a-bad-job-1423613936.

the boss, another possibility is to use **360-degree feedback**. In this approach, feedback comes from four sources: the boss, subordinates, peers and coworkers, and the employees themselves. The data, which are obtained anonymously (except for the boss's), are compiled into a feedback report comparing the employee's self-ratings with those of the boss, subordinates, and peers and coworkers. Usually, a consultant or human resource specialist discusses the results with the employee. The advantage of 360-degree programs is that negative feedback ("You don't listen") is often more credible when it comes from several people.

Herbert Meyer, who has been studying performance appraisal feedback

360-degree feedback a performance appraisal process in which feedback is obtained from the boss, subordinates, peers, and coworkers, and the employees themselves

for more than 30 years, recommends a list of topics to discuss in performance appraisal feedback sessions (see the bottom half of Exhibit 11.10).[130] Furthermore, managers can do three different things to make performance reviews more comfortable and productive. First, they should separate developmental feedback, which is designed to improve future performance, from administrative feedback, which is used as a reward for past performance, such as for raises. When managers give developmental feedback, they're acting as coaches, but when they give administrative feedback, they're acting as judges. These roles, coaches and judges, are clearly incompatible. As coaches, managers encourage, pointing out opportunities for growth and improvement, and employees are typically open and receptive to feedback. But as judges, managers are evaluative, and employees are typically defensive and closed to feedback.

Second, Meyer suggests that performance appraisal feedback sessions be based on self-appraisals, in which employees carefully assess their own strengths, weaknesses, successes, and failures in writing. Because employees play an active role in the review of their performance, managers can be coaches rather than judges. Also, because the focus is on future goals and development, both employees and managers are likely to be more satisfied with the process and more committed to future plans and changes. Because the focus is on development and not administrative assessment, studies show that self-appraisals lead to more candid self-assessments than traditional supervisory reviews.[131]

Job search website **Monster.com** has put self-appraisals at the center of its performance feedback system by asking managers to conduct quarterly check-ins with their direct reports. Prior to the meetings, employees must complete a short template that includes one to three professional goals for the upcoming period, what kind of results they hope to achieve in that time frame, and how they plan to achieve them. Monster.com chief human resources officer Kim Mullaney says that "by communicating professional aspirations with their superiors, staffers will be more engaged. Knowing that you're in direct control of your goals is extremely important – as is knowing that your boss is a stakeholder in the plan."[132]

Finally, what people do with the performance feedback they receive really matters. A study of 1,361 senior managers found that managers who reviewed their 360-degree feedback with an executive coach (hired by the company) were more likely to set specific goals for improvement, ask their bosses for ways to improve, and subsequently improve their performance.[133] A five-year study of 252 managers found that their performance improved dramatically if they met with their subordinates to discuss their 360-degree feedback ("You don't listen") and how they were going to address it ("I'll restate what others have said before stating my opinion"). Performance was dramatically lower for managers who never discussed their 360-degree feedback with subordinates and for managers who did not routinely do so.

Why is discussing 360-degree feedback with subordinates so effective? These discussions help managers understand their weaknesses better, force them to develop a plan to improve, and demonstrate to the subordinates the managers' public commitment to improving.[134] In short, it helps to have people discuss their performance feedback with others, but it particularly helps to have them discuss their feedback with the people who provided it.

11-6 COMPENSATION AND EMPLOYEE SEPARATION

Taco Bell typically pays general managers $50,000 to $80,000 a year in company-owned restaurants. However, it announced plans to "test" a salary of $100,000 a year in job markets where finding and keeping managers is difficult. Ferril Onyett, senior director of global training and international human resources, said, "As we grow the Taco Bell business, we're really focused on managers. They have a huge impact on restaurant performance. We hope through this test we can evaluate the effect on not only restaurant performance but team morale, customer experience and recruitment and retention."[135] Neil Saunders, managing director of retail at GlobalData, a market research firm, said, "I think it's a necessary move because I think the labor market is now extremely tight. In order to attract good talent, companies have to pay for it and give good benefits."[136]

Compensation includes both the financial and the nonfinancial rewards that organizations give employees in exchange for their work. **Employee separation** is a broad term covering the loss of an employee for any reason. *Involuntary separation* occurs when employers terminate or lay off employees. *Voluntary separation* occurs when employees quit or retire. Because employee separations affect recruiting, selection, training, and compensation, organizations should forecast the number of employees they expect to lose through terminations, layoffs, turnover, or retirements when doing human resource planning.

Let's learn more about compensation by examining the **11-6a compensation decisions that managers must make** *as well as* **11-6b termination, 11-6c downsizing, 11-6d retirement**, *and* **11-6e turnover**.

11-6a Compensation Decisions

There are three basic kinds of compensation decisions: pay level, pay variability, and pay structure.[137] *Pay-level decisions* concern whether to pay workers at a level that is below, above, or at current market wages. Companies use job evaluation to set

> **Compensation** the financial and nonfinancial rewards that organizations give employees in exchange for their work
>
> **Employee separation** the voluntary or involuntary loss of an employee

their pay structures. **Job evaluation** determines the worth of each job by determining the market value of the knowledge, skills, and abilities needed to perform it. After conducting a job evaluation, most companies try to pay the going rate, meaning the current market wage. There are always companies, however, whose financial situation causes them to pay considerably less than current market wages.

Some companies choose to pay above-average wages for key management and technical positions where it's difficult to attract and keep people. *Above-market wages* can attract a larger, more qualified pool of job applicants, increase the rate of job acceptance, decrease the time it takes to fill positions, and increase the time that employees stay.[138] Many managers, however, are reluctant to pay above-average wages because of budget concerns or resentment from lower-paid employees. Patty McCord, Netflix's former chief talent officer, says:

> *In that case I suggest identifying the positions with the greatest potential to boost your performance and paying top dollar to fill them with the very best people you can get. Think about it this way: What if by paying top of market you could bring in one supremely talented person who could do the job of two people or add even more value than that? Consider the 80/20 rule about sales teams: that 20 percent of your salespeople will generate 80 percent of your revenue. It may apply to other employees. I've seen a similar effect on team after team.[139]*

Pay-variability decisions concern the extent to which employees' pay varies with individual and organizational performance. Linking pay to performance is intended to increase employee motivation, effort, and job performance. Piecework, sales commissions, profit sharing, employee stock ownership plans, and stock options are common pay-variability options. For instance, under **piecework** pay plans, employees are paid a set rate for each item produced up to some standard (for example, $3 per item produced for output up to 100 units per day). After productivity exceeds the standard, employees are paid a set amount for each unit of output over the standard (e.g., $4.50 for each unit above 100 units). Under a sales **commission** plan, salespeople are paid a percentage of the purchase price of items they sell. The more they sell, the more they earn. At inventory software company **Fishbowl**, every employee's pay is determined in part by how much he or she contributes to company sales. Employees receive a base salary discounted from the market rate, as well as a monthly commission based on how much they were able to directly influence sales. Since a company needs more than just salespeople, the significance of the commission is relative to the function within the company. Programmers receive 80 percent of their pay as base salary and 20 percent as commission, whereas salespeople receive 10 percent of their pay as base salary and 90 percent as commission. Even administrative employees earn commission. In lean months, no commissions are paid, but in good months, employees can double their base salaries through commission payouts. Overall, commissions increase Fishbowl employees' compensation by 19 percent per year.[140]

Because pay plans such as piecework and commissions are based on individual performance, they can reduce the incentive that people have to work together. Therefore, companies also use group rewards (discussed in Chapter 10) and organizational incentives, such as profit sharing, employee stock ownership plans, and stock options, to encourage teamwork and cooperation.

With **profit sharing**, employees receive a portion of the organization's profits over and above their regular compensation. In 2019, before the coronavirus pandemic of 2020, Delta Airlines posted a profit of $6.2 billion.[141] Delta pays 10 percent of the first $2.5 billion in profits and 20 percent of all profits above $2.5 billion to employees.[142] Thanks to the company's generous profit sharing plan, $1.6 billion of that was distributed to employees – "marking the sixth year in a row that Delta's profit sharing has exceeded $1 billion," said CEO Ed Bastian.[143]

Employee stock ownership plans (ESOPs) compensate employees by awarding them shares of the company stock in addition to their regular compensation. Central States Manufacturing, a steel-cutting firm in Lowell, Arkansas, is 100 percent owned by its 517 employees. Six and a half percent of each employee's annual pay goes into a tax-deferred ESOP account. Aaron King, a 60-year-old truck driver with the company for 23 years, has accumulated $1.25 million in his ESOP account. Because of the ESOP, he says, "We hold one another accountable. Somebody leaving a bundle of metal where

---

Job evaluation a process that determines the worth of each job in a company by evaluating the market value of the KSAs needed to perform it

Piecework a compensation system in which employees are paid a set rate for each item they produce

Commission a compensation system in which employees earn a percentage of each sale they make

Profit sharing a compensation system in which a company pays a percentage of its profits to employees in addition to their regular compensation

Employee stock ownership plan (ESOP) a compensation system that awards employees shares of company stock in addition to their regular compensation

it could be run over – a $3,000 bundle – we go and get that guy and talk to him. (Because) It's going to come out of all of our paychecks."[144] Not all ESOPs are 100 percent employee owned, however. Employees at yogurt company **Chobani** receive stock grants from founder and majority owner Hamdi Ulukaya enabling them to own up to 10 percent of the $3 billion company.[145]

Stock options give employees the right to purchase shares of stock at a set price. Options work like this. Let's say you are awarded the right (or option) to buy 100 shares of stock from the company for $5 a share. If the company's stock price rises to $15 a share, you can exercise your options, sell the stock for $15 a share, come out with $1,000. When you exercise your options, you pay the company $500 (100 shares at $5 a share), but because the stock is selling for $15 in the stock market, you can sell your 100 shares for $1,500 and make $1,000. Of course, as the company's profits and share values increase, stock options become even more valuable to employees. Stock options have no value, however, if the company's stock falls below the option "grant price," the price at which the options have been issued to you. The options you have on 100 shares of stock with a grant price of $5 aren't going to do you a lot of good if the company's stock is worth $2.50. Proponents of stock options argue that this gives employees and managers a strong incentive to work hard to make the company successful. If they do, the company's profits and stock price increase, and their stock options increase in value. If they don't, profits stagnate or turn into losses, and their stock options decrease in value or become worthless. To learn more about ESOPs and stock options, see the National Center for Employee Ownership (www.nceo.org).

The incentive from ESOPS and stock options has to be more than just a piece of paper, however. It has to motivate employees with the real opportunity to grow the value of the company and their wealth. **Publix Super Markets**, with 200,000+ employees and annual sales approaching $40 billion, is the largest ESOP in the United States. Dain Rusk, Publix's vice president of pharmacy says, "Oftentimes, you hear the phrase, 'Think like a customer, act like an owner.' We actually can live that every day because of our employee ownership."[146]

Publix Supermarkets ranked number 1 in US ESOPs in 2019, according to the National Center for Employee Ownership.

Felix Mizioznikov/Shutterstock.com

With typical employees earning 3.5 shares of stock each week, equivalent to roughly 8 percent of their salary, someone starting at Publix out of high school can retire early with more than $1 million in Publix stock.[147] In the United States, 6,600 employee-owned businesses, worth $1.4 trillion, are owned by 14.2 million employees.[148]

Pay-structure decisions are concerned with internal pay distributions, meaning the extent to which people in the company receive very different levels of pay.[149] With *hierarchical pay structures*, there are big differences from one pay level to another. The highest pay levels are for people near the top of the pay distribution. The basic idea behind hierarchical pay structures is that large differences in pay between jobs or organizational levels should motivate people to work harder to obtain those higher-paying jobs. Many publicly owned companies have hierarchical pay structures, paying huge salaries to their top managers and CEOs. For example, CEOs of the 350 largest US firms now make an average of $17.2 million per year, which is 278 times the salary of the average employee.[150]

By contrast, *compressed pay structures* typically have fewer pay levels and smaller differences in pay between levels. Pay is less dispersed and more similar across jobs in the company. The basic idea behind compressed pay structures is that similar pay levels should lead to higher levels of cooperation, feelings

Stock options a compensation system that gives employees the right to purchase shares of stock at a set price, even if the value of the stock increases above that price

of fairness and a common purpose, and better group and team performance.

So, should companies choose hierarchical or compressed pay structures? The evidence isn't straightforward, but studies seem to indicate that there are significant problems with the hierarchical approach. The most damaging finding is that there appears to be little link between organizational performance and the pay of top managers.[151] Furthermore, studies of professional athletes indicate that hierarchical pay structures (e.g., paying superstars 40 to 50 times as much as the lowest-paid athlete on the team) hurt the performance of teams and individual players.[152] Likewise, managers are twice as likely to quit their jobs when their companies have very strong hierarchical pay structures (i.e., when they're paid dramatically less than the people above them).[153] For now, it seems that hierarchical pay structures work best for independent work, where it's easy to determine the contributions of individual performers, and little coordination with others is needed to get the job done. In other words, hierarchical pay structures work best when clear links can be drawn between individual performance and individual rewards. By contrast, compressed pay structures, in which everyone receives similar pay, seem to work best for interdependent work, which requires employees to work together. Some companies are pursuing a middle ground: combining hierarchical and compressed pay structures by giving ordinary workers the chance to earn more through ESOPs, stock options, and profit sharing.

11-6b Terminating Employees

The words "You're fired!" may have never been directed at you, but lots of people hear them, as more than 400,000 people a year get fired from their jobs. Getting fired is a terrible thing, but many managers make it even worse by bungling the firing process, needlessly provoking the person who was fired and unintentionally inviting lawsuits. Manager Craig Silverman had to fire the head of a company whom his organization had just acquired. He was specifically instructed to invite her to a meeting, which would require her to travel halfway across the country, and then fire her immediately on arrival. He said, "I literally had to tell the car service to wait. I don't think it ever entered (her) mind that (she) would be terminated."[154] When Zynga terminated almost all of the employees from OMGPOP, a startup company it had acquired a year before, one of the employees tweeted, "I learned via Facebook I was laid off today and @omgpop office is closed. Thanks @zynga for again reminding me how not to operate a business."[155] A computer systems engineer was fired on "Take Your Daughter to Work Day," with his eight-year-old daughter sitting next to him in the human resource manager's office. He and his daughter were both escorted from the building.[156] How would you feel if you had been fired in one of these ways? Though firing is never pleasant (and managers hate firings nearly as much as employees do), managers can do several things to minimize the problems inherent in firing employees.

To start, in most situations, firing should not be the first option. Instead, employees should be given a chance to change their behavior. When problems arise, employees should have ample warning and must be specifically informed as to the nature and seriousness of the trouble they're in. After being notified, they should be given sufficient time to change their behavior. Ron Cohen is CEO and founder of **Acorda Therapeutics**, a company that develops therapies to restore neurological function for people with multiple sclerosis and spinal cord injuries. Cohen first fired an employee when he was 31 years old. He says it was painful, and, "I wound up hugging the employee, and she was crying on my shoulder." Since then, however, when he fires someone, they've had plenty of opportunities to address performance issues. Says Cohen, "I've learned over the years that if the employee doesn't expect it and know it's coming, you're not doing your job as a manager."[157]

Dos and Don'ts of Conducting Layoffs in the Digital Age

» **DO** conduct layoffs in person. If that's not possible, conduct the layoff live over the phone or via Skype. Email should only be used as a last resort if the employee is perpetually absent and unresponsive.

» **DON'T** announce a mass layoff via chat, IM, or other collaborative networking platform.

» **DO** shut down access to internal communication systems at the same time employees are being summoned to the meeting or call during which they will learn of the layoff.

» **DON'T** let employees figure out that they've been laid off by seeing that their access to email, Slack, IM, or other digital platforms has been disabled.

» **DO** keep communication brief and to the point to minimize time for speculation and suspense.

» **DON'T** conduct a layoff without a representative from human resources present.

» **DO** gather the remaining team and let them know who is no longer with the company. Remember to alert remote employees and freelancers.

» **DON'T** discuss specifics about why an employee was let go with remaining employees.

» Most of all, **DO** be kind, **DO** treat people decently, and **DO** act with integrity.

iStock.com/WillSelarep

Source: L. Dishman, "The New Etiquette of Firing in the Digital Age," *Fast Company*, November 19, 2015, accessed May 1, 2016, www.fastcompany.com/3053763/the-future-of-work/the-new-etiquette-of-firing-in-the-digital-age.

If problems continue, the employees should again be counseled about their job performance, what could be done to improve it, and the possible consequences if things don't change (such as a written reprimand, suspension without pay, or firing). Sometimes this is enough to solve the problem. If the problem isn't corrected after several rounds of warnings and discussions, however, the employee may be terminated.[158]

Second, employees should be fired only for a good reason. Employers used to hire and fire employees under the legal principle of employment at will, which allowed them to fire employees for a good reason, a bad reason, or no reason at all. (Employees could also quit for a good reason, a bad reason, or no reason whenever they desired.) As employees began contesting their firings in court, however, the principle of wrongful discharge emerged. **Wrongful discharge** is a legal doctrine that requires employers to have a job-related reason to terminate employees. In other words, like other major human resource decisions, termination decisions should be made on the basis of job-related factors such as violating company rules or consistently poor performance. And with former employees winning 68 percent of wrongful

discharge cases and the average wrongful termination award at \$532,000 and climbing, managers should record the job-related reasons for the termination, document specific instances of rule violations or continued poor performance, and keep notes and documents from the counseling sessions held with employees.[159]

11-6c Downsizing

Downsizing is the planned elimination of jobs in a company (see box "Dos and Don'ts of Conducting Layoffs in the Digital Age"). Two-thirds of companies that downsize will downsize a second time within a year. HSBC, Europe's largest bank, which does much of its business in Hong Kong and China, announced in August 2019 that it would layoff 4,000 employees, mostly in senior positions, to reduce costs by 4 percent.[160] In October 2019, it announced plans to lay off an additional 10,000 employees.[161] In

Wrongful discharge a legal doctrine that requires employers to have a job-related reason to terminate employees

Downsizing the planned elimination of jobs in a company

February 2020, HSBC announced plans to lay off 35,000 more employees.[162] CEO Noel Quinn explained, "Parts of our business are not delivering acceptable returns."[163]

Does downsizing work? In theory, downsizing is supposed to lead to higher productivity and profits, better stock performance, and increased organizational flexibility. However, numerous studies demonstrate that it doesn't. For instance, a 15-year study of downsizing found that downsizing 10 percent of a company's workforce produced only a 1.5 percent decrease in costs; that downsizing firms increased their stock price by only 4.7 percent over three years, compared with 34.3 percent for firms that didn't; and that profitability and productivity were generally not improved by downsizing. Likewise, a five-year study of 4,710 firms in 83 industries found that the 24 percent of firms that laid off at least 3 percent of their workforce were twice as likely to declare bankruptcy.[164] One reason could be the loss of skilled workers who would be expensive to replace when the company grows again.[165] These results make it clear that the best strategy is to conduct effective human resource planning and avoid downsizing altogether. Downsizing should always be a last resort.[166]

If companies do find themselves in financial or strategic situations where downsizing is required for survival, however, they should train managers how to break the news to downsized employees, have senior managers explain in detail why downsizing is necessary, and time the announcement so that employees hear it from the company and not from other sources, such as TV, online reports or social media.[167] Finally, companies should do everything they can to help downsized employees find other jobs. One of the best ways to do this is to use **outplacement services** that provide employment counseling for employees faced with downsizing. Outplacement services often include advice and training in preparing résumés, getting ready for job interviews, and even identifying job opportunities in other companies. Sixty-nine percent of companies provide outplacement services for laid-off employees, 61 percent provide extended health coverage, and most offer up to 26 weeks of severance payments.[168] Offering this kind of assistance can soften the blow from being laid off, preserve goodwill, and lower the risk of future lawsuits.[169]

Companies also need to pay attention to the survivors, the employees remaining after layoffs have occurred. Professor Kenneth Freeman says, "No one knows where this is going to end…The survivors are going to be worried about their jobs."[170] According to author Sylvia Ann Hewlett, the impact of layoffs on remaining employees' morale is severe: 64 percent of employees who survived a layoff felt demotivated, 73 percent felt demoralized, and 74 percent said they simply shut down. "In other words," she says, "just when a company needs its top performers to charge the hill, they retreat to the bunkers."[171] The key to working with layoff survivors, according to Barry Nickerson, president of Dallas-based Marlow Industries, which downsized from 800 to 200 employees, is "Communicate. Communicate. Communicate." Nickerson says, "Every time we had a change we had a meeting to explain exactly what we were doing. We were very open with our employees about where we were financially. We would explain exactly the current status and where we were."[172]

11-6d Retirement

Early retirement incentive programs (ERIPs) offer financial benefits to employees to encourage them to retire early. Companies use ERIPs to reduce the number of employees in the organization, to lower costs by eliminating positions after employees retire, to lower costs by replacing high-paid retirees with lower-paid, less-experienced employees, or to create openings and job opportunities for people inside the company. Verizon offered early retirement to 44,000 employees. Incentives included three weeks of pay for every year with the company, up to a maximum of 60 weeks of salary, benefits, and a $50,000 bonus. Everyone received 6 months of health-care benefits, with the option to pay for 18 months of continued coverage. Over 10,000 Verizon employees accepted the early retirement offer.[173]

Although ERIPs can save companies money, they can pose a big problem for managers if they fail to accurately predict which employees will retire – the good performers or the poor performers – and how many will retire early. When Progress Energy, in Raleigh, North Carolina, identified 450 jobs it wanted to eliminate with an ERIP, it carefully shared the list of jobs with employees, indicated that layoffs would follow if not enough

Albert Pego/Shutterstock.com

Early Retirement

Outplacement services employment-counseling services offered to employees who are losing their jobs because of downsizing

Early retirement incentive programs (ERIPs) programs that offer financial benefits to employees to encourage them to retire early

people took early retirement, and then held 80 meetings with employees to answer questions. Despite this care, an extra 1,000 employees, for a total of 1,450, took the ERIP offer and applied for early retirement![174]

Because of the problems associated with ERIPs, 14 percent of companies are now offering **phased retirement**, in which employees transition to retirement by working reduced hours over a period of time before completely retiring. The advantage for employees is that they have more free time but continue to earn salaries and benefits without changing companies or careers. The advantage for companies is that it allows them to reduce salaries and hiring and training costs and retain experienced, valuable workers.[175] Paul Irving, chairman of the Milken Institute Center for the Future of Aging, said, "There's a need for more companies to do this if they want to preserve their best practices, innovations, and customer relations. And there's receptivity among older workers, a majority of whom want to stay engaged and keep working, but in new ways."[176]

11-6e Employee Turnover

With record low unemployment, as many as 80 percent of workers with a job were either actively seeking or open to a new job.[177] Twenty-seven percent actually quit their jobs.[178] Why? Because taking a job with another company typically raises pay by 15 percent, compared to 2 to 3 percent in one's current job.[179] **Employee turnover** is the loss of employees who voluntarily choose to leave the company. In general, most companies try to keep the rate of employee turnover low to reduce recruiting, hiring, training, and replacement costs. It's estimated that employee turnover cost companies $617 billion a year.[180]

Not all kinds of employee turnover are bad for organizations, however. In fact, some turnover can actually be good. **Functional turnover** is the loss of poor-performing employees who choose to leave the organization.[181] Functional turnover gives the organization a chance to replace poor performers with better workers. In fact, one study found that simply replacing poor-performing workers with average workers would increase the revenues produced by retail salespeople in an upscale department store by $112,000 per person per year.[182] By contrast, **dysfunctional turnover**, the loss of high performers who choose to leave, is a costly loss to the organization. To minimize dysfunctional turnover, **VoloMetrix, Inc.** uses algorithms to identify so-called flight risks – employees who are gearing up to quit. Software examines anonymized data from employee emails and calendars to identify patterns of communication that indicate the employee is spending less time interacting with colleagues and attending only required meetings. The analysis helps the company predict a departure up to a year in advance, which is important, as the median cost of turnover for most jobs is 21 percent of the employee's annual salary.[183]

Employee turnover should be carefully analyzed to determine whether good or poor performers are choosing to leave the organization. If the company is losing too many high performers, managers should determine the reasons and find ways to reduce the loss of valuable employees. The company might have to raise salary levels, offer enhanced benefits, or improve working conditions to retain skilled workers. One of the best ways to influence functional and dysfunctional turnover is to link pay directly to performance. A study of four salesforces found that when pay was strongly linked to performance via sales commissions and bonuses, poor performers were much more likely to leave (that is, functional turnover). By contrast, poor performers were much more likely to stay when paid large, guaranteed monthly salaries and small sales commissions and bonuses.[184]

Phased retirement employees transition to retirement by working reduced hours over a period of time before completely retiring

Employee turnover loss of employees who voluntarily choose to leave the company

Functional turnover loss of poor-performing employees who voluntarily choose to leave a company

Dysfunctional turnover loss of high-performing employees who voluntarily choose to leave a company

12 | Managing Individuals and a Diverse Workforce

LEARNING OUTCOMES

12-1 Describe diversity and explain why it matters.

12-2 Summarize the special challenges that the dimensions of surface-level diversity pose for managers.

12-3 Explain how the dimensions of deep-level diversity affect individual behavior and interactions in the workplace.

12-4 Explain the basic principles and practices that can be used to manage diversity.

12-1 DIVERSITY: DIFFERENCES THAT MATTER

Workplace diversity as we know it is changing. Exhibit 12.1 shows predictions from the US Census Bureau of how the US population will change over the next 40 years. The percentage of white, non-Hispanic Americans in the general population is expected to decline from 61.3 percent in 2016 to 44.3 percent by 2060. By contrast, the fastest-growing group is Hispanics, who are expected to increase from 17.8 percent of the total population in 2016 to 27.5 percent by 2060. The percentage of black Americans will increase (from 13.3 to 15 percent), as will the percentage of Asian Americans (from 5.7 to 9.1 percent), people of two or more races (from 2.6 to 6.2 percent), and American Indians and Alaska Natives (from 1.3 to 1.4 percent). Other significant changes have already occurred. For example, today women hold 46.8 percent of the jobs in the United States, up from 38.2 percent

in 1970.[1] Furthermore, white males, who composed 63.9 percent of the workforce in 1950, hold just 42.4 percent of today's jobs.[2]

These rather dramatic changes have taken place in a relatively short time. As these trends clearly show, the workforce of the near future will be increasingly Hispanic, Asian American, and female.

With low birth rates, longer life spans, and many baby boomers (born between 1946 and 1964) postponing retirement to work into their 70s, the workforce will also be older.[3] For instance, between 1996 and 2026, 16- to 24-year-olds (15.8 to 11.7 percent), 25- to 34-year-olds (25.3 to 22.1 percent), 35- to 44-year-olds (27.3 to 22.2 percent) and 45- to 54-year-olds (19.7 to 19.2 percent) will have become a smaller part of the US labor force. By contrast, 55- to 64-year-olds (9.1 to 16.2 percent), 65- to 74-year-olds (2.4 to 6.8 percent), and 75 years and older (0.5 to 1.9 percent) will all have become larger parts of the US labor force.[4]

Diversity means variety. Therefore, **diversity** exists in organizations when there is a variety of demographic, cultural, and personal differences among the people who work there and the customers who do business there. With 5,700 locations in 110 countries, few businesses have the diversity of locations and customers that **Marriott International** has.[5] But Marriott's Executive Global Diversity and Inclusion Council still expects each hotel to have diversity in terms of its local workforce, customer, and vendor communities. For instance, the Marriott Marquis Washington, DC, two years after opening, filled 58 percent of its jobs with applicants from eight inner-city neighborhoods, hired 200 disadvantaged applicants with limited work experience who completed a joint Marriott/Goodwill Jobs Training Partnership, and was already doing millions of dollars of business with women- and minority-owned businesses.[6] CEO and Chairman Bill Marriott says that everywhere Marriott does business, "We are broadening how we think about global diversity and inclusion, reaching across cultural borders to compete for customers and talent worldwide."[7] Marriott is regularly recognized as one of the top-10 most diverse firms in

> **Diversity** a variety of demographic, cultural, and personal differences among an organization's employees and customers

Exhibit 12.1

Percent of the Projected Population by Race and Hispanic Origin for the United States: 2016–2060

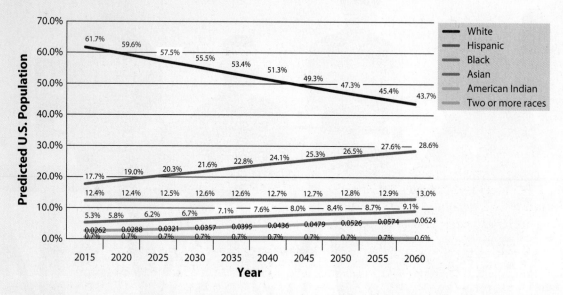

Source: "Race and Hispanic Origin of the Native and Foreign Born: Main Projections Series for the United States, 2017–2060," US Census Bureau, accessed May 9, 2020, www2.census.gov/programs-surveys/popproj/tables/2017/2017-summary-tables/np2017-t11.xlsx.

the world and was ranked #2 on DiversityInc's. Top 50 Companies for Diversity List in 2019.[8]

*You'll begin your exploration of diversity by learning **12-1a** that diversity is not affirmative action and **12-1b** that diversity makes good business sense.*

12-1a Diversity Is Not Affirmative Action

A common misconception is that workplace diversity and affirmative action are the same, yet these concepts differ in several critical ways, including their purpose and how they are practiced. To start, **affirmative action** refers to purposeful steps taken by an organization to create employment opportunities for minorities and women.[9] By contrast, diversity has a broader focus that includes demographic, cultural, and personal differences.

A second difference is that affirmative action is a policy for actively

Affirmative action purposeful steps taken by an organization to create employment opportunities for minorities and women

creating diversity, but diversity can exist even if organizations don't take purposeful steps to create it. A local restaurant located near a university in a major city is likely to have a more diverse group of employees than one located in a small town. So, organizations can achieve diversity without affirmative action. Conversely, affirmative action does not guarantee diversity. An organization can create employment opportunities for women and minorities yet not have a diverse workforce.

A third important difference is that affirmative action is required by law for private employers with 50 or more employees, whereas diversity is not. Affirmative action originated with Executive Order 11246 but is also related to the 1964 Civil Rights Act, which bans discrimination in voting, public places, federal government programs, federally supported public education, and employment. Title VII of the Civil Rights Act (www.eeoc.gov/laws/statutes/titlevii.cfm) requires that workers have equal employment opportunities when being hired or promoted. More specifically, Title VII prohibits companies from discriminating on the basis of race, color, national origin, religion, sex, sexual orientation, or gender identity. Title VII also created the Equal Employment Opportunity Commission, or EEOC (www.eeoc.gov), to administer these laws. By contrast, there is no federal law or agency to oversee diversity. Organizations that pursue diversity goals and programs do so voluntarily.

bikeriderlondon/Shutterstock.com

Fourth, affirmative action programs and diversity programs have different purposes. The purpose of affirmative action programs is to:

» compensate for past discrimination, which was widespread when legislation was introduced in the 1960s;

» prevent ongoing discrimination;

» and provide equal opportunities to all, regardless of race, color, religion, sex, sexual orientation or gender identity, or national origin.

Organizations that fail to uphold affirmative action laws may be required to

» hire, promote, or give back pay to those not hired or promoted;

» reinstate those who were wrongly terminated;

» pay attorneys' fees and court costs for those who bring charges against them; or

» take other actions that make individuals whole by returning them to the condition or place they would have been had it not been for discrimination.[10]

Consequently, affirmative action is basically a punitive approach.[11]

By contrast, the general purpose of diversity programs is to create a positive work environment where no one is advantaged or disadvantaged, where "we" is everyone, where everyone can do his or her best work, where differences are respected and not ignored, and where everyone feels comfortable.[12] So, unlike affirmative action, which punishes companies for not achieving specific sex and race ratios in their workforces, diversity programs seek to benefit both organizations and their employees by encouraging organizations to value all kinds of differences.

Despite affirmative action making workplaces much fairer than they used to be, many people argue that affirmative action programs only establish surface-level diversity and offer unconstitutional preferential treatment to females and minorities at the expense of other employees, a view accepted by some courts.[13] The American Civil Rights institute successfully campaigned via state ballot initiatives to ban race- and sex-based affirmative action in college admissions, government hiring, and government contracting programs in California (1996), Washington (1998), and Michigan (2006). Today, voters in five other states have banned the use of affirmative action, Nebraska (2008), Arizona (2010), New Hampshire (2012), Oklahoma (2012), and Idaho (2020). In Washington, affirmative action was banned again in 2019 after opposition from WA Asians for Equality representing Chinese Americans.[14] In a 2014 decision, the US Supreme Court ruled 6–2 that state ballot initiatives banning race- and sex-based action are constitutional.[15]

Research shows that people who have gotten a job or promotion as a result of affirmative action are commonly viewed as unqualified, *even* when clear evidence of their qualifications exists.[16] Thirty-year-old Travis Montaque is the African American founder and CEO of **Holler**, a tech-based marketing company with clients like McDonald's, Universal Pictures, and Ikea. Before starting Holler, he was hired at a Wall Street firm. He says, "…the problem with affrmative action is that the people coming in feel stigmatized immediately. I experienced firsthand from my time on Wall Street that individuals who get access to jobs via this route are often labeled by their peers as underqualified. You see similar treatment in programs for women and LGBTQ people."[17] This effect is so robust that many benefiting from affirmative action experience doubts about their competence.[18]

So, while affirmative action programs have created opportunities for minorities and women, they may unintentionally produce persistent doubts and self-doubts regarding the qualifications of those who are believed to have obtained their jobs as a result of affirmative action.

12-1b Diversity Makes Good Business Sense

Those who support the idea of diversity in organizations often ignore its business aspects altogether, claiming instead that diversity is simply the right thing to do. Yet diversity actually makes good business sense in several ways: cost savings, attracting and retaining talent, and driving business growth.[19]

Diversity helps companies with *cost savings* by reducing turnover, decreasing absenteeism, and avoiding expensive lawsuits.[20] Because of lost productivity and the cost of recruiting and selecting new workers, companies lose substantial amounts of money when employees quit their jobs. In fact, turnover costs typically amount to more than 90 percent of employees' salaries. By this estimate, if an executive who makes $200,000 leaves, the organization will have to spend approximately $180,000 to find a replacement; even the lowest-paid hourly workers can cost the company as much as $10,000 when they quit. Because turnover rates for African Americans average 40 percent higher than for whites, and since women quit their jobs at twice the rate men do, companies that manage diverse workforces well can cut costs by reducing the turnover rates of these employees.[21] With women absent from work 60 percent more often than men, primarily because of family responsibilities, diversity programs that address the needs of female workers can also reduce the substantial costs of absenteeism.

Diversity programs also save companies money by helping them avoid discrimination lawsuits, which have increased by a factor of 20 since 1970 and quadrupled just since 1995. In one survey conducted by the Society for Human Resource Management (SHRM), 78 percent of respondents reported that diversity efforts helped them avoid lawsuits and litigation costs.[22] In fact, because companies lose two-thirds of all discrimination cases that go to trial, the best strategy from a business perspective is not to be sued for discrimination at all. When companies lose, the average individual settlement amounts to more than $600,000.[23] However, settlement costs can be substantially higher in class-action lawsuits in which individuals join together to sue a company as a group. For example **Qualcomm**, a maker of computer chips, reached a court settlement to pay $19.5 million to 3,300 women in science, technology and engineering positions who accused the company of giving them lower pay and chances for promotion than men.[24]

Diversity also makes business sense by helping companies *attract and retain talented* workers.[25] Female employees at **Alphabet** (Google is a division of Alphabet) were once twice as likely as male employees to quit the company. Company data revealed that many of the women who left were young mothers. Former Alphabet head of human resources Laszlo Bock responded by substantially increasing parental leave at the company. Biological mothers now get 18 weeks of fully paid leave for the birth of a child, and mothers who experience complications during childbirth receive 22 weeks. Primary caregivers, adoptive caregivers, and surrogate caregivers are also eligible for 12 weeks of fully paid time off. Now, a new mother is no more likely to leave Alphabet than the average employee.[26] Diversity-friendly companies tend to attract better *and* more diverse job applicants. Very simply, diversity begets more diversity. Companies that make *Fortune* magazine's list of the 50 best companies for minorities or are recognized by *Working Women* and *DiversityInc.* magazine have already attracted a diverse and talented pool of job applicants. But, after being recognized for their efforts, they subsequently experience big increases in both the quality and the diversity of people who apply for jobs. Research shows that companies with acclaimed diversity programs not only attract more talented workers but also have higher performance in the stock market.[27]

The third way that diversity makes business sense is by *driving business growth*. In the United States today, there are 46 million African Americans,

60 million Hispanic Americans, and 22 million Asian Americans with, respectively, $1.4 trillion, $1.7 trillion, and $1.2 trillion in purchasing power.[28] Given the size of those markets, it shouldn't be surprising that a survey conducted by the SHRM found that tapping into "diverse customers and markets" was the number-one reason managers gave for implementing diversity programs.[29] **Fidelity Investments** CEO Abby Johnson says, "We have a real need in our business right now to recruit more women. (When women come into a Fidelity branch,) very often, the first thing they say when we're trying to get them paired up with a rep is, 'I'd like to work with a woman.'"[30] Because of those requests, says Kathleen Murphy, president of Fidelity's Personal Investing unit, says, "…we've had an effort over the last three years or so or longer to increase the diversity in our branches. This year half of the new hires in our branches are women, and that's in an industry where less than 25 percent of licensed professionals are women."[31] Murphy explains, "What we wanted to do was increase diversity in general in our branches, really to serve our customers more broadly. We serve millions and millions of women, both through the workplace and through personal investing."[32]

Diversity *might* also help companies grow through higher-quality problem solving. For example, a McKinsey & Co. study of 1,000+ companies in 12 countries found that organizations with more diverse executive teams and boards of directors report larger profits.[33] Why might this happen? It's generally assumed that diverse teams have more perspectives, which leads to more cognitive conflict and better problem solving (see Deep-Level Diversity: The Key to Team Problem Solving). However, more scientifically rigorous studies show that executive team diversity and board diversity have little to no relationship with company profits.[34] Over the last decade, many studies across different disciplines have shown that the problem solving gains from diversity are *not* automatic.[35]

So what do we know about diversity and problem-solving? We know that diverse groups initially have more difficulty working together than homogeneous groups, but that they can eventually establish rapport and do a better job of identifying problems and generating alternative solutions, the two most important steps in problem solving.[36] But, that doesn't happen unless the diverse members speak up in group discussions (those in the minority often don't) and influence other group members (who have to be open to different perspectives).[37] Those with different views and perspectives must be heard and considered for diversity to lead to better problem solving.[38]

Research conducted by McKinsey & Co. found that in order for teams to be successful, it is important for diverse members to speak up during group discussions.

SDI Productions/E+/Getty Images

 12-2

SURFACE-LEVEL DIVERSITY

A survey that asked managers "What is meant by diversity to decision makers in your organization?" found that they most frequently mentioned race, culture, sex, national origin, age, religion, and regional origin.[39] When managers describe workers this way, they are focusing on surface-level diversity. **Surface-level diversity** consists of differences that are immediately observable, typically unchangeable, and easy to measure.[40] In other words, independent observers can usually agree on dimensions of surface-level diversity, such as another person's age, sex, race/ethnicity, or physical capabilities.

Most people start by using surface-level diversity to categorize or stereotype other people. But those initial categorizations typically give way to deeper impressions formed from knowledge of others' behaviors and psychological characteristics such as personality and attitudes.[41] When you think of others this way, you are focusing on deep-level diversity. **Deep-level diversity** consists of differences that are communicated through verbal and nonverbal behaviors and are learned only through extended interaction with others.[42] Examples of deep-level diversity include personality differences, attitudes, beliefs, and values. In other words, as people in diverse workplaces get to know each

Surface-level diversity
differences such as age, sex, race/ethnicity, and physical disabilities that are observable, typically unchangeable, and easy to measure

Deep-level diversity
differences such as personality and attitudes that are communicated through verbal and nonverbal behaviors and are learned only through extended interaction with others

other, the initial focus on surface-level differences such as age, race/ethnicity, sex, and physical capabilities is replaced by deeper, more complex knowledge of coworkers.

If managed properly, the shift from surface- to deep-level diversity can accomplish two things.[43] First, 95 percent of studies on this issue show that getting to know and understand each other reduces prejudice and conflict.[44] Second, it can lead to stronger social integration. **Social integration** is the degree to which group members are psychologically attracted to working with each other to accomplish a common objective, or, as one manager put it, "working together to get the job done."

Because age, sex, race/ethnicity, and disabilities are usually immediately observable, many managers and workers use these dimensions of surface-level diversity to form initial impressions and categorizations of co-workers, bosses, customers, or job applicants. While not always immediately known, sexual orientation and gender identity (often referred to as LGBT, meaning lesbian, gay, bisexual, or transgender) may also be a form of surface-level diversity. Whether intentional or not, sometimes those initial categorizations and impressions lead to decisions or behaviors that discriminate. Consequently, these dimensions of surface-level diversity pose special challenges for managers who are trying to create positive work environments where everyone feels comfortable, and no one is advantaged or disadvantaged.

*Let's learn more about those challenges and the ways that **12-2a age**, **12-2b sex**, **12-2c sexual orientation and gender identity**, **12-2d race/ethnicity**, and **12-2e mental or physical disabilities** can affect decisions and behaviors in organizations.*

12-2a Age

Age discrimination is treating people differently (e.g., in hiring and firing, promotion, and compensation decisions) because of their age. The victims of age discrimination are almost always older workers, and the discrimination is based on the assumption that "you can't teach an old dog new tricks." Perhaps this is why, according to comedian Bill Maher, "Ageism is the last acceptable prejudice."[45] Indeed, it's commonly believed that older workers are less motivated, less productive, more prone to illness and accidents, not

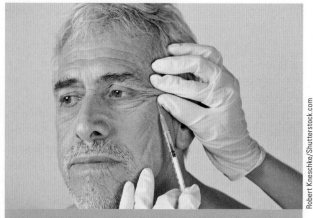

Ageism in the tech sector has caused plastic surgery to surge in Silicon Valley.

Robert Kneschke/Shutterstock.com

interested in learning new things, cost more, and make greater—more expensive—use of health care benefits.[46]

Facebook founder and CEO Mark Zuckerberg once said, "I want to stress the importance of being young and technical . . . Young people are just smarter."[47] Consistent with that stereotype, older job applicants accused **PricewaterhouseCoopers (PwC)**, a "Big Four" accounting firm, of "substantial evidence of age disparities in hiring" through nearly exclusive use of college campus recruiting not available to older applicants.[48] PwC, which reported on its website that 80 percent of its then 220,000 employees were younger than 40, settled an age discrimination class action lawsuit with 3,500 older job applicants for $11.6 million.[49] Using data that PwC submitted to the court, the lawsuit showed that PwC hired 18 percent of applicants under 40, but only 3 percent of those over 40.[50] Google settled a similar age discrimination lawsuit for $11 million.[51] On average, according to the EEOC, 19,000 age discrimination claims are filed each year, resulting in $71 million in EEOC-awarded damages.[52]

So, what's reality and what's myth? Do older employees actually cost more? In some ways, they do. The older people are and the longer they stay with a company, the more the company pays for salaries, pension plans, and vacation time. But older workers cost companies less, too, because they show better judgment, care more about the quality of their work, and are less likely to quit, show up late, or be absent, the costs of which can be substantial.[53] A meta-analysis combining the results of 118 individual studies also found that older workers are more likely to help others at work and are much less likely to use drugs or alcohol at work, engage in workplace aggression, or be involved in accidents. The authors of this study concluded, "The stereotype of older workers as difficult colleagues, then, seems largely unfounded."[54]

Social integration the degree to which group members are psychologically attracted to working with each other to accomplish a common objective

Age discrimination treating people differently (for example in hiring and firing, promotion, and compensation decisions) because of their age

1 + 1 = DIVERSITY

If there is only one woman or minority candidate in the finalist pool (usually those who get on site interviews), that person stands out as different, which makes them less likely to be hired. For example, in a study of 598 finalists for university teaching positions, when just one of the four finalists was a woman or minority, not one woman or minority was hired. When there were two, half the positions were filled by a woman or minority. When there were three, 67 percent of the jobs were filled by a woman or minority. Similar results were found in the National Football League (NFL). In 22 head coaching searches where there was one black finalist, only one black coach was hired (4.5 percent). But in 12 other head coaching searches where two black coaches were finalists, four black coaches were hired (33 percent). One may be the loneliest number, but when it comes to position finalists, 1 + 1 = diversity.

Source: S. Johnson, "What Amazon's Board Was Getting Wrong About Diversity and Hiring," *Harvard Business Review*, May 14, 2018, accessed May 16, 2020, hbr.org/2018/05/what-amazons-board-is-getting-wrong-about-diversity-and-hiring; S. Johnson, D. Hekman & E. Chan, "If There's Only One Woman in Your Candidate Pool, There's Statistically No Chance She'll Be Hired," *Harvard Business Review*, April 26, 2016, accessed May 16, 2020, hbr.org/2016/04/if-theres-only-one-woman-in-your-candidate-pool-theres-statistically-no-chance-shell-be-hired.

As for the widespread belief that job performance declines with age, the scientific evidence clearly refutes this stereotype. Performance does not decline with age, regardless of the type of job.[55] Which is why the New York-based **PKF O'Connor Davies LLP** accounting firm hires experienced accountants who were available because of mandatory retirement policies, typically at age 60, in many accounting firms. PKF O'Connor Davies partner Christopher Petermann said, "There are a lot of people at other organizations who 'time out' based on age that still have tremendous value,"[56]

What can companies do to reduce age discrimination?[57] To start, managers need to recognize that age discrimination is much more pervasive than they probably think. Whereas "old" used to mean mid-50s, in today's workplace "old" is closer to 40. When 773 CEOs were asked, "At what age does a worker's productivity peak?" the average age they gave was 43, which is concerning because the median age (half above, half below) of US workers is 42.[58] Thus, age discrimination may be affecting more workers because perceptions about age have changed. In addition, with the aging of the baby boomers, age discrimination is more likely to occur simply because there are millions more older workers than there used to be. And, because studies show that interviewers rate younger job candidates as more qualified (even when they aren't), companies need to train managers and recruiters to make hiring and promotion decisions on the basis of qualifications, not age.

Companies also need to monitor the extent to which older workers receive training. The US Bureau of Labor Statistics found that the number of training courses and number of hours spent in training drop dramatically after employees reach the age of 44.[59] Finally, companies need to ensure that younger and older workers interact with each other. One study found that younger workers generally hold positive views of older workers, such as "responsible," "hard-working," and "mature," and that the more time they spent working with older coworkers, the more positive their attitudes became.[60]

12-2b Sex

Sex discrimination, *not* to be confused with discrimination based on sexual orientation and gender identity (discussed in Section 12-2c), occurs when people are treated differently because of their sex. Sex discrimination and racial/ethnic discrimination (discussed in Section 12-2d) are often associated with the so-called **glass ceiling**, the invisible barrier that prevents women and minorities from advancing to the top jobs in organizations.

To what extent do women face sex discrimination in the workplace? Almost every year, the EEOC receives between 23,000 and 30,000 charges of sex-based discrimination.[61] In some ways, there is much less sex discrimination than there used to be. For example, whereas women held only 17 percent of

Sex discrimination treating people differently because of their sex

Glass ceiling the invisible barrier that prevents women and minorities from advancing to the top jobs in organizations

Does Scrubbing Résumés to Remove Bias Work?

In an effort to reduce hiring biases and improve workplace diversity, some companies have begun using blind hiring where a person's name, sex, age, ethnic background and alma mater are removed from his or her résumé and work sample before reviewing them. This way, hiring managers can evaluate candidates based solely on their potential. The goal is to reduce unconscious biases that may result in preferential treatment for candidates of a particular sex or ethnicity, or with work experience at a prominent company or a degree from an elite school, things that are not always accurate predictors of job performance.

But does it work? The most famous study, comparing blind and nonblind orchestra auditions, is widely cited as supporting the effectiveness of blind hiring, but it's not clear that it does. The authors stated, "Women are about 5 percentage points more likely to be hired than are men in a completely blind audition, although the effect is not statistically significant. The effect is nil [meaning no difference]…." Other studies show a variety of results. Some indicate blind hiring leads to more interviews for women and minorities. Others show fewer interviews. And some indicate no differences at all. Two studies indicate that hiring managers still draw conclusions about the age or gender of applicants' blind resumes or job applications forms, which may make them pay more attention to gender or age stereotypes, which is what blind hiring is supposed to prevent. Finally, more studies than not show that blind hiring does not lead to more job offers for women and minorities (see section 12-2d for an extensive review of studies on resumes and racial discrimination).

What can we conclude? It depends on how you define success. In terms of procedural fairness, blind hiring is clearly meant to make job interview and hiring decisions fairer. And that's important for applicants and hiring managers. But in terms of outcome fairness, results are clearly mixed. Some argue, ironically, that mixed results show that discrimination maybe less prevalent than believed. In all, it's too early to conclude that blind hiring doesn't work. But, so far, it's not the magic wand that many had hoped for.

Creativa Images/Shutterstock.com

Source: O. Aslund & O. Nordsrom Skans, "Do Anonymous Job Application Procedures Level the Playing Field?" *Industrial and Labor Relations Review* 65, no. 1 (2012): 82-107; L. Behaghel, B. Crepon & T. Le Barbanchon, "Unintended Effects of Anonymous Résumés," *American Economic Journal: Applied Economics* 7, no. 3 (2015): 1-27; E. Derous & J. Decoster, "Implicit Age Cues in Resumes: Subtle Effects on Hiring Discrimination, *Frontiers in Psychology*, August 10, 2017, https://www.frontiersin.org/articles/10.3389/fpsyg.2017.01321/full; R. Feintzeig, "Tossing Out the Résumé in Favor of 'Blind Hiring,'" *Wall Street Journal*, January 6, 2016, B1; M. Foley & S. Williamson, "Does Anonymizing Job Applications Reduce Gender Bias?: Understanding Managers' Perspectives," *Gender in Management: An International Journal* 8 (2018): 623-635; C. Goldin & C. Rouse, "Orchestrating Impartiality: The Impact of "Blind" Auditions on Female Musicians," *The American Economic Review* 90, no. 4 (2000): 715-741; M. Hiscox, T. Oliver, M. Ridgway, L. Arcos-Holzinger, A. Warren & A. Willis, "Going Blind to See More Clearly: Unconscious Bias in Australian Public Service Shortlisting Processes," Behavioral Economics Team of the Australian Government, June 2017, accessed May 17, 2020, https://www.5050foundation.edu.au/assets/reports/documents/2017-Unconscious-Bias-BETA-copy.pdf; S. Johnson & J. Kirk, "Dual-anonymization Yields Promising Results for Reducing Gender Bias: A Naturalistic Field Experiment of Applications for Hubble Space Telescope Time," *Publication of the Astronomical Society of the Pacific*, March 2020, accessed May 17, 2020, https://iopscience.iop.org/article/10.1088/1538-3873/ab6ce0/pdf; A. Krause, U. Rinne & K. Zimmerman, "Anonymous job applications in Europe | *IZA Journal of European Labor Studies* 1 (2012), https://izajoels.springeropen.com/articles/10.1186/2193-9012-1-5; U. Rinne, "Anonymous Job Applications and Hiring Discrimination," *IZA World of Labor* 48 (2014), https://econpapers.repec.org/article/izaizawol/journl_3ay_3a2014_3an_3a48.htm.

---

managerial jobs in 1972, today they hold 40 percent of managerial jobs and 47 percent of all jobs in the workplace.[62] Likewise, women own 42 percent of all US businesses. Although women owned 2.8 million businesses in 1982 and 5.4 million businesses in 1997, today they own 13 million businesses, generating $1.9 trillion in sales and employing more than 9.4 million people![63] Finally, though women still earn less than men on average, the differential is narrowing. Women today earn 81 percent of what men do, up from 62 percent in 1979.[64]

Although progress is being made across many fronts, sex discrimination continues to operate via the glass ceiling at higher levels in organizations, as shown in Exhibit 12.2. For instance, while the trends are upward, women were the top earners in just 11 percent of companies in 2019.[65] Likewise, only 26.5 percent of corporate officers (i.e., top management) were women, and the numbers were even lower for women of color. Vertex Pharmaceuticals' Reshma Kewalramani, Gap's Sonia Syngal, Arista Networks' Jayshree Ullal, and Yum China's Joey Wat are the only women of color heading *Fortune* 500 or Standard & Poor's 500 companies.[66] In fact, just 37 of the 500 largest companies in the United States have women CEOs.[67] Similarly, only 26.1 percent of the members of US corporate boards of directors are women.[68]

Finally, a meta-analysis of 97 studies covering 378,850 employees in multiple industries over three decades found that, "Across occupations ranging from bank tellers to accountants, industries ranging from IT to health care, and jobs ranging from mundane to challenging, our results show

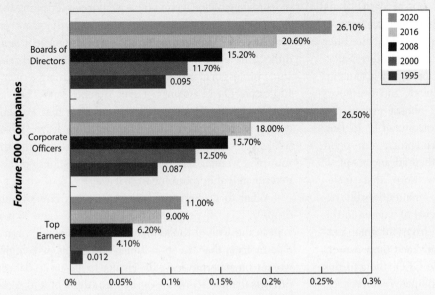

Exhibit 12.2
Women at *Fortune* 500 and 1000 Companies

Fortune 500 Companies

Legend:
- 2020
- 2016
- 2008
- 2000
- 1995

Boards of Directors:
- 26.10% (2020)
- 20.60% (2016)
- 15.20% (2008)
- 11.70% (2000)
- 0.095 (1995)

Corporate Officers:
- 26.50% (2020)
- 18.00% (2016)
- 15.70% (2008)
- 12.50% (2000)
- 0.087 (1995)

Top Earners:
- 11.00% (2020)
- 9.00% (2016)
- 6.20% (2008)
- 4.10% (2000)
- 0.012 (1995)

(x-axis: 0%, 0.05%, 0.1%, 0.15%, 0.2%, 0.25%, 0.3%)

Sources: "Women in S&P 500 Companies," Catalyst, March 1, 2017, accessed April 23, 2017, www.catalyst.org /knowledge/women-sp-500-companies; J. Lublin, "Dozens of Boards Excluded Women for Years," *Wall Street Journal*, December 27, 2016, accessed April 23, 2017, www.wsj.com/articles/dozens-of-boards-excluded-women-for -years-1482847381; B. Darrow, "Nearly All Fortune 1000 Companies Are Still Led by Men," *Fortune*, September 6, 2016, accessed April 23, 2017, fortune.com/2016/09/06/fortune-1000-still-led-by-men/; V. Zarya, "Female Fortune 500 CEOs Set to Break Records in 2017," *Fortune*, December 22, 2016, accessed April 23, 2017, fortune.com/2016/12/22 /female-fortune-500-ceos-2017/. "U.S. Women in Business," Catalyst, June 10, 2014, accessed July 11, 2014, www .catalyst.org/knowledge/us-women-business-0.

that sex differences in organizational rewards were almost 14 times larger than sex differences in performance evaluations. Moreover, performance differences did not explain reward differences between men and women."[69] In other words, when men and women performed their jobs equally well, men received 14 times the rewards in terms of salary, bonuses, and promotions compared to women.

Is sex discrimination the sole reason for the slow rate at which women have been rewarded and promoted to middle and upper levels of management and corporate boards? Some studies indicate that it's not.[70] Historically, men's career and job choices were often driven by the search for higher pay and advancement, while women were more likely to choose jobs or careers that gave them a greater sense of accomplishment, more control over their work schedules, and easier movement in and out of the workplace.[71] For, example, a study of Massachusetts Bay Transportation Authority train and bus operators, where a union contract guaranteed that men and women were paid the same, found that women worked 83 percent less overtime (which pays 50 percent more), took 48 percent more unpaid hours for which they were eligible under the Family Medical Leave Act, and, as they gained control of their schedules via seniority, regularly chose conventional weekly schedules

rather than weekend, holiday and split shifts (for example, 5:00–9:00 a.m., then 2:00–6:00 p.m.) that conflicted with family responsibilities.[72] Similarly, after examining 47,000 resumes over seven years, jobs site Glassdoor.com found, "Many college majors that lead to high-paying roles in tech and engineering are male dominated, while majors that lead to lower-paying roles in social sciences and liberal arts tend to be female dominated, placing men in higher-paying career pathways, on average. Nine of the 10 highest paying majors we examined are male dominated. By contrast, 6 of the 10 lowest-paying majors are female dominated."[73]

As these studies suggest, whether by choice or by need, women have historically been much more likely than men to prioritize family over work at some time in their careers. Beyond these reasons, however, sex discrimination has slowed women's progress into higher levels of management. And even if you don't think so, many of the women you work with probably do.[74] In fact, studies indicate that 90 percent of women believe the glass ceiling hurts their careers, and 80 percent said they left their last job because of the glass ceiling and that starting a business allows them to avoid the career limitations of the glass ceiling.[75] Discrimination is widely believed to be the most significant factor behind the lack of women in management.[76]

So, what can companies do to make sure that women have the same opportunities for development and advancement as men, especially since a meta-analysis of 43 studies with over 13,000 people found no difference between men and women in desire to lead (see Chapter 14 section 14-2a on leadership traits)?[77]

One strategy is mentoring, or pairing promising female executives with senior ex-ecutives from whom they can seek advice and support.[78] **Salesforce**, a leading customer relationship management software company, has a mentoring program for women. So, co-founder

Parker Harris, who encourages Salesforce managers to speak up about their ambitions, was surprised when he discovered that Leyla Seka, who ran their mobile apps unit, was preparing to leave. Seka wanted to lead a larger division but thought her bosses didn't think she was capable, so she didn't share her aspirations. In fact, her bosses found her so capable, they hired her to run Desk.com, a company recently acquired by Salesforce, and coached her as she developed her leadership skills. "I've never had more fun at work, and I've never felt more challenged," she says. "I almost missed this opportunity by shutting the doors on myself."[79] In fact, 91 percent of female executives had a mentor at some point and felt their mentor was critical to their advancement.

Another strategy is to make sure that male-dominated social activities don't unintentionally exclude women. Nearly half (47 percent) of women in the workforce believe that "exclusion from informal networks" makes it more difficult to advance their careers (by contrast, just 18 percent of male CEOs thought this was a problem). For instance, at company conferences, **Rockwell Automation** has replaced cocktail receptions (that is, hanging out at the bar), which are a traditional social function at conferences, with alternative activities, such as chili cook-offs.[80] Another is to designate a go-to person other than their supervisors that women can talk to if they believe that they are being held back or discriminated against because of their sex. That person, of course, must have the knowledge and authority to conduct a fair, confidential internal investigation.[81]

Finally, in many instances, longer maternity leaves (6–12 months), which were expanded to help women address work–life challenges associated with having children, may actually increase the chances of lower career pay (because of more time away from work), *not* being promoted, *not* moving into management, and *not* returning to work.[82] Professors Ivona Hideg, Anja Krstic and Raymand Trau and consultant Tanya Zarina found that, "Evidence from a variety of countries reveals that the longer new mothers are away from paid work, the less likely they are to be promoted, move into management, or receive a pay raise once their leave is over. They are also at greater risk of being fired or demoted.

Length of leave can be a factor in the perceptions of co-workers as well—women who take longer leaves are often seen as less committed to their jobs than women who take much shorter leaves. This trade-off undercuts a major goal of legislating national parental leave policies: ensuring that women don't have to choose between motherhood and career success."[83] Longer maternity leaves also make it more difficult to reestablish professional relationships and reassume professional responsibilities upon returning to work. Professors David Collings, Yseult Freeney, and Lisa van der Werff said, "Our interviews found signs that women's careers were derailed after returning from leave [26–42 weeks], that colleagues held unconscious biases against the returning women, and that professional relationships also deteriorated after returning from leave."[84]

What to do, especially since women's employment drops by 28 to 40 percent in the United States and 38 percent in the United Kingdom after having a child?[85] Early data indicate that "Keep-in-Touch" programs, which give women on maternity leave the chance to stay up-to-date on projects *without work responsibilities* (think of it as social media lurking) and to remain in contact with colleagues and clients, addresses these issues.[86] Phased returns in which women return to work starting with three days, then four, and then full-time can also help.[87] Finally, it may be that maternity leaves under six months represent a better work/life balance for new mothers. Fifty percent fewer new mothers quit their jobs when Google increased paid maternity leave from 12 to 18 weeks. Likewise, 40 percent fewer new mothers quit their jobs when Accenture increased paid maternity leave from 8 to 16 weeks.[88]

12-2c Sexual Orientation and Gender Identity

Sexual orientation indicates an individual's attraction to people of the same and/or different sex. **Sexual orientation discrimination** occurs when people are treated differently because of their sexual orientation. Usually, sexual orientation discrimination occurs toward lesbians, gays, or bisexuals. Though less frequent, straight or heterosexual people can be discriminated against, too. According to the EEOC, examples of sexual orientation discrimination include not hiring, not promoting, firing, awarding a lower salary, denying spousal health insurance, or making derogatory, sexually oriented, or disparaging comments because of someone's sexual orientation.[89]

A **transgender person** is someone whose personal and gender identity differ from the person's birth sex—for example, someone born female who identifies as male. **Gender identity discrimination** occurs when people

Sexual orientation an individual's attraction to people of the same and/or different sex

Sexual orientation discrimination treating people differently because of their sexual orientation

transgender person someone whose personal and gender identity differ from the person's birth sex—for example, someone born female who identifies as male

Gender identity discrimination treating people differently because of their gender identity

are treated differently because of their gender identity. According to the EEOC, in addition to typical discriminatory acts, examples of gender identity discrimination include firing an employee who is planning, making, or has completed a gender transition, denying equal access to a common restroom corresponding to the employee's gender identity, or intentionally not using the name and gender pronoun corresponding to the person's gender identity.[90]

Federal, state, and city laws regarding workplace discrimination in terms of age, sex, race/ethnicity, and mental or physical disabilities have been in place for 20 to 50 years (See Exhibit 11.2, Summary of Major Federal Employment Laws in Chapter 11). By contrast, laws and regulations regarding sexual orientation and gender identity discrimination were new, in question from a legal perspective, or were not yet in place in many states or at the federal level. Since Title VII of the Civil Rights Act explicitly prohibits employment discrimination on the basis of race, color, religion, sex, or national origin, the strict interpretation was that Title VII did not cover sexual orientation or gender identity.[91] However, in 2015 the EEOC ruled that Title VII's sex discrimination provision prohibits, "discrimination against employees on the basis of sexual orientation and gender identity."[92] That was confirmed by a US Supreme Court decision in June 2020 in response to three different cases, thus expanding workplace protections for sexual orientation and gender identity from 22 to 50 states.[93]

Before the Supreme Court ruling in 2020, many companies proactively changed their policies to prohibit sexual orientation and gender identity discrimination. Todd Sears, who founded Out Leadership, a nonprofit organization that partners with companies to develop LGBT-inclusive workplaces, says, "Big business was way out ahead of government when it came to creating domestic partner benefits for their teams—and they remain way out in front when it comes to nondiscrimination policies."[94]

To what extent do LGBT individuals face sexual orientation discrimination or gender identity discrimination in the workplace? Fifty-three percent of LGBT employees hide their sexual orientation or gender identity at work, while 35 percent lie about their personal lives.[95] Studies find similar results in Australia and the United Kingdom.[96] Thirty-five percent who were open about their sexual or gender identity have reported being harassed at work.[97] Sixty-two percent of LGBT employees have heard disparaging jokes about gays or lesbians, 42 percent have heard jokes about bisexuals, and 40 percent have heard jokes about transgender people.[98] In 2019, the EEOC received 1,868 charges of sexual identity or gender identity discrimination, up 70 percent from 1,100 charges in 2014.[99] A national survey of nearly 28,000 transgender people

John Arehart/Shutterstock.com

In June 2020, the US Supreme Court expanded workplace protections for sexual orientation and gender identity to include all 50 states.

found that 27 percent were fired, not promoted, or not hired because of sexual identity; 15 percent were verbally harassed, physically attacked, or sexually assaulted at work; 15 percent were unemployed; 13 percent had lost a job because of gender identity; and that 77 percent took steps at work to hide or delay their gender transition.[100]

What can companies do to make sure that LGBT individuals have the same opportunities as others?[101] Start by including sexual orientation and gender identity in nondiscrimination and equal opportunity policies. Ben Hladilek, executive director of human resources at JPMorgan Chase, said, "What we have found in our recruiting efforts is that individuals will often look for signals about what a culture is like; having gender identity protection signals we are a diversity leader and are serious about providing an inclusive environment."[102] Organizations can reduce the isolation that LGBT employees often feel at work by connecting LGBT employees to mentors and creating employee resource groups where LGBT employees can learn from and support each other.[103] Most organizations are unable to track whether LGBT employees are treated fairly because they don't ask employees about LGBT status. Companies can fix this by giving LGBT employees the opportunity to confidentially self-identify their sexual orientation or gender identity as part of the normal gathering of demographic information.[104]

A few additional steps are required to be sure that transgender employees are treated the same as other employees. A small but critical step is changing the employee's name on all official records, including badge, office and phone numbers, email, corporate directory, business cards, and anywhere else the employee's name appears. When Michael DuVally transitioned to Maeve DuVally at investment bank **Goldman Sachs**, she, "got new business cards, a new ID badge, a new email address, … a new profile in Goldman's internal directory, so that when she joined work discussions digitally, the meeting software would display… her smiling, feminine face."[105] A co-worker kindly changed her name in all previous internal company communications and the security team let her come in for a new photo for her new ID before she told anyone about transitioning.[106]

Companies can also publish guidelines and protocols for gender transitions that make clear the responsibilities for the transitioning employee, as well as their subordinates, colleagues and managers.[107] For example, EY, a global accounting firm, has a set of transition guidelines that specify everything from appearance (dressing consistent with one's new gender and unisex restroom and locker access), to identifying a support team, medical leave, and health benefits.[108] Finally, the World Professional Association for Transgender Health has published Standards of Care to assist companies in providing medical care for transitioning transgender employees.[109]

12-2d Race/Ethnicity

Racial and ethnic discrimination occurs when people are treated differently because of their race or ethnicity. To what extent is racial and ethnic discrimination a factor in the workplace? Every year, the EEOC receives between 26,000 and 36,000 charges of racial discrimination, which is more than any other type of charge of discrimination.[110] However, since the passage of the 1964 Civil Rights Act and Title VII, there is much less racial and ethnic workplace discrimination than there used to be.[111] For example, 27 *Fortune* 500 firms had an African American (3), Hispanic (8), or Asian (16) CEO in 2020 whereas none did in 1988.[112] Nonetheless, strong racial and ethnic disparities still exist. For instance, whereas 12.3 percent of employed Americans are black, only 7.8 percent of managers and 4.1 percent of CEOs are black. Similarly, 17.6 percent of employed Americans are Hispanic, but only 10.7 percent are managers and 6.2 percent are CEOs. By contrast, Asians, who constitute 6.5 percent of employed workers, are better represented, holding 6.1 percent of management jobs and 5.8 percent of CEO jobs.[113]

While progress has been made in terms of racial and ethnic workplace discrimination since the passage of the 1964 Civil Rights Act and Title VII, many studies provide strong direct evidence of continuing racial or ethnic discrimination in the workplace that cannot be discounted.[114]

For example, one study directly tested hiring discrimination by sending pairs of black and white males and pairs of Hispanic and non-Hispanic males to apply for the same jobs. Each pair had résumés with identical qualifications, and all were trained to present themselves in similar ways to minimize differences during interviews. The researchers found that the white males got three times as many job offers as the black males, and that the non-Hispanic males got three times as many offers as the Hispanic males.[115] Another study, which used similar methods to test hiring procedures at 149 different companies, found that whites received 10 percent more interviews than blacks. Half of the whites interviewed then received job offers, but only 11 percent of the blacks. And when job offers were made, blacks were much more likely to be offered lower-level positions, while whites were more likely to be offered jobs at higher levels than the jobs they had applied for.[116]

Critics of these studies point out that it's nearly impossible to train different applicants to give identical responses in job interviews and that differences in interviewing skills may have somehow accounted for the results. However, researchers at the University of Chicago mailed thousands of résumés to employers that were identical except for the candidate's name, which was either stereotypically black, such as "Jamal," or stereotypically white, such as "Brendan." Applicants with the "white" name were called back for interviews 50 percent more often those with "black" names.[117] Comparable studies in the United Kingdom with Indian and Pakistani applicants and in Australia with Greek and Vietnamese applicants produced similar results.[118] A meta-analysis of 97 such studies with 200,000 job applicants finds similar results in nine countries in Europe and North America.[119] In short, the evidence indicates that there is strong and persistent racial and ethnic discrimination in the hiring processes of many organizations around the world.

What can companies do to make sure that people of all racial and ethnic backgrounds have the same opportunities.[120] Start by looking at the numbers. Compare the hiring rates of whites with the hiring rates for racial and ethnic applicants. Do the same thing for promotions within the company. See if nonwhite workers quit the company at higher rates than white workers. Also, survey employees to compare white and nonwhite employees' satisfaction with jobs, bosses, and the company as well as their perceptions concerning equal treatment. Next, if the numbers indicate racial or ethnic disparities, consider employing a private firm to test your hiring system by having applicants of different races with identical qualifications apply for jobs in your company, by data mining your application criteria and by validating artificial intelligence algorithms used to screen applicants in early stages.[121] Data analysis software showed **Xerox** that customer-service employees with the shortest daily commutes stayed with

Racial and ethnic discrimination treating people differently because of their race or ethnicity

the company the longest. Nevertheless, managers stopped screening job applicants for commute times because they thought that doing so would put applicants from minority neighborhoods, which were generally farther from Xerox offices, at a disadvantage.[122]

Another step companies can take is to eliminate unclear selection and promotion criteria.[123] Vague criteria allow decision makers to focus on nonjob-related characteristics that may unintentionally lead to employment discrimination. Instead, selection and promotion criteria should spell out the specific knowledge, skills, abilities, education, and experience needed to perform a job well. As explained in Chapter 11, "Managing Human Resource Systems," it is also important to train managers and others who make hiring and promotion decisions.

Finally, because racial and ethnic disparities in general employment and managerial jobs shrink dramatically when there are equal opportunities for skill development, training and education, companies and wealthy individuals need to do more to address those key differences. Examples include **Netflix** CEO Reed Hasting and his wife, Patty Quillin, who donated $120 million for academic scholarships split three ways between the United Negro College Fund, Morehouse College, and Spelman College, the latter two being historically black colleges.[124] Robert F. Smith, the African American founder and CEO of **Vista Equity Partners**, donated $34 million to pay off the college debts of Morehouse College's entire 2019 graduating class.[125] **Apple** committed $100 million to racial equity and justice initiative that will increase Apple's spending with minority-owned suppliers, create developer camps for black developers and entrepreneurs, and support underfunded historically black colleges and universities.[126] Finally, **Facebook** is investing $100 million in 2020 in black-owned small businesses, will spend $1 billion a year with diverse suppliers, and will provide free digital skills training to 1 million black and 1 million Hispanic people, along with 100,000 scholarships for black students seeking digital skills certification.[127]

12-2e Mental or Physical Disabilities

According to the Americans with Disabilities Act (www.ada.gov), a **disability** is a mental or physical impairment that substantially limits one or more major life activities.[128] Approximately 41 million Americans—12.7 percent of the population—are disabled.[129] **Disability discrimination** occurs when people are treated differently because of their disabilities. To what extent is disability discrimination a factor in the workplace? Similar to studies examining racial discrimination, researchers sent out 6,000 fictitious résumés and cover letters for jobs (in accounting). One résumé was for a highly qualified candidate with six years of experience, and another was for an inexperienced candidate a year out of college. One of three different cover letters accompanied each résumé: one for an applicant with no disabilities, one for an applicant with an injured spinal cord, and one for an applicant with Asperger syndrome, which makes interpersonal relationships and communication difficult. Overall, applicants with disabilities were 26 percent less likely to be contacted by an employer for further steps in the hiring process. Interestingly, experienced applicants were 34 percent less likely to be contacted by employers.[130] Indeed, while 74.6 percent of the US population was employed in 2019, only 30.9 percent of disabled people had jobs. Individuals with sensory disabilities, such as visual disabilities (44.2 percent) or hearing disabilities (53.4 percent), had the highest employment rates; those with self-care disabilities (16.3 percent), who can't dress or bathe themselves, or with independent living disabilities (17.8 percent), who can't do basic errands such as shopping or go to the doctor without assistance, were the least likely to work.[131]

What accounts for the disparities between those with and without disabilities? Contrary to popular opinion, it has nothing to do with how well people with disabilities can do their jobs. Studies show that as long as companies make reasonable accommodations for disabilities (e.g., changing procedures or equipment), people with disabilities perform their jobs just as well as people without disabilities. Furthermore, they have better safety records and are not any more likely to be absent or quit their jobs.[132]

What can companies do to make sure that people with disabilities have the same opportunities as everyone else? Beyond educational efforts to address incorrect stereotypes and expectations, a good place to start is to commit to reasonable workplace accommodations such as changing work schedules, reassigning jobs, acquiring or modifying equipment, or providing assistance when needed. Accommodations for disabilities needn't be expensive. According to the Job Accommodation Network, 59 percent of accommodations don't cost anything at all, while those with costs are typically just $500.[133]

For about $1,200, the JAWS (Job Access With Speech) app uses Braille and speech to "read" the contents of a computer screen to a blind employee. JAWS can also be paired with

Disability a mental or physical impairment that substantially limits one or more major life activities

Disability discrimination treating people differently because of their disabilities

screen magnification software or a keyboard with large font, boldfaced easy-to-read letters. Color identification apps and currency identification apps also help blind employees. Lee Huffman, editor of *AccessWorld* magazine, says, "You simply wave your phone camera over the piece of clothing [for color identification] or the currency, and it tells you what it is. Five years ago, these programs might have cost $125 or more, but now you can download these apps at low or no cost and have all that accessible technology on one device in your pocket."[134]

Some of the accommodations just described involve *assistive technology* that gives workers with disabilities the tools they need to overcome their disabilities. Providing workers with assistive technology is also an effective strategy to recruit, retain, and enhance the productivity of people with disabilities. According to the National Council on Disability, 92 percent of workers with disabilities who use assistive technology report that it helps them work faster and better, 81 percent indicate that it helps them work longer hours, and 67 percent say that it is critical to getting a job.[135] To learn about assistive technologies that can help workers with disabilities, see AbleData (https://abledata.acl.gov), which lists 40,000 products, or the National Rehabilitation Information Center (www.naric.com), which provides information for specific disabilities.

Finally, companies should actively recruit qualified workers with disabilities. Numerous organizations, such as Mainstream, Kidder Resources, the American Council of the Blind (www.acb.org), the National Federation of the Blind (nfb.org), the National Association of the Deaf (www.nad.org), the Epilepsy Foundation (www.epilepsy.com), and the National Amputation Foundation (www.nationalamputation.org), actively work with employers to find jobs for qualified people with disabilities. Companies can also place advertisements in publications, such as *Careers and the disABLED*, or on online job boards, such as abilityJOBS.com or RecruitDisability.org, that specifically target workers with disabilities.

New apps and software use Braille and speech to "read" computer screens to vision-impaired employees.

12-3 DEEP-LEVEL DIVERSITY

As you learned in Section 12-2, people often use the dimensions of surface-level diversity to form initial impressions about others. Over time, however, as people have a chance to get to know each other, initial impressions based on age, sex, race/ethnicity, and mental or physical disabilities give way to deeper impressions based on behavior and psychological characteristics. When we think of others this way, we are focusing on deep-level diversity. *Deep-level diversity* represents differences that can be learned only through extended interaction with others. Hall of famer Bob Gibson is a two-time World Series MVP, and one of the best pitchers in Major League Baseball (MLB) history with 3,117 strikeouts, a career earned run average of 2.91 and a 251–174 win–loss record in his 17 seasons with the St. Louis, Cardinals. Gibson, who is African American, experienced racism growing up and through the first part of his MLB career. Gibson, however, describes the deep-level diversity that can happen in MLB locker rooms, "Black people and white people and people from other countries, we all get thrown into this [pro baseball] life, thrown together on buses and planes and in clubhouses, and then we spend more time with each other than we do with our own families. We're forced to find out who we all are and what we're all about. And it can be the best education in the world."[136] For example, says Gibson, "(Catcher) Tim McCarver (who is white) has been my friend for 60 years. I came out of housing projects. He came out of Memphis. But we learned from each other."[137]

Examples of deep-level diversity include differences in personality, attitudes, beliefs, and values. In short, recognizing deep-level diversity requires getting to know and understand one another better. And that matters, because it can result in less prejudice, discrimination, and conflict in the workplace. These changes can then lead to better *social integration*, the degree to which organizational or group members are psychologically attracted to working with each other to accomplish a common objective.

Stop for a second and think about your boss (or the boss you had in your last job). What words would you use to describe him or her? Is your boss introverted or extraverted? Emotionally stable or unstable? Agreeable or disagreeable? Organized or disorganized? Open or closed to new experiences? When you describe your boss or others in this way, what you're really doing is describing dispositions and personality.

A **disposition** is the tendency to respond to situations and events in a predetermined manner. **Personality** is the relatively stable set of behaviors, attitudes, and emotions displayed over time that makes people different from each other.[138] For example, which of your aunts or uncles is a little offbeat, a little out of the ordinary? What were they like when you were small? What are they like now? Chances are that she or he is pretty much the same wacky person. In other words, the person's core personality hasn't changed. For example, as a child, Kip Tindell, former CEO of the Container Store, would reorganize the pantry or closets when his parents were out of the house. "If your house is unbelievably messy, I probably won't come back to visit. I'll meet you at a restaurant. I'm just not comfortable around mess."[139] Research conducted in different cultures, different settings, and different languages has shown that five basic dimensions of personality account for most of the differences in peoples' behaviors, attitudes, and emotions (or why your boss is the way he or she is!). The *Big Five Personality Dimensions* are extraversion, emotional stability, agreeableness, conscientiousness, and openness to experience.[140]

Extraversion is the degree to which someone is active, assertive, gregarious, sociable, talkative, and energized by others. In contrast to extraverts, introverts tend to be focused, thoughtful, quiet, reserved, and energized by ideas. For the best results in the workplace, introverts and extraverts should be correctly matched to their jobs. Research shows that being talkative and assertive is not correlated with greater insight, and that those who speak first and more often (usually extraverts) are not more capable than less talkative people.[141] Professor Stephen Garras is often frustrated by the premium placed on extraversion, saying, "I worry that there are people who are put in positions of authority because they're good talkers,

bram janssens/123RF

but they don't have good ideas. It's so easy to confuse schmoozing ability with talent . . . we put too much of a premium on presenting and not enough on substance and critical thinking.[142]

Emotional stability is the degree to which someone is not angry, depressed, anxious, emotional, insecure, or excitable. People who are emotionally stable respond well to stress. In other words, they can maintain a calm, problem-solving attitude in even the toughest situations (for example, conflict, hostility, dangerous conditions, or extreme time pressures). By contrast, emotionally unstable people find it difficult to handle the most basic demands of their jobs under only moderately stressful situations and become distraught, tearful, self-doubting, and anxious. Emotional stability is particularly important for high-stress jobs such as police work, firefighting, emergency medical treatment, piloting planes, or commanding. When a flock of geese flew into the engines of US Airways Flight 1549 departing New York's LaGuardia airport, Captain "Sully" Sullenberger and First Officer Jeffrey Skiles had less than 4 minutes to save their passengers' lives. Sullenberger said, "Realizing that we were without engines, I knew that this was the worst aviation challenge I'd ever faced. It was the most sickening, pit-of-your-stomach, falling-through-the-floor feeling I had ever experienced."[143] Sullenberger said, "I was aware of my body. I could feel an adrenaline rush. I'm sure that my blood pressure and pulse spiked."[144] Three and a half minutes later, after a dozen instantaneous decisions, Sullenberger and Skiles beat the odds by "landing" their plane in the middle of the frigid Hudson River, a nearly impossible task. Nearby boats and ferries rescued the crew and passengers minutes before the plane sank. When asked whether it was difficult to stay calm, Sullenberger replied, "No. It just took some concentration."[145] That's emotional stability.

Agreeableness is the degree to which someone is cooperative, polite,

---

Disposition the tendency to respond to situations and events in a predetermined manner

Personality the relatively stable set of behaviors, attitudes, and emotions displayed over time that makes people different from each other

Extraversion the degree to which someone is active, assertive, gregarious, sociable, talkative, and energized by others

Emotional stability the degree to which someone is not angry, depressed, anxious, emotional, insecure, and excitable

Agreeableness the degree to which someone is cooperative, polite, flexible, forgiving, good-natured, tolerant, and trusting

DEEP-LEVEL DIVERSITY: THE KEY TO TEAM PROBLEM SOLVING

While diverse groups initially have difficulty working together, they eventually do a better job of identifying problems and generating alternative solutions.

But that doesn't come from surface-level diversity—that is, people of different ages, sexes, or ethnicities. It comes from cognitive diversity, that is, differences in experience, knowledge, and thinking styles (engineers vs. artists). It's the clash of ideas, assumptions, or approaches that makes cognitively diverse teams better at solving problems. Professors Alison Reynolds and David Lewis explain that the difficulty is that, "Someone being from a different culture or of a different generation gives no clue as to how that person might process information, engage with, or respond to change."

So create diverse teams using knowledge of peoples' deep-level diversity, which only comes from working closely with them. Select people with different functional backgrounds, personalities (introverts vs. extroverts), and thinking styles, and you'll greatly increase the chances of successful team problem solving.

Rawpixel.com/Shutterstock.com

Sources: M. Amini, M. Ekstrom, T. Ellingsen, M. Johannesson, F. Stromsten, "Does Gender Diversity Promote Nonconformity?" *Management Science* 63, no. 4 (2017): 1085–1096; S. Bell, A. Villado, M. Lukasik, L. Belau & A. Briggs, "Getting Specific about Demographic Diversity Variable and Team Performance Relationships: A Meta-Analysis," *Journal of Management* 37, no. 3 (2011): 709–743; A. Eagly, "When Passionate Advocates Meet Research on Diversity, Does the Honest Broker Stand a Chance?" *Journal of Social Issues* 72 no. 1 (2016): 199–222; A. Reynolds and D. Lewis, "Teams Solve Problems Faster When They're More Cognitively Diverse," *Harvard Business Review*, March 30, 2017, accessed April 26, 2017, hbr.org/2017/03/teams-solve-problems-faster-when-theyre-morecognitively -diverse; F. Shi, M. Teplitskiy, E. Duede & J. Evans, "Are Politically Diverse Teams More Effective?" *Harvard Business Review*, July 15, 2019, accessed May 17, 2020, hbr.org/2019/07/are-politically-diverse-teams-more-effective.

flexible, forgiving, good-natured, tolerant, and trusting. Basically, agreeable people are easy to work with and be around, whereas disagreeable people are distrusting and difficult to work with and be around. A number of companies have made general attitude or agreeableness the most important factor in their hiring decisions.

Conscientiousness is the degree to which someone is organized, hardworking, responsible, persevering, thorough, and achievement oriented. One management consultant wrote about his experiences with a conscientious employee: "He arrived at our first meeting with a typed copy of his daily schedule, a sheet bearing his home and office phone numbers, addresses, and his email address. At his request, we established a timetable for meetings for the next four months. He showed up on time every time, day planner in hand, and carefully listed tasks and due dates. He questioned me exhaustively if he didn't understand an assignment and returned on schedule with the completed work or with a clear explanation as to why it wasn't done."[146] Conscientious employees are also more likely to engage in positive behaviors, such as helping new employees, coworkers, and supervisors, and are less likely to engage in negative behaviors, such as verbally or physically abusing coworkers or stealing.[147]

Openness to experience is the degree to which someone is curious, broadminded, and open to new ideas, things, and experiences; is spontaneous; and has a high tolerance for ambiguity. Most companies need people who are strong in terms of openness to experience to fill certain positions, but for other positions, this dimension is less important. People in marketing, advertising, research, or other creative jobs need to be curious, open to new ideas, and spontaneous. By contrast, openness to experience is not particularly important to accountants, who need to apply stringent rules and formulas consistently to make sense out of complex financial information.

Which of the Big Five Personality Dimensions has the largest impact on behavior in organizations? The cumulative results of multiple studies indicate that conscientiousness is related to job performance across five different occupational groups (professionals, police,

Conscientiousness the degree to which someone is organized, hardworking, responsible, persevering, thorough, and achievement oriented

Openness to experience the degree to which someone is curious, broad-minded, and open to new ideas, things, and experiences; is spontaneous; and has a high tolerance for ambiguity

managers, salespeople, and skilled or semiskilled workers).[148] In short, people "who are dependable, persistent, goal directed, and organized tend to be higher performers on virtually any job; viewed negatively, those who are careless, irresponsible, low achievement striving, and impulsive tend to be lower performers on virtually any job."[149] A lifetime study measured the personality traits of high IQ (top 0.5 percent) students in grades 1 through 8 in 1921 and 1922, tracking them till 1991. Over those 70 years, it found that men who were above average in conscientiousness earned $16.7 percent more ($567,000) over their working lives.[150] The results also indicate that extraversion is related to performance in jobs, such as sales and management, that involve significant interaction with others. In people-intensive jobs like these, it helps to be sociable, assertive, and talkative and to have energy and be able to energize others. That same lifetime study found that extraverts earned $760,000 more over their working lives compared to introverts.[151] Finally, people who are extraverted and open to experience seem to do much better in training. Being curious and open to new experiences as well as sociable, assertive, talkative, and full of energy helps people perform better in learning situations.[152]

 MANAGING DIVERSITY

How much should companies change their standard business practices to accommodate the diversity of their workers? What do you do when a talented top executive has a drinking problem that seems to affect his behavior only at company business parties (for entertaining clients), where he has made inappropriate advances toward female employees? What do you do when, despite aggressive company policies against racial discrimination, employees continue to tell racist jokes or post racist comments on social media? And, because many people confuse diversity with affirmative action, what do you do to make sure that your company's diversity practices and policies are viewed as benefiting all workers and not just some workers?

No doubt about it, questions like these make managing diversity one of the toughest challenges that managers face. Nonetheless, there are steps companies can take to begin to address these issues.

As discussed earlier, diversity programs try to create a positive work environment where no one is advantaged or disadvantaged, where "we" is everyone, where everyone can do his or her best work, where differences are respected and not ignored, and where everyone feels comfortable.

Let's begin to address those goals by learning about **12-4a different diversity paradigms, 12-4b diversity**

principles, 12-4c diversity training and practices, and **12-4d what works**

12-4a Diversity Paradigms

There are several different methods or paradigms for managing diversity: the discrimination and fairness paradigm, the access and legitimacy paradigm, and the learning and effectiveness paradigm.[153]

The *discrimination and fairness paradigm*, which is the most common method of approaching diversity, focuses on equal opportunity, fair treatment, recruitment of minorities, and strict compliance with the equal employment opportunity laws. Under this approach, success is usually measured by how well companies achieve recruitment, promotion, and retention goals for women, people of different racial/ethnic backgrounds, or other underrepresented groups. According to a workplace diversity practices survey conducted by the Society for Human Resource Management, 66 to 91 percent of companies use specialized strategies to recruit, retain, and promote talented women and minorities. The percentages increase with company size, and companies of more than 500 employees are the most likely to use these strategies. Of companies with more than 500 employees, 77 percent systematically collect measurements on diversity-related practices.[154] Joelle Emerson, founder and CEO of **Paradigm**, a diversity consulting firm, says, "What I always come back to is approach diversity and inclusion as you would any other business challenge. That starts with measurement. So take a look at where gaps exist. Actually dig in to where barriers are emerging in your systems....Let's look at promotion rates, let's look at performance scores. Let's look at how work is distributed. Starting by looking at some of those outcomes, and looking at how they might differ based on people's identities, is a really helpful first place to start."[155] The primary benefit of the discrimination and fairness paradigm is that it generally brings about fairer treatment of employees and increases demographic diversity. The primary limitation is that the focus of diversity remains on the surface-level diversity dimensions of sex, race, and ethnicity.[156]

The *access and legitimacy paradigm* focuses on the acceptance and celebration of differences to ensure that the diversity within the company matches the diversity found among primary stakeholders, such as customers, suppliers, and local communities. This is similar to the *business growth* advantage of diversity discussed earlier in the chapter. The basic idea behind this approach is to create a demographically diverse workforce that attracts a broader customer base.[157] For example, the diversity strategy at **Oshkosh**, a maker of specialty trucks and truck bodies, states, "We operate and sell our products and services in over 100 countries on six continents, each with its own culture, customs, and business practices. We seek employees who are passionate about serving customers and who reflect our diverse customer base so that we can truly understand our customers to better serve and delight them."[158]

The primary benefit of this approach is that it establishes a clear business reason for diversity. Like the discrimination and fairness paradigm, however, it focuses only on the surface-level diversity dimensions of sex, race, and ethnicity. Furthermore, employees who are assigned responsibility for customers and stakeholders on the basis of their sex, race, or ethnicity may eventually feel frustrated and exploited.

Although the discrimination and fairness paradigm focuses on assimilation (having a demographically representative workforce), and the access and legitimacy paradigm focuses on differentiation (having demographic differences inside the company match those of key customers and stakeholders), the *learning and effectiveness paradigm* focuses on integrating deep-level diversity differences, such as personality, attitudes, beliefs, and values, into the actual work of the organization. Global accounting and consulting firm **Deloitte** practices the learning and effectiveness paradigm by integrating diversity of thinking into how it runs its business.

Our view is that the goal is to create workplaces that leverage diversity of thinking. Why? Because research shows that diversity of thinking is a wellspring of creativity, enhancing innovation by about 20 percent. It also enables groups to spot risks, reducing these by up to 30 percent. And it smooths the implementation of decisions by creating buy-in and trust. So how can leaders make this insight practical, and not neglect demographic diversity? The answer lies in keeping an eye on both. Deloitte's research reveals that high-performing teams are both cognitively and demographically diverse.[159]

And how does that happen? Deloitte says, "A complex problem typically requires input from six different mental frameworks or 'approaches': evidence, options, outcomes, people, process, and risk. In reality, no one is equally good at all six; hence, the need for complementary team members."[160]

The learning and effectiveness paradigm is consistent with achieving organizational plurality.

"We are all on the same team...

Organizational plurality is a work environment where (1) all members are empowered to contribute in a way that maximizes the benefits to the organization, customers, and themselves, and (2) the individuality of each member is respected by not segmenting or polarizing people on the basis of their membership in a particular group.[161]

The learning and effectiveness diversity paradigm offers four benefits.[162] First, it values common ground. Former Harvard Business School professor David Thomas explains:

> *Like the fairness paradigm, it promotes equal opportunity for all individuals. And like the access paradigm, it acknowledges cultural differences among people and recognizes the value in those differences. Yet this new model for managing diversity lets the organization internalize differences among employees so that it learns and grows because of them. Indeed, with the model fully in place, members of the organization can say, "We are all on the same team, with our differences—not despite them."*[163]

Second, this paradigm makes a distinction between individual and group differences. When diversity focuses only on differences between groups, such as females versus males, large differences within groups are ignored.[164] For example, think of the women you know at work. Now, think for a second about what they have in common. After that, think about how they're different. If your situation is typical, the list of differences should be just as long as the list of commonalties, if not longer. In short, managers can achieve a greater understanding of diversity and their employees by treating them as individuals and by realizing that not all African Americans, Hispanics, women, or white males want the same things at work.[165]

Third, because the focus is on individual differences, the learning and effectiveness paradigm is less likely to encounter the conflict, backlash, and divisiveness sometimes associated with diversity programs that focus only on group differences. Taylor Cox, one of the leading management writers on diversity, says, "We are concerned here with these more destructive forms of conflict which may be present with diverse workforces due to language barriers, cultural clash, or resentment by majority-group members of what they

> **Organizational plurality** a work environment where (1) all members are empowered to contribute in a way that maximizes the benefits to the organization, customers, and themselves, and (2) the individuality of each member is respected by not segmenting or polarizing people on the basis of their membership in a particular group

with our differences—not despite them."

DIVERSITY APPS

Information technology has helped us in countless ways, but we're just beginning to discover how it can help us create a workforce that is talented, capable, and diverse. Check out these three new apps developed to increase diversity in the workplace:

» **Textio** is a diversity spell checker that scans job listings for biased language that might discourage a diverse applicant pool. And just like a regular spell checker, Textio suggests different wordings to help increase the number and diversity of applicants.

» **GapJumpers** helps companies review job applications without knowing candidates' sex or race. GapJumpers also provides companies with a number of online performance auditions so they can see how candidates perform tasks that pertain to the job in question.

» **Mentorloop** is a mentoring matching program that signs employees up for your mentoring program, uses algorithms to match mentors and mentees on experience, skills, interests, location, and desired outcomes. The My Match function allows employees to browse and connect with the potential mentors or mentees. Mentor loop also tracks the extent to which mentors and mentees actually engage with each other.

Source: "Mentorloop Mentoring Software | Features," Mentorloop.com, accessed May 17, 2020, mentorloop.com/features/; R. Silverman and L. Gellman, "Apps Take on Workplace Bias," *Wall Street Journal*, September 30, 2015, accessed May 9, 2016, www.wsj.com/articles/apps-take-on-workplace-bias-1443601027.

the best organizational decisions and to produce innovative, competitive products and services.

12-4b Diversity Principles

Diversity paradigms are general approaches or strategies for managing diversity. Whatever diversity paradigm a manager chooses, diversity principles will help managers do a better job of *managing company diversity programs.*[168]

Begin by *carefully and faithfully following and enforcing federal and state laws regarding equal opportunity employment.* Diversity programs can't and won't succeed if the company is being sued for discriminatory actions and behavior. Faithfully following the law will also reduce the time and expense associated with EEOC investigations or lawsuits. Start by learning more at the EEOC website (www.eeoc.gov). Following the law also means strictly and fairly enforcing company policies.

Treat group differences as important but not special. Surface-level diversity dimensions such as age, sex, gender orientation and sexual identity, and race/ethnicity should be respected but should not be treated as more important than other kinds of differences (i.e., deep-level diversity). Remember, the shift in focus from surface- to deep-level diversity helps people know and understand each other better, reduces prejudice and conflict, and leads to stronger social integration with people wanting to work together and get the job done. Also, *find the common ground.* Although respecting differences is important, it's just as important, especially with diverse workforces, to actively find ways for employees to see and share commonalties.

Tailor opportunities to individuals, not groups. Special programs for training, development, mentoring, or promotion should be based on individual strengths and weaknesses, not on group status. Instead of making mentoring available for just one group of workers, create mentoring opportunities for everyone who wants to be mentored. At Deloitte and the DuPont Corporation, mentoring programs are open to all employees. Through candid and

may perceive as preferential and unwarranted treatment of minority-group members."[166] And Ray Haines, a consultant who has helped companies deal with the aftermath of diversity programs that became divisive, says, "There's a large amount of backlash related to diversity training. It stirs up a lot of hostility, anguish, and resentment but doesn't give people tools to deal with (the backlash). You have people come in and talk about their specific ax to grind."[167] Not all diversity programs are divisive or lead to conflict. But by focusing on individual rather than group differences, the learning and effectiveness paradigm helps minimize these potential problems.

Finally, unlike the other diversity paradigms that simply focus on surface-level diversity, the learning and effectiveness paradigm focuses on bringing different talents and perspectives (that is deep-level diversity) *together* to make

confidential conversations, Deloitte and DuPont mentors help younger workers and managers with problem solving and career and leadership development.[169]

Maintain high standards. Companies have a legal and moral obligation to make sure that their hiring and promotion procedures and standards are fair to all. At the same time, in today's competitive markets, companies should not lower standards to promote diversity. This not only hurts the organizations but also feeds the stereotype that applicants who are hired or promoted in the name of affirmative action or diversity are less qualified. When Gregg Popovich, coach of the NBA's San Antonio Spurs, discussed hiring former WNBA All-Star player and Olympic Medalist Becky Hammon, he told her, "As cool as it would be to hire you [as a full-time assistant coach], you'd have to be qualified, and I'd have to make sure you're qualified." She agreed. When Popovich hired her after a one-year coaching internship, Hammon said, "Honestly, I don't think he gives two cents that I'm a woman. And, I don't want to be hired because I'm a woman . . . I'm getting hired because I'm capable."[170] San Francisco 49ers receivers' coach, Katie Sowers, the first woman and openly LGBT coach in the NFL, said, "I'm not here to be the token female. I'm here to help us win."[171] After hiring two women to serve as the NFL Tampa Bay Buccaneers' assistant defensive-line and strength-and-conditioning coaches, Buc's coach Bruce Ariens said, "They're good fits for what we need. The fact that their gender's different – who gives a s***."[172]

Solicit negative as well as positive feedback. Diversity is one of the most difficult management issues. No company or manager gets it right from the start. Consequently, companies should aggressively seek positive and negative feedback about their diversity programs. One way to do that is to use a series of measurements to see if progress is being made.

Set high but realistic goals. Just because diversity is difficult doesn't mean that organizations shouldn't try to accomplish as much as possible. The general purpose of diversity programs is to try to create a positive work environment where no one is advantaged or disadvantaged, where "we" is everyone, where everyone can do his or her best work, where differences are respected and not ignored, and where everyone feels comfortable. Even if progress is slow, companies should not shrink from these goals.

12-4c Diversity Training and Practices

Organizations use diversity training and several common diversity practices to manage diversity. There are two basic types of diversity training programs, skills-based and awareness. **Skills-based diversity training** teaches employees the practical skills they need for managing a diverse workforce, skills such as flexibility and adaptability, negotiation, problem solving, and conflict resolution.[173] By contrast, **awareness training** is designed to raise employees' awareness of diversity issues and to challenge underlying assumptions or stereotypes we may have about others. **Dell Inc.** enrolled several male executives in a six-month program run by Catalyst, a nonprofit group that tracks and advocates for women's advancement. The program teaches managers to recognize the hurdles facing women in the workplace. As a result of the training, Doug Hillary, a Dell vice president, checked in with a female staff member with two young children and asked her if he was adequately accommodating her family needs. She told him that, actually, he was regularly scheduling staff conference calls at an hour when she was dropping her children off at school. He changed the meeting times, saying that, previously, "He didn't pay as much attention."[174]

Some companies use the Implicit Association Test (IAT) for awareness training.[175] The IAT measures the extent to which people associate positive or negative thoughts (that is underlying assumptions or stereotypes) with blacks or whites, men or women, homosexuals or heterosexuals, young or old, or other groups. For the race IAT (versions

Cal Sport Media/Alamy Stock Photo

Katie Sowers is the first woman to coach in the NFL.

> **Skills-based diversity training** training that teaches employees the practical skills they need for managing a diverse workforce, such as flexibility and adaptability, negotiation, problem solving, and conflict resolution

> **Awareness training** training that is designed to raise employees' awareness of diversity issues and to challenge the underlying assumptions or stereotypes they may have about others

also exist for weight, age, sexuality, and other ethnic groups), test takers are shown black or white faces that they must instantly pair with various words. IAT proponents argue that shorter responses generally indicate stronger associations and that the patterns of associations indicate the extent to which people are biased. For example, an early study showed that 88 percent of whites have a more positive mental association toward whites than toward blacks, but surprisingly, 48 percent of blacks showed the same bias. Do the biases measured by the IAT mean we're likely to discriminate against others? Thankfully, no, according to the results of a growing number of critical studies that indicate that IAT scores are *not* consistent over time, and, as admitted by its authors, are *not* related to discriminatory behavior.[176] But the IAT may help us become aware of potential biases and therefore increase awareness of diversity issues. However, *if* IAT training changes attitudes, those changes – at best – last no more than a few days.[177] IAT codeveloper Professor Anthony Greenwald says IAT training "appears to be the right thing to do, but this training hasn't been shown to be effective, and… is not likely to change anything."[178]

Companies also use diversity audits, diversity pairing, and minority experiences for top executives to better manage diversity. **Diversity audits** are formal assessments that measure employee and management attitudes, investigate the extent to which people are advantaged or disadvantaged with respect to hiring and promotions, and review companies' diversity-related policies and procedures. Writing in *The New York Times* against age discrimination, Ashton Applewhite says that any manager serious about diversity should start with the "shoe test." She says, "Look under the table, and if everyone's wearing the same kind of shoes, whether wingtips or flip-flops, you've got a problem." In other words, measurement and data are at the core of diversity audits.[179] According to Harvard Professor Iris Bohnet, "Using data to learn about the possible disparate treatment of employees shouldn't be controversial. No company runs its finances

Mentoring and the newer trend of "reverse mentoring" provides different aged workers with the opportunity of tapping into new resources for learning.

based just on intuition, and the same should hold for personnel decisions."[180] One manager whose company uses metrics for assessing diversity says that he has asked his team, "'How come, in the last month, you've gone after a large number of new people, and you haven't interviewed one woman for the position?' I started asking questions like this — I am not expecting them to have the answers. I'm expecting them to know that the next time I ask these questions, you better have the answers because I already have the data."[181]

Earlier in the chapter, you learned that *mentoring* is a common strategy for creating learning and promotional opportunities for women. Diversity pairing is a special kind of mentoring. In **diversity pairing**, people of different ages, cultural backgrounds, sexes, or races/ethnicities are paired for mentoring. The hope is that stereotypical beliefs and attitudes will change as people get to know each other as individuals.[182] Phyllis Korkki, a *New York Times* assignment editor in her mid-50s approached Talya Minsberg, age 27, and asked, "Will you mentor me?"[183] Minsberg said, "Korkki is a longtime *Times* employee, an accomplished journalist and an author. So the fact that she was approaching me for mentorship was unexpected."[184] Korkki wanted Minsberg to "reverse mentor" her so she could learn SnapChat. Minsberg leads the *Times'* efforts to attract younger readers via SnapChat stories. Korkki said, "I sought a mentor to help me develop a specific new skill—and something entirely outside my comfort zone—namely, how to use Snapchat, the smartphone-based photo and video service that is popular among teenagers and young adults."[185] While awkward at first, both benefited from

Diversity audits formal assessments that measure employee and management attitudes, investigate the extent to which people are advantaged or disadvantaged with respect to hiring and promotions, and review companies' diversity-related policies and procedures

Diversity pairing a mentoring program in which people of different ages, cultural backgrounds, sexes, or races/ethnicities are paired together to get to know each other and change stereotypical beliefs and attitudes

the relationship. Minsberg said, "I realized our mentorship provided me with something unexpected: a chance to take what amounts to a leadership position I had not seen coming."[186] Korkki said that being mentored, ". . . made me realize that organizations and individual workers could do a lot more to bridge the gaps between generations. Each age group has untapped resources that can benefit others at a different stage of life."[187]

Because top managers are still overwhelmingly white and male, a number of companies believe that it is worthwhile to *have top executives experience what it is like to be in the minority*. This can be done by having top managers go to places or events where nearly everyone else is of a different sex or racial/ethnic background. For example, managers at Raytheon are required to spend an entire day in the office in a wheelchair so that they have a better understanding of the challenges faced by their disabled colleagues. Managers and executives at Sodexho Alliance are asked to spend time working with organizations that represent minorities. One male manager became the sponsor of a women employees group at **Sodexho** and accompanied a female colleague to a meeting of the Women's Food Service Forum. The manager called the experience, in which he was at a conference with 1,500 women, "profound" and said that it taught him what it feels like to be different. He also described how his experiences working with women made him more sensitive to women's feelings and even led him to change the social activities that he plans with coworkers from golf to dinner cruises. Rohini Anand, Sodexho's chief diversity officer, endorses this experiential approach, saying, "To really engage people, you have to create a series of epiphanies and take leaders through those epiphanies.[188]

12-4d Diversity: What Works?

Finally, while there's a wealth of data on what is being done to address diversity issues, there's not much clear, consistent, scientifically rigorous evidence on effectiveness.[189] So what do we know at this time?

Let's start with what does *not* work. In general, it's difficult to have confidence in diversity training. A review of 985 studies examining ways to reduce prejudice or bias toward others (similar to awareness training) concluded, "Psychologists are a long way from demonstrating the most effective ways to reduce prejudice," and that the evidence, so far, "does not reveal whether, when, and why interventions reduce prejudice in the world."[190] We also know that the Implicit Association Test (IAT) scores are not related to discriminatory behavior, that *if* IAT training changes attitudes, those changes – at best – last no more than a few days, and that one of the IAT's developers admits that IAT training isn't effective. However, a meta-analysis of 260 studies found that diversity training improves learning (what is known about diversity), attitudes, and behavior, but only learning about diversity lasts over time. That same study found that diversity training works best as part of an overall approach to diversity in which companies conduct skills *and* awareness training in combination with other diversity initiatives.[191]

The other downside to diversity training is that it may produce negative effects.[192] According to professors Frank Dobbin and Alexandra Kalev, who studied 30 years of data across 800 companies, "The positive effects of diversity training rarely last beyond a day or two, and a number of studies suggest that it can activate bias or spark a backlash. Nonetheless, nearly half of midsize companies use it, as do nearly all the *Fortune* 500."[193] Why? Because training is required, and the message is, "We don't trust you to treat people fairly." As a result, Dobbin and Kaley say, "Trainers tell us that people often respond to compulsory courses with anger and resistance – and many participants actually report more animosity toward other groups afterward."[194] Expanding the focus to specific workplace situations, such as recruiting/hiring, team dynamics and career development, and, exploring practical actions, like structured interviews (so everyone gets asked the same questions), clarifying what job qualifications are most important, and making sure that quieter voices are heard in group and team discussions, can significantly reduce defensiveness that may accompany some diversity training.[195]

A survey of 829 companies suggests that the most popular programs, diversity training, diversity performance audits (assessing how well managers are addressing diversity issues), and network programs (company sponsored affinity groups for women and minorities) "have no positive effects in the average workplace."[196]

So what *does* work? Ironically, the two least frequently used programs, diversity mentoring and appointing diversity managers responsible for diversity programs, "were among the most effective."[197] Finally, focusing on deep-level diversity appears to have strong positive effects. According to professors Jonathan Haidt and Lee Jussim, "In a review of more than 500 studies, published in the *Journal of Personality and Social Psychology*, authors Thomas Pettigrew and Linda Tropp concluded that when people of different races and ethnicities mix together and get to know each other, the effect is generally to reduce prejudice on all sides. This is a good justification for increasing diversity."[198]

13 | Motivation

13-1 BASICS OF MOTIVATION

What makes people happiest and most productive at work?[1] Is it money, benefits, opportunities for growth, interesting work, or something else altogether? And if people desire different things, how can a company keep everyone motivated? It takes insight and hard work to motivate workers to join the company, perform well, and then stay with the company.

In a 2018 study, Gallup found that only 34 percent of US employees are "engaged" or motivated at work, whereas 53 percent are "not engaged," meaning they are unmotivated, not interested in organizational goals or outcomes, or, as Gallup reports, "they're just there." For example, *The New York Times* reporter Erin Griffith confessed, "Never once at the start of my workweek – not in my morning coffee shop line; not in my crowded subway commute; not as I begin my bottomless inbox slog – have I paused, looked to the heavens, and whispered: #ThankGodIt'sMonday."[2] Even worse, 13 percent of employees are "actively disengaged."[3] Says Gallup, "They are miserable in the workplace and destroy what the most engaged employees build."[4]

Gallup examined the results of 1.9 million people across 49 countries employed in 82,000 work units for 230 companies to see how engagement, or motivation, matters. "Business/work units scoring in the top half on employee engagement nearly double their odds of success compared with those in the bottom half. Those at the 99th percentile have four times the success rate of those at the first percentile. Median differences between

top-quartile and bottom-quartile units were 10 percent in customer ratings, 21 percent in profitability, 20 percent in sales production, 17 percent in production records, 24 percent in turnover (high-turnover organizations), 59 percent in turnover (low-turnover organizations), 70 percent in safety incidents, 28 percent in shrinkage, 41 percent in absenteeism, 58 percent in patient safety incidents, and 40 percent in quality (defects)."[5]

So what is motivation? **Motivation** is the set of forces that initiates, directs, and makes people persist in their efforts to accomplish a goal.[6] *Initiation of effort* is concerned with the choices that people make about how much effort to put forth in their jobs. ("Do I really knock myself out or just do a decent job?") *Direction of effort* is concerned with the choices that people make in deciding where to put forth effort in their jobs. ("I should be spending time with my high-dollar accounts instead of learning this new computer system!") *Persistence of effort* is concerned with the choices that people make about how long they will put forth effort in their jobs before reducing or eliminating those efforts. ("I'm only halfway through the project, and I'm exhausted. Do I

plow through to the end, or just call it quits?") Initiation, direction, and persistence are at the heart of motivation.

One of the ways in which researchers determine what motivates different workers is to ask them how much of a pay increase they'd be willing to give up in order to get something else, like paid time off. A National Bureau of Economic Research (NBER) study found that people would be willing to give up a 23 percent pay raise to get 20 days of paid time off (PTO) or a 16.4 percent raise for 10 days of PTO. Would you? If your job required "heavy physical activity," would you give up a 14.9 percent raise for a job with only "moderate physical activity," or a 12 percent raise for a job where you mostly sat? Would you forgo a 9 percent raise to set your own schedule (instead of your boss), or an 8.4 percent raise to work by yourself (instead of on a team)?[7]

Under which of these conditions would you be more motivated? Or, in Gallup's terms, in which conditions would you be more engaged,

> **Motivation** the set of forces that initiates, directs, and makes people persist in their efforts to accomplish a goal

disengaged, or actively engaged at work? What parts of the job really interest and energize you? Or your co-workers? Which don't, and why? Answering questions like these is at the heart of figuring out how best to motivate people at work.

*Let's learn more about motivation by building a basic model of motivation out of **13-1a effort and performance, 13-1b need satisfaction,** and **13-1c extrinsic and intrinsic rewards** and then discussing **13-1d how to motivate people with this basic model of motivation.***

13-1a Effort and Performance

When most people think of work motivation, they think that working hard (effort) should lead to a good job (performance). Exhibit 13.1 shows a basic model of work motivation and performance, displaying this process. The first thing to notice about Exhibit 13.1 is that this is a basic model of work motivation *and* performance. In practice, it's almost impossible to talk about one without mentioning the other. Not surprisingly, managers often assume motivation is the only determinant of performance, saying things such as "Your performance was really terrible last quarter. What's the matter? Aren't you as motivated as you used to be?" In fact, motivation is just one of three primary determinants of job performance. In industrial psychology, job performance is frequently represented by this equation:

Job Performance = Motivation × Ability × Situational Constraints

In this formula, *job performance* is how well someone performs the requirements of the job. *Motivation*, as defined previously, is effort, the degree to which someone works hard to do the job well. *Ability* is the degree to which workers possess the knowledge, skills, and talent needed to do a job well. And *situational constraints* are factors beyond the control of individual employees, such as tools, policies, and resources that have an effect on job performance.

Because job performance is a multiplicative function of motivation times ability times situational constraints, job performance will suffer if any one of these components is weak. This doesn't mean that motivation doesn't matter. It just means that all the motivation in the world won't translate into high performance when an employee has little ability and high situational

Needs the physical or psychological requirements that must be met to ensure survival and well-being

Exhibit 13.1
A Basic Model of Work Motivation and Performance

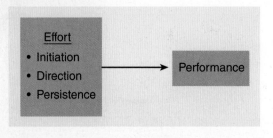

constraints. So, even though we will spend this chapter developing a model of work motivation, it is important to remember that ability and situational constraints affect job performance as well.

13-1b Need Satisfaction

In Exhibit 13.1, we started with a very basic model of motivation in which effort leads to job performance. But managers want to know, "What leads to effort?" Determining employee needs is the first step to answering that question.

Needs are the physical or psychological requirements that must be met to ensure survival and well-being.[8] As shown on the left side of Exhibit 13.2, a person's unmet need creates an uncomfortable, internal state of tension that must be resolved. For example, if you normally skip breakfast but then have to work through lunch, chances are you'll be so hungry by late afternoon that the only thing you'll be motivated to do is find something to eat. So, according to needs theories, people are motivated by unmet needs. But a need no longer motivates once it is met. When this occurs, people become satisfied, as shown on the right side of Exhibit 13.2. For example, **Weifield Group Electrical Contracting** was so busy it asked its 400 employees to work 50-hour weeks. But, says CEO Seth Anderson, after two or three consecutive 50-hour weeks, workers get tired and don't install wiring and fixtures as fast as they normally would. At that point, he says, "There are some guys that will not work overtime. You can't pay 'em enough to work overtime."[9] Why not? Because the extra money, which motivated them at first and is now in their bank accounts, no longer motivates them, especially given the fatigue and time away from family.

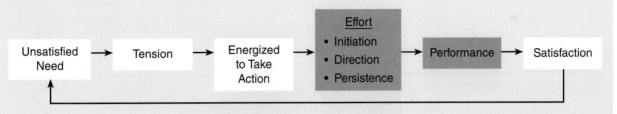

Exhibit 13.2
A Basic Model of Work Motivation and Performance

| Unsatisfied Need | → | Tension | → | Energized to Take Action | → | **Effort**
• Initiation
• Direction
• Persistence | → | Performance | → | Satisfaction |

As shown on the left side of this exhibit, a person's unsatisfied need creates an uncomfortable internal state of tension that must be resolved. So, according to needs theories, people are motivated by unmet needs. But after a need is met, it no longer motivates. When this occurs, people become satisfied, as shown on the right side of the exhibit.

Note: Throughout the chapter, as we build on this basic model, the parts of the model that we've already discussed will appear shaded in color. For example, because we've already discussed the effort → performance part of the model, those components are shown with a colored background. When we add new parts to the model, they will have a white background. We're adding need satisfaction to the model at this step, so the need-satisfaction components of unsatisfied need, tension, energized to take action, and satisfaction are shown with a white background. This shading convention should make it easier to understand the work motivation model as we add to it in each section of the chapter.

Marta Design/Shutterstock.com

Because people are motivated by unmet needs, managers must learn what those unmet needs are and address them. This is not always a straightforward task, however, because different needs theories suggest different needs categories. Consider three well-known needs theories. Maslow's hierarchy of needs suggests that people are motivated by *physiological* (food and water), *safety* (physical and economic), *belongingness* (friendship, love, and social interaction), *esteem* (achievement and recognition), and *self-actualization* (realizing your full potential) needs.[10] Alderfer's ERG theory collapses Maslow's five needs into three: *existence* (safety and physiological needs), *relatedness* (belongingness), and *growth* (esteem and self-actualization).[11] McClelland's acquired-needs theory suggests that people are motivated by the need for *affiliation* (to be liked and accepted), the need for *achievement* (to accomplish challenging goals), or the need for *power* (to influence others).[12]

Things become even more complicated when we consider the different predictions made by these theories. According to Maslow, needs are arranged in a hierarchy from low (physiological) to high (self-actualization). Within this hierarchy, people are motivated by their lowest unsatisfied need. As each need is met, they work their way up the hierarchy from physiological to self-actualization needs. By contrast, Alderfer says that people can be motivated by more than one need

Exhibit 13.3
Adding Rewards to the Model

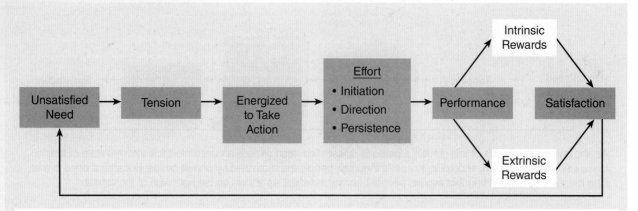

Performing a job well can be rewarding intrinsically (the job itself is fun, challenging, or interesting) or extrinsically (as you receive better pay, promotions, and so on). Intrinsic and extrinsic rewards lead to satisfaction of various needs.

at a time. Furthermore, he suggests that people are just as likely to move down the needs hierarchy as up, particularly when they are unable to achieve satisfaction at the next higher need level. McClelland argues that the degree to which particular needs motivate varies tremendously from person to person, with some people being motivated primarily by achievement and others by power or affiliation. Moreover, McClelland says that needs are learned, not innate. For instance, studies show that children whose parents own a small business or hold a managerial position are much more likely to have a high need for achievement.[13]

So, with three different sets of needs and three very different ideas about how needs motivate, how do we provide a practical answer to managers who just want to know what leads to effort? Fortunately, the research evidence simplifies things a bit. To start, studies indicate that there are two basic kinds of needs categories.[14] *Lower-order needs* are concerned with safety and with physiological and existence requirements, whereas *higher-order needs* are concerned with relationships (belongingness, relatedness, and affiliation), challenges and accomplishments (esteem, self-actualization, growth, and achievement), and influence (power). Studies generally show that higher-order needs will not motivate people as long as lower-order needs remain unsatisfied.[15]

For example, imagine that you graduated

from college six months ago and are still looking for your first job. With money running short (you're probably living on your credit cards), and the possibility of having to move back in with your parents looming (if this doesn't motivate you, what will?), your basic needs for food, shelter, and security drive your thoughts, behavior, and choices at this point. But after you land that job, find a great place (of your own!) to live, and put some money in the bank, these basic needs should decrease in importance as you begin to think about making new friends and taking on challenging work assignments. In fact, after lower-order needs are satisfied, it's difficult for managers to predict which higher-order needs will motivate behavior.[16] Some people will be motivated by affiliation, while others will be motivated by growth or esteem. Also, the relative importance of the various needs may change over time but not necessarily in any predictable pattern. So, what leads to effort? In part, needs do. After we discuss rewards in Subsections 13-1c and 13-1d we discuss how managers can use what we know from need-satisfaction theories to motivate workers.

13-1c Extrinsic and Intrinsic Rewards

No discussion of motivation would be complete without considering rewards. Let's add two kinds of rewards, extrinsic and intrinsic, to the model in Exhibit 13.3.[17]

Extrinsic rewards are tangible and visible to others and are given to employees contingent on the

Extrinsic reward a reward that is tangible, visible to others, and given to employees contingent on the performance of specific tasks or behaviors

Syda Productions/Shutterstock.com

Gym members who have a fun workout experience are more likely to exercise longer and stay on goal.

performance of specific tasks or behaviors.[18] External agents (managers, for example) determine and control the distribution, frequency, and amount of extrinsic rewards, such as pay, company stock, benefits, and promotions. For example, 91 percent of large- and medium-sized US companies surveyed by Hewitt Associates offer incentives or bonuses to reward employees, as do 82 percent of smaller companies.[19]

Lincoln Electric, a manufacturer of arc welding tools and technology, has paid annual profit sharing bonuses to its factory workers for 86 straight years. In 2019, Lincoln paid out 32 percent of its pretax profits, $100.4 million, to employees who received bonuses of $35,850, each, worth approximately 33 percent of total wages. In the 86 years in which Lincoln has paid profit-sharing bonuses, the percentage has never dropped below 25 percent of total wages and has been as high as 120 percent. Over the past decade, bonuses have averaged 40 percent of total salary.[20]

Why do companies need to offer extrinsic rewards? To get people to do things they wouldn't otherwise do. Companies use extrinsic rewards to motivate people to perform four basic behaviors: join the organization, regularly attend their jobs, perform their jobs well, and stay with the organization.[21] Think about it. Would you show up at work every day to do the best possible job that you could just out of the goodness of your heart? Very few people would.

Intrinsic rewards are the natural rewards associated with performing a task or activity for its own sake. For example, aside from the external rewards management offers for doing something well, employees often find the activities or tasks they perform interesting and enjoyable. Examples of intrinsic rewards include a sense of accomplishment or achievement, a feeling of responsibility, the chance to learn something new or interact with others, or simply the fun that comes from performing an interesting, challenging, and engaging task.

Across five studies with 449 people, Professors Kaitlin Woolley and Ayelet Fishbach found that the immediate rewards from performing a task (i.e., intrinsic rewards) predicted long-term task persistence.[22] For example, people who work out do so to get subsequent rewards, such as losing weight, getting fit, or better health. But Woolley and Fishbach found that gym goers kept going to the gym *only* if they enjoyed their workouts. In other words, people only kept working toward their long-term goals when the tasks or steps to accomplish those goals were intrinsically rewarding. They concluded, "Gym-goers who cared more about having a fun workout exercised longer than those who cared less about having fun."[23] The potential downside to intrinsically rewarding tasks, however, is that employees find them so rewarding that they become much less motivated to perform less interesting tasks well.[24]

Which types of rewards are most important to workers in general? A number of surveys suggest that both extrinsic and intrinsic rewards are important and that employee preferences for either intrinsic or extrinsic rewards are relatively stable.[25] A Society for Human Resource Management (SHRM) national survey found that three extrinsic factors—pay, benefits, and job security/organizational financial stability—and four intrinsic factors—respectful treatment of employees, trust in senior management, relationships with immediate supervisors, and the chance to use one's skills and abilities in your work—were among the top factors rated as "very important" by employees.[26]

13-1d Motivating with the Basics

So, given the basic model of work motivation in Exhibit 13.3, what practical steps can managers take to motivate employees to increase their effort?

The first step is to *start by asking people what their needs are.* One way to do that is via *stay interviews.* Unlike exit interviews, which find out why employees are leaving, stay interviews ask current employees what it would take to get them to *stay* in their job or with the company. Questions such as, "What do you look forward to when coming to work?" "What did you love in your last position that you're not doing now?" or "What's bothering you most about your job?" can help managers pinpoint what matters to each employee.[27] For example, one employee

> **Intrinsic reward** a natural reward associated with performing a task or activity for its own sake

MEETING EMPLOYEE NEEDS: TIME OR MONEY?

You have a choice: more money or more free time? Most choose money, even in higher-paying jobs. In doing so, we misunderstand need satisfaction theories, which show that *met needs* no longer motivate. The extra money is rewarding only for a short time. Research clearly shows we would be happier choosing more free time, which is a broadly unmet need, as 80 percent of 2.5 million people surveyed lacked enough time to do the things they needed to do. And, feeling "time-poor" has strongly negative effects on health and productivity, even more so than unemployment. So when trying to meet employee needs, give people more time, such as parental leave, flexible paid time off, or a bonus day off. Your employees will be happier and more satisfied.

Source: A. Whillans, "Time for Happiness," *Harvard Business Review*, January 2019, accessed May 26, 2020, hbr.org/cover-story/2019/01/time-for-happiness.

answered, "If you want to do one thing to keep me, let me come in an hour early and then leave an hour early on days when my boy has his Little League games. Then I'll work as hard as I can and stay here a long time."[28] So, if you want to meet employees' needs, just ask.

Next, *satisfy lower-order needs first*. Because higher-order needs will not motivate people as long as lower-order needs remain unsatisfied, companies should satisfy lower-order needs first. In practice, this means providing the equipment, training, and knowledge to create a safe workplace free of physical risks; paying employees well enough to provide financial security; and offering a benefits package that will protect employees and their families through good medical coverage and health and disability insurance. Indeed, the SHRM study mentioned previously found that three of the most important factors in – compensation/pay (63 percent), job security (58 percent), and benefits (60 percent) – were all lower-order needs.[29] During the coronavirus lockdown, trash and recycling collector Waste Management CEO Jim Fish told employees that the company would pay them for 40 hours a week, even if their hours were reduced. Said Fish, "What I did not want is to have any of our 45,000 teammates worry about, how am I going to pay my rent or feed my family? We know it will be costly for the company, but that doesn't matter."[30] Consistent with the idea of satisfying lower-order needs first, a survey of 12,000 employees found that inadequate compensation is the number-one reason employees leave organizations.

Third, managers should *expect people's needs to change*. As needs are satisfied or situations change, what motivated people before may not motivate them now. Likewise, what motivates people to accept a job may not necessarily motivate

them after they have the job. For instance, David Stum, president of the Loyalty Institute, says, "The (attractive) power of pay and benefits is only (strong) during the recruitment stage. After employees take the job, pay and benefits become entitlements to them. They think: 'Now that I work here, you owe me that.'"[31] Managers should also expect needs to change as people mature. For older employees, benefits are as important as pay, which is always ranked as more important by younger employees. Older employees also rank job security as more important than personal and family time, which is more important to younger employees.[32]

Finally, *as needs change and lower-order needs are satisfied, create opportunities for employees to satisfy higher-order needs*. Recall that intrinsic rewards such as accomplishment, achievement, learning something new, and interacting with others are the natural rewards associated with performing a task or activity for its own sake. And, with the exception of influence (power), intrinsic rewards correspond very closely to higher-order needs that are concerned with relationships (belongingness, relatedness, and affiliation) and challenges and accomplishments (esteem, self-actualization, growth, and achievement). Therefore, one way for managers to meet employees' higher-order needs is to create opportunities for employees to experience intrinsic rewards by providing challenging work, encouraging employees to take greater responsibility for their work, and giving employees the freedom to pursue tasks and projects they find naturally interesting.

13-2 EQUITY THEORY

We've seen that people are motivated to achieve intrinsic and extrinsic rewards. However, if employees don't believe that rewards are awarded fairly or don't believe that they can achieve the performance goals the company has set for them, they won't be very motivated.

Fairness, or what people perceive to be fair, is also a critical issue in organizations. **Equity theory** says that people will be motivated at work when they *perceive* that they are being treated fairly. In particular, equity theory stresses the importance of perceptions. So, regardless of the actual level of rewards people receive, they must also perceive that, relative to others, they are being treated fairly. For example, you learned in Chapter 11 that the CEOs of the largest US firms now make $17.2 million per year, which is 278 times their average employee salary.[33] The 10 highest-paid CEOs averaged earnings of $48.09 million per year, led by the late Mark Hurd, the former co-CEO of Oracle, and Safra Catz, Oracle's other co-CEO, both of whom made $108 million.[34] By contrast, in 2019, CEOs of companies with less than $1 billion a year in revenues averaged $234,690 in earnings, or 3.79 times what the average worker makes.[35]

Many people believe that CEO pay is obscenely high and unfair. Others believe that CEO pay is fair because the supply and demand for executive talent largely determine what CEOs are paid. They argue that if it were easier to find good CEOs, then CEOs would be paid much less. Equity theory doesn't focus on objective equity (that is, that CEOs make 278 times or 3.79 times more than average workers). Instead, equity theory says that equity, like beauty, is in the eye of the beholder.

*Let's learn more about equity theory by examining **13-2a the components of equity theory, 13-2b how people react to perceived inequity, and 13-2c how to motivate people using equity theory.***

13-2a Components of Equity Theory

The basic components of equity theory are inputs, outcomes, and referents. **Inputs** are the contributions employees make to the organization. They include education and training, intelligence, experience, effort, number of hours worked, and ability. **Outcomes** are what employees receive in exchange for their contributions to the organization. They include pay, fringe benefits, status symbols, and job titles and assignments. And, because perceptions of equity depend on comparisons, **referents** are other people with whom people compare themselves to determine if they have been treated fairly. The referent can be a single person (comparing yourself with a coworker), a generalized other (comparing yourself with "accountants in general," for example), or even yourself over time ("I was better off last year than I am this year"). Usually, people choose to compare themselves with referents who hold the same or similar jobs or who are otherwise similar in gender, race, age, tenure, or other characteristics.[36]

Copywriter Lucy Bayly says, "You think you're satisfied (with your pay) and then all of a sudden, you find out someone is paid a little more, and it ruins your day."[37] That's what happened to Olivia Wainhouse, an account executive at New York social media analytics firm SumAll. When Wainhouse learned that a new hire was earning $10,000 more than she was, she felt betrayed: "My competitive drive kicked in. I thought, 'What's going on here?'"[38]

According to equity theory, employees compare their outcomes (the rewards they receive from the organization) with their inputs (their contributions to the organization). This comparison of outcomes with inputs is called the **outcome/input (O/I) ratio**. After an internal comparison in which they compare their outcomes with their inputs, employees then make an external comparison in which they compare their O/I ratio with the O/I ratio of a referent.[39] With "pay secrecy" a standard organizational policy, how are employees finding the information they need to make these comparisons? Kevin Hallock, dean of Cornell University's College of Business, says, "People are much more willing to talk about pay than they were even 10 years ago."[40] A survey by Robert Half global staffing agency found that 54 percent of workers exchange salary information with coworkers and that 73 percent have used online websites, like Glassdoor.com, a recruiting website, to see how their salaries compare. Paul McDonald, senior executive director for Robert Half, said, "Workers have more access to information about their

Equity theory a theory that states that people will be motivated when they perceive that they are being treated fairly

Inputs in equity theory, the contributions employees make to the organization

Outcomes in equity theory, the rewards employees receive for their contributions to the organization

Referents in equity theory, others with whom people compare themselves to determine if they have been treated fairly

Outcome/input (O/I) ratio in equity theory, an employee's perception of how the rewards received from an organization compare with the employee's contributions to that organization

salaries, roles, and career options than ever before, arming them for conversations with current and potential employers."[41]

When people perceive that their O/I ratio is equal to the referent's O/I ratio, they conclude that they are being treated fairly. But when people perceive that their O/I ratio is different from their referent's O/I ratio, they conclude that they have been treated inequitably or unfairly.

Inequity can take two forms, underreward and overreward. **Underreward** occurs when a referent's O/I ratio is better than your O/I ratio. In other words, you are getting fewer outcomes relative to your inputs than the referent you compare yourself with is getting. Many people believe they are underpaid, even when they're not. A PayScale survey of 71,000 employees found that among people who actually had *average salaries* (at market), 64 percent thought they were underpaid, 30 percent thought they were paid fairly, and just 6 percent thought they were overpaid. Among people who actually had *higher than average* salaries (above market), 35 percent thought they were underpaid, 45 percent thought they were paid fairly, and 21 percent thought they were overpaid.[42] People who perceive that they have been underrewarded tend to experience anger or frustration. When University of California employees were made aware of a public website containing every employee's salary, the pay satisfaction and job satisfaction of those with salaries *below* their department's median salary dropped after learning their coworker's salaries.[43]

By contrast, **overreward** occurs when a referent's O/I ratio is worse than your O/I ratio. In this case, you are getting more outcomes relative to your inputs than your referent is. In theory, when people perceive that they have been overrewarded, they experience guilt. But, not surprisingly, people have a very high tolerance for overreward. It takes a tremendous amount of overpayment before people decide that their pay or benefits are more than they deserve. When University of California employees with salaries *above* their department's

pathdoc/Shutterstock.com

median salary checked their coworker's salaries (on the public website), their pay satisfaction and job satisfaction were unaffected.[44]

13-2b How People React to Perceived Inequity

So what happens when people perceive that they have been treated inequitably at work? Exhibit 13.4 shows that perceived inequity affects satisfaction. In the case of underreward, this usually translates into frustration or anger; with overreward, the reaction is guilt. These reactions lead to tension and a strong need to take action to restore equity in some way. At first, a slight inequity may not be strong enough to motivate an employee to take immediate action. If the inequity continues, or there are multiple inequities, however, tension may build over time until a point of intolerance is reached and the person is energized to take action to restore equity by reducing inputs, increasing outcomes, rationalizing inputs or outcomes, changing the referent, or simply leaving. We will discuss these possible responses in terms of the inequity associated with underreward, which is much more common than the inequity associated with overreward.

People who perceive that they have been underrewarded may try to restore equity by *decreasing or withholding their inputs (that is, effort)*. **American Airlines** mechanics, represented by the Transport Workers and the International Association of Machinists and Aerospace Workers unions, were frustrated with the company after four years of unsuccessful contract negotiations in which they sought significant pay increases. Those frustrations resulted in a "sickout" in the summer of 2019

Underreward a form of inequity in which you are getting fewer outcomes relative to inputs than your referent is getting

Overreward a form of inequity in which you are getting more outcomes relative to inputs than your referent

Exhibit 13.4
Adding Equity Theory to the Model

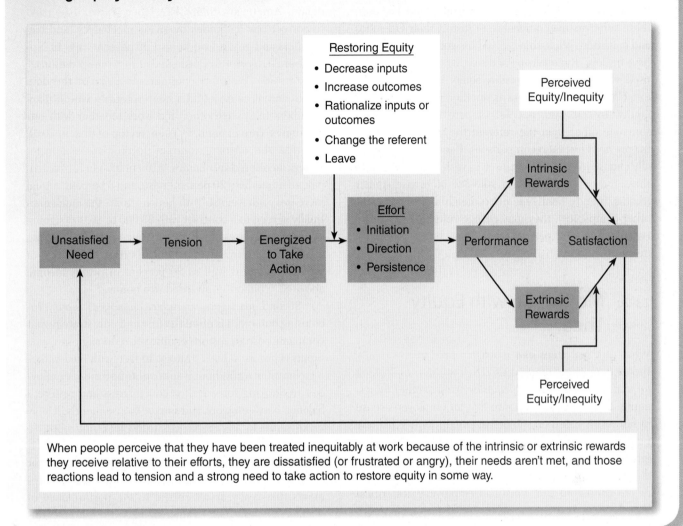

Restoring Equity
- Decrease inputs
- Increase outcomes
- Rationalize inputs or outcomes
- Change the referent
- Leave

Perceived Equity/Inequity

Unsatisfied Need → Tension → Energized to Take Action → **Effort** • Initiation • Direction • Persistence → Performance → Intrinsic Rewards → Satisfaction

Extrinsic Rewards

Perceived Equity/Inequity

When people perceive that they have been treated inequitably at work because of the intrinsic or extrinsic rewards they receive relative to their efforts, they are dissatisfied (or frustrated or angry), their needs aren't met, and those reactions lead to tension and a strong need to take action to restore equity in some way.

in which just enough mechanics would call in "sick" to significantly slow down the company's operations. At its peak, the sickout forced American to cancel 80 flights, delaying 11,000 passengers, each day. Attorney Mike Green said, "I was on a flight recently that was delayed two hours because of mechanical issues. It was clear that the pilot was frustrated, too."[45]

Increasing outcomes is another way people try to restore equity. This might include asking for a raise or pointing out the inequity to the boss and hoping that he or she takes care of it. Sometimes, however, employees may go to external organizations such as labor unions, federal agencies, or the courts for help in increasing outcomes to restore equity. For instance, the US Department of Labor estimates that 10 percent of

workers are not getting the extra overtime pay they deserve when they work more than 40 hours a week. These are known as Fair Labor Standards Act (FLSA) violations.[46] After a US Department of Labor ruling, Halliburton, a global oil field services company, agreed to pay $18.2 million in back wages to 1,106 oil and gas employees who were at first denied overtime pay after incorrectly being classified as exempt employees (who are ineligible for overtime).[47] In 2019, 11,018 FLSA cases resulted in companies paying $186 million in back wages to 215,000 employees.[48]

Another method of restoring equity is to *rationalize or distort inputs or outcomes*. Instead of decreasing inputs or increasing outcomes, employees restore equity by making mental or emotional adjustments in their O/I ratios or the O/I ratios of their referents. For example, suppose that a company downsizes 10 percent of its workforce. It's likely that the people who still have jobs will be angry or frustrated with company management because of the layoffs. If alternative jobs are difficult to find, however, these survivors may rationalize or distort their O/I ratios and conclude, "Well, things could be worse. At least I still have my job." Rationalizing or distorting outcomes may be used when other ways to restore equity aren't available.

Changing the referent is another way of restoring equity. In this case, people compare themselves with someone other than the referent they had been using for previous O/I ratio comparisons. Because people usually choose to compare themselves with others who hold the same or similar jobs or who are otherwise similar (that is, friends, family members, neighbors who work at other companies), they may change referents to restore equity when their personal situations change, such as a decrease in job status or pay.[49]

13-2c Motivating with Equity Theory

What practical steps can managers take to use equity theory to motivate employees? They can *start by looking for and correcting major inequities*. Among other things, equity theory makes us aware that an employee's sense of fairness is based on subjective perceptions. What one employee considers grossly unfair may not affect another employee's perceptions of equity at all. Although these different perceptions make it difficult for managers to create conditions that satisfy all employees, it's critical that they do their best to take care of major inequities that can energize employees to take disruptive, costly, or harmful actions such as decreasing inputs or leaving. So,

People who perceive that they have been underrewarded at the office may withhold their efforts until they feel they are fairly compensated.

whenever possible, managers should look for and correct major inequities.

Ironically, prior to that summer 2019 American Airlines mechanics' sickout causing flight cancellations and delays, American's then-CEO Doug Parker had tried to correct pay inequities by giving mechanics (and bag handlers and ground workers) a 22 percent raise in November 2016 *prior* to finishing contract renegotiations.[50] Parker said, "We must continue moving past the days of discontent as we build a new American where team members trust each other and work together with our customers' care in mind."[51] Then, on top of that, in 2019, to break the ongoing contract negotiations stalemate, American offered mechanics "$160 million in retroactive pay, an immediate 20 percent raise, and 3 percent annual increases each August."[52] In January 2020, the mechanics finally agreed to a contract with $3,000 to $6,000 signing bonuses, pay raises of 4 to 18 percent, and profit-sharing in which "10 percent of American's first $2.5 billion of pretax income as well as 20 percent of pretax income above $2.5 billion" is awarded as a bonus.[53]

Second, managers can *reduce employees' inputs*. Increasing outcomes is often the first and only strategy that companies use to restore equity, yet reducing employee inputs is just as viable a strategy. In fact, with dual-career couples working 50-hour weeks, more and more employees are looking for ways to reduce stress and restore a balance between work and family. Consequently, it may make sense to ask employees to do less, not more; to have them identify and eliminate the 20 percent of their jobs that doesn't increase productivity or add value for customers; and to eliminate company-imposed requirements that really aren't critical to the performance of managers, employees, or the company (for example, unnecessary meetings and reports).

Another way to reduce employee inputs is by committing to 40-hour workweeks. Mortgage lender United Shore Financial Services calls this the "firm 40." The deal, says chief people officer Laura Lawson, is that "You give us 40. Everything else is yours."[54] That means no online shopping at work, and no checking Facebook or Twitter. CEO Mat Isbia tells employees that they need to work as hard at 5:55 p.m. on Friday as they do on Tuesday at 10:55 a.m. But then, at 6 p.m. sharp, the office empties. Ahmed Haider, who works in client relations at USFS, says that "the parking lot is pretty much empty" by 6:05 p.m.[55] At first, Haider doubted whether the commitment to "firm 40" was real. But now, he always leaves at 6 p.m. and rarely sends emails or phones colleagues after work hours. "There's nobody to call. Everyone's at home," he says.[56] CEO Mat Ishbia says, "Our people work to live, they don't live to work."[57]

Rommel Canlas/Shutterstock.com

Finally, managers should *make sure decision-making processes are fair*. Equity theory focuses on **distributive justice**, the perceived degree to which outcomes and rewards are fairly distributed or allocated. However, **procedural justice**, the perceived fairness of the procedures used to make reward allocation decisions, is just as important.[58]

Procedural justice matters because even when employees are unhappy with their outcomes (i.e., low pay), they're much less likely to be unhappy with company management if they believe that the procedures used to allocate outcomes were fair. For example, employees who are laid off tend to be hostile toward their employer when they perceive that the procedures leading to the layoffs were unfair. When Air France announced a plan to reduce costs by $2 billion over two years – partly by cutting 2,900 jobs – angry employees interrupted a work council meeting attended by key members of management and leaders representing the workers. Five irate employees stormed into the meeting, knocking a security guard unconscious as they attempted to assault two top managers by ripping the shirts and jackets off their backs. Ultimately, the executives were forced to climb a fence to avoid further harm.[59]

By contrast, employees who perceive layoff procedures to be fair tend to continue to support and trust their employers.[60] Also, if employees perceive that their outcomes are unfair (i.e., distributive injustice) but that the decisions and procedures leading to those outcomes were fair (i.e., procedural justice), they are much more likely to seek constructive ways of restoring equity, such as discussing these matters with their manager. If, however, employees perceive both distributive and procedural injustice, they may resort to more destructive tactics, such as withholding effort, absenteeism, tardiness, or even sabotage and theft.[61]

13-3 EXPECTANCY THEORY

One of the hardest things about motivating people is that not everyone is attracted to the same rewards. **Expectancy theory** says that people will be motivated to the extent to which they believe that their efforts will lead to good performance, that good performance will be rewarded, and that they will be offered attractive rewards.[62]

Let's learn more about expectancy theory by examining **13-3a the components of expectancy theory** *and* **13-3b how to use expectancy theory as a motivational tool.**

13-3a Components of Expectancy Theory

Expectancy theory holds that people make conscious choices about their motivation. The three factors that affect those choices are valence, expectancy, and instrumentality.

Valence is simply the attractiveness or desirability of various rewards or outcomes. Expectancy theory recognizes that the same reward or outcome – say, a promotion – will be highly attractive to some people, will be highly disliked by others, and will not make much difference one way or the other to still others. Accordingly, when people are deciding how much effort to put forth, expectancy theory says that they will consider the valence of all possible rewards and outcomes that they can receive from their jobs. The greater the sum of those valences, each of which can be positive, negative, or neutral, the more effort people will choose to put forth on the job.

Each year, companies review benefits packages, weighing costs against attractiveness. Health/dental/disability insurance and 401(k) retirement packages typically top the lists of employers and employees. But according to insurer MetLife's 2019 Employee Benefits Trend Study, the most popular "emerging" benefit is unlimited paid time off (PTO), which only 4 percent of workers currently have.[63] One-third of workers can use PTO for anything, sickness, funerals, vacation, but have a limited number of PTO days, while 33 million workers have no PTO at all.[64]

Unlimited PTO frees employees from having to decide whether to come into work sick in order to "save" PTO for taking a child to the doctor at a later date. And, unlimited PTO sends a powerful message that the firm values and trusts employees. Still, some employees prefer having a limited or fixed number of PTO days because in many firms unused PTO can be banked and paid as a cash benefit when employees leave the firm. In other words, despite its growing popularity, unlimited PTO isn't an attractive award for all employees, which is why companies review benefits packages each year.

Distributive justice the perceived degree to which outcomes and rewards are fairly distributed or allocated

Procedural justice the perceived fairness of the process used to make reward allocation decisions

Expectancy theory the theory that people will be motivated to the extent to which they believe that their efforts will lead to good performance, that good performance will be rewarded, and that they will be offered attractive rewards

Valence the attractiveness or desirability of a reward or outcome

Cut CEO Pay to Raise Worker Pay: Results Five Years Later and Coronavirus Update

In 2015, CEO Dan Price of Gravity Payments, a credit-card processing company, cut his salary from $1 million to $70,000 to raise minimum employee salaries from $48,000 to $70,000. Although viewed positively by labor activists, others were skeptical. So, what's happened?

» Early on, two of his best employees quit, believing that paying everyone the same was unfair.

» But after 15 months, surveys indicated employees were happier, turnover was at a six-year low, profits doubled, client retention was up, and new accounts increased 60 percent. Thirty thousand people applied for jobs and 50 new employees were hired.

» After five years, Gravity has twice as many employees. Credit card payments, from which it earns its fees, have grown from $3.8 billion a year to $10.2 billion. Employees bought Price a new Tesla as a show of their appreciation.

» March 2020, the coronavirus hit and Gravity's revenue drops 55 percent. Ten of 200 employees volunteered to work for free, while 186 volunteered to take a 50 percent pay cut. That slashed Gravity's monthly losses from $1.5 to $0.5 million per month. With unemployment at near record levels, Gravity did not lay off any employees.

» Price's pay cut was supposed to be temporary. "When I made the announcement, I said I would just put my salary back where it was once the company's profits had gone back to where they were." But, five years later, despite the company's growth, he has yet to increase his salary. If he ever does, how will his business and employees be affected?

Source: Gravity Payments

Sources: P. Cohen, "A Company Copes With Backlash Against the Raise That Roared - The New York," *New York Times*, July 31, 2015, accessed April 28, 2017, www.nytimes.com/2015/08/02/business/a-company-copes-with-backlash-against-the-raise-that-roared.html; S. Hegarty, "The Boss Who Put Everyone on 70K, *BBC News*, February 28, 2020, accessed May 26, 2020, www.bbc.com/news/stories-51332811; C. Lin, "Stories from Seattle: Surviving the COVID-19 Crisis Without Layoffs Is No Easy Feat," *Seattle Magazine*, April 27, 2020, accessed May 26, 2020, www.seattlemag.com/city-life/stories-seattle-surviving-covid-19-crisis-without-layoffs-no-easy-feat; R. Murray, "Gravity Payments' $70K Minimum Salary: CEO Dan Price Shares Result Over a Year Later," Today, August 11, 2016, accessed April 28, 2017, www.today.com/money/gravity-payments-70k-minimum-salary-ceo-dan-price-shares-results-t101678; "The Gravity of 70k," *Gravity Payments*, accessed April 28, 2017, gravitypayments.com/thegravityof70k/.

Expectancy is the perceived relationship between effort and performance. When expectancies are strong, employees believe that their hard work and efforts will result in good performance, so they work harder. By contrast, when expectancies are weak, employees figure that no matter what they do or how hard they work, they won't be able to perform their jobs successfully, so they don't work as hard.

Instrumentality is the perceived relationship between performance and rewards.

When instrumentality is strong, employees believe that improved performance will lead to better and more rewards, so they choose to work harder. When instrumentality is weak, employees don't believe that better performance will result in more or better rewards, so they choose not to work as hard.

Expectancy theory holds that for people to be highly motivated, all three variables—valence, expectancy, and instrumentality—must be high. Thus, expectancy theory can be represented by the following simple equation:

$$\text{Motivation} = \text{Valence} \times \text{Expectancy} \times \text{Instrumentality}$$

Expectancy the perceived relationship between effort and performance

Instrumentality the perceived relationship between performance and rewards

Exhibit 13.5
Adding Expectancy Theory to the Model

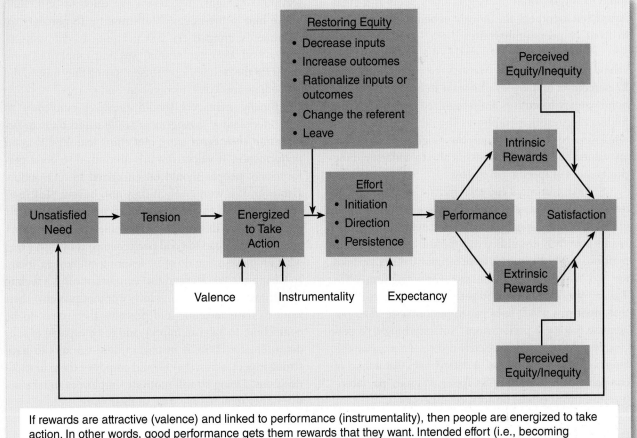

Restoring Equity
- Decrease inputs
- Increase outcomes
- Rationalize inputs or outcomes
- Change the referent
- Leave

Effort
- Initiation
- Direction
- Persistence

Unsatisfied Need → Tension → Energized to Take Action → Effort → Performance

Valence — Instrumentality — Expectancy

Perceived Equity/Inequity → Intrinsic Rewards → Satisfaction

Performance → Extrinsic Rewards → Satisfaction

Perceived Equity/Inequity

If rewards are attractive (valence) and linked to performance (instrumentality), then people are energized to take action. In other words, good performance gets them rewards that they want. Intended effort (i.e., becoming energized to take action) turns into actual effort when people expect that their hard work and efforts will result in good performance. After all, why work hard if that hard work is wasted?

If any one of these variables (valence, expectancy, or instrumentality) declines, overall motivation will decline, too.

Exhibit 13.5 incorporates the expectancy theory variables into our motivation model. Valence and instrumentality combine to affect employees' willingness to put forth effort (that is, the degree to which they are energized to take action), while expectancy transforms intended effort ("I'm really going to work hard in this job") into actual effort. If you're offered rewards that you desire and you believe that you will in fact receive these rewards for good performance, you're highly likely to be energized to take action. However, you're not likely to actually exert effort unless you also believe that you can do the job (that is, that your efforts will lead to successful performance).

13-3b Motivating with Expectancy Theory

What practical steps can managers take to use expectancy theory to motivate employees? First, they can *systematically gather information to find out what employees want from their jobs*. In addition to individual managers directly asking employees what they want from their jobs (see Subsection 13-1d, "Motivating with the Basics"), companies need to survey their employees regularly to determine their wants, needs, and dissatisfactions. Because people consider the valence of all the possible rewards and outcomes that they can receive from their jobs, regular identification of wants, needs, and dissatisfactions gives companies the chance to turn negatively valent rewards and outcomes into positively valent rewards and outcomes, thus raising overall motivation and effort. Mark Peterman, vice president of client solutions at **Maritz Incentives**, says that individual employees are motivated in vastly different ways: "For some, being honored in front of one's peers is a great award, but for others, the thought of being put on display in front of peers embarrasses them." And companies have a long way to go to ensure that their employees feel valued, Peterman says. A Maritz survey found that only 27 percent of employees who want to be recognized by nonmonetary incentives are recognized that way.[65] Such findings suggest that employers should routinely survey employees to identify not only the range of rewards that are valued by most employees but also to understand the preferences of specific employees.

Second, managers can *take specific steps to link rewards to individual performance in a way that is clear and understandable to employees*. Unfortunately, most employees are extremely dissatisfied with the link between pay and performance in their organizations, and their companies are, too. A survey by compensation consulting firm Willis Towers Watson found that 80 percent of companies report that merit pay, which links pay to performance, does not increase employee performance. Not surprisingly, 68 percent report that pay is not clearly tied to performance differences, either.[66] Of course, it doesn't help that a third of companies, according to Willis Towers Watson, "pay incentives to employees who do *not* meet expectations."[67]

One way to establish a clear connection between pay and performance (see Chapter 11 for a discussion of compensation strategies) is for managers to publicize the way in which pay decisions are made.[68] This is especially important given that only 52 percent of employees know how their pay increases are determined.[69] Inspired by fantasy sports leagues, **Clayton Homes** director of inside sales, David Schwall, had his sales managers become team "owners" who drafted sales representatives onto their sales teams, which competed against each other in a rotating schedule, with the best four teams moving on to the "championships." Sales reps (players) scored points by making more calls to sales leads, by increasing the percentage of leads who made appointments at Clayton Homes retail stores, and upping the percentage of leads whose phone calls were successfully transferred to a local store. Scores were tallied in real time, and the best scores were posted on TVs for everyone to see (poor scores were only visible within teams). Each sales rep's theme music played when they reached sales milestones. The connection between efforts and results was clear, prompting one sales rep to say, "When I saw one of my colleagues leaving, I thought, 'Yes, now I can catch up and climb above him in the ranks.'" Calls rose by 18 percent, appointments jumped by 200 percent, as did visits to stores. And, after the "season" was over, employees were eager for the next season to begin, saying they missed the immediate feedback, recognition, and energy.[70]

Finally, managers should *empower employees to make decisions if management really wants them to believe that their hard work and effort will lead to good performance*. If valent rewards are linked to good performance, people should be energized to take action. However, this works only if they also believe that their efforts will lead to good performance. One of the ways that managers destroy the expectancy that hard work and effort will lead to good performance is by restricting what employees can do or by ignoring employees' ideas. In Chapter 9, you learned that *empowerment* is a feeling of intrinsic motivation in which workers perceive their work to have meaning and perceive themselves to be competent, to have an impact, and to be capable of self-determination.[71] So, if managers want workers to have strong expectancies, they should empower them to make decisions. Doing so will motivate employees to take active rather than passive roles in their work.

13-4 REINFORCEMENT THEORY

Reinforcement theory says that behavior is a function of its consequences, that behaviors followed by positive consequences (that is, reinforced) will occur more frequently, and that behaviors either followed by negative consequences or not followed by positive consequences will occur less frequently.[72] Two interesting examples show how this works.

When **Domino's Pizza** announced its "Domino's Forever" promotion, offering 100 free pizzas per year for 100 years to any Russian who got tattooed with the Domino's logo, it had to stop the two-month promotion after only half a day because 381 people had already tatted up for free pizza. Russian Natalia Koshkina, whose Domino's tattoo is just above her left knee, said, "More than a million people would have come to demand pizzas. After all, this is Russia."[73] Turning from positive to

Reinforcement theory the theory that behavior is a function of its consequences, that behaviors followed by positive consequences will occur more frequently, and that behaviors followed by negative consequences, or not followed by positive consequences, will occur less frequently

negative consequences, every holiday season, thousands of Christmas trees are cut down and stolen from private and public property. The city of Lincoln, Nebraska, is fighting back by spraying evergreen trees with fox urine. This urine produces no smell in cold weather, but emits a strong, skunklike smell once the tree is brought into a warm home. Thanks to the noxious smell, along with prominently posted signs warning that the trees have been sprayed, thieves are no long cutting down Lincoln's evergreen trees.[74] As these examples show, **reinforcement** is the process of changing behavior by changing the consequences that follow behavior.[75]

Reinforcement has two parts: reinforcement contingencies and schedules of reinforcement. **Reinforcement contingencies** are the cause-and-effect relationships between the performance of specific behaviors and specific consequences. For example, if you get docked an hour's pay for being late to work, then a reinforcement contingency exists between a behavior (being late to work) and a consequence (losing an hour's pay). A **schedule of reinforcement** is the set of rules regarding reinforcement contingencies such as which behaviors will be reinforced, which consequences will follow those behaviors, and the schedule by which those consequences will be delivered.[76]

Exhibit 13.6 incorporates reinforcement contingencies and reinforcement schedules into our motivation model. First, notice that extrinsic rewards and the schedules of reinforcement used to deliver them are the primary methods for creating reinforcement contingencies in organizations. In turn, those reinforcement contingencies directly affect valences (the attractiveness of rewards), instrumentality (the perceived link between rewards and performance), and effort (how hard employees will work).

Let's learn more about reinforcement theory by examining **13-4a the components of reinforcement theory, 13-4b the different schedules for delivering reinforcement, and 13-4c how to motivate with reinforcement theory.**

13-4a Components of Reinforcement Theory

As just described, *reinforcement contingencies* are the cause-and-effect relationships between the performance of specific behaviors and specific consequences. There are four kinds of reinforcement contingencies: positive reinforcement, negative reinforcement, punishment, and extinction.

Positive reinforcement strengthens behavior (i.e., increases its frequency) by following behaviors with desirable consequences. **Walmart** now reinforces employee attendance with a 25 percent larger quarterly store bonus for employees with perfect attendance. Drew Holler, Vice President of Associate Experience for Walmart US, said, "Our associates told us they wanted to be rewarded for their dedication, and we couldn't agree more."[77] Walmart made the attendance bonus even more rewarding (and achievable) by simultaneously introducing a new "protected" paid time off (PTO) program, up to 48 hours for part-time workers and 80 hours for full time employees. "Protected" PTO does *not* count as an absence and does *not* affect quarterly bonuses.[78]

Negative reinforcement strengthens behavior by withholding an unpleasant consequence when employees perform a specific behavior. Negative reinforcement is also called *avoidance learning* because workers perform a behavior to *avoid* a negative consequence. A study at the University of Pennsylvania shows how well negative reinforcement works. Over three months, 281 employees were given a daily walking goal of 7,000 steps. Thirty percent of those who were not rewarded for walking (the control group) met the daily goal. Thirty-five percent of those who were positively reinforced with a $1.40 per day for walking 7,000 steps met the goal. Finally, the negative reinforcement group was given $42 at the start of the study and was told they'd lose $1.40 each day they didn't walk 7,000 steps. Achieving the goal avoided the unpleasant consequence of losing money. Fifty-five percent who were negatively reinforced met the daily goal. Professor Mitesh Patel said, "It was surprising how

Reinforcement the process of changing behavior by changing the consequences that follow behavior

Reinforcement contingencies cause-and-effect relationships between the performance of specific behaviors and specific consequences

Schedule of reinforcement rules that specify which behaviors will be reinforced, which consequences will follow those behaviors, and the schedule by which those consequences will be delivered

Positive reinforcement that strengthens behavior by following behaviors with desirable consequences

Negative reinforcement that strengthens behavior by withholding an unpleasant consequence when employees perform a specific behavior

Exhibit 13.6
Adding Reinforcement Theory to the Model

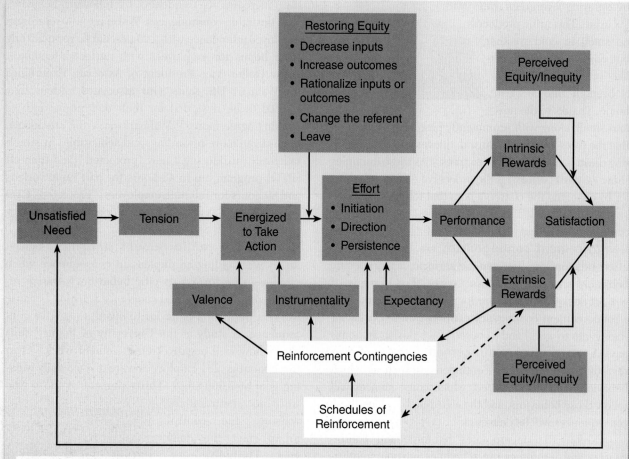

Extrinsic rewards and the schedules of reinforcement used to deliver them are the primary methods for creating reinforcement contingencies in organizations. In turn, those reinforcement contingencies directly affect valence (the attractiveness of rewards), instrumentality (the perceived link between rewards and performance), and effort (how hard employees will work).

dramatically effective loss aversion [negative reinforcement] was."[79]

By contrast, punishment weakens behavior (that is, decreases its frequency) by following behaviors with undesirable consequences. For example, the standard disciplinary or punishment process in most companies is an oral warning ("Don't ever do that again"), followed by a written warning ("This letter is to discuss the serious problem you're having with . . ."), followed by three days off without pay ("While you're at home not being paid, we want you to think hard about . . ."), followed by

being fired ("That was your last chance"). **Citigroup**'s London bond trading office suspended a senior trader earning $1.32 million a year for allegedly stealing food from the cafeteria.[80] You might be thinking that the punishment is disproportionate, But it seems more reasonable if we assume that the suspension occurred after repeated warnings and in consideration of the UK's Financial Conduct Authority, under which financial firms must comply with strict guidelines regarding their employees' honesty and competence. For example, a London fund manager for BlackRock, the world's

Bloomberg/Getty Images

David Joyce, head of GE's aviation business, was the only top executive to receive a bonus for 2017.

largest investment firm, was banned for life by the UK's Financial Conduct Authority after repeatedly failing to pay $60,000 in rail fares from his suburban home into central London over five years. "The FCA does not consider that this is fit and proper behavior for an approved person."[81] Though punishment can weaken behavior, managers must be careful to avoid the backlash that sometimes occurs when employees are punished at work.

Extinction is a reinforcement strategy in which a positive consequence is no longer allowed to follow a previously reinforced behavior. By removing the positive consequence, extinction weakens the behavior, making it less likely to occur. Based on the idea of positive reinforcement, most companies give company leaders and managers substantial financial rewards when the company performs well. Based on the idea of extinction, you would then expect that leaders and managers would not be rewarded (i.e., the positive consequence would be removed) when companies perform poorly. That's what happened at **General Electric**, the US-based conglomerate, when GE's board of directors decided to not pay top executives a cash bonus for the first time in 125 years. After the company's poor financial performance resulted in thousands of layoffs and a cut in its stock dividend, GE's board withheld cash bonuses and canceled stock awards.[82] If companies really want pay to reinforce the right kinds of behaviors, rewards have to be removed, like at GE, when company management doesn't produce successful performance.

13-4b Schedules for Delivering Reinforcement

As mentioned earlier, a *schedule of reinforcement* is the set of rules regarding reinforcement contingencies, such as which behaviors will be reinforced, which consequences will follow those behaviors, and the schedule by which those consequences will be delivered. There are two categories of reinforcement schedules: continuous and intermittent.

With **continuous reinforcement schedules**, a consequence follows every instance of a behavior. For example, employees working on a piece-rate pay system earn money (consequence) for every part they manufacture (behavior). The more they produce, the more they earn. By contrast, with **intermittent reinforcement schedules**, consequences are delivered after a specified or average time has elapsed or after a specified or average number of behaviors has occurred. As Exhibit 13.7 shows, there are four types of intermittent reinforcement schedules. Two of these are based on time and are called *interval reinforcement schedules*; the other two, known as *ratio schedules*, are based on behaviors.

With **fixed interval reinforcement schedules**, consequences follow a behavior only after a fixed time has elapsed. For example, most people receive their paychecks on a fixed interval schedule (e.g., once or twice per month). As long as they work (behavior) during a specified pay period (interval), they get a paycheck (consequence). With **variable interval reinforcement schedules**, consequences follow a behavior after different times, some shorter and some longer, that vary around a specified average time. On a 90-day variable interval reinforcement schedule, you might receive a bonus after 80 days or perhaps after 100 days, but the average interval between performing your job well (behavior) and receiving your bonus (consequence) would be 90 days.

Extinction reinforcement in which a positive consequence is no longer allowed to follow a previously reinforced behavior, thus weakening the behavior

Continuous reinforcement schedule a schedule that requires a consequence to be administered following every instance of a behavior

Intermittent reinforcement schedule a schedule in which consequences are delivered after a specified or average time has elapsed or after a specified or average number of behaviors has occurred

Fixed interval reinforcement schedule an intermittent schedule in which consequences follow a behavior only after a fixed time has elapsed

Variable interval reinforcement schedule an intermittent schedule in which the time between a behavior and the following consequences varies around a specified average

Exhibit 13.7
Intermittent Reinforcement Schedules

	Fixed	**Variable**
INTERVAL (TIME)	Consequences follow behavior after a fixed time has elapsed.	Consequences follow behavior after different times, some shorter and some longer, that vary around a specific average time.
RATIO (BEHAVIOR)	Consequences follow a specific number of behaviors.	Consequences follow a different number of behaviors, sometimes more and sometimes less, that vary around a specified average number of behaviors.

With **fixed ratio reinforcement schedules**, consequences are delivered following a specific number of behaviors. For example, a car salesperson might receive a $1,000 bonus after every 10 sales. Therefore, a salesperson with only nine sales would not receive the bonus until finally selling that tenth car.

With **variable ratio reinforcement schedules**, consequences are delivered following a different number of behaviors, sometimes more and sometimes less, that vary around a specified average number of behaviors. With a 10-car variable ratio reinforcement schedule, a salesperson might receive the bonus after 7 car sales, or after 12, 11, or 9 sales, but the average number of cars sold before receiving the bonus would be 10 cars.

Which reinforcement schedules work best? In the past, the standard advice was to use continuous reinforcement when employees were learning new behaviors because reinforcement after each success leads to faster learning. Likewise, the standard advice was to use intermittent reinforcement schedules to maintain behavior after it is learned because intermittent rewards are supposed to make behavior much less subject to extinction.[83] Research shows, however, that except for interval-based systems, which usually produce weak results, the effectiveness of continuous reinforcement, fixed ratio, and variable ratio schedules differs very little.[84] In organizational settings, all three consistently produce large increases over noncontingent reward schedules. So managers should choose whichever of these three is easiest to use in their companies.

Fixed ratio reinforcement schedule an intermittent schedule in which consequences are delivered following a specific number of behaviors

Variable ratio reinforcement schedule an intermittent schedule in which consequences are delivered following a different number of behaviors, sometimes more and sometimes less, that vary around a specified average number of behaviors

13-4c Motivating with Reinforcement Theory

What practical steps can managers take to use reinforcement theory to motivate employees? University of Nebraska business professor Fred Luthans, who has been studying the effects of reinforcement theory in organizations for more than a quarter of a century, says that there are five steps to motivating workers with reinforcement theory: *identify*, *measure*, *analyze*, *intervene*, and *evaluate* critical performance-related behaviors.[85]

Identify means singling out critical, observable, performance-related behaviors. These are the behaviors that are most important to successful job performance. In addition, they must also be easily observed so that they can be accurately measured. *Measure* means determining the baseline frequencies of these behaviors. In other words, find out how often workers perform them. *Analyze* means studying the causes and consequences of these behaviors. Analyzing the causes helps managers create the conditions that produce these critical behaviors, and analyzing the consequences helps them determine if these behaviors produce the results that they want. *Intervene* means changing the organization by using positive and negative reinforcement to increase the frequency of these critical behaviors. *Evaluate* means assessing the extent to which the intervention actually changed workers' behavior. This is done by comparing behavior after the intervention to the original baseline of behavior before the intervention.

In addition to these five steps, managers should remember three other key things when motivating with reinforcement theory. First, *don't reinforce the wrong behaviors*. Although reinforcement theory sounds simple, it's actually very difficult to put into practice. One of the most common mistakes is accidentally reinforcing the wrong behaviors. Sometimes organizations reinforce

FIXED INTERVAL REINFORCEMENT SCHEDULES: SAME DAY PAY?

Most people receive paychecks on a fixed interval reinforcement schedule of once or twice per month. But what if the fixed interval was one day? Some companies are doing that with the DailyPay app. DailyPay is not a loan. Employees pay $2.99 if they want immediate access to earned wages between pay checks, or $1.99 if they want them the next day. Ann Sizemore, vice president of human resources for Captain D's restaurants, says, "We have seen it used for medical expenses, including for their children—that's a big one..." Captain D's uses DailyPay for recruiting and retention. Sizemore says, "Leaving their job means leaving their daily payment option." DailyPay's Jeanniey Mullen says, "Employers may not be able to pay more, but if they want to be competitive, they need to differentiate themselves by offering same-day pay." DailyPay seems to be valuable as Kroger, McDonald's, Arby's, Domino's, and Panera Bread have signed on to make it available to their employees. Fixed interval reinforcement schedules typically have little effect on employee performance. But DailyPay should increase regular attendance because if you don't show up for work today you can't take out any more money via DailyPay tomorrow.

doomu/Shutterstock.com

Sources: K. Mayer, "Why Instant Pay Benefits Are Showing Growth, *"Human Resource Executive*, November 15, 2019, accessed May 26, 2020, hrexecutive.com/why-instant-pay-benefits-are-showing-growth/; C. Morris, "Can Early Pay Help Restaurants Retain Employees?" *QSR Magazine*, August 2019, accessed May 26, 2020, www.qsrmagazine.com/employee-management/can-early-pay-help-restaurants-retain-employees; K. Webster, "Is It Time to Offer All Employees Same-Day Pay?" *Employee Benefit News*, May 13, 2020, accessed May 26, 2020, www.benefitnews.com/news/is-it-time-to-offer-all-employees-same-day-pay.

behaviors that they don't want! To encourage green driving, Norway exempted electric cars from toll road, tunnel, ferry, and parking fees. Arne Nordbo drives an electric car and avoids $6,000 in annual tolls for the undersea tunnel leading in and out of Finnoy, an island-locked town.[86] Finnoy borrowed $70 million to dig the tunnel, expecting drivers like Nordbo to pay off the loan via tunnel fees. But with electric cars having grown from 25 to 50 percent of all tunnel traffic, "We won't be able to pay down the tunnel," says Gro Skartveit, head of the company that operates the tunnel.[87] The Norwegian government loses nearly a billion dollars a year in forgone tax revenue and tunnel/ferry fees. Electric car owner Hans Halvorsen admitted, "The reason for buying this was a little bit about the environment, but mostly the savings," the same reason given by 72 percent of Norwegian electric car owners.[88] The significant loss of revenue led Norway to raise fees for electric car owners from zero to 50 percent of what gas/diesel cars owners are charged.[89] Be careful what you reward!

Managers should also *correctly administer punishment at the appropriate time*. Many managers believe that punishment can change workers' behavior and help them improve their job performance. Furthermore, managers believe that fairly punishing workers also lets other workers know what is or isn't acceptable.[90] A danger of using punishment is that it can produce a backlash against managers and companies. But, if administered properly, punishment can weaken the frequency of undesirable behaviors without creating a backlash.[91] To be effective, the punishment must be strong enough to stop the undesired behavior and must be administered objectively (same rules applied to everyone), impersonally (without emotion or anger), consistently and contingently (each time improper behavior occurs), and quickly (as soon as possible following the undesirable behavior). In addition, managers should clearly explain what the appropriate behavior is and why the employee is being punished. Employees typically respond well when punishment is administered this way.[92]

Finally, managers should *choose the simplest and most effective schedule of reinforcement*. When choosing a schedule of reinforcement, managers need to balance effectiveness against simplicity. In fact, the more complex the schedule of reinforcement, the more likely it is to be misunderstood and resisted by managers and employees.

Performance feedback—information about the quality or quantity of past performance—is key to attaining goals.

For example, a forestry and logging company experimented with a unique variable ratio schedule. When tree-planters finished planting a bag of seedlings (about 1,000 seedlings per bag), they got to flip a coin. If they called the coin flip correctly (heads or tails), they were paid $4, double the regular rate of $2 per bag. If they called the coin flip incorrectly, they got nothing. The company began having problems when several workers and a manager, who was a part-time minister, claimed that the coin flip was a form of gambling. Then another worker found that the company was taking out too much money for taxes from workers' paychecks. Because the workers didn't really understand the reinforcement schedule, they blamed the payment plan associated with it and accused the company of trying to cheat them out of their money. After all of these problems, the researchers who implemented the variable ratio schedule concluded that "the results of this study may not be so much an indication of the relative effectiveness of different schedules of reinforcement as they are an indication of the types of problems that one encounters when applying these concepts in an industrial setting."[93] In short, choose the simplest, most effective schedule of reinforcement. Because continuous reinforcement, fixed ratio, and variable ratio schedules are about equally effective, continuous reinforcement schedules may be the best choice in many instances by virtue of their simplicity.

13-5 GOAL-SETTING THEORY

The basic model of motivation with which we began this chapter showed that individuals feel tension after becoming aware of an unfulfilled need. When they experience tension, they search for and select courses of action that they believe will eliminate this tension. In other words, they direct their behavior toward something. This something is a goal. A **goal** is a target, objective, or result that someone tries to accomplish. **Goal-setting theory** says that people will be motivated to the extent to which they accept specific, challenging goals and receive feedback that indicates their progress toward goal achievement.

*Let's learn more about goal setting by examining **13-5a the components of goal-setting theory** and **13-5b how to motivate with goal-setting theory**.*

13-5a Components of Goal-Setting Theory

The basic components of goal-setting theory are goal specificity, goal difficulty, goal acceptance, and performance feedback.[94] **Goal specificity** is the extent to which goals are detailed, exact, and unambiguous. Specific goals, such as "I'm going to have a 3.0 average this semester," are more motivating than general goals, such as "I'm going to get better grades this semester."

Goal difficulty is the extent to which a goal is hard or challenging to accomplish. Difficult goals, such as "I'm going to have a 3.5 average and make the dean's list this semester," are more motivating than easy goals, such as "I'm going to have a 2.0 average this semester."

Goal acceptance, which is similar to the idea of goal commitment discussed in Chapter 5, is the extent to which people consciously understand and agree to goals. Accepted goals, such as "I really want to get a 3.5 average this semester to show my parents how much I've improved," are more motivating than unaccepted goals, such as "My parents really want me to get a 3.5 average this semester, but there's so much more I'd rather do on campus than study!"

Goal a target, objective, or result that someone tries to accomplish

Goal-setting theory the theory that people will be motivated to the extent to which they accept specific, challenging goals and receive feedback that indicates their progress toward goal achievement

Goal specificity the extent to which goals are detailed, exact, and unambiguous

Goal difficulty the extent to which a goal is hard or challenging to accomplish

Goal acceptance the extent to which people consciously understand and agree to goals

Performance feedback is information about the quality or quantity of past performance and indicates whether progress is being made toward the accomplishment of a goal. GE managers now use a smartphone app to give employees immediate performance feedback. The app prompts managers to provide detailed feedback using categories such as *Insights* (for current challenges), *Consider* (for changes to make), and *Continue* (for actions to keep doing). Leonardo Baldassarre and Brien Finken, of GE's Oil & Gas Turbomachinery Solutions explain, "For example, an engineer was asked to 'consider' being more open to supplier recommendations and to visit the supplier for a day. He did, and in GE's Real-Time Performance Development the following weeks the change was apparent. He championed a new approach that doubled our overall savings rate on budgeted project costs. Similarly, a procurement specialist was told to 'continue' encouraging volume pricing and other such practices among vendors to increase savings."[95]

How does goal setting work? To start, challenging goals focus employees' attention (that is, direction of effort) on the critical aspects of their jobs and away from unimportant areas. Goals also energize behavior. When faced with unaccomplished goals, employees typically develop plans and strategies to reach those goals. Goals also create tension between the goal, which is the desired future state of affairs, and where the employee or company is now, meaning the current state of affairs. This tension can be satisfied only by achieving or abandoning the goal. Finally, goals influence persistence. Because goals only go away when they are accomplished, employees are more likely to persist in their efforts in the presence of goals, especially with performance feedback. Exhibit 13.8 incorporates goals into the motivation model by showing how

> **Performance feedback**
> information about the quality or quantity of past performance that indicates whether progress is being made toward the accomplishment of a goal

Exhibit 13.8
Adding Goal-Setting Theory to the Model

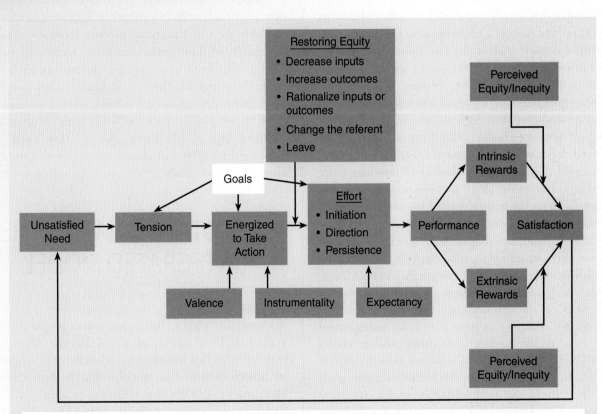

Goals create tension between the goal, which is the desired future state of affairs, and where the employee or company is now, meaning the current state of affairs. This tension can be satisfied only by achieving or abandoning the goal. Goals also energize behavior. When faced with unaccomplished goals, employees typically develop plans and strategies to reach those goals. Finally, goals influence persistence.

goals directly affect tension, effort, and the extent to which employees are energized to take action.

13-5b Motivating with Goal-Setting Theory

What practical steps can managers take to use goal-setting theory to motivate employees? Managers can do five things, beginning with *assigning specific, challenging goals*. One of the simplest, most effective ways to motivate workers is to give them specific, challenging goals. When the chief of staff of a CEO received feedback that he micromanaged and didn't listen, he and his executive coach set specific, challenging goals to track his progress. Because changing work habits is difficult, he started with just three long-term goals, each accompanied by one short-term goal. For his "listen better" goal, the short-term goal was "attending one meeting a day without devices (smartphone, tablet, or laptop)." The short-term goal then increased to "two meetings a day," and so on, until, after four months, he no longer took devices to meetings.[96]

Second, don't set too many goals for employees.[97] Remember, goals work by focusing attention away from less important parts of a job to the most important parts. Having too many goals is just the opposite of focusing! In a five-year study of 5,000 top performing managers, sales representatives, doctors, lawyers, engineers and software programmers, Professor Morten Hansen found what distinguished these high performers from their colleagues. "It wasn't a better ability to organize or delegate. Instead, top performers mastered selectivity. Whenever they could, they carefully selected which priorities, tasks, meetings, customers, ideas, or steps to undertake and which to let go. They then applied intense, targeted effort on those few priorities in order to excel."[98]

Third, managers should *make sure workers truly accept organizational goals*. Specific, challenging goals won't motivate workers unless they really accept, understand, and agree to the organization's goals. For this to occur, people must see the goals as fair and reasonable. Employees must also trust management and believe that managers are using goals to clarify what is expected from them rather than to exploit or threaten them ("If you don't achieve these goals . . ."). Participative goal setting, in which managers and employees generate goals together, can help increase trust and understanding and thus acceptance of goals. Furthermore, providing workers with training can help increase goal acceptance, particularly when workers don't believe they are capable of reaching the organization's goals.[99]

Fourth, don't just set goals; figure out how to remove the obstacles that could prevent achieving those goals.[100] Goals work because they focus attention, energize behavior, *and* influence persistence, that is, sustaining efforts to achieve a goal. But the path to achieving goals is rarely smooth and without problems. Taking the time to think about the obstacles that get in the way of goal achievement directly affects persistence by prompting employees to develop contingency plans for overcoming those problems. Contingency plans, in turn, make employees even more committed to achieving their goals, even when they encounter difficulties. So, for each goal, have employees take two additional steps, identifying obstacles (What might stop you from achieving this goal?) and ways of removing them (Identify steps you can take to overcome this obstacle).[101]

Finally, managers should *provide frequent, specific, performance-related feedback*. After employees have accepted specific, challenging goals, they should receive frequent performance-related feedback so that they can track their progress toward goal completion. Feedback leads to stronger motivation and effort in three ways.[102] Receiving specific feedback about the quality of their performance can encourage employees who don't have specific, challenging goals to set goals to improve their performance. After people meet goals, performance feedback often encourages them to set higher, more difficult goals. Moreover, feedback lets people know whether they need to increase their efforts or change strategies in order to accomplish their goals.

13-6 MOTIVATING WITH THE INTEGRATED MODEL

We began this chapter by defining motivation as the set of forces that initiates, directs, and makes people persist in their efforts to accomplish a goal. We also asked the basic question that managers ask when they try to figure out how to motivate their workers: What leads to effort? The answer to that question is likely to be somewhat different for each employee. So, if you're having difficulty figuring out why people aren't motivated where you work, check your Review Card for a useful, theory-based starting point.

14 | Leadership

14-1 LEADERS VERSUS MANAGERS

Whether you construct buildings, create and innovate to bring new products to markets, or help a company gain competitive advantage to better serve customers, **leadership** is the process of influencing others to achieve group or organizational goals. If you've ever been in charge, or even just thought about it, chances are you've considered questions such as these: Do I have what it takes to lead? What are the most important things leaders do? How can I transform a poorly performing department, division, or company? Do I need to adjust my leadership depending on the situation and the employee? Why doesn't my leadership inspire people? If you feel overwhelmed at the prospect of being a leader, you're not alone – millions of leaders in organizations across the world struggle with these fundamental leadership issues on a daily basis.

Leadership the process of influencing others to achieve group or organizational goals

Why? Because leadership is incredibly difficult! Whether measured by subordinate surveys, leader behaviors, unit performance, company finances, or the short tenures of company CEOs replaced by frustrated corporate boards, half a century of research show that the base rate of leadership incompetence is between 60 percent and 75 percent.[1] Similar research by **Gallup** of 2.5 million leaders in 195 countries revealed that "18 percent of those currently in management roles demonstrate a high level of talent for managing others, while another 20 percent show a basic talent for it," leaving 62 percent who lack even the basic talent for leadership.[2] Gallup concludes that "just 1 in 10 have the natural, God-given talent to manage a team of people," and "that another 2 in 10 people have some characteristics of functioning managerial talent and can perform at a high level if their company coaches and supports them."[3]

While we know from Chapter 1 that basic management practices significantly improve individual and company performance, studies also show that who leads matters just as much. The leadership skills of CEOs and other top managers explain 14 to 45 percent of the differences between high- and low-performing companies.[4] In short, leadership makes a huge difference, but achieving good leadership is incredibly difficult. The knowledge and skills you'll learn in this chapter won't make the task of leadership less daunting, but they will help you navigate your journey as a leader. Let's start by examining the differences between leaders and managers.

According to late business professor Warren Bennis, the primary difference between leaders and managers is that leaders are concerned with doing the right thing, while managers are concerned with doing things right.[5] In other words, leaders begin with the question "What should we be doing?" while managers start with "How can we do what we're already doing better?" Jochen Zeitz became the new CEO of motorcycle manufacturer **Harley-Davidson** during the global coronavirus pandemic. His focus was on making sure Harley-Davidson did the right things moving forward. Zeitz said:

During this extraordinary time of crisis, my first priority is the well-being of our H-D community as I execute our COVID-19 response plan efforts to stabilize the business, resume operations, and recover. I am also leading a necessary and comprehensive overhaul of the company structure, operating model, and strategy as we adjust to the new post COVID-19 realities. Over the next few months, we will rewire the business and define a new five-year strategic plan later this year. I will then oversee the implementation of these changes and reignite Harley-Davidson as one of the most revered and iconic brands in the world.[6]

Leaders focus on vision, mission, goals, and objectives, while managers focus on productivity and efficiency. Managers see themselves as preservers of the status quo, while leaders see themselves as promoters of change and challengers of the status quo in that they encourage creativity and risk taking. For example, by creating incentives to reward restaurants with the fastest drive-through lanes and offering a limited nighttime menu (to reduce complexity and increase speed), **McDonald's** is *managing* productivity and efficiency to improve its average drive-through time of nearly four minutes, the slowest in the fast-food industry.[7] That's a quantum leap from **General Electric** changing its vision and mission by selling the 129-year-old lightbulb business started by company founder Thomas Edison. GE also sold its appliance, locomotive, oil equipment, and biopharma businesses over the last few years.[8] GE CEO Larry Culp said that the sale of the lightbulb business "is another important step in the transformation of GE into a more focused industrial company."[9] CEOs pursuing "transformation" are *leading*, not managing.

Another difference is that managers have a relatively short-term perspective, while leaders take a long-term view. Managers are concerned with control and limiting the choices of others, while leaders are more concerned with expanding people's choices and options.[10] Managers also solve problems so that others can do their work, while leaders inspire and motivate others to find their own solutions. Finally, managers are also more concerned with *means*, how to get things done, while leaders are more concerned with *ends*, what gets done.

Although leaders are different from managers, organizations need them both.[11] Managers are critical to getting out the day-to-day work, and leaders are critical to inspiring employees and setting the

organization's long-term direction. The key issue for any organization is the extent to which it is properly led and properly managed. As Bennis said in summing up the difference between leaders and managers, "American organizations [and probably those in the industrialized world] are underled and overmanaged. They do not pay enough attention to doing the right thing, while they pay too much attention to doing things right."[12]

14-2 WHO LEADERS ARE AND WHAT LEADERS DO

Jack Dorsey (@Jack), CEO of **Twitter**, once a micromanager, has become a listener who asks questions to facilitate discussion and strategic direction with his leadership team.[13] Mark Donegan, CEO of **Precision Castparts**, which makes complex parts for aircrafts and aircraft engines, is known for being a hard-nosed businessperson, focused more on tasks than people. His predecessor and mentor, Bill McCormick, says, "I was relatively relentless. But he was a lot more relentless."[14]

Which one is likely to be successful as a CEO? According to a survey of 1,542 senior managers, it's the extrovert. Of those 1,542 senior managers, 47 percent felt that extroverts make better CEOs, while 65 percent said that being an introvert hurts a CEO's chances of success.[15] So clearly, senior managers believe that extroverted CEOs are better leaders. But are they? Not necessarily. In fact, a relatively high percentage of CEOs, 40 percent, are introverts. Elena Lytkina Botelho, a partner at executive consulting firm **ghSmart**, says, "The biggest aha, overall, is that some of the things that make CEOs attractive to the board have no bearing on their performance. Like most human beings, they get seduced by (extroverts, who are) charismatic, polished presenters. They simply do better in interviews."[16]

So, what makes a good leader? Does leadership success depend on who leaders are, such as introverts or extroverts, or on what leaders do and how they behave?

*Let's learn more about who leaders are by investigating **14-2a leadership traits** and **14-2b leadership behaviors**.*

14-2a Leadership Traits

Trait theory is one way to describe who leaders are. **Trait theory** says that effective leaders possess a similar set of traits or characteristics. **Traits** are relatively stable characteristics such as abilities, psychological motives, or consistent patterns of behavior. For example, trait theory holds that leaders are taller and more confident and have greater physical stamina (that is, higher energy levels) than nonleaders. In fact, studies show we perceive those in authority as being taller than they actually are, and that taller people see themselves as more qualified to lead.[17] Indeed, while just 14.5 percent of men are six feet tall, 58 percent of *Fortune* 500 CEOs are six feet or taller. Author Malcolm Gladwell says, "We have a sense, in our minds, of what a leader is supposed to look like, and that stereotype is so powerful that when someone fits it, we simply become blind to other considerations."[18] Likewise, in terms of physical stamina, companies whose CEOs have run and finished a marathon have a stock valuation that is 5 percent larger than those whose CEO had not.[19] Another study found a small relationship between *Fortune* 500 CEO face width (thought to indicate a leader's dominance, ambition, and power) and company profitability.[20] Trait theory is also known as the "great person" theory because early versions of the theory stated that leaders are born, not made. In other words, you either have the right stuff to be a leader or you don't. And if you don't, there is no way to get it.

For some time, it was thought that trait theory was wrong and that there were no consistent trait differences between leaders and nonleaders, or between effective and ineffective leaders. However, more recent evidence shows that "successful leaders are not like other people," that successful leaders are indeed different from the rest of us.[21] More specifically, leaders are different from nonleaders in the following traits: drive, the desire to lead, honesty/integrity, self-confidence, emotional stability, cognitive ability, and knowledge of the business.[22]

Drive refers to high levels of effort and is characterized by achievement, motivation, initiative, energy, and tenacity. In terms of achievement and ambition, leaders always try to make improvements or achieve success in what they're doing. Because of their initiative, they have strong desires to promote change or solve problems. At **Amazon**, founder Jeff Bezos calls this "high-velocity decision-making." Bezos says, ". . . most decisions should probably be made with somewhere around 70 percent of the information you wish you had. If you wait for 90 percent, in most cases, you're probably being slow.

Leaders are tenacious and better able to overcome obstacles that might deter others.

Plus, either way, you need to be good at quickly recognizing and correcting bad decisions. If you're good at course correcting, being wrong may be less costly than you think, whereas being slow is going to be expensive for sure."[23] Leaders who possess drive typically have more energy – they have to, given the long hours they put in and followers' expectations that they be positive and upbeat. Thus, leaders must have physical, mental, and emotional vitality. Leaders are also more tenacious than nonleaders and are better at overcoming obstacles and problems that would deter most of us.

Successful leaders also have a stronger *desire to lead*.[24] They want to be in charge and think about ways to influence or convince others about what should or shouldn't be done. The importance of a strong desire to lead becomes clear, according to Scott Gregory, CEO of **Hogan Assessment Systems**, in *absentee leaders* who don't possess it:

> *A young friend recently remarked that the worst boss he*

Trait theory a leadership theory that holds that effective leaders possess a similar set of traits or characteristics

Traits relatively stable characteristics, such as abilities, psychological motives, or consistent patterns of behavior

wavebreakmedia/Shutterstock.com

ever had would provide him with feedback that always consisted of "You're doing a great job." But they both knew it wasn't true – the organization was in disarray, turnover was excessive, and customers were not happy. My friend was giving it his all, but he needed more support and better feedback than he received. He wanted a leader who would be around when he needed them, and who would give him substantive advice, not platitudes. As a measure of his frustration, he said, "I would rather have had a boss who yelled at me or made unrealistic demands than this one, who provided empty praise."[25]

Honesty/integrity is also important to leaders. *Honesty*, being truthful with others, is a cornerstone of leadership. Without it, leaders won't be trusted. When leaders are honest, subordinates are willing to overlook other flaws. Bezos says, "If you have conviction on a particular direction even though there's no consensus, it's helpful to say, 'Look, I know we disagree on this but will you gamble with me on it? Disagree and commit?'"[26] He cites the example of a new **Amazon Studios** TV show that he didn't like, but which was still approved for funding. "I told the team my [negative] view. . . They had a completely different opinion and wanted to go ahead. I wrote back right away with, "I disagree and commit and hope it becomes the most watched thing we've ever made."[27] *Integrity* is the extent to which leaders do what they say they will do. Leaders may be honest and have good intentions, but if they don't consistently deliver on what they promise, they won't be trusted.

Self-confidence, or believing in one's abilities, also distinguishes leaders from nonleaders. Self-confident leaders are more decisive and assertive and are more likely to gain others' confidence. Moreover, self-confident leaders will admit mistakes because they view them as learning opportunities rather than as refutations of their leadership capabilities. That, in turn, according to a study of 161 teams, makes employees more likely to admit mistakes and give credit to others, rather than to themselves.[28]

Leaders also have *emotional stability*. Even when things go wrong, they remain even-tempered and consistent in their outlook and in the way they treat others. Consultants David Maxfield and Justin Hale describe this leader who, unfortunately, *lacked* emotional stability: "One executive we worked with was adamant and deliberate about creating a fun and supportive atmosphere where his team felt safe to try new things. He saw his role as supporting people and developing talent. And

yet, to his surprise, most of his team labeled him a jerk." Maxwell and Hale explain that as they described to him a time when his team found him to be especially "jerky," he said, "I know what you're thinking: you're thinking I'm some sort of hypocrite. But I'm not. Ninety-five percent of the time, I'm the fun, supportive guy I've described. It's only 5 percent of the time when I lose my temper or forget what I should be doing and I say stupid things like that. Those statements are not an accurate reflection of who I am."[29] Except, according to his followers, they were.

Leaders are also smart – they typically have strong *cognitive abilities*. This doesn't mean that leaders are necessarily geniuses – far from it. But it does mean that leaders have the capacity to analyze large amounts of seemingly unrelated, complex information and see patterns, opportunities, or threats where others might not see them. Finally, leaders also know their stuff, which means they have superior technical knowledge about the businesses they run. Leaders who have a good *knowledge of the business* understand the key technological decisions and concerns facing their companies. More often than not, studies indicate that effective leaders have long, extensive experience in their industries. CEO Michelle Buck has been with **Hershey's** for 15 years and was chief operating officer prior to becoming CEO. She had 17 years of experience in snack foods at Kraft/Nabisco and the Frito-Lay division of PepsiCo before Hershey's.[30] Says Buck, "One of the most important lessons I've learned is to weigh the perspectives of those around me with my north star. Then, I listen to my gut, which to me isn't just natural instinct, it's been built through years of experience, successes, failures, and everything in between."[31]

14-2b Leadership Behaviors

Thus far, you've read about who leaders *are*. But traits alone are not enough to make a successful leader. They are, however, a precondition for success. After all, it's hard to imagine a truly successful leader who lacks most of these qualities. Leaders who have these traits (or many of them) must then take actions that encourage people to achieve group or organizational goals.[32] Both leader traits *and* behaviors are essential for successful leadership.[33] Accordingly, we now examine what leaders *do*, meaning the behaviors they perform or the actions they take to influence others to achieve group or organizational goals.

Researchers at the University of Michigan, the Ohio State University, and the University of Texas examined the specific behaviors that leaders use to improve

CONSIDERATE LEADER BEHAVIOR: SHOULD YOU BE AN OVERSHARING BOSS?

Accounting software company **inDinero's** 31-year-old CEO Jessica Mah says, "What haven't I shared?" Mah has told employees about fighting with her mom, bad dates, barfing at Burning Man, and jokingly offered $100,000 to whoever finds her a husband. Mah overshares as the boss, but should you?

Fuse/Corbis/Getty Images

While being close to employees has benefits, like promoting better understanding of employees' needs and potentially stronger relationships, it also has costs. Being too close might contaminate the fair assessments, judgments, and decisions that leaders need to make about individual and company performance. Also, not everyone wants an oversharing boss. While employees want bosses who understand them, they also want bosses who provide the guidance and resources they need to do their jobs.

Also, are you oversharing for yourself or for those who work for you? Professor Brene Brown, whose Ted Talk on the power of vulnerability has been seen 48 million times, says oversharing "is dangerous when things become misunderstood. For leaders, sharing without the intention of developing other people or processes is not courageous."

Be humble. Let people see your humanity. But, you're the boss, not a co-worker. Share, but be careful about oversharing. "Did I ever tell you about the time my roommates and I…. Oh, wait, never mind."

Source: R. Feintzeig, "Now Emoting in the Corner Office: The Oversharing CEO," *Wall Street Journal*, May 1, 2018, accessed June 5, 2020, https://www.wsj.com/articles/now-emoting-in-the-corner-office-the-oversharing-ceo-1525193113; Z. Liao, W. Liu & Z. Song, "Research: When Being Close to Your Employees Backfires," *Harvard Business Review*, January 14, 2019, accessed June 5, 2020, https://hbr.org/2019/01/research-when-being-close-to-your-employees-backfires..

---

subordinate satisfaction and performance. Hundreds of studies were conducted, and hundreds of leader behaviors were examined. At all three universities, two basic leader behaviors emerged as central to successful leadership: initiating structure (called *job-centered leadership* at the University of Michigan and *concern for production* at the University of Texas) and considerate leader behavior (called *employee-centered leadership* at the University of Michigan and *concern for people* at the University of Texas).[34] These two leader behaviors, which are strongly associated with positive leadership results, form the basis for many of the leadership theories discussed in this chapter.[35]

Initiating structure is the degree to which a leader structures the roles of followers by setting goals, giving directions, setting deadlines, and assigning tasks. A leader's ability to initiate structure primarily affects subordinates' job performance.[36] The CEO of **Precision Castparts,** Mark Donegan, described earlier as focused more on tasks than people, initiated structure in terms of the performance goals and directions (lower costs) for its 150+ factories. AeroDynamic Advisory's Kevin Michaels says, "They're maniacs about operational improvement. That comes right from Mark Donegan." Donegan has regular on-site reviews at every factory every three months, meeting with the factory's plant manager, head of finance, the business segment president to whom the plant manager reports, and the factory's head of operations. Prior to each meeting, 26 identical charts, used across all 150 factories, are used to track productivity, plant earnings, product market share, and fixed costs per employee. When once asked how the company could keep costs so low, he responded, "We're a different breed. We're kind of a blue-collar, in-your-face, slug-it-out, down-in-the-trenches type of company. And I take great pride in that."[37]

Consideration is the extent to which a leader is friendly, approachable, and supportive and shows concern for employees. Consideration primarily affects subordinates' job satisfaction.[38] Specific leader consideration behaviors include listening to employees' problems and concerns, consulting with employees before making decisions, and treating employees as equals. Hershey's CEO

> **Initiating structure** the degree to which a leader structures the roles of followers by setting goals, giving directions, setting deadlines, and assigning tasks
>
> **Consideration** the extent to which a leader is friendly, approachable, and supportive and shows concern for employees

Hershey's CEO Michelle Buck believes that as a leader, it's important to listen to the experts around you, including those that are on the outside of the decision making domain.

tupungato/iStock Editorial/Getty Images

Michelle Buck, who practices considerate leader behavior, says, "I find immense value in seeking diverse perspectives when I'm making an important business decision. I want to hear from people who are deep in the organization, closest to the work, as well as those outside the decision domain who may see things a bit differently. As a leader, it's important to set direction and impart your knowledge to others; but you have to balance that with listening to the expertise and point of views of those around you. Intentional listening, and the learning associated with that, has undoubtedly been key to my success."[39]

Although researchers at all three universities generally agreed that initiating structure and consideration were basic leader behaviors, their interpretation differed on how these two behaviors are related to one another and which are necessary for effective leadership.

The University of Michigan studies indicated that initiating structure and consideration were mutually exclusive behaviors on opposite ends of the same continuum. In other words, leaders who wanted to be more considerate would have to do less initiating of structure (and vice versa). The University of Michigan studies also indicated that only considerate leader behaviors (that is, employee-centered behaviors) were associated with successful leadership. By contrast, researchers at the Ohio State University and the University of Texas found that initiating structure and consideration were independent behaviors, meaning that leaders can be considerate and initiate structure at the same time. Additional evidence confirms this finding.[40] The same researchers also concluded that the most effective leaders were strong on both initiating structure and considerate leader behaviors.

This "high–high" approach can be seen in the upper-right corner of the Blake/Mouton leadership grid, as shown in Exhibit 14.1. Blake and Mouton used two leadership behaviors, concern for people (that is, consideration) and concern for production (that is, initiating structure), to categorize five different leadership styles. Both behaviors are rated on a nine-point scale, with 1 representing "low" and 9 representing "high." Blake and Mouton suggest that a "high–high," or 9,9 leadership style is the best. They call this style *team management* because leaders who use it display a high concern for people (9) and a high concern for production (9).

By contrast, leaders use a 9,1 *authority-compliance* leadership style when they have a high concern for production and a low concern for people. A 1,9 *country club* style occurs when leaders care about having a friendly, enjoyable work environment but don't really pay much attention to production or performance. The worst leadership style, according to the grid, is the 1,1 *impoverished* leader, who shows little concern for people or production and does the bare minimum needed to keep his or her job. Finally, the 5,5 *middle-of-the-road* style occurs when leaders show a moderate amount of concern for both people and production.

Is the team management style, with a high concern for production and a high concern for people, the best leadership style? Logically, it would seem so. Why wouldn't you want to show high concern for both people and production? Nonetheless, nearly 75 years of research indicates that there isn't one best leadership style. The best leadership style depends on the situation. In other words, no one leadership behavior by itself and no one combination of leadership behaviors work well across all situations and employees.

Exhibit 14.1
Blake/Mouton Leadership Grid

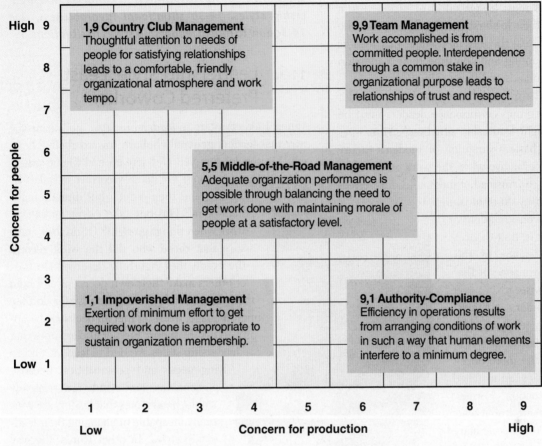

High 9 **1,9 Country Club Management** Thoughtful attention to needs of people for satisfying relationships leads to a comfortable, friendly organizational atmosphere and work tempo.

9,9 Team Management Work accomplished is from committed people. Interdependence through a common stake in organizational purpose leads to relationships of trust and respect.

5,5 Middle-of-the-Road Management Adequate organization performance is possible through balancing the need to get work done with maintaining morale of people at a satisfactory level.

1,1 Impoverished Management Exertion of minimum effort to get required work done is appropriate to sustain organization membership.

9,1 Authority-Compliance Efficiency in operations results from arranging conditions of work in such a way that human elements interfere to a minimum degree.

Concern for people — High 9, 8, 7, 6, 5, 4, 3, 2, Low 1

Concern for production — 1 2 3 4 5 6 7 8 9 — Low ... High

Source: R. R. Blake and A. A. McCanse, "The Leadership Grid", Leadership Dilemmas – Grid Solutions (Houston: Gulf Publishing Company), 21.

14-3 PUTTING LEADERS IN THE RIGHT SITUATION: FIEDLER'S CONTINGENCY THEORY

After leader traits and behaviors, the situational approach to leadership is the third major method used in the study of leadership. We'll review four major situational approaches to leadership – Fiedler's contingency theory, path–goal theory, Hersey and Blanchard's Situational Leadership® theory, and Vroom, Yetton, and Jago's normative decision model. All assume that the effectiveness of any **leadership style**, the way a leader

generally behaves toward followers depends on the situation.[41] A study of 130 restaurants in a pizza franchise examined the interaction between how extroverted store managers were and how involved employees were in trying "to bring about improved procedures [in the store.]" Profits were 16 percent *above* average in stores with extroverted managers and less involved employees. In those instances, the strengths of the more outgoing boss fit well with the less involved employees. By contrast, profits were 14 percent *below* average in stores with extroverted leaders and highly involved employees. Why? Because the extroverted leaders were less comfortable with employees who wanted a say in making improvements. Again, leadership success depends on the situation.[42]

Leadership style the way a leader generally behaves toward followers

According to situational leadership theories, there is no one best leadership style. But one of these situational theories differs from the other three in one significant way. Fiedler's contingency theory assumes that leadership styles are consistent and difficult to change. Therefore, leaders must be placed in or matched to a situation that fits their leadership style. By contrast, the other three situational theories all assume that leaders are capable of adapting and adjusting their leadership styles to fit the demands of different situations.

Fiedler's **contingency theory** states that in order to maximize work group performance, leaders must be matched to the right leadership situation.[43] More specifically, the first basic assumption of Fiedler's theory is that leaders are effective when the work groups they lead perform well. So, instead of judging leaders' effectiveness by what they do (that is, initiating structure and consideration) or who they are (that is, trait theory), Fiedler assesses leaders by the conduct and performance of the people they supervise.

Second, Fiedler assumes that leaders are generally unable to change their leadership styles and that they will be more effective when their styles are matched to the proper situation. Former business CEO Robert Rubin who served as the US Treasury secretary, explains, "Some people… operate on the assumption that they've had success in business and can do the same in government. But Washington is just a different world."[44] For example, Paul O'Neill, then CEO of **Alcoa**, an aluminum manufacturer where worker safety was critical, was appointed Treasury Secretary. When O'Neill met with his predecessor Larry Summers, he asked about the office-based Treasury Department's safety programs. Rubin says that Summers, "didn't have a clue about workplace safety – not a clue." Author Charles Duhigg explains that, "At Alcoa, he [O'Neill] was lionized for his focus on safety. At Treasury, it didn't really matter." Treasury employees joked their greatest risk was paper cuts. O'Neill was forced out of Treasury after just one year for repeatedly clashing with the Bush Whitehouse that appointed him. O'Neil admitted, "I thought I knew the players well enough, and that we were like-minded about fact-based policy making. It turned out that was all wrong."[45]

*Let's learn more about Fiedler's contingency theory by examining **14-3a the least preferred coworker and leadership styles, 14-3b situational favorableness, and 14-3c how to match leadership styles to situations**.*

14-3a   Leadership Style: Least Preferred Coworker

When Fiedler refers to *leadership style*, he means the way that leaders generally behave toward their followers. Do the leaders yell and scream and blame others when things go wrong? Or do they correct mistakes by listening and then quietly but directly make their point? Do they take credit for others' work when things go right? Or do they make sure that those who did the work receive the credit they rightfully deserve? Do they let others make their own decisions and hold them accountable for the results? Or do they micromanage, insisting that all decisions be approved first by them? Fiedler also assumes that leadership styles are tied to leaders' underlying needs and personalities. Because personalities and needs are relatively stable, he assumes that leaders are generally incapable of changing their leadership styles. In other words, the way that leaders treat people now is probably the way they've always treated others. So, according to Fiedler, if your boss's first instinct is to yell and scream and blame others, chances are he or she has always done that.

Fiedler uses a questionnaire called the Least Preferred Coworker (LPC) scale to measure leadership style. When completing the LPC scale, people are instructed to consider all of the people with whom they have ever worked and then to choose the one person with whom they have worked *least* well. Fiedler explains, "This does not have to be the person you liked least well, but should be the one person with whom you have the most trouble getting the job done."[46]

Would you describe your LPC as pleasant, friendly, supportive, interesting, cheerful, and sincere? Or would you describe the person as unpleasant, unfriendly, hostile, boring, gloomy, and insincere? People who describe their LPC in a positive way (scoring 64 and above) have *relationship-oriented* leadership styles. After all, if they can still be positive about their least preferred

iStock.com/David Franklin

Contingency theory a leadership theory states that to maximize work group performance, leaders must be matched to the situation that best fits their leadership style

How LPC is described	Leadership style
Positively	Relationship-oriented
Negatively	Task-oriented
Moderately	Flexible

Image Source/Getty Images

coworker, they must be people-oriented. By contrast, people who describe their LPC in a negative way (scoring 57 or below) have *task-oriented* leadership styles. Given a choice, they'll focus first on getting the job done and second on making sure everyone gets along. Finally, those with moderate scores (from 58 to 63) have a more *flexible* leadership style and can be somewhat relationship-oriented or somewhat task-oriented.

14-3b Situational Favorableness

Fiedler assumes that leaders will be more effective when their leadership styles are matched to the proper situation. More specifically, Fiedler defines **situational favorableness** as the degree to which a particular situation either permits or denies a leader the chance to influence the behavior of group members.[47] In highly favorable situations, leaders find that their actions influence followers. But in highly unfavorable situations, leaders have little or no success influencing the people they are trying to lead.

Three situational factors determine the favorability of a situation: leader–member relations, task structure, and position power. The most important situational factor is **leader–member relations**, which refers to how well followers respect, trust, and like their leaders. When leader–member relations are good, followers trust the leader, and there is a friendly work atmosphere. **Task structure** is the degree to which the requirements of a subordinate's tasks are clearly specified. With highly structured tasks, employees have clear job responsibilities, goals, and procedures. **Position power** is the degree to which leaders are able to hire, fire, reward, and punish workers. The more influence leaders have over hiring, firing, rewards, and punishments, the greater their power.

Exhibit 14.2 shows how leader–member relations, task structure, and position power can be combined into eight situations that differ in their favorability to leaders. In general, Situation I, on the left side of Exhibit 14.2, is the most favorable leader situation. Followers like and trust their leaders and know what to do because their tasks are highly structured. Also, the leaders have the formal power to influence workers through hiring, firing, rewarding, and punishing them. Therefore, it's relatively easy for a leader to influence followers in Situation I. By contrast, Situation VIII, on the right side of Exhibit 14.2, is the least favorable situation for leaders. Followers don't like or trust their leaders. Plus, followers are not sure what they're supposed to be doing, given that their tasks or jobs are highly unstructured.

Situational favorableness the degree to which a particular situation either permits or denies a leader the chance to influence the behavior of group members

Leader–member relations the degree to which followers respect, trust, and like their leaders

Task structure the degree to which the requirements of a subordinate's tasks are clearly specified

Position power the degree to which leaders are able to hire, fire, reward, and punish workers

Exhibit 14.2
Situational Favorableness

Leader–Member Relations	Good	Good	Good	Good	Poor	Poor	Poor	Poor
Task Structure	High	High	Low	Low	High	High	Low	Low
Position Power	Strong	Weak	Strong	Weak	Strong	Weak	Strong	Weak
Situation	I	II	III	IV	V	VI	VII	VIII
	Favorable		**Moderately Favorable**				**Unfavorable**	

Finally, leaders find it difficult to influence followers because they don't have the ability to hire, fire, reward, or punish the people who work for them. In short, it's very difficult to influence followers given the conditions found in Situation VIII.

14-3c Matching Leadership Styles to Situations

After studying thousands of leaders and followers in hundreds of different situations, Fiedler found that the performance of relationship- and task-oriented leaders followed the pattern displayed in Exhibit 14.3.

Relationship-oriented leaders with high LPC scores were better leaders (that is, their groups performed more effectively) under moderately favorable situations. In moderately favorable situations, the leader may be liked somewhat, tasks may be somewhat structured, and the leader may have some position power. In this situation,

a relationship-oriented leader improves leader–member relations, which is the most important of the three situational factors. In turn, morale and performance improve.

By contrast, as Exhibit 14.3 shows, task-oriented leaders with low LPC scores are better leaders in highly favorable and unfavorable situations. Task-oriented leaders do well in favorable situations where leaders are liked, tasks are structured, and the leader has the power to hire, fire, reward, and punish. In these favorable situations, task-oriented leaders effectively step on the gas of a well-tuned car. Their focus on performance sets the goal for the group, which then charges forward to meet it. But task-oriented leaders also do well in unfavorable situations where leaders are disliked, tasks are unstructured, and the leader doesn't have the power to hire, fire, reward, and punish. In these unfavorable situations, the task-oriented leader sets goals that focus attention on performance and clarify what needs to be done, thus overcoming low task structure. This is enough to jump-start performance even if workers don't like or trust the leader.

Exhibit 14.3
Matching Leadership Styles to Situations

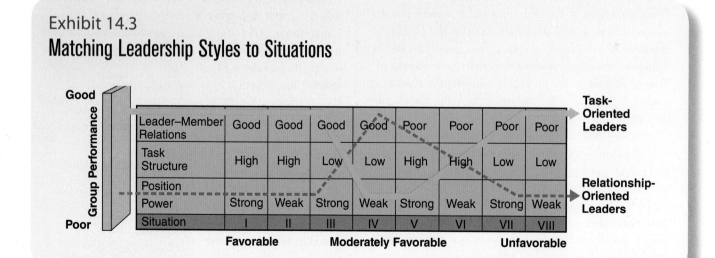

Finally, though not shown in Exhibit 14.3, people with moderate LPC scores, who can be somewhat relationship-oriented or somewhat task-oriented, tend to do fairly well in all situations because they can adapt their behavior. Typically, though, they don't perform quite as well as relationship-oriented or task-oriented leaders whose leadership styles are well matched to the situation.

Recall, however, that Fiedler assumes leaders to be incapable of changing their leadership styles. Accordingly, the key to applying Fiedler's contingency theory in the workplace is to accurately measure and match leaders to situations or to teach leaders how to change situational favorableness by changing leader-member relations, task structure, or position power. When powerful Hollywood producer Jeffrey Katzenberg realized that people were wary of approaching him (due to poor leader–member relations), he tried to change situational favorableness by making a practice of sharing meals with subordinates multiple times a day. "Suddenly, the relaxed nature of sitting at a table with somebody coming and bringing food and eating just gave me an ability to connect with people way, way, way better than I could across a desk in an office or sitting on the other side of a couch."[48]

Although matching or placing leaders in appropriate situations works particularly well, practicing managers have had little luck reengineering situations to fit their leadership styles. The primary problem, as you've no doubt realized, is the complexity of the theory. In a study designed to teach leaders how to reengineer their situations to fit their leadership styles, Fiedler found that most of the leaders simply did not understand what they were supposed to do to change their situations. Furthermore, if they didn't like their LPC profile (perhaps they felt they were more relationship-oriented than their scores indicated), they arbitrarily changed it to better suit their view of themselves. Of course, the theory won't work as well if leaders are attempting to change situational factors to fit their perceived leadership style rather than their real leadership style.[49]

14-4 ADAPTING LEADER BEHAVIOR: HERSEY AND BLANCHARD'S SITUATIONAL LEADERSHIP® THEORY

Have you ever had a new job that you didn't know how to do and your boss was not around to help you learn it? Conversely, have you ever known exactly how to do your job but your boss kept treating you like you didn't? Hersey and Blanchard's Situational Leadership theory is based on the idea of follower readiness. Hersey and Blanchard argue that employees have different levels of readiness for handling different jobs, responsibilities, and work assignments. Accordingly, Hersey and Blanchard's **situational theory** states that leaders need to adjust their leadership styles to match followers' readiness.[50]

Let's learn more about Hersey and Blanchard's situational theory by examining 14-4a worker readiness and 14-4b different leadership styles.

14-4a Worker Readiness

Performance readiness is the ability and willingness to take responsibility for directing one's behavior at work. Readiness is composed of two components. *Job readiness* consists of the amount of knowledge, skill, ability, and experience people have to perform their jobs. As you would expect, people with greater skill, ability, and experience do a better job of supervising their own work. *Psychological readiness,* on the other hand, is a feeling of self-confidence or self-respect. Likewise, confident people do a better job of guiding their own work than do insecure people. Job readiness and psychological readiness are combined to produce four different levels of readiness in Hersey and Blanchard's Situational Leadership theory.

The lowest level, R1, represents insecure people who are neither willing nor able to take responsibility for guiding their own work. R2 represents people who are confident and are willing but not able to take responsibility for guiding their own work. R3 represents people who are insecure and are able but not willing to take responsibility for guiding their own work. And R4 represents people who are confident and willing and able to take responsibility for guiding their own work. It's important to note that a follower's readiness is usually task specific. For example, you may be highly confident and capable when it comes to social media marketing, but know nothing about setting up budgets for planning purposes. Thus, you would possess readiness (R4) with respect to social media marketing but not (R1) with respect to budgets.

Situational theory theory that says leaders need to adjust their leadership styles to match followers' readiness

Performance readiness the ability and willingness to take responsibility for directing one's behavior at work

14-4b Leadership Styles

Similar to Blake and Mouton's managerial grid, situational theory defines leadership styles in terms of task behavior (that is, concern for production) and relationship behavior (that is, concern for people). As shown in Exhibit 14.4, these two behaviors can be combined to form four different leadership styles: telling, selling, participating, and delegating. Leaders choose one of these styles, depending on the readiness a follower has for a specific task.

A *telling* leadership style (high task behavior and low relationship behavior) is based on one-way communication, in which followers are told what, how, when, and where to do particular tasks. Telling is used when people are insecure and neither willing nor able to take responsibility for guiding their own work (R1). For instance, someone using a telling leadership style might say, "We're going to start a company e-newsletter that goes out once a week to our customers, pointing them to new content on our website. I want you to contact bulk email services, like MailChimp for cost estimates. Then get together with each product manager and then get a list of product feature and usability updates. Don't write these yourself. Have the product managers write them and we'll edit them as we see fit. Also, call the CEO's assistant to remind her that we need her comments. Finally, have this all assembled in a draft email for me next Friday."

A *selling* leadership style (high task behavior and high relationship behavior) involves two-way communication and psychological support to encourage followers to "own" or "buy into" particular ways of doing things. Selling is used when confident people are willing but not able to take responsibility for guiding their own work (R2). For instance, someone using a selling leadership style might say, "We're going to start a company e-newsletter that goes out once a week to our customers, pointing them to new content on our website. I really think that's a great idea, don't you? We're going to need some cost estimates from bulk email services, like MailChimp, and a list of product feature and usability updates from each product manager. But that's pretty straightforward. Oh, don't forget that we need the CEO's comments, too. She's expecting you to call. I know that you'll do a great job on this. We'll meet next Tuesday to see if you have any questions once you've dug into this. I'd like to see a draft email at that time. By the way, we need to have this done by next Friday."

A *participating* style (low task behavior and high relationship behavior) is based on two-way communication and shared decision-making. Participating is used when

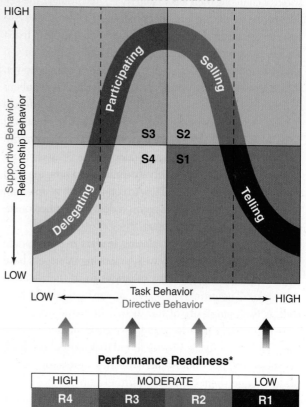

Exhibit 14.4
Hersey and Blanchard's Situational Leadership Model

Source: https://situational.com/the-cls-difference/situational-leadership-what-we-do/.

insecure people are able but not willing to take responsibility for guiding their own work (R3). Since the problem is with motivation and not ability, someone using a participating leadership style might say, "What do you think about starting a company e-newsletter that goes out once a week to our customers, pointing them to new content on our website? Uh-huh, uh-huh (listening). Ok, I think so, too. What kind of stuff do you hate in company e-newsletters? Un-huh (listening). Ok, I agree. That stuff drives me nuts, too. Well, what do you think we should put in ours? Uh-huh (listening). Those are great ideas. I'd like to see you implement them. We've got about 10 days to put it together. Why don't you put together a first draft, based on what we talked about here today, get the product managers involved to generate web content, touch base with the CEO's assistant, and we can meet on Tuesday to review those ideas. Great!"

A *delegating* style (low task behavior and low relationship behavior) is used when leaders basically let workers "run their own show" and make their own decisions. Delegating is used when people are willing and able to take responsibility for guiding their own work (R4). For instance, someone using a delegating leadership style might say, "We're going to start a company e-newsletter that goes out once a week to our customers, pointing them to new content on our website generated by the product managers. You've got 10 days to do it. Run with it. Let me know when you've got it done. I'll email you a couple of ideas, but other than that, do what you think is best. Thanks."

In general, as people become more "ready," and thus more willing and able to guide their own behavior, leaders should become less task oriented and more relationship oriented. Then, as people become even more "ready," leaders should become both less task oriented and less relationship oriented until people eventually manage their own work with little input from their leaders.

How well does Hersey and Blanchard's situational theory work? Despite its intuitive appeal (managers and consultants tend to prefer it over Fiedler's contingency theory because of its underlying logic and simplicity), most studies don't support situational theory.[51] While managers generally do a good job of judging followers' readiness levels, the theory doesn't seem to work well, except at lower levels, where a telling style is recommended for people who are insecure and neither willing nor able to take responsibility for guiding their own work.[52]

Delegating is used when people are willing and able to take responsibility for guiding their own work.

14-5 ADAPTING LEADER BEHAVIOR: PATH–GOAL THEORY

Just as its name suggests, **path–goal theory** states that leaders can increase subordinate satisfaction and performance by clarifying and clearing the paths to goals and by increasing the number and kinds of rewards available for goal attainment. Said another way, leaders need to clarify how followers can achieve organizational goals, take care of problems that prevent followers from achieving goals, and then find more and varied rewards to motivate followers to achieve those goals.[53]

Leaders must meet two conditions for path clarification, path clearing, and rewards to increase followers' motivation and effort. First, leader behavior must be a source of immediate or future satisfaction for followers. The things you do as a leader must either please your followers today or lead to activities or rewards that will satisfy them in the future. One of the key cultural principles followed by Charlie Kim, CEO of New York-based **Next Jump**, which runs web-based reward programs for 90,000 companies, is "Better Me + Better You = Better Us," Kim says, "The culture we're building is predicated on the concept of long-term, sustained happiness."[54] This is why Next Jump's leadership frequently asks its people what *would* make them happier. Because of the long hours they put in, employees were spending half a day per weekend in a New York City laundromat doing their laundry. So they asked if washers and dryers could be installed at work to be used (and which they would pay for) when working late hours. Recognizing the problem (not laundry, but the secondary effect of long hours resulting in lost weekend time), Next Jump now pays for laundry service. Employees bring in laundry on Fridays and it returns done on Mondays in a bag with Next Jump's logo and this phrase: "My company gets my laundry. I get my weekends back."[55] Next Jump's culture is so positive, rewarding, and satisfying that 18,000 people applied for 35 openings last year. Furthermore, while the quit rate in the tech industry is 22 percent per year, Next Jump has an incredibly low 1 percent quit rate.

Second, while providing the coaching, guidance, support, and rewards necessary for effective work performance, leader behaviors

Path–goal theory a leadership theory states that leaders can increase subordinate satisfaction and performance by clarifying and clearing the paths to goals and by increasing the number and kinds of rewards available for goal attainment

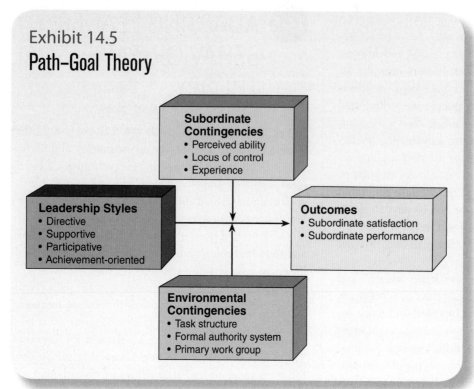

Exhibit 14.5
Path–Goal Theory

Subordinate Contingencies
• Perceived ability
• Locus of control
• Experience

Leadership Styles
• Directive
• Supportive
• Participative
• Achievement-oriented

Outcomes
• Subordinate satisfaction
• Subordinate performance

Environmental Contingencies
• Task structure
• Formal authority system
• Primary work group

must complement and not duplicate the characteristics of followers' work environments. Thus, leader behaviors must offer something unique and valuable to followers beyond what they're already experiencing as they do their jobs or what they can already do for themselves.

In contrast to Fiedler's contingency theory, path–goal theory assumes that leaders *can* change and adapt their leadership styles. Exhibit 14.5 illustrates this process, showing that leaders change and adapt their leadership styles contingent on their subordinates or the environment in which those subordinates work.

*Let's learn more about path–goal theory by examining **14-5a the four kinds of leadership styles that leaders use, 14-5b the subordinate and environmental contingency factors that determine when different leader styles are effective**, and **14-5c the outcomes of path–goal theory in improving employee satisfaction and performance.***

Directive leadership a leadership style in which the leader lets employees know precisely what is expected of them, gives them specific guidelines for performing tasks, schedules work, sets standards of performance, and makes sure that people follow standard rules and regulations

Supportive leadership a leadership style in which the leader is friendly and approachable to employees, shows concern for employees and their welfare, treats them as equals, and creates a friendly climate

Participative leadership a leadership style in which the leader consults employees for their suggestions and input before making decisions

14-5a Leadership Styles

As illustrated in Exhibit 14.5, the four leadership styles in path–goal theory are directive, supportive, participative, and achievement oriented.[56] **Directive leadership** involves letting employees know precisely what is expected of them, giving them specific guidelines for performing tasks, scheduling work, setting standards of performance, and making sure that people follow standard rules and regulations. These activities are especially important during economic downturns and periods during which a company is struggling. Recent research suggests that in more challenging economic environments (such as recessions), a more directive and authoritarian approach to leadership may produce stronger financial results for the company. More directive leaders reinforce discipline, effective coordination, and operational efficiency, so they are more likely to increase revenues during short-term crises and economic downturns.[57] Directive leadership is very similar to initiating structure.

Supportive leadership involves being approachable and friendly to employees, showing concern for them and their welfare, treating them as equals, and creating a friendly climate. Supportive leadership is very similar to considerate leader behavior. Supportive leadership often results in employee satisfaction with the job and with leaders. This leadership style may also result in improved performance when it increases employee confidence, lowers employee job stress, or improves relations and trust between employees and leaders.[58]

Participative leadership involves consulting employees for their suggestions and input before making decisions. Participation in decision-making should help followers understand which goals are most important and clarify the paths to accomplishing them. Furthermore, when people participate in decisions, they become more committed to making them work. San Antonio, Texas-based **H-E-B Grocery** regularly is frequently honored as a "best place to work." President and COO Craig Boyan says there is a culture of "restless dissatisfaction" to reduce costs, satisfy customers, and keep employees engaged. Listening to and empowering employees is central to those efforts. Boyan says, "Our store leaders run their business the way they know best, and each store and each department in each store is always looking to improve and evolve how we do things. The key is pushing decision-making to those who know best –partners in our stores – and having great leaders and partners to be constantly learning and working to evolve our business."[59] H-E-B employees are even more committed now that the company awarded 15 percent of its stock to 55,000+ employees (who must be over 21 and have worked at least 1,000 hours in the last year). Veronica Solis, who started with H-E-B after high school and manages store payroll, says, "I'm going to retire from here. I'm not going anywhere."[60]

Achievement-oriented leadership means setting challenging goals, having high expectations of employees, and displaying confidence that employees will assume responsibility and put forth extraordinary effort. **Airbnb** growth product manager Lenny Rachitsky says, "At the end of each year, looking at our growth charts we were often shocked at how close we came to hitting our wildly ambitious, seemingly impossible, goals. And when I say wildly ambitious, I'm making an understatement – Brian, Airbnb's CEO, is (in)famous for doubling our proposed goals, and often pushing us to 10 times the goal. Either he knew something we didn't, or the wildly ambitious goals pushed teams to think bigger and rise to the occasion. It was absolutely the latter."[61] Once the challenging goal was set, he says, leaders should, "Align a cross-functional team behind that goal, and give that team ownership of HOW to achieve it. Your #1 job as a leader is to assemble the right team, point them in the right direction, and stay vigilant in unblocking them [that is, removing obstacles to their success]."[62]

14-5b Subordinate and Environmental Contingencies

As shown in Exhibit 14.5, path–goal theory specifies that leader behaviors should be adapted to subordinate characteristics. The theory identifies three kinds of subordinate contingencies: perceived ability, experience, and locus of control. *Perceived ability* is simply how much ability subordinates believe they have for doing their jobs well. Subordinates who perceive that they have a great deal of ability will be dissatisfied with directive leader behaviors. Experienced employees are likely to react in a similar way. Because they already know how to do their jobs (or perceive that they do), they don't need or want close supervision. By contrast, subordinates with little experience or little perceived ability will welcome directive leadership.

Locus of control is a personality measure that indicates the extent to which people believe that they have control over what happens to them in life. *Internals* believe that what happens to them, good or bad, is largely a result of their choices and actions. *Externals*, on the other hand, believe that what happens to them is caused by external forces beyond their control. Accordingly, externals are much more comfortable with a directive leadership style, whereas internals greatly prefer a participative leadership style because they like to have a say in what goes on at work.

Path–goal theory specifies that leader behaviors should complement rather than duplicate the characteristics of followers' work environments. There are three kinds of environmental contingencies: task structure, the formal authority system, and the primary work group. As in Fiedler's contingency theory, *task structure* is the degree to which the requirements of a subordinate's tasks are clearly specified. When task structure is low and tasks are unclear, directive leadership should be used because it complements the work environment. When task structure is high and tasks are clear, however, directive leadership is not needed because it duplicates what task structure provides. Alternatively, when tasks are stressful, frustrating, or dissatisfying, leaders should respond with supportive leadership.

The *formal authority system* is an organization's set of procedures, rules, and policies. When the formal authority system is unclear, directive leadership complements the situation by reducing uncertainty and increasing clarity. But when the formal authority system is clear, directive leadership is redundant and should not be used.

Primary work group refers to the amount of work-oriented participation or emotional support that is provided by an employee's immediate work group. Participative leadership should be used when tasks are complex, and there is little existing work-oriented participation in the primary work group. When tasks are stressful, frustrating, or repetitive, supportive leadership is called for.

Finally, because keeping track of all of these subordinate and environmental contingencies can get a bit confusing, Exhibit 14.6 provides a summary of when directive, supportive, participative, and achievement-oriented leadership styles should be used.

14-5c Outcomes

Does following path–goal theory improve subordinate satisfaction and performance? More and more evidence suggests that it does.[63] In particular, people who work for supportive leaders are much more satisfied with

> **Achievement-oriented leadership** a leadership style in which the leader sets challenging goals, has high expectations of employees, and displays confidence that employees will assume responsibility and put forth extraordinary effort

Exhibit 14.6

Path–Goal Theory: When to Use Directive, Supportive, Participative, or Achievement-Oriented Leadership

Directive Leadership	Supportive Leadership	Participative Leadership	Achievement-Oriented Leadership
Unstructured tasks	Structured, simple, repetitive tasks Stressful, frustrating tasks	Complex tasks	Unchallenging tasks
Workers with external locus of control	Workers lack confidence	Workers with internal locus of control	
Unclear formal authority system	Clear formal authority system	Workers not satisfied with rewards	
Inexperienced workers		Experienced workers	
Workers with low perceived ability		Workers with high perceived ability	

Are Angry Half-Time Motivational Speeches Good or Bad Leadership? Yes.

Team sports movies often have a half-time scene where the team's coach angrily criticizes the players because they're losing. Of course, in the movies, the team rallies to win in the second half. But do angry half-time motivational speeches actually work? A study of 304 half-time locker-room speeches made by 23 high school and college basketball coaches found that negative, critical speeches work up to a point. Coaches who are overly negative and critical or are barely negative or critical hurt second-half effort and team performance. But coaches who are moderately negative or critical are able to get their teams to focus on playing harder and better, which they do by significantly outscoring their competition in the second half. Barry Staw, one of the study's authors, says that moderately critical half-time speeches work because they get teams to realize, "you can play better than this." He warns, however, that "Our results do not give leaders a license to be a jerk."

Cory Thoman/Shutterstock.com

Sources: B. Staw, K. DeCelles & P. de Goey, "Leadership in the Locker Room: How the Intensity of Leaders' Unpleasant Affective Displays Shapes Team Performance," *Journal of Applied Psychology* 104, no. 12 (2019): 1547–1557; B. Renner, "For Coaches, Anger More Effective Than Positivity When It Comes to Halftime Speeches," *Study finds*, August 19, 2019, accessed June 5, 2020, www.studyfinds.org/for-coaches-anger-more-effective-than-positivity-when-it-comes-to-halftime-speeches/.

their jobs and their bosses. Likewise, people who work for directive leaders are more satisfied with their jobs and bosses (but not quite as much as when their bosses are supportive) and perform their jobs better, too. Does adapting one's leadership style to subordinate and environmental characteristics improve subordinate satisfaction and performance? Earlier editions of this textbook indicated that it was too early to tell.[64] But more recent research solidly indicates that following the path–goal theory's ideas for adapting one's leadership style to the situation works.[65] Finally, because so much leadership research shows that it makes sense for leaders to be both supportive (that is, consideration) *and* directive (that is, initiating structure), it also makes sense that leaders can improve subordinate satisfaction and performance by adding participative and achievement-oriented leadership styles to their capabilities as leaders.

14-6 ADAPTING LEADER BEHAVIOR: NORMATIVE DECISION THEORY

Many people believe that making tough decisions is at the heart of leadership. Yet experienced leaders will tell you that deciding *how* to make decisions is just as important. The **normative decision theory** (also known as the *Vroom-Yetton-Jago model*) helps leaders decide how much employee participation (from none to letting employees make the entire decision) should be used when making decisions.[66]

Let's learn more about normative decision theory by investigating 14-6a decision styles and 14-6b decision quality and acceptance.

14-6a Decision Styles

Unlike nearly all of the other leadership theories discussed in this chapter, which have specified *leadership* styles, that is, the way a leader generally behaves toward followers, the normative decision theory specifies five different *decision* styles, or ways of making decisions. (See Chapter 5 for a more complete review of decision-making in organizations.) As shown in Exhibit 14.7, those styles vary from *autocratic decisions* (AI or AII) on the left, in which leaders make the decisions by themselves, to *consultative decisions* (CI or CII), in which leaders share problems with subordinates but still make the decisions themselves, to *group decisions* (GII) on

> **Normative decision theory**
> a theory that suggests how leaders can determine an appropriate amount of employee participation when making decisions

---

Exhibit 14.7
Normative Theory, Decision Styles, and Levels of Employee Participation

Leader solves the problem or makes the decision

Leader is willing to accept any decision supported by the entire group

AI	AII	CI	CII	GII
Using information available at the time, the leader solves the problem or makes the decision.	The leader obtains necessary information from employees and then selects a solution to the problem. When asked to share information, employees may or may not be told what the problem is.	The leader shares the problem and gets ideas and suggestions from relevant employees on an individual basis. Individuals are not brought together as a group. Then the leader makes the decision, which may or may not reflect their input.	The leader shares the problem with employees as a group, obtains their ideas and suggestions, and then makes the decision, which may or may not reflect their input.	The leader shares the problem with employees as a group. Together, the leader and employees generate and evaluate alternatives and try to reach an agreement on a solution. The leader acts as a facilitator and does not try to influence the group. The leader is willing to accept and implement any solution that has the support of the entire group.

Source: Table 2.1, "Decision Methods for Group and Individual Problems," in *Leadership and Decision-Making* (Pittsburgh: University of Pittsburgh Press, 1973), by V. H. Vroom and P. W. Yetton.

Exhibit 14.8
Normative Theory Decision Rules

Decision Rules to Increase Decision Quality

Quality Rule. If the quality of the decision is important, then don't use an autocratic decision style.

Leader Information Rule. If the quality of the decision is important, and if the leader doesn't have enough information to make the decision on his or her own, then don't use an autocratic decision style.

Subordinate Information Rule. If the quality of the decision is important, and if the subordinates don't have enough information to make the decision themselves, then don't use a group decision style.

Goal Congruence Rule. If the quality of the decision is important, and subordinates' goals are different from the organization's goals, then don't use a group decision style.

Problem Structure Rule. If the quality of the decision is important, the leader doesn't have enough information to make the decision on his or her own, and the problem is unstructured, then don't use an autocratic decision style.

Decision Rules to Increase Decision Acceptance

Commitment Probability Rule. If having subordinates accept and commit to the decision is important, then don't use an autocratic decision style.

Subordinate Conflict Rule. If having subordinates accept the decision is important and critical to successful implementation, and subordinates are likely to disagree or end up in conflict over the decision, then don't use an autocratic or consultative decision style.

Commitment Requirement Rule. If having subordinates accept the decision is absolutely required for successful implementation, and subordinates share the organization's goals, then don't use an autocratic or consultative style.

Sources: Adapted from V. H. Vroom, "Leadership," in *Handbook of Industrial and Organizational Psychology*, ed. M. D. Dunnette (Chicago: Rand McNally, 1976); V. H. Vroom and A. G. Jago, *The New Leadership: Managing Participation in Organizations* (Englewood Cliffs, NJ: Prentice Hall, 1988).

the right, in which leaders share the problems with subordinates and then have the group make the decisions.

GE Aircraft Engines in Durham, North Carolina, uses a similar approach when making decisions. According to *Fast Company* magazine, "At GE/Durham, every decision is either an 'A' decision, a 'B' decision, or a 'C' decision. An 'A' decision is one that the plant manager makes herself, without consulting anyone.[67] One plant manager said, "I don't make very many of those, and when I do make one, everyone at the plant knows it. I make maybe 10 or 12 a year."[68] "B" decisions are also made by the plant manager but with input from the people affected. "C" decisions, the most common type, are made by consensus, by the people directly involved, with plenty of discussion. With "C" decisions, the view of the plant manager doesn't necessarily carry more weight than the views of those affected.[69]

14-6b Decision Quality and Acceptance

Management consultant John Canfield says, "Leaders are responsible for improving the performance of organizations. Two significant components of (a leader's) decisions are the quality of the decision and the level of buy-in associated with it. Effective leaders want them

both."[70] According to the normative decision theory, using the right degree of employee participation improves the quality of decisions and the extent to which employees accept and are committed to decisions (that is, buy-in). Exhibit 14.8 lists the decision rules that normative decision theory uses to increase the quality of a decision and the degree to which employees accept and commit to it.

The quality, leader information, subordinate information, goal congruence, and problem structure rules are used to increase decision quality. For example, the leader information rule states that if a leader doesn't have enough information to make a decision on his or her own, then the leader should not use an autocratic decision style. The commitment probability, subordinate conflict, and commitment requirement rules shown in Exhibit 14.8 are used to increase employee acceptance and commitment to decisions. For example, the commitment requirement rule says that if decision acceptance and commitment are important, and the subordinates share the organization's goals, then you shouldn't use an autocratic or consultative style. In other words, if followers want to do what's best for the company, and you need their acceptance and commitment to make a decision work, then use a group decision style and let them make the decision.

As you can see, these decision rules help leaders improve decision quality and follower acceptance and commitment by eliminating decision styles that don't fit the particular decision or situation they're facing. Normative decision theory, like path–goal theory, is situational in nature. The abstract decision rules in Exhibit 14.8 are framed as yes/no questions, which makes the process of applying these rules more concrete. These questions are shown in the decision tree displayed in Exhibit 14.9. You start at the left side of the tree and answer the first question, "How important is the technical quality of this decision?" by choosing "high" or "low." Then you continue by answering each question as you proceed along the decision tree until you get to a recommended decision style.

Let's use the model to make the decision of whether to change from private offices to open offices and cubicles. The problem sounds simple, but it is actually more complex than you might think. Follow the yellow line in Exhibit 14.9 as we work through the decision in the bottom half of the exhibit (see Problem: Change to Open Offices and Cubicles).

How well does the normative decision theory work? A prominent leadership scholar has described it as the best supported of all leadership theories.[71] In general, the more managers violate the decision rules in Exhibit 14.8, the less effective their decisions are, especially with respect to subordinate acceptance and commitment.[72]

14-7 VISIONARY LEADERSHIP

In Chapter 5, we defined a purpose statement, which is often referred to as an organizational mission or vision, as a statement of a company's purpose or reason for existing. Similarly, **visionary leadership** creates a positive image of the future that motivates organizational members and provides direction for future planning and goal setting.[73]

*Two kinds of visionary leadership are **14-7a charismatic leadership** and **14-7b transformational leadership**.*

14-7a Charismatic Leadership

Charisma is a Greek word meaning "divine gift." The ancient Greeks saw people with charisma as inspired by the gods and capable of incredible accomplishments. German sociologist Max Weber viewed charisma as a special bond between leaders and followers.[74] Weber wrote that the special qualities of charismatic leaders enable them to strongly influence followers. Weber also noted that charismatic leaders tend to emerge in times of

crisis and that the radical solutions they propose enhance the admiration that followers feel for them. In fact, charismatic leaders tend to have incredible influence over followers who may be inspired by their leaders and become fanatically devoted to them. From this perspective, charismatic leaders are often seen as larger than life.

Charismatic leaders have strong, confident, dynamic personalities that attract followers and enable the leaders to create strong bonds with their followers. Followers trust charismatic leaders, are loyal to them, and are inspired to work toward the accomplishment of the leader's vision. Followers who become devoted to charismatic leaders may go to extraordinary lengths to please them. Therefore, we can define **charismatic leadership** as the behavioral tendencies and personal characteristics of leaders that create an exceptionally strong relationship between them and their followers. Charismatic leaders also:

» articulate a clear vision for the future that is based on strongly held values or morals;

» model those values by acting in a way consistent with the vision;

» communicate high performance expectations to followers; and

» display confidence in followers' abilities to achieve the vision.[75]

Does charismatic leadership work? Studies indicate that it often does. In general, the followers of charismatic leaders are more committed and satisfied, are better performers, are more likely to trust their leaders, and simply work harder.[76] Nonetheless, charismatic leadership also has risks that are at least as large as its benefits. The problems are likely to occur with ego-driven charismatic leaders who take advantage of fanatical followers. In other words, to the detriment of themselves, their followers, and their organizations, leaders can be too charismatic.[77]

In general, there are two kinds of charismatic leaders, ethical charismatics and unethical charismatics.[78] **Ethical charismatics** provide developmental opportunities for followers,

Visionary leadership leadership that creates a positive image of the future that motivates organizational members and provides direction for future planning and goal setting

Charismatic leadership the behavioral tendencies and personal characteristics of leaders that create an exceptionally strong relationship between them and their followers

Ethical charismatics charismatic leaders who provide developmental opportunities for followers, are open to positive and negative feedback, recognize others' contributions, share information, and have moral standards that emphasize the larger interests of the group, organization, or society

Exhibit 14.9

Normative Decision Theory Tree for Determining the Level of Participation in Decision-Making

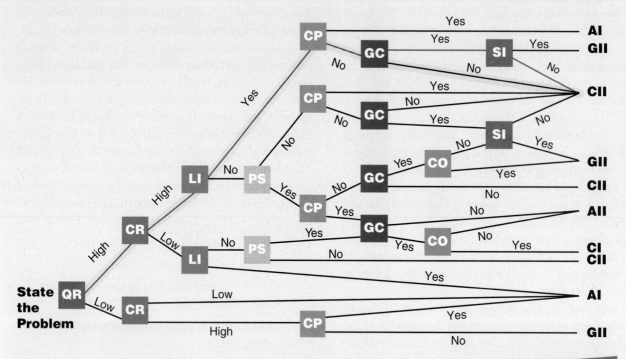

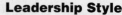

Leadership Style

PROBLEM: CHANGE TO OPEN OFFICES AND CUBICLES?

1. *Quality requirement: How important is the technical quality of this decision?* High. This question has to do with whether there are quality differences in the alternatives and whether those quality differences matter. In other words: Is there a lot at stake in this decision? People have incredibly strong reactions to giving up private offices for cubicles. While companies use open offices to increase communication, workers will see this as a loss of privacy and status. Yes, there is a lot at stake.

2. *Commitment requirement: How important is subordinate commitment to the decision?* High. Changes in offices, from private to open settings, require subordinate commitment or they fail. In fact, it's not uncommon for companies to abandon open offices after trying them.

3. *Leader's information: Do you have sufficient information to make a high-quality decision?* Yes. Let's assume that you've done your homework. Much has been written about open offices and cubicles, from how to make the change to the effects it has in companies (which are mixed, sometimes positive and sometimes negative).

4. *Commitment probability: If you were to make the decision by yourself, is it reasonably certain that your subordinate(s)*

would be committed to the decision? No. Studies of companies that change from private offices to open offices find that employees' initial reactions are almost uniformly negative. Employees are likely to be angry if you change something as personal as their offices without consulting them.

5. *Goal congruence: Do subordinates share the organizational goals to be attained in solving this problem?* Probably not. The goals that usually accompany a change to open offices are a more informal culture, better communication, and less money spent on renting or buying office space (because open offices and cubicles take less square footage than private offices), none of which will matter much to employees who are losing their private offices.

6. *CII is the answer:* With a CII, or consultative decision process, the leader shares the problem with employees as a group, obtains their ideas and suggestions, and then makes the decision, which may or may not reflect their input. So, given the answers to these questions (remember, different managers won't necessarily answer these questions the same way), the normative decision theory recommends that leaders consult with their subordinates before deciding whether to change from private offices to open offices and cubicles.

Source: "Figure 9.3, Decision-Process Flow Chart for Both Individual and Group Problems," in *Leadership and Decision-Making* (Pittsburgh: University of Pittsburgh Press, 1973), by V. H. Vroom and P. W. Yetton.

are open to positive and negative feedback, recognize others' contributions, share information, and have moral standards that emphasize the larger interests of the group, organization, or society. Leadership consultant Liz Wiseman distinguishes between two kinds of leaders, "multipliers" and "diminishers."[79] Both, she says, welcome conflict, are brutally direct, and challenge accepted wisdom.[80] But Wiseman, CEO of the **Wiseman Group**, says they have different goals. "A multiplier's goal is to light a fire that helps people think big... A diminisher uses disruption as a means of self-aggrandizement, which can lower performance."[81] She says, "Sometimes you need someone who's a bit of a wrecking ball, but we also need leaders who can draw on the capability of the team."[82] Wiseman's multiplier is an ethical charismatic. CEO John Legere, who transformed **T-Mobile** from an also-ran to the most innovative and competitive cell phone service provider, is a multiplier. Said Legere, "I'm outspoken and loud – and yes, sometimes I call out the other guys [T-Mobile's competitors] and point out their bad behavior. [But] everything I do is about one thing: inspiring people to be better and constantly pushing for innovation. It's been that way from day one, and I won't change."[83]

By contrast, **unethical charismatics** control and manipulate followers, do what is best for themselves instead of their organizations, want to hear only positive feedback, share information that is only beneficial to themselves, and have moral standards that put their interests before everyone else's. Steven Cohen, the billionaire owner of **SAC Capital Advisers**, was renowned for being acerbic and impatient with his staff of financial analysts and managers. One of his standard responses when portfolio managers couldn't answer a question about a stock was, "Do you even know how to do your f***ing job?" Once, during the first week of January, he yelled at an employee for not having come up with any good trading ideas so far that year. Cohen routinely pitted traders against each other by displaying their profits and losses in real time. He also pushed them to compete to have their picks included in his personal portfolio. Under his leadership, SAC Capital pleaded guilty to insider trading, paying $1.8 billion in fines.[84]

Because followers can become just as committed to unethical charismatics as to ethical charismatics, unethical characteristics pose a tremendous risk for companies. Professor Diane Chandler explains, "By being greatly influenced by charismatic leaders, followers are apt to agree with, feel affection for, and obey them. With charismatic leaders fostering a sense of strong identification with followers, they may

Steven Cohen, founder and chief executive officer of SAC Capital Advisors, speaks during a Robin Hood Veterans Summit in New York City.

Bloomberg/Getty Images

likewise curry followers' inordinate allegiance to them in the face of unethical or moral leadership indiscretion."[85] Indeed, one study shows that companies led by unethical charismatics are much more likely to be sued.[86]

Exhibit 14.10 shows the stark differences between ethical and unethical charismatics on several leader behaviors: exercising power, creating the vision, communicating with followers, accepting feedback, stimulating followers intellectually, developing followers, and living by moral standards. For example, ethical charismatics account for the concerns and wishes of their followers when creating a vision by having followers participate in the development of the company vision. By contrast, unethical charismatics develop a vision by themselves solely to meet their personal agendas. One unethical charismatic said, "The key thing is that it is my idea; and I am going to win with it at all costs."[87]

> **Unethical charismatics** charismatic leaders who control and manipulate followers, do what is best for themselves instead of their organizations, want to hear only positive feedback, share only information that is beneficial to themselves, and have moral standards that put their interests before everyone else's

Exhibit 14.10
Ethical and Unethical Charismatics

Charismatic Leader Behaviors	Ethical Charismatics . . .	Unethical Charismatics . . .
Exercising power	. . . use power to serve others.	. . . use power to dominate or manipulate others for personal gain.
Creating the vision	. . . allow followers to help develop the vision.	. . . are the sole source of vision, which they use to serve their personal agendas.
Communicating with followers	. . . engage in two-way communication and seek out viewpoints on critical issues.	. . . engage in one-way communication and are not open to suggestions from others.
Accepting feedback	. . . are open to feedback and willing to learn from criticism.	. . . have inflated egos, thrive on attention and admiration of sycophants, and avoid candid feedback.
Stimulating followers intellectually	. . . want followers to think and question status quo as well as leader's views.	. . . don't want followers to think but instead want uncritical acceptance of leader's ideas.
Developing followers	. . . focus on developing people with whom they interact, express confidence in them, and share recognition with others.	. . . are insensitive and unresponsive to followers' needs and aspirations.
Living by moral standards	. . . follow self-guided principles that may go against popular opinion and have three virtues: courage, a sense of fairness or justice, and integrity.	. . . follow standards only if they satisfy immediate self-interests, manipulate impressions so that others think they are doing the right thing, and use communication skills to manipulate others to support their personal agendas.

Source: J. M. Howell and B. J. Avolio, "The Ethics of Charismatic Leadership: Submission or Liberation?" *Academy of Management Executive 6*, no. 2 (1992): 43–54.

14-7b Transformational Leadership

While charismatic leadership involves articulating a clear vision, modeling values consistent with that vision, communicating high performance expectations, and establishing very strong relationships with followers, **transformational leadership** goes further by generating awareness and acceptance of a group's purpose and mission and by getting employees to see beyond their own needs and self-interest for the good of the group.[88] Like charismatic leaders, transformational leaders are visionary, but they transform their organizations by getting their followers to accomplish more than they intended and even more than they thought possible.

Transformational leaders are able to make their followers feel that they are a vital part of the organization and help them see how their jobs fit with the organization's vision. By linking individual and organizational interests, transformational leaders encourage followers to make sacrifices for the organization because they know that they will prosper when the organization prospers. **Edwards Lifesciences**, a medical technology company, connects individual and organizational interests by frequently bringing patients to its offices to "meet the employees who hand-stitched their heart valves."[89] CEO Michael Mussalem says, "It fills our employees with a tremendous amount of joy. It doesn't matter what role you might have in the company – we make the point that it takes all of us together to do this."[90]

Transformational leadership has four components: charismatic leadership or idealized influence, inspirational motivation, intellectual stimulation, and individualized consideration.[91]

Charismatic leadership or idealized influence means that transformational leaders act as role models for their followers. Because transformational leaders put others' needs ahead of their own and share risks with their

Transformational leadership leadership that generates awareness and acceptance of a group's purpose and mission and gets employees to see beyond their own needs and self-interests for the good of the group

followers, they are admired, respected, and trusted, and followers want to emulate them. When the coronavirus lockdown hit and business revenues dropped suddenly and dramatically, Disney's Chairman and former CEO Robert Iger, Front Burner Restaurants CEO Randy DeWitt, Delta Airlines CEO Ed Bastian, Qantas Airlines CEO Alan Joyce, and Yum Brands CEO David Gibbs all gave up 100 percent of their salaries to support worker salaries and benefits.[92] Among the 1,500 largest US public companies, the average reduction was 50 percent.[93] Yum Brands' David Gibbs said it "was simply the right thing to do in this unprecedented time."[94] Thus, in contrast to purely charismatic leaders (especially unethical charismatics), transformational leaders can be counted on to do the right thing and maintain high standards for ethical and personal conduct.

Inspirational motivation means that transformational leaders motivate and inspire followers by providing meaning and challenge to their work. By clearly communicating expectations and demonstrating commitment to goals, transformational leaders help followers envision future states, such as the organizational vision or mission. In turn, this leads to greater enthusiasm and optimism about the future.

Intellectual stimulation means that transformational leaders encourage followers to be creative and innovative, to question assumptions, and to look at problems and situations in new ways even if their ideas are different from those of leaders. **Airbnb's** "Project Snow White" was created after CEO and cofounder Brian Chesky read a Walt Disney biography in which storyboarding was used to plan the very first animated film, *Snow White*.[95] Chesky said, "When you have to storyboard something, the more realistic it is, the more decisions you have to make, Like, are these hosts men or women? Are they young, are they old? Where do they live? The city or the countryside? ...[Guests] show up to the house, how many bags do they have? ...At that point you start designing for stuff for a very particular

use case."[96] Airbnb teams created storyboards for the hosting process and the guest process with the intention of improving every frame or step in those processes. For example, as part of the post-a-listing step for new hosts, Airbnb can now connect new hosts to 3,000 professional photographers around the world.[97]

Individualized consideration means that transformational leaders pay special attention to followers' individual needs by creating learning opportunities, accepting and tolerating individual differences, encouraging two-way communication, and being good listeners.

Finally, a distinction needs to be drawn between transformational leadership and transactional leadership. While transformational leaders use visionary and inspirational appeals to influence followers, **transactional leadership** is based on an exchange process in which followers are rewarded for good performance and punished for poor performance. When leaders administer rewards fairly and offer followers the rewards that they want, followers will often reciprocate with effort. A problem, however, is that transactional leaders often rely too heavily on discipline or threats to bring performance up to standards. This may work in the short run, but it's much less effective in the long run. Also, as discussed in Chapters 11 and 13, many leaders and organizations have difficulty successfully linking pay practices to individual performance. As a result, studies consistently show that transformational leadership is much more effective on average than transactional leadership. In the United States, Canada, Japan, and India at all organizational levels, from first-level supervisors to upper-level executives, followers view transformational leaders as much better leaders and are much more satisfied when working for them. Furthermore, companies with transformational leaders have significantly better financial performance.[98]

> **Transactional leadership**
> leadership based on an exchange process in which followers are rewarded for good performance and punished for poor performance

15 | Managing Communication

LEARNING OUTCOMES

15-1 Explain the role that perception plays in communication and communication problems.

15-2 Describe the communication process and the various kinds of communication in organizations.

15-3 Explain how managers can manage effective one-on-one communication.

15-4 Describe how managers can manage effective organizationwide communication.

15-1 PERCEPTION AND COMMUNICATION PROBLEMS

It's estimated that managers spend over 80 percent of their day communicating with others.[1] Indeed, much of the basic management process – planning, organizing, leading, and controlling – cannot be performed without effective communication. If this weren't reason enough to study communication, consider that effective oral communication – achieved by listening, following instructions, conversing, and giving feedback – is the most important skill for college graduates who are entering the workforce.[2] **Communication** is the process of transmitting information from one person or place to another. While some bosses sugarcoat bad news, smart managers understand that effective, straightforward communication between managers and employees is essential for success.

Communication the process of transmitting information from one person or place to another

One study found that when *employees* were asked whether their supervisor gave recognition for good work, only 13 percent said their supervisor gave a pat on the back, and a mere 14 percent said their supervisor gave sincere and thorough praise. But when the *supervisors* of these employees were asked if they gave recognition for good work, 82 percent said they gave pats on the back, while 80 percent said that they gave sincere and thorough praise.[3] Given that these managers and employees worked closely together, how could they have had such different perceptions of something as simple as praise?

*Let's learn more about perception and communication problems by examining **15-1a the basic perception process, 15-1b perception problems, 15-1c how we perceive others, and 15-1d how we perceive ourselves.** We'll also consider how all of these factors make it difficult for managers to communicate effectively.*

15-1a   Basic Perception Process

As shown in Exhibit 15.1, **perception** is the process by which individuals attend to, organize, interpret, and retain information from their environments. And because communication is the process of transmitting information from one person or place to another, perception is obviously a key part of communication. Yet perception can also be a key obstacle to communication.

As people perform their jobs, they are exposed to a wide variety of informational stimuli such as emails, direct conversations with the boss or coworkers, rumors heard over lunch, stories about the company in the press, or a video broadcast of a speech from the CEO to all employees. Just being exposed to an informational stimulus, however, is no guarantee that an individual will pay attention or attend to that stimulus. People experience stimuli through their own **perceptual filters** – the personality-, psychology-, or experience-based differences that influence them to ignore or pay attention to particular stimuli. Because of filtering, people exposed to the same information will often disagree about what they saw or heard. As shown in Exhibit 15.1, perceptual filters affect each

> **Perception** the process by which individuals attend to, organize, interpret, and retain information from their environments
>
> **Perceptual filters** the personality-, psychology-, or experience-based differences that influence people to ignore or pay attention to particular stimuli

Exhibit 15.1
Basic Perception Process

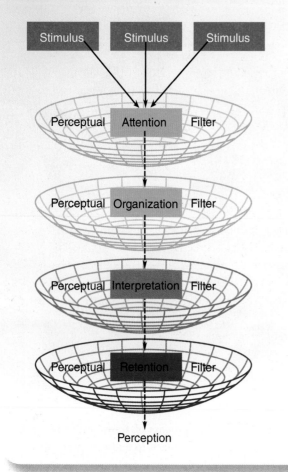

part of the *perception process*: attention, organization, interpretation, and retention.

Attention is the process of noticing, or becoming aware of, particular stimuli. Because of perceptual filters, we attend to some stimuli and not others. For instance, a study at the University of Illinois asked viewers to watch people in black shirts and white shirts toss a basketball back and forth and to count the number of times someone in a black shirt tossed the basketball. Because their perceptual filters had narrowed to track the activities of people in black shirts, half of the viewers did not notice when the experimenters had someone in a gorilla suit walk through the midst of the people tossing the basketball back and forth.[4] *Organization* is the process of incorporating new information (from the stimuli that you notice) into your existing knowledge. Because of perceptual filters, we are more likely to incorporate new knowledge that is consistent with what we already know or believe. *Interpretation* is the process of attaching

meaning to new knowledge. Because of perceptual filters, our preferences and beliefs strongly influence the meaning we attach to new information (e.g., "This decision must mean that top management supports our project"). Finally, *retention* is the process of remembering interpreted information. Retention affects what we recall and commit to memory after we have perceived something. Of course, perceptual filters affect retention as much as they do organization and interpretation.

For instance, imagine that you miss the first 10 minutes of a TV show and turn on your TV to see two people talking to each other in a living room. As they talk, they walk around the room, picking up and putting down various items. Some items, such as a ring, watch, and credit card, appear to be valuable, while others appear to be drug-related, such as a water pipe for smoking marijuana. In fact, this situation was depicted on videotape in a well-known study that manipulated people's perceptual filters.[5] Before watching the video, one-third of the study participants were told that the people were there to rob the apartment. Another third were told that police were on their way to conduct a drug raid and that the people in the apartment were getting rid of incriminating evidence. The remaining third of the participants were told that the people were simply waiting for a friend.

After watching the video, participants were asked to list all of the objects from the video that they could remember. Not surprisingly, the different perceptual filters (theft, drug raid, and waiting for a friend) affected what the participants attended to, how they organized the information, how they interpreted it, and ultimately which objects they remembered. Participants who thought a theft was in progress were more likely to remember the valuable objects in the video. Those who thought a drug raid was imminent were more likely to remember the drug-related objects. There was no discernible pattern to the items remembered by those who thought that the people in the video were simply waiting for a friend.

In short, because of perception and perceptual filters, people are likely to pay attention to different things, organize and interpret what they pay attention to differently, and, finally, remember things differently. Consequently, even when people are exposed to the same communications (e.g., organizational announcements, discussions with managers or customers), they can end up with very different perceptions and understandings. This is why communication can be so difficult and frustrating for managers. Let's review some of the communication problems created by perception and perceptual filters.

BROKEN RIBS, A PUNCTURED LUNG, AND A BRONZE MEDAL: THE POWER OF PERCEPTION

While warming up for her race at the winter Olympic Games, Slovenian cross-country skier Petra Majdic fell 10 feet to a rocky creek, breaking one ski and both ski poles. Despite shrieking in pain with every breath, she asked the onsite doctor, "Can I go?" He said, "I don't know, but it looks like everything is OK." After performing well enough to reach the quarterfinals, semifinals, and the finals, she won the bronze medal. At the hospital that night, doctors confirmed four broken ribs and a punctured lung, which collapsed, ending her Olympics. Veteran Canadian skier Sara Renner said, "The fact she pulled off a bronze medal…, she was digging into something superhuman there. I can't imagine how she was able to do it." Perception is a powerful influence on human behavior.

Alexander Hassenstein/Bongarts/Getty Images

Source: A. Hutchinson, "The Mental Tricks of Athletic Endurance," *Wall Street Journal,* February 2, 2018, accessed June 15, 2020, www.wsj.com/articles/the-mental-tricks-of-athletic-endurance-1517583851; M. Beamish, "Slovenia's Petra Majdic's determination, Grit Wins Her Olympic Cross-Country Bronze," *Vancouver Sun,* February 18, 2010, accessed June 15, 2020, www.vancouversun.com/sports/Olympic+cross+country+Slovenia+Petra+Majdic+determination+grit+wins+bronze/2583221/story.html.

15-1b Perception Problems

Perception creates communication problems for organizations because people exposed to the same communication and information can end up with completely different ideas and understandings. Two of the most common perception problems in organizations are selective perception and closure.

At work or when working from home, we are constantly bombarded with sensory stimuli: phones ringing, the dog barking or children playing loudly in the background, computers dinging as new email arrives, coworkers, spouses, or roommates calling our names, and so forth. As limited processors of information, we cannot possibly notice, receive, and interpret all of this information. As a result, we attend to and accept some stimuli but screen out and reject others. This isn't a random process.

Selective perception is the tendency to notice and accept objects and information consistent with our values, beliefs, and expectations, while ignoring or screening out inconsistent information. For example, in a research study, pedestrians are stopped on a sidewalk by a man who asks for directions. Ten seconds into giving directions, two people carrying a door walk between the man who asked for directions, on the left, and the pedestrian, on the right. When the door goes by, the man who asked for directions quickly switches places with one of the young men carrying the door. The pedestrian, however, doesn't see this switch because the door blocks the view. Like the invisible gorilla example cited earlier, 50 percent of the time people don't even notice that they're talking to a different man and go right back to giving directions. Selective perception is one of the biggest contributors to misunderstandings and miscommunication, because it strongly influences what people see, hear, read, and understand at work.[6]

After we have initial information about a person, event, or process, **closure** is the tendency to fill in the gaps where information is missing, that is, to assume that what we don't know is consistent with what we already do know. If employees are told that budgets must be cut by 10 percent, they may automatically assume that 10 percent of employees will lose their jobs, too, even if that isn't the case. Not surprisingly, when closure occurs, people sometimes fill in the gaps with inaccurate information, which can create problems for organizations.

15-1c Perceptions of Others

Attribution theory says that we all have a basic need to understand and explain the causes of other people's behavior.[7] In other words, we need to know why people do what they do. According to attribution theory, we use two general reasons or attributions to explain people's behavior: an *internal attribution,* in which behavior

Selective perception the tendency to notice and accept objects and information consistent with our values, beliefs, and expectations, while ignoring or screening inconsistent information

Closure the tendency to fill in gaps of missing information by assuming that what we don't know is consistent with what we already know

Attribution theory the theory that we all have a basic need to understand and explain the causes of other people's behavior

Exhibit 15.2
Defensive Bias and Fundamental Attribution Error

The Coworker

How can they expect us to make sales if they don't have hot-selling inventory in stock? We can't sell what's not there.

The Employee

That's the third sale I've lost this week because company management doesn't keep enough inventory in stock. I can't sell it if we don't have it.

The Boss

That new employee isn't very good. I may have to get rid of him if his sales don't improve.

Defensive Bias—
the tendency for people to perceive themselves as personally and situationally similar to someone who is having difficulty or trouble

Defensive Bias—
the tendency for people to perceive themselves as personally and situationally similar to someone who is having difficulty or trouble

Fundamental Attribution Error—
the tendency to ignore external causes of behavior and to attribute other people's actions to internal causes

is thought to be voluntary or under the control of the individual, and an *external attribution*, in which behavior is thought to be involuntary and outside of the control of the individual.

If you've ever seen someone changing a flat tire on the side of the road and thought to yourself, "What rotten luck – somebody's having a bad day," you perceived the person through an external attribution known as the defensive bias. The **defensive bias** is the tendency for people to perceive themselves as personally and situationally similar to someone who is having difficulty or trouble.[8] When we identify with the person in a situation, we tend to use external attributions (i.e., features related to the situation) to explain the person's behavior. For instance, because flat tires are common, it's easy to perceive ourselves in that same situation and put the blame on external causes such as running over a nail.

Now, let's assume a different situation, this time in the workplace:

A utility company worker puts a ladder

on a utility pole and then climbs up to do his work. As he's doing his work, he falls from the ladder and seriously injures himself.[9]

Answer this question: Who or what caused the accident? If you thought, "It's not the worker's fault. Anybody could fall from a tall ladder," then you interpreted the incident with a defensive bias in which you saw yourself as personally and situationally similar to someone who is having difficulty or trouble. In other words, you made an external attribution by attributing the accident to an external cause or some feature of the situation.

Most accident investigations, however, initially blame the worker (i.e., an internal attribution) and not the situation (i.e., an external attribution). Typically, 60 to 80 percent of workplace accidents each year are blamed on "operator error," that is, on the employees themselves. In reality, more complete investigations usually show that workers are responsible for only 30 to 40 percent of all workplace accidents.[10] Why are accident investigators so quick to blame workers? The reason is that they are committing the **fundamental attribution error**, which is the tendency to ignore external causes of behavior and to attribute other people's actions to internal causes.[11] In other words, when investigators examine the possible

Defensive bias the tendency for people to perceive themselves as personally and situationally similar to someone who is having difficulty or trouble

Fundamental attribution error the tendency to ignore external causes of behavior and to attribute other people's actions to internal causes

causes of an accident, they're much more likely to assume that the accident is a function of the person and not the situation.

Which attribution – the defensive bias or the fundamental attribution error – are workers likely to make when something goes wrong? In general, as shown in Exhibit 15.2, employees and coworkers are more likely to perceive events and explain behavior from a defensive bias. Because they do the work themselves and see themselves as similar to others who make mistakes, have accidents, or are otherwise held responsible for things that go wrong at work, employees and coworkers are likely to attribute problems to external causes such as failed machinery, poor support, or inadequate training. By contrast, because they are typically observers (who don't do the work themselves) and see themselves as situationally and personally different from workers, managers tend to commit the fundamental attribution error and blame mistakes, accidents, and other things that go wrong on workers (i.e., an internal attribution).

Consequently, workers and managers in most workplaces can be expected to take different views when things go wrong. Therefore, the defensive bias, which is typically used by workers, and the fundamental attribution error, which is typically made by managers, together present a significant challenge to effective communication and understanding in organizations.

15-1d Self-Perception

The **self-serving bias** is the tendency to overestimate our value by attributing successes to ourselves (internal causes) and attributing failures to others or the environment (external causes).[12] The self-serving bias can make it especially difficult for managers to talk to employees about performance problems. In general, people have a need to maintain a positive self-image. This need is so strong that when people seek feedback at work, they typically want verification of their worth (rather than information about performance deficiencies) or assurance that mistakes or problems weren't their fault.[13] People can become defensive and emotional when managerial communication threatens their positive self-image. They quit listening, and communication becomes ineffective. In the second half of the chapter, which focuses on improving communication, we'll explain ways in which managers can minimize this self-serving bias and improve effective one-on-one communication with employees.

15-2 KINDS OF COMMUNICATION

There are many kinds of communication – formal, informal, coaching/counseling, and nonverbal – but they all follow the same fundamental process.

*Let's learn more about the different kinds of communication by examining **15-2a the communication process, 15-2b formal communication channels, 15-2c informal communication channels, 15-2d coaching and counseling, or one-on-one communication,** and **15-2e nonverbal communication.***

15-2a The Communication Process

At the beginning of this chapter, we defined *communication* as the process of transmitting information from one person or place to another. Exhibit 15.3 displays a model of the communication process and its major components: the sender

Self-serving bias the tendency to overestimate our value by attributing successes to ourselves (internal causes) and attributing failures to others or the environment (external causes)

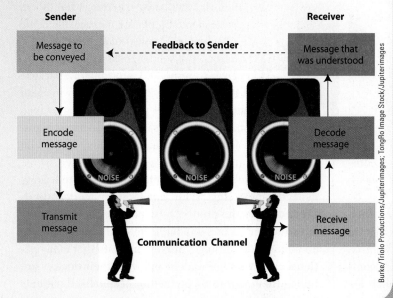

Exhibit 15.3
The Interpersonal Communication Process

Sender | Receiver

Message to be conveyed → ← Feedback to Sender → Message that was understood

Encode message → Decode message

Transmit message → Receive message

NOISE   NOISE   NOISE

Communication Channel

Burke/Triolo Productions/Jupiterimages; TongRo Image Stock/Jupiterimages

(message to be conveyed, encoding the message, transmitting the message); the receiver (receiving message, decoding the message, and the message that was understood); and noise, which interferes with the communication process.

The communication process begins when a *sender* thinks of a message he or she wants to convey to another person. For example, you had a flu shot and a pneumonia shot, and yet you've had an unexplainable fever for nine days, so you visit the doctor. The doctor asks a series of questions regarding your appetite, fatigue, tenderness in your abdomen, and whether your fever comes and goes during the day. The doctor, the sender, runs some tests and then has you, the receiver, come back the next day to give you a diagnosis and recommend a treatment.

The next step is to encode the message. **Encoding** means putting a message into a written, verbal, or symbolic form that can be recognized and understood by the receiver. In our example, this means the doctor has to take the technical language of medicine and lab test results and communicate it in a way that patients can understand. This is not easy to do. The difficulty of doing this well is compounded by the average doctor's visit lasting less than 15 minutes. And, while your visit might be 15 minutes, you're not getting a full 15 minutes to talk to the doctor. Indeed, one study showed that doctors give patients 11 seconds on average to describe their medical issue before cutting them off to comment or ask questions.[14] Not surprisingly, 60 percent of patients feel as if their doctor is rushing through their exam. Despite this, 58 percent of surveyed patients say their doctors do a good job of explaining things to them. But, as we'll see in a few steps, that doesn't mean communication has been effective.[15]

The sender then *transmits the message* via *communication channels*. The traditional communication channel for doctors and patients is face-to-face discussion in the doctor's office. Ironically, though, the introduction of electronic health records may be interfering with that. Dr. Rita Redberg, at the University of California San Francisco Medical Center, says, "The recent introduction of electronic health records in the office, for example, requires many doctors to spend much of a patient exam looking at a computer screen instead of the patient in order to record information." Doctors now spend 45 percent of their day on the computer, making as many as 4,000 digital clicks per day in electronic health records.[16] Not surprisingly, studies show that one-third of the time, doctors forget to give patients critical information. Another critical study found that across 30 different medical conditions, patients only received all the information they needed from their doctors about 55 percent of the time.[17] Why? In an average 15-minute doctor's visit, the doctor will spend just 1.3 minutes telling the patient about his or her condition, prognosis, and treatment. Furthermore, as we will see, that 1.3 minutes is filled with information that is too complex and technical for the typical patient to understand.[18]

With some communication channels such as the telephone, face-to-face communication, or video-conferencing, the sender receives immediate feedback, whereas with others such as email (or text messages and file attachments), voice mail, memos, and letters, the sender must wait for the receiver to respond. Unfortunately, because of technical difficulties (e.g., fax down, dead battery in the cell phone, inability to read email attachments) or people-based transmission problems (e.g., forgetting to pass on the message), messages aren't always transmitted.

If the message is transmitted and received, however, the next step is for the receiver to decode it. **Decoding** is the process by which the receiver translates the verbal or symbolic form of the message into an understood message. Surveys indicate that many patients clearly do not understand what their doctors are telling them. Up to 85 percent of hospitalized patients

FEEDBACK

Ditty_about_summer/Shutterstock.com

Encoding putting a message into a written, verbal, or symbolic form that can be recognized and understood by the receiver

Decoding the process by which the receiver translates the written, verbal, or symbolic form of a message into an understood message

don't even know the name of the doctor in charge of their treatment. As many as 58 percent don't know why they were admitted to the hospital. Likewise, in a typical 15-minute doctor's appointment, half of patients will leave without understanding what their doctor has told them to do to get better.[19] Unfortunately, even when patients seem to understand what their doctors are telling them in their 15-minute visit, it turns out that they immediately forget 80 percent of that medical information, and then half of what they do remember is wrong![20]

The last step of the communication process occurs when the receiver gives the sender feedback. **Feedback to sender** is a return message to the sender that indicates the receiver's understanding of the message (of what the receiver was supposed to know, to do, or not to do). Feedback makes senders aware of possible miscommunications and enables them to continue communicating until the receiver understands the intended message. Because of the difficulties of communicating complex medical information in too little time, many doctors now employ the "teach-back" method at the end of a patient visit, where they ask patients to explain in their own words what they've heard the doctor say regarding their problem (diagnosis), whether they'll get better (prognosis), and what the patient is supposed to do after they leave the doctor's office (i.e., treatment plan and managing medications).[21] Even so, much progress needs to be made, as about half of patients are not even asked if they have questions.[22]

Unfortunately, feedback doesn't always occur in the communication process. Complacency and overconfidence about the ease and simplicity of communication can lead senders and receivers to simply assume that they share a common understanding of the message and, consequently, to not use feedback to improve the effectiveness of their communication. This is a serious mistake, especially as messages and feedback are always transmitted with and against a background of noise. Part of the background noise in medicine is how well medical information is communicated between medical professionals. After all, medicine is a "team sport" involving various doctors, physician assistants, nurses, and other care professionals for each patient. Medical mistakes kill an estimated 5,200 people per year, and a large percentage of those deaths are caused by miscommunication that occurs when patients are transferred from one set of caregivers to another – for instance, the night-shift nurses not communicating key information to the day-shift nurses, or one doctor not being aware

of the diagnosis and treatment plan of another doctor on a case.[23]

Noise is anything that interferes with the transmission of the intended message. Noise can occur in any of the following situations:

» The sender isn't sure what message to communicate.

» The message is not clearly encoded.

» The wrong communication channel is chosen.

» The message is not received or decoded properly.

» The receiver doesn't have the experience or time to understand the message.

Emotional outbursts are an often-unrecognized type of noise. Whether yelling, crying, sulking, or table pounding, strong emotions interfere with the transmission of intended messages. The outburst itself, however, is a signal that what's being discussed touches strongly held beliefs or values. The first step in addressing noise related to strong emotions is spotting early indicators, such as body language not matching words. Acknowledge the difficulty of the issue, and then ask them to share their views. Next, listen to the response, and ask follow-up questions. Finally, work toward resolution by helping them articulate their core issues.[24] We'll cover listening and asking questions in greater detail in Section 15-2d on coaching and counseling.

Jargon, which is vocabulary particular to a profession or group, is another form of noise that interferes with communication in the workplace. When *Bloomberg* reporter Brandon Presser spent a week as a cruise director on **Royal Caribbean**'s largest ship, he learned code words (jargon) that crew members used but passengers would not:

A "30–30" means the crew is asking maintenance to clean up a mess; three times during my stint I called in a "PVI" (public vomiting incident). An "Alpha" is a medical emergency, a "Bravo" is a fire, and "Kilo" is a request for all personnel to report to their emergency posts, which happens in the event of, say, a necessary evacuation. Be wary of "Echo," which is called if the ship is starting to

Feedback to sender in the communication process, a return message to the sender that indicates the receiver's understanding of the message

Noise anything that interferes with the transmission of the intended message

Jargon vocabulary particular to a profession or group that interferes with communication in the workplace

drift, or "Oscar," which means someone's gone overboard. A crew member told me he's had only four or five Oscars in 10 years of cruising.[25]

Medical jargon is a common cause of misunderstandings between doctors and patients. Brian Jack, chief of family medicine at Boston Medical Center, says, "We throw papers and throw words at patients. It is crazy to think they would understand."[26] The result, says Dr. David Langer, chief of neurosurgery at Lenox Hill Hospital in New York City, is that patients, "would go home and call back and say they didn't understand, and then ask me the same questions . . . Doctors often do a terrible job at educating their patients."[27] To combat this problem, Dr. Langer and his colleagues have begun using digital videos to explain computed tomography (CT) scans and magnetic resonance imaging (MRIs), as well as to provide detailed post-visit medical instructions. While preparing for an upcoming surgery, Emily Monato watched the video of her brain MRI several times to better "grasp these big chunks of information."[28] She had her children, father, and friends watch it, too.

15-2b Formal Communication Channels

An organization's **formal communication channel**, is the system of official channels that carry organizationally approved messages and information. Organizational objectives, rules, policies, procedures, instructions, commands, and requests for information are all transmitted via the formal communication system or channel. There are three formal communication channels: downward communication, upward communication, and horizontal communication.[29]

Downward communication flows from higher to lower levels in an organization. Downward communication is used to issue orders down the organizational hierarchy, to give organizational members job-related information, to give managers and workers performance reviews from upper managers, and to clarify organizational objectives and goals.[30] Michael Beer, professor emeritus at Harvard Business School, says, "You can never overcommunicate. When you think you've

Formal communication channel the system of official channels that carry organizationally approved messages and information

Downward communication communication that flows from higher to lower levels in an organization

Upward communication communication that flows from lower to higher levels in an organization

Horizontal communication communication that flows among managers and workers who are at the same organizational level

Marc Benioff ✔
@Benioff

〔 Follow 〕 ∨

My favorite internal salesforce group is Airing of Grievances! #salesforce1selfie

Airing of Grievances
4,037 Members · Public · Active

● ● ●

Salesforce.com CEO Marc Benioff encourages upward communication by regularly participating in the "Airing of Grievances" chat group.

communicated well, go out three or four more times and communicate again."[31] At 500+ Apple Stores around the world, 70,000 employees start each day with the Hello apps. Former vice president of retail Angela Ahrendts explains that Hello, which is a means of downward communication from Ahrendts and her retail store leadership team, briefs employees on the "need to knows" of the day in terms of new products or promotions.[32]

Upward communication flows from lower levels to higher levels in an organization. Upward communication is used to give higher-level managers feedback about operations, issues, and problems; to help higher-level managers assess organizational performance and effectiveness; to encourage lower-level managers and employees to participate in organizational decision-making; and to give those at lower levels the chance to share their concerns with higher-level authorities. Salesforce.com, the largest customer relationship marketing platform in the world, is used by companies to find, manage, and close more sales leads and to better manage and monitor existing customer relationships. CEO and founder Marc Benioff and his senior leadership team encourage upward communication by regularly participating in the "Airing of Grievances" chat group that is open to everyone in the company.[33] Salesforce's Jody Kohner, vice president of employee marketing and engagement, says that Airing of Grievances is based on a communication philosophy of "'bring it out into the open, let's talk about it and solve it' – because that's what the world's most innovative companies do, they solve problems."[34]

Horizontal communication flows among managers and workers who are at the same organizational level, such as when a day shift nurse comes in at 7:30 a.m. for a half-hour discussion with the midnight nurse supervisor who leaves at 8:00 a.m. Horizontal communication helps facilitate coordination and cooperation between different parts of a company and allows coworkers to share relevant information. It also helps people at the same level resolve conflicts and solve problems without involving high levels of management. Many hospitals now use bedside shift reports for horizontal communication during shift changes. Both nurses, one leaving and the other coming on, discuss the patient's status at their bedside with family members present. Beverly Johnson, CEO of the Institute for Patient-and-Family-Centered Care, says bedside shift reports "ensure that complete and accurate information is shared and there is mutual understanding of the care plan and other priorities."[35] Shift reports usually take three to seven minutes per patient and nurses typically hand off three to six patients per shift.

In general, what can managers do to improve formal communication? First, decrease reliance on downward communication. Second, increase chances for upward communication by increasing personal contact with lower-level managers and workers. Third, encourage much better use of horizontal communication.

15-2c Informal Communication Channels

An organization's **informal communication channel**, sometimes called the **grapevine**, is the transmission of messages from employee to employee outside of formal communication channels. The grapevine arises out of curiosity, that is, the need to know what is going on in an organization and how it might affect you or others.[36] To satisfy this curiosity, employees need a consistent supply of relevant, accurate, in-depth information about what is going on in the company and why. Some companies using tracking technology to measure how well informal communication functions in their organizations and how it can be improved. As it prepared to move to new offices, BCG, a global consulting firm, had one in five employees wear badges that tracked where they went in the office and who they talked to (but not their conversations). BCG managing partner Ross Love, who headed the research, said the firm learned that employees were spending too much time with their bosses and subordinates, thus hurting cross-team communication. However, employees who spoke to a wider variety of people within the office spent five fewer hours in meetings each week because, he thinks, they were obtaining and sharing information much more effectively – just as informal grapevines should.[37] As a result of what BCG learned, it created a town-square lounge in its new offices, offering free breakfast, lunch, and snacks to increase informal interactions and reduce formal meetings.[38]

Grapevines arise out of informal communication networks such as the gossip or cluster chains shown in

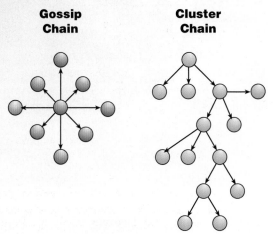

Exhibit 15.4
Grapevine Communication Networks

Gossip Chain   **Cluster Chain**

Source: K. Davis and J. W. Newstrom, *Human Behavior at Work: Organizational Behavior*, 8th ed. (New York: McGraw-Hill, 1989).

Exhibit 15.4. In a *gossip chain*, one highly connected individual shares information with many other managers and workers. By contrast, in a *cluster chain*, numerous people simply tell a few of their friends. The result in both cases is that information flows freely and quickly through the organization.

Some believe that grapevines are a waste of employees' time, that they promote gossip and rumors that fuel political speculation, and that they are sources of highly unreliable, inaccurate information. Yet studies clearly show that grapevines are highly accurate sources of information for a number of reasons.[39] First, because grapevines typically carry "juicy" information that is interesting and timely, information spreads rapidly. During **Allstate**'s annual Leaders Forum, a gathering of 2,000 agents and employees, CEO Thomas Wilson announced plans for reducing the company's sales force and changing sales commission rates. Later that evening, a group of employees were at the hotel bar, complaining about the changes and about Wilson, when the president of Allstate's home and auto insurance division, was allegedly overheard using two expletives in reference to Wilson. By the next day, nearly all conference attendees had heard the critical remarks. The president of that division was abruptly let go just a few weeks later.[40]

Second, because information is typically spread by face-to-face conversation, receivers can send feedback to make sure they understand the message that is being communicated. This reduces

Informal communication channel (grapevine) the transmission of messages from employee to employee outside of formal communication channels

There is a fine line between news and gossip. At some point, you might find yourself a target of the rumor mill.

misunderstandings and increases accuracy. Third, because most of the information in a company moves along the grapevine rather than through formal communication channels, people can usually verify the accuracy of information by checking it out with others.

What can managers do to manage organizational grapevines? The very worst thing they can do is withhold information or try to punish those who share information with others. The grapevine abhors a vacuum, so rumors and anxiety will flourish in the absence of information from company management. Why does this occur? According to workplace psychologist Nicholas DiFonzo, "The main focus of rumor is to figure out the truth. It's the group trying to make sense of something that's important to them."[41] A better strategy is to embrace the grapevine and keep employees informed about possible changes and strategies. Failure to do so will just make things worse. And, in addition to using the grapevine to communicate with others, managers should not overlook the grapevine as a tremendous source of valuable information and feedback. In fact, research shows that, contrary to popular belief, grapevines are fast, accurate, and focused on information more than gossip.[42]

15-2d Coaching and Counseling: One-on-One Communication

When the **Wyatt Company** surveyed 531 US companies undergoing major changes and restructuring, it asked the CEOs, "If you could go back and change one thing, what would it be?" The answer: "The way we communicated with our employees." The CEOs said that instead of flashy videos, printed materials, or formal meetings, they would make greater use of one-on-one communication, especially with employees' immediate supervisors instead of with higher-level executives whom employees didn't know.[43]

Coaching and counseling are two kinds of one-on-one communication. **Coaching** is communicating with someone for the direct purpose of improving the person's on-the-job performance or behavior.[44] Managers tend to make several mistakes when coaching employees. First, they wait for a problem to arise before coaching. Why? Because similar to performance appraisals, most managers also dislike giving employees feedback. Peggy Klaus, an executive trainer, says that managers "worry that the person will go to HR and get into a big kerfuffle."[45] When she told an executive she was working with that he needed to give employees more feedback, he responded, "I'd rather have a colonoscopy."[46] Indeed, a survey of 616 managers found that 69 percent are uncomfortable communicating with employees and that 37 percent are distressed about criticizing performance when they fear that employees will respond badly to the feedback.[47]

Second, when mistakes *are* made, managers wait much too long before talking to the employee about the problem. Management professor Ray Hilgert said, "A manager must respond as soon as possible after an incident of poor performance. Don't bury your head. . . . When employees are told nothing, they assume everything is okay."[48] Jack Welch, who was CEO at GE for two decades, said, "I've spoken to more than 500,000 people around the world, and I always ask audiences, 'How many of you know where you stand in your organization?'" He said, "Typically no more than 10 percent raise their hands. That's criminal! As a manager, you owe candor to your people. They must not be guessing about what the organization thinks of them. My experience is that most employees appreciate this reality check, and today's millennials practically demand it."[49] In short, said Welch, "You have no right to be a leader if someone who works for you doesn't know where they stand."[50] So coach your employees about their job performance.

Coaching communicating with someone for the direct purpose of improving the person's on-the-job performance or behavior

> When one executive was told that he needed to give employees more feedback, he responded, "I'd rather have a colonoscopy."

In contrast to coaching, **counseling** is communicating with someone about non-job-related issues such as stress, child care, health issues, retirement planning, or legal issues that may be affecting or interfering with the person's performance. But counseling does not mean that managers should try to be clinicians, even though an estimated 20 percent of employees are dealing with personal problems at any one time. Dana Kiel, regional director in Account Management at Magellan Health, says, "We call it the quicksand. If you're a good supervisor, you do care about your employees, but it's not your job to be a therapist."[51]

Instead, managers should discuss specific performance problems, listen if the employee chooses to share personal issues, and then recommend that the employee call the company's *Employee Assistance Program (EAP)*. EAPs are typically free when provided as part of a company's benefit package. In emergencies or times of crisis, EAPs can offer immediate counseling and support; they can also provide referrals to organizations and professionals that can help employees and their family members address personal issues. On the first day of her new job, Wendy Wolfson was called to pick up her first grader from school. Worried she might have to quit unless she could find child care, Wolfson called her employer's EAP for help with this problem.

Despite their proven effectiveness and a wide variety of assistance services (including mental health, substance abuse, financial counseling, and elder care services), less than 10 percent of employees use EAPs.[52] Christopher Calvert, Sibson Consulting's vice president for health, says, "Usage is abysmal. Most companies aren't communicating their EAPs well. It wouldn't occur to employees to call."[53] Employees, like Wendy Wolfson, who use EAPs, value them. A study of nearly 25,000 employees found that when employees used EAPs for personal problems, absenteeism dropped 27 percent while work engagement increased 8 percent and life satisfaction rose 22 percent.[54]

15-2e Nonverbal Communication

Nonverbal communication is any communication that doesn't involve words. Nonverbal communication almost always accompanies verbal communication and may

Consultant Suzanne Bates says that some of her CEO clients check their phones so much during meetings, "it's the equivalent of not showing up for half of the meeting."

either support and reinforce the verbal message or contradict it. The importance of nonverbal communication is well established. Researchers have estimated that as much as 93 percent of any message is transmitted nonverbally, with 55 percent coming from body language and facial expressions, and 38 percent coming from the tone and pitch of the voice.[55] Because many nonverbal cues are unintentional, receivers often consider nonverbal communication to be a more accurate representation of what senders are thinking and feeling than the words they use.

Kinesics and paralanguage are two kinds of nonverbal communication.[56] **Kinesics** (from the Greek word *kinesis*, meaning "movement") are movements of the body and face.[57] These movements include arm and hand gestures, facial expressions, eye contact, folding arms, crossing legs, and leaning toward or away from another person. For example, people tend to avoid eye contact when they are embarrassed or unsure of the message they are sending. Crossed arms or legs usually indicate defensiveness or that the person is not receptive to the message or the sender. Also, people tend to smile frequently when they are seeking someone's approval.

It turns out that kinesics play an incredibly

Counseling communicating with someone about non-job-related issues that may be affecting or interfering with the person's performance

Nonverbal communication any communication that doesn't involve words

Kinesics movements of the body and face

Monkey Business Images/Shutterstock.com

important role in communication. One of the most powerful ways is *mirroring*, in which people in conversations mimic or mirror physical gestures, facial expressions, or pitch and tone of voice. Brain scanning studies indicate that when mirroring occurs during conversations, peoples' brains react in similar positive ways at the same time. Mirroring, while usually done unconsciously, can be used intentionally by managers as a positive nonverbal behavior. David Hoffied, author of *The Science of Selling*, says, "It's not something you do to someone. It's something you do with someone. The very process of mirroring will help you keep your focus where it should be – on the other person."[58]

Kinesics provide clues about people's true feelings, over and above what they say (or don't say). Unfortunately, not making or maintaining eye contact is an increasingly frequent and negative occurrence in today's workplace. Consultant Suzanne Bates, author of *Speak Like a CEO*, says that some of her CEO clients check their phones so much during appointments that "it's the equivalent of not showing up for half of the meeting." And that, she says, breeds resentment in others who think, "I'm just as busy as the CEO. I just have different things to juggle."[59]

In fact, a survey of business professionals found that strong majorities think it is inappropriate to answer phone calls (86 percent) or write texts or emails (84 percent) in meetings or at business lunches (66 percent). The kinesics related to checking smartphones in these situations communicate a lack of respect, attention, listening, and self-control.[60] United Wholesale Mortgage's CEO, Mat Ishbia also tells his executive team and company managers not to check their phones as they walk the halls to and from meetings. "Don't act like we're too important to say hello. Make eye contact with people."[61]

Paralanguage includes the pitch, rate, tone, volume, and speaking pattern (use of silences, pauses, or hesitations) of one's voice. When people are unsure of what to say, for example, they tend to decrease their communication effectiveness by speaking softly. When people are nervous, they tend to speak faster and louder. How much does paralanguage matter? A study in which 1,000 people listened to 120 different speeches found that the tone of the speaker's voice accounted for 23 percent of the difference in listener's evaluations of the speech, compared to speech content, which accounted for only 11 percent.[62] So paralanguage was twice as important as what was actually said.

Paralanguage the pitch, rate, tone, volume, and speaking pattern (i.e., use of silences, pauses, or hesitations) of one's voice

Communication medium the method used to deliver an oral or written message

Call centers have begun using Cogito software, which monitors the paralanguage of customers and agents. At the call center for insurer **MetLife**, a coffee cup appears on agents' screens when their voice tone turns less than positive. But, it also helps call agents monitor the emotion shown in caller's voices. MetLife's Emily Baker says, "If a call becomes not so positive, it lets the associate to know to offer a little bit of hope" to customers.[63] Cogito also tracks whether agents talk to quickly, how long callers are silent, or how often customers and agents talk over each other.

In short, because nonverbal communication is so informative, especially when it contradicts verbal communication, managers need to learn how to monitor and control their nonverbal behaviors.

15-3 MANAGING ONE-ON-ONE COMMUNICATION

When it comes to improving communication, managers face two primary tasks, managing one-on-one communication and managing organizationwide communication.

On average, first-line managers spend 57 percent of their time with people, middle managers spend 63 percent of their time directly with people, and top managers spend as much as 78 percent of their time dealing with people.[64] These numbers make it clear that managers spend a great deal of time in one-on-one communication with others.

Let's learn more about managing one-on-one communication by reading how to 15-3a choose the right communication medium, 15-3b be a good listener, and 15-3c give effective feedback.

15-3a Choosing the Right Communication Medium

Sometimes messages are poorly communicated simply because they are delivered using the wrong **communication medium**, which is the method used to deliver a message. For example, the wrong communication medium is being used when an employee returns from lunch, picks up the note left on her office chair, and learns she has been fired. The wrong communication medium is also being used when an employee pops into your office every 10 minutes with a simple request. (An email or text message would be better.)

There are two general kinds of communication media: oral and written communication. *Oral communication* includes face-to-face interactions and group meetings through telephone calls, videoconferencing, or any other means of sending and receiving spoken messages. Studies show that managers generally prefer oral communication over written because it provides the opportunity to ask questions about parts of the message that they don't understand. Oral communication is also a rich communication medium because it allows managers to receive and assess the nonverbal communication that accompanies spoken messages (i.e., body language, facial expressions, and the voice characteristics associated with paralanguage). While videoconferencing via Zoom, Microsoft Teams, and Google Chat exploded because of the sudden shift to working-from-home caused by the coronavirus, face-to-face meetings are often the richest oral communication medium.

A&E Network executive Mel Berning travels two weeks a month, and when he is at headquarters, he forgoes what he calls "antiseptic" formal meetings and instead prefers impromptu informal meetings in which he breezes into the offices of direct reports in the morning. "You have a conversation that is less hurried and less guarded," he says. "Face-to-face encounters are so much more revealing than a text or an email.[65] Amit Singh, president of **Palo Alto Networks**, a digital security firm, agrees. He says that because "so much gets lost in translation in emails," companies should make greater use of face-to-face discussions, where there is "a clash of ideas, but a respectful clash."[66]

Former *Wall Street Journal* columnist Jason Fry worries that voice mail and email and messaging have made managers less willing to engage in meaningful, face-to-face oral communication than before. In fact, 67 percent of managers admit to using email as a substitute for face-to-face conversations. While there are advantages to email or messaging (e.g., they create a history of what's been said), it's often better to talk to people instead of just emailing them. Fry writes, "If you're close enough that the person you're emailing uses the plonk of your return key as a cue to look for the little Outlook envelope, [it's] best [to] think carefully about whether you should be typing instead of talking."[67] But the oral medium should not be used for *all* communication. In general, when the message is simple, such as a quick request or a presentation of straightforward information, a text or email is often the better communication medium.

Written communication includes letters, email, and messaging (including discussion channels and chat rooms, discussed later in the chapter). Although most managers still like and use oral communication, digital communication via email and messaging have changed how they communicate with workers, customers, and each other. Email and messaging are the dominant forms of communication in organizations primarily because of convenience and speed. The average adult spends more than an hour each day reading and sending emails and, depending on whether messaging supplements or replaces email in their companies, they spend another 30 to 60 minutes reading and sending messages.[68] By 2023, nearly 350 billion emails will be sent around the world every year every day.[69] The numbers for workplace messaging will likely be similar, if not slightly larger.

Part of the reason for the dominance of email and messaging is that, as written communication, they are well suited for delivering straightforward messages and information. Furthermore, with email and messaging accessible at the office, at home, and on the road (by laptop computer, cell phone, or web-based platforms), managers can use them to stay in touch from anywhere at almost any time. And, because digital communications don't have to be sent and received simultaneously, they can be sent and stored for reading at any time. Consequently, managers can send and receive much more information via messages and emails than they could by using oral communication, which requires people to get together in person or by phone or videoconference.

Email and messaging have serious drawbacks, however. One is that they lack the formality of paper memos and letters. It is easy to fire off a rushed email or text message that is not well written or fully thought through. The opportunity to lash out with an angry reply is incredibly tempting. To avoid that temptation and the damage it does to your work relationships, Pamela Rutledge of the Media Psychology Research Center recommends asking yourself, "Do I want an outcome where someone throws a cup of coffee at me? Or do I want an outcome where we work toward a solution"[70]

Another drawback is the lack of nonverbal cues, making emails and messages very easy to misinterpret. When communications consultant Nick Morgan asked a neuroscientist how to make email better, the response was, "Pick up the phone and read your email to the other person." Morgan said, "That's better because at least you could stop and say, 'Did you understand that? How did that affect you?'"[71]

A final drawback is the sheer volume that employees receive each day. The day after Christmas, Taylor Lorenz, a former technology reporter for *The Atlantic*, spent 7 hours dealing with 2,700 unread emails she received in the last month! And that's not counting the emails she had already dealt with. She says, "There is simply no way for anyone with a full-time job and multiple inboxes to keep up with the current email climate. Even after deleting and sorting my 2,700 unread messages, I awoke the next day to more than 400 more."[72] Likewise, on average, users of the Slack workplace messaging app receive 200 messages a day.[73]

Although written communication is well suited for delivering straightforward messages and information, it is not well suited to complex, ambiguous, or emotionally laden messages, which are better delivered through oral communication. At software company **Autodesk**, 62 percent of managers have at least one remote employee. Because of this, all employees are trained to makes sure that the medium fits the message. For sharing information and ideas, employees use email. For brainstorming or problem solving, they use video calls or video conferencing. For making difficult decisions or resolving conflicts, they meet face to face.[74]

15-3b Listening

Are you a good listener? You probably think so. In fact, most people, including managers, are terrible listeners. A recent study from Stanford Graduate School of Business showed that listening was among the least mentioned strengths in CEO performance evaluations.[75] You qualify as a poor listener if you frequently interrupt others, jump to conclusions about what people will say before they've said it, hurry the speaker to finish his or her point, are a passive listener (not actively working at your listening), or simply don't pay attention to what people are saying.[76] On this last point – attentiveness – college students were periodically asked to record their thoughts during a psychology course. On average, 20 percent of the students were paying attention (only 12 percent were actively working at being good listeners), 20 percent were thinking about sex, 20 percent were thinking about things they had done before, and the remaining 40 percent were thinking about other things unrelated to the class (e.g., worries, religion, lunch, daydreaming).[77]

How important is it to be a good listener? In general, about 45 percent of the total time you spend communicating with others is spent listening. Furthermore, listening is important for managerial and business success, even for those at the top of an organization. Former **T-Mobile** CEO John Legere says that when he took the top job at the telecommunications company, he needed *Wireless for Dummies*. His response to his lack of familiarity with the industry was simple – listen. He listened to customer service calls, visited stores to listen to customers and employees, and even interacted with users over social media. Legere says, "My business philosophy is to listen to your employees, listen to your customers. Shut up and do what they tell you. And each of our uncarrier moves and the way I run my company is completely aligned with that."[78] Andrew Glincer, CEO of law firm Nixon Peabody LLP, agrees, "I ask a lot of questions. I don't learn much by what comes out of my mouth."[79]

Listening is a more important skill for managers than ever because generation X and millennial employees tend to expect a high level of interaction with their supervisors. They want feedback on their performance, but they also want to offer feedback and know that it is heard. In fact, managers with better listening skills are rated more highly by their employees and are much more likely to be promoted.[80]

So, what can you do to improve your listening ability? First, understand the difference between hearing and listening. According to *Webster's New World Dictionary*, **hearing** is the "act or process of perceiving sounds," whereas **listening** is "making a conscious effort to hear." In other words, we react to sounds, such as bottles breaking or music being played too loud, because hearing is an involuntary physiological process. By contrast, listening is a voluntary behavior. So, if you want to be a good listener, you have to choose to be a good listener. Typically, that means choosing to be an active, empathetic listener.[81]

Simon Mulcahy, chief marketing officer at **Salesforce**, is deliberate in meetings about listening, with "this sort of background music playing [in my head] all the time: Don't tell. Ask questions. Don't tell. Ask questions."[82]

Active listening means assuming half the responsibility for successful communication by actively giving the speaker nonjudgmental feedback that shows you've accurately heard what he or she said. Active listeners make it clear from their behavior that they are listening carefully to what the speaker has to say. Active listeners put the speaker at ease, maintain eye contact, and show the speaker that they are attentively listening by nodding and making short statements.

Several specific strategies can help you be a better active listener. First, engage in immediacy behaviors, such as putting your phone away, blanking screens on nearby electronic devices, leaning forward and making eye contact, and using short words such as "yes," "uh-huh," and "okay," to encourage the speaker to continue

Hearing the act or process of perceiving sounds

Listening making a conscious effort to hear

Active listening assuming half the responsibility for successful communication by actively giving the speaker nonjudgmental feedback that shows you've accurately heard what he or she said

Exhibit 15.5
Immediacy Behaviors, and Paraphrasing and Summarizing Responses for Active Listeners

Immediacy Behaviors	Clarifying Responses	Paraphrasing Responses	Summarizing Responses
Put your phone away.	Could you explain that again?	What you're really saying is	Let me summarize . . . .
Turn off electronic devices.	I don't understand what you mean.	If I understand you correctly	Okay, your main concerns are . . . .
Sit close and lean forward.	I'm not sure how	In other words	To recap, what you've said . . . .
Make eye contact.	I'm confused. Would you run through that again?	So your perspective is that	Thus far, you've discussed . . . .
Use "yes," "uh-huh," "okay," and other short words to encourage the speaker to continue.		Tell me if I'm wrong, but what you seem to be saying is	

Source: E. Atwater, *I Hear You*, rev. ed. (New York: Walker, 1992); E. Bernstein, "How 'Active Listening' Makes Both Participants in a Conversation Feel Better," *Wall Street Journal*, January 12, 2015, accessed May 13, 2015, www.wsj.com/articles/how-active-listening-makes-both-sides-of-a-conversation-feel-better-1421082684.

and to demonstrate that you're listening.[83] In group settings, that means *not* following the "rule of three," which is that in a group of five or six people, it's acceptable to look at your phone as long as three people have their heads up and appear to be paying attention.[84] The "rule of three" is not active listening. Second, clarify responses by asking the speaker to explain confusing or ambiguous statements. Third, when there are natural breaks in the speaker's delivery, use this time to paraphrase or summarize what has been said. *Paraphrasing* is restating what has been said in your own words. *Summarizing* is reviewing the speaker's main points or emotions. Paraphrasing and summarizing give the speaker the chance to correct the message if the active listener has attached the wrong meaning to it. Paraphrasing and summarizing also show the speaker that the active listener is interested in the speaker's message.

Exhibit 15.5 reviews immediacy behaviors and lists specific statements that listeners can use to clarify responses, paraphrase, or summarize what has been said. Active listeners also avoid evaluating the message or being critical until the message is complete. They recognize that their only responsibility during the transmission of a message is to receive it accurately and derive the intended meaning from it. Evaluation and criticism can take place after the message is accurately received. Finally, active listeners recognize that a large portion of any message is transmitted nonverbally and thus pay very careful attention to nonverbal cues (i.e., immediacy behaviors) transmitted by the speaker.

Empathetic listening means understanding the speaker's perspective and personal frame of reference and giving feedback that conveys that understanding to the speaker. Empathetic listening goes beyond active listening because it depends on our ability to set aside our own attitudes or relationships to be able to see and understand things through someone else's eyes. Empathetic listening is just as important as active listening, especially for managers, because it helps build rapport and trust with others. Unfortunately, an analysis of 14,000 college students across 72 studies found a 40 percent decrease in empathy over the last 30 years.[85] Since most of that decline occurred between 2000 and today, it's clear that companies need to focus on developing their managers' ability to empathize.

Thankfully, one interesting study suggests that empathy and listening skills can quickly improve. Two groups of children were asked to accurately identify peoples' emotions in pictures and videotapes. The first group attended a five-day device-free camp (no phones, tablets, or computers), while the second group did not. After the camp, the two groups were tested again. There was little difference in the second group's scores, but the first group improved nearly 40 percent. Why? Students at camp weren't watching TV or playing video games five hours a day. Aggie Chamlin, who attends a no-device

Empathetic listening
understanding the speaker's perspective and personal frame of reference and giving feedback that conveys that understanding to the speaker

camp, said, "I think a cell phone's a virtual wall that you put up for yourself."[86] Yalda Uhls, lead author of the study and senior researcher with the UCLA's Children's Digital Media Center, Los Angeles, commented, "You can't learn nonverbal emotional cues from a screen in the way you can learn it from face-to-face communication."[87] MIT Professor Sherry Turkle, author of *Reclaiming Conversation: The Power of Talk in a Digital Age*, explained the results this way: "They talked to one another. In conversation, things go best if you pay close attention and learn how to put yourself in someone else's shoes."[88]

The key to being a more empathetic listener is to show your desire to understand and to reflect people's feelings. You can *show your desire to understand* by listening, that is, asking people to talk about what's most important to them and then by giving them sufficient time to talk before responding or interrupting.

Reflecting feelings is also an important part of empathetic listening because it demonstrates that you understand the speaker's emotions. Unlike active listening, in which you restate or summarize the informational content of what has been said, the focus is on the affective part of the message. As an empathetic listener, you can use the following statements to *reflect the speaker's emotions*:

» So, right now it sounds like you're feeling . . . .

» You seem as if you're . . . .

» Do you feel a bit . . . ?

» I could be wrong, but I'm sensing that you're feeling . . . .

In the end, says management consultant Terry Pearce, empathetic listening can be boiled down to these three steps. First, wait 10 seconds before you respond. It will seem an eternity, but waiting prevents you from interrupting others and rushing your response. Second, to be sure you understand what the speaker wants, ask questions to clarify the speaker's intent. Third, only then should you respond first with feelings and then facts (notice that facts *follow* feelings).[89]

A word of caution, however: Not everyone appreciates having what they said repeated back to them. Manager Candy Friesen says that whenever she did that, "I seemed to engender animosity or hostility. . . . the person to whom you're speaking may not appreciate having his thoughts paraphrased one little bit."[90] So, when applying these listening techniques, pay attention

Destructive feedback
feedback that disapproves without any intention of being helpful and almost always causes a negative or defensive reaction in the recipient

Constructive feedback
feedback intended to be helpful, corrective, and/or encouraging

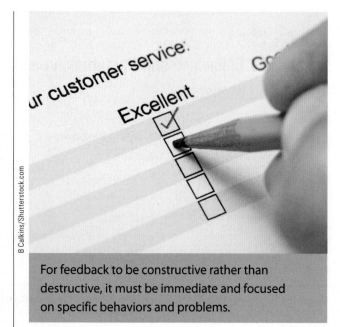

For feedback to be constructive rather than destructive, it must be immediate and focused on specific behaviors and problems.

to the body language and tone of voice of the people you're communicating with to make sure they appreciate your attempts to be a better listener.

15-3c Giving Feedback

In Chapter 11, you learned that performance appraisal feedback (i.e., judging) should be separated from developmental feedback (i.e., coaching).[91] We can now focus on the steps needed to communicate feedback one-on-one to employees.

To start, managers need to recognize that feedback can be constructive or destructive. **Destructive feedback**, what some call *feedsmack*, is disapproving without any intention of being helpful and almost always causes a negative or defensive reaction in the recipient.[92] By contrast, **constructive feedback** is intended to be helpful, corrective, and/or encouraging. It is aimed at correcting performance deficiencies and motivating employees. But finding the fine line between the two can be difficult. Ranstad, a global HR services company, adopted a philosophy of radical candor out of concerns that managers and employees were not having honest, constructive discussions about performance. A recipient of radically candid feedback said it "cut me to the bone." Wendy Finlason Seymour, a director of talent management, said the candid feedback is "not there to destroy," but "sometimes the truth can hurt."[93]

For feedback to be constructive rather than destructive, it must be immediate, focused on specific behaviors, and problem-oriented. *Immediate feedback* is much more effective than delayed feedback because manager

Coaching and Crying: There's No "P" in Hamster

Destructive feedback, or **feedsmack,** is being critical without any intention of being helpful. It almost always causes negative or defensive reactions. By contrast, constructive feedback is intended to be helpful, corrective, and/or encouraging. It is aimed at correcting performance deficiencies and motivating employees. But finding the fine line between the two can be difficult. So what if you're providing constructive feedback and the person cries?

Like the late-20ish employee who cried when her boss corrected her spelling, telling her, "I don't know why you corrected that because I spell it with the P in it." The boss calmly responded, "But that's not how the word is spelled. There is no P in hamster." When the boss suggested looking at the dictionary, she said spelling hamster with a P was how she "wanted to spell it." To make things worse, she texted Mom so Mom called, she put the call on speaker for all to hear, complained about her boss with Mom's encouragement, and asked Mom to call the boss for being "mean."

So what do you do? Stay calm. Take a quick break. Ask if there was something more you needed to know about what happened. Other things may be going on in their work or personal lives. It's OK to say, "I'm sorry you were upset," but don't overly sympathize or commiserate. Getting constructive feedback is a normal part of any job. Announce a conclusion: "Here's what we're going to do. You'll do X. I'll do Y. That will take care of it. Thanks."

Eric Isselee/Shutterstock.com

Will this always work? No. Welp,* it is a constructive approach to dealing with difficult workplace emotions like crying.
*(Welp is the nonstandard spelling of **well,** but with a P.)

Source: C. Blymire, "Here Is a Hopefully Short Synopsis of Something That Happened This Week That I Still Don't Understand (1/?)," Twitter, July 12, 2019, accessed June 15, 2020, twitter.com/CarolBlymire/status/1149805563674583040; L. Kislik, "How to Manage an Employee Who Cries Easily," Harvard Business Review, March 23, 2018, accessed June 15, 2020, hbr.org/2018/03/how-to-manage-an-employee-who-cries-easily.

and worker can recall the mistake or incident more accurately and discuss it in detail before it's too late to have a meaningful conversation. Employees at **PwC** use an app called Snapshot to request short, immediate assessments from their managers on everything from overall business acumen to specific technical capabilities. The feedback is visible to the employee, career coach, direct supervisor, HR manager, and the partner in charge of the team, and analytics tools assess the quality of the feedback and how quickly the manager responded. PwC vice chairman Tim Ryan says that the goal is to develop employees in real time: "We analogize it to athletes. They get feedback every time they come off the court."[94]

Specific feedback focuses on particular acts or incidents that are clearly under the control of the employee. For instance, instead of telling an employee that he or she is "always late for work," it's much more constructive to say, "In the last three weeks, you have been 30 minutes late on four occasions and more than an hour late on two others." Furthermore, specific feedback isn't very

helpful unless employees have control over the problems that the feedback addresses. Giving negative feedback about behaviors beyond someone's control is likely to be seen as unfair. Similarly, giving positive feedback about behaviors beyond someone's control may be viewed as insincere.

Last, *problem-oriented feedback* focuses on the problems or incidents associated with the poor performance rather than on the worker or the worker's personality. Giving feedback does not give managers the right to personally attack workers. Although managers may be frustrated by a worker's poor performance, the point of problem-oriented feedback is to draw attention to the problem in a nonjudgmental way so that the employee has enough information to correct it. Executive coach Deborah Bright says, "As an example, consider someone who cares about being respected by peers but is habitually 10 minutes late to weekly staff meetings and often blames her tardiness on her busy schedule. A manager might simply reprimand her—either nicely

("Please make more of an effort to be on time") or sharply ("Do we need to get you a new watch?"). But a more effective strategy is to say something like: "How do you think coming in late affects your reputation with your colleagues?"[95]

15-4 MANAGING ORGANIZATIONWIDE COMMUNICATION

Although managing one-on-one communication is important, managers must also know how to communicate effectively with a larger number of people throughout an organization.

Let's learn more about organizationwide communication by reading the following sections about 15-4a improving transmission by getting the message out and 15-4b improving reception by finding ways to hear what others feel and think.

15-4a Improving Transmission: Getting the Message Out

Several methods of electronic communication – email, messaging via discussion channels and chat rooms, and real-time broadcasting of announcements speeches and meetings – now make it easier for managers to communicate with people throughout the organization and get the message out.

Although we normally think of email, the transmission of messages via computers, as a means of one-on-one communication, it also plays an important role in organizationwide communication. With the click of a button, managers can send an email to everyone in the company via distribution lists. John Rae-Grant, lead product manager for Gmail, says, "People have been forecasting the death of email for the last 25 years," yet, "there's no sign that email usage is abating. It's certainly changing, but in the working world, email is still the baseline glue that pretty much carries everything."[96]

But, as a communication tool, email is a huge burden for most managers and employees, with 40 percent of white-collar employees devoting a minimum of

Discussion channels and chat rooms the use of web- or app-based communication tools to hold department-based, topic/project/client-based, team, or private discussions

three hours per workday to email. Forty-three percent of employees have felt so controlled by their email that they've put themselves in "detox," completely avoiding touching their email for three to four days.[97] The most overwhelmed emailers declare email bankruptcy by deleting all their unanswered email. Via an email blast to all of their contacts, or using auto reply, they communicate that they've deleted all email and that if you urgently needed something from them, you should send your message again. With a now-empty inbox and the likelihood that most deleted emails won't be resent to them, they can start over.[98] When people are overwhelmed with email, and most are, email becomes a much less effective way to get an organizationwide message out.

Collaborative communication tools are another means of electronically promoting organizationwide communication. **Discussion channels and chat rooms** use web- or app-based communication tools to hold department, team or private discussions based on topics, projects, or clients. Team room channels are often restricted to team members working together, while private discussions are typically invitation-only for teams or for one-to-one work sessions. Discussion channels and chat rooms, all of which are standard features in Slack, Microsoft Teams, or Google Chat, allow the sharing of expertise, avoid duplicating solutions already discovered by others, and provide a historical database for people dealing with particular problems. They promote collaborative discussion via participant comments and through document sharing and editing. To better understand discussion channels and chat rooms, let's take a closer look at Slack.

Slack is a robust group communication platform (on computers, smartphones, and tablets) that includes automatic archiving, a powerful search engine, and more informal and accessible online collaboration. Slack increases communication transparency by making messages, files, comments, images, and video visible to everyone else in the team, project or department. David Maddocks, chief marketing officer of footwear company **Cole Haan,** says, "We now have people all over the world using Slack. We communicate in multiple languages and virtually every time zone."[99] Vice president of brand design, Andrew Enright, uses seasonal channels like "#campaign_spring," "So when we pick up spring, for example, we'll pick up right where we left off last spring. Looking back at how we've worked (in the #campaign_spring channel) just gives us a lot of information that we can leverage as we begin to repeat certain cycles."[100]

With everything searchable in Slack, anyone can quickly catch up to find out where projects or discussions stand. Technology guru Walt Mossberg says, "It's sort

"Subject" Your Email with Key Words for Quick Responses

Author, financial executive, entrepreneur, Grammy award-winning producer and former military officer Kabir Sehgal, says, "The first thing that your email recipient sees is your name and subject line, so it's critical that the subject clearly states the purpose of the email, and specifically, what you want them to do with your note."

He suggests these key words:

» ACTION – Something needs to be done.
» SIGN – A signature is needed.
» INFO – For informational purposes with no response needed.
» DECISION – Please make a decision about this.
» REQUEST – Permission or approval is needed.
» COORD – Coordination with you is needed.

Emails with keywords stand out in people's inboxes. They don't have to guess what you want – or how to reply. For example, no one will be confused if you send an email with this subject line:

SIGN – Submitted attached travel expense report for San Francisco trip.

Subject line relevance

bearsky23/Shutterstock.com

TRY IT: Write emails with keywords in the subject line to get results.

Source: K. Sehgal, "How to Write Email with Military Precision," *Harvard Business Review*, November 22, 2016, accessed June 15, 2020, hbr.org/2016/11/how-to-write-email-with-military-precision.

---

of like a combination of Facebook, Twitter, iMessage, and Dropbox, but just for you and your co-workers.[101] Companies have adopted Slack primarily because it increases communication effectiveness so much that email usage within teams or companies often drops by 70 or 80 percent. That said, Slack messaging overload, like email overload, is a problem in many companies.

Real-time broadcasting is a third electronic method of organizationwide communication. **Real-time broadcasting** allows announcements, speeches, and meetings made to smaller in-person audiences to be livestreamed to broader company audiences and stored on demand for subsequent viewing and interactive discussion. Broadcast voice mail and Yammer are examples of real-time broadcasting.

Voice messaging, or voice mail, is a telephone answering system that records audio messages. Most people, however, are unfamiliar with the ability to broadcast voice mail by sending a recorded message to everyone in the company. While *broadcast voice mail* isn't real-time (it is stored on demand, however), it gives top managers

a quick, convenient way to address their workforces via oral communication – but only if people actually listen to the message, and that turns out to be a challenge with today's workers, who are much more likely to use their smartphones for social media rather than phone calls. Consequently, company leaders are increasingly using real-time broadcasting platforms like **Microsoft**'s *Yammer* to broadcast livestreamed video to their entire workforces.

Think of Yammer as for companywide announcements, information, and discussion, whereas Microsoft Teams, Slack, or Google Chat are for daily project or team communication.[102] Yammer allows companies to engage up to 10,000 people in live events with video and interactive discussion. On-demand viewing and companywide discussion channels are available for those who miss livestreamed events and announcements.[103]

> **Real-time broadcasting** allows announcements, speeches and meetings made to smaller in-person audiences to be livestreamed to broader company audiences and stored on demand for subsequent viewing and interactive discussion

Organization silence can isolate a manager if employees are reluctant to tell managers things they don't think they will want to hear.

thoughts and feelings with top managers. Surveys indicate that only 29 percent of first-level managers feel that their companies encourage employees to express their opinions openly. Another study of 22 companies found that 70 percent of the people surveyed were afraid to speak up about problems they knew existed at work.

Withholding information about organizational problems or issues is called **organizational silence**. Organizational silence occurs when employees believe that telling management about problems won't make a difference or that they'll be punished or hurt in some way for sharing such information.[106] A survey of executives – not employees, executives – found that 85 percent had at some point kept quiet when they saw a serious problem at work.[107] Financial company Charles Schwab CEO Walt Bettinger explains that organizational silence isolates managers in two ways: "people telling you what they think you want to hear, and people being fearful to tell you things they believe you don't want to hear."[108] Nandan Nilekani, a co-founder of Infosys, the India-based global information technology consulting firm, agrees, saying, "If you're a leader, you can put yourself in a cocoon – a good-news cocoon," he notes. "Everyone tells you, 'It's all right – there's no problem.' And the next day, everything's wrong."[109]

Beyond fear of punishment or the assumption that telling management won't make a difference, another reason for organizational silence is the **bystander effect**.[110] A bystander will ignore widely known organizational problems under the assumption that someone else who knows about the problem will fix it. Professors Insya Hussain and Subra Tangirala said, "So if you're wondering why that particular boss seems to get away with bad behavior, or why no one has spoken up about an obvious glitch in the company product, consider whether everyone – including yourself – might be waiting for someone else to take action."[111]

Company hotlines, survey feedback, frequent informal meetings, surprise visits, and townhalls are additional ways of overcoming organizational silence and the bystander effect. **Company hotlines** are phone numbers that anyone in the company can call anonymously to

Microsoft uses Yammer for CEO Satya Nadella and his leadership team to communicate companywide to 150,000 employees who can hear/view his messages and post questions and comments for discussion.[104] Senior Program Manager Frank Delia says, "If you're trying to reach a large audience, then Yammer is a good interactive platform to do that. Our CEO sponsors a Yammer community that brings people across all levels of the company into conversations about our company strategy."[105]

15-4b Improving Reception: Hearing What Others Feel and Think

When people think of "organizationwide" communication, they think of the CEO and top managers getting their message out to people in the company. But organizationwide communication also means finding ways to hear what people throughout the organization are thinking and feeling. This is important because most employees and managers are reluctant to share their

Organizational silence when employees withhold information about organizational problems or issues

Bystander effect ignoring widely known organizational problems under the assumption that someone else will fix them

Company hotlines phone numbers that anyone in the company can call anonymously to leave information for upper management

BLIND: THE SOLUTION TO ORGANIZATIONAL SILENCE?

Organizational silence, withholding information about organizational problems or issues, happens when telling management about problems doesn't make a difference or people fear punishment for sharing such information. When that happens, problems go unidentified and unsolved, companies squander workers' experience and knowledge, and the benefits of cognitive conflict that advance understanding are lost.

Blind (teamblind.com) may represent a solution. Blind's 3.5 million users are completely and securely anonymous. But to join a company channel (i.e., a discussion), users must authenticate a valid work email. So everyone in the Microsoft (71,000 people), Amazon (63,000), Google (27,000), and Facebook (22,000) channels works in those companies. But Amazonians don't get to join the Microsoft channel, for example. Anonymity within Blind's workplace communities leads to free, candid discussions that are the antithesis of organizational silence.

TechCrunch's John Chen says, "With Blind, for the first time, HR and executives will have a pulse on

employee sentiment that is both real-time and authentic. As [cofounder Sunguk] Moon puts it, "no company is perfect, and if it was, Blind would not need to exist."

Source: "Anonymous Professional Network," Blind, accessed June 16, 2020, https://www.teamblind.com/whyBlind; J. Chen, "Blind Loyalty," TechCrunch, August 11, 2018, accessed June 16, 2020, techcrunch.com/2018/08/11/blind-loyalty/.

leave information for upper management. Company hotlines are incredibly useful, as 41 percent of the calls placed to them result in an investigation and some form of corrective action within the organization. Anonymity is critical, too, because as those investigations proceeded, 59 percent of the callers did not want their identities revealed.[112]

Survey feedback is information that is collected by survey from organization members and then compiled, disseminated, and used to develop action plans for improvement. Many organizations make use of survey feedback by surveying their managers and employees several times a year. **Microsoft** asks a small sample of employees to complete a "daily pulse" survey that takes "a snapshot of how employees are feeling about the company, its culture, and other timely topics."[113] There are 20 core questions asked each time, five additional questions determined by Microsoft's senior leadership, plus a series of rotating open-ended questions such as, "In what ways do you think Microsoft is different today than it was one year ago?" or "What is the biggest change you'd recommend your leadership make to allow you to be more effective in your job?"[114]

Frequent *informal meetings* between top managers and lower-level employees are one of the best ways for top managers to hear what others think and feel. Many people assume that top managers are at the center of everything that goes on in organizations, but top managers commonly feel isolated from most of their lower-level managers and employees.[115] Consequently, more and more top managers are scheduling frequent informal meetings with people throughout their companies.

The World Bank, with 10,000 people in 120 offices worldwide, is a nongovernmental organization that aims to end extreme poverty and promote "income growth for the bottom 40 percent of every country."[116] When James Wolfensohn became president of the World Bank, "he went on fact-finding trips to developing countries to understand the kinds of projects that the bank was doing. After several visits he realized that he was only being shown successful projects, smiling villagers, and grateful government officials." He told consultant and author Ron Ashkenas that "he eventually learned to stray from his tour guides so that he could meet people who hadn't been prepped for his visit, to see what was really happening. This dramatically changed his assessment of how much

> **Survey feedback** information that is collected by surveys from organizational members and then compiled, disseminated, and used to develop action plans for improvement

of the bank's aid was getting through the local government, to the people who really needed it."[117]

Have you ever been around when a supervisor learns that upper management is going to be paying a visit? First, there's shock. Next, there's anxiety. And then there's panic, as everyone is told to drop what he or she is doing to polish, shine, and spruce up the workplace so that it looks perfect for the visit. Of course, when visits are conducted under these conditions, top managers don't get a realistic look at what's going on in the company. Consequently, one of the ways to get an accurate picture is to pay *surprise visits* to various parts of the organization. These visits should not just be surprise inspections but should also be used as opportunities to encourage meaningful upward communication from those who normally don't get a chance to communicate with upper management.

Monitoring social media, such as blogs, Twitter, and Facebook, written by people outside the company, can be a good way to find out what others are saying or thinking about your organization or its products or actions. This is why **American Airlines** (AA), which normally gets 4,500 mentions per hour, has a dedicated social media hub with 40 employees and a variety of screens showing flight numbers, maps displaying real time flight locations, social media mentions of AA travel hubs, geo-tagged mentions that can quickly highlight trouble spots, and trending breaking news hashtags to identify disruptions to airline travel.[118] When Nikki-Colette Manzie missed her connecting flight from Los Angeles to Flint, Michigan, instead of waiting helplessly in a long line at the AA customer service desk, she used Twitter to direct message @AmericanAir. Two minutes later, someone from AA social media team responded, "What's your record locator (the unique six letter code associated with your travel itinerary)?"[119] Three minutes after that, she was booked on a new flight. She tweeted, "Shout out to @AmericanAir for the fastest customer service I've ever received."[120]

Finally, in addition to being a way to deliver organizational communication, so-called *town hall meetings* can be an effective way for companies to hear feedback from employees. Earlier you learned that CEO Satya Nadella and his leadership team use Yammer to communicate with Microsoft's 150,000 employees who view his video messages and post questions and comments for discussion. Nadella's monthly townhall meetings are broadcast live and are then available on demand. Yammer is used to measure real-time reactions via polls, instant surveys, or simply counting how many people are viewing the townhall. There is always a question-and-answer period to address live questions posted by employees. Conversations continue afterward via Nadella's CEO Connection page on Yammer.[121] Of course, the most important part of townhalls is for managers to listen and respond. Microsoft's Angus Florance explains, "Every day, Satya's team reviews the most active conversations and starts to collate questions that can be addressed in the next all company Q&A event."[122] The leadership team also responds to ongoing conversations in the CEO Connection discussion groups.[123]

16 | Control

LEARNING OUTCOMES

16-1 Describe the basic control process.

16-2 Discuss the various methods that managers can use to maintain control.

16-3 Describe the behaviors, processes, and outcomes that today's managers are choosing to control in their organizations.

16-1 THE CONTROL PROCESS

For all companies, past success is no guarantee of future success. Even successful companies fall short or face challenges and have to make changes. **Control** is a regulatory process of establishing standards to achieve organizational goals, comparing actual performance to the standards, and taking corrective action when necessary to restore performance to those standards. Control is achieved when behavior and work procedures conform to standards and when company goals are accomplished.[1] Control is not just an after-the-fact process, however. Preventive measures are also a form of control.

Control a regulatory process of establishing standards to achieve organizational goals, comparing actual performance against the standards, and taking corrective action when necessary

Mark Rober's "Porch Pirate vs. Glitter Bomb" You-Tube videos have been seen by 100+ million people. Why? Because 1.7 million delivered packages are stolen every day by porch pirates. Amazon, the world's biggest shipper of packages, bought Ring, the video doorbell company, to deter thefts and control the cost of replacing stolen packages.[2] Professor Read Hayes, director of the Loss Prevention Research Council supported by 70 retail chains, says, "There's an incredible cost of replacing [a stolen] item: Somebody has to understand it's missing; it has to be processed, picked, staged, packed, mailed, and delivered."[3] Since Ring doorbells

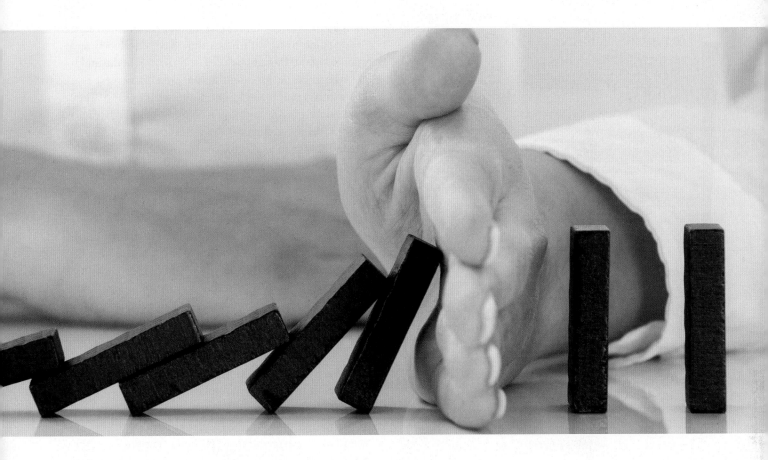

are everywhere, porch pirates are often caught on multiple Ring videos shared on Ring's Neighbors app, which notifies users as local thefts are reported.[4] Amazon also tries to control package theft via real-time tracking, secure, self-service hub lockers in stores and apartments, and Amazon Key, which uses a smart lock and/or Ring security camera to allow secure delivery inside your locked home, garage, or car trunk.[5]

*The basic control process **16-1a begins with the establishment of clear standards of performance; 16-1b involves a comparison of performance to those standards; 16-1c takes corrective action, if needed, to repair performance deficiencies; 16-1d is a dynamic, cybernetic process; and 16-1e consists of three basic methods: feedback control, concurrent control, and feedforward control.** However, as much as managers would like, **16-1f control isn't always worthwhile or possible.***

16-1a Standards

The control process begins when managers set goals such as satisfying 90 percent of customers or increasing sales by 5 percent. Companies then specify the performance standards that must be met to accomplish those goals. **Standards** are a basis of comparison for measuring the extent to which organizational performance is satisfactory or unsatisfactory. For example, many pizzerias use 30 to 40 minutes as the standard for delivery time. Because anything longer is viewed as unsatisfactory, they'll typically reduce the price if they can't deliver a hot pizza to you within that time period.

So how do managers set standards? How do they decide which levels of performance are satisfactory and which are unsatisfactory? The first criterion for a good standard is that it must enable goal achievement. If you're meeting the standard but still not achieving company goals, then the standard may have to be changed. While the hotel industry already had rigorous cleanliness standards, the American Hotel & Lodging Association (AHLA) developed improved "SafeStay" standards because of the coronavirus pandemic.[6] **Hilton**, a global hotel and hospitality company, plans to exceed AHLA's coronavirus standards by partnering with RB, maker of Lysol and Dettol disinfecting products, and the Mayo Clinic, the top-ranked hospital system in the United States.[7]

> **Standards** a basis of comparison for measuring the extent to which various kinds of organizational performance are satisfactory or unsatisfactory

PHONE-FREE PERFORMANCES! THANKS YONDR!

Comedian Dave Chappelle hates it when people in the audience record him on their smartphones. Fan-posted videos on Facebook and YouTube also limit his ability to develop new material. Comedians like Chappelle can take months to craft, edit, and finely hone new material in small venues before playing larger performance halls.

Chappelle, however, now has his audiences put their smartphones in Yondr pouches, which fans hold onto during performance. Yondr automatically locks, preventing access and recording. If your phone buzzes, indicating a call, you leave the performance area and unlock the Yondr pouch by tapping it on an unlocking pod in the lobby.

Chappelle says, "I know my show is protected, and it empowers me to be more honest and open with the audience." He also says, "People actually watch the show, they're in the moment, and they're vastly more fun to speak to." Most fans agree, finding that without the distraction of their phones they enjoy the performance much more, except for a drunk fan at one performance who chewed off the bottom of his Yondr pouch.

Source: "Yondr: Be Here Now," Yondr, accessed June 29, 2020, www.overyondr.com/; J. Morrissey, "Your Phone's on Lockdown. Enjoy the Show," *New York Times*, October 15, 2016, accessed May 5, 2017, www.nytimes.com/2016/10/16/technology/your-phones-on-lockdown-enjoy-the-show.html; J. Stern, "The Night They Locked Up All the Smartphones," *Wall Street Journal*, February 28, 2017, accessed May 5, 2017, www.wsj.com/articles/thenight-they-locked-up-all-the-smartphones-1488306868.

Hilton's CleanStay program includes "a seal to indicate when a room has been deep-cleaned; a checklist of 10 high-touch areas (from light switches to remotes and thermostats) that will receive extra disinfection; the removal of clutter like pens, paper, and guest directories; new cleaning and occupancy limits for fitness centers; contactless check-ins and digital room keys; and the addition of cleaning technologies like ultraviolet light."[8]

Companies also determine standards by listening to customers' comments, complaints, and suggestions or by observing competitors. You might know that squirrels destroy car wires, gnawing them to control the size of their fast-growing teeth. But unless you live in Germany, you've probably not heard of stone marten weasels, which destroyed the wiring in 200,000 cars last year. German car companies, reacting to customer complaints, work with biologist Susann Parlow, who says, "They come to us with hoses they have developed and want to know if they are safe."[9] The torn wires in the building where she keeps stone martin weasels suggest not. Daimler AG staff biologist Karl Kugelschafter says, "They go absolutely insane and tear everything apart."[10] Because it's so difficult to design car weasel-resistant wires, Kugelschafter designed an electric grid surrounding the engine to zap the varmints. Not to be left behind, German automaker Audi sells a *Marderabwehrsystem* (translation: Weasel Defense System) with this tag line, "My Audi, My Territory."[11]

Standards can also be determined by benchmarking other companies. **Benchmarking** is the process of determining how well other companies (not just competitors) perform business functions or tasks. In other words, benchmarking is the process of determining other companies' standards. When setting standards by benchmarking, the first step is to determine what to benchmark. Organizations can benchmark anything from cycle time (how fast) to quality (how well) to price (how much). For example, based on national benchmarking studies of thousands of fire departments, many firefighters are expected to respond to an alarm within 15 seconds, 95 percent of the time. Additionally, 90 percent of the time, it should take no more than 60 seconds to leave the firehouse for emergency medical responses and no more than 80 seconds for fires. It should also take no more than four minutes to arrive at the scene.[12]

After setting standards, the next step is to identify the companies *against which* to benchmark those standards. The last step is to collect data to determine other companies' performance standards. Intuit, maker of financial software and websites such as QuickBooks, Intuit Payroll, and TurboTax, gets nearly 40 percent of its revenues by selling its products and services to tens of thousands of small- to medium-sized businesses in different industries. Fred Shilmover, CEO of InsightSquared, which sells data-analytic tools to those businesses, says, "Intuit figured out how to leverage its internal data team for their customers, when those companies couldn't gather enough data on their own to understand the bigger [industry and business] trends."[13] And because Intuit also sells add-on products and services to help manage payroll, inventory, financing, customers, point of sale trends, and online/social media marketing, he says those businesses "can now benchmark their costs [and organizational performance in all of those areas] against each other." This benchmarking shows them whether they perform at, above, or below thousands of other companies on a number of critical dimensions.[14]

Benchmarking the process of identifying outstanding practices, processes, and standards in other companies and adapting them to your company

16-1b Comparison to Standards

The next step in the control process is to compare actual performance to performance standards. Although this sounds straightforward, the quality of the comparison depends largely on the measurement and information systems a company uses to keep track of performance. The better the system, the easier it is for companies to track their progress and identify problems that need to be fixed.

Last year, European spruce bark beetles destroyed more trees in Sweden than forest fires. The beetles prefer the most mature trees, which typically grow for 50 years or more before being harvested. If left uncontrolled, they could destroy 15 percent of Sweden's annual logging production at a loss of $625 million a year.[15] The best way to minimize beetle damage is to find and remove trees infested with the spruce bark beetles. But for **Sveaskog AB**, Sweden's largest forestry company with 9.6 million forested acres, that's an extraordinarily difficult task. So Sveaskog AB is working with Sogeti to identify infected areas using Geo Satellite Intelligence (GSI). Sogeti's Joakim Wahlqvist explains, "The GSI solution enables us to produce detailed maps that visualize the movements of the bark beetle in selected areas. We've been able to point out areas in the forest that are currently under attack and successively point out new affected areas. Fredrik Klang, forestry director at Sveaskog, says that they have verified the 100 percent accuracy of these areas with the help of drones. This is enabling Sveaskog to move fast to contain the beetles' progress in affected forest areas and to reduce their spread."[16]

16-1c Corrective Action

The next step in the control process is to identify performance deviations, analyze those deviations, and then develop and implement programs to correct them. This is similar to the planning process discussed in Chapter 5. Regular, frequent performance feedback allows workers and managers to track their performance and make adjustments in effort, direction, and strategies.

Customer visits to bank branches dropped by 30 percent when the coronavirus struck. Many customers, who rarely used bank apps and websites, finally tried and liked mobile banking, with mobile banking transactions rising by 85 percent.[17] Now just 40 percent of bank customers expect to visit their local bank branch. Maria Schuld of Fidelity National Information Services, which provides software for the world's 50 largest banks, says, "Once people begin favoring mobile-based account access, there's no going back."[18] Because of these changes, banks will take corrective action by closing 10 to 15 percent of their 83,000 branches within the next year.[19]

16-1d Dynamic, Cybernetic Process

As shown in Exhibit 16.1, control is a continuous, dynamic, cybernetic process. Control begins by setting standards, measuring performance, and then comparing performance to the standards. If the performance deviates from the standards, then managers and employees analyze the deviations and develop and implement corrective programs that (they hope) achieve the desired performance by meeting the standards. Managers must repeat the entire process again and again in an endless feedback loop (a continuous process). Thus, control is not a one-time achievement or result. It continues over time (i.e., it is dynamic) and requires daily, weekly, and monthly attention from managers to maintain performance levels at the standard (i.e., it is cybernetic). **Cybernetic** derives from the Greek word *kubernetes*, meaning "steersman," that is, one who steers or keeps on course.[20] The control process shown in Exhibit 16.1 is cybernetic because constant attention to the feedback loop is necessary to keep the company's activity on course.

When the coronavirus struck in early 2020, many people turned to mobile banking for all of their banking needs, including those who had rarely used this form of banking in the past.

Ivan Marc Sanchez/Alamy Stock Photo

> **Cybernetic** the process of steering or keeping on course

Exhibit 16.1
Cybernetic Control Process

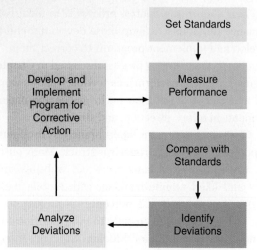

Source: H. Koontz and R. W. Bradspies, "Managing through Feedforward Control: A Future Directed View," *Business Horizons*, June 1972, pp. 25–36.

16-1e Feedback, Concurrent, and Feedforward Control

The three basic control methods are feedback control, concurrent control, and feedforward control. **Feedback control** is a mechanism for gathering information about performance deficiencies *after* they occur. This information is then used to correct or prevent performance deficiencies. Study after study has clearly shown that feedback improves both individual and organizational performance. In most instances, any feedback is better than no feedback.

If feedback has a downside, it's that feedback always comes after the fact. Within minutes of rescuing a snowmobiler stranded in a whiteout, an Alaska Department of Public Safety helicopter crashed, killing all on board. Video footage from a cockpit camera recovered from the rubble revealed that the pilot had incorrectly reset the device that indicates that the craft is flying level. National Transportation Safety Board chief aviation investigator John DeLisi said, "Without that video, we would have been looking at a pile of burned-up wreckage, trying to figure out what caused the erratic flight path that led to this crash."[21] The black box data and voice recorder required on all jets and helicopters could not have provided that information. Because of this video footage, the Alaska Department of Public Safety now requires pilots to receive instrument training every 90 days. This better prepares pilots to navigate in whiteout conditions, which are common in the state. By contrast, the pilot of the crashed helicopter hadn't received instrument training in more than 10 years.[22] While pilots object to cockpit video recorders because of privacy concerns, the National Traffic Safety Board (NTSB) is now recommending that manufacturers make "crash-protected cockpit image recorders" standard on all new turbine-powered helicopters and offer kits to retrofit existing models.[23] Dana Schulze, director of the NTSB's office of aviation safety, says, "The more information we have, the better we can understand not only the circumstances of a crash but what can be done to prevent future accidents."[24]

Concurrent control addresses the problems inherent in feedback control by gathering information about performance deficiencies *as* they occur. Thus, it is an improvement over feedback because it attempts to eliminate or shorten the delay between performance and feedback about the performance. Over a five-year period, 1 out of 50 homeowners filed water damage insurance claim from burst pipes, leaky hoses, or loose plumbing connections. With an average cost of $10,000, the insurance industry spends $13 billion a year repairing homeowners' internal water damage. Insurer USAA executive Jon-Michael Kowall says, "Wildfires, hurricanes, and tornadoes catch headlines, but the reality is that the No. 1 kind of risk that the everyday consumer has is a water claim."[25] So insurers are incentivizing customers to install water sensors—near water heaters, washers, dishwashers, toilets, sinks, and basement pipes—that detect and report leaks within minutes of starting.[26] Chubb, which insures expensive homes, also pays for the installation of water shutoff systems that automatically turn off the water supply to the entire house when leaks are detected.[27]

Feedforward control is a mechanism for gathering information about performance deficiencies *before* they occur. In contrast to feedback and concurrent control, which provide feedback on the basis of outcomes and results, feed-forward control provides information about performance deficiencies by monitoring inputs rather than outputs. Thus, feedforward control seeks to prevent or minimize performance deficiencies before they happen.

Feedback control a mechanism for gathering information about performance deficiencies after they occur

Concurrent control a mechanism for gathering information about performance deficiencies as they occur, thereby eliminating or shortening the delay between performance and feedback

Feedforward control a mechanism for monitoring performance inputs rather than outputs to prevent or minimize performance deficiencies before they occur

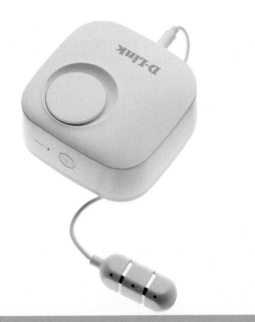

Some insurance companies are incentivizing customers to install water sensors, which will detect and report leaks within minutes of starting.

Power companies have traditionally relied on consumers to call in power outages (i.e., provide feedback). Then, when repair crews arrive, fault detectors displaying a flag or a light can tell them which line is out, but the crews still have to visually inspect miles of power lines, often in weather with poor visibility, to find the precise cause of the outage. Tollgrade makes sensors the size of a loaf of bread, which sit on and are powered by the electricity flowing through the wires, that can notify power companies about problems *before* they happen (i.e., feedforward). With Global Positioning System (GPS) (location) and wireless (communication) capabilities, the sensors monitor the fluctuations in the flow of electricity—from outages to drops to normal transmissions to surge overloads—and instantaneously alert power company engineers when there are problems.[28] Pennsylvania's Orange & Rockland Utilities were alerted to an electrical line problem over a Fourth of July weekend, and the advanced notice of the outage offered ample time for repair crews to fix the issue *before* a

single customer could complain.[29] Sensors can also trigger reclosers that automatically turn off the energy to a power line when there is a surge or some other problem. If the problem can't be fixed remotely, a switcher kicks in to reroute power around the problem area. When Hurricane Florence hit the United States in 2018, reclosers and switchers helped prevent 80,000 outages for Duke Energy.[30]

16-1f Control Isn't Always Worthwhile or Possible

Control is achieved when behavior and work procedures conform to standards, and goals are accomplished. By contrast, **control loss** occurs when behavior and work procedures do not conform to standards.[31] Globally, one-third of food is wasted each year. In North America, that amounts to 650 pounds of wasted food a year per person at a cost of $218 billion.[32] McDonald's uses data analytic strategies to minimize food waste through *inventory management*, only having on hand the food ingredients and supplies it needs, and *demand management*, predicting the amount and kind of food that will be sold each day. But when food waste occurs, it partners with charities to donate fresh food to those in need, makes animal food when excess food is out of date, converts food waste into energy or compost for food production, and, as a last resort, sends food waste to landfills.[33]

Maintaining control is important because control loss prevents organizations from achieving their goals. When control loss occurs, managers need to find out what, if anything, they could have done to prevent it. Usually, that means identifying deviations from standard performance, analyzing the causes of those deviations, and taking corrective action. Even so, implementing controls isn't always worthwhile or possible. Let's look at regulation costs and cybernetic feasibility to see why this is so.

To determine whether control is worthwhile, managers need to carefully assess **regulation costs**, that is, whether the costs and unintended consequences of control exceed its benefits. If a

Control loss the situation in which behavior and work procedures do not conform to standards

Regulation costs the costs associated with implementing or maintaining control

control process costs more than it benefits, it may not be worthwhile.

For several decades, city and state recycling programs paid for themselves as the cost of collecting recyclables was exceeded by the revenue from reselling millions of tons of glass, aluminum, and plastic. But with China no longer accepting contaminated recyclables, higher recycling costs because of "single-stream" recycling where glass, metal, paper, and plastic are mixed together (recycling is much cheaper when they are separated), and much lower prices for recycled metal, glass, paper, and plastic, recycling costs have risen significantly.[34] Because regulation costs now exceed regulation benefits, cities are closing recycling services and centers and burning recycling to generate energy. Facing an additional $25,000 in monthly costs, the small city of Deltona, Florida, shut down its recycling program. Mayor Heidi Herzberg said, "We all did recycling because it was easy, but the reality is that not much was actually being recycled [any way]." California State Treasurer Fiona Ma says, "We are in a crisis moment in the recycling movement right now."[35]

Another factor to consider is **cybernetic feasibility**, the extent to which it is possible to implement each of the three steps in the control process. If one or more steps cannot be implemented, then maintaining effective control may be difficult or impossible.

16-2 CONTROL METHODS

What happens if a crew member sleeps with a cruise ship passenger? According to **Royal Caribbean** cruise director Dru Pavlov, the answer is, "Chicken or beef?" Because, "That's what a flight attendant asks you when you're put on the first flight home."[36] Despite what's shown on reruns of *The Love Boat* TV show, Pavlov says there's zero tolerance in the cruise industry for sleeping with passengers. He says, "Whenever I take photos with people, I always give a thumbs up. My hands are visible, so no one can claim any inappropriate behavior."[37] "Chicken or beef?" that is, firing crew members who sleep with passengers, is an example of bureaucratic, top-down control.

Let's review the five different methods managers can use to achieve control in their organizations: **16-2a bureaucratic, 16-2b objective, 16-2c normative, 16-2d concertive,** and **16-2e self-control.**

16-2a Bureaucratic Control

When most people think of managerial control, what they have in mind is bureaucratic control. **Bureaucratic control** is top-down control, in which managers try to influence employee behavior by rewarding or punishing employees for compliance or noncompliance with organizational policies, rules, and procedures.

When the coronavirus emptied offices, many companies enacted bureaucratic controls via software to monitor employees' keystrokes and computer screens as they logged in from home. In an email to employees at **Axios Financial,** CEO Gregory Garrabrants said, "We have seen individuals taking unfair advantage of flexible work arrangements by essentially taking vacations … If daily tasks aren't completed, workers will be subject to disciplinary action, up to and including termination."[38] Consistent with this example, most employees would argue that bureaucratic managers emphasize punishment of noncompliance much more than rewards for compliance.

As you learned in Chapter 2, bureaucratic management and control were created to prevent just this type of managerial behavior. By encouraging managers to apply well-thought-out rules, policies, and procedures in an impartial, consistent manner to everyone in the organization, bureaucratic control is supposed to make companies more efficient, effective, and fair. Ironically, it frequently has just the opposite effect. Managers who use bureaucratic control often emphasize following the rules above all else.

Another characteristic of bureaucratically controlled companies is that, due to their rule- and policy-driven decision-making, they are highly resistant to change and slow to respond to customers and competitors. Recall from Chapter 2 that even Max Weber, the German philosopher who is largely credited with popularizing bureaucratic ideals in the late nineteenth century, referred to bureaucracy as the "iron cage." He said, "Once fully established, bureaucracy is among those social structures that are the hardest to destroy."[39]

Professor Gary Hamel and consultant Michele Zanini, citing the view of leading executives, agree with Weber:

> *Bureaucracy has few fans. Walmart CEO Doug McMillon calls it a villain. Berkshire Hathaway vice chair Charlie Munger says its tentacles should be treated like "the cancers they so much*

Cybernetic feasibility the extent to which it is possible to implement each step in the control process

Bureaucratic control the use of hierarchical authority to influence employee behavior by rewarding or punishing employees for compliance or noncompliance with organizational policies, rules, and procedures

Working from Home: The Boss Knows You're on TikTok

The *New York Time's* Adam Satariano wrote, "I started work at 8:49 a.m., reading and responding to emails, browsing the news and scrolling Twitter. At 9:14 a.m., I made changes to an upcoming story and read through interview notes. By 10:09 a.m., work momentum lost, I read about the Irish village where Matt Damon was living out the quarantine. All of these details—from the websites I visited to my GPS coordinates—were available for my boss to review," *even though he was working from home.* How? Because he and his boss were trying out **Hubstaff,** one of the popular programs used for time tracking and productivity monitoring of employees. After three weeks of daily reports, including hundreds of screenshots of Satariano's computer, his boss's response was, "Ick."

Hubstaff's founder says that since workers know they are being monitored, no one's privacy is being violated. Legally, that's true. If you're using company-provided technology on company systems, the boss has the right to see what you're doing.

But, what if, as Satariano points out, you log on to your bank account or to health information and forget that Hubstaff is cataloging that information? As his boss said, "Ick."

The only solution is having your own technology for personal use, like designer and researcher Diana Hubbard. Hubbard always carries a second, personal smartphone. She also owns two laptops for personal use, one for travel and the other for gaming.

Chesnot/Getty Images Entertainment/Getty Images

So, working from home and need a break? Reach for an old personal tablet. Buy a used laptop for personal use. But don't check out the latest TikTok video on your work laptop or smartphone.

Source: C. Cutter, T-P Chen & S. Krouse, "You're Working From Home, but Your Company Is Still Watching You," *The Wall Street Journal,* April 18, 2020, accessed June 29, 2020, www.wsj.com/articles/youre-working-from-home-but -your-company-is-still-watching-you-11587202201; S. Krouse, "The New Ways Your Boss Is Spying on You," *Wall Street Journal,* July 19, 2019, accessed June 29, 2020, www.wsj.com/articles/the-new-ways-your-boss-is-spying-on-you -11563528604?mod=article_inline; A. Satariano, "How My Boss Monitors Me While I Work From Home," *The New York Times,* May 7, 2020, accessed June 29, 2020, www. nytimes.com/2020/05/06/technology/employee-monitoring-work-from -home-virus.html.

---

resemble." *Jamie Dimon, the CEO of JPMorgan Chase, agrees that bureaucracy is a disease. These leaders understand that bureaucracy saps initiative, inhibits risk taking, and crushes creativity. It's a tax on human achievement.*[40]

So why does bureaucracy persist? Despite significant disadvantages, say Hamel and Zanini, "… it works, at least to a degree. With its clear lines of authority, specialized units, and standardized tasks, bureaucracy facilitates efficiency at scale."[41]

16-2b Objective Control

In many companies, bureaucratic control has evolved into **objective control**, which is the use of observable measures of employee behavior or output to assess performance and influence behavior. However, bureaucratic control focuses on whether policies and rules are followed, objective control focuses on observing and measuring worker behavior or output.

There are two kinds of objective control: behavior control and output control. **Behavior control** is regulating behaviors and actions that workers perform on the job. The basic assumption of behavior control is that if you do the right things (i.e., the right behaviors) every day, then those things should lead to goal achievement. Behavior control is still management-based, however, which means that managers are responsible for monitoring and then rewarding or punishing workers for exhibiting desired or undesired behaviors.

Algorithmic management, or using computer algorithms to measure and regulate employees, is behavioral

> **Objective control** the use of observable measures of worker behavior or outputs to assess performance and influence behavior
>
> **Behavior control** the regulation of the behaviors and actions that workers perform on the job

control. Uber's algorithms track drivers' locations, the percentage of rides that accepted or canceled, hours logged into the app (when driving), completed trips, and drivers' acceleration and cornering (via the accelerometers and gyroscopes in drivers' phones).[42] Furthermore, Uber's app tells drivers where to pick up customers and how to get to customers' destinations. Drivers that don't follow the app's behavioral instructions can be penalized or fired.[43]

Instead of measuring what managers and workers do, **output control** measures the results of their efforts. While behavioral control regulates, guides, and measures how workers behave on the job, output control gives managers and workers the freedom to behave as they see fit as long as they accomplish prespecified, measurable results. Output control is often coupled with rewards and incentives.

Three things must occur for output control to lead to improved business results. First, output control measures must be reliable, fair, and accurate. Second, employees and managers must believe that they can produce the desired results. If they don't, then the output controls won't affect their behavior. Third, the rewards or incentives tied to output control measures must truly be dependent on achieving established standards of performance. Common forms of output control measures include production levels in manufacturing, sales, customer satisfaction, and on-time performance (deliveries, airlines, and trucking, for example).

In a unique form of output control, Aetna will reward employees who get extra sleep. CEO Mark Bertolini said, "If they can prove they get 20 nights of sleep for seven hours or more in a row [via Fitbit fitness trackers], we will give them $25 a night, up [to] $500 a year." Bertolini says, "If we can make … business fundamentals better by investing in our people, then that's going to show up in our revenue."[44] Arianna Huffington, cofounder of the *Huffington Post*, said, "It really changes the cultural delusion that most businesses have been operating under, which has been . . . the more exhausted and burned out the employees are, the more productive they are."[45]

16-2c Normative Control

Rather than monitoring rules, behavior, or output, another way to control what goes on in organizations is to use normative control to shape the beliefs and values of the people who work there. With

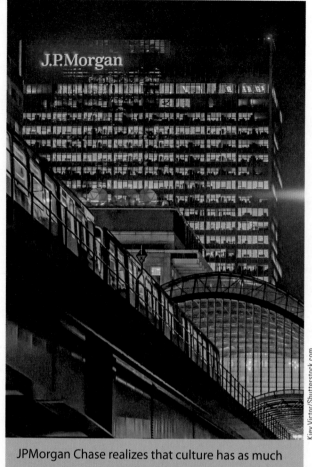

JPMorgan Chase realizes that culture has as much to do with control as algorithms, so it has added and designated more than 300 executives as "cultural ambassadors."

Kiev.Victor/Shutterstock.com

normative controls, a company's widely shared values and beliefs guide workers' behavior and decisions.

JPMorgan Chase realizes that culture has as much to do with control as algorithms, so it has designated more than 300 executives as "cultural ambassadors" who focus on standards. The company published a memo that encouraged employees to flag any compliance concerns and emphasized that poor compliance and scandals damage the bank's reputation and affect everyone, both professionally and financially. The goal of the program is to reshape the beliefs and values of the bank's employees so that compliance and ethical financial stewardship are part of the company culture.[46]

Normative controls are created in two ways. First, companies that use normative controls are very careful about whom they hire. While many companies screen potential applicants on the basis of their abilities, normatively controlled companies are just as likely to screen potential applicants based on their attitudes and values.

Mark Fitzsimmons, president of Psychometrics Canada, which is in the business of helping organizations select and develop their workforces, says, "Finding a suitable employee is not simply about adequate performance. It involves selecting a candidate who also upholds the carefully fostered organizational climate. An employee who doesn't quite gel can be detrimental to these efforts and can in some cases equate to damaging toxicity in the workplace. To avoid this, [we] use time-saving and objective personality assessments that measure a candidate's organizational values early in the selection process."[47]

Second, with normative controls, managers and employees learn what they should and should not do by observing experienced employees and by listening to the stories they tell about the company. We learned the importance of storytelling and organizational culture in Chapter 3. For normative controls to work, however, managers must not only select the right people, they must reward employees who honor those attitudes and values, and deal with those who don't. Tinuiti (formerly Elite SEM) is a New York City-based search engine marketing firm that helps *Fortune* 500 companies increase their profile when potential customers do web searches. Elite SEM values hiring people with advanced technical skills and cooperative attitudes. More specifically, the company prides itself on being a "jerk-free workplace." So, there are consequences for employees and managers who, as founder Ben Kirshner says, "don't embrace our core values." When a new employee refused to work late his first week on the job, he was let go. Kirshner says, "He was a bad seed!" And, because of the long hours people put in to meet client needs, Elite SEM has a free meal policy. So when another new employee ordered himself groceries and $30 breakfasts, Kirshner says, "Everyone jumped on him."[48]

16-2d Concertive Control

Although normative controls are based on beliefs that are strongly held and widely shared throughout a company, **concertive controls** are based on beliefs that are shaped and negotiated by work groups.[49] While normative controls are driven by strong organizational cultures, concertive controls usually arise when companies give work groups complete autonomy and responsibility for task completion (see Chapter 10, "Managing Teams," for a complete discussion of the role of autonomy in teams and groups). The most autonomous groups operate without managers and are completely responsible for controlling work group processes, outputs, and behavior. Such groups do their own hiring, firing, worker discipline, scheduling, materials ordering, budget making and meeting, and decision-making.

Concertive control is not established overnight. Highly autonomous work groups evolve through two phases as they develop concertive control. In phase one, group members learn to work with each other, supervise each other's work, and develop the values and beliefs that will guide and control their behavior. And because they develop these values and beliefs themselves, work group members feel strongly about following them.

An active form of concertive control is used by the teams at The Other Side Movers (TOSM), a moving company run by The Other Side Academy, a nonprofit in Salt Lake City, Utah, that "helps former felons, substance abusers, and others get clean, stay clean, and learn how to live successful, productive lives."[50] The TOSM website explains, "Our guys might have some wild tattoos, but they will be the hardest working, friendliest, and most careful movers you have ever hired. Hard work is part of our healing process."[51] TOSM team members are to be "200 percent accountable," meaning 100 percent accountable for their own work and—here's the concertive control – 100 percent accountable for the work of everyone else on the team. TOSM team member enforce accountability through "pull-ups." When they see a mistake being made, they're expected to stop, "pull up" the person making the mistake by explaining how to correct the mistake, and then inform the crew leader about the mistake. Team members on the receiving end of a pull-up are expected to be open to the feedback by responding, "OK."[52] Finally, after owning up to a mistake, other team members "patch up" with the "pulled-up" team member by expressing their support and respect for them and their efforts. In its first year, TOSM became the top-ranked moving company in Salt Lake City.[53]

The second phase in the development of concertive control is the emergence and formalization of objective rules to guide and control behavior. The beliefs and values developed in phase one usually develop into more objective rules as new members join teams. The clearer those rules, the easier it becomes for new members to figure out how and how not to behave.

Ironically, concertive control may lead to even more stress for workers to conform to expectations than bureaucratic control. Under bureaucratic control, most workers only have to worry about pleasing the boss. But with concertive control, their behavior has to satisfy the rest of their team members. For example, one team member says, "I don't have to sit there and look for the boss to be around; and if the boss is not around, I can sit there and talk to my neighbor or do what I want. Now the whole team is around me

Concertive control the regulation of workers' behavior and decisions through work group values and beliefs

and the whole team is observing what I'm doing."[54] Plus, with concertive control, team members have a second, much more stressful role to perform: that of making sure that their team members adhere to team values and rules.

16-2e Self-Control

Self-control, also known as **self-management**, is a control system in which managers and workers control their own behavior.[55] Self-control does not result in anarchy, in which everyone gets to do whatever he or she wants. In self-control, or self-management, leaders and managers provide workers with clear boundaries within which they may guide and control their own goals and behaviors.[56] Leaders and managers also contribute to self-control by teaching others the skills they need to maximize and monitor their own work effectiveness. In turn, individuals who manage and lead themselves establish self-control by setting their own goals, monitoring their own progress, rewarding or punishing themselves for achieving or for not achieving their self-set goals, and constructing positive thought patterns that remind them of the importance of their goals and their ability to accomplish them.[57]

For example, let's assume you need to do a better job of praising and recognizing the good work that your staff does for you. You can use goal setting, self-observation, and self-reward to manage this behavior on your own. For self-observation, write "praise/recognition" on a three-by-five-inch card. Put the card in your pocket. Put a check on the card each time you praise or recognize someone. (Wait until the person has left before you do this.) Keep track for a week. This serves as your baseline, or starting point. Simply keeping track will probably increase how often you do this. After a week, assess your baseline, or starting point, and then set a specific goal. For instance, if your baseline was twice a day, you might set a specific goal to praise or recognize others' work five times a day. Continue monitoring your performance with your cards. After you've achieved your goal every day for a week, give yourself a reward (perhaps a movie or lunch with a friend at a new restaurant) for achieving your goal.[58]

As you can see, the components of self-management, self-set goals, self-observation, and self-reward have their roots in the motivation theories you read about in Chapter 13. The key difference, though, is that the goals, feedback, and rewards originate from employees themselves and not from their managers or organizations.

> **Self-control (self-management)** a control system in which managers and workers control their own behavior by setting their own goals, monitoring their own progress, and rewarding themselves for goal achievement

Alexmillos/Shutterstock.com

16-3 WHAT TO CONTROL?

In the first section of this chapter, we discussed the basics of the control process and the fact that control isn't always worthwhile or possible. In the second section, we looked at the various ways in which control can be achieved. In this third and final section, we address an equally important issue: What should managers control? Costs? Quality? Customer satisfaction? The way managers answer this question has critical implications for most businesses.

If you control for just one thing, such as costs, then other dimensions such as marketing, customer service, and quality are likely to suffer. But if you try to control for too many things, then managers and employees become confused about what's really important. In the end, successful companies find a balance that comes from doing three or four things right, such as managing costs, providing value, and keeping customers and employees satisfied.

After reading this section, you should be able to explain **16-3a the balanced scorecard approach to control** *and how companies can achieve balanced control of company performance by choosing to control* **16-3b budgets, cash flows, and economic value added; 16-3c customer defections; 16-3d quality;** *and* **16-3e waste and pollution.**

16-3a The Balanced Scorecard

Most companies measure performance using standard financial and accounting measures such as return on capital, return on assets, return on investments, cash

Exhibit 16.2
Barclays Bank–Balanced Scorecard

Balanced Scorecard	Barclays Bank	Objectives	Measures	Targets	Initiatives
Financial	Financial	Sustainable Returns above Cost of Equity	Group Return on Equity	10%	Invest and Grow, Reposition, Transition, or Exit Key Businesses
		Control Operating Expenses	Cost to Income Ratio	60% or Less	Keep Costs at 60% or Less of Income
Customer	Customer & Client	Bank of Choice	Net Promoter Score (Ratio of Delighted vs. Dissatisfied Customers)	#1	Improve Customer Exerience via Technology
			Digital Engagement	70% or More	Simplify and Extend Range of Digital Products & Services
Internal	Colleague & Conduct	Colleagues Fully Engaged	Sustained Engagement Scores	87–91%	Purpose and Value Program
		Diverse, Inclusive Environment	% of Women in Senior Leadership	28%	Two New Flagship Leadership Development Programs
Learning	Society	Preservation of Our Environment and Progress of Our Communities	Social and Environmental Financing	$200 Billion	Loans Made for Social Innovation and Environmental Sustainability
			Connect with Work Program	250,000 Job Placements	Vital Work Skills Training or People in Overlooked Communities

Source: "Delivering for Our Stakeholders: Strategic Report 2019," Barclays, accessed June 28, 2020, https://home.barclays/content/dam/home-barclays/documents/investor -relations/reports-and-events/annual-reports/2019/Barclays%20PLC%20Strategic%20Report%202019.pdf.

flow, net income, and net margins. The **balanced scorecard** encourages managers to look beyond such traditional financial measures to four different perspectives on company performance. How do customers see us (the customer perspective)? At what must we excel (the internal perspective)? Can we continue to improve and create value (the innovation and learning perspective)? How do we look to shareholders (the financial perspective)?[59]

The balanced scorecard has several advantages over traditional control processes that rely solely on financial measures. First, it forces managers at each level of the company to set specific goals and measure performance in each of the four areas. For example, Exhibit 16.2 shows that the UK-based Barclays Bank uses eight different measures in its balanced scorecard to determine whether it is meeting the standards it has set for itself in the control process. Of those, only two—group return on equity and its cost-to-income ratio—are standard financial measures of performance. In addition, Barclays measures the ratio of delighted versus dissatisfied customers and digital engagement via the percentage of clients who use Barclay's digital banking apps and website (customer perspective); employee engagement over time, and the percentage of women in senior leadership positions (internal perspective); and benefits to society, measured by the level of funding provided to support social innovation and

environmental projects, as well as job placements resulting from vital work skills training in overlooked communities (innovation and learning perspective).

The second major advantage of the balanced scorecard approach to control is that it minimizes the chances for **suboptimization**, which occurs when performance improves in one area at the expense of decreased performance in others. Jon Meliones, medical director of pediatric cardio ICU at Duke Children's Hospital, says, "We explained the [balanced scorecard] theory to clinicians and administrators like this: if you sacrifice too much in one quadrant to satisfy another, your organization as a whole is thrown out of balance. We could, for example, cut costs to improve the financial quadrant by firing half the staff, but that would hurt quality of service, and the customer quadrant would fall out of balance. Or we could increase productivity in the internal business quadrant by assigning more patients to a nurse, but doing so would raise the likelihood of errors – an unacceptable trade-off."[60]

Let's examine some of the ways in which companies are controlling the four basic parts of the balanced scorecard:

Balanced scorecard measurement of organizational performance in four equally important areas: finances, customers, internal operations, and innovation and learning

Suboptimization performance improvement in one part of an organization but only at the expense of decreased performance in another part

the financial perspective (budgets, cash flows, and economic value added), the customer perspective (customer defections), the internal perspective (total quality management), and the innovation and learning perspective (sustainability).

16-3b The Financial Perspective: Controlling Budgets, Cash Flows, and Economic Value Added

The traditional approach to controlling financial performance focuses on accounting tools such as cash flow analysis, balance sheets, income statements, financial ratios, and budgets. **Cash flow analysis** predicts how changes in a business will affect its ability to take in more cash than it pays out. **Balance sheets** provide a snapshot of a company's financial position at a particular time (but not the future). **Income statements**, also called profit and loss statements, show what has happened to an organization's income, expenses, and net profit (income less expenses) over a period of time. **Financial ratios** are typically used to track a business's liquidity (cash), efficiency, and profitability over time compared with other businesses in its industry. For example, **Aetna**, a health insurance provider, uses a metric called the medical loss ratio. This financial ratio expresses the percentage of premiums used to pay patient medical costs—the lower the ratio, the higher the company's profits. So when the ratio dropped from 82.3 to 81.1 percent, it represented a 1.2 percent increase in profitability.[61] Finally, **budgets** are used to project costs and revenues, prioritize and control spending, and ensure that expenses don't exceed available funds and revenues. Soon after Marne Levine became Instagram's chief operating officer, she attended a meeting with other top managers and asked to see the annual budget. The room went silent until one top executive responded, "What do you mean, 'the budget'?"[62] Which is all you need to know to understand why she was hired!

In a typical budgeting process, a manager uses the previous year's budget and adjusts it to reflect the current situation, but **zero-based budgeting** (ZBB) requires managers to outline a budget from scratch each year. In doing so, they must justify every expenditure—down to the number of company cell phones issued—every year. Roughly 300 multinational companies use ZBB, including drugstore chain **Walgreens Boots Alliance**, which aims to cut annual costs by $1 billion.[63] On average, ZBB saves the company $280 million a year. At **Welch's**, the farming coop famous for its grape jams and grape juice, finance chief Chris Caswell says that ZBB "… is allowing the organization to understand where all of its spending is. Every piece of spending is being supported by a business reason to make sure we don't have any stale spend."[64] Caswell says, "For the first time, we asked, 'Why are we in this trade group, and is there a benefit going to that conference?'"[65] Twenty-six percent of chief financial officers indicated their companies would use ZBB to reduce costs to adjust to revenue shortfalls caused by the coronavirus.[66]

By themselves, none of these tools—cash flow analyses, balance sheets, income statements, financial ratios, or budgets—tell the whole financial story of a business. They must be used together when assessing a company's financial performance. Because these tools are reviewed in detail in your accounting and finance classes, only a brief overview is provided here. Still, these are necessary tools for controlling organizational finances and expenses, and they should be part of your business toolbox. Unfortunately, most managers don't have a good understanding of these accounting tools even though they should.[67]

Though no one would dispute the importance of cash flow analyses, balance sheets, income statements, financial ratios, or budgets for determining the financial health of a business, accounting research also indicates that the complexity and sheer amount of information contained in these accounting tools can shut down the brain and glaze over the eyes of even the most experienced manager.[68] Sometimes there's simply too much information to make sense of. The balanced scorecard simplifies things by focusing on one simple question when it comes to finances: How do we look to shareholders? One way to answer that question is through something called economic value added.

Cash flow analysis a type of analysis that predicts how changes in a business will affect its ability to take in more cash than it pays out

Balance sheets accounting statements that provide a snapshot of a company's financial position at a particular time

Income statements accounting statements, also called "profit and loss statements," that show what has happened to an organization's income, expenses, and net profit over a period of time

Financial ratios calculations typically used to track a business's liquidity (cash), efficiency, and profitability over time compared to other businesses in its industry

Budgets quantitative plans through which managers decide how to allocate available money to best accomplish company goals

Zero-based budgeting a budgeting technique that requires managers to justify every expenditure every year

Exhibit 16.3
Calculating Economic Value Added (EVA)

1. Calculate net operating profit after taxes (NOPAT).	$3,500,000
2. Identify how much capital the company has invested (i.e., spent).	$16,800,000
3. Determine the cost (i.e., rate) paid for capital (usually 5–8%).	10%
4. Multiply capital used (Step 2) times cost of capital (Step 3).	(10% × $16,800,000) = $1,680,000
5. Subtract the total dollar cost of capital from net profit after taxes.	$3,500,000 NOPAT −$1,680,000 Total cost of capital $1,820,000 EVA

Conceptually, **economic value added (EVA)** is not the same thing as profits. It is the amount by which profits exceed the cost of capital in a given year. It is based on the simple idea that capital is necessary to run a business and that capital comes at a cost. Although most people think of capital as cash, after it is invested (i.e., spent), capital is more likely to be found in a business in the form of computers, manufacturing plants, employees, raw materials, and so forth. And just like the interest that a homeowner pays on a mortgage or that a college student pays on a student loan, there is a cost to that capital.

The most common costs of capital are the interest paid on long-term bank loans used to buy all those resources, the interest paid to bondholders (who lend organizations their money), and the dividends (cash payments) and growth in stock value that accrue to shareholders. EVA is positive when company profits (revenues minus expenses minus taxes) exceed the cost of capital in a given year. In other words, if a business is to truly grow, its revenues must be large enough to cover both short-term costs (annual expenses and taxes) and long-term costs (the cost of borrowing capital from bondholders and shareholders). If you're a bit confused, the late Roberto Goizueta, the former CEO of Coca-Cola, explained it this way: "You borrow money at a certain rate and invest it at a higher rate and pocket the difference. It is simple. It is the essence of banking."[69]

Exhibit 16.3 shows how to calculate EVA. First, starting with a company's income statement, you calculate the net operating profit after taxes (NOPAT) by subtracting taxes owed from income from operations. The NOPAT shown in Exhibit 16.3 is $3,500,000. Second, identify how much capital the company has invested (i.e., spent). Total liabilities (what the company owes) less accounts payable and less accrued expenses, neither of which you pay interest on, provides a rough approximation of this amount. In Exhibit 16.3, total capital invested is $16,800,000. Third, calculate the cost (i.e., rate) paid for capital by determining the interest paid to bondholders (who lend organizations their money), which is usually somewhere between 2 and 4 percent, and the return that stockholders want in terms of dividends and stock price appreciation, which is historically between 9 and 12 percent. Take a weighted average of the two to determine the overall cost of capital. In Exhibit 16.3, the cost of capital is 10 percent. Fourth, multiply the total capital ($16,800,000) from Step 2 by the cost of capital (10 percent) from Step 3. In Exhibit 16.3, this amount is $1,680,000. Fifth, subtract the total dollar cost of capital in Step 4 from the NOPAT in Step 1. In Exhibit 16.3, this value is $1,820,000, which means that our example company has created economic value or wealth this year. If our EVA number had been negative, meaning that the company didn't make enough profit to cover the cost of capital from bondholders and shareholders, then the company would have destroyed economic value or wealth by taking in more money than it returned.[70]

Why is EVA so important? First and most importantly, because it includes the cost of capital, it shows whether a business, division, department, profit center, or product is really paying for itself. The key is to make sure that managers and employees can see how their choices and behaviors affect the company's EVA. For example, because of EVA

Economic value added (EVA) the amount by which company profits (revenues minus expenses minus taxes) exceed the cost of capital in a given year

training and information systems, factory workers at **Herman Miller**, a leading office furniture manufacturer, understand that using more efficient materials, such as less expensive wood-dust board instead of real wood sheeting, contributes an extra dollar of EVA from each desk the company makes. On its website, Herman Miller explains, "Under the terms of the EVA plan, we shifted our focus from budget performance to long-term continuous improvements and the creation of economic value. When we make plans for improvements around here, we include an EVA analysis. When we make decisions to add or cut programs, we look at the impact on EVA. Every month, we study our performance in terms of EVA, and this measurement system is one of the first things new recruits to the company learn."[71] "The result is a highly motivated and business-literate workforce that challenges convention and strives to create increasingly greater value for both customers and owners. Every month the company and all employees review performance in terms of EVA, which has proven to be a strong corollary to shareholder value."[72]

Second, because EVA can easily be determined for subsets of a company such as divisions, regional offices, manufacturing plants, and sometimes even departments, it makes managers and workers at all levels pay much closer attention to their segment of the business. In other words, EVA motivates managers and workers to think like small-business owners who must scramble to contain costs and generate enough business to meet their bills each month. And, unlike many kinds of financial controls, EVA doesn't specify what should or should not be done to improve performance. Thus, it encourages managers and workers to be creative in looking for ways to improve EVA performance.

Remember that EVA is the amount by which profits exceed the cost of capital in a given year. So the more that EVA exceeds the total dollar cost of capital, the better a company has used investors' money that year. For example, Apple had an EVA of $45.8 billion in 2019, by far the largest EVA in the world. The next-closest companies were Microsoft at $26 billion and Alphabet (parent company of Google) at $20.6 billion. Apple's EVA financial performance in 2019 was extraordinary and the second largest ever achieved by any company.[73]

> **Customer defections** a performance assessment in which companies identify which customers are leaving and measure the rate at which they are leaving

> Apple had an EVA of $45.8 billion in 2019, by far the largest EVA in the world.

Rose Carson/Shutterstock.com

16-3c The Customer Perspective: Controlling Customer Defections

The second aspect of organizational performance that the balanced scorecard helps managers monitor is customers. It does so by forcing managers to address the question, "How do customers see us?" Unfortunately, most companies try to answer this question through customer satisfaction surveys, but these are often misleadingly positive. Most customers are reluctant to talk about their problems because they don't know who to complain to or think that complaining will not do any good. In fact, a study by the Australian Federal Office of Consumer Affairs found that 96 percent of unhappy customers never complain to anyone in the company.[74]

One reason that customer satisfaction surveys can be misleading is that sometimes even very satisfied customers will leave to do business with competitors. Rather than poring over customer satisfaction surveys from current customers, studies indicate that companies may do a better job of answering the question, "How do customers see us?" by closely monitoring **customer defections**, that is, by identifying which customers are leaving the company and measuring the rate at which they are leaving. Unlike the results of customer satisfaction surveys, customer defections and retention have a great effect on profits.

Because most accounting systems measure the financial impact of a customer's current activity (sales), rather than the lifetime value of each customer, few managers realize the financial impact that even a low rate of customer defection can have on a business. Businesses frequently lose 15 to 20 percent of their customers each year, so even a small improvement in retention can have a significant impact on profits. In fact, retaining just 5 percent more customers per year can increase annual profits 25 to 100 percent. Managers, therefore, should pay closer attention to customer defections. John Tschohl, an author and business consultant, worked with a network of 17 blood plasma donation centers to determine the financial impact of defections. With 40,600 donors each year, analysis of the network showed that the "lifetime" of a typical donor—the time when the donor was active—was 3.4 years. During that time, each lifetime donor contributed roughly $6,000 in profits to the company. Each year, however, a cohort of 2,340 donors defected, making the network's annual customer defection rate 6 percent. While the defection rate was modest, the financial impact was considerable, resulting in more than $100 million in lost revenue and $60 million less in profits each year, or $200 million in profits over the lifetime (3.4 years) of a single cohort (2,430 people) of defectors.[75]

Beyond the clear benefits to the bottom line, the second reason to study customer defections is that customers who have left are much more likely than current customers to tell you what you are doing wrong. Perhaps the best way to tap into this source of good feedback is to have top-level managers from various departments talk directly to customers who have left. It's also worthwhile to have top managers talk to dissatisfied customers who are still with the company. Finally, companies that understand why customers leave can not only take steps to fix ongoing problems but also identify which customers are likely to leave and make changes to prevent them from leaving.

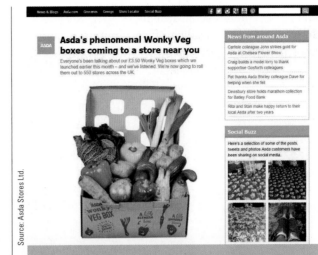

Source: Asda Stores Ltd.

British supermarket chain Asda recently began packaging misshapen, cracked, blemished, and unusually sized vegetables into reduced-price Wonky Veg Boxes.

16-3d The Internal Perspective: Controlling Quality

The third part of the balanced scorecard, the internal perspective, consists of the processes, decisions, and actions that managers and workers make within the organization. In contrast to the financial perspective of EVA and the outward-looking customer perspective, the internal perspective focuses on internal processes and systems that add value to the organization. For McDonald's, it could be processes and systems that enable the company to provide consistent, quick, low-cost food. For Toyota, it could be reliability—when you turn on your car, it starts, regardless of whether it has 20,000 or 200,000 miles on it. Yet, no matter what area a company chooses, the key is to excel in that area. Consequently, the internal perspective of the balanced scorecard usually leads managers to a focus on quality.

Quality is typically defined and measured in three ways: excellence, value, and conformance to expectations.[76] When the company defines its quality goal as *excellence*, managers must try to produce a product or service of unsurpassed performance and features. *Condé Nast Traveler* magazine has been ranking global airlines for 31 years. For 30 of those years, **Singapore Airlines** was named the best airline in the world.[77] Although many airlines try to cram passengers into every available inch on a plane, Singapore Airlines delivers creature comforts to encourage repeat business and lure customers willing to pay premium prices. On its newer planes, the first-class cabin is divided into eight private mini-rooms, each with an unusually wide leather seat that folds down flat for sleeping, a 24-inch HD TV with Bose noise-canceling headphones and over 1,000 choices in movies, TV shows, music, games, and apps.[78]

These amenities and services are common for private jets but truly unique in the commercial airline industry. Singapore Airlines was the first airline, in the 1970s, to introduce a choice of meals, complimentary drinks, and earphones in coach class. It was the first to introduce worldwide video, news, telephone, and fax services; was the first to feature personal video monitors for movies, news, and documentaries; and has had AC power outlets and on-board high-speed internet for some time —well ahead of other airlines.

Value is the customer perception that the product quality is excellent for the price offered. At a higher price, for example, customers may perceive the product to be less of a value. When a company emphasizes value as its quality goal, managers must simultaneously control excellence, price, durability, and any other features of a product or service that customers strongly associate with value. Fresh fruits and vegetables are categorized according to size, uniformity, and appearance. The most attractive produce (about 85 percent) goes to supermarkets, while the nonconforming produce ends up in processed foods, animal feed, and landfills. British supermarket chain **Asda** recently loosened its produce appearance specifications and began packaging misshapen, cracked, blemished, and unusually sized vegetables into five kilogram boxes. Asda's so-called Wonky Veg Box sells for £3.50 (about $5.00), a 30 percent discount, which 95 percent of Asda's customers think is a tremendous value. Sales quadrupled in the first two months after the box launched.[79] Ian Harrison, Asda's produce

Value customer perception that the product quality is excellent for the price offered

Exhibit 16.4
Conformance to Specifications Checklist for Buying Fresh Fish

Fresh Whole Fish	Acceptable	Not Acceptable
Gills	✓ Bright red, free of slime, clear mucus	✗ Brown to grayish, thick, yellow mucus
Eyes	✓ Clear, bright, bulging, black pupils	✗ Dull, sunken, cloudy, gray pupils
Smell	✓ Inoffensive, slight ocean smell	✗ Ammonia, putrid smelll
Skin	✓ Opalescent sheen, scales adhere tightly to skin	✗ Dull or faded color, scales missing or easily removed
Flesh	✓ Firm and elastic to touch, tight to the bone	✗ Soft and flabby, separating from the bone
Belly cavity	✓ No viscera or blood visible, lining intact, no bone protruding	✗ Incomplete evisceration, cuts or protruding bones, off-odor

iStock.com/Valeriy Evlakhov

Sources: "A Closer Look: Buy It Fresh, Keep It Fresh," *Consumer Reports Online*, accessed June 20, 2005, www.seagrant.sunysb.edu/SeafoodTechnology/SeafoodMedia/CR02-2001/CR-SeafoodII020101.htm; "How to Purchase: Buying Fish," *About Seafood*, accessed June 20, 2005, www.aboutseafood.com/faqs/purchase1.html.

technical director, said that the Wonky Veg Box "was always meant as a trial to see how customers reacted to slightly scruffier produce, but this has also enabled us to flex our specifications across a wide variety of our standard produce lines."[80] He adds, "we now deliver 20 boxes to 300 of our larger stores every Thursday, helping an additional 300 tonnes of misshapen veg make it on to our shelves [each year]."[81] Harrison says, "We've got a real hit on our hands with Wonky!"[82]

When a company defines its quality goal as conformance to specifications, employees must base decisions and actions on whether services and products measure up to the standard. In contrast to excellence and value-based definitions of quality that can be somewhat ambiguous, measuring whether products and services are "in spec" is relatively easy. Furthermore, while conformance to specifications (e.g., precise tolerances for a part's weight or thickness) is usually associated with manufacturing, it can be used equally well to control quality in nonmanufacturing industries like supermarkets. Exhibit 16.4 shows a checklist that a cook or restaurant owner would use to ensure quality when buying fresh fish.

The way in which a company defines quality affects the methods and measures that workers use to control quality. Accordingly, Exhibit 16.5 shows the advantages and disadvantages associated with the excellence, value, and conformance to specification definitions of quality.

16-3e The Innovation and Learning Perspective: Sustainability

The last part of the balanced scorecard, the innovation and learning perspective, addresses the question, "Can we continue to improve and create value?" Thus, the innovation and learning perspective involves continuous improvement in ongoing products and services (discussed in Chapter 18), as well as relearning and redesigning the processes by which products and services are created (discussed in Chapter 7). Because these are discussed in more detail elsewhere in the text, this section reviews an increasingly important topic, sustainability. Exhibit 16.6 shows the four levels of sustainability, ranging from waste disposal, which produces the smallest minimization of waste, to waste prevention and reduction, which produces the greatest minimization.[83]

The goals of the top level, *waste prevention and reduction*, are to prevent waste and pollution before they occur or to reduce them when they do occur. It took 10 years to accomplish, but Apple's headquarters, stores, distribution centers, and massive data centers are all powered by renewable, green energy. From the solar panels on top of Apple Park Headquarters to the 20 megawatt Fort Churchill, Nevada, solar farm that powers Apple's Reno, Nevada, data center, Apple currently has 25 renewable energy projects, with 15 additional sources under construction.[84] Since inception, Apple's use of renewable energy has prevented the release of 2.2 million

Exhibit 16.5
Advantages and Disadvantages of Different Measures of Quality

Quality Measure	Advantages	Disadvantages
Excellence	Promotes clear organizational vision.	Provides little practical guidance for managers.
	Being/providing the "best" motivates and inspires managers and employees..	Excellence is ambiguous. What is it? Who defines it?
Value	Appeals to customers who know excellence "when they see it."	Difficult to measure and control.
	Customers recognize differences in value.	Can be difficult to determine what factors influence whether a product/service is seen as having value.
	Easier to measure and compare whether products/services differ in value.	Controlling the balance between excellence and cost (i.e., affordable excellence) can be difficult.
Conformance to Specifications	If specifications can be written, conformance to specifications is usually measurable.	Many products/services cannot be easily evaluated in terms of conformance to specifications.
	Should lead to increased efficiency.	Promotes standardization, so may hurt performance when adapting to changes is more important.
	Promotes consistency in quality.	May be less appropriate for services, which are dependent on a high degree of human contact.

Source: Briar Cliff Manor, NY, 10510-8020; C. A. Reeves and D. A. Bednar, "Defining Quality: Alternatives and Implications," *Academy of Management Review* 19 (1994): 419–445.

metric tons of greenhouse gas emissions.[85] Apple could have achieved its goal much sooner by simply purchasing already existing green energy. But it followed the principle of "additionality" by creating new green energy sources. Vice president of environment, policy, and social initiatives Lisa Jackson says, "We want to put new, clean power on the grid so that we're not sucking up all the clean energy that's [already] there."[86]

The following are three strategies for waste prevention and reduction:

1. *Good housekeeping.* Perform regularly scheduled preventive maintenance for offices, plants, and equipment. Examples of good housekeeping include fixing leaky valves quickly to prevent wasted water and making sure machines are running properly so that they don't use more fuel than necessary. Aquarius Spectrum, in Tel Aviv, Israel, uses thousands of sensors to listen to the sounds water creates as it passes through or leaks from pipes. Cloud servers analyzing the data pinpoint leaks to within 1 foot

Exhibit 16.6 Four Levels of Sustainability

- Waste Prevention & Reduction
- Recycle & Reuse
- Waste Treatment
- Waste Disposal

iStock.com/0g-vision

Source: D. R. May and B. L. Flannery, "Cutting Waste with Employee Involvement Teams," *Business Horizons*, September–October 1995, pp. 28–38.

of their actual location. CEO Oded Fruchtman says, "We can tell if the leak's in an office building or a flat, or if the problem is with the water meter, a pressure reduce valve—anything that creates a noise that should not be creating a noise. When you can find leaks that small, you don't have to react in an emergency manner, or work on weekends or holidays."[87]

2. *Material/product substitution. Replace* toxic or hazardous materials with less harmful materials.

3. *Process modification. Change inefficient* steps or procedures to eliminate or reduce waste.

At the second level of sustainability, *recycle and reuse*, wastes are reduced by reusing materials as long as possible or by collecting materials for on- or off-site recycling. **Primark**, a worldwide clothing retailer based in the United Kingdom, has an annual revenue of £7.79 billion and is growing roughly 25 percent per year. The company's flagship store has 44 fitting rooms, 104 cash registers, and can—and often does—hold 3,200 customers. When delivery trucks arrive at the back of the store, merchandise is unpacked and sent straight onto the floor. The cardboard boxes used to ship the merchandise go right back onto the truck to be recycled and later return to the store as Primark's iconic brown paper shopping bags.[88]

A growing trend in recycling is *design for disassembly*, where products are designed from the start for easy disassembly, recycling, and reuse after they are no longer usable. **Samsung Electronics** used design for disassembly principles to redesign a 55-inch TV with a curved screen, replacing 30 out of 38 screws with plastic snaps so that it only takes 10 minutes to disassemble the TV. Likewise, **Apple** has built robots with 29 arms. Each Robot, which Apple has named "Liam,"

CONTROL: MORE FUN WITH ANIMALS

The chapter already has several animal examples, squirrels, and stone marten weasels that destroy car wiring, European spruce bark beetles that destroy trees, and quality specifications used when buying fresh fish. But none of those show how organizations use animals to achieve control and meet goals. So let's have more fun with animals!

» The Puy du Fou is a French historical theme park with 2.2 million visitors a year. Six trained crows receive a tasty treat each time they pick up and then deposit cigarette ends and small items of trash in a specially designed box.

» Unimaginably aggressive flies known as screwworms, which emerge from larvae after females lay eggs in living animals, used to kill millions of cattle each year. Adult flies and larvae eat animals *alive* down to the bone. It took decades to wipe them out by releasing sterile males in the southernmost parts of the United States. Since females only breed once, the weekly release of 15 million sterile flies over a 50-mile section of the Panama-Columbia border prevents the screwworm population from growing and moving north into Mexico and the United States. The annual $15 million cost saves US farmers $800 million a year in potential losses.

» A Dutch company, Guard From Above, uses birds of prey (such as eagles) to take down drones that are too close to protected air spaces like airports, or that are being used for illegal surveillance.

» With nearly 500,000 people in attendance, the Wimbledon Grand Slam tennis tournament at the All England Club in greater London uses a hawk named Rufus to prevent—and thus control—pigeon problems, such as pigeon droppings and play interrupted by pigeons landing on the courts. Owner Wayne Davis says, "The pigeons learned he [Rufus] was in charge. Other than a few stragglers, they stopped coming around like they did before. He scares them away."

OLI SCARFF/AFP/Getty Images

Sources: S. Castle, "Dutch Firm Trains Eagles to Take Down High-Tech Prey: Drones," *The New York Times*, May 28, 2016, accessed June 29, 2020, www.nytimes.com/2016/05/29/world/europe/drones-eagles.html; L. Holson, "Latest Attraction at French Theme Park: Crows That Pick Up Trash," *The New York Times*, August 17, 2018, accessed June 29, 2020, www.nytimes.com/2018/08/17/science/Crows-trash-puy-du-fou.html; K. Streeter, "On Pigeon Patrol, Rufus the Hawk Rules the Skies Over Wimbledon," *The New York Times*, July 12, 2019, accessed June 29, 2020, www.nytimes.com/2019/07/12/sports/tennis/wimbledon-hawk-pigeons-rufus.html; S. Zhang, "The 'Wall' That Keeps Flesh-Eating Worms Out of America," *The Atlantic*, May 26, 2020, accessed June 29, 2020, www.theatlantic.com/science/archive/2020/05/flesh-eating-worms-disease-containment-america-panama/611026/.

is capable of disassembling and recycling every part in 1.2 million iPhones a year. Liam's successor, Daisy, which can recycle 200 iPhones an hour (1.75 million a year), not only recycles parts, it helps Apple recycle and reuse 14 minerals that, like lithium, would otherwise have to be obtained from mining.[89] Apple's long-term goal is to become a "closed-loop" manufacturer that relies completely on recycled parts, minerals, and components.[90]

At the third level of sustainability, waste treatment, companies use biological, chemical, or other processes to turn potentially harmful waste into harmless compounds or useful by products. Finland-based **Neste Oil** converts animal fat and plant oil wastes, which are regulated by the Environmental Protection Agency, into green diesel fuel and jet fuel that reduce greenhouse-gas emissions by 60 percent and 80 percent, respectively.[91] Unlike many other treated fuels, Neste's diesel and jet fuels do not require modifications to existing diesel or jet engines. Neste partnered with McDonald's Netherlands to convert 384,000 gallons of used cooking oil each year into renewable diesel "to fuel the trucks that supply the restaurants, as well as those that pick up the [used oil] waste."[92]

The fourth and lowest level of sustainability is *waste disposal*. Wastes that cannot be prevented, reduced, recycled, reused, or treated should be safely disposed of in processing plants or in environmentally secure landfills that prevent leakage and contamination of soil and underground water supplies. Contrary to common belief, all businesses, not just manufacturing firms, have waste disposal problems. For example, with the average computer lasting just three years, approximately 60 million computers come out of service each year, creating disposal problems for offices all over the world. But organizations can't just throw old computers away because they have lead-containing cathode ray tubes in the monitors, toxic metals in the circuit boards, paint-coated plastic, and metal coatings that can contaminate groundwater.[93] Many companies give old computers and computer equipment to local computer recycling centers that distribute usable computers to nonprofit organizations or safely dispose of lead and other toxic materials. A number of retailers and electronics manufacturers operate recycling programs to keep electronics out of landfills. Dell's Reconnect program partners with Goodwill Industries. Find your local Goodwill location (www.dellreconnect.com) and drop off all of your electronics for recycling.[94] **Best Buy** recycles everything from TVs to ink and toner cartridges for printers to digital cameras to fitness equipment, no matter where you bought them or how old the items.[95] Finally, the US Environmental Protection Agency (EPA) has an online database (www.epa.gov/recycle/electronics-donation-and-recycling) to find out what companies have recycling programs for a variety of electronic items.

17 | Managing Information

LEARNING OUTCOMES

17-1 Explain the strategic importance of information.

17-2 Describe the characteristics of useful information (i.e., its value and costs).

17-3 Explain the basics of capturing, processing, and protecting information.

17-4 Describe how companies can access and share information and knowledge.

Jack Hollingsworth/Photodisc/Getty Images

17-1 STRATEGIC IMPORTANCE OF INFORMATION

A generation ago, computer hardware and software had little to do with managing business information. Rather than storing information on networked hard drives in cloud-based, data warehouses, managers stored it in filing cabinets. Instead of real-time tracking of daily sales and inventory levels via high-speed broadband connecting headquarters to warehouses to trucks to retail stores and web sales, print summaries were sent to top management at the end of each month. Instead of graphical displays of real-time company data in continuously updated digital dashboards, reports were typed on electric typewriters. Instead of auto-updating spreadsheets that pull live data from internal or external data sources, calculations were made by hand on adding machines. Managers communicated by sticky notes, not email or group chat. Phone messages were written down by assistants and coworkers, not forwarded in your email as a sound file with the message converted

to text. Workers did not use desktop, laptop, or tablet computers or smartphones as daily tools to get work done. Instead, they scheduled limited access time to run batch jobs on the mainframe computer (and prayed that the batch job computer code they wrote would work).

Today, computer hardware and software are an integral part of managing business information. This is due mainly to something called **Moore's law**. Gordon Moore is one of the founders of Intel Corporation, one of the largest designers and manufacturers of semiconductor chips used in computers. In 1965, Moore predicted that computer-processing power would double and that its cost would drop by 50 percent every two years.[1] As Exhibit 17.1 shows, Moore was right. Computer power, as measured by chip density, the number of transistors per computer chip, *has* more than doubled every few years, as have hard drive sizes and pixel density (i.e., screen resolution). Consequently, the computing device sitting in your lap or on your desk (or in your hand!) is not only smaller but also much cheaper and more powerful than the

large mainframe computers used by *Fortune* 500 companies 40 years ago. For instance, your iPhone replaces 13 of the 15 items, such as a desktop computer, mobile phone, CD player, camcorder, and so on, commonly sold by Radio Shack in 1991, items that would have cost you $3,071.21 then, or, after adjusting for inflation, $5,781.50 today. So your $750 iPhone not only replaces a trunkful of 1991 electronics gear, it does so for only 13 percent of the cost.[2] Of course, that doesn't include things invented since 1991 that iPhones can also replace, such as digital cameras, eBook readers, gaming devices, barcode scanners, and DVD players.[3] That's Moore's law in action. Likewise, in

> **Moore's law** the prediction that about every two years, computer processing power would double and its cost would drop by 50 percent

Exhibit 17.1
Moore's Law & Computer Chip Density (# of Transistors)

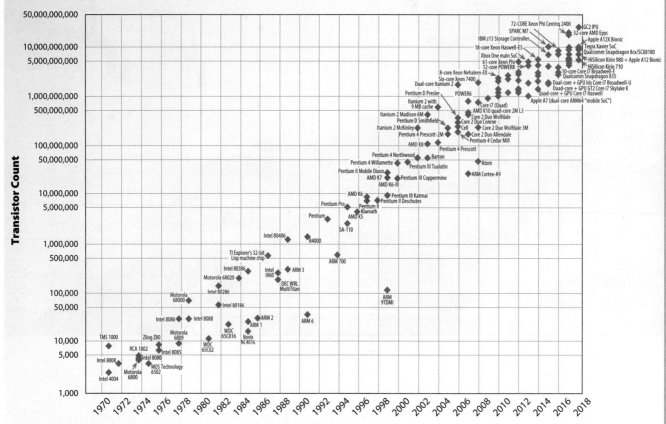

M. Roser, "Moore's Law—The Number of Transistors on Integrated Circuit Chips (1971–2018)," Our World in Data, accessed July 4, 2020, https://ourworldindata.org/technological-progress.

2001, the cost of sequencing one human genome was $100 million. Thanks to Moore's law, that cost is only $1,000 in 2020.[4]

Will Moore's law eventually fail and technological progress eventually slow? Perhaps, as the physics and costs of developing faster, more powerful chips (today's chips are already based on circuitry 1 billionth of a meter thin) may eventually slow the rate of development. For now, chip producers are meeting Moore's law two ways. First, tasks are offloaded from the main CPU to dedicated chips that only handle video, photography, or security. For that reason, a typical smart-phone uses a dozen or more specialized chips.[5] Second, stacking specialized chips on top of each other reduces temperatures and speeds data flow between chips.[6] Godfrey Cheng, of Taiwan Semiconductor Manufacturing Company, which makes the chips Apple uses in iPhones and iPads, says, "Moore's law is not dead; there are many different paths to continue to increase [chip] density."[7]

Raw data are facts and figures. For example, 26, $204, 128, and 57,171 are some data that I used the day I wrote this section of the chapter. However, facts and figures aren't particularly useful unless they have meaning. For example, you probably can't guess what these four pieces of raw data represent, can you? If you can't, these data are useless. That's why researchers

Raw data facts and figures

make the distinction between raw data and information. However, raw data consist of facts and figures, **information** is useful data that can influence someone's choices and behavior. One way to think about the difference between data and information is that information has context. Everywhere you go, your smartphone leaves behind digital breadcrumbs. **Thasos Group** founder Greg Skibiski says, "It's creating this data all the time, even if it's not ringing."[8] While those digital breadcrumbs can't identify you, they do show where millions of people are going – and that context means information. For example, if a new Whole Foods store opens, Thasos can track whether grocery shoppers left Kroger or Walmart to shop there. MIT researcher Alex Pentland says, "You can look at this blood flow of people moving around."[9]

So what did those four pieces of data mean to me? Well, 26 stands for Channel 26, ESPN, on which I watched the qualifying rounds for the next day's Formula 1 race; $204 (a crazy good price) is how much it would cost to fly to the West Coast to visit family; 128 is for the 128-gigabyte storage card that I want to add to my digital camera (prices are low, so I'll probably buy it); and 57,171 means that it's time to get the oil changed in my truck.

In today's hypercompetitive business environments, information is as important as capital (i.e., money) for business success, whether it's about product inventory, pricing, or costs. It takes money to get businesses started, but businesses can't survive and grow without the right information.

*Information has strategic importance for organizations because it can be used to **17-1a obtain first-mover advantage** and **17-1b sustain competitive advantage after it has been created.***

17-1a First-Mover Advantage

First-mover advantage is the strategic advantage that companies earn by being the first in an industry to use new information technology to substantially lower costs or to differentiate a product or service from that of competitors. Pandora, for example, pioneered music streaming and used to lead this highly competitive market. Pandora's most popular option, which is advertising-supported and free to listeners, has 65 million active listeners, down from 79.4 million in 2016. Pandora has just 7.1 million paying subscribers.[10]

While first-mover advantage typically leads to above average profits and market share, it doesn't immunize a company from competition. Pandora faces three primary competitors: Spotify (130 million subscribers), Apple Music (68 million subscribers), and Amazon's Prime Music (55 million subscribers), which is free for Amazon's estimated 133 million Prime members (who pay $119 a year for Prime membership, which includes two-day shipping and a number of other benefits), or $9.99 per month for non-Prime members.[11]

Many first-movers have failed to capitalize on their strategic advantages. BlackBerry lost first-mover advantage in smartphones (to Apple and Android), as did Taxi

> The key to sustaining a competitive advantage is using information technology to continuously improve and support the core functions of a business.

iStock.com/ManuelBurgos

Information useful data that can influence people's choices and behavior

First-mover advantage the strategic advantage that companies earn by being the first to use new information technology to substantially lower costs or to make a product or service different from that of competitors

Magic (to Uber and Lyft) and HomeAway (to Airbnb).[12] A study of 30 first-movers found two key factors mattered in terms of sustaining first-mover advantage: the pace at which product technology is changing and how fast the market is growing.[13] As these examples show, if better technology is quickly being introduced by new market entrants, and the market is quickly growing (which attracts new competitors who want a share of that growing market), it can be difficult to sustain first-mover advantage.

17-1b Sustaining Competitive Advantage

As described earlier, companies that use information technology to establish first-mover advantage usually have higher market shares and profits. According to the resource-based view of information technology, shown in Exhibit 17.2, companies need to address three critical questions to sustain a competitive advantage through information technology. First, does the information technology create value for the firm by lowering costs or providing a better product or service? If an information technology doesn't add value, then investing in it would put the firm at a competitive disadvantage relative to companies that choose information technologies that do add value.

Second, is the information technology the same or different across competing firms? If all the firms have access to the same information technology and use it in the same way, then no firm has an advantage over another (i.e., there is competitive parity).

Third, is it difficult for another company to create or buy the information technology used by the firm? If so, then the firm has established a sustainable competitive advantage over competitors through information technology. If not, then the competitive advantage is just temporary, and competitors should eventually be able to duplicate the advantages the leading firm has gained from information technology. *The Wall Street Journal's* Christopher Mims explains, "Sure, you can start a business that uses Amazon's cloud-computing services and taps into its logistics platform by selling on its site, but the software Amazon developed to enable Amazon Web Services and its retail marketplace are not themselves available for other firms. [Likewise] Walmart built an elaborate logistics system around bar code scanners, which allowed it to beat out smaller retail rivals. Notably, it never sold this technology to any competitors."[14]

In short, the key to sustaining a competitive advantage is not faster computers, more memory, or larger hard drives. The key is using information technology to continuously improve and support the core functions of a business.

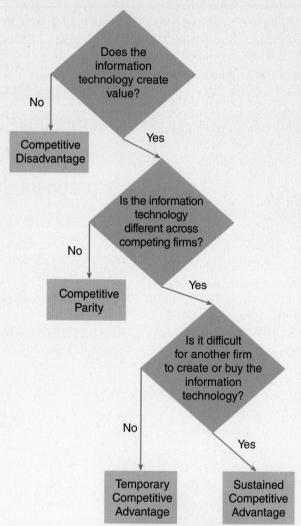

Exhibit 17.2
Using Information Technology to Sustain a Competitive Advantage

Source: Adapted from F. J. Mata, W. L. Fuerst, and J. B. Barney, "Information Technology and Sustained Competitive Advantage: A Resource-Based Analysis," *MIS Quarterly* 19, no. 4 (December 1995): 487–505.

17-2 CHARACTERISTICS AND COSTS OF USEFUL INFORMATION

Information and data are more abundant today than ever before. Seven years ago, British Airways (BA) began providing pilots with iPads to replace the huge binders containing printouts of standard procedures, and emergency protocols required in every cockpit. Today, those iPads have become an indispensable tool. Pilots click the "There's Go Fly" app for inflight information, "Yammer" to communicate with others at BA, "ESP-PIL" to see information on every passenger on board – whether they've been delayed and their status with BA's frequent-flyer program. Since crews can be large, for example, 22 crew members on an Airbus A380, an app shows names, pictures and profiles for every crew member on board. Pilot Spencer Norton says, "When you're opening the flight deck door, you've got a good idea who you're operating with..."[15] Before leaving for the airport, pilots check their BA iPads for alerts, such as bad weather or labor strikes (common in parts of Europe). If one of those operational alerts suggests in-flight delays, Pilots can order more fuel to account for the delay with a finger-controlled slider that shows how many more minutes of flight time they need (the amount of fuel is automatically calculated using BA algorithms). Finally, as they near destinations, pilots can review standard flight approach paths, runway layouts, and on-the-ground taxi paths to arrival gates.[16]

*As British Airways use of iPads demonstrates, information is useful when it is **17-2a accurate, 17-2b complete, 17-2c relevant, and 17-2d timely**. However, there can be significant **17-2e acquisition, 17-2f processing, 17-2g storage, 17-2h retrieval,** and **17-2i communication costs** associated with useful information.*

17-2a Accurate Information

Information is useful when it is accurate. Before relying on information to make decisions, you must know that the information is correct. But what if it isn't?

Or, what if it's not the data you need? A study of 300 companies by big-four accounting firm

PricewaterhouseCoopers (PwC) found that only 15 percent had the right data they needed to use digital tools to cut costs, remain competitive, and increase sales.[17] PwC's report concluded that most company data were "acquired haphazardly" and lacked "the detail and demonstrable accuracy needed for use with AI and other advanced automation."[18] How important are accurate data? The firms in PwC's study estimated that cleaning up data to ensure accuracy would cut costs by 33 percent and grow revenues by 31 percent. For the typical Fortune 1000 multinational firm, increasing data accuracy by just 10 percent increases revenues by $2 billion a year.[19] There's an old saying regarding data, data analysis, and decision-making: "Garbage in. Garbage Out." At a minimum, companies should consider hiring a chief data officer to oversee data management and data analytics.[20]

17-2b Complete Information

Information is useful when it is complete. Incomplete or missing information makes it difficult to recognize problems and identify potential solutions. Grocery customers assume the mangoes they buy are fresh and safe – until the US Food and Drug Administration (FDA) issues a mango recall for salmonella or listeria contamination, both of which cause fever, diarrhea, fatigue, muscle aches, and sometimes more serious complications. When this happens, grocers stop selling mangoes supplied by firms on the FDA recall list. But they still have to check for contamination from other mango suppliers. Incomplete information, however, makes this difficult, as contamination could occur when mangoes are harvested from farms, packed at distribution warehouses, transported to wholesalers, repackaged by wholesalers for grocery stores, transported to grocery store distribution centers, and transported to grocery stores and placed on shelves for customers. Without complete data at each step, it would take **Walmart** almost seven days to trace the origin of a bag of mangoes in one of its stores.[21]

Walmart now uses an app with a blockchain ledger system to track and collect those data. At each step of the supply chain, Walmart's mango suppliers use the app to record dates, location, fruit images, and transaction approvals. Because blockchain ledgers are encrypted, those data cannot be changed once approved, time-stamped, and added via Walmart's app. This also ensures that the data are always up to date. What's the advantage for Walmart? It takes just 2.2 seconds to trace the origin and supply chain steps of a bag of mangoes![22] Frank Yiannas, vice president of food safety at Walmart, says, "You're capturing real-time data at every point...It's the equivalent of FedEx tracking for food."[23] Complete information matters.

17-2c Relevant Information

You can have complete, accurate information, but it's not very useful if it doesn't pertain to the problems you're facing. The dairy industry is a low-margin, highly competitive industry where small changes in productivity make a big difference. Keeping cows healthy and managing pregnancies so that each cow has a calf every year are fundamental to a well run dairy farm. Austin Knowles, a dairy farmer in Worcestershire, England, in the United Kingdom, has relevant information thanks to notifications sent to his phone from sensors inserted in his cow's stomachs. The sensors, which last about four years, act as an early warning signal by letting him know the cow's temperature, how much she's had to drink, how many steps she's taken, and the pH content of her stomach. Stefan Rosenkranz, cofounder of SmaXtec, which makes the devices that upload information to cloud servers for analysis, said, "It's easier, after all, to look at the situation from inside the cow than in the lab."[24] The real-time data save farmers from having a vet examine the cows for vital signs. And that information is 95 percent accurate in predicting when calves will be born. Farmer Knowles said, "The crux of any dairy farm is fertility. We are trying to have a calf per cow every year. Everything we do on the farm

JIANG HONGYAN/ Shutterstock.com

comes back to that."[25] Farmer Paul Doble says, "I use smaXtec as an early warning system, to pick up issues early, take preventive measures, and reduce use of antibiotics."[26]

17-2d Timely Information

Finally, information is useful when it is timely. To be timely, the information must be available when needed to define a problem or to begin to identify possible solutions. If you've ever thought, "I wish I had known that earlier," then you understand the importance of timely information and the opportunity cost of not having it.

Schwebel Baking Company, in Cleveland, Ohio, makes 1 million packages of bread, buns, rolls, bagels, and stuffing every day for delivery in Ohio, Pennsylvania, West Virginia, and New York. An hour after a delivery truck left its Cleveland bakery on its way to Rochester, New York, truck sensors triggered messages that led the driver to turn back to Cleveland. Why? He'd picked up the wrong trailer and had the wrong order. One of Schwebel's truck dispatchers, who was tracking 78 trucks and 100 trailers on a live map, was notified by a pop-up message saying the trailer was heading to the wrong location. Vice president of operations Adam Schwebel said, "Had that not taken place, it would have been eight hours or more of lost time, and our sales team would have been very upset."[27]

17-2e Acquisition Costs

Acquisition cost is the cost of obtaining data that you don't have. For example, a startup cookie company expands to a small facility to set up a production line with 10 ovens running 24 hours a day. To keep costs down and quality high, oven temperatures, timers, and conveyor speeds need to be monitored and controlled. Full-time staff could be hired to do that. Or, you could automate data acquisition by buying a data logger (which records data over time) connected to a thermocouple thermometer (which turns the temperature reading into recordable data) and a frequency input from a magnetic pickup (for measuring conveyor speed). You'll also need software to record and analyze the data. At a minimum, figure $5,000 per oven, or $50,000 to get started.[28] And that doesn't include data acquisition costs for raw materials, industrial dough mixers, extruders, and moulders for sizing and shaping cookie dough prior to baking, oil-spray machines to spray additional flavors on the just-baked cookies, and machines to package and box the cookies for distribution.[29]

17-2f Processing Costs

Companies often have massive amounts of data but not in the form or combination they need. **Processing cost** is the cost of turning raw data into usable information. A **data silo** is an isolated data set that is difficult to obtain, combine, or use with other company data.[30] Data silos often have high processing costs because of **data variety**, that is, data that are formatted or structured in different ways. Making differently formatted and structured data, such as numbers, words, pictures, and social media, compatible is difficult and costly.[31]

Pilot Flying J runs 750 travel centers in 44 states and Canada where truckers can stop to refuel themselves and their trucks, shop, shower, play video games, do laundry, or have truck maintenance or repairs performed. When it decided to create an app that truckers could use to reserve parking spots, it had data variety and data silo problems because of incompatible data stored in a variety of different IT systems. Tyler Tanaka, Pilot Flying J's director of digital, loyalty, and innovation, said, "We had all this disparate data in silos and homegrown systems that we were trying to get to talk back to the app, and realized that we were really hamstrung."[32] It took three years to fix these problems.

17-2g Storage Costs

Storage cost is the cost of physically or electronically archiving information for later retrieval and use. Besides the networked computer servers on which data reside, the costs of data storage facilities include power, backup power, high-speed data feeds to the data center, cooling solutions to prevent computer, network

---

Acquisition cost the cost of obtaining data that you don't have

Processing cost the cost of turning raw data into usable information

Data silo is an isolated data set that is difficult to obtain, combine or use with other company data

Data variety data that are formatted or structured in different ways

Storage cost the cost of physically or electronically archiving information for later retrieval and use

Juice Jacking: Don't Charge Your Phone at a Public Charging Station

Your phone, tablet, or laptop is about to die from a low battery, so you plug into a public charging station with already attached charging cords. Aren't they thoughtful! But Los Angeles County District Attorney Luke Sisak says, "A free charge could end up draining your bank account." How? *Juice jacking*. Hackers put minuscule hardware into charging cables that loads malware to log keystrokes or remotely lock you out of your device.

But what if you have your own cable? Well, hackers are now putting similar hacking hardware into public USB charging ports. But there's no way to tell if a public USB charging port is safe. So buy a USB condom (yes, that's really a thing) with a disabled data pin that charges but doesn't transmit data. No data means no malware and no hacking. Plug your charging wire into the USB condom and then plug the USB condom into the public USB charging port. Voila! Safe charging.

lakshmiprasada S/Shutterstock.com

Source: Cox, "These Legit-Looking iPhone Lightning Cables Will Hijack Your Computer," *Vice*, April 10, 2019, accessed July 9, 2020 www.vice.com /en_us/article/evj4qw/these-iphone-lightning-cables-will-hack-your-computer; A. Ortiz, "Stop! Don't Charge Your Phone This Way," *The New York Times*, November 18, 2019, accessed July 9, 2020, www.nytimes.com/2019/11/18/technology /personaltech/usb-warning-juice-jacking.html.

and power equipment from overheating, onsite and online security to protect data, and network and software engineers to run it.[33]

This makes sense for large companies like Walmart, but most small and mid-sized businesses rent cloud data storage and services from Amazon, Google, or Microsoft. For example, **ClubCorp**, which manages 200+ country clubs, city clubs, athletic clubs, and stadium clubs nationwide, abandoned the networked storage servers it had run for 18 years to move to the cloud. Chief Information Officer Patrick Benson said, "IT spending was escalating out of control. If we looked at bringing our IT systems up to date, without moving to the cloud, we would have had to purchase all new data center hardware. We would have had to up[date] the licensing to current licensing for that hardware."[34]

17-2h Retrieval Costs

Retrieval cost is the cost of accessing already-stored and processed information. One of the most common misunderstandings about information is that it is easy and cheap to retrieve after the company has it. Not so. First, you have to find the

> **Retrieval cost** the cost of accessing already-stored and processed information

information. Then, you've got to convince whoever has it to share it with you. Then the information has to be processed into a form that is useful for you. By the time you get the information you need, it might not be timely anymore.

For example, as companies move toward paperless office systems, how will employees quickly and easily retrieve archived emails, file records, website information, word processing documents, or images? Likewise, how will managers and employees quickly and easily retrieve information about costs, inventory, and sales going back months and years? Think about it. At home could you easily access the information found on 5¼ inch or 3.5-inch floppy disks? Have you got computers with drives to read them? Would the file formats still be readable? Is the software for those files available and still running? Have you got time to sort through them file by file and disk by disk to find what you need?[35]

Retrieval cost is also a big factor for firms moving their data to the cloud. Which is why **Amazon Web Services (AWS)**, the largest cloud service in the world, offers its Snowmobile service to transport huge amounts of corporate data to its AWS servers. Despite the name, Amazon's Snowmobile uses a long-haul truck trailer, 45 feet long, that is stuffed with hard drives and servers capable of holding 100 petabytes of data (a petabyte is 1 million gigabytes). Since it's not uncommon for large

Amazon Web Services estimate it would take 20 years to transfer an exabyte of data from a corporate data warehouse to AWS servers. It takes just two weeks plus drive time using 10 of the company's Snowmobile data trucks.

17-3 CAPTURING, PROCESSING, AND PROTECTING INFORMATION

In 1907, **Metropolitan Life Insurance** built a huge office building in New York City for its brand-new, state-of-the-art information technology system. What was this great breakthrough in information management? Card files. That's right, the same card file system that every library in America used before computers. Metropolitan Life's information technology consisted of 20,000 separate file drawers that sat in hundreds of file cabinets more than 15 feet tall. This filing system held 20 million insurance applications, 700,000 accounting books, and 500,000 death certificates. Metropolitan Life employed 61 workers who did nothing but sort, file, and climb ladders to pull files as needed.[39]

How we get and share information has clearly changed. The cost, inefficiency, and ineffectiveness of using this formerly state-of-the-art system would put an insurance company out of business within months. Today, if storms, fire, or accidents damage a policyholder's property, he or she can use the insurance company's smartphone app to photograph and describe the damage and upload receipts and relevant documents. A company representative will then show up and write a check on the spot to cover the losses. As the claims process unfolds, the policyholder can ask questions, fill out forms, and access documents on the company's personalized web portal. From card files to internet files in just under a century, the rate of change in information technology is spectacular.

*In this section, you will learn about the information technologies that companies use to **17-3a capture, 17-3b process**, and **17-3c protect information.***

17-3a Capturing Information.

There are two basic methods of capturing information: manual and electronic.

Manual capture of information is a slow, costly, labor-intensive, and often inaccurate process, which entails recording and entering data by hand into a data storage device. When you applied for your first driver's license,

> **Communication cost** the cost of transmitting information from one place to another

firms to have exabyte-sized amounts of data (an exabyte is 1 billion gigabytes), Amazon estimates that it would take 20+ years to transfer an exabyte of data from a corporate data warehouse to AWS servers.[36] However, it takes two weeks plus driving using 10 Snowmobile data trucks. At a cost of $500,000 per month per truck, the total cost of retrieval from one system to another would be $5 million for an exabyte of data.[37]

17-2i Communication Costs

Communication cost is the cost of transmitting information from one place to another. While Moore's law has significantly increased communication speeds and reduced communication costs, those costs aren't insignificant. Typically, each office, warehouse, manufacturing facility, and store needs broadband internet, dedicated office phones, wired ethernet access to each desk, Wi-Fi, smartphones with data plans, tablets, and computers. And that's without factoring in the super-high-speed options needed for data-intensive companies like technology, design, engineering, or manufacturing firms. When the coronavirus pandemic forced computer chip maker **Micron Technology**'s 3,500 managers and employees to work from home, the company had to purchase 700 laptops, 800 computer monitors, and nearly 3,000 virtual machine accounts permitting secure offsite access to company networks and data. Micron also quadrupled its monthly high-speed internet data cap to handle the higher data volumes associated with everyone working from home.[38]

you manually entered personal information about yourself by typing it into an electronic form. Then, after you passed your driver's test, that information was electronically transferred from the department of motor vehicles' database to the statewide database used by local and state police who could access it from their patrol cars in the event they pulled you over for speeding. (Isn't information great?) To avoid incomplete information and data entry errors that plague manual information capture, companies have turned to *electronic capture*, using bar codes, radio frequency identification (RFID) tags, sensors, document scanners, and robotic data automation to electronically capture and record data.

Bar codes represent numerical data by varying the thickness and pattern of vertical bars. The primary advantage of bar codes is that the data they represent can be read and recorded in an instant with a handheld or pen-type scanner. One pass of the scanner (okay, sometimes several) and "beep!" the information has been captured. Bar codes cut checkout times in half, reduce data entry errors by 75 percent, and save stores money because stockers don't have to go through the labor-intensive process of putting a price tag on each item in the store.[40] And, with mobile phone apps, bar codes are becoming ubiquitous in travel (mobile boarding passes), for customer loyalty and payment programs (Starbucks), and in entertainment, such as movies (Fandango) and live events (LiveNation or TicketMaster).

QR (quick response) codes are bar codes with black and white patterns scanned with your smartphone. Chinese consumers can quickly pay for taxi rides by scanning the taxi driver's QR code using Alipay Wallet (China-based Alibaba's PayPal equivalent).[41] Replicon's CloudClock system works by having employees scan a QR code that prompts a camera to take and time-stamp their picture, indicating when they started and stopped work.[42] Finally, BMO Harris Bank uses cardless ATM machines where customers use their bank app to indicate how much money they want to withdraw. The app generates a QR code that the ATM machine scans and authorizes before dispensing cash in just 15 seconds, or just one-third of the time of a card-based transaction. Also, QR codes eliminate the risk of card skimming in which hackers tap into the card-reading device in the ATM machine.[43]

With mobile phone apps, bar codes are becoming ubiquitous in travel (mobile boarding passes), for customer loyalty, payment programs and in entertainment, such as movies (Fandango), and live events (TicketMaster).

Radio frequency identification (RFID) tags contain minuscule microchips and antennas that transmit information via radio waves.[44] Unlike bar codes, which require direct line-of-sight scanning, RFID tags are read by turning on an RFID reader that, like a radio, tunes into a specific frequency to determine the number *and* location of products, parts, or anything else to which the RFID tags are attached. Turning on an RFID reader sends out an electromagnetic energy pulse that activates every RFID tag within the reader's range (from several hundred to several thousand feet).

Because they are now so inexpensive, RFID tags and readers are being put to thousands of uses in all kinds of businesses. When Johnson Controls, a $37 billion manufacturer, realized that it was missing thousands of shipping containers and racks used to transport parts and finished products, it bought 830,000 RFID tags and attached them to its remaining equipment. Thanks to the RFID tag readers installed in all of its factories and warehouses, **Johnson Controls** can now track the location of its 830,000 containers and racks—down to which door they exited the factory from and which customers they got shipped to. Brian Kelly, Johnson Controls' director of supply-chain management, said, "We could get to a point that we not only know where all of our containers are but what is in each one without ever opening them up."[45]

Sensors detect an event or change and actively transmit that information to other electronic devices. An event, for example, could be someone entering or leaving a space, while a change could be temperature increasing or decreasing. In Sydney, Australia, park benches and

Bar code a visual pattern that represents numerical data by varying the thickness and pattern of vertical bars

Radio frequency identification (RFID) tags tags containing minuscule microchips that transmit information via radio waves and can be used to track the number and location of the objects into which the tags have been inserted

Sensors instruments that detect events or changes and actively transmit that information to other electronic devices

tables with sensors detect and report how often they are used, which tells the park department whether they might be broken (no one uses them) or whether more need to be added (they're used all the time).[46] Sensors are also being used to track passenger line lengths at airports, whether hailstorms have damaged cars at auto dealerships, and whether social distancing guidelines are being disregarded in the workplace.[47] In manufacturing, sensors are frequently used to monitor machine vibrations (indicating when maintenance is needed), power monitoring (for detecting when power stops or power use surges), or temperatures (for monitoring whether temperatures fall in or out of acceptable ranges).[48]

Document scanners, which convert printed text and pictures into digital images, have become an increasingly popular method of capturing data electronically because they are inexpensive and easy to use. The first requirement for a good scanner is a document feeder that automatically feeds document pages into the scanner or turns the pages (often with a puff of air) when scanning books or bound documents. Text that has been digitized cannot be searched or edited like the regular text in your word processing software, however, so the second requirement for a good scanner is **optical character recognition** software to scan and convert original or digitized documents into American Standard Code for Information Interchange (ASCII) text or Adobe PDF documents. ASCII text can be searched, read, and edited with standard word processing, email, desktop publishing, database management, and spreadsheet software, and PDF documents can be searched and edited with Adobe's Acrobat software.

After data or documents have been entered, captured, or scanned with OCR, **robotic data automation**, also known as software bots, can be taught to recognize specific data patterns, such as dates, costs, and product numbers, in files, reports, or data silos. Once a pattern has been recognized, bots automatically scan, locate, and extract those data, compiling them into more useful forms and combinations. For instance, the customer service division of media giant **AT&T** needs to know which network traffic issues prompt its cellphone and home internet customers to call for assistance. Those data, which used to be processed by hand, are now handled by bots. Network design engineer Michael Martuccio says, "My time isn't spent compiling and conditioning data anymore; it's spent analyzing it."[49]

17-3b Processing Information

Processing information means transforming raw data into meaningful information that can be applied to

> Data mining is carried out using complex algorithms such as neural networks, rule induction, and decision trees. If you don't know what those are, that's okay. With data mining, you don't have to.

business decision-making. Evaluating sales data to determine the best- and worst-selling products, examining repair records to determine product reliability, and monitoring costs (of any kind) are all examples of processing raw data into meaningful information. And with automated, electronic capture of data, increased processing power, and cheaper and more plentiful ways to store data, managers no longer worry about getting data. Instead, they scratch their heads about how to use the overwhelming amount of data that pours into their businesses every day. Furthermore, most managers know little about statistics and have neither the time nor the inclination to learn how to use them to analyze data.

One promising tool to help managers dig out from under the avalanche of data is data mining. **Data mining** is the process of discovering patterns and relationships in large amounts of data.[50] Data mining is carried out using complex algorithms such as neural networks, rule induction, and decision trees. If you don't know what those are, that's okay. With data mining, you don't have to. Most managers only need to know that data mining looks for patterns that are already in the data but are too complex for them to spot on their own.

Many **Airbnb** hosts who rent their rooms or homes to travelers have

Document scanner an electronic device that converts printed text and pictures into digital images

Optical character recognition the ability of software to convert digitized documents into American Standard Code for Information Interchange (ASCII) text that can be searched, read, and edited by word processing and other kinds of software

Robotic data automation software robots are taught to recognize specific data patterns and then automatically scan, locate, and extract those data

Processing information transforming raw data into meaningful information

Data mining the process of discovering unknown patterns and relationships in large amounts of data

trouble deciding how much to charge per night. Data mining showed Airbnb that adjusting prices for *similarity, recency,* and *location* could maximize profits and occupancy rates. Similarity measured factors such as a home versus a private room, the number of bedrooms, the uniqueness of the property (are you renting a room in a castle or in an apartment?), and the number of reviews. Why reviews? They give potential renters confidence regarding the property and its host. Travel is seasonal, and demand for rentals is affected by major events like holidays, trade shows, and sporting events. Taking these and other recency factors into consideration, Airbnb can decide whether last week's, last month's, or last year's pricing should guide how much to charge today. Finally, data mining revealed that a rental's location was critical to renters. Is it safe? Is it near transportation, restaurants, and tourist sites? To measure the value of rentals' locations, Airbnb hired cartographers to "map the boundaries of every neighborhood in our top cities all over the world."[51]

Data mining typically splits a data set in half, finds patterns in one half, and then tests the validity of those patterns by trying to find them again in the second half of the data set. The data typically come from a **data warehouse**, which stores huge amounts of data that have been prepared for data mining analysis by being cleaned of errors and redundancy. The data in a data warehouse can then be analyzed using two kinds of data mining. **Supervised data mining** usually begins with the user telling the data mining software to look and test for specific patterns and relationships in a data set. Typically, this is done through a series of "what-if?" questions or statements. For instance, a grocery store manager might instruct the data mining software to determine if Facebook ads shown to local shoppers increase or decrease sales.

By contrast, with **unsupervised data mining**, the user simply tells the data mining software to uncover whatever patterns and relationships it can find in a data set. **Castlight Healthcare** conducts unsupervised data mining to identify nonmedical data that are related to employees having diabetes, or heart disease, for example. Harry Greenspun, director of Deloitte LLP's Center for Health Solutions, which does health-related data mining like Castlight, says, "I bet I could better predict your risk of a heart attack by where you shop and where you eat than by your genome."[52] Someone who regularly buys things at a bike shop will likely be in better shape than someone who regularly buys video games online or at GameStop. Castlight then "nudges" employees with personalized messages regarding medical services or healthier behavior related to their medical issues.[53] Unsupervised data mining is particularly good at identifying association or affinity patterns, sequence patterns, and predictive patterns. It can also identify what data-mining technicians call data clusters.[54]

Association or affinity patterns occur when two or more database elements tend to occur together in a significant way. **Castlight Healthcare** has a new data-mining tool that it uses to determine which female employees are likely to get pregnant. The idea is to identify them early in their pregnancy to make sure mothers and babies are healthy from the start. It typically finds that the earliest predictors of pregnancy are whether women have searched for pregnancy-related information on the Castlight Healthcare website (which helps employees search for medical information and providers) and if they have stopped filling birth-control prescriptions. When those two pieces of data are combined with a woman's age and ages of her children (if any), Castlight can accurately predict whether a woman is pregnant. At that point, unbeknown to employers who are not privy to this confidential information, Castlight sends female employees information to help them choose an obstetrician and begin prenatal care. And, if the data mining was wrong, they can opt out of receiving the messages.[55]

Sequence patterns appear when two or more database elements occur together in a significant pattern in which one of the elements precedes the other. Hospitals employ the Modified Early Warning Score (MEWS), which uses commonly measured vital signs, such as blood pressure, temperature, and heart rate, to predict the likelihood of a patient going Code Blue—that is, respiratory or cardiac arrest. Patients with higher MEWS scores are monitored more closely. Doctors at Chicago's NorthShore University HealthSystem used data mining to see how well 72 medical variables predicted the likelihood of a patient going Code Blue. On a data set of 133,000 patients, data mining correctly predicted Code Blues 72 percent of the time—four hours before they happened. By contrast, MEWS scores accurately predicted Code Blues just 30 percent of the time.[56]

Data warehouse a database that stores huge amounts of data that have been prepared for data-mining analysis by being cleaned of errors and redundancy

Supervised data mining the process when the user tells the data-mining software to look and test for specific patterns and relationships in a data set

Unsupervised data mining the process when the user simply tells the data mining software to uncover whatever patterns and relationships it can find in a data set

Association or affinity patterns when two or more database elements tend to occur together in a significant way

Sequence patterns when two or more database elements occur together in a significant pattern in which one of the elements precedes the other

Predictive patterns are just the opposite of association or affinity patterns. While association or affinity patterns look for database elements that seem to go together, **predictive patterns** help identify database elements that are different. Banks and credit card companies use data mining to find predictive patterns that distinguish customers who are good credit risks from those who are less likely to pay their loans and monthly bills. Lending money to people with poor credit or without bank accounts (one out of four adults worldwide) is risky. To better assess that risk, some startup companies are going beyond standard credit scores and are using social media to separate good borrowers from bad ones. For example, you're a better candidate if you access the internet via an expensive smartphone (versus an internet cafe where you pay by the hour); don't let your phone battery run down; and you get more phone calls than you make. You are also more likely to get a loan if your phone stays in the same place every day (indicating that you're at work) and you regularly interact with a group of close friends who are good credit risks (meaning that you probably are as well).[57]

Data clusters are the last kind of pattern found by data mining. **Data clusters** occur when three or more database elements occur together (i.e., cluster) in a significant way. If you're injured at work, workers' compensation insurance pays for lost wages and medical care. Since opioid pain killers were frequently prescribed for even minor injuries, since 20 percent of those prescribed opioids become addicted (with severe consequences), and since incorrectly prescribed opioids triple how long injured workers are out of work, **Hartford Financial** uses data mining to find data clusters that identify injured workers most at risk of opioid addiction. Hartford's workers' compensation insurance databases are scanned daily to examine new claims for workers' comp, looking for things such as insomnia (first element), heart disease (second element), anxiety (third element), a recent divorce (fourth element), or a recent death in the family (fifth element). When matches are found, Hartford's nurses contact doctors and patients if pain killer dosages are too strong or if the prescriptions are for too long.[58]

Traditionally, data mining has been very expensive and very complex. Today, however, data-mining services and analyses are much more affordable and within reach of most companies' budgets. And, if it follows the path of most technologies, data mining will become even easier and cheaper to use in the future.

17-3c Protecting Information

Protecting information is the process of ensuring that data are reliably and consistently retrievable in a

usable format for authorized users but no one else. Unfortunately, data breaches are occurring at record levels. According to IBM, 8.5 billion records, such as credit cards, personal identification, passwords, and health information, were compromised via hacking in 2019, a 200 percent increase over 2018.[59] The average data breach costs a company $8.2 million. It typically takes 206 days to identify the breach and 73 days to contain it, meaning the hackers are long gone before the breach was realized and stopped.[60] Marriott Hotels (383 million guests' passport numbers and credit cards), Facebook (540 million usernames, IDs, and passwords on unprotected servers!!!), and Capital One (100 million credit card applications, 80,000 bank accounts, and 140,000 social security numbers) were some of the worst and largest breaches in the last year.[61] Hackers also got to Amazon founder and CEO Jeff Bezos's phone via the WhatsApp messaging app.[62] If they can get to Bezos, the world's richest person, they can get to anyone.

People inside and outside companies can steal or destroy company data in various ways, including denial-of-service web server attacks that can bring down some of the busiest and best-run sites on the internet; malware and viruses, spyware, or adware that spread quickly and can result in data loss and business disruption; keystroke monitoring, in which every mouse click and keystroke you make is monitored, stored, and sent to unauthorized users; password-cracking software that steals supposedly secure passwords; and phishing, where fake but real-looking emails and websites trick users into sharing personal information (user names, passwords, account numbers) leading to unauthorized account access; and ransomware in which data are encrypted and made

Predictive patterns patterns that help identify database elements that are different

Data clusters when three or more database elements occur together (i.e., cluster) in a significant way

Protecting information the process of ensuring that data are reliably and consistently retrievable in a usable format for authorized users but no one else

WHAT HAPPENED WHEN CHRISTOPHER MIMS GAVE THE WORLD HIS TWITTER PASSWORD

Wall Street Journal reporter Christopher Mims published his Twitter password, "christophermims," in one of his columns. Mims wrote, "Knowing that won't help you hack it, however." And he was right. Despite hundreds of attempts, no one accessed his account.

The reason they couldn't? Mims had enabled two-factor authentication, a second form of authentication, which in this case was based on codes good for just 60 seconds that were randomly generated by the Google Authenticator app linked to his Twitter account.

Mims concluded, "I think I proved my point: Even when I exposed my password in as public a fashion as possible, my account remained secure."

So, protect your accounts. Enable two-factor authentication. But, don't give the world your password.

Sources: C. Mims, "The Password Is Finally Dying. Here's Mine," *The Wall Street Journal*, July 13, 2014, accessed May 7, 2017, https://www.wsj.com/articles/the-password-is-finally-dying-heres-mine-1405298376; C. Mims, "Commentary: What I Learned, and What You Should Know, After I Published My Twitter Password," Digits, *The Wall Street Journal*, July 15, 2014, accessed May 7, 2017, blogs.wsj.com/digits/2014/07/15/commentary-what-i-learned-and-what-you-should-know-after-i-published-my-twitter-password/.

Rawpixel.com/Shutterstock.com

unusable until a ransom is paid to hackers to unlock the data. Studies show that the threats listed in Exhibit 17.3 are so widespread that automatic attacks will begin on an unprotected computer 60 seconds after it connects to the internet, potentially affecting it with malware or viruses.[63]

As shown in the right-hand column of Exhibit 17.3, numerous steps can be taken to secure data and data networks. Some of the most important are authentication and authorization, firewalls, anti-malware and antivirus software for corporate servers and personal devices, data encryption, virtual private networks, secure sockets layer encryption, and ensuring security on home and public Wi-Fi.[64] We will review those steps and then finish this section with a brief review of white-hat hacking and the threat of social engineering.

Two critical steps are required to make sure that data can be accessed by authorized users and no one else. One is **authentication**, that is, making sure users are who they claim to be.[65] The other is **authorization**, that is, granting authenticated users approved access to data, software, and systems.[66] When an ATM prompts you to enter your personal identification number (PIN), the bank is authenticating that you are you. After you've been authenticated, you are authorized to access your funds and no one else's. Of course, as anyone who has lost a PIN or password or had one stolen knows, user authentication systems are not foolproof. In particular, users create security risks by not changing their default account passwords (such as birthdates) or by using weak passwords such as names ("Larry") or complete words ("football") that are quickly guessed by password-cracking software.[67]

This is why many companies are now turning to **two-factor authentication**, which is based on what users know, such as a password, and what they have, in their possession, such as a secure ID card, their phones, or unique information that only they would know.[68] When logging in, users are first asked for their passwords. But then they must provide a second authentication factor, such as an answer to a security question (i.e., unique information) or a validation code that has been sent to their mobile phone.

Authentication making sure potential users are who they claim to be

Authorization granting authenticated users approved access to data, software, and systems

Two-factor authentication authentication based on what users know, such as a password and what they have in their possession, such as a secure ID card or key

Exhibit 17.3
Security Threats to Data and Data Networks

Security Problem	Source	Affects	Severity	The Threat	The Solution
Denial of service; web server attacks and corporate network attacks	Internet hackers	All servers	High	Loss of data, disruption of service, and theft of service.	Implement firewall, password control, server-side review, threat monitoring, and bug fixes; turn PCs off when not in use; reroute data traffic to weed out and block malicious packets.
Password cracking software and unauthorized access to PCs	Local area network, internet	All users, especially digital subscriber line and cable internet users	High	Hackers take over PCs. Privacy can be invaded. Corporate users' systems are exposed to other machines on the network.	Close ports and firewalls, disable file and print sharing, and use strong passwords.
Viruses, worms, Trojan horses, and rootkits	Email, downloaded and distributed software	All users	Moderate to high	Monitor activities and cause data loss and file deletion; compromise security by sometimes concealing their presence.	Use antivirus software and firewalls; control internet access.
Malware, spyware, adware, malicious scripts, and applets	Rogue web pages	All users	Moderate to high	Invade privacy, intercept passwords, and damage files or file system.	Disable browser script support; use security, blocking, and anti-malware software.
Email snooping	Hackers on your network and the internet	All users	Moderate to high	People read your email from intermediate servers or packets, or they physically access your machine.	Encrypt messages, ensure strong password protection, and limit physical access to machines.
Keystroke monitoring	Trojan horses, people with direct access to PCs	All users	High	Records everything typed at the keyboard and intercepts keystrokes before password masking or encryption occurs.	Use anti-malware and antivirus software to catch Trojan horses, control internet access to transmission, and implement system monitoring and physical access control.
Phishing	Hackers on your network and the internet	All users, including customers	High	Fake but real-looking emails and websites that trick users into sharing personal information on what they wrongly think is a company's website. This leads to unauthorized account access.	Educate and warn users and customers about the dangers. Encourage both not to click on potentially fake URLs, which might take them to phishing websites. Instead, have them type your company's URL into the web browser.
Spam	Email	All users and corporations	Mild to high	Clogs and overloads email servers and inboxes with junk mail. HTML-based spam may be used for profiling and identifying users.	Filter known spam sources and senders on email servers; have users create further lists of approved and unapproved senders on their PCs.
Ransomware	Hackers on your network and the internet	All users and corporations	High	Encrypts personal or corporate data so it can't be accessed. Attacked individuals or corporations must pay a ransom of hundreds to tens of thousands of dollars using bitcoin (an anonymous method of payment) within a specified time or the data will be permanently locked or destroyed.	Educate managers and employees about phishing, close open ports, patch and update unpatched and outdated applications.

Sources: "X-Force Threat Intelligence Index 2020," IBM Security, accessed July 7, 2020, www.ibm.com/security/data-breach/threat-intelligence; L. Newman, "A 1.3Tbs DDoS Hit GitHub, the Largest Yet Recorded," *Wired*, March 4, 2018, accessed July 8, 2020, www.wired.com/story/github-ddos-memcached; M. Ali, "Is Your Company Ready for a Ransomware Attack?," *Harvard Business Review*, October 3, 2016, accessed May 6, 2017, hbr.org/2016/10/is-your-company-ready-for-a-ransomware-attack; "The 11 Most Common Computer Security Threats . . . And What You Can Do to Protect Yourself from Them," *Symantec-Norton*, accessed May 12, 2015, www.symantec-norton.com/11-most-common-computer-security-threats_k13.aspx; K. Bannan, "Look Out: Watching You, Watching Me," *PC Magazine*, July 2002, 99; A. Dragoon, "Fighting Phish, Fakes, and Frauds," *CIO*, September 1, 2004, 33; B. Glass, "Are You Being Watched?" *PC Magazine*, April 23, 2002, 54;; B. Machrone, "Protect & Defend," *PC Magazine*, June 27, 2000, 168–181; "Top 10 Security Threats," *PC Magazine*, April 10, 2007, 66; M. Sarrel, "Master End-User Security," *PC Magazine*, May 2008, 101.

Home Depot paid $19.5 million to settle a class-action lawsuit brought by customers affected by a massive online security breach at the company.

Google, for example, requires two-factor authentication for its Google Apps (Gmail, Calendar, Drive, Docs, and so on). After entering their passwords, users can either use the code sent via text to their phone or a code generated by Google's Authenticator app. Google Authenticator, which requires a mobile phone or internet connection, gives you the ability to generate authentication codes for multiple accounts (including non-Google accounts), and generates codes that are only good for 60 seconds.[69]

Unfortunately, stolen or cracked passwords are not the only way for hackers and electronic thieves to gain access to an organization's computer resources. Unless special safeguards are put in place, every time corporate users are online, there's literally nothing between their PCs and the internet (home users with high-speed internet access face the same risks). Hackers can access files, run programs, and control key parts of computers if precautions aren't taken. To reduce these risks, companies use **firewalls**, hardware or software devices that sit between the computers in an internal organizational network and outside networks such as

Firewall a protective hardware or software device that sits between the computers in an internal organizational network and outside networks, such as the internet

Malware a program or piece of code that, without your knowledge, attaches itself to other programs on your computer and can trigger anything from a harmless flashing message to the reformatting of your hard drive to a system-wide network shutdown

Virus a special kind of malware that copies itself and spreads to other devices

Data encryption the transformation of data into complex, scrambled digital codes that can be decrypted only by authorized users who possess unique decryption keys

the internet. Firewalls filter and check incoming and outgoing data. They prevent company insiders from accessing unauthorized sites or from sending confidential company information to people outside the company. Firewalls also prevent outsiders from identifying and gaining access to company computers and data. If a firewall is working properly, the computers behind the company firewall literally cannot be seen or accessed by outsiders.

Malware is a program or piece of code that, without your knowledge, attaches itself to other programs on your computer and can trigger anything from a harmless flashing message to the reformatting of your hard drive to a systemwide network shutdown. Malware includes viruses, spyware, ransomware, and other damaging software. A **virus** is a specific kind of malware that copies itself and spreads to other devices. You used to have to do something or run something to get malware or a virus, such as double-clicking an infected email attachment from someone you don't know (Don't!). Today's malware and viruses are much more threatening. In fact, with some malware and viruses, just being connected to a network can infect your computer. *Anti-malware* and *antivirus software for PCs* scan email, downloaded files, and computer hard drives, disk drives, and memory to detect and stop computer malware and viruses from doing damage. However, this software is effective only to the extent that users of individual computers have and use up-to-date versions. With new malware and viruses appearing all the time, users should update their anti-malware and antivirus software weekly or, even better, configure their software to automatically check for, download, and install updates. By contrast, *corporate anti-malware and antivirus software* automatically scan email attachments such as Microsoft Word documents, graphics, or text files as they come across the company email server. It also monitors and scans all file downloads across company databases and network servers. So, while anti-malware and antivirus software for PCs prevent individual computers from being infected, corporate anti-malware and antivirus software for email servers, databases, and network servers adds another layer of protection by preventing infected files from multiplying and being sent to others.

Another way of protecting information is to encrypt sensitive data. **Data encryption** transforms data into complex, scrambled digital codes that can be decrypted only by authorized users who possess unique decryption keys. Corporate data encryption is needed to encrypt the files stored on network servers and databases. Indeed, after being hit by a major security breach in which

GongTo/Shutterstock.com

Give Out Your Cell Phone Number: Get Hacked

Because you may never change your cell phone number—ever—it may be easier to identify who you are with your phone number than by your name. Do a Google search with your cell phone number (really, do this). Here's what you might find:

» Your name and birth date.

» Your home address, what you paid for your house and property, and your annual property taxes.

» Previous addresses from the last 10 years.

» If you own a business, the business name and estimated annual revenue.

» Previous telephone numbers, landline, and cell phone.

» Names and ages of people who live with you, and their previous addresses.

» Your children (including adult children), mother and father, brothers and sisters, and their detailed information.

This information is scarily accurate. And it's dangerous. Hackers can use previous addresses and your mother's maiden name, which are often used as answers to security questions, to reset account passwords. What to do?

» Reset security question answers on key accounts, such as your mobile phone provider, email provider, bank, social security, Google, Apple, etc. Use a password manager to randomly generate a 10-character answer like VELrnVQNgj. Substitute that, for example, for your mother's maiden name. Record the new answers for each account in your secure password manager.

» Call your cell provider and set up a separate password to prevent a SIM hack in which hackers, using your publicly

Marynchenko Oleksandr/Shutterstock.com

available information, transfer your account to a SIM chip/number under their control.

» Turn off SMS codes sent to your phone.

» Set up two-factor authentication using an app like Google Authenticator or use a physical security key (see Yubico Security Key).

» Use the Google Voice or Burner apps to set up alternative phone numbers. Only give out those numbers when setting up accounts.

» Freeze your credit reports at Experian, Equifax, and Trans Union.

» Knock on wood. Good luck. You'll need it.

Sources: B. Chen, "I Shared My Phone Number. I Learned I Shouldn't Have," *The New York Times*, August 15, 2019, accessed July 9, 2020, www.nytimes.com/2019/08/15/technology/personaltech/i-shared-my-phone-number-i-learned-i-shouldnt-have.html; D. O'Sullivan, "One Man Lost His Life Savings in a SIM Hack. Here's How You Can Try to Protect Yourself," *CNN*, March 13, 2020, accessed July 9, 2020, www.cnn.com/2020/03/13/tech/sim-hack-million-dollars/index.html.

---

56 million customers' unencrypted credit card numbers were stolen by hackers, The Home Depot now spends $7 million a year to encrypt data at its 2,285 stores.[70] Likewise, to encrypt data on personal computers, use BitLocker, which comes with Windows 10, or FileVault, which comes with Mac OS. This is especially important with laptop computers, which are easily stolen.

With people increasingly gaining unauthorized access to email messages—email snooping—it's also important to encrypt sensitive email messages and file attachments. You can use a system called *public key encryption* to do so. First, give copies of your "public key" to anyone who sends you files or email. Have the sender use the public key, which is actually a piece of software, to encrypt files, before sending them to you. The only

way to decrypt the files is with a companion "private key" that you keep to yourself.

Although firewalls can protect PCs and network servers directly connected to the corporate network, people away from their offices (e.g., salespeople, business travelers, telecommuters) who interact with their company networks via the i]nternet face a security risk. Because internet data are not encrypted, "packet sniffer" software easily allows hackers to read everything sent or received except files that have been encrypted before sending.

Previously, the only practical solution was to have employees dial in to secure company phone lines for direct access to the company network. Of course, with international and long-distance phone calls, the costs quickly added up. Now, **virtual private networks (VPNs)** have solved this problem by using software to encrypt all internet data at both ends of the transmission process. Unlike typical internet connections in which data packets are decrypted, the VPN encrypts the data sent by employees outside the company computer network, decrypts the data when they arrive within the company network, and does the same when data are sent back to the computer outside the network. VPN connections provide secure access to everything on a company's network. If your employer or university doesn't provide a VPN, you can purchase VPN services for personal use and protection from well-known providers, such as ExpressVPN or NordVPN, for about $3 a month. VPN services should be used when connecting to corporate networks or databases and to public Wi-Fi systems, such as in hotels, airports, or coffee shops, where anyone on the public network can monitor or spy on what you're doing.

Alternatively, many companies use web-based **secure sockets layer (SSL) encryption** to provide secure offsite access to data and programs. If you've ever entered your credit card in a web browser to make an online purchase, you've used SSL technology to encrypt and protect that information. You can tell if SSL encryption is being used on a website if you see a padlock icon or if the URL begins with "https." SSL encryption works the same way in the workplace. Managers and employees who aren't at the office simply connect to the internet, open a web browser, and then enter a user name and password to gain access to SSL-encrypted data and programs. *Wall Street Journal* technology reporter David Pierce explains, "When you visit an https-enabled website, you immediately open an encrypted connection. Even if I could intercept all the data you are sending and receiving, all I could figure out is the site you're on, not what you're doing there."[71]

Finally, while wireless networks come equipped with security and encryption capabilities that, in theory, permit only authorized users to access the wireless network, those capabilities are easily bypassed with the right tools. Compounding the problem, many wireless network routers are shipped with outdated firmware susceptible to hacking and with encryption capabilities turned off for ease of installation.[72] When working from home or on the go, extra care is critical because Wi-Fi networks in homes and public places such as hotel lobbies are among the most targeted by hackers.[73] See the Wi-Fi Alliance site at www.wi-fi.org for the latest information on wireless security and encryption protocols that provide much stronger protection for your company's wireless network.

Finally, companies are combating security threats by hiring *white-hat hackers*, so-called good guys, who test security weak points in information systems so that they can be fixed. While this is typically done using traditional hacking tools, as discussed in Exhibit 17.3, white-hat hackers also test security via *social engineering*, in which they trick people into giving up passwords and authentication protocols or unknowingly providing unauthorized access to company computers.

One test involves emailing a picture of a cat with a purple mohawk and the subject line "Check out these kitties!" to employees with a link to more cute kitty photos. When you click an embedded link to "more cute kitty photos," you're taken to a company website warning about the dangers of phishing scams. Think that you wouldn't fall for this? Forty-eight percent of employees receiving this email click the link.[74] Former hacker Kevin Mitnick, whose company now helps corporations and governments protect their data from hackers, says, "You can have the best technology in the world, but if I can call or email or somehow communicate with a target in your company, I can usually bypass all of that technology by manipulating the target."[75]

Another test involves "lost or left-behind" USB thumb drives, ostensibly belonging to competitors. When the person who picked up the thumb drive inserts it into a computer, it installs software that uses the webcam to snap a picture of the employee, who then receives a visit from the IT security team.[76]

 17-4 ACCESSING AND SHARING INFORMATION AND KNOWLEDGE

Today, information technologies are letting companies communicate data, share data, and provide data access to workers, managers, suppliers, and customers in ways that were unthinkable just a few years ago.

After reading this section, you should be able to explain how companies use information technology to improve **17-4a internal access and sharing of information, 17-4b external access and sharing of information,** *and* **17-4c the sharing of knowledge and expertise.**

Virtual private network (VPN) software that securely encrypts data sent by employees outside the company network, decrypts the data when they arrive within the company computer network, and does the same when data are sent back to employees outside the network

Secure sockets layer (SSL) encryption Internet browser–based encryption that provides secure offsite web access to some data and programs

Daniel Koh, chief of staff for Boston Mayor Marty Walsh, updates the mayor and staff on City Score performances.

17-4a Internal Access and Sharing

Executives, managers, and workers inside the company use three kinds of information technology to access and share information: executive information systems, intranets, and portals. An **executive information system (EIS)** uses internal and external sources of data to provide managers and executives the information they need to monitor and analyze organizational performance.[77] The goal of an EIS is to provide accurate, complete, relevant, and timely information to managers. With just a few mouse clicks and basic commands such as *find*, *compare*, and *show*, the EIS displays costs, sales revenues, and other kinds of data in color-coded charts and graphs. Managers can drill down to view and compare data by global region, country, state, time period, and product.

Boston Mayor Marty Walsh tracks the performance of the city's various departments on a huge display in his office. The dashboard, called City Score, monitors 21 quality of life measures, from response time on 911 calls, to cleaning up graffiti, to collecting trash, to crime. Every measure is scaled so a score of 1.00 or above, shown in white, indicates meeting or exceeding goals. A score below 1.00, shown in red, indicates below-targeted performance. Daniel Koh, the mayor's chief of staff, says, "Everybody knows that he is looking at this."[78] For instance, says Koh, "the mayor could see over and over that EMS [Emergency Medical Services] response time was in the red." Mayor Walsh's phone call with the head of EMS revealed that the number of ambulances had not increased as Boston's population had grown. So, the city bought 10 more. Says Koh, "It's not a stretch to say. . . [this] will save lives because of improved response times."[79] City Score can be viewed at www.boston.gov/cityscore.

Intranets are private company networks that allow employees to easily access, share, and publish information. Intranets are often designed to look like external websites, but the firewall separating the internal company network from the internet permits only authorized internal access.[80]

Intranets typically include:[81]

» Online publishing of company information (such as benefits and policies) and online forms (to replace paper forms)

» Scheduling and coordinating company events, including invitations, RSVPs, and reservations for public spaces, from small conference rooms to large meeting rooms

» Directories to find and contact people, including whether they are in the office, in a meeting, or working from home

» Collaboration tools, such as instant messaging, discussion chats and channels, document sharing, and task management

» Companywide news, events, and communications

Dormakaba, a global provider of security and business access solutions (keys, locks, automatic doors, door and controls), has 16,000 employees in 130 countries speaking multiple languages. It needed an intranet that promoted collaboration and sharing of information. Its intranet was designed so that employees could easily create corporate blogs, disseminate company news and videos, and promote events and announcements. What's more, it made all of this content readily accessible in each user's native language. Dormakaba's intranet has other advanced features as well. SmartFeed, which sits on the intranet home page, automatically finds the most important and relevant news for each user. Collaboration is facilitated via Yammer, a corporate social networking function, directly into the intranet. Within months of launch, more than 500 conversations on new products had taken place on Yammer, allowing global sales and operational teams to answer questions and share best practices. To reach employees no matter where they're located or what devices they're using, Dormakaba's intranet is synchronized across PCs and Macs and there are native applications for iOS, Android, and Windows phones and tablets.[82]

Executive information system (EIS) a data processing system that uses internal and external data sources to provide the information needed to monitor and analyze organizational performance

Intranets private company networks that allow employees to easily access, share, and publish information

> A number of information technologies—electronic data interchange, extranets, web services, and the internet—are making it easier to share company data with external groups such as suppliers and customers.

iStock.com/AMR Image

Self-service kiosks have sped up check-in times for the more than 34 million passengers who pass through Gatwick Airport every year.

Finally, **corporate portals** are a hybrid of executive information systems and intranets. While an EIS provides managers and executives with the information they need to monitor and analyze organizational performance, and intranets help companies distribute and publish information and forms within the company, corporate portals allow company managers and employees to access customized information *and* complete specialized transactions using a web browser.

17-4b External Access and Sharing

Historically, companies have been unable or reluctant to let outside groups have access to corporate information. Now, however, a number of information technologies—electronic data interchange, extranets, web services, and the internet—are making it easier to share company data with external groups such as suppliers and customers. They're also reducing costs, increasing productivity by eliminating manual information processing (70 percent of the data output from one company, such as a purchase order, ends up as data input at another company, such as a sales invoice or shipping order), reducing data entry errors, improving customer service, and speeding communications. As a result, managers are scrambling to adopt these technologies.

With **electronic data interchange,** or **EDI,** two companies convert purchase and ordering information to a standardized format to enable direct electronic transmission of that information from one company's computer system to the other company's system. For example, when a Walmart checkout clerk drags an Apple iPad across the checkout scanner, Walmart's computerized inventory system automatically reorders another iPad through the direct EDI connection that its computer has with Apple's manufacturing and shipping computer. No one at Walmart or Apple fills out paperwork. No one makes phone calls. There are no delays to wait to find out whether Apple has the iPad in stock. The transaction takes place instantly and automatically because the data from both companies were translated into a standardized, shareable, compatible format.

Web services are another way for companies to directly and automatically transmit purchase and ordering data from one company's computer system to another company's computer system. **Web services** use standardized protocols to describe and transfer data from one company in such a way that those data can automatically be read, understood, transcribed, and processed by different computer systems in another company.[83] Route One, which helps automobile dealers process loans for car buyers, was started by the financing companies of Daimler AG, Ford, General Motors, and Toyota. Not surprisingly, each auto company had a different computer system with different operating systems, different programs, and different data structures. RouteOne relies on web services to connect these different computer systems to 135+ different databases and software used by various auto dealers, credit bureaus, banks, and other auto financing companies.

Corporate portal a hybrid of executive information systems and intranets that allows managers and employees to use a web browser to gain access to customized company information and to complete specialized transactions

Electronic data interchange (EDI) when two companies convert their purchase and ordering information to a standardized format to enable the direct electronic transmission of that information from one company's computer system to the other company's computer system

Web services software that uses standardized protocols to describe data from one company in such a way that those data can automatically be read, understood, transcribed, and processed by different computer systems in another company

WE'VE GOT YOUR DATA! PAY UP OR ELSE!

Ransomware is a malicious code that encrypts data and locks out users. The only way to regain access is by paying a ransom, usually via bitcoin, within a time period specified by the hackers. If you don't, they destroy your data. By the beginning of 2020, the average ransom was $190,000. If your company falls victim to a ransomware attack, literally run to turn off computers, servers, and your network. Call everyone you can. Have them do the same. Assume everything is contaminated. Wipe and reinstall all of your computers and network devices. Then upgrade your internet security protection and buy cyberattack insurance. A $20 million policy cost the city of Baltimore an annual premium of $850,000. Or, do what the small city of Lakeland, Florida did – pay the $460,000 ransom, which turned out to be significantly cheaper than rebuilding all of its systems. Still, says Audrey Sikes, Lakeland's city clerk, "It put us years and years and years behind." Thousands of digitized documents may have to be scanned again because all of its files were not recovered.

Sources: S. Calvert, "Baltimore to Buy $20 Million in Insurance in Case of Another Cyber Attack," *The Wall Street Journal*, October 16, 2019, accessed July 10, 2020, www.wsj.com/articles/baltimore-to-buy-20-million-in-insurance-in-case-of-another-cyber-attack-11571246605; M. Fernandez, D. Sanger, M. Trahan Martinez, "Ransomware Attacks Are Testing Resolve of Cities Across America," *The New York Times*, August 23, 2019, accessed July 10, 2020, www.nytimes.com/2019/08/22/us/ransomware-attacks-hacking.html; N. Popper, "Ransomware Attacks Grow, Crippling Cities and Businesses," *The New York Times*, February 9, 2020, accessed July 10, 2020, www.nytimes.com/2020/02/09/technology/ransomware-attacks.html.

Without web services, there's no way these different companies and systems could share information.[84]

Now, what's the difference between web services and EDI? For EDI to work, the data in different companies' computer, database, and network systems must adhere to a particular set of standards for data structure and processing. For example, company X, which has a seven-digit parts numbering system, and company Y, which has an eight-digit parts numbering system, would agree to convert their internal parts numbering systems to identical 10-digit parts numbers when their computer systems talk to each other. By contrast, the tools underlying web services such as extensible markup language (or XML) automatically do the describing and transcribing so that data with different structures can be shared across very different computer systems in different companies. (Don't worry if you don't understand how this works, just appreciate what it does.) As a result, by automatically handling those differences, web services allow organizations to communicate data without special knowledge of each other's computer information systems.

In EDI and web services, the different purchasing and ordering applications in each company interact automatically without any human input. No one has to lift a finger to click a mouse, enter data, or hit the Enter key. An **extranet**, by contrast, allows companies to exchange information and conduct transactions by purposely providing outsiders with direct, password-protected, web browser–based access to authorized parts of a company's intranet or information system.[85]

Emerson is a global, US-based technology and engineering company that makes products for a wide variety of markets. Emerson's Automation Solutions division helps manufacturers run factories and control energy and operating costs. The MyEmerson extranet (www.emerson.com/en-us/automation/digital) allows industrial customers to size and select the proper tools, obtain detailed computer-aided-design drawings and diagrams, and use engineering calculators to estimate costs and product life under various conditions. Customers can also get price quotes and make orders, manage lead times (paying more for quicker manufacturing and delivery in emergency situations), access technical documents, order replacement parts, and monitor all of the digital installed devices purchased from Emerson in use in their factories.[86]

Finally, companies are reducing paperwork and manual information processing by using the internet to electronically automate transactions with customers; this is similar to the way in which extranets are used to handle transactions with suppliers and distributors. For example, most airlines have automated the ticketing process by eliminating paper tickets altogether. Simply buy an e-ticket and then check yourself in online via an app on your smart phone, or by printing your boarding pass from your PC or an airport kiosk. Internet

> **Extranets** networks that allow companies to exchange information and conduct transactions with outsiders by providing them direct, web-based access to authorized parts of a company's intranet or information system

purchases, ticketless travel, and automated check-ins have together fully automated the purchase of airline tickets. Use of self-service kiosks is expanding, too.

At London's Gatwick airport, self-service kiosks now offer "self bag drop," which travelers use to check in, weigh, and tag their luggage – all without the help of an agent. The self-service kiosks can process excess, oversized, and overweight baggage, even taking credit card payments for modified or extra charges. After check-in and bag tagging, customers place their luggage on baggage conveyor belts immediately adjacent to the kiosks. While the kiosks are speeding up check-in, some customers still prefer checking bags with gate agents.[87] New Yorker Mark Rosenthal says, "I don't work for the airline. Why should I do their job? If something goes wrong or I have a question, the self-tagging machine isn't going to have an answer."[88]

In the long run, the goal is to link customer internet sites with company intranets (or EDI) and extranets so that everyone—all the employees and managers within a company as well as the suppliers and distributors outside the company—involved in providing a service or making a product for a customer are automatically notified when a purchase is made. Companies that use EDI, web services, extranets, and the internet to share data with customers and suppliers achieve increases in productivity 2.7 times larger than those that don't.[89]

17-4c Sharing Knowledge and Expertise

At the beginning of the chapter, we distinguished between raw data, which consist of facts and figures, and information, which consists of useful data that influence someone's choices and behavior. One more important distinction needs to be made, namely, that data and information are not the same as knowledge. **Knowledge** is the understanding that one gains from information. Importantly, knowledge does not reside in information. Historically, knowledge has resided in people. That's why companies hire consultants and why family doctors refer patients to specialists. Unfortunately, it can be quite expensive to employ consultants, specialists, and experts. So companies have used two information technologies to capture and share the knowledge of consultants, specialists, and experts with other managers and workers: decision support systems and expert systems. Thanks to cheap computing power and the availability of "big data," companies are now in the early stages of using systems in which knowledge resides in machines or computers via artificial intelligence.

Although an executive information system speeds up and simplifies the acquisition of information, a **decision support system (DSS)** helps managers understand problems and potential solutions by acquiring and analyzing information with sophisticated models and tools.[90] Furthermore, whereas EIS programs are broad in scope and permit managers to retrieve all kinds of information about a company, DSS programs are usually narrow in scope and targeted toward helping managers solve specific kinds of problems. DSS programs have been developed to help managers pick the shortest and most efficient routes for delivery trucks, select the best combination of stocks for investors, and schedule the flow of inventory through complex manufacturing facilities. It's important to understand that DSS programs don't replace managerial decision-making; they *improve* it by furthering managers' and workers' understanding of the problems they face and the solutions that might work.

Expert systems are created by capturing the specialized knowledge and decision rules used by experts and experienced decision makers. They permit nonexpert employees to draw on this expert knowledge base to make decisions. Most expert systems work by using a collection of "if–then" rules to sort through information and recommend a course of action. For example, let's say that you're using your American Express card to help your spouse celebrate a promotion. After dinner and a movie, the two of you stop for an ice cream and start scrolling your Instagram feed, filled with Las Vegas pictures. Thirty minutes later, caught up in the moment, you find yourselves at the airport ticket counter trying to purchase last-minute tickets to Vegas. But there's just one problem. American Express didn't approve your purchase. In fact, the ticket counter agent is now on the phone with an American Express customer service agent. So what put a temporary halt to your weekend escape to Vegas? An expert system that American Express calls Authorizer's Assistant.[91]

The first "if–then" rule that prevented your purchase was the rule "*if* a purchase is much larger than the cardholder's regular spending habits, *then* deny approval of the purchase." This if–then rule, just one of 3,000, is built into American Express's transaction-processing system that handles thousands of purchase requests per second. Now that the American Express customer service agent

Knowledge the understanding that one gains from information

Decision support system (DSS) an information system that helps managers understand specific kinds of problems and potential solutions

Expert system an information system that contains the specialized knowledge and decision rules used by experts and experienced decision makers so that nonexperts can draw on this knowledge base to make decisions

IBM's Watson has been used in myriad industries, from finance to cancer research.

then have the AI system make decisions (do this or that) or categorical distinctions (this is a picture of a wolf, not a dog), letting the system know when it was wrong or right. That feedback helps the AI system "learn" and become more accurate over time.

For example, **H&R Block** is using IBM's "Watson" AI system to analyze tax returns for 11 million people at 10,000 branch offices. Former CEO Bill Cobb says that when H&R Block approached IBM with the idea to use Watson in its business, they told him, "This is not magic. You have to teach Watson over time."[93] To do that, they started by feeding Watson 74,000 pages of the US federal tax code, along with thousands of tax questions that H&R Block's tax preparers asked clients over 60 years of business. Watson was eventually given thousands of tax filings, already handled by H&R Block tax preparers, from which to learn. Watson would suggest a question for a particular tax situation and then learn, via feedback from H&R Block's tax specialists, who indicated whether the question was appropriate. The advantage of using Watson, says H&R Block's George Gaustello, is that it makes their people better. Gaustello said, "We have 70,000 experts, but let's say 500 of those are very knowledgeable about firefighters, or they know every credit deduction a farmer can get." If Watson learns what those 500 experts know, then, he says, we're "making our experts even smarter."[94] Former CEO Bill Cobb said, "Our clients will benefit from an enhanced experience and our tax pros will have the latest technology to help them ensure every deduction and credit is found."[95]

is on the line, he or she is prompted by the Authorizer's Assistant to ask the ticket counter agent to examine your identification. You hand over your driver's license and another credit card to prove you're you. Then the ticket agent asks for your address, phone number, and your mother's maiden name and relays the information to American Express. Finally, your ticket purchase is approved. Why? Because you met the last series of "if–then" rules. *If* the purchaser can provide proof of identity and *if* the purchaser can provide personal information that isn't common knowledge, *then* approve the purchase.

Artificial intelligence, or **AI**, is the capability of computerized systems to learn and adapt through experience.[92] Devices and applications that have this capability are said to possess artificial intelligence. A common way to develop AI is to feed information into an AI system, have it analyze that information for patterns, and

> **Artificial intelligence (AI)**
> the capability of computerized systems to learn and adapt through experience

18 | Managing Service and Manufacturing Operations

LEARNING OUTCOMES

18-1 Discuss the kinds of productivity and their importance in managing operations.

18-2 Explain the role that quality plays in managing operations.

18-3 Explain the essentials of managing a service business.

18-4 Describe the different kinds of manufacturing operations.

18-5 Explain why and how companies should manage inventory levels.

18-1 PRODUCTIVITY

Furniture manufacturers, hospitals, restaurants, automakers, airlines, and many other kinds of businesses struggle to find ways to produce quality products and services efficiently and then deliver them in a timely manner. Managing the daily production of goods and services, or **operations management**, is a key part of a manager's job. But an organization depends on the quality of its products and services as well as its productivity.

Operations management
managing the daily production of goods and services

After a 10-hour flight from Los Angeles to London's Heathrow airport, an arriving Boeing 787 Dreamliner has only 2 hours before leaving for Shanghai. Prior to touchdown, a tow vehicle (which pushes the plane back from the terminal), gallery food truck, luggage loaders (drivable ramps with conveyor belts), ground power carts, and fuel, air-conditioning and potable water trucks are positioned to connect to the plane in a choreographed sequence as the arriving passengers and crew disembark. While cleaners work from the front and back toward the middle, emptying trash bins and cleaning high-touch surfaces, a lavatory truck underneath the plane empties the waste tanks. Clean blankets and pillows, food carts with 400 hot meals, 185 gallons of water, and 60 tons of jet fuel are replenished. Luggage, loaded front and back into five pressurized cargo holds, is secured and balanced for safety and stability. Engineers, ground crew,

pilots, and air crew check off detailed flight preparation lists, including loading the route into the Flight Management Computer. With 45 minutes left, passengers begin boarding. If all goes as planned, the boarding doors close, the air bridges pull back, and the tow vehicle pushs the plane back from the gate with seven minutes to spare for the 11-hour flight to Shanghai.[1]

At their core, organizations are production systems. Companies combine inputs such as labor, raw materials, capital, and knowledge to produce outputs in the form of finished products or services. **Productivity** is a measure of performance that indicates how many inputs it takes to produce or create an output.

$$Productivity = \frac{Outputs}{Inputs}$$

The fewer inputs it takes to create an output (or the greater the output from one input), the higher the productivity. On calm weather days, London's Heathrow airport lands 40 to 45 planes every hour. Strong headwinds drop that rate to just 32 to 38 planes per hour, however. How could Heathrow be more productive on windy days? Based on a safety concept called "miles-in-trail," arriving planes are typically spaced 3 to 7 miles apart, depending on jet size.[2] Heathrow, however, now uses time-based plane separation to improve arrival efficiency. *The Wall Street Journal's* Scott McCartney explains: "If a plane normally needs to be five miles behind the one it's following, but the headwind at 3,000 feet above sea level is 50 knots, or 58 miles an hour, now the plane might move a mile closer. Time between touchdowns remains the same, even with the headwinds slowing down the flight." How well does this work? On a blustery March day with nearly 60-miles-per-hour headwinds, 60 more planes than normal landed at Heathrow. Indeed, delays and circling patterns have dropped significantly, and the airport reports a 50 percent increase in landing productivity on windy days.[3]

Let's examine **18-1a** *why productivity matters,* **18-1b** *the different kinds of productivity,* and **18-1c** *productivity and automation.*

> **Productivity** a measure of performance that indicates how many inputs it takes to produce or create an output

"OH, LOOK, IT'S THE UPS... TRICYCLE?"

UPS spends billions automating package sorting and developing mapping algorithms to shave seconds from the routes its drivers take delivering packages. But in congested cities, UPS trucks sit in traffic, lowering productivity and counteracting those billion dollar investments. To fix that, UPS is piloting package delivery via an electric tricycle in Seattle. The UPS "cargo eBike" pulls a brown UPS cargo box, which looks like a miniature UPS truck, sans the cab and engine. The cargo eBikes are dual-powered, by the driver's pedal-power and by battery-powered electric motors. The eBike's cargo box holds up to 40 packages weighing 350 pounds and has an 18-mile range. Scott Phillippi, UPS's head of maintenance and engineering, said, "While we have launched cycle logistic projects in other cities, this is the first one designed to meet a variety of urban challenges. The modular boxes and trailer allow us to expand our delivery capabilities and meet the unique needs of our Seattle customers." Their small size allows them to move while stalled traffic sits, and to go where its larger trucks can't, particularly on pedestrian-friendly corporate and college campuses. So next time the UPS delivery person comes, ask them when they're getting a UPS tricycle.

Source: D. Byron, "UPS Is Testing Delivery Tricycles in Traffic-Choked Seattle," *Wired*, December 6, 2018, accessed July 20, 2020, www.wired.com /story/ups-delivery-tricycle-seattle/?mod=djemCFO_h.

18-1a Why Productivity Matters

Why does productivity matter? For companies, higher productivity – that is, doing more with less – results in lower costs for the company, lower prices, faster service, higher market share, and higher profits. **United Parcel Service (UPS)**, which delivered 850+ million packages between Thanksgiving and New Year's last year, started decades ago with hand sorting. Employees trained for two weeks on computers to memorize 120 ZIP codes before working in sorting facilities, handling thousands of packages per shift. UPS boosted productivity by 15 percent with its "Next Generation Sort Aisle," where sorters manually scanned a package barcode, heard a beep (indicating a successful scan), and then read the name of a color-coded chute to which the packages needed to go.[4] A three-year $20 billion investment has now fully automated package sorting so it is 10 times faster than hand sorting and 30 to 35 percent faster than hand scanning.[5] The conveyor belts at sorting facilities move at 600 feet per minute so that each package spends just 7 minutes in the building. After a package is offloaded from a truck to a conveyor belt, it enters a "scanning tunnel" where six high-speed cameras take pictures of every side of the box, all without the conveyor belt slowing. Image processing software instantly decodes the address, say Austin, Texas, and wirelessly pairs it with six digital "smart shoes," black rectangles, that are roughly a foot in front of the package. When a scanner looking for Austin, Texas, packages detects the right smart shoes, the package is diverted down an exit chute, where another worker loads it onto the truck bound for Austin.[6]

Productivity matters because it results in a higher standard of living in terms of higher wages, charitable giving, and making products more affordable. When companies can do more with less, they can raise employee wages without increasing prices or sacrificing normal profits. Recent government economic data indicated that US companies were paying workers 2.8 percent more than in the previous year. But because workers were only producing 0.7 percent more than they had the year before, real labor costs actually increased.[7]

The median US family income was $78,646 in 2018. If productivity grows 1 percent per year, that family's income will increase to $97,892 in 2040. But if productivity grows 2 percent per year, their income in 2040 will be $121,585, an increase of $23,693, and that's without working longer hours.[8]

Thanks to long-term increases in business productivity, the typical American family today earns 28.6 percent more than the average family in 1980 and 50.4 percent more than the average family in 1967 – and that's after accounting for inflation.[9] Productivity increased an average of 1.5 percent from 1979 to 1990, 2.2 percent from 1990 to 2000, 2.7 percent from 2000 to 2007, and 1.4 percent from 2007 to 2019.[10] However, from 2007 to 2019, the US economy created nearly 11.5 million new jobs.[11]

And when more people have jobs that pay more, they give more to charity. For example, in 2018 Americans donated more than $427 billion to charities, compared to $358 million in 2014, $261 billion in 2009, and $230 billion in 2000.[12] Did Americans become more thoughtful, caring, conscientious, and giving? Probably not. Yet, because of increases in productivity during this time, the average American's income (which is different from family income) increased by 79.6 percent, from $36,335 in 2000 to $65,281 in 2019.[13] Because people earned more money, they were able to share their good fortune with others by giving more to charity.[14]

Another benefit of productivity is that it makes products more affordable or better. One way to demonstrate this is by comparing how many work hours it would take to earn enough money to buy a product now versus in the past. For instance, in 1964, a 21-inch color TV sold for $750, or $6,237 in 2020 dollars. With that much money, you could buy a 20.2 cubic foot refrigerator ($598), a five-burner gas stove/oven ($549), a built-in dishwasher ($386), an over-the-range microwave ($199), a 4.1 cubic foot top-load washer ($549) and a 7-cubic-foot gas dryer ($599) at Lowes; a 55-inch 4k TV ($430) and a 7 + 2.1 channel home theater sound system with a subwoofer ($130) at Amazon; and, a 4k Apple TV for streaming ($199), an iPhone 11 w/128 GB ($749), a 13-inch, 8GB memory, 256GB SSD Apple MacBook Air laptop ($999), two Apple Home-Pods for streaming music ($598) at home and a pair of noise-cancelling AirPods Pro ($249) for listening to music and podcasts on the go, all at Apple. And while the average American would work 293 hours in 1964 to pay off a $6,237 bill, it would take just 199 hours in 2020.[15] People like to reminisce about the "good ol' days," when things were "cheaper." But, mostly, they really weren't. Thanks to steady increases in productivity, most goods become better and more affordable over time.

18-1b Kinds of Productivity

Two common measures of productivity are partial productivity and multifactor productivity. **Partial productivity** indicates how much of a particular kind of input it takes to produce an output.

$$\text{Partial Productivity} = \frac{\text{Outputs}}{\text{Single Kind of Inputs}}$$

Labor is one kind of input that is frequently used when determining partial productivity. *Labor productivity* typically indicates the cost or number of hours of labor it takes to produce an output. In other words, the lower the cost of the labor to produce a unit of output, or the less time it takes to produce a unit of output, the higher the labor productivity. In the aviation industry, output is typically measured in available seat miles (ASM), which are calculated by multiplying the number of seats on a plane (capacity) by the number of miles a plane flies (distance). More seats and longer flight distances generate more revenue per flight. The labor cost per available seat mile is a basic measure of labor productivity in the airline industry. Airlines with lower labor costs per ASM have higher labor productivity. In the United States, Delta (5.5 cents per ASM), United (5.2 cents),

Southwest (4.8 cents), and American (4.7) have the highest labor costs and worst labor productivity. Hawaiian and JetBlue (both with 3.6 cents per ASM) and Alaska (3.4 cents) have average labor costs and labor productivity. Not surprisingly, low-cost airlines Allegiant (2.7 cents per ASM) and Spirit and Frontier (both 1.7 cents) have the lowest labor costs and highest labor productivity.[16]

Partial productivity assesses how efficiently companies use only one input, such as labor, when creating outputs. Multifactor productivity is an overall measure of productivity that assesses how efficiently companies use all the inputs it takes to make outputs. More specifically, **multifactor productivity** indicates how much labor, capital, materials, and energy it takes to produce an output.[17]

$$\frac{\text{Multifactor}}{\text{Productivity}} = \frac{\text{Outputs}}{(\text{Labor} + \text{Capital} + \text{Materials} + \text{Energy})}$$

Exhibit 18.1 shows the trends in multifactor productivity across a number of US industries since 1987. With a 6.4-fold increase since 1987, the growth in multifactor productivity in the computer and electronic products industry far exceeded the productivity growth in mining, utilities, auto manufacturing, retail stores, air transportation, and financial and insurance services, as well as most other industries tracked by the US government.

Should managers use multiple or partial productivity measures? In general, they should use both. Multifactor productivity indicates a company's overall level of productivity relative to its competitors. In the end, that's what counts most. However, multifactor productivity measures don't indicate the specific contributions that labor, capital, materials, or energy make to overall productivity. To analyze the contributions of these individual components, managers need to use partial productivity measures. Doing so can help them determine what factors need to be adjusted or in what areas adjustment can make the most difference in overall productivity.

18-1c Productivity and Automation

Automation isn't new. Consider these jobs that no longer exist: Bowling alley pinsetter, window knockers (who used long poles to tap on windows to wake people up for work before alarm clocks and now smartphones), ice cutters,

Partial productivity a measure of performance that indicates how much of a particular kind of input it takes to produce an output

Multifactor productivity an overall measure of performance that indicates how much labor, capital, materials, and energy it takes to produce an output

Exhibit 18.1
Multifactor Productivity Growth Across Industries, 1987–2018

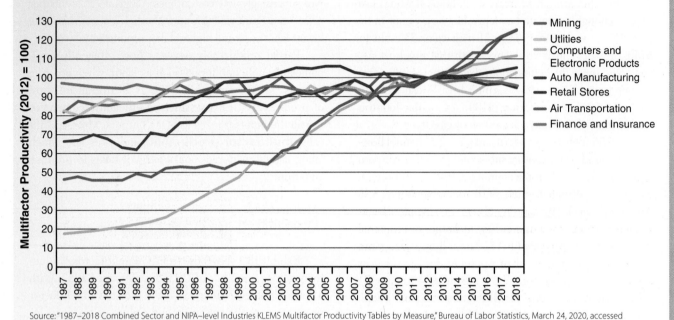

Source: "1987–2018 Combined Sector and NIPA–level Industries KLEMS Multifactor Productivity Tables by Measure," Bureau of Labor Statistics, March 24, 2020, accessed July 16, 2020, www.bls.gov/mfp/special_requests/klemscombinedbymeasure.xlsx.

street lamplighters, and switchboard operators. All have long been automated.[18] At home, would you give up your dishwasher to handwash dishes, your clothes dryer and washing machine to handwash and dry your clothes, and your furnace to cut logs for the wood stove to heat your house? Indeed, thanks to productivity-enhancing automation, we spend roughly 12.5 hours a week on housework compared to 26 hours in 1965.[19] From the Industrial Revolution, to the telegraph, to the car, to the internet, computers, and, yes, home appliances, automation has long made life easier and tasks more productive.

Thanks to advances in robotics design and artificial intelligence, we are at the beginning of another surge in automation, this one driven by **robots**, which are machines or programs capable of completing complex tasks. The McKinsey Global Institute estimates that robot-driven automation could raise global productivity 0.8 to 1.4 percent a year.[20] Let's look at the three ways in which work can be automated with robots: robotic process automation, intelligent recognition, and collaborative/social robotics.[21]

Process automation is using robots to automate routine, highly repetitive, low complexity, or single-purpose tasks. This works well in work environments, such as factories, where a robot is dedicated to one task or a limited set of tasks, or in the automation of data collection and processing.[22] FarmWise's agribot, which uses artificial intelligence to identify and pick weeds, is an example of process automation.[23] So are Brain Corp's autonomous floor-scrubbing robots, which are used by Walmart and Kroger. Brain Corp. CEO Eugene Izhikevich says, "Every day, we give back 8,000 hours to essential workers to do other stuff, for example . . . to precision clean, [disinfect] handles, restocking or just taking a break they need. So the robots aren't doing all the cleaning, they are the doing the most monotonous work."[24]

Intelligent recognition is using automation programming to recognize and react to patterns of speech, written language, images, and other items. When you say, "Hey Google," or "Hey Siri," to your smartphone, followed by a command such as finding something on the Web, figuring out when your next appointment is, or getting directions, you're using intelligent recognition automation. Target is using Tally, a 30-pound, 38-inch-tall robot built

Robots machines or programs capable of completing complex tasks

Process automation using robots to automate routine, highly repetitive, low-complexity, or single-purpose tasks

Intelligent recognition using automation programming to recognize and react to patterns of speech, written language, images, and other items

by Simbe Robotics to analyze product inventory on retail store shelves. Tally rolls down store aisles, even when customers are shopping, using a dozen high-resolution cameras to determine how many of each product are on the shelf, whether items are misplaced on the wrong shelves or not facing toward the aisle, and whether items need to be restocked or reordered.[25] Tally also does radio frequency identification scanning (see Chapter 17) at the rate of 700 RFID tags per second.[26] According to Simbe, Tally can inventory all of the items in a medium-sized store in 30 minutes with 97 percent accuracy, compared to a person who would take 25 hours at 65 percent accuracy.[27]

Collaborative/social automation is using robots to automate tasks while working directly with or near people. Worker safety was one of the earliest concerns with using robots in factories. Because robots were typically used for physically demanding tasks requiring high levels of force, they were surrounded by steel cages or industrial fencing so that people couldn't be harmed by walking into the robot's workspace. By contrast, collaborative/social automation puts workers and robots side by side. Rick Faulk, CEO of Locus, which makes robots that work with warehouse workers, said, "The first trend was to try to replace humans. Now it's about humans and robots working collaboratively." [28]Amazon, which bought Kiva Systems several years ago (it's now Amazon Robotics), has Kiva robots zip down the aisles of its massive warehouses to retrieve and deliver packages directly to warehouse workers, who used to walk 15 to 20 miles a day finding the items needed to complete orders. With the help of Kiva robots (which will slow as they get near people and stop if they make contact), Amazon warehouse employees can now fill an order in 15 minutes instead of 90 minutes because the Kiva robots deliver items to them. Overall, thanks to its collaborative/social robots, warehouse productivity is up 20 percent and Amazon can put 50 percent more items in each warehouse.[29]

⬤18-2 QUALITY

With the average car costing $38,940 car buyers want to make sure that they're getting good quality for their money.[30] Fortunately, as indicated by the number of problems per 100 cars (PP100), today's cars are of much higher quality than earlier models. In 1981, Japanese cars averaged 240 PP100. GM's cars averaged 670, Ford's averaged 740, and Chrysler's averaged 870 PP100! In other words, as measured by PP100, the quality of American cars was two to three times worse than that of Japanese cars. By 1992, however, US carmakers had

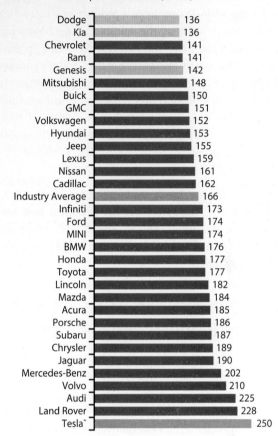

Exhibit 18.2
2020 J. D. Power Initial Quality Survey

Problems per 100 Vehicles (PP100)

Brand	PP100
Dodge	136
Kia	136
Chevrolet	141
Ram	141
Genesis	142
Mitsubishi	148
Buick	150
GMC	151
Volkswagen	152
Hyundai	153
Jeep	155
Lexus	159
Nissan	161
Cadillac	162
Industry Average	166
Infiniti	173
Ford	174
MINI	174
BMW	176
Honda	177
Toyota	177
Lincoln	182
Mazda	184
Acura	185
Porsche	186
Subaru	187
Chrysler	189
Jaguar	190
Mercedes-Benz	202
Volvo	210
Audi	225
Land Rover	228
Tesla^	250

Source: Press Release, "New-Vehicle Quality Mainly Dependent on Trouble-Free Technology," J.D. Power, June 24, 2020, accessed July 16, 2020, www.jdpower.com/business/press-releases/2020-initial-quality-study-iqs.

made great strides, significantly reducing the number of problems to an average of 155 PP100. Japanese vehicles had improved, too, averaging just 125 PP100. According to the 2020 J. D. Power and Associates survey of initial car quality, as shown in Exhibit 18.2, overall quality has backtracked to 166 problems per 100 vehicles, largely because of infotainment problems (voice recognition, Bluetooth connectivity, touch screens, etc.), which account for 25 percent of all issues, and significant quality problems at four luxury brands, Mercedes-Benz (202 PP100), Volvo (210 PP100), Audi (225 PP100), and Tesla, which had the worst quality at 250 PP100. In contrast to 20 years ago, 7 of the 14 above

Collaborative/social automation using robots to automate tasks while working directly with or near people

average cars were built by US automakers: Dodge, Chevrolet, Ram, Buick, GMC, Jeep, and Cadillac. Three were Korean: Kia, Genesis, and Hyundai. Three were Japanese: Mitsubishi, Lexus, and Nissan. One was German, Volkswagen.[31]

The American Society for Quality gives two meanings for **quality**. It can mean a product or service free of deficiencies, such as the number of problems per 100 cars, or it can mean the characteristics of a product or service that satisfy customer needs.[32] Today's cars are of higher quality than those produced 20 years ago in both senses. Not only do they have fewer problems per 100 cars, they also have a number of additional standard features (power brakes and steering, Bluetooth connectivity, power windows and locks, keyless entry, cruise control).

*In this part of the chapter, you will learn about **18-2a quality-related characteristics for products and services, 18-2b ISO 9000, 14000, and 27000, 18-2c the Baldrige National Quality Award,** and **18-2d total quality management.***

18-2a Quality-Related Characteristics for Products and Services

Quality products usually possess three characteristics: reliability, serviceability, and durability.[33] A breakdown occurs when a product quits working or doesn't do what it was designed to do. The longer it takes for a product to break down, or the longer the time between breakdowns, the more reliable the product. Consequently, many companies define *product reliability* in terms of the average time between breakdowns. *Serviceability* refers to how easy or difficult it is to fix a product. The easier it is to maintain a working product or fix a broken product, the more serviceable that product is.

A product breakdown assumes that a product can be repaired. However, some products don't break down; they fail. *Product failure* means products can't be repaired. They can only be replaced. *Durability* is defined as the mean time to failure. A typical incandescent lightbulb, for example, has a mean time of failure of 1,000 hours. By contrast, LED bulbs, which use the same technology that lights up HDTVs and cell phone screens, typically have a mean time to failure of 114,000 hours. Furthermore, the energy savings from one $7 LED bulb means it will pay for itself in less than one year and then, assuming three hours per day of use, provide 12 more years of lighting while saving $136 in energy costs over the longer lifetime of the bulb.[34]

While high-quality products are characterized by reliability, serviceability, and durability, services are different. There's no point in assessing the durability of a service because services are consumed the minute they're performed. For example, after a lawn service has mowed your lawn, the job is done until the mowers come back next week to do it again. Services also don't have serviceability. You can't maintain or fix a service. If a service wasn't performed correctly, all you can do is perform it again. Rather than serviceability and durability, the quality of service interactions often depends on how the service provider interacts with the customer. Was the service provider friendly, rude, or helpful? Five characteristics typically distinguish a quality service: reliability, tangibles, responsiveness, assurance, and empathy.[35]

Service reliability is the ability to consistently perform a service well. Studies clearly show that reliability matters more to customers than anything else when buying services. When you take your clothes to the dry cleaner, you don't want them returned with cracked buttons or wrinkles down the front. If your dry cleaner gives you perfectly clean and pressed clothes every time, it's providing a reliable service.

Also, although services themselves are not tangible (you can't see or touch them), services are provided in tangible places. Thus, *tangibles* refer to the appearance of the offices, equipment, and personnel involved with the delivery of a service. One of the best examples of the effect of tangibles on the perception of quality is the restroom. When you eat at an expensive restaurant, you expect upscale restrooms with marble floors, expensive sinks, specialty soaps, and cloth rather than paper towels. But even at fast-food restaurants, we expect cleanliness. How different is your perception of a fast-food restaurant if it has a filthy restroom rather than a clean one?

Responsiveness is the promptness and willingness with which service providers give good service. *Assurance* is the confidence that service providers are knowledgeable, courteous, and trustworthy. *Empathy* is the extent to which service providers give individual attention and care to customers' concerns and problems.

When Apple first launched its retail stores, they were widely predicted to fail given all of the locations where consumers could already buy computer and electronics equipment. Those predictions were wrong, however, as more than 400 million people visit Apple stores every year. Apple's average annual revenue tops $50 million per store, and malls with Apple stores

Quality a product or service free of deficiencies, or the characteristics of a product or service that satisfy customer needs

To improve customer service at its retail stores, Apple recently redesigned the Genius Bar customer service desk to be more welcoming and rebranded it as the Genius Grove. Here, Genius Grove employees help customers solve problems at the company's flagship store in San Francisco.

average 10 percent more overall customer traffic than those without.[36] Why have Apple stores achieved these extraordinary results? In addition to great products, the stores are great at delivering responsiveness, assurance, and empathy.

At Apple stores, responsiveness manifests itself in a sales philosophy of not selling. Instead, Apple store employees are trained to help customers solve problems. An Apple training manual says, "Your job is to understand all of your customers' needs – some of which they may not even realize they have." David Ambrose, a former Apple store employee, says, "You were never trying to close a sale. It was about finding solutions for a customer and finding their pain points."

Apple store employees demonstrate assurance through the high level of training that they receive. Apple "geniuses," who staff the Genius Bar in each Apple store, are trained at Apple headquarters and, according to Apple's website, "can take care of everything from troubleshooting your problems to actual repairs." Geniuses are regularly tested on their knowledge and problem-solving skills to maintain their certification. Other Apple store employees are highly trained, too, and are not allowed to help customers until they've spent two to four weeks shadowing experienced store employees.

The acronym APPLE instructs employees on how to empathetically engage with customers: "Approach customers with a personalized warm welcome," "Probe politely to understand all the customer's needs," "Present a solution for the customer to take home today," "Listen for and resolve any issues or concerns," and "End with a fond farewell and an invitation to return." And when customers are frustrated and become emotional, the advice is to "listen and limit your responses to simple reassurances that you are doing so. 'Uh-huh,' 'I understand,' etc."

The results from Apple's retail approach speak for themselves, as Apple retail sales average $5,546 per square foot, higher than Tiffany & Co. jewelry stores ($2,951), Lululemon Athletica ($1,560), or Michael Kors ($1,466).[37]

18-2b 9000, 14000, and 27000

ISO, pronounced *eye-so*, comes from the Greek word *isos*, meaning "equal, similar, alike, or identical" and is also an acronym for the International Organization for Standardization, which helps set standards for 165 countries. The purpose of this agency is to develop and publish standards that facilitate the international exchange of goods and services.[38] **ISO 9000** is a series of five international standards, from ISO 9000 to ISO 9004, for achieving consistency in quality management and quality assurance in companies throughout the world.[39] **ISO 14000** is a series of international standards for managing, monitoring, and minimizing an organization's harmful effects on the environment.[40] (For more on environmental quality and issues, see Subsection 16-3e of Chapter 16 on sustainability.) **ISO 27000** is a series of 12 international standards for managing and monitoring security techniques for information technology.[41] (For more in information technology security issues, see Subsection 17-3c of Chapter 17 on protecting information.)

The ISO 9000, 14000, and 27000 standards publications, which are available from the American National Standards Institute (see the end of this section), are general and can be used for manufacturing any kind of product or delivering any kind of service. Importantly, the ISO 9000 standards don't describe how to make a better-quality car, computer, or widget. Instead, they describe how companies can extensively document (and thus standardize) the steps they take to create and improve the quality of their products. Why should companies go to the trouble to achieve ISO 9000 certification?

ISO 9000 a series of five international standards, from ISO 9000 to ISO 9004, for achieving consistency in quality management and quality assurance in companies throughout the world

ISO 14000 a series of international standards for managing, monitoring, and minimizing an organization's harmful effects on the environment

ISO 27000 a series of 12 international standards for managing and monitoring security techniques for information technology

"What Do You Mean I'm Not a Medium?"

Do you find that the clothes you've ordered online don't fit? Consumer Madison Price, says, "Sometimes, I'll be an extra small, sometimes I'll be a medium. The sizing is all over the place." While the International Organization for Standardization publishes clothing size standards (ISO 8559), no one seems to follow them. The idea behind standards is to fit clothes to people. But when no one adheres to standards, the better answer might be fitting people to clothes.

For example, the MySizeID app uses smartphone sensors (not the camera) and patented algorithms to measure customer sizes. Short videos show you where to hold and move your smartphone to measure your chest, hips, waist, and forearm. It's simple and takes two minutes. Once your MySizeID is determined, click "Go Shopping" to see which retailers have clothes that fit. This works because MySizeID matches your personal measurement with retailers' size charts. Just remember, a medium in one store might be a large or a small in another.

So, when buying clothes online, instead of looking for a Medium, which probably won't fit, look for clothes that fit your personalized MySizeID.

Sources: "Faq – MYSIZE," MySizeID, accessed July 20, 2020, www.mysizeid .com/faq/#null; "ISO – ISO 8559-1:2017 – Size Designation of Clothes—Part 1: Anthropometric Definitions for Body Measurement," *International Organization for Standardization*, accessed July 20, 2020, https://www.iso.org/standard/61686. html?browse=tc; S. Kapner, "It's Not You. Clothing Sizes Are Broken," *The Wall Street Journal*, December 16, 2019, accessed July 20, 2020, www.wsj.com/articles /its-not-you-clothing-sizes-are-broken-11576501384.

Because their customers increasingly want them to. In fact, studies show that customers clearly prefer to buy from companies that are ISO certified. Companies, in turn, believe that being ISO certified helps them keep customers who might otherwise switch to an ISO certified competitor.[42]

To become ISO certified, a process that can take months, a company must show that it is following its own procedures for improving production, updating design plans and specifications, keeping machinery in top condition, educating and training workers, and satisfactorily dealing with customer complaints.[43] An accredited third party oversees the ISO certification process, just as a certified public accountant verifies that a company's financial accounts are up to date and accurate. After a company has been certified as ISO compliant, the accredited third party will issue an ISO certificate that the company can use in its advertising and publications. This is the quality equivalent of a "buy" recommendation from *Consumer Reports* or the *Wirecutter*. But continued ISO certification is not guaranteed. Accredited third parties typically conduct periodic audits to make sure the company is still following quality procedures. If it is not, its certification is suspended or canceled.

To get additional information on ISO guidelines and procedures, see the American National Standards Institute (www.webstore.ansi.org; the ISO 9000, 14000, and 27000 (27000 to 27010) standards publications are available here for about $599, $499, and $1,199, respectively), the American Society for Quality (www.asq.org), and the IOS (www.iso.org).

18-2c Baldrige National Quality Award

The Malcolm Baldrige National Quality Award, which is administered by the US government's National Institute of Standards and Technology, is given "to recognize US companies for their achievements in quality and business performance and to raise awareness about the importance of quality and performance excellence as a competitive edge."[44] Each year, awards may be given in the categories of manufacturing, education, health care, service, small business, and nonprofit.

The cost of applying for the Baldrige Award includes a $400 eligibility fee for all organizations. Manufacturing, service and large health care or nonprofit organizations also pay an application fee of $20,000 and a site visitation fee of $58,000 to $69,000. Small businesses and small health care, nonprofit, and education organizations also pay an application fee of $10,800 and a site visitation fee of $35,000 to $40,500. K–12 education organizations also pay an application fee of $4,800 and a site visitation fee of $17,000.[45]

Why does it cost so much? Because you get a great deal of useful information about your business even if you don't win. At a minimum, each company that applies receives an extensive report based on 300 hours of assessment from at least eight business and quality experts.

At $125 an hour for small organizations and about $215 an hour for manufacturing, service, and large organizations, the *Journal for Quality and Participation* called the Baldrige feedback report "the best bargain in consulting in America."[46] Arnold Weimerskirch, former chair of the Baldrige Award panel of judges and former vice president of quality at Honeywell, says, "The application and review process for the Baldrige Award is the best, most cost-effective, and comprehensive business health audit you can get."[47]

Businesses that apply for the Baldrige Award are judged on the seven criteria shown in Exhibit 18.3: leadership; strategy; customers; measurement, analysis, and knowledge management; workforce; operations; and results.[48] Results are typically the most important category. In other words, in addition to the six other criteria, companies must show that they have achieved superior quality when it comes to products and process, its customers, workforce, leadership, governance (and societal contributions), and financial and market results. This emphasis on results is what differentiates the Baldrige Award from the ISO standards. The Baldrige Award indicates the extent to which companies have actually achieved world-class quality. The ISO standards simply indicate whether a company is following the management system it put into place to improve quality. In fact, ISO certification covers less than 10 percent of the requirements for the Baldrige Award.[49]

Why should companies go to the trouble of applying for the Baldrige National Quality Award? Baldrige program examiner Betsy Beam explains that it's not just about winning the award; it's about the opportunity to improve. "Ritz-Carlton has won the Baldrige Award twice," Beam says. "Even in . . . the years they won, there were 35 opportunities for improvement identified. This is a very difficult journey for any organization, but it's well worth it as changes [that are needed] become obvious."[50]

18-2d Total Quality Management

Total quality management (TQM) is an integrated, organizationwide strategy for improving product and service quality.[51] TQM is not a specific tool or technique. Rather, TQM is a philosophy or overall approach to management that is characterized by three principles: customer focus and satisfaction, continuous improvement, and teamwork.[52]

Although most economists, accountants, and financiers argue that companies exist to earn profits for shareholders, TQM suggests that customer focus and customer satisfaction

should be a company's primary goals. **Customer focus** means that the entire organization, from top to bottom, should be focused on meeting customers' needs. The result of that customer focus should be **customer satisfaction**, which occurs when the company's products or services meet or exceed customers' expectations.

Exhibit 18.3
Criteria for the Baldrige National Quality Award

2019–2020 Categories/Items

1 Leadership
1.1 Senior Leadership
1.2 Governance and Societal Contributions

2 Strategy
2.1 Strategy Development
2.2 Strategy Implementation

3 Customers
3.1 Customer Listening
3.2 Customer Engagement

4 Measurement, Analysis, and Knowledge Management
4.1 Measurement, Analysis, and Improvement of Organizational Performance
4.2 Information and Knowledge Management

5 Workforce
5.1 Workforce Environment
5.2 Workforce Engagement

6 Operations
6.1 Work Processes
6.2 Operational Effectiveness

7 Results
7.1 Product and Process Results
7.2 Customer-Focused Results
7.3 Workforce-Focused Results
7.4 Leadership and Governance Results
7.5 Financial, Market, and Strategy Results

Source: "Baldrige Criteria Commentary: Baldrige Criteria for Performance Excellence Categories and Items," Baldrige Performance Excellence Program, November 15, 2019, accessed July 17, 2020, www.nist.gov/baldrige/baldrige-criteria-commentary.

Total quality management (TQM) an integrated, principle-based, organizationwide strategy for improving product and service quality

Customer focus an organizational goal to concentrate on meeting customers' needs at all levels of the organization

Customer satisfaction an organizational goal to provide products or services that meet or exceed customers' expectations

At companies where customer satisfaction is taken seriously, such as **Alaska Airlines**, paychecks depend on keeping customers satisfied. Everyone at Alaska Airlines, from the CEO to pilots to people who handle baggage, gets a monthly bonus, 70 percent of which is based on earnings, with the remaining 30 percent split among costs, safety, and customer satisfaction. Alaska Airlines employees received $130 million in monthly bonuses (roughly an extra month's pay for each employee) for their 2019 performance in those four categories.[53] In 2019, Alaska ranked third in on-time arrivals (81.5 percent) and third in the J.D. Power Airline Satisfaction Study for short-haul airlines.[54] Based on millions of customer ratings, Alaska Airlines was also named travel website Kayak's 2019 best overall airline, topping the rankings in every category, including best boarding, best comfort, best crew, best entertainment, and best food.[55]

Continuous improvement is an ongoing commitment to increase product and service quality by constantly assessing and improving the processes and procedures used to create those products and services. How do companies know whether they're achieving continuous improvement? Invented in 1885, **Dr Pepper** is the oldest soft drink in the United States. While soft drink sales have dropped 15 years in a row, the Dr Pepper Snapple Group is increasing profits and lowering costs through rapid continuous improvement (RCI). Former Chief Financial Officer Marty Ellen said, "RCI is about taking the existing baseline and improving it by finding the waste. We walk by waste every day. A team watched the process of fountain-syrup bags being assembled and packed into the cardboard boxes used to ship the bags. Somebody asked, 'Why does that box have the maroon Dr Pepper logo on it when the box isn't a consumer package?' You immediately call on the box supplier and ask, if we took that off, how much could we save a year? They said $60,000, and we said great. Put it in the bank."[56] Ellen notes that in the first two years of the RCI program, the company saved $200 million in expenses, reducing inventory by 41 percent, transportation and warehouse expenses by $30 million, and back office costs by $9 million, all while reducing customer complaints by 13 percent.[57]

Besides higher customer satisfaction, continuous improvement is usually associated with a

Everyone at Alaska Airlines, from the CEO to the pilots to the people who handle baggage, gets a monthly bonus based, in part, on customer satisfaction.

reduction in variation. **Variation** is a deviation in the form, condition, or appearance of a product from the quality standard for that product. The less a product varies from the quality standard, or the more consistently a company's products meet a quality standard, the higher the quality. No one likes cold, soggy French fries, but that's what you get when you have them delivered. Fries stay crunchy for about five minutes, but delivery drivers make things worse by putting fries next to cold drinks. Deb Dihel, the vice president of innovation for **Lamb Weston**, the leading provider of potato products for McDonald's and Yum Brands, says, "If you put a French fry next to a shake, neither of them benefit."[58] That variation in form, condition (taste) and appearance means lower quality. So, Lamb Weston, which produces a million pounds of potato products every day, is experimenting with six different kinds of potatoes, tracking temperatures, nutrients, and how much water they receive, all to make a fry that stays crisp longer. Troy Emmerson, Lamb Weston's director of agricultural services, said, "It's like you're going every week to the doctor. We treat them better than ourselves."[59] Lamb Weston also developed a new French fry batter that instantly forms a crispy outer layer when dropped into hot oil. That keeps fries crispy for 12 minutes. But, using a new package with just the right amount of ventilation (plastic bags and containers turn fries soggy) means the fries stay crisp for 30 minutes.[60] Lamb Weston's patented "Crispy Technology" fry cups – think of a French fry container with hole punches in the sides – are now available in shoestring, concertina, regular cut skin-on, and regular cut fries.[61]

The third principle of TQM is teamwork. **Teamwork** means collaboration between managers and nonmanagers, across business functions, and between

Continuous improvement an organization's ongoing commitment to constantly assess and improve the processes and procedures used to create products and services

Variation a deviation in the form, condition, or appearance of a product from the quality standard for that product

Teamwork collaboration between managers and nonmanagers, across business functions, and between companies, customers, and suppliers

the company and its customers and suppliers. In short, quality improves when everyone in the company is given the incentive to work together and the responsibility and authority to make improvements and solve problems. The **ArcellorMittal** plant in Gent, Belgium, needs only needs 1.3 labor-hours to make a ton of steel, or one-third less than average. One of ArcellorMittal's practices is to "twin" its best plants, such as Gent, with its poor-performing plants, such as its Burns Harbor, Indiana, plant. Then, it uses teamwork – and competition – to improve both. So it flew 100 Burns Harbor engineers and managers to Gent and told them, "Do as the Belgians do," whereas the Belgians were told to maintain their advantage. Founder Lakshmi Mittal says, "The process doesn't change: melt iron, cast, roll [steel]. But there are always incremental improvements you can make. We wanted Burns Harbor to be more like Gent."[62] Teamwork comes into play as teams from both plants meet regularly to discuss plant performance and share the steps they're taking to improve it. Following practices at Gent, Burns Harbor began using a different high pressure water nozzle to remove flakes (i.e., imperfections) from super-heated steel. Not only did steel quality improve, the nozzle used less water and power, saving $1.4 million in annual energy costs. Likewise, Burns Harbor workers began trimming less steel off the sides of steel coils, saving 725 coils of steel per year, the equivalent of 17,000 cars. Today, thanks to twinning and teamwork, Burns Harbor now produces 900 tons of steel per employee each year, close to Gent's 950.

Customer focus and satisfaction, continuous improvement, and teamwork mutually reinforce each other to improve quality throughout a company. Customer-focused, continuous improvement is necessary to increase customer satisfaction. At the same time, continuous improvement depends on teamwork from different functional and hierarchical parts of the company.

18-3 SERVICE OPERATIONS

At the start of this chapter, you learned that operations management means managing the daily production of goods and services. Then you learned that to manage production, you must oversee the factors that affect productivity and quality. In this half of the chapter, you will learn about managing operations in service and manufacturing businesses. The chapter ends with a discussion of inventory management, a key factor in a company's profitability.

Imagine that your trusty Roku streaming player breaks down as you try to watch favorite TV show. You've got two choices. You can run to Walmart and spend $50 to $80 purchase a new Roku 4K HDR streaming player, or you can ship it back to Roku to have it fixed. Either way, you end up with the same thing, a working Roku. However, the first choice, getting a new Roku, involves buying a physical product (a good), while the second, getting repairs, involves buying a service.

Services differ from goods in several ways. First, goods are produced or made, but services are performed. In other words, services are almost always labor-intensive in that someone typically has to perform the service for you. A computer repair shop could give you the parts needed to repair a laptop computer with a broken screen, but unless you're a do-it-yourself techie, you're still going to have a broken laptop screen without the technician to perform the repairs. Second, goods are tangible, but services are intangible. You can touch and see that replacement laptop screen, but you can't touch or see the service provided by the technician who fixed your laptop. All you can "see" is that the laptop screen has been replaced and works. Third, services are perishable and unstorable. If you don't use them when they're available, they're wasted. For example, if your computer repair shop is backlogged on repair jobs, then you'll just have to wait until next week to get your laptop repaired. You can't store an unused service and use it when you like. By contrast, you can purchase a good, such as motor oil, and store it until you're ready to use it.

Because services are different from goods, managing a service operation is different from managing a manufacturing or production operation.

*Let's look at **18-3a the service-profit chain** and **18-3b service recovery and empowerment**.*

18-3a The Service–Profit Chain

One of the key assumptions in the service business is that success depends on how well employees – that is, service providers – deliver their services to customers. But success actually begins with how well management treats service employees, as the service–profit chain, depicted in Exhibit 18.4, demonstrates.[63] The key concept behind the service–profit chain is **internal service quality**, meaning the quality of treatment that employees receive from a company's internal service providers, such

> **Internal service quality** the quality of treatment employees receive from management and other divisions of a company

Exhibit 18.4
Service–Profit Chain

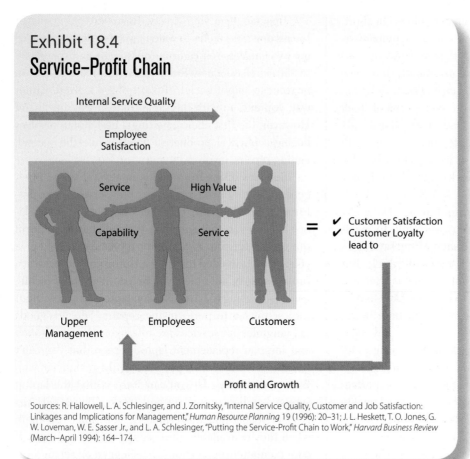

Sources: R. Hallowell, L. A. Schlesinger, and J. Zornitsky, "Internal Service Quality, Customer and Job Satisfaction: Linkages and Implications for Management," *Human Resource Planning* 19 (1996): 20–31; J. L. Heskett, T. O. Jones, G. W. Loveman, W. E. Sasser Jr., and L. A. Schlesinger, "Putting the Service-Profit Chain to Work," *Harvard Business Review* (March–April 1994): 164–174.

as management, payroll and benefits, human resources, and so forth.

As depicted in Exhibit 18.4, good internal service leads to employee satisfaction and service capability. *Employee satisfaction* occurs when companies treat employees in a way that meets or exceeds their expectations. In other words, the better employees are treated, the more satisfied they are, and the more likely they are to give high-value service that satisfies customers. How employers treat employees is important because it affects service capability. *Service capability* is an employee's perception of his or her ability to serve customers well. When an organization serves its employees in ways that help them to do their jobs well, employees, in turn, are more likely to believe that they can and ought to provide high-value service to customers.

A study of 293 large companies in 13 industries over 10 years examined the link between **Glassdoor.com** employee satisfaction scores (1–5 stars) and ratings from the American Customer Satisfaction Index (ACSI), which measures customers satisfaction (on a 0–100 scale) across 46 different industries.[64] A one-star increase on Glassdoor's employee satisfaction measure was associated with a 1.3-point increase in the ACSI.[65] In health

care, food service, and retail industries, where employees and customers interact every day, a one-star increase in employee satisfaction was associated with a 3.2-point increase in customer satisfaction.[66] This strongly supports the core idea of the service–profit chain: customers are more satisfied when dealing with happier employees.

According to the service–profit chain shown in Exhibit 18.4, *high-value service* leads to *customer satisfaction* and *customer loyalty*, which, in turn, lead to *long-term profits and growth*.[67] What's the link between customer satisfaction and profits? While the 1.3-point and 3.2-point increases in ACSI customer satisfaction scores associated with more satisfied employees might seem small, they're not. A 1 percent increase in ACSI customer satisfaction scores is associated with a sizable 4.6 percent increase in a firm's stock value. The study authors said, "Applying this to our findings, we can calculate the possible impact of a one-star improvement in Glassdoor employer ratings, given the expected knock-on improvement in customer satisfaction scores: an increase of 7.8 to 18.9 percent in long-term market valuation."[68]

What about the link to customer loyalty? A meta-analysis of 126+ studies and over 61,000 people supported every link in the service–profit chain, finding very strong relationships between how customers were treated, customer satisfaction, customer loyalty, and profitability.[69] In practice, how much does this matter? The average business keeps only 70 to 90 percent of its existing customers each year. No big deal, you say? Just replace leaving customers with new customers. Well, there's one significant problem with that solution. It costs 10 times as much to find a new customer as it does to keep an existing customer. Also, new customers typically buy only 20 percent as much as established customers. In fact, keeping existing customers is so cost-effective that most businesses could double their profits by simply keeping 5 percent more customers per year![70] Imagine that keeping more of your customers turns some of those customers into customers for life (i.e., repurchasers). This is a reasonable assumption as customer satisfaction and customer loyalty are strongly linked with customers who come back time and time again to repurchase services.[71] How much of a difference would that make to company profits? Consider that just one lifetime customer spends $9,600 on pizza and over $395,000 on luxury cars![72]

18-3b Service Recovery and Empowerment

When mistakes are made, when problems occur, and when customers become dissatisfied with the service they've received, service businesses must switch from the process of service delivery to the process of **service recovery**, or restoring customer satisfaction to strongly dissatisfied customers.[73] Or as business consultant Barry Moltz explains, "When a customer says they are dissatisfied, the company gets a chance to fix it and turn them into a more loyal customer."[74] Service recovery sometimes requires service employees to not only fix whatever mistake was made but also perform heroic service acts that delight highly dissatisfied customers by far surpassing their expectations of fair treatment. Jason Friend, co-founder of Basecamp.com, which makes web-based collaboration software, bought a custom bike via the Web from **Mission Bicycle Company** in San Francisco. When the bike arrived, he found a large gash on the side of the bike's frame. He described what happened when he contacted Mission: "They said sending the whole bike back would be over-kill since the only thing that was damaged was the frame. Further, the bike was rideable – it was just a paint problem – so sending the bike back would mean I didn't have a bike for a week or so. They didn't feel good about that. So here's what they did: They called up a local shop (On The Route) and arranged to ship a new frame to them. Then one of their bike techs would drive down to my office and swap the frames and reassemble the bike for me while I waited. All of this at Mission's expense." He concluded by saying, "That's incredible customer service. I'm a happy customer for life. If you're in the market for a great custom bike, check out the good people and products at Mission Bicycle Company."[75]

Unfortunately, when mistakes occur, service employees often don't have the discretion to resolve customer complaints. Customers who want service employees to correct or make up for poor service are frequently told, "I'm not allowed to do that," "I'm just following company rules," or "I'm sorry, only managers are allowed to make changes of any kind." In other words, company rules prevent them from engaging in acts of service recovery

meant to turn dissatisfied customers back into satisfied customers. The result is frustration for customers and service employees and lost customers for the company.

Now, however, many companies are empowering their service employees.[76] In Chapter 9, you learned that *empowering workers* means permanently passing decision-making authority and responsibility from managers to workers. With respect to service recovery, empowering workers means giving service employees the authority and responsibility to make decisions that immediately solve customer problems.[77] For example, when customers call into Nicor National, an energy utility, to ask for credits to their accounts, they are not transferred to a billing department. They are not put on hold while the call rep looks for a supervisor or manager. Instead, the call rep, who is empowered to make this decision, simply awards the credit without having to check with anyone. According to Barbara Porter, the company's vice president of business development and customer service, empowering the call centers in this way results in a quick, easy resolution. "They're professionals and we trust them to make the right decisions," says Porter.[78]

When things go wrong for customers, how well does service recovery work? Sixty-nine percent of customers see quick resolution of their problems as central to good customer service. Furthermore, about half of customers will stop buying from a company when bad customer service is not resolved. Either way, roughly 9 out of 10 customers will tell others about their poor customer service or how you fixed their problem.[79]

18-4 MANUFACTURING OPERATIONS

Tesla makes cars, and Dell does computers. BP produces gasoline, whereas Sherwin-Williams makes paint. Airbus makes jet planes, but Anheuser-Busch makes beer. Western Digital makes hard drives, and Whirlpool makes appliances. The *manufacturing operations* of these companies all produce physical goods. But not all manufacturing operations, especially these, are the same.

*Let's learn how various manufacturing operations differ in terms of **18-4a the amount of processing that is done to produce and assemble a product** and **18-4b the flexibility to change the number, kind, and characteristics of products that are produced.***

Service recovery restoring customer satisfaction to strongly dissatisfied customers

18-4a Amount of Processing in Manufacturing Operations

Manufacturing operations can be classified according to the amount of processing or assembly that occurs after a customer order is received. The highest degree of processing occurs in **make-to-order operations**. A make-to-order operation does not start processing or assembling products until it receives a customer order. In fact, some make-to-order operations may not even order parts until a customer order is received. Not surprisingly, make-to-order operations produce or assemble highly specialized or customized products for customers.

Midwest Precision, Inc., in Tulsa, Oklahoma, uses computer-controlled lasers and waterjet machining to fabricate sheet metal into parts for health and fitness equipment, cars and trucks, and aerospace, agricultural, and architectural customers. Because it serves so many industries, it doesn't design and produce parts until they are ordered. For example, its make-to-order deadlines ranged from 24 hours to two weeks for the exterior metal signs, gutters, window jambs, corner panels, decorative details and large perforated weathered steel panels it manufactured for Tulsa's Hardesty Arts center. Likewise, its computer-controlled waterjets cut 2.25-inch-thick custom titanium alloy parts for an aerospace customer needing them two to three weeks after they were ordered.[80]

A moderate degree of processing occurs in **assemble-to-order operations**. A company using an assemble-to-order operation divides its manufacturing or assembly process into separate parts or modules. The company orders parts and assembles modules ahead of customer orders. Then, based on actual customer orders or on research forecasting what customers will want, those modules are combined to create semicustomized products. For example, when a customer orders a new car, GM may have already ordered the basic parts or modules it needs from suppliers. In other words, based on sales forecasts, GM may already have ordered enough tires, air-conditioning compressors, brake systems, and seats from suppliers to accommodate nearly all customer orders on a particular day. Special orders from customers and car dealers are then used to determine the final assembly checklist for particular cars as they move down the assembly line.

The lowest degree of processing occurs in **make-to-stock operations** (also called build-to-stock). Because the products are standardized, meaning each product is exactly the same as the next, a company using a make-to-stock operation starts ordering parts and assembling finished products before receiving customer orders. Customers then purchase these standardized products – such as Rubbermaid storage containers, microwave ovens, and vacuum cleaners – at retail stores or directly from the manufacturer. Because parts are ordered and products are assembled before customers order the products, make-to-stock operations are highly dependent on the accuracy of sales forecasts. If sales forecasts are incorrect, make-to-stock operations may end up building too many or too few products, or they may make products with the wrong features or without the features that customers want.

18-4b Flexibility of Manufacturing Operations

A second way to categorize manufacturing operations is by **manufacturing flexibility**, meaning the degree to which manufacturing operations can easily and quickly change the number, kind, and characteristics of products they produce. Flexibility allows companies to respond quickly to changes in the marketplace (i.e., in response to competitors and customers) and to reduce the lead time between ordering and final delivery of products. There is often a trade-off between flexibility and cost, however, with the most flexible manufacturing operations frequently having higher costs per unit, and the least flexible operations having lower costs per unit. Some common manufacturing operations, arranged in order from the least flexible to the most flexible, are continuous-flow production, line-flow production, batch production, and job shops.

Most production processes generate finished products at a discrete rate. A product is completed, and then – perhaps a few seconds, minutes, or hours later– another is completed, and so on. For instance, if

Make-to-order operation a manufacturing operation that does not start processing or assembling products until a customer order is received

Assemble-to-order operation a manufacturing operation that divides manufacturing processes into separate parts or modules that are combined to create semicustomized products

Make-to-stock operation a manufacturing operation that orders parts and assembles standardized products before receiving customer orders

Manufacturing flexibility the degree to which manufacturing operations can easily and quickly change the number, kind, and characteristics of products they produce

MANUFACTURING FLEXIBILITY: FROM CARS TO VENTILATORS

Manufacturing flexibility is the degree to which manufacturing operations can easily and quickly change the number, kind, and characteristics of products they produce. When coronavirus demand surges emptied warehouses of ventilators, masks and hand sanitizer, companies around the world pivoted to meet demand. Fashion house Christian Dior's perfume factories and Pernon Ricard's Absolut Vodka and Jameson Irish whiskey facilities began manufacturing hand sanitizer. Apple made face shields for health care workers. Ferrari, maker of super-fast, expensive cars, produced respirator valves and mask fittings.

But the biggest changes in manufacturing flexibility involved ventilators, which have 700 components. Ford Motor engineers, who weeks before had finished their work on the factory launch of its new Ford Bronco, used Post-It notes to lay out all of the production steps and locations involved in making ventilators designed by Airon Corporation. Airon, which has been making ventilators for 40 years, makes 10 ventilators a week – by hand. Ford, running two shifts a day, employed 260 workers to manufacture 7,200 ventilators a week. General Motors, partnering with ventilator maker Ventec Life Systems, plans to match Ford's production.

How difficult is it for automakers to switch to ventilators? Gerald Johnson, GM's global manufacturing chief, explains, "You've got to bring 1,200 people up to speed on processes that they've not ever done before." That's manufacturing flexibility.

Sources: "Ferrari's Maranello Factory Now Building Respirator Parts to Help Coronavirus Fight," Formula 1®, April 17, 2020, accessed July 21, 2020, www.formula1.com/en/latest/article.ferraris-maranello-factory-%E2%80%A6ding-respirator-parts-to-help-coronavirus.6NykgmRMptrerPefAnxxzX.html; T. Buckley, "Companies Revamp to Make Hand Sanitizer and Coronavirus Products," Bloomberg, March 24, 2020, accessed July 21, 2020, www.bloomberg.com/news/articles/2020-03-24/companies-revamp-to-make-hand-sanitizer-and-coronavirus-products?sref=xXo7CWym; M. Colias, "Auto Giants Trade Drills for Tweezers in Bid to Rush Coronavirus Ventilators," The Wall Street Journal, April 12, 2020, accessed July 21, 2020, www.wsj.com/articles/ford-and-gm-try-mass-producing-ventilators-can-they-move-fast-enough-11586711800; M. Dalton, R. Bender & J. Douglas, "Companies Retool Operations to Assist in Coronavirus Fight," Wall Street Journal, March 19, 2020, accessed July 21, 2020, www.wsj.com/articles/companies-retool-operations-to-assist-in-coronavirus-fight-11584637831; M. Maidenberg, "Ford Working With 3M, GE to Produce Medical Supplies," The Wall Street Journal, March 24, 2020, accessedJuly 21, 2020,www.wsj.com/articles/ford-working-with-3m-ge-to-produce-medical-supplies-11585053318.

you stood at the end of an automobile assembly line, nothing much would seem to be happening for 55 seconds of every minute. In that last five seconds, however, a new car would be started and driven off the assembly line, ready for its new owner. By contrast, in **continuous-flow production**, products are produced continuously rather than at a discrete rate. Like a water hose that is never turned off and just keeps on flowing, production of the final product never stops. Until recently, drug companies used discrete production operations to make drugs, mixing ingredients in huge vats at separate factories. But to cut costs and increase quality, many are switching to continuous-flow production where the raw materials used to make drugs are "fed into a single, continuously running process."[81]

Johnson & Johnson, GlaxoSmithKline, and Novartis are building continuous-flow factories, which should reduce operating costs by 30 percent and increase quality because corrections can be made immediately and not after large batches have been produced. Furthermore, continuous-flow pharmaceutical factories are much smaller, at 4,000 square feet compared to the typical 100,000 square foot drug making facility, and thus, much less costly to build. Finally, production speeds and output can be dramatically higher. For instance, while it takes four to six weeks to make 100,000 tablets of Vertex's new cystic-fibrosis drug, its new continuous-flow factory will be able to make that many tablets in an hour![82] Despite their many advantages, continuous-flow production processes are the most standardized and least flexible manufacturing operations. In other words, a continuous-flow factory dedicated to making cystic-fibrosis drugs could not be used to make another kind of drug.

Line-flow production processes are preestablished, occur in a serial or linear manner, and are dedicated to making one type of product. In this way, the 10 different steps required to make product X can be completed in a separate manufacturing process (with separate machines, parts, treatments, locations, and workers) from the 12 different steps required to make product Y. Line-flow production processes are inflexible because they are typically dedicated to manufacturing

> **Continuous-flow production**
> a manufacturing operation that produces goods at a continuous, rather than a discrete, rate
>
> **Line-flow production**
> manufacturing processes that are preestablished, occur in a serial or linear manner, and are dedicated to making one type of product

one kind of product. The machines that make toilet paper are four stories tall and as big as a football field. Plus, it takes four months to get them running. But they can only make one kind of toilet paper.[83] There are two similarly sized markets for toilet paper, the soft, cushy kind consumers buy for home and the thin, scratchy kind businesses buy for their facilities (no pun intended). Scott Luton, founder and CEO of **Supply Chain Now**, a digital media company, explains that toilet paper manufacturing "is not built for dramatic shifts and seasonal demand changes. It's not like pumpkins during the fall and chicken wings during the Super Bowl."[84] So, if you blamed hoarding for the toilet paper shortage during the coronavirus, you'd only be half right. It was also because of inflexible line-flow production, which prevented companies like Kimberly-Clark from switching their office toilet paper factories over to consumer toilet paper.[85]

The next most flexible manufacturing operation is **batch production**, which involves the manufacture of large batches of different products in standard lot sizes. A worker in a batch production operation will perform the same manufacturing process on 100 copies of product X, followed by 200 copies of product Y, and then 50 copies of product Z. Furthermore, these batches move through each manufacturing department or process in identical order. So, if the paint department follows chemical treatment, and chemical treatment is now processing a batch of 50 copies of product Z, then the paint department's next task will be to paint 50 copies of product Z. Batch production is finding increasing use among restaurant chains. To ensure consistency in the taste and quality of their products, many restaurant chains have central kitchens, or commissaries, that produce batches of food such as mashed potatoes, stuffing, macaroni and cheese, rice, quiche filling, and chili, in volumes ranging from 10 to 200 gallons. These batches are then delivered to the individual restaurant locations, which in turn serve the food to customers.

Next in terms of flexibility is the job shop. **Job shops** are typically small manufacturing operations that handle special manufacturing processes or jobs. In contrast to batch production, which handles large batches of different products, job shops typically handle very small batches, some

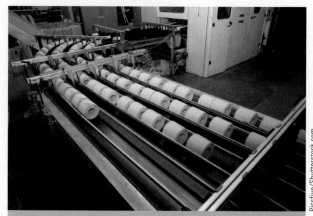

Machines that make toilet paper are four stories tall and as big as a football field. However, they can only make one type of toilet paper.

Picsfive/Shutterstock.com

as small as one product or process per batch. Basically, each job in a job shop is different, and after a job is done, the job shop moves on to a completely different job or manufacturing process for, most likely, a different customer. **Kenworthy Machine LLC** in Duvall, Washington, is a job shop with six employees that uses CNC (computer numerical control) machine tools to make high-quality parts from plastics to the hardest carbon, alloy tool steels. Owner Mark Kenworthy says, "When it comes to part design, we have various types of customers."[86] It made 90,000 parts last year, with orders as small as just two parts to as large as several thousand of the same parts.[87] The addition of a 3-D printer has allowed the company to expand its business by "printing" one-off parts when needed. For example, it used 3-D printing to make metal shelf brackets, a metal kitchen wall rack, and replacement plastic buttons for the machines it runs in its job shop.

18-5 INVENTORY

Inventory is the amount and number of raw materials, parts, and finished products that a company has in its possession. After switching chicken suppliers, **Kentucky Fried Chicken (KFC)** temporarily closed 900 of its 1,800 restaurants in the United Kingdom and Ireland because it ran out of most important raw material, chicken! KFC tweeted, "The chicken crossed the road, just not to our restaurants. We've brought a new delivery partner onboard, but they've had a couple of teething problems – getting fresh chicken out to 900

Batch production a manufacturing operation that produces goods in large batches in standard lot sizes

Job shops manufacturing operations that handle custom orders or small-batch jobs

Inventory the amount and number of raw materials, parts, and finished products that a company has in its possession

restaurants across the country is pretty complex! We won't compromise on quality, so no deliveries has meant some of our restaurants are closed, and others are operating a limited menu or shortened hours... The Colonel is working on it."[88] After restaurants reopened a week later, many had no gravy. A KFC spokesperson said, "We're working as hard as we can to get this sorted out. We know that our gravy is a big favourite!"[89] So many customers contacted London's Metropolitan Police Department about the shortages that it tweeted, "Please do not contact us about the #KFCCrisis – it is not a police matter..."[90]

In this section, you will learn about **18-5a the different types of inventory, 18-5b how to measure inventory levels, 18-5c the costs of maintaining an inventory, and 18-5d the systems for managing inventory.**

18-5a Types of Inventory

Exhibit 18.5 shows the four kinds of inventory a manufacturer stores: raw materials, component parts, work-in-process, and finished goods. The flow of inventory through a manufacturing plant begins when the purchasing department buys raw materials from vendors. **Raw material inventories** are the basic inputs in the manufacturing process. For example, to begin making a car, automobile manufacturers purchase raw materials such as steel, iron, aluminum, copper, rubber, and unprocessed plastic.

Next, raw materials are fabricated or processed into **component parts inventories**, meaning the basic parts used in manufacturing a product. For example, in an automobile plant, steel is fabricated or processed into a car's body panels, and steel and iron are melted and shaped into engine parts such as pistons or engine blocks. Some component parts are purchased from vendors rather than fabricated in-house.

The component parts are then assembled to make unfinished **work-in-process inventories**, which are also known as partially finished goods. This process is also called *initial assembly*. For example, steel body panels are welded to each other and to the frame of the car to make a "unibody," which comprises the unpainted interior frame and exterior structure of the car. Likewise, pistons, camshafts, and other engine parts are inserted into the engine block to create a working engine.

Next, all the work-in-process inventories are assembled to create **finished goods inventories**, which are the final outputs of the manufacturing process.

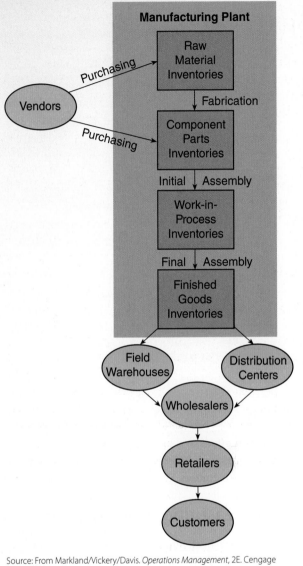

Exhibit 18.5
Types of Inventory

Source: From Markland/Vickery/Davis. *Operations Management*, 2E. Cengage Learning, Inc.

This process is also called *final assembly*. For a car, the engine, wheels, brake system, suspension, interior, and electrical system are assembled into a car's painted unibody to make the working automobile, which is the

Raw material inventories the basic inputs in a manufacturing process

Component parts inventories the basic parts used in manufacturing that are fabricated from raw materials

Work-in-process inventories partially finished goods consisting of assembled component parts

Finished goods inventories the final outputs of manufacturing operations

Popeye's Spicy Chicken Sandwich Stockouts? Nooooooooooo!!!

Popeyes Louisiana Kitchen is famous for its Cajun fried chicken and shrimp. But nothing is more popular at its 2,700 restaurants than its $3.99 Spicy Chicken Sandwich (SCC). Franchise owner, Brian Smith, sold 1,200 SCCs a day the week they were introduced. Popeyes ran out of three months' worth of chicken breasts in just two weeks! Popeyes US president, Felipe Athayde, said, "We had very aggressively forecasted the demand, and we thought we wouldn't have any problems at all.... And then two weeks go by, and we're out of the product on a national level."

What happened? Suppliers couldn't keep up with demand for the small, quarter-pound chicken breasts that are perfect for chicken sandwiches. Chicken suppliers have focused on increasing the size of chickens, from 2.5 pounds in 1925 to 6 pounds today. But breasts from larger chickens are just too big (and tasteless).

It took Popeyes two months to find adequate supplies of the smaller chicken breasts needed for its SCCs. Guillermo Perales, CEO of Sun Holdings, which owns 165 Popeyes, said, "We definitely weren't ready last time." But this time, "We're getting trained, ready, and having the systems in place this time for everything." Will supplies last? Economist Will Sawyers says there's no new supply to meet growing industry demand. He says, "Everyone wants a bite out of that market."

Carmen K. Sisson/Alamy Stock Photo

Sources: H. Haddon, "Supplies in Hand, Popeyes to Bring Back Its Spicy Chicken Sandwich," *The Wall Street Journal*, October 27, 2019, accessed July 21, 2020, www.wsj.com/articles/supplies-in-hand-popeyes-to-bring-back-its-spicy-chicken-sand-wich-11572181201; L. Patton & L. Mulvany, "Chick-Fil-A's War With Popeyes Drains Little-Chicken Supply," *Bloomberg*, January 28, 2020, accessed July 21, 2020, www.bloomberg.com/news/articles/2020-01-28/chick-fil-a-s-war-with-popeyes-drains-supply-of-little-chickens?sref=xXo7CWym; D. Yaffe-Bellany & M. Sedacca, "15 Minutes to 'Mayhem': How a Tweet Led to a Shortage at Popeyes," *New York Times*, August 29, 2019, accessed July 21, 2020, www.nytimes.com/2019/08/29/business/popeyes-chicken-sandwich-shortage.html?mod=article_inline.

factory's finished product. In the last step in the process, the finished goods are sent to field warehouses, distribution centers, or wholesalers, and then to retailers for final sale to customers.

18-5b Measuring Inventory

As you'll learn next, uncontrolled inventory can lead to huge costs for any organization. Consequently, managers need good measures of inventory to prevent inventory costs from becoming too large. Three basic measures of inventory are average aggregate inventory, weeks of supply, and inventory turnover.

If you've ever worked in a retail store and had to take inventory, you probably weren't too excited about the process of counting every item in the store and storeroom. It's an extensive task that's a bit easier today because of bar codes that mark items and computers that can count and track them. Nonetheless, inventories still differ from day to day. An inventory count taken at the beginning of the month will likely be different from a count taken at the end of the month. Similarly, an inventory count taken on a Friday will differ from a count taken on a Monday. Because of such differences, companies often measure **average aggregate inventory**, which is the average overall inventory during a particular time period. Average aggregate inventory for a month can be determined by simply averaging the inventory counts at the end of each business day for that month. One way companies know whether they're carrying too much or too little inventory is to compare their average aggregate inventory with the industry average for aggregate inventory. For example, 67 days of finished goods inventory (completed cars and trucks) was the average for the automobile industry in 2019.[91]

The automobile industry records inventory in terms of days of supply, but most other industries measure inventory in terms of *weeks of supply*, meaning the number of weeks it would take for a company to run out of its current supply of inventory. In general, there is an acceptable number of weeks of inventory for a particular kind of business. Too few weeks of

Average aggregate inventory average overall inventory during a particular time period

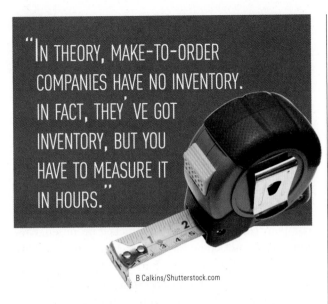

"IN THEORY, MAKE-TO-ORDER COMPANIES HAVE NO INVENTORY. IN FACT, THEY'VE GOT INVENTORY, BUT YOU HAVE TO MEASURE IT IN HOURS."

B Calkins/Shutterstock.com

inventory on hand, and a company risks a **stockout** – running out of inventory. With low interest rates, fast growth in Asia, and aging jet fleets needing replacement, the largest makers of passenger jets, Airbus and Boeing, experienced record orders that raised production 30 percent a year. Pratt & Whitney, which makes jet engines, and Zodiac, which makes $100,000 business-class seats, experienced stockouts as they struggled to keep up with rising production levels. Airbus, in particular, had so many finished planes – without engines – that a frustrated Qatar Airlines canceled its orders.[92]

Another common inventory measure, **inventory turnover**, is the number of times per year that a company sells, or "turns over," its average inventory. For example, if a company keeps an average of 100 finished widgets in inventory each month, and it sold 1,000 widgets this year, then it turned its inventory ten times this year.

In general, the higher the number of inventory turns, the better. In practice, a high turnover means that a company can continue its daily operations with just a small amount of inventory on hand. For example, let's take two companies, A and B, which have identical inventory levels of 520,000 widget parts and raw materials over the course of a year. If company A turns its inventories 26 times a year, it will completely replenish its inventory every two weeks and have an average inventory of 20,000 widget parts and raw materials. By contrast, if company B turns its inventories only two times a year, it will completely replenish its inventory every 26 weeks and have an average inventory of 260,000 widget parts and raw materials. So, by turning its inventory more often, company A has 92 percent less inventory on hand at any one time than company B.

The average number of inventory turns across all kinds of manufacturing plants is approximately eight per year, although the average can be higher or lower for different industries.[93] For example, whereas the average automobile or truck manufacturer turns its entire inventory 11.9 times per year, truck manufacturer Paccar turns its inventory 22.34 times a year–roughly once every 2.3 weeks.[94] Turning inventory more frequently than the industry average can cut an auto company's costs by several hundred million dollars per year.

18-5c Costs of Maintaining Inventory

Maintaining an inventory incurs four kinds of costs: ordering, setup, holding, and stockout. **Ordering cost** is not the cost of the inventory itself but the costs associated with ordering the inventory. It includes the costs of completing paperwork, manually entering data into a computer, making phone calls, getting competing bids, correcting mistakes, and simply determining when and how much new inventory should be reordered.

Twenty years ago, ordering costs in the restaurant business were estimated at $14 billion to $20 billion because 80 percent of foodservice orders (in which restaurants reorder food supplies) were processed manually.[95] Today, however, ordering costs have dropped dramatically thanks to services like FoodBAM, a web- and app-based electronic ordering system. "Search through all of the items on your order guides, select the food and supplies that you need to add, stay informed about your up-to-date prices, and click send. Your orders are automatically routed to distributors in a standard format…"[96] And, since most restaurants order similar ingredients over and over again, reordering is as simple as reloading and editing previous orders. FoodBAM makes it easy to search and sort across dozens of suppliers, provides real-time pricing, and shows restaurant owners when their orders were received. Richard Dennis, the owner and chef at Stars on Hingham Harbor in Hingham, Massachusetts, said, "It used to take me hours to do my ordering, now I have it down to 15 minutes thanks to FoodBAM!"[97]

Stockout the point when a company runs out of finished product

Inventory turnover the number of times per year that a company sells, or "turns over," its average inventory

Ordering cost the costs associated with ordering inventory, including the cost of data entry, phone calls, obtaining bids, correcting mistakes, and determining when and how much inventory to order

Setup cost is the cost of changing or adjusting a machine so that it can produce a different kind of inventory.[98] For example, 3M uses the same production machinery to make several kinds of industrial tape, but it must adjust the machines whenever it switches from one kind of tape to another. There are two kinds of setup costs: downtime and lost efficiency. *Downtime* occurs whenever a machine is not being used to process inventory. If it takes five hours to switch a machine from processing one kind of inventory to another, then five hours of downtime have occurred. Downtime is costly because companies earn an economic return only when machines are actively turning raw materials into parts or parts into finished products. The second setup cost is *lost efficiency*. Recalibrating a machine to its optimal settings after a switchover typically takes some time. It may take several days of fine-tuning before a machine finally produces the number of high-quality parts that it is supposed to. So, each time a machine has to be changed to handle a different kind of inventory, setup costs (downtime and lost efficiency) rise.

Holding cost, also known as *carrying* or *storage cost*, is the cost of keeping inventory until it is used or sold. Holding cost includes the cost of storage facilities, insurance to protect inventory from damage or theft, inventory taxes, the cost of obsolescence (holding inventory that is no longer useful to the company), and the opportunity cost of spending money on inventory that could have been spent elsewhere in the company. When demand for oil dropped to record lows because of the coronavirus, oil producers were slow to cut production, resulting in a record oil glut. With land-based oil storage tanks full, oil producers rented 100 very large crude carriers (VLCC), each holding 2 million barrels of crude oil. While the typical cost to rent a VLCC for shipping oil is $10,000 per day, prices jumped to $150,000 per day after floating oil storage surged from 23 million barrels to 150 million barrels in just one week.[99] Robert Macleod, CEO of Norway-based Frontline Management AS, one of the world's largest tanker owners, said, "The world is oversupplied and oil basically only has one place to go when land based is full, and that is tankers. (Charter) periods are mainly six months and more."[100]

Stockout cost is the cost incurred when a company runs out of a product. There are two basic kinds of stockout costs. First, the company incurs the transaction costs of overtime work, shipping, and the like in trying to quickly replace out-of-stock inventories with new inventories. The second and perhaps more damaging cost is the loss of customers' goodwill when a company cannot deliver the products it promised. Customers may not come back when a store doesn't have the products they're looking for. In a typical year, it's estimated that stockouts cost retailers $634 billion a year in lost sales.[101] However, it's estimated that stockout costs to retailers tripled to $1.8 trillion a year in 2020 due to widespread stockouts caused by coronavirus surge buying.[102]

18-5d Managing Inventory

Inventory management has two basic goals. The first is to avoid running out of stock and thus angering and dissatisfying customers. This goal seeks to increase inventory to a safe level that won't risk stockouts. The second is to efficiently reduce inventory levels and costs as much as possible without impairing daily operations. This goal seeks a minimum level of inventory. The following inventory management techniques – economic order quantity (EOQ), just-in-time inventory (JIT), and materials requirement planning (MRP) – are different ways of balancing these competing goals.

Economic order quantity (EOQ) is a system of formulas that helps determine how much and how often inventory should be ordered. EOQ takes into account the overall demand (D) for a product while trying to minimize ordering costs (O) and holding costs (H). The formula for EOQ is

$$EOQ = \sqrt{\frac{2DO}{H}}$$

For example, if a factory uses 40,000 gallons of paint a year (D), ordering costs (O) are $75 per order, and holding costs (H) are $4 per gallon, then the optimal quantity to order is 1,225 gallons:

$$EOQ = \sqrt{\frac{2(40,000)(75)}{4}} = 1,225$$

Setup cost the costs of downtime and lost efficiency that occur when a machine is changed or adjusted to produce a different kind of inventory

Holding cost the cost of keeping inventory until it is used or sold, including storage, insurance, taxes, obsolescence, and opportunity costs

Stockout cost the cost incurred when a company runs out of a product, including transaction costs to replace inventory and the loss of customers' goodwill

Economic order quantity (EOQ) a system of formulas that minimizes ordering and holding costs and helps determine how much and how often inventory should be ordered

With 40,000 gallons of paint being used per year, the factory uses approximately 110 gallons per day:

$$\frac{4,000 \text{ gallons}}{365 \text{ days}} = 110$$

Consequently, the factory would order 1,225 new gallons of paint approximately every 11 days:

$$\frac{1,225 \text{ gallons}}{110 \text{ gallons per days}} = 11.1 \text{ days}$$

In general, EOQ formulas do a good job of letting managers know what size or amount of inventory they should reorder to minimize ordering and holding costs. Mark Lore, former founder of Diapers.com (now an Amazon brand), explains how it used EOQ formulas to decide precisely how much inventory to keep on hand. He says, "We built software with computational algorithms to determine what the optimal number of boxes to have in the warehouse is and what the sizes of those boxes should be. Should we stock five different kinds of boxes to ship product in? Twenty kinds? Fifty kinds? And what size should those boxes be? Right now, it's 23 box sizes, given what we sell, in order to minimize the cost of dunnage (those little plastic air-filled bags or peanuts), the cost of corrugated boxes, and the cost of shipping. We rerun the simulation every quarter."[103] As this example makes clear, EOQ formulas and models can become much more complex as adjustments are made for price changes, quantity discounts, setup costs, and many other factors.[104]

While EOQ formulas try to minimize holding and ordering costs, the just-in-time (JIT) approach to inventory management attempts to eliminate holding costs by reducing inventory levels to near zero. With a **just-in-time (JIT) inventory system**, component parts arrive from suppliers just as they are needed at each stage of production. By having parts arrive just in time, the manufacturer has little inventory on hand and thus avoids the costs associated with holding inventory. Thanks to its strict JIT inventory system, Apple carries the smallest amount of inventory among technology companies, averaging just eight days of inventory of iPhones, iPad Pro tablets, and Mac computers waiting to be shipped. That eight days of inventory is equivalent to an inventory turn of 44.55 times a year (remember, more turns is better). For comparison, Dell Technologies has 19.2 days of inventory or 19.01 turns a year. Amazon has 39.8 days of inventory or 9.17 turns. Hewlett-Packard (HP) has 45.2 days of inventory or 8.07 turns a year.[105]

To have just the right amount of inventory arrive at just the right time requires a tremendous amount of coordination between manufacturing operations and suppliers. One way to promote tight coordination under JIT is close proximity. Most parts suppliers for Toyota's JIT system at its Georgetown, Kentucky, plant are located within 200 miles of the plant. Furthermore, parts are picked up from suppliers and delivered to Toyota as often as 16 times a day.[106] A second way to promote close coordination under JIT is to have a shared information system that allows a manufacturer and its suppliers to know the quantity and kinds of parts inventory the other has in stock. Generally, factories and suppliers facilitate information sharing by using the same part numbers and names. Ford's seat supplier accomplishes this by sticking a bar code on each seat, and Ford then uses the sticker to route the seat through its factory.

Manufacturing operations and their parts suppliers can also facilitate close coordination by using the system of kanban. **Kanban**, which is Japanese for "sign," is a simple ticket-based system that indicates when it is time to reorder inventory. Suppliers attach kanban cards to batches of parts. Then, when an assembly-line worker uses the first part out of a batch, the kanban card is removed. The cards are then collected, sorted, and quickly returned to the supplier, who begins resupplying the factory with parts that match the order information on the kanban cards. Glenn Uminger, former manager of production control and logistics at Toyota's Georgetown, Kentucky, plant, said they would place, "orders for new parts as the first part is used out of a box." Because prices and batch sizes are typically agreed to ahead of time, kanban tickets greatly reduce paperwork and ordering costs.[107]

A third method for managing inventory is **materials requirement planning (MRP)**. MRP is a production and inventory system that, from beginning to end, precisely determines the production schedule, production batch sizes, and inventories needed to complete final products. The three key parts of MRP systems are the master production schedule, the bill of materials, and the inventory records. The *master production schedule* is a detailed schedule that indicates the quantity of each item to be produced, the planned delivery dates for those items, and the time by which each step of the

Just-in-time (JIT) inventory system an inventory system in which component parts arrive from suppliers just as they are needed at each stage of production

Kanban a ticket-based JIT system that indicates when to reorder inventory

Materials requirement planning (MRP) a production and inventory system that determines the production schedule, production batch sizes, and inventory needed to complete final products

production process must be completed to meet those delivery dates. Based on the quantity and kind of products set forth in the master production schedule, the *bill of materials* identifies all the necessary parts and inventory, the quantity or volume of inventory to be ordered, and the order in which the parts and inventory should be assembled. *Inventory records* indicate the kind, quantity, and location of inventory that is on hand or that has been ordered.

When inventory records are combined with the bill of materials, the resulting report indicates what to buy, when to buy it, and what it will cost to order. Today, nearly all MRP systems are available in the form of powerful, flexible computer software.[108]

Independent demand system an inventory system in which the level of one kind of inventory does not depend on another

Dependent demand system an inventory system in which the level of inventory depends on the number of finished units to be produced

Which inventory management system should you use? Economic order quantity (EOQ) formulas are intended for use with **independent demand systems**, in which the level of one kind of inventory does not depend on another. For example, because inventory levels for automobile tires are unrelated to the inventory levels of women's dresses, Costco could use EOQ formulas to calculate separate optimal order quantities for dresses and tires. By contrast, JIT and MRP are used with **dependent demand systems**, in which the level of inventory depends on the number of finished units to be produced. For example, if Yamaha makes 1,000 motorcycles a day, then it will need 1,000 seats, 1,000 gas tanks, and 2,000 wheels and tires each day. So, when optimal inventory levels depend on the number of products to be produced, use a JIT or MRP management system.

1

1. S. Kapner, "How Sears Lost the American Shopper," *Wall Street Journal*, March 15, 2019, accessed January 16, 2020, https://www.wsj.com/articles/how-sears-lost-the-american-shopper-11552647601.

2. Sears Archives Home Page, accessed January 16, 2020, http://www.searsarchives.com/.

3. Kapner, "How Sears Lost the American Shopper."

4. S. Kapner, "Sears Buys Time With Craftsman Brand Sale, Store Closures," *Wall Street Journal*, January 5, 2017, accessed March 2, 2017, https://www.wsj.com/articles/sears-sells-craftsman-brand-to-stanley-black-decker-1483623215; "Advance Auto Parts Announces Purchase of the DieHard Brand from Transformco," Transformco, December 23, 2019, accessed January 16, 2020, https://transformco.com/press-releases/pr/2144; "Sears Holdings Reports Fourth Quarter and Full Year 2016 Results", Sears Holding, March 9, 2017, https://transformco.com/docs/investor/eap/q4-2016-shc-earnings-release.pdf, accessed January 16, 2020. M. Corkery, "Sears, the Original Everything Store, Files for Bankruptcy," *New York Times*, October 14, 2018, https://www.nytimes.com/2018/10/14/business/sears-bankruptcy; "What Is a Sears Modern Home?" *Sears Archives*, accessed January 15, 2020, http://www.searsarchives.com/homegs/index.htm.

5. S. Kapner, "Sears Owner Says It Will Close an Additional 96 Stores by February," *Wall Street Journal*, November 7, 2019, accessed January 16, 2020, https://www.wsj.com/articles/sears-owner-says-it-will-close-another-96-stores-by-february-11573161195; N. Bomey and K. Tyko, "Struggling Retailers 2020: Forever 21, JCPenney, David's Bridal," *USA Today*, December 27, 2019, accessed January 16, 2020, https://www.usatoday.com/story/money/2019/12/27/struggling-retailers-2020-forever-21-jcpenney-davids-bridal/4386889002/.

6. "Forecast: Industry Revenue of 'Management Consulting Services' in the United States 2011–2023, *Statista*, accessed January 16, 2020, https://www-statista-com.ezproxy.butler.edu/forecasts/409755/management-consulting-services-revenue-in-the-us.

7. "What Do Managers Do?" Adapted from "The Wall Street Journal Guide to Management" by Alan Murray. *Wall Street Journal*, accessed March 2, 2017, http://guides.wsj.com/management/developing-a-leadership-style/what-do-managers-do/.

8. C. Paris and M. Sudal, "With Container Ships Getting Bigger, Maersk Focuses on Getting Faster," *Wall Street Journal*, December 20, 2018, accessed January 17, 2020, https://www.wsj.com/articles/with-container-ships-getting-bigger-maersk-focuses-on-getting-faster-11545301800?mod=hp_minor_pos1.

9. D. Hambling, "Here's How to Unload the World's Biggest Container Ship," *Popular Mechanics*, September 30, 2016, accessed January 17, 2020, https://www.popularmechanics.com/technology/infrastructure/g2787/unloading-the-worlds-biggest-container-ship/.

10. Ibid.

11. S. McCartney, "Finally, Tracking for the Hotel Shuttle Van," *Wall Street Journal*, August 7, 2019, accessed January 17, 2020, https://www.wsj.com/articles/wheres-that-darn-airport-hotel-van-finally-an-answer-11565170200?mod=djemwhatsnew.

12. Ibid.

13. Ibid.

14. D. A. Wren, A. G. Bedeian, and J. D. Breeze, "The Foundations of Henri Fayol's Administrative Theory," *Management Decision* 40 (2002): 906–918.

15. A. Bryant, "Google's Quest to Build a Better Boss," *New York Times*, March 12, 2011, accessed February 23, 2012, http://www.nytimes.com/2011/03/13/business/13hire.html?_r=0; B. Hall, "Google's Project Oxygen Pumps Fresh Air into Management," *The Street*, February 11, 2014, accessed June 11, 2014, http://www.thestreet.com/story/12328981/1/googles-project-oxygen-pumps-fresh-air-into-management.html; J. Bariso, "The Best Bosses Do These Things, According to Google," *Business Insider*, December 18, 2019, accessed January 17, 2020, https://www.businessinsider.com/the-best-bosses-do-these-things-according-to-google-2019.

16. H. Fayol, *General and Industrial Management* (London: Pittman & Sons, 1949).

17. R. Stagner, "Corporate Decision Making," *Journal of Applied Psychology* 53 (1969): 1–13.

18. D. W. Bray, R. J. Campbell, and D. L. Grant, *Formative Years in Business: A Long-Term AT&T Study of Managerial Lives* (New York: Wiley, 1993).

19. K. Naughton, "Tesla Created Demand for Electric Cars, But Only for Teslas," *Bloomberg*, January 21, 2020, accessed January 27, 2020, https://www.bloomberg.com/news/articles/2020-01-21/tesla-created-demand-for-electric-vehicles-but-only-for-tesla?sref=xXo7CWym; S. Nicola, "Tesla Gigafactory 4: Elon Musk's Attack on BMW, VW, Mercedes-Benz," *Bloomberg*, January 18, 2020, accessed January 18, 2020, https://www.bloomberg.com/news/features/2020-01-17/tesla-gigafactory-4-elon-musk-s-attack-on-bmw-vw-mercedes-benz?sref=xXo7CWym; No author., "Our Eye Is on Tesla with a 10-Year Production Forecast - Target Price: $655.72," *Seeking Alpha*, January 17, 2020, accessed January 18, 2020, https://seekingalpha.com/article/4317618-eye-is-on-tesla-10-year-production-forecast-target-price-655_7.

20. A. Roberts, "Driving? The Kids Are So Over It," *Wall Street Journal*, April 20, 2019, accessed January 18, 2020, https://www.wsj.com/articles/driving-the-kids-are-so-over-it-1155573281.

21. I. Khrennikov, "Here Is the Future of Car Sharing, and Carmakers Should Be Terrified," *Bloomberg*, February 8, 2019, accessed January 18, 2020, https://www.bloomberg.com/news/articles/2019-02-08/here-is-the-future-of-car-sharing-and-carmakers-should-be-terrified.

22. J. Cusano and M.Costonis, "Driverless Cars Will Change Auto Insurance. Here's How Insurers Can Adapt," *Harvard Business Review*, December 5, 2017, accessed January 18, 2020, https://hbr.org/2017/12/driverless-cars-will-change-auto-insurance-heres-how-insurers-can-adapt.

23. M. Colias, T. Higgins and W. Boston, " Will Tech Leave Detroit in the Dust?" *Wall Street Journal*, October 20, 2018, accessed January 17, 2020, https://www.wsj.com/articles/can-detroit-become-a-software-business-1540008107?mod=hp_lead_pos.

24. J. Nassauer, "Welcome to Walmart. The Robot Will Grab Your Groceries," *Wall Street Journal*, January 8, 2020, accessed January 18, 2020, https://www.wsj.com/articles/welcome-to-walmart-the-robot-will-grab-your-groceries-11578499200?mod=djemCI.

25. Ibid.

26. Ibid.

27. Ibid.

28. J. Stallbaumer, "How Walmart's Alphabot is Helping to Revolutionize Online Grocery Pickup and Delivery," Walmart, January 8, 2020, accessed January 18, 2020, https://corporate.walmart.com/newsroom/2020/01/08/how-walmarts-alphabot-is-helping-to-revolutionize-online-grocery-pickup-and-delivery.

29. T. Mickle, "Apple Was Headed for a Slump. Then It Had One of the Biggest Rallies Ever," *Wall Street Journal*, January 26, 2020, accessed January 27, 2020, https://www.wsj.com/articles/apple-was-headed-for-a-slump-then-it-had-one-of-the-biggest-rallies-ever-11580034601?mod=djemCF.

30. J. Bezos, "2018 Letter to Shareholders," *The Amazon Blog: Day One*, April 11, 2019, accessed January 19, 2020, https://blog.aboutamazon.com/company-news/2018-letter-to-shareholders?mod=djemCIO.

31. No author, "Fatal Falls From Heights Are at a Five Year Low, but Not for the Nation's Tower Techs," *Wireless Estimator*, December 20, 2019, accessed January 19, 2020, http://wirelessestimator.com/articles/2019/fatal-falls-from-heights-are-at-a-five-year-low-but-not-for-the-nations-tower-techs/; News Release, "National Census of Fatal Occupational Injuries in 2018," Bureau of Labor Statistics, U.S. Department of Labor, December 17, 2019, accessed January 19, 2020, https://www.bls.gov/news.release/pdf/cfoi.pdf.

32. J. Pitcher, "Drones Do Deadly Work So You Don't Have To," *Bloomberg*, July 26, 2019, accessed January 19, 2020, https://www.bloomberg.com/news/articles/2019-07-26/drones-do-deadly-work-so-you-don-t-have-to.

33. Ibid.

34. H. S. Jonas III, R. E. Fry, and S. Srivastva, "The Office of the CEO: Understanding the Executive Experience," *Academy of Management Executive* 4 (1990): 36–47.

35. H. Haddon, "America's Biggest Supermarket Company Struggles with Online Grocery Upheaval," *Wall Street Journal*, April 21, 2019, accessed January 19, 2020, https://www.wsj.com/articles/americas-biggest-supermarket-company-struggles-with-online-grocery-upheaval-1155587712.

36. R. Redman, "Kroger, Microsoft Partner on Retail-As-a-Service Platform," *Supermarket News*, January 7, 2019, accessed January 19, 2020, https://www.supermarketnews.com/retail-financial/kroger-microsoft-partner-retail-service-platform; No author, "EDGE Shelf Technology," EdgeShelf, accessed January 19, 2020, https://www.edgeshelf.com/lang/en/index.html.

37. H. Haddon, "America's Biggest Supermarket Company Struggles with Online Grocery Upheaval."

38. Jonas et al., "The Office of the CEO."

39. A. Carr and D. Bass, "Satya Nadella Remade Microsoft as World's Most Valuable Company," *Bloomberg*, May 2, 2019, accessed January 19, 2020, https://www.bloomberg.com/features /2019-05-02/satya-nadella-remade-microsoft-as -world-s-most-valuable-company?sref=xXo7CWym.

40. Ibid.

41. Ibid.

42. D. Bass, "How Amy Hood Won Back Wall Street and Helped Reboot Microsoft," *Bloomberg*, July 16, 2018, accessed January 20, 2020, https:// www.bloomberg.com/news/articles/2018-07-16 /how-amy-hood-won-back-wall-street-and-helped -reboot-microsoft?sref=xXo7CWym.

43. Ibid.

44. M. Porter, J. Lorsch, and N. Nohria, "Seven Surprises for New CEOs," *Harvard Business Review* (October 2004): 62.

45. Q. Huy, "In Praise of Middle Managers," *Harvard Business Review*. September 2001, 72–79.

46. "Using Their Own Words, Middle Managers Describe the Nature of Their Jobs," *Wall Street Journal*, August 6, 2013, accessed June 12, 2014, www.wsj.com/articles/SB10001424127887323420 60 4578652110485397972.

47. R. Feintzeig, "Radical New Idea: Middle Managers," *Wall Street Journal*, August 19, 2015, B5.

48. "Using Their Own Words, Middle Managers Describe the Nature of Their Jobs."

49. R. Silverman, "Some Tech Firms Ask: Who Needs Managers?" *Wall Street Journal*, August 6, 2013, accessed June 12, 2014, http://www.wsj.com /articles/SB10001424127887323420604578652051 466314748.

50. Feintzeig, "Radical New Idea: Middle Managers."

51. S. Tully, "What Team Leaders Need to Know," *Fortune*, February 20, 1995, 93.

52. B. Francella, "In a Day's Work," *Convenience Store News*, September 25, 2001, 7.

53. L. Liu and A. McMurray, "Frontline Leaders: The Entry Point for Leadership Development in the Manufacturing Industry," *Journal of European Industrial Training* 28, no. 2–4 (2004): 339–352.

54. M. Boyle, "Walmart's New Workplace: Gold Stars, 'Attitude Cards' and Cheers," *Bloomberg*, May 2, 2019, accessed January 20, 2020, https:// www.bloomberg.com/news/articles/2019-05-02 /walmart-s-new-workplace-gold-stars-attitude -cards-and-cheers?sref=xXo7CWym.

55. Ibid.

56. S. Nassauer, "Walmart to Try Thinning Store Manager Ranks," *Wall Street Journal*, May 2, 2019, accessed January 20, 2020, https://www.wsj.com /articles/walmart-to-try-thinning-store-manager -ranks-1155680742.

57. M. Boyle, "Walmart's New Workplace: Gold Stars, 'Attitude Cards' and Cheers."

58. C. Porath, "How Rudeness Stops People from Working Together," *Harvard Business Review*, January 20, 2017, accessed March 8, 2017, https:// hbr.org/2017/01/how-rudeness-stops-people-from -working-together.

59. N. Steckler and N. Fondas, "Building Team Leader Effectiveness: A Diagnostic Tool," *Organizational Dynamics*, Winter 1995, 20–34.

60. H. Mintzberg, *The Nature of Managerial Work* (New York: Harper & Row, 1973).

61. C. P. Hales, "What Do Managers Do? A Critical Review of the Evidence," *Journal of Management Studies* 23, no. 1 (1986): 88–115.

62. M. Porter and N. Nohria, "The Leader's Calendar: How CEOs Manage Time," *Harvard Business Review*, July–August 2018, accessed January 21, 2020, https://hbr.org/2018/07/the -leaders-calendar?

63. M. Dalton, "Why Your Next Louis Vuitton Bag May Hail From Texas," *Wall Street Journal*, October 17, 2019, accessed January 21, 2020, https://www.wsj.com/articles/why-your-next-louis -vuitton-bag-may-hail-from-texas-11571332220.

64. Porter and Nohria, "The Leader's Calendar: How CEOs Manage Time."

65. J. Jargon and E. Morath, "Short of Workers, Fast-Food Restaurants Turn to Robots," *Wall Street Journal*, June 24, 2018, accessed January 21, 2020, https://www.wsj.com/articles/short-of-workers -fast-food-restaurants-turn-to-robots -1529868693?mod=djem10poin.

66. R. Zemmel, M. Cuddihy and D. Carey, "How Successful CEOs Manage the Middle of Their Tenure," *Harvard Business Review*, May–June 2018, accessed January 21, 2020, https://hbr.org/2018/05 how-successful-ceos-manage-their-middle-act.

67. Ibid.

68. "News by Industry," *Business Wire*, accessed January 21, 2020, http://www.businesswire.com /portal/site/home/news/industries/.

69. "Media Monitoring and Analysis Services," Glean.info, accessed January 21, 2020,, https:// glean.info/glean-info-media-monitoring-and -analysis-services/.

70. "Complete Media Monitoring Services," Glean.info, accessed January 21, 2020, https://glean .info/media-monitoring/.

71. "U.S. Congress Bill Tracking | Federal Bill Tracking | FiscalNote," FiscalNote, accessed January 21, 2020, https://fiscalnote.com/products/cq-federal.

72. A. Purbasari Horton, "How 3 Tech CEOs Practice Transparency in the Workplace," *Fast Company*, November 6, 2018, accessed January 22, 2020, https://www.fastcompany.com/90259898 /why-these-ceos-think-transparency-is-crucial-for -workplace-success.

73. Ibid.

74. Ibid.

75. S. McCartney, "At Southwest Airlines, the Minutes After Disaster Struck," *Wall Street Journal*, April 24, 2018, accessed January 22, 2020, https:// www.wsj.com/articles/at-southwest-airlines-the -minutes-after-disaster-struck-1524586032?mod=dj emRiskComplianc.

76. D. Primack and K. Korosec, "GM Buying Self-Driving Tech Startup for More Than $1 Billion," *Fortune*, March 11, 2016, accessed January 23, 2020, https://fortune.com/2016/03/11 /gm-buying-self-driving-tech-startup-for-more -than-1-billion/.

77. T. Higgins and M. Colias, "GM's Cruise Reveals New Robot Taxi: Toaster-Shaped, No Steering Wheel," *Wall Street Journal*, January 22, 2019, accessed January 23, 2020, https://www.wsj.com /articles/gms-cruise-reveals-new-robot-taxi-toaster -shaped-no-steering-wheel-11579670413?mod =djemCF.]

78. Ibid.

79. Ibid.

80. A. Hawkins, "Cruise, GM- Backed Self-Driving Company, Teases Life 'Beyond the Car,'" *The Verge*, December 11, 2019, accessed January 23, 2020, https://www.theverge. com/2019/12/11/21011297/cruise-gm-self-driving -division-tease-beyond-car.

81. T. Higgins and M. Colias, "GM's Cruise Reveals New Robot Taxi: Toaster-Shaped, No Steering Wheel."

82. S. Andrew, "How Waffle House Became the Unofficial Authority for Disaster-Affected Areas," *CNN*, September 4, 2019, accessed January 23, 2020, https://www.cnn.com/2019/09/04/us/waffle -house-hurricane-dorian-trnd/index.html.

83. Fox News, "Waffle House Won't Stop Slinging Waffles During Hurricane Matthew," Fox News, October 5, 2016, accessed March 9, 2017, http:// www.foxnews.com/food-drink/2016/10/05/waffle -house-wont-stop-slinging-waffles-during-hurricane -matthew.html.

84. L. Rao, "The Wall Street Veteran Who's Helping Google Get Disciplined," *Fortune*, September 12, 2016, accessed March 9, 2017, http://fortune .com/google-cfo-ruth-porat-most-powerful-women/.

85. Ibid.

86. "About the HTA," The Health Transformation Alliance, accessed January 24, 2020, http:// www.htahealth.com/about/.

87. Press Release, "Leading US Companies Announce Plan to Transform the Corporate Health Care System," Health Transformation Alliance, February 5, 2016, accessed March 9, 2017, http:// htahealth.com/docs/press/Leading_US_Companies _Announce_Plan_to_Transform_the_Corporate _Health_Care_System.pdf.

88. J. Walker, "Health Costs Get a Rethink," *Wall Street Journal*, March 8, 2017, B8.

89. L. A. Hill, *Becoming a Manager: Mastery of a New Identity* (Boston: Harvard Business School Press, 1992).

90. R. L. Katz, "Skills of an Effective Administrator," *Harvard Business Review*, September–October 1974, 90–102.

91. C. A. Bartlett and S. Ghoshal, "Changing the Role of Top Management: Beyond Systems to People," *Harvard Business Review*, May–June 1995, 132–142.

92. F. L. Schmidt and J. E. Hunter, "Development of a Causal Model of Process Determining Job Performance," *Current Directions in Psychological Science* 1 (1992): 89–92.

93. J. B. Miner, "Sentence Completion Measures in Personnel Research: The Development and Validation of the Miner Sentence Completion Scales," in *Personality Assessment in Organizations*, ed. H. J. Bernardin and D. A. Bownas (New York: Praeger, 1986), 145–176.

94. M. W. McCall, Jr., and M. M. Lombardo, "What Makes a Top Executive?" *Psychology Today*, February 1983, 26–31; E. van Velsor and J. Brittain, "Why Executives Derail: Perspectives Across Time and Cultures," *Academy of Management Executive*, November 1995, 62–72.

95. Ibid.

96. J. Lublin, "How to Delegate the Right Way," *Wall Street Journal*, March 13, 2014, accessed June 3, 2014, http://www.wsj.com/articles/SB10001424052 7023041851045794356408033453898.

97. A. K. Naj, "Corporate Therapy: The Latest Addition to Executive Suite Is Psychologist's Couch," *Wall Street Journal*, August 29, 1994, A1.

98. Ibid.

99. P. Wallington, "Leadership: How to Spot a Toxic Boss," *CIO*, April 26, 2006, accessed June 13, 2014, http://www.cio.com/article/20139 /Leadership_How_to_Spot_a_Toxic_Boss; P. Wallington, "Management2 Toxic!" *Financial Mail*, July 28, 2006, 48.

100. R. Ashkenas, "First-Time Managers, Don't Do Your Team's Work for Them," *Harvard Business Review*, September 21, 2015, accessed April 16, 2016, https://hbr.org/2015/09/first-time-managers -dont-do -your-teams-work-for-them.

101.   J. Sandberg, "Overcontrolling Bosses Aren't Just Annoying; They're Also Inefficient," *Wall Street Journal*, March 30, 2005, B1.

102.   P. Drexler, "Managing Up: When Your Boss Is an Obsessive Micromanager," *Forbes*, June 13, 2013, accessed June 3, 2014, http://www.forbes.com/sites/peggydrexler/2013/06/13/managing-up-when-your-boss-is-an-obsessive-micromanager/.

103.   Hill, *Becoming a Manager*, p. 17.

104.   Ibid., p. 55.

105.   Ibid., p. 57.

106.   Ibid., p. 64.

107.   Ibid., p. 67.

108.   Ibid., p. 161.

109.   J. McGregor, "Tim Cook, the Interview: Running Apple 'Is Sort of a Lonely Job,'" *Washington Post*, August 13, 2016, accessed March 2, 2017, http://www.washingtonpost.com/sf/business/2016/08/13/tim-cook-the-interview-running-apple-is-sort-of-a-lonely-job/?utm_term=.0fe4524234b2.

110.   J. Pfeffer, *The Human Equation: Building Profits by Putting People First* (Boston: Harvard Business School Press, 1996); J. Pfeffer, *Competitive Advantage Through People: Unleashing the Power of the Work Force* (Boston: Harvard Business School Press, 1994).

111.   M. A. Huselid, "The Impact of Human Resource Management Practices on Turnover, Productivity, and Corporate Financial Performance," *Academy of Management Journal* 38 (1995): 635–672.

112.   D. McDonald and A. Smith, "A Proven Connection: Performance Management and Business Results," *Compensation & Benefits Review* 27, no. 6 (January 1, 1995): 59.

113.   J. Combs, Y. Liu, A. Hall, and D. Ketchen, "How Much Do High-Performance Work Practices Matter? A Meta-Analysis of Their Effects on Organizational Performance," *Personnel Psychology* 59 (2006): 501–528.

114.   B. Becker and M. Huselid, "Strategic Human Resources Management: Where Do We Go from Here?" *Journal of Management* 32 (2006): 898–925; M. Huselid and B. Becker, "Comment On "measurement Error in Research on Human Resources and Firm Performance: How Much Error Is There and How Does It Influence Effect Size Estimates?" *Personnel Psychology* 53 (2000): 835–854.

115.   Fulmer, B. Gerhart, and K. Scott, "Are the 100 Best Better? An Empirical Investigation of the Relationship between Being a 'Great Place to Work' and Firm Performance," *Personnel Psychology*, Winter 2003, 965–993.

116.   B. Schneider and D. E. Bowen, "Employee and Customer Perceptions of Service in Banks: Replication and Extension," *Journal of Applied Psychology* 70 (1985): 423–433; B. Schneider, J. J. Parkington, and V. M. Buxton, "Employee and Customer Perceptions of Service in Banks," *Administrative Science Quarterly* 25 (1980): 252–267.

117.   "How Investing in Intangibles – Like Employee Satisfaction – Translates into Financial Returns," *Knowledge@Wharton*, January 9, 2008, accessed January 24, 2010, http://knowledge.wharton.upenn.edu/article.cfm?articleid=1873.

2

1.   C. S. George Jr., *The History of Management Thought* (Englewood Cliffs, NJ: Prentice-Hall, 1972).

2.   C. Ingraham, "Ancient Data, Modern Math and the Hunt for 11 Lost Cities of the Bronze Age," The Washington Post, November 13, 2017, accessed January 30, 2020, https://www.washingtonpost.com/news/wonk/wp/2017/11/13/ancient-data-modern-math-and-the-hunt-for-11-lost-cities-of-the-bronze-age/.

3.   D. Schmandt-Besserat, *How Writing Came About* (Austin: University of Texas Press, 1997).

4.   Ingraham, "Ancient Data, Modern Math and the Hunt for 11 Lost Cities of the Bronze Age."

5.   A. Erman, *Life in Ancient Egypt* (London: Macmillan & Co., 1984).

6.   J. Burke, *The Day the Universe Changed* (Boston: Little, Brown, 1985).

7.   S. A. Epstein, *Wage Labor and Guilds in Medieval Europe* (Chapel Hill: University of North Carolina Press, 1991).

8.   R. Braun, *Industrialization and Everyday Life*, trans. S. Hanbury-Tenison (Cambridge: Cambridge University Press, 1990).

9.   J. B. White, "The Line Starts Here: Mass-Production Techniques Changed the Way People Work and Live Throughout the World," *Wall Street Journal*, January 11, 1999, R25.

10.   R. B. Reich, *The Next American Frontier* (New York: Time Books, 1983).

11.   J. Mickelwait and A. Wooldridge, *The Company: A Short History of a Revolutionary Idea* (New York: Modern Library, 2003).

12.   H. Kendall, "Unsystematized, Systematized, and Scientific Management," in *Scientific Management: A Collection of the More Significant Articles Describing the Taylor System of Management*, ed. C. Thompson (Easton, PA: Hive Publishing, 1972), 103–131.

13.   United States Congress, House, Special Committee, *Hearings to Investigate the Taylor and Other Systems of Shop Management*, vol. 3 (Washington, DC: Government Printing Office, 1912).

14.   Ibid.

15.   Ibid.

16.   A. Derickson, "Physiological Science and Scientific Management in the Progressive Era: Frederic S. Lee and the Committee on Industrial Fatigue," *Business History Review* 68 (1994): 483–514.

17.   US Congress, House, Special Committee, 1912.

18.   F. W. Taylor, *The Principles of Scientific Management* (New York: Harper, 1911).

19.   C. D. Wrege and R. M. Hodgetts, "Frederick W. Taylor's 1899 Pig Iron Observations: Examining Fact, Fiction, and Lessons for the New Millennium," *Academy of Management Journal* 43 (December 2000): 1283; J. R. Hough and M. A. White, "Using Stories to Create Change: The Object Lesson of Frederick Taylor's 'Pig-tale,'" *Journal of Management* 27, no. 5 (October 2001): 585–601; E. A. Locke, "The Ideas of Frederick W. Taylor: An Evaluation," *Academy of Management Review* 7, no. 1 (1982) 14–24.

20.   Locke, "The Ideas of Frederick W. Taylor."

21.   George, *The History of Management Thought*.

22.   F. Gilbreth and L. Gilbreth, "Applied Motion Study," in *The Writings of the Gilbreths*, ed. W. R. Spriegel and C. E. Myers (1917; reprint, Homewood, IL: Irwin, 1953), 207–274.

23.   Ibid.

24.   D. Ferguson, "Don't Call It 'Time and Motion Study,'" *IIE Solutions* 29, no. 5 (1997): 22–23.

25.   H. Gantt, "A Graphical Daily Balance in Manufacture," *Transactions of the American Society of Mechanical Engineers* 24 (1903): 1325.

26.   P. Peterson, "Training and Development: The View of Henry L. Gantt (1861–1919)," *SAM Advanced Management Journal*, Winter 1987, 20–23.

27.   Gantt, H. L. (1910). Work, wages, and profits: Their influence on the cost of living. New York: The Engineering magazine.

28.   Ibid.

29.   M. Weber, *The Theory of Social and Economic Organization*, trans. A. Henderson and T. Parsons (New York: Free Press, 1947).

30.   M. Weber, *The Protestant Ethic and the Spirit of Capitalism* (New York: Scribner's, 1958).

31.   George, *The History of Management Thought*.

32.   D. A. Wren, "Henri Fayol as Strategist: A Nineteenth Century Corporate Turnaround," *Management Decision* 39, no. 6 (2001): 475–487; D. Reid, "Fayol: From Experience to Theory," *Journal of Management History* (Archive) 1, no. 3 (1995): 21–36.

33.   Ibid.

34.   Ibid.

35.   Ibid.

36.   F. Blancpain, "Les cahiers inédits d'Henri Fayol," trans. D. Wren, *Extrait du bulletin de l'institut international d'administration publique* 28–29 (1974): 1–48.

37.   D. A. Wren, A. G. Bedeian, and J. D. Breeze, "The Foundations of Henri Fayol's Administrative Theory," *Management Decision* 40 (2002): 906–918.

38.   H. Fayol, *General and Industrial Management* (London: Pittman & Sons, 1949); Wren, Bedeian, and Breeze, "Foundations."

39.   P. Graham, ed., *Mary Parker Follett—Prophet of Management: A Celebration of Writings from the 1920s* (Boston: Harvard Business School Press, 1995).

40.   D. Linden, "The Mother of Them All," *Forbes*, January 16, 1995, 75.

41.   J. H. Smith, "The Enduring Legacy of Elton Mayo," *Human Relations* 51, no. 3 (1998): 221–249.

42.   E. Mayo, *The Human Problems of an Industrial Civilization* (New York: Macmillan, 1933).

43.   Ibid.

44.   "Hawthorne Revisited: The Legend and the Legacy," *Organizational Dynamics*, Winter 1975, 66–80.

45.   E. Mayo, *The Social Problems of an Industrial Civilization* (Boston: Harvard Graduate School of Business Administration, 1945).

46.   "Hawthorne Revisited: The Legend and the Legacy."

47.   Mayo, *The Social Problems of an Industrial Civilization*, 45.

48.   George, *The History of Management Thought*.

49.   C. I. Barnard, *The Functions of the Executive* (Cambridge, MA: Harvard University Press, 1938), 4.

50.   C. I. Barnard, *The Functions of the Executive: 30th Anniversary Edition* (Cambridge, MA: Harvard University Press, 1968), 5.

51.   J. Fuller and A. Mansour, "Operations Management and Operations Research: A Historical and Relational Perspective," *Management Decision* 41 (2003): 422–426.

52.   D. Wren and R. Greenwood, "Business Leaders: A Historical Sketch of Eli Whitney," *Journal of Leadership & Organizational Studies* 6 (1999): 131.

53.   "Monge, Gaspard, comte de Péluse," *Britannica Online*, accessed January 9, 2005, http://www.britannica.com/biography/Gaspard-Monge-comte-de-Peluse.

54.   M. Schwartz and A. Fish, "Just-in-Time Inventories in Old Detroit," *Business History* 40, no. 3 (July 1998): 48.

55. D. Ashmos and G. Huber, "The Systems Paradigm in Organization Theory: Correcting the Record and Suggesting the Future," *Academy of Management Review* 12 (1987): 607–621; F. Kast and J. Rosenzweig, "General Systems Theory: Applications for Organizations and Management," *Academy of Management Journal* 15 (1972): 447–465; D. Katz and R. Kahn, *The Social Psychology of Organizations* (New York: Wiley, 1966).

56. R. Mockler, "The Systems Approach to Business Organization and Decision Making," *California Management Review* 11, no. 2 (1968): 53–58.

57. F. Luthans and T. Stewart, "A General Contingency Theory of Management," *Academy of Management Review* 2, no. 2 (1977): 181–195.

3

1. No author, "The Numbers - Movie Market Summary 1995 to 2020," *The Numbers*, accessed February 2, 2020, https://www.the-numbers.com/market/.

2. E. Schartzel, "Comfiest Seat in the House: Struggling Movie Theaters Go Upscale to Survive," *Wall Street Journal*, April 9, 2018, https://www.wsj.com/articles/comfiest-seat-in-the-house-struggling-movie-theaters-go-upscale-to-survive-1523285886.

3. Ibid.

4. Ibid.

5. "AMC Stubs A-List," AMC, accessed February 2, 2020, https://www.amctheatres.com/amcstubs/alist; No author, "AMC Stubs A-List Just Passed Another Big Milestone," *Cinema Blend*, March 1, 2019, https://www.cinemablend.com/news/2467721/amc-stubs-a-list-just-passed-another-big-milestone.

6. "AMC Stubs A-List Just Passed Another Big Milestone."

7. "Statistics: General Funeral Service Facts/ Costs/Rates of Cremation and Burial," National Funeral Directors Association (NFDA), accessed February 2, 2020, https://nfda.org/news/statistics#2; D. Herbert "Rest in Peace for Less with Caskets Made in China," *Bloomberg Businessweek*, February 20, 2015, accessed April 24, 2015, http://www.bloomberg.com/news/features/2015-02-20/casket-industry-fends-off-chinese-imports-favored-by-vegas-entrepreneur; P. Cain, "The Living Dead: New Embalming Method Aids Surgical Training," *BBC News*, June 15, 2013, accessed April 24, 2015, http://www.bbc.com/news/health-22908661.

8. R. Dezember, "Behind Lumber's Collapse: A Perfect Storm of Housing and Trade," *Wall Street Journal*, January 2, 2019, accessed February 2, 2020, https://www.wsj.com/articles/behind-lumbers-collapse-a-perfect-storm-of-housing-and-trade-11546437601.

9. E. Romanelli and M. L. Tushman, "Organizational Transformation as Punctuated Equilibrium: An Empirical Test," *Academy of Management Journal* 37 (1994): 1141–1166.

10. H. Banks, "A Sixties Industry in a Nineties Economy," *Forbes*, May 9, 1994, 107–112.

11. L. Cowan, "Cheap Fuel Should Carry Many Airlines to More Record Profits for 1st Quarter," *Wall Street Journal*, April 4, 1998, B17A.

12. "Annual Revenues and Earnings: US Airlines – All Services," *Air Transport Association*, accessed January 15, 2005, http://www.airlines.org; S. Carey, "Carrier Makes Deeper Cuts as It Seeks Federal Backing Needed to Exit Chapter 11," *Wall Street Journal*, November 27, 2002, A3; S. Carey, "UAL Will Lay Off 1,500 Workers as Part of Cost-Cutting Strategy," *Wall Street Journal*, January 6, 2003, A3; D. Carty, "Oral Testimony of Mr. Donald J. Carty, Chairman and CEO, American Airlines: United States Senate, Committee on Commerce, Science, and Transportation," accessed January 9, 2003, http://www.amrcorp.com; S. McCartney, M. Trottman, and S. Carey, "Northwest, Continental, America West Post Losses as Delta Cuts Jobs," *Wall Street Journal*, November 18, 2002, B4.

13. "Airlines Still in Upheaval, 5 Years after 9/11," *CNNMoney.com*, September 8, 2006, accessed July 25, 2008, http://money.cnn.com/2006/09/08/news/companies/airlines_sept11/?postversion=2006090813&eref=yahoo.

14. "Economic Performance of the Airline Industry," International Air Transport Association (IATA), 2019 End-Year Report, December 11, 2019, accessed February 2, 2020, https://www.iata.org/en/iata-repository/publications/economic-reports/airline-industry-economic-performance---december-2019---report/; "Net Income (In Thousands of Dollars $000 All U.S. Carriers - All Regions," Bureau of Transportation Statistics, accessed February 2, 2020,, Data Elements - Financial, https://www.transtats.bts.gov/Data_Elements_Financial.aspx?Data=6.

15. J. Mouawad, "Airlines Reap Record Profits, and Passengers Get Peanuts," *New York Times*, February 6, 2016, accessed August 4, 2016, http://www.nytimes.com/2016/02/07/business/energy-environment/airlines-reap-record-profits-and-passengers-get-peanuts.html.

16. D. Cameron, "Coronavirus Sends Airlines Toward Record Annual Loss," *Wall Street Journal*, June 9, 2020, accessed June 10, 2020, https://www.wsj.com/articles/boeing-adds-cargo-orders-as-max-deals-decline-11591714801?mod=djemHL_t; N. Chokshi, "As Passengers Disappeared, Airlines Filled Planes With Cargo," *New York Times*, May 25, 2020, accessed June 9, 2020, https://www.nytimes.com/2020/05/25/business/coronavirus-airlines-cargo-passengers.html; A. Sider, "Airlines Got $25 Billion in Stimulus; Industry Still Expected to Shrink," *Wall Street Journal*, June 7, 2020, accessed June 9, 2020, https://www.wsj.com/articles/airlines-got-25-billion-in-stimulus-industry-still-expected-to-shrink-11591527600; S. Tully, "Coronavirus Travel: Will the Airlines Survive COVID-19? Yes – and Here's How," *Fortune*, May 24, 2020, accessed June 9, 2020, https://fortune.com/2020/05/24/airlines-coronavirus-travel-flying-after-covid-19/; V. Walt, "Airline Industry Facing Long, Slow Recovery After Coronavirus Pandemic Ends Travel Boom," *Fortune*, April 19, 2020, accessed June 9, 2020, https://fortune.com/2020/04/19/airlines-coronavirus-travel-industry-bailout/.

17. No author. "U.S. Recreational Boating Industry Sees Seventh Consecutive Year of Growth in 2018, Expects Additional Increase in 2019," National Marine Manufacturers Association, January 1, 2019, accessed February 2, 2020, https://www.nmma.org/press/article/22428; No author. "Recreational boating in the U.S.," Statista, 2018, accessed February 2, 2020, https://www-statista-com.ezproxy.butler.edu/study/10744/recreational-boating-in-the-us-statista-dossier/.

18. T. Black, "As Millennials 'Buy Everything Online,' Truckers Reap Riches," *Bloomberg*, January 9, 2019, accessed February 3, 2020, https://www.bloomberg.com/news/articles/2019-01-09/big-and-bulky-e-commerce-opens-new-road-to-riches-for-truckers?sref=xXo7CWym.

19. B. Morris, "E-Commerce Boom Roils Trucking Industry," *Wall Street Journal*, March 31, 2016, accessed March 5, 2017, https://www.wsj.com/articles/e-commerce-boom-roils-trucking-industry-1459442027.

20. Ibid.

21. J. Smith, "Truckers Seek New Routes Into 'Last Mile'," *Wall Street Journal*, April 13, 2018, accessed February 3, 2020, https://www.wsj.com/articles/truckers-seek-new-routes-into-last-mile-1523611801.

22. J. Bunge & H. Haddon, "Fast Food Embraces Meatless Burgers, but There Aren't Enough to Go Around," *Wall Street Journal*, June 4, 2019, accessed February 3, 2020, https://www.wsj.com/articles/fast-food-embraces-meatless-burgers-but-there-arent-enough-to-go-around-11559640601.

23. Ibid.

24. M. Burton, "There's an Impossible Burger 2.0 Shortage and Restaurants Are Losing Out," *Eater*, April 29, 2019, accessed February 3, 2020, https://www.eater.com/2019/4/29/18522717/impossible-burger-impossible-foods-expansion-restaurants-demand.

25. J. Bunge & H. Haddon, "Fast Food Embraces Meatless Burgers, but There Aren't Enough to Go Around."

26. G. Wearden, "Chinese Economic Boom Has Been 30 Years in the Making," *The Guardian*, August 16, 2016, accessed April 17, 2016, http://www.theguardian.com/business/2010/aug/16/chinese-economic-boom; "The Economist Explains: Why China's Economy Is Slowing," *The Economist*, March 11, 2015, accessed April 17, 2016, http://www.economist.com/blogs/economist-explains/2015/03/economist-explains-8.

27. C. Paris, "Dry-Bulk Shipping Firms Face Unprecedented Crisis; Companies Selling Vessels to Survive," *Wall Street Journal*, January 20, 2016, accessed April 17, 2016, http://www.wsj.com/articles/dry-bulk-shipping-firms-face-unprecedented-crisis-1453293892.

28. C. Paris, "Economic Slump Sends Big Ships to Scrap Heap," *Wall Street Journal*, August 14, 2016, accessed March 5, 2017, https://www.wsj.com/articles/economic-slump-sends-big-ships-to-scrap-heap-1471192256.

29. B. Einhorn and C. Matlack, "The Shipping Industry Is Suffering from China's Trade Slowdown," *Bloomberg BusinessWeek*, February 11, 2016, accessed April 17, 2016, http://www.bloomberg.com/news/articles/2016-02-11/shipping-industry-suffering-from-china-s-trade-slowdown; "Baltic Dry Index," accessed April 17, 2016, http://www.bloomberg.com/quote/BDIY:IND.

30. Paris, "Dry-Bulk Shipping Firms Face Unprecedented Crisis; Companies Selling Vessels to Survive."

31. No author, "Demolition Market," *Go Shipping*, accessed February 3, 2020, https://www.go-shipping.net/demolition-market.

32. R. Silverman, J. Lublin & R. Fentzeig, "In Uncertain Times, CEOs Lose Faith in Forecasts," *Wall Street Journal*, July 12, 2016, accessed March 5, 2017, https://www.wsj.com/articles/in-uncertain-times-ceos-lose-faith-in-forecasts-1468315801.

33. Ibid.

34. "CEO Confidence Rebounded in Q4," The Conference Board, January 7, 2020, accessed February 3, 2020, https://www.conference-board.org/data/ceoconfidence.cfm.

35. A. Petrik, "Economic Pessimism Declines, Buoying Small Business Confidence in November 2019 *Wall Street Journal*/Vistage Survey," *Vistage*, November 27, 2019, accessed February 3, 2020, https://www.vistage.com/research-center/business-financials/economic-trends/20191126-economic-pessimism-declines-buoying-small-business-confidence-in-nov-2019-wsj-vistage-survey/.

36. C. Dawson, K. Naughton & G. Coppola, "GM Strike: United Auto Workers Fear Electric Vehicle

Unrest," *Bloomberg*, September 27, 2019, accessed February 3, 2020, https://www.bloomberg.com/news/articles/2019-09-27/-they-don-t-need-us-anymore-auto-workers-fear-electric-unrest?sref=xXo7CWym.

37. Ibid.

38. No author, "Chinese Cruise Tourism Market to Flourish with Massive Growth Potential," *China Daily*, June 17, 2019, accessed February 3, 2020, https://www.chinadaily.com.cn/a/201906/17/WS5d0702f3a3103dbf143289d0_1.html.

39. F. Kuo, "Cruise Industry Looks to Growing Market from China," *CGTN*, August 16, 2019, accessed February 3, 2020, https://america.cgtn.com/2019/08/16/cruise-industry-looks-to-growing-market-from-china.

40. C. Ingraham, "Boomers Have Outgrown Real Christmas Trees," *The Washington Post*, December 5, 2019, accessed February 4, 2020, https://www.washingtonpost.com/business/2019/12/05/boomers-have-outgrown-real-christmas-trees.

41. E. Newburger, "Christmas Tree Prices Rise as Drought and Fire Hit Crops, Farms Close," *CNBC*, November 29, 2019, accessed February 4, 2020, https://www.cnbc.com/2019/11/29/christmas-tree-prices-rise-as-drought-and-fire-hit-crops-farms-close.html.

42. C. Ingraham, "Boomers Have Outgrown Real Christmas Trees."

43. E. Newburger, "Christmas Tree Prices Rise as Drought and Fire Hit Crops, Farms Close"; C. Ingraham, "Boomers Have Outgrown Real Christmas Trees."

44. "The Civil Rights Act of 1991," US Equal Employment Opportunity Commission, accessed April 17, 2016, http://www.eeoc.gov/policy/cra91.html.

45. "Compliance Assistance – Family and Medical Leave Act (FMLA)," U.S. Department of Labor: Employment Standards Administration, Wage and Hour Division, accessed April 17, 2016, http://www.dol.gov/.

46. A Loten, "Small Business Owners Scramble to Prepare for New Tax Form," *Wall Street Journal*, March 4, 2015, B5.

47. R. J. Bies and T. R. Tyler, "The Litigation Mentality in Organizations: A Test of Alternative Psychological Explanations," *Organization Science* 4 (1993): 352–366.

48. M. Orey, "Fear of Firing," *BusinessWeek*, April 23, 2007, 52–62.

49. S. Gardner, G. Gomes, and J. Morgan, "Wrongful Termination and the Expanding Public Policy Exception: Implications and Advice," *SAM Advanced Management Journal* 65 (2000): 38.

50. "Bases by Issue: FY 2010 - FY 2019," U.S. Equal Employment Opportunity Commission, accessed February 4, 2020, https://www.eeoc.gov/eeoc/statistics/enforcement/bases_by_issue.cfm.

51. J. Mundy, "Wrongful Termination Lawsuits on the Rise," *LawyersandSettlements.com*, January 5, 2011, accessed June 4, 2014, http://www.lawyersandsettlements.com/articles/wrongful-termination/wrongful-termination-law-11-15747.html#.U48_GvldWSp.

52. Orey, "Fear of Firing."

53. Ibid.

54. S. Chaudhuri, "Inside IKEA's Strategy to Stay Relevant as Consumers Change," *Wall Street Journal*, February 22, 2019, accessed February 4, 2020, https://www.wsj.com/articles/inside-ikeas-strategy-to-stay-relevant-as-consumers-change-11550852828?mod=hp_jr_pos.

55. S. Chaudhuri & E. Brown, "IKEA Jumps Into 'Gig Economy' With Deal for TaskRabbit," *Wall Street Journal*, September 29, 2017, accessed February 9, 2020, https://www.wsj.com/articles/ikea-to-acquire-online-freelancer-marketplace-taskrabbit-150661842.

56. R. Johnston and S. Mehra, "Best-Practice Complaint Management," *Academy of Management Experience* 16 (November 2002): 145–154.

57. D. Smart and C. Martin, "Manufacturer Responsiveness to Consumer Correspondence: An Empirical Investigation of Consumer Perceptions," *Journal of Consumer Affairs* 26 (1992): 104.

58. S. Warwick, "124 Million of You Now Subscribe to Spotify," *iMore*, February 5, 2020, accessed February 5, 2020, https://www.imore.com/124-million-you-now-subscribe-spotify.

59. No author, "Rounding up 2019's Spotify for Artists Updates," *Spotify for Artists*, December 18, 2019, accessed February 4, 2020, https://artists.spotify.com/blog/rounding-up-2019s-spotify-for-artists-updates.

60. "Spotify Launches Tool to Let Artists Track their Biggest Fans," *Fact*, November 18, 2015, accessed April 17, 2016, http://www.factmag.com/2015/11/18/spotify-fan-insights-tool-artists-track-biggest-fans/.

61. Ibid.

62. S.T. Downing, J-S Kang & G.D. Markman, "What You Don't See Can Hurt You: Awareness Cues to Profile Indirect Competitors," *Academy of Management Journal* 62 (2019): 1872-1900; S. A. Zahra and S. S. Chaples, "Blind Spots in Competitive Analysis," *Academy of Management Executive* 7 (1993): 7–28.

63. S. Blanco, "Honda, Volkswagen Make Wildly Different Bets on the EV Future," *Car & Driver*, December 28, 2019, accessed February 8, 2020, https://www.caranddriver.com/news/a30350065/honda-vw-electric-cars-future/.

64. C. Rauwals & F. Lacqua, "Volkswagen CEO Confident He Can Catch Tesla in E-Car Race," *Bloomberg*, January 24, 2020, accessed February 8, 2020, https://www.bloomberg.com/news/articles/2020-01-24/volkswagen-ceo-confident-he-can-catch-tesla-in-electric-car-race?sref=xXo7CWym.

65. K. G. Provan, "Embeddedness, Interdependence, and Opportunism in Organizational Supplier-Buyer Networks," *Journal of Management* 19 (1993): 841–856.

66. No author, "U.S. Dependence on China's Rare Earth: Trade War Vulnerability," *Reuters*, June 27, 2019, accessed February 4, 2020, https://www.reuters.com/article/us-usa-trade-china-rareearth-explainer/u-s-dependence-on-chinas-rare-earth-trade-war-vulnerability-idUSKCN1TS3AQ; Opinion, "China's Rare-Earths Bust," *Wall Street Journal*, July 18, 2016, accessed March 6, 2017, https://www.wsj.com/articles/chinas-rare-earths-bust-1468860856; Press Release, "Rare Earth Metals Market Forecast By End-use Industry 2016-2026," openPR, February 27, 2017, accessed March 6, 2017, http://www.openpr.com/news/449519/Rare-Earth-Metals-Market-Forecast-By-End-use-Industry-2016-2026.html.

67. K. Young-won, "Samsung increases OLED supply for Apple's latest iPhones," *The Investor*, October 22, 2019, accessed February 4, 2020, http://www.theinvestor.co.kr/view.php?ud=20191022000805.

68. E. Niu, "Apple Is About to Add a Third OLED Supplier," *The Motley Fool*, December 31, 2019, accessed February 4, 2020, https://www.fool.com/investing/2019/12/31/apple-is-about-to-add-a-third-oled-supplier.aspx.

69. K. Wiese, "Prime Power: How Amazon Squeezes the Businesses Behind Its Store," *New York Times*, December 19, 2019, accessed February 5, 2020, https://www.nytimes.com/2019/12/19/technology/amazon-sellers.html.

70. Ibid.

71. Ibid.

72. Ibid.

73. "Viewpoint: Antecedents and Outcomes of Employee Perspective Taking," *Academy of Management Journal* 44 (2001): 1085–1100; B. K. Pilling, L. A. Crosby, and D. W. Jackson, "Relational Bonds in Industrial Exchange: An Experimental Test of the Transaction Cost Economic Framework," *Journal of Business Research* 30 (1994): 237–251.

74. J. Bennett, "GM Loosens Terms for Some Parts Suppliers," June 17, 2016, accessed March 6, 2017, https://www.wsj.com/articles/gm-loosens-terms-for-some-suppliers-1466185855.

75. Ibid.

76. A. Sachs, "In France, Airbnb and Others Move to Enforce Rental Caps," *Washington Post*, February 26, 2019, accessed February 5, 2020, https://www.washingtonpost.com/lifestyle/travel/in-france-airbnb-and-others-move-to-enforce-rental-caps/2019/02/26/656b424e-36f0-11e9-a400-e481bf264fdc_story.html.

77. "Responsible Hosting in France," *Airbnb Help Center*, accessed February 5, 2020, https://www.airbnb.com/help/article/2108/night-limits-in-france-frequently-asked-questions; "Réglementation location saisonnière Airbnb," *LegalPlace*, accessed February 5, 2020, https://www.legalplace.fr/questionnaire/location-tourisme.

78. "Following an Additional Child Fatality, IKEA Recalls 29 Million MALM and Other Models of Chests and Dressers Due to Serious Tip-Over Hazard; Consumers Urged to Anchor Chests and Dressers or Return for Refund," U.S. Consumer Product Safety Commission, June 28, 2016, accessed March 6, 2017, https://www.cpsc.gov/Recalls/2016/following-an-additional-child-fatality-ikea-recalls-29-million-malm-and-other-models-of.

79. J. Bromwich, "Ikea Reaches $50 Million Settlement Over Deadly Furniture Accidents," *New York Times*, December 22, 2016, accessed February 5, 2020, https://www.nytimes.com/2016/12/22/business/ikea-settlement-dresser-tip-over.html.

80. No author, "IKEA Introduces New Safety App," *Ikea*, October 8, 2019, accessed February 5, 2020, https://www.ikea.com/us/en/this-is-ikea/newsroom/ikea-us-introduces-new-child-safety-app-as-part-of-safer-homes-initiative-pub97e7fc90.

81. No author, "The Unkindest Clip of All," *The Sydney Morning Herald*, March 11, 2005, accessed February 5, 2020, https://www.smh.com.au/national/the-unkindest-clip-of-all-20050311-gdkwjf.html.

82. S. Williams & J. Melocco, "Telling the Real Yarn," *The Daily Telegraph* (Australia), June 14, 2008, 115. http://images.wool.com/pub/AWI0595_Flystrike_Road_Map_Leaflet_271109.pdf.

83. No author, "Flystrike R&D Update," Australian Wool Innovation Limited, October 9, 2018, accessed February 5, 2020, https://www.wool.com/globalassets/wool/sheep/research-publications/welfare/flystrike-research-update/btb-june2018-flystrike-rde-update.pdf

84. Ibid.

85. No author, "Nude Alicia Silverstone Anti-Wool Billboard Now Up in Boston," *PETA*, December 13, 2018, accessed February 5, 2020, https://www.peta.org/media/news-releases/nude-alicia-silverstone-anti-wool-billboard-now-up-in-boston/.

86. Q. McEwen, "Dear Lucky Brand, My name is Quintin...," Cedar Grove Farm | Facebook, December 2, 2018, accessed February 5, 2020, https://www.facebook.com/1218667178211762/posts/dear

-lucky-brandmy-name-is-quintin-mcewen
-and-i-am-the-owner-operator-of-a-canad
/1985784191500053/.

87. S. Nassaer, "Fiber Optics: Wool Lovers Battle Animal-Rights Crowd Over Sheep Shearing," *Wall Street Journal*, January 7, 2019, accessed February https://www.wsj.com/articles/fiber-optics-wool -lovers-battle-animal-rights-crowd-over-sheep -shearing-11546884830?mod=djemlogistics_h.

88. M. Evans & L. Stevens, "Amazon's Latest Ambition: To Be a Major Hospital Supplier," *Wall Street Journal*, February 13, 2018, accessed February 6, 2020, https://www.wsj.com/articles /amazons-latest-ambition-to-be-a-major-hospital -supplier-1518517802?mod=djemCIO_.

89. Ibid.

90. Ibid.

91. D. F. Jennings and J. R. Lumpkin, "Insights Between Environmental Scanning Activities and Porter's Generic Strategies: An Empirical Analysis," *Journal of Management* 4 (1992): 791–803.

92. A. DeBarros & J. Adamy, "U.S. Births Fall to Lowest Level Since 1980s," *Wall Street Journal*, May 15, 2019, accessed February 6, 2020, https:// www.wsj.com/articles/u-s-births-fall-to-lowest-rates -since-1980s-1155789286.

93. J. Adamy, "Baby Lull Promises Growing Pains for Economy," *Wall Street Journal*, May 10, 2016, accessed March 7, 2017, https://www.wsj.com /articles/baby-lull-promises-growing-pains-for -economy-1462894211.

94. Ibid.

95. Ibid.

96. E. Jackson and J. E. Dutton, "Discerning Threats and Opportunities," *Administrative Science Quarterly* 33 (1988): 370–387.

97. B. Thomas, S. M. Clark, and D. A. Gioia, "Strategic Sensemaking and Organizational Performance: Linkages Among Scanning, Interpretation, Action, and Outcomes," *Academy of Management Journal* 36 (1993): 239–270.

98. R. Daft, J. Sormunen, and D. Parks, "Chief Executive Scanning, Environmental Characteristics, and Company Performance: An Empirical Study," *Strategic Management Journal* 9 (1988): 123–139; V. Garg, B. Walters, and R. Priem, "Chief Executive Scanning Emphases, Environmental Dynamism, and Manufacturing Firm Performance," *Strategic Management Journal* 24 (2003): 725–744; D. Miller and P. H. Friesen, "Strategy-Making and Environment: The Third Link," *Strategic Management Journal* 4 (1983): 221–235.

99. A. Gasparro and A. Prior, "Kellogg's Profit Falls 16% as Cereal Sales Drop," *Wall Street Journal*, July 31, 2014, accessed April 25, 2015, http:// www.wsj.com/articles/kelloggs-profit-pressured-by -cereal -sales-1406809902.

100. M. Maidenberg & J. Kang, "Cereal Makers Try Again to Jump-Start Stale Sales," *Wall Street Journal*, August 20, 2019, accessed February 7, 2020, https:// www.wsj.com/articles/cereal-makers-try-again-to-jump -start-stale-sales-11566293404?mod=djem10poin.

101. A. Gasparro, "Kellogg Lowers Expectations for 2020," *Wall Street Journal*, February 6, 2020, accessed February 7, 2020, https://www.wsj.com /articles/kelloggs-snacks-help-results-but-cereal -sales-weaken-1158099737.

102. "Happy Inside™," Kellogg's, accessed February 7, 2020, https://www.kelloggs.com/en_US /brands/happy-inside.html#num=12.

103. T. Warekar, "Kellogg's NYC Cafe in Union Square Has Closed," *Eater NY*, December 5, 2019, accessed February 7, 2020, https://ny.eater.com /2019/12/5/20995793/kelloggs-nyc-union-square -store-closure.

104. J. Bunge, "Tastes Like Chicken: The Race Is on to Breed Better Birds as Chicken Emerges as the Protein of the Masses," *Wall Street Journal*, December 4, 2015, 2016, accessed April 17, 2016, http://www.wsj.com/articles/how-to-satisfy-the -worlds-surging-appetite-for-meat-1449238059.

105. K. Paris, "How Cargill Plans to Help Feed the World," *Foodonline.com*, September 25, 2014, accessed April 17, 2016, http://www.foodonline. com/doc/how-cargill-plans-to-help-feed-the -world-0001; S. Lewis, "Cargill's New Poultry Processing Facility Is Up and Running, September 16, 2014, 2016, accessed April 17, 2016, http://www .foodonline.com/doc/cargill-s-new-poultry-processing -facility-is-up-and-running-0001.

106. Bunge, "Tastes Like Chicken: The Race Is On to Breed Better Birds as Chicken Emerges as the Protein of the Masses."

107. A. Dizik, "The Relationship Between Corporate Culture and Performance," *Wall Street Journal*, February 21, 2016, accessed March 7, 2017, WSJ, https://www.wsj.com/articles/the-relationship -between-corporate-culture-and-performance -1456110320.

108. Ibid.

109. A. Boyce, L. Nieminen, M. Gillespie, A. Ryan & D. Denison, "Which Comes First, Organizational Culture or Performance? A Longitudinal Study of Causal Priority with Automobile Dealerships," *Journal of Organizational Behavior* 36 (2015): 339-359.

110. Dizik, "The Relationship Between Corporate Culture and Performance."

111. S. Berfield, "Container Store: Conscious Capitalism and the Perils of Going Public," Bloomberg Business, February 19, 2015, accessed April 25, 2015, http://www.bloomberg.com/news /articles/2015-02-19/container-store-conscious -capitalism-and-the-perils-of-going-public.

112. Ibid.; K. Gustafson, "Retail's Turnover a Plus for Economy but Challenge for Stores," CNBC, September 23, 2014, accessed April 25, 2015, http://www.cnbc.com/id/102021496.

113. D. M. Boje, "The Storytelling Organization: A Study of Story Performance in an Office-Supply Firm," *Administrative Science Quarterly* 36 (1991): 106–126.

114. S. Blank, "Hacking a Corporate Culture: Stories, Heroes and Rituals in Startups and Companies," *Mission*, May 7, 2018, accessed February 8, 2020, https://medium.com/the-mission/hacking -a-corporate-culture-stories-heroes-and-rituals-in -startups-and-companies-a8c3360ef7da.

115. Ibid.

116. Ibid.

117. Ibid.

118. D. R. Denison and A. K. Mishra, "Toward a Theory of Organizational Culture and Effectiveness," *Organization Science* 6 (1995): 204–223.

119. J. Carreyrou, "Blood-Testing Firm Theranos to Dissolve," *Wall Street Journal*, September 5, 2018, accessed February 9, 2020, https://www.wsj .com/articles/blood-testing-firm-theranos-to -dissolve-1536115130?mod=djem10poin.

120. Carreyrou, "Blood-Testing Firm Theranos to Dissolve."; U.S. Attorneys, "U.S. v. Elizabeth Holmes, et al."; The United States Attorney's Office, Northern District of California, November 19, 2019, accessed February 9, 2020, https://www .justice.gov/usao-ndca/us-v-elizabeth-holmes-et -al.; Press Release, "Theranos, CEO Holmes, and Former President Balwani Charged With Massive Fraud," U.S. Securities and Exchange Commission," March 14, 2019, accessed February 9, 2020, https://www.sec.gov/news/press-release/2018-41.

121. Press Release, "Theranos, CEO Holmes, and Former President Balwani Charged with Massive Fraud."

122. J. Carreyrou, "A New Look Inside Theranos' Dysfunctional Corporate Culture," *Wired*, May 21, 2018, accessed February 9, 2020, https://www .wired.com/story/a-new-look-inside-theranos -dysfunctional-corporate-culture/.

123. "Our Philosophy," *BPV Capital Management*, June 18, 2014, accessed June 18, 2014, http://www .backporchvista.com/about-bpv/our-philosophy/.

124. T. Agins, "With a Glance Backward, Brooks Brothers Looks to the Future," *New York Times*, April 21, 2018, accessed February 7, 2020, https:// www.nytimes.com/2018/04/21/business/brooks -brothers-looks-to-the-future.html.

125. A. Zuckerman, "Strong Corporate Cultures and Firm Performance: Are There Tradeoffs?" *Academy of Management Executive*, November 2002, 158–160.

126. E. Schein, *Organizational Culture and Leadership*, 2nd ed. (San Francisco: Jossey-Bass, 1992).

127. S. Albert & D.A. Whetten, "Organizational Identity," *Research in Organizational Behavior* 7 (1985): 263–295. C.M. Fiol, "Managing Culture as a Competitive Resource: An Identity-Based View of Sustainable Competitive Advantage," *Journal of Management* 17 (1991): 191–211.

128. R. Fentzeig, "Companies Rethink Sales Rewards," *Wall Street Journal*, November 8, 2016, accessed March 8, 2017, https://www.wsj.com/articles /companies-rethink-sales-rewards-1478620745.

129. E. Glazer and C. Rexrode, "Wells Fargo CEO Defends Bank Culture, Lays Blame with Bad Employees," *Wall Street Journal*, September 13, 2016, accessed March 8, 2017, https://www.wsj .com/articles/wells-fargo-ceo-defends-bank-culture -lays-blame-with-bad-employees-1473784452.

130. Ibid.

131. E. Flitter & S. Cowley, "Wells Fargo Says Its Culture Has Changed. Some Employees Disagree," *New York Times*, March 9, 2019, accessed February 9, 2020, https://www.nytimes.com/2019/03/09/business /wells-fargo-sales-culture.html?emc=edit_th_19031 0&nl=todaysheadlines&nlid=729027500310.

132. Ibid.

133. Ibid.

134. Ibid.

135. "Michael O'Leary's Most Memorable Quotes," *The Telegraph*, September 5, 2012, accessed April 17, 2016, http://www.telegraph.co.uk /travel/lists/Michael-OLearys-most-memorable- quotes/.

136. Ryanair: How the Airline Is Trying to Change Its Image," *The Telegraph*, February 4, 2016, accessed April 17, 2016, http://www.tele- graph.co.uk/travel/galleries/Ryanair-how-the -airline-is-trying-to-change-its-image/ryanair4/; C. Osborne, "Ryanair CEO Admits His Loudmouth Ways Are Affecting Carrier's Growth," ZDNet, November 22, 2013, accessed April 17, 2016, http:// www.zdnet.com/article/ryanair-ceo-admits-personal -behavior-is-affecting-carriers-growth/#!; A. Tovey, "Being Nice Pays Off for Ryanair as Passenger Numbers Soar," *The Telegraph*, September 2, 2015, accessed April 17, 2016, http://www.telegraph.co .uk/finance/newsbysector/transport/11839609/Being -nice-pays-off-for-Ryanair as-passenger-numbers -soar.html.

137. Tovey, "Being Nice Pays Off for Ryanair as Passenger Numbers Soar."

138. G. Bensinger, "Amazon Recruits Face 'Bar Raisers,'" *Wall Street Journal*, January 8, 2014, B1.

139. Day One Staff, "How Amazon Hires: Learn More about Amazon's Bar Raiser Program," About

Amazon, January 9, 2019, accessed February 9, 2020, https://blog.aboutamazon.com/working-at-amazon/how-amazon-hires.

140. B. Groysberg, J. Lee, J. Price and J. Cheng, "The Leader's Guide to Corporate Culture," *Harvard Business Review*, January–February 2018, accessed February 9, 2020, https://hbr.org/2018/01/the-culture-factor#context-conditions-and-culture.

4

1. T. Zhang, F. Gino and J. Margolis, "Does 'Could' Lead to Good? On the Road to Moral Insight," *Academy of Management Journal* 61 (2018): 857–895.

2. "2019 Edelman Trust Barometer: Expectations for CEOs," Edelman, accessed February 17, 2020, https://www.edelman.com/sites/g/files/aatuss191/files/2019-04/2019_Edelman_Trust_Barometer_CEO_Trust_Report.pdf.

3. D. Meinhert, "Creating an Ethical Workplace," *HR Magazine* 59 (April 2014): 4, accessed June 4, 2014, https://www.shrm.org/Publications/hrmagazine/EditorialContent/2014/0414/Pages/0414-ethical-workplace-culture.aspx.

4. "Global Business Ethics Survey: 2018 Global Benchmark on Workplace Ethics," Ethics Research Center of the Ethics & Compliance Initiative, accessed February 17, 2020, https://www.ethics.org/knowledge-center/interactive-maps/.

5. "2013 National Business Ethics Survey of the US Workforce," Ethics Research Center of the Ethics & Compliance Initiative, accessed March 18, 2017, http://www.ethics.org/research/nbes/nbes-reports/nbes-2013.

6. C. Smith, "The Ethical Workplace," *Association Management* 52 (2000): 70–73.

7. "Trust in the Workplace: 2010 Ethics & Workplace Survey," *Deloitte LLP*, 2010, accessed June 4, 2014, http://www.deloitte.com/assets/Dcom-United-States/Local%20Assets/Documents/us_2010_Ethics_and_Workplace_Survey_report_071910.pdf.

8. "Communication, Honesty Among Traits Most Desired and Lacking in Corporate Leaders, ASQ Survey Says," *Reuters.com*, February 11, 2014, accessed April 11, 2015, http://www.reuters.com/article/2014/02/11/idUSnGNX91ymYv+1c2+GNW20140211.

9. A. Bryant, "Michael Gould of Bloomingdale's, on Passion and Compassion," *New York Times*, October 5, 2013, accessed March 18, 2017, http://www.nytimes.com/2013/10/06/business/michael-gould-of-bloomingdales-on-passion-and-compassion.html?smid=tw-share&_r=0.

10. Association of Certified Fraud Examiners, "Report to the Nations: 2018 Global Study on Occupational Fraud and Abuse," Association of Certified Fraud Examiners, accessed February 17, 2020, https://s3-us-west-2.amazonaws.com/acfepublic/2018-report-to-the-nations.pdf; K. Gibson, "Excuses, Excuses: Moral Slippage in the Workplace," *Business Horizons* 43, no. 6 (2000): 65; S. L. Robinson and R. J. Bennett, "A Typology of Deviant Workplace Behaviors: A Multidimensional Scaling Study," *Academy of Management Journal* 38 (1995): 555–572.

11. Harvard Management Update, "Learn by 'Failing Forward,'" *Globe & Mail*, October 31, 2000, B17.

12. A. Gouveia, "2014 Wasting Time at Work Survey," Salary.com, accessed March 18, 2017, http://www.salary.com/2014-wasting-time-at-work/slide/2/.

13. C. Conner, "Wasting Time at Work: The Epidemic Continues," *Forbes*, July 31, 2015, accessed March 18, 2017, https://www.forbes.com/sites/cherylsnappconner/2015/07/31/wasting-time-at-work-the-epidemic-continues/#13c222031d94.

14. C. Zakrzewski, "Workplace Technology (A Special Report) – The Key to Getting Workers to Stop Wasting Time Online," *Wall Street Journal*, March 14, 2016, R4.

15. C. Mele, "Self-Service Checkouts Can Turn Customers into Shoplifters, Study Says," *New York Times*, August 10, 2016, accessed March 18, 2017, https://www.nytimes.com/2016/08/11/business/self-service-checkouts-can-turn-customers-into-shoplifters-study-says.html.

16. "The Sensormatic Global Shrink Index: Results & Executive Summary," Tyco Retail Solutions, February 2018, accessed February 17, 2020, https://shrinkindex.sensormatic.com/wp-content/uploads/2018/05/Sensormatic-Global-Shrink-Index.pdf.

17. M. Gold, "Worker Stole $90,000 in 'Lady M' Cakes and Resold Them, Lawsuit Says," *New York Times*, September 9, 2019, accessed February 17, 2020, https://www.nytimes.com/2019/09/09/nyregion/lady-m-cake-thief.html; L. Jany, "Police: Andover man stole $240k worth of printer ink, tried to sell it on eBay," *StarTribune*, February 11, 2019, accessed February 17, 2020, http://www.startribune.com/police-plymouth-man-stole-240-000-worth-of-printer-ink-tried-to-sell-it-on-ebay/505668952/.

18. "The Sensormatic Global Shrink Index: Results & Executive Summary."; R. Hollinger, "2019 National Retail Security Survey," National Retail Federation, accessed February 17, 2020, https://cdn.nrf.com/sites/default/files/2019-06/NRSS%202019.pdf; A. Fisher, "US Retail Workers are No. 1 … In Employee Theft," *Fortune*, January 26, 2015, accessed March 18, 2017, http://fortune.com/2015/01/26/us-retail-worker-theft.

19. J. L. Hayes, "31st Annual Retail Theft Survey," *Hayes International* press release, February 17, 2020, accessed February 17, 2020, http://hayesinternational.com/news/annual-retail-theft-survey/.

20. G. Bangs, "Nothing Sweet About It," *Risk & Insurance*, September 12, 2017, accessed February 17, 2020, https://riskandinsurance.com/nothing-sweet-about-it/.

21. A. Wren, "Sweethearting: A Bottom Line Drain for Retailers," *Chain Store Age*, June 21, 2012, accessed April 11, 2015, http://www.chainstoreage.com/article/sweethearting-bottom-line-drain-retailers; M. K. Brady, C. M. Voorhees, and M. J. Brusco, "Service Sweethearting: Its Antecedents and Customer Consequences," *Journal of Marketing* 76 (2012): 81–98.

22. J. Norman, "Cultivating a Culture of Honesty," *The Orange County [California] Register*, October 23, 2006.

23. News Release, "Employer-Reported Workplace Injuries and Illnesses – 2018," Bureau of Labor Statistics, US Department of Labor, November 7, 2019, accessed February 17, 2020, https://www.bls.gov/news.release/pdf/osh.pdf.

24. News Release, "National Census of Fatal Occupational Injuries in 2018," Bureau of Labor Statistics, US Department of Labor, December 17, 2019, accessed February 17, 2020, https://www.bls.gov/news.release/pdf/cfoi.pdf; US Economic News Release, "Fatal Occupational Injuries by Major Event, 2015, in Census of Fatal Occupations Injuries Charts, 1992–2015 (final data)," US Bureau of Labor Statistics, accessed March 18, 2017, https://www.bls.gov/iif/oshwc/cfoi/cfch0014.pdf.

25. D. Palmer and A. Zakhem, "Bridging the Gap Between Theory and Practice: Using the 1991 Federal Sentencing Guidelines as a Paradigm for Ethics Training," *Journal of Business Ethics* 29, no. 1/2 (2001): 77–84.

26. K. Tyler, "Do the Right Thing: Ethics Training Programs Help Employees Deal with Ethical Dilemmas," *HR Magazine*, February 2005, accessed March 13, 2009, http://www.shrm.org/publications/hrmagazine/editorialcontent/pages/0205tyler.aspx.

27. D. R. Dalton, M. B. Metzger, and J. W. Hill, "The 'New' US Sentencing Commission Guidelines: A Wake-up Call for Corporate America," *Academy of Management Executive* 8 (1994): 7–16.

28. G. Marcias, "Q&A: Gayle Macias, World Vision," interview by B. DiPietro, *Wall Street Journal*, June 12, 2013, accessed June 4, 2014, http://blogs.wsj.com/riskandcompliance/2013/06/12/qa-gayle-macias-world-vision/.

29. B. Ettore, "Crime and Punishment: A Hard Look at White-Collar Crime," *Management Review* 83 (1994): 10–16.

30. F. Robinson and C. C. Pauze, "What Is a Board's Liability for Not Adopting a Compliance Program?" *Healthcare Financial Management* 51, no. 9 (1997): 64.

31. United States Sentencing Commission, *Guidelines Manual*, §3E1.1 (November 2015), accessed February 18, 2020, http://www.ussc.gov/sites/default/files/pdf/guidelines-manual/2015/GLMFull.pdf.

32. Ibid.

33. "Quick Facts: Organizational Offenders," United States Sentencing Commission, accessed February 18, 2020, https://www.ussc.gov/sites/default/files/pdf/research-and-publications/quick-facts/Organizational-Offenders_FY18.pdf.

34. Robinson and Pauze, "What Is a Board's Liability?"

35. B. Schwartz, "The Nuts and Bolts of an Effective Compliance Program," *HR Focus* 74, no. 8 (1997): 13–15.

36. C. Chen, "The CEO Who Saved a Life and Lost His Job," *Bloomberg Businessweek*, January 22, 2015, accessed April 18, 2016, http://www.bloomberg.com/news/articles/2015-01-22/biotech-drug-approvals-social-media-storm-hits-chimerix.

37. S. Morris and R. McDonald, "The Role of Moral Intensity in Moral Judgments: An Empirical Investigation," *Journal of Business Ethics* 14 (1995): 715–726; B. Flannery and D. May, "Environmental Ethical Decision Making in the US Metal-Finishing Industry," *Academy of Management Journal* 43 (2000): 642–662.

38. K. Bode, "The Rise of Netflix Competitors Has Pushed Consumers Back Toward Piracy," *VICE*, October 2, 2018, accessed February 18, 2020, https://www.vice.com/en_us/article/d3q45v/bittorrent-usage-increases-netflix-streaming-sites.

39. E. Gardner, "Piracy Crackdown May Be Next Front in Streaming Wars," *Hollywood Reporter*, November 5, 2019, accessed February 18, 2020, https://www.hollywoodreporter.com/thr-esq/piracy-crackdown-may-be-next-front-streaming-wars-1252309; A. Weprin, "Streaming Services Prepare for Password-Sharing 'Havoc,'" *Hollywood Reporter*, January 8, 2020, accessed February 18, 2020, https://www.hollywoodreporter.com/news/streaming-services-prepare-password-sharing-havoc-1267728.

40. L. Kohlberg, "Stage and Sequence: The Cognitive-Developmental Approach to Socialization," in *Handbook of Socialization Theory and Research*, ed. D. A. Goslin (Chicago: Rand McNally, 1969); L. Trevino, "Moral Reasoning and Business

Ethics: Implications for Research, Education, and Management," *Journal of Business Ethics* 11 (1992): 445–459.

41. E. Gruenwedel, "Report: Global Online Video Piracy Costs U.S. Economy $29.2B Annually," *Media Play News*, June 25, 2019, https://www.mediaplaynews.com/report-global-online-video-piracy-costs-u-s-economy-29-2b-annually/.

42. L. Trevino and M. Brown, "Managing to Be Ethical: Debunking Five Business Ethics Myths," *Academy of Management Executive* 18 (May 2004): 69–81.

43. L. T. Hosmer, "Trust: The Connecting Link Between Organizational Theory and Philosophical Ethics," *Academy of Management Review* 20 (1995): 379–403.

44. J. DiMasi, H. Grabowski, and R. Hansen, "Innovation in the Pharmaceutical Industry: New Estimates of R&D Costs," *Journal of Health Economics* 47 (2016): 20–33.

45. C. Chen, "The CEO Who Saved a Life and Lost His Job," *Bloomberg BusinessWeek*, January 22, 2015, accessed April 18, 2016, http://www.bloomberg.com/news/articles/2015-01-22/biotech-drug-approvals-social-media-storm-hits-chimerix.

46. Ibid; "Chimerix Announces Final Data from AdVise Trial of Brincidofovir at BMT Tandem Meetings," Chimeriz, February 22, 2017, accessed March 19, 2017, http://ir.chimerix.com/releasedetail.cfm?ReleaseID=1013907.

47. C. Chen, "The CEO Who Saved a Life and Lost His Job."

48. Ibid.

49. "Josh Hardy, Va. Boy Who Inspired Social Media Campaign, Dies," NBC4 Washington, October 22, 2016, accessed March 19, 2017, http://www.nbcwashington.com/news/local/Josh-Hardy-Va-Boy-Who-Inspired-Social-Media-Campaign-Dies-394586831.html.

50. "Global Business Ethics Survey: Measuring the Impact of Ethics & Compliance Programs," *Ethics & Compliance Initiative*, June 2018, accessed February 19, 2020, https://www.ethics.org/knowledge-center/2018-gbes-2/; "2013 National Business Ethics Survey of the US Workforce."

51. H. J. Bernardin, "Validity of an Honesty Test in Predicting Theft Among Convenience Store Employees," *Academy of Management Journal* 36 (1993): 1097–1108.

52. J. M. Collins and F. L. Schmidt, "Personality, Integrity, and White Collar Crime: A Construct Validity Study," *Personnel Psychology* (1993): 295–311.

53. W. C. Borman, M. A. Hanson, and J. W. Hedge, "Personnel Selection," *Annual Review of Psychology* 48 (1997): 299–337.

54. "303A.10 Code of Business Conduct and Ethics," *NYSE Listed Company Manual*, November 25, 2009, accessed February 19, 2020, http://nysemanual.nyse.com/lcm/Help/mapContent.asp?sec=lcm-sections&title=sx-ruling-nyse-policymanual_303A.09&id=chp_1_4_3_11.

55. P. E. Murphy, "Corporate Ethics Statements: Current Status and Future Prospects," *Journal of Business Ethics* 14 (1995): 727–740.

56. "ADP's Commitment to Ethics and Compliance," ADP, April 3, 2019, accessed February 19, 2020, https://www.adp.com/about-adp/corporate-social-responsibility/ethics.aspx#D.

57. "ADP Anti-Bribery Policy," ADP, April 3, 2019, accessed February 19, 2020, https://www.adp.com/about-adp/corporate-social-responsibility/ethics/anti-bribery-policy.aspx.

58. "Global Business Ethics Survey: Measuring the Impact of Ethics & Compliance Programs."

59. "More Corporate Boards Involved in Ethics Programs; Ethics Training Becoming Standard Practice," *PR Newswire*, October 16, 2006.

60. S. J. Harrington, "What Corporate America Is Teaching About Ethics," *Academy of Management Executive* 5 (1991): 21–30.

61. Y. Feldman, "Companies Need to Pay More Attention to Everyday Unethical Behavior," *Harvard Business Review*, March 1, 2019, accessed February 19, 2020, https://hbr.org/2019/03/companies-need-to-pay-more-attention-to-everyday-unethical-behavior.

62. L. A. Berger, "Train All Employees to Solve Ethical Dilemmas," *Best's Review–Life-Health Insurance Edition* 95 (1995): 70–80.

63. Meinhert, "Creating an Ethical Workplace."

64. L. Trevino, G. Weaver, D. Gibson, and B. Toffler, "Managing Ethics and Legal Compliance: What Works and What Hurts," *California Management Review* 41, no. 2 (1999): 131–151.

65. J. Katz, "Making Compliance Training Stick," *Compliance Week*, November 5, 2013, accessed March 19, 2017, https://www.complianceweek.com/news/news-article/making-compliance-training-stick#.WM73NBiZNhE.

66. "Leader's Guide: A Culture of Trust 2008," *Lockheed Martin*, accessed July 17, 2008, http://www.lockheedmartin.com/data/assets/corporate/documents/ethics/2008_EAT_Leaders_Guide.pdf.

67. Meinhert, "Creating an Ethical Workplace."

68. E. White, "Theory & Practice: What Would You Do? Ethics Courses Get Context; Beyond Checking Boxes, Some Firms Start Talking About Handling Gray Areas," *Wall Street Journal*, June 12, 2006, B3.

69. "Global Business Ethics Survey: Interpersonal Misconduct in the Workplace – What It Is, How It Occurs and What You Should Do About It," *Ethics & Compliance Initiative*, December 2018, accessed February 19, 2020, https://www.ethics.org/knowledge-center/2018-gbes-2/; "2019 Global Business Ethics Survey: The Impact of Organizational Values and Ethical Leadership on Misconduct - A Global Look," *Ethics & Compliance Initiative*, 2019, accessed February 19, 2020, https://www.ethics.org/knowledge-center/2018-gbes-2/.

70. "The State of Ethics in Large Companies: A Research Report from the National Business Ethics Survey (NBES)," Ethic Research Center of the Ethics & Compliance Initiative, 2015, accessed April 11, 2015, http://www.ethics.org/nbes/wp-content/uploads/2015/03/LargeCompanies ExecSummary.pdf;

71. G. Weaver and L. Trevino, "Integrated and Decoupled Corporate Social Performance: Management Commitments, External Pressures, and Corporate Ethics Practices," *Academy of Management Journal* 42 (1999): 539–552; Trevino, et al., "Managing Ethics and Legal Compliance."

72. "2013 National Business Ethics Survey of the US Workforce."

73. J. Salopek, "Do the Right Thing," *Training & Development* 55 (July 2001): 38–44.

74. J. Sahadi, "When Your Job Is to Teach Corporations to Do the Right Thing," *CNN* , June 26, 2019, accessed February 19, 2020, https://www.cnn.com/2019/06/26/success/business-chief-ethics-officer/index.html/

75. M. Gundlach, S. Douglas, and M. Martinko, "The Decision to Blow the Whistle: A Social Information Processing Framework," *Academy of Management Executive* 17 (2003): 107–123.

76. R. Carucci, "Why Ethical People Make Unethical Choices," *Harvard Business Review*, December 16, 2016, accessed March 19, 2017, https://hbr.org/2016/12/why-ethical-people-make-unethical-choices.

77. "2013 National Business Ethics Survey of the US Workforce"; "The State of Ethics in Large Companies: A Research Report from the National Business Ethics Survey (NBES)."

78. M. Colias & A. Roberts, "Head of Fiat Chrysler's US Sales Sues, Claiming He Was Punished for Cooperating With SEC," *MarketWatch*, June 5, 2019, accessed February 19, 2020, https://www.marketwatch.com/story/head-of-fiat-chryslers-us-sales-sues-claiming-he-was-punished-for-cooperating-with-sec-2019-06-05?ref=streamer.ai.

79. Press Release, "Automaker to Pay $40 Million for Misleading Investors," US Securities and Exchange Commission, September 27, 2019, accessed February 19, 2020, https://www.sec.gov/news/press-release/2019-196.

80. N. Bunkley & V. Bond Jr., "Bigland plans to refile lawsuit against FCA in December," *Automotive News Europe*, November 5, 2019, accessed February 19, 2020, https://europe.autonews.com/retail/bigland-plans-refile-lawsuit-against-fca-december; E. Lawrence, "The Head of Ram Who Filed Whistleblower Suit Against FCA Is Quitting," *Detroit Free Press*, March 4, 2020, accessed March 23, 2020, https://www.freep.com/story/money/cars/chrysler/2020/03/04/reid-bigland-leaving-fca-whistleblower-lawsuit/4951238002/; D. Szatkowski, "FCA Says Sales Chief Bigland Doesn't Merit Whistleblower Status," *Automotive News*, July 12, 2019, accessed February 19, 2020, https://www.autonews.com/executives/fca-says-sales-chief-bigland-doesnt-merit-whistleblower-status.

81. J. Deschenaux, "High Court Extends Employee Whistle-blower Protections," *Society for Human Resource Management*, March 5, 2014, accessed June 4, 2014, http://www.shrm.org/LegalIssues/FederalResources/Pages/High-Court-Extends-Employee-Whistle-blower-Protections.aspx.

82. A. Ackerman, "Supreme Court Curbs Protections for Whistleblowers," *Wall Street Journal*, February 21, 2019, accessed February 20, 2020, https://www.wsj.com/articles/supreme-court-curbs-protections-for-whistleblowers-1519235827?mod=djemRiskCompliance; H. Cutter, "Whistleblower Ruling Adds a Risk for Companies," *Wall Street Journal*, February 23, 2019, accessed February 20, 2020, https://blogs.wsj.com/riskandcompliance/2018/02/23/whistleblower-ruling-adds-a-risk-for-companies/.

83. "Reporting Ethical Violations Globally (except Europe), ADP, accessed February 20, 2020, https://www.adp.com/about-adp/corporate-social-responsibility/ethics/reporting-ethical-violations.aspx; "EthicsPoint - ADP," EthicsPoint, accessed March 20, 2017, https://secure.ethicspoint.com/domain/media/en/gui/48099/index.html.

84. "2016 Global Business Ethics Survey: Measuring Risk and Promoting Workplace Integrity," Ethics Research Center of the Ethics & Compliance Initiative, accessed March 18, 2017, http://www.ethics.org/research/ethics.org/gbes/gbes-form.

85. M. P. Miceli and J. P. Near, "Whistleblowing: Reaping the Benefits," *Academy of Management Executive* 8 (1994): 65–72.

86. G. Millman, "Compliance Without Compliance Officer: Q&A with Martin Mucci of Paychex," *Wall Street Journal*, February 6, 2014, accessed February 20, 2020, https://blogs.wsj.com/riskandcompliance/2014/02/06/compliance

-without-a-chief-compliance-officer-qa-with-martin-mucci-of-paychex/.

87.   Ibid.

88.   "Global Business Ethics Survey: Measuring the Impact of Ethics & Compliance Programs."

89.   M. Master and E. Heresniak, "The Disconnect in Ethics Training," *Across the Board* 39 (September 2002): 51–52.

90.   H. R. Bower, *Social Responsibilities of the Businessman* (New York: Harper & Row, 1953).

91.   J. Nicas, "Does the F.B.I. Need Apple to Hack Into iPhones?" *New York Times*, January 17, 2020, accessed February 20, 2020, https://www.nytimes.com/2020/01/17/technology/fbi-iphones.html.

92.   M. Apuzzo, J. Goldstein, and E. Lichtblau, "Apple's Line in the Sand Was Over a Year in the Making," *New York Times*, February 18, 2016, accessed March 20, 2017, https://www.nytimes.com/2016/02/19/technology/a-yearlong-road-to-a-standoff-with-the-fbi.html.

93.   S. L. Wartick and P. L. Cochran, "The Evolution of the Corporate Social Performance Model," *Academy of Management Review* 10 (1985): 758–769.

94.   J. Nocera, "The Paradox of Businesses as Do-Gooders," *New York Times*, November 11, 2006, C1.

95.   S. Waddock, C. Bodwell, and S. Graves, "Responsibility: The New Business Imperative," *Academy of Management Executive* 16 (2002): 132–148.

96.   T. Donaldson and L. E. Preston, "The Stakeholder Theory of the Corporation: Concepts, Evidence, and Implications," *Academy of Management Review* 20 (1995): 65–91.

97.   R. King, "The Week Ahead: At Tech Confab, a Social Component," *Wall Street Journal*, October 3, 2016, B2.

98.   M. Langley, "The Many Stakeholders of Salesforce.Com: They Go Well Beyond Shareholders, Says the Company's CEO, Marc Benioff," *Wall Street Journal*, October 27, 2015, R2.

99.   Press Release, "Adoption of Salesforce.com's 1/1/1 Model Accelerates Around the World, February 23, 2010, accessed March 20, 2017, http://www.prnewswire.com/news-releases/adoption-of-salesforcecoms-111-model-accelerates-around-the-world-85034902.html.

100.   M. Benioff, "Pledge 1% - Salesforce.org," Salesforce, accessed February 22, 2020, https://www.salesforce.org/pledge-1/. Q. Hardy, "Marc Benioff, SalesForce Chief, on the Strategic Benefits of Corporate Giving," *New York Times*, November 2, 2015, accessed March 20, 2017, https://www.nytimes.com/2015/11/08/giving/marc-benioff-salesforce-chief-on-the-strategic-benefits-of-corporate-giving.html.

101.   Ibid.

102.   M. B. E. Clarkson, "A Stakeholder Framework for Analyzing and Evaluating Corporate Social Performance," *Academy of Management Review* 20 (1995): 92–117.

103.   B. Agle, R. Mitchell, and J. Sonnenfeld, "Who Matters to CEOs? An Investigation of Stakeholder Attributes and Salience, Corporate Performance, and CEO Values," *Academy of Management Journal* 42 (1999): 507–525.

104.   No author, "Council of Institutional Investors Responds to Business Roundtable Statement on Corporate Purpose," Council of Institutional Investors, August 19, 2019, accessed February 20, 2020, https://www.cii.org/content.asp?contentid=277.

105.   M. Mauboussin and A. Rappaport, "Reclaiming the Idea of Shareholder Value," *Harvard Business Review*, July 1, 2016, accessed February 20, 2020, https://hbr.org/2016/07/reclaiming-the-idea-of-shareholder-value.

106.   R. Wartzman, "The Tricky Role of the CEO in a New Era of Social Responsibility," *Wall Street Journal*, December 12, 2019, accessed February 20, 2020, https://www.wsj.com/articles/the-tricky-role-of-the-ceo-in-a-new-era-of-social-responsibility-11576170755.

107.   No author, "Statement on the Purpose of a Corporation," *Business Roundtable*, August 19, 2019, accessed February 20, 2020, https://opportunity.businessroundtable.org/wp-content/uploads/2020/02/BRT-Statement-on-the-Purpose-of-a-Corporation-with-Signatures-Feb2020.pdf.

108.   Ibid.

109.   Wartzman, "The Tricky Role of the CEO in a New Era of Social Responsibility."

110.   E. W. Orts, "Beyond Shareholders: Interpreting Corporate Constituency Statutes," *George Washington Law Review* 61 (1992): 14–135; K. Wu & J. Hua Ye, "Do Constituency Statutes Deter Tax Avoidance?" University of Waterloo, July 2019, accessed February 20, 2020, https://scholarspace.manoa.hawaii.edu/bitstream/10125/64926/1/HARC_2020_paper_270.pdf.

111.   A. B. Carroll, "A Three-Dimensional Conceptual Model of Corporate Performance," *Academy of Management Review* 4 (1979): 497–505.

112.   J. Lublin and M. Murray, "CEOs Leave Faster Than Ever Before as Boards, Investors Lose Patience," *Wall Street Journal Interactive*, October 27, 2000.

113.   "CEO Dismissals in the US at the Lowest Level in a Decade, The Conference Board Finds," The Conference Board, April 14, 2015, accessed April 18, 2016, http://www.prnewswire.com/news-releases/ceo-dismissals-in-the-us-at-the-lowest-level-in-a-decade-the-conference-board-finds-300065351.html.

114.   Press Release, "Report: Number of Women CEOs Declines, and Personal Misconduct Leads to Record CEO Firings," *The Conference Board*, November 20, 2019, accessed February 20, 2020, https://www.conference-board.org/press/women-ceos-declines.

115.   J. Ewing and N. Boudette, "As VW Pleads Guilty in US Over Diesel Scandal, Trouble Looms in Europe," *New York Times*, March 10, 2017, accessed March 20, 2017, https://www.nytimes.com/2017/03/10/business/volkswagen-europe-diesel-car-owners.html.

116.   G. Kable, "Volkswagen's Dieselgate Costs Top $33.6 Billion," *Wards Auto*, May 2, 2019, accessed February 20, 2020, https://www.wardsauto.com/industry/volkswagen-s-dieselgate-costs-top-336-billion; K. Matussek & E. Behrmann, "VW Can't Escape the Diesel Scandal Fallout," *Bloomberg Businessweek*, September 12, 2018, accessed February 20, 2020, https://www.bloomberg.com/news/articles/2018-09-12/vw-can-t-escape-the-diesel-scandal-fallout?sref=xXo7CWym.

117.   M. Simon, "Why the $29 iPhone Battery Replacement Is Apple's Best Move of the Year," *Macworld*, December 29, 2017, accessed February 21, 2020, https://www.macworld.com/article/3245067/apple-iphone-battery-replacement-program.html.

118.   S. Ovide, "Apple iPhone Battery Fix Is Gonna Hurt," *Bloomberg*, January 4, 2018, accessed February 21, 2020, https://www.bloomberg.com/opinion/articles/2018-01-04/apple-iphone-battery-fix-is-gonna-hurt?sref=xXo7CWym.

119.   Ibid.

120.   Ibid.

121.   B. Weber, "Costs of Alberta Wildfire Reach $9.5 Billion: Study," BNN, January 17, 2017, accessed March 20, 2017, http://www.bnn.ca/costs-of-alberta-wildfire-reach-9-5-billion-study-1.652292.

122.   S. Horwitz, "In Natural Disasters, Companies Operate Like Neighbors," *Wall Street Journal*, June 7, 2016, accessed March 20, 2017, https://www.wsj.com/articles/in-natural-disasters-companies-operate-like-neighbors-1465338881.

123.   Ibid.

124.   D. MacMillan & R. McMillan, "Google Exposed User Data, Feared Repercussions of Disclosing to Public," *Wall Street Journal*, October 8, 2018, accessed February 21, 2020, https://www.wsj.com/articles/google-exposed-user-data-feared-repercussions-of-disclosing-to-public-1539017194?mod=djemCIO_h.

125.   Ibid.

126.   Amazon, "Product Safety and Compliance in Our Store," *The Amazon Blog*, August 23, 2019, accessed February 21, 2020, https://blog.aboutamazon.com/company-news/product-safety-and-compliance-in-our-store.

127.   "Amazon Services LLC FIFRA Settlement," Enforcement – United States Environmental Protection Agency, February 25, 2018, accessed February 21, 2020, https://www.epa.gov/enforcement/amazon-services-llc-fifra-settlement.

128.   A. Berzon, S. Shifflett & J. Scheck, "Amazon Has Ceded Control of Its Site. The Result: Thousands of Banned, Unsafe or Mislabeled Products," *Wall Street Journal*, August 23, 2019, accessed February 21, 2020, https://www.wsj.com/articles/amazon-has-ceded-control-of-its-site-the-result-thousands-of-banned-unsafe-or-mislabeled-products-11566564990.

129.   Ibid.

130.   Ibid.

131.   J. Dastin, "Amazon to Ramp Up Counterfeit Reporting to Law Enforcement," *Reuters*, January 13, 2020, accessed February 21, 2020, https://www.reuters.com/article/us-amazon-com-counterfeit/amazon-to-ramp-up-counterfeit-reporting-to-law-enforcement-idUSKBN1ZC25U.

132.   G. Suthivarakom, "Welcome to the Era of Fake Products," *Wirecutter*, February 11, 2020, accessed February 21, 2020, https://thewirecutter.com/blog/amazon-counterfeit-fake-products/#amazon-fights-back.

133.   A. McCall, "Navigating Amazon's Neutral Patent Evaluation in Real Life: Part I," IP Watchdog, "February 11, 2020, accessed February 21, 2020, https://www.ipwatchdog.com/2020/02/11/navigating-amazons-neutral-patent-evaluation-real-life-part/id=118736/.

134.   D. Kesmodel, J. Bunge, and A. Gasparro, "McDonald's to Curb Antibiotics Use," *Wall Street Journal*, March 5, 2015, B1, B2.

135.   J. Jargon, "McDonald's to Trim Antibiotics from Its Beef," *Wall Street Journal*, December 11, 2018, accessed February 22, 2020, https://www.wsj.com/articles/mcdonalds-to-trim-antibiotics-from-its-beef-11544550260?mod=searchresults&page=1&pos=1&mod=djemCFO_h.

136.   "Knowledgebase: Age of animals slaughtered," Aussie Farms, October 12, 2017, accessed February 22, 2020, https://www.aussiefarms.org.au/kb/48-age-animals-slaughtered.

137.   McDonald's to Trim Antibiotics from Its Beef."

138.   A. McWilliams and D. Siegel, "Corporate Social Responsibility: A Theory of the Firm Perspective," *Academy of Management Review* 26, no.1 (2001): 117–127; H. Haines, "Noah Joins Ranks of Socially Responsible Funds," *Dow Jones News Service*, October 13, 1995. A meta-analysis of 41 different studies also found no relationship between corporate social responsibility and profitability. Though not reported in the meta-analysis, when

confidence intervals are placed around its average sample-weighted correlation of .06, the lower confidence interval includes zero, leading to the conclusion that there is no relationship between corporate social responsibility and profitability. See M. Orlitzky, "Does Firm Size Confound the Relationship Between Corporate Social Responsibility and Firm Performance?" *Journal of Business Ethics* 33 (2001): 167–180; S. Ambec and P. Lanoie, "Does It Pay to Be Green? A Systematic Overview," *Academy of Management Perspectives*, 22 (2008): 45–62.

139.   M. Orlitzky, "Payoffs to Social and Environmental Performance," *Journal of Investing* 14 (2005): 48–51.

140.   M. Orlitzky, F. Schmidt, and S. Rynes, "Corporate Social and Financial Performance: A Meta-analysis," *Organization Studies* 24 (2003): 403–441.

141.   Orlitzky, "Payoffs to Social and Environmental Performance."

142.   D. Kesmodel, "Beef's Meaty Profits Slow Effort to Boost Antibiotic-Free Production," *Wall Street Journal*, September 15, 2015, accessed March 20, 2017, https://www.wsj.com/articles/beefs -meaty-profits-slow-effort-to-boost-antibiotic-free -production-1442309400.

143.   Orlitzky, et al., "Corporate Social and Financial Performance."

144.   M. Reyes, "Why Didn't the Panera Cares Social Experiment Pay Off?" *The Boston Globe*, February 7, 2019, accessed February 22, 2020, https://www.bostonglobe.com/business/2019/02/07 /why-didn-panera-social-experiment-pay-off /xLBOWbLo5VyndijDGQ1CyN/story.html.

145.   D. Neman, "Panera's Pay-What-You-Can-Afford Community café in Clayton Closes," *St. Louis Post-Dispatch*, January 4, 2018, accessed February 22, 2020, https://www.stltoday.com/entertainment/dining /restaurants/off-the-m%e2%80%a6-community-caf-in /article_e997deef-8892-5789-92f2-e63c14a23b70.html.

146.   Ibid.

5

1.   L. A. Hill, *Becoming a Manager: Master a New Identity* (Boston: Harvard Business School Press, 1992).

2.   J. Carpenter, "The World's Top 10 Retailers," Investopedia, May 16, 2019, accessed February 26, 2020, https://www.investopedia.com/articles/markets /122415/worlds-top-10-retailers-wmt-cost.asp; "Corporate Profile: Costco Wholesale Corporation," Costco Wholesale, November 15, 2019, accessed February 26, 2020, https://investor.costco.com /corporate-profile-2.

3.   N. Gabler, "Inside Costco: The Magic in the Warehouse," *Fortune*, December 2, 2016, accessed February 26, 2020, https://fortune.com/longform /costco-wholesale-shopping/.

4.   B. Lehrer, "Costco Capitalism," BryanLehrer. com, December 16, 2019, accessed February 26, 2020, https://www.bryanlehrer.com/entries/costco/.

5.   "Corporate Profile: Costco Wholesale Corporation."

6.   E. A. Locke and G. P. Latham, *A Theory of Goal Setting & Task Performance* (Englewood Cliffs, NJ: Prentice Hall, 1990).

7.   M. E. Tubbs, "Goal-Setting: A Meta-Analytic Examination of the Empirical Evidence," *Journal of Applied Psychology* 71 (1986): 474–483.

8.   J. Bavelas and E. S. Lee, "Effect of Goal Level on Performance: A Trade-Off of Quantity and Quality," *Canadian Journal of Psychology* 32 (1978): 219–240.

9.   D. Turner, "Ability, Aspirations Fine, But Persistence Is What Gets Results," *Seattle Times*, February 13, 2005, http://community.seattletimes.nwsource .com/archive/?date=20030215&slug=dale15m.

10.   K. Allen, "The Former CEO of DHL Express on Leading the Company Through an Existential Crisis," *Harvard Business Review*, March 28, 2019, accessed February 26, 2020, https://hbr .org/2019/03/the-former-ceo-of-dhl-express-on -leading-the-company-through-an-existential-crisis.

11.   Ibid.

12.   C. C. Miller, "Strategic Planning and Firm Performance: A Synthesis of More Than Two Decades of Research," *Academy of Management Performance* 37 (1994): 1649–1665.

13.   H. Mintzberg, "Rethinking Strategic Planning: Part I: Pitfalls and Fallacies," *Long Range Planning* 27 (1994): 12–21, and "Part II: New Roles for Planners," 22–30; H. Mintzberg, "The Pitfalls of Strategic Planning," *California Management Review* 36 (1993): 32–47.

14.   W. Duggan, "Swiss Watch Makers Aren't Worried About the Apple Watch," *Benzinga*, May 18, 2015, accessed March 23, 2017, https://www.benzinga .com/analyst-ratings/analyst-color/15/05/5520111/swiss -watch-makers-arent-worried-about-the-apple-watch.

15.   "The Swiss and World Watchmaking Industries in 2016," Federation of the Swiss Watch Industry FH, accessed March 23, 2017, http://www .fhs.swiss/file/59/Watchmaking_2016.pdf.

16.   S. Wilmot, "No Time for Joy in Swiss Watches," *Wall Street Journal*, December 21, 2016.

17.   D. Reisinger, "Here's How Popular Apple Watch Was Last Quarter," *Fortune*, February 8, 2017, accessed March 23, 2017, http://fortune .com/2017/02/08/apple-watch-2016-sales/.

18.   "Exports of Swiss Watches Electronic and Mechanical," Federation of the Swiss Watch Industry FH, accessed February 26, 2020, https://www .fhs.swiss/scripts/getstat.php?file=histo_elec_mec _200101_a.pdf.

19.   O. Haslam, "Apple Watch Reportedly Sold More Units Than Every Swiss Watchmaker Combined," *iMore*, February 6, 2020, accessed February 26, 2020, https://www.imore.com/apple -watch-reportedly-sold-more-units-every-swiss -watchmaker-combined.

20.   M. Cogley, "Apple Watch Outsells Entire Swiss Watch Industry," *The Telegraph*, February 6, 2020, accessed February 26, 2020, https://www. telegraph.co.uk/technology/2020/02/06/apple -watch-o…utm_medium=Edi_Tec_New _TechIntel20200207&utm_campaign=DM1193213.

21.   G. Ip, "China, Oil Show Peril of Faulty Assumptions," *Wall Street Journal*, January 13, 2016, accessed May 7, 2016, http://www.wsj.com /articles/china-oil-show-peril-of-faulty-assumptions -1452705708.

22.   G. Ip, "Economists Got the Decade All Wrong. They're Trying to Figure Out Why," *Wall Street Journal*, December 14, 2019, accessed February 26, 2020, https://www.wsj.com/articles /economists-got-the-decade-all-wrong-theyre -trying-to-figure-out-why-11576346400.

23.   Mintzberg, "The Pitfalls of Strategic Planning."

24.   S. Musaji, W. Schulze & J. De Castro, "How Long Does It Take to Get to the Learning Curve?" *Academy of Management Journal* 63 No. 1 (2020): 205-223.

25.   Locke and Latham, *A Theory of Goal Setting & Task Performance.*

26.   King, B. Oliver, B. Sloop, and K. Vaverek, *Planning & Goal Setting for Improved Performance: Participant's Guide* (Cincinnati, OH: Thomson Executive Press, 1995).

27.   M. Prior, "Lafly: P&G Getting into Shape," *WWD*, February 20, 2015, 9, *P&G 2014 Annual Report*, accessed April 26, 2015, http://www.pginvestor .com/interactive/lookandfeel/4004124/PG_Annual_ Report_2014.pdf; J. Hawkins, "Procter & Gamble Looking to Trim Its Brand Portfolio by Exiting Over 100 Brands," *Mainenewsonline*, February 23, 2015, accessed April 26, 2015, http://mainenewsonline .com/content/15022993-procter-gamble-looking -trim-its-brand-portfolio-exiting-over.

28.   Ibid.

29.   Ibid; A. Steele, "Coty Profits Hit by Costs of Merger with PG Brands," *Market Watch*, February 4, 2016, accessed May 7, 2016, http://www.marketwatch .com/story/coty-profit-hit-by-costs-of-merger -with-pg-brands-2016-02-04; "P&G Accepts Coty's Offer of $12.5 Billion to Merge 43 P&G Beauty Brands with Coty," *Business Wire*, July 9, 2015, accessed May 7, 2016, http://www.businesswire .com/news/home/20150709005357/en/PG-Accepts -Coty%e2%80%99s-Offer-12.5-Billion-Merge.

30.   Procter & Gamble, "Our Brands," accessed July 8, 2020, http://us.pg.com/our-brands.

31.   "P&G is Executing a Strategy that is Working," P&G, September 2017, accessed February 26, 2020, https://www.pginvestor.com/interactive /newlookandfeel/4004124/Strategy_Slides.pdf,

32.   C. Loomis, J. Schlosser, J. Sung, M. Boyle, and P. Neering, "The 15% Delusion: Brash Predictions about Earnings Growth Often Lead to Missed Targets, Battered Stock, and Creative Accounting – and That's When Times Are Good," *Fortune*, February 5, 2001, 102; H. Paster, "Manager's Journal: Be Prepared," *Wall Street Journal*, September 24, 2001, A24; P. Sellers, "The New Breed: The Latest Crop of CEOs Is Disciplined, Deferential, Even a Bit Dull," *Fortune*, November 18, 2002, 66; H. Klein and M. Wesson, "Goal and Commitment and the Goal-Setting Process: Conceptual Clarification and Empirical Synthesis," *Journal of Applied Psychology* 84 (1999): 885–896.

33.   Locke and Latham, *A Theory of Goal Setting & Task Performance.*

34.   S. Kapner, "Bed Bath & Beyond Boss Tries to Declutter Stores," *Wall Street Journal*, February 18, 2020, accessed February 26, 2020, https://www .wsj.com/articles/bed-bath-beyond-boss-tries-to -declutter-its-stores-11582059600?mod =djemwhatsnews.

35.   Bandura and D. H. Schunk, "Cultivating Competence, Self-Efficacy, and Intrinsic Interest Through Proximal Self-Motivation," *Journal of Personality & Social Psychology* 41 (1981): 586–598.

36.   W. Boston & T. Higgins, "Tesla's Post-China Challenge: Bats and Bombs in Germany," *Wall Street Journal*, January 21, 2020, accessed February 27, 2020, https://www.wsj.com/articles/tesla-aims -to-replicate-china-success-with-german-factory -11579602602?mod=djemCFO; K. Naughton, "Tesla Created Demand for Electric Cars, But Only for Teslas," *Bloomberg*, January 21, 2020, accessed January 27, 2020, https://www.bloomberg.com/news /articles/2020-01-21/tesla-created-demand-for -electric-vehicles-but-only-for-tesla?sref =xXo7CWym; S. Nicola, "Tesla Gigafactory 4: Elon Musk's Attack on BMW, VW, Mercedes-Benz," *Bloomberg*, January 18, 2020, accessed January 18, 2020, https://www.bloomberg.com/news /features/2020-01-17/tesla-gigafactory-4-elon-musk -s-attack-on-bmw-vw-mercedes-benz?sref =xXo7CWym; No author., "Our Eye Is on Tesla With A 10-Year Production Forecast - Target Price: $655.72," *Seeking Alpha*, January 17, 2020, accessed January 18, 2020, https://seekingalpha.com /article/4317618-eye-is-on-tesla-10-year-production -forecast-target-price-655_7.

37. Locke and Latham, *A Theory of Goal Setting & Task Performance.*

38. M. J. Neubert, "The Value of Feedback and Goal Setting over Goal Setting Alone and Potential Moderators of This Effect: A Meta-Analysis," *Human Performance* 11 (1998): 321–335.

39. E. H. Bowman and D. Hurry, "Strategy Through the Option Lens: An Integrated View of Resource Investments and the Incremental-Choice Process," *Academy of Management Review* 18 (1993): 760–782; F. Mallette & J. Goddard, "Why Companies Are Using M&A to Transform Themselves, Not Just to Grow," *Harvard Business Review*, May 16, 2018, accessed February 27, 2020, https://hbr.org/2018/05/why-companies-are-using-ma-to-transform-themselves-not-just-to-grow.

40. L. Feiner, "Apple Buys a Company Every Few Weeks, Says CEO Tim Cook," CNBC, May 6, 2019, accessed February 27, 2020, https://www.cnbc.com/2019/05/06/apple-buys-a-company-ever-few-weeks-says-ceo-tim-cook.html.

41. G. Burnett, "ANALYSIS: Google, Apple Focus M&A Activity on Tech Startup Takeovers," *Bloomberg Law*, September 16, 2019, accessed February 27, 2020, https://news.bloomberglaw.com/bloomberg-law-analysis/analysis-google-apple-focus-m-a-activity-on-tech-startup-takeovers.

42. J. Horwitz, "Apple reportedly acquires Stamplay, Visa API development contest winner," Transform 2020, March 21, 2019, accessed February 27, 2020, https://venturebeat.com/2019/03/21/apple-reportedly-acquires-stamplay-visa-api-development-contest-winner/; A. Tilley, "Apple Acquires AI Device Startup Silk Labs," *The Information*, November 20, 2019, accessed February 27, 2020, https://www.theinformation.com/articles/apple-acquires-ai-device-startup-silk-labs.

43. J. Porter, "Apple Buys Intel's Smartphone Modem Business," *The Verge*, July 25, 2019, accessed February 27, 2020, https://www.theverge.com/2019/7/25/8909671/apple-intel-5g-smartphone-modems-acquisition.

44. F. S. Bentley & R. Kehoe, "Give Them Some Slack – They're Trying to Change! The Bene-Fits of Excess Cash, Excess Employees, and Increased Hu-Man Capital in the Strategic Change Context," Academy of Management Journal 63 (2020): 181-204; M. Lawson, "In Praise of Slack: Time Is of the Essence," *Academy of Management Executive* 15 (2000): 125–135.

45. R. Smith, "Utilities Seek to Stockpile Essential Parts for Disasters," *Wall Street Journal*, April 7, 2016, accessed May 7, 2016, http://www.wsj.com/articles/utilities-seek-to-stockpile-essential-parts-for-disasters-1460076194.

46. C. Galford, "Grid Assurance Enhances Catastrophe Response as Critical Electric Equipment Readied for Service, October 30, 2019, accessed February 27, 2020, https://www.gridassurance.com/os/resources/media/Grid_Assurance_enhances_catastrophe_response_as_critical_electric_equipment_readied_for_service_-_Da.pdf.

47. No author, "The Vision Council: Organizational Overview," The Vision Council, 2018, accessed February 27, 2020, https://www.thevisioncouncil.org/sites/default/files/TVC_OrgOverview_sheet_0419.pdf.

48. N. Redd, "The Best Places to Buy Glasses Online for 2020," *Wirecutter*, December 5, 2019, accessed February 27, 2020, https://thewirecutter.com/reviews/best-places-to-buy-glasses-online/.

49. Ibid.

50. Ibid.

51. J. C. Collins and J. I. Porras, "Organizational Vision and Visionary Organizations," *California Management Review*, Fall 1991: 30–52.

52. "Avon Mission, Vision & Values," *Comparably*, accessed February 27, 2020, https://www.comparably.com/companies/avon/mission.

53. Collins and Porras, "Organizational Vision and Visionary Organization"; "About Us," *Highlights for Children*, accessed March 24, 2017, https://www.highlights.com/about-us.

54. Collins and Porras, "Organizational Vision and Visionary Organizations"; J. A. Pearce II, "The Company Mission as a Strategic Goal," *Sloan Management Review*, Spring 1982: 15–24.

55. "About us," *Edwards Lifesciences*, accessed February 27, 2020, https://www.edwards.com/aboutus/home.

56. "What We Do," *Edwards Lifesciences*, accessed February 28, 2020, https://www.edwards.com/aboutus/what-we-do.

57. T. Malnight, I. Buche & C. Dhanaraj, "Put Purpose at the Core of Your Strategy," *Harvard Business Review*, September-October 2019, accessed February 28, 2020, https://hbr.org/2019/09/put-purpose-at-the-core-of-your-strategy?autocomplete=true.

58. "Our History," Edwards Lifesciences, accessed February 28, 2020, https://www.edwards.com/aboutus/OurHistory.

59. "Arby's | About," Arby's, accessed February 28, 2020, https://arbys.com/about.

60. Dan, "How Arby's Carved A Successful Brand Message by Staying True to Itself," *Forbes*, April 29, 2019, accessed February 28, 2020, https://www.forbes.com/sites/avidan/2019/04/29/how-arbys-carved-a-successful-brand-message-by-staying-true-to-itself/#714108a82e4d.

61. Bruell, "Arby's Pivots to Sandwiches, Looks to Shed Roast Beef Image," *Wall Street Journal*, September 6, 2018, accessed February 28, 2020, https://www.wsj.com/articles/arbys-pivots-to-sandwiches-looks-to-shed-roast-beef-image-1536231600?mod=hp_minor_pos1.

62. Ibid.

63. J. Jargon, "New Plan at Hostess: Cupcakes Everywhere," *Wall Street Journal*, September 18, 2015, B1.

64. "Products | Hostess Ice Cream," Hostess, accessed February 28, 2020, http://www.hostesscakes.com/icecream.

65. M. Maidenberg, "Food Makers Crowd Snack Aisle Despite Uneven Growth," *Wall Street Journal*, July 1, 2019, accessed February 28, 2020, https://www.wsj.com/articles/food-makers-crowd-snack-aisle-despite-uneven-growth-11561973400.

66. L. Weber, "At Kimberly-Clark, 'Dead Wood' Workers Have Nowhere to Hide," *Wall Street Journal*, August 21, 2016, accessed March 24, 2017, https://www.wsj.com/articles/focus-on-performance-shakes-up-stolid-kimberly-clark-1471798944.

67. Ibid.

68. S. Oda, "End of an Era for Tokyo's Iconic Tsukiji Fish Market," *Bloomberg*, October 5, 2018, accessed February 28, 2020, https://www.bloomberg.com/news/features/2018-10-05/end-of-an-era-for-tokyo-s-iconic-tsukiji-fish-market?sref=xXo7CWym.

69. Katayama, "The World Biggest Fish Market Tsukiji Moved to Toyosu. How Is the New Market Doing?" *Forbes*, February 25, 2019, accessed February 28, 2020, https://www.forbes.com/sites/akikokatayama/2019/02/25/the-world-biggest-fish-market-tsukiji-moved-to-toyosu-how-is-the-new-market-doing/#74c75e9226c8.

70. Ibid.

71. S. McCartney, "Inside an Airline's Winter War Room," *Wall Street Journal*, February 5, 2015, D1.

72. J. Paterson, "Presenteeism on the Rise Among UK Workforce," *Employee Benefits*, May 2013, 3.

73. J. Weed, "Airlines, Now More Proactive on Weather, Allow Fliers to Shift Own Travel Plans," *New York Times*, January 2, 2017, accessed March 23, 2017, https://www.nytimes.com/2017/01/02/business/flight-weather-delay-change-itinerary.html.

74. S. McCartney, "The Trouble With Keeping Commercial Flights Clean," *Wall Street Journal*, September 18, 2014, D1.

75. "Volume VII, Book A Medical Staff, Chapter 1: Medical Staff Approved Policies," The University of Texas MD Anderson Cancer Center, accessed March 24, 2017, www.palliativedrugs.com/download/med%20brought%20into%20hospital3.pdf.

76. K. R. MacCrimmon, R. N. Taylor, and E. A. Locke, "Decision Making and Problem Solving," in *Handbook of Industrial & Organizational Psychology*, ed. M. D. Dunnette (Chicago: Rand McNally, 1976), 1397–1453.

77. M. Evans, "Hospitals Alter Routines to Control Drug Spending," *Wall Street Journal*, December 18, 2016, accessed March 24, 2017, https://www.wsj.com/articles/hospitals-alter-routines-to-control-drug-spending-1482062403.

78. MacCrimmon, et al., "Decision Making and Problem Solving."

79. G. Kress, "The Role of Interpretation in the Decision Process," *Industrial Management* 37 (1995): 10–14.

80. K. Inoue, "The "Quiet Life" Hypothesis Is Real: Managers Will Put Off Hard Decisions If They Can," *Harvard Business Review*, January 9, 2018, accessed February 28, 2020, https://hbr.org/2018/01/the-quiet-life-hypothesis-is-real-managers-will-put-off-hard-decisions-if-they-can.

81. V. Lipman, "Under-Management Is the Flip Side of Micromanagement – and It's a Problem Too," *Harvard Business Review*, November 8, 2019, accessed February 28, 2020, https://hbr.org/2018/11/under-management-is-the-flip-side-of-micromanagement-and-its-a-problem-too.

82. R. Carucci, "Leaders, Stop Avoiding Hard Decisions," *Harvard Business Review*, April 13, 2018, accessed February 28, 2020, https://hbr.org/2018/04/leaders-stop-avoiding-hard-decisions.

83. M. Evans, "Hospitals Alter Routines to Control Drug Spending," *Wall Street Journal*, December 18, 2016, accessed March 24, 2017, https://www.wsj.com/articles/hospitals-alter-routines-to-control-drug-spending-1482062403.

84. J. Bartlett & G. Shenhar, "How Consumer Reports Tests Cars," *Consumer Reports*, February 14, 2017, accessed March 24, 2017, http://www.consumerreports.org/cars-how-consumer-reports-tests-cars/; M. Rechtin, "A Better Way to Find Your Next Car," *Consumer Reports*, February 23, 2016, accessed March 24, 2017, http://www.consumerreports.org/new-car-buying/a-better-way-to-find-your-next-car/.

85. P. Djang, "Selecting Personal Computers," *Journal of Research on Computing in Education* 25 (1993): 327.

86. J. Ellenberg, "How Not to Be Misled by Data," *Wall Street Journal*, June 26, 2015, accessed March 25, 2017, https://www.wsj.com/articles/how-not-to-be-misled-by-data-1435258933.

87. "European Cities Monitor," Cushman & Wakefield, 2010, http://www.europeancitiesmonitor.eu/wp-content/uploads/2010/10/ECM-2010-Full-Version.pdf.

88. J. Clement, "Global Instagram User Age & Gender Distribution 2020," *Statista*, February 14, 2020, accessed February 29, 2020, https://www.statista.com/statistics/248769/age-distribution-of

-worldwide-instagram-users/; J. Clement, "Favorite Social Networks of U.S. Teens 2012-2019," Statista, October 15, 2019, accessed February 29, 2020, https://www.statista.com/statistics/250172/social-network-usage-of-us-teens-and-young-adults/; J. Clement, "U.S. Social Media Activities by Platform 2019," Statista, August 21, 2019, accessed February 29, 2020, https://www-statista-com.ezproxy.butler.edu/statistics/200843/social-media-activities-by-platform-usa/; J. Stiff, "6 Tips to Build Your Social Media Strategy," CIO, May 8, 2013, accessed May 26, 2013, http://www.cio.com/article/732975/6_Tips_to_Build_Your_Social_Media_Strategy; D. Steiner, "How to Choose the Right Social Media for your ecommerce Business," CIO, October 19, 2016, accessed March 25, 2017, http://www.cio.com/article/3132468/social-networking/how-to-choose-the-right-social-media-for-your-ecommerce-business.html.

89.   "The Critical Role of Teams," The Ken Blanchard Companies, March 23, 2006, accessed June 5, 2014, http://www.kenblanchard.com/img/pub/pdf_critical_role_teams.pdf.

90.   L. Janis, *Groupthink* (Boston: Houghton Mifflin, 1983).

91.   P. Neck and C. C. Manz, "From Groupthink to Teamthink: Toward the Creation of Constructive Thought Patterns in Self-Managing Work Teams," *Human Relations* 47 (1994): 929–952; J. Schwartz and M. L. Wald, "'Groupthink' Is 30 Years Old, and Still Going Strong," *New York Times*, March 9, 2003, 5.

92.   Almandoz & A. Tilcsik, "When Experts Become Liabilities: Domain Experts on Boards and Organizational Failure," *Academy of Management Journal* 59 no. 4 (2016): 1124-1149.

93.   McIntosh, "Assumptions of Quality Could Hinder Group Decision-Making Ability," Medical News Today, March 10, 2015, accessed April 27, 2015, http://www.medicalnewstoday.com/articles/290618.php.

94.   E. Livni, "Troublemakers Are Underrated and Highly Necessary, Says a Berkeley Professor," *Quartz*, May 6, 2018, accessed March 1, 2020, https://qz.com/1269977/a-berkeley-professor-explains-why-society-needs-more-troublemakers/; C. Nemeth, *In Defense of Troublemakers: The Power of Dissent in Life and Business* (New York: Basic Books, 2018)

95.   Mason, W.A. Hochwarter, and K.R. Thompson, "Conflict: An Important Dimension in Successful Management Teams," *Organizational Dynamics* 24 (1995): 20.

96.   Taylor, "True Leaders Believe Dissent Is an Obligation," *Harvard Business Review*, January 12, 2017, accessed March 25, 2017, https://hbr.org/2017/01/true-leaders-believe-dissent-is-an-obligation.

97.   Fernandez, "TED 2018: Netflix Sees Itself as the Anti-Apple," *Wired*, April 15, 2018, accessed March 1, 2020, https://www.wired.com/story/reed-hastings-at-ted/?CNDID=49330717&mbid=nl_041618_daily_list1_p2.

98.   Mason, et al., "Conflict: An Important Dimension in Successful Management Teams."

99.   R. Cosier and C. R. Schwenk, "Agreement and Thinking Alike: Ingredients for Poor Decisions," *Academy of Management Executive* 4 (1990): 69–74.

100.   K. Jenn and E. Mannix, "The Dynamic Nature of Conflict: A Longitudinal Study of Intragroup Conflict and Group Performance," *Academy of Management Journal* 44, no. 2 (2001): 238–251; R. L. Priem, D. A. Harrison, and N. K. Muir, "Structured Conflict and Consensus Outcomes in Group Decision Making," *Journal of Management* 21 (1995): 691–710.

101.   J. Fairley, "How A No. 1 Fund Survived, Learned from Great Recession," *Financial Advisor*, March 6, 2019, accessed March 1, 2020, https://www.fa-mag.com/news/how-a-no--1-fund-survived--learned-from-great-recession-43670.html.

102.   Ibid.

103.   Priem, Harrison, & Muir, "Structured Conflict and Consensus Outcomes in Group Decision Making."

104.   Van De Ven and A. L. Delbecq, "Nominal versus Interacting Group Processes for Committee Decision Making Effectiveness," *Academy of Management Journal* 14 (1971): 203–212.

105.   P. Gilbert, "Hearing Every Voice in the Room: How IBM Brings Ideas Forward from Its Teams," *New York Times*, December 6, 2014, BU8.

106.   R. Dennis and J. S. Valicich, "Group, Sub-Group, and Nominal Group Idea Generation: New Rules for a New Media?" *Journal of Management* 20 (1994): 723–736.

107.   R. B. Gallupe, W. H. Cooper, M. L. Grise, and L. M. Bastianutti, "Blocking Electronic Brainstorms," *Journal of Applied Psychology* 79 (1994): 77–86.

108.   Fisher, "Shy at Work? 7 Ways to Speak Up," *Fortune*, May 31, 2013, accessed March 25, 2017, http://fortune.com/2013/05/31/shy-at-work-7-ways-to-speak-up/.

109.   R. B. Gallupe and W. H. Cooper, "Brainstorming Electronically," *Sloan Management Review*, Fall 1993, 27–36.

110.   Ibid.

111.   G. Kay, "Effective Meetings through Electronic Brainstorming," *Management Quarterly* 35 (1995): 15.

6

1.   A. Neeley, "Apple Has More Than 1.5B Active Devices in the Wild, up 100M in Last Year," *AppleInsider*, January 28, 2020, accessed March 9, 2020, https://appleinsider.com/articles/20/01/28/apple-has-more-than-15b-active-devices-in-the-wild-up-100m-in-last-year.

2.   F. Richter, "Digital Camera Sales Dropped 87% Since 2010," *Statista*, February 7, 2020, accessed March 9, 2020, https://www-statista-com.ezproxy.butler.edu/chart/5782/digital-camera-shipments/.

3.   S. O'Dea, "iPhone Unit Sales as Share of Global Smartphone Sales from 3Q'07 to 4Q'19," *Statista*, February 28, 2020, accessed March 9, 2020, https://www-statista-com.ezproxy.butler.edu/statistics/216459/global-market-share-of-apple-iphone/; Statista Research Department, "Tablet Shipments Market Share by Vendor Worldwide From 2nd Quarter 2011 to 4th Quarter 2019," *Statista*, March 2, 2020, accessed March 9, 2020, https://www-statista-com.ezproxy.butler.edu/statistics/276635/market-share-held-by-tablet-vendors/; B. Thompson, "Integration and Monopoly," *Stratechery*, November 18, 2019, accessed March 9, 2020, https://stratechery.com/2019/integration-and-monopoly/.

4.   J. Snell, "Fun with Charts: When Apple Was in the Red," *Six Colors*, February 12, 2020, accessed March 9, 2020, https://sixcolors.com/post/2020/02/fun-with-charts-when-apple-was-in-the-red/.

5.   Ibid.

6.   T. Martin & S. Krouse, "The Big Hangup: Why the Future Is Not Just Your Phone," *Wall Street Journal*, January 12, 2019, accessed March 9, 2020, https://www.wsj.com/articles/the-big-hangup-why-the-future-is-not-just-your-phone-11547269202?mod=hp_lead_pos.

7.   J. Barney, "Firm Resources and Sustained Competitive Advantage," *Journal of Management* 17 (1991): 99–120; J. Barney, "Looking Inside for Competitive Advantage," *Academy of Management Executive* 9 (1995): 49–61.

8.   S. Warwick, "Apple Developers Have Earned Over $155 Billion Since the App Store's Launch in 2008," *iMore*, March 13, 2020, accessed March 15, 2020, https://www.imore.com/developers-have-earned-over-155-billion-app-stores-launch-2008.

9.   V. Savov, "Apple and Samsung Feel the Sting of Plateauing Smartphones," *The Verge*, January 3, 2019, accessed March 9, 2020, https://www.theverge.com/2019/1/3/18166399/iphone-android-apple-samsung-smartphone-sales-peak.

10.   B. Thompson, "Integration and Monopoly," *Stratechery*, November 18, 2019, accessed March 10, 2020, https://stratechery.com/2019/integration-and-monopoly/.

11.   G. Rosenberg, "Apple: A Misunderstood Giant," *Seeking Alpha*, October 6, 2015, accessed March 10, 2020, https://seekingalpha.com/instablog/8125221-gregg-rosenberg/4427186-apple-misunderstood-giant.

12.   R. Holly & C. Lynch, "Can I use a Galaxy Watch or Watch Active Even if I Don't Have a Galaxy Phone?" *Android Central*, January 7, 2020, accessed March 10, 2020, https://www.androidcentral.com/can-i-use-galaxy-watch-even-if-i-dont-have-galaxy-phone; "Device-compatibility | Samsung Galaxy Watch," *The Official Samsung Galaxy Site*, accessed March 10, 2020, https://www.samsung.com/global/galaxy/galaxy-watch/device-compatibility/.

13.   A. Kingley-Hughs, "Apple: Wearables Is Now the Size of a Fortune 150 Company, and Tim Cook Dodges a Question about the Future," ZDNet, January 29, 2020, accessed March 10, 2020, https://www.zdnet.com/article/apple-wearables-is-now-the-size-of-a-fortune-150-company-and-tim-cook-dodges-a-question-about-the-future/.

14.   J. Snell, "Apple Results: $64B in Revenue on Record Services Income," *Six Colors*, October 30, 2019, accessed March 11, 2020, https://sixcolors.com/post/2019/10/apple-results-64b-in-revenue-on-record-services-income/; T. Spangler, "Apple Services Up 17% in Fiscal Q1 2020, Record Revenue and Earnings," *Variety*, January 28, 2020, accessed March 11, 2020, https://variety.com/2020/digital/news/apple-q1-2020-results-apple-tv-plus-1203484288/; ;

15.   O. Malik, "An Exclusive Look Inside Apple's A13 Bionic Chip," *Wired*, September 19, 2019, accessed March 10, 2020, https://www.wired.com/story/apple-a13-bionic-chip-iphone/; K. Carlon, "Why Apple's A10 Chip 'Blows Away the Competition" *AndroidAuthority*, October 22, 2016, accessed March 26, 2017, http://www.androidauthority.com/apple-a10-fusion-chip-performance-723918/; V. Savov, "The iPhone's New Chip Should Worry Intel," *The Verge*, September 16, 2016, accessed March 26, 2017, http://www.theverge.com/2016/9/16/12939310/iphone-7-a10-fusion-processor-apple-intel-future.

16.   R. McMillan & E. Brown, "Intel Agrees to Sell Smartphone-Chip Assets to Apple," *Wall Street Journal*, July 25, 2019, accessed March 10, 2020, https://www.wsj.com/articles/intel-agrees-to-sell-smartphone-chip-assets-to-apple-11564086391?mod=djemRiskCompliance.

17.   "U.S. Market Reach of the Most Popular iPhone Apps in March 2012," Statista, accessed April 20, 2016, http://www.statista.com/statistics/243757/us-market-reach-of-the-most-popular-iphone-app/.

18.   N. Carlson, "Apple Has ~7,000 Fewer People Working on Maps Than Google," *Business Insider*,

September 21, 2012, accessed April 20, 2016, http://www.businessinsider.com/apple-has-7000-fewer-people-working-on-maps-than-google-2012-9?op=1.

19. D. Goldman, "Apple CEO: 'We Are Extremely Sorry' for Maps Frustration," *CNN Money*, September 28, 2012, accessed April 20, 2016, http://money.cnn.com/2012/09/28/technology/apple-maps-apology/index.html.

20. P. Elmer-DeWitt, "How Apple Maps Overtook Google Maps," *Fortune*, June 16, 2015, accessed April 20, 2016, http://fortune.com/2015/06/16/apple-google-maps-ios/.

21. M. Panzarino, "Apple is Rebuilding Maps from the Ground Up," *TechCrunch*, June 29, 2018, accessed March 10, 2020, https://techcrunch.com/2018/06/29/apple-is-rebuilding-maps-from-the-ground-up/.

22. R. Christoffel, "Apple Maps in iOS 13: Sights Set on Google," *MacStories*, July 31, 2019, accessed March 10, 2020, https://www.macstories.net/stories/apple-maps-in-ios-13-sights-set-on-google/; J. O'Beirne, "Apple's New Map," JustinObeirne.com, 2020, accessed March 10, 2020, https://www.justinobeirne.com/new-apple-maps.

23. W. Hilliard, "Apple Maps versus Google Maps – Which Is the Best for Your iPhone?" *AppleInsider*, February 16, 2020, accessed March 10, 2020, https://appleinsider.com/articles/20/02/16/apple-maps-vs-google-maps---smartphone-mapping-titans-battle-it-out-in-2020.

24. B. Thompson, "Apple's Error," *Stratechery*, January 7, 2019, accessed March 11, 2020, https://stratechery.com/2019/apples-errors/.

25. S. Hart and C. Banbury, "How Strategy-Making Processes Can Make a Difference," *Strategic Management Journal* 15 (1994): 251–269.

26. R. A. Burgelman, "Fading Memories: A Process Theory of Strategic Business Exit in Dynamic Environments," *Administrative Science Quarterly* 39 (1994): 24–56; R. A. Burgelman and A. S. Grove, "Strategic Dissonance," *California Management Review* 38 (Winter 1996): 8–28.

27. F. Gillette, "AT&T Is Dragging HBO's Streaming Strategy Out of the Dark Ages," *Bloomberg*, March 7, 2019, accessed March 11, 2020, https://www.bloomberg.com/news/features/2019-03-07/at-t-is-dragging-hbo-s-streaming-strategy-out-of-the-dark-ages?sref=xXo7CWym.

28. Ibid.

29. A. Watson, "Number of HBO Now Subscribers 2015-2019," *Statista*, September 17, 2019, accessed March 11, 2020, https://www.statista.com/statistics/539290/hbo-now-subscribers/; A. Watson, "Number of Netflix Subscribers 2019," *Statista*, January 22, 2020, accessed March 11, 2020, https://www.statista.com/statistics/250934/quarterly-number-of-netflix-streaming-subscribers-worldwide/.

30. A. Nicolaou & A. Barker, "How HBO Took on the Streaming Wars," *Financial Times*, May 20, 2020, accessed June 17, 2020, https://www.ft.com/content/1e1fa894-9969-11ea-8b5b-63f7c5c86bef.

31. R. A. Burgelman and A. S. Grove, "Strategic Dissonance," *California Management Review* 38 (Winter 1996): 8–28.

32. B. Halligan, "The Art of Strategy Is About Knowing When to Say No," *Harvard Business Review*, January 26, 2018, accessed March 12, 2020, https://hbr.org/2018/01/the-art-of-strategy-is-about-knowing-when-to-say-no.

33. Ibid.

34. Ibid.

35. Ibid.

36. R. Wall, "Airbus Cuts A380 Production Plans in 2017," *Wall Street Journal*, December 27, 2016, accessed March 26, 2017, *Wall Street Journal*, https://www.wsj.com/articles/airbus-cuts-a380-production-plans-in-2017-1482860279; R. Wall, "Airports Worried the A380 Was Too Big. Turns Out, That Wasn't the Problem," *Wall Street Journal*, February 14, 2019, accessed March 12, 2020, https://www.wsj.com/articles/airports-worried-the-a380-was-too-big-turns-out-that-wasnt-the-problem-11550171293?mod=djem10point.

37. A. Tsang & D. Segal, "Airbus Retiring Its Jaw-Dropping Giant, the A380, in an Industry Gone Nimble," *New York Times*, February 14, 2109, accessed March 12, 2020, https://www.nytimes.com/2019/02/14/business/airbus-a380.html.

38. A. Fiegenbaum, S. Hart, and D. Schendel, "Strategic Reference Point Theory," *Strategic Management Journal* 17 (1996): 219–235.

39. "Best Cars, SUVs, and Trucks for 2020," *Consumer Reports*, accessed March 12, 2020, https://www.consumerreports.org/cro/cars/best-cars-suvs-autos-spotlight/index.htm.

40. K. Yakal, "The Best Tax Software for 2020," *PC Magazine*, February 27,2020, accessed March 12, 2020, https://www.pcmag.com/picks/the-best-tax-software.

41. "Fairway Market - Why We're Like No Other Market," Fairway Market, accessed March 13, 2020, https://www.fairwaymarket.com/about-fairway/.

42. J. Kang, "Specialty Grocers Lose Their Edge," *Wall Street Journal*, March 1, 2020, accessed March 13, 2020, https://www.wsj.com/articles/upscale-specialty-grocers-lose-their-edge-11583058601.

43. A. Fiegenbaum and H. Thomas, "Strategic Groups as Reference Groups: Theory, Modeling and Empirical Examination of Industry and Competitive Strategy," *Strategic Management Journal* 16 (1995): 461–476.

44. "4.1% Growth Projected for 2019 Home Improvement Products Market," Home Improvement Research Institute, September 16, 2019, accessed March 13, 2020, https://www.hiri.org/index.php?option=com_dailyplanetblog&view=entry&year=2019&month=09&day=15&id=42:4-1-growth-projected-for-2019-home-improvement-products-market.

45. R. K. Reger and A. S. Huff, "Strategic Groups: A Cognitive Perspective," *Strategic Management Journal* 14 (1993): 103–124.

46. "The Home Depot Announces Fourth Quarter and Fiscal 2019 Results; Reiterates Fiscal 2020 Business Outlook; Increases Quarterly Dividend by 10 Percent," Home Depot, February 25, 2020, accessed March 13, 2020, https://ir.homedepot.com/news-releases/2020/02-25-2020-105936546; "Lowe's Reports Fourth Quarter Sales And Earnings Results," Lowe's, February 26, 2020, accessed March 13, 2020, https://newsroom.lowes.com/news-releases/q4-2019-sales-earnings/; "Investor Fact Sheet," Lowe's, February 1, 2019, accessed March 13, 2020, https://lowes.gcs-web.com/static-files/180edcad-7d04-4511-a4d8-8c33ebf8066d.

47. "About Ace Hardware," Ace Corporate, accessed March 13, 2020, https://www.myace.com/invest/about-ace; "2019 Financial Report," February 12, 2020, accessed March 13, 2020, https://newsroom.acehardware.com/download/828760/2019financialreport.pdf.

48. "About Aubuchon Hardware," Aubuchon Hardware, accessed March 13, 2020, https://www.hardwarestore.com/about-us.

49. "About Us | Hardware Opportunities with Ace," Ace, accessed March 13, 2020, https://www.myace.com/about-us/.

50. "About 84 Lumber," 84 Lumber, April 1, 2019, accessed March 13, 2020, https://www.84lumber.com/media/4558/84-lumber-about-fact-sheet-2019-april-01.pdf.

51. R. Kestenbaum, "Amazon and Whole Foods after a Year: Supermarkets Will See Massive Changes," *Forbes*, December 16, 2018, accessed March 14, 2020, https://www.forbes.com/sites/richardkestenbaum/2018/12/16/amazon-whole-foods-supermarkets-grocery-massive-change/#1b9319369cc9.

52. M. Boyle, "Walmart to Redesign Produce Section in Bid to Fend Off Amazon," *Bloomberg*, November 20, 2019, accessed March 14, 2020, https://www.bloomberg.com/news/articles/2019-11-20/walmart-to-redesign-produce-section-in-bid-to-fend-off-amazon?sref=xXo7CWym.

53. Ibid.

54. R. Redman, "Walmart launches 'Refresh' of Produce Department," *Supermarket News* November 20, 2019, accessed March 14, 2020, https://www.supermarketnews.com/produce-floral/walmart-launches-refresh-produce-department.

55. "Purpose, Vision, Values, and Mission," Southwest Airlines, accessed March 15, 2020, http://investors.southwest.com/our-company/purpose-vision-values-and-mission.

56. "Our Organization," TED, accessed March 15, 2020, https://www.ted.com/about/our-organization.

57. "Dr Pepper History," Dr Pepper Snapple Group, accessed March 15, 2020, https://www.drpeppersnapplegroup.com/brands/dr-pepper.

58. M. Lubatkin, "Value-Creating Mergers: Fact or Folklore?" *Academy of Management Executive* 2 (1988): 295–302; M. Lubatkin and S. Chatterjee, "Extending Modern Portfolio Theory into the Domain of Corporate Diversification: Does It Apply?" *Academy of Management Journal* 37 (1994): 109–136; M. H. Lubatkin and P. J. Lane, "Psst . . . The Merger Mavens Still Have It Wrong!" *Academy of Management Executive* 10 (1996): 21–39.

59. "About 3M - Investor Overview," 3M, accessed March 15, 2020, https://investors.3m.com/about-3m/investor-overview/default.aspx; "Why 3M Company Finds It Hard to Keep Up with Investor Expectations," *The Motley Fool*, October 24, 2018, accessed March 15, 2020, https://www.fool.com/investing/2018/10/24/premium-3m-company.aspx.

60. J. McNish, "Bombardier Shed Snowmobiles for Jetliners, Trains. Now, It's Giving Up Both," *Wall Street Journal*, February 18, 2018, accessed March 15, 2020, https://www.wsj.com/articles/bombardier-shed-snowmobiles-for-jetliners-trains-now-its-giving-up-both-11582055596?mod=hp_lead_pos7.

61. S. Terllep, "A Megadeal Joined Sharpie Markers and Crock-Pots. What Could Go Wrong? A Lot," *Wall Street Journal*, May 2, 2018, accessed March 15, 2020, https://www.wsj.com/articles/a-megadeal-joined-sharpie-markers-and-crock-pots-what-could-go-wrong-a-lot-1525280516.

62. M. Reeves, S. Moose, and T. Venema, "BCG Classics Revisited: The Growth Share Matrix," *BCG Perspectives*, June 4, 2014, accessed April 25, 2016, https://www.bcgperspectives.com/content/articles/corporate_strategy_portfolio_management_strategic_planning_growth_share_matrix_bcg_classics_revisited/.

63. M. Lubatkin & P.J. Lane, "Psst! . . . The Merger Mavens Still Have it Wrong,"*Academy of Management Executive* 10 (1996) 21–39; L. Palich, L. Cardinal & C. Miller, "Curvilinearity in the Diversification–Performance Linkage: An Examination of Over Three Decades of Research," *Strategic Management Journal* 21 (2000): 155-174; G. Ahuja & E. Novelli, "Redirecting Research Efforts on the Diversification-Performance Linkage: The Search for Synergy," *Academy of Management Annals* v. 11 no. 1 (2017): 342-390.

64. "A Megadeal Joined Sharpie Markers and Crock-Pots. What Could Go Wrong? A Lot."

65. D. Hambrick, I. MacMillan, and D. Day, "Strategic Attributes and Performance in the BCG Matrix—A PIMS-based Analysis of Industrial Product Businesses," *Academy of Management Journal* 25 (1982): 510–531.

66. J. Armstrong and R. Brodie, "Effects of Portfolio Planning Methods on Decision Making: Experimental Results," *International Journal of Research in Marketing* 11 (1994): 73–84.

67. D. Welch, "Chevy Silverado Pickup Trucks Will Pay for GM's Electric Future," *Bloomberg*, February 5, 2019, accessed March 15, 2020, http://www.bloomberg.com/news/features/2019-02-05/chevy-silverado-pickup-trucks-will-pay-for-gm-s-electric-future?sref=xXo7CWym.

68. Ibid.

69. Ibid.

70. P. Eisenstein, "Chevy Is Working on What Could Be the First Pickup to Top $100,000," CNBC, June 26, 2019, accessed March 15, 2020, https://www.cnbc.com/2019/06/25/chevy-is-working-on-what-could-be-the-first-pickup-to-top-100000.html.

71. D. Klein, "Arby's to Buy Buffalo Wild Wings in $2.9B Deal," *QSR Magazine*, November 2017, accessed March 15, 2020, https://www.qsrmagazine.com/finance/arbys-buy-buffalo-wild-wings-29b-deal.

72. J. Jargon, "Arby's Parent to Buy Sonic for $2.3 Billion," *Wall Street Journal*, September 25, 2018, accessed March 15, 2020, https://www.wsj.com/articles/arbys-parent-to-buy-sonic-for-2-3-billion-1537884264?mod=hp_lista_pos2.

73. J. A. Pearce II, "Selecting Among Alternative Grand Strategies," *California Management Review* (Spring 1982): 23–31.

74. Associated Press, "Marriott Buys Starwood, Becoming World's Largest Hotel Chain," CNBC, September 23, 2016, accessed March 29, 2017, http://www.cnbc.com/2016/09/23/marriott-buys-starwood-becoming-worlds-largest-hotel-chain.html.

75. A. Bhattaria, "'Size Matters': Marriott to Buy Starwood, Creating the World's Largest Hotel Company," *Washington Post*, November 16, 2015, accessed March 29, 2017,https://www.washingtonpost.com/business/capitalbusiness/marriott-to-buy-starwood-creating-the-worlds-largest-hotel-company/2015/11/16/acb40a20-8c6f-11e5-acff-673ae-92ddd2b_story.html?utm_term=.e8bc5773d6b5.

76. Press Release, "Marriott International Reports Fourth Quarter 2019 Results," *Marriott International*, February 26, 2020, accessed March 15, 2020, https://marriott.gcs-web.com/news-releases/news-release-details/marriott-international-reports-fourth-quarter-2019-results.

77. J. Creswell, "How Amazon Steers Shoppers to Its Own Products," *New York Times*, June 23, 2018, accessed March 16, 2020, https://www.nytimes.com/2018/06/23/business/amazon-the-brand-buster.html.

78. "Amazon Steps Up Its Private Label Strategy," ScrapeHero, July 4, 2019, accessed March 16, 2020, https://www.scrapehero.com/amazon-step-up-its-private-label-strategy/.

79. G. Anderson, "Are Amazon's Private Labels Falling Short or Just Getting Started?" *RetailWire*, March 19, 2019, accessed March 16, 2020, https://retailwire.com/discussion/are-amazons-private-labels-falling-short-or-just-getting-started/.

80. "Benefits of Lower Costs at Vanguard: Why Cost Matters," Vanguard, accessed March 16, 2020, https://about.vanguard.com/what-sets-vanguard-apart/the-benefits-of-lower-costs/.

81. J. A. Pearce II, "Retrenchment Remains the Foundation of Business Turnaround," *Strategic Management Journal* 15 (1994): 407–417.

82. C. Morgan, "Will GameStop Survive in a Digital Future?" *Business Insider*, May 20, 2019, accessed March 16, 2020, https://www.businessinsider.com/gamestop-video-games-gaming-survive-digital-future-2019-5.

83. N. Statt, "Sony Confirms It Will Stop Letting GameStop and Other Retailers Sell PS4 Download Codes," *The Verge*, March 25, 2019, accessed March 16, 2020, https://www.theverge.com/2019/3/25/18281538/sony-playstation-4-gamestop-stop-selling-game-download-codes-retailers; L. Sun, "Microsoft's "All Digital" Xbox One S Raises Red Flags for GameStop," *The Motley Fool*, April 17, 2019, accessed March 16, 2020, https://www.fool.com/investing/2019/04/17/microsofts-all-digital-xbox-one-s-raises-red-flags.aspx.

84. News Release, "GameStop Reports Fourth Quarter and Fiscal 2019 Results Ahead of Earnings Expectations," GameStop Corp., March 26, 2020, accessed June 17, 2020, http://news.gamestop.com/news-releases/news-release-details/gamestop-reports-fourth-quarter-and-fiscal-2019-results-ahead; P. Thomas, "GameStop Shares Fall as Company Turns to Store Closures," *Wall Street Journal*, September 11, 2019, accessed March 16, 2020, https://www.wsj.com/articles/gamestop-shares-fall-as-company-turns-to-store-closures-11568230146?mod=djemRiskCompliance.

85. A. Al-Muslim, "Hilton Plays Catch-Up in Luxury-Travel Market," *Wall Street Journal*, July 15, 2019, accessed March 17, 2020, https://www.wsj.com/articles/hilton-plays-catch-up-in-luxury-travel-market-11563163381?mod=djemwhatsnews.

86. L. Ingrassia, "They Changed the Way You Buy Your Basics," *New York Times*, January 23, 2020, accessed March 17, 2020, https://www.nytimes.com/2020/01/23/business/Billion-Dollar-Brands.html.

87. M. Ramsey, "Tesla Is Hiring Fast as Rivals Loom," *Wall Street Journal*, December 29, 2015, B1; M. Ramsey, "Tesla Rival Plans $1 Billion Plant," *Wall Street Journal*, November 6, 2015, B6; D. Wakabayashi and M. Ramsey, "Apple Secretly Gears Up to Create Car," *Wall Street Journal*, February 14–16, 2015, A1; "Best Cars: 2015 Tesla Model S," *U.S. News and World Report*, April 25, 2016, http://usnews.rankingsandreviews.com/cars-trucks/Tesla_Model-S/.

88. D. Primack & K. Korosec, "GM Buying Self-Driving Tech Startup for More Than $1 Billion," *Fortune*, March 11, 2016, accessed January 23, 2020, https://fortune.com/2016/03/11/gm-buying-self-driving-tech-startup-for-more-than-1-billion/.

89. L. Ellis and L. Stevens, "UPS Tries On 3-D Printing in Bet to Stem New Threat," *Wall Street Journal*, September 19–20, 2015, B1.

90. Ibid.

91. "3D Printing | 3D Print Services," The UPS Store, accessed March 17, 2020, https://www.theupsstore.com/print/3d-printing.

92. G. Bensinger & L. Stevens, "Amazon's Newest Ambition: Competing Directly with UPS and FedEx," *Wall Street Journal*, September 27, 2016, accessed March 30, 2017, https://www.wsj.com/articles/amazons-newest-ambitioncompeting-directly-with-ups-and-fedex-1474994758; D. Leonard, "Will Amazon Kill FedEx?" *Bloomberg-Businessweek*, August 31, 2016, accessed March 30, 2017, https://www.bloomberg.com/features/2016-amazon-delivery/.

93. News Release, "Amazon.com Announces Fourth Quarter Sales up 21% to $87.4 Billion," Amazon.com, Inc., January 30, 2020, accessed March 17, 2020, https://ir.aboutamazon.com/news-releases/news-release-details/amazoncom-announces-fourth-quarter-sales-21-874-billion.

94. J. Brumley, "43 Companies Amazon Could Destroy (Including One for a Second Time)," *Kiplinger*, November 27, 2019, accessed March 17, 2020, https://www.kiplinger.com/slideshow/investing/T052-S001-43-companies-amazon-amzn-could-destroy/index.html.

95. P. Ziobro, "Fred Smith Created FedEx. Now He Has to Reinvent It," *Wall Street Journal*, October 17, 2019, accessed March 17, 2020, https://www.wsj.com/articles/fred-smith-created-fedex-now-he-has-to-reinvent-it-11571324050?mod=djemwhatsnews.

96. D. Sax, "A $99.99 Surfboard Upends the Industry," *Bloomberg Businessweek*, October 29, 2015, April 26, 2016, http://www.bloomberg.com/news/articles/2015-10-29/wavestorm-s-99-99-surfboard-upends-the-industry.

97. Ibid.

98. S. Kurtz, "The Last Great Clothing Store," *New York Times*, March 29, 2018, accessed March 17, 2020, https://www.nytimes.com/2018/03/29/style/the-last-great-clothing-store-boyds.html.

99. Ibid.

100. Ibid.

101. Ibid.

102. Ibid.

103. G. Smith, "HGTV Will Never Upset You: How the Network Beat CNN in 2016," *Bloomberg*, December 28, 2016, accessed March 30, 2017, https://www.bloomberg.com/news/articles/2016-12-28/hgtv-will-never-upset-you-how-the-network-beat-cnn-in-2016.

104. R. E. Miles and C. C. Snow, *Organizational Strategy, Structure, & Process* (New York: McGraw-Hill, 1978); S. Zahra and J. A. Pearce, "Research Evidence on the Miles-Snow Typology," *Journal of Management* 16 (1990): 751–768; W. L. James and K. J. Hatten, "Further Evidence on the Validity of the Self Typing Paragraph Approach: Miles and Snow Strategic Archetypes in Banking," *Strategic Management Journal* 16 (1995): 161–168.

105. A. Carr & N. Grant, "Xerox and HP Are in a $35 Billion Fight Over Ink Cartridges," *Bloomberg*, February 27, 2020, accessed March 18, 2020, https://www.bloomberg.com/news/features/2020-02-27/xerox-and-hp-are-in-a-35-billion-fight-over-ink-cartridges?sref=xXo7CWym.

106. B. Stone, "Toyota Invests $394 Million in Joby Aviation's Flying Taxis," *Bloomberg*, January 15, 2020, accessed March 18, 2020, https://www.bloomberg.com/news/articles/2020-01-15/toyota-invests-394-million-in-joby-aviation-s-flying-taxis?sref=xXo7CWym.

107. B. Gallagher, "Copycat: How Facebook Tried to Squash Snapchat," *Wired*, February 16, 2018, accessed March 18, 2020, https://www.wired.com/story/copycat-how-facebook-tried-to-squash-snapchat/.

108. S. Frier, "Facebook Mimics Snapchat Stories in Its Main Application, Copying Snap for a Fourth Time," *Bloomberg*, March 28, 2017, accessed March 31, 2017, https://www.bloomberg.com/news/articles/2017-03-28/facebook-mimics-snapchat-stories-in-its-main-application-copying-snap-for-a-fourth-time; C. Newton, "Facebook Launches Stories to Complete Its All-Out Assault on Snapchat," The Verge, March 28, 2017, accessed March 31, 2017, http://www.theverge.com/2017/3/28/15081398/facebook-stories-snapchat-camera-direct; D. Seetharaman, "Facebook, Eye on Snapchat, Adds Camera Features," Wall Street Journal, March 28, 2017, accessed March 31, 2017, Facebook launches stories to complete its all-out assault on Snapchathttps://www.wsj.com/articles/facebook-eye-on-snapchat-adds-camera-features-1490702404.

109.   D. Jagielski, "Facebook Is Copying Some of Snap's Key Features, Again," *The Motley Fool*, October 9, 2019, accessed March 18, 2020, https://www.fool.com/investing/2019/10/09/facebook-is-copying-some-of-snaps-key-features-aga.aspx.

110.   "Instagram by the Numbers (2020): Stats, Demographics & Fun Facts," Omnicore Agency, February 10, 2020, accessed March 18, 2020, https://www.omnicoreagency.com/instagram-statistics/; "Snapchat by the Numbers (2020): Stats, Demographics & Fun Facts," Omnicore Agency, February 7, 2020, accessed March 18, 2020, https://www.omnicoreagency.com/snapchat-statistics/.

111.   W. Boston, "In Luxury Race, Profits Get Dented," *Wall Street Journal*, March 13, 2015, B1.

112.   M. Chen, "Competitor Analysis and Interfirm Rivalry: Toward a Theoretical Integration," *Academy of Management Review* 21 (1996): 100–134; J. C. Baum and H. J. Korn, "Competitive Dynamics of Interfirm Rivalry," *Academy of Management Journal* 39 (1996): 255–291.

113.   M. Chen, "Competitor Analysis and Interfirm Rivalry: Toward a Theoretical Integration," *Academy of Management Review* 21 (1996): 100–124.

114.   H. Haddon, "McDonald's Falls Short on Profit," *Wall Street Journal*, October 22, 2019, accessed March 18, 2020, https://www.wsj.com/articles/mcdonalds-falls-short-on-profit-11571745670?mod=djemCFO.

115.   J. Jargon, "McDonald's Decides to Embrace Fast-Food Identity," *Wall Street Journal*, March 1, 2017, accessed March 31, 2017, https://www.wsj.com/articles/mcdonalds-to-expand-mobile-delivery-as-it-plots-future-1488390702; K. Samuelson, "McDonald's to Test UberEATS Delivery Service in Three Florida Cities," *Fortune*, December 16, 2016, accessed March 31, 2017, http://fortune.com/2016/12/16/mcdonalds-delivery-service-florida-cities/.

116.   J. White, "Wendy's Wendy Gets a Makeover," *Wall Street Journal*, October 11, 2012, accessed June 5, 2014. http://blogs.wsj.com/corporate-intelligence/2012/10/11/wendy/?KEYWORDS=wendy%27s+strategy.

117.   H. Haddon, "Wendy's Puts Breakfast on the Menu," *Wall Street Journal*, September 9, 2019, accessed March 18, 2020, https://www.wsj.com/articles/wendys-puts-breakfast-on-the-menu-11568066269?mod=djemCFO; "Wendy's Breakfast | Breakfast Worth Waking Up For," Wendy's, accessed March 18, 2020, https://www.wendys.com/breakfast.

118.   "Fresh Beef Burgers," McDonald's, accessed March 18, 2020, https://www.mcdonalds.com/us/en-us/about-our-food/fresh-beef.html.

119.   J. Jargon, "McDonald's to Switch to Fresh Beef in Quarter Pounders," *Wall Street Journal*, March 30, 2017, accessed March 31, 2017, https://www.wsj.com/articles/mcdonalds-to-switch-to-fresh-beef-in-quarter-pounders-1490878800; R. Leadem, "Wendy's Trolls McDonald's Over Its Fresh Beef Announcement," *Entrepreneur*, March 31, 2017, accessed March 31, 2017, https://www.entrepreneur.com/article/292265.

120.   L. Lavelle, "The Chickens Come Home to Roost, and Boston Market Is Prepared to Expand," *The Record*, October 6, 1996.

121.   "Subway Franchise Information," *Entrepreneur*, accessed March 18, 2020, http://www.entrepreneur.com/franchises/subway/282839; "McDonald's Franchise Information," *Entrepreneur*, accessed March 18, 2020, https://www.entrepreneur.com/franchises/mcdonalds/282570; "Explore Our World | SUBWAY.com – United States (English)," Subway, accessed March 18, 2020, https://www.subway.com/en-US/ExploreOurWorld; "Around the World | McDonald's," McDonald's, accessed March 18, 2020, https://corporate.mcdonalds.com/corpmcd/about-us/around-the-world.html.

122.   "Our People, Our Communities," *Subway*, accessed March 18, 2020, https://www.subway.com/en-GD/AboutUs/SocialResponsibility/OurPeopleOurCommunities#HeartHealth. s

123.   N. Rossolillo, "There Are Only Two Catches to This One-Cent Whopper Deal," *The Motley Fool*, December 7, 2018, accessed March 19, 2020, https://www.fool.com/investing/2018/12/07/there-are-only-2-catches-to-this-one-cent-whopper.aspx.

124.   A. Davies, "Burger King's 1-Cent Whopper Is a Taste of the Robocar Future," *Wired*, December 11, 2018, accessed March 19, 2020, https://www.wired.com/story/burger-king-whopper-detour-mcdonalds-self-driving-car-advertising/.

125.   D. Ketchen Jr., C. Snow, and V. Street, "Improving Firm Performance by Matching Strategic Decision – Making Process to Competitive Dynamics," *Academy of Management Executive* 18 (2004) 29–43.

126.   T. Rivias, "McDonald's 1-Cent Big Mac Isn't as Cheap as It Seems," *Barron's*, October 3, 2019, accessed March 19, 2020, https://www.barrons.com/articles/mcdonalds-1-cent-big-mac-penny-51570055563.

127.   M. Gottfried, "T-Mobile's Shine Dims Sprint's Deal Hopes," *Wall Street Journal*, March 1, 2014, B14.

128.   Press Release, "T-Mobile Adds 7.0 Million Customers in 2019 – the Sixth Year in a Row with More Than 5 Million Net Customers Joining the Un-carrier Movement," T-Mobile Newsroom, January 7, 2020, accessed March 19, 2020, https://www.t-mobile.com/news/t-mobile-customer-results-q4-2019; S. O'Dea, "US Wireless Carrier Market Share 2019," *Statista*, February 27, 2020, accessed March 19, 2020, https://www.statista.com/statistics/199359/market-share-of-wireless-carriers-in-the-us-by-subscriptions/.

129.   "Investor Factbook: Q4 and Full-Year 2016," T-Mobile, accessed March 31, 2017, http://investor.t-mobile.com/Cache/1001220063.PDF?O=PDF&T=&Y=&D=&FID=1001220063&iid=4091145; "US Wireless Carrier Market Share 2016," Statista, accessed March 31, 2017, https://www-statista-com.ezproxy.butler.edu/statistics/199359/market-share-of-wireless-carriers-in-the-us-by-subscriptions/; R. Karpinski, "Un-Carrier at Three Years: Assessing T-Mobile's Disruptive Impact," 451 Research, March 28, 2016, accessed April 26, 2016, https://newsroom.t-mobile.com/content/1020/files/NEWImpactReport.pdf.

130.   "Investor Factbook: Q4 and Full-Year 2016," T-Mobile, accessed March 31, 2017, http://investor.t-mobile.com/Cache/1001220063.PDF?O=PDF&T=&Y=&D=&FID=1001220063&iid=4091145. "US Wireless Carrier Market Share 2016," Statista, accessed March 31, 2017, https://www-statista-com.ezproxy.butler.edu/statistics/199359/market-share-of-wireless-carriers-in-the-us-by-subscriptions/; "Now More Than 100 Services Stream Free with T-Mobile's Binge On and Music Freedom," *T-Mobile*, April 5, 2016, accessed April 26, 2016, https://newsroom.t-mobile.com/news-and-blogs/binge-on-music-freedom-new-services.htm; "T-Mobile Introduces 'Mobile without Borders': Extends Coverage & Calling Across North America at No Extra Charge," T-Mobile, July 9, 2015, accessed April 26, 2016, https://newsroom.t-mobile.com/media-kits/mobile-without-borders.htm; M. Gottfried, "T-Mobile Takes Toll on Verizon," *Wall Street Journal*, April 25, 2014, C8; E. Mason, "T-Mobile's Loss Widens as Costs Press Higher," *Wall Street Journal*, February 26, 2014, B4; T Gryta and B. Rubin, "T-Mobile Posts Big Gain in Subscribers," *Wall Street Journal*, May 1, 2014, accessed June 26, 2014, http://www.wsj.com/articles/SB10001424052702304677904579535292125406530 8; Z. Epstein, "The Most Important Wireless Carrier in America," *BGR*, October 10, 2013, accessed June 26, 2014, http://bgr.com/2013/10/10/t-mobile-free-international-roaming-analysis/; T. Gryta, "T-Mobile will Waive Data Fees for Music Services," *Wall Street Journal*, June 18, 2014, accessed June 26, 2014, http://online.wsj.com/articles/t-mobile-will-waive-data-fees-for-music-service-1403142678.

131.   R. Wall and J. Chow, "Europe's Top Airlines to Spend Billions in Battle to Win Back Passengers," *Wall Street Journal*, June 4, 2015, accessed April 26, 2016, http://www.wsj.com/articles/europes-top-airlines-to-spend-billions-in-battle-to-win-back-passengers-1433425762.

132.   Ibid.

133.   S. Nassauer & L. Stevens, "Star Shower Price War Shakes Up Retailers," *Wall Street Journal*, December 14, 2016, accessed April 1, 2017, https://www.wsj.com/articles/star-shower-price-war-shakes-up-retailers-1481657498.

134.   J. Del Rey, "Amazon and Walmart Are in an All-Out Price War that Is Terrifying America's Biggest Brands," *Recode*, March 30, 2017, accessed April 1, 2017, https://www.recode.net/2017/3/30/14831602/amazon-walmart-cpg-grocery-price-war.

135.   Ibid.

7

1.   R. Van Hooijdonk, "The Smartest, Greenest Office Building on Earth – the Edge – Is Like a Computer With a Roof," Richardvanhoojidonk.com, January 25, 2019, accessed March 24, 2020, https://www.richardvanhoojidonk.com/blog/en/the-smartest-greenest-office-building-on-earth-the-edge-is-like-a-computer-with-a-roof.

2.   T. Randall, "Inside the Connected Future of Architecture," *Bloomberg Businessweek*, September 23, 2015, 72–77.

3.   A. Kessler, "In Tech Years, 2010 Was Eons Ago," *Wall Street Journal*, December 20, 2019, accessed March 24, 2020, https://www.wsj.com/articles/in-tech-years-2010-was-eons-ago-11577648410.

4.   A. Pasztor and R. Wall, "Air Taxis and Self-Driving Aircraft: Aviation Industry Faces Its Future," *Wall Street Journal*, July 21, 2018, accessed March 24, 2020, https://www.wsj.com/articles/air-taxis-and-self-driving-aircraft-aviation-industry-faces-its-future-1532174400.

5.   A. VanderMey, "Elon's Hyperloop May Have as Much to Offer Suburbs as Cities," *Bloomberg*, December 17, 2018, accessed March 24, 2020, https://www.bloomberg.com/news/articles/2018-12-17/elon-s-hyperloop-may-have-as-much-to-offer-suburbs-as-cities?sref=xXo7CWym.

6.   P. Anderson and M. L. Tushman, "Managing Through Cycles of Technological Change," *Research/Technology Management* 34(3) (May–June 1991): 26–31.

7.   R. N. Foster, *Innovation: The Attacker's Advantage* (New York: Summit, 1986).

8.   "The Silicon Engine: A Timeline of Semiconductors in Computers," *Computer History Museum*, accessed April 22, 2001, http://www.computerhistory.org/semi-conductor/; "Transistor Count," *Wikipedia*, March 2, 2020, accessed March 25, 2020, https://en.wikipedia.org/wiki/Transistor_count;

9. J. Burke, *The Day the Universe Changed* (Boston: Little, Brown, 1985).

10. A. Ferriman, "BMJ Readers Choose the "Sanitary Revolution" as Greatest Medical Advance Since 1840," *The British Medical Journal* 334 (January 20, 2007), accessed March 25,2020, https://www.bmj.com/content/334/7585/111.2.

11. F. Richter, "Digital Camera Sales Dropped 87% Since 2010," *Statista*, February 7, 2020, accessed March 9, 2020, https://www-statista-com.ezproxy.butler.edu/chart/5782/digital-camera-shipments/.

12. D. Wakabayashi, "The Point-and-Shoot Camera Faces Its Existential Moment," *Wall Street Journal*, July 30, 2013, accessed June 30, 2014, http://online.wsj.com/news/articles/SB10001424127887324251504578580263719432252.

13. J. Osawa, "Phones Imperil Fancy Cameras," *Wall Street Journal*, November 7, 2013, accessed June 13, 2014, http://online.wsj.com/news/articles/SB10001424052702304672404579183643696236868?KEYWORDS=high-end+camera&mg=reno64-wsj.

14. P. Holland, "iPhone 11 and 11 Pro, 2 Months Later: The Ultrawide Camera Is Still Our Favorite Thing," *CNET*, January 3, 2020, accessed March 25, 2020, https://www.cnet.com/news/iphone-11-and-11-pro-review-2-months-later-its-ultrawide-camera-is-our-favorite/; R. Wong, "iPhone 11 Pro and 11 Pro Max Review: The Ultimate Camera," *Mashable*, November 7, 2019, accessed March 25, 2020, https://mashable.com/feature/apple-iphone-11-pro-max-review/.

15. M. L. Tushman, P. C. Anderson, and C. O'Reilly, "Technology Cycles, Innovation Streams, and Ambidextrous Organizations: Organization Renewal Through Innovation Streams and Strategic Change," in *Managing Strategic Innovation and Change*, ed. M. L. Tushman and P. Anderson (New York: Oxford Press, 1997), 3–23.

16. L. Grush, "Magnetically Levitating Elevators Could Reshape Skylines—They Go Up, Down, and All Around," *Popular Science*, April 14, 2015, accessed April 26, 2015, http://www.popsci.com/elevator-will-reshape-skylines; "ThyssenKrupp Develops the World's First Rope-Free Elevator System to Enable the Building Industry to Face the Challenges of Global Urbanization," *ThyssenKrupp*, November 27, 2014, accessed May 4, 2015, http://www.thyssenkrupp-elevator.com/Show-article.104.0.html?&L=1&cHash=08b38cb686f00ec874ad82c44c737427&tx_ttnews%5Btt_news%5D=546.

17. A. Zappia, "Thyssenkrupp's MULTI Elevator Will Change the Future of Skyscrapers," *Metropolis*, April 11, 2018, accessed March 25, 2020, https://www.metropolismag.com/homepage/thyssenkrupp-horizontal-elevator-multi/.

18. "50 Things Your Smartphone Replaced [Or Will Replace In The Future]," *Gecko & Fly*, January 3, 2020, accessed March 25, 2020, https://www.geckoandfly.com/13143/50-things-smartphone-replaced-will-replace-future/; T. Haselton, "Everything the iPhone Has Destroyed in the Last 10 Years," *CNBC*, June 29, 2017, accessed March 25, 2020, https://www.cnbc.com/2017/06/29/everything-the-iphone-has-destroyed-in-the-last-10-years.html; C. Queen, "Ten Things That Are Practically Obsolete Now that We Have Smartphones," *PJ Media*, November 13, 2018, accessed March 25, 2020, https://pjmedia.com/lifestyle/10-things-that-are-practically-obsolete-now-that-we-have-smartphones/.

19. E. Schlossberg, *Interactive Excellence: Defining and Developing New Standards for the Twenty-First Century* (New York: Ballantine, 1998).

20. W. Abernathy and J. Utterback, "Patterns of Industrial Innovation," *Technology Review* 2 (1978): 40–47.

21. C. Welch, "The PlayStation 3: Blu-ray's Ultimate Trojan Horse," *The Verge*, December 4, 2019, accessed March 25, 2020, https://www.theverge.com/2019/12/4/20992215/playstation-3-ps3-blu-ray-disc-hd-dvd-sony-25th-anniversary.

22. R. Triggs, "Wireless Charging Technology: What You Need to Know," *Android Authority*, January 11, 2019, accessed March 25, 2020, http://www.androidauthority.com/wireless-charging-qi-pad-technology-580015/.

23. Press Release, "Powermat joins the Wireless Power Consortium," *Powermat*, January 3, 2018, accessed March 25, 2020, https://www.powermat.com/news/press-releases/powermat-joins-the-wpc/.

24. Statista Research Department, "Wireless Charging Market Value Worldwide, 2017 and 2023," Statista, February 19, 2020, accessed March 25, 2020, https://www.statista.com/statistics/1005101/worldwide-wireless-charging-market-size/.

25. "5G - Fifth Generation of Mobile Technologies," *International Telecommunication Union*, December 2019, accessed March 25, 2020, https://www.itu.int/en/mediacentre/backgrounders/Pages/5G-fifth-generation-of-mobile-technologies.aspx.

26. C. McGarry, "5G Speed: 5G vs 4G Performance Compared," *Tom's Guide*, December 16, 2019, accessed March 25, 2020, https://www.tomsguide.com/features/5g-vs-4g.

27. T. Gryta, "Wireless Players Tout 5G as They Await Next Smartphone Wave," *Wall Street Journal*, February 26, 2017, accessed April 3, 2017, https://www.wsj.com/articles/wireless-players-tout-5g-as-they-await-next-smartphone-wave-1488024006.

28. M. Schilling, "Technological Lockout: An Integrative Model of the Economic and Strategic Factors Driving Technology Success and Failure," *Academy of Management Review* 23 (1998): 267–284; M. Schilling, "Technology Success and Failure in Winner-Take-All Markets: The Impact of Learning Orientation, Timing, and Network Externalities," *Academy of Management Journal* 45 (2002): 387–398.

29. R. McMillan, "Tech World Prepares Obituary for Adobe Flash," *Wall Street Journal*, July 20, 2015, B1.

30. "Chromium Blog: Roll-out plan for HTML5 by Default," *Chromium Blog*, December 9, 2016, accessed April 3, 2017, https://blog.chromium.org/2016/12/roll-out-plan-for-html5-by-default.html.

31. "Flash & The Future of Interactive Content," *Adobe Blog*, July 25, 2017, accessed March 25, 2020, https://theblog.adobe.com/adobe-flash-update/; "Adobe Flash End of Support," *Microsoft Support*, September 9, 2019, accessed March 25, 2020, https://support.microsoft.com/en-us/help/4520411/adobe-flash-end-of-support.

32. T. M. Amabile, R. Conti, H. Coon, J. Lazenby, and M. Herron, "Assessing the Work Environment for Creativity," *Academy of Management Journal* 39 (1996): 1154–1184.

33. Ibid.

34. M. Csikszentmihalyi, *Flow: The Psychology of Optimal Experience* (New York: Harper & Row, 1990).

35. Press Release, "Gen Z Says They Are Most Productive When Working Around Noise; Baby Boomers Say "SHHHH!" They Need Quiet to Get Work Done," *PR Newswire*, May 13, 2019, accessed March 25, 2020, https://www.prnewswire.com/news-releases/gen-z-says-they-are-most-productive-when-working-around-noise-baby-boomers-say-shhhh-they-need-quiet-to-get-work-done-300848446.html.

36. R. Feintzeig, "Can Furniture Help Workers Stay Focused?" *Wall Street Journal*, April 22, 2015, B7.

37. R. Silverman, "GE Re-Engineers Performance Reviews, Pay Practices," *Wall Street Journal*, June 8, 2016, accessed April 3, 2017, https://www.wsj.com/articles/ge-re-engineers-perfor-mance-reviews-pay-practices-1465358463.

38. C. Dougherty, "They Promised Us Jet Packs. They Promised the Bosses Profit," *New York Times*, July 23, 2016, accessed April 3, 2017, https://www.nytimes.com/2016/07/24/technology/they-promised-us-jet-packs-they-promised-the-bosses-profit.html?_r=0.

39. A. Teller, "More Moonshot Secrets: Making Audacity the Path of Least Resistance," *Back Channel*, April 15, 2016, accessed April 3, 2017, https://backchannel.com/the-head-of-x-explains-how-to-make-audacity-the-path-of-least-resistance-fac53c3338d.

40. A. Ahrendts, "The Experts: How Should Leaders Spur Innovation?" interview by C. Wiens, March 12, 2013, accessed June 13, 2014, http://online.wsj.com/news/articles/SB10001424127887323826704578352921473825316?mg=reno64-wsj&url=http%3A%2F%2Fonline.wsj.com%2Farticle%2FSB10001424127887323826704578352921473825316.html.

41. L. Collins, "Google X Spin-Off Malta Could Change World, but Lags Behind Rivals," *Recharge*, August 9, 2019, accessed March 26, 2020, https://www.rechargenews.com/transition/google-x-spin-off-malta-could-change-world-but-lags-behind-rivals/2-1-651240.

42. M. Chediak and M. Bergen, "Gates Among Billionaires Backing Alphabet Energy Spinoff," *Bloomberg*, December 19, 2018, accessed March 26, 2020, https://www.bloomberg.com/news/articles/2018-12-19/gates-bezos-among-billionaires-backing-alphabet-energy-spinoff?sref=xXo7CWym.

43. D. Hodari and E. Ballard, "To Store the Wind and Sun, Energy Startups Look to Gravity," *Wall Street Journal*, February 14, 2020, accessed March 26, 2020, https://www.wsj.com/articles/to-store-the-wind-and-sun-energy-startups-look-to-gravity-11581657948.

44. S. Antony, P. Cobban, R. Nair and N. Painchaud, "Breaking Down the Barriers to Innovation," *Harvard Business Review*, November-December 2019, accessed March 26, 2020, https://hbr.org/2019/11/breaking-down-the-barriers-to-innovation.

45. Ibid.

46. K. M. Eisenhardt, "Accelerating Adaptive Processes: Product Innovation in the Global Computer Industry," *Administrative Science Quarterly* 40 (1995): 84–110.

47. Ibid.

48. "Attract and Trap Flying Insects in Your Home With Zevo," Zevo, accessed March 27, 2020, https://zevoinsect.com/pages/flying-insect-traps.

49. T. Kary, "P&G Is Developing Its Next Big Thing in a Room Buzzing With Flies," *Bloomberg*, February 13, 2020, accessed March 27, 2020, https://www.bloomberg.com/news/features/2020-02-13/p-g-is-developing-its-next-big-thing-in-a-room-buzzing-with-flies?sref=xXo7CWym.

50. E. Byron, "Bugs, the New Frontier in Housecleaning," *Wall Street Journal*, July 15, 2017, accessed March 27, 2020, https://www.wsj.com/articles/bugs-the-new-frontier-in-housecleaning-1500116400.

51. A. Davies, "Inside X, the Moonshot Factory Racing to Build the Next Google," *Wired*, July 11, 2018, accessed March 27, 2020, https://www.wired.com/story/alphabet-google-x-innovation-loon-wing-graduation/.

52. Teller, "More Moonshot Secrets: Making Audacity the Path of Least Resistance."

53. M. Gurman and G. De Vynck, "Apple Said to Develop Car Operating System in BlackBerry Country," *Bloomberg*, October 25, 2016, accessed April 4, 2017, https://www.bloomberg.com/news/articles/2016-10-25/apple-develops-car-operating-system-in-blackberry-country; M. Gurman and A. Webb, "How Apple Scaled Back Its Titanic Plan to Take on Detroit," *Bloomberg*, October 17, 2016, accessed April 4, 2017, https://www.bloomberg.com/news/articles/2016-10-17/how-apple-scaled-back-its-titanic-plan-to-take-on-detroit.

54. MacRumors Staff, "Apple Car: It's No Secret, Apple's Actively Working on Car Tech," *MacRumors*, March 10, 2020, accessed March 27, 2020, https://www.macrumors.com/roundup/apple-car/.

55. A. Stoklosa, "Mazda Skyactiv-X Compression-Ignition-Capable Engine Europe-Market Fuel Economy," *Car and Driver*, June 5, 2019, accessed March 27, 2020, https://www.caranddriver.com/news/a27750433/mazda-skyactiv-x-engine-europe-mpg/.

56. R. Truett, "Internal Combustion Engine Keeps Improving as EV Hype Grows,"

57. L. Kraar, "25 Who Help the US Win: Innovators Everywhere are Generating Ideas to Make America a Stronger Competitor. They Range from a Boss Who Demands the Impossible to a Mathematician with a Mop," *Fortune*, March 22, 1991.

58. M. W. Lawless and P. C. Anderson, "Generational Technological Change: Effects of Innovation and Local Rivalry on Performance," *Academy of Management Journal* 39 (1996): 1185–1217.

59. J. Kastrenakes, "Wi-Fi Now Has Version Numbers, and Wi-Fi 6 Comes Out Next Year," *The Verge*, October 3, 2018, accessed March 27, 2020, https://www.theverge.com/2018/10/3/17926212/wifi-6-version-numbers-announced.

60. R. Crist and S. Conaway, "How Fast Is Wi-Fi 6? Here Are Our Latest Speed Test Results," *CNET*, February 23, 2020, accessed March 27, 2020, https://www.cnet.com/news/how-fast-is-wi-fi-6-our-latest-speed-test-results/; J. Kastrenakes, "Wi-Fi 6, explained: how fast it really is," *The Verge*, February 21, 2019, accessed March 27, 2020, https://www.theverge.com/2019/2/21/18232026/wi-fi-6-speed-explained-router-wifi-how-does-work.

61. Apple, Inc., "Form 10-K, 2019," Apple Investor Relations, October 31, 2019, accessed March 27, 2020, https://investor.apple.com/sec-filings/sec-filings-details/default.aspx?FilingId=13709514. A. Satariano, "Apple Gets More Bank for Its R&D Buck," *Bloomberg BusinessWeek*, November 30–December 6, 2015, 38–39.

62. J. Kang, "Food Companies Add AI to Their Recipes," *Wall Street Journal*, October 9, 2019, accessed March 28, 2020, https://www.wsj.com/articles/food-companies-add-ai-to-their-recipes-11570662421?mod=article_inline.

63. C. Doering, "McCormick Turns to Artificial Intelligence to Spice Up Product Development," *Food Dive*, February 5, 2019, accessed March 28, 2020, https://www.fooddive.com/news/mccormick-turns-to-artificial-intelligence-to-spice-up-product-development/547613/.

64. J. Brustein, "Inside RadioShack's Collapse—How Did the Electronics Retailer Go Broke? Gradually, Then All at Once," *Bloomberg Businessweek*, February 9–15, 2015, 56. "Table 13–AT&T Interstate Residential Tariff Rates for 10-Minute Calls," *The Industry Analysis Division's Reference Book of Rates, Price Indices, and Household Expenditures for Telephone Service*, March 1997, Federal Trade Commission, 69, accessed April 25, 2015, http://transition.fcc.gov/Bureaus/Common_Carrier/Reports/FCC-State_Link/IAD/ref97.pdf.

65. Brustein, "Inside RadioShack's Collapse."

66. P. Strebel, "Choosing the Right Change Path," *California Management Review* 36(2) (Winter 1994): 29–51.

67. E. Steel, "Netflix Refines Its DVD Business, Even as Streaming Unit Booms," *New York Times*, July 27, 2015, B1.

68. D. Fitzgeral and M. Jarzemsky, "Besieged RadioShack Spirals into Bankruptcy," *Wall Street Journal*, February 6, 2015, accessed May 4, 2015, http://www.wsj.com/articles/SB2181097287747776469470458044181413975 1730.

69. P. Brickley and D. FitzGerald, "RadioShack Is Dead, Long Live RadioShack," *Wall Street Journal*, April 2, 2015, B1.

70. D. Fitzgerald and R. Knutson, "RadioShack to Seek Bankruptcy Protection, Again," *Wall Street Journal*, March 6, 2017, accessed April 4, 2017, https://www.wsj.com/articles/radioshack-to-seek-bankruptcy-protection-again-1488843485; "Bankruptcy Announcement – RadioShack," General Wireless Operations, March 8, 2017, accessed April 4, 2017, https://www.radioshack.com/pages/bankruptcy-announcement.

71. L. Fickenscher, "RadioShack's Comeback Is Taking Shape," *New York Post*, July 13, 2018, accessed March 28, 2020, https://nypost.com/2018/07/13/radioshacks-comeback-is-taking-shape/.

72. K. Lewin, *Field Theory in Social Science: Selected Theoretical Papers* (New York: Harper & Brothers, 1951).

73. S. Shellenbarger, "Do You Resist New Tech at the Office?" *Wall Street Journal*, June 10, 2019, accessed March 28, 2020, https://www.wsj.com/articles/do-you-resist-new-tech-at-the-office-11560159001?mod=hp_lead_pos8.

74. Lewin, *Field Theory in Social Science*.

75. A. B. Fisher, "Making Change Stick," *Fortune*, April 17, 1995, 121.

76. J. P. Kotter and L. A. Schlesinger, "Choosing Strategies for Change," *Harvard Business Review* (March–April 1979): 106–114.

77. S. Giessner, G. Viki, T. Otten, S. Terry, and D. Tauber, "The Challenge of Merging: Merger Patterns, Premerger Status, and Merger Support," *Personality and Social Psychology Bulletin* 32, no. 3 (2006): 339–352.

78. E. Cassano, "How Vince Donnelly Led PMA Companies Through an Acquisition by Involving Everyone," *Smart Business*, February 1, 2012, accessed March 7, 2012, http://www.sbnonline.com/article/how-vince-donnelly-led-pma-companies-through-an-acquisition-by-involving-everyone/.

79. J. Dean, "Why Digital Transformations Are Hard," *Wall Street Journal*, March 6, 2017, accessed April 4, 2017, https://www.wsj.com/articles/why-digital-transformations-are-hard-1488856200.

80. D. Meinert, "An Open Book," *HR Magazine*, April 2013, 42–46.

81. J. P. Kotter, "Leading Change: Why Transformation Efforts Fail," *Harvard Business Review* 73, no. 2 (March–April 1995): 59.

82. K. Allen, "The Former CEO of DHL Express on Leading the Company Through an Existential Crisis," *Harvard Business Review*, March 28, 2019, accessed February 26, 2020, https://hbr.org/2019/03/the-former-ceo-of-dhl-express-on-leading-the-company-through-an-existential-crisis.

83. "Our History - About Us | Stora Enso," Stora Enso, accessed March 28, 2020, https://www.storaenso.com/en/about-stora-enso/our-history.

84. A. Enders and L. Haggstrom, "How the World's Oldest Company Reinvented Itself," *Harvard Business Review*, January 30, 2019, accessed March 28, 2020, https://hbr.org/2018/01/how-the-worlds-oldest-company-reinvented-itself.

85. M. Galbraith, "Don't Just Tell Employees Organizational Changes Are Coming — Explain Why," *Harvard Business Review*, October 5, 2018, accessed March 28, 2020, https://hbr.org/2018/10/dont-just-tell-employees-organizational-changes-are-coming-explain-why; FMC, "FMC Corporation: 2018 Annual Report," FMC, February 28, 2019, accessed March 28, 2020, https://materials.proxyvote.com/default.aspx?docHostID=385968.

86. "Don't Just Tell Employees Organizational Changes Are Coming — Explain Why."

87. S. Cramm, "A Change of Hearts," *CIO*, April 1, 2003, May 20, 2003, http://www.cio.com/archive/040103/hsleadership.html.

88. K. Safdar, "As Gap Struggles, Its Analytical CEO Prizes Data Over Design," *Wall Street Journal*, November 27, 2016, accessed April 5, 2017, https://www.wsj.com/articles/as-gap-struggles-its-analytical-ceo-prizes-data-over-design-1480282911.

89. S. Baker, "Zara's Recipe for Success: More Data, Fewer Bosses," *Bloomberg*, November 23, 2016, accessed April 5, 2017, https://www.bloomberg.com/news/articles/2016-11-23/zaras-recipe-for-success-more-data-fewer-bosses.

90. D. Rigby, J. Sutherland and H. Takeuchi, "Embracing Agile," *Harvard Business Review*, May 2016, accessed March 29, 2020, https://hbr.org/2016/05/embracing-agile.

91. S. Castellanos, "Campbell Goes Agile, From Soup to Snacks," *Wall Street Journal*, July 8, 2019, accessed March 29, 2020, https://www.wsj.com/articles/campbell-goes-agile-from-soup-to-snacks-11562579556.

92. R. Clough, "General Electric Wants to Act Like a Startup," *BloombergBusinessweek*, August 11, 2014, pp. 22-24.

93. "Embracing Agile."

94. "General Electric Empowers Employees to Act Like Entrepreneurs," *Business Because*, November 24, 2014, accessed April 5, 2017, http://www.businessbecause.com/news/mba-careers/2933/general-electric-empowers-employees-to-act-like-entrepreneurs.

95. B. Power, "How GE Applies Lean Startup Practices," *Harvard Business Review Digital Articles*, April 23, 2014, pp. 2-4.

96. W. J. Rothwell, R. Sullivan, and G. M. McLean, *Practicing Organizational Development: A Guide for Consultants* (San Diego, CA: Pfeiffer & Co., 1995).

97. Ibid.

8

1. D. Barboza, "An iPhone's Journey, From the Factory Floor to the Retail Store," *New York Times*, December 29, 2016, accessed April 6, 2017, https://www.nytimes.com/2016/12/29/technology/iphone-china-apple-stores.html.

2. "Facility Locations," Harley-Davidson, accessed April 3, 2020, https://www.harley-davidson.com/us/en/about-us/careers/locations.html.

3. "About Harley-Davidson | Harley-Davidson USA," Harley-Davidson, accessed April 3, 2020, https://www.harley-davidson.com/us/en/about-us/company.html; "Facility Locations," Harley-Davidson, accessed April 6, 2017, http://www.harley-davidson.com/content/h-d/en_US/company/locations.html.

4. "Harley-Davidson Announces Fourth Quarter, Full-Year 2019 Results," Harley-Davidson, January 28, 2020, accessed April 3, 2020, https://investor.harley-davidson.com/news-releases/news-release-details/harley-davidson-announces-fourth-quarter-full-year-2019-results.

5. "World Investment Report, 2016: Investor Nationality – Policy Challenges," United Nations Conference on Trade and Development, accessed April 6, 2017, http://unctad.org/en/Publications Library/wir2016_en.pdf; "Web Table 34. Number of Parent Corporations and Foreign Affiliates, by Region and Economy," World Investment Report 2011, United Nations Conference on Trade and Development, accessed April 28, 2016, http://unctad.org/Sections/dite_dir/docs/WIR11_web tab 34.pdf.

6. I. Kim and H. Milner, "Multinational Corporations and Their Influence Through Lobbying on Foreign Policy," *Brookings Institute*, December 2, 2019, accessed April 3, 2020, https://www.brookings.edu/wp-content/uploads/2019/12/Kim_Milner _manuscript.pdf

7. S. Chaudhuri and A. Gasparro, "Nestlé Sells Butterfinger and BabyRuth Unit to Italian Candy Maker," *Wall Street Journal*, January 16, 2018, accessed April 3, 2020, https://www.wsj.com /articles/ferrero-purchases-nestles-u-s-chocolate -business-1516125150.

8. M. de la Merced, "Coca-Cola Bets on Coffee with $5.1 Billion Deal for Costa," *New York Times*, August 31, 2018, accessed April 3, 2020, https://www.nytimes.com/2018/08/31/business/dealbook /coca-cola-costa-coffee.html.

9. Ibid.

10. "China – Automotive Industry," US International Trade Administration, July 30, 2019, accessed April 3, 2020, https://www.export.gov/apex /article2?id=China-Automotive-Components -Market.

11. T. Moss, C. Dawson, and W. Mauldin, "Auto Makers Target China as New U.S. Trade Rules Loom," *Wall Street Journal*," March 22, 2017, accessed April 6, 2017, https://www.wsj.com/articles /auto-makers-target-china-as-new-u-s-trade-rules -loom-1490175002.

12. " Global Dynamics: Total Number of Implemented Interventions Since November 2008," Global Trade Alert, accessed April 3, 2020, https://www.globaltradealert.org/global_dynamics/day -to_0403/flow_all.

13. J. Zumbrun, "US Consumers Hit Hardest by Trade Tariffs, Studies Find," *Wall Street Journal*, March 5, 2019, accessed April 3, 2020, https://www .wsj.com/articles/u-s-consumers-hit-hardest-by -trade-tariffs-studies-find-11551820951.

14. J. Tankersley, "Trump's Washing Machine Tariffs Stung Consumers While Lifting Corporate Profits," *New York Times*, April 21, 2019, accessed April 3, 2020, https://www.nytimes.com/2019/04/21 /business/trump-tariffs-washing-machines.html.

15. K. Jun & W. Mauldin, "Quotas Make a Comeback as Countries Seek U.S. Tariff Exemptions," *Wall Street Journal*, May 11, 2018, accessed April 4, 2020, https://www.wsj.com/articles/quotas -make-a-comeback-as-countries-seek-u-s-tariff -exemptions-1526031000.

16. P. Lei and M. Martina, "Hollywood's China Dreams Get Tangled in Trade Talks," *Reuters*, May 19, 2018, accessed April 4, 2020, https://www .reuters.com/article/us-usa-trade-china-movies /hollywoods-china-dreams-get-tangled-in-trade -talks-idUSKCN1IK0W0; L. Lin and E. Schwartzel, "China Lets More Foreign Films Slip In," *Wall Street Journal*, November 2, 2016, accessed April 6, 2017, https://www.wsj.com/articles/china-lets -more-foreign-films-slip-in-1478083587; B. Fritz and L. Burkitt, "Chinese Film Company Takes Role in Hollywood," *Wall Street Journal*, April 20, 2015, B1.

17. Reuters, "Mexico Bows to Brazilian Pressure on Auto Exports," *Reuters*, March 15, 2012, accessed June 8, 2013, http://www.reuters .com/article/2012/03/16/mexico-brazil-autos -idUSL2E8EF3G420120316.

18. "Understanding the WTO," World Trade Organization, accessed April 28, 2016, http://www.wto .org/english/thewto_e/whatis_e/tif_e/agrm9_e.htm.

19. C. Tate, "Dispute over Europe's Ban on US Beef Could Mean Tariffs on Imports," *McClatchy DC*, December 22, 2016, accessed April 6, 2017, http://www.mcclatchydc.com/news/nation-world /national/economy/article122427524.html.

20. A. Alper & S. Holland, "Trump, EU Officials Announce Deal to Sell More American Beef to Europe," *Reuters*, August 2, 2019, accessed April 4, 2020, https://www.reuters.com/article/us-usa-trade -europe/trump-eu-officials-announce-deal-to-sell -more-american-beef-to-europe-idUSKCN1US1A3.

21. R. Wall & D. Cameron, "EU Failed to Cut Off Illegal Subsidies to Airbus, WTO Rules," *Wall Street Journal*, September 22, 2016, accessed April 6, 2017, https://www.wsj.com/articles/eu -gave-billions-in-illegal-subsidies-to-airbus-wto -rules-1474554683.

22. Ibid.

23. "EU Rapped by WTO for $10bn a Year Airbus Subsidies," BBC News, September 22, 2016, accessed April 6, 2017, http://www.bbc.com/news /business-37444780.

24. A. Swanson, "US to Tax European Aircraft, Agriculture and Other Goods," *New York Times*, October 2, 2019, accessed April 4, 2020, https://www.nytimes.com/2019/10/02/us/politics/airbus -tariffs-wto.html.

25. "Santa Suit Items Excluded from Tariff Classification," KPMG United States, April 29, 2019, accessed April 4, 2020, https://home.kpmg /us/en/home/insights/2019/04/tnf-federal-circuit -santa-suit-items-excluded-from-tariff-classification -as-festive-articles.html; T. Shields, "'Costumes or Clothes?' H.R. 3128 Department of Homeland Security Appropriations, 2016," *Bloomberg Businessweek*, October 19–25, 2015, 35.

26. "GATT/WTO," Duke Law: Library & Technology, June 2014, accessed April 7, 2017, https://law .duke.edu/lib/researchguides/gatt/.

27. "Third Anniversary of Trade Facilitation Agreement Sees Increasing Implementation Rate," World Trade Organization, February 22, 2020, accessed April 4, 2020, https://www.wto.org/english /news_e/news20_e/fac_22feb20_e.htm; R. Azevêdo, "WTO Press Conference — Entry into Force of Trade Facilitation Agreement," World Trade Organization, February 27, 2017, accessed April 7, 2017, https://www.wto.org/english/news_e/spra_e /spra157_e.htm.

28. "Music Listening 2019," International Federation of the Phonographic Industry, September 24, 2019, accessed April 4, 2020, https://www.ifpi.org /downloads/Music-Listening-2019.pdf.

29. "Software Management: Security Imperative, Business Opportunity: 2018 BSA Global Software Survey," BSA The Software Alliance, June 5, 2018, accessed April 4, 2020, https://gss.bsa.org/.

30. D. Blackburn, J. Eisenach & D. Harrison, "Impacts of Digital Video Piracy on the U.S. Economy," US Chamber of Commerce Global innovation Policy Center, June 2019, accessed April 4, 2020, https://www.theglobalipcenter.com/wp-content /uploads/2019/06/Digital-Video-Piracy.pdf.

31. T. Kika, "Piracy Crackdown: FBI Shut Down Two Massive Illegal Film and TV Streaming Sites," *International Business Times*, December 16, 2019, accessed April 4, 2020, https://www.ibtimes.com /piracy-crackdown-fbi-shut-down-two-massive -illegal-film-tv-streaming-sites-2886525.

32. "Dispute Settlement – Appellate Body," World Trade Organization, accessed April 4, 2020, https://www.wto.org/english/tratop_e/dispu_e /appellate_body_e.htm.

33. A. Gale & E. Peker, "Japan, EU Sign Trade Deal: 'We Stand Together Against Protectionism,'" *Wall Street Journal*, July 17, 2018, accessed April 4, 2020, https://www.wsj.com/articles/japan-european -union-sign-major-trade-deal-1531826380; I. Reynolds, J. Jacobs & J. Wingrove, "Trump-Abe Trade Deal Helps U.S. Farmers, Staves Off Auto Tariffs," *Bloomberg*, August 25, 2019, accessed April 4, 2020, https://www.bloomberg.com/news /articles/2019-08-25/trump-says-very-close-to-japan -trade-deal-before-abe-meeting?sref=xXo7CWym.

34. "What Is the Euro Area?" European Commission, accessed April 4, 2020, https://ec.europa.eu /info/business-economy-euro/euro-area/what-euro -area_en#whos-already-in.

35. L. Hughes, K. McCann and G. Rayner, "Theresa May Triggers Article 50 with Warning over Security as EU Leaders Rule Out Key Brexit Demand," *Telegraph*, March 30, 2017, accessed April 7, 2017, http://www.telegraph.co.uk /news/2017/03/29/article-50-triggered-brexit-eu -theresa-may-watch-live/.

36. No Author, "Brexit: All you need to know about the UK leaving the EU," *BBC News*, February 17, 2020, accessed April 4, 2020, https://www .bbc.com/news//uk-politics-32810887.

37. M. Villarreal & I. Fergusson, "NAFTA and the United States-Mexico-Canada Agreement (USMCA)," Congressional Research Service, March 2, 2020, accessed April 4, 2020, https://fas .org/sgp/crs/row/R44981.pdf.

38. M. Villarreal & I. Ferguson, "The North American Free Trade Agreement (NAFTA)," Congressional Research Service, February 22, 2017, accessed April 7, 2017, https://fas.org/sgp/crs/row /R42965.pdf.

39. T. Budd, "Got Trade? Dairy Farmers Stand to Gain From the USMCA," *Wall Street Journal*, December 13, 2019, accessed April 5, 2020, https://www.wsj.com/articles/got-trade-dairy-farmers -stand-to-gain-from-the-usmca-11576276775; A. Swanson & J. Tankersley, "What Is the USMCA? Here's What's in the New NAFTA," *New York Times*, January 29, 2020, accessed April 5, 2020, https://www.nytimes.com/2020/01/29/business /economy/usmca-deal.html.

40. "CAFTA-DR (Dominican Republic-Central America FTA)," United States Trade Representative, accessed April 5, 2020, https://ustr.gov/trade -agreements/free-trade-agreements/cafta-dr -dominican-republic-central-america-fta; "Trade in Goods with CAFTA-DR," U.S. Census Bureau, accessed April 5, 2020, https://www.census.gov /foreign-trade/balance/c0017.html; "Population by Country (2020)," Worldometer, accessed April 5, 2020, https://www.worldometers.info/world -population/population-by-country/.

41. No Author, "Uruguay Abandons Unasur and Rejoins the TIAR Reciprocal Assistance Treaty," *MercoPress*, March 11, 2020, accessed April 5, 2020, https://en.mercopress.com/2020/03/11 /uruguay-abandons-unasur-and-rejoins-the-tiar-reciprocal -assistance-treaty; "La Región en Cifras: UNASUR: Espacio de Cooperación e Integración para al Desarrollo," accessed April 28, 2016, http://unasursg. org/; "Union of South American Nations – Wikipedia," *Wikipedia*, April 5, 2017, accessed April 7, 2017, https://en.wikipedia.org/wiki/Union _of_South_American_Nations.

42. C. Felter, D. Renwick and A. Chatzky, "Mercosur: South America's Fractious Trade Bloc," Council on Foreign Relations, July 10, 2019, ac-

cessed April 5, 2020, https://www.cfr.org/backgrounder/mercosur-south-americas-fractious-trade-bloc;

43. "MERCOSUR – Official website," MERCOSUR, accessed April 5, 2020, https://www.mercosur.int/en/; "Mercosur: South America's Fractious Trade Bloc."

44. "ASEAN Member States: Selected Basic Indicators, 2018," AseanStats, accessed April 5, 2020, https://cdn.aseanstats.org/public/data/statics/table1.xls; "Almost $100 Billion of US Goods and Services Exports Go to ASEAN," US-ASEAN, September 16, 2016, accessed April 7, 2017, https://www.usasean.org/why-asean/trade.

45. "Almost $100 Billion of US Goods and Services Exports Go to ASEAN," US-ASEAN, accessed April 7, 2017, https://www.usasean.org/why-asean/trade; "ASEAN 2025 – Forging Ahead Together," US-ASEAN, November 2015, accessed April 28, 2016, https://asean.org/?static_post=asean-2025-forging-ahead-together

46. "Trade Raises Living Standards in APEC Region: Report," Asia-Pacific Economic Cooperation, accessed April 7, 2017, http://www.apec.org/Press/News-Releases/2016/0331_development.aspx; "StatsAPEC – Data for the Asia-Pacific Region – Economic and Social Statistics & Bilateral Trade and Investment Flows," StatsAPEC, accessed April 5, 2020, http://statistics.apec.org/index.php/apec_psu/index.

47. "Member Economies," Asia Pacific Economic Cooperation, accessed August 6, 2008, http://www.apec.org/About-Us/About-APEC/Member-Economies.aspx; "Frequently Asked Questions (FAQs)," Asia-Pacific Economic Cooperation, accessed August 6, 2008, http://www.apec.org/FAQ.aspx.

48. "The Institutional Arrangements of the Tripartite Free Trade Area," Tralac Trade Law Centre, September 13, 2019, accessed April 5, 2020, https://www.tralac.org/blog/article/14248-the-institutional-arrangements-of-the-tripartite-free-trade-area.html; "African integration: Facing up to Emerging Challenges," Tralac Trade Law Centre, January 9, 2017, accessed April 8, 2017, https://www.tralac.org/news/article/11045-african-integration-facing-up-to-emerging-challenges.html; C. Ligami, "East African Countries to Ratify TFTA Agreement before March," The East African, December 20, 2016, accessed April 8, 2017, http://www.theeastafrican.co.ke/business/East-African-countries-to-ratify-TFTA-agreement-before-March/2560-3493016-as7c5xz/index.html.

49. M. Xuequan, "SADC-EAC-COMESA Tripartite Free Trade Area Legal Texts and Policy Documents," Tralac Trade Law Centre, accessed April 5, 2020, https://www.tralac.org/resources/by-region/comesa-eac-sadc-tripartite-fta.html.

50. "GNI per capita, Atlas method (Current US$) | Data," The World Bank, accessed April 5, 2020, https://data.worldbank.org/indicator/NY.GNP.PCAP.CD; "GNI per capita, PPP (Current International $) | Data," The World Bank, accessed April 5, 2020, https://data.worldbank.org/indicator/NY.GNP.PCAP.PP.CD.

51. Ibid.

52. Ibid.

53. "The Global Competitiveness Report: 2019," World Economic Forum, accessed April 5, 2020, http://www3.weforum.org/docs/WEF_TheGlobalCompetitivenessReport2019.pdf.

54. Q. Bui and K. Russell, "How Much Will the Trade War Cost You by the End of the Year?" New York Times, September 1, 2019, accessed April 5, 2020, https://www.nytimes.com/interactive/2019/business/economy/trade-war-costs.html; J. Zumbrun, "US Collected $63 Billion in Tariffs Through June," Wall Street Journal, August 7, 2019, accessed April 5, 2020, https://www.wsj.com/articles/u-s-collects-63-billion-in-chinese-tariffs-through-june-11565168400.

55. G. Hufbauer and Z. Lu, "The Payoff to America from Globalization: A Fresh Look with a Focus on Costs to Workers," Peterson Institute for International Economics, May 2017, accessed April 5, 2020, https://www.piie.com/publications/policy-briefs/payoff-america-globalization-fresh-look-focus-costs-workers; "The Benefits of International Trade," U.S. Chamber of Commerce, accessed April 5, 2020, https://www.uschamber.com/international/international-policy/benefits-international-trade. J. Furman, "Ten Facts about U.S. Trade," The White House, May 1, 2015, accessed April 8, 2017, https://obamawhitehouse.archives.gov/blog/2015/05/01/ten-facts-about-us-trade; B. Lomborg, "The Free-Trade Miracle," Project Syndicate, October 21, 2016, accessed April 8, 2017, https://www.project-syndicate.org/commentary/free-trade-benefits-for-global-poor-by-bjorn-lomborg-2016-10.

56. J. Boak and E. Swanson, "AP-GfK Poll: Americans Prefer Low Prices to Items 'Made in the USA,'" Associated Press GfK Poll, April 14, 2016, accessed April 8, 2017, http://ap-gfkpoll.com/featured/ap-gfk-poll-americans-prefer-low-prices-to-items-made-in-the-usa.

57. L. Saad, "Americans' Vanishing Fear of Foreign Trade," Gallup, February 26, 2020, accessed April 6, 2020, https://news.gallup.com/poll/286730/americans-vanishing-fear-foreign-trade.aspx.

58. A. Percival, "Love Island Is Taking over the World – See How The UK Show Is Being Replicated Across the Globe," HuffPost UK, June 16, 2019, accessed April 6, 2020, https://www.huffingtonpost.co.uk/entry/love-island-global-international-versions.

59. L. Abend, "'Love Island' in the Land of Gender Equality," New York Times, November 6, 2018, accessed April 6, 2020, https://www.nytimes.com/2018/11/06/arts/television/love-island-denmark-sweden-norway-finland.html.

60. S. Ramachandran, "Netflix, Amazon Take Divergent Paths to Reach Indian Audience," Wall Street Journal, November 1, 2016, accessed April 8, 2017, https://www.wsj.com/articles/netflix-amazon-take-divergent-paths-to-reach-indian-audience-1477954726.

61. P. Arora, "In 2019, Netflix and Amazon Set Their Sights on India," New York Times, December 30, 2019, accessed April 6, 2020, https://www.nytimes.com/2019/12/30/arts/television/indian-tv-amazon-netflix.html.

62. S. Pearson & S. Nassauer, "Wal-Mart Doubles Down in Brazil Despite Sluggish Sales," Wall Street Journal, March 12, 2017, accessed April 8, 2017, WSJ, https://www.wsj.com/articles/wal-mart-doubles-down-in-brazil-despite-sluggish-sales-1489327201.

63. C. Mandl, "Walmart Brand to Be Dropped from Supermarkets in Brazil," Reuters, August 12, 2019, accessed April 6, 2020, https://www.reuters.com/article/us-walmart-brazil-advent/walmart-brand-to-be-dropped-from-supermarkets-in-brazil-idUSKCN1V214H.

64. I. Lunden, "Walmart Sells 80% of Its Brazilian Operation to Advent Intl, Will Record $4.5B Loss as a Result," TechCrunch, June 4, 2018, accessed April 6, 2020, https://techcrunch.com/2018/06/04/walmart-brazil-advent/.

65. A. Sundaram and J. S. Black, "The Environment and Internal Organization of Multinational Enterprises," Academy of Management Review 17 (1992): 729–757.

66. J. Wheeler, "McDonald's Fries Around the World," Chowhound, April 1, 2019, accessed April 6, 2020, https://www.chowhound.com/food-news/223736/mcdonalds-fries-around-the-world/.

67. T. Grove, "In Russia, McDonald's Serves Local Fries and a Side of Realpolitik," Wall Street Journal, November 8, 2018, accessed April 6, 2020, https://www.wsj.com/articles/in-russia-mcdonalds-serves-local-fries-and-a-side-of-realpolitik-1541678402?reflink=djem_BrexitBeyond.

68. H. S. James Jr. and M. Weidenbaum, When Businesses Cross International Borders: Strategic Alliances & Their Alternatives (Westport, CT: Praeger Publishers, 1993).

69. "Record Production Year for BMW Manufacturing: South Carolina Plant Produces 411,620 Units in 2019," BMW Group Plant Spartanburg, January 15, 2020, accessed April 6, 2020, https://www.bmwgroup-plants.com/spartanburg/en/news/2020/record-production-year-for-bmw-manufacturing.html#sectioncontainer_sectionparsys_layoutcontainer_layoutcontainercontent_nachricht.

70. "Welcome to BMW Group Plant Spartanburg," BMW Group Plant Spartanburg, accessed April 6, 2020, https://www.bmwgroup-plants.com/spartanburg/en.html.

71. No Author, "Kilcoy's Airfreight Beef Charter to China Keeps Product Moving During Difficult Times," Beef Central, March 2, 2020, accessed April 6, 2020, https://www.beefcentral.com/trade/kilcoys-airfreight-beef-charter-to-china-keeps-product-moving-during-difficult-times/; A. Whitley, "Giving a New Meaning to Cattle Class," Bloomberg Businessweek, November 23–29, 2015, 24–25.

72. M. Maidenberg, "Hasbro Picks Up Peppa Pig in $4 Billion Deal," Wall Street Journal, August 22, 2019, accessed April 7, 2020, https://www.wsj.com/articles/hasbro-picks-up-peppa-pig-in-4-billion-deal-11566510461.

73. T. McLean, "eOne Expands 'Peppa Pig' Licensing in U.S., Canada," Animation World Network, January 4, 2018, accessed April 6, 2020, https://www.awn.com/news/eone-expands-peppa-pig-licensing-us-canada.

74. K. Chu and M. Fujikawa, "Burberry Gets Grip on Brand in Japan," Wall Street Journal, August 15–16, 2015, B4.

75. "#1 on the Franchise 500: How McDonald's Evolved with Its Customer," Entrepreneur.com, January 15, 2019, accessed April 7, 2020, https://www.entrepreneur.com/article/325691; "Buying a Franchise," McDonald's.com, accessed April 7, 2020, https://www.mcdonalds.com/us/en-us/about-us/franchising/acquiring-franchising.html.

76. B. Gruley and L. Patton, "McRevolt: The Frustrating Life of the McDonald's Franchisee—Not Lovin' it," Bloomberg BusinessWeek, September 16, 2015, accessed April 28, 2016, http://www.bloomberg.com/features/2015-mcdonalds-franchises/.

77. C. Abrams, "McDonald's Buys Out Rogue Licensee in India," Wall Street Journal, May 9, 2019, accessed April 7, 2020, https://www.wsj.com/articles/mcdonalds-buys-out-rogue-licensee-in-india-11557418978?mod=djemCFO.

78. L. Stampler, "16 Bizarre Fast Food Items That Should Have Never Been," Time, March 25, 2015, accessed April 9, 2017, http://time.com/3752903/ridiculous-fast-food-items/; People Staff, "The Weirdest International Fast Foods," People, December 8, 2016, accessed April 9, 2017, http://people.com/food/weirdest-international-fast-foods/black-burger/.

79. S. Shead, "Airbnb China President Says Localization Is Key for Success," CNBC, November 19, 2019, accessed April 7, 2020,

https://www.cnbc.com/2019/11/19/airbnb-china-president-localization-abiyang.html.

80. S. Nassauer and M. Negishi, "Wal-Mart Has a New Ally in Fight with Amazon: Japan's Rakuten," *Wall Street Journal*, January 26, 2018, accessed April 7, 2020, https://www.wsj.com/articles/wal-mart-has-a-new-ally-in-fight-with-amazon-japans-rakuten-1516930260.

81. E. Fung, "U.S. Mall Developers Face Hurdles in China," *Wall Street Journal*, January 3, 2017, accessed April 9, 2017, https://www.wsj.com/articles/u-s-mall-developers-face-hurdles-in-china-1483459559.

82. J. Hagerty, "In Alabama, Chinese Firm Struggles to Fit In," *Wall Street Journal*, February 29, 2016, B1.

83. O. Sachgau & K. Naughton, "Ford Will Close Six European Plants as Part of Global Downsizing," *Bloomberg*, June 27, 2019, accessed April 7, 2020, https://www.bloomberg.com/news/articles/2019-06-27/ford-to-eliminate-20-of-european-workforce-in-sweeping-overhaul?sref=xXo7CWym.

84. Ibid.

85. W. Hordes, J. A. Clancy, and J. Baddaley, "A Primer for Global Start-Ups," *Academy of Management Executive*, May 1995, 7–11.

86. P. Dimitratos, J. Johnson, J. Slow, and S. Young, "Micromultinationals: New Types of Firms for the Global Competitive Landscape," *European Management Journal* 21, no. 2 (April 2003): 164; B. M. Oviatt and P. P. McDougall, "Toward a Theory of International New Ventures," *Journal of International Business Studies*, Spring 1994, 45–64; S. Zahra, "A Theory of International New Ventures: A Decade of Research," *Journal of International Business Studies*, January 2005, 20–28.

87. "Stripe: Countries – Find Stripe in Your Country," Stripe, accessed April 7, 2020, https://stripe.com/global.

88. E. Huet, "Globalization Helped Make Stripe a $23 Billion Company. Here's What Comes Next," *Bloomberg*, February 6, 2019, accessed April 7, 2020, https://www.bloomberg.com/news/articles/2019-02-06/globalization-helped-make-stripe-a-23-billion-company-here-s-what-comes-next?sref=xXo7CWym.

89. S. Binsted, "Finder's Starbucks Index 2019 – Finder US, September 30, 2019, accessed April 7, 2020, https://www.finder.com/starbucks-index.

90. S. Pham, "China's Car Sales Fell 8% in 2019 and the Slump Is Entering Its Third Year," *CNN*, January 13, 2020, accessed April 8, 2020, https://www.cnn.com/2020/01/13/business/china-car-sales/index.html.

91. J. Qian, "Forget Love: In China, I'll Marry You for Your License Plate," *Wall Street Journal*, March 20, 2017, accessed April 9, 2017, https://www.wsj.com/articles/forget-love-in-china-ill-marry-you-for-your-license-plate-1490001303; "New PC Registrations or Sales," The International Organization of Motor Vehicle Manufacturers, accessed April 9, 2017, www.oica.net/wp-content/uploads//pc-sales-2016.pdf; "Global Sector Report: Automotive," Euler Hermes Economic Research, February 2017, accessed April 9, 2017, www.eulerhermes.com/economic-research/blog/EconomicPublications/automotive-global-sector-report-feb17.pdf.

92. L. Sanchez, "Why Starbucks Is Betting Big on China," *The Motley Fool*, April 10, 2019, accessed April 8, 2020, https://www.fool.com/investing/2019/02/08/why-starbucks-is-betting-big-on-china.aspx.

93. A. Chen, "How Can Coke Coffee Gain Ground in China?" *EqualOcean*, May 5, 2019, accessed April 8, 2020, https://equalocean.com/retail/20190505-how-can-coke-coffee-gain-ground-in-china.

94. L. Craymer, "China's Changing Tastes Offer Upside for Coffee," *Wall Street Journal*, September 6, 2015, accessed April 28, 2016, http://www.wsj.com/articles/chinas-changing-tastes-offer-upside-for-coffee-1442431980; D. Harashima, "China's Coffee Market: Cafe Competition Perks Up Amid Slowdown," *Nikkei Asian Review*, October 31, 2015, accessed April 28, 2016, http://asia.nikkei.com/Business/Trends/Cafe-competition-perks-up-amid-slowdown.

95. J. Arlidge, "How Singapore sucked in James Dyson," *The Sunday Times*, January 27, 2019, accessed April 8, 2020, https://www.thetimes.co.uk/article/how-singapore-sucked-in-james-dyson-kwdtjzfpw.

96. Ibid.

97. "Table II.1. Statutory Corporate Income Tax Rate," Organisation for Economic Co-operation and Development (OECD), April 8, 2020, accessed April 8, 2020, https://stats.oecd.org/index.aspx?DataSetCode=Table_II1.

98. "Special Eurobarometer 386: Europeans and Their Languages," European Commission, June 2012, accessed April 28, 2016, http://ec.europa.eu/public_opinion/archives/ebs/ebs_386_en.pdf.

99. "IMD World Talent Ranking 2019," *IMD Institute for Management Development*, November 2019, accessed April 8, 2020, https://www.imd.org/globalassets/wcc/docs/release-2019/talent/imd_world_talent_ranking.pdf.

100. C. Passariello and S. Kapner, "Search for Cheaper Labor Leads to Africa," Wall Street Journal, July 13, 2015, B1.

101. S. Adams, "2015's Most and Least Reliable Countries to Do Business In," *Forbes*, March 31, 2015, accessed April 28, 2016, http://www.forbes.com/sites/susanadams/2015/03/31/2015s-most-and-least-reliable-countries-to-do-business-in/; "Resilience Index," FM Global, http://www.fmglobal.com/assets/pdf/Resilience_Methodology.pdf.

102. J. Oetzel, R. Bettis, and M. Zenner, "How Risky Are They?" *Journal of World Business* 36, no. 2 (Summer 2001): 128–145.

103. K. D. Miller, "A Framework for Integrated Risk Management in International Business," *Journal of International Business Studies*, 2nd Quarter 1992, 311.

104. C. Abrams, "Products Yanked from Amazon in India to Comply with New E-Commerce Rules," *Wall Street Journal*, February 1, 2019, accessed April 8, 2020, https://www.wsj.com/articles/products-yanked-from-amazon-in-india-to-comply-with-new-e-commerce-rules-11549046283; N. Purnell, "U.S. Tech Giants Bet Big on India. Now It's Changing the Rules," *Wall Street Journal*, December 3, 2019, accessed April 8, 2020, https://www.wsj.com/articles/u-s-tech-giants-bet-big-on-india-now-the-rules-are-changing-11575386675?mod=hp_lead_pos5.

105. A. Kotoky, R. Singh & D. Chakraborty, "Billionaire Adani Woos Amazon, Google With Indian Data Hubs," *Bloomberg*, July 10, 2019, accessed April 8, 2020, https://www.bloomberg.com/news/articles/2019-07-10/coal-billionaire-adani-woos-amazon-google-with-indian-data-hubs?sref=xXo7CWym.

106. "U.S. Tech Giants Bet Big on India. Now It's Changing the Rules."

107. "BMI Research: United Arab Emirates Country Risk Report, 2020 Q1, Issue 1," *Fitch Solutions*, accessed April 9, 2020; "BMI Research: Israel Country Risk Report, 2020 Q1, Issue 1," *Fitch Solutions*, accessed April 9, 2020.

108. J. Zumbrun, A. DeBarros & C. Day, "At 10,000 and Counting, This Company Is Flooding

the U.S. with Tariff Appeals," *Wall Street Journal*, September 22, 2019, accessed April 9, 2020, https://www.wsj.com/articles/at-10-000-and-counting-this-company-is-flooding-the-u-s-with-tariff-appeals-11569144600.

109. Ibid.

110. C. Alessi, "India Invests in Germany's Family Firms," *Wall Street Journal*, April 11–12, 2015, B4.

111. G. Hofstede, "The Cultural Relativity of the Quality of Life Concept," *Academy of Management Review* 9 (1984): 389–398; G. Hofstede, "The Cultural Relativity of Organizational Practices and Theories," *Journal of International Business Studies*, Fall 1983, 75–89; G. Hofstede, "The Interaction Between National and Organizational Value Systems," *Journal of Management Studies*, July 1985, 347–357; M. Hoppe, "An Interview with Geert Hofstede," *Academy of Management Executive*, February 2004, 75–79.

112. Alessi, "India Invests in Germany's Family Firms."

113. Ibid.

114. Ibid.

115. R. Hodgetts, "A Conversation with Geert Hofstede," *Organizational Dynamics*, Spring 1993, 53–61.

116. T. Lenartowicz and K. Roth, "Does Subculture within a Country Matter? A Cross-Cultural Study of Motivational Domains and Business Performance in Brazil," *Journal of International Business Studies* 32 (2001): 305–325.

117. K. Lahrichi, "An Expat's Guide to the Latin American Concept of Time," *Wall Street Journal*, September 26, 2016, accessed April 10, 2017, http://blogs.wsj.com/expat/2016/09/06/an-expats-guide-to-the-latin-american-concept-of-time.

118. Ibid.

119. Ibid.

120. J. S. Black, M. Mendenhall, and G. Oddou, "Toward a Comprehensive Model of International Adjustment: An Integration of Multiple Theoretical Perspectives," *Academy of Management Review* 16 (1991): 291–317; R. L. Tung, "American Expatriates Abroad: From Neophytes to Cosmopolitans," *Columbia Journal of World Business*, June 22, 1998, 125; A. Harzing, "The Persistent Myth of High Expatriate Failure Rates," *International Journal of Human Resource Management* 6 (1995): 457–475; A. Harzing, "Are Our Referencing Errors Undermining Our Scholarship and Credibility? The Case of Expatriate Failure Rates," *Journal of Organizational Behavior* 23 (2002): 127–148; N. Forster, "The Persistent Myth of High Expatriate Fai lure Rates: A Reappraisal," *International Journal of Human Resource Management* 8 (1997): 414–433.

121. J. Black, "The Right Way to Manage Expats," *Harvard Business Review* 77 (March–April 1999): 52; C. Joinson, "No Returns," *HR Magazine*, November 1, 2002, 70.

122. "International Assignment Perspectives: Critical Issues Facing the Globally Mobile Workforce," *PricewaterhouseCoopers*, Vol. 5, November 2011, accessed June 13, 2014, http://www.pwc.com/en_US/us/hr-international-assignment-services/publications/assets/ny-12-0258_ias_journal_volume_5_new_images.pdf.

123. R. Feintzeig, "After Stints Abroad, Re-Entry Can Be Hard," *Wall Street Journal*, September 17, 2013, accessed June 14, 2014, http://online.wsj.com/news/articles/SB10001424127887323342404579081382781895274?KEYWORDS=after+stints+abroad&mg=reno64-wsj.

124. S. Banjo, "It's Becoming Harder to Use Cash in China: Fully Charged," *Bloomberg reprinted in The Economic Times*, February 13, 2018, accessed

April 9, 2020, https://economictimes.indiatimes
.com/news/international/business/its-becoming
-harder-to-use-cash-in-china-fully-charged
/articleshow/62902490.cms.

125. M. Russon, "Beggars in China Now Accepting Donations via Mobile Payments and QR Codes," *International Business Times*, April 24, 2017, accessed April 9, 2020, https://www.ibtimes .co.uk/beggars-china-now-accepting-donations-via -mobile-payments-qr-codes-1618396.

126. J. S. Black and M. Mendenhall, "Cross-Cultural Training Effectiveness: A Review and Theoretical Framework for Future Research," *Academy of Management Review* 15 (1990): 113–136.

127. K. Essick, "Executive Education: Transferees Prep for Life, Work in Far-Flung Lands," *Wall Street Journal*, November 12, 2004, A6.

128. Ibid.

129. E. Meyer, "When Culture Doesn't Translate," *Harvard Business Review*, October 2015, accessed April 10, 2017, https://hbr.org/2015/10 /when-culture-doesnt-translate.

130. S. Hamm, "Aperian: Helping Companies Bridge Cultures," *BusinessWeek*, September 8, 2008, 16.

131. W. Arthur, Jr. and W. Bennett, Jr., "The International Assignee: The Relative Importance of Factors Perceived to Contribute to Success," *Personnel Psychology* 48 (1995): 99–114; B. Cheng, "Home Truths About Foreign Postings; To Make an Overseas Assignment Work, Employers Need More Than an Eager Exec with a Suitcase. They Must Also Motivate the Staffer's Spouse," *BusinessWeek Online*, accessed March 20, 2009, http://www .businessweek.com/careers/content/jul2002 /ca20020715_9110.htm.

132. B. Groysberg and R. Abrahams, "A Successful International Assignment Depends on These Factors," *Harvard Business Review* (blog), February 13, 2014, 10:00, accessed June 15, 2014, http://blogs .hbr.org/2014/02/a-successful-international -assignment-depends-on-these-factors/.

133. "OAI: Overseas Assignment Inventory," *Prudential Real Estate and Relocation Services Intercultural Group*, accessed April 10, 2017, http:// www.performance programs.com/self-assessments/ work-across-cultures/overseas-assignment-inventory/.

134. S. P. Deshpande and C. Viswesvaran, "Is Cross-Cultural Training of Expatriate Managers Effective? A Meta-Analysis," *International Journal of Intercultural Relations* 16, no. 3 (1992): 295–310.

135. D. M. Eschbach, G. Parker, and P. Stoeberl, "American Repatriate Employees' Retrospective Assessments of the Effects of Cross-Cultural Training on Their Adaptation to International Assignments," *International Journal of Human Resource Management* 12 (2001): 270–287; "Culture Training: How to Prepare Your Expatriate Employees for Cross-Cultural Work Environments," *Managing Training & Development*, February 1, 2005.

136. I. Driscoll, "You Love Going Abroad for Work. Your Spouse Hates It." *BBC*, November 11, 2014, accessed May 5, 2015, http://www.bbc.com /capital/story/20141110-the-reluctant-expat-spouse.

137. Ibid.

9

1. T. Shumsky, "ABB Bets Simplified Structure Will Cut Costs, Boost Profit," *Wall Street Journal*, January 9, 2019, accessed April 12, 2020, https:// www.wsj.com/articles/abb-bets-simplified-structure -will-cut-costs-boost-profit-11547075162.

2. "Our Businesses - ABB Group," ABB, accessed April 12, 2020, https://new.abb.com/about/our-businesses;

"ABB Fact Sheets," ABB Group, February 2020 update, accessed April 12, 2020, https://new.abb. com/docs/default-source/investor center-docs/abb-fact-sheets.pdf.

3. Shumsky, "ABB Bets Simplified Structure Will Cut Costs, Boost Profit."

4. M. Hammer and J. Champy, *Reengineering the Corporation: A Manifesto for Business Revolution* (New York: Harper & Row, 1993).

5. "Windows Insider Program | Get the Latest Windows Features," Microsoft, accessed April 13, 2020, https://insider.windows.com/en-us/.

6. "Good Feedback Makes Windows Better | Windows 10 Insider Previews," Microsoft, accessed April 13, 2020, https://insider.windows.com/en-us /how-to-feedback/#submit-feedback-on-behalf-of -your-organization.

7. "Microsoft by the Numbers," Microsoft, accessed April 13, 2020, https://news.microsoft.com /bythenumbers/en/windowsdevices; E. Bott, "It's 2020: How many PCs are still running Windows 7?" *ZDNet*, January 7, 2020, accessed April 13, 2020, https://www.zdnet.com/article/how-many-pcs-are -still-running-windows-7-today/.

8. D. Halfin, "Windows Insider Program for Business Frequently Asked Questions," Microsoft, April 7, 2017, accessed April 11, 2017, https:// technet.microsoft.com/en-us/itpro/windows/update /waas-windows-insider-for-business-faq; A. Patrizio, "Microsoft's Windows Insider Program Surpasses 10 Million Users," *Network World*, March 28, 2017, accessed April 11, 2017, http://www.networkworld. com/article/3185461/windows/windows-insider -program-surpasses-10-million-users.html.

9. J. G. March and H. A. Simon, *Organizations* (New York: John Wiley & Sons, 1958).

10. A. Prang, "Pfizer to Reorganize Business Units," *Wall Street Journal*, July 11, 2018, accessed April 13, 2020, https://www.wsj.com /articles/pfizer-to-reorganize-business-units -1531310957?mod=djemCFO_h.

11. "Global Human Capital Trends 2016-The New Organization: Different by Design," *Deloitte University Press*, accessed April 29, 2016, http:// www2.deloitte.com/content/dam/Deloitte/global /Documents/HumanCapital/gx-dup-global-human -capital-trends-2016.pdf.

12. Note: Raytheon and United Technologies merged in 2019, so these revenue and profit numbers were obtained from the United Technologies annual report. "Annual Report 2019," United Technology, accessed April 13, 2020, https:// investors.rtx.com/static-files/5612ce4a-a018-4f37 -adc6-a154069a68f3. .

13. "Annual Report 2019," Verizon, accessed April 13, 2020, https://www.verizon.com/about /sites/default/files/2019-Verizon-Annual-Report.pdf; "Verizon Fact Sheet," Verizon, February 7, 2020, accessed April 13, 2020, https://www.verizon .com/about/our-company/verizon-fact-sheet; S. Krouse, "Verizon to Break Up Wireless Unit in Reorganization," *Wall Street Journal*, November 5, 2018, accessed April 13, 2020, https://www.wsj .com/articles/verizon-to-break-up-wireless-unit-in -reorganization-1541420253.

14. "2019 Annual Report," AB InBev, February 27, 2020, accessed April 13, 2020, https://www.ab -inbev.com/content/dam/abinbev/news-media /press-releases/2020/02/final-full-ab-inbev-annual -report/Full_AB-INBEV%20AR%20EN.pdf.

15. Ibid.

16. Ibid.

17. "¿Quiénes somos?" Grupo Modelo, accessed April 13, 2020, xhttps://www.gmodelo.mx/en /quienes-somos; "About Ambev," Cervejaria Ambev,

accessed April 13, 2020, https://www.ambev.com .br/sobre/.

18. "P&G Corporate Structure," Procter & Gamble, accessed April 13, 2020, https://us.pg.com /structure-and-governance/corporate-structure/; A. Al-Muslim, "P&G Moves to Streamline Its Structure," *Wall Street Journal*, November 8, 2018, accessed April 14, 2020, https://www.wsj .com/articles/p-g-moves-to-streamline-its -structure-1541713822.

19. Ibid.

20. L. R. Burns, "Adoption and Abandonment of Matrix Management Programs: Effects of Organizational Characteristics and Interorganizational Networks," *Academy of Management Journal* 36 (1993): 106–138.

21. H. Fayol, *General and Industrial Management*, trans. C. Storrs (London: Pitman Publishing, 1949).

22. M. Weber, *The Theory of Social and Economic Organization*, trans. and ed. A. M. Henderson and T. Parsons (New York: Free Press, 1947).

23. Fayol, *General and Industrial Management*.

24. C. Zillman, "With Co-CEOs, Companies Flirt with Disaster," *Fortune*, September 20, 2014, accessed April 29, 2016, http://fortune. com/2014/09/20/oracle-two-ceos-disaster/.

25. A. Gasparro, "CEO Revamp Raises Questions About Whole Foods' Strategy," *Wall Street Journal*, November 3, 2016, accessed April 12, 2017, https://www.wsj.com/articles/ceo-revamp-raises -questions-about-whole-foods-strategy -1478197430.

26. E. Henning, D. Enrich, & J. Strasburg, "Deutsche Bank Co-CEOs Jain and Fitschen Resign," *Wall Street Journal*, June 7, 2016, accessed April 12, 2017, https://www.wsj.com/articles /deutsche-bank-co-ceos-to-announce-resignations -1433674815.

27. M. Armental, "Oracle Won't Return to Dual-CEO Structure," *Wall Street Journal*, December 19, 2019, accessed April 14, 2020, https://www.wsj. com/articles/oracle-reports -higher-profit-11576186408; S. Kapner, "Erik Nordstrom Named Sole CEO of Nordstrom," *Wall Street Journal*, March 3, 2020, accessed April 14, 2020, https:// www.wsj.com/articles/erik-nordstrom-named-sole -ceo-of-nordstrom-11583273545; S. Needleman, "Salesforce Co-CEO Keith Block Steps Down," *Wall Street Journal*, February 26, 2020, accessed April 14, 2020, https://www.wsj.com/articles/salesforce -co-ceo-keith-block-steps-down-11582666066.

28. A. Lashinsky, "Inside Apple, from Steve Jobs Down to the Janitor: How America's Most Successful – and Most Secretive – Big Company Really Works," *Fortune*, May 23, 2011, 125–134.

29. M. Mamet, "Directly Responsible Individuals," *Medium*, November 13, 2016, accessed April 12, 2017, https://medium.com/@mmamet/directly -responsible-individuals-f5009f465da4.

30. B. Borzykowski, "Why You Can't Delegate and How to Fix It," *BBC Capital*, April 2, 2015, accessed April 18, 2016, http://www.bbc.com/capital/ story/20150401-why-you-find-it-hard-to-delegate.

31. D. Riegel, "8 Ways Leaders Delegate Successfully," *Harvard Business Review*, August 15, 2019, accessed April 14, 2020, https://hbr. org/2019/08/8-ways-leaders-delegate-successfully.

32. Ibid.

33. I. Brat, "Whole Foods Reworks Approach," *Wall Street Journal*, February 16, 2016, B2.

34. H. Haddon & L. Stevens, "New Era at Amazon's Whole Foods Grates on Some Suppliers, Employees," *Wall Street Journal*, July 2, 2018, accessed April 14, 2020,

https://www.wsj.com/articles/new-era-at-amazons-whole-foods-grates-on-some-suppliers-employees-1530526964.

35. C. Faulkner, "Amazon Now Has More Than 150 Million Prime Members After Huge Holiday Season," *The Verge*, January 30, 2020, accessed April 14, 2020, https://www.theverge.com/2020/1/30/21115823/amazon-q4-19-earnings-prime-membership-fresh-one-day-shipping.

36. "New Benefit for Prime Members at Whole Foods Market," *Amazon Prime Insider*, June 26, 2018, accessed April 14, 2020, https://www.amazon.com/primeinsider/tips/whole-foods-perks.html; "Prime at Whole Foods Market," Whole Foods Market, accessed April 14, 2020, https://www.wholefoodsmarket.com/amazon.

37. K. Safdar, "As Gap Struggles, Its Analytical CEO Prizes Data over Design," *Wall Street Journal*, November 27, 2016, accessed April 12, 2017, https://www.wsj.com/articles/as-gap-struggles-its-analytical-ceo-prizes-data-over-design-1480282911.

38. E. E. Lawler, S. A. Mohrman, and G. E. Ledford, *Creating High Performance Organizations: Practices and Results of Employee Involvement and Quality Management in Fortune 1000 Companies* (San Francisco: Jossey-Bass, 1995).

39. "Portrait & Production Plants," Volkswagen Group, December 31, 2019, accessed April 14, 2020, https://www.volkswagenag.com/en/group/portrait-and-production-plants.html.

40. C. Rauwald & C. Reiter, "At Volkswagen, Engineering Change in the Eye of the Diesel Storm," *Bloomberg*, December 8, 2016, accessed April 12, 2017, https://www.bloomberg.com/news/articles/2016-12-08/at-volkswagen-engineering-change-in-the-eye-of-the-diesel-storm.

41. "Employee Turnover Rate Tops 70% in 2015," National Restaurant Association, March 22, 2016, accessed April 29, 2016, http://www.restaurant.org/News-Research/News/Employee-turnover-rate-tops-70-in-2015.

42. R. W. Griffin, *Task Design* (Glenview, IL: Scott, Foresman, 1982).

43. F. Herzberg, *Work and the Nature of Man* (Cleveland, OH: World Press, 1966).

44. R. Hackman and G. R. Oldham, *Work Redesign* (Reading, MA: Addison-Wesley, 1980).

45. T. Burns and G. M. Stalker, *The Management of Innovation* (London: Tavistock, 1961).

46. Hammer and Champy, *Reengineering the Corporation*.

47. Ibid.

48. R. Ritchie, "From 10 Days to 30 Minutes: BDC's iOS Apps Revolutionize Loans for Canadian Entrepreneurs," iMore, November 15, 2019, accessed April 15, 2020, https://www.imore.com/10-days-30-minutes-bdcs-ios-apps-revolutionize-loans-canadian-entrepreneurs.

49. R. Huising, "Can You Know Too Much About Your Organization?" *Harvard Business Review*, December 4, 2019, accessed April 15, 2020, https://hbr.org/2019/12/can-you-know-too-much-about-your-organization.

50. Ibid.

51. J. D. Thompson, *Organizations in Action* (New York: McGraw-Hill, 1967).

52. G. James, "World's Worst Management Fads," *Inc.*, May 10, 2013, accessed May 1, 2015 http://www.inc.com/geoffrey-james/worlds-worst-management-fads.html.

53. J. B. White, "'Next Big Thing': Re-Engineering Gurus Take Steps to Remodel Their Stalling Vehicles," *Wall Street Journal Interactive*, November 26, 1996.

54. C. Tuna, "Remembrances: Champion of 'Re-Engineering' Saved Companies, Challenged Thinking,"

Wall Street Journal, September 6, 2008, A12.

55. G. M. Spreitzer, "Individual Empowerment in the Workplace: Dimensions, Measurement, and Validation," *Academy of Management Journal* 38 (1995): 1442–1465.

56. O. Stanley, "Warby Parker is Getting Better Results by Getting Better Results," *Quartz*, September 15, 2016, accessed April 12, 2017, https://qz.com/749863/warby-parker-is-getting-better-results-by-reducing-managers-control-over-workers/.

57. K. W. Thomas and B. A. Velthouse, "Cognitive Elements of Empowerment," *Academy of Management Review* 15 (1990): 666–681.

58. No Author, "The Power of Empowerment," Ritz-Carlton Leadership Center, March 19, 2019, accessed April 15, 2020, https://ritzcarltonleadershipcenter.com/2019/03/19/the-power-of-empowerment/.

59. C. Gallo, "How Wegmans, Apple Store and Ritz-Carlton Empower Employees to Offer Best-in-Class Service," Retail Customer Experience, December 27, 2012, accessed June 12, 2013, http://www.retailcustomerexperience.com/article/205849/How-Wegmans-Apple-Store-and-Ritz-Carlton-empower-employees-to-offer-best-in-class-service.

60. R. Nelsen, "Why Giving Your Employees More Freedom Will Improve Your Customer Experience," *Qualtrics*, October 26, 2015, accessed April 12, 2017, https://www.qualtrics.com/blog/why-giving-your-employees-more-freedom-will-improve-your-customer-experience/.

61. J. Lee, "Finding Gooey Goodness in Nutella's Huge Supply Chain," *Triple Pundit*, January 10, 2014, accessed April 29, 2016, http://www.triplepundit.com/2014/01/nutella-supply-chain/; D. Mitzman, "Nutella, How the World Went Nuts for a Hazelnut Spread," *BBC News*, May 18, 2014, accessed May 19, 2016; http://www.bbc.com/news/magazine-27438001.

62. L. Weber, "The End of Employees," *Wall Street Journal*, February 2, 2017, accessed April 13, 2017, https://www.wsj.com/articles/the-end-of-employees-1486050443.

63. C. Lecher, "How Amazon Automatically Tracks and Fires Warehouse Workers for 'Productivity,'" *The Verge*, April 25, 2019, accessed April 15, 2020, https://www.theverge.com/2019/4/25/18516004/amazon-warehouse-fulfillment-centers-productivity-firing-terminations; S. Soper, "Amazon Doubles Holiday Hiring to 200,000 Temporary Workers," *Bloomberg*, November 27, 2019, accessed April 15, 2020, https://www.bloomberg.com/news/articles/2019-11-27/amazon-doubles-holiday-hiring-to-200-000-temporary-workers?sref=xXo7CWym.

64. A. Satariano and S. Soper, "Yuletemps," *Bloomberg Businessweek*, December 14–20, 2015, 30–31; "Amazon.com Announces Fourth Quarter Sales up 22% to $35.7 Billion," *Business Wire*, January 28, 2016, accessed April 29, 2016, http://www.businesswire.com/news/home/20160128006357/en/Amazon.com-Announces-Fourth-Quarter-Sales-22-35.7.

65. C. C. Snow, R. E. Miles, and H. J. Coleman, Jr., "Managing 21st Century Network Organizations," *Organizational Dynamics* 20 (Winter 1992): 5–20.

66. J. H. Sheridan, "The Agile Web: A Model for the Future?" *Industry Week*, March 4, 1996, 31.

10

1. B. Dumaine, "The Trouble With Teams," *Fortune*, September 5, 1994, 86–92.

2. K. C. Stag, E. Salas, and S. M. Fiore, "Best Practices in Cross Training Teams," in *Workforce Cross Training Handbook*, ed. D. A. Nembhard (Boca Raton, FL: CRC Press), 156–175.

3. M. Marks, "The Science of Team Effectiveness," *Psychological Science in the Public Interest* 7 (December 2006): pi–i.

4. J. R. Katzenbach and D. K. Smith, *The Wisdom of Teams* (Boston: Harvard Business School Press, 1993).

5. S. G. Cohen and D. E. Bailey, "What Makes Teams Work: Group Effectiveness Research from the Shop Floor to the Executive Suite," *Journal of Management* 23, no. 3 (1997): 239–290.

6. J. Mathieu, J. Hollenbeck, D. van Knippenberg & D. Ilgen, "A Century of Work Teams in the *Journal of Applied Psychology*," *Journal of Applied Psychology* 102 (2017): 452–467.

7. S. E. Gross, *Compensation for Teams* (New York: American Management Association, 1995); B. L. Kirkman and B. Rosen, "Beyond Self-Management: Antecedents and Consequences of Team Empowerment," *Academy of Management Journal* 42 (1999): 58–74; G. Stalk and T. M. Hout, *Competing Against Time: How Time-Based Competition Is Reshaping Global Markets* (New York: Free Press, 1990); S. C. Wheelwright and K. B. Clark, *Revolutionizing New Product Development* (New York: Free Press, 1992).

8. D. A. Harrison, S. Mohamed, J. E. McGrath, A. T. Florey, and S. W. Vanderstoep, "Time Matters in Team Performance: Effects of Member Familiarity, Entrainment, and Task Discontinuity on Speed and Quality," *Personnel Psychology* 56, no. 3 (August 2003): 633–669.

9. R. Cross, R. Rebele, and A. Grant, "Collaborative Overload," *Harvard Business Review*, January–February 2016, accessed April 30, 2016, https://hbr.org/2016/01/collaborative-overload.

10. L. Chao, "Auto Makers, Others Explore New Roles for 3-D Printing," *Wall Street Journal*, April 25, 2016, accessed April 30, 2016, http://www.wsj.com/articles/auto-makers-others-explore-new-roles-for-3-d-printing-1461626635; "Hunton & Williams Launches 3D Printing Team to Guide Clients Through Emerging Technology's Legal Complexities," *Business Wire*, April 30, 2016, accessed May 19, 2016, http://www.businesswire.com/news/home/20160420006044/en/Hunton-Williams-Launches-3D-Printing-Team-Guide.

11. R. D. Banker, J. M. Field, R. G. Schroeder, and K. K. Sinha, "Impact of Work Teams on Manufacturing Performance: A Longitudinal Field Study," *Academy of Management Journal* 39 (1996): 867–890.

12. L. Chao, "Trucker Teams Drive to the Rescue of Online Shipping," *Wall Street Journal*, December 24, 2015, accessed April 30, 2016, http://www.wsj.com/articles/trucker-teams-drive-to-the-rescue-of-online-shipping-1450953001.

13. Ibid.

14. J. L. Cordery, W. S. Mueller, and L. M. Smith, "Attitudinal and Behavioral Effects of Autonomous Group Working: A Longitudinal Field Study," *Academy of Management Journal* 34 (1991):464–476; T. D. Wall, N. J. Kemp, P. R. Jackson, and C. W. Clegg, "Outcomes of Autonomous Workgroups: A Long-Term Field Experiment," *Academy of Management Journal* 29 (1986): 280–304.

15. S. Crowley, "Open-Book Management at Atomic," Atomic Objects, March 14, 2016, accessed April 13, 2017, Object, https://spin.atomicobject.com/2016/03/14/open-book-management/.

16. L. Tjapkes, "Atoms on 'Give a Shit' – the Quintessential Atomic Value," Atomic Objects, January 31, 2015, accessed April 13, 2017, https://spin.atomicobject.com/2015/01/31/atomic-values-part-5-give-a-shit/.

17. R. Silverman, "At Zappos, Some Employees Find Offer to Leave Too Good to Refuse," *Wall*

Street Journal, May 7, 2015, accessed May 8, 2015, http://www.wsj.com/articles/at-zappos-some -employees-find-offer-to-leave-too-good-to-refuse -1431047917?KEYWORDS=zappos; D. Gelles, "The Zappos Exodus Continues after a Radical Management Experiment," *New York Times*, January 13, 2016,accessed April 30, 2016, http://bits .blogs.nytimes.com/2016/01/13/after-a-radical-man-agement-experiment-the-zappos-exodus-continues/.

18. R. Liden, S. Wayne, R. Jaworski, and N. Bennett, "Social Loafing: A Field Investigation," *Journal of Management* 30 (2004): 285–304.

19. J. George, "Extrinsic and Intrinsic Origins of Perceived Social Loafing in Organizations," *Academy of Management Journal* 35 (1992): 191–202.

20. T. T. Baldwin, M. D. Bedell, and J. L. Johnson, "The Social Fabric of a Team-Based M.B.A. Program: Network Effects on Student Satisfaction and Performance," *Academy of Management Journal* 40 (1997): 1369–1397.

21. S. Perry, N. Lorinkova, E. Hunter, A Hubbard, and J. McMahon, "When Does Virtuality Really Work? Examining the Role of Work-Family and Virtuality in Social Loafing," *Journal of Management* 42 (2016), 449–479.

22. K. H. Price, D. A. Harrison, and J. H. Gavin, "Withholding Inputs in Team Contexts: Member Composition, Interaction Processes, Evaluation Structure and Social Loafing," *Journal of Applied Psychology* 91(6) (2006): 1375–1384.

23. L. P. Tost, F. Gino, and R. P. Larrick, "When Power Makes Others Speechless: The Negative Impact of Leader Power on Team Performance," *Academy of Management Journal* 35, no. 5 (October 1, 2013): 1465–1486.

24. C. Joinson, "Teams at Work," *HR Magazine*, May 1, 1999, 30.

25. R. Wageman, "Critical Success Factors for Creating Superb Self-Managing Teams," *Organizational Dynamics* 26, no. 1 (1997): 49–61.

26. R. Etherington, "Audi Announces New Design Strategy," *Dezeen*, December 19, 2012, accessed June 13, 2013, http://www.dezeen.com/2012/12/19 /audi-announces-new-car-design-strategy/.

27. B. L. Kirkman and B. Rosen, "Beyond Self-Management: Antecedents and Consequences of Team Empowerment," *Academy of Management Journal* 42 (1999): 58–74;

28. K. Kelly, "Managing Workers Is Tough Enough in Theory. When Human Nature Enters the Picture, It's Worse," *BusinessWeek*, October 21, 1996, 32.

29. S. Easton and G. Porter, "Selecting the Right Team Structure to Work in Your Organization," in *Handbook of Best Practices for Teams*, vol. 1, ed. G. M. Parker (Amherst, MA: Irwin, 1996).

30. S. Wilhelm, "Quadrupling 787 Production Won't Be Easy for Boeing, Just Necessary," *Puget Sound Business Journal*, February 10, 2012, accessed March 12, 2012, http://www.bizjournals .com/seattle/print-edition/2012/02/10/quadrupling -787-production-wont-be.html?page=all.

31. R. M. Yandrick, "A Team Effort: The Promise of Teams Isn't Achieved Without Attention to Skills and Training," *HR Magazine* 46, no. 6 (June 2001): 136–144.

32. S. Boyd, "Spotify | An Emergent Organization – Work Futures," *Medium*, July 30, 2019, accessed April 20, 2020, https://medium.com/work-futures/ spotify-an-emergent-organization-df9da1125c; M. Mankins & E. Garton, "How Spotify Balances Employee Autonomy and Accountability," *Harvard Business Review*, February 9, 2017, accessed April 14, 2017, https://hbr.org/2017/02/how-spotify-balances -employee-autonomy-and-accountability;

AC. Hardy, "Agile Team Organisation: Squads, Chapters, Tribes and Guilds," *Full-Stack Agile*, February 14, 2016, accessed April 14, 2017, http:// www.full-stackagile.com/2016/02/14/team -organisation-squads-chapters-tribes-and-guilds/.

33. R. Williams, "Self-Directed Work Teams: A Competitive Advantage," *Quality Digest*, accessed November 18, 2009, http://www.qualitydigest.com.

34. Yandrick, "A Team Effort."

35. "People at Valve – Valve Corporation," *Valve*, accessed April 20, 2020, https://www .valvesoftware.com/en/people.

36. "Valve: Handbook for New Employees," *Valve*, accessed May 8, 2015, http://media.steam-powered.com/apps/valve/Valve_Handbook _LowRes.pdf.

37. Ibid.

38. R. Silverman, "Who's the Boss? There Isn't One," *Wall Street Journal*, June 19, 2012, accessed May 8, 2015, http://www.wsj.com/articles/SB100014 24052702303379204577474953586383604.

39. R. J. Recardo, D. Wade, C. A. Mention, and J. Jolly, *Teams* (Houston: Gulf Publishing Co., 1996).

40. D. R. Denison, S. L. Hart, and J. A. Kahn, "From Chimneys to Cross-Functional Teams: Developing and Validating a Diagnostic Model," *Academy of Management Journal* 39, no. 4 (1996): 1005–1023.

41. S. Shellenbarger, "Are You Agile Enough for Agile Management?" *Wall Street Journal*, August 12, 2019, accessed April 20, 2020, https://www .wsj.com/articles/are-you-agile-enough-for-agile -management-11565607600.

42. A. M. Townsend, S. M. DeMarie, and A. R. Hendrickson, "Virtual Teams: Technology and the Workplace of the Future," *Academy of Management Executive* 13, no. 3 (1998): 17–29.

43. F. Rendón, "Understanding the Proliferation of Virtual Teams in the Global Economy," *Huffington Post*, April 28, 2014, accessed June 16, 2014, http://www.huffingtonpost.com/frankie-rendon /understanding-the-prolife_b_5212366.html.

44. J. Stoll, "Impossible Foods CEO on Running a $4 Billion Startup From Children's Bedroom," *Wall Street Journal*, March 19, 2020, accessed April 20, 2020, https://www.wsj.com/articles/impossible -foods-ceo-on-running-a-4-billion-startup-from -childrens-bedroom-11584627688.

45. M.E. Slater, "How to Effectively Delegate to Your Remote Team," Startup Collective, accessed May 8, 2015, http://startupcollective.com/effectively -delegate-remote-team/.

46. C. Kane, "Virtual Offices: What Happens When All Employees Telecommute," *Fortune*, May 15, 2015, accessed April 14, 2017, http://fortune .com/2015/05/15/office-less-virtual-companies/.

47. N. Radley, "Survey: How Team Members Prefer to Communicate on Virtual Projects," *Software Ad-vice*, July 17, 2014, accessed May 8, 2015, http:// blog.softwareadvice.com/articles/project-manage -ment/survey-communication-virtual-proj-ects -0714/.

48. Slater, "How to Effective Delegate to Your Remote Team."

49. Ibid.

50. D. Mankin, S. G. Cohen, and T. K. Bikson, *Teams and Technology: Fulfilling the Promise of the New Organization* (Boston: Harvard Business School Press, 1996).

51. A. P. Ammeter and J. M. Dukerich, "Leadership, Team Building, and Team Member Characteristics in High Performance Project Teams," *Engineering Management* 14, no. 4 (December 2002): 3–11.

52. K. Lovelace, D. Shapiro, and L. Weingart, "Maximizing Cross-Functional New Product Teams' Innovativeness and Constraint Adherence: A Conflict Communications Perspective," *Academy of Management Journal* 44 (2001): 779–793.

53. L. Holpp and H. P. Phillips, "When Is a Team Its Own Worst Enemy?" *Training*, September 1, 1995, 71.

54. S. Asche, "Opinions and Social Pressure," *Scientific American* 193 (1995): 31–35.

55. J. Corsello & D. Minor, "Want to Be More Productive? Sit Next to Someone Who Is," *Harvard Business Review*, February 14, 2017, accessed April 14, 2017, https://hbr.org/2017/02/want-to-be-more -productive-sit-next-to-someone-who-is.

56. S. G. Cohen, G. E. Ledford, and G. M. Spreitzer, "A Predictive Model of Self-Managing Work Team Effectiveness," *Human Relations* 49, no. 5 (1996): 643–676.

57. C. Duhigg, "Group Study: What Google Learned from Its Quest to Build the Perfect Team," *New York Times*, February 28, 2016, MM20.

58. A. Edmondson, "Psychological Safety and Learning Behavior in Work Teams," *Administrative Science Quarterly* 44 (1999): 350–383.

59. A. Wooley, C. Chabris, A. Pentland, N. Hashmi, and T. Malone, "Evidence for a Collective Intelligence Factor in the Performance of Human Groups," *Science* 330 (2010): 686–688.

60. K. Bettenhausen and J. K. Murnighan, "The Emergence of Norms in Competitive Decision-Making Groups," *Administrative Science Quarterly* 30 (1985): 350–372.

61. M. E. Shaw, *Group Dynamics* (New York: McGraw Hill, 1981).

62. F. Rees, *Teamwork from Start to Finish* (San Francisco: Josey-Bass, 1997).

63. R. E. Silverman, "Tracking Sensors Invade the Workplace," *Wall Street Journal*, March 7, 2013, accessed June 16, 2014, http://online.wsj.com/news /articles/SB1000142412788732403480457834303 429080678.

64. S. M. Gully, D. S. Devine, and D. J. Whitney, "A Meta-Analysis of Cohesion and Performance: Effects of Level of Analysis and Task Interdependence," *Small Group Research* 26, no. 4 (1995): 497–520.

65. K. Kahler, "Vikings' Donut Club Is NFL Tradition Like No Other," *The MMQB with Peter King*, October 20, 2015, accessed April 14, 2017, http://mmqb.si.com/mmqb/2015/10/20/nfl-minneso-ta-vikings-donut-club.

66. J. Bersin, J. Geller, N. Wakefield & B. Walsh, *Global Human Capital Trends 2016 – The New Organization: Different by Design*, eds. B. Pelster and J. Schwartz (Deloitte University Press), 20.

67. Gully, et al., "A Meta-Analysis of Cohesion and Performance." F. Tschan and M. V. Cranach, "Group Task Structure, Processes and Outcomes," in *Handbook of Work Group Psychology*, ed. M. A. West (Chichester, UK: Wiley, 1966).

68. D. E. Yeatts and C. Hyten, High-Performing Self-Managed Work Teams (Thousand Oaks, CA: SAGE Publications, 1998).

69. S. Shellenbarger, "A Manifesto to End Boring Meetings," December 20, 2016, accessed April 14, 2017, https://www.wsj.com/articles/a-manifesto -to-end-boring-meetings-1482249683.

70. Ibid.

71. J. Lublin, "Smaller Boards Get Bigger Returns," *Wall Street Journal*, August 26, 2014, accessed April 30, 2016, 8, 2015, http://www.wsj.com /articles/smaller-boards-get-bigger-returns -1409078628.

72. Yeatts and Hyten, *High-Performing Self-Managed Work Teams*; J. Colquitt, R. Noe, and C. Jackson, "Justice in Teams: Antecedents and Consequences of Procedural Justice Climate," *Personnel Psychology*, April 1, 2002, 83.

73. D. S. Kezsbom, "Re-Opening Pandora's Box: Sources of Project Team Conflict in the '90s," *Industrial Engineering* 24, no. 5 (1992): 54–59.

74. A. C. Amason, W. A. Hochwarter, and K. R. Thompson, "Conflict: An Important Dimension in Successful Management Teams," *Organizational Dynamics* 24 (1995): 20.

75. A. C. Amason, "Distinguishing the Effects of Functional and Dysfunctional Conflict on Strategic Decision Making: Resolving a Paradox for Top Management Teams," *Academy of Management Journal* 39, no. 1 (1996): 123–148.

76. K. M. Eisenhardt, J. L. Kahwajy, and L. J. Bourgeois III, "How Management Teams Disagree," *California Management Review* 39, no. 2 (Winter 1997): 42–62.

77. K. M. Eisenhardt, J. L. Kahwajy, and L. J. Bourgeois III, "How Management Teams Can Have a Good Fight," *Harvard Business Review* 75, no. 4 (July–August 1997): 77–85.

78. S. Shellenbarger, "Meet the Meeting Killers," *Wall Street Journal*, May 15, 2012, accessed May 8, 2015, http://www.wsj.com/articles/SB100014240527 02304192704577404434001058726.

79. C. Nemeth and P. Owens, "Making Work Groups More Effective: The Value of Minority Dissent," in *Handbook of Work Group Psychology*, ed. M. A. West (Chichester, UK: Wiley, 1996).

80. J. M. Levin and R. L. Moreland, "Progress in Small Group Research," *Annual Review of Psychology* 9 (1990): 72–78; S. E. Jackson, "Team Composition in Organizational Settings: Issues in Managing a Diverse Work Force," in *Group Processes and Productivity*, ed. S. Worchel, W. Wood, and J. Simpson (Beverly Hills, CA: SAGE, 1992).

81. Eisenhardt, et al., "How Management Teams Can Have a Good Fight."

82. Ibid.

83. J. Lublin, "Arguing with the Boss: A Winning Career Strategy," *Wall Street Journal*, August 9, 2012, accessed May 8, 2015, http://www.wsj.com/articles/SB 10000872396390443991704577579201122821724.

84. A. Pittampalli, "Why Groups Struggle to Solve Problems Together," *Harvard Business Review*, November 7, 2019, accessed April 21, 2020, https://hbr.org/2019/11/why-groups-struggle-to-solve-problems-together.

85. B. W. Tuckman, "Development Sequence in Small Groups," *Psychological Bulletin* 63, no. 6 (1965): 384–399.

86. Gross, *Compensation for Teams*.

87. J. F. McGrew, J. G. Bilotta, and J. M. Deeney, "Software Team Formation and Decay: Extending the Standard Model for Small Groups," *Small Group Research* 30, no. 2 (1999): 209–234.

88. Ibid.

89. J. Case, "What the Experts Forgot to Mention: Management Teams Create New Difficulties, But Succeed for XEL Communication," *Inc.*, September 1, 1993, 66.

90. J. R. Hackman, "The Psychology of Self-Management in Organizations," in *Psychology and Work: Productivity, Change, and Employment*, ed. M. S. Pallak and R. Perloff (Washington, DC: American Psychological Association, 1986), 85–136.

91. A. O'Leary-Kelly, J. J. Martocchio, and D. D. Frink, "A Review of the Influence of Group Goals on Group Performance," *Academy of Management Journal* 37, no. 5 (1994): 1285–1301.

92. A. Zander, "The Origins and Consequences of Group Goals," in *Retrospections on Social Psychology*, ed. L. Festinger (New York: Oxford University Press, 1980), 205–235.

93. M. Erez and A. Somech, "Is Group Productivity Loss the Rule or the Exception? Effects of Culture and Group-Based Motivation," *Academy of Management Journal* 39, no. 6 (1996): 1513–1537.

94. S. Sherman, "Stretch Goals: The Dark Side of Asking for Miracles," *Fortune*, November 13, 1995.

95. S. Ramakrishnan & S. John, "We Don't Want to Waste a Crisis: Tata Steel MD TV Narendran," *The Economic Times*, February 29, 2016, accessed April 14, 2017, http://economictimes.indiatimes.com/opi nion/interviews/we-dont-want-to-waste -a-crisis-tata-steel-md-tv-narendran/articleshow /51180585.cms.

96. K. Leigh, "At Hormel, Growth Means Doing Deals," *Star Tribune*, November 27, 2016, 1D.

97. K. R. Thompson, W. A. Hochwarter, and N. J. Mathys, "Stretch Targets: What Makes Them Effective?" *Academy of Management Executive* 11, no. 3 (1997): 48–60.

98. J. Baskin, "Innovation at Experian: Build, Don't Just Buy," *Forbes*, March 2, 2016, accessed April 14, 2017, https://www.forbes.com/sites /jonathansalem-baskin/2016/03/02/innovation-at -experian-build-dont-just-buy/#34c1a22f520e.

99. Ibid.

100. M. Freeman, "How Experian is Turning Big Data into Big Dollars," *Los Angeles Times*, September 28, 2016, http://www.latimes.com/business/la-fi -experian-big-data-20160928-snap-story.html.

101. Dumaine, "The Trouble With Teams."

102. J.E. Mathieu, S.I. Tanenbaum, J.S. Donsbach and G.M. Alliger, "A Review and Integration of Team Composition Models: Moving Toward a Dynamic and Temporal Framework," *Journal of Management* 40, no. 1 (2014): 130-160; G. A. Neuman, S. H. Wagner, and N. D. Christiansen, "The Relationship Between Work-Team Personality Composition and the Job Performance of Teams," *Group & Organization Management* 24, no. 1 (1999): 28–45.

103. M. A. Campion, G. J. Medsker, and A. C. Higgs, "Relations Between Work Group Characteristics and Effectiveness: Implications for Designing Effective Work Groups," *Personnel Psychology* 46, no. 4 (1993): 823–850.

104. B. L. Kirkman and D. L. Shapiro, "The Impact of Cultural Values on Employee Resistance to Teams: Toward a Model of Globalized Self-Managing Work Team Effectiveness," *Academy of Management Review* 22, no. 3 (1997): 730–757.

105. J. Pavlus, "SAP Looks to XRX for R&D Inspiration," *Bloomberg Businessweek*, February 2–8, 2015, p. 32.

106. A. Galinsky, "Is Your Team Too Talented," *Columbia Ideas at Work*, October 30, 2014, accessed May 8, 2015, http://www8.gsb.columbia.edu /ideas-at-work/publication/1700.

107. J. Bunderson and K. Sutcliffe, "Comparing Alternative Conceptualizations of Functional Diversity in Management Teams: Process and Performance Effects," *Academy of Management Journal* 45 (2002): 875–893.

108. S. Woo, "In Search of a Perfect Team at Work," *Wall Street Journal*, April 4, 2017, accessed April 15, 2017, https://www.wsj.com/articles/in -search-of-a-perfect-team-at-work-1489372003.

109. P. Leonardi & N. Contractor, "Better People Analytics: Measure Who They Know, Not Just Who They Are," *Harvard Business Review*, November–December 2018, accessed April 21, 2020, https:// hbr.org/2018/11/better-people -analytics?autocomplete=true.

110. J. Hackman, "New Rules for Team Building – The Times Are Changing – And So Are the Guide-lines for Maximizing Team Performance," *Optimize*, July 1, 2002, 50.

111. Joinson, "Teams at Work."

112. Strozniak, "Teams at Work."

113. Ibid.

114. L. Davey, "If Your Team Agrees on Everything, Working Together Is Pointless," *Harvard Business Review*, January 31, 2017, accessed April 15, 2017, https://hbr.org/2017/01/if-your-team -agrees-on-everything-working-together-is-pointless.

115. Wellins, et al., *Inside Teams*.

116. E. Salas, D. DiazGranados, C. Klein, C. Burke, K. Stagl, G. Goodwin, and S. Halpin, "Does Team Training Improve Team Performance? A Meta-Analysis," *Human Factors* 50, no. 6 (2008): 903–933.

117. A.M. Hughes, M.E. Gregory, D.L. Joseph, S. C. Sonesh, S.L. Marlow, C. N. Lacerenza, L.E. Benishek, H.B.King and E. Salas, "Saving Lives: A Meta-Analysis of Team Training in Healthcare," *Journal of Applied Psychology* 101, no. 9 (2016): 1266-1304.

118. S. Caudron, "Tie Individual Pay to Team Success," *Personnel Journal* 73, no. 10 (October 1994): 40.

119. Ibid.

120. A. Mitra, N. Gupta, & J. Shaw, "A Comparative Examination of Traditional and Skill-Based Pay Plans," *Journal of Managerial Psychology* 26, no. 4 (2011): 278-296.

121. G. Ledford, "Three Case Studies on Skill-Based Pay: An Overview," *Compensation & Benefits Review* 23, no. 2 (1991): 11–24.

122. T. Law, "Where Loyalty Is Rewarded," *The Press*, September 29, 2008, *Business Day* 4.

123. J. R. Schuster and P. K. Zingheim, *The New Pay: Linking Employee and Organizational Performance* (New York: Lexington Books, 1992).

124. Cohen and Bailey, "What Makes Teams Work."

125. R. Allen and R. Kilmann, "Aligning Reward Practices in Support of Total Quality Management," *Business Horizons* 44 (May 2001): 77–85.

126. S. Devaraj and K. Jiang, "It's About Time – A Longitudinal Adaptation Model of High-Performance Work Teams, " *Journal of Applied Psychology* 104, no. 3 (2019): 433–447.

11

1. No Author, "A Running List of States and Localities That Have Outlawed Pay History Questions," *HR Dive*, February 28, 2020, accessed April 26, 2020, https://www.hrdive.com/news/salary -history-ban-states-list/516662/.

2. K. Gee, "Cities Push Employers to Ignore Pay History," *Wall Street Journal*, April 15, 2017, accessed April 16, 2017, https://www.wsj.com /articles/cities-push-employers-to-ignore-pay -history-1492254003.

3. J. Sammer, "Employers Adjust to Salary-History Bans," *Society for Human Resource Management*, June 5, 2019, accessed April 26, 2020, https://www. shrm.org/resourcesandtools/hr-topics /compensation/pages/employers-adjust-to-salary -history-bans.aspx.

4. Ibid.

5. "Genetic Information Discrimination," *US Equal Employment Opportunity Commission*, accessed May 6, 2016, http://www.eeoc.gov/laws /types/genetic.cfm.

6. K. McGowan, "Barring Male Guards for Female Inmates Might Violate Title VII, Ninth Circuit Rules," *Bloomberg BNA*, July 8, 2014, accessed May 6, 2016, http://www.bna.com/barring-male-guards-n17179891923/.

7. J. Hyman, "No Matter What the Producers of #Hamilton Tell You, Race is Never a BFOQ," Ohio Employer's Law Blog, April 5, 2016, http://www.ohioemployerlawblog.com/2016/04/no-matter-what-producers-of-hamilton.html, accessed August 25, 2017.

8. P. S. Greenlaw and J. P. Kohl, "Employer 'Business' and 'Job' Defenses in Civil Rights Actions," *Public Personnel Management* 23, no. 4 (1994): 573.

9. A. Martyn, "Boxed In: Dollar Tree, the Giant Discount Chain, Cited for Job Safety Violations at Dozens of Stores," *FairWarning*, December 11, 2019, accessed April 26, 2020, https://www.fairwarning.org/2019/12/dollar-tree-cited-for-job-safety-violations/.

10. OSHA National News Release, "US Department of Labor Cites Dollar Tree for Exposing Employees to Exit and Storage Hazards at Pennsylvania Store – US Department of Labor," Occupational Safety and Health Administration, March 3, 2020, accessed April 26, 2020, https://www.osha.gov/news/newsreleases/region3/03032020; OSHA National News Release, "US Labor Department, Dollar Tree Reach Settlement Agreement to Implement Enhanced Safety Measures Nationwide – US Department of Labor," Occupational Safety and Health Administration, December 10, 2015, accessed April 26, 2020, https://www.osha.gov/news/newsreleases/national/12102015.

11. Ibid.

12. Greenlaw and Kohl, "Employer 'Business' and 'Job' Defenses in Civil Rights Actions."

13. City News Service, "66-Year-Old Man Awarded $26 Million in Age Discrimination Lawsuit," *Los Angeles Daily News*, February 27, 2014, accessed May 6, 2016, http://www.dailynews.com/general-news/20140227/66-year-old-man-awarded-26-million-in-age-discrimination-lawsuit-against-staples.

14. P. Lee and C. Hymowitz, "No Place for Old Waiters at Texas Roadhouse?" *Bloomberg Businessweek*, September 28–October 4, 2015, 23–24.

15. L. Nagele-Piazza, "Texas Roadhouse Agrees to $12 Million Age Bias Settlement," Society for Human Resource Management, April 17, 2017, accessed April 26, 2020, https://www.shrm.org/resourcesandtools/legal-and-compliance/employment-law/pages/texas-roadhouse-agrees-to-$12-million-age-bias-settlement.aspx.

16. E. Coe, "Steakhouse Chain Says EEOC Age Bias Suit Too Vague," *Law 360*, accessed April 30, 2016, http://www.law360.com/articles/305259/steakhouse-chain-says-eeoc-age-bias-suit-too-vague.

17. A. Carlsen, M. Salam, C. Cain Miller, D. Lu, A. Ngu, J. Patel & Z. Wichter, "#MeToo Brought Down 201 Powerful Men. Nearly Half of Their Replacements Are Women," *New York Times*, October 29, 2018, accessed April 26, 2020, https://www.nytimes.com/interactive/2018/10/23/us/metoo-replacements.html.

18. W. Peirce, C. A. Smolinski, and B. Rosen, "Why Sexual Harassment Complaints Fall on Deaf Ears," *Academy of Management Executive* 12, no. 3 (1998): 41–54.

19. "Jury Awards $2,323,505.48 to Former Employee in Her Tennessee State Action Alleging Quid Pro Quo Sexual Harassment and Sexual Discrimination," LexisNexis, February 16, 2017, accessed April 17, 2017, https://www.lexisnexis.com/jvsubmission/b/case_of_week/archive/2017/02/16/jury-awards-2-323-505-48-to-former-employee-in-her-tennessee-state-action-alleging-quid-pro-quo-sexual-harassment-and-sexual-discrimination.aspx.

20. B. Frank, "Zillow accused of 'adult frat house' culture, sales manager fired after sexual harassment investigation," *Geek Wire*, December 2, 2014, accessed April 17, 2017, http://www.geekwire.com/2014/zillow-accused-adult-frat-house-culture-sales-manager-fired-sexual-harassment-investigation/.

21. R. Smith, "Zillow Settles Several Suits Alleging Sexual Harassment, Discrimination," *Mortgage Professional America*, June 7, 2016, accessed April 17, 2017, http://www.mpamag.com/news/zillow-settles-several-suits-alleging-sexual-harassment-discrimination-32939.aspx.

22. Peirce, et al., "Why Sexual Harassment Complaints Fall on Deaf Ears."

23. Ibid.

24. L. Weber, "After #MeToo, Those Who Report Harassment Still Risk Retaliation," *Wall Street Journal*, December 12, 2018, accessed April 27, 2020, https://www.wsj.com/articles/after-metoo-those-who-report-harassment-still-risk-retaliation-11544643939.

25. E. Larson, "The Economic Costs of Sexual Harassment," *The Freeman 46*, August 1996, accessed May 6, 2016, http://fee.org/freeman/the-economic-costs-of-sexual-harassment.

26. "The Little Annual Employer Survey," *Littler*, May 8 2019, accessed April 27, 2020, https://www.littler.com/files/2019_littler_employer_survey.pdf.

27. P. McCord, "How to Hire," *Harvard Business Review*, January-February 2018, accessed April 27, 2020, https://hbr.org/2018/01/how-to-hire.

28. Ibid.

29. R. D. Gatewood and H. S. Field, *Human Resource Selection* (Fort Worth, TX: Dryden Press, 1998).

30. Ibid.

31. P. McCord, "Hiring the Best People," *HBR IdeaCast [Transcript]*, January 2, 2018, accessed April 27, 2020, https://hbr.org/podcast/2018/01/hiring-the-best-people.

32. W. Johnson, "Write a Job Description That Attracts the Right Candidate," *Harvard Business Review*, March 30, 2020, accessed April 27, 2020, https://hbr.org/2020/03/write-a-job-description-that-attracts-the-right-candidate.

33. "Machine Learning," SAP, accessed April 17, 2017, https://www.sap.com/solution/machine-learning.what-is-machine-learning.html#benefits.

34. T. Greenwald, "How AI Is Transforming the Workplace," *Wall Street Journal*, March 10, 2017, accessed April 17, 2017, https://www.wsj.com/articles/how-ai-is-transforming-the-workplace-1489371060.

35. "Machine Learning."

36. *Griggs v. Duke Power Co.*, 401 US 424, 436 (1971); *Albemarle Paper Co. v. Moody*, 422 US 405 (1975).

37. R. E. Silverman and N. Waller, "The Algorithm That Tells the Boss Who Might Quit," *Wall Street Journal*, March 13, 2015, accessed May 6, 2016, http://www.wsj.com/articles/the-algorithm-that-tells-the-boss-who-might-quit-1426287935.

38. P. Cappelli, "Your Approach to Hiring Is All Wrong," *Harvard Business Review*, May–June 2019, accessed April 27, 2020, https://hbr.org/2019/05/recruiting.

39. J. A. Breaugh, *Recruitment: Science and Practice* (Boston: PWSKent, 1992).

40. R. Albergotti, "LinkedIn Wants to Help You Stay at Your Company," *Wall Street Journal* (blog), April 10, 2014, accessed May 6, 2016, http://blogs.wsj.com/atwork/2014/04/10/linkedin-wants-to-help-you-stay-at-your-company/.

41. Ibid.

42. L. Klaff, "New Internal Hiring Systems Reduce Cost and Boost Morale," *Workforce Management* 83 (March 2004): 76–79.

43. R. Silverman and L. Weber, "An Inside Job: More Firms Opt to Recruit from Within," *Wall Street Journal*, May 29, 2012, accessed May 6, 2016, http://online.wsj.com/article/SB10001424052702303395604577434563715828218.html.

44. M. Bidwell, "Paying More to Get Less: The Effects of External Hiring versus Internal Mobility," *Administrative Science Quarterly* 56 no. 3 (2011): 369–407.

45. R. E. Silverman, "Climbing the Career Ladder with Help," *Wall Street Journal*, January 14, 2015, B6.

46. Ibid.

47. J. Stoll, "KitchenAid's Key Ingredient: Investing in Workers. 'It's Not a Dead-End Job Anymore,'" *Wall Street Journal*, February 22, 2019, accessed April 27, 2020, https://www.wsj.com/articles/a-kitchenaid-recipe-for-a-tight-job-market-11550840415.

48. Ibid.

49. L. Lambert, "US Unemployment Rate Passes 20% With 4.4 Million Weekly Jobless Claims, 26.5 Million Total Claims for Bene-Fits, Insurance," *Fortune*, April 23, 2020, accessed April 27, 2020, https://fortune.com/2020/04/23/us-unemployment-rate-numbers-claims-this-week-total-job-losses-april-23-2020-benefits-claims/.

50. L. Weber, "50,000 Jobs, 900,000 Resumes: Coronavirus Is Redeploying Workers at Record Pace," *Wall Street Journal*, April 15, 2020, accessed April 27, 2020, https://www.wsj.com/articles/inside-the-push-to-redeploy-workers-quickly-11586943000.

51. Ibid.

52. J. Breaugh and M. Starke, "Research on Employee Recruitment: So Many Studies, So Many Remaining Questions," *Journal of Management* 26 (2000): 405–434.

53. J. J. Colao, "The Facebook Job Board Is Here: Recruiting Will Never Look the Same," *Forbes*, November 14, 2012, accessed May 6, 2016, http://www.forbes.com/sites/jjcolao/2012/11/14/the-facebook-job-board-is-here-recruiting-will-never-look-the-same/; J. Zappe, "Now Almost Gone: The Decline of Print-Based Help-Wanted Ads," *Source Con*, March 20, 2012, accessed May 5, 2015, http://www.sourcecon.com/news/2012/03/20/now-almost-gone-the-decline-of-print-based-help-wanted-ads/.

54. "2016 Jobvite Job Seeker Nation Study," *Jobvite*, accessed May 1, 2016, http://www.jobvite.com/wp-content/uploads/2016/03/Jobvite_Jobseeker_Nation_2016.pdf.

55. K. Krader, "Restaurants Are Using the Pared App to Staff Their Kitchens," *Bloomberg*, April 18, 2019, accessed April 27, 2020, https://www.bloomberg.com/news/articles/2019-04-18/restaurants-are-using-the-pared-app-to-staff-their-kitchens?sref=xXo7CWym.

56. R. E. Silverman, "New Year, New Job? Read This First," *Wall Street Journal*, January 2, 2015, B1, B4.

57. T. Greenwald," How AI Is Transforming the Workplace.

58. N. Buhayar, "Be a Grand Pooh-Bah of Probability," *Bloomberg Businessweek*, March 16–22, 2015, 34–35.

59. S. Shellenbarger, "How to Deal with a Long Hiring Process," *Wall Street Journal*, January 19, 2016,

B1; R. Feintzeig, "Hiring on the Fast Track," *Wall Street Journal*, September 17, 2015, B1.

60. C. Cutter, "Yes, You're Hired. No, We Don't Need to Meet You First," *Wall Street Journal*, November 15, 2018, accessed April 28, 2020, https://www.wsj.com/articles/youre-hired-no-we-dont-need-to-meet-you-first-1542298757?mod=djemwhatsnews.

61. Cappelli, "Your Approach to Hiring Is All Wrong."

62. C. Camden and B. Wallace, "Job Application Forms: A Hazardous Employment Practice," *Personnel Administrator* 28 (1983): 31–32.

63. R. Maurer, "Screening Candidates' Social Media May Lead to TMI, Discrimination Claims," Society for Human Resource Management, April 23, 2018, accessed April 28, 2020, https://www.shrm.org/resourcesandtools/hr-topics/talent-acquisition/pages/screening-social-media-discrimination-claims.aspx; J. Valentino-Devries, "Bosses May Use Social Media to Discriminate Against Job Seekers," *Wall Street Journal*, November 20, 2013, accessed May 6, 2016, http://online.wsj.com/news/articles/SB10001424052702303775504579208304255139392.

64. "Fifty-Eight Percent of Employers Have Caught a Lie on a Résumé, According to a New Career-Builder Survey," *CareerBuilder.com*, August 7, 2014, accessed May 6, 2016, http://www.careerbuilder.com/share/aboutus/pressreleasesdetail.aspx?sd=8%2F7%2F2014&id=pr837&ed=12%2F31%2F2014.

65. D. Papandrea, "The Biggest Resume Lies to Avoid," *Monster.com*, accessed April 28, 2020, https://www.monster.com/career-advice/article/the-truth-about-resume-lies-hot-jobs.

66. S. Adler, "Verifying a Job Candidate's Background: The State of Practice in a Vital Human Resources Activity," *Review of Business* 15, no. 2 (1993/1994): 3–8.

67. "The Background Check Is Taking Longer Than Expected. Can Checkr Expedite the Process? – Checkr Help Center, April 23, 2020, accessed April 28, 2020, https://help.checkr.com/hc/en-us/articles/216553118-The-background-check-is-taking-longer-than-expected-Can-Checkr-expedite-the-process-; R. Feintzeig & R. Silverman, "In the Uber Age, a Boom in Background Checks," *Wall Street Journal*, May 11, 2016, accessed April 18, 2017, https://www.wsj.com/articles/background-checks-are-booming-1462926915.

68. L. Chao, "Driver-Screening Firms Draw Scrutiny," *Wall Street Journal*, October 19, 2016, accessed April 18, 2017, https://www.wsj.com/articles/driver-screening-firms-draw-scrutiny-1476869402.

69. W. Woska, "Legal Issues for HR Professionals: Reference Checking/Background Investigations," *Public Personnel Management* 36 (Spring 2007): 79–89.

70. "More Than 70 Percent of HR Professionals Say Reference Checking Is Effective in Identifying Poor Performers," *Society for Human Resource Management*, accessed May 6, 2016, http://www.shrm.org/press_published/CMS_011240.asp.

71. P. Babcock, "Spotting Lies: The High Cost of Careless Hiring," *HR Magazine* 48, no. 10 (October 2003).

72. E. Leizerman, "Oregon Jury Renders $5.2M Verdict Against Trucking Broker and Driver in Negligent Hiring Case," *PRWeb*, March 6, 2012, accessed May 6, 2016, http://www.prweb.com/releases/2012/3/prweb9258166.htm.

73. M. Le, T. Nguyen, and B. Kleiner, "Legal Counsel: Don't Be Sued for Negligent Hiring," *Nonprofit World*, May 1, 2003, 14–15.

74. J. Calmes, "Hiring Hurdle: Finding Workers Who Can Pass a Drug Test," *New York Times*, May 17, 2016, accessed April 19, 2017, https://www.nytimes.com/2016/05/18/business/hiring-hurdle-finding-workers-who-can-pass-a-drug-test.html?_r=0.

75. "Best Practices and Model Policies: Creating a Fair Chance Policy," National Employment Law Project," April 2015, accessed April 28, 2020, https://www.nelp.org/publication/best-practices-model-fair-chance-policies/; Emshwiller and Fields, "Decades-long Arrest Wave Vexes Employers"; S. Thurm, "Background Checks Fuel Jobs Debate," *Wall Street Journal*, June 11, 2013, accessed May 6, 2016, http://www.wsj.com/articles/SB10001424127887323495604578539283518855020.

76. C. Ciaramella, "Trump Will Sign Federal 'Ban the Box' Bill into Law as Part of Massive Spending Bill," *Reason*, December 20, 2019, accessed April 28, 2020, https://reason.com/2019/12/20/trump-will-sign-federal-ban-the-box-bill-into-law-as-part-of-massive-spending-bill/.

77. Ibid.

78. C. Cohen, "Reference Checks," *CA Magazine*, November 2004, 41.

79. Keith J. Winstein, "Inflated Credentials Surface in Executive Suite," *Wall Street Journal*, November 13, 2008, accessed May 6, 2016, http://online.wsj.com/article/SB122652836844922165.html.

80. B. Ellis, "For Hire: Professional Liars for Job Seekers," *CNN Money*, July 17, 2013, accessed May 6, 2016, http://money.cnn.com/2013/07/17/pf/professional-liars/.

81. L. Weber, "To Get a Job, New Hires Are Put to the Test," *Wall Street Journal*, April 15, 2015, A1, A10.

82. N. Kuncel & P. Sackett, "The Truth About the SAT and ACT," *Wall Street Journal*, March 8, 2018, accessed April 28, 2020, https://www.wsj.com/articles/the-truth-about-the-sat-and-act-1520521861; J. Piereson and N. Schaefer Riley, "Here's Why Tests Matter," *Wall Street Journal*, March 31, 2016, accessed May 6, 2016, http://www.wsj.com/articles/heres-why-tests-matter-1459379670.

83. J. Hunter, "Cognitive Ability, Cognitive Aptitudes, Job Knowledge, and Job Performance," *Journal of Vocational Behavior* 29 (1986): 340–362.

84. F. L. Schmidt, "The Role of General Cognitive Ability and Job Performance: Why There Cannot Be a Debate," *Human Performance* 15 (2002): 187–210.

85. "D. Hambrick and C. Chabris, "Yes, IQ Really Matters," *Slate*, April 14, 2014, accessed July 10, 2014, http://www.slate.com/articles/health_and_science/science/2014/04/what_do_sat_and_iq_tests_measure_general_intelligence_predicts_school_and.html.

86. E. E. Cureton, "Comment," in *Research Conference on the Use of Autobiographical Data as Psychological Predictors*, ed. E. R. Henry (Greensboro, NC: The Richardson Foundation, 1965), 13.

87. J. R. Glennon, L. E. Albright, and W. A. Owens, *A Catalog of Life History Items* (Greensboro, NC: The Richardson Foundation, 1966).

88. Gatewood and Field, *Human Resource Selection*.

89. J. M. Digman, "Personality Structure: Emergence of the Five-Factor Model," *Annual Review of Psychology* 41 (1990): 417–440; M. R. Barrick and M. K. Mount, "The Big Five Personality Dimensions and Job Performance: A Meta-Analysis," *Personnel Psychology* 44 (1991): 1–26.

90. N. Schmitt, "Beyond the Big Five: Increases in Understanding and Practical Utility," *Human Performance* 17 (2004): 347–357.

91. T. Cower, "Personality Affects Pay: Extroverts Earn More Than Introverts," *Bloomberg*, August 9, 2018, accessed April 29, 2020, https://www.bloomberg.com/opinion/articles/2018-08-09/personality-affects-pay-extroverts-earn-more-than-introverts?sref=xXo7CWym; M. Gensowski, M. "Personality, IQ, and Lifetime Earnings," *Labour Economics* 51 (2018): 170-183.

92. L. Weber, "Today's Personality Tests Raise the Bar for Job Seekers," *Wall Street Journal*, April 15, 2015, accessed April 19, 2017, https://www.wsj.com/articles/a-personality-test-could-stand-in-the-way-of-your-next-job-1429065001.

93. L.J. Brock & J. Pinchback, "Why We Modeled Our Hiring Process on the NFL and NASA," *Harvard Business Review*, January 25, 2018, accessed April 29, 2020, https://hbr.org/2018/01/why-we-modeled-our-hiring-process-on-the-nfl-and-nasa.

94. Ibid.

95. S. Nassauer & C. Cutter, "Walmart Turns to VR to Pick Middle Managers," *Wall Street Journal*, June 30, 2019, accessed April 29, 2020, https://www.wsj.com/articles/walmart-turns-to-vr-to-pick-middle-managers-11561887001.

96. L. Weber, "Today's Personality Tests Raise the Bar for Job Seekers," *Wall Street Journal*, April 14, 2015, accessed May 6, 2016, http://www.wsj.com/articles/a-personality-test-could-stand-in-the-way-of-your-next-job-1429065001.

97. M. S. Taylor and J. A. Sniezek, "The College Recruitment Interview: Topical Content and Applicant Reactions," *Journal of Occupational Psychology* 57 (1984): 157–168.

98. M. Harris, "Reconsidering the Employment Interview: A Review of Recent Literature and Suggestions for Future Research," *Personnel Psychology* 42 (Winter 1989): 691–726.

99. Taylor and Sniezek, "The College Recruitment Interview."

100. M. Wilson, "Here's Google's Secret to Hiring the Best People," *Wired*, April 7, 2015, accessed April 19, 2017, https://www.wired.com/2015/04/hire-like-google/.

101. R. Burnett, C. Fan, S. J. Motowidlo, and T. DeGroot, "Interview Notes and Validity," *Personnel Psychology* 51, (1998): 375–396; M. A. Campion, D. K. Palmer, and J. E. Campion, "A Review of Structure in the Selection Interview," *Personnel Psychology* 50, no. 3 (1997): 655–702.

102. T. Judge, "The Employment Interview: A Review of Recent Research and Recommendations for Future Research," *Human Resource Management Review* 10, no. 4 (2000): 383–406.

103. J. Cortina, N. Goldstein, S. Payne, K. Davison, and S. Gilliland, "The Incremental Validity of Interview Scores Over and Above Cognitive Ability and Conscientiousness Scores," *Personnel Psychology* 53, no. 2 (2000): 325–351; F. L. Schmidt and J. E. Hunter, "The Validity and Utility of Selection Methods in Personnel Psychology: Practical and Theoretical Implications of 85 Years of Research Findings," *Psychological Bulletin* 124, no. 2 (1998): 262–274.

104. K. Tyler, "Training Revs Up," *HR Magazine* (April 2005), *Society for Human Resource Management*, accessed March 23, 2009, http://www.shrm.org.

105. D. Belkin, "More Companies Teach Workers What Colleges Don't," *Wall Street Journal*, March 22, 2018, accessed April 29, 2020, https://www.wsj.com/articles/more-companies-teach-workers-what-colleges-dont-1521727200.

106. E. Mazareanu, "Market Size of the Global Workplace Training Industry From 2007 to 2018

(In Billion US Dollars)," Statista, September 12, 2019, accessed April 29, 2020, https://www.statista.com/statistics/738399/size-of-the-global-workplace-training-market/.

107. L. Weber, "Why Companies Are Failing at Reskilling," *Wall Street Journal*, April 19, 2019, accessed April 29, 2020, https://www.wsj.com/articles/the-answer-to-your-companys-hiring-problem-might-be-right-under-your-nose-11555689542.

108. S. Lupkin, "Texas Health Workers Use Tabasco to Help Train for Ebola," *Good Morning America*, October 23, 2014, accessed May 7, 2015, http://abcnews.go.com/Health/texas-health-workers-tabasco-train-ebola/story?id=26385702.

109. Ibid.

110. M. Fenlon & S. McEneaney, "How We Teach Digital Skills at PwC," *Harvard Business Review*, October 15, 2018, accessed April 29, 2020, https://hbr.org/2018/10/how-we-teach-digital-skills-at-pwc.

111. A. Fisher, "Online training: Tips From Adobe on Making Your Company's Training Digital," *Fortune*, April 3, 2020, accessed April 29, 2020, https://fortune.com/2020/04/03/employee-training-online-advice-adobe-coronavirus/.

112. Ibid.

113. Ibid.

114. Ibid.

115. D. L. Kirkpatrick, "Four Steps to Measuring Training Effectiveness," *Personnel Administrator* 28 (1983): 19–25.

116. L. Bassi, J. Ludwig, D. McMurrer, and M. van Buren, "Profiting from Learning: Do Firms' Investments in Education and Training Pay Off?" *American Society for Training and Development*, accessed August 14, 2008, https://www.td.org/Publications/Research-Reports/2000/Profiting-from-Learning

117. Daley, "It's Shaping Up to Be a Good Year," *Entrepreneur*, January 2014, 92.

118. D. Meinert, "Is It Time to Put the Performance Appraisal on a PIP?," Society of Human Resource Management, April 1, 2015, accessed May 6, 2016, https://www.shrm.org/publications/hrmagazine/editorialcontent/2015/0415/pages/0415-qualitative-performance-reviews.aspx; J. McGregor, "This Big Change Was Supposed to Make Performance Reviews Better. Could It Be Making Them Worse?" Washington Post, June 7, 2016, accessed April 19, 2017, https://www.washingtonpost.com/news/on-leadership/wp/2016/06/07/this-big-change-was-supposed-to-make-performance-reviews-better-could-it-be-making-them-worse/?utm_term=.9476cc57671d.

119. M. Nisen, "Why GE Had to Kill Its Annual Performance Reviews after More than Three Decades," *Quartz*, August 13, 2015, accessed May 6, 2016, http://qz.com/428813/ge-performance-review-strategy-shift/

120. Ibid.

121. J. McGregor, "This Big Change Was Supposed to Make Performance Reviews Better. Could It Be Making Them Worse?"

122. K. R. Murphy and J. N. Cleveland, *Understanding Performance Appraisal: Social, Organizational and Goal-Based Perspectives* (Thousand Oaks, CA: SAGE, 1995).

123. L. Goler, J. Gale & A. Grant, "Let's Not Kill Performance Reviews Yet," *Harvard Business Review*, November 2016, accessed April 20, 2017, https://hbr.org/2016/11/lets-not-kill-performance-evaluations-yet.

124. W. Demere, K. Sedatole and A. Woods, "Why Managers Shouldn't Have the Final Say in

Performance Reviews," *Harvard Business Review*, June 11, 2018, accessed April 30, 2020, https://hbr.org/2018/06/why-managers-shouldnt-have-the-final-say-in-performance-reviews.

125. U. J. Wiersma and G. P. Latham, "The Practicality of Behavioral Observation Scales, Behavioral Expectation Scales, and Trait Scales," *Personnel Psychology* 39 (1986): 619–628; U. J. Wiersma, P. T. Van Den Berg, and G. P. Latham, "Dutch Reactions to Behavioral Observation, Behavioral Expectation, and Trait Scales," *Group & Organization Management* 20 (1995): 297–309.

126. D. J. Schleicher, D. V. Day, B. T. Mayes, and R. E. Riggio, "A New Frame for Frame-of-Reference Training: Enhancing the Construct Validity of Assessment Centers," *Journal of Applied Psychology* (August 2002): 735–746.

127. R. Feintzeig, "Everything Is Awesome! Why You Can't Tell Employees They're Doing a Bad Job," *Wall Street Journal*, February 10, 2015, accessed May 6, 2016, http://www.wsj.com/articles/everything-is-awesome-why-you-cant-tell-employees-theyre-doing-a-bad-job-1423613936.

128. R. Feintzeig, "The Trouble with Grading Employees," *Wall Street Journal*, April 22, 2015, B1, B7.

129. K. Heanery, "Everyone Hates Performance Reviews," *The Cut*, January 28, 2019, accessed April 30, 2020, https://www.thecut.com/2019/01/everyone-hates-performance-reviews.html.

130. H. H. Meyer, "A Solution to the Performance Appraisal Feedback Enigma," *Academy of Management Executive* 5, no. 1 (1991): 68–76; G. C. Thornton, "Psychometric Properties of Self-Appraisals of Job Performance," *Personnel Psychology* 33 (1980): 263–271.

131. Thornton, "Psychometric Properties of Self-Appraisals of Job Performance."

132. K. Mullaney, "It's Not OK to 'Rate' Employees," *CNBC*, April 18, 2016, accessed May 6, 2016, http://www.cnbc.com/2016/04/18/its-not-ok-to-rate-employees-commentary.html.

133. J. Smither, M. London, R. Flautt, Y. Vargas, and I. Kucine, "Can Working with an Executive Coach Improve Multisource Feedback Ratings Over Time? A Quasi-Experimental Field Study," *Personnel Psychology* (Spring 2003): 21–43.

134. A. Walker and J. Smither, "A Five-Year Study of Upward Feedback: What Managers Do with Their Results Matters," *Personnel Psychology* 52 (Summer 1999): 393–422.

135. D. Tayler, "Taco Bell to Test Paying Managers $100,000 a Year," *New York Times*, January 11, 2020, accessed April 30, 2020, https://www.nytimes.com/2020/01/10/business/taco-bell-manager-salary.html.

136. Ibid.

137. G. T. Milkovich and J. M. Newman, *Compensation*, 4th ed. (Homewood, IL: Irwin, 1993).

138. M. L. Williams and G. F. Dreher, "Compensation System Attributes and Applicant Pool Characteristics," *Academy of Management Journal* 35, no. 3 (1992): 571–595.

139. "How to Hire."

140. D. K. Williams and M. M. Scott, "Why We Pay All Our Employees a Commission," *Harvard Business Review*, March 26, 2013, accessed May 6, 2016, https://hbr.org/2013/03/why-we-pay-all-our-employees-a/.

141. "Form 10-k, 2019 Annual Report," Delta Airlines, February 13, 2020, accessed April 30, 2020, https://d18rn0p25nwr6d.cloudfront.net/CIK-0000027904/1fe7420e-4781-437f-92c3-08991a2d6695.pdf.

142. Ibid.

143. Staff Writer, "Following $1.6B Profit Sharing Payout, Delta Unveils 'Thank You' Plane Featuring all 90,000 Employee Names," *Delta News Hub*, February 14, 2020, accessed April 30, 2020, https://news.delta.com/following-16b-profit-sharing-payout-delta-unveils-thank-you-plane-featuring-all-90000-employee-0. R. Solomon, "Delta Pays Out Biggest Profit Sharing in US History," *Delta*, February 12, 2016, accessed May 6, 2016, http://news.delta.com/delta-pays-out-biggest-profit-sharing-us-history.

144. M. Josephs, "The Millionaire Truck Driver and Other ESOP Miracles," *Forbes*, April 30, 2014, accessed May 6, 2016, http://www.forbes.com/site/maryjosephs/2014/04/30/the-millionaire-truck-driver-and-other-esop-miracles/.

145. S. Strom, "At Chobani, Now It's Not Just the Yogurt That's Rich," *New York Times*, April 26, 2016, accessed July 26, 2016, http://www.nytimes.com/2016/04/27/business/a-windfall-for-chobani-employees-stakes-in-the-company.html?_r=0.

146. D. Salazar, "The Secret Sauce: How Publix Finds and Keeps Top Talent," *Drug Store News*, December 12, 2019, accessed May 1, 2020, https://drugstorenews.com/secret-sauce-how-publix-finds-and-keeps-top-talent.

147. E. McKnight, "Retire as a Millionaire, College Degree Not Required," *Atlanta Journal Constitution*, March 25, 2016, accessed May 1, 2020, https://www.ajc.com/business/employment/retire-millionaire-from-this-company-college-degree-not-required/PWg5SAhU4jRy78tCnwdLlN/.

148. "Employee Ownership by the Numbers, "National Center for Employee Ownership," September 2019, accessed April 30, 2020, https://www.nceo.org/articles/employee-ownership-by-the-numbers.

149. M. Bloom, "The Performance Effects of Pay Dispersion on Individuals and Organizations," *Academy of Management Journal* 42, no. 1 (1999): 25–40.

150. L. Mischel & J. Scheider, "CEO compensation has grown 940% since 1978," Economic Policy Institute, August 14, 2019, accessed May 1, 2020, https://www.epi.org/publication/ceo-compensation-2018/.

151. W. Grossman and R. E. Hoskisson, "CEO Pay at the Crossroads of Wall Street and Main: Toward the Strategic Design of Executive Compensation," *Academy of Management Executive* 12, no. 1 (1998): 43–57.

152. Bloom, "The Performance Effects of Pay Dispersion."

153. M. Bloom and J. Michel, "The Relationships Among Organizational Context, Pay Dispersion, and Managerial Turnover," *Academy of Management Journal* 45 (2002): 33–42.

154. S. Needleman, "Bad Firings Can Hurt Firm's Reputation," *Wall Street Journal*, July 8, 2008, D4.

155. J. Strickland, "Zynga Layoffs: The Aftermath," *Inc*, June 3, 2013, accessed May 6, 2016, http://www.inc.com/julie-strickland/zynga-lay-off-eighteen-percent-staff-close-three-offices.html.

156. A. Rupe, "Horrors from the Bad-Firing File," *Workforce Management*, November 2003, 16.

157. D. Mattel, J. Lublin, and R. Silverman, "Bad Call: How Not to Fire a Worker," *Wall Street Journal*, September 9, 2011, B2.

158. P. Michal-Johnson, *Saying Good-Bye: A Manager's Guide to Employee Dismissal* (Glenview, IL: Scott, Foresman & Co., 1985).

159. M. Bordwin, "Employment Law: Beware of Time Bombs and Shark-Infested Waters," *HR*

Focus, April 1, 1995, 19; D. Jones, "Fired Workers Fight Back . . . and Win; Laws, Juries Shift Protection to Terminated Employees," *USA Today*, April 2, 1998, 01B.

160. K. Kumar, "HSBC Layoffs 2019: 4,000 Lose Jobs After CEO's Exit," *International Business Times*, August 5, 2019, accessed May 1, 2020, https://www.ibtimes.com/hsbc-layoffs-2019-4000-lose-jobs-after-ceos-exit-2810978.

161. J. Kelly, "HSBC Plans to Axe 10,000 Jobs – Bringing the Total to 60,000 Banking Employees Downsized Just This Year," *Forbes*, accessed May 1, 2020, https://www.forbes.com/sites/jackkelly/2019/10/07/hsbc-plans-to-axe-10000-jobsbringing-the-total-to-60000-banking-employees-downsized-just-this-year/#5e76b174186f.

162. S. Clark & M. Patrick, "HSBC to Cut 35,000 Jobs and $100 Billion of Assets," *Wall Street Journal*, February 18, 2020, accessed May 1, 2020, https://www.wsj.com/articles/hsbc-2019-net-profit-plunged-53-11582001092.

163. A. Stevenson & M. de la Merced, "HSBC Plans to Cut 35,000 Jobs, Weighed Down by Virus and Hong Kong Unrest," *New York Times*, February 18, 2020, accessed May 1, 2020, https://www.nytimes.com/2020/02/18/business/hsbc-job-cuts.html.

164. M. Zorn, P. Norman, F. Butler & M. Bhussar, "If You Think Downsizing Might Save Your Company, Think Again," *Harvard Business Review*, April 26, 2017, accessed May 1, 2020, https://hbr.org/2017/04/if-you-think-downsizing-might-save-your-company-think-again.

165. C. Luan, C. Tien & Y. Chi, "Downsizing to the Wrong Size? A Study of the Impact of Downsizing on Firm Performance During an Eco-Nomic Downturn," *The International Journal of Human Resource Management* 24, no. 7 (2013): 1519-1535.

166. W. F. Cascio, "Employment Downsizing and Its Alternatives: Strategies for Long-Term Success," *SHRM Foundation's Effective Practice Guideline Series, Society for Human Resource Management Foundation*, accessed May 6, 2016, http://www.shrm.org/about/foundation/products/Documents/Downsizing%20EPG-%20Final.pdf.

167. K. E. Mishra, G. M. Spreitzer, and A. K. Mishra, "Preserving Employee Morale During Downsizing," *Sloan Management Review* 39, no. 2 (1998): 83–95.

168. K. Frieswick, "Until We Meet Again?" *CFO*, October 1, 2001, 41; Cascio, "Employment Downsizing and Its Alternatives: Strategies for Long-Term Success"; L. Weber and R. Feintzeig, "Assistance for Laid-Off Workers Gets Downsized," *Wall Street Journal*, February 18, 2013, accessed May 6, 2016, http://www.wsj.com/news/articles/SB10001424052702304899704579391254047535652

169. Cascio, "Employment Downsizing and Its Alternatives: Strategies for Long-Term Success."

170. R. Knight, "How to Manage Coronavirus Layoffs With Compassion," *Harvard Business Review*, April 7, 2020, accessed May 1, 2020, https://hbr.org/2020/04/how-to-manage-coronavirus-layoffs-with-compassion?ab=hero-main-text.

171. C. Jones and L. Scott, "Layoffs Are Awful, but Don't Forget the Survivors," *Oilweek*, January 14, 2016, accessed May 6, 2016, http://www.oilweek.com/index.php/columnists/699-layoffs-are-awful-but-don-t-forget-the-survivors.

172. J. Ackerman, "Helping Layoff Survivors Cope: Companies Strive to Keep Morale High," *Boston Globe*, December 30, 2001, H1.

173. S. Salinas, "Verizon Says 10,000 Employees Have Accepted Its Buyout Offer," *CNBC*, December 10, 2018, accessed May 1, 2020, https://www.cnbc.com/2018/12/10/verizon-says-10400-employees-have-been-accepted-as-a-part-of-a-voluntary-program-to-leave-the-business.html.

174. J. Lublin and S. Thurm, "How Companies Calculate Odds in Buyout Offers," *Wall Street Journal*, March 27, 2009, B1.

175. M. Willett, "Early Retirement and Phased Retirement Programs for the Public Sector," *Benefits & Compensation Digest*, April 2005, 31.

176. C. Hymowitz, "American Firms Want to Keep Older Workers a Bit Longer," *Bloomberg*, December 16, 2016, accessed April 20, 2017, https://www.bloomberg.com/news/articles/2016-12-16/american-firms-want-to-keep-older-workers-a-bit-longer.

177. Accounting Principals, "Over Eighty Percent of Full-time Workers are Actively Seeking or Passively Open to New Job Opportunities," *Cision PR Newswire*, July 18, 2018, accessed May 1, 2020, https://www.prnewswire.com/news-releases/over-eighty-percent-of-full-time-workers-are-actively-seeking-or-passively-open-to-new-job-opportunities-300682881.html.

178. T. Mahan, D. Nelms, C. Bearden & B. Pearce, "2019 Retention Report," *Work Institute*,

179. K. Dill, "Companies Step Up Efforts to Keep Workers From Quitting," *Wall Street Journal*, March 1, 2020, accessed May 1, 2020, https://www.wsj.com/articles/companies-step-up-efforts-to-keep-workers-from-quitting-11583058602.

180. Ibid.

181. D. R. Dalton, W. D. Todor, and D. M. Krackhardt, "Turnover Overstated: The Functional Taxonomy," *Academy of Management Review* 7 (1982): 117–123.

182. J. R. Hollenbeck and C. R. Williams, "Turnover Functionality versus Turnover Frequency: A Note on Work Attitudes and Organizational Effectiveness," *Journal of Applied Psychology* 71 (1986): 606–611.

183. Silverman and Waller, "The Algorithm That Tells the Boss Who Might Quit."

184. C. R. Williams, "Reward Contingency, Unemployment, and Functional Turnover," *Human Resource Management Review* 9 (1999): 549–576.

12

1. "Table 3.4. Civilian Labor Force by Age, Sex, Race, and Ethnicity, 1996, 2006, 2016, and Projected 2026," *Bureau of Labor* Statistics, October 24, 2017, accessed May 8, 2020, https://www.bls.gov/emp/tables/civilian-labor-force-detail.htm;

2. "Table 3.4. – Civilian Labor Force by Age, Sex, Race, and Ethnicity, 1996, 2006, 2016, and Projected 2026;" "Labor Force Projections to 2020: A More Slowly Growing Workforce," *Monthly Labor Review,* January 2012, 43–64.

3. A. DeBarros and J. Adamy, "US Births Fall to Lowest Level Since 1980s," *Wall Street Journal*, May 15, 2019, accessed May 9, 2020, https://www.wsj.com/articles/u-s-births-fall-to-lowest-rates-since-1980s-11557892860; D. Dougherty, R. Rigdon & P. Overberg, "How America Has Changed Since the Last Census," *Wall Street Journal*, March 9, 2020, accessed May 9, 2020, https://www.wsj.com/articles/how-america-has-changed-since-the-last-census-11583703849.

4. "Table 3.4. Civilian Labor Force by Age, Sex, Race, and Ethnicity, 1996, 2006, 2016, and Projected 2026."

5. "Marriott Facts: Prepare for your Interview and Learn about Marriott," Marriott, accessed April 22, 2017, http://www.marriott.com/careers/business-facts.mi.

6. B. Marriott, "Diversity & Inclusion Matters," *Marriott on the Move*, February 6, 2017, accessed April 22, 2017, http://www.blogs.marriott.com/marriott-on-the-move/2017/02/diversity-matters.html.

7. "Diversity & Inclusion Global Fact Sheet, Marriott International, Spirit to Serve Our Diverse World," *Marriott*, accessed April 22, 2017, www.marriott.com/Multimedia/PDF/Corporate/DiversityFactSheet.pdf.

8. Press Release, "Marriott International Ranks #2 on 2019 DiversityInc Top 50 Companies for Diversity List," *Cision PR Newswire*, May 9, 2019, accessed May 9, 2020, https://www.prnewswire.com/news-releases/marriott-international-ranks-2-on-2019-diversityinc-top-50-companies-for-diversity-list-300847650.html.

9. Equal Employment Opportunity Commission, "Affirmative Action Appropriate Under Title VII of the Civil Rights Act of 1964, as Amended. Chapter XIV – Equal Employment Opportunity Commission, Part 1608," *Government Publishing Office*, accessed May 8, 2016, http://www.access.gpo.gov/nara/cfr/waisidx_04/29cfr1608_04.html.

10. Equal Employment Opportunity Commission, "Federal Laws Prohibiting Job Discrimination: Questions and Answers," *Equal Employment Opportunity Commission*, accessed May 8, 2016, http://www.eeoc.gov/facts/qanda.html.

11. A. P. Carnevale and S. C. Stone, *The American Mosaic: An In-Depth Report on the Future of Diversity at Work* (New York: McGraw-Hill, 1995).

12. T. Roosevelt, "From Affirmative Action to Affirming Diversity," *Harvard Business Review* 68, no. 2 (1990): 107–117.

13. A. M. Konrad and F. Linnehan, "Formalized HRM Structures: Coordinating Equal Employment Opportunity or Concealing Organizational Practices?" *Academy of Management Journal* 38, no. 3 (1995): 787–820; see, for example, *Hopwood v. Texas*, 78 F.3d 932 (5th Cir., March 18, 1996). The US Supreme Court has upheld the principle of affirmative action but has struck down some specific programs.

14. J. O'Sullivan, "Washington Voters Narrowly Rejecting Affirmative Action in Referendum 88," *The Seattle Times*, November 5, 2019, accessed May 9, 2020, https://www.seattletimes.com/seattle-news/politics/election-results-2019-referendum-88-affirmative-action-washington-state/.

15. J. Bravin, "Court Backs Affirmative Action Ban – Justices Uphold State Initiative to End Race-Based Admissions, But Are Divided on Broader Issue," *Wall Street Journal*, April 23, 2014, A1.

16. M. E. Heilman, C. J. Block, and P. Stathatos, "The Affirmative Action Stigma of Incompetence: Effects of Performance Information Ambiguity," *Academy of Management Journal* 40, no. 3 (1997): 603–625; D. Evans, "A Comparison of the Other Directed Stigmatization Produced by Legal and Illegal Forms of Affirmative Action," *Journal of Applied Psychology* 88, no. 1 (2003): 121–130.

17. T. Montaque, "Diversity and Inclusion: How to End Today's Corporate Culture," *Fortune*, June 10, 2020, accessed June 21, 2020, https://fortune.com/2020/06/10/black-ceo-corporate-diversity-inclusion/.

18. L. Leslie, D. Mayer, and D. Kravitz, "The Stigma of Affirmative Action: A Stereotyping-Based Theory and Meta-Analytic Test of the Consequences for Performance." *Academy of Management Journal* 57, no. 4 (2014): 964–989.

19. E. Orenstein, "The Business Case for Diversity," *Financial Executive*, May 2005, 22–25; G. Robinson and K. Dechant, "Building a Business Case for Diversity," *Academy of Management Executive* 11, no. 3 (1997): 21–31.

20. E. Esen, "2005 Workplace Diversity Practices: Survey Report," *Society for Human Resource Management*, accessed March 24, 2009, http://www.shrm.org/research; M. Reinwald & F. Kunze, "Being Different, Being Absent? A Dynamic Perspective on Demographic Dissimilarity and Absenteeism in Blue-Collar Teams," *Academy of Management Journal* (In-Press), Published Online April 30, 2019, accessed May 10, 2020, https://journals.aom.org/doi/10.5465/amj.2018.0290.

21. Orenstein, "Business Case for Diversity."

22. Esen, "2005 Workplace Diversity Practices: Survey Report."

23. Orenstein, "Business Case for Diversity."

24. S. Randazzo, "Qualcomm to Pay $19.5 Million to Settle Claims of Bias Against Women," *Wall Street Journal*, July 26, 2016, accessed April 22, 2017, https://www.wsj.com/articles/qualcomm-to-pay-19-5-million-to-settle-claims-of-bias-against-women-1469571756.

25. P. Wright and S. P. Ferris, "Competitiveness Through Management of Diversity: Effects on Stock Price Valuation," *Academy of Management Journal* 38 (1995): 272–285.

26. I. Bohnet, "Real Fixes for Workplace Bias," *Wall Street Journal*, March 12–13, 2016, C3; K. Lachance Shandrow, "10 US Companies with Radically Awesome Parental Leave Policies," *Entrepreneur*, August 11, 2015, accessed May 8, 2016, https://www.entrepreneur.com/slideshow/249467.

27. P. Wright and S. P. Ferris, "Competitiveness Through Management of Diversity: Effects on Stock Price Valuation."

28. "Buying Power: Quick Take," Catalyst, April 27, 2020, accessed May 10, 2020, https://www.catalyst.org/research/buying-power/; American Community Survey, "Table DP05, Total Population, 2018: ACS 1-Year Estimates Data Profiles, ACS Demographic and Housing Estimates," US Census Bureau, accessed May 10, 2020, https://data.census.gov/cedsci/table?q=Total%20Population%20in%20the%20United%20States&hidePreview=false&tid=ACSDP1Y2018.DP05&vintage=2018; J. Humphreys, "The Multicultural Economy 2019," Selig Center for Economic Growth, Terry College of Business, University of Georgia, accessed May 10, 2020, https://www.terry.uga.edu/about/selig/publications.php.

29. "QuickFacts: United States," Census Bureau, July 1, 2015, accessed April 22, 2017, https://www.census.gov/quickfacts/table/RHI125215/00#head note-js-a; M. Weeks & J. Humphreys, "Asians, Hispanics Driving US Economy Forward, According to UGA Study," *UGA Today*, September 24, 2015, accessed April 22, 2017, http://news.uga.edu/releases/article/2015-multicultural-economy-report/.

30. S. Willmer, "Fidelity Has 'Real Need' to Recruit More Women, Johnson Says," *Bloomberg*, September 27, 2017, accessed May 10, 2020, https://www.bloomberg.com/news/articles/2017-09-27/fidelity-has-real-need-to-recruit-more-women-johnson-says?sref=xXo7CWym.

31. P. Collins & C. Stein, "The Most Powerful Woman in Investing: Abby Johnson Opens Up," *Bloomberg*, November 17, 2018, accessed May 10, 2020, https://www.bloomberg.com/news/features/2018-11-17/fidelity-s-abby-johnson-opens-up-about-crypto-and-index-funds?sref=xXo7CWym.

32. Ibid.

33. V. Fuhrmans, "Companies With Diverse Executive Teams Posted Bigger Profit Margins, Study Shows," *Wall Street Journal*, January 18, 2018, accessed May 10, 2020, https://www.wsj.com/articles/companies-with-diverse-executive-teams-posted-bigger-profit-margins-study-shows-1516322484.

34. J. Pletzer, R. Nikolova, K. Kedzior, S. Voelpel, "Does Gender Matter? Female Representation on Corporate Boards and Firm Financial Performance - A Meta-Analysis," *PLOS One* (June 18, 2015), accessed May 10, 2020, https://www.ncbi.nlm.nih.gov/pmc/articles/PMC4473005/; C. Post & K. Byron, "Women on Boards and Firm Financial Performance: A Meta-Analysis," *Academy of Management Journal* 58, no. 5 (2015): 1546-1571; S. Tasheva & A. Hillman, "Integrating Diversity at Different Levels: Multilevel Human Capital, Social Capital, and Demographic Diversity and Their Implications for Team Effectiveness," *Academy of Management Review* 44, no. 4 (2019): 746–765.

35. S. Bell, A. Villado, M. Lukasik, L. Belau & A. Briggs, "Getting Specific about Demographic Diversity Variable and Team Performance Relationships: A Meta-Analysis," *Journal of Management* 37, no. 3 (2011): 709-743; S. Harvey, S. Currall & T. Hammer, "Decision Diversion in Diverse Teams: Findings From Inside a Corporate Boardroom," *Academy of Management Discoveries* 3, no. 4 (2017): 358–381.

36. W. W. Watson, K. Kumar, and L. K. Michaelsen, "Cultural Diversity's Impact on Interaction Process and Performance: Comparing Homogeneous and Diverse Task Groups," Academy of Management Journal 36 (1993): 590–602; K. A. Jehn, G. B. Northcraft, and M. A. Neale, "Why Differences Make a Difference: A Field Study of Diversity, Conflict, and Performance in Workgroups," Administrative Science Quarterly 44 (1999): 741–763; E. Kearney, D. Gebert, and S. Voelpel, "When and How Diversity Benefits Teams: The Importance of Team Members' Need for Cognition," Academy of Management Journal 52 (2009): 581–598.

37. S. Creary, M. McDonnell, S. Ghai & J. Scruggs, "When and Why Diversity Improves Your Board's Performance," *Harvard Business Review*, March 27, 2019, accessed May 11, 2020, https://hbr.org/2019/03/when-and-why-diversity-improves-your-boards-performance; A. Mayo, A. Wooley, R. Chow, "Unpacking Participation and Influence: Diversity's Countervailing Effects on Expertise Use in Groups," *Academy of Management Discoveries* (In-press, published online January 8, 2019,) accessed May 11, 2020, https://journals.aom.org/doi/10.5465/amd.2018.0044.

38. "Women on Boards and Firm Financial Performance: A Meta-Analysis;" K. Klein, "Does Gender Diversity on Boards Really Boost Company Performance?" *Knowledge@Wharton*, May 18, 2017, accessed May 11, 2020, https://knowledge.wharton.upenn.edu/article/will-gender-diversity-boards-really-boost-company-performance/.

39. M. R. Carrell and E. E. Mann, "Defining Workplace Diversity Programs and Practices in Organizations," *Labor Law Journal* 44 (1993): 743–764.

40. D. A. Harrison, K. H. Price, and M. P. Bell, "Beyond Relational Demography: Time and the Effects of Surface-and Deep-Level Diversity on Work Group Cohesion," *Academy of Management Journal* 41 (1998): 96–107.

41. D. Harrison, K. Price, J. Gavin, and A. Florey, "Time, Teams, and Task Performance: Changing Effects of Surface-and Deep-Level Diversity on Group Functioning," *Academy of Management Journal* 45 (2002): 1029–1045.

42. Harrison, et al., "Beyond Relational Demography."

43. Ibid.

44. J. Haidt and L. Jussim, "Hard Truths About Race on Campus," *Wall Street Journal*, May 6, 2016, accessed May 8, 2016, http://www.wsj.com/articles/hard-truths-about-race-on-campus-1462544543; T. Pettigrew and L. Tropp, "A Meta-Analytic Test of Intergroup Contact Theory," *Journal of Personality and Social Psychology* 90 (2006): 751–783.

45. S. Levy, "How Can We Achieve Age Diversity in Silicon Valley?" *BackChannel*, October 19, 2015, accessed April 23, 2017, https://backchannel.com/how-can-we-achieve-age-diversity-in-silicon-valley-11a847.

46. R. Alsop, "Why Your Grandfather Might Land a Job Before You Do," BBC, October 25, 2013, accessed May 8, 2016, http://www.bbc.com/capital/story/20131024-older-workers-fogey-or-find; E. White, "The New Recruits: Older Workers," *Wall Street Journal*, January 14, 2008, B3.

47. M. Kane, "Say What? 'Young People are Just Smarter,'" *CNET*, March 28, 2007, accessed May 9, 2015, http://www.cnet.com/news/say-what-young-people-are-just-smarter/.

48. P. Barnes, "Proposed Settlement Of Age Discrimination Case Hardly Onerous For PricewaterhouseCoopers," *Forbes*, March 16, 2020, accessed May 11, 2020, https://www.forbes.com/sites/patriciagbarnes/2020/03/16/proposed-settlement-of-age-discrimination-case-hardly-onerous-for-pricewaterhousecoopers/#161e733a5d7f; R. Mauer, "PwC Settles Age Discrimination in Hiring Claim," *Society for Human Resources Management*, March 18, 2020, accessed May 11, 2020, https://www.shrm.org/resourcesandtools/hr-topics/talent-acquisition/pages/pwc-settles-age-discrimination-hiring-claim.aspx.

49. Ibid.

50. K. Gee, "Campus Recruiting Hurts Older Workers, Suit Against PricewaterhouseCoopers Claims," *Wall Street Journal*, February 28, 2018, accessed May 11, 2020, https://www.wsj.com/articles/suit-claims-pwcs-campus-recruiting-disadvantages-older-job-seekers-1519850508.

51. P. Barnes, "Deja Vu: Google Settles Age Discrimination Lawsuit For $11 Million," *Forbes*, July 20, 2019, accessed May 11, 2020, https://www.forbes.com/sites/patriciagbarnes/2019/07/20/deja-vu-google-settles-age-discrimination-lawsuit-for-11-million/#5178f31171f1.

52. "Age Discrimination in Employment Act (Charges filed with EEOC) (includes Concurrent Charges with Title VII, ADA and EPA) FY 1997–FY 2019," *US Equal Employment Opportunity Commission*, accessed May 11, 2020,, http://www.eeoc.gov/eeoc/statistics/enforcement/adea.cfm.

53. S. R. Rhodes, "Age-Related Differences in Work Attitudes and Behavior," *Psychological Bulletin* 92 (1983): 328–367.

54. T. Ng and D. Feldman, "The Relationship of Age to Ten Dimensions of Job Performance," *Journal of Applied Psychology* 93, no. 2 (2008): 392–423.

55. G. M. McEvoy and W. F. Cascio, "Cumulative Evidence of the Relationship Between Employee Age and Job Performance," *Journal of Applied Psychology* 74 (1989): 11–17; T. Ng and D. Feldman, "The Relationship of Age to Ten Dimensions of Job Performance," *Journal of Applied Psychology* 93, no. 2 (2008): 392–423; A. Tergesen, "Why Everything You Think about Aging May Be Wrong," *Wall Street Journal*, November 30, 2014, accessed May 9, 2015, http://www.wsj.com/articles/why-everything-you-think-about-aging-may-be-wrong-1417408057; A. Tergesen, "Five Myths About Landing a Good Job Later in Life," *Wall Street Journal*, November 29, 2016, accessed April 23, 2017, tell application "Safari" to return URL of front dochttps://www.wsj.com/articles/five-myths-about-landing-a-good-job-later-in-life-1480302842.

56. L. Weber, "One Accounting Firm Wants to Hire Retirees," *Wall Street Journal*, January 17, 2018, accessed May 12, 2020, https://www.wsj.com/articles/one-accounting-firm-wants-to-hire-retirees-1516201200.

57. S. E. Sullivan and E. A. Duplaga, "Recruiting and Retaining Older Workers for the Millennium," *Business Horizons* 40 (November 12, 1997): 65; E. Townsend, "To Keep Older Workers, Consider New Responsibilities and Guard Against Discrimination," SHRM Foundation, accessed May 3, 2016, http://www.shrm.org/about/foundation/pages/researchthatmatters.aspx.

58. C. Hymowitz and R. Burnson, "It's Tough Being Over 40 in Silicon Valley," *Bloomberg*, September 8, 2016, accessed April 23, 2017, https://www.bloomberg.com/news/articles/2016-09-08/silicon-valley-s-job-hungry-say-we-re-not-to-old-for-this.

59. T. Maurer and N. Rafuse, "Learning, Not Litigating: Managing Employee Development and Avoiding Claims of Age Discrimination," *Academy of Management Executive* 15, no. 4 (2001): 110–121.

60. D. Brady, "The Bottom-Line Reasons for \ Mixing the Young and Old at Work," *Bloomberg Businessweek*, April 10, 2014, accessed July 11, 2014, http://www.businessweek.com/articles/2014-02-10/workplaces-boost-profits-when-young-and-old-workers-mentor-each-other; B. L. Hassell and P. L. Perrewe, "An Examination of Beliefs About Older Workers: Do Stereotypes Still Exist?" *Journal of Organizational Behavior* 16 (1995): 457–468; E. King, L. Finkelstein, C. Thomas & A. Corrington, "Generational Differences At Work Are Small. Thinking They're Big Affects Our Behavior," *Harvard Business Review*, August 1, 2019, accessed May 12, 2020, https://hbr.org/2019/08/generational-differences-at-work-are-small-thinking-theyre-big-affects-our-behavior.

61. "Charge Statistics: FY 1997 Through FY 2019," *Equal Employment Opportunity Commission*, accessed May 12, 2020, http://eeoc.gov/eeoc/statistics/enforcement/charges.cfm.

62. "Women in the Labor Force: A Databook," *Bureau of Labor Statistics,* December 2019, accessed May 12, 2020, https://www.bls.gov/opub/reports/womens-databook/2019/pdf/home.pdf .

63. "The 2019 State of Women-Owned Businesses Report: Summary of Key Trends," *Commissioned by American Express* , with the assistance of the Economic Census Branch of the Company Statistics Division of the US Census Bureau, September 23, 2019, accessed May 12, 2020, http://www.womenable.com/content/userfiles/2016_State_of_Women-Owned_Businesses_Executive_Report.pdf; Press Release, "Woman-Owned Businesses Are Growing 2X Faster On Average Than All Businesses Nationwide | Business Wire," *BusinessWire*, September 23, 2019, accessed May 12, 2020, https://www.businesswire.com/news/home/20190923005500/en/Woman-Owned-Businesses-Growing-2X-Faster-Average-Businesses.

64. "Women in the Labor Force: A Databook," *Bureau of Labor Statistics*.

65. "Pyramid: Women in S&P 500 Companies," Catalyst, January 15, 2020, accessed May 12, 2020, https://www.catalyst.org/research/women-in-sp-500-companies/.

66. Women CEOs of the S&P 500," *Catalyst*, May 1, 2020, accessed May 12, 2020, https://www.catalyst.org/research/women-ceos-of-the-sp-500/; D. Rabouin, "Only 1 Fortune 500 Company Is Headed by a Woman of Color," *Axios*, January 14, 2019, accessed May 12, 2020, https://www.axios.com/fortune-500-no-women-of-color-ceos-3d42619c-967b-47d2-b94c-659527b22ee3.html.

67. E. Hinchliffe, "Female Fortune 500 CEOs Reach 7.4%, a Record High," *Fortune*, May 18, 2020, accessed May 19, 2020, https://fortune.com/2020/05/18/women-run-37-fortune-500-companies-a-record-high/?utm_source=email&utm_medium=newsletter&utm_campaign=data-sheet&utm_content=2020051913pm.

68. " Women on Corporate Boards: Quick Take," *Catalyst*, March 13, 2020, accessed May 12, 2020, https://www.catalyst.org/research/women-on-corporate-boards/.

69. A. Joshi, J. Son, and H. Roh, "When Can Women Close the Gap? A Meta-Analytic Test of Sex Differences in Performance and Rewards," *Academy of Management Journal* 58 (2015): 1516–1545.

70. M. Bertrand and K. Hallock, "The Gender Gap in Top Corporate Jobs," *Industrial & Labor Relations Review* 55 (2001): 3–21.

71. J. R. Hollenbeck, D. R. Ilgen, C. Ostroff, and J. B. Vancouver, "Sex Differences in Occupational Choice, Pay, and Worth: A Supply-Side Approach to Understanding the Male-Female Wage Gap," *Personnel Psychology* 40 (1987): 715–744.

72. V. Bolotnyy & N. Emanuel, "Why Do Women Earn Less Than Men? Evidence from Bus and Train Operators (Working Paper)," *Harvard University Department of Economics*, July 5, 2019, accessed May 12, 2020, https://scholar.harvard.edu/files/bolotnyy/files/be_gender_gap.pdf.

73. A. Chamberlain & J. Jayaraman, "The Pipeline Problem: How College Majors Contribute to the Gender Pay Gap - Glassdoor Economic Research," Glassdoor, April 19, 2017, accessed April 23, 2017, https://www.glassdoor.com/research/studies/pipeline-problem-college-majors-gender-pay-gap/.

74. M. McCord, D. Joseph, L. Dhanani & J. Beus, "A Meta-Analysis of Sex and Race Differences in Perceived Workplace Mistreatment," *Journal of Applied Psychology* 103, no. 2 (2018): 137–163.

75. Department of Industry, Labor and Human Relations, Report of the Governor's Task Force on the Glass Ceiling Commission (Madison, WI: State of Wisconsin, 1993); S. Devillard, S. Sancier, C. Werner, I. Maller, and C. Kossoff, "Women Matter 2013, Gender Diversity in Top Management: Moving Corporate Culture, Moving Boundaries," *McKinsey & Company*, November 2013, 10–11; E. O. Wright and J. Baxter, "The Glass Ceiling Hypothesis: A Reply to Critics," *Gender & Society* 14 (2000): 814–821.

76. M. Fix, G. C. Galster, and R. J. Struyk, "An Overview of Auditing for Discrimination," in *Clear and Convincing Evidence: Measurement of Discrimination in America*, ed. M. Fix and R. Struyk (Washington, DC: Urban Institute Press, 1993), 1–68; V. Fuhrmans, "Where Women Fall Behind at Work: The First Step Into Management," *Wall Street Journal*, October 15, 2019, accessed May 12, 2020, https://www.wsj.com/articles/where-women-fall-behind-at-work-the-first-step-into-management-11571112361?mod=djemwhatsnews; "A Meta-Analysis of Sex and Race Differences in Perceived Workplace Mistreatment," *Journal of Applied Psychology*.

77. K. Badura, E. Grijalva, B. Galvin, B. Owens & D. Joseph, "Motivation to Lead: A Meta-Analysis and Distal-Proximal Model of Motivation and Leadership," *Journal of Applied Psychology* 105, no. 4 (2019): 311–354.

78. S. Devillard, S. Sancier, C. Werner, I. Maller, and C. Kossoff, "Women Matter 2013, Gender Diversity in Top Management: Moving Corporate Culture, Moving Boundaries," *McKinsey & Company*, November 2013, 13–14.

79. S. Shellenbarger, "One Way to Get Unstuck and Move Up? All You Have to Do Is Ask" *Wall Street Journal*, April 15, 2015, D3.

80. J. Lublin, "Men Enlist in Fight for Gender Equality," *Wall Street Journal*, March 11, 2015, B7.

81. "How to Report Sexual Harassment at Work," *Schwin Law*, accessed August 17, 2016, http://www.schwinlaw.com/uncategorized/how-to-report-sexual-harassment-at-work.

82. I. Hideg, A. Krstic, R. Trau & T. Zarina, "Do Longer Maternity Leaves Hurt Women's Careers?" *Harvard Business Review*, September 14, 2018, accessed May 13, 2020, https://hbr.org/2018/09/do-longer-maternity-leaves-hurt-womens-careers; I. Hideg, A. Krstic, R. Trau & T. Zarina, "The Unintended Consequences of Maternity Leaves: How Agency Interventions Mitigate the Negative Effects of Longer Legislated Maternity Leaves," *Journal of Applied Psychology* 103, no. 10 (2018): 1155-1164; D. Collings, Y. Freeney, & L. van der Werff, "How Companies Can Ensure Maternity Leave Doesn't Hurt Women's Careers," *Harvard Business Review*, September 11, 2019, accessed May 13, 2020, https://hbr.org/2018/09/how-companies-can-ensure-maternity-leave-doesnt-hurt-womens-careers.

83. "Do Longer Maternity Leaves Hurt Women's Careers?" *Harvard Business Review*.

84. "How Companies Can Ensure Maternity Leave Doesn't Hurt Women's Careers," *Harvard Business Review*.

85. I. Kuziemko, J. Pan, J. Shen & E. Washington, "The Mommy Effect: Do Women Anticipate the Employment Effects of Motherhood? (Working Paper)" *National Bureau of Economic Research*, June 2018, accessed May 13, 2020, https://www.nber.org/papers/w24740.pdf; L. Weber, "Working Women Often Underestimate Motherhood Costs," *Wall Street Journal*, June 26, 2018, accessed May 13, 2020, https://www.wsj.com/articles/working-women-often-underestimate-motherhood-costs-1530024789?mod=hp_major_pos13.

86. "Do Longer Maternity Leaves Hurt Women's Careers?" *Harvard Business Review*; "The Unintended Consequences of Maternity Leaves: How Agency Interventions Mitigate the Negative Effects of Longer Legislated Maternity Leaves," *Journal of Applied Psychology*.

87. "How Companies Can Ensure Maternity Leave Doesn't Hurt Women's Careers," *Harvard Business Review*.

88. Ibid.

89. "What You Should Know: EEOC and Enforcement Protections for LGBT Workers," US Equal Employment Opportunity Commission, accessed April 24, 2017, https://www.eeoc.gov/eeoc/newsroom/wysk/enforcement_protections_lgbt_workers.cfm.

90. Ibid.

91. K. Sangha, "LGBT Protection in the Workplace – A Survey of State and Local Laws," *Employment Relations Today* 42 no. 2 (2015): 57–68.

92. "What You Should Know: EEOC and Enforcement Protections for LGBT Workers," US Equal Employment Opportunity Commission.

93. *Bostock v. Clayton County, Georgia*, 17–1618 (US Supreme Court, June 15, 2020); *Altitude Express v. Zarda and Moore, Jr.*, 17–1623 (US Supreme Court, June 15, 2020); *Harris Funeral Homes v. Equal Employment Opportunity Commission*, 18-107 (US Supreme Court, June 15, 2020); J. Bravin & B. Kendall, "Supreme Court Rules for Gay and Transgender Rights in the Workplace," *Wall Street Journal*, June 15, 2020, accessed June 22, 2020, https://www.wsj.com/articles/supreme

-court-rules-for-gay-rights-in-the-workplace-11592230310?mod=djemwhatsnews; Non-Discrimination Laws," Movement Advancement Project, May 5, 2020, accessed May 13, 2020, http://www.lgbtmap.org/equality-maps/non_discrimination_laws; N. Scheiber, "US Agency Rules for Gays in Workplace Discrimination," *New York Times*, July 17, 2015, accessed April 24, 2017, https://www.nytimes.com/2015/07/18/business/us-agency-rules-for-gays-in-workplace-discrimination.html.

94. M. Bianco, "Pride 2016: The Simple Reason More and More Businesses Openly Support LGBT Rights," *Quartz*, June 26, 2016, accessed April 24, 2017, https://qz.com/710643/the-business-sense-of-supporting-lgbt-rights/.

95. D. Fidas and L. Cooper, The Cost of the Closet and the Rewards of Inclusion: Why the Workplace Environment for LGBT People Matters to Employees," Human Rights Campaign, May 2015, accessed April 24, 2017, http://hrc-assets.s3-website-us-east-1.amazonaws.com//files/assets/resources/Cost_of_the_Closet_May2014.pdf.

96. R. Trau, J. O'Leary & Cathy Brown, "7 Myths About Coming Out at Work," *Harvard Business Review*, October 19, 2018, accessed May 13, 2020, https://hbr.org/2018/10/7-myths-about-coming-out-at-work.

97. B. Sears and C. Mallory, "Documented Evidence of Employment Discrimination & Its Effects on LGBT People," The Williams Institute, UCLA Law School, July 2011, accessed April 24, 2017, https://williamsinstitute.law.ucla.edu/wp-content/uploads/Sears-Mallory-Discrimination-July-20111.pdf.

98. D. Fidas and L. Cooper, The Cost of the Closet and the Rewards of Inclusion: Why the Workplace Environment for LGBT People Matters to Employees," Human Rights Campaign, May 2015, accessed April 24, 2017, http://hrc-assets.s3-website-us-east-1.amazonaws.com//files/assets/resources/Cost_of_the_Closet_May2014.pdf.

99. "LGBT-Based Sex Discrimination Charges," US Equal Employment Opportunity Commission, accessed May 13, 2020, https://www.eeoc.gov/enforcement/lgbt-based-sex-discrimination-charges.

100. "The Report of the 2015 US Transgender Survey," National Center for Transgender Equality, December 2016, accessed April 24, 2017, http://www.transequality.org/sites/default/files/docs/usts/Executive%20Summary%20-%20FINAL%201.6.17.pdf.

101. C. Thoroughgood, K. Sawyer & J. Webster, "Creating a Trans-Inclusive Workplace," *Harvard Business Review*, March-April 2020, accessed May 13, 2020, https://hbr.org/2020/03/creating-a-trans-inclusive-workplace.

102. "Building LGBT-Inclusive Workplaces: Engaging Organizations and Individuals in Change," Catalyst, 2009, accessed April 24, 2017, http://www.catalyst.org/system/files/Building_LGBT_Inclusive_Workplaces_Engaging_Organizations_and_Individuals_in_Change.pdf.

103. "Building LGBT-Inclusive Workplaces: Engaging Organizations and Individuals in Change," Catalyst.

104. "Transgender Inclusion in the Workplace: A Toolkit for Employers," Human Rights Campaign Foundation, 2016, accessed April 24, 2017, http://assets.hrc.org//files/assets/resources/Transgender_Inclusion_in_the_Workplace_A_Toolkit_for_Employers_Version_10_14_2016.pdf?_ga=1.40958882.1697316505.1493052696.

105. E. Flitter, "Being Transgender at Goldman Sachs," *New York Times*, June 21, 2019, accessed May 13, 2020, https://www.nytimes.com/2019/06/21/business/goldman-transgender.html.

106. Ibid.

107. "First Step: Gender Identity in the Workplace," *Catalyst*, June 22, 2015, accessed April 24, 2017, http://www.catalyst.org/knowledge/first-step-gender-identity-workplace.

108. "Workplace Gender Transition Guidelines at Ernst & Young," EY, accessed May 13, 2020, https://assets2.hrc.org/files/assets/resources/ErnstYoung-TransitionGuidelines.pdf.

109. Standards of Care for the Health of Transsexual, Transgender, and Gender Nonconforming People, Version 7," The World Professional Association for Transgender Health, September 14, 2011, accessed May 13, 2020, https://www.wpath.org/media/cms/Documents/SOC%20v7/Standards%20of%20Care_V7%20Full%20Book_English.pdf.

110. "Charge Statistics: FY1997 Through FY 2019," Equal Employment Opportunity Commission, accessed May 14, 2020, https://www.eeoc.gov/enforcement/charge-statistics-charges-filed-eeoc-fy-1997-through-fy-2019.

111. "A Meta-Analysis of Sex and Race Differences in Perceived Workplace Mistreatment," *Journal of Applied Psychology*.

112. L. Fraser, "4 Latino CEOs You Should Know," *Diversity Best Practices*, September 23, 2019, accessed May 14, 2020, https://www.diversitybestpractices.com/latino-ceos-you-should-know; S. Kalita, "Opinion: 9 reasons the Indian CEO keeps coming to the rescue," *CNN Business*, February 4, 2020, accessed May 14, 2020, https://www.cnn.com/2020/02/02/perspectives/indian-ceo-perspectives/index.html; E. McGirt, "Waiting for Corporate America's 'Crazy Rich Asians' Moment," *Fortune*, November 7, 2019, accessed May 14, 2020, https://fortune.com/2019/11/07/waiting-for-corporate-americas-crazy-rich-asians-moment/.

113. "Household Data Annual Averages: Table 11. Employed Persons by Detailed Occupation, Sex, Race, and Hispanic or Latino Ethnicity," *Bureau of Labor Statistics, Department of Labor*, January 22, 2020, accessed May 14, 2020, https://www.bls.gov/cps/cpsaat11.htm.

114. "A Meta-Analysis of Sex and Race Differences in Perceived Workplace Mistreatment," *Journal of Applied Psychology*.

115. Fix, et al., "An Overview of Auditing for Discrimination."

116. M. Bendick, Jr., C. W. Jackson, and V. A. Reinoso, "Measuring Employment Discrimination through Controlled Experiments," in *African-Americans* and *Post-Industrial Labor Markets*, ed. James B. Stewart (New Brunswick, NJ: Transaction Publishers, 1997), 77–100.

117. S. Mullainathan, "Racial Bias Even When We Have Good Intentions," *New York Times*, January 3, 2015, BU6.

118. P. B. Riach and J. Rich, "Measuring Discrimination by Direct Experimental Methods: Seeking Gunsmoke," *Journal of Post Keynesian Economics* 14, no. 2 (Winter 1991–1992): 143–150.

119. A. Heath & V. Di Stasio, "Racial Discrimination in Britain, 1969–2017: A Meta-Analysis of Field Experiments on Racial Discrimination in the British Labour Market," *The British Journal of Sociology* 70, no. 5 (2019): 1774–1798; L. Quilliam, A. Heath, D. Pager, A. Midtboen, F. Fleischmann & O. Hexel, "Do Some Countries Discriminate More than Others? Evidence from 97 Field Experiments of Racial Discrimination in Hiring," *Sociological Science* 6, no. 18, (2019): 467–496, https://www.sociologicalscience.com/articles-v6-18-467/.

120. A. P. Brief, R. T. Buttram, R. M. Reizenstein, and S. D. Pugh, "Beyond Good Intentions: The Next Steps Toward Racial Equality in the American Workplace," *Academy of Management Executive* 11 (1997): 59–72.

121. S. Mullainathan," Biased Algorithms Are Easier to Fix Than Biased People," *New York Times* December 6, 2019, accessed May 14, 2020, https://www.nytimes.com/2019/12/06/business/algorithm-bias-fix.html; L. E. Wynter, "Business & Race: Federal Agencies, Spurred on by Nonprofit Groups, Are Increasingly Embracing the Use of Undercover Investigators to Identify Discrimination in the Marketplace," *Wall Street Journal*, July 1, 1998, B1; E. Dwoskin, "Social Bias Creeps into New Web Technology," *Wall Street Journal*, August 21, 2015, B1, B4.

122. E. Dwoskin, "Social Bias Creeps into New Web Technology," *Wall Street Journal*, August 21, 2015, B1, B4.

123. J. Williams & S. Mihaylo, "How the Best Bosses Interrupt Bias on Their Teams," *Harvard Business Review*, November-December 2019, accessed May 15, 2020, https://hbr.org/2019/11/how-the-best-bosses-interrupt-bias-on-their-teams.

124. M. Korn, "Netflix CEO and Wife Give $120 Million to Historically Black Colleges," *Wall Street Journal*, June 17, 2020, accessed June 22, 2020, https://www.wsj.com/articles/netflix-ceo-and-wife-give-120-million-to-historically-black-colleges-11592399700;

125. Ibid.

126. J. Kastrenakes, "Apple launches $100 million Racial Equity and Justice Initiative," *The Verge*, June 11, 2020, accessed June 22, 2020, https://www.theverge.com/2020/6/11/21287999/apple-racial-equity-justice-initiative-amount-cook-lisa-jackson.

127. S. Sandberg, "Supporting Black and Diverse Communities," About Facebook, June 18, 2020, accessed June 22, 2020, https://about.fb.com/news/2020/06/supporting-black-and-diverse-communities/.

128. "Americans with Disabilities Act Questions and Answers," *US Department of Justice*, accessed April 25, 2017, http://www.ada.gov/qandaeng.htm.

129. "Disability Statistics," Disability Statistics, accessed May 14, 2020, https://www.disabilitystatistics.org/reports/acs.cfm?statistic=1.

130. N. Scheiber, "Fake Cover Letters Expose Discrimination Against Disabled," *New York Times*, November 2, 2015, accessed May 8, 2016, http://www.nytimes.com/2015/11/02/upshot/fake-cover-letters-expose-discrimination-against-disabled.html.

131. "Disability Statistics," Disability Statistics; Economic News Release, "Persons with a Disability: Labor Force Characteristics Summary," Bureau of Labor Statistics, February 26, 2020, accessed May 14, 2020, https://www.bls.gov/news.release/disabl.nr0.htm.

132. R. Greenwood and V. A. Johnson, "Employer Perspectives on Workers with Disabilities," *Journal of Rehabilitation* 53 (1987): 37–45.

133. B. Loy, "Accommodation and Compliance Series Workplace Accommodations: Low Cost, High Impact," *Job Accommodation Network*, September 1, 2016, accessed April 25, 2017, https://askjan.org/media/downloads/LowCostHighImpact.pdf.

134. D. Zielinski, "New Assistive Technologies Aid Employees With Disabilities," Society for *Human Resource Management*, December 20, 2016, accessed April 25, 2017, https://www.shrm.org/resourcesandtools/hr-topics/technology/pages/new-assistive-technologies-aid-employees-with-disabilities.aspx.

135. "Study on the Financing of Assistive Technology Devices and Services for Individuals With Disabilities: A Report to the President and the

Congress of the United States," *National Council on Disability*, accessed May 8, 2016, http://www.ncd.gov/newsroom/publications/assistive.html.

136.   M. Lupica, "Bob Gibson on Race, Baseball and What Is Next," *MLB News*, June 17, 2020, accessed June 21, 2020, https://www.mlb.com/news/bob-gibson-on-race-baseball.

137.   Ibid.

138.   R. B. Cattell, "Personality Pinned Down," *Psychology Today* 7 (1973): 40–46; C. S. Carver and M. F. Scheier, *Perspectives on Personality* (Boston, MA: Allyn & Bacon, 1992).

139.   S. Berfield, "Will Investors Put the Lid on the Container Store's Generous Wages," *Bloomberg BusinessWeek*, February 19, 2015, accessed May 8, 2016, http://www.bloomberg.com/news/articles/2015-02-19/container-store-conscious-capitalism-and-the-perils-of-going-public.

140.   J. M. Digman, "Personality Structure: Emergence of the Five-Factor Model," *Annual Review of Psychology* 41 (1990): 417–440; M. R. Barrick and M. K. Mount, "The Big Five Personality Dimensions and Job Performance: A Meta-Analysis," *Personnel Psychology* 44 (1991): 1–26.

141.   C. Anderson and G. Kilduff, "Why Do Dominant Personalities Attain Influence in Face-to-Face Groups? The Competence Signaling Effects of Trait Dominance," *Journal of Personal and Social Psychology* 96, no. 2 (2001): 1160–1175.

142.   K. D. Lassila, "A Brief History of Groupthink: Why Two, Three, or Many Heads Aren't Always Better Than One," *Yale Alumni Magazine*, January/February 2008, accessed May 8, 2016, http://yalealumnimagazine.com/articles/1947.

143.   J. Bariso, "10-Year Anniversary of the 'Miracle on the Hudson': How a Pilot and His Crew Used 208 Seconds to Save Over 100 Lives," *Inc.*, January 15, 2019, accessed June 21, 2020, https://www.inc.com/justin-bariso/10-year-anniversary-of-miracle-on-hudson-how-a-pilot-his-crew-used-208-seconds-to-save-over-100-lives.html.

144.   Ibid.

145.   Ibid.

146.   O. Behling, "Employee Selection: Will Intelligence and Conscientiousness Do the Job?" *Academy of Management Executive* 12 (1998): 77–86.

147.   R. S. Dalal, "A Meta-Analysis of the Relationship Between Organizational Citizenship Behavior and Counterproductive Work Behavior," *Journal of Applied Psychology* 90 (2005): 1241–1255.

148.   Barrick and Mount, "The Big Five Personality Dimensions and Job Performance"; M. K. Mount and M. R. Barrick, "The Big Five Personality Dimensions: Implications for Research and Practice in Human Resource Management," *Research in Personnel & Human Resources Management* 13 (1995): 153–200; M. K. Mount and M. R. Barrick, "Five Reasons Why the 'Big Five' Article Has Been Frequently Cited," *Personnel Psychology* 51 (1998): 849–857; D. S. Ones, M. K. Mount, M. R. Barrick, and J. E. Hunter, "Personality and Job Performance: A Critique of the Tett, Jackson, and Rothstein (1991) Meta-Analysis," *Personnel Psychology* 47 (1994): 147–156.

149.   Mount and Barrick, "Five Reasons Why the 'Big Five' Article Has Been Frequently Cited."

150.   T. Cower, "Personality Affects Pay: Extroverts Earn More Than Introverts," *Bloomberg*, August 9, 2018, accessed April 29, 2020, https://www.bloomberg.com/opinion/articles/2018-08-09/personality-affects-pay-extroverts-earn-more-than-introverts?sref=xXo7CWym; M. Gensowski, M. "Personality, IQ, and Lifetime Earnings," *Labour Economics* 51 (2018): 170–183.

151.   Ibid.

152.   J. A. Lopez, "Talking Desks: Personality Types Revealed in State Workstations," *Arizona Republic*, January 7, 1996, D1.

153.   D. A. Thomas and R. J. Ely, "Making Differences Matter: A New Paradigm for Managing Diversity," *Harvard Business Review* 74 (September–October 1996): 79–90.

154.   Esen, "2005 Workplace Diversity Practices."

155.   L. Stevens, "Small Changes Can Increase Corporate Diversity," *Wall Street Journal*, March 13, 2018, accessed May 14, 2020, https://www.wsj.com/articles/small-changes-can-increase-corporate-diversity-1520993340.

156.   E. Esen, "2007 State of Workplace Diversity Management. A Survey Report by the Society for Human Resource Management," 2008.

157.   M. Cardador & M. Pratt, "Becoming Who We Serve: A Model of Multi-Layered Employee-Customer Identification," *Academy of Management Journal* 61, no. 6 (2018): 2053–2080.

158.   "Oshkosh Corporation – Diversity & Inclusion," *Oshkosh*, accessed July 12, 2014, http://www.oshkoshcorporation.com/about/diversity.html.

159.   J. Bourke & B. Dillon, "Eight Truths About Diversity and Inclusion at Work," *Deloitte Insights* 22, January 22, 2018, accessed June 23, 2020, https://www2.deloitte.com/us/en/insights/deloitte-review/issue-22/diversity-and-inclusion-at-work-eight-powerful-truths.html.

160.   Ibid.

161.   J. R. Norton and R. E. Fox, *The Change Equation: Capitalizing on Diversity for Effective Organizational Change* (Washington, DC: American Psychological Association, 1997).

162.   Ibid.

163.   Thomas and Ely, "Making Differences Matter."

164.   R. Thomas, Jr., *Beyond Race and Gender: Unleashing the Power of Your Total Workforce by Managing Diversity* (New York: AMACOM, 1991).

165.   Ibid.

166.   T. Cox Jr., "The Multicultural Organization," *Academy of Management Executive* 5 (1991): 34–47.

167.   S. Lubove, "Damned If You Do, Damned If You Don't: Preference Programs Are on the Defensive in the Public Sector, but Plaintiffs' Attorneys and Bureaucrats Keep Diversity Inc. Thriving in Corporate America," *Forbes*, December 15, 1997, 122.

168.   L. S. Gottfredson, "Dilemmas in Developing Diversity Programs," in *Diversity in the Workplace*, ed. S. E. Jackson and Associates (New York: Guilford Press, 1992).

169.   A. Wittenberg-Cox, "Deloitte's Radical Attempt to Reframe Diversity," *Harvard Business Review*, August 3, 2017, accessed May 15, 2020, https://hbr.org/2017/08/deloittes-radical-attempt-to-reframe-diversity; J. Graham and S. Kerr, "Mentoring," in *Diversity in Engineering: Managing the Workforce of the Future* (Washington, DC: National Academies Press, 2002), accessed June 16, 2013, http://www.nap.edu/openbook.php?record_id=10377&page=99.

170.   J. Longman, "Pioneer of a Crossover Move: How Becky Hammon Became NBA's First Full-Time Female Assistant Coach," New York Times, August 12, 2014, B8.

171.   M. Jacobs, "Katie Sowers: The 49ers Didn't Hire Me as a Coach to Make a Point,'" *The Guardian*, January 16, 2020, accessed May 15, 2020, https://www.theguardian.com/sport/2020/jan/16/katie-sowers-san-francisco-49ers-coach-nfl.

172.   Ibid.

173.   Carnevale and Stone, *The American Mosaic*.

174.   J. Lublin, "Men Enlist in Fight for Gender Equality," *Wall Street Journal*, March 11, 2015, B7.

175.   A. Greenwald, B. Nosek, and M. Banaji, "Understanding and Using the Implicit Association Test: I. An Improved Scoring Algorithm," *Journal of Personality & Social Psychology* (August 2003): 197–206; J. S. Lublin, "Bringing Hidden Biases into the Light," *Wall Street Journal*, January 9, 2014, accessed May 9, 2016, http://online.wsj.com/news/articles/SB100014240527023037544045793085626908696896; "The IAT The Blind Spot," *The Blind Spot*, accessed July 13, 2014, http://spottheblindspot.com/the-iat/.

176.   T. Bartlett, "Can We Really Measure Implicit Bias? Maybe Not," *The Chronicle of Higher Education*, January 5, 2017, accessed May 15, 2020, https://www.chronicle.com/article/Can-We-Really-Measure-Implicit/238807; H. Blanton, J. Jaccard, E. Strauts, G. Mitchell and P. Tetlock, "Toward a Meaningful Metric of Implicit Prejudice," *Journal of Applied Psychology* 100 (2015): 1468–1481; F. Oswald, G. Mitchell, H. Blanton, J. Jaccard, and P. Tetlock, "Predicting Ethnic and Racial Discrimination: A Meta-Analysis of IAT Criterion Studies," *Journal of Personality and Social Psychology* 105 (2013): 171–192; H. Blanton, J. Jaccard, J. Klick, B. Mellers, G. Mitchell, and P. Tetlock, "Strong Claims and Weak Evidence: Reassessing the Predictive Validity of the IAT," *Journal of Applied Psychology* 94 (2009): 567–582; T. Bartlett, "Can We Really Measure Implicit Bias? Maybe Not," *Chronicle of Higher Education*, January 5, 2017, accessed April 25, 2017, http://www.chronicle.com/article/Can-We-Really-Measure-Implicit/238807.

177.   P. Forscher, C. Lai, J. Axt, C. Ebersole, M. Herman, P. Devine & B. Nosek, "A Meta-Analysis of Procedures to Change Implicit Measures," *Journal of Personality and Social Psychology*, 117, no. 3 (2019): 522–559.

178.   K. Herzog, "Is Starbucks Implementing Flawed Science in Their Anti-Bias Training?" Slog - The Stranger, April 17, 2018, accessed May 15, 2020, https://www.thestranger.com/slog/2018/04/17/26052277/is-starbucks-implementing-flawed-science-in-their-anti-bias-training.

179.   A. Applewhite, "You're How Old? We'll Be in Touch - The New York," *New York Times*, September 3, 2016, accessed April 25, 2017, https://www.nytimes.com/2016/09/04/opinion/sunday/youre-how-old-well-be-in-touch.html.

180.   Bohnet, "Real Fixes for Workplace Bias.'"

181.   A. Valerio and K. Sawyer, "The Men Who Mentor," *Harvard Business Review*, December 7, 2016, accessed April 25, 2017, https://hbr.org/2016/12/the-men-who-mentor-women.

182.   R. Joplin and C. S. Daus, "Challenges of Leading a Diverse Workforce," *Academy of Management Executive* 11 (1997): 32–47.

183.   Korkki, "What Could I Possibly Learn from a Mentor Half My Age? Plenty," *New York Times*, September 10, 2016, accessed April 25, 2017, https://www.nytimes.com/2016/09/11/business/what-could-i-possibly-learn-from-a-mentor-half-my-age.html?_r=0.

184.   T. Minsberg, "In a Reverse Mentorship, Seeing Age Though a New Lens," *New York Times*, September 10, 2016, accessed April 25, 2017, https://www.nytimes.com/2016/09/11/business/in-a-reverse-mentorship-seeing-age-though-a-new-lens.html.

185.   Korkki, "What Could I Possibly Learn from a Mentor Half My Age? Plenty."

186. Minsberg, "In a Reverse Mentorship, Seeing Age Though a New Lens."

187. Korkki, "What Could I Possibly Learn from a Mentor Half My Age? Plenty."

188. P. Dvorak, "How Executives Are Pushed to Foster Diversity," *Wall Street Journal,* December 18, 2006, accessed May 8, 2016, http://online.wsj.com/article/SB116640764543853102.html?mod=rss_build.

189. A. Kalev, F. Dobbin, and E. Kelly. "Best Practices or Best Guesses? Diversity Management and the Remediation of Inequality." *American Sociological Review* 71 (2006): 589–617; A. Eagly, "When Passionate Advocates Meet Research on Diversity, Does the Honest Broker Stand a Chance," *Journal of Social Issues* 72 (2016): 199–122; C. Moss-Racusin, J. van der Toorn, J. Dovidio, V. Brescoll, M. Graham, and J. Handelsman, "Scientific Diversity Interventions," *Science* 343 (2014): 615–616.

190. F. Dobbin, A. Kalev, and E. Kelley, "Diversity Management in Corporate America," *Contexts* 6 (2007): 21–27.

191. K. Bezrukova, C. Spell, J. Perry & K. Jehn, "A Meta-Analytical Integration of Over 40 Years of Research on Diversity Training Evaluation," *Psychological Bulletin* 142, no. 11 (2016): 1227–1274.

192. L. Leslie "Diversity Initiative Effectiveness: A Typological Theory of Unintended Consequences," *Academy of Management Review* 44, no. 3 (2019): 538–563.

193. F. Dobbin and A. Kalev, "Why Diversity Program," *Harvard Business Review*, July–August 2016, accessed April 25, 2017, https://hbr.org/2016/07/why-diversity-programs-fail.

194. Ibid.

195. J. Emerson, "Don't Give Up on Unconscious Bias Training – Make It Better," *Harvard Business Review*, April 28, 2017, accessed July 8, 2020, https://hbr.org/2017/04/dont-give-up-on-unconscious-bias-training-make-it-better.

196. E. Paluck and D. Green, "Prejudice Reduction: What Works? A Review and Assessment of Research and Practice," *Annual Review of Psychology* 60 (2009): 339–367.

197. Dobbin, A. Kalev, and E. Kelley, "Diversity Management in Corporate America."

198. Haidt and Jussim, "Hard Truths About Race on Campus."

13

1. R. Kanfer, M. Frese and R. Johnson, "Motivation Related to Work: A Century of Progress," *Journal of Applied Psychology* 102, no. 3 (2017): 338–355.

2. E. Griffith, "Why Are Young People Pretending to Love Work?" *New York Times*, January 26, 2019, accessed May 21, 2020, https://www.nytimes.com/2019/01/26/business/against-hustle-culture-rise-and-grind-tgim.html.

3. J. Harter, "Employee Engagement on the Rise in the U.S.," Gallup, August 26,2018, accessed May 21, 2020, https://news.gallup.com/poll/241649/employee-engagement-rise.aspx.

4. "State of the American Workplace," Gallup, April 12, 2017, accessed April 26, 2017, http://www.gallup.com/reports/199961/state-american-workplace-report-2017.aspx.

5. J. Harter, F. Schmidt, S. Agrawal, S. Plowman, and A. Blue, "The Relationship Between Engagement at Work and Organizational Outcomes 2016 Q 12® Meta-Analysis: Ninth Edition," Gallup, April 2016, http://www.gallup.com/services/191558/q12-meta-analysis-ninth-edition-2016.aspx.

6. P. Campbell and R. D. Pritchard, "Motivation Theory in Industrial and Organizational Psychology," in *Handbook of Industrial and Organizational Psychology*, ed. M. D. Dunnette (Chicago: Rand McNally, 1976).

7. N. Maestas, K. Mullen, D. Powell, T. Von Wachter and J. Wenger, "The Value of Working Conditions in the United States and Implications for the Structure of Wages (Working Paper)," National Bureau of Economic Research, October 2018, accessed May 22, 2020, https://www.nber.org/papers/w25204.pdf; J. Yadoo, "Americans Willing to Forgo a 56% Pay Raise for Best Job Perks," *Bloomberg*, October 31, 2018, accessed May 22, 2020, https://www.bloomberg.com/news/articles/2018-10-31/americans-willing-to-forgo-a-56-pay-raise-for-best-job-perks?sref=xXo7CWym.

8. A. Locke, "The Nature and Causes of Job Satisfaction," in *Handbook of Industrial and Organizational Psychology*, ed. M. D. Dunnette (Chicago: Rand McNally, 1976).

9. R. Fentzeig and L. Weber, "Companies Pressured to Pay More in Overtime Wonder If It's Worth It," *Wall Street Journal*, April 13, 2018, accessed May 22, 2020, https://www.wsj.com/articles/daily-grind-gets-longer-and-now-some-companies-wonder-if-its-worth-it-1523620801.

10. H. Maslow, "A Theory of Human Motivation," *Psychological Review* 50 (1943): 370–396.

11. P. Alderfer, *Existence, Relatedness, and Growth: Human Needs in Organizational Settings* (New York: Free Press, 1972).

12. C. McClelland, "Toward a Theory of Motive Acquisition," *American Psychologist* 20 (1965): 321–333; D. C. McClelland and D. H. Burnham, "Power Is the Great Motivator," *Harvard Business Review* 54, no. 2 (1976): 100–110.

13. J. H. Turner, "Entrepreneurial Environments and the Emergence of Achievement Motivation in Adolescent Males," *Sociometry* 33 (1970): 147–165.

14. L. W. Porter, E. E. Lawler III, and J. R. Hackman, *Behavior in Organizations* (New York: McGraw-Hill, 1975).

15. C. Ajila, "Maslow's Hierarchy of Needs Theory: Applicability to the Nigerian Industrial Setting," *IFE Psychology* 5 (1997): 162–174.

16. M. A. Wahba and L. B. Birdwell, "Maslow Reconsidered: A Review of Research on the Need Hierarchy Theory," *Organizational Behavior and Human Performance* 15 (1976): 212–240; J. Rauschenberger, N. Schmitt, and J. E. Hunter, "A Test of the Need Hierarchy Concept by a Markov Model of Change in Need Strength," *Administrative Science Quarterly* 25 (1980): 654–670.

17. E. E. Lawler III and L. W. Porter, "The Effect of Performance on Job Satisfaction," *Industrial Relations* 7 (1967): 20–28.

18. Porter, et al., *Behavior in Organizations*.

19. P. Cohen, "One-Time Bonuses and Perks Muscle Out Pay Raises for Workers," *New York Times*, May 25, 2016, accessed May 4, 2016, http://www.nytimes.com/2015/05/26/business/one-time-bonuses-and-perks-muscle-out-pay-raises-for-workers.html?_r=0; S. Miller, "Short-Term Pay Incentives Offered to More Workers at Private and Smaller Companies," Society for Human Resource Management, May 25, 2018, accessed May 22, 2020, https://www.shrm.org/resourcesandtools/hr-topics/compensation/pages/short-term-pay-incentives-at-private-and-smaller-companies.aspx.

20. "2020 Proxy Statement and 2019 Annual Report with 10K (combined report)," Lincoln Electric, March 17, 2020, accessed May 22, 2020, https://ir.lincolnelectric.com/static-files/70f999ff

-3718-46f4-bb97-af58e3b27336; F. Koller, "2017 at Lincoln Electric – No Layoffs for 69 years and 84 Years of Amazing Profit-Sharing Bonuses," *Frank Koller*, April 30, 2018, accessed May 22, 2020, http://www.frankkoller.com/2018/04/2017-at-lincoln-electric-no-layoffs-for-69-years-and-84-years-of-amazing-profit-sharing-bonuses/.

21. Porter, et al., *Behavior in Organizations*.

22. K. Woolley and A. Fishbach, "Immediate Rewards Predict Adherence to Long-Term Goals," *Personality and Social Psychology Bulletin* 43 no. 2 (2017): 151–162.

23. K. Woolley and A. Fishbach, "What Separates Goals We Achieve From Goals We Don't," *Harvard Business Review*, April 26, 2017, accessed April 27, 2017, https://hbr.org/2017/04/what-separates-goals-we-achieve-from-goals-we-dont.

24. J. Shin and A. Grant, "Bored by Interest: How Intrinsic Motivation in One Task Can Reduce Performance on Other Tasks," *Academy of Management Journal* 62, no. 2 (2019): 415–436.

25. C. Caggiano, "What Do Workers Want?" *Inc.*, November 1992, 101–104; "National Study of the Changing Workforce," *Families and Work Institute*, accessed May 31, 2005, http://www.familiesandwork.org/summary/nscw.pdf.

26. C. Lee, A. Alonso, E. Esen, J. Coombs, T. Mulvey, K. Wessels, and H. Ng, "Employee Job Satisfaction and Engagement: Revitalizing a Changing Workforce," *Society for Human Resource Management*, April 18, 2016, accessed May 4, 2016, https://www.shrm.org/Research/SurveyFindings/Articles/Documents/2016-Employee-Job-Satisfaction-and-Engagement-Report.pdf.

27. B. Conerly, "Retain More Employees With Stay Interviews," *Forbes*, July 21, 2018, accessed May 22, 2020, https://www.forbes.com/sites/billconerly/2018/07/21/retain-more-employees-with-stay-interviews/#489bbd51f18c; D. DeZube, "11 Great Stay Interview Questions," *Monster*, December 20, 2019, accessed May 22, 2020, https://hiring.monster.com/employer-resources/recruiting-strategies/interviewing-candidates/stay-interview-questions/; R. Finnegan, "Stay Interviews vs. Millennials? Stay Interviews Work!" *C-Suite Analytics*, March 16, 2017, accessed May 22, 2020, https://c-suiteanalytics.com/stay-interviews-vs-millennials/.

28. "Stay Interviews vs. Millennials? Stay Interviews Work!" *C-Suite Analytics*.

29. Lee, et. al., "Employee Job Satisfaction and Engagement."

30. L. Weber, "During Coronavirus Crisis, Big Companies Display Largess – But for How Long?" *Wall Street Journal*, March 22, 2020, accessed May 23, 2020, https://www.wsj.com/articles/during-coronavirus-crisis-big-companies-display-largessbut-for-how-long-11584893891.

31. J. Laabs, "Satisfy Them with More Than Money," *Personnel Journal* 77, no. 11 (1998): 40.

32. R. Kanfer and P. Ackerman, "Aging, Adult Development, and Work Motivation," *Academy of Management Review* (2004): 440–458.

33. L. Mishel and J. Schieder, "CEO Compensation Has Grown 940% Since 1978," *Economic Policy Institute*, August 14, 2019, accessed May 23, 2020, https://www.epi.org/publication/ceo-compensation-2018/.

34. M. Sauter, "The Highest-Paid CEOs at the Largest US Companies," *USA Today*, May 3, 2019, accessed May 23, 2020, https://www.usatoday.com/story/money/2019/04/30/highest-paid-ceos-at-americas-largest-companies-tim-cook-robert-iger/39389897/ .

35. "Occupational Employment and Wages, May 2019: 11-1011 Chief Executives," *Bureau of Labor*

Statistics, March 31, 2020, accessed May 23, 2020, http://www.bls.gov/oes/current/oes111011.htm.

36.   C. T. Kulik and M. L. Ambrose, "Personal and Situational Determinants of Referent Choice," *Academy of Management Review* 17 (1992): 212–237.

37.   L. Weber and R. Silverman, "Worker Share Their Secret Salaries," *Wall Street Journal*, April 6, 2013, accessed May 4, 2016, http://www.wsj.com/articles/SB10001424127887324345804578426744168583824.

38.   S. Shellenbarger, "Open Salaries: The Good, the Bad and the Awkward," *Wall Street Journal*, January 12, 2016, accessed May 4, 2016, http://www.wsj.com/articles/open-salaries-the-good-the-bad-and-the-awkward-1452624480.

39.   J. S. Adams, "Toward an Understanding of Inequity," *Journal of Abnormal Social Psychology* 67 (1963): 422–436.

40.   S. Shellenbarger, "Open Salaries: The Good, the Bad and the Awkward," *Wall Street Journal*, January 12, 2016, accessed May 4, 2016, http://www.wsj.com/articles/open-salaries-the-good-the-bad-and-the-awkward-1452624480.

41.   "Money Matters: Survey Finds Workers Are Scrutinizing Salaries; Feelings Split," Robert Half, August 28, 2019, accessed May 23, 2020, https://www.multivu.com/players/English/8217352-robert-half-2020-salary-guides/?mod=article_inline.

42.   D. Burkus, "Why Being Transparent About Pay Is Good for Business," *Wall Street Journal*, May 30, 2016, accessed April 27, 2017, https://www.wsj.com/articles/why-being-transparent-about-pay-is-good-for-business-1464660062.

43.   D. Card, A. Mas, E. Moretti and E. Saez, "Inequality at Work: The Effect of Peer Salaries on Job Satisfaction (Working Paper), National Bureau of Economic Research, September 2010, accessed May 23, 2020, http://ceg.berkeley.edu/research_67_1067483490.pdf.

44.   Ibid.

45.   K. Arnold, "American Airlines Says Mechanics Are Causing Delays. Now, a Judge Could Force the Union to Pay for It," *The Dallas Morning News*, June 30, 2019, accessed May 23, 2020, https://www.dallasnews.com/business/local-companies/2019/06/30/american-airlines-says-mechanics-are-causing-delays-now-a-judge-could-force-the-union-to-pay-for-it/.

46.   "General Information on the Fair Labor Standards Act (FLSA)," *Department of Labor*, July 2009, accessed April 27, 2017, https://www.dol.gov/whd/regs/compliance/mwposter.htm; "Overtime Pay – Wage and Hour Division (WHD)," *Department of Labor*, accessed May 4, 2016, https://www.dol.gov/whd/overtime_pay.htm.

47.   News Release, "Halliburton Pays Nearly $18.3 Million in Overtime Owed to More Than 1,000 Employees Nationwide After US Labor Department Investigation, *Department of Labor*, September 22, 2015, accessed May 4, 2016, https://www.dol.gov/opa/media/press/whd/whd20151647.htm.

48.   "Fair Labor Standards Act Enforcement Statistics," United States Department of Labor Wage and Hour Division, accessed May 23, 2020,US https://www.dol.gov/agencies/whd/data/charts/fair-labor-standards-act.

49.   C. Chen, J. Choi, and S. Chi, "Making Justice Sense of Local-Expatriate Compensation Disparity: Mitigation by Local Referents, Ideological Explanations, and Interpersonal Sensitivity in China – Foreign Joint Ventures," *Academy of Management Journal* 45 (2002): 807–817.

50.   C. Shine, "American Airlines Offering Raises of Up to 8 Percent for Pilots, Flight Attendants,"

Dallas News, April 26, 2017, accessed April 27, 2017, https://www.dallasnews.com/business/american-airlines/2017/04/26/american-airlines-offering-raises-8-percent-pilots-flight-attendants.

51.   Ibid.

52.   "American Airlines Says Mechanics Are Causing Delays. Now, a Judge Could Force the Union to Pay for It," *The Dallas Morning News*.

53.   T. Reed, "American Airlines Reaches $4.2 Billion Deal With Mechanics And Fleet Service That Boosts Profit Sharing And Caps Offshore Work," *Forbes*, January 30, 2020, accessed May 23, 2020, https://www.forbes.com/sites/tedreed/2020/01/30/american-airlines-reaches--42-billion-deal-with-mechanics-and-fleet-service/#63d650b2159b.

54.   R. Feintzeig, "Radical Idea at the Office: A 40-Hour Workweek," *Wall Street Journal*, October 13, 2015, accessed May 4, 2016, http://www.wsj.com/articles/radical-idea-at-the-office-a-40-hour-wor kweek-1444754956.

55.   Ibid.

56.   Ibid.

57.   United Shore, "'Work to Live': Why One Metro Detroit Company Embraces a People-First Mentality," *Crain's Detroit Business*, July 16, 2018, accessed May 24, 2020, https://www.crainsdetroit.com/article/20180716/custom/665766/work-to-live-why-one-metro-detroit-company-embraces-a-people-first.

58.   R. Folger and M. A. Konovsky, "Effects of Procedural and Distributive Justice on Reactions to Pay Raise Decisions," *Academy of Management Journal* 32 (1989): 115–130; M. A. Konovsky, "Understanding Procedural Justice and Its Impact on Business Organizations," *Journal of Management* 26 (2000): 489–512.

59.   "Four Air France Employees Sacked Over Violent Protest," *BBC News*, November 12, 2015, accessed May 4, 2016, http://www.bbc.com/news/world-europe-34804611.

60.   E. Barret-Howard and T. R. Tyler, "Procedural Justice as a Criterion in Allocation Decisions," *Journal of Personality and Social Psychology* 50 (1986): 296–305; Folger and Konovsky, "Effects of Procedural and Distributive Justice on Reactions to Pay Raise Decisions." M. Richter, C. Konig, C. Koppermann and M. Schilling, "Displaying Fairness While Delivering Bad News: Testing the Effectiveness of Organizational Bad News Training in the Layoff Context," *Journal of Applied Psychology* 101, no. 6 (2016): 779-792.

61.   R. Folger and J. Greenberg, "Procedural Justice: An Interpretive Analysis of Personnel Systems," in *Research in Personnel and Human Resources Management*, vol. 3, ed. K. Rowland and G. Ferris (Greenwich, CT: JAI, 1985); R. Folger, D. Rosenfield, J. Grove, and L. Corkran, "Effects of 'Voice' and Peer Opinions on Responses to Inequity," *Journal of Personality and Social Psychology* 37 (1979): 2253–2261; E. A. Lind and T. R. Tyler, *The Social Psychology of Procedural Justice* (New York: Plenum, 1988); Konovsky, "Understanding Procedural Justice and Its Impact on Business Organizations."

62.   V. H. Vroom, *Work and Motivation* (New York: John Wiley & Sons, 1964); L. W. Porter and E. E. Lawler III, *Managerial Attitudes and Performance* (Homewood, IL: Dorsey & Richard D. Irwin, 1968).

63.   "MetLife | Employee Benefit Trends Study 2019," Met Life, accessed May 24, 2020, https://www.metlife.com/employee-benefit-trends/ebts-thriving-in-new-work-world-2019/.

64.   K. Dill, "Lack of Sick Time Worries Workers as Coronavirus Looms," *Wall Street Journal*, March 11, 2020, accessed May 24, 2020, https://www.wsj.com/articles/lack-of-sick-time-worries-workers-as-coronavirus-looms-11583938713.

65.   S. Miller, "Countering the Employee Recognition Gap," SHRM Library, *Society for Human Resource Management*, February 2006, accessed March 25, 2009, http://www.shrm.org.

66.   Press Release, "North American Employers Give Pay-for-Performance Programs Low Marks, Willis Towers Watson Survey Finds," Willis Towers Watson, February 4, 2016, accessed April 27, 2017, https://www.willistowerswatson.com/en/press/2016/02/north-american-employers-give-pay-for-performance-programs-low-marks.

67.   L. Wisper, "Purpose-Driven Pay for Performance," Willis Towers Watson, November 15, 2019, accessed May 24, 2020, https://www.willistowerswatson.com/en-US/Insights/2019/11/purpose-driven-pay-for-performance.

68.   J. Shaw and N. Gupta, "Pay System Characteristics and Quit Patterns of Good, Average and Poor Performers," *Personnel Psychology* 60 (2007): 903–928.

69.   E. Bernstein and H. Blunden, "The Sales Director Who Turned Work into a Fantasy Sports Competition," *Harvard Business Review*, March 27, 2015, accessed May 10, 2015, https://hbr.org/2015/03/the-sales-director-who-turned-work-into-a-fantasy-sports-competition.

70.   Ibid.

71.   K. W. Thomas and B. A. Velthouse, "Cognitive Elements of Empowerment," *Academy of Management Review* 15 (1990): 666–681.

72.   E. L. Thorndike, *Animal Intelligence* (New York: Macmillan, 1911).

73.   J. Marson and T. Grove, "Domino's Offered Free Pizza for Life in Exchange for a Logo Tattoo. It Found People Really Like Ink," *Wall Street Journal*, September 17, 2018, accessed May 24, 2020, https://www.wsj.com/articles/dominos-offered-free-pizza-for-life-in-exchange-for-a-logo-tattoo-it-found-people-really-like-ink-1537120377.

74.   "Fox Urine and Christmas Tree Theft," Today I Found Out, December 7, 2015, accessed May 4, 2016, http://www.todayifoundout.com/index.php/2015/12/fox-urine-stops-christmas-tree-theft/.

75.   B. F. Skinner, *Science and Human Behavior* (New York: Macmillan, 1954); B. F. Skinner, *Beyond Freedom and Dignity* (New York: Bantam, 1971); B. F. Skinner, *A Matter of Consequences* (New York: New York University Press, 1984).

76.   A. M. Dickinson and A. D. Poling, "Schedules of Monetary Reinforcement in Organizational Behavior Management: Latham and Huber Revisited," *Journal of Organizational Behavior Management* 16, no. 1 (1992): 71–91.

77.   "Walmart Introduces Increased Rewards and Protected PTO for Associates Nationwide," Walmart, February 1, 2019, accessed May 24, 2020, https://corporate.walmart.com/newsroom/2019/02/01/walmart-introduces-increased-rewards-and-protected-pto-for-associates-nationwide.

78.   "Life Happens. Support for Time Off When It Does," Walmart, accessed May 24, 2020, https://one.walmart.com/content/dam/themepage/pdfs/psl-associate-guide-2018.pdf. M. Boyle, "Walmart Gives Workers Paid Sick Leave to Sweeten Broader Attendance Crackdown," *Bloomberg*, February 1, 2019, accessed May 24, 2020, https://www.bloomberg.com/news/articles/2019-02-01/walmart-gives-workers-paid-sick-leave-to-sweeten-broader-attendance-crackdown?sref=xXo7CWym.

79.   R. Greenfield, "Why Pay Employees to Exercise When You Can Threaten Them?" *Bloomberg*,

February 15, 2016, accessed April 27, 2017, https://www.bloomberg.com/news/articles/2016-02-15/why-pay-employees-to-exercise-when-you-can-threaten-them.

80.   R. Smith, "Citi Suspends Senior Bond Trader Over Alleged Theft From Canteen," *Financial Times*, February 3, 2020, accessed May 24, 2020, https://www.ft.com/content/b7c1952a-467b-11ea-aeb3-955839e06441.

81.   S. Fleming, "Fare Dodger Banned From City Posts," *Financial Times*, December 15, 2014, accessed May 24, 2020, https://www.ft.com/content/4d9073ea-847c-11e4-bae9-00144feabdc0; C. Newlands, "The Curious Case of the Fare Dodger and the FCA," *Financial Times*, January 3, 2015, accessed May 24, 2020, https://www.ft.com/content/6919be24-9277-11e4-b213-00144feabdc0.

82.   T. Gryta and T. Francis, "GE's Top Executives Miss Out on Cash Bonuses for the First Time," *Wall Street Journal*, March 12, 2018, accessed May 25, 2020, https://www.wsj.com/articles/ge-didnt-pay-bonuses-to-ceo-top-executives-in-2017-1520892109.

83.   J. B. Miner, *Theories of Organizational Behavior* (Hinsdale, IL: Dryden, 1980).

84.   Dickinson and Poling, "Schedules of Monetary Reinforcement in Organizational Behavior Management."

85.   F. Luthans and A. D. Stajkovic, "Reinforce for Performance: The Need to Go Beyond Pay and Even Rewards," *Academy of Management Executive* 13, no. 2 (1999): 49–57.

86.   A. Doyle, "Road to Electric Car Paradise Paved With Handouts," *Reuters*, September 21, 2017, accessed May 25, 2020, https://www.reuters.com/article/us-autos-electric-analysis/road-to-electric-car-paradise-paved-with-handouts-idUSKCN1BW1AN; K. Hovland, "Electric-Car Perks Put Norway in a Pinch," Wall Street Journal, September 18, 2015, accessed May 5, 2016, http://www.wsj.com/articles/electric-car-perks-put-norway-in-a-pinch-1442601936.

87.   "Electric-Car Perks Put Norway in a Pinch," *Wall Street Journal*; "Norwegian EV policy: Norway Is Leading the Way for a Transition to Zero Emission in Transport," *Norsk elbilforening*, accessed May 25, 2020, https://elbil.no/english/norwegian-ev-policy/.

88.   R. Milne, "Reality of Subsidies Drives Norway's Electric Car Dream," *Financial Times*, June 14, 2017, accessed May 25, 2020, https://www.ft.com/content/84e54440-3bc4-11e7-821a-6027b8a20f23.

89.   "Norwegian EV policy: Norway Is Leading the Way for a Transition to Zero Emission in Transport," *Norsk elbilforening*.

90.   K. D. Butterfield, L. K. Trevino, and G. A. Ball, "Punishment from the Manager's Perspective: A Grounded Investigation and Inductive Model," *Academy of Management Journal* 39 (1996): 1479–1512.

91.   R. D. Arvey and J. M. Ivancevich, "Punishment in Organizations: A Review, Propositions, and Research Suggestions," *Academy of Management Review* 5 (1980): 123–132.

92.   R. D. Arvey, G. A. Davis, and S. M. Nelson, "Use of Discipline in an Organization: A Field Study," *Journal of Applied Psychology* 69 (1984): 448–460; M. E. Schnake, "Vicarious Punishment in a Work Setting," *Journal of Applied Psychology* 71 (1986): 343–345.

93.   G. A. Yukl and G. P. Latham, "Consequences of Reinforcement Schedules and Incentive Magnitudes for Employee Performance: Problems Encountered in a Field Setting," *Journal of Applied Psychology* 60 (1975): 294–298.

94.   E. A. Locke and G. P. Latham, *Goal Setting: A Motivational Technique That Works* (Englewood Cliffs, NJ: Prentice Hall, 1984); E. A. Locke and G. P. Latham, *A Theory of Goal Setting and Task Performance* (Englewood Cliffs, NJ: Prentice Hall, 1990); E. A. Locke and G. P. Latham, "The Development of Goal Setting Theory: A Half Century Retrospective," *Motivation Science* 5, no. 2 (2019): 93–105.

95.   L. Baldassarre and Brian Finken, "GE's Real - Time Performance Development," *Harvard Business Review*, August 12, 2015, accessed May 5, 2016, https://hbr.org/2015/08/ges-real-time-performance-development.

96.   S. Nawaz, "Break Bad Habits with a Simple Checklist," *Harvard Business Review*, February 10, 2017, accessed April 28, 2017, https://hbr.org/2017/02/break-bad-habits-with-a-simple-checklist.

97.   D. Clark, "Don't Bog Yourself Down with Too Many Goals," *Harvard Business Review*, January 22, 2020, accessed May 25, 2020, https://hbr.org/2020/01/dont-bog-yourself-down-with-too-many-goals.

98.   M. Hansen, "How to Succeed in Business? Do Less," *Wall Street Journal*, January 12, 2018, accessed May 25, 2020, https://www.wsj.com/articles/how-to-succeed-in-business-do-less-1515770816.

99.   G. P. Latham and E. A. Locke, "Goal Setting—A Motivational Technique That Works," *Organizational Dynamics* 8, no. 2 (1979): 68.

100.   J. Constable, "Two Techniques for Helping Employees Change Ingrained Habits," *Harvard Business Review*, March 28, 2018, accessed May 25, 2020, https://hbr.org/2018/03/two-techniques-for-helping-employees-change-ingrained-habits; G. Oettingen and P. Gollwitzer, "Strategies of Setting and Implementing Goals," in J. Maddux and J. Tangney (Eds.), *Social Psychological Foundations of Clinical Psychology* (New York: The Guilford Press, 2010).

101.   "G. Oettingen, "WOOP Kit – Written WOOP Guide," *Woop*, accessed May 25, 2020, https://woopmylife.org/en/practice.

102.   Ibid.

14

1.   J. Hogan, R. Hogan & R. Kaiser, "Management Derailment: Personality Assessment and Mitigation," in *APA Handbook of Industrial and Organizational Psychology*, Volume 3, ed. S. Zedeck (Washington, DC: American Psychological Association, 2011); Hogan, R. "Trouble at the Top: Causes and Consequences of Managerial Incompetence," *Consulting Psychology Journal: Practice and Research*, 46 no. 1 (1994): 9–15; R. Hogan & R. Kaiser, "What We Know About Leadership," *Review of General Psychology* 9, no. 2 (2005): 169–180.

2.   J. Harter & B. Rigoni, "State of the American Manager: Analytics and Advice for Leaders," Gallup, April 21, 2015, accessed May 30, 2020, https://www.gallup.com/services/182216/state-american-manager-report.aspx;

3.   R. Beck & J. Harter, "Managers Account for 70% of Variance in Employee Engagement," Gallup, April 21, 2015, accessed May 30, 2020, https://news.gallup.com/businessjournal/182792/managers-account-variance-employee-engagement.aspx; "State of the American Manager: Analytics and Advice for Leaders," Gallup.

4.   R. Kaider, R. Hogan & S. Craig, "Leadership and the Fate of Organizations," *American Psychologist* 63, no. 2 (2008): 96–110.

5.   W. Bennis, "Why Leaders Can't Lead," *Training & Development Journal* 43, no. 4 (1989): 35–39.

6.   Press Release, "Jochen Zeitz Appointed President and Chief Executive Officer of Harley-Davidson," Harley-Davidson, May 7, 2020, accessed May 31, 2020, https://www.globenewswire.com/news-release/2020/05/07/2029503/0/en/Jochen-Zeitz-Appointed-President-and-Chief-Executive-Officer-of-Harley-Davidson.html.

7.   D. Klein, "How McDonald's Plans to Reinvent the Drive Thru," *QSR Magazine*, May 2019, accessed May 31, 2020, https://www.qsrmagazine.com/fast-food/how-mcdonalds-plans-reinvent-drive-thru.

8.   T. Gryta & C. Lombardo, "GE Exits Lightbulb Business It Pioneered," *Wall Street Journal*, May 27, 2020, accessed May 31, 2020, https://www.wsj.com/articles/ge-sells-lightbulb-business-for-about-250-million-11590585598?mod=searchresults&page=1&pos=2.

9.   M. Egan, "GE Is Saying Goodbye to Its 129-Year-Old Light Bulb Business," *CNN*, May 27, 2020, accessed May 31, 2020, https://www.cnn.com/2020/05/27/business/ge-light-bulbs-sale/index.html.

10.   A. Zaleznik, "Managers and Leaders: Are They Different?" *Harvard Business Review* 55 (1977): 76–78; A. Zaleznik, "The Leadership Gap," *Washington Quarterly* 6 (1983): 32–39.

11.   K. Kniffin, J. Detert & H. Leroy, "On Leading and Managing: Synonyms or Separate (and Unequal)?" *Academy of Management Discoveries* (In-Press), published online September 20, 2019, accessed May 31, 2020, https://journals.aom.org/doi/10.5465/amd.2018.0227.

12.   Bennis, "Why Leaders Can't Lead."

13.   S. Frier, "Jack Dorsey Is Losing Control of Twitter," *Bloomberg*, October 5, 2016, accessed April 29, 2017, https://www.bloomberg.com/features/2016-twitter-dorsey-strategy/.

14.   N. Buhayar, "Warren Buffett Made a Big Bet on an 'In-Your-Face' CEO," *Wall Street Journal*, August 3, 2016, accessed April 29, 2017, https://www.bloomberg.com/news/features/2016-08-03/buffett-s-bet-on-a-relentless-ceo.

15.   D. Jones, "Not All Successful CEOs Are Extroverts," *USA Today*, June 7, 2006, B.1.

16.   J. McGregor, "Introverts Tend to Be Better CEOs – and Other Surprising Traits of Top-Performing Executives," *Washington Post*, April 17, 2017, accessed April 29, 2017, https://www.washingtonpost.com/news/on-leadership/wp/2017/04/17/introverts-tend-to-be-better-ceos-and-other-surprising-traits-of-top-performing-executives/.

17.   G. Murray, "Caveman Politics," *Psychology Today*, December 15, 2011, accessed May 9, 2016, http://www.psychologytoday.com/blog/caveman-politics/201112/are-you-sure-we-prefer-taller-leaders; G. Murray and J. Schmitz, "Caveman Politics: Evolutionary Leadership Preferences and Physical Stature," *Social Science Quarterly* 92 (2011): 1215–1235.

18.   M. Gladwell, "Why Do We Love Tall Men?" Gladwell.com, accessed July 16, 2014, http://gladwell.com/blink/why-do-we-love-tall-men/.

19.   Schumpeter, "The Look of a Leader," *The Economist*, September 27, 2014, accessed May 6, 2016, http://www.economist.com/news/business/21620197-getting-top-much-do-how-you-look-what-you-achieve-look-leader.

20.   E. Wong, M. Ormiston, and M. Haselhuhn, "A Face Only an Investor Could Love: CEO's Facial Structure Predicts Their Firms' Financial Performance," *Psychological Science* 22 (2011):

1478–1483; S. Knapton, "Successful Male Leaders Have Wider Faces than Average Man," *Telegraph*, August 16, 2015, accessed May 9, 2016, http://www.telegraph.co.uk/news/science/science-news/11806360/Successful-male-leaders-have-wider-faces-than-average-man.html.

21. S. Zaccaro, "Trait-Based Perspectives of Leadership," *American Psychologist* 62 (2007): 6-16; R. J. House and R. M Aditya, "The Social Scientific Study of Leadership: Quo Vadis?" *Journal of Management* 23 (1997): 409–473; T. Judge, R. Illies, J. Bono, and M. Gerhardt, "Personality and Leadership: A Qualitative and Quantitative Review," *Journal of Applied Psychology* 89 (August 2002): 765–782; S. A. Kirkpatrick and E. A. Locke, "Leadership: Do Traits Matter?" *Academy of Management Executive* 5, no. 2 (1991): 48–60.

22. House and Aditya, "The Social Scientific Study of Leadership"; Kirkpatrick and Locke, "Leadership: Do Traits Matter?"

23. J. McGregor, "Introverts Tend to Be Better CEOs — and Other Surprising Traits of Top-Performing Executives."

24. K. Badura, E. Grijalva, B. Galvin, B. Owens & D. Joseph, "Motivation to Lead: A Meta-Analysis and Distal-Proximal Model of Motivation and Leadership," *Journal of Applied Psychology* 105, no. 4 (2019): 311–354.

25. S. Gregory, "The Most Common Type of Incompetent Leader," *Harvard Business Review*, March 30, 2018, accessed May 31, 2020, https://hbr.org/2018/03/the-most-common-type-of-incompetent-leader.

26. About Amazon – 2016 Letter to Shareholders," Amazon, April 12, 2017, accessed April 29, 2017, https://www.amazon.com/p/feature/z6o9g6sysxur57t.

27. Ibid.

28. M. Mayo, "If Humble People Make the Best Leaders, Why Do We Fall for Charismatic Narcissists?" *Harvard Business Review*, April 7, 2017, accessed May 31, 2020, https://hbr.org/2017/04/if-humble-people-make-the-best-leaders-why-do-we-fall-for-charismatic-narcissists.

29. D. Maxfield & J. Hale, "When Managers Break Down Under Pressure, So Do Their Teams," *Harvard Business Review*, December 17, 2018, accessed May 31, 2020, https://hbr.org/2018/12/when-managers-break-down-under-pressure-so-do-their-teams.

30. "Leadership | The Hershey Company," The Hershey Company, accessed June 1, 2020, https://www.thehersheycompany.com/en_us/our-story/remarkable-people/leadership.html.

31. Fortune Editors, "International Women's Day: 15 Powerful Women on the Quality That's Key to Their Success," *Fortune*, March 8, 2020, accessed June 1, 2020, https://fortune.com/2020/03/08/15-powerful-women-share-the-personality-trait-thats-key-to-their-success/.

32. Kirkpatrick and Locke, "Leadership: Do Traits Matter?"

33. D. Derue, J. Nahrgang, N. Wellman & S. Humphrey, "Trait and Behavioral Theories of Leadership: An Integration and Meta-Analytic Test of Their Relative Validity," *Personnel Psychology* 64 (2011): 7–52.

34. E. A. Fleishman, "The Description of Supervisory Behavior," *Journal of Applied Psychology* 37 (1953): 1–6; L. R. Katz, *New Patterns of Management* (New York: McGraw-Hill, 1961).

35. T. Judge, R. Piccolo, & R. Ilies, "The Forgotten Ones? The Validity of Consideration and Initiating Structure in Leadership Research," *Journal of Applied Psychology* 89, no. 1 (2004): 36–51.

36. Ibid.

37. N. Buhayar, "Warren Buffett Made a Big Bet on an 'In-Your-Face' CEO."

38. "The Forgotten Ones? The Validity of Consideration and Initiating Structure in Leadership Research," *Journal of Applied Psychology*.

39. "International Women's Day: 15 Powerful Women on the Quality That's Key to Their Success," *Fortune*.

40. P. Weissenberg and M. H. Kavanagh, "The Independence of Initiating Structure and Consideration: A Review of the Evidence," *Personnel Psychology* 25 (1972): 119–130.

41. R. J. House and T. R. Mitchell, "Path-Goal Theory of Leadership," *Journal of Contemporary Business* 3 (1974): 81–97; F. E. Fiedler, "A Contingency Model of Leadership Effectiveness," in *Advances in Experimental Social Psychology*, ed. L. Berkowitz (New York: Academic Press, 1964); V. H. Vroom and P. W. Yetton, *Leadership and Decision Making* (Pittsburgh: University of Pittsburgh Press, 1973); P. Hersey and K. H. Blanchard, The *Management of Organizational Behavior*, 4th ed. (Englewood Cliffs, NJ: Prentice Hall, 1984); S. Kerr and J. M. Jermier, "Substitutes for Leadership: Their Meaning and Measurement," *Organizational Behavior & Human Performance* 22 (1978): 375–403.

42. A. Grant, F. Gino, and D. Hofmann, "The Hidden Advantage of Quiet Bosses," *Harvard Business Review* 88, no. 12 (2010): 28.

43. F. E. Fiedler and M. M. Chemers, *Leadership and Effective Management* (Glenview, IL: Scott, Foresman, 1974); F. E. Fiedler and M. M. Chemers, *Improving Leadership Effectiveness: The Leader Match Concept*, 2nd ed. (New York: Wiley, 1984).

44. M. Bender, "Why CEOs Have Such a Hard Time Moving Into Government," *Wall Street Journal*, March 14, 2018, accessed June 1, 2020, https://www.wsj.com/articles/how-to-move-from-the-boardroom-to-the-beltway-lessons-from-ceos-1521019801.

45. R. Hershey, Jr., "Paul O'Neill, Treasury Secretary Who Clashed With Bush, Dies at 84," *New York Times*, April 18, 2020, accessed June 1, 2020, https://www.nytimes.com/2020/04/18/us/politics/paul-oneill-dead.html.

46. Fiedler and Chemers, *Improving Leadership Effectiveness*.

47. F. E. Fiedler, "The Effects of Leadership Training and Experience: A Contingency Model Interpretation," *Administrative Science Quarterly* 17, no. 4 (1972): 455; F. E. Fiedler, *A Theory of Leadership Effectiveness* (New York: McGraw-Hill, 1967).

48. B. Snyder, "Jeffrey Katzenberg: How Failure Makes a Better Leader," *GSB Insights*, March 13, 2018, accessed June 1, 2020, https://www.gsb.stanford.edu/insights/jeffrey-katzenberg-how-failure-makes-better-leader.

49. L. S. Csoka and F. E. Fiedler, "The Effect of Military Leadership Training: A Test of the Contingency Model," *Organizational Behavior & Human Performance* 8 (1972): 395–407.

50. P. Hersey and K. Blanchard, *Management of Organizational Behavior: Leading Human Resources*, 8th ed. (Escondido, CA: Center for Leadership Studies, 2001).

51. W. Blank, J. Weitzel, and S. Green, "A Test of the Situational Leadership Theory," *Personnel Psychology* 43, no. 3 (1990): 579–597; W. Norris and R. Vecchio, "Situational Leadership Theory: A Replication," *Group & Organization Management* 17, no. 3 (1992): 331–342.

52. Ibid.

53. House and Mitchell, "Path-Goal Theory of Leadership."

54. "Up and Coming Leaders," *Entrepreneur*, March 26, 2014, accessed July 17, 2014, http://www.entrepreneur.com/article/231531.

55. M. Tenney, "More Than Money," *Collector*, October 2013, 26–28.

56. House and Mitchell, "Path-Goal Theory of Leadership."

57. X. Huang, E. Xu, W. Chiu, C. Lam, and J. Farh, "When Authoritarian Leaders Outperform Transformational Leaders: Firm Performance in a Harsh Economic Environment," *Academy of Management Discoveries* 1, no. 2 (2015): 180–200.

58. B. M. Fisher and J. E. Edwards, "Consideration and Initiating Structure and Their Relationships with Leader Effectiveness: A Meta-Analysis," *Proceedings of the Academy of Management*, August 1988, 201–205.

59. Z. Ton and S. Kalloch, "How 4 Retailers Became "Best Places to Work," *Harvard Business Review*, January 2, 2017, accessed April 29, 2017, https://hbr.org/2017/01/how-4-retailers-became-best-places-to-work.

60. H. Tabuchi, "HEB Grocery Chain to Give Stock to 55,000 Employees," *New York Times*, November 2, 2015, accessed April 29, 2017, https://www.nytimes.com/2015/11/03/business/heb-grocery-chain-to-give-stock-to-55000-employees.html.

61. L. Rachitsky, "What Seven Years at Airbnb Taught Me About Building a Business," *Medium*, April 2, 2019, accessed June 2, 2020, https://marker.medium.com/what-seven-years-at-airbnb-taught-me-about-building-a-company-e1d035d49c56.

62. Ibid.

63. C. Farh & G. Chen, "Leadership and Member Voice in Action Teams: Test of a Dynamic Phase Model," *Journal of Applied Psychology* 103, no. 1 (2018): 97–110; J. C. Wofford and L. Z. Liska, "Path-Goal Theories of Leadership: A Meta-Analysis," *Journal of Management* 19 (1993): 857–876.

64. House and Aditya, "The Social Scientific Study of Leadership."

65. "Leadership and Member Voice in Action Teams: Test of a Dynamic Phase Model," *Journal of Applied Psychology*; A. Lee, S. Willia & A. Wei Tian, "When Empowering Employees Works, and When It Doesn't," *Harvard Business Review*, March 2, 2018, accessed June 2, 2020, https://hbr.org/2018/03/when-empowering-employees-works-and-when-it-doesnt; N. Lorinkova, "Examining the Differential Longitudinal Performance of Directive Versus Empowering Leadership in Teams," *Academy of Management Journal* 56, no. 2 (2013): 573–596; S. McClean, C. Barnes, S. Courtright, R. Johnson, "Resetting the Clock on Dynamic Leader Behaviors: A Conceptual Integration and Agenda for Future Research," *Academy of Management Annals* 13, no. 2 (2019): 479–508; R. Wartzman & K. Tang, "The Key to Being a Successful Leader? It's Adaptability," *Wall Street Journal*, March 26, 2020, accessed June 2, 2020, https://www.wsj.com/articles/the-key-to-being-a-successful-leader-its-adaptability-11585242768.

66. V. H. Vroom and A. G. Jago, *The New Leadership: Managing Participation in Organizations* (Englewood Cliffs, NJ: Prentice Hall, 1988).

67. C. Fishman, "How Teamwork Took Flight: This Team Built a Commercial Engine—and Self-Managing GE Plant—from Scratch," *Fast Company*, October 1, 1999, 188.

68. Ibid.

69. Ibid.

70. N. Fallon, "Is Your Management Style Hurting Your Team?" *Business News Daily*, May 14, 2014, accessed May 9, 2016, http://www.businessnewsdaily.com/6409-management-styles-strategies.html.

71. G. A. Yukl, *Leadership in Organizations*, 3rd ed. (Englewood Cliffs, NJ: Prentice Hall, 1995).

72. B. M. Bass, *Bass & Stogdill's Handbook of Leadership: Theory, Research, and Managerial Applications* (New York: Free Press, 1990); N. Luhrs, N. Jager, E. Challies & J. Newig, "How Participatory Should Environmental Governance Be? Testing the Applicability of the Vroom-Yetton-Jago Model in Public Environmental Decision-Making," *Environmental Management* 61 (2018): 249–262.

73. P. Thoms and D. B. Greenberger, "Training Business Leaders to Create Positive Organizational Visions of the Future: Is It Successful?" *Academy of Management Journal*, Best Papers & Proceedings 1995, 212–216.

74. M. Weber, *The Theory of Social and Economic Organizations*, trans. R. A. Henderson and T. Parsons (New York: Free Press, 1947).

75. D. A. Waldman and F. J. Yammarino, "CEO Charismatic Leadership: Levels-of-Management and Levels-of-Analysis Effects," *Academy of Management Review* 24, no. 2 (1999): 266–285.

76. K. B. Lowe, K. G. Kroeck, and N. Sivasubramaniam, "Effectiveness Correlates of Transformational and Transactional Leadership: A Meta-Analytic Review of the MLQ Literature," *Leadership Quarterly* 7 (1996): 385–425.

77. J. Vergauwe, B. Wille, J. Hofmans, R. Kaiser & F. De Fruyt, "Too Much Charisma Can Make Leaders Look Less Effective," *Harvard Business Review*, September 26, 2017, accessed June 4, 2020, https://hbr.org/2017/09/too-much-charisma-can-make-leaders-look-less-effective.

78. J. M. Howell and B. J. Avolio, "The Ethics of Charismatic Leadership: Submission or Liberation?" *Academy of Management Executive* 6, no. 2 (1992): 43–54.

79. L. Wiseman, "Multipliers: How the Best Leaders Make Everyone Smarter," The Wiseman Group, accessed June 4, 2020, https://thewisemangroup.com/books/multipliers/.

80. S. Walker, "One Leader Sent Boeing Into a Hurricane; Landing It Was the Next Guy's Job," *Wall Street Journal*, April 27, 2018, accessed June 4, 2020, https://www.wsj.com/articles/one-leader-sent-boeing-into-a-hurricane-landing-it-was-the-next-guys-job-1524821400.

81. Ibid.

82. Ibid.

83. S. Walker, "T-Mobile's CEO and the Tribal Approach to Management," *Wall Street Journal*, September 7, 2019, accessed June 4, 2020, https://www.wsj.com/articles/t-mobiles-ceo-and-the-tribal-approach-to-management-11567828805?mod=hp_lead_pos9.

84. H. Perlberg and K. Burton, "The Softer Side of Stevie Cohen" *Bloomberg BusinessWeek*, November 6–December 15, 2015, 41–43; A. Viswanatha and J. Chung, "Deal Ends SEC's Pursuit of Steven Cohen," *Wall Street Journal*, January 8, 2016, accessed October 20, 2016, http://www.wsj.com/articles/sec-bars-steven-cohen-from-supervising-hedge-funds-for-two-years-1452278527.

85. D. J. Chandler, "The Perfect Storm of Leaders' Unethical Behavior: A Conceptual Framework," *International Journal of Leadership Studies* 5, no.1 (2009): 69–93.

86. C. O'Reilly, III, B. Doerr & J. Chatman, "'See You in Court': How CEO Narcissism Increases Firms' Vulnerability to Lawsuits," *The Leadership Quarterly* 29 (2018): 365–378.

87. Howell and Avolio, "The Ethics of Charismatic Leadership."

88. B. M. Bass, "From Transactional to Transformational Leadership: Learning to Share the Vision," *Organizational Dynamics* 18 (1990): 19–36.

89. C. Cutter, "The Best-Managed Companies of 2019 – and How They Got That Way," *Wall Street Journal*, November 22, 2019, accessed February 27, 2020, https://www.wsj.com/articles/the-best-managed-companies-of-2019and-how-they-got-that-way-11574437229?mod=hp_lead_pos10.

90. Ibid.

91. B. M. Bass, *A New Paradigm of Leadership: An Inquiry into Transformational Leadership* (Alexandra, VA: US Army Research Institute for the Behavioral and Social Sciences, 1996).

92. K. Chin, "Disney Chair Robert Iger, CEO Bob Chapek to Take Pay Cuts," *Wall Street Journal*, March 30, 2020, accessed April 2, 2020, https://www.wsj.com/articles/disney-chair-robert-ceo-bob-chapek-to-take-pay-cuts-11585603788; R. Feintzeig & P. Thomas, "Companies Try to Preserve Jobs by Cutting Pay Amid Coronavirus Crisis," *Wall Street Journal*, April 3, 2020, accessed June 4, 2020, https://www.wsj.com/articles/companies-try-to-preserve-jobs-by-cutting-pay-amid-coronavirus-crisis-11585906200; A. Murray, "CEO Daily," *Fortune*, May 1, 2020, accessed June 4, 2020, https://fortune.com/newsletter/ceo-daily/; P. Temple-West, "Coronavirus Puts Top Executives' Pay in the Spotlight," *Financial Times*, May 17, 2020, accessed June 4, 2020, https://www.ft.com/content/b8a29cfc-8ac1-11ea-a109-483c62d17528.

93. J. Eaglesham & I. Pacheco, "Coronavirus Crimps Some CEO Salaries but Not All," *Wall Street Journal*, April 24, 2020, accessed June 4, 2020, https://www.wsj.com/articles/coronavirus-crimps-some-ceo-salaries-but-not-all-11587750800.

94. Ibid.

95. Rachitsky, "What Seven Years at Airbnb Taught Me About Building a Business."

96. A. Ha, "Brian Chesky Explains How Snow White Pointed the Way to Airbnb's Future," *TechCrunch*, July 18, 2012, accessed June 4, 2020, https://techcrunch.com/2012/07/18/airbnb-brian-chesky-snow-white/.

97. Ibid.

98. Bass, "From Transactional to Transformational Leadership."

15

1. E. E. Lawler III, L. W. Porter, and A. Tannenbaum, "Manager's Attitudes Toward Interaction Episodes," *Journal of Applied Psychology* 52 (1968): 423–439; H. Mintzberg, *The Nature of Managerial Work* (New York: Harper & Row, 1973).

2. J. D. Maes, T. G. Weldy, and M. L. Icenogle, "A Managerial Perspective: Oral Communication Competency Is Most Important for Business Students in the Workplace," *Journal of Business Communication* 34 (1997): 67–80.

3. E. E. Jones and K. E. Davis, "From Acts to Dispositions: The Attribution Process in Person Perception," in *Advances in Experimental and Social Psychology*, vol. 2, ed. L. Berkowitz (New York: Academic Press, 1965), 219–266; R. G. Lord and J. E. Smith, "Theoretical, Information-Processing, and Situational Factors Affecting Attribution Theory Models of Organizational Behavior," *Academy of Management Review* 8 (1983): 50–60.

4. D. Simons and C. Chabris, "Gorillas in Our Midst: Sustained Inattentional Blindness for Dynamic Events," *Perception* 28 (1999): 1059–1074.

5. J. Zadney and H. B. Gerard, "Attributed Intentions and Informational Selectivity," *Journal of Experimental Social Psychology* 10 (1974): 34–52.

6. M. Beck, "What Cocktail Parties Teach Us," *Wall Street Journal*, April 23, 2012, D1.

7. H. H. Kelly, *Attribution in Social Interaction* (Morristown, NJ: General Learning Press, 1971).

8. J. M. Burger, "Motivational Biases in the Attribution of Responsibility for an Accident: A Meta-Analysis of the Defensive-Attribution Hypothesis," *Psychological Bulletin* 90 (1981): 496–512.

9. D. A. Hofmann and A. Stetzer, "The Role of Safety Climate and Communication in Accident Interpretation: Implications for Learning from Negative Events," *Academy of Management Journal* 41, no. 6 (1998): 644–657.

10. C. Perrow, *Normal Accidents: Living with High-Risk Technologies* (New York: Basic Books, 1984).

11. A. G. Miller and T. Lawson, "The Effect of an Informational Opinion on the Fundamental Attribution Error," *Journal of Personality & Social Psychology* 47 (1989): 873–896; J. M. Burger, "Changes in Attribution Errors Over Time: The Ephemeral Fundamental Attribution Error," *Social Cognition* 9 (1991): 182–193.

12. F. Heider, *The Psychology of Interpersonal Relations* (New York: Wiley, 1958); D. T. Miller and M. Ross, "Self-Serving Biases in Attribution of Causality: Fact or Fiction?" *Psychological Bulletin* 82 (1975): 213–225.

13. J. R. Larson Jr., "The Dynamic Interplay Between Employees' Feedback-Seeking Strategies and Supervisors' Delivery of Performance Feedback," *Academy of Management Review* 14, no. 3 (1989): 408–422.

14. N. Ospina, K. Phillips, R. Rodriguez-Gutierrez, A. Castaneda-Guarderas, M. Gionfriddo, M. Branda & V. Montori, "Eliciting the Patient's Agenda – Secondary Analysis of Recorded Clinical Encounters," *Journal of General Internal Medicine* 34 (2019): 36–40.

15. R. C. Rabin, "15-Minute Visits Take a Toll on the Doctor-Patient Relationship," *Kaiser Health News*, April 21, 2014, accessed May 10, 2016, http://www.kaiserhealthnews.org/Stories/2014/April/21/15-minute-doctor-visits.aspx; S. Wilkins, "The Truth About Those High Patient Satisfaction Scores for Doctor-Patient Communication," *Center For Advancing Health* (Prepared Patient Blog), April 11, 2013, accessed May 10, 2016, http://www.cfah.org/blog/2013/the-truth-about-those-high-patient-satisfaction-scores-for-doctor-patient-communication.

16. R. Wachter, "How Tech Has Undermined – and May Now Save – the Doctor-Patient Relationship," *Wall Street Journal*, April 29, 2018, accessed June 11, 2020, https://blogs.wsj.com/experts/2018/04/29/how-tech-has-undermined-and-may-now-save-the-doctor-patient-relationship/.

17. Ibid.

18. S. Brownlee, "The Doctor Will See You – If You're Quick," *The Daily Beast*, April 16, 2012, accessed May 10, 2016, http://www.thedailybeast.com/newsweek/2012/04/15/why-your-doctor-has-no-time-to-see-you.html.

19. S. Wilkins, "The Truth About Those High Patient Satisfaction Scores for Doctor-Patient Communication."

20. "The Experts: How to Improve Doctor-Patient Communication," *Wall Street Journal*, April 12, 2013, accessed May 10, 2016, http://www.wsj.com/articles/SB10001424127887324050304578411251805908228.

21. Ibid; J. Aleccia, "Never Say 'Die': Why So Many Doctors Won't Break Bad News," *CNBC*, June 12, 2019, accessed June 12, 2020, https://www.nbcnews.com/health/health-news/never-say-die-why-so-many-doctors-won-t-break-n1016876.

22. S. Wilkins, "The Truth About Those High Patient Satisfaction Scores for Doctor-Patient Communication," Center for Advancing Health (Prepared Patient Blog), April 11, 2013, accessed May 10, 2016, http://www.cfah.org/blog/2013/the-truth-about-those-high-patient-satisfaction-scores-for-doctor-patient-communication.

23. D. Gorski, "Are Medical Errors Really the Third Most Common Cause of Death in the US?" *Science-Based Medicine*, February 4, 2019, accessed June 11, 2020, https://sciencebasedmedicine.org/are-medical-errors-really-the-third-most-common-cause-of-death-in-the-u-s-2019-edition/; "The Experts: How to Improve Doctor-Patient Communication."

24. L. Davey, "Managing Emotional Outbursts on Your Team," *Harvard Business Review*, April 30, 2015, accessed May 13, 2015, https://hbr.org/2015/04/handling-emotional-outbursts-on-your-team.

25. B. Presser, "Secrets of Cruise Ships From Crew Codes to Sex to Norovirus," *Bloomberg*, January 31, 2018, accessed June 12, 2020, https://www.bloomberg.com/news/articles/2018-01-31/secrets-of-cruise-ships-from-crew-codes-to-sex-to-norovirus?sref=xXo7CWym.

26. L. Lagnado, "What Patients Need to Remember after Leaving the Hospital," *Wall Street Journal*, November 30, 2015, accessed May 10, 2016, http://www.wsj.com/articles/what-patients-need-to-remember-after-leaving-the-hospital-1448908354.

27. Ibid.

28. Ibid.

29. G. L. Kreps, *Organizational Communication: Theory and Practice* (New York: Longman, 1990).

30. Ibid.

31. J. Jusko, "A Little More Communication," *Industry Week*, March 1, 2010, 19.

32. L. Handley, "Angela Ahrendts: Here's How Apple Store Staff Start Every Single Day," *CNBC*, January 29, 2019, accessed June 12, 2020, https://www.cnbc.com/2019/01/29/angela-ahrendts-heres-how-apple-store-staff-start-every-single-day.html; S. Menkes, "Apple's Angela Ahrendts: How to fix retail," *Vogue Business*, January 28, 2019, accessed June 12, 2020, https://www.voguebusiness.com/companies/angela-ahrendts-apple-retail-strategy.

33. H. Gregersen, "Bursting Out of the CEO Bubble," *Harvard Business Review*, March–April 2017, accessed April 30, 2017, https://hbr.org/2017/03/bursting-the-ceo-bubble.

34. "Employee Engagement in a Digital Business – Technology's Role in Fostering Culture," *Dimension Data*, accessed April 30, 2017, http://www2.dimensiondata.com/en/insights/ambitious-thinking/culture-as-a-business-accelerator/employee-engagement-in-a-digital-business.

35. L. Landro, "The Most Crucial Half-Hour at a Hospital: The Shift Change," *Wall Street Journal*, October 26, 2015, accessed May 1, 2017, https://www.wsj.com/articles/the-most-crucial-half-hour-at-a-hospital-the-shift-change-1445887115.

36. A. Bassuk & C. Lew, "The Antidote to Office Gossip," *Harvard Business Review*, November 11, 2016, accessed June 12, 2020, https://hbr.org/2016/11/the-antidote-to-office-gossip.

37. K. Gee, "The Not-So-Creepy Reason More Bosses Are Tracking Employees," *Wall Street Journal*, March 21, 2017, accessed May 1, 2017, https://www.wsj.com/articles/the-not-so-creepy-reason-more-bosses-are-tracking-employees-1490101200.

38. K. Gee (Dow Jones), "Companies Tracking Employees' Emails, Conversations 'to improve collaboration,'" *Australian Business Review*, March 22,

2017, accessed May 1, 2017, http://www.theaustralian.com.au/business/technology/companies-tracking-employees-emails-conversations-to-improve-collaboration/news-story/1190680b8305cac0a9446884d47285b3.

39. J. Sandberg, "Ruthless Rumors and the Managers Who Enable Them," *Wall Street Journal*, October 29, 2003, B1.

40. E. Holm and J. S. Lublin, "Loose Lips Trip Up a Good Hands Executive," *Wall Street Journal*, August 1, 2011, C1.

41. K. Voight, "Office Intelligence," *Asian Wall Street Journal*, January 21, 2005, P1.

42. A. Aschale, "Review of the Grapevine Communication," June 2013, accessed May 10, 2016, http://www.academia.edu/4362950/Review_of_the_Grapevine_Communication.

43. W. C. Redding, *Communication within the Organization: An Interpretive View of Theory and Research* (New York: Industrial Communication Council, 1972).

44. D. T. Hall, K. L. Otazo, and G. P. Hollenbeck, "Behind Closed Doors: What Really Happens in Executive Coaching," *Organizational Dynamics* 27, no. 3 (1999): 39–53.

45. Shellenbarger, "How to Find Out What the Boss Really Thinks of You," *Wall Street Journal*, June 28, 2016, accessed May 1, 2017, https://www.wsj.com/articles/how-to-find-out-what-the-boss-really-thinks-of-you-1467138157.

46. Ibid.

47. Interact Report, "Many Leaders Shrink from Straight Talk with Employees," *Interact*, February 2016, accessed June 12, 2020, http://interactauthentically.com/articles/research/many-leaders-shrink-straight-talk-employees/; L. Solomon, "Two-Thirds of Managers Are Uncomfortable Communicating with Employees," *Harvard Business Review*, March 9, 2016, accessed June 12, 2020, https://hbr.org/2016/03/two-thirds-of-managers-are-uncomfortable-communicating-with-employees.

48. R. McGarvey, "Lords of Discipline," *Entrepreneur Magazine*, January 1, 2000, page number not available.

49. Jack Welch, "'Rank-and-Yank'? That's Not How It's Done," *Wall Street Journal*, November 15, 2013, A.15.

50. N. Goodman, "Jack Welch on How to Manage Employees," *Entrepreneur*, October 5, 2012, accessed May 10, 2016, http://www.entrepreneur.com/blog/224604.

51. C. Hirschman, "Firm Ground: EAP Training for HR and Managers Improves Supervisor-Employee Communication and Helps Organizations Avoid Legal Quagmires," *Employee Benefit News*, June 13, 2005, accessed May 10, 2016, http://www.highbeam.com/doc/1G1-121455684.html.

52. T. Agovino, "Companies Seek to Boost Low Usage of Employee Assistance Programs," *Society for Human Resource Management*, November 21, 2019, accessed June 12, 2020, https://www.shrm.org/hr-today/news/hr-magazine/winter2019/pages/companies-seek-to-boost-low-usage-of-employee-assistance-programs.aspx.

53. Ibid.

54. Ibid.

55. A. Mehrabian, "Communication without Words," *Psychology Today* 3 (1968): 53; A. Mehrabian, *Silent Messages* (Belmont, CA: Wadsworth, 1971); R. Harrison, *Beyond Words: An Introduction to Nonverbal Communication* (Upper Saddle River, NJ: Prentice Hall, 1974); A. Mehrabian, *Non-Verbal Communication* (Chicago: Aldine, 1972).

56. M. L. Knapp, *Nonverbal Communication in Human Interaction*, 2nd ed. (New York: Holt, Rinehart & Winston, 1978).

57. H. M. Rosenfeld, "Instrumental Affiliative Functions of Facial and Gestural Expressions," *Journal of Personality & Social Psychology* 24 (1966): 65–72; P. Ekman, "Differential Communication of Affect by Head and Body Cues," *Journal of Personality & Social Psychology* 23 (1965): 726–735; A. Mehrabian, "Significance of Posture and Position in the Communication of Attitude and Status Relationships," *Psychological Bulletin* 71 (1969): 359–372.

58. S. Shellenbarger, "Use Mirroring to Connect With Others," *Wall Street Journal*, September 20, 2016, accessed May 1, 2017, https://www.wsj.com/articles/use-mirroring-to-connect-with-others-1474394329.

59. T. Bradberry and K. Kruse, "Why Successful People Never Bring Smartphones Into Meetings," *LinkedIn*, September 22, 2014, accessed May 10, 2016, https://www.linkedin.com/pulse/20140922000 612-50578967-why-successful-people-never-bring-smartphones-into-meetings.

60. Ibid.

61. J. Simons, "'I Lost It': The Boss Who Banned Phones, and What Came Next," *Wall Street Journal*, May 16, 2018, accessed June 13, 2020, https://www.wsj.com/articles/can-you-handle-it-bosses-ban-cellphones-from-meetings-1526470250.

62. S. Shellenbarger, "Is This How You Really Talk?" *Wall Street Journal*, accessed May 10, 2016, accessed June 20, 2014, http://www.wsj.com/news/articles/SB10001424127887323735604578440851083674898.

63. T. Simonite, "Call Centers Tap Voice-Analysis Software to Monitor Moods," *Wired*, March 19, 2018, accessed June 13, 2020, https://www.wired.com/story/this-call-may-be-monitored-for-tone-and-emotion/?CNDID=49330717&mbid=nl_031918_daily_list1_p1.

64. C. A. Bartlett and S. Ghoshal, "Changing the Role of Top Management: Beyond Systems to People," *Harvard Business Review*, May–June 1995, 132–142.

65. J. Lublin, "Managers Need to Make Time for Face Time," *Wall Street Journal*, March 18, 2015, B6.

66. A. Bryant, "Amit Singh of Google for Work: A Respectful Clash of Ideas," *New York Times*, January 22, 2016, BU2.

67. J. Fry, "When Talk Isn't Cheap: Is Emailing Colleagues Who Sit Feet Away a Sign of Office Dysfunction, or a Wise Move?" *Wall Street Journal*, November 28, 2005, accessed May 10, 2016, http://www.wsj.com/articles/SB113293718044406629.

68. J. Milenkovic, "Slack Statistics to Annoy Your Colleagues With," KommandoTech, December 4, 2019, accessed June 13, 2020, https://kommandotech.com/statistics/slack-statistics/.

69. "Email Statistics Report, 2019–2023," The Radicati Group, Inc., accessed June 13, 2020, https://www.radicati.com/wp/wp-content/uploads/2018/12/Email-Statistics-Report-2019-2023-Executive-Summary.pdf.

70. E. Bernstein, "Thou Shalt Not Send in Anger: Recovering from a Snippy Email to Friends, Even the Boss, Is Possible If You Grovel," *Wall Street Journal*, October 14, 2014, D1, D4.

71. S. Green Carmichael, "Avoiding Miscommunication in a Digital World (Transcript)," *HBR IdeaCast from Harvard Business Review*, November 6, 2018, accessed June 13, 2020, https://hbr.org/podcast/2018/11/avoiding-miscommunication-in-a-digital-world.

72. T. Lorenz, "A Case for Inbox Infinity," *The Atlantic*, January 8, 2019, accessed June 13, 2020, https://www.theatlantic.com/technology/archive/2019/01/case-inbox-infinity/579673/.

73. R. Molla, "How Slack Impacts Workplace Productivity," *Vox*, May 1, 2019, accessed June 13, 2020, https://www.vox.com/recode/2019/5/1/18511575/productivity-slack-google-microsoft-facebook.

74. S. Shellenbarger, "The Challenge of Managing a Long-Distance Relationship with Your Boss," *Wall Street Journal*, March 15, 2016, http://www.wsj.com/articles/the-challenge-of-managing-a-long-distance-relationship-with-your-boss-1458065121.

75. D. F. Larcker, S. Miles, B. Tayan, and M. E. Gutman, "2013 CEO Performance Evaluation Survey," *Stanford Graduate School of Business*, accessed May 10, 2016, http://www.gsb.stanford.edu/cldr/research/surveys/performance.html.

76. E. Atwater, *I Hear You*, revised ed. (New York: Walker, 1992).

77. R. G. Nichols, "Do We Know How to Listen? Practical Helps in a Modern Age," in *Communication Concepts and Processes*, ed. J. DeVitor (Englewood Cliffs, NJ: Prentice Hall, 1971); P. V. Lewis, *Organizational Communication: The Essence of Effective Management* (Columbus, OH: Grid Publishing Company, 1975); S. Khan, "Why Long Lectures Are Ineffective," *Time*, October 2, 2012, accessed May 10, 2016, http://ideas.time.com/2012/10/02/why-lectures-are-ineffective/.

78. A. Stevenson, "T-Mobile CEO to Cramer: 'Shut Up and Listen,'" *CNBC*, April 28, 2015, accessed May 10, 2016, http://www.cnbc.com/id/102628529.

79. C. Cutter, "A Law-Firm Veteran Who Leads by Listening," *Wall Street Journal*, June 24, 2019, accessed June 13, 2020, https://www.wsj.com/articles/a-law-firm-veteran-who-leads-by-listening-11561176001.

80. D. A. Kaplan, "Undercover Employee: A Day on the Job at Three Best Companies," *CNNMoney*, January 20, 2011, accessed May 10, 2016, 2012, http://features.blogs.fortune.cnn.com/2011/01/20/undercover-employee-a-day-on-the-job-at-three-best-companies/.

81. L. Gurkow, "The Art of Active Listening," *Jerusalem Post*, May 11, 2014, accessed June 20, 2014, http://www.jpost.com/Jewish-World/Judaism/Active-listening-351878.

82. Gregersen, "Bursting Out of the CEO Bubble."

83. E. Bernstein, "How 'Active Listening' Makes Both Participants in a Conversation Feel Better," *Wall Street Journal*, January 12, 2015, accessed May 10, 2016, http://www.wsj.com/articles/how-active-listening-makes-both-sides-of-a-conversation-feel-better-1421082684.

84. S. Turkle, "Stop Googling. Let's Talk," *New York Times*, September 26, 2015, accessed May 10, 2016, http://www.nytimes.com/2015/09/27/opinion/sunday/stop-googling-lets-talk.html?_r=0.

85. S. Konrath, E. O'Brien, and C. Hsing, "Changes in Dispositional Empathy in American College Students Over Time: A Meta-Analysis," *Personality and Social Psychology Review* 15 (2011): 180–198.

86. T. Smith, "Summer Camps Struggle To Enforce Bans On Screen Time," *NPR*, August 11, 2016, accessed May 1, 2017, http://www.npr.org/2016/08/11/489661961/summer-camps-struggle-to-enforce-bans-on-screen-time.

87. S. Wolpert, "In Our Digital World, Are Young People Losing the Ability to Read Emotions?," *UCLA Newsroom*, August 21, 2014, accessed May 10, 2016, http://newsroom.ucla.edu/releases/in-our-digital-world-are-young-people-losing-the-ability-to-read-emotions; Y. Uhls, M Michikyan, J. Morris, D. Garcia, G. Small, E. Zgourou, and P. Greenfield, "Five Days at Outdoor Education Camp Without Screens Improves Preteen Skills with Nonverbal Emotion Cues," *Computers in Human Behavior* 39 (2014): 387–392.

88. Turkle, "Stop Googling. Let's Talk."

89. Atwater, *I Hear You*.

90. C. Edwards, "Death of a Pushy Salesman," *BusinessWeek*, July 3, 2006, 108.

91. J. Sandberg, "Not Communicating with Your Boss? Count Your Blessings," *Wall Street Journal*, May 22, 2007, B1.

92. J. Grenny, "How to Be Resilient in the Face of Harsh Criticism," *Harvard Business Review*, June 17, 2019, accessed June 13, 2020, https://hbr.org/2019/06/how-to-be-resilient-in-the-face-of-harsh-criticism.

93. R. Feintzeig, "'Nice' Is a Four-Letter Word at Companies Practicing Radical Candor," *Wall Street Journal*, December 30, 2015, accessed May 1, 2017, https://www.wsj.com/articles/nice-is-a-four-letter-word-at-companies-practicing-radical-candor-1451498192.

94. L. Weber and R.E. Silverman, "Workers Get New Tools for Airing Their Gripes," *Wall Street Journal*, August 26, 2015, B1, B4.

95. D. Bright, "How to Deliver Criticism So Employees Pay Attention," *Harvard Business Review*, January 17, 2017, accessed May 1, 2017, https://hbr.org/2017/01/how-to-deliver-criticism-so-employees-pay-attention.

96. Bellis, "Point-Counterpoint: Will Email Ever Disappear From The Workplace?" *Fast Company*, March 29, 2016, accessed May 1, 2017, https://www.fastcompany.com/3058312/point-counterpoint-will-email-ever-disappear-from-the-workplace.

97. R. Holmes, "Why You Should Declare Email Bankruptcy for 2015," *Hootsuite*, January 12, 2015, accessed May 1, 2017, https://blog.hootsuite.com/why-you-should-declare-email-bankruptcy-for-2015/.

98. A. Samuel, "How I Tamed the Email Beast at Work," *Wall Street Journal*, March 14, 2016, accessed May 1, 2017, https://www.wsj.com/articles/how-i-tamed-the-email-beast-at-work-1457921533.

99. "Slack Helps Cole Haan Bring New Footwear to Market Faster," Slack, accessed June 14, 2020, https://slack.com/customer-stories/cole-haan.

100. Ibid.

101. W. Mossberg, "Slack Beats EMail, But Still Needs to Get Better," *The Verge*, April 13, 2016, accessed May 10, 2016, http://www.theverge.com/2016/4/13/11417726/slack-app-walt-mossberg-stewart-butterfield-interview.

102. Intlock Team, "Yammer vs Teams: Which Microsoft Tool Wins the Battle?" CardioLog Analytics, January 1, 2019, accessed June 14, 2020, https://blog.intlock.com/microsoft-teams-vs-yammer-communications-tool-use/.

103. "Live and on-demand events in Microsoft 365," Microsoft.com, accessed June 14, 2020, https://www.microsoft.com/en-us/microsoft-365/live-on-demand-event-solutions.

104. R. Hougaard, J. Carter & K. Hogan, "How Microsoft Builds a Sense of Community Among 144,000 Employees," *Harvard Business Review*, August 28, 2019, accessed June 14, 2020, https://hbr.org/2019/08/how-microsoft-builds-a-sense-of-community-among-144000-employees.

105. M. Stout, "Unpacking How Microsoft Employees Collaborate on Microsoft Teams and Yammer," *Microsoft IT Showcase Blog*, February 13, 2020, accessed June 14, 2020, https://www.microsoft.com/itshowcase/blog/unpacking-how-microsoft-employees-collaborate-on-microsoft-teams-and-yammer/.

106. E. W. Morrison, "Organizational Silence: A Barrier to Change and Development in a Pluralistic World," *Academy of Management Review* 25 (2000): 706–725.

107. M. Heffernan, "Encourage Employees to Speak Up," *Inc*, April 9, 2014, accessed July 21, 2014, http://www.inc.com/margaret-heffernan/encourage-employees-to-speak-up.html.

108. H. Gregersen, "Bursting Out of the CEO Bubble."

109. Ibid.

110. I. Hussain, R. Shu, S. Tangirala, S. Ekkirala, "The Voice Bystander Effect: How Information Redundancy Inhibits Employee Voice," *Academy of Management Journal* 62, no. 3 (2019): 828–849.

111. I. Hussain & S. Tangirala, "Why Open Secrets Exist in Organizations," *Harvard Business Review*, January 14, 2019, accessed June 14, 2020, https://hbr.org/2019/01/why-open-secrets-exist-in-organizations.

112. E. O'Mara, "Three Key Findings from Our 2016 Hotline Benchmark Report," *JD Supra Business Advisor*, April 25, 2016, http://www.jdsupra.com/legalnews/three-key-findings-from-our-2016-67770/. Full NAVEXGlobal 2016 Hotline Benchmark Report available http://trust.navexglobal.com/rs/852-MYR-807/images/NAVEX-Global_2016_Hotline_BenchmarkReport.pdf.

113. Hougaard, Carter, and Hogan, "How Microsoft Builds a Sense of Community Among 144,000 Employees."

114. Ibid.

115. C. Hymowitz, "Sometimes, Moving Up Makes It Harder to See What Goes on Below," *Wall Street Journal*, October 15, 2007, B1.

116. R. Ashkenas, "How to Overcome Executive Isolation," *Harvard Business Review*, February 2, 2017, accessed May 2, 2017, https://hbr.org/2017/02/how-to-overcome-executive-isolation.

117. Ibid.

118. J.T. Genter, "Behind the Scenes at the American Airlines Social Media Hub," *The Points Guy*, October 8, 2017, accessed June 15, 2020, https://thepointsguy.com/2017/10/american-airlines-social-media-hub/.

119. J. Wolfe, "Want Faster Airline Customer Service? Try Tweeting," *New York Times*, November 20, 2018, accessed June 15, 2020, https://www.nytimes.com/2018/11/20/travel/airline-customer-service-twitter.html.

120. Ibid.

121. Hougaard, Carter, and Hogan, "How Microsoft Builds a Sense of Community Among 144,000 Employees."

122. A. Florance, "Connecting Leaders and Employees with Live Events in Yammer," Microsoft Tech Community, August 1, 2018, accessed June 15, 2020, https://techcommunity.microsoft.com/t5/yammer-blog/connecting-leaders-and-employees-with-live-events-in-yammer/ba-p/221959.

123. K. Hogan, "Microsoft's Chief People Officer on Culture and Engaging Employees (Sponsored Content)," *Bloomberg*, March 14, 2018, accessed June 15, 2020, https://sponsored.bloomberg.com/news/sponsors/microsoft/microsofts-chief-people-officer-on-culture-and-engaging-employees/?adv=7971&prx_t=F2ADAX0MaAVykPA&sref=xXo7CWym.

16

1.   R. Leifer and P. K. Mills, "An Information Processing Approach for Deciding Upon Control Strategies and Reducing Control Loss in Emerging Organizations," *Journal of Management* 22 (1996): 113–137.

2.   W. Hu & M. Haag, "90,000 Packages Disappear Daily in N.Y.C. Is Help on the Way?" *New York Times*, December 2, 2019, accessed June 25, 2020, https://www.nytimes.com/2019/12/02/nyregion/online-shopping-package-theft.html?mod=djem10point.

3.   R. Molla, "Amazon Ring Saves Amazon Money on Stolen Packages," – *Vox*, August 12, 2019, accessed June 25, 2020, https://www.vox.com/recode/2019/8/12/20802325/amazon-ring-ecommerce-package-theft.

4.   "Neighbors App by Ring: Real-Time Crime & Safety Alerts," Ring, accessed June 25, 2020, https://store.ring.com/neighbors.

5.   "Everything You Need To Know About Amazon Hub Locker," Amazon, accessed June 25, 2020, https://www.amazon.com/primeinsider/tips/amazon-locker-qa.html; "Amazon Key @ Amazon.com," Amazon, accessed June 25, 2020, https://www.amazon.com/key.

6.   "Safe Stay: AHLA," American Hotel & Lodging Association, accessed June 25, 2020, https://www.ahla.com/safestay.

7.   "Hilton Defining New Standard of Cleanliness," Hilton Press Center, April 27, 2020, accessed June 25, 2020, https://newsroom.hilton.com/corporate/news/hilton-defining-new-standard-of-cleanliness.

8.   S. Ramani, "How Hotels Are Redefining Cleanliness and Safety in the Covid-19 Era," *Robb Report*, May 6, 2020, accessed June 25, 2020, https://robbreport.com/travel/hotels/hotel-cleaning-safety-programs-2919132/.

9.   W. Boston, "'They Go Absolutely Insane and Tear Everything Apart': Weasels Love German Cars," *Wall Street Journal*, December 16, 2019, accessed June 25, 2020, https://www.wsj.com/articles/they-go-absolutely-insane-and-tear-everything-apart-weasels-love-german-cars-11577377251; N. Kurczewski, "Does Your Car Have Wiring That Rodents Think Is Tasty?" *Car and Driver*, June 25, 2018, accessed June 25, 2020, https://www.caranddriver.com/news/a21933466/does-your-car-have-wiring-that-rodents-think-is-tasty/.

10.   Ibid.

11.   Ibid.

12.   "NFPA 1710: Standard for the Organization and Deployment of Fire Suppression Operations, Emergency Medical Operations, and Special Operations to the Public by Career Fire Departments, 2020," National Fire Protection Association, accessed June 25, 2020, https://www.nfpa.org/codes-and-standards/all-codes-and-standards/list-of-codes-and-standards/detail?code=1710.

13.   D. Robb, "Is Big Data Right for Small Business?" *Tech Page One*, June 26, 2014, accessed May 11, 2016, http://techpageone.dell.com/technology/is-big-data-right-for-small-business/.

14.   "Transform Your QuickBooks Data Into Visual Performance Reports and Presentations," Fathom, accessed June 26, 2020, https://www.fathomhq.com/quickbooks.

15.   J. Starn, "This Tiny Bug Could Put a $625 Million Hole in Sweden's Forests," *Bloomberg*, May 7, 2019, accessed June 26, 2020, https://www.bloomberg.com/news/articles/2019-05-07/this-tiny-bug-could-put-a-625-million-hole-in-sweden-s-forests?sref=xXo7CWym.

16.   J. Wahlqvist, "We're Going on a Beetle Hunt," Sogeti, accessed June 26, 2020, https://www.sogeti.com/explore/blog/were-going-on-a-beetle-hunt/.

17.   E. Sheng, "Coronavirus Crisis Mobile Banking Surge Is a Shift Likely to Stick," CNBC.com, May 27, 2020, accessed June 26, 2020, https://www.cnbc.com/2020/05/27/coronavirus-crisis-mobile-banking-surge-is-a-shift-likely-to-stick.html.

18.   Ibid.

19.   O. McCaffrey, "People Aren't Visiting Branches. Banks Are Wondering How Many They Actually Need," *Wall Street Journal*, June 7, 2020, accessed June 26, 2020, https://www.wsj.com/articles/people-arent-visiting-branches-banks-are-wondering-how-many-they-actually-need-11591531200?mod=djemHL_t.

20.   N. Wiener, *Cybernetics; Or Control and Communication in the Animal and the Machine* (New York: Wiley, 1948).

21.   A. Levin, "Pilots Can't Stop Cockpit Video Forever," *Bloomberg Businessweek*, October 12–18, 2015, 27–28.

22.   Ibid.

23.   R. Sumwalt, III., B. Landsberg, J. Homendy & T. Chapman, "Safety Recommendation Report: Install Flight Data, Audio, and Image Recorder Systems on All Turbine-Powered Helicopters," National Transportation Safety Board, May 19, 2020, accessed June 26, 2020, https://www.ntsb.gov/investigations/AccidentReports/Reports/ASR2004.pdf.

24.   A. Pasztor, "NTSB Calls for Cockpit Video Recorders in Helicopters, Faulting FAA," *Wall Street Journal*, June 2, 2020, accessed June 26, 2020, https://www.wsj.com/articles/ntsb-calls-for-cockpit-video-recorders-in-helicopters-faulting-faa-11591136622.

25.   L. Scism, "American Homeowners and Their Insurers Face a Flooding Crisis From Within," *Wall Street Journal*, March 7, 2019, accessed June 26, 2020, https://www.wsj.com/articles/american-homeowners-and-their-insurers-face-a-flooding-crisis-from-within-11551960001?mod=hp_lead_pos7.

26.   Ibid.

27.   "Home Security and Water Defense Overview," Chubb, accessed June 26, 2020, https://www.chubb.com/_global-assets/documents/homesecurityandwaterdefenseoverview.pdf.

28.   M. Griggs, "In Nasty Weather, High-Tech Sensors Get the Lights Back on Faster," *Popular Science*, December 23, 2014, accessed May 11, 2016, http://www.popsci.com/high-tech-power-line-sensors-get-lights-turned-faster.

29.   D. Cardwell, "Grid Sensors Could Ease Disruptions of Power," *New York Times*, February 3, 2015, B4.

30.   E. Ailworth, "What Utilities Can Do to Strengthen the Grid," *Wall Street Journal*, January 22, 2019, accessed June 26, 2020, https://www.wsj.com/articles/what-utilities-can-do-to-strengthen-the-grid-11548170957?mod=djemwhatsnews.

31.   Leifer and Mills, "An Information Processing Approach."

32.   D. Gunders, "Wasted: How America Is Losing up to 40 Percent of Its Food From Farm to Fork to Landfill." *Natural Resources Defense Council*, August 16, 2017, accessed June 27, 2020, https://www.nrdc.org/resources/wasted-how-america-losing-40-percent-its-food-farm-fork-landfill; D. Netburn, "How to Cut Food Waste in Half – and Fight Climate Change Too," *Los Angeles Times*, August 29, 2019, accessed June 27, 2020, https://www.latimes.com/environment/story/2019-08-28/how-to-cut-food-waste-in-half.

33.   "Minimizing Waste," McDonald's, accessed June 27, 2020, https://corporate.mcdonalds.com/corpmcd/scale-for-good/our-planet/eliminating-waste.html.

34.   F. Flam, "The Recycling Game Is Rigged Against Consumers," *Chicago Tribune*, July 3, 2018, accessed June 27, 2020, https://www.chicagotribune.com/opinion/commentary/ct-perspec-recycle-plastic-blue-bin-china-contaminated-nonrecyclable-0705-story.html.

35.   M. Corkery, "As Costs Skyrocket, More US Cities Stop Recycling," *New York Times*, March 16, 2019, accessed June 27, 2020, https://www.nytimes.com/2019/03/16/business/local-recycling-costs.html.

36.   B. Presser, "9 Things I Never Knew About Cruises Until I Ran the World's Largest Ship," *Bloomberg*, January 31, 2018, accessed June 27, 2020, https://www.bloomberg.com/news/articles/2018-01-31/secrets-of-cruise-ships-from-crew-codes-to-sex-to-norovirus?sref=xXo7CWym.

37.   Ibid.

38.   P. Mosendz & A. Melin, "Bosses Panic-Buy Spy Software to Keep Tabs on Remote Workers," *Bloomberg*, March 27, 2020, accessed June 27, 2020, https://www.bloomberg.com/news/features/2020-03-27/bosses-panic-buy-spy-software-to-keep-tabs-on-remote-workers?sref=xXo7CWym.

39.   M. Weber, *The Protestant Ethic and the Spirit of Capitalism* (New York: Scribner's, 1958).

40.   G. Hamel & M. Zanini, "The End of Bureaucracy," *Harvard Business Review*, November–December 2018, accessed June 27, 2020, https://hbr.org/2018/11/the-end-of-bureaucracy?

41.   Ibid.

42.   A. Rosenblat, "When Your Boss Is an Algorithm," *New York Times*, October 12, 2018, accessed June 27, 2020, https://www.nytimes.com/2018/10/12/opinion/sunday/uber-driver-life.html.

43.   M. Mohlmann & O. Henfridsson, "What People Hate About Being Managed by Algorithms, According to a Study of Uber Drivers," *Harvard Business Review*, August 30, 2019, accessed June 27, 2020, https://hbr.org/2019/08/what-people-hate-about-being-managed-by-algorithms-according-to-a-study-of-uber-drivers.

44.   M. Belvedere, "Why Aetna's CEO Pays Workers up to $500 to Sleep," CNBC, April 5, 2016, accessed May 3, 2017, http://www.cnbc.com/2016/04/05/why-aetnas-ceo-pays-workers-up-to-500-to-sleep.html.

45.   Ibid.

46.   H. Son, "'Bob in Accounting Is Going to Fix Currency Rates.' – I'll Tell Jamie Dimon,'" *Bloomberg Businessweek*, April 13–19, 2015, pp. 34–35.

47.   "Capital Question: How Do You Hire People Who Fit Your Company Culture?" *Edmonton Journal* (*Alberta*), January 29, 2014, C11.

48.   A. Kadet, "City News – Metro Money/Jerks Need Not Apply," *Wall Street Journal*, January 18, 2014, accessed May 11, 2016, http://www.wsj.com/articles/SB10001424052702304149404579326730931946454.

49.   J. R. Barker, "Tightening the Iron Cage: Concertive Control in Self-Managing Teams," *Administrative Science Quarterly* 38 (1993): 408–437.

50.   "The Other Side Movers – We Move Lives," The Other Side Movers, accessed May 3, 2017, http://theothersidemovers.com/.

51.   "The Other Side Movers," accessed June 27 2020, https://www.theothersidemovers.com/.

52.   J. Grenny, "How to Make Feedback Feel Normal," *Harvard Business Review*, August 19, 2016,

accessed May 3, 2017, https://hbr.org/2016/08/how-to-make-feedback-feel-normal.

53. Ibid.

54. Barker, "Tightening the Iron Cage."

55. C. Manz and H. Sims, "Leading Workers to Lead Themselves: The External Leadership of Self-Managed Work Teams," *Administrative Science Quarterly* 32 (1987): 106–128.

56. J. Slocum and H. A. Sims, "Typology for Integrating Technology, Organization and Job Design," *Human Relations* 33 (1980): 193–212.

57. C. C. Manz and H. P. Sims, Jr., "Self-Management as a Substitute for Leadership: A Social Learning Perspective," *Academy of Management Review* 5 (1980): 361–367.

58. C. Manz and C. Neck, *Mastering Self-Leadership*, 3rd ed. (Upper Saddle River, NJ: Pearson, Prentice Hall, 2004).

59. R. S. Kaplan and D. P. Norton, "Using the Balanced Scorecard as a Strategic Management System," *Harvard Business Review* (January–February 1996): 75–85; R. S. Kaplan and D. P. Norton, "The Balanced Scorecard: Measures That Drive Performance," *Harvard Business Review* (January–February 1992): 71–79.

60. J. Meliones, "Saving Money, Saving Lives," *Harvard Business Review* (November–December 2000): 57–65.

61. A. Wilde Mathews and A. Steele, "Aetna Lifts Forecast; Net Tops Expectations as Key Measure Falls," *Wall Street Journal*, October 30, 2015, B4.

62. D. Seetharaman, "Instagram Finds Focus Under 'Efficiency Guru,'" *Wall Street Journal*, April 13, 2017, accessed June 28, 2020, https://www.wsj.com/articles/instagram-finds-focus-under-efficiency-guru-1492075801.

63. N. Trentmann, "Global Companies Extend Use of Zero-Based Budgeting to Slash Costs," *Wall Street Journal*, February 27, 2018, accessed June 28, 2020, https://blogs.wsj.com/cfo/2018/02/27/global-companies-extend-use-of-zero-based-budgeting-to-slash-costs/; N. Trentmann, "For Welch's, Zero-Based Budgeting Helps Zero In on Costs," *Wall Street Journal*, December 6, 2019, accessed June 28, 2020, https://www.wsj.com/articles/for-welchs-zero-based-budgeting-helps-zero-in-on-costs-11575671707?mod=djemCFO.

64. N. Trentmann, "For Welch's, Zero-Based Budgeting Helps Zero in on Costs."

65. Ibid.

66. N. Trentmann, "Ryder System Cuts Costs With Zero-Based Budgeting Amid Business Slowdown," *Wall Street Journal*, April 30, 2020, accessed June 28, 2020, https://www.wsj.com/articles/ryder-system-cuts-costs-with-zero-based-budgeting-amid-business-slowdown-11588287239.

67. S. L. Fawcett, "Fear of Accounts: Improving Managers' Competence and Confidence Through Simulation Exercises," *Journal of European Industrial Training* (February 1996): 17.

68. M. H. Stocks and A. Harrell, "The Impact of an Increase in Accounting Information Level on the Judgment Quality of Individuals and Groups," *Accounting, Organizations & Society* (October–November 1995): 685–700.

69. B. Morris, "Roberto Goizueta and Jack Welch: The Wealth Builders," *Fortune*, December 11, 1995, 80–94.

70. G. Colvin, "America's Best & Worst Wealth Creators: The Real Champions Aren't Always Who You Think. Here's an Eye-Opening Look at Which Companies Produce and Destroy the Most Money for Investors – Plus a New Tool for Spotting Future Winners," *Fortune*, December 18, 2000, 207.

71. "About Herman Miller: Operational Excellence," *Herman Miller*, accessed June 20, 2011, http://www.hermanmiller.com/About-Us/About-Herman-Miller/Operational-Excellence.

72. M. Schurman, "A Herman Miller Primer," *Herman Miller*, accessed June 20, 2011, http://www.hermanmiller.com/MarketFacingTech/hmc/about_us/News_Events_Media/Corporate_Backgrounder.pdf.

73. B. Stewart, *Best-Practice EVA: The Definitive Guide to Measuring and Maximizing Shareholder Value* (New York: Wiley Finance, 2013); "Apple, Inc.: Economic Value Added," Stock *Analysis on Net*, accessed June 28, 2020, https://www.stock-analysis-on.net/NASDAQ/Company/Apple-Inc/Performance-Measure/Economic-Value-Added; "Microsoft Corp.: Economic Value Added," *Stock Analysis on Net*, accessed June 28, 2020, https://www.stock-analysis-on.net/NASDAQ/Company/Microsoft-Corp/Performance-Measure/Economic-Value-Added; "Alphabet, Inc.: Economic Value Added," *Stock Analysis on Net*, accessed June 28, 2020, https://www.stock-analysis-on.net/NASDAQ/Company/Alphabet-Inc/Performance-Measure/Economic-Value-Added.

74. "Welcome Complaints," *Office of Consumer and Business Affairs,* Government of South Australia, accessed June 20, 2005, http://www.ocba.sa.gov.au/businessadvice/complaints/03_welcome.html.

75. J. Tschohl, "Cultivate Loyal Customers: The Value of Defection Management," Desk.com, May 23, 2013, accessed May 11, 2016, http://www.desk.com/blog/loyal-customers/.

76. C. A. Reeves and D. A. Bednar, "Defining Quality: Alternatives and Implications," *Academy of Management Review* 19 (1994): 419–445.

77. "The Best International Airlines: 2019 Readers' Choice Awards," *Condé Nast Traveler*, October 7, 2019, accessed June 28, 2020, https://www.cntraveler.com/galleries/2015-10-07/top-international-airlines-readers-choice-awards ; "About Us: *Singapore Airlines*—Our Awards," Singapore Airlines, accessed June 28, 2020, https://www.singaporeair.com/en_UK/us/flying-withus/our-story/awards/.

78. "New First Class," Singapore Airlines, accessed June 28, 2020, https://www.singaporeair.com/en_UK/us/flying-withus/cabins/first-class/new-first-class/.

79. R. Smithers, "Asda Puts UK's First Supermarket Wonky Veg Box on Sale," *The Guardian*, February 5, 2016, accessed May 11, 2016, http://www.theguardian.com/environment/2016/feb/05/asda-puts-uks-first-supermarket-wonky-veg-box-on-sale.

80. L. Neel, "Wonky Veg Introduced in Ongoing Supermarket Price War," *Fresh Business* Thinking, February 9, 2016, accessed May 11, 2016, http://www.freshbusinessthinking.com/wonky-veg-introduced-in-ongoing-supermarket-price-war/.

81. I. Harrison, "How Our Wonky Veg Boxes Have Changed What You'll See in Our Produce Aisles," ASDA, March 28, 2018, accessed June 28, 2020, https://corporate.asda.com/blog/2018/03/28/how-our-wonky-veg-boxes-have-changed-what-youll-see-in-our-produce-aisles.

82. Ibid.

83. D. R. May and B. L. Flannery, "Cutting Waste with Employee Involvement Teams," *Business Horizons*, September–October 1995, 28–38.

84. M. Sullivan, "Apple Now Runs on 100% Green Energy, and Here's How It Got There," *Fast Company*, April 9, 2018.

85. Ibid.

86. Ibid.

87. L. Kaye, "Israeli Startup Prevents Water Leaks Before They Happen," *Triple Pundit*, March 31, 2017, accessed May 4, 2017, http://www.triplepundit.com/2017/03/israeli-startups-advanced-technology-prevent-water-leaks-occur/.

88. M. Campbell, "The Fastest Pants on Earth: Primark Makes Fast-Fashion Look Slow," *Bloomberg Businessweek*, December 21–27, 2015, 46–50.

89. E. Scheyder & S. Nellis, "Apple Pushes Recycling of iPhone with 'Daisy' Robot," *Reuters*, January 10, 2020, accessed June 28, 2020, https://www.reuters.com/article/us-usa-minerals-recycling/apple-pushes-recycling-of-iphone-with-daisy-robot-idUSKBN1Z925S.

90. S. Warwick, "Apple Wants to Become a "Closed-Loop" Manufacturer," *iMore*, January 11, 2020, accessed June 28, 2020, https://www.imore.com/apple-wants-become-closed-loop-manufacturer.

91. "Renewable Aviation," Neste, accessed June 29, 2020, https://www.neste.us/neste-my-renewable-jet-fuel; "Vegetable Oils and Animal Fats: Emergency Response," US Environmental Protection Agency, accessed June 29, 2020, https://www.epa.gov/emergency-response/vegetable-oils-and-animal-fats; S. Kent, "The Key to Big Profits in Clean Energy: Animal Fats," *Wall Street Journal*, August 14, 2018, accessed June 29, 2020, https://www.wsj.com/articles/the-key-to-big-profits-in-clean-energy-animal-fats-1534248000.

92. "Turning Fries Into Miles – How McDonald's, Neste, and HAVI Create a Circular Economy That Uses Cooking Oil to Fuel Logistics," Neste, June 23, 2020, accessed June 29, 2020, https://www.neste.us/neste-in-north-america/news-inspiration/archive/3569-circular-economy/turning-fries-miles-how-mcdonalds-neste-and-havi-create-ci.

93. "The End of the Road: Schools and Computer Recycling," *Intel*, accessed September 5, 2008, http://www.intel.com/education/recycling_computers/recycling.htm.

94. "Goodwill | Donate Computers, Laptops & Electronics | Recycle," Goodwill, accessed June 29, 2020, http://www.goodwillsc.org/donate/computers.

95. "Electronics and Appliances Recycling at Best Buy," Best Buy, accessed June 29, 2020, https://www.bestbuy.com/site/services/recycling/pcmcat149900050025.c?id=pcmcat149900050025.

17

1. R. Lenzner, "The Reluctant Entrepreneur," *Forbes*, September 11, 1995, 162–166.

2. "Inflation Calculator Find US Dollar's Value from 1913-2014," US Inflation Calculator, accessed July 3, 2020, http://www.usinflationcalculator.com/; T. Lee, "Today's iPhone Is More Useful Than $3,000 Worth of Gadgets from a 1991 Radio Shack," *The Washington Post*, January 31, 2014, accessed July 24, 2014, http://www.washingtonpost.com/blogs/the-switch/wp/2014/01/31/todays-iphone-is-more-useful-than-3000-worth-of-gadgets-from-a-1991-radio-shack/.

3. N. Tengyuen, "50 Things Your Smartphone Replaced [Or Will Replace in the Future]," *Gecko&Fly*, January 3, 2020, accessed July 3, 2020, https://www.geckoandfly.com/13143/50-things-smartphone-replaced-will-replace-future/.

4. "The Cost of Sequencing a Human Genome," National Human Genome Research Institute, October 30, 2019, accessed July 3, 2020, https://www.genome.gov/sequencingcosts/.

5. C. Mims, "How Chip Designers Are Breaking Moore's Law," *Wall Street Journal*, March 19, 2017, accessed May 5, 2017, https://www.wsj.com /articles/how-chip-designers-are-breaking-moores -law-1489924804.

6. B. Barrett, "An Intel Breakthrough Rethinks How Chips Are Made," *Wired*, December 12, 2018, accessed July 3, 2020, https://www.wired .com/story/intel-foveros-chips-breakthrough/; C. Mims, "The Secret to Tech's Next Big Break-throughs? Stacking Chips," *Wall Street Journal*, November 19, 2019, accessed July 3, 2020, https:// www.wsj.com/articles/the-secret-to-techs-next-big -breakthroughs-stacking-chips-1511034248.

7. G. Cheng, "Moore's Law is Not Dead," *Taiwan Semiconductor Manufacturing Company Blog*, August 14, 2019, accessed July 3, 2020, https://www. tsmc.com/english/newsEvents/blog _article_20190814.htm.

8. R. Dezember, "Your Smartphone's Location Data Is Worth Big Money to Wall Street," *Wall Street Journal*, November 2, 2018, accessed July 4, 2020, https://www.wsj.com/articles/your -smartphones-location-data-is-worth-big-money -to-wall-street-1541131260?mod=djemwhatsnews.

9. Ibid.

10. "Number of Pandora's Paying Subscribers from 2008 to 2025 (in Millions)," Statista, accessed July 4, 2020, https://www-statista-com.ezproxy. butler.edu/statistics/253850/number-of-pandoras -paying-subscribers/; eMarker Editors, "eMarketer Spotify and Pandora Listeners Forecast Q1 2020," *eMarketer Trends, Forecasts & Statistics*, March 6, 2020, accessed July 4, 2020, https://www.emarketer. com/content/us-spotify-listeners-surpassed -pandora-listeners-in-2019-sooner-than-expected.

11. A. Watson, "Number of Apple Music Sub-scribers Worldwide from October 2015 to December 2019 (in millions)," Statista, accessed July 4, 2020, https://www-statista-com.ezproxy .butler.edu/statistics/604959/number-of-apple -music-subscribers/; A. Watson, "Number of Spotify Premium Subscribers Worldwide from 1st Quarter 2015 to 1st Quarter 2020 (in Millions)," Statista, accessed July 4, 2020, https://www-statista-com. ezproxy.butler.edu/statistics/244995/number-of -paying-spotify-subscribers/; J. Clement, "Number of US Amazon Prime Users 2018–2022 (In Millions)," Statista, accessed July 4, 2020, https:// www-statista-com.ezproxy.butler.edu/statistics/504687 /number-of-amazon-prime-subscription-households -usa/; S. Dredge, "How Many Users Do Spotify, Apple Music and Streaming Services Have?" *Musi-cally*, February 19, 2020, accessed July 4, 2020, https://musically.com/2020/02/19/spotify-apple -how-many-users-big-music-streaming-services/.

12. A. Tabarrok, "How Uber and Airbnb Won," *Wall Street Journal*, January 30, 2017, accessed May 5, 2017, https://www.wsj.com/articles/how-uber -and-airbnb-won-1485821086.

13. F. Suarez and G. Lanzolla, "The Half-Truth of First Mover Advantage," *Harvard Business Review*, April 2005, accessed May 12, 2016, http:// hbr.org/2005/04/the-half-truth-of-first-mover -advantage/ar/1.

14. C. Mims, "Why Do the Biggest Companies Keep Getting Bigger? It's How They Spend on Tech," *Wall Street Journal*, July 26, 2018, accessed July 4, 2020, https://www.wsj.com/articles/why-do -the-biggest-companies-keep-getting-bigger-its -how-they-spend-on-tech-1532610001.

15. J. Stewart, "The Surprisingly Simple iPad Apps Pilots Use to Make Your Flight Better," *Wired*, April 26, 2018, accessed July 4, 2020, https:// www.wired.com/story/pilot-ipad-apps/.

16. Ibid.

17. A. Loten, "AI Efforts at Large Companies May Be Hindered by Poor-Quality Data," *Wall Street Journal*, March 4, 2019, accessed July 4, 2020, https://www.wsj.com/articles/ai-efforts-at -large-companies-may-be-hindered-by-poor -quality-data-11551741634?mod=djemCIO.

18. Ibid.

19. Ibid.

20. T. Davenport & R. Bean, "Are You Asking Too Much of Your Chief Data Officer?" *Harvard Business Review*, February 7, 2020, accessed July 4, 2020, https://hbr.org/2020/02/are-you-asking-too -much-of-your-chief-data-officer.

21. K. Nash, "Business Interest in Blockchain Picks Up While Cryptocurrency Causes Conniptions," *Wall Street Journal*, February 6, 2018, accessed July 5, 2020, https://blogs.wsj.com/cio/2018/02/06/business -interest-in-blockchain-picks-up-while-cryptocurrency -causes-conniptions/?mod=djemCIO_h.

22. Ibid.

23. Ibid.

24. M. Scaturro, "These Cows Will Text You When They're in Heat," Bloomberg, November 4, 2016, accessed May 6, 2017, https://www.bloomberg.com /news/articles/2016-11-04/these-cows-will-text-you -when-they-re-in-heat.

25. Ibid.

26. "smaXtec - Monitor Your Dairy Herd In Real-Time," smaXtec, accessed July 5, 2020, https:// smaxtec.com/en/.

27. E. Phillips, "Trucks Shift Into Higher Gear With New Technology," *Wall Street Journal*, July 25, 2018, accessed July 5, 2020, https://www.wsj .com/articles/trucks-shift-into-higher-gear-with -new-technology-1532527764.

28. "The Hidden Costs of "Low Cost" Data Acquisition Systems," Fluke, 2013, accessed July 5, 2020, https://us.flukecal.com/literature/articles-and -education/data-acquisition-and-test-equipment /application-notes/hidden-costs.

29. I. Davidson, *Biscuit, Cookie and Cracker Produc-tion: Process, Production and Packaging Equipment*, ed. I. Davidson (London: Academic Press, 2018).

30. E. Wilder-James, "Breaking Down Data Si-los," Harvard Business Review, December 5, 2016, accessed May 6, 2017, https://hbr.org/2016/12 /breaking-down-data-silos.

31. R. Bean, "Variety, Not Volume, Is Driving Big Data Initiatives," Sloan Management Review, March 28, 2016, accessed May 6, 2017, http:// sloanreview.mit.edu/article/variety-not-volume -is-driving-big-data-initiatives/.

32. A. Loten, "Companies Eager to Expand Digital Business Learn Value of the Once-Ob-scure API," *Wall Street Journal*, June 12, 2018, accessed July 7, 2020, https://blogs.wsj.com /cio/2018/06/12/companies-eager-to-expand -digital-business-learn-value-of-the-once -obscure-api/?mod=djemCIO_h.

33. R. Bauer, "The Factors to Consider When Choosing a Data Center for Your Business," Back-blaze, March 2, 2018, accessed July 6, 2020, https:// www.backblaze.com/blog/factors-for-choosing-data -center/?u%E2%80%A6content=choosing-data -center-2-i&utm_campaign=Newsletter-20180306.

34. A. Loten, "Q&A: Taking ClubCorp From Filing Cabinets to the Cloud," *Wall Street Journal*, February 20, 2018, accessed July 6, 2020, https:// blogs.wsj.com/cio/2018/02/20/qa-taking-clubcorp -from-filing-cabinets-to-the-cloud/.

35. J. Snell, "Reading Disks From 1988 in 2018," *Six Colors*, January 12, 2018, accessed July 6, 2020, https://sixcolors.com/post/2018/01/reading -disks-from-1988-in-2018/.

36. "AWS Snowmobile: Migrate or Transport Exabyte-Scale Data Sets Into and Out of AWS," Amazon Web Services," accessed July 6, 2020, https://aws.amazon.com/snowmobile/.

37. J. Greene and L. Stevens, "Amazon Uses Trucks to Drive Data Faster," *Wall Street Journal*, November 30, 2016, accessed May 6, 2017, https:// www.wsj.com/articles/amazon-extends-web-based -artificial-intelligence-1480529802.

38. A. Loten, "Businesses Tackle Internet Short-falls as Remote Work Grows More Remote," *Wall Street Journal*, July 2, 2020, accessed July 6, 2020, https://www.wsj.com/articles/businesses -tackle-internet-shortfalls-as-remote-work-grows -more-remote-11593717060.

39. S. Lubar, *Infoculture: The Smithsonian Book of Information Age Inventions* (Boston, MA: Houghton Mifflin, 1993).

40. Ibid.

41. P. Mozur and J. Osawa, "Can Alibab's Taxi App Be New Growth Driver," *Wall Street Journal*, March 17, 2014, B4.

42. Anonymous, "Home & Digital: #ASKWS-JD," *Wall Street Journal*, March 5, 2014, D3.

43. R. Trichur, "Global Finance: No Cards Nec-essary With New ATM Grid," *Wall Street Journal*, March 16, 2015, C3.

44. B. Worthen, "Bar Codes on Steroids," *CIO*, December 15, 2002, 53.

45. J. Bennett, "Johnson Controls Unravels Riddle of Missing Crates," *Wall Street Journal*, April 29, 2016, accessed May 12, 2016, http://www .wsj.com/articles/johnson-controls-unravels-riddle -of-missing-crates-1461943710.

46. M. Cherney, "There Are Park Benches. And Then There Are Smart Park Benches," *Wall Street Journal*, June 25, 2018, accessed July 7, 2020, https://www.wsj.com/articles/there-are-park -benches-and-then-there-are-smart-park-benches -1530064801?mod=djemCIO_h.

47. R. Almgren, "Using Wireless Sensors to Main-tain Social Distancing on the Factory Floor," *Smart Industry*, May 27, 2020, accessed July 7, 2020, https:// www.smartindustry.com/blog/smart-industry-connect /using-wireless-sensors-to-maintain-social-distancing -on-the-factory-floor/; I. Boudway, "How One Startup Is Trying to Help Car Dealers Weather Hailstorms," *Bloomberg*, November 12, 2019, accessed July 7, 2020, https://www.bloomberg.com/news/articles /2019-11-12/how-one-startup-is-trying-to-help-car -dealers-weather-hailstorms?sref=xXo7CWym; J . Weed, "Air Travelers Can't See All of It, but More Tech Is Moving Them Along," *New York Times*, February 25,2020, accessed July 7, 2020, https://www .nytimes.com/2020/02/25/business/artificial -intelligence-airports.html.

48. "Power Monitoring," Fluke, accessed July 7, 2020, https://www.fluke.com/en-us/products /condition-monitoring/power; "Thermocouple Thermometer | Contact Thermometers," Fluke, accessed July 7, 2020, https://www.fluke.com/en-us /products/temperature-measurement/contact -thermometers; "Vibration Monitoring," Fluke, accessed July 7, 2020, https://www.fluke.com/en -us/products/condition-monitoring/vibration.

49. S. Castellanos, "No Coffee Breaks Needed: Companies Add Software Robots to Workforce," *Wall Street Journal*, March 22, 2018, accessed July 5, 2020, https://blogs.wsj.com/cio/2018/03/22 /no-coffee-breaks-needed-companies-add-software -robots-to-workforce/?mod=djemCIO_h.

50. N. Rubenking, "Hidden Messages," *PC Magazine*, May 22, 2001, 86.

51. D. Hill, "The Secret of Airbnb's Pricing Algo-rithm, *IEEE Spectrum*, August 20, 2015, accessed

May 12, 2016, http://spectrum.ieee.org /computing/software/the-secret-of-airbnbs -pricing-algorithm.

52. R. Emma Silverman, "Bosses Tap Outside Firms to Predict Which Workers Might Get Sick," *Wall Street Journal*, February 17, 2016, accessed May 6, 2017, https://www.wsj.com/articles/bosses -harness-big-data-to-predict-which-workers-might -get-sick-1455664940.

53. Ibid.

54. Rubenking, "Hidden Messages."

55. Silverman, "Bosses Tap Outside Firms to Predict Which Workers Might Get Sick."

56. A. Rutkin, "Machine Predicts Heart Attacks 4 Hours Before Doctors," *NewScientist*, August 11, 2014, accessed May 12, 2016, http://www .newscientist.com/article/mg22329814.400 -machine-predicts-heart-attacks-4-hours-before -doctors.html#.VVKi5mBtEkE.

57. S. Yoon, "Lot of Contacts in Your Mobile Phone May Get You Loans," *BloombergBusiness Week*, November 15, 2015, accessed May 12, 2016, http://www.bloomberg.com/news/articles /2015-11-15/lot-of-contacts-in-your-mobile-phone -you-may-qualify-for-a-loan; S. Armour, "Lenders Use Social Media to Screen Borrowers," *Wall Street Journal*, January 8, 2014, accessed May 12, 2016, http://www.wsj.com/articles/SB10001424052702304 77310457926642351930050.

58. L. Scism, "Hartford Financial Takes on the Opioid Epidemic," *Wall Street Journal*, August 8, 2019, accessed July 7, 2020, https://www.wsj.com /articles/hartford-financial-takes-on-the-opioid -epidemic-11565269566?mod=hp_jr_pos1.

59. "X-Force Threat Intelligence Index 2020," IBM Security, accessed July 7, 2020, https://www .ibm.com/security/data-breach/threat-intelligence.

60. "Cost of a Data Breach Report 2019," IBM Security, accessed July 7, 2020, https://www.ibm .com/security/threat-management.

61. R. Hodge, "2019 Data Breach Hall of Shame: These Were the Biggest Data Breaches of the Year," *CNET*, December 27, 2019, accessed July 7, 2020, https://www.cnet.com/news/2019 -data-breach-hall-of-shame-these-were-the-biggest -data-breaches-of-the-year/.

62. S. Frenkel, "How Jeff Bezos' iPhone X Was Hacked," *New York Times*, January 22, 2020, accessed July 7, 2020, https://www.nytimes.com/2020/01/22 /technology/jeff-bezos-hack-iphone.html.

63. "Survival Time," Internet Storm Center, July 7, 2020, accessed July 7, 2020, https://isc.sans.edu /survivaltime.html.

64. D. Yadron, "Five Simple Steps to Protect Corporate Data," *Wall Street Journal*, April 19, 2015, accessed May 6, 2017, https://www.wsj.com /articles/five-simple-steps-to-protect-corporate -data-1429499477.

65. "Authentication," *PC Magazine*, accessed May 12, 2016, http://www.pcmag.com/encyclopedia /term/38192/authentication.

66. "Authorization," *PC Magazine*, accessed May 12, 2016, http://www.pcmag.com/encyclopedia /term/38202/authorization.

67. K. Olmstead and A. Smith, "Americans and Cybersecurity," *Pew Research Center*, January 26, 2017, accessed May 6, 2017, http://www.pewinternet .org/2017/01/26/americans-and-cybersecurity/.

68. "Two-Factor Authentication," *Information Security Glossary*, accessed May 12, 2016, http:// www.rsa.kz/node/glossary/default4b75 .html?id=1056.

69. "Google 2-Step Verification," Google, ac- cessed July 8, 2020, https://www.google.com

/landing/2step/ ; "Install Google Authenticator – iPhone & iPad – Google Account Help," Google, accessed July 8, 2020, https://support.google .com/accounts/answer/1066447?co=GENIE .Platform%3DiOS&hl=en.

70. D. Yadron, "Five Simple Steps to Protect Corporate Data."

71. D. Pierce, "Public Wi-Fi Is Safer Than Ever – But You Still Need to Be Careful," *Wall Street Journal*, August 4, 2019, accessed July 8, 2020, https://www.wsj .com/articles/public-wi-fi-is-safer-than-everbut-you-still -need-to-be-careful-11564923600?mod=djemwhatsnews.

72. J. Valentino-Devries, "Rarely Patched Soft- ware Bugs in Home Routers Cripple Security," *Wall Street Journal*, accessed May 12, 2016, http://www .wsj.com/articles/rarely-patched-software-bugs-in -home-routers-cripple-security-1453136285.

73. J. DeAvila, "Wi-Fi Users, Beware: Hot Spots Are Weak Spots," *Wall Street Journal*, January 16, 2008, D1; J. Vijayan, "Hotel Router Vulnerability a Reminder of Untrusted WiFi Risks," March 27, 2015, Information Week Dark Reading, accessed May 12, 2016, http://www.darkreading .com/perimeter/hotel-router-vulnerability-a -reminder-of-untrusted-wifi-risks/d/d-id/1319668.

74. G. A. Fowler, "You Won't Believe How Ador- able This Kitty Is! Click For More!" *Wall Street Journal*, March 26, 2013, accessed May 12, 2016, http://online.wsj.com/news/articles/SB100014241278 87324373204578373011392662962?mg =reno64-wsj.

75. R. Maniloff, "An 'Old-School Hacker' Fights Cybercrime," *Wall Street Journal*, August 16, 2019, accessed July 8, 2020, https://www.wsj.com /articles/an-old-school-hacker-fights-cybercrime -11565994214?mod=hp_opin_pos_2.

76. Ibid.

77. J. van den Hoven, "Executive Support Systems & Decision Making," *Journal of Systems Management* 47, no. 8 (March–April 1996): 48.

78. "Local Government: How Cities Score," *Economist*, March 23, 2016, accessed May 7, 2017, http://www.economist.com/news/special -report/21695194-better-use-data-could-make -cities-more-efficientand-more-democratic-how -cities-score.

79. C. Mims, "Yelp, Google Hold Pointers to Fix Governments," *Wall Street Journal*, May 9, 2016, accessed May 7, 2017, https://www.wsj.com /articles/yelp-google-hold-pointers-to-fix-governments -1462766463.

80. "Intranet," *PC Magazine*, accessed May 13, 2016, http://www.pcmag.com/encyclopedia /term/45310/intranet.

81. "Intranet Features & Functionality," Jive Software, accessed July 8, 2020, https://www .jivesoftware.com/product/.

82. "2016 Intranet Design Annual Winners," Nielsen Norman Group, January 9, 2016, accessed May 12, 2016, https://www.nngroup.com/news /item/2016-intranet-design-awards/; "DORMA Delivers Access To Innovation For 7000 Global Us- ers With a Unily intranet," Unily, accessed May 12, 2016, https://www.unily.com/insights/dorma-delivers -access-to-innovation-for-7000-global-users-with -unily; "Dorma-Supporting Employees with Access to Innovation," Unily, accessed May 12, 2016, https:// www.unily.com/media/23157/unily-dorma-case -study-2.pdf; M. Gibson, "dorma+kaba Pan-European Intranet Wins Nielsen Norman Best Intranet 2016," Unily, January 11, 2016, accessed May 12, 2016, https://www.unily.com/insights/dormakaba-wins -nielsen-norman-award-for-best-intranet-of-2016.

83. "Web Services," *PC Magazine*, accessed May 13, 2016, http://www.pcmag.com/encyclopedia /term/54345/web-services.

84. "Integration Services RouteOne," RouteO- ne, accessed May 7, 2017, https://www.routeone. com/dealers/integration-services; S. Overby, "This Could Be the Start of Something Small," *CIO*, February 15, 2003, 54.

85. "Extranet," *PC Magazine*, accessed May 13, 2016, http://www.pcmag.com/encyclopedia /term/42945/extranet.

86. "MyEmerson Personalized Digital Experi- ence," Emerson, accessed July 9, 2020, https://www .emerson.com/en-us/automation/digital.

87. "Travelers Embracing Efficiencies of Self- Service Bag Drop," *Airport Business*, April 14, 2016, accessed May 12, 2016, http://www .airport-business.com/2016/04/travellers -embracing-efficiencies-self-service-bag-drop/.

88. J. Nicas and T. Shukla, "The Next Frontier in Airline Baggage: Digital Bag Tags," *Wall Street Journal*, July 1, 2015, accessed May 12, 2016, http:// www.wsj.com/articles/bag-tags-1435340070.

89. S. Hamm, D. Welch, W. Zellner, F. Keenan, and F. Engardio, "Down But Hardly Out: Downturn Be Damned, Companies Are Still Anxious to Expand Online," *BusinessWeek*, March 26, 2001, 126.

90. K. C. Laudon and J. P. Laudon, *Management Information Systems: Organization and Technology* (Upper Saddle River, NJ: Prentice Hall, 1996).

91. R. Hernandez, "American Express Autho- rizer's Assistant," *Business Rules Journal*, August 2001, accessed May 13, 2016, http://bizrules.info /page/art_amexaa.htm.

92. "AI Definition from PC Magazine Encyclo- pedia," *PC Magazine*, accessed May 7, 2017, http:// www.pcmag.com/encyclopedia/term/37613/ai.

93. S. Lohr, "IBM Gives Watson a New Challenge: Your Tax Return," *New York Times*, February 1, 2017, accessed May 7, 2017, https://www.nytimes .com/2017/02/01/technology/ibm-watson-tax-return.html.

94. J. Vincent, "H&R Block Will Use IBM'S Watson to Help Quiz Clients About Their Taxes," *The Verge*, February 1, 2017, accessed May 7, 2017, https://www.theverge.com/2017/2/1/14475054 /ibm-watson-hr-block-tax-preparation.

95. A. Moscaritolo, "H&R Block Enlists IBM Watson to Find Tax Deductions," *PC magazine*, February 7, 2017, accessed May 7, 2017, http:// www.pcmag.com/news/351508/h-r-block-enlists -ibm-watson-to-find-tax-deductions.

18

1. C. Page, "The Aircraft Turnaround: What Goes on Between Flights," *The Points Guy*, August 18, 2019, accessed July 14, 2020, https://thepointsguy .com/guide/the-aircraft-turnaround-what-goes -on-between-flights/; B. Smithson, "How a Major Airline Prepares an Airbus A350 for Its Next Long- Haul Flight," *The Points Guy*, August 21, 2019, accessed July 14, 2020, https://thepointsguy.com /news/how-a-major-airline-prepares-an-airbus-a350 -for-its-next-long-haul-flight/.

2. S. McCartney, "The FAA Is Finding New Tricks to Cut Delays," *Wall Street Journal*, February 20, 2019, accessed July 15, 2020, https://www .wsj.com/articles/the-faa-is-finding-new-tricks-to -cut-delays-11550671200?mod=hp_lead_pos8.

3. S. McCartney, "How Heathrow Airport Cut Down on Flight Delays," *Wall Street Journal*, September 16, 2015, accessed May 5, 2016, http://www.wsj.com/articles/how-heathrow-airport -cut-down-on-flight-delays-1442423115.

4. L. Stevens, "For UPS, E-Commerce Brings Big Business and Big Problems," *Wall Street Jour- nal*, September 11, 2014, accessed May 11, 2015,

http://www.wsj.com/articles/for-ups-e-commerce -brings-big-business-and-big-problems-1410489642.

5. T. Black, "UPS Sees Payoff From $20 Billion Tech Bet Scorned by Wall Street," *Bloomberg*, April 23, 2019, accessed July 15, 2020, https://www .bloomberg.com/news/articles/2019-04-23/ups-sees -payoff-from-20-billion-tech-bet-scorned-by-wall -street?sref=xXo7CWym.

6. A. Pressman, "UPS's $20 Billion Bet on E-Commerce and Its Delivery Strategy Are Paying Off," *Fortune*, December 20, 2019, accessed July 15, 2020, https://fortune.com/longform/ups -ecommerce-strategy-drones-paying-off/.

7. "Employment Cost Index – March 2020," Bureau of Labor Statistics, April 30, 2020, accessed July 15, 2020, http://www.bls.gov/news.release/eci .nr0.htm; "Productivity and Costs: First Quarter 2020, Revised," Bureau of Labor Statistics, June 4, 2020, accessed July 15, 2020, http://www.bls.gov /news.release/prod2.nr0.htm.

8. "Historical Income Tables – Families: Table F-23 – Families by Total Money Income, Race, and Hispanic Origin of Householder: 1967 to 2018," US Census Bureau, Current Population Survey, Annual Social and Economic Supplements, accessed July 15, 2020, https://www2.census.gov /programs-surveys/cps/tables/time-series/historical -income-families/f23.xls.

9. Ibid.

10. "Labor Productivity and Costs: Productivity Change in the Nonfarm Business Sector, 1947–2019," Bureau of Labor Statistics, March 5, 2020, accessed July 15, 2020, https://www.bls.gov /lpc/prodybar.htm.

11. "Labor Force Statistics from the Current Population Survey, 2007 to 2019, Household Data Historical, A-1. Employment Status of the Civilian Noninstitutional Population 16 Years and Over, 1985 to Date," Bureau of Labor Statistics, July 2, 2020, accessed July 15, 2020, https://www.bls.gov /web/empsit/cpseea01.htm.

12. "Charitable Giving Statistics," *National Philanthropic Trust*, accessed July 15, 2020, http://www .nptrust.org/philanthropic-resources/charitable -giving-statistics/; C. Lourosa-Ricardo, "How America Gives to Charity," Wall Street Journal, December 14, 2014, http://www.wsj.com/articles /how-america-gives-to-charity-1418619046, accessed May 11, 2015.

13. "GDP per capita (current US$) – United States," World Bank, accessed July 15, 2020, https:// data.worldbank.org/indicator/NY.GDP.PCAP .CD?locations=US.

14. "Philanthropy in the American Economy," *Council of Economic Advisers*, February 19, 2002, accessed April 13, 2009, http://clinton4.nara.gov /media/pdf/philanthropy.pdf.

15. "GDP per capita (current US$) – United States," World Bank.

16. E. Mazareanu, "US Airline Labor Costs Per Available Seat Mile in Domestic Operations in Q3 2017 and Q3 2018, Ranked by Selected Airlines," *Statista*, April 24, 2019, accessed July 15, 2020, https://www-statista-com.ezproxy.butler. edu/statistics/796399/us-airlines-by-domestic-labor-costs/.

17. "Multifactor Productivity: Frequently Asked Questions," Bureau of Labor Statistics, accessed May 5, 2016, http://www.bls.gov/mfp /mprfaq.htm#1.

18. C. Jandreau, "Jobs That No Longer Exist," Ranker, accessed May 8, 2017, http://www.ranker. com/list/jobs-that-no-longer-exist/coy-jandreau.

19. News Release, "Average Hours Per Day Spent in Selected Activities by Sex and Day, American Time Use Survey" Bureau of Labor Statistics, June 25, 2020, accessed July 16, 2020, https://www.bls.gov/charts/american -time-use/activity-by-sex.htm#; G. Reynolds, "What Housework Has to Do With Waistlines," *New York Times*, February 27, 2013, accessed May 8, 2017, https://well.blogs.nytimes .com/2013/02/27/what-housework-has-to-do -with-waistlines/.

20. J. Manyika, M. Chui, M. Miremadi, J. Bughin, K. George, P. Willmott, and M. Dewhurst, "Harnessing Automation for a Future That Works," McKinsey Global Institute, January 2017, accessed May 8, 2017, http://www.mckinsey.com/global -themes/digital-disruption/harnessing-automation -for-a-future-that-works.

21. G. Zarkadakis, R. Jesuthasan, and T. Malcolm, "The 3 Ways Work Can Be Automated," *Harvard Business Review*, October 13, 2016, accessed May 8, 2017, https://hbr.org/2016/10/the-3-ways -work-can-be-automated.

22. "Harnessing Automation for a Future That Works," McKinsey Global Institute.

23. P. McGee, "Five Robots That Hope to Save the US Food Supply Chain," *Financial Times*, May 18, 2020, accessed July 16, 2020, https:// www.ft.com/content/5dced1f4-2c25-4af6-91e5 -f0ac773ef3c1.

24. Ibid.

25. "Say Hello to Tally," Simbe, accessed July 16, 2020, https://www.simberobotics.com/platform /tally/.

26. K. Shaw, "Simbe Robotics Adds RFID Scanning to Mobile Inventory Robots," *Robotics Business Review*, July 18, 2018, accessed July 16, 2020, https://www.roboticsbusinessreview.com /retail-hospitality/simbe-robotics-adds-rfid-scanning -to-mobile-inventory-robots/.

27. B. Brown, "The Robots Are Coming to Help, May Take Jobs," *Digital Trends*, June 11, 2016, accessed May 8, 2017, https://www.digitaltrends .com/cool-tech/mit-robots-stores-hotels-parking -lots/.

28. P. Clark and K. Bhasin, "Amazon's Robot War Is Spreading," *Bloomberg*, April 5, 2017, accessed May 8, 2017, https://www.bloomberg.com /news/articles/2017-04-05/robots-enlist-humans-to -win-the-warehouse-war-amazon-started.

29. "Harnessing Automation for a Future That Works," McKinsey Global Institute.

30. Press Release, "Average New-Vehicle Prices Up 4% Year-Over-Year in May 2020, According to Kelley Blue Book," *Cision PR Newswire*, June 2, 2020, accessed July 16, 2020, https://www.prnewswire .com/news-releases/average-new-vehicle-prices-up -4-year-over-year-in-may-2020-according-to-kelley -blue-book-301069167.html.

31. Press Release, "New-Vehicle Quality Mainly Dependent on Trouble-Free Technology, J.D. Power Finds," J.D. Power, June 24, 2020, accessed July 16, 2020, https://www.jdpower.com/business /press-releases/2020-initial-quality-study-iqs.

32. "Basic Quality Concepts," *American Society for Quality*, accessed May 8, 2017, http://www.asq .org/learn-about-quality/basic-concepts.html.

33. R. E. Markland, S. K. Vickery, and R. A. Davis, "Managing Quality" (Chapter 7), in *Operations Management: Concepts in Manufacturing and Services* (Cincinnati, OH: South-Western College Publishing, 1998).

34. "GE Refresh 100-Watt EQ A21 Daylight Dimmable LED Light Bulb (2-Pack)," Lowes, accessed July 16, 2020, https://www.lowes.com/pd /GE-Refresh-100-Watt-EQ-A21-Daylight-Dimmable -LED-Light-Bulb-2-Pack/1000444939.

35. L. L. Berry and A. Parasuraman, *Marketing Services* (New York: Free Press, 1991).

36. MacRumors Staff, "Apple Stores: Everything We Know," *MacRumors*, May 12, 2020, accessed July 17, 2020, https://www.macrumors.com/roundup /apple-retail-stores/; S. Kapner, "Apple Gets Sweet Deals From Mall Operators," *Wall Street Journal*, March 10, 2015, accessed May 5, 2016, http://www .wsj.com/articles/apple-gets-sweet-deals-from-mall -operators-1426007804; S. Kovach, "10 Mind-Blowing Facts about the Apple Store," *Business Insider*, March 13, 2015, accessed May 5, 2016, http://www .businessinsider.com/apple-store-facts-2015-3?op=1.

37. L. Eadicicco, "Apple Stores Make Over $5,000 Per Square Foot in Sales," *Time*, accessed May 8, 2017, http://time.com/4339170/apple-store -sales-comparison/.

38. "ISO – About Us," *International Organization for Standardization*, accessed July 17, 2020, https://www.iso.org/about-us.html.

39. "ISO 9000 Family – Quality Management," *International Organization for Standardization*, accessed July 17, 2020, https://www.iso.org/iso -9001-quality-management.html.

40. "ISO 14000 Family – Environmental Management," *International Organization for Standardization*, accessed July 17, 2020, https://www.iso.org /iso-14001-environmental-management.html.

41. "ISO/IEC 27001 – Information Security Management," *International Organization for Standardization*, accessed July 17, 2020, https://www .iso.org/isoiec-27001-information-security.html.

42. J. Briscoe, S. Fawcett, and R. Todd, "The Implementation and Impact of ISO 9000 Among Small Manufacturing Enterprises," *Journal of Small Business Management* 43 (July 1, 2005): 309.

43. R. Henkoff, "The Hot New Seal of Quality (ISO 9000 Standard of Quality Management)," *Fortune*, June 28, 1993, 116.

44. "Baldrige FAQs: Baldrige Performance Excellence Program," *National Institute of Standards and Technology*, accessed July 17, 2020, https:// www.nist.gov/baldrige/how-baldrige-works/about -baldrige/baldrige-faqs.

45. "Baldrige Award Process Fees," *National Institute of Standards and Technology*, November 15, 2019, accessed July 17, 2020, https://www.nist .gov/baldrige/baldrige-award/award-process-fees.

46. "Frequently Asked Questions About the Malcolm Baldrige National Quality Award."

47. Ibid.

48. "Baldrige Criteria Commentary: Baldrige Criteria for Performance Excellence Categories and Items," Baldrige Performance Excellence Program, November 15, 2019, accessed July 17, 2020, https:// www.nist.gov/baldrige/baldrige-criteria -commentary.

49. Ibid.

50. D. C. Moody, "Beam Integral Part of Prestigious Baldrige Program," *theeasleyprogress.com*, June 4, 2014.

51. J. W. Dean, Jr., and J. Evans, *Total Quality: Management, Organization, and Strategy* (St. Paul, MN: West, 1994).

52. J. W. Dean, Jr., and D. E. Bowen, "Management Theory and Total Quality: Improving Research and Practice Through Theory Development," *Academy of Management Review* 19 (1994): 392–418.

53. "Proud of Performance: Our 23,000 Employees Earn Nearly a Month's Extra Pay," *Alaska Airlines Blog*, January 29, 2020, accessed July 17, 2020, https://blog.alaskaair.com/alaska-airlines /company-news/130-million-profit-sharing-payout -alaska-airlines-horizon-air-employees-will-be-paid/.

54. "2020 North America Airline Satisfaction Study," J.D. Power, May 27, 2020, accessed July 17, 2020, https://www.jdpower.com/business /press-releases/2020-north-america-airline-satis-faction-study; D. Reed, "U.S. Airlines' On-Time Arrival Rates Improved Last Year, But The Hidden Reality Is That 30% or More of US Flights Are Still Late," *Forbes*, January 7, 2020, accessed July 17, 2020, https://www.forbes.com/sites/daniel-reed/2020/01/07/us-airlines-on-time-arrival-rates -improved-some-last-year-but-the-hidden -reality-is-that-30-or-more-of-us-flights-are-still -late/#2e10cf5c1517.

55. "2019 KAYAK Travel Awards – Best Airlines in US & Canada," Kayak, accessed July 17, 2020, https://www.kayak.com/travelawards/2019/best -airlines/us-canada/best-airline.

56. M. Esterl, "How Dr Pepper Cuts Costs. And Keeps Cutting," *Wall Street Journal*, February 21, 2016, accessed May 6, 2016, http://www.wsj .com/articles/how-dr-pepper-cuts-costs-and-keeps -cutting-1456110339.

57. M. Ellen, "Dr Pepper: Continuous Improvement – TMAC Success Story," *Texas Lean Six Sigma*, 2017, accessed July 17, 2020, https:// texasleansixsigma.com/dr-pepper/.

58. R. Abrams, "A French Fry Gets Soggy in 5 Minutes. This Company Wants to Keep It Crispy for 60," *New York Times*, June 29, 2018, accessed July 17, 2020, https://www.nytimes.com/2018/06/29 /business/french-fries-delivery.html?emc=edit_th_1 80630&nl=todaysheadlines&nlid=729027500630.

59. Ibid.

60. Ibid.

61. "Lamb Weston® | Crispy on Delivery®," Lamb Weston, accessed July 17, 2020, http:// go.lambweston.com/delivery; "Lamb Weston intro-duces 'Crispy on Delivery': Say Goodbye to Soggy Fries!" *PotatoPro*, February 20, 2018, accessed July 17, 2020, https://www.potatopro.com/news/2018 /lamb-weston-introduces-crispy-delivery-say -goodbye-soggy-fries.

62. J. Miller, "Remade in the USA: Indiana Steel Mill Revived with Lessons from Abroad," *Wall Street Journal*, May 21, 2012, A1.

63. R. Hallowell, L. A. Schlesinger, and J. Zor-nitsky, "Internal Service Quality, Customer and Job Satisfaction: Linkages and Implications for Man-agement," *Human Resource Planning* 19 (1996): 20–31; J. L. Heskett, T. O. Jones, G. W. Loveman, W. E. Sasser, Jr., and L. A. Schlesinger, "Putting the Service-Profit Chain to Work," *Harvard Business Review* (March–April 1994): 164–174.

64. "The American Customer Satisfaction Index Key Findings," *American Customer Satisfaction Index*, accessed July 18, 2020, https://www.theacsi .org/about-acsi/key-acsi-findings.

65. A. Chamberlain and D. Zhao, "The Key to Happy Customers? Happy Employees," *Harvard Business Review*, August 19, 2019, accessed July 18, 2020, https://hbr.org/2019/08/the-key-to-happy -customers-happy-employees.

66. Ibid.

67. J. Paravantis, N. Bouranta, and L. Chitiris, "The Relationship Between Internal and External Service Quality," *International Journal of Contem-porary Hospital Management* 21 (2009): 275–293.

68. "The Key to Happy Customers? Happy Employees," *Harvard Business Review*.

69. J. Hogreve, A. Iseke, K. Derfuss & T. Eller, "The Service–Profit Chain: A Meta-Analytic Test of a Comprehensive Theoretical Framework," *Journal of Marketing* 81 (May 2017): 41–61.

70. G. Brewer, "The Ultimate Guide to Winning Customers: The Customer Stops Here," *Sales &*

Marketing Management 150 (March 1998): 30; F. F. Reichheld, *The Loyalty Effect: The Hidden Force Behind Growth, Profits, and Lasting Value* (Cambridge, MA: Harvard Business School Press, 2001).

71. T. Curtis, R. Abratt, D. Rhoades & P. Dion, "Customer Loyalty, Repurchase and Satisfaction: A Meta-Analytical Review," *Journal of Consumer Sat-isfaction, Dissatisfaction and Complaining Behavior* 24 (2011): 1-26.

72. J. Heskett, T. Jones, G. Loveman, E. Sasser, and L. Schlesinger, "Putting the Service-Profit Chain to Work," *Harvard Business Review* 86 (July–August 2008): 118–129; The lifetime values of a pizza customer, $8,000, and luxury car customer, $330,000, published in 2008 were adjusted for infla-tion using www.usinflationcalculator.com.

73. L. L. Berry and A. Parasuraman, "Listening to the Customer – The Concept of a Service-Quality Information System," *Sloan Management Review* 38, no. 3 (Spring 1997): 65; C. W. L. Hart, J. L. Heskett, and W. E. Sasser, Jr., "The Profitable Art of Service Recovery," *Harvard Business Review* (July–August 1990): 148–156.

74. A. L. Rodgers, "A 5-Point Plan for Making the Most of Customer Complaints," *Inc.*, January 14, 2014, accessed June 25, 2014, http://www.inc.com /the-build-network/a-5-point-plan-for-making -the-most-of-customer-complaints.html.

75. "Great Customer Service from the Mission Bicycle Company," *37signals.com*, August 16, 2011, accessed April 9, 2012, http://37signals.com /svn/posts/2989-great-customer-service-from-the -mission-bicycle-company.

76. D. E. Bowen and E. E. Lawler III, "The Em-powerment of Service Workers: What, Why, How, and When," *Sloan Management Review* 33 (Spring 1992): 31–39; D. E. Bowen and E. E. Lawler III, "Empowering Service Employees," *Sloan Man-agement Review* 36 (Summer 1995): 73–84.

77. Bowen and Lawler, "The Empowerment of Service Workers: What, Why, How, and When."

78. J. Shelly, "Empowering Employees," *Human Resource Executive*, October 2, 2011, accessed April 9, 2012, http://www.hreonline.com/HRE/view /story.jhtml?id=533341639.

79. "Customer Service and Business Results: A Sur-vey of Customer Service From Mid-Size Companies," *ZenDesk*, April 2013, accessed July 28, 2014, http:// cdn.zendesk.com/resources/whitepapers/Zendesk _WP_Customer_Service_and_Business_Results.pdf.

80. "Company Profile for Midwest Precision Inc.," Midwest Precision, accessed July 18, 2020, http://www.mpitulsa.com/company-profile.html; "Fabrication of Architectural Steel Structures for AHHA Project," Midwest Precision, accessed July 18, 2020, http://www.mpitulsa.com/fabrication-of -architectural-steel-structures-for-AHHA-project. html; "Waterjet Cutting & Material Management for Caterpillar Project," Midwest Precision, ac-cessed July 18, 2020, http://www.mpitulsa.com /waterjet-cutting-material-management-for -caterpillar-project.html.

81. J. Rockoff, "Drug Making Breaks Away from Its Old Ways," *Wall Street Journal*, February 8, 2015, ac-cessed May 11, 2015, http://www.wsj.com/articles/drug -making-breaks-away-from-its-old-ways-1423444049.

82. Ibid.

83. S. Terlep, "P&G Toilet Paper Factory Keeps Delivering as Coronavirus Strikes Its Town," *Wall Street Journal*, April 12, 2020, accessed July 19, 2020, https://www.wsj.com/articles/p-g-toilet -paper-factory-keeps-delivering-as-coronavirus -strikes-its-town-11586707201.

84. B. Schrotenboer, "Coronavirus: Why the Toi-let Paper Shortage Is About More Than Hoarding,"

USA Today, April 8, 2020, accessed July 19, 2020, https://www.usatoday.com/story/money/2020/04/08 /coronavirus-shortage-where-has -all-the-toilet-paper-gone/2964143001/.

85. S. Terlep, "Toilet Paper Giant Pivots From Scratchy Office Rolls to Battle Home Shortages," *Wall Street Journal*, April 23, 2020, accessed July 19, 2020, https://www.wsj.com/articles/kimberly -clark-to-reassign-makers-of-office-toilet-paper-to -meet-demand-for-softer-stuff-11587577564.

86. P. Zelinski, "Desktop 3D Printer as Job Shop Resource," *Modern Machine Shop*, March 26, 2015, accessed May 9, 2017, http://www.mmonline .com/articles/desktop-3d-printer-as-job-shop -resource.

87. "About Us: Kenworthy Machine LLC – CNC Production Services," Kenworthy Machine LLC, accessed May 9, 2017, http://www .kenworthymachine.com/.

88. "Chicken Chaos as KFC Closes Outlets," *BBC News*, February 19, 2018, accessed July 19, 2020, https://www.bbc.com/news/business -43110910.

89. "KFC Faces Gravy Shortage as Distribution Problems Continue," *BBC News*, February 28, 2018, accessed July 19, 2020, https://www.bbc.com /news/business-43226105?mod=djemlogistics.

90. A. Smith, "Police Tell People to Stop Calling Them to Report the KFC Crisis," *Metro News*, February 20, 2018, accessed July 19, 2020, https:// metro.co.uk/2018/02/20/police-tell-chicken -lovers-to-stop-calling-them-to-report-the-kfc -crisis-7328291/.

91. "Group 1 Automotive Inc (GPI) Inventory Turn-over Ratio, From First Quarter 2020 to First Quarter 2019, Current and Historic Results, Rankings and More, Quarterly Fundamentals," *CSIMarket*, accessed July 19, 2020, https://csimarket.com/ stocks/singleEfficiencyit.php?code=GPI.

92. R. Wall and D. Cameron, "Where Are the Toilets? Order Glut Stretches Giant Jet Makers to Limit," *Wall Street Journal*, February 23, 2017, accessed May 9, 2017, https://www.wsj.com/articles /where-are-the-toilets-order-glut-stretches-giant -jet-makers-to-limit-1487885428.

93. "Warehouse & Wholesale Inventory Turnover Data," *Strategos*, May 2017, accessed May 9, 2017, http://www.strategosinc.com/articles/inventory /warehouse_inventory_turns.htm.

94. "Paccar Inc's Competition Management Effectiveness Comparisons by Company, ROA, ROI, ROE – CSIMarket," CSIMarket, accessed July 19, 2020, https://csimarket.com/stocks /competitionNO6.php?code=PCAR; "Auto & Truck Manufacturers Industry Efficiency, Revenue per Employee, Inventory and Receivable Turnover Ratios Q1 2020," CSIMarket, accessed July 19, 2020, https://csimarket.com/Industry/industry _Efficiency.php?ind=404.

95. Restaurant Business Staff, "Industry Is Forced to Adopt EFR Standards," *Restaurant Business*, October 30, 2003, accessed July 19, 2020, https://www.restaurantbusinessonline.com/industry -forced-adopt-efr-standards.

96. "Ordering – FoodBAM – Restaurant Inven-tory Management and Ordering," FoodBAM, accessed July 19, 2020, https://foodbam.com /ordering/.

97. Ibid.

98. J. R. Henry, "Minimized Setup Will Make Your Packaging Line S.M.I.L.E.," *Packaging Tech-nology & Engineering*, February 1, 1998, 24.

99. C. Paris, "Oil Traders Are Scrambling to Book Tankers for Storage," *Wall Street Journal*, April 21, 2020, accessed July 19, 2020, https://www.wsj.com

/articles/oil-traders-are-scrambling-to-book
-tankers-for-storage-11587502041.

100. Ibid.

101. IHL Group, "How to Lose Your Customer's
in 1 Easy Step: Retail's $634 Billion Out-of-Stock
Problem," Dynamic Action, accessed May 9, 2017,
http://engage.dynamicaction.com/WS-2015-08-
IHL-Haunting-of-Out-of-Stocks-AR_LP.html.

102. G. Buzek, "Disrupted Retail: How the
Pandemic Exposed Retail's Hidden Inventory Dis-
tortion," IHL Group, July 16, 2020, accessed
July 20, 2020, https://www.ihlservices.com/news
/analyst-corner/2020/07/replay-disrupted-retail
-how-covid-19-exposed-inventory-distortion/.

103. "The Way I Work: Marc Lore of Diapers.
com," *Inc.*, September 1, 2009, accessed March 15,
2010, http://www.inc.com/magazine/20090901/the
-way-i-work-marc-lore-of-diaperscom.html.

104. E. Powell, Jr., and F. Sahin, "Economic
Production Lot Sizing with Periodic Costs and
Overtime," *Decision Sciences* 32 (2001): 423–452.

105. "Apple Inc's Competition Management
Effectiveness Comparisons by Company, ROA,
ROI, ROE," *CSIMarket*, accessed July 20, 2020,
https://csimarket.com/stocks/competitionNO6
.php?code=AAPL; "Apple Inc. (AAPL) Inventory
Turnover Ratio, from Second Quarter 2020 to
Second Quarter 2019, Current and Historic Results,

Rankings and More, Quarterly Fundamentals,"
CSIMarket, accessed July 20, 2020, https://csimarket
.com/stocks/singleEfficiencyit.php?code=AAPL.

106. N. Shirouzu, "Why Toyota Wins Such High
Marks on Quality Surveys," *Wall Street Journal*,
March 15, 2001, A1.

107. Ibid.

108. G. Gruman, "Supply on Demand; Manufacturers Need to Know What's Selling Before
They Can Produce and Deliver Their Wares
in the Right Quantities," *InfoWorld*, April 18,
2005, accessed April 15, 2009, http://www
.infoworld.com/article/2669692/database/supply
-on-demand.html.

Index

Hussain, Insya, 356
Hyatt, 129

I

IBM, 14, 41, 111, 150–151
    Watson AI system, 403
IBM Credit, 202–203
Idealized influence, 334–335
Identify behaviors, 306
Idiosyncratic rater effect, 253–254
IKEA, 53, 57
Immediacy behaviors, 350–351
Immediate feedback, 352–353
Immelt, Jeffrey, 6
Imperfectly imitable resources,
    116–117
Implicit Association Test (IAT),
    285–286, 287
Impossible Burger, 48
Impossible Foods, 91, 219
Impoverished leadership, 318
Inaction stage of decline, 151
In-basket exercises, 247
Income statements, 372
InContext, 204
Increasing outcomes, 297
Incredible Burger, 91
Incremental change, 145
    managing innovation during,
    149–151
*In Defense of Troublemakers: The
Power of Dissent in Life and
Business* (Nemeth), 109–110
Independent demand systems, 426
Index cards, 40
India, foreign owned online stores and,
    177–178
InDinero, 317
Individualism, 180–181
Individualism-collectivism, 227
Individualists, 227
Individualized consideration, 335
Individual rights, principle of, 79
Indulgence, cultural dimension of, 180,
    181
Industrial Revolution, 25
Industry-level strategies, 129–133
    adaptive strategies, 132–133
    five industry forces, 129–131
    positioning strategies, 131–132
Industry regulations, 57
Inequality, perceived, 296–298
Informal communication channels,
    345–346
Informal meetings, 357
Information, 383. *See also* Managing
    information
        accurate, 385–386
        acquisition costs, 387

    capturing, 389–391
    communication costs, 389
    complete, 386
    external access and sharing,
        400–402
    internal access and sharing,
        399–400
    processing, 391–393
    processing costs, 387
    protecting, 393–398
    relevant, 386–387
    retrieval costs, 388–389
    sharing knowledge and expertise,
        402–403
    storage costs, 387–388
    timely, 387
Informational roles, 11–13
Information management, 39–40
Information technology (IT),
    384, 400
Infosys, 356
Initial assembly, 421
Initiating structure, 317
Initiation of effort, 289
Innovation, 138–151
    innovation streams, 141–145
    managing, 145–151
    technology cycles, 140–141
Innovation streams, 141–145
Inputs, 295
InsightSquared, 362
Inspirational motivation, 335
Inspire Brands, 126
Instagram, 372
Institute for Patient-and-Family-
    Centered Care, 345
Instrumentality, 300
Integrated model for motivation,
    310
Integrative conflict resolution, 35
Integrity, 316
Intel Corporation, 140–141, 145, 255,
    381
Intellectual stimulation, 335
Intelligence and management, 15–16
Intelligent recognition, 408–409
Intentional discrimination, 235–236
Interactive Excellence
    (Schlossberg), 143
InterContinental Hotel Group (IHG),
    129
Intermittent reinforcement
    schedules, 305, 306
Internal attribution, 340
Internal environment, 61
Internal motivation, 200
Internal recruiting, 239–241
Internals, 327
Internal service quality, 415–416
International assignment, preparing
    for, 182–185

    language and cross-cultural
        training, 182–184
    spouse, family, and dual-career
        issues, 184–185
International Automotive
    Components Group, 50
International Shipcare, 50
International Telecommunication
    Union (ITU), 143, 144
Internet, 40
Interorganizational processes, 206–209
    modular organizations, 206–207
    virtual organizations, 207–209
Interpersonal communication
    process, 341–342
Interpersonal roles, 10–11
Interpersonal skills, 229
Interpretation, 338
Interval reinforcement
    schedules, 305
Intervening in behaviors, 306
Interviews, 243, 248–249
Intranets, 399
Intraorganizational processes, 202–206
    empowerment, 205–206
    reengineering, 202–205
Intrinsic rewards, 293
Intuit, 362
Intuitive Research and Technology
    Corp., 82
Inventory, 39, 420–426
    costs of maintaining, 423–424
    managing, 424–426
    measuring, 422–423
    types of, 421–422
Inventory records, 426
Inventory turnover, 423
Involuntary separation, 257
Ip, Greg, 95
IPads, 114–115, 116, 385
IPhones, 114, 116, 160, 381
"Iron cage" of Weber, 30, 31
Irving, Paul, 263
Ishbia, Mat, 298, 348
ISO 9000, 411–412
ISO 14000, 411–412
ISO 27000, 411–412
Iteration, 148
Izhikevich, Eugene, 408

J

Jack, Brian, 344
Jackson, Lisa, 377
Jargon, 343–344
J.D. Power Initial Quality
    Survey, 409
Jefferson, Thomas, 39
Jelinek, Craig, 93
Job analysis, 238

Verizon, 191, 192, 262
Vertical loading, 202
Virgin America, 206
Virtual organization agreement, 209
Virtual organizations, 207–209
Virtual private networks (VPNs), 398
Virtual teams, 214, 218–219
Virtual training, 250, 252
Virus, 396
Visible artifacts, 66
Vision, 100, 155
Visionary leadership, 331–335
    charismatic leadership, 331–334
    transformational leadership,
    334–335
Vision-impaired persons, 277, 278
Vista Equity Partners, 277
Vistage Small Business CEO Survey,
    51
Vlastelica, John, 67
Voice mail, 355
Voice messaging, 355
Volkswagen (VW), 55, 70, 87, 198
VoloMetrix, Inc., 263
Voluntary export restraints, 163
Voluntary separation, 257
Voser, Peter, 196
Vroom-Yetton-Jago model, 329. *See
    also* Normative decision theory

W

Waffle House restaurants, 13
Wahlqvist, Joakim, 363
Wakefield, Mark, 52
Walgreens Boots Alliance, 372
Wall Street Journal (WSJ), 245
    assumptions, planning and, 95
    business confidence index of, 51
    managers and, 11
Walmart, 5, 89, 170, 247, 303
    information and, 386
    management structure of, 10
    strategic alternatives of, 122
Walsh, Marty, 399
Walt Disney Company, 132
Warby Parker, 205
Warner, Pat, 13

Warner Media, LLC, 118
Waste disposal, 379
Waste Management, 294
Waste prevention and reduction, 376
Waste treatment, 379
Watch industry, 94–95
Water sensors, 364–365
Watjen, Tom, 11
Watson AI system, 403
Wavestorm, 131
Weber, Max, 30–32, 331, 366
Web services, 400–401
Weifield Group Electrical
    Contracting, 290
Weimerskirch, Arnold, 413
Welch, Jack, 6, 346
Welch's, 372
Wells Fargo, 66
Wendy's, 134–135
West, Mike, 64
Western Electric Company, 35–36
Whirlpool, 241
Whistle-blowing, 84
White-hat hackers, 398
Whitney, Eli, 39
Whole Foods, 196, 198
Wholly owned affiliates, 174
Wi-Fi networks, 398
Wilke, Jeff, 56
Willingness to pay, 91
Wilson, Thomas, 345
Wilson trucking, 48
Wine, Scott, 50
Winkler, Howard, 81
Wiseman, Liz, 333
Wiseman Group, 333
Wolf, William, 240
Wolfensohn, James, 357
Women at Fortune 500 and 1000 Com-
    panies, 273
Wong, Christina, 233
Woodland, Joe, 41
Wool industry of Australia, 58–59
Woolley, Anita, 220–221
Woolley, Kaitlin, 293
Worker readiness, 323
Workforce quality, 176–177
Work group encouragement, 147

Work-in-progress inventories, 421
Workplace deviance, 68–72
Workplace diversity. *See* Diversity
Work sample tests, 247
Work teams, 210, 213. *See also* Teams
    characteristics of, 220–225
World Bank, 357–358
World Management
    Survey (WMS), 21
World Trade Organization (WTO),
    163–165
World Vision, 72
Wozniak, Steve, 151
Wrangler, 177
Wright, Christopher, 181
Written communication, 349–350
Wrongful discharge, 261
Wrongful termination lawsuits, 53
Wyatt Company, 346

X

XEL Communications, 225
Xerox, 276
XPrize, 145

Y

Yammer, 355–356, 358
Yarbrough, Brian, 196
Yondr pouches, 362
Your Gal Friday, 219

Z

Zanini, Michele, 30, 366–367
Zappos, 67, 213
Zara, 157
Zeitz, Jochen, 313–314
Zero-based budgeting, 372
Zilinskas, Matt, 131
Zillow, 237
Zone of indifference, 38
Zoom virtual meetings, 217
Zuckerberg, Mark, 133, 270
Zynga, 260

A GUIDE FOR NEW MANAGERS: SIX STEPS TO BECOME A SUCCESSFUL MANAGER

—ED MUZIO

If you've recently been hired as a manager, you know the dirty secret: Management positions come with surprisingly little guidance. Whether you were promoted internally or brought in from outside, you were probably expected to hit the ground running, toward only the vaguest of goals.

Many of the problems new managers experience stem from that secret. They are faced with an ill-defined job and equally intense pressure from above and below. In addition, as the pivot points in the information revolution, they are barraged with queries about the work of their groups.

It's easy to see why capable, well-meaning managers resort to micromanagement, detachment, grandstanding, or sheer blockheadedness in an effort to find some sort of stability for themselves and their employees.

How can you avoid these pitfalls? The following six steps will help you define your purpose as manager:

1. DEFINE YOUR OWN JOB CLEARLY

If you're a new manager, this is your first and most important step. You need a memorable, meaningful definition, something that you can figuratively (or literally) write across your bathroom mirror so that you see it every morning.

I suggest "engender useful output." Your primary responsibility as a manager is to maximize the likelihood that your employees will be productive; your task is to create an environment in which employee output is clearly defined and realistically achievable. If you're not doing that, then it doesn't matter what data you're gathering, which employees you're monitoring, or whose ear you're bending. You may be busy, you may be stressed, and you may look managerial, but you're not doing your job.

2. DEFINE YOUR GROUP'S OUTPUT

To engender output, you must first define it. This task is easier said than done. Today's workplace changes quickly, and managers at all levels are expected to turn the work of their groups on a dime. Your own manager may not be terribly clear on long-range company plans, so neither of you may fully understand how the work of your group will change in the next quarter, month, or even week.

Uncertainty about the future is not an excuse for lack of productivity in the present. If your plan is to wait around until everything is known before doing anything, you might as well lock the doors and go home for good! Things will change again and again, and only by delivering on current plans will you and your company learn what works, and what changes to make next. Besides, the definition of your group's required output is the definition of YOUR required output as manager. Defining it is one part good management practice and one part career survival.

3. SEEK MOMENTARY CLARITY RATHER THAN PERMANENT ANSWERS

Speak with your leaders about what your group can reasonably produce right now and then agree to task your group with producing it right now. Make it clear that unless you hear otherwise, until the next scheduled check-in you will follow the current plan. Then, verbally summarize the output you are committing to engender in about 90 seconds. During follow-up discussions with your management, use that mini-commercial as a way to gently remind them what you are working on so that they can edit your understanding if needed.

When changes do come, don't fight them. Welcome the new information, openly revise your understanding of what you need to produce, and clearly explain the time and resources you need to accomplish the change. If you can't turn the boat in an hour, say so. It's far better to be up front when something isn't possible than to agree to it under duress but fail to deliver.

4. BECOME AN EXPERT IN DEFINING AND COMMUNICATING EXPECTATIONS

Of course, your definition is only half the story. To engender output from your group, you need to convert from the commitment you made as manager into what each of your employees must do individually.

Contrary to popular opinion, this doesn't mean telling your employees what to do. It means teaching them to discuss what they are doing themselves—to create their own 90-second mini-commercials—and then working with them on a shared understanding of what's needed. You haven't successfully taught an employee his or her expected output until you hear that person say it to you spontaneously, in a way that matches your own understanding. Then you know it's happening.

This also means your employees must be in the habit of speaking openly about what they are doing. To get honesty, avoid using discussions about current objectives as pop quizzes! When you need to adjust an employee's understanding of his or her work, frame your conversation as being about expectations for the future and defining how to succeed. Don't let it degrade into how the employee should already know these things. Remember: When your employees don't know what they're supposed to be doing, it's at least as likely to be your fault as theirs.

5. KEEP TALKING ABOUT OUTPUT

A VSO, or *verbalized summary objective statement*, is a kind of mini-commercial in which you state the output you're trying to deliver at the moment. It should take about 90 seconds and should list about five to seven output goals that together cover about 80 percent of what you are working on. It's yours to change, adjust, and modify whenever you see fit. It's also yours to use as your introduction whenever you're talking to people in or about your workplace. Use VSOs with your management and teach your employees to use them with you.

Why? Your VSO trains people as to what to expect—and not expect—from you. It provides an avenue for a manager to edit an employee's understanding of the job, and a basis for you to accept or decline requests for additional work. As time goes by, and you deliver on your VSO, you also increase your credibility within the organization as people see that you are following through on your commitments.

6. KEEP AT IT

Management is like exercise: It's often difficult, you're never done, and it requires self-discipline.

Get in the habit of having conversations with superiors about the output needed from your group and discussions with your employees about their individual contributions to that output. Then remind yourself that your job is to maximize the chances that your employees will produce. This won't make management easy, but it's the first step in making you better at it.

AUTHOR BIO

Edward G. Muzio, CEO of Group Harmonics, is the author of the award-winning books *Make Work Great: Supercharge Your Team, Reinvent the Culture, and Gain Influence One Person at a Time* and *Four Secrets to Liking Your Work: You May Not Need to Quit to Get the Job You Want*. An expert in workplace improvement and its relationship to individual enjoyment, Muzio has been featured on Fox Business Network, CBS, and other national media. For more information, visit *Make Work Great* and follow the author on Facebook.

1-1 Describe what management is.
Good management is working through others to accomplish tasks that help fulfill organizational objectives as efficiently as possible.

Management getting work done through others (p. 3)

Efficiency getting work done with a minimum of effort, expense, or waste (p. 3)

Effectiveness accomplishing tasks that help fulfill organizational objectives (p. 4)

1-2 Explain the four functions of management.
Henri Fayol's classic management functions are known today as planning, organizing, leading, and controlling. Planning is determining organizational goals and a means for achieving them. Organizing is deciding where decisions will be made, who will do what jobs and tasks, and who will work for whom. Leading is inspiring and motivating workers to work hard to achieve organizational goals. Controlling is monitoring progress toward goal achievement and taking corrective action when needed. Studies show that performing the management functions well leads to better managerial performance.

Planning determining organizational goals and a means for achieving them (p. 4)

Organizing deciding where decisions will be made, who will do what jobs and tasks, and who will work for whom (p. 5)

Leading inspiring and motivating workers to work hard to achieve organizational goals (p. 6)

Controlling monitoring progress toward goal achievement and taking corrective action when needed (p. 6)

1-3 Describe different kinds of managers.
There are four different kinds of managers. Top managers are responsible for creating a context for change, developing attitudes of commitment and ownership, creating a positive organizational culture through words and actions, and monitoring their companies' business environments. Middle managers are responsible for planning and allocating resources, coordinating and linking groups and departments, monitoring and managing the performance of subunits and managers, and implementing the changes or strategies generated by top managers. First-line managers are responsible for managing the performance of nonmanagerial employees, teaching entry-level employees how to do their jobs, and making detailed schedules and operating plans based on middle management's intermediate-range plans. Team leaders are responsible for facilitating team performance, fostering good relationships among team members, and managing external relationships.

Top managers executives responsible for the overall direction of the organization (p. 7)

Middle managers responsible for setting objectives consistent with top management's goals and for planning and implementing subunit strategies for achieving these objectives (p. 7)

First-line managers responsible for training and supervising the performance of nonmanagerial employees who are directly responsible for producing the company's products or services (p. 9)

Team leaders managers responsible for facilitating team activities toward goal accomplishment (p. 9)

1-4 Explain the major roles and subroles that managers perform in their jobs.
Managers perform interpersonal, informational, and decisional roles in their jobs. In fulfilling interpersonal roles, managers act as figureheads by performing ceremonial duties, as leaders by motivating and encouraging workers, and as liaisons by dealing with people outside their units. In performing informational roles, managers act as monitors by scanning their environment for information, as disseminators by sharing information with others in their companies, and as spokespeople by sharing information with people outside their departments or companies. In fulfilling decisional roles, managers act as entrepreneurs by adapting their units to change, as disturbance handlers by responding to larger problems that demand immediate action, as resource allocators by deciding resource recipients and amounts, and as negotiators by bargaining with others about schedules, projects, goals, outcomes, and resources.

Figurehead role the interpersonal role managers play when they perform ceremonial duties (p. 11)

Leader role the interpersonal role managers play when they motivate and encourage workers to accomplish organizational objectives (p. 11)

Liaison role the interpersonal role managers play when they deal with people outside their units (p. 11)

Monitor role the informational role managers play when they scan their environment for information (p. 11)

Disseminator role the informational role managers play when they share information with others in their departments or companies (p. 12)

Spokesperson role the informational role managers play when they share information with people outside their departments or companies (p. 12)

Entrepreneur role the decisional role managers play when they adapt themselves, their subordinates, and their units to change (p. 13)

Disturbance handler role the decisional role managers play when they respond to severe pressures and problems that demand immediate action (p. 13)

Resource allocator role the decisional role managers play when they decide who gets what resources and in what amounts (p. 13)

Negotiator role the decisional role managers play when they negotiate schedules, projects, goals, outcomes, resources, and employee raises (p. 14)

1-5 **Assess managerial potential, based on what companies look for in managers.** Companies do not want one-dimensional managers. They want managers with a balance of skills. Managers need to have the knowledge and abilities to get the job done (technical skills), must be able to work effectively in groups and be good listeners and communicators (human skills), must be able to assess the relationships between the different parts of their companies and the external environment and position their companies for success (conceptual skills), and should want to assume positions of leadership and power (motivation to manage). Technical skills are most important for team leaders and lower-level managers, human skills are equally important at all levels of management, and conceptual skills as well as motivation to manage both increase in importance as managers rise through the managerial ranks.

Technical skills the specialized procedures, techniques, and knowledge required to get the job done (p. 14)

Human skills the ability to work well with others (p. 15)

Conceptual skills the ability to see the organization as a whole, understand how the different parts affect each other, and recognize how the company fits into or is affected by its environment (p. 15)

Motivation to manage an assessment of how enthusiastic employees are about managing the work of others (p. 16)

1-6 **Recognize the top mistakes that managers make in their jobs.** Another way to understand what it takes to be a manager is to look at the top mistakes managers make. Five of the most important mistakes made by managers are being abrasive and intimidating; being cold, aloof, or arrogant; betraying trust; being overly ambitious; and being unable to delegate, build a team, and staff effectively.

1-7 **Describe the transition that employees go through when they are promoted to management.** Managers often begin their jobs by using more formal authority and less people management skills. However, most managers find that being a manager has little to do with "bossing" their subordinates. According to a study of managers in their first year, after six months on the job, the managers were surprised by the fast pace and heavy workload and by the fact that "helping" their subordinates was viewed as interference. After a year on the job, most of the managers had come to think of themselves not as doers but as managers who get things done through others. Because they finally realized that people management was the most important part of their job, most of them had abandoned their authoritarian approach for one based on communication, listening, and positive reinforcement.

Exhibit 1.6
Stages in the Transition to Management

MANAGERS' INITIAL EXPECTATIONS			AFTER SIX MONTHS AS A MANAGER			AFTER A YEAR AS A MANAGER					
JAN	FEB	MAR	APR	MAY	JUN	JUL	AUG	SEP	OCT	NOV	DEC

MANAGERS' INITIAL EXPECTATIONS	AFTER SIX MONTHS AS A MANAGER	AFTER A YEAR AS A MANAGER
◉ Be the boss	◉ Initial expectations were wrong	◉ No longer a doer
◉ Formal authority	◉ Fast pace	◉ Communication, listening, and positive reinforcement
◉ Manage tasks	◉ Heavy workload	◉ Learning to adapt to and control stress
◉ Job is not managing people	◉ Job is to be problem solver and troubleshooter for subordinates	◉ Job is people development

Source: L. A. Hill, *Becoming a Manager: Mastery of a New Identity* (Boston: Harvard Business School Press, 1992).

1-8 **Explain how and why companies can create competitive advantage through people.** Why does management matter? Well-managed companies are competitive because their workforces are smarter, better trained, more motivated, and more committed. Furthermore, companies that practice good management consistently have greater sales revenues, profits, and stock market performance than companies that don't. Finally, good management matters because it leads to satisfied employees who, in turn, provide better service to customers. Because employees tend to treat customers the same way that their managers treat them, good management can improve customer satisfaction.

CHAPTER 2 LEARNING OUTCOMES / KEY TERMS

2-1 Explain the origins of management. Management as a field of study is just 125 years old, but management ideas and practices have actually been used since 5000 BCE. From ancient Sumer to sixteenth-century Europe, there are historical antecedents for each of the functions of management discussed in this textbook: planning, organizing, leading, and controlling. However, there was no compelling need for managers until systematic changes in the nature of work and organizations occurred during the past two centuries. As work shifted from families to factories; from skilled laborers to specialized, unskilled laborers; from small, self-organized groups to large factories employing thousands under one roof; and from unique, small batches of production to standardized mass production; managers were needed to impose order and structure, to motivate and direct large groups of workers, and to plan and make decisions that optimized overall performance by effectively coordinating the different parts of an organizational system.

2-2 Explain the history of scientific management. Scientific management involves studying and testing different work methods to identify the best, most efficient way to complete a job. According to Frederick W. Taylor, the father of scientific management, managers should follow four scientific management principles. First, study each element of work to determine the one best way to do it. Second, scientifically select, train, teach, and develop workers to reach their full potential. Third, cooperate with employees to ensure that the scientific principles are implemented. Fourth, divide the work and the responsibility equally between management and workers. Above all, Taylor believed these principles could be used to align managers and employees by determining a fair day's work (what an average worker could produce at a reasonable pace) and a fair day's pay (what management should pay workers for that effort). Taylor believed that incentives were one of the best ways to align management and employees.

Frank and Lillian Gilbreth are best known for their use of motion studies to simplify work. While Taylor used time study to determine a fair day's work based on how long it took a "first-class man" to complete each part of his job, Frank Gilbreth used motion-picture films and microchronometers to conduct motion studies to improve efficiency by eliminating unnecessary or repetitive motions. Henry Gantt is best known for the Gantt chart, which graphically indicates when a series of tasks must be completed in order to complete a job or project, but he also developed ideas regarding worker training, specifically, that all workers should be trained and their managers should be rewarded for training them.

Scientific management thoroughly studying and testing different work methods to identify the best, most efficient way to complete a job (p. 25)

Soldiering when workers deliberately slow their pace or restrict their work output (p. 26)

Rate buster a group member whose work pace is significantly faster than the normal pace in his or her group (p. 26)

Motion study breaking each task or job into its separate motions and then eliminating those that are unnecessary or repetitive (p. 28)

Time study timing how long it takes good workers to complete each part of their jobs (p. 29)

Gantt chart a graphical chart that shows which tasks must be completed at which times in order to complete a project or task (p. 29)

2-3 Discuss the history of bureaucratic and administrative management. Today, we associate bureaucracy with inefficiency and red tape. Yet German sociologist Max Weber thought that bureaucracy—that is, running organizations on the basis of knowledge, fairness, and logical rules and procedures—would accomplish organizational goals much more efficiently than monarchies and patriarchies, where decisions were based on personal or family connections, personal gain, and arbitrary decision-making. Bureaucracies are characterized by seven elements: qualification-based hiring; merit-based promotion; chain of command; division of labor; impartial application of rules and procedures; recording rules, procedures, and decisions in writing; and separating managers from owners. Nonetheless, bureaucracies are often inefficient and can be highly resistant to change.

The Frenchman Henri Fayol, whose ideas were shaped by his more than 20 years of experience as a CEO, is best known for developing five management functions (planning, organizing, coordinating, commanding, and controlling) and 14 principles of management (division of work, authority and responsibility, discipline, unity of command, unity of direction, subordination of individual interests to the general interest, remuneration, centralization, scalar chain, order, equity, stability of tenure of personnel, initiative, and *esprit de corps*).

Bureaucracy the exercise of control on the basis of knowledge, expertise, or experience (p. 31)

2-4 Explain the history of human relations management. Unlike most people who view conflict as bad, Mary Parker Follett believed that it should be embraced rather than avoided. Of the three ways of dealing with conflict—domination, compromise, and integration—she argued that the latter was the best because it focuses on developing creative methods for meeting conflicting parties' needs.

Elton Mayo is best known for his role in the Hawthorne Studies at the Western Electric Company. In the first stage of the Hawthorne Studies, production went up because both the increased attention paid to the workers in the study and their development into a cohesive work group led to significantly higher levels of job satisfaction and productivity. In the second stage, productivity dropped because the workers had already developed strong negative norms. The Hawthorne Studies demonstrated that workers' feelings and attitudes affect their work, that financial incentives aren't necessarily the most important motivator for workers, and that group norms and behavior play a critical role in behavior at work.

Chester Barnard, president of New Jersey Bell Telephone, emphasized the critical importance of willing cooperation in organizations. In general, Barnard argued that people will be indifferent to managerial directives or orders if they (1) are understood, (2) are consistent with the purpose of the organization, (3) are compatible with the people's personal interests, and (4) can actually be carried out by those people. Acceptance of managerial authority (i.e., cooperation) is not automatic, however.

Domination an approach to dealing with conflict in which one party satisfies its desires and objectives at the expense of the other party's desires and objectives (p. 35)

Compromise an approach to dealing with conflict in which both parties give up some of what they want in order to

reach an agreement on a plan to reduce or settle the conflict (p. 35)

Integrative conflict resolution an approach to dealing with conflict in which both parties indicate their preferences and then work together to find an alternative that meets the needs of both (p. 35)

Organization a system of consciously coordinated activities or forces created by two or more people (p. 38)

2-5 **Discuss the history of operations, information, systems, and contingency management.** Operations management uses a quantitative or mathematical approach to find ways to increase productivity, improve quality, and manage or reduce costly inventories. The manufacture of standardized, interchangeable parts; the graphical and computerized design of parts; and the accidental discovery of just-in-time inventory systems were some of the most important historical events in operations management.

Throughout history, organizations have pushed for and quickly adopted new information technologies that reduce the cost or increase the speed with which they can acquire, store, retrieve, or communicate information. Historically, some of the most important technologies that have revolutionized information management were the invention of machines to produce pulp for paper and the printing press in the fourteenth and fifteenth centuries,

the manual typewriter in 1850, the telephone in the 1880s, the personal computer in the 1980s, and the internet in the 1990s.

A system is a set of interrelated elements or parts (subsystems) that function as a whole. Organizational systems obtain inputs from both general and specific environments. Managers and workers then use their management knowledge and manufacturing techniques to transform those inputs into outputs that, in turn, provide feedback to the organization. Organizational systems must also address the issues of synergy and open versus closed systems.

Finally, the contingency approach to management clearly states that there are no universal management theories. The most effective management theory or idea depends on the kinds of problems or situations that managers or organizations are facing at a particular time. This means that management is much harder than it looks.

System a set of interrelated elements or parts that function as a whole (p. 41)

Subsystems smaller systems that operate within the context of a larger system (p. 41)

Synergy when two or more subsystems working together can produce more than they can working apart (p. 41)

Closed systems systems that can sustain themselves without interacting with their environments (p. 41)

Open systems systems that can sustain themselves only by interacting with their environments, on which they depend for their survival (p. 41)

Contingency approach holds that there are no universal management theories and that the most effective management theory or idea depends on the kinds of problems or situations that managers are facing at a particular time and place (p. 42)

Exhibit 2.7
Systems View of Organizations

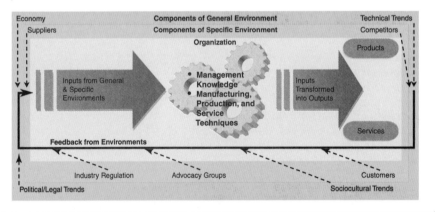

3-1 **Discuss how changing environments affect organizations.** Environmental change, environmental complexity, and resource scarcity are the basic components of external environments. Environmental change is the rate of variation in a company's general and specific environments. Environmental complexity is the number and intensity of factors in the external environment. Resource scarcity is the abundance or shortage of critical resources in the external environment. As the rate of environmental change increases, as the environment becomes more complex, and as resources become more scarce, managers become less confident that they can understand, predict, and effectively react to the trends affecting their businesses. According to punctuated equilibrium theory, companies experience long periods of stability followed by short periods of dynamic, fundamental change, followed by a return to stability.

External environments all events outside a company that have the potential to influence or affect it (p. 45)

Environmental change the rate at which a company's general and specific environments change (p. 46)

Stable environment an environment in which the rate of change is slow (p. 46)

Dynamic environment an environment in which the rate of change is fast (p. 46)

Punctuated equilibrium theory the theory that companies go through long periods of stability (equilibrium), followed by short periods of dynamic, fundamental change (revolutionary periods), and then a new equilibrium (p. 46)

Environmental complexity the number and the intensity of external factors in the environment that affect organizations (p. 47)

Simple environment an environment with few environmental factors (p. 47)

Complex environment an environment with many environmental factors (p. 47)

Resource scarcity the abundance or shortage of critical organizational resources in an organization's external environment (p. 48)

Uncertainty extent to which managers can understand or predict which environmental changes and trends will affect their businesses (p. 48)

3-2 **Describe the four components of the general environment.** The general environment consists of trends that affect all organizations. Because the economy influences basic business decisions, managers often use economic statistics and business confidence indices to predict future economic activity. Changes in technology, which transforms inputs into outputs, can be a benefit or a threat to a business. Sociocultural trends, such as changing demographic characteristics, affect how companies staff their businesses. Similarly, sociocultural changes in behavior, attitudes, and beliefs affect the demand for businesses' products and services. Court decisions and new federal and state laws have imposed much greater political/legal responsibility on companies. The best way to manage legal responsibilities is to educate managers and employees about laws and regulations as well as potential lawsuits that could affect a business.

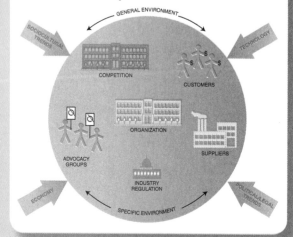

Exhibit 3.2

General and Specific Environments

General environment the economic, technological, sociocultural, and political/legal trends that indirectly affect all organizations (p. 49)

Specific environment the customers, competitors, suppliers, industry regulations, and advocacy groups that are unique to an industry and directly affect how a company does business (p. 49)

Business confidence indices indices that show managers' level of confidence about future business growth (p. 50)

Technology the knowledge, tools, and techniques used to transform inputs into outputs (p. 51)

3-3 **Explain the five components of the specific environment.** The specific environment is made up of five components: customers, competitors, suppliers, industry regulations, and advocacy groups. Companies can monitor customers' needs by identifying customer problems after they occur or by anticipating problems before they occur. Because they tend to focus on well-known competitors, managers often underestimate their competition or do a poor job of identifying future competitors. Suppliers and buyers are very dependent on each other, and that dependence sometimes leads to opportunistic behavior in which one party benefits at the expense of the other. Regulatory agencies affect businesses by creating rules and then enforcing them. Advocacy groups cannot regulate organizations' practices. Nevertheless, through public communications, media advocacy, and product boycotts, they try to convince companies to change their practices.

Competitors companies in the same industry that sell similar products or services to customers (p. 54)

Competitive analysis a process for monitoring the competition that involves identifying competitors, anticipating their moves, and determining their strengths and weaknesses (p. 54)

Suppliers companies that provide material, human, financial, and informational resources to other companies (p. 55)

Supplier dependence the degree to which a company relies on a supplier because of the importance of the supplier's product to the company and the difficulty of finding other sources of that product (p. 55)

Buyer dependence the degree to which a supplier relies on a buyer because of the importance of that buyer to the supplier and the difficulty of finding other buyers for its products (p. 55)

Opportunistic behavior a transaction in which one party in the relationship benefits at the expense of the other (p. 56)

Relationship behavior the establishment of mutually beneficial, long-term exchanges between buyers and suppliers (p. 56)

Industry regulation regulations and rules that govern the business practices and procedures of specific industries, businesses, and professions (p. 57)

Advocacy groups concerned citizens who band together to try to influence the business practices of specific industries, businesses, and professions (p. 57)

Public communications an advocacy group tactic that relies on voluntary participation by the news media and the advertising industry to get the advocacy group's message out (p. 57)

Media advocacy an advocacy group tactic that involves framing issues as public issues; exposing questionable, exploitative, or unethical practices; and forcing media coverage by buying media time or creating controversy that is likely to receive extensive news coverage (p. 57)

Product boycott an advocacy group tactic that involves protesting a company's actions by persuading consumers not to purchase its product or service (p. 57)

3-4 **Apply the process that companies use to make sense of their changing environments.** Managers use a three-step process to make sense of external environments: environmental scanning, interpreting information, and acting on threats and opportunities. Managers scan their environments in order to keep up to date on factors influencing their industries, to reduce uncertainty, and to detect potential problems. When managers identify environmental events as threats, they take steps to protect their companies from harm. When managers identify environmental events as opportunities, they formulate alternatives for taking advantage of them to improve company performance. Using cognitive maps can help managers visually summarize the relationships between environmental factors and the actions they might take to deal with them.

Environmental scanning searching the environment for important events or issues that might affect an organization (p. 59)

Cognitive maps graphic depictions of how managers believe environmental factors relate to possible organizational actions (p. 60)

3-5 **Explain how organizational cultures are created and how they can help companies be successful.** Organizational culture is the set of key values, beliefs, and attitudes shared by members of an organization. Organizational cultures are often created by company founders and then sustained through repetition of organizational stories and recognition of organizational heroes. Companies with adaptable cultures that promote employee involvement, make clear the organization's strategic purpose and direction, and actively define and teach organizational values and beliefs can achieve higher sales growth, return on assets, profits, quality, and employee satisfaction. Organizational cultures exist on three levels: the surface level, where visible artifacts and behaviors can be observed; just below the surface, where values and beliefs are expressed; and deep below the surface, where unconsciously held assumptions and beliefs exist. Managers can begin to change company cultures by focusing on the top two levels. Techniques for changing organizational cultures include using behavioral substitution and behavioral addition, changing visible artifacts, and selecting job applicants who have values and beliefs consistent with the desired company culture.

Internal environment the events and trends inside an organization that affect management, employees, and organizational culture (p. 61)

Organizational culture the values, beliefs, and attitudes shared by organizational members (p. 61)

Organizational stories stories told by organizational members to make sense of organizational events and changes and to emphasize culturally consistent assumptions, decisions, and actions (p. 62)

Organizational heroes people celebrated for their qualities and achievements within an organization (p. 63)

Organizational ceremonies gatherings in which symbolic acts commemorate or celebrate notable achievements or changes (p. 63)

Company mission a company's purpose or reason for existing (p. 64)

Consistent organizational culture a company culture in which the company actively defines and teaches organizational values, beliefs, and attitudes (p. 64)

Behavioral addition the process of having managers and employees perform new behaviors that are central to and symbolic of the new organizational culture that a company wants to create (p. 65)

Behavioral substitution the process of having managers and employees perform new behaviors central to the new organizational culture in place of behaviors that were central to the old organizational culture (p. 66)

Visible artifacts visible signs of an organization's culture, such as the office design and layout, company dress code, and company benefits and perks, such as stock options, personal parking spaces, or the private company dining room (p. 66)

4-1 Identify common kinds of workplace deviance. Ethics is the set of moral principles or values that define right and wrong. Workplace deviance is behavior that violates organizational norms about right and wrong and harms the organization or its workers. There are four different types of workplace deviance. Production deviance and property deviance harm the company, whereas political deviance and personal aggression harm individuals within the company.

Ethics the set of moral principles or values that defines right and wrong for a person or group (p. 69)

Ethical behavior behavior that conforms to a society's accepted principles of right and wrong (p. 70)

Workplace deviance unethical behavior that violates organizational norms about right and wrong (p. 70)

Production deviance unethical behavior that hurts the quality and quantity of work produced (p. 71)

Property deviance unethical behavior aimed at the organization's property or products (p. 71)

Employee shrinkage employee theft of company merchandise (p. 71)

Political deviance using one's influence to harm others in the company (p. 71)

Personal aggression hostile or aggressive behavior toward others (p. 71)

4-2 Describe how the US Sentencing Commission Guidelines Manual for Organizations encourages ethical behavior, including how to calculate fines for unethical behavior. Under the US Sentencing Commission guidelines, companies can be prosecuted and fined up to $600 million for employees' illegal actions. Fines are computed by multiplying the base fine by a culpability score. Companies that establish compliance programs to encourage ethical behavior can reduce their culpability scores and their fines.

4-3 Describe what influences ethical decision-making. Three factors influence ethical decisions: the ethical intensity of the decision, the moral development of the manager, and the ethical principles used to solve the problem. Ethical intensity is high when decisions have large, certain, immediate consequences and when the decision maker is physically or psychologically close to those affected by the decision. There are three levels of moral development. At the preconventional level, decisions are made for selfish reasons. At the conventional level, decisions conform to societal expectations. At the postconventional level, internalized principles are used to make ethical decisions. Each of these levels has two stages. Managers can use a number of different principles when making ethical decisions: long-term self-interest, religious injunctions, government requirements, individual rights, personal virtue, distributive justice, and utilitarian benefits.

Ethical intensity the degree of concern people have about an ethical issue (p. 76)

Magnitude of consequences the total harm or benefit derived from an ethical decision (p. 76)

Social consensus agreement on whether behavior is bad or good (p. 76)

Probability of effect the chance that something will happen that results in harm to others (p. 76)

Temporal immediacy the time between an act and the consequences the act produces (p. 76)

Proximity of effect the social, psychological, cultural, or physical distance between a decision maker and those affected by his or her decisions (p. 76)

Concentration of effect the total harm or benefit that an act produces on the average person (p. 76)

Preconventional level of moral development the first level of moral development, in which people make decisions based on selfish reasons (p. 77)

Conventional level of moral development the second level of moral development, in which people make decisions that conform to societal expectation (p. 78)

Postconventional level of moral development the third level of moral development, in which people make decisions based on internalized principles (p. 78)

Principle of long-term self-interest an ethical principle that holds that you should never take any action that is not in your or your organization's long-term self-interest (p. 79)

Principle of religious injunctions an ethical principle that holds that you should never take any action that is not kind and that does not build a sense of community (p. 79)

Principle of government requirements an ethical principle that holds that you should never take any action that violates the law, for the law represents the minimal moral standard (p. 79)

Principle of individual rights an ethical principle that holds that you should never take any action that infringes on others' agreed-upon rights (p. 79)

Principle of personal virtue an ethical principle that holds that you should never do anything that is not honest, open, and truthful and that you would not be glad to see reported in the newspapers or on TV (p. 79)

Principle of distributive justice an ethical principle that holds that you should never take any action that harms the least fortunate among us: the poor, the uneducated, the unemployed (p. 80)

Principle of utilitarian benefits an ethical principle that holds that you should never take any action that does not result in greater good for society (p. 80)

4-4 Apply the practical steps managers can take to improve ethical decision-making in real-world situations. Employers can increase their chances of hiring ethical employees by testing all job applicants. Most large companies now have corporate codes of ethics. In addition to offering general rules, ethics codes must also provide specific, practical advice. Ethics training seeks to increase employees' awareness of ethical issues; make ethics a serious, credible factor in organizational decisions; and teach employees a practical model of ethical decision-making. The most important factors in creating an ethical business climate are the personal examples set by company managers, the involvement of management in the company ethics program, a reporting system that encourages whistle-blowers to report potential ethics violations, and fair but consistent punishment of violators.

Overt integrity test a written test that estimates job applicants' honesty by directly asking them what they think or feel about theft or about punishment of unethical behaviors (p. 80)

Personality-based integrity test a written test that indirectly estimates job applicants' honesty by measuring psychological traits, such as dependability and conscientiousness (p. 80)

Whistleblowing reporting others' ethics violations to management or legal authorities (p. 84)

4-5 Explain to whom organizations are socially responsible. Social responsibility is a business's obligation to benefit society. According to the shareholder model, a company's only social responsibility is to maximize shareholder wealth by maximizing company profits. According to the stakeholder model, companies must satisfy the needs and interests of multiple corporate stakeholders, not just shareholders. The needs of primary stakeholders, on which the organization relies for its existence, take precedence over those of secondary stakeholders.

Social responsibility a business's obligation to pursue policies, make decisions, and take actions that benefit society (p. 85)

Shareholder model a view of social responsibility that holds that an organization's overriding goal should be profit maximization for the benefit of shareholders (p. 85)

Stakeholder model a theory of corporate responsibility that holds that management's most important responsibility, long-term survival, is achieved by satisfying the interests of multiple corporate stakeholders (p. 85)

Stakeholders persons or groups with a stake, or legitimate interest, in a company's actions (p. 85)

Primary stakeholder any group on which an organization relies for its long-term survival (p. 86)

Secondary stakeholder any group that can influence or be influenced by a company and can affect public perceptions about the company's socially responsible behavior (p. 86)

4-6 Explain for what organizations are socially responsible. Companies can best benefit their stakeholders by fulfilling their economic, legal, ethical, and discretionary responsibilities. Being profitable, or meeting its economic responsibility, is a business's most basic social responsibility. Legal responsibility consists of following a society's laws and regulations. Ethical responsibility means not violating accepted principles of right and wrong when doing business. Discretionary responsibilities are social responsibilities beyond basic economic, legal, and ethical responsibilities.

Economic responsibility a company's social responsibility to make a profit by producing a valued product or service (p. 87)

Legal responsibility a company's social responsibility to obey society's laws and regulations (p. 87)

Ethical responsibility a company's social responsibility not to violate accepted principles of right and wrong when conducting its business (p. 88)

Discretionary responsibilities the social roles that a company fulfills beyond its economic, legal, and ethical responsibilities (p. 88)

4-7 Identify how organizations can respond to societal demands for social responsibility. Social responsiveness is a company's response to stakeholders' expectations concerning socially responsible behavior. There are four social responsiveness strategies. When a company uses a reactive strategy, it denies responsibility for a problem. When it uses a defensive strategy, a company takes responsibility for a problem but does the minimum required to solve it. When a company uses an accommodative strategy, it accepts responsibility for problems and does all that society expects to solve them. Finally, when a company uses a proactive strategy, it does much more than expected to solve social responsibility problems.

Social responsiveness a company's strategy to respond to stakeholders' economic, legal, ethical, or discretionary expectations concerning social responsibility (p. 89)

Reactive strategy a social responsiveness strategy in which a company does less than society expects (p. 89)

Defensive strategy a social responsiveness strategy in which a company admits responsibility for a problem but does the least required to meet societal expectations (p. 89)

Accommodative strategy a social responsiveness strategy in which a company accepts responsibility for a problem and does all that society expects to solve that problem (p. 89)

Proactive strategy a social responsiveness strategy in which a company anticipates a problem before it occurs and does more than society expects to take responsibility for and address the problem (p. 90)

4-8 Explain whether social responsibility hurts or helps an organization's economic performance. Does it pay to be socially responsible? Studies show that there is generally no trade-off between social responsibility and economic performance. In most circumstances, there is generally a small positive relationship between social responsibility and economic performance that becomes stronger when a company or its products have a positive reputation. Social responsibility, however, does not guarantee profitability, as socially responsible companies experience the same ups and downs as other companies.

CHAPTER 5 LEARNING OUTCOMES / KEY TERMS

5-1 **Discuss the benefits and pitfalls of planning.** Planning is choosing a goal and developing a method or strategy for achieving it. Planning is one of the best ways to improve organizational and individual performance. It encourages people to work harder (intensified effort), to work hard for extended periods (persistence), to engage in behaviors directly related to goal accomplishment (directed behavior), and to think of better ways to do their jobs (task strategies). However, planning also has three potential pitfalls. Companies that are overly committed to their plans may be slow to adapt to environmental changes. Planning can create a false sense of security: planning is based on assumptions about the future, and when those assumptions are wrong, plans can fail. Finally, planning can fail when planners are detached from the implementation of their plans.

Planning choosing a goal and developing a strategy to achieve that goal (p. 92)

5-2 **Outline the steps for creating an effective plan.** There are five steps to making a plan that works: (1) Set S.M.A.R.T. goals—goals that are **S**pecific, **M**easurable, **A**ttainable, **R**ealistic, and **T**imely. (2) Develop commitment to the goals. Managers can increase workers' goal commitment by encouraging their participation in goal setting, making goals public, and getting top management to show support for goals. (3) Develop action plans for goal accomplishment. (4) Track progress toward goal achievement by setting both proximal and distal goals and by providing workers with regular performance feedback. (5) Maintain flexibility by keeping options open.

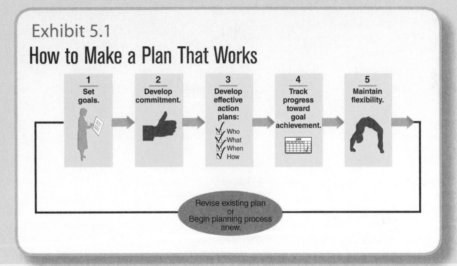

Exhibit 5.1
How to Make a Plan That Works

1 Set goals. → 2 Develop commitment. → 3 Develop effective action plans: ✓ Who ✓ What ✓ When ✓ How → 4 Track progress toward goal achievement. → 5 Maintain flexibility.

Revise existing plan or Begin planning process anew.

S.M.A.R.T. goals goals that are specific, measurable, attainable, realistic, and timely (p. 95)

Goal commitment the determination to achieve a goal (p. 96)

Action plan a plan that lists the specific steps, people, resources, and time period needed to attain a goal (p. 97)

Proximal goals short-term goals or subgoals (p. 97)

Distal goals long-term or primary goals (p. 97)

Options-based planning maintaining planning flexibility by making small, simultaneous investments in many alternative plans (p. 99)

Slack resources a cushion of extra resources that can be used with options-based planning to adapt to unanticipated changes, problems, or opportunities (p. 99)

5-3 **Discuss how companies can use plans at all management levels, from top to bottom.** Proper planning requires that the goals at the bottom and middle of the organization support the objectives at the top of the organization. The goals at the top will be longer range than those at the bottom. Top management develops strategic plans, which start with the creation of an organizational purpose statement and strategic objectives. Middle managers use techniques such as management by objectives to develop tactical plans that direct behavior, efforts, and priorities. Finally, lower-level managers develop operational plans that guide daily activities in producing or delivering an organization's products and services. There are three kinds of operational plans: single-use plans, standing plans (policies, procedures, and rules and regulations), and budgets.

Strategic plans overall company plans that clarify how the company will serve customers and position itself against competitors over the next two to five years (p. 100)

Purpose statement a statement of a company's purpose or reason for existing (p. 100)

Strategic objective a more specific goal that unifies company-wide efforts, stretches and challenges the organization, and possesses a finish line and a time frame (p. 101)

Tactical plans plans created and implemented by middle managers that direct behavior, efforts, and attention over the next six months to two years (p. 102)

Management by objectives a four-step process in which managers and employees discuss and select goals, develop tactical plans, and meet regularly to review progress toward goal accomplishment (p. 102)

Operational plans day-to-day plans, developed and implemented by lower-level managers, for producing or delivering the organization's products and services over a 30-day to six-month period (p. 102)

Single-use plans plans that cover unique, onetime-only events (p. 102)

Standing plans plans used repeatedly to handle frequently recurring events (p. 103)

Policies standing plans that indicate the general course of action that should be taken in response to a particular event or situation (p. 103)

Procedures standing plans that indicate the specific steps that should be taken in response to a particular event (p. 103)

Rules and regulations standing plans that describe how a particular action

should be performed or what must happen or not happen in response to a particular event (p. 104)

Budgeting quantitative planning through which managers decide how to allocate available money to best accomplish company goals (p. 104)

5-4

Use the steps and avoid the limits to rational decision-making. Rational decision-making is a six-step process in which managers define problems, evaluate alternatives, and compute optimal solutions. Step 1 is identifying and defining the problem. Problems are gaps between desired and existing states. Managers won't begin the decision-making process unless they are aware of a gap, are motivated to reduce it, and possess the necessary resources to fix it. Step 2 is defining the decision criteria used to judge alternatives. In Step 3, an absolute or relative comparison process is used to rate the importance of the decision criteria. Step 4 involves generating many alternative courses of action (i.e.,

solutions). Potential solutions are assessed in Step 5 by systematically gathering information and evaluating each alternative against each criterion. In Step 6, criterion ratings and weights are used to compute the weighted average for each alternative course of action. Rational managers then choose the alternative with the highest value.

The rational decision-making model describes how decisions should be made in an ideal world without constraints. However, managers' limited resources, incomplete and imperfect information, and limited decision-making capabilities restrict their decision-making processes in the real world.

Decision-making the process of choosing a solution from available alternatives (p. 104)

Rational decision-making a systematic process of defining problems, evaluating alternatives, and choosing optimal solutions (p. 104)

Problem a gap between a desired state and an existing state (p. 104)

Decision criteria the standards used to guide judgments and decisions (p. 105)

Absolute comparisons a process in which each decision criterion is compared to a standard or ranked on its own merits (p. 105)

Relative comparisons a process in which each decision criterion is

compared directly with every other criterion (p. 106)

Maximize choosing the best alternative (p. 108)

Satisficing choosing a "good-enough" alternative (p. 108)

5-5

Explain how group decisions and group decision-making techniques can improve decision-making. When groups view problems from multiple perspectives, use more information, have a diversity of knowledge and experience, and become committed to solutions they help choose, they can produce better solutions than do individual decision makers. However, group decisions can suffer from several disadvantages: groupthink, slowness, discussions dominated by just a few individuals, and unfelt responsibility for decisions. Group decision-making works

best when group members encourage c-type (cognitive) conflict. Group decision-making doesn't work as well when groups become mired in a-type (affective) conflict. The devil's advocacy approach improves group decisions because it brings structured c-type conflict into the decision-making process. By contrast, the nominal group technique improves decision-making by reducing a-type conflict. Because it overcomes the problems of production blocking and evaluation apprehension, electronic brainstorming is more effective than face-to-face brainstorming.

Groupthink a barrier to good decision-making caused by pressure within the group for members to agree with each other (p. 109)

C-type conflict (cognitive conflict) disagreement that focuses on problem- and issue-related differences of opinion (p. 110)

A-type conflict (affective conflict) disagreement that focuses on individuals or personal issues (p. 110)

Devil's advocacy a decision-making method in which an individual or a subgroup is assigned the role of critic (p. 110)

Dialectical inquiry a decision-making method in which decision makers state

the assumptions of a proposed solution (a thesis) and generate a solution that is the opposite (antithesis) of that solution (p. 110)

Nominal group technique a decision-making method that begins and ends by having group members quietly write down and evaluate ideas to be shared with the group (p. 111)

Delphi technique a decision-making method in which members of a panel of experts respond to questions and to each other until reaching agreement on an issue (p. 111)

Brainstorming a decision-making method in which group members build

on each others' ideas to generate as many alternative solutions as possible (p. 111)

Electronic brainstorming a decision-making method in which group members use computers to build on each others' ideas and generate as many alternative solutions as possible (p. 111)

Production blocking a disadvantage of face-to-face brainstorming in which a group member must wait to share an idea because another member is presenting an idea (p. 112)

Evaluation apprehension fear of what others will think of your ideas (p. 112)

Organizational Strategy

CHAPTER 6 LEARNING OUTCOMES / KEY TERMS

CHAPTER REVIEW

6-1 Explain the steps for creating a sustainable competitive advantage and why having such an advantage is so important. Firms can use their resources to create and sustain a competitive advantage, that is, to provide greater value for customers than competitors can. A competitive advantage becomes sustainable when other companies cannot duplicate the benefits it provides and have, for now, stopped trying. Four conditions must be met if a firm's resources are to be used to achieve a sustainable competitive advantage. The resources must be valuable, rare, imperfectly imitable, and nonsubstitutable.

Resources the assets, capabilities, processes, employee time, information, and knowledge that an organization uses to improve its effectiveness and efficiency and create and sustain competitive advantage (p. 115)

Competitive advantage providing greater value for customers than competitors can (p. 116)

Sustainable competitive advantage a competitive advantage that other companies have tried unsuccessfully to duplicate and have, for the moment, stopped trying to duplicate (p. 116)

Valuable resource a resource that allows companies to improve efficiency and effectiveness (p. 116)

Rare resource a resource that is not controlled or possessed by many competing firms (p. 116)

Imperfectly imitable resource a resource that is impossible or extremely costly or difficult for other firms to duplicate (p. 116)

Nonsubstitutable resource a resource that produces value or competitive advantage and has no equivalent substitutes or replacements (p. 117)

6-2 Describe the steps involved in the strategy-making process. The first step in strategy making is determining whether a strategy needs to be changed to sustain a competitive advantage. The second step is to conduct a situational (SWOT) analysis that examines internal strengths and weaknesses as well as external opportunities and threats. The third step involves choosing a strategy. Strategic reference point theory suggests that when companies are performing better than their strategic reference points, top management will typically choose a risk-averse strategy. When performance is below strategic reference points, risk-seeking strategies are more likely to be chosen.

Competitive inertia a reluctance to change strategies or competitive practices that have been successful in the past (p. 118)

Strategic dissonance a discrepancy between a company's intended strategy and the strategic actions managers take when implementing that strategy. (p. 118)

Situational (SWOT) analysis an assessment of the strengths and weaknesses in an organization's internal environment and the opportunities and threats in its external environment (p. 119)

Distinctive competence what a company can make, do, or perform better than its competitors (p. 119)

Shadow-strategy task force a committee within a company that analyzes the company's own weaknesses to determine how competitors could exploit them for competitive advantage (p. 120)

Core capabilities the internal decision-making routines, problem-solving processes, and organizational cultures that determine how efficiently inputs can be turned into outputs (p. 120)

Strategic group a group of companies within an industry against which top managers compare, evaluate, and benchmark strategic threats and opportunities (p. 120)

Core firms the central companies in a strategic group (p. 121)

Secondary firms the firms in a strategic group that follow strategies related to but somewhat different from those of the core firms (p. 121)

Strategic reference points the strategic targets managers use to measure whether a firm has developed the core competencies it needs to achieve a sustainable competitive advantage (p. 122)

6-3 Explain the different kinds of corporate-level strategies and when each should be used. Corporate-level strategies, consisting of portfolio strategies and grand strategies, help managers determine what businesses they should be in. Portfolio strategy focuses on lowering business risk by being in multiple, unrelated businesses and by investing the cash flows from slow-growing businesses into faster-growing businesses. One portfolio strategy is based on the BCG matrix. The most successful way to use the portfolio approach to corporate strategy is to reduce risk through related diversification. The three kinds of grand strategies are growth, stability, and retrenchment/recovery. Companies can grow externally by merging with or acquiring other companies, or they can grow internally through direct expansion or creating new businesses. Companies choose a stability strategy when their external environment changes very little or after they have dealt with periods of explosive growth. Retrenchment strategy, shrinking the size or scope of a business, is used to turn around poor performance. If retrenchment works, it is often followed by a recovery strategy that focuses on growing the business again.

Corporate-level strategy the overall organizational strategy that addresses the question "What business or businesses are we in or should we be in?" (p. 123)

Diversification a strategy for reducing risk by buying a variety of items (stocks or, in the case of a corporation, types of businesses) so that the failure of one stock or one business does not doom the entire portfolio (p. 123)

Portfolio strategy a corporate-level strategy that minimizes risk by diversifying investment among various businesses or product lines (p. 124)

Acquisition the purchase of a company by another company (p. 124)

Unrelated diversification creating or acquiring companies in completely unrelated businesses (p. 124)

© Cengage

WWW.CENGAGE.COM

BCG matrix a portfolio strategy developed by the Boston Consulting Group that categorizes a corporation's businesses by growth rate and relative market share and helps managers decide how to invest corporate funds (p. 124)

Star a company with a large share of a fast-growing market (p. 124)

Question mark a company with a small share of a fast-growing market (p. 125)

Cash cow a company with a large share of a slow-growing market (p. 125)

Dog a company with a small share of a slow-growing market (p. 125)

Related diversification creating or acquiring companies that share similar products, manufacturing, marketing, technology, or cultures (p. 126)

Grand strategy a broad corporate-level strategic plan used to achieve strategic goals and guide the strategic alternatives that managers of individual businesses or subunits may use (p. 127)

Growth strategy a strategy that focuses on increasing profits, revenues, market

share, or the number of places in which the company does business (p. 127)

Stability strategy a strategy that focuses on improving the way in which the company sells the same products or services to the same customers (p. 128)

Retrenchment strategy a strategy that focuses on turning around very poor company performance by shrinking the size or scope of the business (p. 128)

Recovery the strategic actions taken after retrenchment to return to a growth strategy (p. 128)

6-4 **Describe the different kinds of industry-level strategies and how they affect competition.** The five industry forces determine an industry's overall attractiveness to corporate investors and its potential for long-term profitability. Together, a high level of these elements combine to increase competition and decrease profits. Industry-level strategies focus on how companies choose to compete in their industries. The three positioning strategies can help companies protect themselves from the negative effects of industry-wide competition. The four adaptive strategies help companies adapt to changes in the external environment. Defenders want to defend their current strategic positions. Prospectors look for new market opportunities to bring innovative new products to market. Analyzers minimize risk by following the proven successes of prospectors. Reactors do not follow a consistent adaptive strategy but instead react to changes in the external environment after they occur.

Industry-level strategy a corporate strategy that addresses the question, "How should we compete in this industry?" (p. 129)

Character of the rivalry a measure of the intensity of competitive behavior between companies in an industry (p. 129)

Threat of new entrants a measure of the degree to which barriers to entry make it easy or difficult for new companies to get started in an industry (p. 129)

Threat of substitute products or services a measure of the ease with which customers can find substitutes for an industry's products or services (p. 130)

Bargaining power of suppliers a measure of the influence that suppliers of parts, materials, and services to firms in an industry have on the prices of these inputs (p. 130)

Bargaining power of buyers a measure of the influence that customers have on a firm's prices (p. 130)

Cost leadership the positioning strategy of producing a product or service of acceptable quality at consistently lower production costs than competitors can, so that the firm can offer the product or service at the lowest price in the industry (p. 131)

Differentiation the positioning strategy of providing a product or service that is sufficiently different from competitors' offerings that customers are willing to pay a premium price for it (p. 131)

Focus strategy the positioning strategy of using cost leadership or differentiation to produce a specialized product or service for a limited, specially targeted group of customers in a particular geographic region or market segment (p. 131)

Defenders companies using an adaptive strategy aimed at defending strategic positions by seeking moderate, steady growth and by offering a limited range of high-quality products and services to a well-defined set of customers (p. 132)

Prospectors companies using an adaptive strategy that seeks fast growth by searching for new market opportunities, encouraging risk taking, and being the first to bring innovative new products to market (p. 132)

Analyzers companies using an adaptive strategy that seeks to minimize risk and maximize profits by following or imitating the proven successes of prospectors (p. 133)

Reactors companies that do not follow a consistent adaptive strategy but instead react to changes in the external environment after they occur (p. 133)

6-5 **Explain the components and kinds of firm-level strategies and the ways in which firms attack competitors or respond to competitive attacks.** Firm-level strategies are concerned with direct competition between firms. Market commonality and resource similarity determine whether firms are in direct competition and thus likely to attack each other and respond to each other's attacks. In general, the more markets in which there is product, service, or customer overlap and the greater the resource similarity between two firms, the more intense the direct competition between them will be.

Firm-level strategy a corporate strategy that addresses the question, "How should we compete against a particular firm?" (p. 133)

Direct competition the rivalry between two companies that offer similar products and services, acknowledge each other as rivals, and act and react to each other's strategic actions (p. 134)

Market commonality the degree to which two companies have overlapping products, services, or customers in multiple markets (p. 134)

Resource similarity the extent to which a competitor has similar amounts and kinds of resources (p. 134)

Attack a competitive move designed to reduce a rival's market share or profits (p. 135)

Response a competitive countermove, prompted by a rival's attack, to defend or improve a company's market share or profit (p. 136)

CHAPTER 7 LEARNING OUTCOMES / KEY TERMS

7-1 Explain why innovation matters to companies.

Technology cycles typically follow an S-curve pattern of innovation. Early in the cycle, technological progress is slow, and improvements in technological performance are small. As a technology matures, however, performance improves quickly. Finally, as the limits of a technology are reached, only small improvements occur. At this point, significant improvements in performance must come from new technologies. The best way to protect a competitive advantage is to create a stream of innovative ideas and products. Innovation streams begin with technological discontinuities that create significant breakthroughs in performance or function. Technological discontinuities are followed by discontinuous change, in which customers purchase new technologies, and companies compete to establish the new dominant design. Dominant designs emerge because of critical mass, because they solve a practical problem, or because of the negotiations of independent standards bodies. Because technological innovation both enhances and destroys competence, companies that bet on the wrong design often struggle, while companies that bet on the eventual dominant design usually prosper. When a dominant design emerges, companies focus on incremental change, lowering costs, and making small but steady improvements in the dominant design. This focus continues until the next technological discontinuity occurs.

Organizational innovation the successful implementation of creative ideas in organizations (p. 139)

Technology cycle a cycle that begins with the birth of a new technology and ends when that technology reaches its limits and is replaced by a newer, substantially better technolog (p. 140)

S-curve pattern of innovation a pattern of technological innovation characterized by slow initial progress, then rapid progress, and then slow progress again as a technology matures and reaches its limits (p. 140)

Innovation streams patterns of innovation over time that can create sustainable competitive advantage (p. 142)

Technological discontinuity the phase of an innovation stream in which a scientific advance or unique combination of existing technologies creates a significant breakthrough in performance or function (p. 142)

Discontinuous change the phase of a technology cycle characterized by technological substitution and design competition (p. 142)

Technological substitution the purchase of new technologies to replace older ones (p. 142)

Design competition competition between old and new technologies to establish a new technological standard or dominant design (p. 142)

Dominant design a new technological design or process that becomes the accepted market standard (p. 143)

Technological lockout the inability of a company to competitively sell its products because it relies on old technology or a nondominant design (p. 144)

Incremental change the phase of a technology cycle in which companies innovate by lowering costs and improving the functioning and performance of the dominant technological design (p. 145)

7-2 Outline the steps for the different methods that managers can use to effectively manage innovation in their organizations.

To successfully manage innovation streams, companies must manage the sources of innovation and learn to manage innovation during both discontinuous and incremental change. Because innovation begins with creativity, companies can manage the sources of innovation by supporting a work environment in which creative thoughts and ideas are welcomed, valued, and encouraged. Creative work environments provide challenging work; offer organizational, supervisory, and work group encouragement; allow significant freedom; and remove organizational impediments to creativity.

Discontinuous and incremental change require different strategies. Companies that succeed in periods of discontinuous change typically follow an experiential approach to innovation. The experiential approach assumes that intuition, flexible options, and hands-on experience can reduce uncertainty and accelerate learning and understanding. A compression approach to innovation works best during periods of incremental change. This approach assumes that innovation can be planned using a series of steps and that compressing the time it takes to complete those steps can speed up innovation.

Creative work environments workplace cultures in which workers perceive that new ideas are welcomed, valued, and encouraged (p. 146)

Flow a psychological state of effortlessness, in which you become completely absorbed in what you're doing, and time seems to pass quickly (p. 146)

Experiential approach to innovation an approach to innovation that assumes a highly uncertain environment and uses intuition, flexible options, and hands-on experience to reduce uncertainty and accelerate learning and understanding (p. 148)

Design iteration a cycle of repetition in which a company tests a prototype of a new product or service, improves on that design, and then builds and tests the improved prototype (p. 148)

Product prototype a full-scale, working model that is being tested for design, function, and reliability (p. 148)

Testing the systematic comparison of different product designs or design iterations (p. 148)

Milestones formal project review points used to assess progress and performance (p. 148)

Multifunctional teams work teams composed of people from different departments (p. 149)

Compression approach to innovation an approach to innovation that assumes that incremental innovation can be planned using a series of steps and that compressing those steps can speed innovation (p. 150)

Generational change change based on incremental improvements to a dominant technological design such that the improved technology is fully backward compatible with the older technology (p. 150)

7-3 Discuss why not changing can lead to organizational decline. The five-stage process of organizational decline begins when organizations don't recognize the need for change. In the blinded stage, managers fail to recognize the changes that threaten their organization's survival. In the inaction stage, management recognizes the need to change but doesn't act, hoping that the problems will correct themselves. In the faulty action stage, management focuses on cost cutting and efficiency rather than facing up to the fundamental changes needed to ensure survival. In the crisis stage, failure is likely unless fundamental reorganization occurs. Finally, in the dissolution stage, the company is dissolved through bankruptcy proceedings; by selling assets to pay creditors; or through the closing of stores, offices, and facilities. If companies recognize the need to change early enough, however, dissolution may be avoided.

Organizational decline a large decrease in organizational performance that occurs when companies don't anticipate, recognize, neutralize, or adapt to the internal or external pressures that threaten their survival (p. 151)

7-4 Discuss the different methods that managers can use to better manage change as it occurs. The basic change process involves unfreezing, change intervention, and refreezing. Resistance to change stems from self-interest, misunderstanding, and distrust as well as a general intolerance for change. Resistance can be managed through education and communication, participation, negotiation, top management support, and coercion. Knowing what not to do is as important as knowing what to do to achieve successful change. Managers should avoid these errors when leading change: not establishing a sense of urgency, not creating a guiding coalition, lacking a vision, undercommunicating the vision, not removing obstacles to the vision, not creating short-term wins, declaring victory too soon, and not anchoring changes in the corporation's culture. Finally, managers can use a number of change techniques. Results-driven change and the General Electric fastworks reduce resistance to change by getting change efforts off to a fast start. Organizational development is a collection of planned change interventions (large-system, small-group, person-focused), guided by a change agent, that are designed to improve an organization's long-term health and performance.

Change forces forces that produce differences in the form, quality, or condition of an organization over time (p. 153)

Resistance forces forces that support the existing conditions in organizations (p. 153)

Resistance to change opposition to change resulting from self-interest, misunderstanding and distrust, and a general intolerance for change (p. 153)

Unfreezing getting the people affected by change to believe that change is needed (p. 153)

Change intervention the process used to get workers and managers to change their behaviors and work practices (p. 153)

Refreezing supporting and reinforcing new changes so that they stick (p. 153)

Coercion the use of formal power and authority to force others to change (p. 154)

Results-driven change change created quickly by focusing on the measurement and improvement of results (p. 157)

Agile change using daily standups, or "huddles," to review the progress of multidisciplinary teams or "Scrums," who break problems into small, clearly defined parts that team members work on in sprints (p. 157)

General Electric fastworks quickly experimenting with new ideas to solve customer problems and learn from repeated tests and improvements (p. 157)

Organizational development a philosophy and collection of planned change interventions designed to improve an organization's long-term health and performance (p. 158)

Change agent the person formally in charge of guiding a change effort (p. 158)

Exhibit 7.6
Types of Organizational Development Interventions

Large-System Interventions	
Sociotechnical systems	An intervention designed to improve how well employees use and adjust to the work technology used in an organization.
Survey feedback	An intervention that uses surveys to collect information from the members of the system, reports the results of that survey to the members, and then uses those results to develop action plans for improvement.

Small-Group Interventions	
Team building	An intervention designed to increase the cohesion and cooperation of work group members.
Unit goal setting	An intervention designed to help a work group establish short- and long-term goals.

Person-Focused Interventions	
Counseling/ coaching	An intervention designed so that a formal helper or coach listens to managers or employees and advises them on how to deal with work or interpersonal problems.
Training	An intervention designed to provide individuals with the knowledge, skills, or attitudes they need to become more effective at their jobs.

Source: W. J. Rothwell, R. Sullivan, and G. M. McLean, *Practicing Organizational Development: A Guide for Consultants* (San Diego: Pfeiffer & Co., 1995).

8-1 **Discuss the impact of global business and the trade rules and agreements that govern it.** Today, there are more than 30,000 multinational corporations worldwide; the United States is the second-largest base for multinationals. Global business affects the United States in two ways: through direct foreign investment in the United States by foreign companies and through US companies' investment in businesses in other countries. US direct foreign investment throughout the world amounts to more than $4.9 trillion per year, whereas direct foreign investment by foreign companies in the United States amounts to more than $2.9 trillion per year. Historically, tariffs and nontariff trade barriers such as quotas, voluntary export restraints, government import standards, government subsidies, and customs classifications have made buying foreign goods much harder or more expensive than buying domestically produced products. In recent years, however, worldwide trade agreements such as GATT and the WTO, along with regional trading agreements such as the Maastricht Treaty of Europe, NAFTA, CAFTA-DR, UNASUR, ASEAN, APEC, and TFTA have substantially reduced tariffs and nontariff barriers to international trade. Companies have responded by investing in growing markets in Asia, Eastern Europe, and Latin America. Consumers have responded by purchasing products based on value rather than geography.

Global business the buying and selling of goods and services by people from different countries (p. 160)

Multinational corporation a corporation that owns businesses in two or more countries (p. 161)

Direct foreign investment a method of investment in which a company builds a new business or buys an existing business in a foreign country (p. 162)

Trade barriers government-imposed regulations that increase the cost and restrict the number of imported goods (p. 163)

Protectionism a government's use of trade barriers to shield domestic companies and their workers from foreign competition (p. 163)

Tariff a direct tax on imported goods (p. 163)

Nontariff barriers nontax methods of increasing the cost or reducing the volume of imported goods (p. 163)

Quota a limit on the number or volume of imported products (p. 163)

Voluntary export restraints voluntarily imposed limits on the number or volume of products exported to a particular country (p. 163)

Government import standard a standard ostensibly established to protect the health and safety of citizens but, in reality, is often used to restrict imports (p. 163)

Subsidies government loans, grants, and tax deferments given to domestic companies to protect them from foreign competition (p. 164)

Customs classification a classification assigned to imported products by government officials that affects the size of the tariff and the imposition of import quotas (p. 164)

General Agreement on Tariffs and Trade (GATT) a worldwide trade agreement that reduced and eliminated tariffs, limited government subsidies, and established protections for intellectual property (p. 164)

World Trade Organization (WTO) the successor to GATT; the only international organization dealing with the global rules of trade between nations; its main function is to ensure that trade flows as smoothly, predictably, and freely as possible (p. 164)

Regional trading zones areas in which tariff and nontariff barriers on trade between countries are reduced or eliminated (p. 165)

Maastricht Treaty of Europe a regional trade agreement among most European countries (p. 166)

United States–Mexico–Canada Agreement (USMCA) a regional trade agreement among the United States, Canada, and Mexico (p. 167)

Dominican Republic–Central America Free Trade Agreement (CAFTA-DR) a regional trade agreement among Costa Rica, the Dominican Republic, El Salvador, Guatemala, Honduras, Nicaragua, and the United States (p. 167)

Southern Common Market (MERCOSUR) a regional trade agreement among the primary countries of Argentina, Brazil, Paraguay, and Uruguay, with associated countries, Bolivia, Chile, Colombia, Ecuador, Guyana, Peru, and Surinam (p. 167)

Association of Southeast Asian Nations (ASEAN) a regional trade agreement among Brunei Darussalam, Cambodia, Indonesia, Lao PDR, Malaysia, Myanmar, the Philippines, Singapore, Thailand, and Vietnam (p. 168)

Asia-Pacific Economic Cooperation (APEC) a regional trade agreement among Australia, Canada, Chile, the People's Republic of China, Hong Kong, Japan, Mexico, New Zealand, Papua New Guinea, Peru, Russia, South Korea, Taiwan, the United States, and all the members of ASEAN except Cambodia, Lao PDR, and Myanmar (p. 168)

Tripartite Free Trade Agreement (TFTA) a regional trade agreement among 27 African countries (p. 168)

8-2 **Explain why companies choose to standardize or adapt their business procedures.** Global business requires a balance between global consistency and local adaptation. Global consistency means using the same rules, guidelines, policies, and procedures in each location. Managers at company headquarters like global consistency because it simplifies decisions. Local adaptation means adapting standard procedures to differences in markets. Local managers prefer a policy of local adaptation because it gives them more control. Not all businesses need the same combination of global consistency and local adaptation. Some thrive by emphasizing global consistency and ignoring local adaptation. Others succeed by ignoring global consistency and emphasizing local adaptation.

Global consistency when a multinational company has offices, manufacturing plants, and distribution facilities in different countries and runs them all using the same rules, guidelines, policies, and procedures (p. 169)

Local adaptation modifying rules, guidelines, policies, and procedures to adapt to differences in foreign customers, governments, and regulatory agencies (p. 170)

Explain the different ways that companies can organize to do business globally. The phase model of globalization says that, as companies move from a domestic to a global orientation, they use these organizational forms in sequence: exporting, cooperative contracts (licensing and franchising), strategic alliances, and wholly owned affiliates. Yet, not all companies follow the phase model. For example, global new ventures are global from their inception.

Exporting selling domestically produced products to customers in foreign countries (p. 171)

Cooperative contract an agreement in which a foreign business owner pays a company a fee for the right to conduct that business in his or her country (p. 171)

Licensing an agreement in which a domestic company, the licensor, receives royalty payments for allowing another company, the licensee, to produce the licensor's product, sell its service, or use its brand name in a specified foreign market (p. 171)

Franchise a collection of networked firms in which the manufacturer or marketer of a product or service, the franchisor, licenses the entire business to another person or organization, the franchisee (p. 172)

Strategic alliance an agreement in which companies combine key resources, costs, risks, technology, and people (p. 173)

Joint venture a strategic alliance in which two existing companies collaborate to form a third, independent company or engage in a clearly defined business activity (p. 173)

Wholly owned affiliates foreign offices, facilities, and manufacturing plants that are 100 percent owned by the parent company (p. 174)

Global new ventures new companies that are founded with an active global strategy and have sales, employees, and financing in different countries (p. 174)

Outline the steps for finding a favorable business climate. The first step in deciding where to take your company global is finding an attractive business climate. Be sure to look for a growing market where consumers have strong purchasing power, and foreign competitors are weak. When locating an office or manufacturing facility, consider both qualitative and quantitative factors. In assessing political risk, be sure to examine both political uncertainty and policy uncertainty. If the location you choose has considerable political risk, you can avoid it, try to control the risk, or use a cooperation strategy.

Purchasing power the relative cost of a standard set of goods and services in different countries (p. 175)

Political uncertainty the risk of major changes in political regimes that can result from war, revolution, death of political leaders, social unrest, or other influential events (p. 177)

Policy uncertainty the risk associated with changes in laws and government policies that directly affect the way foreign companies conduct business (p. 177)

Discuss the importance of identifying and adapting to cultural differences. National culture is the set of shared values and beliefs that affects the perceptions, decisions, and behavior of the people from a particular country. The first step in dealing with culture is to recognize meaningful differences such as power distance, individualism, masculinity, uncertainty avoidance, and short-term/long-term orientation. Cultural differences should be interpreted carefully because they are based on generalizations rather than specific individuals. Adapting managerial practices to cultural differences is difficult because policies and practices can be perceived differently in different cultures.

National culture the set of shared values and beliefs that affects the perceptions, decisions, and behavior of the people from a particular country (p. 180)

Explain how to successfully prepare workers for international assignments. Many expatriates return prematurely from international assignments because of poor performance. This is much less likely to happen if employees receive language and cross-cultural training, such as documentary training, cultural simulations, or field experiences, before going on assignment. Adjustment of expatriates' spouses and families, which is the most important determinant of success in international assignments, can be improved through adaptability screening and language and cross-cultural training.

Expatriate someone who lives and works outside his or her native country (p. 182)

9-1 Describe the departmentalization approaches to organizational structure. There are five traditional departmental structures: functional, product, customer, geographic, and matrix. Functional departmentalization is based on the different business functions or types of expertise used to run a business. Product departmentalization is organized according to the different products or services a company sells. Customer departmentalization focuses its divisions on the different kinds of customers a company has. Geographic departmentalization is based on different geographic areas or markets in which the company does business. Matrix departmentalization is a hybrid form that combines two or more forms of departmentalization, the most common being the product and functional forms. There is no single best departmental structure. Each structure has advantages and disadvantages.

Organizational structure the vertical and horizontal configuration of departments, authority, and jobs within a company (p. 186)

Organizational process the collection of activities that transforms inputs into outputs that customers value (p. 187)

Departmentalization subdividing work and workers into separate organizational units responsible for completing particular tasks (p. 188)

Functional departmentalization organizing work and workers into separate units responsible for particular business functions or areas of expertise (p. 189)

Product departmentalization organizing work and workers into separate units responsible for producing particular products or services (p. 189)

Customer departmentalization organizing work and workers into separate units responsible for particular kinds of customers (p. 191)

Geographic departmentalization organizing work and workers into separate units responsible for doing business in particular geographic areas (p. 192)

Matrix departmentalization a hybrid organizational structure in which two or more forms of departmentalization, most often product and functional, are used together (p. 193)

Simple matrix a form of matrix departmentalization in which managers in different parts of the matrix negotiate conflicts and resources (p. 195)

Complex matrix a form of matrix departmentalization in which managers in different parts of the matrix report to matrix managers, who help them sort out conflicts and problems (p. 195)

9-2 Explain organizational authority. Organizational authority is determined by the chain of command, line versus staff authority, delegation, and the degree of centralization in a company. The chain of command vertically connects every job in the company to higher levels of management and makes clear who reports to whom. Managers have line authority to command employees below them in the chain of command but have only staff, or advisory, authority over employees not below them in the chain of command. Managers delegate authority by transferring to subordinates the authority and responsibility needed to do a task; in exchange, subordinates become accountable for task completion. In centralized companies, most authority to make decisions lies with managers in the upper levels of the company. In decentralized companies, much of the authority is delegated to the workers closest to the problems, who can then make the decisions necessary for solving the problems themselves.

Authority the right to give commands, take action, and make decisions to achieve organizational objectives (p. 195)

Chain of command the vertical line of authority that clarifies who reports to whom throughout the organization (p. 196)

Unity of command a management principle that workers should report to just one boss (p. 196)

Line authority the right to command immediate subordinates in the chain of command (p. 196)

Staff authority the right to advise, but not command, others who are not subordinates in the chain of command (p. 196)

Line function an activity that contributes directly to creating or selling the company's products (p. 196)

Staff function an activity that does not contribute directly to creating or selling the company's products but instead supports line activities (p. 196)

Delegation of authority the assignment of direct authority and responsibility to a subordinate to complete tasks for which the manager is normally responsible (p. 197)

Centralization of authority the location of most authority at the upper levels of the organization (p. 198)

Decentralization the location of a significant amount of authority in the lower levels of the organization (p. 198)

Standardization solving problems by consistently applying the same rules, procedures, and processes (p. 198)

9-3 Outline the steps for using the different methods for job design. Companies use specialized jobs because they are economical, easy to learn, and don't require highly paid workers. However, specialized jobs aren't motivating or particularly satisfying for employees. Companies have used job rotation, job enlargement, job enrichment, and the job characteristics model to make specialized jobs more interesting and motivating. The goal of the job characteristics model is to make jobs intrinsically motivating. For this to happen, jobs must be strong on five core job characteristics (skill variety, task identity, task significance, autonomy, and feedback), and workers must experience three critical psychological states (knowledge of results, responsibility for work outcomes, and meaningful work). If jobs aren't internally motivating, they can be redesigned by combining tasks, forming natural work units, establishing client relationships, using vertical loading, and opening feedback channels.

Job design the number, kind, and variety of tasks that individual workers perform in doing their jobs (p. 199)

Job specialization job composed of a small part of a larger task or process (p. 199)

Job rotation periodically moving workers from one specialized job to another to give them more variety and the opportunity to use different skills (p. 199)

Job enlargement increasing the number of different tasks that a worker performs within one particular job (p. 199)

Job enrichment increasing the number of tasks in a particular job and giving workers the authority and control to make meaningful decisions about their work (p. 200)

Job characteristics model (JCM) an approach to job redesign that seeks to formulate jobs in ways that motivate workers and lead to positive work outcomes (p. 200)

Internal motivation motivation that comes from the job itself rather than from outside rewards (p. 200)

Skill variety the number of different activities performed in a job (p. 201)

Task identity the degree to which a job, from beginning to end, requires the completion of a whole and identifiable piece of work (p. 201)

Task significance the degree to which a job is perceived to have a substantial impact on others inside or outside the organization (p. 201)

Autonomy the degree to which a job gives workers the discretion, freedom, and independence to decide how and when to accomplish the job (p. 201)

Feedback the amount of information the job provides to workers about their work performance (p. 201)

9-4 **Explain the methods that companies are using to redesign internal organizational processes (i.e., intraorganizational processes).** Today, companies are using reengineering and empowerment to change their intraorganizational processes. Reengineering changes an organization's orientation from vertical to horizontal and changes its work processes by decreasing sequential and pooled interdependence and by increasing reciprocal interdependence. Reengineering promises dramatic increases in productivity and customer satisfaction, but it has been criticized as simply an excuse to cut costs and lay off workers. Empowering workers means taking decision-making authority and responsibility from managers and giving it to workers. Empowered workers develop feelings of competence and self-determination and believe that their work has meaning and impact.

Mechanistic organization an organization characterized by specialized jobs and responsibilities; precisely defined, unchanging roles; and a rigid chain of command based on centralized authority and vertical communication (p. 202)

Organic organization an organization characterized by broadly defined jobs and responsibilities; loosely defined, frequently changing roles; and decentralized authority and horizontal communication based on task knowledge (p. 202)

Intraorganizational process the collection of activities that take place within an organization to transform inputs into outputs that customers value (p. 202)

Reengineering fundamental rethinking and radical redesign of business processes to achieve dramatic improvements in critical measures of performance, such as cost, quality, service, and speed (p. 202)

Task interdependence the extent to which collective action is required to complete an entire piece of work (p. 204)

Pooled interdependence work completed by having each job or department independently contribute to the whole (p. 204)

Sequential interdependence work completed in succession, with one group's or job's outputs becoming the inputs for the next group or job (p. 204)

Reciprocal interdependence work completed by different jobs or groups working together in a back-and-forth manner (p. 204)

Empowering workers permanently passing decision-making authority and responsibility from managers to workers by giving them the information and resources they need to make and carry out good decisions (p. 205)

Empowerment feeling of intrinsic motivation in which workers perceive their work to have impact and meaning and perceive themselves to be competent and capable of self-determination (p. 206)

9-5 **Describe the methods that companies are using to redesign external organizational processes (i.e., interorganizational processes).** Organizations are using modular and virtual organizations to change interorganizational processes. Because modular organizations outsource all noncore activities to other businesses, they are less expensive to run than traditional companies. However, modular organizations require extremely close relationships with suppliers, may result in a loss of control, and could create new competitors if the wrong business activities are outsourced. Virtual organizations participate in a network in which they share skills, costs, capabilities, markets, and customers. Virtual organizations can reduce costs, respond quickly, and, if they can successfully coordinate their efforts, produce outstanding products and services.

Interorganizational process a collection of activities that take place among companies to transform inputs into outputs that customers value (p. 206)

Modular organization an organization that outsources noncore business activities to outside companies, suppliers, specialists, or consultants (p. 206)

Virtual organization an organization that is part of a network in which many companies share skills, costs, capabilities, markets, and customers to collectively solve customer problems or provide specific products or services (p. 207)

CHAPTER 10 LEARNING OUTCOMES / KEY TERMS

10-1

Explain the good and bad of using teams. In many industries, teams are growing in importance because they help organizations respond to specific problems and challenges. Teams have been shown to increase customer satisfaction (specific customer teams), product and service quality (direct responsibility), and employee job satisfaction (cross-training, unique opportunities, and leadership responsibilities). Although teams can produce significant improvements in these areas, using teams does not guarantee these positive outcomes. Teams and teamwork have the disadvantages of initially high turnover and social loafing (especially in large groups). Teams also share many of the advantages (multiple perspectives, generation of more alternatives, and more commitment) and disadvantages (groupthink, time, poorly run meetings, domination by a few team members, and weak

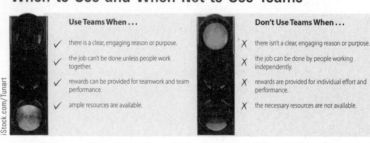

Exhibit 10.1

When to Use and When Not to Use Teams

Use Teams When . . .

✓ there is a clear, engaging reason or purpose.

✓ the job can't be done unless people work together.

✓ rewards can be provided for teamwork and team performance.

✓ ample resources are available.

Don't Use Teams When . . .

✗ there isn't a clear, engaging reason or purpose.

✗ the job can be done by people working independently.

✗ rewards are provided for individual effort and performance.

✗ the necessary resources are not available.

iStock.com/Tunart

Source: R. Wageman, "Critical Success Factors for Creating Superb Self-Managing Teams," *Organizational Dynamics* 26, no. 1 (1997): 49–61.

accountability) of group decision-making. Teams should be used for a clear purpose, when the work requires that people work together, when rewards can be provided for both teamwork and team performance, and when ample resources can be provided.

Work team a small number of people with complementary skills who hold themselves mutually accountable for pursuing a common purpose, achieving performance goals, and improving interdependent work processes (p. 210)

Cross-training training team members to do all or most of the jobs performed by the other team members (p. 212)

Social loafing behavior in which team members withhold their efforts and fail to perform their share of the work (p. 213)

10-2

Summarize the different kinds of teams. Companies use different kinds of teams to make themselves more competitive. Autonomy is the key dimension that makes teams different. Traditional work groups (which execute tasks) and employee involvement groups (which make suggestions) have the lowest levels of autonomy. Semi-autonomous work groups (which control major direct tasks) have more autonomy, while self-managing teams (which control all direct tasks) and self-designing teams (which control membership and how tasks are done) have the highest levels of autonomy. Cross-functional, virtual, and project teams are common but are not easily categorized in terms of autonomy. Cross-functional teams combine employees

from different functional areas to help teams attack problems from multiple perspectives and generate more ideas and solutions. Virtual teams use telecommunications and information technologies to bring coworkers together, regardless of physical location or time zone. Virtual teams reduce travel and work time, but communication may suffer because team members don't work face-to-face. Finally, project teams are used for specific, onetime projects or tasks that must be completed within a limited time. Project teams reduce communication barriers and promote flexibility; teams and team members are reassigned to their departments or to new projects as their current projects are completed.

Traditional work group a group composed of two or more people who work together to achieve a shared goal (p. 215)

Employee involvement team team that provides advice or makes suggestions to management concerning specific issues (p. 215)

Semi-autonomous work group a group that has the authority to make decisions and solve problems related to the major tasks of producing a product or service (p. 217)

Self-managing team a team that manages and controls all of the major tasks of producing a product or service (p. 217)

Self-designing team a team that has the characteristics of self-managing teams but also controls team design, work tasks, and team membership (p. 218)

Cross-functional team a team composed of employees from different functional areas of the organization (p. 218)

Virtual team a team composed of geographically and/or organizationally dispersed coworkers who use telecommunication and information technologies to accomplish an organizational task (p. 218)

Project team a team created to complete specific, onetime projects or tasks within a limited time (p. 219)

10-3 **Identify the general characteristics of work teams.**
The most important characteristics of work teams are team norms, cohesiveness, size, conflict, and development. Norms let team members know what is expected of them and can influence team behavior in positive and negative ways. Positive team norms are associated with organizational commitment, trust, and job satisfaction. Team cohesiveness helps teams retain members, promotes cooperative behavior, increases motivation, and facilitates team performance. Attending team meetings and activities, creating opportunities to work together, and engaging in nonwork activities can increase cohesiveness. Team size has a curvilinear relationship with team performance: teams that are very small or very large do not perform as well as moderate-sized teams of six to nine members. Teams of this size are cohesive and small enough for team members to get to know each other and contribute in a meaningful way but are large enough to take advantage of team members' diverse skills, knowledge, and perspectives. Conflict and disagreement are inevitable in most teams. The key to dealing with team conflict is to maximize cognitive conflict, which focuses on issue-related differences, and minimize affective conflict, the emotional reactions that occur when disagreements become personal rather than professional. As teams develop and grow, they pass through four stages of development: forming, storming, norming, and performing. If a team is not managed well, its performance may decline after a period of time as the team regresses through the stages of de-norming, de-storming, and de-forming.

Norms informally agreed-on standards that regulate team behavior (p. 220)

Cohesiveness the extent to which team members are attracted to a team and motivated to remain in it (p. 221)

Forming the first stage of team development, in which team members meet each other, form initial impressions, and begin to establish team norms (p. 224)

Storming the second stage of development, characterized by conflict and disagreement, in which team members disagree over what the team should do and how it should do it (p. 224)

Norming the third stage of team development, in which team members begin to settle into their roles, group cohesion grows, and positive team norms develop (p. 225)

Performing the fourth and final stage of team development, in which performance improves because the team has matured into an effective, fully functioning team (p. 225)

De-norming a reversal of the norming stage, in which team performance begins to decline as the size, scope, goal, or members of the team change (p. 225)

De-storming a reversal of the storming phase, in which the team's comfort level decreases, team cohesion weakens, and angry emotions and conflict may flare (p. 225)

De-forming a reversal of the forming stage, in which team members position themselves to control pieces of the team, avoid each other, and isolate themselves from team leaders (p. 225)

10-4 **Outline the steps for enhancing work team effectiveness.**
Companies can make teams more effective by setting team goals and managing how team members are selected, trained, and compensated. Team goals provide a clear focus and purpose, reduce the incidence of social loafing, and lead to higher team performance 93 percent of the time. Extremely difficult stretch goals can be used to motivate teams as long as teams have autonomy, control over resources, structural accommodation, and bureaucratic immunity. Not everyone is suited for teamwork. When selecting team members, companies should select people who have a preference for teamwork (i.e., are more collectivists than individualists) and should consider team level (average ability of a team) and team diversity (different abilities of a team). Organizations that use teams successfully provide thousands of hours of training to make sure that teams work. The most common types of team training are for interpersonal skills, decision-making and problem-solving skills, conflict resolution, technical training to help team members learn multiple jobs (i.e., cross-training), and training for team leaders. Employees can be compensated for team participation and accomplishments in three ways: skill-based pay, gainsharing, and nonfinancial rewards.

Structural accommodation the ability to change organizational structures, policies, and practices in order to meet stretch goals (p. 226)

Bureaucratic immunity the ability to make changes without first getting approval from managers or other parts of an organization (p. 226)

Individualism-collectivism the degree to which a person believes that people should be self-sufficient and that loyalty to one's self is more important than loyalty to team or company (p. 227)

Team level the average level of ability, experience, personality, or any other factor on a team (p. 227)

Team diversity the variances or differences in ability, experience, personality, or any other factor on a team (p. 228)

Interpersonal skills skills, such as listening, communicating, questioning, and providing feedback, that enable people to have effective working relationships with others (p. 229)

Skill-based pay compensation system that pays employees for learning additional skills or knowledge (p. 230)

Gainsharing a compensation system in which companies share the financial value of performance gains, such as increased productivity, cost savings, or quality, with their workers (p. 230)

CHAPTER 11 LEARNING OUTCOMES / KEY TERMS

11-1 **Explain how different employment laws affect human resource practice.** Human resource management is subject to numerous major federal employment laws and subject to review by several federal agencies. In general, these laws indicate that sex, age, religion, color, national origin, race, disability, and genetic history may not be considered in employment decisions unless these factors reasonably

qualify as BFOQs. Two important criteria, disparate treatment (intentional discrimination) and adverse impact (unintentional discrimination), are used to decide whether companies have wrongly discriminated against someone. The two kinds of sexual harassment are quid pro quo sexual harassment and hostile work environment.

Human resource management (HRM) the process of finding, developing, and keeping the right people to form a qualified workforce (p. 232)

Bona fide occupational qualification (BFOQ) an exception in employment law that permits sex, age, religion, and the like to be used when making employment decisions, but only if they are "reasonably necessary to the normal operation of that particular business." BFOQs are strictly monitored by the Equal Employment Opportunity Commission (p. 234)

Disparate treatment intentional discrimination that occurs when people are purposely not given the same hiring, promotion, or membership opportunities because of their race, color, sex, sexual orientation,

gender identity, age, ethnic group, national origin, or religious beliefs (p. 235)

Adverse impact unintentional discrimination that occurs when members of a particular race, sex, sexual orientation, gender identity, or ethnic group are unintentionally harmed or disadvantaged because they are hired, promoted, or trained (or any other employment decision) at substantially lower rates than others (p. 236)

Four-fifths (or 80 percent) rule a rule of thumb used by the courts and the EEOC to determine whether there is evidence of adverse impact; a violation of this rule occurs when the impact ratio (calculated by dividing the decision ratio for a protected group by the decision ratio for a nonprotected group) is less than 80 percent, or four-fifths (p. 236)

Sexual harassment a form of discrimination in which unwelcome sexual advances, requests for sexual favors, or other verbal or physical conduct of a sexual nature occurs while performing one's job (p. 236)

Quid pro quo sexual harassment a form of sexual harassment in which employment outcomes, such as hiring, promotion, or simply keeping one's job, depend on whether an individual submits to sexual harassment (p. 237)

Hostile work environment a form of sexual harassment in which unwelcome and demeaning sexually related behavior creates an intimidating and offensive work environment (p. 237)

11-2 **Outline how companies should use recruiting to find qualified job applicants.** Recruiting is the process of finding qualified job applicants. The first step in recruiting is to conduct a job analysis, which is used to write a job description of basic tasks, duties, and responsibilities

and to write job specifications indicating the knowledge, skills, and abilities needed to perform the job. Although internal recruiting involves finding qualified job applicants from inside the company, external recruiting involves finding qualified job applicants from outside the company.

Recruiting the process of developing a pool of qualified job applicants (p. 238)

Job analysis a purposeful, systematic process for collecting information on the important work-related aspects of a job (p. 238)

Job description a written description of the basic tasks, duties, and responsibilities required of an employee holding a particular job (p. 238)

Job specifications a written summary of the qualifications needed to successfully perform a particular job (p. 238)

Internal recruiting the process of developing a pool of qualified job applicants from people who already work in the company (p. 239)

External recruiting the process of developing a pool of qualified job applicants from outside the company (p. 241)

11-3 **Describe the selection techniques and procedures that companies use when deciding which applicants should receive job offers.** Selection is the process of gathering information about job applicants to decide who should be offered a job. Accurate selection procedures are valid, are legally defendable, and improve organizational performance. Application forms and résumés are the most common selection

devices. Managers should check references and conduct background checks even though previous employers are often reluctant to provide such information for fear of being sued for defamation. Unfortunately, without this information, other employers are at risk of negligent hiring lawsuits. Selection tests generally do the best job of predicting applicants' future job performance. The three kinds of job interviews are unstructured, structured, and semistructured.

Selection the process of gathering information about job applicants to decide who should be offered a job (p. 242)

Validation the process of determining how well a selection test or procedure predicts future job performance; the better or more accurate the prediction of future job performance, the more valid a test is said to be (p. 242)

Human resource information system (HRIS) a computerized system for gathering, analyzing, storing, and disseminating information related to the HRM process (p. 243)

Employment references sources such as previous employers or coworkers who can provide job-related

information about job candidates (p. 244)

Background checks procedures used to verify the truthfulness and accuracy of information that applicants provide about themselves and to uncover negative, job-related background information not provided by applicants (p. 244)

Specific ability tests (aptitude tests) tests that measure the extent to which an applicant possesses the particular kind of ability needed to do a job well (p. 245)

Cognitive ability tests tests that measure the extent to which applicants have abilities in perceptual speed, verbal comprehension, numerical aptitude, general reasoning, and spatial aptitude (p. 245)

Biographical data (biodata) extensive surveys that ask applicants questions about their personal backgrounds and life experiences (p. 246)

Personality test an assessment that measures the extent to which an applicant possesses different kinds of job-related personality dimensions (p. 246)

Work sample tests tests that require applicants to perform tasks that are actually done on the job (p. 247)

Assessment centers a series of managerial simulations, graded by trained observers, that are used to determine applicants' capability for managerial work (p. 247)

Interview a selection tool in which company representatives ask job applicants job-related questions to determine whether they are qualified for the job (p. 248)

Unstructured interviews interviews in which interviewers are free to ask the applicants anything they want (p. 248)

Structured interviews interviews in which all applicants are asked the same set of standardized questions, usually including situational, behavioral, background, and job-knowledge questions (p. 248)

11-4 Explain how to align various training needs with the appropriate training methods. Training is used to give employees the job-specific skills, experience, and knowledge they need to do their jobs or improve their job performance. To make sure training dollars are well spent, companies need to determine specific training needs, select appropriate training methods, and then evaluate the training.

Training developing the skills, experience, and knowledge employees need to perform their jobs or improve their performance (p. 250)

Needs assessment the process of identifying and prioritizing the learning needs of employees (p. 250)

11-5 Outline the steps for using performance appraisals to give meaningful performance feedback. The keys to successful performance appraisals are accurately measuring job performance and effectively sharing performance feedback with employees. Organizations should develop good performance appraisal scales; train raters how to accurately evaluate performance; and impress upon managers the value of providing feedback in a clear, consistent, and fair manner, as well as setting goals and monitoring progress toward those goals.

Performance appraisal the process of assessing how well employees are doing their jobs (p. 253)

Objective performance measures measures of job performance that are easily and directly counted or quantified (p. 254)

Subjective performance measures measures of job performance that require someone to judge or assess a worker's performance (p. 254)

Behavior observation scales (BOSs) rating scales that indicate the frequency with which workers perform specific behaviors that are representative of the job dimensions critical to successful job performance (p. 254)

Rater training training performance appraisal raters in how to avoid rating errors and increase rating accuracy (p. 254)

360-degree feedback a performance appraisal process in which feedback is obtained from the boss, subordinates, peers, and coworkers, and the employees themselves (p. 256)

11-6 Describe basic compensation strategies, and discuss the four kinds of employee separations. Compensation includes both the financial and the nonfinancial rewards that organizations provide employees in exchange for their work. There are three basic kinds of compensation decisions: pay level, pay variability, and pay structure. Employee separation is the loss of an employee, which can occur voluntarily or involuntarily. Companies use downsizing and early retirement incentive programs (ERIPs) to reduce the number of employees in the organization and lower costs. However, companies generally try to keep the rate of employee turnover low to reduce costs associated with finding and developing new employees. Functional turnover, on the other hand, can be good for organizations.

Compensation the financial and nonfinancial rewards that organizations give employees in exchange for their work (p. 257)

Employee separation the voluntary or involuntary loss of an employee (p. 257)

Job evaluation a process that determines the worth of each job in a company by evaluating the market value of the KSAs needed to perform it (p. 258)

Piecework a compensation system in which employees are paid a set rate for each item they produce (p. 258)

Commission a compensation system in which employees earn a percentage of each sale they make (p. 258)

Profit sharing a compensation system in which a company pays a percentage of its profits to employees in addition to their regular compensation (p. 258)

Employee stock ownership plan (ESOP) a compensation system that awards employees shares of company stock in addition to their regular compensation (p. 258)

Stock options a compensation system that gives employees the right to purchase shares of stock at a set price, even if the value of the stock increases above that price (p. 259)

Wrongful discharge a legal doctrine that requires employers to have a job-related reason to terminate employees (p. 261)

Downsizing the planned elimination of jobs in a company (p. 261)

Outplacement services employment-counseling services offered to employees who are losing their jobs because of downsizing (p. 262)

Early retirement incentive programs (ERIPs) programs that offer financial benefits to employees to encourage them to retire early (p. 262)

Phased retirement employees transition to retirement by working reduced hours over a period of time before completely retiring (p. 263)

Employee turnover loss of employees who voluntarily choose to leave the company (p. 263)

Functional turnover loss of poor-performing employees who voluntarily choose to leave a company (p. 263)

Dysfunctional turnover loss of high-performing employees who voluntarily choose to leave a company (p. 263)

12-1 Describe diversity and explain why it matters. Diversity exists in organizations when there are demographic, cultural, and personal differences among the employees and the customers. A common misconception is that workplace diversity and affirmative action are the same. However, affirmative action is more narrowly focused on demographics; is required by law; and is used to punish companies that discriminate on the basis of race/ethnicity, religion, sex, or national origin. By contrast, diversity is broader in focus (going beyond demographics); voluntary; more positive in that it encourages companies to value all kinds of differences; and, at this time, substantially less controversial than affirmative action. Thus, affirmative action and diversity differ in purpose, practice, and the reactions they produce. Diversity also makes good business sense in terms of reducing costs (decreasing turnover and absenteeism and avoiding lawsuits), attracting and retaining talent, and driving business growth (improving marketplace understanding and promoting higher-quality problem solving).

Diversity a variety of demographic, cultural, and personal differences among an organization's employees and customers (p. 265)

Affirmative action purposeful steps taken by an organization to create employment opportunities for minorities and women (p. 266)

12-2 Summarize the special challenges that the dimensions of surface-level diversity pose for managers. Age, sex, race/ethnicity, and physical and mental disabilities are dimensions of surface-level diversity. Because those dimensions are (usually) easily observed, managers and workers tend to rely on them to form initial impressions and stereotypes. Sometimes this can lead to age, sex, racial/ethnic, or disability discrimination (i.e., treating people differently) in the workplace. In general, older workers, women, people of color or different national origins, and people with disabilities may be less likely to be hired or promoted than are white males. This disparity is often due to incorrect beliefs or stereotypes such as "job performance declines with age," or "women aren't willing to travel on business," or "workers with disabilities aren't as competent as able workers." To reduce discrimination, companies can determine the hiring and promotion rates for different groups, train managers to make hiring and promotion decisions on the basis of specific criteria, and make sure that everyone has equal access to training, mentors, reasonable work accommodations, and assistive technology. Finally, companies need to designate a go-to person to whom employees can talk if they believe they have suffered discrimination.

Surface-level diversity differences such as age, sex, race/ethnicity, and physical disabilities that are observable, typically unchangeable, and easy to measure (p. 269)

Deep-level diversity differences such as personality and attitudes that are communicated through verbal and nonverbal behaviors and are learned only through extended interaction with others (p. 269)

Social integration the degree to which group members are psychologically attracted to working with each other to accomplish a common objective (p. 270)

Age discrimination treating people differently (for example in hiring and firing, promotion, and compensation decisions) because of their age (p. 270)

Sex discrimination treating people differently because of their sex (p. 271)

Glass ceiling the invisible barrier that prevents women and minorities from advancing to the top jobs in organizations (p. 271)

Sexual orientation an individual's attraction to people of the same and/or different sex (p. 274)

Sexual orientation discrimination treated people differently because of their sexual orientation (p. 274)

transgender person someone whose personal and gender identity differ from the person's birth sex—for example, someone born female who identifies as male (p. 274)

Gender identity discrimination treating people differently because of their gender identity (p. 274)

Racial and ethnic discrimination treating people differently because of their race or ethnicity (p. 276)

Disability a mental or physical impairment that substantially limits one or more major life activities (p. 277)

Disability discrimination treating people differently because of their disabilities (p. 277)

12-3 Explain how the dimensions of deep-level diversity affect individual behavior and interactions in the workplace. Deep-level diversity matters because it can reduce prejudice, discrimination, and conflict while increasing social integration. It consists of dispositional and personality differences that can be recognized only through extended interaction with others. Research conducted in different cultures, settings, and languages indicates that there are five basic dimensions of personality: extraversion, emotional stability, agreeableness, conscientiousness, and openness to experience. Of these, conscientiousness is perhaps the most important because conscientious workers tend to be better performers on virtually any job. Extraversion is also related to performance in jobs that require significant interaction with others.

Disposition the tendency to respond to situations and events in a predetermined manner (p. 279)

Personality the relatively stable set of behaviors, attitudes, and emotions displayed over time that makes people different from each other (p. 279)

Extraversion the degree to which someone is active, assertive, gregarious, sociable, talkative, and energized by others (p. 279)

Emotional stability the degree to which someone is not angry, depressed, anxious, emotional, insecure, and excitable (p. 279)

Agreeableness the degree to which someone is cooperative, polite, flexible, forgiving, good-natured, tolerant, and trusting (p. 279)

Conscientiousness the degree to which someone is organized, hardworking, responsible, persevering, thorough, and achievement oriented (p. 280)

Openness to experience the degree to which someone is curious, broad-minded, and open to new ideas, things, and experiences; is spontaneous; and has a high tolerance for ambiguity (p. 280)

12-4 **Explain the basic principles and practices that can be used to manage diversity.** The three paradigms for managing diversity are the discrimination and fairness paradigm (equal opportunity, fair treatment, strict compliance with the law), the access and legitimacy paradigm (matching internal diversity to external diversity), and the learning and effectiveness paradigm (achieving organizational plurality by integrating deep-level diversity into the work of the organization). Unlike the other paradigms that focus on surface-level differences, the learning and effectiveness paradigm values common ground, distinguishes between individual and group differences, minimizes conflict and divisiveness, and focuses on bringing different talents and perspectives together. What principles can companies use when managing diversity? Follow and enforce federal and state laws regarding equal employment opportunity. Treat group differences as important but not special. Find the common ground. Tailor opportunities to individuals, not groups. Solicit negative as well as positive feedback. Set high but realistic goals. The two types of diversity training are awareness training and skills-based diversity training. Companies also manage diversity through diversity audits and diversity pairing and by having top executives experience what it is like to be in the minority.

Organizational plurality a work environment where (1) all members are empowered to contribute in a way that maximizes the benefits to the organization, customers, and themselves, and (2) the individuality of each member is respected by not segmenting or polarizing people on the basis of their membership in a particular group (p. 283)

Skills-based diversity training training that teaches employees the practical skills they need for managing a diverse workforce, such as flexibility and adaptability, negotiation, problem solving, and conflict resolution (p. 285)

Awareness training training that is designed to raise employees' awareness of diversity issues and to challenge the underlying assumptions or stereotypes they may have about others (p. 285)

Diversity audits formal assessments that measure employee and management attitudes, investigate the extent to which people are advantaged or disadvantaged with respect to hiring and promotions, and review companies' diversity-related policies and procedure (p. 286)

Diversity pairing a mentoring program in which people of different ages, cultural backgrounds, sexes, or races/ethnicities are paired together to get to know each other and change stereotypical beliefs and attitudes (p. 286)

Paradigms for Managing Diversity

Diversity Paradigm	Focus	Success Measured By	Benefits	Limitations
Discrimination & Fairness	Equal opportunity Fair treatment Recruitment of minorities Strict compliance with laws	Recruitment, promotion, and retention goals for underrepresented groups	Fairer treatment Increased demographic diversity	Focus on surface-level diversity
Access & Legitimacy	Acceptance and celebration of differences	Diversity in company matches diversity of primary stakeholders	Establish a clear business reason for diversity	Focus on surface-level diversity
Learning & Effectiveness	Integrating deep-level differences into organization	Valuing people on the basis of individual knowledge, skills, and abilities	Values common ground Distinction between individual and group differences Less conflict, backlash, and divisiveness Bringing different talents and perspectives together	Focus on deep-level diversity, which is more difficult to measure and quantify

13-1 Explain the basics of motivation. Motivation is the set of forces that initiates, directs, and makes people persist in their efforts over time to accomplish a goal. Managers often confuse motivation and performance, but job performance is a multiplicative function of motivation times ability times situational constraints. Needs are the physical or psychological requirements that must be met to ensure survival and well-being. Different motivational theories (Maslow's Hierarchy of Needs, Alderfer's ERG Theory, and McClelland's Learned Needs Theory) specify a number of different needs. However, studies show that there are only two general kinds of needs: lower-order needs and higher-order needs. Both extrinsic and intrinsic rewards motivate people.

Motivation the set of forces that initiates, directs, and makes people persist in their efforts to accomplish a goal (p. 289)

Needs the physical or psychological requirements that must be met to ensure survival and well-being (p. 290)

Extrinsic reward a reward that is tangible, visible to others, and given to employees contingent on the performance of specific tasks or behaviors (p. 292)

Intrinsic reward a natural reward associated with performing a task or activity for its own sake (p. 293)

13-2 Use equity theory to explain how employees' perceptions of fairness affect motivation. The basic components of equity theory are inputs, outcomes, and referents. After an internal comparison in which employees compare their outcomes to their inputs, they then make an external comparison in which they compare their O/I ratio with the O/I ratio of a referent, a person who works in a similar job or is otherwise similar. When their O/I ratio is equal to the referent's O/I ratio, employees perceive that they are being treated fairly. But, when their O/I ratio is lower than or higher than their referent's O/I ratio, they perceive that they have been treated inequitably or unfairly. There are two kinds of inequity: underreward and overreward. Underreward, which occurs when a referent's O/I ratio is higher than the employee's O/I ratio, leads to anger or frustration. Overreward, which occurs when a referent's O/I ratio is lower than the employee's O/I ratio, can lead to guilt but only when the level of overreward is extreme.

Equity theory a theory that states that people will be motivated when they perceive that they are being treated fairly (p. 295)

Inputs in equity theory, the contributions employees make to the organization (p. 295)

Outcomes in equity theory, the rewards employees receive for their contributions to the organization (p. 295)

Referents in equity theory, others with whom people compare themselves to determine if they have been treated fairly (p. 295)

Outcome/input (O/I) ratio in equity theory, an employee's perception of how the rewards received from an organization compare with the employee's contributions to that organization (p. 295)

Underreward a form of inequity in which you are getting fewer outcomes relative to inputs than your referent is getting (p. 296)

Overreward a form of inequity in which you are getting more outcomes relative to inputs than your referent (p. 296)

Distributive justice the perceived degree to which outcomes and rewards are fairly distributed or allocated (p. 299)

Procedural justice the perceived fairness of the process used to make reward allocation decisions (p. 299)

13-3 Use expectancy theory to describe how workers' expectations about rewards, effort, and the link between rewards and performance influence motivation. Expectancy theory holds that three factors affect the conscious choices people make about their motivation: valence, expectancy, and instrumentality. Expectancy theory holds that all three factors must be high for people to be highly motivated. If any one of these factors declines, overall motivation will decline, too.

Expectancy theory the theory that people will be motivated to the extent to which they believe that their efforts will lead to good performance, that good performance will be rewarded, and that they will be offered attractive rewards (p. 299)

Valence the attractiveness or desirability of a reward or outcome (p. 299)

Expectancy the perceived relationship between effort and performance (p. 300)

Instrumentality the perceived relationship between performance and rewards (p. 300)

13-4 Explain how reinforcement theory works, including how it can be used to motivate. Reinforcement theory says that behavior is a function of its consequences. Reinforcement has two parts: reinforcement contingencies and schedules of reinforcement. The four kinds of reinforcement contingencies are positive reinforcement and negative reinforcement, which strengthen behavior, and punishment and extinction, which weaken behavior. There are two kinds of reinforcement schedules—continuous and intermittent; intermittent schedules, in turn, can be divided into fixed and variable interval schedules and fixed and variable ratio schedules.

Reinforcement theory the theory that behavior is a function of its consequences, that behaviors followed by positive consequences will occur more frequently, and that behaviors followed by negative consequences, or not followed by positive consequences, will occur less frequently (p. 302)

Reinforcement the process of changing behavior by changing the consequences that follow behavior (p. 303)

Reinforcement contingencies cause-and-effect relationships between the performance of specific behaviors and specific consequences (p. 303)

Schedule of reinforcement rules that specify which behaviors will be reinforced, which consequences will follow those behaviors, and the schedule by which those consequences will be delivered (p. 303)

Positive reinforcement that strengthens behavior by following behaviors with desirable consequences (p. 303)

Negative reinforcement that strengthens behavior by withholding an unpleasant consequence when employees perform a specific behavior (p. 303)

Extinction reinforcement in which a positive consequence is no longer allowed to follow a previously reinforced behavior, thus weakening the behavior (p. 305)

Continuous reinforcement schedule a schedule that requires a consequence to be administered following every instance of a behavior (p. 305)

Intermittent reinforcement schedule a schedule in which consequences are delivered after a specified or average time has elapsed or after a specified or average number of behaviors has occurred (p. 305)

Fixed interval reinforcement schedule an intermittent schedule in which consequences follow a behavior only after a fixed time has elapsed (p. 305)

Variable interval reinforcement schedule an intermittent schedule in which the time between a behavior and

the following consequences varies around a specified average (p. 305)

Fixed ratio reinforcement schedule an intermittent schedule in which consequences are delivered following a specific number of behaviors (p. 306)

Variable ratio reinforcement schedule an intermittent schedule in which consequences are delivered following a different number of behaviors, sometimes more and sometimes less, that vary around a specified average number of behaviors (p. 306)

13-5 **Describe the components of goal-setting theory, including how managers can use them to motivate workers.**
A goal is a target, objective, or result that someone tries to accomplish. Goal-setting theory says that people will be motivated to the extent to which they accept specific, challenging goals and receive feedback that indicates their progress toward goal achievement. The basic components of goal-setting theory are goal specificity, goal difficulty, goal acceptance, and performance

feedback. Goal specificity is the extent to which goals are detailed, exact, and unambiguous. Goal difficulty is the extent to which a goal is hard or challenging to accomplish. Goal acceptance is the extent to which people consciously understand and agree to goals. Performance feedback is information about the quality or quantity of past performance and indicates whether progress is being made toward the accomplishment of a goal.

Goal a target, objective, or result that someone tries to accomplish (p. 308)

Goal-setting theory the theory that people will be motivated to the extent to which they accept specific, challenging goals and receive feedback that indicates their progress toward goal achievement (p. 308)

Goal specificity the extent to which goals are detailed, exact, and unambiguous (p. 308)

Goal difficulty the extent to which a goal is hard or challenging to accomplish (p. 308)

Goal acceptance the extent to which people consciously understand and agree to goals (p. 309)

Performance feedback information about the quality or quantity of past performance that indicates whether progress is being made toward the accomplishment of a goal (p. 309)

13-6 **Discuss how the entire motivation model can be used to motivate workers.**

Motivating with the Integrated Model

Motivating with	Managers should . . .
The Basics	<ul><li>Ask people what their needs are.</li><li>Satisfy lower-order needs first.</li><li>Expect people's needs to change.</li><li>As needs change and lower-order needs are satisfied, satisfy higher-order needs by looking for ways to allow employees to experience intrinsic rewards.</li></ul>
Equity Theory	<ul><li>Look for and correct major inequities.</li><li>Reduce employees' inputs.</li><li>Make sure decision-making processes are fair.</li></ul>
Expectancy Theory	<ul><li>Systematically gather information to find out what employees want from their jobs.</li><li>Take specific steps to link rewards to individual performance in a way that is clear and understandable to employees.</li><li>Empower employees to make decisions if management really wants them to believe that their hard work and efforts will lead to good performance.</li></ul>
Reinforcement Theory	<ul><li>Identify, measure, analyze, intervene, and evaluate critical performance-related behaviors.</li><li>Don't reinforce the wrong behaviors.</li><li>Correctly administer punishment at the appropriate time.</li><li>Choose the simplest and most effective schedules of reinforcement.</li></ul>
Goal-Setting Theory	<ul><li>Assign specific, challenging goals.</li><li>Make sure workers truly accept organizational goals.</li><li>Provide frequent, specific, performance-related feedback.</li></ul>

CHAPTER 14 LEARNING OUTCOMES / KEY TERMS

14-1 **Explain what leadership is.** Management is getting work done through others; leadership is the process of influencing others to achieve group or organizational goals. Leaders are different from managers. The primary difference is that leaders are concerned with doing the right thing, while managers are concerned with doing things right. Organizations need both managers and leaders. But, in general, companies are overmanaged and underled.

Leadership the process of influencing others to achieve group or organizational goals (p. 312)

14-2 **Describe who leaders are and what effective leaders do.** Trait theory says that effective leaders possess traits or characteristics that differentiate them from nonleaders. Those traits are drive, the desire to lead, honesty/integrity, self-confidence, emotional stability, cognitive ability, and knowledge of the business. These traits alone aren't enough for successful leadership; leaders who have many or all of them must also behave in ways that encourage people to achieve group or organizational goals. Two key leader behaviors are initiating structure, which improves subordinate performance, and consideration, which improves subordinate satisfaction. There is no ideal combination of these behaviors. The best leadership style depends on the situation.

Trait theory a leadership theory that holds that effective leaders possess a similar set of traits or characteristics (p. 315)

Traits relatively stable characteristics, such as abilities, psychological motives, or consistent patterns of behavior (p. 315)

Initiating structure the degree to which a leader structures the roles of followers by setting goals, giving directions, setting deadlines, and assigning tasks (p. 317)

Consideration the extent to which a leader is friendly, approachable, and supportive and shows concern for employees (p. 317)

14-3 **Explain Fiedler's contingency theory.** Fiedler's contingency theory assumes that leaders are effective when their work groups perform well, that leaders are unable to change their leadership styles, that leadership styles must be matched to the proper situations, and that favorable situations permit leaders to influence group members. According to the Least Preferred Coworker (LPC) scale, there are two basic leadership styles. People who describe their LPC in a positive way have a relationship-oriented leadership style. By contrast, people who describe their LPC in a negative way have a task-oriented leadership style. Situational favorableness, which occurs when leaders can influence followers, is determined by leader-member relations, task structure, and position power.

In general, relationship-oriented leaders with high LPC scores are better leaders under moderately favorable situations, whereas task-oriented leaders with low LPC scores are better leaders in highly favorable and highly unfavorable situations. Because Fiedler assumes that leaders are incapable of changing their leadership styles, the key is to accurately measure and match leaders to situations or to teach leaders how to change situational factors. Though matching or placing leaders in appropriate situations works well, reengineering situations to fit leadership styles doesn't because the complexity of the model makes it difficult for people to understand.

Leadership style the way a leader generally behaves toward followers (p. 319)

Contingency theory a leadership theory states that to maximize work group performance, leaders must be matched to the situation that best fits their leadership style (p. 320)

Situational favorableness the degree to which a particular situation either permits or denies a leader the chance to influence the behavior of group members (p. 321)

Leader–member relations the degree to which followers respect, trust, and like their leaders (p. 321)

Task structure the degree to which the requirements of a subordinate's tasks are clearly specified (p. 321)

Position power the degree to which leaders are able to hire, fire, reward, and punish workers (p. 321)

14-4 **Explain Hersey and Blanchard's Situational Leadership theory.** Job readiness and psychological readiness are combined to produce four different levels of readiness in Hersey and Blanchard's Situational Leadership theory. A *telling* leadership style (high task behavior and low relationship behavior) is based on one-way communication, in which followers are told what, how, when, and where to do particular tasks. A *selling* leadership style (high task behavior and high relationship behavior) involves two-way communication and psychological support to encourage followers to "own" or "buy into" particular ways of doing things. A *participating* style (low task behavior and high relationship behavior) is based on two-way communication and shared decision-making. A *delegating* style (low task behavior and low relationship behavior) is used when leaders basically let workers "run their own show" and make their own decisions.

Situational theory theory that says leaders need to adjust their leadership styles to match followers' readiness (p. 323)

Performance readiness the ability and willingness to take responsibility for directing one's behavior at work (p. 323)

14-5 Outline the steps for how path–goal theory works. Path-goal theory states that leaders can increase subordinate satisfaction and performance by clarifying and clearing the paths to goals and by increasing the number and kinds of rewards available for goal attainment. For this to work, however, leader behavior must be a source of immediate or future satisfaction for followers and must complement and not duplicate the characteristics of followers' work environments. In contrast to Fiedler's contingency theory, path-goal theory assumes that leaders can and do change their leadership styles (directive, supportive, participative, and achievement-oriented), depending on their subordinates (experience, perceived ability, and internal or external locus of control) and the environment in which those subordinates work (task structure, formal authority system, and primary work group).

Path–goal theory a leadership theory states that leaders can increase subordinate satisfaction and performance by clarifying and clearing the paths to goals and by increasing the number and kinds of rewards available for goal attainment (p. 325)

Directive leadership a leadership style in which the leader lets employees know precisely what is expected of them, gives them specific guidelines for performing tasks, schedules work, sets standards of performance, and makes sure that people follow standard rules and regulations (p. 326)

Supportive leadership a leadership style in which the leader is friendly and approachable to employees, shows concern for employees and their welfare, treats them as equals, and creates a friendly climate (p. 326)

Participative leadership a leadership style in which the leader consults employees for their suggestions and input before making decisions (p. 326)

Achievement-oriented leadership a leadership style in which the leader sets challenging goals, has high expectations of employees, and displays confidence that employees will assume responsibility and put forth extraordinary effort (p. 327)

14-6 Explain the normative decision theory. The normative decision theory helps leaders decide how much employee participation should be used when making decisions. Using the right degree of employee participation improves the quality of decisions and the extent to which employees accept and are committed to decisions. The theory specifies five different decision styles or ways of making decisions: autocratic decisions (AI or AII), consultative decisions (CI or CII), and group decisions (GII). The theory improves decision quality via decision rules concerning quality, leader information, subordinate information, goal congruence, and problem structure. The theory improves employee commitment and acceptance via decision rules related to commitment probability, subordinate conflict, and commitment requirement. These decision rules help leaders improve decision quality and follower acceptance and commitment by eliminating decision styles that don't fit the decision or situation the group or organization is facing. Normative decision theory operationalizes these decision rules in the form of yes/no questions.

Normative decision theory a theory that suggests how leaders can determine an appropriate amount of employee participation when making decisions (p. 329)

14-7 Explain how visionary (i.e., charismatic or transformational) leadership helps leaders achieve strategic leadership. Strategic leadership requires visionary leadership, which can be charismatic or transformational. Visionary leadership creates a positive image of the future that motivates organizational members and provides direction for future planning and goal setting. Charismatic leaders have strong, confident, and dynamic personalities that attract followers, enable the leader to create strong bonds, and inspire followers to accomplish the leader's vision. Followers of ethical charismatic leaders work harder, are more committed and satisfied, are better performers, and are more likely to trust their leaders. Followers can be just as supportive and committed to unethical charismatics, but these leaders can pose a tremendous risk for companies. Unethical charismatics control and manipulate followers and do what is best for themselves instead of their organizations. Transformational leadership goes beyond charismatic leadership by generating awareness and acceptance of a group's purpose and mission and by getting employees to see beyond their own needs and self-interests for the good of the group. The four components of transformational leadership are charismatic leadership or idealized influence, inspirational motivation, intellectual stimulation, and individualized consideration.

Visionary leadership leadership that creates a positive image of the future that motivates organizational members and provides direction for future planning and goal setting (p. 331)

Charismatic leadership the behavioral tendencies and personal characteristics of leaders that create an exceptionally strong relationship between them and their followers (p. 331)

Ethical charismatics charismatic leaders who provide developmental opportunities for followers, are open to positive and negative feedback, recognize others' contributions, share information, and have moral standards that emphasize the larger interests of the group, organization, or society (p. 331)

Unethical charismatics charismatic leaders who control and manipulate followers, do what is best for themselves instead of their organizations, want to hear only positive feedback, share only information that is beneficial to themselves, and have moral standards that put their interests before everyone else's (p. 333)

Transformational leadership leadership that generates awareness and acceptance of a group's purpose and mission and gets employees to see beyond their own needs and self-interests for the good of the group (p. 334)

Transactional leadership leadership based on an exchange process in which followers are rewarded for good performance and punished for poor performance (p. 335)

CHAPTER 15 LEARNING OUTCOMES / KEY TERMS

15-1 Explain the role that perception plays in communication and communication problems. Perception is the process by which people attend to, organize, interpret, and retain information from their environments. Perception is not a straightforward process. Because of perceptual filters such as selective perception and closure, people exposed to the same information or stimuli often end up with very different perceptions and understandings. Perception-based differences can also lead to differences in the attributions (internal or external) that managers and workers make when explaining workplace behavior. In general, workers are more likely to explain behavior from a defensive bias, in which they attribute problems to external causes (i.e., the situation).

Managers, on the other hand, tend to commit the fundamental attribution error, attributing problems to internal causes (i.e., the worker made a mistake or error). Consequently, when things go wrong, it's common for managers to blame workers and for workers to blame the situation or context in which they do their jobs. Finally, this problem is compounded by a self-serving bias that leads people to attribute successes to internal causes and failures to external causes. So, when workers receive negative feedback from managers, they may become defensive and emotional and not hear what their managers have to say. In short, perceptions and attributions represent a significant challenge to effective communication and understanding in organizations.

Communication the process of transmitting information from one person or place to another (p. 336)

Perception the process by which individuals attend to, organize, interpret, and retain information from their environments (p. 337)

Perceptual filters the personality-, psychology-, or experience-based differences that influence people to ignore or pay attention to particular stimuli (p. 337)

Selective perception the tendency to notice and accept objects and information consistent with our values, beliefs, and expectations, while ignoring or screening inconsistent information (p. 339)

Closure the tendency to fill in gaps of missing information by assuming that what we don't know is consistent with what we already know (p. 339)

Attribution theory the theory that we all have a basic need to understand and explain the causes of other people's behavior (p. 339)

Defensive bias the tendency for people to perceive themselves as personally and situationally similar to someone who is having difficulty or trouble (p. 340)

Fundamental attribution error the tendency to ignore external causes of behavior and to attribute other people's actions to internal causes (p. 340)

Self-serving bias the tendency to overestimate our value by attributing successes to ourselves (internal causes) and attributing failures to others or the environment (external causes) (p. 341)

15-2 Describe the communication process and the various kinds of communication in organizations. Organizational communication depends on the communication process, formal and informal communication channels, one-on-one communication, and nonverbal communication. The major components of the communication process are the sender, the receiver, noise, and feedback. Senders often mistakenly assume that they can pipe their intended messages directly into receivers' heads with perfect clarity. Formal communication channels such as downward, upward, and horizontal communication carry organizationally approved messages and information. By contrast, the informal communication channel, called the *grapevine*, arises out of curiosity and is carried out through gossip or cluster chains. There are two kinds of one-on-one communication. Coaching is used to improve on-the-job performance, while counseling is used to communicate about nonjob-related issues affecting job performance. Nonverbal communication, such as kinesics and paralanguage, accounts for as much as 93 percent of the transmission of a message's content.

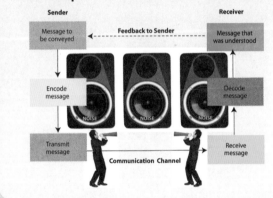

Exhibit 15.3
The Interpersonal Communication Process

Encoding putting a message into a written, verbal, or symbolic form that can be recognized and understood by the receiver (p. 342)

Decoding the process by which the receiver translates the written, verbal, or symbolic form of a message into an understood message (p. 342)

Feedback to sender in the communication process, a return message to the sender that indicates the receiver's understanding of the message (p. 343)

Noise anything that interferes with the transmission of the intended message (p. 343)

Jargon vocabulary particular to a profession or group that interferes with communication in the workplace (p. 343)

Formal communication channel the system of official channels that carry organizationally approved messages and information (p. 344)

Downward communication communication that flows from higher to lower levels in an organization (p. 344)

Upward communication communication that flows from lower to higher levels in an organization (p. 344)

Horizontal communication communication that flows among managers and workers who are at the same organizational level (p. 344)

Informal communication channel (grapevine) the transmission of messages from employee to employee outside of formal communication channels (p. 345)

Coaching communicating with someone for the direct purpose of improving the person's on-the-job performance or behavior (p. 346)

Counseling communicating with someone about non-job-related issues that may be affecting or interfering with the person's performance (p. 347)

Nonverbal communication any communication that doesn't involve words (p. 347)

Kinesics movements of the body and face (p. 347)

Paralanguage the pitch, rate, tone, volume, and speaking pattern (i.e., use of silences, pauses, or hesitations) of one's voice (p. 348)

15-3 **Explain how managers can manage effective one-on-one communication.** One-on-one communication can be managed by choosing the right communication medium, being a good listener, and giving effective feedback. Managers generally prefer oral communication because it provides the opportunity to ask questions and assess nonverbal communication. Oral communication is best suited to complex, ambiguous, or emotionally laden topics. Written communication is best suited for delivering straightforward messages and information. Listening is important for managerial success, but most people are terrible listeners. To improve your listening skills, choose to be an active listener (clarify responses, paraphrase, and summarize) and an empathetic listener (show your desire to understand, reflect feelings). Feedback can be constructive or destructive. To be constructive, feedback must be immediate, focused on specific behaviors, and problem oriented.

Communication medium the method used to deliver an oral or written message (p. 348)

Hearing the act or process of perceiving sounds (p. 350)

Listening making a conscious effort to hear (p. 350)

Active listening assuming half the responsibility for successful

communication by actively giving the speaker nonjudgmental feedback that shows you've accurately heard what he or she said (p. 350)

Empathetic listening understanding the speaker's perspective and personal frame of reference and giving feedback that conveys that understanding to the speaker (p. 351)

Destructive feedback feedback that disapproves without any intention of being helpful and almost always causes a negative or defensive reaction in the recipient (p. 352)

Constructive feedback feedback intended to be helpful, corrective, and/or encouraging (p. 352)

15-4 **Describe how managers can manage effective organizationwide communication.** Managers need methods for managing organization-wide communication and for making themselves accessible so that they can hear what employees throughout their organizations are feeling and thinking. Email, collaborative discussion sites, streamed/videotaped speeches and conferences, and broadcast voice mail make it much easier for managers to improve message transmission and get the message

out. By contrast, anonymous company hotlines, survey feedback, frequent informal meetings, town halls and surprise visits help managers avoid organizational silence and improve reception by giving them the opportunity to hear what others in the organization think and feel. Monitoring internal and external blogs is another way to find out what people are saying and thinking about your organization.

Discussion channels and chat rooms the use of web- or app-based communication tools to hold department-based, topic/project/client-based, team, or private discussions (p. 354)

Real-time broadcasting allows announcements, speeches and meetings made to smaller in-person audiences to be livestreamed to broader company audiences and stored on demand for

subsequent viewing and interactive discussion (p. 355)

Organizational silence when employees withhold information about organizational problems or issues (p. 356)

Bystander effect ignoring widely known organizational problems under the assumption that someone else will fix them (p. 356)

Company hotlines phone numbers that anyone in the company can call anonymously to leave information for upper management (p. 356)

Survey feedback information that is collected by surveys from organizational members and then compiled, disseminated, and used to develop action plans for improvement (p. 357)

CHAPTER 16 LEARNING OUTCOMES / KEY TERMS

16-1 **Describe the basic control process.** The control process begins by setting standards and then measuring performance and comparing performance to the standards. The better a company's information and measurement systems, the easier it is to make these comparisons. The control process continues by identifying and analyzing performance deviations and then developing and implementing programs for corrective action. Control is a continuous, dynamic, cybernetic process, not a onetime achievement or result. Control requires frequent managerial attention. The three basic control methods are feedback control (after-the-fact performance information), concurrent control (simultaneous performance information), and feedforward control (preventive performance information). Control has regulation costs and unanticipated consequences and therefore isn't always worthwhile or possible.

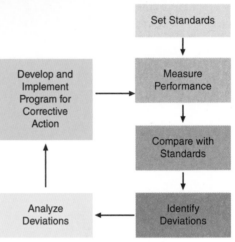

Exhibit 16.1
Cybernetic Control Process

Source: From *Business Horizons*, June 1972, H. Koontz and R. W. Bradspies, "Managing through Feedforward Control: A Future Directed View," pp. 25–36.

Control a regulatory process of establishing standards to achieve organizational goals, comparing actual performance against the standards, and taking corrective action when necessary (p. 360)

Standards a basis of comparison for measuring the extent to which various kinds of organizational performance are satisfactory or unsatisfactory (p. 361)

Benchmarking the process of identifying outstanding practices, processes, and standards in other companies and adapting them to your company (p. 362)

Cybernetic the process of steering or keeping on course (p. 363)

Feedback control a mechanism for gathering information about performance deficiencies after they occur (p. 364)

Concurrent control a mechanism for gathering information about performance deficiencies as they occur, thereby eliminating or shortening the delay between performance and feedback (p. 364)

Feedforward control a mechanism for monitoring performance inputs rather than outputs to prevent or minimize performance deficiencies before they occur (p. 364)

Control loss the situation in which behavior and work procedures do not conform to standards (p. 365)

Regulation costs the costs associated with implementing or maintaining control (p. 365)

Cybernetic feasibility the extent to which it is possible to implement each step in the control process (p. 366)

16-2 **Discuss the various methods that managers can use to maintain control.** There are five methods of control: bureaucratic, objective, normative, concertive, and self-control (self-management). Bureaucratic and objective controls are top down, management based, and measurement based. Normative and concertive controls represent shared forms of control because they evolve from company-wide or team-based beliefs and values. Self-control, or self-management, is a control system in which managers and workers control their own behavior.

Bureaucratic control is based on organizational policies, rules, and procedures. Objective control is based on reliable measures of behavior or outputs. Normative control is based on strong corporate beliefs and careful hiring practices. Concertive control is based on the development of values, beliefs, and rules in autonomous work groups. Self-control is based on individuals setting their own goals, monitoring themselves, and rewarding or punishing themselves with respect to goal achievement.

Each of these control methods may be more or less appropriate, depending on the circumstances.

Bureaucratic control the use of hierarchical authority to influence employee behavior by rewarding or punishing employees for compliance or noncompliance with organizational policies, rules, and procedures (p. 366)

Objective control the use of observable measures of worker behavior or outputs to assess performance and influence behavior (p. 367)

Behavior control the regulation of the behaviors and actions that workers perform on the job (p. 367)

Output control the regulation of workers' results or outputs through rewards and incentives (p. 368)

Normative control the regulation of workers' behavior and decisions through widely shared organizational values and beliefs (p. 368)

Concertive control the regulation of workers' behavior and decisions through work group values and beliefs (p. 369)

Self-control (self-management) a control system in which managers and workers control their own behavior by setting their own goals, monitoring their own progress, and rewarding themselves for goal achievement (p. 370)

16-3

Describe the behaviors, processes, and outcomes that today's managers are choosing to control in their organizations. Deciding what to control is just as important as deciding whether to control or how to control. In most companies, performance is measured using financial measures alone. However, the balanced scorecard encourages managers to measure and control company performance from four perspectives: financial, customer, internal, and innovation and learning. Traditionally, financial control has been achieved through cash flow analysis, balance sheets, income statements, financial ratios, and budgets. (For a refresher on these traditional financial control tools, see the Financial Review Card.) Another way to measure and control financial performance is to evaluate economic value added (EVA). Unlike traditional financial measures, EVA helps managers assess whether they are performing well enough to pay the cost of the capital needed to run the business. Instead of using customer satisfaction surveys to measure performance, companies should pay attention to customer defections, as customers who leave are more likely to speak up about what the company is doing wrong. From the internal perspective, performance is often measured in terms of quality, which is defined in three ways: excellence, value, and conformance to specifications. Sustainability has become an important part of innovation and learning in companies. The four levels of sustainability are waste prevention and reduction, recycling and reuse, waste treatment, and waste disposal.

Exhibit 16.5

Advantages and Disadvantages of Different Measures of Quality

Quality Measure	Advantages	Disadvantages
Excellence	Promotes clear organizational vision.	Provides little practical guidance for managers.
	Being/providing the "best" motivates and inspires managers and employees.	Excellence is ambiguous. What is it? Who defines it?
Value	Appeals to customers who know excellence "when they see it."	Difficult to measure and control.
	Customers recognize differences in value.	Can be difficult to determine what factors influence whether a product/service is seen as having value.
	Easier to measure and compare whether products/services differ in value.	Controlling the balance between excellence and cost (i.e., affordable excellence) can be difficult.
Conformance to Specifications	If specifications can be written, conformance to specifications is usually measurable.	Many products/services cannot be easily evaluated in terms of conformance to specifications.
	Should lead to increased efficiency.	Promotes standardization, so may hurt performance when adapting to changes is more important.
	Promotes consistency in quality.	May be less appropriate for services, which are dependent on a high degree of human contact.

Source: Briar Cliff Manor, NY, 10510-8020; C. A. Reeves and D. A. Bednar, "Defining Quality: Alternatives and Implications," *Academy of Management Review* 19 (1994): 419–445.

Balanced scorecard measurement of organizational performance in four equally important areas: finances, customers, internal operations, and innovation and learning (p. 371)

Suboptimization performance improvement in one part of an organization but only at the expense of decreased performance in another part (p. 371)

Cash flow analysis a type of analysis that predicts how changes in a business will affect its ability to take in more cash than it pays out (p. 372)

Balance sheets accounting statements that provide a snapshot of a company's financial position at a particular time (p. 372)

Income statements accounting statements, also called "profit and loss statements," that show what has happened to an organization's income, expenses, and net profit over a period of time (p. 372)

Financial ratios calculations typically used to track a business's liquidity (cash), efficiency, and profitability over time compared to other businesses in its industry (p. 372)

Budgets quantitative plans through which managers decide how to allocate available money to best accomplish company goals (p. 372)

Zero-based budgeting a budgeting technique that requires managers to justify every expenditure every year (p. 372)

Economic value added (EVA) the amount by which company profits (revenues minus expenses minus taxes) exceed the cost of capital in a given year (p. 373)

Customer defections a performance assessment in which companies identify which customers are leaving and measure the rate at which they are leaving (p. 374)

Value customer perception that the product quality is excellent for the price offered (p. 375)

Basic Accounting Tools for Controlling Financial Performance

Steps for a Basic Cash Flow Analysis

1. Forecast sales (steady, up, or down).
2. Project changes in anticipated cash inflows (as a result of changes).
3. Project anticipated cash outflows (as a result of changes).
4. Project net cash flows by combining anticipated cash inflows and outflows.

Parts of a Basic Balance Sheet (Assets 5 Liabilities 1 Owner's Equity)

1. Assets
   a. Current assets (cash, short-term investment, marketable securities, accounts receivable, and so on)
   b. Fixed assets (land, buildings, machinery, equipment, and so on)
2. Liabilities
   a. Current liabilities (accounts payable, notes payable, taxes payable, and so on)
   b. Long-term liabilities (long-term debt, deferred income taxes, and so on)
3. Owner's Equity
   a. Preferred stock and common stock
   b. Additional paid-in capital
   c. Retained earnings

Basic Income Statement

SALES REVENUE
− sales returns and allowances
+ other income
= NET REVENUE
− cost of goods sold (beginning inventory, costs of goods purchased, ending inventory)
= GROSS PROFIT
− total operating expenses (selling, general, and administrative expenses)
= INCOME FROM OPERATIONS
− interest expense
= PRETAX INCOME
− income taxes
= NET INCOME

Common Kinds of Budgets

Revenue Budgets—used to project or forecast future sales.	• Accuracy of projection depends on economy, competitors, sales force estimates, and so on • Determined by estimating future sales volume and sales prices for all products and services.
Expense Budgets—used within departments and divisions to determine how much will be spent on various supplies, projects, or activities.	• One of the first places that companies look for cuts when trying to lower expenses.
Profit Budgets—used by profit centers, which have "profit and loss" responsibility.	• Combine revenue and expense budgets into one budget. • Typically used in large businesses with multiple plants and divisions.
Cash Budgets—used to forecast how much cash a company will have on hand to meet expenses.	• Similar to cash-flow analyses. • Used to identify cash shortfalls, which must be covered to pay bills, or cash excesses, which should be invested for a higher return.
Capital Expenditure Budgets—used to forecast large, long-lasting investments in equipment, buildings, and property.	• Help managers identify funding that will be needed to pay for future expansion or strategic moves designed to increase competitive advantage.
Variable Budgets—used to project costs across varying levels of sales and revenues.	• Important because it is difficult to accurately predict sales revenue and volume. • Lead to more accurate budgeting with respect to labor, materials, and administrative expenses, which vary with sales volume and revenues. • Build flexibility into the budgeting process.

Common Financial Ratios

Ratios	Formula	What It Means	When to Use
Liquidity Ratios			
Current Ratio	$\dfrac{\text{Current Assets}}{\text{Current Liabilities}}$	• Whether you have enough assets on hand to pay for short-term bills and obligations. • Higher is better. • Recommended level is two times as many current assets as current liabilities.	• Track monthly and quarterly. • Basic measure of your company's health.
Quick (Acid Test) Ratio	$\dfrac{\text{Current Assets} - \text{Inventories}}{\text{Current Liabilities}}$	• Stricter than current ratio. • Whether you have enough (i.e., cash) to pay short-term bills and obligations. • Higher is better. • Recommended level is one or higher.	• Track monthly. • Also calculate quick ratio with potential customers to evaluate whether they're likely to pay you in a timely manner.
Leverage Ratios			
Debt to Equity	$\dfrac{\text{Total Liabilities}}{\text{Total Equity}}$	• Indicates how much the company is leveraged (in debt) by comparing what is owed (liabilities) to what is owned (equity). • Lower is better. A high debt-to-equity ratio could indicate that the company has too much debt. • Recommended level depends on industry.	• Track monthly. • Lenders often use this to determine the creditworthiness of a business (i.e., whether to approve additional loans).
Debt Coverage	$\dfrac{\text{Net Profit} + \text{Noncash Expense}}{\text{Debt}}$	• Indicates how well cash flow covers debt payments. • Higher is better.	• Track monthly. • Lenders look at this ratio to determine if there is adequate cash to make loan payments.
Efficiency Ratios			
Inventory Turnover	$\dfrac{\text{Cost of Goods Sold}}{\text{Average Value of Inventory}}$	• Whether you're making efficient use of inventory. • Higher is better, indicating that inventory (dollars) isn't purchased (spent) until needed. • Recommended level depends on industry.	• Track monthly by using a 12-month rolling average.
Average Collections Period	$\dfrac{\text{Accounts Receivable}}{\text{Annual Net Credit Sales} \div 365}$	• Shows on average how quickly your customers are paying their bills. • Recommended level is no more than 15 days longer than credit terms. If credit is net 30 days, then average should not be longer than 45 days.	• Track monthly. • Use to determine how long company's money is being tied up in customer credit.
Profitability Ratios			
Gross Profit Margin	$\dfrac{\text{Gross Profit}}{\text{Total Sales}}$	• Shows how efficiently a business is using its materials and labor in the production process. • Higher is better, indicating that a profit can be made if fixed costs are controlled.	• Track monthly. • Analyze when unsure about product or service pricing. • Low margin compared to competitors means you're underpricing.
Return on Equity	$\dfrac{\text{Net Income}}{\text{Owner's Equity}}$	• Shows what was earned on your investment in the business during a particular period. Often called "return on investment." • Higher is better.	• Track quarterly and annually. • Use to compare to what you might have earned on the stock market, bonds, or government Treasury bills during the same period.

CHAPTER 17 LEARNING OUTCOMES / KEY TERMS

17-1 Explain the strategic importance of information.

The first company to use new information technology to substantially lower costs or differentiate products or services often gains a first-mover advantage, higher profits, and a larger market share. Creating a first-mover advantage can be difficult, expensive, and risky, however. According to the resource-based view of information technology, sustainable competitive advantage occurs when information technology adds value, is different across firms, and is difficult to create or acquire.

Moore's law the prediction that about every two years, computer processing power would double and its cost would drop by 50 percent (p. 381)

Raw data facts and figures (p. 382)

Information useful data that can influence people's choices and behavior (p. 383)

First-mover advantage the strategic advantage that companies earn by being the first to use new information technology to substantially lower costs or to make a product or service different from that of competitors (p. 383)

17-2 Describe the characteristics of useful information (i.e., its value and costs).

Raw data are facts and figures. Raw data do not become information until they are in a form that can affect decisions and behavior. For information to be useful, it has to be reliable and valid (accurate), of sufficient quantity (complete), pertinent to the problems you're facing (relevant), and available when you need it (timely). Useful information is not cheap. The five costs of obtaining good information are: the costs of acquiring, processing, storing, retrieving, and communicating information.

Acquisition cost the cost of obtaining data that you don't have (p. 387)

Processing cost the cost of turning raw data into usable information (p. 387)

Data silo is an isolated data set that is difficult to obtain, combine or use with other company data (p. 387)

Data variety data that are formatted or structured in different ways (p. 387)

Storage cost the cost of physically or electronically archiving information for later retrieval and use (p. 387)

Retrieval cost the cost of accessing already-stored and processed information (p. 388)

Communication cost the cost of transmitting information from one place to another (p. 389)

17-3 Explain the basics of capturing, processing, and protecting information.

Electronic data capture (using bar codes, radio frequency identification [RFID] tags, scanners, or optical character recognition), is much faster, easier, and cheaper than manual data capture. Processing information means transforming raw data into meaningful information that can be applied to business decision making. Data mining helps managers with this transformation by discovering unknown patterns and relationships in data. Supervised data mining looks for patterns specified by managers, while unsupervised data mining looks for four general kinds of data patterns: association or affinity patterns, sequence patterns, predictive patterns, and data clusters. Protecting information ensures that data are reliably and consistently retrievable in a usable format by authorized users but no one else. Authentication and authorization, firewalls, antivirus software for PCs and corporate email and network servers, data encryption, virtual private networks (VPNs), and web-based secure sockets layer (SSL) encryption are some of the best ways to protect information. Be careful when using wireless networks, which are easily compromised even when security and encryption protocols are in place.

Exhibit 17.3
Security Threats to Data and Data Networks

Security Problem	Source	Affects	Severity	The Threat	The Solution
Denial of service; web server attacks and corporate network attacks	Internet hackers	All servers	High	Loss of data, disruption of service, and theft of service.	Implement firewall, password control, server-side review, threat monitoring, and bug fixes; turn PCs off when not in use; reroute data traffic to weed out and block malicious packets.
Password cracking software and unauthorized access to PCs	Local area network, internet	All users, especially digital subscriber line and cable internet users	High	Hackers take over PCs. Privacy can be invaded. Corporate users' systems are exposed to other machines on the network.	Close ports and firewalls, disable file and print sharing, and use strong passwords.
Viruses, worms, Trojan horses, and rootkits	Email, downloaded and distributed software	All users	Moderate to high	Monitor activities and cause data loss and file deletion; compromise security by sometimes concealing their presence.	Use antivirus software and firewalls; control internet access.
Malware, spyware, adware, malicious scripts, and applets	Rogue web pages	All users	Moderate to high	Invade privacy, intercept passwords, and damage files or file system.	Disable browser script support; use security, blocking, and anti-malware software.
Email snooping	Hackers on your network and the internet	All users	Moderate to high	People read your email from intermediate servers or packets, or they physically access your machine.	Encrypt messages, ensure strong password protection, and limit physical access to machines.
Keystroke monitoring	Trojan horses, people with direct access to PCs	All users	High	Records everything typed at the keyboard and intercepts keystrokes before password masking or encryption occurs.	Use anti-malware and antivirus software to catch Trojan horses, control internet access to transmission, and implement system monitoring and physical access control.
Phishing	Hackers on your network and the internet	All users, including customers	High	Fake but real-looking emails and websites that trick users into sharing personal information on what they wrongly think is a company's website. This leads to unauthorized account access.	Educate and warn users and customers about the dangers. Encourage both not to click on potentially fake URLs, which might take them to phishing websites. Instead, have them type your company's URL into the web browser.
Spam	Email	All users and corporations	Mild to high	Clogs and overloads email servers and inboxes with junk mail. HTML-based spam may be used for profiling and identifying users.	Filter known spam sources and senders on email servers; have users create further lists of approved and unapproved senders on their PCs.
Ransomware	Hackers on your network and the internet	All users and corporations	High	Encrypts personal or corporate data so it can't be accessed. Attacked individuals or corporations must pay a ransom of hundreds to tens of thousands of dollars using bitcoin (an anonymous method of payment) within a specified time or the data will be permanently locked or destroyed.	Educate managers and employees about phishing, close open ports, patch and update unpatched and outdated applications.

Sources: "X-Force Threat Intelligence Index 2020," IBM Security, accessed July 7, 2020; www.ibm.com/security/data-breach/threat-intelligence; L. Newman, "A 1.3Tbs DDoS Hit GitHub, the Largest Yet Recorded," *Wired*, March 4, 2018, accessed July 8, 2020, www.wired.com/story/github-ddos-memcached; M. All, "Is Your Company Ready for a Ransomware Attack?" *Harvard Business Review*, October 3, 2016, accessed May 6, 2017; hbr.org/2016/10/is-your-company -ready-for-a-ransomware-attack; "The 11 Most Common Computer Security Threats … And What You Can Do to Protect Yourself from Them," Symantec-Norton, accessed May 12, 2015; www.symantec-norton.com/11-most-common -computer-security-threats_k13.aspx; K. Bannan, "Look Out: Watching You, Watching Me," *PC Magazine*, July 2002, 99; A. Dragoon, "Fighting Phish, Fakes, and Frauds," *CIO*, September 1, 2004, 33; B. Glass, "Are You Being Watched?" *PC Magazine*, April 23, 2002, 54; B. Machrone, "Protect & Defend," *PC Magazine*, June 27, 2000, 168–181; "Top 10 Security Threats," *PC Magazine*, April 10, 2007, 66; M. Sarrel, "Master End-User Security," *PC Magazine*, May 2008, 101.

Bar code a visual pattern that represents numerical data by varying the thickness and pattern of vertical bars (p. 390)

Radio frequency identification (RFID) tags tags containing minuscule microchips that transmit information via radio waves and can be used to track the number and location of the objects into which the tags have been inserted (p. 390)

Sensors instruments that detect events or changes and actively transmit that information to other electronic devices (p. 390)

Document scanner an electronic device that converts printed text and pictures into digital images (p. 391)

Optical character recognition the ability of software to convert digitized documents into ASCII (American Standard Code for Information Interchange) text that can be searched, read, and edited by word processing and other kinds of software (p. 391)

Robotic data automation software robots are taught to recognize specific data patterns and then automatically scan, locate, and extract those data (p. 391)

Processing information transforming raw data into meaningful information (p. 391)

Data mining the process of discovering unknown patterns and relationships in large amounts of data (p. 391)

Data warehouse a database that stores huge amounts of data that have been prepared for data-mining analysis

by being cleaned of errors and redundancy (p. 392)

Supervised data mining the process when the user tells the data-mining software to look and test for specific patterns and relationships in a data set (p. 392)

Unsupervised data mining the process when the user simply tells the data mining software to uncover whatever patterns and relationships it can find in a data set (p. 392)

Association or affinity patterns when two or more database elements tend to occur together in a significant way (p. 392)

Sequence patterns when two or more database elements occur together in a significant pattern in which one of the elements precedes the other (p. 392)

Predictive patterns patterns that help identify database elements that are different (p. 393)

Data clusters when three or more database elements occur together (i.e., cluster) in a significant way (p. 393)

Protecting information the process of ensuring that data are reliably and consistently retrievable in a usable format for authorized users but no one else (p. 393)

Authentication making sure potential users are who they claim to be (p. 394)

Authorization granting authenticated users approved access to data, software, and systems (p. 394)

Two-factor authentication authentication based on what users know, such as a password and what they have in their possession, such as a secure ID card or key (p. 394)

Firewall a protective hardware or software device that sits between the computers in an internal organizational network and outside networks, such as the internet (p. 396)

Malware a program or piece of code that, without your knowledge, attaches itself to other programs on your computer and can trigger anything from a harmless flashing message to the reformatting of your hard drive to a system-wide network shutdown (p. 396)

Virus a special kind of malware that copies itself and spreads to other devices (p. 396)

Data encryption the transformation of data into complex, scrambled digital codes that can be decrypted only by authorized users who possess unique decryption keys (p. 396)

Virtual private network (VPN) software that securely encrypts data sent by employees outside the company network, decrypts the data when they arrive within the company computer network, and does the same when data are sent back to employees outside the network (p. 398)

Secure sockets layer (SSL) encryption internet browser-based encryption that provides secure offsite web access to some data and programs (p. 398)

17-4 **Describe how companies can access and share information and knowledge.** Executive information systems, intranets, and corporate portals facilitate internal sharing and access to company information and transactions. Electronic data interchange and the internet allow external groups such as suppliers and customers to easily access company information. Both decrease costs by reducing or eliminating data entry, data errors, and paperwork and by speeding up communication. Organizations use decision support systems and expert systems to capture and share specialized knowledge with nonexpert employees.

Executive information system (EIS) a data processing system that uses internal and external data sources to provide the information needed to monitor and analyze organizational performance (p. 399)

Intranets private company networks that allow employees to easily access, share, and publish information (p. 399)

Corporate portal a hybrid of executive information systems and intranets that allows managers and employees to use a web browser to gain access to customized company information and to complete specialized transactions (p. 400)

Electronic data interchange (EDI) when two companies convert their purchase and ordering information to a standardized format to enable the direct

electronic transmission of that information from one company's computer system to the other company's computer system (p. 400)

Web services software that uses standardized protocols to describe data from one company in such a way that those data can automatically be read, understood, transcribed, and processed by different computer systems in another company (p. 400)

Extranets networks that allow companies to exchange information and conduct transactions with outsiders by providing them direct, web-based access to authorized parts of a company's intranet or information system (p. 401)

Knowledge the understanding that one gains from information (p. 402)

Decision support system (DSS) an information system that helps managers understand specific kinds of problems and potential solutions (p. 402)

Expert system an information system that contains the specialized knowledge and decision rules used by experts and experienced decision makers so that nonexperts can draw on this knowledge base to make decisions (p. 402)

Artificial intelligence (AI) the capability of computerized systems to learn and adapt through experience (p. 403)

CHAPTER 18 LEARNING OUTCOMES / KEY TERMS

18-1 **Discuss the kinds of productivity and their importance in managing operations.** Productivity is a measure of how many inputs it takes to produce or create an output. The greater the output from one input, or the fewer inputs it takes to create an output, the higher the productivity. Partial productivity measures how much of a single kind of input, such as labor, is needed to produce an output. Multifactor productivity is an overall measure of productivity that indicates how much labor, capital, materials, and energy are needed to produce an output.

$$\text{Partial Productivity} = \frac{\text{Outputs}}{\text{Single Kind of Input}}$$

Operations management managing the daily production of goods and services (p. 404)

Productivity a measure of performance that indicates how many inputs it takes to produce or create an output (p. 405)

Partial productivity a measure of performance that indicates how much of a particular kind of input it takes to produce an output (p. 407)

Multifactor productivity an overall measure of performance that indicates how much labor, capital, materials, and energy it takes to produce an output (p. 407)

Robots machines or programs capable of completing complex tasks (p. 408)

Process automation using robots to automate routine, highly repetitive, low-complexity, or single-purpose tasks (p. 408)

Intelligent recognition using automation programming to recognize and react to patterns of speech, written language, images, and other items (p. 408)

Collaborative/social automation using robots to automate tasks while working directly with or near people (p. 409)

18-2 **Explain the role that quality plays in managing operations.** Quality can mean that a product or service is practically free of deficiencies or has characteristics that satisfy customer needs. Quality products usually possess three characteristics: reliability, serviceability, and durability. Quality service includes reliability, tangibles, responsiveness, assurance, and empathy. ISO 9000 is a series of five international standards for achieving consistency in quality management and quality assurance, while ISO 14000 is a set of standards for minimizing an organization's harmful effects on the environment. The Baldrige Performance Excellence Program recognizes US companies for their achievements in quality and business performance. Each year, up to three Baldrige National Quality Awards may be given in the categories of manufacturing, service, small business, education, nonprofit, and health care. Total quality management (TQM) is an integrated organization-wide strategy for improving product and service quality. TQM is based on three mutually reinforcing principles: customer focus and satisfaction, continuous improvement, and teamwork.

Quality a product or service free of deficiencies, or the characteristics of a product or service that satisfy customer needs (p. 410)

ISO 9000 a series of five international standards, from ISO 9000 to ISO 9004, for achieving consistency in quality management and quality assurance in companies throughout the world (p. 411)

ISO 14000 a series of international standards for managing, monitoring, and minimizing an organization's harmful effects on the environment (p. 411)

ISO 27000 a series of 12 international standards for managing and monitoring security techniques for information technology (p. 411)

Total quality management (TQM) an integrated, principle-based, organization-wide strategy for improving product and service quality (p. 413)

Customer focus an organizational goal to concentrate on meeting customers' needs at all levels of the organization (p. 413)

Customer satisfaction an organizational goal to provide products or services that meet or exceed customers' expectations (p. 413)

Continuous improvement an organization's ongoing commitment to constantly assess and improve the processes and procedures used to create products and services (p. 414)

Variation a deviation in the form, condition, or appearance of a product from the quality standard for that product (p. 414)

Teamwork collaboration between managers and nonmanagers, across business functions, and between companies, customers, and suppliers (p. 414)

18-3 **Explain the essentials of managing a service business.** Services are different from goods. Goods are produced, tangible, and storable. Services are performed, intangible, and perishable. Likewise, managing service operations is different from managing production operations. The service-profit chain indicates that success begins with internal service quality, meaning how well management treats employees. Internal service quality leads to employee satisfaction and service capability, which, in turn, lead to high-value service to customers, customer satisfaction, customer loyalty, and long-term profits and growth. Keeping existing customers is far more cost-effective than finding new ones. Consequently, to prevent disgruntled customers from leaving, some companies are empowering service employees to perform service recovery—restoring customer satisfaction to strongly dissatisfied customers—by giving employees the authority and responsibility to immediately solve customer problems. The hope is that empowered service recovery will prevent customer defections.

Internal service quality the quality of treatment employees receive from management and other divisions of a company (p. 415)

Service recovery restoring customer satisfaction to strongly dissatisfied customers (p. 417)

18-4 **Describe the different kinds of manufacturing operations.** Manufacturing operations produce physical goods. Manufacturing operations can be classified according to the amount of processing or assembly that occurs after receiving an order from a customer.

Manufacturing operations can also be classified in terms of flexibility, the degree to which the number, kind, and characteristics of products can easily and quickly be changed. Flexibility allows companies to respond quickly to competitors and customers and to reduce order lead times, but it can also lead to higher unit costs.

Make-to-order operation a manufacturing operation that does not start processing or assembling products until a customer order is received (p. 418)

Assemble-to-order operation a manufacturing operation that divides manufacturing processes into separate parts or modules that are combined to create semicustomized products (p. 418)

Make-to-stock operation a manufacturing operation that orders parts and assembles standardized products before receiving customer orders (p. 418)

Manufacturing flexibility the degree to which manufacturing operations can easily and quickly change the number, kind, and characteristics of products they produce (p. 418)

Continuous-flow production a manufacturing operation that produces goods at a continuous, rather than a discrete, rate (p. 419)

Line-flow production manufacturing processes that are preestablished, occur in a serial or linear manner, and are dedicated to making one type of product (p. 419)

Batch production a manufacturing operation that produces goods in large batches in standard lot sizes (p. 420)

Job shops manufacturing operations that handle custom orders or small-batch jobs (p. 420)

18-5 **Explain why and how companies should manage inventory levels.** There are four kinds of inventory: raw materials, component parts, work-in-process, and finished goods. Because companies incur ordering, setup, holding, and stockout costs when handling inventory, inventory costs can be enormous. To control those costs, companies measure and track inventory in three ways: average aggregate inventory, weeks of supply, and turnover. Companies meet the basic goals of inventory management (avoiding stockouts and reducing inventory

without hurting daily operations) through economic order quantity (EOQ) formulas, just-in-time (JIT) inventory systems, and materials requirement planning (MRP). The formula for EOQ is

$$EOQ = \sqrt{\frac{2DO}{H}}$$

Use EOQ formulas when inventory levels are independent, and use JIT and MRP when inventory levels are dependent on the number of products to be produced.

Inventory the amount and number of raw materials, parts, and finished products that a company has in its possession (p. 420)

Raw material inventories the basic inputs in a manufacturing process (p. 421)

Component parts inventories the basic parts used in manufacturing that are fabricated from raw materials (p. 421)

Work-in-process inventories partially finished goods consisting of assembled component parts (p. 421)

Finished goods inventories the final outputs of manufacturing operations (p. 421)

Average aggregate inventory average overall inventory during a particular time period (p. 422)

Stockout the point when a company runs out of finished product (p. 423)

Inventory turnover the number of times per year that a company sells, or "turns over," its average inventory (p. 423)

Ordering cost the costs associated with ordering inventory, including the cost of data entry, phone calls, obtaining bids, correcting mistakes, and determining when and how much inventory to order (p. 423)

Setup cost the costs of downtime and lost efficiency that occur when a machine is changed or adjusted to produce a different kind of inventory (p. 424)

Holding cost the cost of keeping inventory until it is used or sold, including storage, insurance, taxes, obsolescence, and opportunity costs (p. 424)

Stockout cost the cost incurred when a company runs out of a product, including transaction costs to replace inventory and the loss of customers' goodwill (p. 424)

Economic order quantity (EOQ) a system of formulas that minimizes ordering and holding costs and helps determine how much and how often inventory should be ordered (p. 424)

Just-in-time (JIT) inventory system an inventory system in which component parts arrive from suppliers just as they are needed at each stage of production (p. 425)

Kanban a ticket-based JIT system that indicates when to reorder inventory (p. 425)

Materials requirement planning (MRP) a production and inventory system that determines the production schedule, production batch sizes, and inventory needed to complete final products (p. 425)

Independent demand system an inventory system in which the level of one kind of inventory does not depend on another (p. 426)

Dependent demand system an inventory system in which the level of inventory depends on the number of finished units to be produced (p. 426)